Fün Places to go With Kids
and educational
and adults
in Southern California

"My own book of Susan's <u>Fun Place to go With Kids</u> is only kept together by tape. My friends and relatives are constantly asking to borrow what I think is the best tour book in Southern California. Not only does it provide a complete guide to all that Southern California has to offer, but also provides her personal views, which are invaluable when planning time with the family."
Donna Baker   *Producer of Parenting Rollercoaster and Cul-de-Sac Chronicles*

"I have to tell you. I've raved and raved about my new book to everyone who would listen. I am a 'bargain hunting' (OK, cheap) Mom of 3, (one income, private school). I pride myself on finding "fun places" (<cough> that are cheap fun and educational places, LOL!), but was AMAZED by your book. I have lived in So. Cal for 30 years and never heard of half the places mentioned in your book! . . . My book will also be passed on to Grandma who thinks it sounds perfect for her senior club!"
Corby Wagner

"It's 10:30 and I've already had five telephone calls from leaders thanking me for inviting you to the meeting last night, praising your fun-filled presentation, pleasant personality, great ideas, . . . Believe me, Susan, I have never looked so good. It's just not that easy to impress *or* entertain the "been there, done that" woman in Irvine. . . You may be sure that you have substantially improved the quality of Girl Scout field trips in Irvine so I feel confident that I can offer you the appreciation of the 1600 girls affected."
Mary Pearlman   *Membership Development Director for Girl Scouts*
Orange County

"First of all, I absolutely love your book. Your recommendations have all been wonderfully accurate and it's saved me SO much hassle! . . .Thank you for contributing to the sanity of numerous CA moms!!"
Angie Smith   *mother of twins*

"Over 20 copies of <u>Fun and Educational Places to go With Kids</u> are continually checked out in the Orange County Public Library System; we can't keep them on the shelves! Children's librarians feel confident referring parents to this title. It's perfect for planning local inexpensive family outings."
Elke Faraci   *Senior Administrative Librarian*
Orange County Public Library System

"Susan Peterson's book <u>Fun and Educational Places to go with Kids</u> has been a great addition to our children's bookstore. Its extensive collection of family outings makes it a great resource for our customers. It is well organized, making it easy to find wonderful local outings to fit everyone's taste and budget. It has been a big seller, and we recommend it highly."
Ane & David Miller   *Through a Child's Eyes (bookstore)*
Downey

and educational

Fün ^Places to
go With Kids ¬

and adults

in Southern California

A comprehensive guide to Los Angeles, Orange,
Riverside, San Bernardino, San Diego,
Santa Barbara, and Ventura counties

By Susan Peterson

Fun Places Publishing, California
www.funplaces.com

Published by Fun Places Publishing
P.O. Box 376
Lakewood, California 90714-0376
(562) 867-5223
Susan@funplaces.com
www.funplaces.com

ISBN 0-9646737-7-0

Printed in the United States of America

Sixth Edition - June, 2003
Fifth Edition - March, 2001
Fourth Edition - October, 1998
Third Edition - May, 1997
Second Edition - May, 1996
First Edition - May, 1995

ACKNOWLEDGMENTS

Where do I begin to thank my **family** and **friends** who have supported me, prayed with me and for me, and encouraged me when I wanted (desperately, sometimes) to just stop. Exploring places is a fun, vibrant, and exciting activity, but the writing, while enjoyable and challenging, can sometimes be a very solitary enterprise. Thank you all *so* very much!! Many hugs!

A book is <u>never</u> put together alone and there are some special people who have particularly pulled me through and cheered me on:

Lance - my husband and best friend. You are the epitome of a faithful, loving, and upright man. Best of all, after working diligently on this edition together - we are still happily married! It doesn't get any better than this. Thank you, honey, for your hard and oftentimes tedious work on the computer. Without you, there wouldn't be a book. Thank you most of all for listening to me and believing that there is a good purpose in all of this. I adore you.

My three boys (who are still the only kids I know that sometimes ask, "Can we please stay home?") - I love spending time with you guys. You are fun to travel with and I have been privileged to get to know you better all the time. I love the fact that we spend so much time in the car talking, or sharing, as I like to say.

Kellan (age 16) - Pretty soon *you* will be driving *me* places - eeks! That said, you are a great traveling companion; interesting to talk with and definitely coming into your own. You are my favorite.

Bryce (age 13) - You are so passionate about life and quick-witted, and you make me laugh. You are my favorite.

T.J. (age 11) - You truly enjoy most of the places we visit and are thankful for the opportunity. I appreciate that and your compassionate heart. You are my favorite.

My wonderful editors - without you this book would be rife with ~~eros! erors!~~ errors! Thank you for taking the time to read, edit, and redirect my writing efforts. And I actually do appreciate comments such as, "I have no idea what you are trying to say" and "Did you make this word up?" (Well, a new word has to start somewhere!) A special thanks to **Jim Birge**, **Chuck and Linda Clark**, **Jan Davidson**, **Joe and Jan Gallagher**, **Pauline Hirabayashi**, **Gail Karon**, **Cathy Martinez**, and **Kathleen Yanelli**,

My cauliflowered-eared phone mates who spent countless hours helping me call every single blessed place (sometimes more than once!) to verify facts: **Jewelene Pate** - I am sooo thankful for your help, your belief that the book is a valuable resource, and for your precious friendship; and **Jane Stuart** - You are awesome! Welcome aboard and <u>many</u> thanks, Jane.

All of the people associated with places mentioned in this book that were so willing to talk with me, send me information, and enable my family to come and visit - thank you, THANK YOU, **<u>THANK YOU!!</u>**.

TABLE OF CONTENTS

INTRODUCTION and LEGEND EXPLANATION

In this world there are specifically fun places to go with kids, and there are places we go and bring our kids, anyhow. I think going shopping is great, but when my boys were younger, while I was looking at clothes, they thought it was fun to climb in the clothing racks and maybe even pull off a ticket or two to bring home as "prizes." That did not make for a fun family outing. I've tried to do the weeding for you so that anywhere you choose to go in this guidebook, whether it's an all-day outing or just for an hour, would be an enjoyable time for you and your child. Some places are obvious choices; some are places you might have simply forgotten about; some are hidden treasures; and some are new attractions.

The book is set up by county. Under each county, categories are listed alphabetically; and under each category, attractions are listed alphabetically. Note: The names of places in all capital letters used in a description (e.g. DISNEYLAND) are attractions listed separately elsewhere in the book and usually referenced by a page number. An explanation of what each category means is on the following pages simply titled, "What Do the Categories Mean?" If you still have a hard time figuring out what category I have placed an attraction (and that is a strong possibility), look it up in the one of the four indexes in the back of the book: alphabetical, city, price, or theme.

Each attraction has a set of directions in parenthesis. The "**TG**" at the end of the directions is the *Thomas Guide* map page and grid reference number.

Next to most of the places described are symbols, meant to be at-a-glance guidelines. The **sun** indicates the average amount of time needed to see this attraction. You might decide you need more or less time - this is just a guideline. The **dollar signs and exclamation mark** are price guidelines. They incorporate *the entrance cost for one adult, a 10-year-old child, and the parking fee* (if there is one). If you have more than one child, or one who gets in for free, your cost will vary. "**Ages**" stands for recommended ages. It is meant to be an aid to help you decide if an attraction is appropriate and/or meaningful for your child. Some of the age restrictions, however, are designated by the place you are visiting. The **birthday cake** symbol represents an attraction that is a good place to 1) have a birthday party (the place may or may not have a separate party room), or 2) incorporate with a birthday party.

☼	= 15 minutes to 1 hour	!	= FREE!
☼	= 1½ hours to half a day	!/$	= FREE, but bring spending money.
☼	= all day	$	= 1¢ - $5
▦	= good for birthday parties	$$	= $5.01 - $10
		$$$	= $10.01 - $20
		$$$$	= $20.01 - $40
		$$$$$	= over $40

***   Discounts: Look for discount coupons for main attractions in hotel lobbies and visitors centers. Check the attraction's website for on-line discounts. Also, if you belong to AAA   ***
(i.e. Auto Club), check if the attraction offers discount admission for members.

WHAT DO THE CATEGORIES MEAN?
(and other helpful information)

Each attraction in every county is listed under one, or more, of the following categories. The information below is to help you understand what the categories mean so that you can find a place to visit that interests you.

AMUSEMENT PARKS
Webster's definition of amusement is: "To cause to laugh or smile; entertainment; a pleasant diversion." So, from roller coasters to water slides - have fun!

ARTS AND CRAFTS
Children have creative urges and need a place to express themselves. Since art classes are offered in a dizzying array and fluctuating times and prices, most of the places listed in these sections are paint-it-yourself ceramic studios to assist your young artists in developing their talents - move over Monet! Note: Museums are also great resources for arts and crafts workshops.

BEACHES
Beaches are a "shore" bet for a day of fun in the sun. Along with sand and water play, inline skating, and/or biking, some beaches have playgrounds, picnic tables, and waveless waters that make them particularly younger-kid friendly. These sections includes *just a few* suggestions of where to go beaching. A great resource for information on beaches is www.beachcalifornia.com.

On a sad note, some beaches' waters get polluted, either temporarily or longer term. Before your visit, please contact Heal the Bay at (800) 432-5229 / www.healthebay.org and see the rating/report card for that particular beach.

EDIBLE ADVENTURES
"Eatertainment" abounds in Southern California. From themed restaurants to high tea, to farmer's markets to a fun place to get an ice-cream cone, the Edible Adventures sections cover some of the best.

FAMILY PAY AND PLAY
The family that plays together, stays together! Indoor play areas, outdoor miniature golf courses, rock climbing centers, laser tag arenas, paint ball fields, indoor skate parks, and more are great places to go to spend some special bonding time.

GREAT OUTDOORS
Contrary to popular belief, Southern California consists not only of concrete buildings, but also of the great outdoors. Explore the region's natural beauty by visiting open-space preserves, botanic gardens, nature centers, and a plethora of designed parks. Go take a hike - with your kids! For a complete listing of state-run parks call (916) 653-6995 / www.parks.ca.gov. Also listed under the Great Outdoors sections are outdoor skate parks, which are sprouting up all over. Tip: Check this website - www.skateboardparks.com - or call your city hall to keep up on new skate parks.

MALLS
These sections are not necessarily to tell you where to go shopping, but rather to inform you of free kids' clubs, programs, events, and "shoppertainment" features that your local mall has to offer. We included just a few of our favorite, unique malls, also. Be entertained, enjoy, and create - and maybe get in a little shopping, too!

MUSEUMS

There is a whole world of learning in the huge variety of museums in Southern California. Captivate kids' imaginations, hearts, and even their hands by treating them to a visit. Here are a few tips about museums:

* Exhibits rotate, so be flexible in your expectations.
* If you really like the museum, become a member. Besides supporting the foundation, you'll reap benefits such as visiting the museum year round at no additional fee, being invited to members-only events, receiving newsletters, getting discounts on store merchandise, and lots more. Sometimes membership is reciprocal with other similar museums. For instance, museum membership at the California Science Center in Los Angeles allows entrance to the Discovery Science Center in Santa Ana and the Reuben H. Fleet Science Center in San Diego, as well as almost 200 other science museums in the United States.
* If you're looking for a special present, most museum gift shops carry unique merchandise that is geared towards their specialty.
* Museums offer a fantastic array of special calendar events. Check their websites or get on a mailing list.
* Take a guided tour! You and your kids will learn a lot about the exhibits this way.

PIERS AND SEAPORTS

It ap*piers* that walking around seaport villages, looking at boats, fishing off piers, taking a cruise, and maybe going on some rides, is a delightful way to spend a few hours with your child.

POTPOURRI

The dictionary defines potpourri as: "A miscellaneous mixture; a confused collection." This accurately describes these sections! Unique stores, cemeteries, libraries, Catalina Island, Tijuana, and more fill these pages. Whatever you do, there are a potpourri of ideas to explore.

SHOWS AND THEATERS

How about a day (or evening) at the theater? The listings here range from theaters that have productions specifically for children, to planetarium shows, dinner and show combinations, and musical extravaganzas!

TOURS

Take a tour of a place to gain insight into ordinary and unique places. Many tours are offered under the Museums sections, too, as well as a few other sections. Note: See the Ideas / Resources section toward the back of the book for general tour ideas regarding a particular profession or subject.

Tip: Many restaurants, especially chain restaurants, offer tours of their facility. The tours usually require a minimum number of participants (usually school-aged children), and could include a tour of the kitchen, plus a partial or full meal. These tours are usually free. Participating restaurants that I know of (although there are no guarantees) include Bristol Farms (I know it's not really a restaurant, but it does have food), California Pizza Kitchen, Chevy's Restaurant, Krispy Kreme Doughnuts (I know, another "not-restaurant", but you get milk and one of their incredible doughnuts), and Outback Steakhouse. I suggest that if you see a place you're interested in taking a tour of, call and ask! They might not be set up to do it for the general public, but they might be willing to take your group around.

TRANSPORTATION

Take a journey with your child by bike, plane, train, automobile, boat, carriage, etc., for a truly "moving" experience. Note: There are numerous boating companies up and down the coastline. I've mentioned only a few, giving just some pertinent facts. Anchors away!

Trains are a great alternative to driving. By incorporating a train trip into your day's excursion, it makes the journey almost as much fun as the destination whether you're visiting a park, a special restaurant, or a major attraction. TheAmtrak phone number and website - (800) USA RAIL (872-7245) / www.amtrak.com - gives fares and other pertinent information. For example, from Union Station in Los Angeles to San Juan Capistrano, the fare is $24 for adults; $12 for children ages 2 through 15. Ask about AAA discounts. Contact www.dot.ca.gov/hq/rail for money-saving rail rates. Also, contact this last website, then click on to the Amtrak California link to find out information on the Kid's 'N Trains Program. This program, offered mid-September through mid-May, allows teachers and students (minimum of twenty) to ride the rails of Pacific Surfliner (a division of Amtrak) during the week (except Fridays) for as little as $5 per person round trip. **Metrolink**, (800) 371-5465 / www.metrolinktrains.com, offers another fairly hassle-free mode of transportation that links the counties of Ventura, Los Angeles (mostly in Antelope Valley), San Bernardino, Riverside, and Orange. These trains run Monday through Friday; only a few counties run on weekends, too. Trains do not run on major holidays. One-way tickets start at about $4.25; round trip, $6.75. Kids 5 and under ride for free. Information on the **Metro Rail** (for Los Angeles County) and the **Coaster** (for San Diego County) is listed in the Transportation section for those respective counties.

Bike riding is a pollution-free (and exhilarating!) way of getting around. There are many bike trails in Southern California (not everyone drives a car everywhere!). I have just written up a few. One of the best ways I can be of service to you is to give you the contacts so you can order bike trail maps for a specific area and choose your own route. Look in the Transportation section, under BIKE MAPS, for each county for phone numbers and websites. One of our favorite contacts is www.labikepaths.com. Many beaches and parks have bike paths, too, so look in the Beaches sections and the Great Outdoors sections, also. Be wise when biking. Carry water bottles, a cell phone, change for snacks, a small bike pump, a patch kit, sun screen, a small first aid kit, and anything else useful. Most pathways are safe, but bike with a buddy, just in case. Note that many of the bike trails that I've listed are paved pathways also great for strollers, roller bladers, joggers, and others.

ZOOS AND ANIMALS
Kids and animals seem to go hand-in-hoof - both are adorable and neither is easy. Zoos, aquariums, farms, animal rescue facilities, and more are listed here. Animals lovers - these sections are for you!

NEVER LEAVE HOME WITHOUT THESE ESSENTIALS

1) **SNACKS**: Always carry snacks and a water bottle with you and/or in the car. Listening to a child whine because he is hungry or thirsty can drive any sane parent over the edge. (And kids will not stop this endearing behavior until they actually get their food or drink!)

2) **MAP**: I would be lost without it! Invest in a street-finder map such as *The Thomas Guide* or *Rand McNally Streetfinder*.

3) **TISSUES AND/OR WIPES**: For obvious reasons.

4) **QUARTERS**: A few quarters tucked away in a container in the car can come in handy for phone calls, those snacks I told you to pack but you forgot, metered parking, or arcade games.

5) **TOYS/BOOKS/GAMES**: Keeping little fingers busy helps keep little hands out of trouble. (Check out Educational Toys, Books, and Games under the IDEAS/RESOURCES section.)

6) **TAPES**: Audio tapes can get kids singing instead of fussing. (And if kids cry really loud, just turn up the volume of the tape even louder!) We've found story tapes to be a real blessing, too. (See Audio Tapes under the IDEAS / RESOURCES section.)

7) **FIRST AID KIT**: Fill it with the essentials including band aids, ointment, adhesive tape, scissors, an ice pack, Benedryl®, disposable gloves, a sewing kit, and Tylenol™ (both children's and adults').

8) **ROADSIDE EMERGENCY KIT**: This kit should contain jumper cables (know how to use them!), flares, a flashlight, batteries, extra drinking water, tools, matches, screwdrivers, wrenches, etc.

9) **JACKET**: Pack a light jacket or sweater for the unexpected change in weather or change of plans. Throw in a change of clothes, too, for little ones who don't always make it to the bathroom in time. (This last tip could save your outing from being cut short.)

10) **BLANKET**: We use ours mainly for picnics, but it doubles as an "I'm cold" helper, and is handy for other emergencies.

11) **FANNY PACK**: Even if your kids are still in the diaper/stroller stage, a fanny pack is great for storing snacks and water bottles, and keeping your hands free to either help your children or grab them before they dart away.

12) **SUNSCREEN**: With our weather, we almost always need it.

13) **CAMERA AND FILM**: Capture those precious moments in a snap!

14) **GROCERY BAG**: It holds trash, excuse me, I mean treasures, that kids collect such as rocks, sticks, and creepy crawly things. The bag helps keep your car clean (and makes it easier to throw everything away once you get home!).

15) **A SENSE OF HUMOR!**

MISCELLANEOUS TIDBITS

OTHER HELPFUL ITEMS TO BRING:
1. **Cell phone**
2. **Walkie talkies** - Instead of just hoping that you'll actually meet up with your spouse, friend, kids, etc. at the appointed place and time, communicate! Most walkie talkies have a two-mile radius.
3. **Video camera**
4. **Tape recorder** - Carry a hand-size tape recorder and press "record" anytime. This is a great way to document trips (remember to state the date and location) and interview kids, as well as get genuine reactions and impromptu stories, songs, and arguments.

MATCHING ARTICLES OF CLOTHING: Dress your kids in the same shirt (no, I don't mean one big shirt), or at least shirts of the same color (orange, yellow, and red are bright choices) when you go on an outing. I thought this would look silly, but while we do get stares and comments, I can find my kids at just a glance. If kids balk at wearing the same-colored shirt, invest in solid color baseball caps. Not only can you spot your children quickly, but hats help shade their faces from the sun.

SAFETY PRECAUTIONS (just a few to get you started):
1. Dress kids in brightly colored or easily identifiable shoes. If someone should try to snatch your child, shoes are the hardest thing to change.
2. Carry your child's picture for easy identification purposes.
3. Instruct your child where to meet or who to talk to in case you get separated from each other.

EXPECTATIONS:
1. Be Aware - Simply because you have a fun outing planned, whether it's going to the "happiest place on earth" or just an hour of play, please don't expect your child to necessarily enjoy every moment of it. Know and expect that your child will probably fuss about something, or seemingly nothing. Beware of the fun-stealers - tiredness and hunger. Visit places before or after nap time, and always bring food, even if you just ate.
2. Be Prepared - Call ahead and make sure the place you want to visit is open, especially if there is something that you particularly want to see; check off your list of essentials; set realistic expectations for all participants; be flexible; and go for it!
3. Family Mottos - We no longer promise our kids that we'll take them on an outing. A promise, as any parent knows, cannot be broken; it is an absolute. A plan, however, can be altered depending on weather, circumstance, and/or attitude! One of our family mottos is, "It's a plan, not a promise." Another one is, "Oh well." Feel free to use either or both as the situation warrants.

SOME IDEAS TO EXTEND THE MEMORIES OF YOUR OUTING

1. **PHOTO ALBUMS** - Buy your child an inexpensive 35mm camera (even a disposable one) and let him document the fun you have together. Keep ticket stubs and brochures. Have your older child keep a journal of his travels; where he went, when, and what he liked best. (See information on ordering the FUN PLACES TO GO JOURNAL.) Give younger children duplicate pictures (or ones that aren't going in the family album) so each child can put together his/her own album. Use craft scissors with patterned blades for creative cutting. Have kids use acid-free construction paper and stickers for decorations. Coming up with captions can be lots of fun - and funny! Spending this time together is a great way to extend a trip and continue making special memories. Note: Photo albums with magnetic pages will discolor your pictures eventually, but ones that use acid-free paper will not. See "Photo Albums" under the IDEAS / RESOURCES section in back of the book.

2. **COLLECTIONS** - Collect key chains, refrigerator magnets, mugs, pencils, decks of cards, or something else inexpensive from each place you go, and display them.
   A. Patches - I collect patches and sew them on a quilt, for each child. Using a twin-size, colored flannel sheet and thin batting, I folded the sheet in half with the batting in between, and "quilted" it. (i.e. sewed the edges together and a few semi-straight lines, both vertically and horizontally.) Of course, just buying a quilt is a lot easier. I sew, or iron, on the patches as we get them. My kids love their "travel blankets."
   B. Postcards - Ask your younger children, "What's the most fun thing you remember about this place?" and jot down the answers on the back of this inexpensive memory-keeper. Make older kids write out the answers the themselves. Be sure you date the postcard, too. Keep all the postcards in a small, three-ring binder. Another option: If you're going away on a trip, bring stamps and mail the postcards home. Kids love to receive mail..

3. **EDUCATION** - Spend some time doing a little (or a lot) of research about a particular place (or time period) before you visit. It will make your outing more meaningful and make a lasting impression upon your child. Think of your field trip as curriculum supplement! Call the attraction to get a brochure on it or use an encyclopedia to look up pertinent information, or do some on-line research. Other educational activities to enhance your outing include:
   A. Read stories - If you're going apple picking, for instance, read stories that have something to do with apples such as Johnny Appleseed, William Tell, Snow White, Adam and Eve, Sir Isaac Newton, and specifically, *The Giving Tree* by Shel Silverstein or *Ten Apples on Top* by Theo LeSieg.
   B. Theme books - There are thematic study books for almost every subject written. Teacher Created Materials, Inc. at (800) 662-4321 / www.teachercreated.com has over fifty thematic unit study books available. Each book includes lessons and projects that incorporate math, arts and crafts, history, science, language arts, and cooking, into a study about one particular subject. (i.e. weather, birds, the human body, holidays, and more.)
   C. Spelling words - Give your child a spelling list pertaining to the attraction you are visiting.
   D. Maps - Have older children use a map to track your way to and from your outing - this is an invaluable skill, especially if they learn to do it correctly!
   E. Flash cards - Take pictures of the places you go. Put the picture on a piece of construction paper and write the facts about the attraction on the back. "Laminate" it with contact paper. Use the cards as flash cards. Tip: If you're not a picture taker, buy postcards instead.

F. Bingo - Get duplicate pictures made of the places you go. Make bingo boards and cards. If the kids get a match, however, they have to tell you at least one fact about the place before they can put their chip on the board.
G. Use my FUN PLACES TO GO JOURNAL.

4. **LISTEN TO YOUR AUDIO TAPE** - Nothing refreshes your memory about a trip like playing back on-the-road commentary. (See Miscellaneous Tidbits.)

These are just a few ideas - I'm sure you'll come up with many of your own!

5. **YOUR IDEAS -**

ROAD GAMES

"Are we almost there yet?" and "I'm bored!" (along with "I have to go to the bathroom!") are common cries from children (and adults) who are traveling. Tapes, books, toys, and snacks all help to keep kids entertained, as do car games. Here are just a few of our favorites with brief explanations on how to play:

FOR THE YOUNGER SET:
MISSING LETTER ABC SONG - Sing the ABC song, leaving out a letter. See if your child can figure out what letter is missing. Now let your child sing (or say) the alphabet, leaving out a letter. Suggest correct (and incorrect) letters and see if your child agrees with you on what letter is missing. (Tip: Know your alphabet!)

MISSING NUMBER GAME - Count up to a certain number and stop. See if your child can figure out what number comes next. Now let your child do the counting. See if he/she agrees with what you say the next number should be.

COLOR CAR GAME - Look out the window for just red cars (or just blue or just green, etc.). Each time your child sees a red car, he/she can shout "red!" (or "blue!" or "green!", etc.) Count together the number of cars of a particular color you see on your trip. Your child can eagerly share at night, "Daddy, we had a fifteen-red-car day!" A variation of this game is to count a particular type of car; VW Bugs is the popular choice for our family.

ABC WORD GAME - A is for apple; B is for bear; etc. Encourage your child to figure out words that start with each letter of the alphabet.

FOR OLDER CHILDREN:
ALPHABET SIGN GAME - Each person, or team, looks for a word outside the car (i.e. billboards, freeway signs, bumper stickers, etc.) that begins with each letter of the alphabet. When the words are found, the person, or team, shouts it out. The words must be found in alphabetical order, starting with the letter A. Since words beginning with a Q, X, or Z are hard to find (unless you're near a Quality Inn, X-Ray machine, or a Zoo), players may find these particular letters used <u>in</u> any word. A word on a sign, billboard, etc., can only be used once, by one player or team member. Other players must find their word in another sign, billboard, etc. The first one to get through the alphabet wins! Warning #1: Try to verify that the word has been seen by more than just the player who shouted it out, or learn to trust each other. Warning #2: From personal experience: If the driver is competitive and wants to play, make sure he/she keeps his/her eyes on the road!

ALPHABET WORD GAME - This is a variation on the above game. Instead of finding words that begin with each letter of the alphabet, each player must look outside the car and describe his surroundings using letters of the alphabet, in sequential order. This game can be played fast and gets creative, depending on the quick-thinking skills of the people playing. Example: Someone who is on the letter D might look at the land and see dirt; a person looking for an S might say soil; someone else who is on the letter G might say ground. All are correct. Players may use the same point of reference as long as the exact same word is not used. Whoever gets through the alphabet first wins.

GHOST - (Or whatever title you choose.) The object of this game is to add one letter per turn and be in the process of spelling a word, without actually spelling out a word. Players take turns adding letters until someone either spells a word, or can't think of another letter to add without spelling a word. A player may try to bluff and add a letter that doesn't seem like it spells a word. If he gets challenged by someone asking what he is spelling, he must come up with a legitimate word. If he doesn't, he loses the round. (If he does have a word, however, than the challenger loses that round.) Whoever spells a word or can't think of a letter to add, gets a G. The second time he loses a round, he gets an H, etc. Whoever earns G-H-O-S-T (i.e. loses 5 rounds) is eliminated from the game. Example: Player 1 says the letter "B." Player 2 adds the letter "E." (Words must be at least 3 letters long to count as a word.) Player 3 says "T." Player 3 gets a G, or whatever letter-round he is on. He loses the round even if his intent was to spell the word "better" because "bet" is a word.

WORD SCRAMBLE - Make sure players have a piece of paper and a writing implement. Using a word on a sign or billboard, or using the name of the place you are visiting, see how many other words players can make. To spice up the game, and add stress, set a time limit. Whoever has the most words wins. A variation is that letters are worth points: 2 letter words are worth 2 points, 3 letter words are worth 5 points, 4 letter words are worth 8 points, etc. The player with the most points wins. (Although a player may have fewer words, he/she could win the game by being long-worded.) Note: This game can be played for only a brief period of time by players who are prone to motion sickness.

FOR ALL AGES:

BINGO - This is the only game that you have to prepare for ahead of time. Make up bingo-type cards for each child. Cards for younger children can have pictures of things kids would typically see on their drive (although this depends on where you are traveling, of course): a blue car, McDonalds, a cow, a pine tree, etc. Cards for older children can have pictures, signs, license plates, and/or words that they would typically see on their drive: exit, stop, a traffic light, curvy road ahead, etc. Use magazines, newspapers, etc., and glue the pictures and words onto posterboard, one card per child. Tip: Have your kids help you prepare the cards as it's a fun project. Use raisins (or M&M's®) as markers and when your child has bingo (or has seen a certain number of objects on his card), he can eat his reward. For those parents who intend to use the bingo boards more than once, "laminate" them with contact paper. Put small pieces of velcro on a part of each picture or sign on the card and make (non-edible) markers that have the other part of velcro on them. (This will keep markers from sliding off the cards during sudden turns!) Keep the cards and markers together in a plastic baggy in the car.

20 QUESTIONS - This time-honored game has many variations. (Our version is usually called 40 Questions.) The basic rules are for one player to think of a well-known person, or at least someone well-known to your children, and for other players to ask questions about the person to try to find out his/her identity. Only yes or no answers can be given. Whoever figures out the mystery person, in 20 questions or less, wins. Tip: Encourage players to ask general questions first to narrow down the field. (Inevitably, my youngest one's first question was, "Is it George Washington?") Teach them to ask, for instance: "Is it a man?"; "Is he alive?"; "Is he real?"; "Is he a cartoon?"; "Is he on T.V.?"; "Is he an historical figure?"; "Is it someone I know personally?" You get the picture. For a variation of the game, think of an object instead of a person. (Tip: Tell the others players first, though, about the switch in subject matter.)

3 THINGS IN COMMON - This is a great thinking game that is easily adaptable for kids of all ages. One person names 3 words (or things) that have something in common. Everyone else takes turns guessing what that something is. Examples for younger children: #1) sky, ocean, grandpa's eyes (or whomever). Answer: Things that are blue. #2) stop sign, fire truck, Santa's suit. Answer: Things that are red. Examples for older kids and adults: #1) house, butter, horse. Answer: Things that have the word fly at the end of them. #2) chain, missing, sausage. Answer: Things that can end with the word link. #3) tiger, nurse, sand. Answer: Kinds of sharks.

I'M GOING ON A PICNIC. . . . - This game tests a player's abilities to remember things and remember them in order. Player 1 starts with the words, "I'm going on a picnic" and then adds a one-word item that he will bring. The next player starts with the same phrase, repeats player 1's item, and then adds another item, and so on. Play continues until one of the players can't remember the list of things, in order, to bring on a picnic. Example: Player 1 says, "I'm going on a picnic and I am going to bring a ball." Player 2 says, "I'm going on a picnic and I'm going to bring a ball and a kite." Variations of the game include adding items in alphabetical order or adding items beginning with the same letter.

PLEASE be aware that although the facts recorded in this book are accurate and current as of June, 2003:

- HOURS CHANGE!
- EXHIBITS ROTATE!
- ADMISSION COSTS ARE RAISED WITHOUT FANFARE!
- PLACES CLOSE, EITHER TEMPORARILY OR PERMANENTLY!

To avoid any unexpected (and unpleasant) surprises:

Always, ALWAYS, *ALWAYS*
CALL BEFORE YOU VISIT AN ATTRACTION!!!

xx

LOS ANGELES COUNTY

Ciudad de Los Angeles; City of Los Angeles; "City of Angels": This international city of Mexican heritage is one of extremes with its concrete jungles, acres of parkland, pockets of poverty, and renown cultural meccas. Almost 10 million people live in this county, which is a sprawling metropolis that encompasses the glitz of Hollywood, the incredible wealth of Beverly Hills, the quirkiness of Venice, the beach-city attitudes of Manhattan Beach and Malibu, the charm of Pasadena, the deserts of Lancaster, and the daily living of families in every community.

Brave the freeways to reach mainstream attractions such as Universal Studios Hollywood, California Science Center, Aquarium of the Pacific, Huntington Library, Magic Mountain, and the Music Center, as well as the numerous "smaller" jewels that make L.A. a gem of a place to visit.

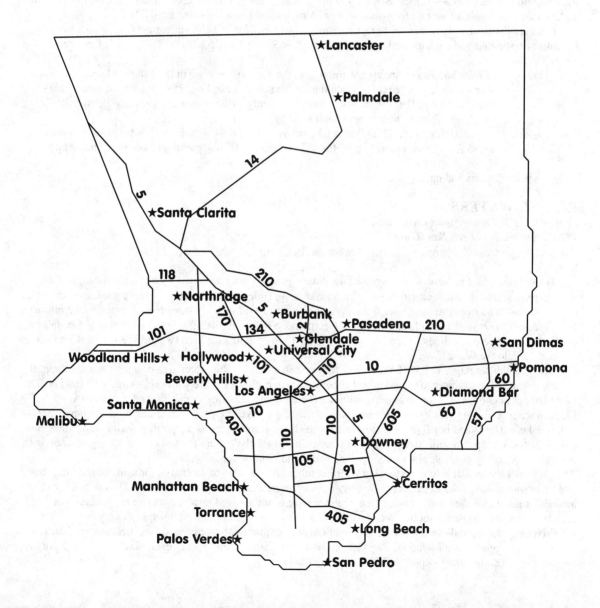

-----*AMUSEMENT PARKS*-----

PACIFIC PARK
(310) 260-8744 / www.pacpark.com
At the western end of Colorado Boulevard, on Santa Monica Pier, Santa Monica
(Exit Santa Monica Fwy [10] N. on 4th St., L. on Colorado Blvd. It dead-ends at the pier. There is limited parking on the pier. From Colorado Blvd., other parking is available by turning L. on Oceanside, R. on Seaside, R. on Appian Way. [TG: 671 E3])

The major kid-attraction on the Santa Monica pier is Pacific Park. It has thirteen family amusement rides, including six kiddie rides at the nautically-themed Kids Cove. Some of the rides include a huge Ferris wheel, which gives a great view at the top for miles around; a historic carousel (with horses, camels, and lions); a roller coaster; bumper cars; a ship that swings back and forth like a giant pendulum; Pier Patrol trucks that ride on a track around re-created beach scenes; Sea Fury, which spins riders in a 360 degree rotation; a scrambler; a mini biplane ride; and a submarine ride for young sailors. A rock climbing wall is also available.

Nineteen carnival-style games are here, as are arcade games. If your belly starts rumbling, grab a bite at oceanfront restaurants, snack bars, and ice cream shops. See SANTA MONICA PIER (pg. 127) for details about the pier.

Hours: All rides and games are up and running in the summer, Sun. - Thurs., 11am - 11pm; Fri. - Sat., 10am - midnight. The park is open during the school year, Fri., 6pm - midnight; Sat., 11am - midnight; Sun., 11am - 9pm. Some games and only a ride or two are open during the school year, Mon. - Thurs., noon - 6pm. Call first!

Admission: Individual tickets are $2 and rides take between 1 - 3 tickets each. An all-day rides wristband is $19.95 for 42" and taller; $10.95 for 41" and under. All-day parking prices range between $5 - $7.

Ages: 2 years and up.

RAGING WATERS
(909) 802-2200 / www.ragingwaters.com
111 Raging Waters Drive, San Dimas
(Exit San Bernardino Fwy [10] N. on the 210 Fwy, or follow the Orange Fwy [57] where it turns into the 210 Fwy; exit at Raging Waters Dr. [TG: 600 B4])

What a cool place to be on a hot day! Raging Waters is out*rage*ous with its fifty acres of chutes, white-water rapids, slides, drops, enclosed tubes (which make these slides dark and scary), a wave pool, lagoons, and sandy beaches. The rides run the gamut from a peaceful river raft ride in only three feet of water, to the ultimate for daredevils, such as plunging headfirst on High Extreme, a 600-foot ride off a 100-foot tower, or free falling off the Wedge where a feeling of near-zero gravity is terrifyingly fun. Ride high (well, three-feet high) on waves that roll out into the Wave Cove.

The younger set reigns at Kids Kingdom as they splash around in this water area designed just for them. It has a big water play structure to climb on that shoots out water, plus tyke-size water slides and a tire swing. The Little Dipper Lagoon is also for youngsters with its wading pools, shooting fountains, and waterfalls. Elementary-school-aged kids have their own, separate, fantastic, activity pool with slides, a ropes course, and Splash Island. The Island is a five-story treehouse with slides, water cannons, cargo nets, swinging bridges, and a huge bucket on top that spills over gallons of water. Holy smoke! Volcano Fantasia is a smoking volcano with several slides oozing down its sides into hip-deep water and more water activities.

Life vests are available at no extra charge. Inner tubes are available at no charge for some of the rides, but you must wait in long lines to get them. On busy days I recommend renting a tube ($4 to $7). A picnic area is available just outside the main entrance gate. Outside food is not allowed inside, but there are several food outlets throughout the park. Hot tip: Wear water shoes or sandals because the walkways get very hot.

Hours: Open mid-April through May, and Labor Day through September, on weekends only, 10am - 6pm. Open Memorial Day through mid-June daily, 10am - 6pm. Open mid-June through August daily, 10am - 8pm. Call first as hours fluctuate.

Admission: $27.99 for 48" and taller; $17.99 for seniors; $16.99 for 47" and under; children 2 and under are free. After 4pm, prices are $19.99 for 48" and taller; $11.99 for seniors and kids 47" and under. Purchase season passes by May and save $! Parking is $7.

Ages: 1½ years and up.

SIX FLAGS HURRICANE HARBOR

(661) 255-4111 / www.sixflags.com

Magic Mountain Parkway, Valencia

(Exit Golden State Fwy [5] W. on Magic Mountain Pkwy. It's right next to Magic Mountain. [TG: 4550 A1])

$$$$$

Pirates and lost tropical islands are the themes creatively integrated throughout every attraction in this twenty-two-acre water park. Older kids enjoy the swashbuckling thrill of the vertical drops, speed slides, open tube rides, and two of the tallest enclosed speed slides this side of the Mississippi. Taboo Tower is sixty-five-feet high!! Bamboo Racer pits six contestants against each other as they race down the slide into the water. The wave pool, with two-foot waves, is a hit for those practicing surfing techniques. The five-person raft ride is fun without being too scary, and the lazy, looping river ride in only three feet of water is great for everyone in the family.

Relax in lounge chairs while your younger children play in Castaway Cove, a shallow pool with mini-slides, cement aquatic creatures, and a wonderful fortress-like water play structure with waterfalls, swings, water-spurting gadgets, and more. The next harbor over is ideal for elementary-school-aged mateys to get wet and play on board the "floating" pirate ship. Watch out for the huge skull - it dumps thousands of gallons of water every few minutes on unsuspecting crew members. An adult activity pool is great for swimming, plus it has a net for water volleyball and, of course, it also has several slides. Sand volleyball is available, too - outside the pool!

Tube rentals run between $6 and $8, although tubes are included in some of the rides. Food is available to purchase inside the Harbor as outside food is not allowed in. Hot tip: Wear water shoes or sandals as the walkways get very hot. Note: The Harbor shares the same parking lot as Magic Mountain.

Hours: Open May and September on weekends only, 10am - 6pm. Open June through Labor Day daily, 10am - 7pm.

Admission: $21.99 for 49" and taller; $14.99 for seniors and kids 48" and under; children 2 and under are free. Parking is $8. Combo tickets for Hurricane Harbor and Magic Mountain are available.

Ages: 1½ years and up.

SIX FLAGS MAGIC MOUNTAIN

(661) 255-4111 / www.sixflags.com

Magic Mountain Parkway, Valencia

(Exit Golden State Fwy [5] W. on Magic Mountain Pkwy. [TG: 4550 A1])

$$$$$

Thrill seekers and/or roller-coaster aficionados consider action-packed Magic Mountain the most daring place to go. Sixteen roller coasters range from the classic, wooden Colossus, to some of the world's tallest and fastest rides - Superman and Goliath, which is a 255-foot drop! Try the ultimate of Scream, a floorless coaster that has a 150-foot initial drop, seven loops, and a top speed of 65 m.p.h. This extreme theme park also has DejaVu, a suspended coaster ride that plummets riders down a hill and, with a boomerang-style turn, back up. Riders are going forward and backward, so they don't know if they are coming or going! X, yet another ripping coaster ride, spins its vehicles independently of one another while going along the tracks. My stomach and I just like to watch these rides and not actually participate. Magic Mountain has over forty-five rides and attractions geared mostly for kids 8 years and older.

Other highlights here include the Log Ride and Jet Stream (both wet rides), bumper cars, and a visit to Pirate's Cove, where a fifteen-foot-tall volcano erupts. The Sky Tower is a "must-do" for all ages because it affords a 360-degree view of the park and the surrounding area. Bugs Bunny World is ideal for the younger crowd (2 to 8 year olds). Looney Tunes characters are often here for hugs and pictures. The rides include a pint-size free fall, train ride, Bigfoot truck ride, balloon ride, roller coasters (of course), and Tweety's Escape, which is a ride in an oversized bird cage. Another high-ranking attraction in this section is the Looney Tunes Lodge, a two-story funhouse. Visitors in here use cannons and other creative gadgets to shoot, drop, or hurl hundreds of foam balls through the air at one another. To complete this world is a petting zoo and a fountain area where Looney Tunes statues spew out water.

Magic Mountain has entertainment such as live music and spectacular special events in its 3,200-seat theater; stunt shows, such as the Batman and Robin Live Action special effects show; water shows; a truly exciting free-flight bird show; and interactive shows for younger kids such as Kids World, with Bugs Bunny presiding. Catch the nighttime extravaganza in the summer as Looney Tunes characters and DC Comic Book superheroes participate in a parade through the park that ends with a fireworks display.

Cyclone Bay is toward the back of the park, where specialty shops are the specialty. Coastal Candy Company is an especially sweet stop as kids can watch fudge, caramel apples, and all sorts of mouth-watering delights being made before their very eyes. If it's real food that you're hankering for try Mooseburger Lodge. In a forest-like setting waiters and waitresses sometimes sing, a moose talks, and the dessert - chocolate "moose" - is served in an edible chocolate shell.

Although there are lots of grassy, shady areas to rest, Magic Mountain is spacious and hilly, so wear walking shoes. Tip: Visit this Mountain on a Monday or Tuesday, if possible, as it is normally less crowded then. Note: If you want wet, summertime fun, check out SIX FLAGS HURRICANE HARBOR (pg. 3), which is right next door to Magic Mountain.

Hours: Open April through October daily, 10am - 6pm. Call for extended summer hours, usually 10am - 10pm or later. Open the rest of the year weekends and holidays only, 10am - 6pm.

Admission: $44.99 for 49" and taller; $29.99 for seniors and kids 48" and under; children 2 and under are free. Certain discounts available through AAA. Parking is $8. Combo tickets for Magic Mountain and Hurricane Harbor are available.

Ages: 1½ years and up.

UNIVERSAL STUDIOS HOLLYWOOD

☼
$$$$$
🎂

(818) 508-9600 / www.universalstudioshollywood.com
Universal Center Drive, Universal City
(Going NW on Hollywood Fwy [101], exit NE on Universal Center Dr. Going SE on 101, exit R. on Lankershim. At the end of the off ramp, turn L. on Cahuenga Blvd., L. on Universal Center Dr. [TG: 563 C6])

This huge, unique, Hollywood-themed amusement park is really one of the world's biggest and busiest motion picture and television studios. Personal advice is to go on the forty-five-minute, guided studio tram tour first, as lines get long later on. Each tram on the tour is outfitted with monitors that shows film clips as well as how various sets and sound stages have been used in productions over the years. You'll go behind the scenes and through several of Hollywood's original and most famous backlots; see sound stages and lots of props; and learn about the shows currently being filmed at Universal. Along the way, some of the elaborate special effects that you'll encounter are: A confrontation with King Kong; the shark from *Jaws*; Earthquake - The Big One, where buildings collapse and a run-away big-rig crashes within inches of you, followed by fire and a flood coming toward you; and more disasters, such as the collapsing bridge and the flash flood. Some of it can get a bit overwhelming for younger kids.

Want to go Back to the Future? Be prepared in this ride for an intense, jolting, simulated experience through the Ice Ages, into the mouth of a Tyrannosaurus Rex, and forward to the year 2015. Take the Starway to the lower lot where, if you are at least 46" tall, you can enter through the gates of Jurassic Park to river raft through the primordial forest. It starts off as a peaceful ride, but it ends up as a very wet, terrifying, face-to-face encounter with bellowing dinosaurs! You will get drenched. Ponchos are available for purchase at a nearby vending machine. Follow up this ride with Backdraft, where you literally feel the heat of the hottest attraction here. (You'll dry off from the Jurassic waters.) This sound stage becomes a fiery furnace, ablaze with ruptured fuel lines and melting metal. Note that some of the rides at Universal have height and age restrictions. The Special Effects Stage reveals how sleight-of-sight effects were created and used in various Universal movies, such as *How the Grinch Stole Christmas*, *Gladiator*, and *Incredible Hulk*. See behind-the-camera work with make-up, computer graphics, green screen technology, and the art of sound effects. Be a part of the half-hour show through audience participation. Tip: Watch out for monsters. Lovers of Lucy can visit the heart-shaped facility and "walk through" her career with the aid of photos, videos, costumes, and other memorabilia.

Walk through a labyrinth reminiscent of *The Mummy Returns* featuring over 200 original props. Watch out for the moving scarabs, waterfall of scorpions, and the giant cobra - this attraction is not for the faint hearted. Revenge of the Mummy ride, opening 2004, hurtles thrill-seeking passengers through Egyptian chambers and passageways as a ceiling of flame, skeleton warriors and other ghoulish robotic figures, pyrotechnics, and laser images seek to terrify. The ride jostles visitors in a backwards and forwards motion.

The Nickelodeon-themed Blast Zone has several components including a kids water play area where a rocket ship shoots out water, fountains spurt up from the ground, water target streamers can be aimed at friends and friends-yet-to-be, 500-gallon water buckets dump over to shower unsuspecting bystanders, and Sponge Bob hangs out. Bring a change of clothing. The Wild Thornberrys-themed temple here is filled with soft foam balls to shoot everywhere and at everyone - it's like letting the kids loose in a ball pit! A "backyard" resembles segments of the *Blue's Clues* show, and Rugrats characters are often on hand to greet young visitors.

As Universal Studios is synonymous with quality productions, the live shows here are entertaining and highlighted with special effects. Animal Planet Live employs a lot of humor with a variety of well-trained animals. Waterworld, the "coolest" production here, has explosive stunts and special effects that blow you out of the water. Terminator 2: 3-D mostly follows the storyline of the *Terminator 2* movie. This version is very intense, often violent, definitely action-packed, and a combination of a 3-D action movie projected onto a huge screen and live actors that pop in and out of the scenery. In a castle-like building plays Shrek 4-D, a fifteen-minute animated show that incorporates quite a few special effects to keep participants really feeling a part of the presentation, right down to their theater seats. The twenty-minute Spiderman Rocks features the real-life comic book hero in high-flying stunts while fighting the Green Goblin, plus singing, dancing, and pyrotechnics. Some of Universal's shows are seasonal, and/or performed on weekends and holidays only.

Get an early start for your adventure at Universal Studios, and don't forget to bring your camera for some wonderful photo opportunities. Check out the adjacent UNIVERSAL CITYWALK (pg. 140), for unusual shopping and dining experiences.

If you're interested in "edutainment," ask about the educational and the recreational programs. Third through twelfth grade students are introduced to a variety of subjects which incorporate lesson plans on location or technical tours. Field trips here could include learning about dinosaurs, sound effects, and careers in advertising and entertainment. Other programs include assemblies at Universal for seventh through twelfth graders, where speakers and one-hour live performances address important issues facing today's youth. Both the field trips and the programs invited students to spend the remainder of the day at Universal Studios. The recreational programs are pretty much student discount days. Call (800) 959-9688 / www.universalstudios.com/education for more information on these programs.

Hours: Open the majority of the year daily, 9am - 6pm. Summer hours are Mon. - Fri., 9am - 9pm; Sat. - Sun., 9am - 10pm. Call to verify the hours for the day of your visit. Tours in Spanish are available Sat. and Sun. Closed Thanksgiving and Christmas.

Admission: $47 for adults; $45 for seniors; $37 for ages 3 - 9; children 2 and under are free. Certain discounts available through AAA. Parking is $8. Annual passes are a really good deal here. In the beginning of the year, Universal sometimes offers buy-a-day, get-a-year-free deal. The educational programs range from $25 - $35 per person.

Ages: 3 years and up.

-----*ARTS AND CRAFTS*-----

CERAMIC ART SPACE

(888) CERAMIX (237-2649) or (818) 752-9767 / www.ceramicartspace.com

12532 Riverside Drive, Studio City

$$$$

(Going W. on Ventura Fwy [101], exit N. on Laurel Canyon, L. on Riverside Dr. Going E. on 101, exit N. on Coldwater Canyon, R. on Riverside Dr. [TG: 562 F3])

This older ceramic store is one of our favorite places to paint ceramic and plastercraft pieces because of the selection and the price. (i.e. The place is packed with inventory and there is no hourly fee.) Choose from ornaments, plates, mugs, banks, figurines, and lots more. Sit at a table and use the paints, brushes, smocks, etc. for your take-home masterpiece. Products range from clay, greenware, bisque, and plaster to kiln supplies, glazes, ceramic pens, and ceramic crayons. Note: The store sells prepackaged kits so kids can take an item home. It also sells paints, brushes, and everything else needed to complete their project. Buy a kit for a friend, too and share the messy fun!

Hours: Open Tues. - Sat., 10:30am - 5pm; Sun., 11am - 4pm. Closed Mon.
Admission: Items range from $3 - $90, plus $6 for glazing. There is no hourly fee.
Ages: 4 years and up.

CLAY BISQUE

(310) 316-5669
1704 S. Catalina Avenue, Redondo Beach
(Exit Harbor Fwy [110] W. on Pacific Coast Hwy., L. on Ave I (second L. after Palos Verdes Blvd.), L. on Catalina. [TG: 792 J1])

This airy, paint-it-yourself ceramic art studio is located on a main shopping strip, not far from the beach. The small intimate setting, coupled with brightly colored walls and high and low tables (for kids) adds up to a friendly atmosphere. The selection of ceramic items ranges from cups, plates, and picture frames to knickknacks, tiles, vases, and everything in between. Included in the per-hour price are unlimited usage of paints, glaze, brushes, sponges, stencils, and assistance. After glazing, your piece will be ready in about three days for pick up.

Hours: Open Mon. - Wed., 10am - 7pm; Thurs. - Sat., 10am - 9pm; Sun., noon - 5pm.
Admission: The price of your item, which ranges between $3 - $30, plus $5.50 per hour for adults, pro-rated every 15 minutes after the first hour; $4 per hour for children 10 and under. Ask about special rates on certain dates and hours. Metered street parking is available.
Ages: 4 years and up.

CLAY CLUB

(818) 716-6340 / www.clayclub.com
20929 Ventura Boulevard, Woodland Hills
(Exit Ventura Fwy [101] S. on DeSoto, R. on Ventura and into the first shopping center on the R. [TG: 560 C2])

Come to this inviting store to make a keepsake designed with a personal touch. Figurines, frames, mugs, and vases are just some of the items to choose from in painting your own ceramic masterpiece. Be prepared to spend some time here - it takes kids (and adults) a while to choose what they want to paint and to then actually paint it. But what a fun time to share together! Ask about their art, mosaic, and decoupage classes.

Hours: Open daily, 10am - 6pm; open Thurs. until 9pm.
Admission: The cost of the item, plus a flat studio fee of $7 for adults; $5 for ages 14 and under.
Ages: 4 years and up.

COLOR ME MINE (Los Angeles County)

(877) COLOR ME (265-6763) - for a listing of all locations. Beverly Hills - (310) 247-1226; Encino - (818) 784-0400; Ladera Heights - (310) 310-9700; Long Beach - (562) 433-4177; Los Angeles - (323) 465-1680; North Hollywood - (818) 505-2112; Pasadena - (626) 844-7173; Santa Monica - (310) 393-0069; Studio City - (818) 762-4434; Torrance - (310) 325-9968; and Whittier - (562) 789-5600. / www.colormemine.com

Do your kids have an artistic flair? Or think they do? Color Me Mine is a delightful, cozy, paint-your-own ceramic store. Kids can express themselves by first choosing their own ceramic piece, and then their own palette. White dinosaurs, dolphins, mugs, plates, and more will be transformed into vibrant works of art that will be treasured forever, or at least a while. My boys were so intent on their artistry that the hours just flew by. Warning: This recreational activity can become quite addicting! Pieces are glazed and fired, then ready to be picked up in a day or two. Each store has a computer that has 25,000 drawings that can be printed out and traced.

Some stores also offer wood works and iron works. Note: The Encino and San Diego stores offer glass works and mosaics. Ask about Color Me Mine's specialty classes. My kids took an eight-week class in the Long Beach store that focused on master painters. The kids learned who the painter was and about his/her style, then they painted plates according to that style. Other series of classes focus on geography around the world, endangered animals, and more.

Hours: Most stores are open Sun. - Thurs., 11am - 10pm; Fri. - Sat., 11am - 11pm.
Admission: Prices for mugs and vases start at $6. Painting rates fluctuate depending on the store; some charge $10 for the day for adults and $6 for ages 11 and under, while others charge by the hour, usually $6 for adults and $4 for kids.
Ages: 4 years and up.

KAR-LAN'S KRAFTS

(661) 251-7924 $$$$
17743 Sierra Highway, Canyon Country
(Exit Golden State Fwy [5] N. on Antelope Valley Fwy [14], N. on Via Princessa, R. on Sierra Hwy. [TG: 4552 A1])

Kids kan kultivate their kreativity at Kar-Lan's Krafts. Both plastercraft and ceramics are available to paint and glaze at this roomy and well-lit krafts store. Please note that plastercraft items are more fragile than ceramic pieces, but they are also less expensive. This is a wonderful way to spend an hour or so together!

Hours: Open Tues., 10am - 5:30pm; Wed. - Thurs., 10:30am - 9pm; Fri. - Sat., 11am - 5pm. Closed Sun. and Mon.
Admission: Prices start at $2 for a piece of unfinished art, plus $5 a day for paint and brushes. Firing costs extra, depending on the size of the piece.
Ages: 4 years and up.

PAINT A DREAM

(661) 274-7800 $$$$
39332 10th Street West, Palmdale
(Going N. on Antelope Valley Fwy [14], exit W. on Ave 'P', L. on 10th St. W. Going S. on 14, exit S. on 10th St W. It's in the shopping center. [TG: 4195 G6])

Tucked away in an expansive shopping center, artists (and even the artistically challenged) can paint their own dreams choosing from a large variety of ceramic pieces. Paints and brushes, plus the tools to stencil, trace, or sponge are all included in the price. Take an hour or two, or take all day and get creative. The glazed and fired pieces are ready for pick up after just a few days. Ask about children's classes and birthday parties.

Hours: Open Mon. - Thurs., 11am - 8pm; Fri. - Sat., 11am - 9pm; Sun., 11am - 7pm.
Admission: The price of the piece plus a $6 flat fee for adults; $4 for ages 10 and under.
Ages: 4 years and up.

SANTA MONICA MUDD

(310) 315-9155 / www.smmudd.com $$$$$
2918 Santa Monica Boulevard, suite 2, Santa Monica
(Exit San Diego Fwy [405] W. on Santa Monica Blvd. [TG: 631 H6])

Make mirror frames, masks, sculptures, mugs, plates, and more out of clay, then paint it, and have it fired. Walk-ins are welcome, but taking a series of classes, based on a once-a-week, four-week program, is highly recommended as most projects take more than just a day to create and finish. Fees include materials, including paints, plus instruction and the usage of the pottery wheel, if desired. After-school programs are available.

Hours: Kid's classes are offered after school. Call for a schedule.

Admission: $35 - $40 per class for adults; $100 for a series of four classes for kids. Walk-ins pay $25 for one hour; $40 for two hours.

Ages: Children must be at least 8 years old.

SWIRLRAMICS

(562) 425-3553 / www.esitemakers.com/swirlramics/swirlramics.html

4154 Norse Way, Long Beach

(Exit Artesia Fwy [91] S. on Lakewood Blvd., L. on Norse Way. [TG: 766 A6])

Swirls, twirls, stripes, or dots - at Swirlramics you can paint your own ceramic piece any way you want. Although the store is intimate (i.e. small), the prices are reasonable and the selection is terrific. We perused dragon cups, sunflower picture frames, car banks, a wide variety of figurines, bowls, and lots more. If your time (and/or money) is tight, a shelf contains small ceramic items that can be purchased and painted relatively quickly for only $5, inclusive. Tip: Ask about monthly specials or sale items.

Need direction on decorating your item? Stencils and carbon paper are some of the available artistic aids. As there is a flat rate charged to paint - brushes, a colorful array of paints, and glazing are included in the price - you can stay for hours and not feel rushed!

Hours: Open Tues - Thurs., 12:30pm - 8pm, Fri., 12:30pm - 9pm; Sat., 11am -9pm; Sun., 11am - 4pm. Closed Mon.

Admission: The price of the item plus $8 per painter. Ask about weekday specials.

Ages: 4 years and up.

-----BEACHES-----

CABRILLO BEACH

(310) 548-2645 or (310) 548-7554 / www.sanpedro.com

3720 Stephen M White Drive, San Pedro

(Take Harbor Fwy [110] to the end, L. on Gaffey St., L. on 9th St., R. on Pacific Ave., almost to the end, L. on 36th St., which turns into Stephen M White Dr. [TG: 854 C2])

This sometimes windy beach has a gated entrance, wonderful sandy stretches, a playground, picnic tables, a snack bar, rock jetties to climb out on, a short fishing pier, and several fire rings. Beyond the breakwater is ocean surf; inside the breakwater is a gentle harbor. The water quality is not always the best, however. A paved, wheelchair-accessible trail runs from the parking lot to the aquarium, across the beach, and to the water's edge at the tidepools. See CABRILLO MARINE AQUARIUM (pg. 179), as this terrific museum is adjacent to the beach (and it's free!). Ask about the seasonal grunion runs.

Hours: Open daily, sunrise - 10:30pm.

Admission: $7 per vehicle in the summer; discounted the rest of the year. Very little street parking is available.

Ages: All

COLORADO LAGOON

(562) 570-3215 / www.lbparks.org

E. Colorado Street & E. Appian Way, Long Beach

(Exit San Diego Fwy [405] S. on Bellflower Blvd., R. on Colorado Blvd. As the road forks, keep along the lagoon on Appian Wy. [TG: 796 B7])

This half-mile stretch of lagoon water is fed through a large pipe from the ocean. The water quality is tested daily and usually deemed good, except after rain. Kids can swim the length of the lagoon, or a much shorter distance across it, from shore to shore. They can also jump off a wooden dock that spans across the water. Just beyond the sandy beach area is a grassy area. A playground, featuring a large plastic boat, is shaded by a canopy. A few scattered picnic tables, shade trees, and barbecue pits make this an ideal location for a picnic.

Although the lagoon has residential quarters and a fairly busy street on one side of it, and a golf course on the other, we found it to be a relatively quiet place to spend the day. Lifeguards are on duty daily, mid-June through mid-September. See the Calendar entry (pg. 583) for information on the Colorado Lagoon Model Boat Shop for a first-rate, boat-building opportunity.

Hours: Open daily, 8am - dusk.

Admission: Free

Ages: All

LEO CARRILLO STATE BEACH

(805) 986-8591 or (805) 488-1827 - state beach; (818) 880-0350 - camping info; (800) 444-7275 - camping reservations / parks.ca.gov

36000 Pacific Coast Highway, Malibu

(Exit Ventura Fwy [101] S. on Westlake Blvd. [Hwy 23], which turns into Mulholland Hwy., which turns into Decker Rd. Go to the end, and turn R. on Pacific Coast Hwy. [TG: 626 B6])

Leo Carrillo combines the best of everything that's enjoyable about the beach - a beautiful, sandy beach; good swimming and surfing; sea caves to carefully explore; tidepools; a playground; lifeguards; and nature trails. Camping near the beach (campsites are a five-minute walk from the beach) makes this one of our favorite campgrounds. Each campsite has a fire pit and picnic table. Pack a sweater!

Hours: Open daily, 7am - dusk.

Admission: $5 per vehicle for day use. Camping is $12 a night, plus a $7.50 camping reservation fee. There are no hook-ups.

Ages: All

MARINA BEACH or "MOTHER'S BEACH"

(562) 570-3215 or (562) 431-6866 / www.greaterlongbeachrc.org

5839 Appian Way, Long Beach

(Take San Gabriel River Fwy [605] to Garden Grove Fwy [22] W., exit on Studebaker and eventually head S., R. on Westminster, R. on Appian Way, which is just over a bridge. It's across from the Long Beach Marina. [TG: 826 D2])

This beach is aptly nicknamed because it is a mother/child hang out. There are waveless waters in this lagoon-type setting, lifeguards, a nice grassy playground, and barbecues. Single and double kayak rentals are available daily during the summer, and weekends only the rest of the year.

Hours: Open daily, sunrise - 10:30pm.

Admission: Bring either lots of quarters for parking - 25¢ for each half hour - or get here early to park on the street for free. Kayak rentals are $5 an hour for a single; $15 an hour for a double.

Ages: All

MOTHER'S BEACH

(310) 306-3344 / beaches.co.la.ca.us

4142 Via Marina/Washington, Marina Del Rey

(Exit the San Diego Fwy [405] W. on Washington, L. on Via Marina. It's in back of the Cheesecake Factory. [TG: 671 J7])

This tiny patch of waveless water where younger children can swim is adjacent to a large marina. A half circle of sand has play equipment, such as a big play boat, several swings, a tire swing, and slides. There are numerous picnic tables set up under a covered area right on the beach, near volleyball nets. It's pleasant scenery. Tip: A visit to the adjoining Cheesecake Factory makes it an extra fun (and tasty) excursion.

Hours: Open daily, sunrise - sunset.

Admission: Free. Parking is about $2.75.

Ages: Toddler to 8 years old.

ROYAL PALMS STATE BEACH

beaches.co.la.ca.us

Western Avenue and Paseo Del Mar, San Pedro

(Take Harbor Fwy [110] to the end, continue S. on Gaffey St., R. on 25th St., L. on Western to the end. [TG: 853 G1])

Park on the top of the bluff or drive down to the "beach." I put this word in quotes because there is precious little sand here, as the shoreline is composed of tons of rocks. Numerous tidepools are just beyond the parking lot, so you'll have a great day of exploring and searching for small marine organisms. My boys, of course, also loved climbing out on the rocks and the jetty. Note: A lifeguard is on duty here, too. Tip: Come during low tide. We've also come during high tide, though, and watched the waves slam into the rocks and shoot high into the sky. Bring your camera!

One side of the beach has a cement patio with picnic tables (and restrooms) under the palm trees (hence the name of the park) that are snug up against the cliffs - very picturesque.

Hours: Open daily, sunrise - sunset.
Admission: Free, although a toll booth is located here, too.
Ages: 4 years and up.

SEASIDE LAGOON

(310) 318-0681 / www.redondo.org/depts/recreation/facilities
200 Portofino Way, Redondo Beach
(Exit San Diego Fwy [405] S. on Western, R. on 190th St., which turns into Anita St., which then turns into Herondo St., L. on Harbor Dr. It's on the S.W. corner of Harbor Dr. and Portofino Way. Park in the lot on Harbor Blvd. [TG: 762 H4])

Have a swimmingly good time at the gated, Seaside Lagoon. This large saltwater lagoon, next to an ocean inlet and rock jetties, is heated by a nearby steam generating plant, so the average water temperature is seventy-five degrees. Warm waveless waters, plus a lifeguard, make it an ideal swimming spot for little ones. A large water fountain sprays out water in the shallow end of the lagoon and there are a few slides in the deeper end. There is also a beach area, grass areas that ring the sand, playgrounds with a big plastic pirate ship and swings, barbecues, picnic tables, and volleyball courts. Tips: Bring your own beach chair and pack a picnic lunch. An easily-accessible snack bar is sponsored by Ruby's. Several other restaurants are in the immediate vicinity.

Hours: Open Memorial Day through Labor Day daily, 10am - 5:45pm. Open in September on weekends only, 10am - 5:45pm.
Admission: $4 for adults; $3 for ages 2 - 17; children under 2 are free. Parking is $3 with validation.
Ages: All

VENICE BEACH

(310) 399-2775 / www.laparks.org
1800 Ocean Front Walk, between Washington Boulevard and Rose Avenue, Venice
(Exit San Diego Fwy [405] W. on Venice Blvd. Park at the end of Venice or Washington blvds., or in lots along Speedway. [TG: 671 G6])

I think Southern California's reputation of being offbeat, quirky, funky, etc., comes directly from Venice Beach. This area actually has a three-mile stretch of beach, but visitors come here mainly to gawk at and mingle with the eclectic Venice population of street performers. They include jugglers (one juggler specializes in chain saws), musicians, artists, magicians, mimes, and fortune tellers, as well as people sporting unusual and colorful haircuts, and numerous tattoos, plus bikini-clad women (and men), skaters, and more - self expression reigns. Two hot spots here are Muscle Beach, where weight lifters of all levels pump iron, and the International Chess Park. This park, south of Santa Monica pier and north of Venice pier, has rows of picnic tables where players run the gamut of older, scruffy-looking men to teens in street clothing. Watch and learn strategies as players compete in traditional play or speed chess. Venice Beach also has a bike path, playground, basketball courts, pagodas, volleyball courts, handball courts, shuffleboard, souvenir shops, a boardwalk, and restaurants. A cement skate park is here, too, complete with bowl, ramps, rails, and other street elements. A helmet and pads are required in the skate park.

Hours: Open daily, sunrise - sunset.
Admission: Free, although parking may cost.
Ages: All

ZUMA BEACH

beaches.co.la.ca.us

30000 Pacific Coast Highway, Malibu

(Exit the Ventura Fwy [101] S. on Kanan Rd., which turns in to Kanan Dume Rd. Take this to the end and turn R on P.C.H. [TG: 667 C3])

This is one of the busiest and biggest beaches in Southern California. Besides the miles of sand, good swimming, lifeguard stations, volleyball courts, a swing set, and ample parking, these ocean waters are often home to schools of dolphins that ride the waves.

Hours: Open daily, sunrise - sunset.
Admission: $5 per vehicle.
Ages: All

-----*EDIBLE ADVENTURES*-----

BEN BOLLINGER'S CANDLELIGHT PAVILION

(909) 626-1254 / www.candlelightpavilion.com

455 W. Foothill Boulevard, Claremont

See the entry for BEN BOLLINGER'S CANDLELIGHT PAVILION on page 142 for details.

BENIHANA OF TOKYO (Los Angeles County)

Beverly Hills - (323) 655-7311; City of Industry - (626) 912-8784; Encino - (818) 788-7121;
Santa Monica - (310) 260-1423; Torrance - (310) 316-7777 / www.benihana.com

Beverly Hills - 38 N. La Cienega Boulevard; City of Industry - 17877 Gale Avenue; Encino - 16226 Ventura Boulevard; Santa Monica - 1447 Fourth Street; Torrance - 21327 Hawthorne Boulevard

Enjoy the "show" and the food at Benihana. With their choreographed cooking, the chefs prepare the food on a grill right in front of you, hibachi-style. Knives flash as the food is chopped up seemingly in mid-air, as well as on the frying table, with lightning speed - this is the show part. (Don't try this at home.) Although my kids are not normally prone to trying new foods, they readily taste new entrees here because the food is fixed in such an intriguing way!

The atmosphere is unique. The choices of food includes chicken, seafood, steak and fresh vegetables. Sushi is also available. The communal tables seat up to ten people. Adult lunch prices range from $8.50 to $16; dinners, from $17 to $32. Kids' meals range from $6.50 to $8 for a choice of chicken, teriyaki steak, or shrimp. Their meals also come with soup or salad, shrimp appetizer, rice, and ice cream. Several Benihana locations have a koi pond and a traditional Japanese arched bridge as part of their outside decor.

Hours: Most locations are open daily for lunch, 11:30am - 2pm; for dinner, 5pm - 10:30pm.
Ages: 5 years and up.

THE CANDY FACTORY

(818) 766-8220

12508 Magnolia Boulevard, N. Hollywood

(Exit Ventura Fwy [101] N. on Laurel Canyon Blvd., L. on Magnolia. The cross street is Whitsett. [TG: 562 F2])

How sweet it is! The Candy Factory is one of the largest and oldest candy-making suppliers on the West Coast. The store does not actually have a lot of the finished product to purchase, but it has an abundance of the supplies needed, such as a wide variety of molds, flavorings, chocolates (to melt), and lollipop sticks. Hour-and-a-half candy-making classes are offered for families on Saturdays three times a month. Classes often focus on a theme that the whole family can work on together, such as making a chocolate house, trimmed with assorted candies ($30 per house); creating chocolate heart-shaped boxes and chocolates to fit in them for Valentine's Day ($17.50 per box); and concocting a bouquet of chocolate flowers for Mother's Day ($25). Note: This type of candy-making doesn't involve the use of an oven, so it's a safe project for most ages.

Groups of fifteen to forty people can create edible projects to take home on weekdays. Groups can request a particular theme and learn additional parts of the candy business, such as making clusters and soft centers, hand-dipped candies, and more. Prices begin at $12.50 per person. Two-hour birthday parties are people-pleasers as the kids get deliciously messy making about a dozen candies, using molds and candy coatings, to sample and bring home. Cake and punch (more sugar!) are also included in the $17.50 per-child price. My children offered (begged) to live at the Factory for a while - imagine that!

Hours: The store is open Mon. - Fri., 10am - 5pm; Sat., 10am - 4pm. Open Sun. for private parties only. Closed major holidays. Family classes are offered on Sat. afternoons. Call to schedule a group class.

Admission: Some prices are listed above - call for more information.

Ages: 6 years and up.

CARNEY'S

$$$

Studio City - (818) 761-8300; West Hollywood - (323) 654-8300 / www.carneytrain.com

Studio City - 12601 Ventura Blvd.; West Hollywood - 8351 Sunset Blvd

(Studio City: Exit Ventura Fwy [101] S. on Laurel Canyon Blvd., R. on Ventura. [TG: 562 F5] West Hollywood: From Hollywood Fwy [101], exit W. on Sunset Blvd. From Santa Monica Fwy [10], exit N. on La Cienega, R. on Sunset. [TG: 593 A5])

Railroad the kids and take them to Carney's for a bite to eat on board passenger train cars. The West Hollywood location has a 1920's Union Pacific dining car. The Studio City location has two 1940's train cars and a caboose. Grab a burger ($3.95), hot dog ($1.65), chicken breast filet sandwich ($3.60), beef or chicken soft taco ($1.75 each), or tuna melt ($3.60).

Hours: Open daily, 11am. Closing times vary from 10pm - 2am.

Admission: Prices listed above.

Ages: All

CHUCK E. CHEESE

$$$

Check your yellow pages or this website for a local listing. / www.chuckecheese.com

These popular indoor eateries and play lands for young kids offer token-taking kiddie rides and video and arcade games, as well as the all-important prize redemption centers. Many facilities also have play areas with tubes, slides, and ball pits. Chuck E. Cheese, the costumed rat mascot, is usually walking around giving hugs and high fives. An electronic version of Chuck E. performs several stage shows throughout the day.

Every child's favorite food is served here - pizza! A large pizza is between $14 to $18, and a one-time trip to the salad bar is about $3.50. All purchases come with a few tokens, but kids always want more. Bring in their report cards (especially if they have good grades!) to redeem for extra tokens and check out the website for on-line coupons. Note: This place is often noisy at peak lunch and dinner times, especially on weekends when crowds descend.

Hours: Most locations are open Sun. - Thurs., 10am - 10pm; Fri. - Sat., 10am - 11pm. Call for a particular location's hours.

Admission: Free admission, but count on spending money on pizza and tokens.

Ages: 2 - 11 years.

DALE'S DINER

$$$

(562) 425-7285

4339 E. Carson Street, Long Beach

(Exit Riverside Fwy [91] S. on Lakewood Blvd., L. on Carson St. It's on the corner of Carson and Norse Way. [TG: 766 A6])

Hey daddy-o! This small 50's diner is a really happenin' place. It's decorated with black and white checkered tile floor, turquoise vinyl seats, and a few special booths that look like they were made from the back section of cars from this era. Each table has its own small jukebox. At 25¢ for two songs, your kids can now be introduced to such classics as *Chantilly Lace* and *Purple People Eater*.

For breakfast, try a five-egg omelette stuffed with bacon and cheese and served with hash browns or fruit, and toast or a cinnamon roll, for $6.85. Blueberry flapjacks ($4.85) or cinnamon raisin french toast ($4.85) make tasty morning choices, too. Kids' meals, for ages 9 and younger, include two oreo pancakes (about $4.50), or one egg and one pancake and a piece of bacon ($3.25). The lunch and dinner menu offers a Cobb salad ($7.95), pork chops ($7.95), sirloin tip steak kabob ($7.95), deli sandwiches (average $7), hamburgers (average $6), and more. Top off your meal with a chocolate, vanilla, or cherry soda. Kids can choose a burger and fries, grilled cheese with fries, chili, or a pepperoni pizza for about $3.95. Beverages are extra. Come in just for dessert sometime and try a piece of fresh-baked pie ($3.25), or a scrumptious Brownie Saturday, which is alternating layers of brownies with vanilla ice cream, topped with hot fudge and whipped cream ($4.95).

Hours: Open Mon. - Fri., 6am - 10; Sat. - Sun., 7am - 10pm. Closed Christmas.
Ages: All

EMERALD BBQ GARDEN

(310) 534-5492

$$$$

2795 Pacific Coast Highway in Airport Plaza, Torrance

(Exit San Pedro Fwy [110] W. on Pacific Coast Highway. It's one block west of Crenshaw Blvd. [TG: 793 F4])

The phrase "have it your way" takes on a new meaning at this Korean-style barbeque buffet restaurant that features interactive dining. For lunch, choose from marinated portions of beef, pork, chicken, and beef ribs. Dinner selections also include crab legs, rib eye steak, shrimp, fish, and more exotic items such as beef tongue and octopus. (Might as well be adventuresome!) Cook these items on a grill that's built into the middle of your table. While the main course is grilling, go back to buffet tables to fill up your plate with sushi, white rice, tempura, noodles, salads, pastas, soups, fresh fruit, Jell-O, and soft serve ice cream. Parents, this is a night off from cooking, kind of.

Hours: Open daily, 11am - 10pm.
Admission: Lunch during the week for adults is $8.95; Sat. - Sun., it's $11.95. Daily lunch prices for kids are $5.95 for ages 8 -12; $3.95 for ages 5 - 7; children 4 and under are free. Dinner is $15.95 for adults; $7.95 for ages 8 - 12; $5.95 for ages 5 - 7; children 4 and under are free. Beverages are extra.
Ages: 4 years and up.

ENCOUNTER RESTAURANT

(310) 215-5151

$$$$

209 World Way, Los Angeles

(Exit Century Fwy [105] N. on Sepulveda Blvd. and follow the signs that say "arrivals." It's at L.A.X. [airport]. [TG: 702 F5])

Seemingly from a galaxy far, far away comes (a close) Encounter Restaurant that looks like a space station. It is located at the hub of the Los Angeles airport. Earthlings need to take the elevator, with its mood lighting and other-worldly music, up to the restaurant which overlooks the immediate L.A. area. Note: The nighttime ambiance is almost surreal as hundreds of twinkling lights fill the skyline.

I can't decide if the interior decor, designed by Walt Disney Engineering, is futuristic or from the 60's. The carpet's predominant colors are lime green, dark red, and blue. The booths are white and oblong. The ceiling has blue and purple lights shining through oval and odd-shaped holes. My boys and I sat around the bar and were entertained by the lava lamps. (We are easily amused!) The servers used hand held drink dispensers shaped like laser guns (even emitting lights and sounds). A main attraction in this circular restaurant is the windows which are slanted outward, from the floor to the ceiling. Although looking down out the window made me dizzy, my boys thought it was cool (and a little scary).

The food (and prices) are out of this world. The lunch menu includes fried calamari ($11), turkey club sandwich ($11.50), grilled Ahi tuna steak sandwich ($15.50), linguini with tiger shrimp ($25.50), or pan roasted chicken breast with rice and sauteed spinach ($21.95). Dinner entrees include the linguini or chicken breast or open-faced steak sandwich ($17), grilled salmon fillet ($27), twelve-ounce New York steak ($29), and more. Sophisticated children's meals included linguine ($8), filet of beef ($10), or chicken breast ($11). Desserts are $8 and include a choice of vanilla creme brulee with a chocolate dipped cookie, or white chocolate and cranberry brioche bread pudding.

Hours: The restaurant is open daily, 11am - 4pm for lunch; 4pm - 5pm for cocktails and a light dinner. Open for dinner Sun. - Thurs., 5pm - 10pm; Fri. - Sat., 5pm - 11pm.
Admission: Prices are mentioned above.
Ages: 3 years and up.

FAIR OAKS PHARMACY AND SODA FOUNTAIN

(626) 799-1414 / www.fairoakspharmacy.net

$$

1526 Mission Street, Pasadena

(Exit the Pasadena Fwy [110] S. on Fair Oaks Blvd., R. on Mission. [TG: 595 H2])

Fair Oaks is a small "store" with a quaint ambiance, located in the midst of Old Town Pasadena, which has lots of shops and restaurants. It is part pharmacy, that also sells retro collectables, jewelry, and home accents, and part 1900's restaurant and soda fountain, complete with a marble counter top and antique fixtures. Both sides of the store are decorated with memorabilia, unique toys, and fun stuff to look at.

Lunch items include grilled chicken sandwiches ($7.50), deli sandwiches ($6.96), burgers ($6.25), chili cheese dogs ($4.95), and either chicken Caesar salads or Cobb salads ($7.95). Now for the good stuff - dessert. Ask the soda jerk (who is actually quite nice) to fix you an old-fashioned phosphate ($1.95); a chocolate, pineapple, or raspberry ice cream soda ($3.95); a clown sundae ($2.95); a hot fudge brownie topped with ice cream and whipped cream ($5.50); or a specialty drink, like a New York egg cream ($1.95). There is a small eating area inside, as well as a few tables and chairs outside.

Hours: Open Mon. - Fri., 11am - 9pm; Sat., 11am - 10pm; Sun., 11pm - 7pm. Lunch is served Sun. - Fri., 11am - 5pm; Sat., 11am - 7pm. Closed Easter, Thanksgiving, and Christmas.
Admission: Prices are mentioned above.
Ages: All

FARMERS MARKET

(323) 933-9211 / www.farmersmarketla.com

!/$$

6333 W. 3rd Street, Los Angeles

(Going S. on Hollywood Fwy [101], exit S. on Vermont Ave., R. on 3rd. Going N. on 101, exit E. on Beverly Blvd., L. on Vermont, R. on 3rd. From the Santa Monica Fwy [10], exit N. on Fairfax. From the San Diego Fwy [405], exit E. on Santa Monica Blvd., R. on Wilshire Blvd., L. on Robertson Blvd., R. on 3rd. It's on the corner of Fairfax and 3rd. [TG: 633 B1])

This unique outdoor market, originally founded in 1934 and almost unchanging in its "small-town" ambiance, is an eclectic mixture of more than sixty fresh food and produce vendors, and over twenty kitchens that make and sell all sorts of homemade domestic and international favorites. The market can be crowded, but it is a fun place to shop or enjoy lunch. Patrons can order their favorite ethnic food and eat at an outdoor table. Kids love stopping by Littlejohn's English Toffee House stall to watch (and sample) mouth-watering candy being made. At Magee's House of Nuts, they can see peanuts steadily pouring into a large machine behind glass, being churned around to make very fresh-tasting peanut butter. Across the way from the main marketplace, more than sixty-five retail stores offer unique clothing items and specialty gifts. See the entry for THE GROVE (pg. 73), for details about the uptown mall just across the road.

Hours: Open Mon. - Fri., 9am - 9pm; Sat., 9am - 8pm; Sun., 10am - 7pm. Closed major holidays.
Admission: Free, but bring spending money.
Ages: 2½ years and up.

FARMER'S MARKETS

www.cafarmersmarkets.org; www.cafarmersmarkets.com; www.farmersmarkets.net; www.farmernet.com

Many cities host a weekly farmer's market. These markets usually consist of open-air (outside) booths set up for customers to purchase fresh produce, bakery goods, meats, and more - taste the difference! Freshly-cut flowers are often available, too, as is entertainment of some sort. Indulge yourself and let your kids pick out a "new" foods to try. We think the food and ambiance of a market is much more enticing than a grocery store. Call your local city hall or chamber of commerce or check the above websites to see if there is a farmer's market near you. Here are just a few of the cities that I know of that host a market: Beverly Hills, Burbank, Calabasas, Coronado, Costa Mesa, Culver City, Encino, Gardena, Julian, Long Beach, Los Angeles, Malibu, Mission Valley, Monrovia, Montrose, Northridge, Ocean Beach, Oceanside (with llama rides!), Ojai, Oxnard, Pacific Beach, Palm Springs, Pasadena, Pomona, Redondo Beach, Riverside, San Dimas, Santa Barbara, Santa Maria, Santa Monica, Studio City, Temecula, Tustin, Ventura, Vista, Westwood, and Woodland Hills.

FRILLS

(626) 303-3201
504 S. Myrtle Avenue, Monrovia
(Exit Foothill Fwy [210] N. on Myrtle Ave. [TG: 567 G4])

$$$$

Entering through the doors of Frills is like taking a step back in time. The front Victorian boutique sells vintage clothing and a variety of hats, plus gift items like cards and unusual buttons.

The back part of Frills is a tea room. If you feel inappropriately attired, choose a feather boa and/or a glamorous hat from the dress-up trunk. What fun! The room is charmingly decorated with lacy tablecloths, old-fashioned clothing and hats, and tea sets that are for sale. There are over forty types of tea to choose from, with cinnamon vanilla and cherry being the two most popular with the younger set. Order a meal fit for a king with King's Tea, which includes a hearty meat pie or sausage roll, a variety of tea sandwiches, fresh fruit, cheese, dessert, and of course, tea - $15.50. Other teas (meals) fit for a queen, princess, or peasant are available. Children's Tea - a peanut butter sandwich, shortbread, fresh fruit, and tea, costs $10.50. Ask about Frills' special children's programs. Reservations for all teas are recommended.

    Hours: Open Tues. - Sat., 11am - 4pm; Fri., 11am - 7:30pm. Closed Sun. and Mon.
Admission: Prices range from $10.50 - $15.50.
    Ages: 4 years and up.

FRISCO'S CAR HOP DINER (City of Industry)

(626) 913-FOOD (3663) / www.friscos.com
18065 Gale Avenue, City of Industry
(Exit Pomona Fwy [60] N. on Fullerton Rd., L. on Gale. [TG: 678 J4])

$$$

Pop quiz: What are skateresses? Answer: Waitresses on skates! Frisco's has them and lots more. The restaurant's prominent colors are hot pink and cool turquoise, along with white and black checked flooring. The walls and ceilings are painted blue with clouds that feature artists from the 50's (i.e. Jimmy Dean, Elvis, Marilyn Monroe, and others) with wings, as in heavenly angels. There are also some neon thunderbolts and a few 3-D images popping out. Other decor includes parking meters, traffic signals, dice, drive-in movie speakers, a juke box, and an old gas pump. Many of the booths have the front or back end of a car incorporated in them.

The food is a combination of American and Greek, served in a fifties-themed restaurant - and somehow it works! Breakfast selections include three eggs, bacon or sausage, home fries or hash browns or fresh fruit, a toast or muffin for about $5.50; ribeye steak and eggs, $7.50; breakfast burrito, $5.95; and Belgian waffles, $4.50. Kids 12 years and under can choose from two pancakes or french toast, eggs, and bacon or sausage plus a small drink for $3.95. Lunch options include a variety of burgers starting at $5.25; Greek salad, $6.95; pepperoni pizza, $5.95; turkey avocado melt, $6.95; chicken souvlaki, $6.75; beef fajita pita, $6.50, and more. Kid's meal are $4.95 for a choice of burger, hot dog or corn dog, chicken strips, or grilled cheese, plus fries and a soft drink. Adult dinner choices, which are served with soup or salad, baked potato or rice or french fries, vegetable, and either garlic bread or pita bread, include half rack baby back ribs, $9.95; Grecian platter for two, $23.95; spaghetti with meat balls, $6.95; chicken or beef shish kabob, $10.95; and a carne asada burrito, $6.95. Desserts include blueberry sundaes, $4.45; hot fudge and banana sundae, $4.50; and freezes and floats, $3.95. Keep on cruisin'! Note: There is another Frisco's in Downey.

    Hours: Open Sun. - Thurs., 7am - 10pm; Fri. - Sat., 7am - midnight. Ask about specials.
Admission: Menu prices are mentioned above.
    Ages: All

FRISCO'S CAR HOP DINER (Downey)

(562) 928-FOOD (3663) / www.friscos.com   *$$$*

12050 Woodruff Avenue, Downey

(From the Glenn Anderson Fwy [105], exit N. on Bellflower Blvd., R. on Imperial Hwy, L. on Woodruff. From the San Gabriel River Fwy [605], exit W on Imperial, R. on Woodruff. [TG: 706 D7])

   See the entry for FRISCO'S CAR HOP DINER (City of Industry) on page 15 for details. This Downey location is much smaller.

GOSPEL BRUNCH (Hollywood)

(323) 848-5100 / www.hob.com   *$$$$$*

8430 Sunset Boulevard, Hollywood

(From the Hollywood Fwy [101], exit W. on Sunset Blvd. From the Santa Monica Fwy [10], exit N. on La Cienega, R. on Sunset. [TG: 593 A5])

   Got the blues? Gospel Brunch at the renown House of Blues is the cure. With its corrugated tin roof and weathered walls this unique building looks (deceptively) like an old shack, like something found in the deep South. The three-story house's eclectic decor consists of bottlecaps imbedded in the walls, folk art done in various mediums, African designs on the wood beams, 3-D reliefs on the ceiling depicting Blues' artists (e.g. Aretha Franklin, Billy Holiday, and others), earth-tone colors mixed with splashes of bright colors, broken-in wooden tables and chairs, and lots more ambiance. The bars also have African masks and other cultural renderings.

   The two-hour gospel brunch is a feast for the body, mind, and spirit. Indulge in eating some of the finest Mississippi Delta cuisine this side of, well, the Mississippi. The buffet includes roast beef, shrimp, biscuits and gravy, fried chicken, macaroni and cheese, omelettes fixed any way you like 'em, mini waffles with a variety of toppings, and desserts. Finger-licking good!

   The food is a precursor to the uplifting, high energy, hour-long concert that follows. The stage is on the first floor with a curtain that resembles a patchwork quilt. Above it are symbols of world religions. The upstairs section actually separates (think parting of the Red Sea) so visitors can look down onto the stage. If you are seated on the second floor towards the buffet area, you can either view the concert on the monitors, or get up and move toward the center railing that oversees the stage. Most people do not remain seated throughout the concert, anyway. They are standing up, dancing around, clapping their hands, singing along, and at times, even joining the musicians on stage.

   Every week features different artists or groups, from traditional ensembles and choirs to contemporary gospel; from nationally known singers to locally famous ones. It's a great way for a family to spend a Sunday afternoon.

   The House of Blues is home to numerous headliner concerts during the week. Check out the BLUES SCHOOLHOUSE (Hollywood) on page 128 for information on a school program.

   Hours: Brunch is every Sun. at 10am and 1pm. On holiday Sun., such as Easter and Mother's Day, it's
                      served at 9:30am, noon, and 2:30pm. Reservations are highly recommended.
   Admission: $33 for adults; $16.50 for ages 6 - 12; children 5 and under are free. Parking is $5.
   Ages: 3 years and up.

GOURMET CAROUSEL RESTAURANT / OCEAN SEA FOOD

(323) 721-0774 - Chinatown Center event planner / www.chinatowncenter.com   *$$$$*

911 N. Broadway / 747 N. Broadway, Los Angeles

(Going N.W. on Hollywood Fwy [101], exit N. on Alameda, L. on Alpine, R. on Broadway. Going S.E. on 101, exit N. on Broadway. [TG: 634 G2])

   Get ready for China Night, a wonderful dinner show that is a cultural and culinary experience offered at least once a month. Dinner begins around 7pm and consist of a delicious nine-course Chinese meal, including soup, orange chicken, shrimp and snowpeas, Chinese pork chops, fried rice, and dessert. The show begins around 8pm. You'll be entertained by colorful folk dances (such as the lion dance), meeting the "Emperor of

China," live instrumental music, and the highlight, the amazing acrobats. The dinner shows are held at the Ocean Sea Food. Admission is $42 for adults; $28 for ages 11 and under. If your birthday is in the month of your visit, you pay only $25, but you need to prove it.

Bruncheons are held at the Gourmet Carousel Restaurant once a month, or so. A nine-course meal is served about 11:30am. Enjoy egg rolls, barbecue pork, orange chicken, fried rice, noodles, broccoli and mushrooms, dessert, and more. A forty-minute show, beginning around 12:30pm, features the lion dance, live music, and Magic Castle magicians. Admission is $25 for adults; $12.50 for ages 11 and under. Look up CHINATOWN TOURS (pg. 160) for information on the educational walking tours combined with lunch and entertainment.

Hours: Call for a schedule. Reservations are suggested.
Admission: Prices are given above.
Ages: 4 years and up.

GRAND CENTRAL MARKET

(213) 624-2378 / www.grandcentralsquare.com
317 S. Broadway Street, Los Angeles
(Exit Hollywood Fwy [101] S. on Spring St., R. on 3rd St., then a quick L. on Hill. The parking structure is between 3rd St. and Hill St. [TG: 634 F4])

This is a fun, aromatic, cultural experience for kids who are used to shopping at a regular grocery store. There are over forty stalls inside this covered structure that spans a city block. Everything from exotic fruits and vegetables to octopus, chicken feet, honeycomb tripe, chiles, fresh tortillas (made on-site), birch bark, shrimp powder, and lambs' heads are sold here. There are also meat stalls, restaurants, and bakeries. Stop here to shop and/or eat on your way to visit other fun and educational places listed in this book!

Hours: Open daily, 9am - 6pm.
Admission: Parking is $1.25 for every fifteen minutes; $8 maximum. Parking is free for an hour if you purchase merchandise worth $10 or more. Closed New Year's Day, Thanksgiving, and Christmas.
Ages: 3 years and up.

HARD ROCK CAFE (Los Angeles County)

Los Angeles - (310) 276-7605; Universal City - (818) 622-7625 / www.hardrock.com
Los Angeles - 8600 Beverly Boulevard; Universal City - 1000 Universal Center Drive, at Universal CityWalk
(Los Angeles: From San Diego Fwy [405], exit E. on Santa Monica Blvd., R. on Beverly Blvd. From Santa Monica Fwy [10], exit N. on La Cienega, L. on Beverly. [TG: 632 J1] Universal City: Going N.W. on Hollywood Fwy [101], exit N. at Universal Center Dr. Going SE on 101, exit at Lankershim Blvd., L. on Cahuenga, L. on Universal Center Dr. [TG: 563 C6])

This has become the "in" place to eat and hang out if you are a rock 'n roll fan. Each Cafe has its own unique memorabilia displayed in glass cases on the walls, but the essence of all the cafes is the same; to pay tribute to music industry legends and the hot artists of today, and promote the environmental motto, "Save the Planet." Hard Rock Cafe is part restaurant and part museum, so before or after your meal take a walk around to see your favorite musician's guitar, record album, or stage costume on exhibit. And, oh yes, rock music is played constantly. Souvenir T-shirts and glasses bearing the Cafe's logo and location (as there are restaurants throughout the world) have become collectible items among Hard Rock Cafe enthusiasts.

The Cafe at UNIVERSAL CITYWALK (see pg. 140), for instance, fetures a gigantic neon electric guitar out front. Inside are numerous guitars (one is covered with snake skin), a few saxophones, a cool-looking '57 Cadillac convertible spinning on a pedestal, a gleaming Harley Davidson motorcycle, gold records, autographed items, and an outfit worn by Elton John.

Menu items include Chinese chicken salad ($9.19), burgers (average $8.50), barbeque ribs ($15), fajitas ($13), T-bone steaks ($18), and sandwiches (average $8.50). Personal dessert favorites include chocolate chip cookie pie ($4.25) and Heath Bar rain forest nut crunch sundae ($4.99). Kids' meals are $6.99 each for a pizza, burger, hotdog, chicken tenders (shaped like guitars), or spaghetti. Most meals also come with applesauce, fries, and a beverage in a souvenir cup.

Hours: Open Sun. - Thurs., 11:30am - 11pm; Fri. - Sat., 11:30am - 12am.
Admission: Certain discounts are available through AAA.
Ages: 5 years and up.

JOE'S CRAB SHACK (Los Angeles County)

City of Industry - (626) 839-4116; Long Beach - (562) 594-6551; Redondo Beach - (310) 406-1999 / $$$
www.joescrabshack.com

City of Industry - 1420 Azusa; Long Beach - 6550 Marina Drive; Redondo Beach - 230 Portofino Way

If you're in a *crab*by mood, this is the restaurant for you! Most of the shacks really do resemble tacky-looking shacks - it's part of the charm. And the servers must have fun because they sometimes dance on the table and break out into song.

Outside the Newport Beach restaurant, for instance, is a collage of large, marine-related items such as a life-size carved wooden captain, a whale's tail, a surfboard, fishing nets, and a wooden alligator. Inside, a lot of stuff fills the walls and ceiling. From the corrugated tin roof hangs plastic seagulls, netting, crab and lobster decorations, animals made out of shells, surfer clothing, and small boats - you get the picture. The wall is completely covered with photographs of everyday people, some holding fish, some not. At almost any of the wooden tables, the waterfront view of the harbor is terrific.

Most of the meals are large enough to be shared; even the kid's meals are more than adequate. Crab is the featured specialty, but other foods are available. My oldest son fell in love with the crab cake sandwiches ($8.99). Other entrees include top sirloin ($11.99), coconut shrimp ($10.99), one pound of snow crab ($16.99), lobster tail ($21.99), appetizer of fried calamari with marinara ($5.99), and a delicious salad with fried chicken strips ($7.99). Kids' meals come with fries and are $3.99 for a choice of chicken fingers, corn dog, burger, popcorn shrimp, pizza, or mac and cheese. Drinks are extra.

Hours: Open Sun. - Mon., 11am - 9pm; Tues. - Thurs., 11am - 10pm; Fri. - Sat., 11am - 11pm.
Admission: Prices are listed above.
Ages: All

JOHNNY REB'S SOUTHERN SMOKEHOUSE (Los Angeles County)

Bellflower - (562) 866-6455; Long Beach - (562) 423-7327 $$$

Bellflower - 16639 Bellflower Boulevard; Long Beach - 4663 Long Beach Boulevard

(Bellflower: Exit Artesia Fwy [91] N. on Bellflower. [TG: 736 C6]; Long Beach: Exit Long Beach Fwy [710], E. on Del Amo Blvd., R. on Long Beach Blvd. [TG: 765 D4])

This roadhouse restaurant serves up southern hospitality, as well as good ol' southern cookin'. Walk past the bales of hay and cow bells into the main room with its wood-beam ceilings, wooden tables and benches, and rustic ambiance. Large U.S. (and a few other) flags hang from the ceiling. The walls and counter tops are decorated with straw hats, old wash basins, musical instruments, license plates, old-fashioned kitchen gadgets and tools, and pictures of farms framed by shutters. Bluegrass music plays in the background.

The immediate attraction for kids (and adults) is the bowl of peanuts on each table because peanut shells are to be thrown on the floor! (My floor looks like this too, sometimes. The only difference is that kids are allowed to do it here.) I have to mention that even the bathrooms fit into the Ma and Pa Kettle theme because they look like (nice) outhouses, and barnyard noises are piped in.

Our waiter, who wore a long johns shirt, served our beverages in canning jars. Breakfast items include grits ($1.89), omelettes (average $6.95), pancakes (average $4.25), and country ham and eggs ($7.99). Meals come with all the fixing's. The children's menu offers an egg and toast, french toast, pancakes, or bacon and egg biscuit, for $2.50 each. The lunch menu is the same as the following dinner menu, only the portions are smaller, so prices are lower. Going along with the southern attitude toward food - anything tastes better when fried - choices include fried green tomatoes, okra, fried sweet potatoes, hushpuppies (i.e. fried cornbread), catfish, and chicken fried steak. Y'all may also select ribs, hamburger, blackened T-bone steak, stuffed Cajun sausage sandwich, chicken salad, and more. Dinner prices range from $8 to $21. The homemade desserts are delicious, especially the peach cobbler. Personal advice - don't even think about dieting, at least for the meal you eat here.

The kids' menu offers chicken, catfish, or beef ribs from $4 to $5.50. Beverages are extra. "Put some south in your mouth" and grab some grub at Johnny Reb's! Note: The Long Beach location is the smallest one.

Hours: Open Sun. - Thurs., 7am - 9pm; Fri. - Sat., 7am - 10pm.
Admission: Prices are listed above.
Ages: 2 years and up.

MEL'S DRIVE-IN

(323) 465-3111 / www.melsdrive-in.com
1650 N. Highland Avenue, Hollywood
(Exit Hollywood Fwy [101] W. on Hollywood Blvd., L. on Highland. [TG: 593 E4])

$$$

Mel's is a very hip, very 50's place to go and eat. The atmosphere harkens back to that time period with its interior decor, memorabilia, old photographs everywhere, the background music, and the way the waiters and waitresses are dressed. Listen to *Johnny B. Goode*, *Rock Around the Clock*, and other oldies, but goodies on the jukebox. Order a burger, fries, and a milkshake (and/or a soup or salad) that just tastes plain good. Meals average between $6 to $10. A choice of kid's meals is available for about $5 for a burger, hot dog, or macaroni and cheese, plus fries.

Hours: Open daily, 6am - 3am.
Admission: Call for prices.
Ages: All

THE OLD SPAGHETTI FACTORY (Los Angeles County)

Duarte - (626) 358-2115; Hollywood - (323) 469-7149 / www.osf.com
Duarte - 1431 Buena Vista; Hollywood - 5939 Sunset Boulevard
(Duarte: Exit Foothill Fwy [210], N. on Buena Vista. [TG: 568 A5]; Hollywood: Exit Hollywood Fwy [101] W. on Sunset. [TG: 593 G4])

$$$

These elegant "factories" have posh, velvet seats in a variety of colors. The overhead fabric lamps are from a more genteel era. The old world antiques and the dark, rich furniture exudes a quiet, classy atmosphere. Yet, the restaurants are also very kid friendly. Old Spaghetti factories usually have a train or trolley car to eat in - this is a highlight. The franchised restaurants differ only in regional decor. For instance, the one in Riverside, being in a citrus city, has orange crate labels on the walls.

The food selection is focused on (what a surprise!) - spaghetti, with a large selection of sauces to choose from, as well as lasagna, tortellini, and ravioli. Prices range from $4 to $9.95. Kids' meals are $3.65 for a choice of mac and cheese, grilled cheese sandwich, and six 'sghetti meals with different sauces. The meal comes with a salad, beverage, and dessert.

Hours: Open Mon. - Fri., 11:30am - 2pm and 5pm - 10pm (plus Fri., noon - 3pm); Sat. - Sun., 11:30am - 10pm.
Admission: Prices are listed above.
Ages: 4 years and up.

OLIVIA'S DOLL HOUSE and TEA ROOM (Los Angeles County)

(661) 252-1404 - general number; Newhall - (661) 222-7331; West Hollywood - (310) 273-6631
Newhall - 22700 Lyons Avenue; West Hollywood - 8804 Rosewood Avenue
(Newhall: Exit Golden State Fwy [5] E. on Lyons. [TG: 464- J1]; West Hollywood: From the Hollywood Fwy [101], exit W. on Santa Monica Blvd., L. on N. Robertson, R. on Rosewood Ave. [TG: 592 H7])

$$$$$

These small, Victorian-style house-like buildings are beautifully decorated with flowers and lace - a little girl's dream come true. Young ladies can dress up in gowns and accessorize with feather boas, hats, gloves, parasols, and jewelry. Next comes a hair style befitting the new look, plus make-up, and even having the nails done. (Forget about little girls - this sounds like a mom's dream come true!) Each party-goer then participates in a fashion show and gets her picture taken. In the dining room, "tea" (lemonade) is served along with hors d'oeuvres (bite-size pizza and cocktail wienies), finger sandwiches (turkey, tuna, and peanut butter and jelly), and dessert (candy assortments, brownies, and a cookie). Then party favors are doled out. What a memorable party for young ladies! New houses are in the works to open in Irvine, Ontario, and Pasadena.

> **Hours:** Open for parties by reservation only.
> **Admission:** Parties start at $250 for 7 girls; additional children are $25 each.
> **Ages:** 4 years and up.

PETER PIPER PIZZA (Los Angeles County)

Bell - (323) 773-5502; Covina - (626) 858-0202; Pacoima - (818) 899-4848; Sylmar - (818) 837-5996;
Whittier - (562) 692-5563 / www.peterpiperpizza.com
Bell - 6207 Atlantic Boulevard; Covina - 1459 N. Citrus Avenue; Pacoima - 13200 Osborne Street;
Sylmar - 12902 Foothill Boulevard; Whittier - 11885 Whittier Boulevard

$$$

This huge, fun-filled pizza place is very similar to Chuck E. Cheese. Obviously the main food offered here is pizza (a large cheese pizza is about $10.50), but chicken wings and a salad bar are also available. For entertainment, there are ball pits, arcade games, lots of skee ball lanes, and a merry-go-round that is free (yea!). The mascot, a green-spotted purple dinosaur, comes on stage a few times throughout the day/night to put on a show. You will have to purchase tokens for the games - twenty tokens for $5. Bring in a good report card for extra, free tokens. The kids love coming here - just cover your ears to block out the din. Note that for a minimum of fifteen kids, tours are offered where youngsters see the kitchens, learn about dough and oven temperature, and most importantly, top their own 7" pizza. A drink and two tokens are included in the $2.99 per child price. Adults, you're on your own!

> **Hours:** Open Sun. - Thurs., 10am - 10pm; Fri. - Sat., 10am - 11pm.
> **Admission:** Free, but bring money for food and tokens.
> **Ages:** 1½ years and up.

PROUD BIRD RESTAURANT

(310) 670-3093
11022 Aviation Boulevard, Los Angeles
(Exit Imperial Fwy [105] N. on Aviation. [TG: 702 J6])

$$$$

Several airplanes have landed outside this restaurant, which is fittingly located just a stone's throw from the Los Angeles International Airport. The planes include a P-38 Lightning, P-51 Mustang, and Bell X-I. Inside this elegant restaurant are hallways lined with aviation pictures and flight artifacts. The rectangular-shaped main dining room has windows to see the field of planes in the "backyard," as well as planes actually landing and taking off from the airport. Tip: Choose a table near a window for the view.

Adult entree lunches include blackened chicken, grilled salmon, hamburgers, and club sandwiches. Prices range from $7.95 to $14.95. Lunch buffets have themes that change daily. Dinner choices include catfish, filet mignon, salmon, London broil, shrimp, lamb shank, chicken, ribs, and lobster. Prices range from $16.95 to $54.95. Appetizers include oysters, crab-stuffed mushrooms or escargot for $7.95 each. The kids' menu has grilled cheese sandwiches, hamburger, or chicken strips for $4.95. Their meals include an ice-cream cone. Beverages are extra.

> **Hours:** Open for lunch, Mon. - Sat., 11am to 3pm. Open for dinner, Mon. - Thurs., 4pm - 10pm; Fri. - Sat., 4pm to 11pm. Open for Sun. brunch, 9am - 3pm.
> **Admission:** Menu prices are listed above.
> **Ages:** 5 years and up.

QUEEN MARY

(562) 435-3511 / www.queenmary.com
Pier J, Long Beach

See the entry for QUEEN MARY on page 114 for details.

RUBY'S (Los Angeles County)

(800) HEY RUBY (439-7829); Marina Del Rey - (310) 574-RUBY; Pasadena - (626) 796-RUBY; Redondo Beach - (310) 376-RUBY; Rolling Hills Estates - (310) 544-RUBY; Whittier - (562) 947-RUBY; Woodland Hills - (818) 340-RUBY / www.rubys.com

Marina Del Rey - 13455 Maxella Avenue; Pasadena - 45 S. Fair Oaks Avenue; Redondo Beach - 245 N. Harbor Drive; Rolling Hills Estates - 550 Deep Valley Drive; Whittier -10109 Whittwood Lane; Woodland Hills - 6100 Topanga Canyon Boulevard

See the entry for RUBY'S (Orange County) on page 206 for details.

SHOGUN

(626) 351-8945

470 N. Halstead Street, Pasadena

(Exit Foothill Fwy [210] N. on Rosemead Blvd. It's on the corner of Rosemead and Halstead St. [TG: 566 G3])

This Japanese-style restaurant has built-in tabletop grills where chefs prepare the food with rapid slicing and dicing movements (and cool tricks) in front of your eyes. (See BENIHANA on page 11, as it is a similar type of restaurant.) The "entertainment" is great and the food is delicious. Kids get a real kick out of the presentation, and are more likely to try "new" foods now that they've seen the unique way it has been prepared. Chicken, seafood, and steak are some of the menu selections. Lunch ranges from $6 to $12; dinners from $14 to $31. Kids' meals usually run between $7.95 to $9.95. (Kids are served the same meals as adults, just smaller portions.)

Hours: Open Mon. - Fri., 11:30am - 10pm; Sat., noon - 10:30pm; Sun., noon - 9:30pm.
Admission: Prices listed above.
Ages: 4 years and up.

SPEEDZONE

(626) 913-9663 / www.speedzone.com

17871 Castleton Street, City of Industry

See the entry for SPEEDZONE on page 32 for details.

VINTAGE TEA LEAF

(562) 435-5589 / www.vintagetealeaf.com

969 E. Broadway, Long Beach

(Exit the Long Beach Fwy [710] E. on Broadway. [TG: 825 F1])

Classical music, bone china, lacy tablecloths, and a homey atmosphere make an afternoon tea at Vintage Tea Leaf a real treat. Offerings here include eighteen different kinds of tea "meals." The staples include soup, fresh-baked scones, cakes, and more than ten varieties of dainty sandwiches. Only at tea places do you find such sandwich combinations as salmon, cream cheese, and lemon capers; mayonnaise and mixed berry jam on cranberry bread; etc. I need to be more adventurous while making sandwiches at home! Ask about specific teas for young children, such as the Teddy Bear Tea, with its chocolate tea (de-caf), baloney and cheese and peanut butter and jelly sandwiches, and biscuits, served with honey of course. If kids (or perhaps adults) feel underdressed, they may select a fancy hat or feather boa. The Leaf also features almost 100 kinds of tea to drink, each brewed just right, and a gift shop with tea-related items.

Hours: Open Thurs. - Mon., 11:30am - 6pm. Closed New Year's Day, the week of the Long Beach Grand Prix, Thanksgiving, and Christmas.
Admission: Prices range, depending on the tea, between $15 - $20 per person.
Ages: 3 years and up.

-----*FAMILY PAY AND PLAY*-----

ADVENTURE PLEX

(310) 546-7708 / www.adventureplex.org
1701 Marine Avenue, Manhattan Beach
(Exit San Diego Fwy [405] N. on Inglewood Ave., L. on Marine. [TG: 732 J5])

Let's get physical! This adventure complex offers numerous classes for kids of all ages, including fitness programs, sports psychology, rock climbing, karate, pop star dance, coaching skills for teens, arts and crafts, homework tutoring, Mad Science programs, and more. Drop-ins are also welcome. For instance, come with your child to the Sports Court so he/she can pick up a game of basketball or volleyball. Two, twenty-eight-foot-tall rock walls are other appealing options. Kids learn skills, confidence, and even strategy planning by literally climbing the walls. A staff belayer is provided and so is the safety equipment. An adjacent ropes course is equally fun and challenging. A fitness center offers cardio equipment and free weights set up for youths. The four-story indoor play structure is just plain fun for you and your child; mainly your child. Crawl through tunnels, go down slides, climb up ladders, play in the ball pit, bounce on the air bounces, and just get good and tired. An arts and crafts room, a classroom with internet access, and a cafe with outdoor seating complete this complex.

Hours: Call for a schedule of classes. Drop-in sessions for the Sports Center and play structure are in two-hour increments the same hours as the complex is open: Mon. - Fri., 9am - 9pm; Sat., 10am - 7pm; Sun., 10am - 6pm. Rock climbing drop-ins are in two hour increments Mon. - Fri., 3pm - 6:30pm; Sat., 11am - 6:30pm; Sun., 11am - 6pm.

Admission: Call for a class price list. Sports Courts drops-ins are $5 per child per two hours. Rock wall drop-ins are $15 for two hours. The play structure is $10 for one child and one parent for two hours.

Ages: 2 years and up, depending on the class or activity.

ARROYO MINIATURE GOLF

(323) 255-1506 / www.arroyoseco.com
1055 Lohman Lane, South Pasadena
(Going S. on Golden State Fwy [5], exit S. on Orange Grove, R. on Mission. Go straight past Arroyo onto Stoney Dr. Going N. on Pasadena Fwy [110], exit N. on Marmion Way, R. on Pasadena, L. on Arroyo, L. on Stoney Dr. From Mission St., Stoney Dr. winds around to the (big) Arroyo golf course. [TG: 595 F2])

This miniature golf course, adjacent to a real golf course, is very simple (i.e. no fancy castles, difficult obstacles, etc.). It does, however, offer itself as a good little course for practicing your short stroke game at an inexpensive price. So, for the price, practice, and fun of it, why not bring the kids and come play a couple of rounds?!

Hours: Open daily, 7am - 9:30pm.
Admission: $1.50 per person per round.
Ages: 4 years and up.

BRIGHT CHILD (Rolling Hills)

(310) 544-9409 / www.brightchild.com
5550 Deep Valley Drive in Avenue Mall, Rolling Hills Estates
(Exit San Diego Fwy [405] S. on Crenshaw Blvd., R. on Indian Peak Rd., R. on Avenue of the Peninsula. It's on the 3rd level, opposite the movie theaters. [TG: 823 A1])

Please see the following BRIGHT CHILD entry for details.

Hours: Open Mon. - Sat., 10am - 7pm; Sun., 10am - 6pm. Closed major holidays.

BRIGHT CHILD (Santa Monica)

(310) 393-4844 / www.brightchild.com   *$$*

1415 4th Street, Santa Monica

(Exit Santa Monica Fwy [10] N. on Lincoln, L. on Wilshire, L. on 4th. It's next door to Toys R Us. Parking is available in structure #5 and #3, on 4th St. [TG: 671 E2])

This large indoor play land offers big time fun for your little ones. One of the best of its kind, Bright Child has six slides, four zip lines, a few themed ball pits, a wind tunnel, a mini putting green, a basketball court (with an adjustable rim height), an arts and crafts room, a music room with a karaoke stage and several keyboards, and a toddler room. Whew! Your kids will not want to leave. Classes, geared for particular age groups, are available throughout the week. Instructors encourage learning and agility through activities, games, and using equipment. Outside food is not allowed in, but the cafe here serves good food, such as fresh sandwiches that range between $3.50 to $6.50, and kids' meals that include a sandwich and a drink. Socks must be worn by everyone, including adults. I hope a visit here *bright*ens your day!

Hours: Open daily, 10am - 6pm.

Admission: $8 per child for up to two hours of play; each additional hour is $4. One adult is free with one paid child's admission; additional adults are $4 each. Children 20 months and younger are $4. Parking is free for the first two hours in structure #5 or #3.

Ages: 6 months to 9 years.

CALIFORNIA PAINTBALL PARK

(818) 893-5290 / paintballpark.net   *$$$$$*

Charley Canyon Road, Castaic

(Exit Golden State Fwy [5] W. on Parker Rd., R. on Castaic which turns into Tapia Canyon, L. on Charley Canyon. [TG: 4459 J1])

Line up your sights to play paintball at one of these ten playing fields sprawled over thirty-seven acres. Choose urban warfare, trenches, bunkers, or speedball fields with theme-appropriate obstacles used to take cover. Playing fields accomodate both beginner and advanced paintballers. Full face shields and ear protection are required. Old jeans, a long sleeve shirt, or camouflage clothing are suggested. A parental waiver, available on-line, for youths 17 and under must be signed.

Hours: Open Sat. - Sun., 9am - 4pm.

Admission: $20 for walk ons with their own equipment; $39 for half-day play with full rental equipment - semi-automatic machine airgun, camouflage outfit, battle mask, and 100 paintballs; $49 for the full day, plus 500 paintballs. Jr. warriors (ages 10 - 17) are $35 for all day and all the equipment, including 100 paintballs.

Ages: Must be 10 years and up.

CHILD'S PLAY

(310) 470-4997   *$$*

2299 Westwood Boulevard, Los Angeles

(From San Diego Fwy [405], exit E. on Santa Monica Blvd., R. on Westwood. From Santa Monica Fwy [10], exit N. on Overland Ave., L. on Pico Blvd., R. on Westwood. [TG: 632 C5])

Child's Play consists of one large room with a few side smaller rooms or play areas for young kids. Socks are a must for the soft play area that has a ball pit, slides, and other fun amenities. A bounce house, dress up stage, Thomas the Train, and other ride toys are all here. Classes such as art, music, and dance are offered and oftentimes storytelling or other special activities are on the schedule as well.

Hours: Open Mon., Wed., and Fri., 10am - 6pm; Tues. and Thurs., 10am - 8pm. Open on weekends for private parties only.

Admission: $8 per child; adults are free with a paid child.

Ages: 1 - 7 years.

CHUCK E. CHEESE
See the entry for CHUCK E. CHEESE on page 12 for details.

CLOSE ENCOUNTERS PAINT BALL

(800) 919-9237 or (323) 656-9179 / www.paintballusa.org   *$$$$$*
22400 The Old Road, Newhall

(Exit Golden State Fwy [5] L. on Roxford St., under the freeway to the dead end. Turn R. on Sepulveda Blvd. and follow it along the freeway for 1 mile to the first stop sign. Turn L. on San Fernando Rd., which turns into The Old Road. Travel a little over 2 miles and on the R. above a ranch, look for the field, not necessarily the address. [TG: 4641 B7])

Play this version of Capture the Flag while armed with markers (i.e. guns) filled with paint. This makes the game a bit more colorful! You'll be placed on one of two teams. The object of the game is to get the flag from your opponent's base, while dodging paintballs by hiding behind bunkers and trees. The three-a-half-acres of mountainside is a perfect setting to play this rugged game. A referee is on the playing field to insure fair play and help out. Each game lasts about twenty minutes. After you're rested, go for another round. Food is available to purchase, or bring your own, as there is a shaded grove of trees with picnic tables. Tip: Wear pants and other clothing you don't care about, and shoes with good traction. Getting hit stings, so wear a padded shirt or multiply layers to help absorb the hits. Participants 17 and under must have a waiver, which is available on-line, signed by a parent or guardian.

- **Hours:** Open to the public, Sat. - Sun. and holiday Mon., 9am - 4pm. Groups of thirty or more can reserve play time during the week.
- **Admission:** $40 for all-day play, which includes a pistol, goggles, and face mask. There are two types of upgraded guns to rent - constant-air pump rifles at $20 a day, or a semi-automatic, constant-air machine gun at $25, which includes free CO_2 for the day. Paintballs cost $10 for 100 or $25 for 500. Call to inquire about discount packages for junior players, ages 10 to 15, such as a Ninja Special. This special includes all-day play, an air rifle, and 100 paintballs for $30.
- **Ages:** 10 years and up.

FIELD OF FIRE

(661) 297-7948 / www.fieldoffire.com   *$$$$$*
23925 The Old Road, Newhall

(Exit Golden State Fwy [5] W. on Calgrove, L. on The Old Rd. - look for signs. [TG: 4640 G5])

Utilizing about eight acres, Field of Fire hits the mark with its two paintball fields studded with obstacles. Tanks, eighty foxholes, bushes, shacks, sand bags, and bunkers litter the field, while a 1,000 foot tunnel system goes under the field - how cool is that! A snack bar that serves hamburgers or sandwiches is also on the premises. Wear long sleeve shirts and jeans or camouflage clothing. A parental waiver, available on-line, must be signed for ages 17 and under.

- **Hours:** Open Sat. - Sun., 9am - 4:30pm.
- **Admission:** $20 for walk ons with own equipment; $35 for half a day of play with full equipment rental, including paintballs.
- **Ages:** Must be 10 years and up.

FUNLAND U.S.A.
(661) 273-1407 / www.funlandusa.com   *$$$*
525 W. Avenue P-4, Palmdale

(Exit Antelope Valley Fwy [14] W. on Ave. P, L. on 10th St. W., L. on Marketplace, which turns into Ave. P-4. [TG: 4195 H5])

This land of fun offers three, themed, ten-hole **miniature golf** courses - $5.95 per course for adults; children 5 years and under play for free with a paying adult. **Go-karts** are $5.95 for a five-minute ride; drivers must be at least 10 years old. **Bumper boats** are $5.95 per ride and drivers must be at least 4 years old and 44" tall. Other attractions here include **batting cages**, a large game arcade area, a toddler ball pit and kiddie rides, and a snack bar.

Hours: Open Sun. - Thurs., 10am - 10pm; Fri. - Sat., 10am - 11pm. Open in the summer one hour later.
Admission: Individual attractions are listed above, or purchase a park pass - one round of golf, two rides, twelve tokens, and a soda for $16 per person.
Ages: 4 years and up.

GO KART WORLD AND SLICK CART RACING

(310) 834-3800 or (310) 834-3700
21830 Recreation Road, Carson
(Exit San Diego Fwy [405] E. on Carson, take an immediate R. on Recreation Rd. [TG: 764 F6])

Go full speed ahead on the six race tracks here. The Kiddie Track has battery-operated cars that go about three m.p.h. on an L-shaped track. This ride is for children over 3 years old and under 75 pounds. Mini Indie is for drivers at least 45" tall and goes about nine m.p.h. on a B-shaped track. A double-seater car can hold a driver who is at least 16 years old with a passenger who is at least 32" tall. The Bumper Car track is for drivers at least 45" tall. These cars can be individually manipulated to go forwards, backwards, and even spin all the way around. For a slick ride, drivers at least 54" tall can race on the Slick Track. We vote the Turbo Track the most-like-a-real-race-track ride. Race over and under passes and around banked hairpin turns. Drivers must be at least 58" tall. The one-third mile track is for drivers at least 18 years old, as the cars go thirty-five m.p.h. All rides last four minutes. If you have a group of ten or more, you may rent the track for a private party. A large video and arcade game area, with redemption-playing games, are inside.
Hours: Open daily, 11:30am - 11pm.
Admission: Each of the rides listed cost $3.50 per ride, or purchase 7 rides for $20.
Ages: 3 years and up.

GOLFLAND ARCADE

(626) 444-5163
1181 N. Durfee Avenue, South El Monte
(Exit Pomona Fwy [60] S. at Peck Ave., R. on Durfee. [TG: 637 C5])

What course of action will you take? Choose from four, well-kept miniature golf courses with lots of fun holes designed with whimsical buildings and challenging obstacles. The inside arcade area is clean and has games, such as air hockey, as well as video games. Tip: McDonald's is only a few buildings away.
Hours: Open Sun. - Thurs., 10am - 11pm; Fri. - Sat., 10am - 1am.
Admission: Miniature golf is $5 for adults; $2 for seniors; $3 for ages 7 - 12; $2 for children 6 and under.
Ages: 4 years and up.

GOLF 'N STUFF - FAMILY FUN CENTER (Norwalk)

(562) 863-8338 / www.golfnstuff.com
10555 E. Firestone Boulevard, Norwalk
(Exit San Gabriel River Fwy [605] E. on Firestone. [TG: 706 D7])

This big family fun center offers several different ways to have fun, with three themed **miniature golf** courses - $7 for adults, 6.50 for seniors, children 4 years and under are free with a paying adult. Other attractions include **Li'l Indy** race cars - $5.50 for drivers; **bumper boats - $5** for drivers; and **bumper cars** - $5 for drivers. On these rides passengers cost $2.75 per and there are height restrictions. Yes, there are also lots of arcade games to be played here. I actually enjoy some of the interactive virtual reality games. This can keep you and the kids busy for hours - just bring quarters! A snack bar is on the premises, too.
Hours: Open Mon - Thurs., 10am - 10pm (rides are open 2pm - 9pm); Fri. - Sat., 10am - midnight; Sun., 10am - 11pm.
Admission: Attractions are individually priced above, or buy an all-park pass for $18.50 per person that entitles you to a round of miniature golf, 4 rides, and 4 tokens.
Ages: 4 years and up.

HIGH DESERT PAINTBALL

(661) 943-6788 / www.highdesertpaintball.com

Avenue E, Lancaster

(Exit Antelope Valley Fwy [14] W. on Avenue I, which turns into Lancaster Rd., R. on 170th, R. on Avenue E - it's a dirt road, so look for signs. [TG: n/a])

$$$$$

You're on target with these six paintball fields, the largest one being the two-and-a-half acre "Battle Zone." The dirt fields are enclosed with tall mesh wire and have bunkers, piles of tires, plywood cutouts, cans, and other such obstacles all set in a hilly desert backdrop. Your object, after you suit up, is to aim, fire, and splat - nail your opponent with paint. Games usually last about twenty minutes, unless you get tagged out before that time. Wear long sleeves, pants, and boots or running shoes. Kids 17 and under must have a signed parental waiver, which is available on-line.

Hours: Open Sat. - Sun., 9am - 4pm.

Admission: $10 for players who have their own equipment; $35 for players who need to rent all the equipment - gun, air, mask, and even 200 paintballs. Ask about "Young Guns" special pricing for ages 10 - 17 years old.

Ages: Must be 10 years and up.

HOLLYWOOD SPORTS COMPLEX

(562) 867-9600 / www.hollywoodsports.com

9030 Somerset Boulevard, Bellflower

(Exit Artesia Fwy [91] N. on Lakewood Blvd., R. on Somerset. [TG: 736 A4])

$$$$

This thirty-acre extreme sports complex is definitely designed with teens in mind, although other age groups (and this means adults) enjoy it, too. Note that proper safety equipment is required for all sports activities and a parental waiver (available on-line) for ages 17 and under must be signed. Rental equipmental is available.

The paintball area looks like something out of a *Terminator* movie (without even entering the fields!) with its futuristic/techno look. The field names speak for themselves: Lunar Wars, Forbidden City, Mad Max World, and Apocalypse. The arenas feature scenarios from actual movie sets with stone walls, buses, beat up automobiles, cargo nets, buildings, piles of tires, and much more. Warriors, I mean players, run, hide, and generally try to ambush and shoot the enemy with paintballs while rock music plays in the background. (Getting hit <u>can</u> hurt.) Spectators can watch the action from a second-story observation deck. Another paintball area features inflatable obstacles. There is a target range for practice here, too. A pro shop is on the premises for purchasing supplies. Note that all paintballs must be purchased on site. Wear old pants, a long sleeve sweatshirt, and high-top boots or old tennis shoes.

Past a large grass area, towards the back of the complex, is a skate park that's 30,000 square-feet big! It has a full size vert ramp, plus mini ramps, rails, pyramids, and other street course elements. It's awesome and we saw some incredible moves here. The BMX track is well kept up and ready for action with all of its curves and hills. The forty-foot rock climbing wall, which looks more like a mountain, offers a different kind of challenge. It features several routes, ranging from easy (kind of) to difficult, including various angles of the rock face to climb. Staff members belay. Play volleyball on a sand court that is encased by a semi-circle of palm trees and thatched-roof covered "umbrellas" over round tables with chairs. A scenic beach mural and waterfall complete the ambiance in this section.

The two-story arcade, set in a warehouse-type atmosphere, has games like Time Crisis 2, L.A. Machine Guns, and Virtual Cop. There are also more interactive, virtural reality games as well as an air hockey table and pool table in here. The upper story is a cyber cafe. The wall murals are of inner city street scapes and dark images. The decor of the adjacent restaurant and full bar is an actual set from the film, *The Haunted*. It looks like a gothic theater room with huge pillars, graphic paintings, and griffins. Burgers, pastas, and other food choices are available to purchase. The outdoor cafe is open year round and offers typical fast food fare.

Tennis courts have been converted to basketball courts and to fast-play soccer fields. Grab a friend to come and play.

Hours: Open most of the year, Mon. - Thurs., 3pm - 10pm; Fri., 3pm - 11:30pm; Sat., 8am (paintball only), 9am (everything else) - 11:30pm; Sun., 8am (paintball only), 9am (everything else) - 10pm. Summer, spring break, and holidays the gates open daily at 8am.

Admission: General admission includes all day rock climbing, soccer, basketball, and volleyball: $7 per person. Paintball field admission: $15 all day (Mon. - Thurs.) - $25 per session of 9am - 4pm or 4pm - 11:30pm (weekends). Gear rental costs are $13 for semi automatic gun, $5 for a full face mask; $8.50 for 200 paintballs; etc. Skate park: $10 for the day (Mon. - Thurs.) - $12 per session (weekends). BMX: $10 all day (Mon. - Thurs.) - $15 all day (weekends).

Ages: Must be 10 years and up for paintball; 7 years and up for skate park; at least 45 pounds for rock climbing.

IRWINDALE SPEEDWAY

$$$

(626) 358-1100 / www.irwindalespeedway.com

13300 Live Oak Avenue, Irwindale

(Going N. on San Gabriel Fwy [605], exit W. on Live Oak Ave. Going S. on 605, exit W. on Arrow Hwy., L. on Live Oak Ave. [TG: 597 J2])

If your family likes fast cars, speed on over to a NASCAR, Speed Truck, Winston West, or USAC Midget and Sprint Cars event. This banked one-half mile super speedway track packs in thrills a minute for the racing enthusiast.

Hours: The season runs mid-March through November. Races are held on Saturdays.

Admission: Admission fees for regular events are $15 for adults; $5 for ages 6 - 12; children 5 and under free. Special event nights are $20 - $35 for adults; $10 for ages 6 - 12; children 5 and under are free.

Ages: 5 years and up.

JUNGLE GYM ARCADIA

$$$$

(626) 446-5014 / www.junglegymclimbing.com

305 N. Santa Anita, Arcadia

(Exit Foothill Fwy [210] S. on Santa Anita, R. on St. Joseph St. to park behind the gym. [TG: 567 D5])

Does your child climb like a monkey? Let him loose in this indoor rock climbing facility which offers 4,500 feet for bouldering, as well as twenty top ropes and a high ropes course. Inexperienced and experienced climbers alike find the protruding rocks a challenge to grab and climb, but doable and exciting. The aptly-named Jungle Gym also offers a portable climbing wall and an obstacle course that can come to you.

Hours: Open Mon. - Thurs., noon - 10pm (plus Tues. and Thurs., 6am - 9pm); Fri - Sun., noon - 8pm.

Admission: $15 for a day pass. Shoe rentals and equipment are an additional $7. Ask about membership.

Ages: 6 years and up.

KID CONCEPTS U.S.A.

$$

(310) 465-0075 / www.kidconceptsusa.com

22844 Hawthorne Boulevard, Torrance

(Exit San Diego Fwy [405] S. on Crenshaw Blvd., R. on Sepulveda, L. on Hawthorne. It's on the L., beyond the buildings located right on the street. [TG: 793 D1])

What a concept! The main feature within this 9,000 square-foot room is a multi-level play structure. It has tubes (large enough for adults to crawl through), slides, ball pits, a bounce room, a mini-zip line, a small room with huge balls to roll on, and lots of nooks and crannies to discover. Note: The black slide is <u>really</u> fast. Kids can also sit in a child-sized rocket ship or helicopter and "fly" away to parts unknown. (Doesn't that sound appealing sometimes?!) Although this area is well-ventilated, my kids got sweaty having such a good time. Wearing socks is a must!

The large room has several other sections distinguished by various play equipment and/or colorful murals that represent different regions of the U.S. The toddler area, for ages 3 and under, has a tot-sized ball pit, a short slide, and large foam blocks. Under the dinosaur and rock mural, children can unearth "fossils" in the archaeological sand pit. A Hollywood backdrop showcases a stage, complete with karaoke and costumes. The "quiet room" has two computer terminals and a nice selection of children's books. Drive to the little market, that has lots of play food, using pedal cars. For nominal additional fees, guests can play air hockey, work on a craft project, or climb up the four-foot-high, rock-climbing wall that rotates vertically and can tilt at various angles.

The sitting area is centrally located with themed red, white, and blue tables. The restaurant serves up delicious food including regular pizzas ($4.95 for an individual pan), specialty pizzas such as barbecue chicken ($13.95 for a twelve inch), a variety of salads, hamburger or turkey burgers with fries ($6.25), angel hair pasta ($7.99), bagels ($1), and brownies (65¢). Kid's meals are about $5 for their choice of pizza, ham and cheese sandwich, chicken strips, burger, or a hot dog, plus fries and a drink.

Two other features worth mentioning are the cutely-decorated party rooms (party-goers can create their own sundaes) and the separate room for gym classes which contains all the latest equipment for future gymnasts. Ask about the numerous classes and special events hosted here.

Hours: Open Mon. - Sat., 10am - 8pm; Sun., 10am - 6pm. Closed major holidays.
Admission: Two-hour sessions are $8 for ages 2 and up, with one free adult per child; additional adults are $4; $5 for 1 year olds; children under 1 are free. Ask about prices for gym classes.
Ages: 9 months - 10 years.

KIDDYLAND

(626) 308-0588 / www.pakmannkiddyland.com
247 E. Main Street, Alhambra
(Exit San Bernardino Fwy [10] N. on Garfield Ave., R. on Main. [TG: 596 C4])

Colorful, bright, and fun - that's Kiddyland! The 5,000 square-foot, multi-story, giant soft play area has large tunnels to crawl through, curvy slides to whoosh down, a bounce house, a large ball pit, and a fun climbing area for younger ones. Play Skeeball, Wacky Gator, air hockey, dancing games, and more, at the arcade area that dispenses redemption tickets. These games and video games will keep both younger and older patrons happily busy. Kiddieland also offers kiddie rides and a full-service snack bar that serves pizza, hot dogs, juice, and other snack items. (No outside food is allowed inside.) There are two, themed rooms for birthday parties, too. Bring socks for the soft play area!

Hours: Open Mon. - Wed., noon - 7pm; Thurs. - Sun., 11am - 7pm.
Admission: $5.95 for ages 3 years and up; $3.95 for ages 2 and under; adults are free.
Ages: 2 years and up.

L.A. ROCK GYM

(310) 973-3388 / www.larockgym.com
4926 W. Rosecrans Avenue, Hawthorne
(Exit San Diego Fwy [405] E. on Rosecrans Ave. Just past the cross-street of Ocean Gate Ave., pull into the second driveway on the R. The gym is located towards the back. [TG: 733 B4])

Climb every mountain - or, at least every indoor rock wall at the Rock Gym. This nice-sized facility has realistic-looking boulders and high walls, two of which are at intense angles, plus multi-colored hand and foot holds that create over 100 different routes. Beginners to experienced rock climbers will be challenged here, as well as enjoy the physical excursion. (Have you ever noticed how most rock climbers don't have an ounce of fat on their bodies? After attempting the sport - I know why!) Harnesses and helmets are the norm here. The gym holds classes in basic climbing, intermediate techniques, and advanced lead climbing techniques. Birthday parties can utilize the provided tables and chairs for the really important stuff like cake and gifts.

Hours: Open Mon. - Thurs., 11am - 10pm; Fri., 11am - 8pm; Sat. - Sun., 9am - 6pm.
Admission: A day pass is $15 for adults; $13 for ages 12 and under. An introductory lesson is $25. A supervised climb, with a belayer, is $12 an hour for a minimum of 2 people. Ask about class and membership rates. Equipment rental is $5.
Ages: Children must be 6 years old to climb.

LASER STORM (Torrance)

(310) 373-8470 / www.gablehousebowl.com

$$

22535 Hawthorne Boulevard, Torrance

(Going S. on San Diego Fwy [405], exit S. on Hawthorne Blvd. Going N. on 405, exit W. on Sepulveda Blvd., L. on Hawthorne Blvd. [TG: 763 D7])

Laser tag is taking kids (and adults) by storm! Power up your laser gun as two teams of up to thirty people compete against each other and "shoot" it out in a darkened room. Take cover behind neon-colored partitions, decorated with gak splats, as an opponent aims at you. Or, use the partitions as cover to stealthily sneak up on someone. The ten-minute games are action-packed, and all the running around can literally take your breath away! Note that there are two arenas here and that they are located right next to Gable House Bowl. A full-service snack bar and arcade games are here, too.

Hours: Open during the school year, Mon. - Wed., 3pm - 9pm; Thurs., 3pm - 10pm; Fri., 3pm - 11pm; Sat., 10am - 11pm; Sun., 10am - 8pm. Open in the summer, Sun. - Thurs., 10am - 10pm; Fri. - Sat., 10am - 11pm.

Admission: $4 per game, Mon. - Fri.; $5, Sat. - Sun. Ask about specials.

Ages: 6 years and up.

LASERTREK

(310) 325-7710

$$

2755 Pacific Coast Highway, #D, Torrance

(Exit Harbor Fwy [110] W. on Pacific Coast Highway. It's just past Crenshaw Blvd., in a shopping center. [TG: 793 F5])

Unlike most laser tag lobbies, which are usually dark and filled with loud video games, LaserTrek's lobby is brightly lit and has just a few games. It also has two birthday party rooms. A space theme is prevalent throughout the actual playing arena. Astronauts, rocket ships, and other-world cities, painted with glow-in-the-dark paint, decorate the walls, angled partitions, and ramps. Even so, it's dark in here. Fog swirls around the up to twenty-five players as they run after (and from) opposing team members who are likewise trying to "shoot" them with laser guns. Each "hit" registers on that person's vest and he/she is out of the game for a few seconds. Then the action, enhanced by mood music, picks back up again. Each pulse-pounding game lasts ten minutes.

Hours: Open Mon. - Thurs., 11am - 10pm; Fri., 11am - midnight; Sat., 10am - midnight; Sun., 10am, - 10pm.

Admission: $5 for one game; $9 for two.

Ages: 6 years and up.

LAZERSTAR

(626) 963-9444 / www.hottaco.com/lazerstar

$$$

1365 S. Grand Avenue, Glendora

(Exit Foothill Fwy [210] S. on Grand Ave. It's in a mall. [TG: 599 D1])

Two teams, of up to twenty individuals each, compete against each other armed with laser guns and a lighted vest. The foggy 5,000 square-foot arena, illuminated by black lights, accompanied by pulsating background music, and interspersed with large tubes decorated in bands of color as just some of the obstacles, is an awesome place to play hide and seek (and zap!). When your mission is completed, return to Mission Command Center to pick up your score sheet because it details who scored on who and how many times. Tip: Ask Lazerstar about their great deals for team parties and their various monthly specials. The lobby has several video and arcade games, including virtual reality games. The full-service snack bar sells hot dogs, pizza, and other food.

Hours: Open Mon. - Thurs., noon - 10pm; Fri., noon - midnight; Sat., 10am - midnight; Sun., 10am - 10pm. Open extended hours in the summer.

Admission: $6.25 per player for one game. Ask about specials.

Ages: 7 years and up.

MALIBU CASTLE

(310) 643-5167 / www.malibugrandprix.com   *$$$*

2410 Marine Avenue, Redondo Beach

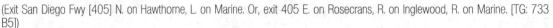

(Exit San Diego Fwy [405] N. on Hawthorne, L. on Marine. Or, exit 405 E. on Rosecrans, R. on Inglewood, R. on Marine. [TG: 733 B5])

    Hold court at Malibu castle as your little subjects play either one of the two wonderful **miniature golf** courses here. There are video and arcade games inside the castle walls, plus a ticket redemption area, a full-service snack bar, and party rooms. **Batting cages** just outside.

    Hours: Open Mon. - Thurs., 11am - 9pm; Fri., 11am - 11pm; Sat., 10am - 11pm; Sun., 10am - 9pm. Call for summer hours.

    Admission: Miniature golf is $6.25 a round for adults; $3 for seniors; $5.25 for children 12 and under.

    Ages: 4 years and up.

MOUNTASIA FUN CENTER

(661) 253-4FUN (4386) / www.mountasiafuncenter.com   *$$$*

21516 Golden Triangle Road, Santa Clarita

(Exit Golden State Fwy [5] E. on Valencia Blvd. which turns into Soledad Canyon Rd., R. on Golden Oak Rd., L. on Golden Triangle Rd. [TG: 4551 B3])

    Mountasia offers a mountain of fun for your family! Play either one of two **miniature golf** courses that feature a cascading waterfall. (Note: The zebra course has a hole that goes under the waterfall and inside a cave.) Prices are $6.25 for ages 4 and up; $5.25 for seniors; children 3 years and under are free. Note that there are some holes that are wheelchair friendly. Zip around the race track in **go karts** - $4.75 for a single or double car. Drivers must be at least 54" tall and passengers must be 42". Try to avoid getting wet (or go for it) in the **bumper boats** - $4.75 a ride; a passenger can ride for free. Height and age restrictions apply. Kids at least 48" tall and 6 years old can improve their batting average at the **batting cages**.

    Inside Mountasia are family-oriented video and arcade games, a redemption center, a spacious **laser tag arena** where players put on vests and use their laser guns to "tag" opponents and score points (about $5 per game), a **rock climbing wall**, and **Farrell's Ice Cream Parlour and Restaurant**. This restaurant has a wholesome and fun atmosphere, just like the "old" Farrell's from the 70's and 80's (so I've heard). Besides hamburgers, club sandwiches, salads, and kid's meal of grilled cheese, hot dog, and chicken nuggets, they serve dessert favorites. This include the Trough, which is two banana splits piled high with goodies, eaten from a trough as the waiter exclaims, "This person made a pig of himself at Farrell's." There are, of course, numerous other, single-serving choices, such as a Tin Roof, malts, and clown sundaes. This is a great place for a birthday party. Good luck getting the kids past the tempting candy counter!

    Hours: Open in the summer, Sun. - Fri., 10am - 10pm; Sat., 10am - midnight. Open the rest of the year, Mon. - Thurs., noon - 9pm; Fri., noon - 11pm; Sat., 11am - 11pm; Sun., 11am - 9pm.

    Admission: Attractions are individually priced above, or purchase a $12 pass that includes one round of miniature golf, one ride on the go-karts, and one ride on the bumper cars. Ask about other specials.

    Ages: 4 years and up.

MULLIGAN FAMILY FUN CENTER (Torrance)

(310) 325-3950 / www.mulliganfun.com   *$$$*

1351 Sepulveda Boulevard, Torrance

(Exit Harbor Fwy [110] W. on Sepulveda past Normandie. It's on the R. Look for the sign, as it is easy to miss. [TG: 793 J1])

    This center features **batting cages** - $1 for twenty pitches; two wonderful **miniature golf** courses - $6 for adults, $4.50 for seniors and kids ages 5 to 10, children 4 years and under play for free; **go-kart slic track** racing - $5.25 for a five-minute ride (height restrictions apply); **rookie go-karts** for ages 6 to 12 - $4; **mini grand prix** for ages 2 to 6 - $3; a Jungle Gym **play area** with tubes, slides, and ball pits just for young children - $2; **laser tag** - a hi-tech battle game in a 2,200 square foot arena - $5; and the ever-present arcade games. A

glow range is also here so you can take practice swings with a real golf club and ball at night because the distance targets are lit up - forty-five balls for $5. A full-service snack bar is here with nachos, pizza, hot dogs, and more.

Hours: Open Mon. - Thurs., noon - 10pm; Fri., noon - 11pm; Sat., 10am - 11pm; Sun., 10am - 10pm.
Admission: Attractions are individually priced above.
Ages: 2 years through 60" tall for the play area; 4 years and up for miniature golf.

POWER STATION

(562) 497-1197 / www.powerstationgames.com
7589 Carson Boulevard at the Long Beach Town Center, Long Beach
(Going N. on San Gabriel River Fwy [605], exit W. on Carson Blvd. Going S. on 605, exit at Carson and proceed across Carson into the Long Beach Towne Center. It's near the movie theaters. [TG: 766 G6])

Power up at the laser tag arena inside this very noisy (and dark) arcade. Games last ten, pulse-pounding minutes as opponents search for one another in over 1,000 square feet of playing room. The room is set up like a maze, making it challenging to find your way in and out of different sections. The walls are decorated with neon colors that show up under the black lights. My boys and I love these fast action games. Note: The Power Station is part of a large outdoor mall which includes Edwards Cinemas, plenty of restaurants and a food court, and lots of fun shops.

Hours: Open Mon. - Thurs., 11am - 10pm; Fri., 11am - midnight; Sat., 10am - 1am, Sun., 10am - 10pm.
Admission: $5 per person; $7 for two games with eight or more people
Ages: 6 years and up.

THE ROCK GYM

(562) 981-3200 / www.therockgym.com
2599 E. Willow Street, Signal Hill
(Exit San Diego Fwy [405] S. on Cherry/Temple, L. on Temple, R. on Willow. [TG: 795 H3])

Go rock climbing at the beach, Long Beach, that is. The Rock Gym is one of Southern California's largest indoor rock climbing facilities. The huge lead climbing roof, unique bouldering tunnel, and walls jutting out at various angles prove a fitting challenge for your young athletes, and for those who are not so athletically inclined. Both seasoned climbers and those new to the sport will experience a sense of accomplishment as they conquer the rocky obstacles and terrain. Staff is on hand to harness, belay, and encourage climbers. Classes are offered where you can learn to belay your kids and other people. Belay means to stand on the ground, as an anchor, attached to the climber. The multi-colored rocks, embedded in the realistic-looking granite walls, are marked so they can be used as trail guides, though the routes are changed every few months to stimulate your mind and body. Ask about the variety of classes and programs offered. So, if you're feeling caught between a rock and a hard place, come to the Rock Gym for safe, fun exercise for the whole family!

Hours: The gym is open Mon. - Thurs., noon - 11pm; Fri., noon - 8pm; Sat. - Sun., 10am - 7pm.
Admission: $15 for adults for an all-day pass; $12 for ages 11 and under (non-belaying). Equipment rental is an additional $6 a day. A safety orientation class is $7. An two-hour introduction class for belaying for kids 12 and up (this includes adults) is $35, which also includes a week pass to the gym.
Ages: 5 years and up.

ROCKREATION (Los Angeles)

(310) 207-7199 / www.rockreation.com
11866 La Grange Avenue, Los Angeles
(Exit San Diego Fwy [405] W. on Olympic Ave., N. on Bundy, R. on La Grange. [TG: 632 A6])

See the entry for ROCKREATION (Costa Mesa) on page 214 for details.

Hours: The gym is open Mon. and Wed., noon - 11pm; Tues. and Thurs., 6am - 11pm; Fri., noon - 10pm; Sat. - Sun., 10am - 6pm. Kids' Climb, for ages 6 - 11, is offered Mon., Wed., Sat., and Sun., 4pm - 6pm.

Admission: $15 for adults for a day pass; $10 for ages 11 and under, but they must have a belayer. Rental equipment - shoes, harness, and chalk - is an additional $5. Kids Climb is $25 per participant, which includes the necessary equipment. Reservations are needed.

Ages: 5 years and up.

SHERMAN OAKS CASTLE PARK

(818) 756-9459 / www.shermanoakscastle.com

4989 Sepulveda Blvd., Sherman Oaks

(Going E. on Ventura Fwy [101], exit N. on Sepulveda. From San Diego Fwy [405], exit E. on Ventura Blvd., L. on Sepulveda. [TG: 561 H3])

This Castle Park offers royal fun for the whole family. There are three majestic **miniature golf** courses to putt around on, nine **batting cages** (kids must be 8 years old, or at least 54" tall), over 100 arcade games, a redemption center, and a full-service snack bar.

Hours: Open Mon. - Thurs., 10am - 11pm; Fri., 10am - midnight; Sat., 9am - midnight; Sun., 9am - 11pm.

Admission: Miniature golf is $6 for the first round for adults; $5 for seniors and for children 12 and under; $2 for replays for all ages. Pay only $2 a round for early bird specials on Sat. and Sun. morning, 9am - 10am.

Ages: 4 years and up.

SPEEDZONE

(626) 913-9663 / www.speedzone.com

17871 Castleton Street, City of Industry

(Exit Pomona Fwy [60] S. on Fullerton Rd., R. on Colima, R. on Stoner Creek. It's on the corner of Stoner Creek and Castleton. [TG: 678 H4])

Ahhhh, the smell of gasoline and the sound of engines being revved! Although SpeedZone is advertised as a racing park for adults, kids can go full throttle here, too. The huge mural and formula race cars on the outside of the massive black and white checkered building reinforce the park's intentions of being dedicated to speed, racing, and competition. Drivers must be at least five feet tall and have a valid driver's license. If you do not have a license, but are at least 58" tall, you may drive a two-seater sidewinder racer on the Turbo Track during daytime hours. The four tracks consist of Top Eliminator Dragsters, with cars powered by 300 hp; Grand Prix, with custom-scale-designed Formula One Racers; Turbo Track, which allows wheel-to-wheel racing with up to nineteen other drivers; and Slick Trax, for a spin around the concrete track. SpeedZone is the closest thing to professional racing available to the public.

Two, eighteen-hole miniature golf courses are done in the racing theme motif and include paraphernalia such as gas pumps, tires, and guard rails, plus waterways and bridges. Inside, SpeedZone decor consists of racing flags, murals, photos, a few cars (on the floor and suspended from the ceiling), and signed memorabilia such as helmets and jumpsuits. Even the restaurant table tops are designed to look like race tracks!

The Terrace Bar and outdoor grill offer open seating, or enjoy full-service dining in the Cafe. For about $7 each, your menu choices include burgers, turkey or cheddar melt sandwiches, hoagies, Cobb salads, and individual pizzas. A chicken or steak meal is available for a few more dollars.

Keep the adrenaline pumping with over 100 video, virtual reality, and arcade games in the Electric Alley, plus a prize redemption area. Play basketball or skee ball, or try virtual jetskiing, motocross, or downhill skiing. At the Daytona simulators up to eight drivers can race against each other on the same track. A day at SpeedZone is not just another day at the races!

Hours: Open Sun. - Thurs., 11am - 11pm; Fri. - Sat., 11am - 1am. Open one hour earlier in the summer. All visitors at SpeedZone after 10pm must have a valid California driver's license.

Admission: Free entrance. Top Eliminator - $12 for 3 runs; Grand Prix - $3 a lap with a 2 lap minimum; Turbo Track and Slick Trax are $6.50 for 5 minutes. Speedway miniature golf is $6.50 a round for adults; $5.50 for children 12 and under.

Ages: 4 years and up for the restaurant and miniature golf; see above restrictions for driving cars.

ULTRAZONE (Alhambra)

(626) 282-6178 / www.ultrazonealhambra.com

231 E. Main Street, Alhambra

(Exit San Bernardino Fwy [10] N. on Garfield Ave., R. on Main St. [TG: 596 B4])

See the below entry details. This facility also has a simulated rock climbing wall that rotates, moves, and tilts as you climb according to the level you set.

Hours: Open most of the year, Thurs., 3pm - 9pm; Fri., 3pm - midnight; Sat., 11am - midnight; Sun., noon - 10pm. Summer hours are Mon. - Thurs., 2pm - 9pm; Fri., 2pm - midnight; Sat., 11am - midnight; Sun., noon - 8pm. Open extended hours during school breaks. Closed most major holidays.

Admission: $6 a game. The rock climbing wall is $2 for 3 minutes.

Ages: 5 years and up.

ULTRAZONE (Sherman Oaks)

(818) 789-6620 / www.zonehead.com/shermanoaks

14622 Ventura Boulevard, suite 208, Sherman Oaks

(Exit Ventura Fwy [101] S. on Van Nuys Blvd., R. on Ventura Blvd. It's on the S. side of the street, upstairs. Two hours of parking free with validation. [TG: 561 J4])

It's almost pitch black. You're going through mazes and tunnels trying to find your way to the enemy's base before your enemy finds you. Suddenly, ZAP - you get hit! You realize you've lost your power and now you have to recharge. Where *is* the recharging site? After getting lost several times you find it, and now your infrared sighting helps spy one of "them"! You fire, hit, and score one for your team!

Ultrazone, with over 5,000 square feet of excitement, is the ultimate in laser tag. You carry your own equipment - a vest and laser gun - and play with up to thirty people, or three teams. After a five-minute briefing, you'll play for fifteen intense minutes. The first game will wear you out, but it's just practice. Now that you've got a handle on how the game is played, go for a second round. Or, just play some video games and grab a bite to eat from the full-service snack bar. Three party rooms are available. Laser tag - there is fun to be had with a game this rad!

Hours: Open Tues. - Thurs., 3pm - 10pm; Fri., 3pm - midnight; Sat., 10am - midnight; Sun., 10am - 10pm. Closed Mon.

Admission: Games are $7 each. Volume discounts, role playing, and advanced access membership are also available.

Ages: 6 years and up, or not afraid of the dark.

UNDER THE SEA (Burbank)

(818) 567-9945 / ww3.choicemall.com/underthesea

2424 Victory Boulevard, Burbank

(Going S. on Golden State Fwy [5], exit S.E. on San Fernando Blvd, R. on Buena Vista St., L. on Victory. Going N. on 5, exit E. on Burbank Blvd., angle R. on Victory Blvd. at corner of Burbank. [TG: 533 E7])

See the entry for UNDER THE SEA (Woodland Hills) on page 34 for details.

UNDER THE SEA (Northridge)

(818) 772-7003 / ww3.choicemall.com/underthesea

19620 Nordhoff Street, Northridge

(From San Diego Fwy [405], exit W. on Nordhoff, stay R. on Nordhoff St. as Nordhoff Wy. goes L. From the Ventura Fwy [101], exit N. on Winnetka Ave., R. on Nordhoff St., L. on Corbin Ave., R. again on Nordhoff St. [TG: 500 F7])

    See the below entry for details.

UNDER THE SEA (Woodland Hills)

(818) 999-1533 / ww3.choicemall.com/underthesea
20929 Ventura Boulevard, Woodland Hills
(Exit Ventura Fwy [101] S. on De Soto Ave., R. on Ventura. [TG: 560 C3])

    Murals of mermaids and octopuses submerge your children in a world of play at Under the Sea. This indoor play area has a bounce house, a ball pit, soft play mats, Little Tykes™ cars, a playhouse, free standing slides, and a Baby Corner. Socks are required in the play area. Ask about classes, including modern dance and Mommy & Me. You are welcome to bring your own food in and enjoy a meal at the picnic tables toward the entrance. There are three other UNDER THE SEA locations.

      Hours: Open Mon. - Fri., 10am - 6pm. Open Sat. and Sun. for private parties only.
 Admission: $6 per child; adults are free.
       Ages: 6 months to 7 years.

-----GREAT OUTDOORS-----

ABALONE COVE SHORELINE PARK

(310) 377-1222 - park; (310) 377-0360 ext. 309 - guided hikes /
www.palosverdes.com/rpv/recreationparks
5907 Palos Verdes Drive South, Rancho Palos Verdes
(Exit Harbor Fwy [110] W. on Pacific Coast Hwy., L. on Western Ave., R. on Palos Verdes Dr. S. [TG: 823 A4])

    This beautiful cliff-side park on the Palos Verdes Peninsula has a grassy park area at the top and plenty of picnic tables. The ocean view (and sighting of Catalina on a clear day) is spectacular. This park is the only way down to Abalone Cove and the great tidepools at Portuguese Point, which you are welcome to explore on your own. (Ask for a tidepool map at the entrance.) A paved pathway follows along the street for a short while before veering downward. The quarter mile dirt path is a bit more direct, as well as a bit steeper. Be prepared to carry your gear (chairs, towels, food, fishing poles, etc.). Fishing is allowed as long as participants ages 16 years and up have a California fishing license, which is not sold here. Bring your own bait, too. Lifeguards are on duty at the cove during the summer months. Note: The WAYFARERS CHAPEL (on pg. 141) is directly across the street.

    A variety of outdoor, educational, guided tours and hikes are offered, including a two-hour tidepool tour to discover small creatures native to California waters. Wear shoes with good tread as you must first hike down the trail, then cross a cobblestone beach to get to the rocky tidepool. And remember - wet rocks are slippery rocks! Your guide will explain all about the animals you see and ones that you may gently touch. Look for sea stars, sea slugs, sea urchins, crabs, octopuses, and mussels, and scan the ocean for seals and sea lions. Tours are given on days when low tides are one foot above sea level, or lower. Tips: Wear sunscreen and bring a water bottle.

    Other two-hour habitat hikes include a good amount of hiking and information about the environment. Topical hikes deal with native animals, geology, plants, ecology, and the Native American's usage of natural resources, or any combination thereof. Depending on the topic emphasized or being studied, hikers will see and learn about coastal sage scrub, bluffs, and active landslides.

      Hours: Gates are open most of the year, Mon. - Fri., noon - 4pm; Sat., Sun., and holidays, 9am - 4pm. Gates are open Memorial Day through Labor Day daily, 9am - 4pm. Tours are given by reservation only and require a three-week advance notice. Closed New Year's Day, Thanksgiving, Christmas Eve, and Christmas Day.
 Admission: Parking is $5 per car; $15 per bus. Tours are $2 for adults; $1 for children 13 and under; with a minimum of $15.
       Ages: 6 years and up.

APOLLO PARK

William J. Barnes Avenue, Lancaster
(Exit Antelope Valley Fwy [14] W. at Ave. 'G', R. on William Barnes Ave. [across from 50th St. W.], past the General Fox Airfield, into the park. [TG: 3924 J7])

This *space*ious park has three man-made lakes that are named after the astronauts from Apollo XI: Lake Aldrin, Lake Armstrong, and Lake Collins. The lakes are stocked with trout, and while there is not a fee for fishing, a California state fishing license is needed for those over 16 years of age. The park, though surrounded by the desert, is picturesque with its shade trees, bridges over portions of water, and plenty of run-around room. There is also a small playground. My kids were intrigued by the glass-enclosed, well-built mock-up of a command module. The placard describes the dedication of the park to the Apollo program. (Don't you love sneaking in a history lesson?) Tip: Bring bread to feed the relentlessly friendly ducks and geese. This ritual alone took us over half an hour!

Hours: Open daily, dawn - dusk.
Admission: Free
Ages: All

BLUFF'S PARK / PAPA JACK'S SKATE PARK

(310) 317-1364 / ci.malibu.ca.us
24250 Pacific Coast Highway, Malibu
(Exit Ventura Fwy [101] S. on Las Virgenes Rd., which turns in to Malibu Cyn Rd. Malibu Cyn ends at Bluff's Park on P.C.H. [TG: 628 H7])

Bluff's Park overlooks the Pacific Ocean. Besides the gorgeous view, it also has multi-purpose fields, soccer fields, two baseball diamonds (the concession stands are open on game days), picnic tables, and a pathway that leads down to the beach.

Skateboarders and bladers must come to the park office at Bluff's first to sign up for a skate session at Papa Jack's, just down the road at 23415 Civic Center Way, next to city hall. This 10,000 square-foot paved park has fun boxes, a half pipe, a capsule, pyramid, grind rails, and a smooth surface to just skate around. All participants 17 years and under must have a signed parental waiver and wear safety equipment - helmet and knee and elbow pads.

Hours: Bluff's Park is open daily, dawn - dusk. The skate park is open Mon. and Wed., 3pm - 5pm; Fri. - Sat., noon - 5pm. Tues. and Thurs. are reserved for lessons. Call for summer hours.
Admission: Free to Bluff's Park. The skate park is $2 per two-hour session.
Ages: All for the park; 7 years and up for the skate park.

BRAND PARK

1601 W. Mountain Street, Glendale
(Exit Golden State Fwy [5] N. on Western Ave., R. on Mountain. [TG: 534 B7])

The front part of this thirty-acre park is comprised of green lawns, playgrounds, a few basketball courts, volleyball courts, and picnic tables. The back part, behind the museum and library, is a huge hilly area with miles of dirt and asphalt hiking trails (and for mountain bikers who like a real workout) that lead through chaparral into the Verdugo Mountains and around a reservoir. A two-and-a-half-mile fire road "trail" starts on the asphalt road up the hill and to the left of the fire road fork. Great view from the top.

The park sees a lot of action on the weekends. Look up THE DOCTORS' HOUSE MUSEUM (on pg. 86), as it and the beautiful adjacent Glendale Library are located in the park.

Hours: The park is open daily, sunrise - sunset.
Admission: Free
Ages: All

CARUTHERS PARK / BELLFLOWER SKATE PARK

(562) 866-5684

10500 Flora Vista Street at Caruthers Park, Bellflower

(Exit Artesia Fwy [91] N. on Bellflower Blvd., R. on Flower St., which turns into Flora Vista. [TG: 736 D6])

This 8,000 square-foot, supervision-free park features benches, ramps, rails, a curb, pyramid, snake run, hips, and bowls. A helmet and pads are encouraged. The adjacent, frequently-used Caruthers Park offers access to the bike path that runs along the riverbed (see BIKE TRAIL: LOS ANGELES RIVER TRAIL on page 170); large grassy areas; picnic tables; barbecue pits; and swing sets and other playground equipment.

Hours: Open daily, sunrise - sunset.

Admission: Free

Ages: All

CASTAIC LAKE RECREATION AREA

(661) 257-4050 - lake information; (661) 775-6232 - boat rentals / parks.co.la.ca.us

32100 Ridgeroute Road and Lake Hughes, Castaic

(Exit Golden State Fwy [5] E. on Lake Hughes. It's about 7 miles N. of Magic Mountain. [TG: 4279 G4])

There are so many ways to play in the great outdoors at the massive (8,000 acres) Castaic Lake Recreation Area. The lake and lagoon are stocked with trout and bass. A California state fishing license is needed for those who are over 16 years old. All kinds of boating activities are available. A lifeguarded swimming area at the lagoon (available seasonally), picnicking, and playgrounds can all be found in the park. Ask about their Jr. lifeguard program. The scenery is beautiful with shade and pine trees, plenty of grassy areas, and of course, the lake. Nature trails, for both hiking and biking, are as short as one mile and as long as seven miles. The trails range from an easy stroll to rugged hikes. Maps are available. Come spend the night in sites reserved for RV and tent camping. However long you choose to visit, an escape to Castaic Lake fits all your recreational desires!

Hours: Open daily, sunrise - sunset.

Admission: March through October, $6 per vehicle per day. November through February, $6 per vehicle on weekends and holidays only. Camping starts at $12 a night. A fourteen-foot aluminum, nine-horse-power boat rents for $25 for the first two hours and $5 an hour thereafter during the week; $30 for the first two hours and $8 an hour thereafter on the weekends.

Ages: All

CASTRO CREST

(818) 880-0367 / www.csp-angeles.com

Corral Canyon Road, Malibu

(Exit Pacific Coast Highway N. on Corral Canyon Rd., go about 5.2 very windy miles until it dead-ends. It's a part of Malibu Creek State Park. [TG: 628 B1])

My kids jumped out of the almost-stopped car and made a bee-line for the rock formations directly in front of us, the tallest of which they dubbed Pride Rock. A variety of moderately difficult trails lead hikers past just a few more formations. The trails roller-coaster either along the ridgeline offering panoramic views, on fire roads, or on roads that cut through a gorge. Although the green velvety-looking hills were covered with trees when we visited, we found relatively little shade along the trails we walked. Note: There are no restroom facilities here, but there are some off the main entrance at Los Virgenes. Tip: Bring your own water.

Hours: Open daily, 8am - sunset.

Admission: Free

Ages: 6 years and up.

CERRITOS REGIONAL PARK / SPORTS COMPLEX

(562) 924-5144 - regional park; (562) 916-8590 - sports complex;
(562) 403-7498 - pool / www.ci.cerritos.ca.us

19900 & 19700 Bloomfield Avenue, Cerritos

(From the San Gabriel Fwy [605], exit E. on Del Amo, L. on Bloomfield. From the Artesia Fwy [91], exit S. on Carmenita, R. on Del Amo, R. on Bloomfield. From Bloomfield, turn R. in the driveway where the sign states "Sports Complex," just N. of Target. [TG: 767 A3])

Thirteen lighted tennis courts, several baseball diamonds with stadium seating and lights, soccer fields, playgrounds, a small lake, a swimming pool (open seasonally), large open grassy areas, cement pathways throughout, and a large, outdoor skate park make this park a delight for the whole family. The gated, 10,000-square-foot concrete skate park has a grinding pole, pools, ramps, bowls, and a small fish bowl. The posted rules (enforced by patrolling policemen who <u>do</u> give out citations) state that skaters (no bikes allowed) must wear helmets and elbow and knee pads. Aluminum benches are available for visitors and tired skaters. My kids love to skate and blade here - I just don't like the foul language that is often prevalent.

Hours: The park is open daily, dawn - dusk. The skate park is open Wed. - Mon., 8am - dusk; Tues., 10am - dusk. The pool is open in the summer.

Admission: Free. The pool is free for Cerritos residents. Non-residents need to call and ask about an admission fee.

Ages: All

CHANTRY FLAT / STURTEVANT FALLS

(818) 790-1151 or (626) 574-5200 / www.r5.fs.fed.us/angeles

Santa Anita Avenue, Los Angeles

(Exit Foothill Fwy [210] N. on Santa Anita Ave., drive 6 miles to Chantry Flat picnic area. [TG: 537 E4])

Take the Gabrielino Trail about a mile and a half into the tree-lined Big Santa Anita Canyon. Cross the Winter Creek Bridge up the trail and go straight through the three-way junction. Ford the creek, then re-cross it where it takes a sharp bend to the left, and scramble over boulders to reach the foot of Sturtevant Falls, a fifty-five foot cascading waterfall. Caution: Climbing up the waterfall can be dangerous! The small rocky pool at the falls end is just right for wading or even a dip. The canyon is beautiful - oak trees line the streambed, along with maples and spruce trees. There are numerous other hiking trails to take in the immediate area, depending on how far you want to go. Note: The Lonergan Pack Station, just up the road, has very limited parking.

Hours: Open daily, dawn - dusk.

Admission: $5 per vehicle for an Adventure Pass.

Ages: 5 years and up.

CHARLES WILSON PARK / TORRANCE SKATEPARK

(310) 618-2930 - park; (310) 328-6069 - skatepark / www.tprd.torrnet.com; www.torranceskatepark.com

2200 Crenshaw Boulevard, Torrance

(From San Diego Fwy [405], exit S. on Crenshaw Blvd. Going S. on Harbor Fwy [110], exit W. on Carson St., L. on Crenshaw Blvd. Going N. on 110, exit at 220th, L. on Figuroa St., L. on Carson St., L. on Crenshaw Blvd. [TG: 763 F7])

This large, elongated park has a delightful playground for younger children, four baseball diamonds, grassy "fields," gently rolling hills lined with shade trees, stroller-friendly pathways that crisscross throughout, a horseshoe court in the northeast corner, several tennis courts, and a fountain in the middle. A roller hockey rink is available by reservation. On the first Sunday of each month, the Southern California Live Steamers Club offers free rides on their scale electric, steam, or diesel-powered trains. Call (310) 530-3153 for more train information. Every Tuesday and Saturday a Farmer's Market is held in the main parking lot.

A 23,000-square foot, stadium-lit street style skatepark is fabulous for intermediate and advanced skaters and in liners. It also has a beginner's area. Designed for skaters by skaters, the supervised park features a seven-foot bowl, a roof gap, planter boxes, hand rails, and a seven-foot pyramid - all satellite surfaced. A signed parental waiver, available on-line, must be on the records for participants 17 and under. Helmet, knee, and elbow pads are required. Rentals are available here. Skate sessions are two hours long. The first session on Sundays is reserved for kids 12 and under. Ask about special events. Note that the skatepark is located in the rear of the park, off Jefferson Street.

Hours: The park is open daily, 6am - 10pm. Train rides are offered on the first Sun., 11am - 3pm. The skatepark is open Mon. - Fri., 3:30pm - 7:45pm; Sat., 11am - 10pm; Sun., 11am - 7:45pm. Ask about extended summer hours. Closed Thanksgiving and Christmas.

Admission: The park is free. Skatepark sessions are $8 for non-members. Membership is available for $35 a year for an individual; $50 for a family. Sessions for members cost $5 per.

Ages: All for the park; 7 years and up for the skatepark.

CHATSWORTH PARK

(818) 341-6595

22360 Devonshire (South) or 22300 Chatsworth (North), Chatsworth

(Exit Simi Valley/San Fernando Valley Fwy [118] S. on Topanga Canyon Blvd., R. on Devonshire for the south park, or R. on Chatsworth for the north park. [TG: 499 H3/J3])

There are two Chatsworth parks; a north and a south. The north park has shade trees, baseball diamonds with stadium lights, a play area, a basketball court, volleyball court, and some pathways to explore.

My family is partial, however, to Chatsworth Park South. It has two tennis courts, a basketball court, a playground, open grassy areas, a community center building that offers lots of activities (including a wheelchair hockey league), a small natural stream running throughout, and picnic tables. Best of all, it has several hiking trails around the perimeter of the park with our favorite ones leading up to, through, and on top of the surrounding rocks. Note that you do have to go past working railroad tracks to hike up on the rocks and that this back part of the park is huge! Accompany your kids and don't be up there after dark. I love climbing rocks and my kids share this passion, so we think this park is "boulderdacious."

At the southern end of the south park, at 10385 Shadow Oak Drive, is the historic Hill-Palmer House. Take a tour through the old house while visiting the park. It is open the first Sunday of every month from 1pm to 4pm, and admission is free.

Hours: The parks are open daily, sunrise - 10pm.

Admission: Free

Ages: All

CHESEBRO CANYON

(818) 597-9192 / www.nps.gov/samo

Chesebro Canyon Road, Agoura Hills

(Going E. on Ventura Fwy [101], exit at Agoura Rd., L. on Palo Comado Canyon Rd., R. on Chesebro. Going W. on 101, exit N. on Chesebro Rd. When you're on Chesebro Rd., look for Chesebro Canyon Road on your R., after you pass Old Agoura Park. [TG: 558 E4])

Hike or bike on the numerous dirt trails here that go through canyons, grasslands, and riparian areas. The road most traveled is the one immediately accessible, the Chesebro Canyon Trail. The hike starts off moderately easy along a streambed and through a valley of oak trees. A picnic area is about a mile-and-a-half from the parking lot. Stop here, or continue on to more strenuous hiking. Bring your own water! You'll reach Sulphur Springs (almost another two miles), where the smell of rotten eggs lets you know you've arrived. This particular trail goes on for another mile through a variety of terrain. Several trails branch off and connect to the Chesebro Trail. Pick up a trail map at the SANTA MONICA MOUNTAINS NATIONAL PARK HEADQUARTERS (pg. 538), which is down the road a bit.

Hours: Open daily, sunrise - sunset.

Admission: Free

Ages: 3 years (for shorter hikes) and up.

CHEVIOT HILLS RECREATION AREA

(310) 837-5186 - park; (310) 202-2844 - pool

2551 Motor Avenue, Los Angeles

(Going W. on Santa Monica Fwy [10], exit at National. Drive past National, up Manning and go R. on Motor Ave. Going E. on 10, exit N. on Overland, R. on Pico, R. on Motor. Going S. on San Diego Fwy [405], exit E. on Pico, R. on Motor. [TG: 632 E5])

This large park really fits the bill of a recreation area with its basketball courts, baseball diamonds, tennis courts, and nice playground. During the hot summer months, when kids have played hard and need to cool off, they can take a dip in the municipal swimming pool.

Hours: The park is open Mon. - Fri., 9am - 10pm; Sat. - Sun., 9am - 6pm. Summer sessions for the pool are Mon. - Fri., 10am - 1pm and 2pm - 5pm; Sat. - Sun., 1pm - 5pm.

Admission: The park is free. Each swim session costs $1.25 for adults; ages 17 and under are free.

Ages: All

CHILDREN'S NATURE INSTITUTE (Los Angeles)

(310) 364-3591 / www.childrensnatureinstitute.org $

Children's Nature Institute provides guided walking tours for groups and families with babies, toddlers, and children up to 10 years old. With over sixty locations throughout the Los Angeles and Ventura counties, you're almost guaranteed to find a walk at a park near you. Some of the hikes are very easy, while others are longer and more strenuous. Tour guides usually encourage strollers, and they gear exploratory walks specifically towards kids. This is a tremendous opportunity for young children to be exposed to the beauty of nature, and to learn to respect the environment at a tender age. Note: Slightly older children who have gone on several Nature Adventures for Kids walks can help lead their peers, with adult assistance, on walks, too.

Bring your camera, sunscreen, and snacks, and enjoy the pitter patter of little feet next to yours on the nature trails!

Hours: Nature walks are given almost daily at various locations, and usually start at 10am.

Admission: $5 per family. Some parks also have parking fees.

Ages: Birth up to 10 years.

CLAREMONT SKATE PARK

www.ci.claremont.ca.us   !

1717 N. Indian Hill Boulevard, Claremont

(Exit San Bernardino Fwy [10] N. on Indian Hill. Or take the 30 Fwy E. to the end and continue E. on Foothill Blvd., L. on Wheeler Ave., R. on Base Line Rd. [30], R. on Indian Hill. [TG: 601 C1])

This medium-sized, concrete skate park has a bowl, grinding poles, grinding boxes, and some flat area to skate and gain momentum. Lights make it one of the few skate parks available at nighttime. Wearing helmet and knee and elbow pads is required. The rest of the park offers shade trees, picnic areas, and other amenities.

Hours: Open daily, 6am - 10pm.

Admission: Free

Ages: 7 years and up.

COLDWATER CANYON PARK / TREEPEOPLE

(818) 753-4600 or (818) 753-4631 / www.treepeople.org   !

12601 Mulholland Drive, Los Angeles

(Exit Ventura Fwy [101] S. on Coldwater Cyn Ave., which merges with Mulholland Dr. near the park. [TG: 562 F7])

Coldwater Canyon Park is beautiful, with large oak and California Bay Laurel trees shading the meandering trails. Most of the five miles of hiking trails are covered with sawdust and small broken twigs, making it bumpy for strollers. Picnic tables are available toward the park entrance.

If you and your kids are concerned about environmental issues, come visit the TreePeople, whose headquarters are in the park. This organization is dedicated to replenishing the diminishing number of trees and to encouraging recycling. Visit the small garden and the adjacent compost pile, which is a smelly, but a fascinating resource tool. Look for an educational center to be opening here soon.

Hour-long guided hikes and tours of the park are scheduled, such as the full-moon hike. Tours include in-depth information about conservation, as well as the importance of planting trees in areas damaged by pollution.

Interactive games are sometimes offered to children as they explore and hike the trails. Tours are also given specifically for school groups or other organizations, such as scouts, with advanced reservations. Other activities include nursery plantings and transplanting trees.

Hours: The park is open daily. Call to make a reservation for a TreePeople tour.

Admission: The park is free. Tours usually cost $5 for nonmembers; some activities are free.

Ages: 6 years and up.

DESCANSO GARDENS

(818) 949-4200 / www.descanso.com

1418 Descanso Drive, La Canada

(Exit Foothill Fwy [210] S. on Angeles Crest Hwy, R. on Foothill Blvd., L. on Verdugo Blvd., L. on Alta Canyada Rd., which turns into Descanso Dr. [TG: 535 A4])

$$

Descanso Gardens is over sixty acres of incredible beauty. It's not just a bed of roses here as lilacs, camellias, tulips, dogwood, and other flowers, also bloom. Although flowers bloom here year round, you can call for a specific bloom schedule. A network of stroller-friendly trails wind through the grounds. One trail that is particularly delightful goes through a forest of California oaks. There are also open grassy areas to run around.

The Japanese garden is intriguing because of its unique, maze-like layout. It also has ponds and a stream. Be on the lookout for squirrels, and land and water birds, as this is a haven for more than 150 species.

Take the forty-five-minute narrated tram tour to see and learn about all of Descanso Gardens. Hop aboard the five-minute model train ride for a more kid-oriented trip. Either way, bring your camera and enjoy your fragrant outing. Food is available at the cafe daily, 10am to 3pm; at the Japanese Tea Garden on weekends from 11am to 3pm (the restaurant is closed August, December, and January); or bring your own and use the picnic grounds adjacent to the parking lot. Ask about the numerous educational programs offered throughout the year and camps for kids in the summer. Hour-and-a-half guided tours are offered for school groups Monday through Friday at 10am.

Hours: The gardens are open daily, 9am - 5pm. Closed Christmas. Tram tours are offered Tues. - Fri. at 1pm, 2pm, and 3pm; Sat. - Sun. at 11am, 1pm, 2pm, and 3pm. Train rides are available every Sat. and Sun. from 10am - noon and 1pm - 4pm.

Admission: $6 for adults; $4 for seniors and students; $1.50 for ages 5 - 12; children 4 and under are free. On the third Tuesday of each month, admission is half price. The tram tour and train ride each cost $2 per person.

Ages: 2½ years and up.

DEVIL'S PUNCHBOWL

(661) 944-2743 / parks.co.la.ca.us

28000 Devil's Punchbowl Road, Pearblossom

(Exit Antelope Valley Fwy [14] E. on Ave S., R. on Pearblossom Hwy [138], R. on Longview, L. on Tumbleweed Rd., which turns into Devil's Punchbowl Rd. [TG: 4559 F3])

The "punchbowl" is a spectacular geological formation that looks like a huge, jagged bowl created from rocks. The 1,310-acre park consists of rugged wilderness rock formations along the San Andreas Fault, plus a seasonal stream. The hiking trails vary in degrees of difficulty. We hiked down into the punchbowl and back up along a looping trail in about half an hour. The terrain is diverse, ranging from desert plants to pine trees, as the elevation changes from 4,200 feet to 6,500 feet. Rock climbing is a popular sport here, whether you prefer climbing on boulders or scaling sheer rock walls.

The small nature center museum contains a few taxidermied animals and displays that pertain to this region. Outside the center a few live birds, such as owls and hawks, live in cages. The park also offers picnic areas and equestrian trails, and is host to many special events throughout the year. Ask about school field trips.

Hours: The park is open daily, sunrise - sunset. The nature center is open daily, 8am - 4pm. Closed Christmas.

Admission: Free
     Ages: 5 years and up.

DOUGLAS PARK

(310) 458-8310 / www.santa-monica.org
Wilshire Boulevard and 25th Street, Santa Monica
(Exit San Diego Fwy [405] W. on Wilshire Blvd. [TG: 591 G6])

This pleasant respite is just off a busy street. At the northern end is a wonderful playground for young children with a tennis court on either side. In the center of the park is a little nature area with a pond (and ducks, of course) and a cluster of trees. An expanse of lawn, a smaller pond, shaded concrete pathways throughout, and bridges add to the specialness of this park. Another unique feature is a shallow concrete "pool" used for trikes and skaters, although not at the same time. In the summer, a few fountains shoot water up here at unexpected intervals, providing a refreshing way to cool off and eliciting giggles.

Hours: Open daily, sunrise - sunset.
Admission: Free
     Ages: All

EARL BURNS MILLER JAPANESE GARDENS

(562) 985-8885 / www.csulb.edu/~jgarden
Earl Warren Drive at California State Long Beach, Long Beach
(Exit San Diego Fwy [405] S. on Bellflower, L. on State University Dr. Or, take Garden Grove Fwy [22] to the end, turn R. on Bellflower, R. on State University Dr. From State University Dr., go through the campus gates, turn L. on Earl Warren. The garden is on the L. [TG: 796 D5])

This beautiful one-acre Japanese garden has two waterfalls, a meditation rock garden, a quaint teahouse (to look in), and a koi pond. Kids can help feed the koi, so bring 25¢ for the food dispenser. As you cross over the zig-zag bridge into the gardens, share with your kids that it was built in this shape to side-step spirits because, according to Japanese tradition, spirits can only travel in straight lines! Free guided tours are provided for school and community groups.

Hours: Open Tues - Fri., 8am - 3:30pm; Sun., noon - 4pm. Closed Mon., Sat., spring break,
               Thanksgiving, and winter break.
Admission: Free. There is metered parking (to your right) in Student Lot 16 on weekdays; free parking on
               weekends.
     Ages: 3 years and up.

EAST AND RICE CANYONS

(661) 255-2974 / ceres.ca.gov/smmc/eastrice.htm
Off The Old Road, Newhall
(Exit Golden State Fwy [5] on Calgrove and go W. back under the freeway, S. on The Old Road about 1 mile. The trailhead is S. of the entrance to Towsley Canyon, just past the Church of Nazarene - look for signs. [TG: 4640 G5])

A year-round stream and a wide variety of plants and trees line trails that lead hikers away from city life and straight into nature. The Rice Canyon trail is a little over two miles round trip. It is a moderate walk that gets harder toward the end as it goes uphill. The trail follows along the stream and crosses over it a few times. If you smell petroleum, it's not coming from cars, but from natural oil seeps near the creek. This area was once part of an oil boom town. The East Canyon trail is almost four miles round trip. As you go steadily up in elevation, you'll pant harder, but you'll also see big-cone Douglas-fir trees and vistas of the Santa Clarita Valley. Be on the lookout for wildlife such as deer, foxes, skunks, and an abundance of birds. Neither trail loops, so I hope you like the way you came, because you get the opportunity to see it all again! Also look up TOWSLEY CANYON (pg. 70).

Hours: Open daily, sunrise - sunset.
Admission: Free
     Ages: 3 years and up.

EATON CANYON COUNTY PARK

(626) 398-5420 or (626) 794-1866 / www.ecnca.org

1750 N. Altadena Drive, Pasadena

(Going W. on Foothill Fwy [210], exit at Sierra Madre Blvd. The off ramp turns into Maple. Stay on Maple and turn R. on N. Altadena Dr. Or, going E. on 210, exit N. on Altadena Dr. [TG: 536 E6])

    Located in the foothills of the mountains, this 190-acre wilderness park has several rugged dirt trails leading up into the mountains. One of the most popular hikes starts at the nature center and continues a little over a mile on an easy trail through oak and sycamore trees to the Mt. Wilson toll bridge. If you feel like pushing it a bit, take the ½ mile stretch past the bridge up to Eaton Falls. Hardy hikers can take a trail up to Mt. Wilson, a "mere" ten-mile hike. Approximately two-thirds of this park was burned in a 1993 brush fire. As the slopes and flats recover from the fire, new plant growth continues to restore the park's beauty.

    There are shorter trails in the immediate vicinity of the nature center. One such trail is only a quarter of a mile and has a self-guiding pamphlet (pick it up from the nature center) that helps identify the plants. The first, and most important, plant to recognize is poison oak.

    The Eaton Canyon Wash (river bed) is filled with rocks and is fun to explore - when it's dry, of course. Eaton Creek flows through the canyon, except during the summer months. Pretty, shaded, and almost hidden picnic areas are found just off the parking lot. Remember to B.Y.O.W. - Bring Your Own Water.

    The nicely laid-out nature center contains display cases that hold rocks and animal skulls, mounted insects, and stuffed birds such as a great horned owl, quail, and a hummingbird. A diorama of the area is complete with a (stuffed) crouching mountain lion peering down. There are also several cases of live critters - snakes, including a rattlesnake, plus lizards, tree frogs, scorpions, and more. A few cubicles contain books, animal puppets, and some games. A 3-D map of the park shows the area's trails. Outside, a 150-seat amphitheater is the setting for environmental programs. The park offers many special events, such as free family nature walks which are given every Saturday from 9am to 11am.

    Hours: The park is open daily, sunrise - sunset. The nature center is open daily, 9am - 5pm. Closed New Year's Day and Christmas.

    Admission: Free

    Ages: 3 years and up.

ECHO PARK

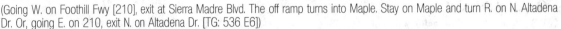

(213) 250-3578

1632 Bellevue Avenue, Los Angeles

(Going N. on Hollywood Fwy [101], exit on Echo Park Ave./N. Glendale Ave. Going S. on 101, exit L. on Alvarado, R. on Santa Ynez which runs into the lake on Glendale Blvd. [TG: 634 E1])

    This long lake, which is occasionally stocked with trout, is between the freeway and an older, lower income Los Angeles neighborhood. Paddle boat rentals are available daily during the summer and on weekends only the rest of the year. Beside the cement pathway all around Echo Lake, there are some shade trees, a few palm trees, a small playground, picnic tables, and some run-around space. The north end also has a bridge with Chinese-looking decorations on it that reaches over to a small island. The real reason I'm writing about this park is that this end also holds huge seasonal lotus plants that are contained in this area by a rope. Every July, Echo Lake, actually one of the largest lotus ponds in the United States, undergoes a spectacular transformation as the lotus flowers explode into blossom. See information about the Lotus Festival on page 591.

    Across the street and right next to the freeway is the Echo Park Recreation Center and a park. The park boasts a large sand box, a playground, an old basketball court, a few picnic tables with shade trees, a small lifeguarded swimming pool open for lap swim and recreational swim, and six lighted tennis courts. Note: Just down the street at 1419 Colton Street, (213) 481-2640, is an indoor swimming pool that is open year round.

    Hours: The park is open daily, sunrise - sunset. Call for hours for a specific activity.

    Admission: Free. The pool cost $1.25 for adults per session; ages 16 and under are free.

    Ages: All

EL DORADO EAST REGIONAL PARK

(562) 570-1771 / www.lbparks.org

7550 E. Spring Street, Long Beach

(Exit San Gabriel River Fwy [605] W. on Spring St. El Dorado Park is on the N. side; the Nature Center on the S. side. If going E. on Spring, use the Nature Center entrance and drive around to park. [TG: 796 G2])

El Dorado has 450 acres of lush green park with lots for kids to do! There are three stocked fishing lakes, that also have ducks clamoring for handouts; pedal boat rentals at $7 per half hour - open daily in the summer and 11am to 4pm on weekends the rest of the year; an archery range where targets are provided, but you must bring your own equipment; a model glider field; several playgrounds; four-and-a-half miles of biking trails, including access to the San Gabriel River cement embankment; and a one-mile, gasoline-powered scale train ride that runs Friday through Sunday year round (weather permitting) from 10:30am to 4pm. The cost is $2 for ages 4 and up; $1 for ages 3 and under. Call (562) 496-4228 for more information. One-hour hayrides are also available in the park for $150 for up to ten people, $7.50 for each additional person, and a maximum of twenty-five people. Call Larry's at (562) 865-3290 / www.ponyrides4u.net for information and reservations. Larry's also provides pony rides ($3) and a petting zoo ($1.25) on Sundays, March through September from 11am to 4pm. Organized youth groups are invited to camp at the park overnight. You can be as active or relaxed as you want (or as the kids let you!) at El Dorado Park. Also see EL DORADO NATURE CENTER and EL DORADO PARK WEST.

Hours: Open daily, 7am - dusk.

Admission: $3 per vehicle Mon. - Fri.; $5 on Sat. - Sun. and holidays. Entrance fee is good for a same-day visit to the Nature Center located across the street. Annual passes are $35.

Ages: All

EL DORADO NATURE CENTER

(562) 570-1745 / www.lbparks.org

7550 E. Spring Street, Long Beach

(Exit San Gabriel Fwy [605] W. on Spring St. El Dorado Park is on the N. side, the Nature Center is on the S. side. If going W. on Spring, use the park entrance and drive around to the nature center. [TG: 796 G2])

The eighty-five-acre El Dorado Nature Center is part of the El Dorado East Regional Park. When crossing over the wooden bridge leading to the museum and trail-heads, look down to see the many ducks and turtles swimming in the water below.

The Nature Center Museum has skulls, antlers, and other artifacts to touch; bugs to look at under a magnifier; a few cases of live insects and reptiles; a display of feathers and wings; and a huge book depicting various animal habitats. Contact the Center for information on their many special programs, such as the Turtle and Reptile Show, or summer camps.

Walk on a short, quarter-mile paved trail, or hike a two-mile, stroller-friendly dirt trail that goes under the pine trees. The longer trail winds around two lakes and a stream. I love being in God's beautiful creation! Picnicking is not allowed inside the Nature Center, but picnic tables and shade trees can be found outside the gates at the end of the parking lot. The Nature Center is truly "an oasis of greenery and woodland in the middle of Long Beach." Also see EL DORADO EAST REGIONAL PARK and EL DORADO PARK WEST.

Hours: The trails and park are open Tues. - Sun., 8am - 5pm. The museum is open Tues. - Fri., 10am - 4pm; Sat. - Sun., 8:30am - 4pm. The Nature Center is closed on Christmas.

Admission: $3 per vehicle, Tues. - Fri.; $5 on Sat. - Sun. and holidays. Walk in or bicyclists are free. Entrance fee is good for a same-day visit to El Dorado Regional Park located across the street. Annual passes are $35.

Ages: All

EL DORADO PARK WEST

(562) 570-3225 - park; (562) 425-0553 - tennis courts / www.lbparks.org

2800 Studebaker Road, Long Beach

(Exit San Gabriel River Fwy [605] W. on Spring St., L. on Studebaker. [TG: 796 F2])

This city park is just around the corner from its neighbors, EL DORADO EAST REGIONAL PARK and EL DORADO NATURE CENTER. Sprawling across both sides of Willow Street, this park features lots of grassy areas, picnic tables under shade trees, a Frisbee golf course, a couple of ponds with ducks, baseball diamonds, playgrounds, a large library, fifteen tennis courts, and an outdoor skate park. The concrete skate park offers street type of skating with ramps, bowls, grinding boxes, and more. Wearing safety equipment - helmet and elbow and knee pads - is enforced.

Hours: Open daily, sunrise - sunset. The tennis courts are open Mon. - Fri., 7am - 9pm; Sat. - Sun., 7am - 7pm.

Admission: Free to the park and skate park. Tennis courts are $4 per hour during day light hours; $6 per hour after 4pm and on weekends. (No additional fee if lights are used.)

Ages: All

EXPOSITION PARK

Exposition Park, Los Angeles

(Exit the Harbor Fwy [110] W. on Exposition Blvd., L. on Flower, L. on Figueroa. Or, exit Santa Monica Fwy [10] S. on Vermont, L. on Exposition, R. on Figueroa. Parking is available by entering the first driveway on the right. [TG: 674 A2])

The expansive Exposition Park encompasses the AIR AND SPACE GALLERY (pg. 80), CALIFORNIA AFRICAN AMERICAN MUSEUM (pg. 84), CALIFORNIA SCIENCE CENTER (pg. 85), IMAX THEATER (pg. 148), and NATURAL HISTORY MUSEUM OF LOS ANGELES (pg. 109). Up until now, most of park has simply been grassy areas surrounding these attractions. Exposition Park is currently undergoing development that is transforming it into a more family-oriented park. The perimeters of the park will be lined with trees and each of the four corners of Exposition Park will become distinct parks in their own right, with picnic table, barbecue grills, and playgrounds, as well as open grassy areas. A Community Center, with recreational facilities, will be located in the Southwest quadrant of the park. While paved pedestrian areas will provide easy access to and from the Coliseum, spacious lawns will provide a great place for picnics and tailgate parties.

The sunken Rose Garden, adjacent to the California Science Center, has always been a *scent*ral part of the park. Enjoy its seven acres of beauty where 16,000 specimens of 190 varieties of roses are cultivated. (I bet your kids didn't know there are so many different varieties.) The gardens are wonderful for walking, smelling the perfumed air, and picture taking, plus it's stroller accessible. There is also a huge fountain in the middle of this park. Often on weekends, people of various nationalities have their wedding ceremonies in the garden. (We like looking at the different types of wedding attire.)

Hours: Open daily, 8:30am - 5:30pm. Closed January - mid-March.

Admission: Free

Ages: 3 years and up.

FORT TEJON STATE HISTORIC PARK

(661) 248-6692 / www.forttejon.org

Fort Tejon Road, Lebec

(Exit Golden State Fwy [5] on Fort Tejon Rd. The park is on the W. side of the fwy, about 30 miles S. of Bakersfield.)

A long time ago battles were fought, and the U.S. Dragoons were garrisoned at this fort. Near the entrance is very small museum with several informational panels and a few military uniforms. Come and explore the long barracks building, walk through the officers' quarters that display war time memorabilia, and pretend to shoot the cannons at unseen enemies. Portions of the fort are still intact, such as a few foundational remains of buildings and a small cemetery. There are plenty of picnic tables and wide open grass areas, plus a few trails for hiking. Note: Primitive overnight camping is permitted here.

I highly recommend coming here when Dragoon Era Programs/Living History Days are presented or during Civil War Reenactments. Dragoon program activities include adobe brick making, playing old-fashioned games, participating in chores from days of yore, and more. Visitors will also see a blacksmith in action, open hearth cooking, military drills, and the everyday life of a soldier. During Civil War reenactment days troops of the Union and Confederate armies are authentically uniformed and equipped. Meet soldiers and civilians and tour their camps. See demonstrations of weapons and watch battle skirmishes at 10:30am and 1:30pm. Guided tours of the fort are given in between battles. Come see history in action. Come <u>live</u> history in action by participating in a day and/or overnight program for students. Kids will live life as it was in the 1800's.

Hours: The grounds are open daily, sunrise - sunset. The buildings are open daily, 8am - 4pm. Closed New Year's Day, Thanksgiving, and Christmas. Dragoon Era Programs are the first Sun. of most months, 10am - 4pm. Civil War Reenactments are held April through October on the third Sun. of the month, 10am - 4pm.

Admission: $2 for adults; ages 16 and under are free. Special programs and reenactments are $5 for adults; $3 for ages 6 - 12; children 5 and under are free. Call for student programs. Call for camping prices.

Ages: 3 years and up.

FOX HILLS PARK

(310) 253-6650 / www.culvercity.org
6161 Buckingham Parkway, Culver City
(Exit San Diego Fwy [405] N. on Sepulveda Blvd., R. on Green Valley Circle. It's on the corner of Birmingham and Green Valley. [TG: 672 H6])

This attractive little park, surrounded on the street level by office buildings and condos, is tucked away on a hill and offers a pleasant respite from city life. The hillside is landscaped with flowers, bushes, and trees and has a packed-dirt jogging/walking trail winding all around it. Exercise equipment, such as pull up bars and rings, are along the track. For kids, and those who work nearby and have extended lunchtime, the top of the hill has a playground, sand volleyball court, a basketball court, several tennis courts, a large flat grassy area (baseball field!), climbing trees, and picnic tables. My boys enjoyed the playground with its slides, climbing structures, and a cement dolphin. When the recreation center building is open, the staff offers board games and sometimes arts and crafts activities.

Hours: The park is open daily, 7am - 10pm. The rec center building is open daily in the summer, 10am - 7pm. It's open the rest of the year, Mon. - Fri., 3pm - 6pm; Sat. - Sun., 10am - 6pm. The tennis courts are open park hours, except Wed., 6am - noon and Tues., 3:30pm - 5:30pm, when they are closed.

Admission: Free

Ages: All

FRANK G. BONELLI REGIONAL COUNTY PARK / PUDDINGSTONE LAKE

(909) 599-8411- park information / parks.co.la.ca.us
120 E. Via Verde, San Dimas
(Take San Bernardino Fwy [10] or Orange Fwy [57] to the Foothill Fwy [210], exit on Raging Waters Dr. It's just S. of Raging Waters. [TG: 600 D6])

This sprawling park (almost 2,000 acres!) is centered around the huge man-made Puddingstone Reservoir, which is an ideal water hole for all your fishing and boating desires. A fishing license is required for those over 16 years old. If the fish are biting, catch bass, catfish, and trout. Boat rentals, (866) 677-3687, are available daily during the summer and on weekends the rest of the year. Reservations are required at any time of the year. Rental prices start at about $15 an hour for a four-passenger boat. You can also launch your own boat here, but it must pass an inspection here first. Jet skiing, fast boating, and water skiing are allowed on alternate days. Part of the lake is sectioned off in the summer months for swimming. Lifeguards are here then, too. Visitors can also feed the ducks and observe the wildlife at the lake area. We saw a heron and a crane, which my kids thought was pretty cool. Picnic areas are plentiful. There are a few playgrounds.

There are over fourteen miles of hiking trails here, or you can rein in your children with a horseback ride. Horse rentals are available Wednesday through Sunday, 10am to 5pm (later on weekends), for $20 an hour for ages 7 and up. Younger children can take a pony ride around the compound for $5. Horse rentals are closed most major holidays. Call (909) 599-8830 for more information. The scenery along the equestrian trail changes and ranges from cacti to pine trees - only in California! If you prefer riding bikes to horses, check out Wheel Fun Rentals which has three locations throughout the park. Bike rentals are open daily during the summer from 10am to dusk and on weekends only the rest of the year. Call (909) 592-6645 / www.wheelfunrentals.com for prices and more information.

Just outside the park grounds, treat yourself and the kids to a relaxing time in a hot tub. (Or just indulge yourself after spending a day with the kids!) Choose from fifteen private, hilltop tubs. Tub rentals are available Sunday through Thursday from noon to midnight for $30 an hour for two people; Friday and Saturday, it's $40 an hour. Call Puddingstone Hot Tubs Resort at (909) 592-2222 / www.hottubsresort.com for reservations. To reach the hot tubs, exit the 10 freeway at Fairplex Drive, turn left on Via Verde Drive and right on Camper View Drive.

    Hours: Open March 1 through October 31 daily, 6am to 10pm. Open November 1 through February 28, sunrise - 7pm. Closed Christmas. Boat rentals are available Fri., 7am - 4pm; Sat. - Sun., 6:30am - 4pm.

    Admission: $6 per vehicle; $3 for seniors during the week. A daily boat permit is $6.

    Ages: All

FRANKLIN CANYON

(310) 858-3834 / www.smmc.ca.gov

2600 Franklin Canyon Drive, Beverly Hills

(From L.A., exit San Diego Fwy [405] E. on Sunset Blvd., L. on Beverly Dr. [past Beverly Glen Blvd.], follow signs "to Coldwater Canyon Drive" to the stoplight at Beverly Hills Fire Station #2, turn L. - staying on Beverly Dr. Go 1 mile to Franklin Cyn. Dr., turn R. and go 1½ miles to Lake Dr., and follow signs to the canyon. From the Valley, exit Ventura Fwy [101] S. on Coldwater Cyn. Dr., R. on Franklin Cyn. Dr. [passing over Mulholland Dr.] to the canyon. [TG: 592 E1])

Franklin Canyon, almost 600 acres large, proves that there is more to Los Angeles than just skyscrapers. The lower canyon is the site of an old ranch house, which is now an office. A big green lawn and a few picnic tables are the only things down here. Follow the creek along the mile-and-a-half trail leading to the Upper Canyon and the Nature Center. Inside the Sooky Goldman Nature Center are mounted displays of the type of animals that live in the canyon, such as mountain lions, plus a scale model of the Santa Monica Mountains, an interactive exhibit and dioramas on Native Americans, and an exhibit on the importance of water conservation. For your tactile child, there are fossils, antlers, furs, bones, and even a few bird's nests to touch.

This Center is also the headquarters of the William O. Douglas Outdoor Classroom, which is really the name for numerous, on-going, free nature programs. Docent-led tours are open for the general public daily. There are several programs for all ages that range from Babes in the Woods, which is a stroller-friendly walk on a paved trail, to Nearly Full Moon Hikes, geared for older kids to have a howling good time. Tours are available for school groups Wednesday through Friday between 10am and noon.

The canyon has a variety of trees such as California live oaks, black walnuts, and sycamores. Wildlife here includes deer, bobcats, coyotes, rabbits, and lizards. The Upper Reservoir has reverted to a natural lake and is a wetland area for herons and other waterfowl. Enjoy your day in the wilds of L.A.!

    Hours: The canyon entrance is open daily, sunrise - sunset. The Nature Center is open daily, 10am - 4pm. The center is closed on major holidays.

    Admission: Free

    Ages: All

GANESHA PARK

(909) 620-2321

1600 N. White Avenue, Pomona

(Exit San Bernardino Fwy [10] N. on Garey Ave., L. on McKinley. [TG: 600 H6])

Just down the street from the Pomona fairgrounds and the NATIONAL HOT ROD ASSOCIATION

MOTORSPORTS MUSEUM (see pg. 109) is this nice neighborhood park. It has a half basketball court, a good-sized playground with a tall lighthouse slide, other slides, swings, picnic tables, barbecue grills, two tennis courts, a picnic pavilion, and some grassy run-around area. The pool here is open seasonally and has a diving board, a shallow end (although not where the diving board is), and a twisty water slide. The snack bar is usually open the same hours as the pool.

    Hours: Open daily, sunrise - sunset. Call for pool hours.

Admission: Free. Pool admission is $1.50 per person.

    Ages: All

GARDEN OF THE GODS

(310) 589-3200 or (310) 455-1030 / www.smmc.ca.gov

Red Mesa Drive, Chatsworth

(Exit Ronald Reagan Fwy [118] S. on Topanga Canyon, R. Santa Susana Pass, R. on Red Mesa. [TG: 499 J2])

    I'm not really sure if the gods would use this twenty-three-acre garden, but it's a great one for mortals to visit. Sandstone rock formations dot the park and make it a delight for kids who like to climb. A short, easy trail leads westward towards the rocks. On a clear day, you've got a good view of the valley. There are other, longer trails to hike, too. History buffs might appreciate knowing that portions of an old stage coach route that once ran over the Santa Susana Pass run through this park.

    Hours: Open daily, sunrise - sunset.

Admission: Free

    Ages: 3 years and up.

GATES CANYON

(818) 880-6461

25801 Thousand Oaks Boulevard, Calabasas

(Exit Ventura Fwy [101] N. on Las Virgenes Rd., R. on Thousand Oaks. [TG: 558 J3])

    Besides the playground, tennis courts, basketball court, and picnic area here, skateboarders have their own little haven here. The portable skate park (i.e. wooden ramps and other skate elements on top of asphalt) is available at certain times throughout the week. Parental waivers are required and all participants must wear a helmet and elbow and knee pads.

    Hours: The park is open daily, sunrise - sunset. The skate park is open Tues. and Thurs., 3pm - 6pm; Sat., 1pm - 5pm. Call for summer hours.

Admission: The park is free. Skating is $2 a day or $20 a month.

    Ages: All

GLENDALE SKATEPARK

(818) 548-6420 / parks.ci.glendale.ca.us

229 S. Orange Street, Glendale

(Exit Golden State Fwy [5] E. on Colorado St., L. on Orange. It's near the Glendale Galleria. [TG: 564 E5])

    This good-sized skate park has two bowls, a kidney-shaped pool, ramps, slide rails, and more all on a concrete surface. The park is fenced-in and staff is on hand at all times. Skaters under 18 years must have a parent or legal guardian sign a waiver. Wearing helmet and knee and elbow pads is a requirement. No rentals are available. This is supposed to be temporary location, while a permanent facility is being built at Verdugo Park. The above number works for both facilities.

    Hours: Open during the school year, Mon. - Fri., 3pm - dark; Sat., 10am - noon for 12 year olds and under; noon - dark for all ages; Sun., noon - dark. Open longer hours during the summer.

Admission: Free

    Ages: 7 years and up.

GREYSTONE MANSION AND PARK

(310) 550-4654 / www.beverlyhills.org

905 Loma Vista, Beverly Hills

(Exit Santa Monica Fwy [10] N. on Robertson Blvd., R. on Santa Monica Blvd., L. on San Vicente Blvd., L. on Sunset Blvd., R. on Mountain Dr., R. on Loma Vista. Look for park signs. [TG: 592 G5])

Edward Doheny made an oil discovery that enabled him to become one of the world's largest oil producers. In 1927 he put a great deal of his wealth into constructing the fifty-five room Greystone mansion, designed in Gothic and neo-classical styles. It was built using mainly grey stones (hence the name), plus limestone facing, a slate roof, and seven magnificent brick chimneys. Opened, iron gates at the end of a stone driveway lead to an outside porch that's made of marble. The basement used to house a bowling alley and billiards room. This multi-story, castle-like mansion is the epitome of opulence and, although you may not go into it, you are welcome to peer through the windows. We looked and saw an elegant entry way with black and white checkered tiles, a gorgeous chandelier, elaborately carved wooden banisters, and several archways that are followed by incredibly long hallways. There isn't any furniture inside. Quite a few shows have been filmed here including episodes of *Murder She Wrote* and the movie, *Ghostbusters II*. Walk around to the front sundeck for a gorgeous view of Beverly Hills and the Los Angeles area.

Behind the mansion is a dungeon (according to my boys) built into the hillside. The adjacent, closed, control room has levers and a high voltage sign, which clinched the dungeon notion. Imagination definitely reigns here!

Tiered, lush gardens and extensive grounds lavishly landscaped into and around the hillside are immaculately maintained. Go up the stone steps or walk the pathways to see the acres of grassy areas, courtyards surrounded by trimmed hedges, shade trees, some koi fish and turtles in the ponds, reflecting pools, fountains, and a few park benches. A highlight for my kids was simply running down the long, sloping stone driveway - then panting their way back up.

Hours: Open April through October, 10am - 6pm. Open November through March, 10am - 5pm. Closed New Year's Day and Christmas.

Admission: Free

Ages: All

GRIFFITH PARK

(323) 913-4688 or (323) 913-7390 or (213) 485-5501 / www.laparks.org

4730 Crystal Springs Drive, Los Angeles

(Going N. on Golden State Fwy [5] or W. on Ventura Fwy [134], exit at Zoo Dr. and follow the signs. Going E. on 134, exit S. on Victory Blvd., L. on Zoo Dr. Going S. on 5 Fwy, exit S. on Western, L. on Victory Blvd. to Zoo Dr. [TG: 564 B4])

The vast 4,100 acres of the eastern Santa Monica Mountains, known as Griffith Park, is really several parks in one. One part consists of enormous stretches of grassy lawns with several picnic areas and children's attractions, such as the merry-go-round and playground equipment near Park Center. A particularly interesting picnic area is the Old Zoo Picnic area on Griffith Park Drive. It has tables near obsolete caves and cages that were once part of the original zoo. The caves, or concrete and stone outcroppings, were small "natural" settings for lions and tigers and bears. Kids can prowl and roar around inside them. At the back of the shallow caves are locked, steep, stony steps leading up to other cages. There are several barred cages, too, along the same row of enclosures as the caves. More cages, a large empty building, and hiking trails are just steps away on a pathway that hairpins back over the caves. Explore away!

Another part of the park incorporates the zoo, an observatory, and two museums. Look up LOS ANGELES ZOO (pg. 183), GRIFFITH OBSERVATORY AND PLANETARIUM (pg. 92), AUTRY MUSEUM OF WESTERN HERITAGE (pg. 82), and TRAVEL TOWN (pg. 121) for more information. Note: The Greek Theater, a nationally-renown venue for concerts and other events, is just down the road.

The largest part of the park, two-thirds of it, is the wilderness area with fifty-three miles of trails for hiking and horseback riding. Be on the lookout for deer, red-tailed hawks, opossums, coyotes, and other critters. One of the most popular hikes is three miles round trip, beginning at the observatory and extending up to the one of highest points in the park - Mt. Hollywood. On a clear day the view is unbeatable. The famous Hollywood sign is easily seen from the observatory, too. Rugged wilderness trails as well as easy walking trails network throughout this gigantic park located in the middle of L.A. Call or visit the ranger station in the park for all trail information. Also check out the LA. Orienteering Club which offers monthly nature walks for all skill levels. They incorporate learning survival skills such as map and compass reading with their hikes.

Bike riding is another exercise alternative. A bike trail runs along a portion of the LA. River that passes by Griffith Park, or just ride along the fairly level roads inside the park. Rentals are available at 4730 Crystal Spring Drive, in the park, for $8 an hour. The rental place is open Saturdays and Sundays, year-round, from 11am to 6pm (open until 7pm in the summer). Call (323) 662-6593 for more information.

Other noteworthy attractions, from the northern end of the park to the southern end, include: 1) **Los Angeles Live Steamers** - located west of the Victory Boulevard entrance to the park, next to TRAVEL TOWN. This club offers free, twelve-minute, large-scale model train rides on Sundays from 11am to 3pm. Call (323) 661-8958 or (818) 762-0272 for more information. Note that the barn-like structure at the edge of the Live Steamers site once belonged to Walt Disney. It is the place he built model trains and brainstormed about Disneyland. The barn contains pictures, memorabilia, and model trains. It is open to tour through the third Sunday of every month from 11am to 3pm - and, unlike anything else Disney, it's free. 2) **Merry-go-round** - located off Griffith Park Drive, south of the Zoo. The **antique carousel**, with its sixty-eight carved horses, offers rides daily in the summer, and on weekends and holidays the rest of the year, from 11am to 5pm. Rides are $1.50 for everyone over 11 months old. Call (323) 665-3051 for more information. Non-fee **tennis courts** are here, too. **Shane's Inspiration Playground**, a large boundless playground, is also located here. It was constructed for physically-challenged children and has several age-appropriate play areas with paved pathways, lowered monkey bars, high-backed swings, rocket ship and airplane apparatuses, signs in Braille, ramps to interconnect the play areas, raised sand tables to accommodate wheelchairs, courts with lowered basketball hoops, and stainless steel slides for hearing-impaired kids. At Shane's Inspiration, able-bodied and disabled children can play side-by-side. 3) **Pony rides** and **covered wagon rides** - located at the Los Feliz entrance to the park. Each ride is $2 for kids 1 years old to 100 pounds, and available Tuesday through Sunday from 10am to 4pm. Call (323) 664-3266 for more information. 4) **Train rides** and **simulator** - located at the Los Feliz entrance to the park. The eight-minute, mini-train ride chugs past weathered Western town facades. (During Christmas season, it makes a stop in the "North Pole" and kids can visit with Santa.) The train costs $2 for ages 19 months and older; $1.50 for seniors; children 18 months and under are free. The simulator, which simulates bobsledding, riding a roller coaster, or being in an airplane, costs $2 per person. Both are open daily from 10am to 4:30pm. Call (323) 664-6903 for more information on either attraction. 5) **Tennis courts**, **soccer fields**, **rugby fields**, a **swimming pool**, and **golf course** - located at the Los Feliz entrance to the park. (The cross street is Riverside.) The twelve tennis courts are open during the week at no charge and open Saturday to Sunday from 7am to 7pm. It cost $8 an hour to play. Call (323) 661-5318 for more information. The pool is open mid-June to September, Monday through Friday, 2pm to 6pm; Saturday and Sunday, noon to 3pm and 4pm to 7pm. Adults are $1.50 per session; kids 17 years and under are $1. Call (323) 644-6878 seasonally, for pool information. This area also has the well-used Los Feliz par-three course, which is great for beginners. Call (323) 663-7758 for more information. 6) **Bird Sanctuary** - located on Vermont Canyon Road, northeast of the Observatory. This verdant area has a short, stroller-friendly nature trail that crosses over a creek and loops around. A wide variety of birds flock here and make it their home. It's open daily from 10am to 5pm. 7) **Ferndell** - located near the Western Avenue entrance. This is a pretty spot to rest and picnic. Ferns and flowers growing along the brook make it an attractive, cool haven on hot days and nature trails take you into the heart of the park. A snack stand, open seasonally, is also available here. There are refreshment stands located throughout the park, as well as restaurants at golf courses and at the Autry Museum.

Some of the equestrian centers around the park include: **Bar S. Stables**, (818) 242-8443 - located at 1850 Riverside Drive in Glendale. It's open Monday through Friday, 8am to 4pm; Saturday through Sunday, 8am to 4:30pm. During the winter, the stables are closed Wednesdays and Thursdays. Riding, available on a first come-first served basis, costs $18 per hour per person; $25 for an hour-and-a-half. The minimum age is 7. A twenty-minute school or scout presentation is available on horse care and safety for an additional $30 for the group.

Special evening rides begin at 4:30pm and include a half-hour of riding, an hour dinner break at Viva Fresh (www.vivacantina.com), followed by another hour-and-a-half of riding. The cost is $45 per person with a minimum of two people. Dinner is not included in this price. **J.P. Stables**, (818) 843-9890 is located at 1914 Mariposa Street in Burbank. It's open daily, 8am to 5pm. Riding costs $18 for one hour; $30 for an hour-and-a-half. The minimum age is 7 years old. **L.A. Equestrian Center**, (818) 840-8401 / www.la-equestriancenter.com, is located at 480 Riverside Drive in Burbank. It's open daily, 8am to 4pm; an hour later in the summer. Riding costs $20 an hour; $30 for an hour-and-a-half. The minimum age is 6 years old (and four feet tall). Ask about the sunset/barbeque rides that operate April through October every other Friday evening. After an hour-and-a-half horseback ride, guests come back to the ranch/center for a dinner of barbecue chicken, beans, potato salad, and rolls. The sunset rides begin at 6pm and cost $40 per person. **Sunset Ranch Hollywood Stables**, (323) 464-9612 / www.sunsetranchhollywood.com, is located at 3400 N. Beachwood Drive in Los Angeles. It's open daily, 9am - 3:30pm. Riding is $20 an hour, with a minimum age limit of 7 years. The much-acclaimed sunset rides begin around 5:30pm. Ride over the hills, enjoy dinner at Viva Fresh (www.vivacantina.com), and then leisurely head back to the stables to arrive around 10:30pm, or so. The sunset rides are $40 per person during the week for a group of at least 10 people; minimum age 16 years. Friday nights the rides are open to individuals and cost $45. The price of dinner is not included in the cost of the rides.

      Hours: The park is open daily, 6am - 10pm.

  Admission: Free

      Ages: All

HANSEN DAM RECREATION AREA

(323) 906-7953 or (213) 236-2357; (818) 899-3779 aquatics center / www.laparks.org

11798 Foothill Boulevard, Lake View Terrace

(Exit Golden State Fwy [5] E. on Osborne St., R. on Foothill, R. on Dronfield Ave. [TG: 502 J1])

    This large, somewhat run-down park offers a few hiking trails, a picnic area, ball fields, and a few scattered playgrounds. Its best features are a small man-made lake and an adjacent year-round swimming pool. The recreation lake, with cement sides, offers paddle boat and kayak rentals. Kayakers must first take a safety class to be eligible to rent the boats. Catfish and bass fishing are also available. A fishing license is needed for ages 16 years and up.

    The non-heated, gated pool, which is referred to as the swimming lake, is four-feet deep all around, very large, and extremely long. Lifeguards are on duty when it's open. Coarse sand all around the pool, a sand volleyball court, and no shade offers a quasi beach-like atmosphere. A snack stand is open in the summertime. Note: The Los Angeles Children's Museum is planning to open a 60,000 square foot, hands-on museum in this recreation area sometime soon. It should be absolutely wonderful!

      Hours: The park is open daily, dawn - dusk. The pool is open in the summer daily, 9am - 7pm; open the rest of the year, Sat. - Sun., noon - 4pm. Pedal boat rentals are usually open 10am - one hour before sunset.

  Admission: Park entrance is free. Pool admission is $1.25 for adults; free for seniors, and ages 17 and under. Youths 7 and under must be accompanied by an adult. Pedal boat rentals are $9 a half hour, $12 an hour.

      Ages: 3 years and up.

HERITAGE PARK (Cerritos)

(562) 916-8570 / www.ci.cerritos.ca.us

18600 Bloomfield, Cerritos

(From San Gabriel Fwy [605], exit E. on South St., L. on Bloomfield. From Artesia Fwy [91], exit S. on Bloomfield. [TG: 767 A1])

    One if by land, two if by sea . . . . The most unique feature of this noteworthy park is an island with a kid-size version of an old New England town. Cross the covered bridge and be transported back in time. (Not literally, it's just the atmosphere of the island.) This "town" has a replica of Paul Revere's house, a cemetery, and the North Church Tower, which has two slides. (Creative parents can reinforce a Paul Revere history lesson here.) The town is also comprised of a series of little buildings with play space and more slides in them, small cannons to sit on or "fire", and small replicas of British ships harbored in the water. They're designed for pint-sized sailors to climb aboard. The island has a brook running through it and plenty of shade trees, so it is refreshingly cool even on hot days.

The ducks swimming in the "moat" surrounding the island are always looking for a handout, so be sure to bring old bread. Across the water is a wonderful, large play area with swings, slides, and climbing aparatus. The park also has picnic tables, a few barbecues, basketball courts, large grass areas, climbing trees, and a baseball diamond with stadium-type benches.

Hours: The park is Mon. - Fri., 9am - 10pm; Sat. - Sun., 8am - 6pm (until 8pm in the summer.)
Admission: Free
Ages: All

HOPKINS WILDERNESS PARK

(310) 318-0668 / www.redondo.org
1102 Camino Real, Redondo Beach
(Exit Harbor Fwy [110] W. on Sepulveda, which turns into Camino Real. [TG: 763 A7])

Escape to the wilderness of Redondo Beach. This gated, eleven-acre hilltop park has two streams running through it, two ponds, and a wonderful view of the city. Hike along the nature trail that takes you through California Redwood and pine trees; through a meadow - be on the lookout for butterflies and lizards; and to the small waterfall and pond where turtles, crayfish, and bullfrogs have made their homes. Wilderness Park also has a campground and is a popular spot for local, overnight camping.

Hours: Open Thurs. - Tues., 10am - 4:30pm. Closed Wed., New Year's Day, Thanksgiving, Christmas, and in bad weather. No overnight camping on Tues. or Wed.
Admission: The park is free. Tent camping (no stakes allowed) is $5 a night for non-resident adults (residents are $4); $3 a night for non-resident kids 17 and under (residents are $2). Residency is proven by bringing a utility bill or photo I.D. Picnic tables and barbecue pits are available for campers.
Ages: 3 years and up.

HUNTINGTON LIBRARY, ART COLLECTIONS AND BOTANICAL GARDENS

(626) 405-2125 / www.huntington.org
1151 Oxford Road, San Marino

See the entry for HUNTINGTON LIBRARY, ART COLLECTIONS AND BOTANICAL GARDENS on page 98 for details.

JOHNNY CARSON PARK

Bob Hope Drive and Parkside Avenue, Burbank
(Going W. on Ventura Fwy [134], exit N. at Hollywood Wy., go R. at end of the off ramp on Alameda Ave., R. on Bob Hope Dr. Going E. on 134, exit N. on Bob Hope Dr. It's across the street from NBC Studio and just down the street from Warner Bros. Studio. [TG: 563 E4])

Despite the proximity of the freeway, this pleasant park offers a refuge, of sorts, in downtown Burbank. Kids enjoy the large grassy areas, small woods, climbing and shade trees, and stroller-friendly dirt pathways that run throughout the park. The Tonight Show Playground, for today's kids, has slides, swings, and climbing apparatus. Picturesque bridges go over what I first thought was a seasonal stream, but it is only a drainage "creek." Come enjoy a picnic here before or after you take the NBC (pg. 165) or WARNER BROS. (pg. 167) studio tours.

Hours: Open daily, sunrise - sunset.
Admission: Free
Ages: All

KENNETH HAHN STATE RECREATION AREA

(323) 298-3660 / parks.co.la.ca.us

4100 S. La Cienega Boulevard, Los Angeles

(Exit Santa Monica Fwy [10] S. on La Cienega Blvd., exit E. at the turnoff with signs for Kenneth Hahn. [TG: 673 A2])

This spacious, 320-acre natural parkland in the heart of Baldwin Hills has hilly grasslands, forest areas, and several dirt hiking trails. It also features a large lake that is stocked with trout in the winter, and catfish, bluegill, and bass in the summer. The fishing is free, but ages 11 and up need a license. Swimming in the water is not allowed. You may, however, feed the ducks who are always looking for a handout. There are seven picnic areas (which were a bit run down when we visited), complete with barbecue grills, for families to enjoy as well as a few scattered playgrounds and basketball and volleyball courts.

Hours: Open daily, sunrise - sunset. Closed Christmas.

Admission: Free during the week; $3 per vehicle on weekends and on county holidays.

Ages: All

LACY PARK

(626) 304-9648 / www.ci.san-marino.ca.us

3300 Monterey Road, San Marino

(Exit Foothill Fwy [210] S. on Sierra Madre Blvd., R. on Huntington Dr., R. on Virginia Rd. The park is on the L. [TG: 596 B1])

This is one of the prettiest parks we've visited - it's so well maintained and beautifully landscaped. In the center is a large expanse of immaculately-kept grass. Encircling it are several varieties of trees, including oak, pine, and palm. An outside dirt loop track, which is about a mile long, is designated for joggers and walkers. An inside paved loop trail is designated for cyclists and rollerskaters. The playground has the normal play equipment plus talking tubes (i.e. where two people can talk to each other through a long tube) and a few patches of trees to play hide and seek. There are also a few scattered benches and picnic tables. The west entrance has several rose arbors blooming seasonally. Six tennis courts, operated by the San Marino Tennis Foundation, are also on the grounds. Call (626) 793-1622 for playing times and prices.

Hours: Open year-round, Mon. - Fri., 6:30am - sunset. Open May through October on weekends, 8am - 8pm; November through April, 8am - 6pm. Closed New Year's Eve, New Year's Day, Thanksgiving, Christmas Eve, and Christmas Day.

Admission: Free on weekdays for everyone, and on weekends for residents, too. Entrance is $3 for ages 5 and up on weekends for non-residents.

Ages: All

LADERA LINDA COMMUNITY CENTER

(310) 541-7073 - park; (310) 544-5264 / www.palosverdes.com/rpv/recreationparks

3201 Forrestal Drive, Rancho Palos Verdes

(Exit Harbor Fwy [110] W. on Pacific Coast Hwy., L. on Western Ave., R. on Palos Verdes Dr. S. (NOT Palos Verdes Dr. N.), R. on Forrestal. [TG: 823 D5])

This park features wilderness areas, two grass volleyball courts, a basketball court, a small playground, and, closer to where the additional parking lot is located, two paddle tennis courts and (up the wooden stairs) soccer and baseball fields. There are picnic tables and a few shade trees, too. The community center building is home to Montessori school classes, game rooms, and a Discovery Room. The small Discovery Room has a few live animals, displays of rocks and fossils, and information about and photos of this area. Ask about the REACH programs for the developmentally disabled.

Two-hour, docent-led hikes offered by the center enable groups of kids, minimum ten, to explore the coastal habitat of the Palos Verdes Peninsula. Look out for and learn about coastal sage scrub, native trees, and wildflowers, as well as important critters such as lizards, butterflies, and birds. Hikes are moderately difficult, so bring a water bottle and wear sunscreen. The hike/tours can focus on a topic of your choice, such as plants, animals, fossils, or the geology of the area, including a visit to a rock quarry. A visit to the Discovery Room, with explanations about the exhibits, is included in your time here.

Hours: The park and Discovery Room are open Memorial Day through Labor Day, Mon. - Fri., 1pm - 5pm; Sat. - Sun., 10am - 5pm. It's open the rest of the year, Mon., Wed., and Fri. - Sun., 1pm - 5pm. Closed New Year's Day and Christmas. Tours are set up by reservation.

Admission: Free to the park. Tours are $2 for adults; $1 for children 13 and under.

Ages: All for the park; 7 years and up for the tours.

LIBERTY PARK (Cerritos)

(562) 916-8565 / www.ci.cerritos.ca.us
19211 Studebaker Road, Cerritos
(Exit San Gabriel River Fwy [605] W. on South St., L. on Studebaker Rd. [TG: 766 F2])

Experience the freedom at Liberty Park to do almost anything. The park offers long grassy areas to run around, three playground areas, picnic tables, barbeque pits, three picnic shelters, three sand volleyball courts, a 330-yard walking/jogging track, a softball field, a disc (Frisbee) golf course, outside exercise clusters equipped with pull up bars and more, and six lighted tennis courts. Tennis is free for Cerritos residents (show a driver's license or utility bill for proof of residency) and $5 per hour for non-residents. A bike path runs along the Los Angeles River just outside the park gates. (See BIKE TRAIL: SAN GABRIEL RIVER TRAIL on page 170 for more information.)

Inside the community building are four racquetball courts ($5 per hour for residents, $8 for non-residents); a weight room (free to residents, $2 per day for non-residents); and a Walleyball court (indoor volleyball that uses walls) on Monday nights ($10 per hour for residents, $15 for non-residents). Summertime offers the refreshing pleasures of a wading pool that has a water sprayer, Monday night family time at the movies ('G' rated), and Wednesday night family entertainment consisting of puppets, magicians, or storytellers.

Hours: Open Mon. - Fri., 9am - 10pm; Sat. - Sun., 9am - 6pm. Call for times for special programs.

Admission: Free to the park. Fees for activities are listed above.

Ages: All

LINCOLN PARK / PLAZA DE LA RAZA

(213) 847-1726 - park; (323) 906-7953 - aquatic center / www.angelfire.com/ca4/lincolnpark
3501 Valley Boulevard, Los Angeles
(From Golden State [5] (just above the 10 Fwy) exit E. on N. Main St., R. on Marengo, L. on Mission, R. on Selig. Park entrance is a block east of the intersection of Valley Blvd. and Mission Rd. at Plaza de la Raza. [TG: 635 B2])

This older park in an older section of town has an Aztec-themed playground with two slides coming down from a temple. The really tall slide is made of cement, so it's not very slick. An adjacent playground has more slides and swings. There are rows of picnic tables here under huge pine and oak trees. Other features of the park include paved pathways that crisscross throughout, a big lake with a large fountain that is stocked with fish (a license is needed for ages 15 and over) and home to numerous ducks, four nice tennis courts, another playground with a sand base for younger children, grassy expanses, a community building, and a swimming pool that is open seasonally. We also enjoyed the large, grass-covered hill - walking up it and running back down Kamikaze-style! For those who like even more action, try the skate park which has ramps, quarter and half pipes, and other skateboarding elements.

Hours: The park and community center are open daily, 9am - 9pm. The skate park is open Mon. - Fri., 3pm - dusk; Sat., 10am - 5pm; Sun., noon - 5pm. Ask about extended summer hours. The pool is open mid-June to Labor Day.

Admission: The park is free, as are several of the classes offered at the center. Admission to the pool is $1.25 for adults; free for seniors, people with disabilities, and ages 17 and under.

Ages: All

LINDBERG PARK

(310) 558-9114 / www.culvercity.org
5401 Rhoda Way, Culver City

(Going N. on San Diego Fwy [405], exit N. on Sepulveda Blvd., L. on Cota St., R. on Rhoda. Going S. on 405, exit E. on Culver Blvd., R. on Overland Ave., R. on Virginia Ave. The park is at the end of the street. [TG: 672 G4])

If you're in the neighborhood, this tucked-away park is a good one to visit. There are ball fields on each end of the park, exercise stations, a basketball court, outside handball courts, a lighted tennis court, grassy areas, picnic tables, barbecues, a recreation building, and most, notably, a good-sized playground with lots of fun play equipment all built in a sand base. Besides the typical slides and swings, there is a small pile of tires to climb up, a short rope wall, a small railcar and boat structure, monkey bars, and a pulley system with a bucket for the sand. And yes, the restroom is usually open.

Hours: Open daily, sunrise - sunset.
Admission: Free
Ages: All

LIVE OAK PARK (Manhattan Beach)

(310) 545-5621 / www.citymb.info/parksrec
Valley Drive N. and 21st Street, Manhattan Beach
(Exit San Diego Fwy [405] W. on Rosecrans Ave., L. on Pacific Coast Highway, next R. on Valley Dr. [TG: 732 F5])

This park is formed around a bend in the road and is divided into various, gated sections. The northern section has baseball diamonds, picnic tables, and some short, bent gnarled trees. One particular threesome of trees bends in and down so much that they form a kind of hideout. Other sections have playground equipment, a lighted basketball court, soccer fields, places just to run and play, and tennis courts. The six courts are open weekdays and holidays from 7am to 4pm ($4 per court), and weekdays 5pm to 10pm and all day on weekends ($5 per court). Non-residents are $6 an hour at all times. Call (310) 545-0888 to make reservations.

Hours: Open daily, dawn - dusk.
Admission: Free
Ages: All

LOS ANGELES COUNTY ARBORETUM & BOTANIC GARDEN

(626) 821-3222 / www.lacountybotanicgarden.org
301 N. Baldwin Avenue, Arcadia
(Going W. on Foothill Fwy [210], exit S. on Baldwin. Going E. on 210, exit E. on Foothill Blvd., R. on Baldwin. [TG: 567 B4])

Do you have a budding horticulturalist in your family? Come visit this awesome arboretum and explore the more than 127 acres of plants and trees from around the world. The blooming flowers and the variety of gardens are astounding. We walked along the southern (and most interesting) route first. There are numerous paved pathways as well as several dirt pathways leading through trees, bushes, and jungle-like landscape which makes the walk an adventure for kids. Ducks and geese loudly ask for handouts at Baldwin Lake. (Look for the turtles in the lake's water.)

For your history lesson for the day, peek into the spacious Hugo Reid Adobe house where each room is furnished with period furniture. The adobe grounds are beautiful and reflective of the mid-1800's. Peer into the gracious Queen Anne "Cottage" for another glimpse of the past. You'll see mannequins dressed in old-fashioned clothes, elegantly furnished rooms, and a harp in the music room. The nearby immaculate Coach Barn has stalls ornately decorated with wood paneling and iron grillwork. Instead of horses, they now hold farm tools, blacksmith tools, and a coach. Also see the Santa Anita Depot with a train master's office and railroad paraphernalia.

The lush greenery around the waterfall makes it one of the most enchanting spots in the arboretum. Walk up the wooden stairs for a panoramic view and "discover" a lily pond. Back down on Waterfall Walk you'll see a serene woodland area and rock-lined stream. I was utterly content to sit while the kids let their imaginations kick into gear and play. Colorful Koi fish are just around the "corner" at the Tule Pond.

The northern section has a few greenhouses with exotic flowers and plants. An African and Australian section at this end has an abundance of trees.

Peacocks are everywhere - strutting their stuff and calling out in plaintive-sounding wails. (Peacock feathers are available at the gift shop for $1 each.)

Picnicking is not allowed on the grounds, but there is a shaded, grassy area between the parking lots. Or, eat at the Peacock Cafe which has reasonably priced food. Tip 1: Take a half-hour tram ride around and through the extensive arboretum, or get off at any one of the seven stops along the way and reboard at a later time. Trams run from 11am to 3:30pm. Passes cost $2 for ages 3 and up. Tip 2: It gets hot here during the summer, so bring water bottles (and look for the sprinklers to run through).

Wonderful, family-geared events are held here several times throughout the year. In the summer, Science Adventure Day Camps, which include classes on space and rocketry, magic, and more, are offered.

Hours: Open in the summer, Mon. - Fri., 9am - 6:30pm; Sat. - Sun., 9am - 4:30pm. Open the rest of the year daily, 9am - 4:30pm. Closed Christmas.

Admission: $6 for adults; $4 for seniors, students with ID, and ages 13 - 17; $1.50 for ages 5 - 12; children 4 and under are free. The third Tues. of every month is free. Free parking.

Ages: 2 years and up.

MADRONA MARSH

(310) 32 MARSH (326-2774) or (310) 782-3989 / www.friendsofmadronamarsh.com !/$$

3201 Plaza Del Amo, Torrance

(From San Diego Fwy [405], exit S. on Crenshaw Blvd., R. on Carson St., L. on Madrona Ave., L. on Plaza Del Amo. Going S. on Harbor Fwy [110], exit W. on Carson St., L. on Madrona Ave., L. on Plaza Del Amo. Going N. on 110, exit at 220th, L. on Figuroa St., L. on Carson St., L. on Madrona Ave., L. on Plaza Del Amo. [TG: 763 E7])

The Madrona Marsh is a vernal marsh, meaning that it's a depression flooded by runoff water from surrounding upland slopes. There is a seasonal pond here and four different plant habitats that are home to small mammals (namely squirrels); insects, such as dragonflies and butterflies; and numerous bird species. Educational nature walks for kids (and adults) of all ages are given throughout the year. During the hour, or so, guided tour you'll see and learn mostly about birds, plus ground animals, like tree frogs, and varieties of plant life. Ask about the numerous other programs offered, such as junior naturalist, astronomy, art classes, and habitat restoration. (It does my heart good to see kids pulling weeds.) Bring snacks or a water bottle.

The handicapped-accessible Nature Center contains pictures of animals and plants, information panels, a classroom, a project lab, and furs to touch such as raccoon, possum, and squirrel. The forty-three acre marsh and pond is located in the middle of an industrial section, but somewhat hidden from sight. If it's not big enough to make you feel like you've gotten away from it all, it's at least big enough to make you feel like you've gotten away from some of it.

Hours: The marsh is open daily, sunrise - sunset to explore on your own. Guided walks are given the fourth weekend of every month, and field study tours are given at various times. Call for details. The nature center is open daily, 10am - 5pm.

Admission: Free; donations gladly accepted. Summer field study tours are $5 per person or $10 per family.

Ages: 6 years and up.

MALIBU CREEK STATE PARK

(818) 880-0350 - park; (800) 444-7275 - camping reservations / parks.ca.gov $

1925 Las Virgenes Road, Calabasas

(Exit Ventura Fwy [101] S. at Las Virgenes Rd. The park is S. of Mulholland Hwy. [TG: 588 G5])

Of the many hiking, mountain bike, and horseback riding trails to choose from in the Santa Monica Mountains, one of our favorites is the Malibu Creek Trail. Starting at the broad fire road, veer to the right as the trail forks onto Cragg Road. The scenery keeps getting better the further in you hike. Oak trees shade part of the trail as you follow the high road along the creek. Man-made Century Lake is a great place to stop for a picnic, take in the beauty of your surroundings, and/or fish. This spot marks a four-mile round trip. Continue on an additional two miles (round trip) to the former M*A*S*H* set. Being here might not have any meaning for your kids, but they'll at least think the rock formation, named Goat Buttes and used in the opening scene of the show, is worth a "wow."

A mile in from the parking lot is the Visitor's Center, which also has a small museum. Each room in the museum is different. One contains taxidermied animals, another contains M*A*S*H* memorabilia, and yet another is a room for school groups to work on craft projects.

Feel like taking a dip in cool, refreshing water? Just beyond the Visitor's Center, over the bridge to the left and over a short trail of rocks, is a rock-lined swimming hole. It's like a hidden oasis. My boys thought jumping off the boulders into the "pool" formed by the creek was the ultimate.

Take advantage of all that the park offers by spending a night or two here. Each of the sixty-two campsites, some of which are shaded, has a picnic table and charcoal-use fire pit. Eight people per campsite are allowed.

Hours: The park is open daily, 8am - 10pm. The Visitor's Center is open Sat. - Sun., noon - 4pm.

Admission: $6 per vehicle. Camping prices are seasonal, and start at $12, plus a reservation fee of $7.50.

Ages: 3 years and up.

MARIE KERR SKATEPARK

(661) 267-5611 / www.cityofpalmdale.org

39700 30th Street West, Palmdale

(Exit Antelope Valley Fwy [14], W. on Ave. P., R. 30th St. [TG: 4195 C5])

Airborne! At least my kids keep hoping for this state when they skate. I just hope they land unharmed. This 8,500 square foot skatepark has all the necessary ramps, grinding boxes, and other street elements to make it fun. A helmet and knee and elbow pads are required. A parent or guardian must sign a waiver if the participant is under 18 years old.

The surrounding park has tennis courts, basketball courts, a playground, soccer field, baseball diamonds, and picnic areas. For the free summer Starlight concert series, B.Y.O.B. (Bring Your Own Blanket, or lawn chair) and bring a picnic dinner, or purchase something from the food vendors.

Hours: The park is open daily. The skatepark is open Mon. - Fri., 3pm - 9pm; Sat. - Sun., 10am - 9pm. Both are closed New Year's Day, Thanksgiving, and Christmas.

Admission: Free

Ages: 7 years and up.

MATHIAS BOTANICAL GARDEN AT U.C.L.A.

(310) 825-3620 / www.botgard.ucla.edu

U.C.L.A. Campus, Westwood

See the entry for U.C.L.A., on page 139, for details.

MAYFAIR PARK

(562) 866-9771 - park; (562) 804-4256 - pool (in season) / www.lakewoodcity.org

5720 Clark Street, Lakewood

(Exit Artesia Fwy [91] S. on Lakewood Blvd., L. on South St. It's on the corner of South and Clark sts. [TG: 766 B2])

Mayfair Park is a very fair park indeed! The two enclosed playgrounds have fun equipment for younger children. The best attractions (judging by my kids playing on them for a long time) are the wooden train to climb on and in, and a sand play area that has a small climbing structure with buckets attached to pulleys. Open grassy fields are plentiful here, plus there are basketball courts, tennis courts, baseball diamonds with lights and stadium seating, barbecue pits, a swimming pool, a wading pool, and an Express McDonald's that's usually open in the summer and during special events.

Hours: The park is open daily. The pools are open mid-May through mid-June, weekends only; open daily in the summer. Swim sessions are 1pm - 2:30pm and 2:45pm - 4:15pm. Call for extended nighttime hours.

Admission: Free to the park. Each pool session costs $1.25 for adults; 75¢ for children 17 and under. The wading pool is free.

Ages: All

MENTRYVILLE / PICO CANYON

(661) 259-2701 / ceres.ca.gov/smmc/mentry.html
Pico Canyon Road, Santa Clarita
(Exit Golden State Fwy [5] W. on Lyons Ave. which turns into Pico Canyon Road. Go about 3 miles, staying to the L. at the Y intersection when the road forks, up a bumpy, semi-paved road. [TG: 4640 A1])

Mentryville was once an oil boom town. Of the few old buildings that remain, the Felton schoolhouse, originally built in 1885, is the only one open to the public. Inside are wooden school desks, a pot bellied stove, blackboards, and a very small library room that no longer contains books. A dual-seat outhouse is just outside. Other structures on the grounds include Mr. Mentry's house, a barn and chicken coop, and a jail that was built just a few years ago for a movie. Please note that the entire "town" is currently undergoing a restoration that's expected to be completed in 2005. Short, guided tours of town, where visitors learn the history of it and the area, are given by appointment.

Picnic tables are set up under shade trees. A seasonal creek runs through this area. Take a short hike on a service road that is stroller/wheelchair accessible. The road leads to Johnson Park, a picnic spot featuring a replica of a wood oil derrick. Hike a bit further through the surrounding hills of Pico Canyon, past foundation remains and up to some overlooks. Head south for about three miles on the service road which has a gentle grade. After that, the trail changes and only experienced hikers should continue as there are several very steep and strenuous sections. Tip: Bring your own water.

Hours: The park is open daily, sunrise - sunset.
Admission: Free
Ages: All

MILLARD CANYON FALLS

(818) 899-1900 / www.r5.fs.fed.us/angeles
Chaney Trail, Los Angeles
(Exit Foothill Fwy [210] N. on Lincoln Ave., R. on Loma Alta Dr., L. on Chaney Tr., continue as it curves until it ends at Millard campground. [TG: 535 H2])

Past the picnic tables and camping area is a fire road. Follow it for about a mile - the walk is fairly easy. There are some boulders to climb over, but that's part of the fun. The falls are beautiful. The pool at the bottom is not very deep, so use caution if you want to get wet.

Hours: Open daily, dawn - dusk.
Admission: $5 per vehicle for an Adventure Pass.
Ages: 5 years and up.

MONROVIA CANYON PARK

(626) 256-8246 - park; (626) 256-8282 - nature center / www.ci.monrovia.ca.us
Canyon Boulevard, Monrovia
(Exit Foothill Fwy [210] N. on Myrtle, R. on Foothill, L. on Canyon, stay to the R. [TG: 537 H7])

This canyon park, bordering on the Angeles National Forest, backs into the wildlife corridor. The twenty developed acres contain a lovely nature center and several grassy and wooded picnic areas. Note that there is a cabin to rent near the nature center that sleeps up to twenty-eight people. It comes with a fireplace, kitchenette, and other amenities. Prices range from $135 to $260 per night.

The nature center contains stuffed animals such as foxes, coyotes, two small black bears, raccoons, a mule deer, and more. There are live lizards and walking sticks in here as well as gopher snakes, rosy boas, and king snakes. A mural depicts animals in their natural habitat. An historical display features the story of the original settlers to this area, a reproduction of some of their tombstones, and remnants from Deer Park lodge, which was a supply cabin just up the road.

The sixty other acres are woodland nature at its best, supporting wildlife like deer, mountain lions, and bears, as well as small mammals and lizards and such. One of the most popular and beautiful trails, which is only one-and-a-half miles round trip from the nature center, leads to a year-round, thirty-foot-high waterfall that's fed by springs. For a longer hike, take the trail from the entrance station of the park, or go another route completely and hike the Ben Overturff Trail. Take the fireroad a portion of the way on this trail or go all the way on the footpath. The trail is a moderate grade of seven miles that leads through virtually undisturbed wilderness, including an overlook, and ends at the Deer Park lodge site.

Hours: The park is open Wed. - Mon., 8am - 5pm. Closed Tues., July 4th weekend, and Christmas. The nature center is usually open (if staffing is available) Wed. - Sat., 11am - 1pm; Sun., 9am - 5pm.
Admission: $2 per vehicle.
Ages: 4 years and up.

NEW OTANI HOTEL AND GARDENS

!

(213) 629-1200 / www.newotani.com
120 S. Los Angeles Street, Los Angeles
(Exit Harbor Fwy [110] E. on 4th St., L. on Los Angeles. Going W. on Hollywood Fwy [101], exit at Alameda, stay straight to the next street, L. on Los Angeles. Going E. on 101, exit S. on Los Angeles. [TG: 634 G4])

Amid the hustle and bustle of downtown Los Angeles, take a quick breather at the New Otani Hotel gardens. Ride the elevator up to the small, but beautiful, Japanese garden located just outside the Thousand Cranes Restaurant. The garden's waterfall give it a sense of serenity. We loved its unique location - on top of a roof! Enjoy your short break from the busy world not far below.

Hours: Open daily the same hours as the hotel.
Admission: Free; metered parking is available.
Ages: 2 years and up.

NORTHRIDGE SKATE PARK

$$$

(818) 341-4758 / www.northridgeskatepark.com
9305 Shirley Avenue, Northridge
(From San Diego Fwy [405], exit E. on Nordhoff St., R. on Shirley. From Ventura Fwy [101], exit N. on Tampa Ave., L. on Nordhoff, R. on Shirley. [TG: 500 F6])

Awesome dude! This 20,000 square-foot park has lights for nighttime skating. The street course features a twelve- by forty-foot halfpipe (whew!), an eight-foot start box leading to a thirteen-foot wall, plus ledges, rails, spine, boxes, and banks. There are also three- by five- foot minis with stairs and a rail. Parental waivers, available on-line, must be signed for participants 17 years and under. Sessions are three hours long. BMX riders are welcome at certain sessions.

Hours: Open Mon. - Tues., 7pm - 10pm; Wed. - Thurs., 4pm - 7pm for BMX only, 7pm - 10pm skaters; Fri., 4pm - 1am; Sat., 10am - 1pm for BMX only, 1pm - 1am for skaters; Sun., 10am - 10pm. Open extended hours during holidays and the summer.
Admission: $14 for non-member skaters; $18 for non-members BMX riders. Membership is $20 a year. Member prices are $7 for skaters; $11 for BMX riders.
Ages: 7 years and up.

NORWALK PARK

!

(562) 929-5702 / www.ci.norwalk.ca.us/parksandrec2.asp
12203 Sproul Street, Norwalk
(Exit Santa Ana Fwy [5] S. on Pioneer Blvd., L. on Firestone Blvd., L. on San Antonio Dr., R. on Sproul. [TG: 736 J2])

This park has a nature center/mini farm located in the back corner, near the freeway. A little stream and benches under shade trees, make it a nice place to visit the farm friends living here. The animals, all in pens, include spotted goats, sheep, a donkey, pot-bellied pigs, geese, and steer.

The park itself is spacious with lots of open grassy areas, a playground for younger kids, tennis courts, basketball courts, and a small museum. The Sproul Museum and Hargitt House contain artifacts from early Norwalk, including pictures, a few articles of clothing, and some furniture. A pool with a shallow end, and a diving board at the deep end, is open seasonally. A snack bar is in the pool area.

Hours: The park is open daily, sunrise - 10pm. The nature center/mini-farm is open Sat. - Sun., 1pm - 4pm. Call for hours during the week when it is open by appointment for tours for younger children. Call for museum/house hours. The pool and snack bar are usually open daily, mid-June through August. Swim sessions are daily, 1pm - 2:45pm and 3:15pm - 5pm. An additional Sunday session is 11am - 12:30pm.

Admission: Free to the park. Swim sessions are $1 per person.

Ages: All

ORANGEWOOD PARK / SKATEPARK

(626) 939-8430 or (626) 939-8439 / www.westcov.org

1615 W. Merced Avenue, West Covina

(Exit San Bernardino Fwy [10] S. on Azusa Ave., R. on Merced. [TG: 638 J3])

Orangewood Park has a playground, basketball court, baseball field, plenty of picnic tables and barbecues, and two covered roller rinks for open-play most days, but used by leagues in the evenings. The unsupervised 12,000 square-foot skate park is lighted for night use. In-line bladers and skaters are welcome to get some big air at the park. Participants must wear safety gear.

Hours: Open daily, 6am - 10pm.

Admission: Free

Ages: All

ORCUTT RANCH HORTICULTURE CENTER

(818) 883-6641 / www.laparks.org

23600 Roscoe Boulevard, West Hills

(Exit Ventura Fwy [101] N. on Valley Circle Ave., R. on Roscoe Blvd. [TG: 529 F2])

The horticultural center was originally created in the early 1900's. A stroll through these nostalgic gardens is a delightful way to pass a half an hour or so. A short, wide, stroller-friendly, dirt trail leads into a grove of shady oak trees and through grounds that are lush with greenery and wildflowers. The adjacent pathway along Dayton Creek, which borders one side of the Ranch's perimeters, is not for strollers. It does have stone benches for resting and leads to a few bridges that extend over the water. On the other side of the creek is a cozy picnic area. Look for ancient live oaks throughout the ranch; one is over 700 years old (and still growing)! Also on the grounds are a picnic table in the small bamboo grove and more formal gardens consisting of maze-like hedges around the rose gardens. Note: Visitors may not walk through the adjacent acres of citrus trees.

The adobe building, once the Orcutt's home, is now used for park offices and group rental functions. A quick walk around and through the mostly unfurnished building allows you to see the Mexican-influence architecture and hand-painted, South-of-the-Border tiles.

Hours: The grounds are open daily, sunrise - sunset. Many private functions are held here, however, so call first. (But you would do that anyhow, right?) Docent-guided tours are given the last Sun. of the month, except in the summer, between 1pm - 4pm.

Admission: Free

Ages: All

PALOS VERDES PENINSULA LAND CONSERVANCY

(310) 541-7613 / www.pvplc.org

Various locations throughout the Palos Verdes and San Pedro areas.

Once-a-month guided Nature Walks, most of them family oriented and suitable for children, are given by naturalists, historians, and geologists. Tour guides share information about the history of the area, wildlife, plants, and more. The walks range from one to three hours and from easy to more difficult. All are on dirt paths. Starting points include Abalone Cove, the Cabrillo Marine Aquarium, Ladera Linda, Madrona Marsh, and Malaga Dunes, most of which are listed separately in this section. Call for a calendar of events.

Hours: Tours are usually given on the second Sat. of each month.

Admission: Free, but donations are often requested.

PARAMOUNT RANCH

(805) 370-2300 or (805) 370-2301 / www.nps.gov/samo

On Cornell Road, Agoura Hills

(Exit Ventura Fwy [101] S. on Kanan Rd., L. on Troutdale Dr., L. on Mulholland Hwy., L. on Cornell Rd. [TG: 588 B3])

Howdy partners! You've come to the right ranch if you're looking for some action. Western Town, in Paramount Ranch, was once owned by Paramount Studios and used as a western movie set. The "town" still stands. The most recent television show filmed here was *Dr. Quinn, Medicine Woman.* Walk the dusty roads and inspect the town buildings from the outside. These buildings include a blacksmith shop, general store, a jail, and even a train depot with railroad tracks. It all looks so real! Dress up your cowboy or cowgirl and bring your camera. Better yet, bring your video camera, props, and script and do your own western mini-movie. Note that this section of the park is sometimes used for filming and there is a possibility that if the town is completely overhauled for a new show, it might stay that way. Free, guided walking tours that describe the set and history of the area are usually given on the first and third Saturdays of each month at 9:30am.

Over the bridge next to the main part of town, is a huge meadow with a few picnic tables. At the end of the meadow is a wonderful, wooded trail that follows along a creek. It's only one-eighth of a mile round trip. If the kids are in the mood for hiking into the mountains, go up Coyote Canyon Trail, just behind Western Town. This uphill, half-mile, round-trip trail goes through green chaparral-covered canyons overlooking the valley. The picnic spot up here has a view that is worth the effort. Ranger-led naturalist programs are also offered at the park. Call regarding the many special and seasonal events that the ranch hosts.

Hours: The park is open daily, 8am - sunset. The visitors center is open daily, 9am - 5pm. Closed New Year's Day and Christmas.

Admission: Free

Ages: All

PETER STRAUSS RANCH

(805) 370-2300 / www.nps.gov/samo

3000 Mulholland Highway, Agoura

(Exit Ventura Fwy [101] S. on Kanan Rd., L. on Troutdale Dr., L. on Mulholland Hwy. [TG: 599 D4])

This sprawling park, once owned by actor Peter Strauss, goes for miles and miles, with great hiking trails amongst the chaparral and oak trees. One of the smaller trails is only a three-quarter-mile loop, but there are several other trails for more ambitious walkers.

Hours: Open daily, 8am - sunset.

Admission: Free

Ages: 4 years and up.

PIONEER PARK

(909) 394-6230 / www.cityofsandimas.com

225 S. Cataract Avenue, San Dimas

(Going S.E. on Foothill Fwy [210], exit E. on Arrow Hwy., L. on Cataract. Going N.W. on 210, exit E. on Covina Blvd. and stay on it as it bends to the left and turns into Cataract. [TG: 600 B2])

This park offers a playground, basketball courts, picnic tables, and, most importantly for my boys, an 8,000 square-foot concrete skate park. It has all the elements of a good skate park - ramps, a grinding box, and more. A helmet, and knee and elbow pads, are required.

Hours: Open daily, dawn - dusk.

Admission: Free

Ages: All

PLACERITA CANYON NATURE CENTER AND PARK

(661) 259-7721 / www.placerita.org; parks.co.la.ca.us

19152 Placerita Canyon Road, Newhall

(Exit Golden State Fwy [5] N. on Antelope Valley Fwy [14], S. on Placerita Canyon Rd. [TG: 4641 G1])

Placerita Canyon was the site of one of the first gold discoveries, small though it was, in California. In fact, the famed oak tree where gold was first discovered, "Oak of the Golden Dream", is just a short walk from the parking lot. There is a wealth of history and wilderness to be found at this Nature Center and park.

The Center has live animals, such as snakes and lizards, on display outside. One of the rooms inside has exhibits regarding the circle of life - predators, prey, and plants. Other exhibits include equipment that monitors weather conditions; dirt samples comparing texture and content; and taxidermied animals. Another room has live snakes and spiders (in glass cases), and a touch table with nests, pine cones, and bones.

The hiking is great here, especially for more experienced hikers. Canyon Trail is a gradual climb, following along a stream. The left fork leads to the Scout campground. The right fork leads to the Waterfall Trail, where yes, about two-thirds of a mile back, is a waterfall. Canyon Trail also hooks up to Los Pinetos Trail, which is a hardy, eight-mile hike.

A large picnic area on the hillside of the park is nestled in a huge grove of oak trees. Play equipment is here, although the main attractions are the beauty of the area and a small hiking trail. Call to find out more about the Saturday nature hikes, the animal demonstrations, astronomy club, summer camps, and other special programs.

Hours: Open daily, 9am - 5pm. Closed Christmas.
Admission: Free
Ages: 2 years and up.

POINT FERMIN PARK

(310) 548-7756 / www.sanpedrochamber.com
807 S. Paseo del Mar, San Pedro
(Take Harbor Fwy [110] to the end, turn L. on Gaffey St., L. on 9th St., R. on Pacific Ave. to the end, then R. on Paseo del Mar. [TG: 854 B2])

This corner park has lots of green grassy areas, shade trees, and a few play structures. Its two best features are the wonderful view of the California coastline and a nineteenth-century lighthouse. The lighthouse is not open for tours, but it is very picturesque, with a wide variety of flowers and other plants surrounding it. I mention this park mainly because its large size and its proximity to several fun places in San Pedro makes it ideal for picnicking.

Hours: Open daily, sunrise - sunset.
Admission: Free
Ages: All

POLLIWOG PARK

(310) 545-5621 - park; (310) 374-7575 - museum / www.citymb.info/parksrec/facilities; www.geocities.com/history90266
Corner of Manhattan Beach Boulevard and Redondo Avenue, Manhattan Beach
(Exit San Diego Fwy [405] S. on Inglewood, R. on Manhattan Beach Blvd. [TG: 732 J6])

This expansive park is wonderfully deceptive. The part seen from the street is beautiful, with a play area and lots of grass and trees. Some of the trees have low branches that beckon to climbers. There is also an exercise area, with wood benches and handles for pull-ups, sit-ups, and other physical activities. A huge portion of the lawn is graded for summer concerts. The original red beach cottage in the park is a small historic museum. It features photos, old-fashioned bathing suits, and other artifacts of the olden days. Nearby is a rose garden.

As you take the stroller-friendly pathway leading down toward the interior of the park, you'll discover some "hidden" delights, such as a pond where marshy reeds and ducks abound. (Signs ask that you don't feed the ducks.) Tip: Watch your children around the water as there are no guard rails. Children have a large play area with climbing structures. Younger kids, ages 2 to 5, have a playground designed especially for them with rope bridges, tires, slides, and swings.

Across the street from the main park is a baseball diamond and four lighted tennis courts. On the campus of Manhattan Beach Transition School, adjacent to the park, is Begg Pool. The pool is open during the summer for recreation swim and at other times during the year for lessons and classes.

Hours: The park is open daily, dawn - dusk. The museum is open weekends, noon - 3pm; closed on major holidays. The pool is open daily in the summer, 1:30pm - 3:20pm.

Admission: Free to the park and museum. The pool is $2 per person.

Ages: All

PRIME DESERT WOODLAND PRESERVE

(661) 723-6070

43201 35th Street West, Lancaster

(Exit Antelope Valley Fwy [14] W. on Ave. 'L', R. on 35th W. The entrance is at the bend of 35th and K-8. [TG: 4105 B3])

This stretch of desert preserve is carved out of the surrounding suburbia, which is within eyesight. Easy-walking, rope-lined, hard-packed dirt/sand trails meander through desert topography while interpretative signs allow visitors to learn about the plant and animal life they see. The longest trail is one mile, round trip.

The small nature center building displays a few taxidermied animals, pictures of old Lancaster, and a touch table with lots of great objects - fossils, feathers, an ostrich egg, and several replicas of dinosaur parts such as skin, claws, and a tooth.

Hours: The trails are open daily, dawn - dusk. The building is open Mon. - Fri., 3pm - sunset; Sat. - Sun., 10am - 3pm.

Admission: Free

Ages: All

PYRAMID LAKE

(661) 295-1245 - lake; (661) 257-2892 - bait shop; (661)248-6575 - campground

Off Interstate 5, 20 miles N. of Santa Clarita Valley.

(Exit Golden State Fwy [5] W. on Smokey Bear Rd.)

This huge sparkling reservoir lake, surrounded by hills, offers a myriad of activities for families. Year-round boating, including waterskiing, canoeing, rowboating, and rubber rafting, is allowed. B.Y.O.B. (Bring Your Own Boat) as only aluminum fishing boats, which seat up to four people, are available to rent. Shaded picnic shelters and barbeques are near the docks. Some of the beach and picnic sites across the lake are reachable only by boat. Fish for seasonal bass, trout, catfish, crappie, and bluegill. A bait and tackle shop is on the grounds. A California state fishing license is required for those 16 years old or older. The waveless swim beach is open during the summer and is patrolled by lifeguards on the weekends. Meander on trails along the lake, enjoy a picnic meal, visit the nearby VISTA DEL LAGO VISITOR CENTER (see pg. 122), and/or camp at your choice of two campgrounds near the lake. Los Alamos Campground, two miles up the road, has room for ninety-three family units and three group units. Hard Luck Campground, on Piru Creek, has twenty-two family units.

Hours: The lake is open November through March daily, 7am - 5pm; April through October, 6am - 8pm. The swim beach is open the same hours, seasonally. The park is closed New Year's Day and Christmas.

Admission: $7 per vehicle, which includes the swim beach. Pay an additional $7 if you are bringing in your own boat. Fishing boat rentals are open year round for $55 for the day. Camping is $12 per night.

Ages: All

RANCHO SANTA ANA BOTANIC GARDEN

(909) 625-8767 / www.rsabg.org

1500 N. College Avenue, Claremont

(Exit San Bernardino Fwy [10] N. on Indian Hill Blvd., R. on Foothill. Go 3 blocks, then turn L. on College Ave. [TG: 571 D7])

This eighty-six-acre botanic garden is beautiful in scope and sequence, and abundant with plants native only to California. Thousands of different kinds of plants grow in our state, so this garden covers a lot of ground with its giant sequoias, fan palms, California live oak, manzanitas, cacti, wildflowers, and more.

The numerous trails, many of which are stroller friendly, afford good walking opportunities. Since the diverse vegetation attracts a wide variety of birds, bird lovers can pick up a bird check list at the gift shop, or join an organized bird walk on the first Sunday of each month. I don't know how much horticulture my kids take in when we visit botanic gardens, but it's a good introduction to the variety and importance of plant life, plus a beautiful walk is always enjoyable.

Hours: Open daily, 8am - 5pm. Closed New Year's Day, July 4th, Thanksgiving, and Christmas.
Admission: Free; donations of $2 per person or $5 per family are suggested.
Ages: 3 years and up.

RECREATION PARK / MONROVIA SK8 PARK

(626) 256-8246 / www.ci.monrovia.ca.us
843 East Olive Avenue, Monrovia
(Exit Foothill Fwy [210] N. on Myrtle Ave., R. on Colorado Blvd. Park is the end of the street. [TG: 567 J4])

This nice-sized park features a playground, picnic areas with shade trees, ball fields, tennis courts, basketball courts, a roller hockey rink, sand volleyball courts, and a youth center. A supervised skate park here offers over 10,000 square feet of skating fun! The concrete skate park has two sections; a street side with rails, stairs, ramps, kickers, and ledges, and a bowl side with a kidney-shape pool with roll-overs. Areas to watch the skaters are available. All participants are required to wear safety protection.

Hours: Open daily, sunrise - sunset.
Admission: Free
Ages: All for the park; 7 years and up for the skate park.

ROBERT E. RYAN PARK

(310) 377-2290 - park site; (310) 541-4566 - city parks / www.palosverdes.com/rpv/recreationparks
30359 Hawthorne Boulevard, Rancho Palos Verdes
(Exit Pacific Coast Highway [1] S. on Hawthorne Blvd. It's S. of Crest Rd., near Vallon Dr. [TG: 822 H3])

From the parking lot of this nine-acre park, you get a glimpse of the California coastline, and on a clear day, Catalina Island. Steps lead down into the park itself. Note: Strollers and wheelchairs can take a ramp that leads all the way down to the playground. The play equipment is ADA approved and wheelchair accessible. Set sail on a large ship-like structure with slides and swings or on a smaller ship with similar apparatus. Play in the tot area on a climbing structure shaped like a car, swing on swings, and ride on cement whales. Stroll under shade trees on cement pathways that go through a good portion of the park. Bring a sack lunch to enjoy at the picnic tables, or grill food at the barbecues.

The community center has some play equipment to check out, as long as you leave your driver's license in exchange. Play a game of basketball or baseball or romp around on the large, open, grassy areas.

Hours: Open July through Labor Day daily, and on holidays, 10am - dusk. Open the rest of the year usually Mon. - Fri. and Sun., noon - dusk; Sat., 10am - dusk. Closed New Year's Day, Thanksgiving, Christmas Eve, and Christmas Day.
Admission: Free
Ages: All

ROXBURY PARK

(310) 550-4761 - park; (310) 550-4979 - tennis / www.beverlyhills.org
471 S. Roxbury Drive, Beverly Hills
(Exit Santa Monica Fwy [10] N. on Robertson, L. on Olympic. It's on the corner of Olympic and Roxbury. [TG: 632 F3])

This beautiful park fits right in with its surroundings of well-manicured lawns and stately homes. Although it is off a main street, it still seems somewhat removed from city life. The park offers a wealth of activities to choose from such as tennis (four lighted courts, plus backboards), sand volleyball, and basketball. Along with a few picnic tables, barbecue pits, and some large shaded grassy areas, there is a good-sized playground. One of the areas is designed for slightly older kids with a big slide to go down, bridges to cross, and ropes to climb. The other is designed with younger kids in mind. It has swings and slides, too.

Hours: The park is open daily, 6am - 11pm. The community center is open Mon. - Fri., 9am - 10pm; Sat. - Sun., 9am - 5pm.

Admission: Free. Tennis courts are $6 an hour for residents; $8 an hour for non-residents.

Ages: All

RUNYON CANYON PARK

(323) 666-5004 / www.laparks.org

2000 Fuller Street, Hollywood

(Exit Hollywood Fwy [101] W. on Sunset Blvd., N. on Franklin St. all the way to the top. [TG: 593 C3])

Hike the hills of Hollywood in the popular Runyon Canyon. The dirt trail starts off at an upward slant, leading past ruins where house foundations and a few chunks of wall still remain. We walked the scenic, mostly woodland, main trail all the way up the mountain, as it affords a spectacular view of the famed city. The hike is strenuous as it goes up and along the rim of the hills. The trail eventually levels off, then loops back down. The two-mile round-trip hike is not stroller/wheelchair accessible. Nor is the slightly longer hike out to Mulholland. Bring water! Note: Look where you walk as this is a popular park for walking dogs. Inquire about periodic guided hikes.

Hours: Open daily, dawn - dusk.

Admission: Free

Ages: 5 years and up.

RUSTIC CANYON RECREATION CENTER

(310) 454-5734

601 Latimer Road, Pacific Palisades

(Exit San Diego Fwy [405] W. on Wilshire Blvd., R. on 7th St., which turns into Entrada Dr., R. on Mesa Rd., L. on Latimer Rd. [TG: 631 B6])

This pretty park is nestled in a somewhat secluded area of Pacific Palisades, but it's worth making the effort to visit here. Shade trees line the perimeter of a paved pathway that leads down into the park. A baseball field, basketball court, playground, grassy area, climbing trees (always a hit with my family), a wooden pyramid structure (to climb on and around), two picnic areas, and barbeque pits make up the central part of the park. Several tennis courts are located in one corner. Up near the parking lot is an older-style recreation center which offers a variety of classes. An adjacent, medium-sized community swimming pool is open seasonally.

Hours: The park is open daily, sunrise - sunset. Closed Thanksgiving and Christmas. The pool is open the mid-June through Labor Day. Swim sessions are Mon. - Fri., 10am - noon and 1pm - 5pm; Sat. - Sun., 1pm - 5pm.

Admission: Free to the park. Swim sessions are $1.25 for adults; 75¢ for kids 17 and under.

Ages: All

SADDLEBACK BUTTE STATE PARK

(661) 942-0662 / www.calparksmojave.com

17102 Avenue 'J' East, Lancaster

(Going N. on Antelope Valley Fwy [14], exit N. on 20th St. W., N. to Ave. 'J'. Going S. on 14, exit E. on Ave. 'J'. It's quite a few miles out to the park. [TG: 4109 H1])

This state park is 3,000 acres of desert landscape, with Joshua trees scattered throughout and a huge granite mountain top, Saddleback Butte, jutting up almost a 1,000 feet above the valley. Be on the lookout for wildlife such as desert tortoises, rabbits, coyotes, kit foxes, kangaroo rats, and lots of reptiles and birds. Several hiking trails are available here, including a two-and-a-half-mile trail that leads to the top of the Butte, and a view that makes the hike worthwhile. Springtime is particularly beautiful at the park because the wildflowers are in bloom. Near the entrance and park headquarters are several covered picnic areas, complete with barbecues. Please remember that desert weather is hot in the summer and cold in the winter, so dress accordingly. Overnight camping is available here. Saddleback is located just a few miles down the road from the ANTELOPE VALLEY INDIAN MUSEUM (see pg. 81).

      Hours: Open daily, sunrise - sunset.
Admission: Day use is $3 per vehicle. Camping is $9 per night.
       Ages: 5 years and up.

SALT LAKE MUNICIPAL PARK / HUNTINGTON SKATEBOARD PARK

(323) 584-6218 / www.huntingtonpark.org
3401 Florence Avenue, Huntington Park
(Exit Long Beach Fwy [710] W. on Florence Ave. [TG: 675 B7])

    This twenty-three-acre park comes fully equipped for a day of sports fun. It has four fenced-in baseball diamonds, basketball courts, racquetball/handball courts, a soccer field, tennis courts, a gym, picnic area with grills, a playground, and a skate park. The lighted skate park has rails, pyramids, ledges, ramps, and a few smooth "open" sections for skating. Safety gear - a helmet and pads - is required.

      Hours: The park is open daily, sunrise - sunset. The skate park is open Mon. - Fri., 1pm - 9pm; Sat. - Sun. and holidays, 9am - 9pm.
Admission: Free
       Ages: All

SAND DUNE PARK

(310) 545-5621 / www.citymb.info/parksrec
At the corner of 33rd Street and Bell Avenue, Manhattan Beach
(Exit San Diego Fwy [405] W. on Rosecrans Ave., L. on Bell. [TG: 732 F4])

    This little park has a big surprise. While there is a small playground for younger children, the park is really "beachy" because of its steep wall of sand (100 feet high) that is perfect for running, jumping, or rolling down. 200 steps on the switchback lead to the top of the hill, or just climb up it. Bring your own bucket and shovel to play with at the bottom. Here is a local's favorite tip: After it rains, take a snow sled down the hill!

    Behind the playground is a green grassy stretch. Picnic tables and a few barbecue pits under a shelter are also available. Parking is limited.

      Hours: Open daily, dawn - dusk.
Admission: Free
       Ages: All

SAN DIMAS COUNTY PARK

(909) 599-7512 / parks.co.la.ca.us
1628 Sycamore Canyon Road, San Dimas
(From Foothill Fwy [210], take the 30 Fwy E., go N.W. on Foothill Blvd., R. on San Dimas Canyon Dr., L. on Sycamore Canyon Rd., up the hill to the park office. [TG: 570 D6])

    Nestled in the foothills of the San Gabriel Mountains, adjacent to Angeles National Forest, is a wonderful county park/museum/wildlife sanctuary. The nature museum is fairly comprehensive. It contains live snakes, such as a California king and gopher snakes; taxidermied animals, such as California gray squirrels, birds, and raccoons; and several small collections including rocks, arrowheads, insects, and butterflies.

    The outside wildlife sanctuary offers a caged home to several injured or non-releasable native animals. Hawks, heart-faced barn owls, and great-horned owls are part of the bird rehabilitation area; not part of the bird "rebellion" area as my son misread the sign. (Hmm - could be something to do with his childhood. . . .) Other live animals here include a deer, raccoon (his little paws were busily cleaning his food when we saw him), possum, and tortoises, plus many squirrels running around freely.

A one-mile, self-guiding nature trail begins in the oak woodland just behind the nature center building and loops around. There are plenty of picnic tables here under the cover of shady oak trees. Some of the picnic areas have barbeques. The area below the museum has a baseball diamond, a few playgrounds, and large grassy areas. An equestrian center is next to the park, and a portion of a long bike route goes through part of the park. Come visit the park on your own, or via a Jr. Ranger Program which is offered through the park system. A visit to the San Dimas County Park is great for temporarily escaping city life.

Hours: The park is open daily, 8am - sunset. The nature center is open daily, 10am - 4pm. Closed Christmas.

Admission: Free

Ages: All

SANTA FE DAM RECREATIONAL AREA

(626) 334-1065 - park; (626) 334-9049 - boat rental / parks.co.la.ca.us

15501 Arrow Highway, Irwindale

$$

(North entrance: Exit Foothill Fwy [210], S. on Irwindale, R. on 1st St. [TG: 568 C7]; South entrance: From San Gabriel River Fwy [605], exit E. on Live Oak Ave. which turns into Arrow Hwy. From Foothill Fwy [210], exit S. on Irwindale, R. on Arrow Highway. [TG: 598 E2])

Though located in the middle of an industrial section, city sounds fade away while at this enormous recreational area that sports a mountainous backdrop. Our first stop was at the nature center trail, at the northern end of the park. The rock-lined, three-quarter-mile looping trail is paved, level, and a delight to walk. Desert is the predominant theme. We observed an abundance of cacti and other plant life, and animals such as jackrabbits, lizards, roadrunners, and hummingbirds.

The huge lake toward the entrance offers a nice-sized beach with a lifeguarded swimming area. A small water play area for children 52" and under is located by the picnic area. It has a few slides and some colorful climbing apparatus in shallow waters. Other attractions in the park include a playground; fishing - a California state license is required for those 16 years of age and older; quiet boating activities (no gasoline powered boats allowed), with rentals of kayaks and paddle boats available; a snack bar (usually open in the summer); picnic facilities; and unpaved walking trails. This lakeside area, with its shade trees and acres of green grass, is vastly different from the northern desert area.

Ready for a bike ride? Choose your route and go the distance all the way north to San Gabriel Canyon, or south to Long Beach, using various trails that go through this park. Parts of the trail are paved, while other parts are not.

Hours: Open daily, sunrise - sunset. The swim beach and water play areas are open seasonally. Boat rentals are usually available on weekends most of the year, and daily during the summer.

Admission: $6 per vehicle; $3 for a senior citizen's or a disabled person's vehicle. There is no extra charge to use the swim beach. The water play area, however, is $1 per person for each hour-and-a-half session. Rowboats are $10 an hour. Paddle boats are $8 an hour.

Ages: All

SCHABARUM REGIONAL COUNTY PARK

(626) 854-5560 / parks.co.la.ca.us

17250 E. Colima Road, Rowland Heights

!/$

(Exit Pomona Fwy [60] S. on Azusa Ave., L. on Colima. [TG: 678 G4])

650 acres huge with lots of green rolling hillsides, this country park is seemingly removed from city life. Towards the entrance are scattered picnic tables, barbeque pits, a playground featuring a pirate ship, shade trees, and open space to run around. About a mile of paved trail follows along a creek as it winds through part of the park. There are twenty miles of dirt hiking and equestrian trails that weave through the rest of the sprawling countryside, leading past shrub, groves of trees, wild flowers (in the spring), and cherry trees, which are beautiful in bloom.

Ray's Equestrian Center, located inside the park, (626) 810-4229, offers guided horseback rides at $20 an hour. Pony rides, for younger children, are $20 for a half hour, although this time may be split between kids. (i.e. Three kids get ten minutes each.)

Hours: The park is open May through September, Mon. - Fri., 6am - 8pm; weekends 8am - 8pm. Open October through April, Mon. - Fri., 6am - 6pm; weekends, 8am - 8pm. Closed Christmas. The equestrian center is open in the summer, Wed., Thurs., Fri., 11am - 5:30pm; Sat. - Sun., 9am - 5:30pm. It's open the rest of the year, Wed. - Fri., 11am - 4pm; Sat. - Sun., 9am - 4pm. Closed New Year's Day, Thanksgiving, and Christmas.

Admission: The park is free during the week. $3 per vehicle is charged on weekends and holidays.

Ages: All

SEPULVEDA DAM RECREATION AREA - BALBOA PARK and BALBOA LAKE

(818) 756-9743 - Balboa Lake and boat rentals; (818) 756-9642 - sports center;
(818) 266-6991 - skate park / www.laparks.org/dos/aquatic/balboa.htm
6300 Balboa Boulevard, Van Nuys
(Exit Ventura Fwy [101] N. on Balboa Blvd. It's between Burbank Blvd. and Victory Blvd. [TG: 531 D7])

Is there anything you can't do at the massive Sepulveda Dam area? Balboa Park, which comprises a major portion of the area is very spread out: On the east side of the street are three golf courses; on the west side is an enormous field with sixteen soccer fields, four lighted baseball diamonds, sixteen lighted tennis courts (and a backboard), lighted basketball courts, and lots of open space and gently sloping hills. The Encino Velodrome is also in this vicinity. A paved, relatively easy, ten-mile round-trip bike trail encompasses the east and west side of the park

Our favorite place to play is a little further north, just south of Victory Boulevard, at Balboa Lake. The huge playground has large flat rocks around its perimeters (which is almost all my boys need) and a few play areas for both toddlers and older kids. The play grounds feature slides, climbing apparatus (some with steering wheels), and wooden bridges, plus large (relatively speaking) model camels, elephants, and turtles to climb on. The twenty-seven-acre man-made lake, made from reclaimed water and patrolled by lifeguards, offers pedal boat rentals. The boats hold up to four passengers and take some muscle power, but are a lot of fun. Bring some old bread for the always-hungry ducks swimming around here. Numerous walkers take advantage of the cement pathway that loops around the scenic lake - no bikes, blades, or skateboards are allowed. Fishing is allowed, though. A license is required for those 17 years and older.

At Pedlow Field, on Victory Boulevard, an enclosed 8,500 square-foot cement skate park is another highlight. It includes handrails, steps, a funbox, plenty of ramps, a pyramid, and a waterfall (which is just the name of a ramp - there is no actual water.) Safety gear - a helmet and knee and elbow pads - are required. Plans for the skate park include doubling it's size and adding an exhibition area and a concession stand.

Drive east through the park, past a golf course and you'll reach the adjacent Anthony Beilenson Park. Its outstanding feature is a model aircraft flying field. Members of the San Fernando Valley Flyers club are often seen here, using (and fixing) their remote-controlled aircraft on a scale runway, and then flying them. See if you can tell the difference in the air between the models and the real planes coming to and from the nearby Van Nuys airport.

Hours: Most parts of the park are open daily, sunrise - sunset. Pedal boat rentals are available daily during the summer, 11am - 6:45pm; available the rest of the year on weekends and holidays only, 11am - ninety minutes prior to sunset. The skate park is open Mon. - Fri., noon - dark; Sat. - Sun., 10am - dark. The sports center is open Mon. - Fri., 9am - 10pm; Sat. - Sun., 9am - 5pm.

Admission: Free to the park. Pedal boats are $9 a half hour; $12 an hour. Note that seniors receive a discount.

Ages: All

SMITH PARK

(626) 308-2875 / www.sangabrielcity.com/comlivng/parknrec
232 W. Broadway, San Gabriel

(Exit San Bernardino Fwy [10], N. on Del Mar Ave., L. on Broadway. [TG: 596 E4])

Six lighted tennis courts, basketball courts, handball courts, youth and toddler playground areas sitting atop a beautiful and intricate tile wall, a swimming pool, a wading pool, picnic areas, grassy run-around space, and more are yours for coming to Smith Park. Another play area, based on Native American Tongva peoples, incorporates a picnic area, rolling green lawns, and a few concrete animals, such as dolphins. Take a look at the large concrete compass at this spot, too. Walkways crisscross throughout the park.

Hours: Open daily, 7:30am - 10pm. The swim pool is open seasonally for recreation swim.

Admission: Free to the park. Swim sessions are $1.75 for adults; 75¢ for ages 17 and under. The wading pool is free.

Ages: All

SOLSTICE CANYON

(805) 370-2301 / www.nps.gov/samo

Corral Canyon Road, Malibu

(Exit Pacific Coast Highway N. on Corral Canyon Rd. It's through a gated entry, just off the highway. [TG: 628 C7])

This canyon offers a variety of trail lengths and terrain, from huge shady oak woodlands to shrubs to an intermittent stream. Short easy trails include the 1.2 mile round trip on Dry Canyon Trail which ends near a seasonal waterfall, or the Solstice Canyon Trail, a 2.1 mile round-trip paved road for bikers as well as hikers. Longer trails include the 3.9 miles Sostomo Trail/Deer Valley Loop. We found the canyon to be a peaceful and beautiful place to explore nature. A few picnic tables are located near the parking lot. Note: There are restroom facilities. Tip: Bring your own water.

Hours: Open daily, 8am - sunset.

Admission: Free

Ages: 4 years and up.

SOUTH COAST BOTANICAL GARDENS

(310) 544-6815 / parks.co.la.ca.us

26300 S. Crenshaw Boulevard, Rolling Hills Estates

(Exit San Diego Fwy [405] S. on Crenshaw Blvd. It's a few miles to Rolling Hills Estates. [TG: 793 D6])

This attractive, eighty-seven-acre garden is a breath of fresh air for Southern Californians. It's planted with exotic trees (redwoods, palms, and others), shrubs, and flowers from Africa, New Zealand, and all over the world. There are several different specialty areas here including a cactus garden, a rose garden (we love taking pictures of roses here - such color and variety), a woodland walk, and a Garden for the Senses. In the latter, vegetation with unique fragrances, textures, and color schemes flourish. A fanciful children's garden features fairy tales figures and structures as well as plants.

Stroll along the cement and dirt pathways through the gardens, under shade trees, and up and down the gently rolling hills and grassy areas. It feels good to be surrounded by such beauty! Feed ducks at the man-made lake and look for koi, turtles, and heron and other waterfowl who make their home here. Outside food can't be brought in, but a picnic area is just outside the gates.

Hours: Open daily, 9am - 5pm. Closed on Christmas.

Admission: $6 for adults; $4 for seniors and students; $1.50 for ages 5 - 12; children 4 and under are free. Admission is free the third Tues. of every month.

Ages: 3 years and up.

STONEY POINT

Topanga Canyon Boulevard, Chatsworth

(Exit Simi Valley/San Fernando Valley Fwy [118] S. on Topanga Canyon Blvd. It's the first big rock on your left. [TG: 500 A2])

Do you have a rock-climber wannabe in your household? Stoney Point, so named for the large boulder perched at the top of the hill, is a famous (at least locally) rock climbers' delight. Practice repelling on this small mountain of stone, or just hike the trail up to the top. Either way, it can be an exhilarating way to spend part of the day. Be on the lookout for the numerous alcoves and caves to crawl into, but use caution, too. There is a dirt path towards the "back" of the hill that visitors can hike for a bit.

Hours: Open daily, sunrise - sunset.

Admission: Free

Ages: 4 years and up to hike; your discretion about rock climbing.

STOUGH CANYON NATURE CENTER / WILDWOOD CANYON PARK

(818) 238-5440 / www.burbank.com/nature.shtml

2300 Walnut Avenue, Burbank

(Exit Golden State Fwy [5] E. on Burbank Blvd., L. on San Fernando Blvd., R. on Delaware, R. on Glenoaks, L. on Walnut. [TG: 533 H4])

Snuggled right into the mountains, this nature center offers a variety of displays around the perimeters and some in the center, as well as a few classrooms. The exhibits include stuffed animals, such as bobcat, raccoons, deer, quail, and an owl; a few live tarantulas and snakes (which visitors can touch) and a few non-living ones; a touch table with animals skins and bones; a beekeeping display; and several colorful information panels. Ask about the numerous educational programs and recreational opportunities, ranging from organized nature hikes to astronomy workshops. Tip: Pick up a trail map here.

The fire road behind the nature center winds its way up the mountain and leads to a main trail, the Verdugo Mountainway Trail, which traverses the Verdugo Mountains. Taken in the other direction, where the road branches, and the path eventually leads to Brand fire road and BRAND PARK (see pg. 35).

Just down the street from the nature center is Wildwood Canyon Park, at 1701 Wildwood Canyon Drive. A two-mile trail system here snakes around on the Burbank side of the Verdugo Mountains and a steep, three-plus mile Vital Link Trail hooks up with the Verdugo Mountainway. There are a few places at Wildwood to park, picnic, and play, with some grassy areas to run around.

Hours: The nature center is open Tues. - Fri. and Sun., 11am - 5pm; Sat., 9am - 5pm. Open extended hours in the summer. Closed Mon. The trails are open daily, dawn - dusk.

Admission: Free

Ages: 3 years and up.

SWITZER FALLS

(818) 899-1900 / www.r5.fs.fed.us/angeles

Angeles Crest Highway, Los Angeles

(Exit Foothill Fwy [210] N.E. on Angeles Crest Hwy [State 2], go about 10 miles and Switzer Picnic area will be on your R. Drive down a somewhat steep road to park. You'll pass by a ranger station - stop to purchase an Adventure Pass. [TG: 505 H1])

Ah - the rewards of a hike! Follow the moderately-graded Gabrielino Trail on the west end of the picnic area about a mile to the remnants of Switzer's Camp, which is a backpacker's campground, to reach the top of the falls; a fifty-foot chute. To reach the bottom, and your destination of a refreshing, rock-line swimming hole, continue hiking on the Gabrielino Trail, along the right-hand side (or west) of the canyon wall and over some boulders. Note: Please use caution around any waterfall - wet rocks are slippery rocks.

Another alternative is to take the three mile or so hike to Bear Canyon. Once you've hiked down the initial trail and reached Switzer's Camp, go up the canyon to Bear Canyon trail. A primitive campsite, a seasonal stream, and careful boulder hopping await. Bring a water bottle. Note: The small parking lot fills up early on the weekends.

Hours: Open daily, 8am - dusk.

Admission: $5 per vehicle for an Adventure Pass.

Ages: 5 years and up.

TEMESCAL GATEWAY PARK

(310) 454-1395 / www.smmc.ca.gov

15601 Sunset Boulevard, Pacific Palisades

(Exit Pacific Coast Highway [1] N. on Temescal Canyon Rd., cross Sunset Blvd. into the park. [TG: 631 A4])

This comely wilderness park is particularly pretty in the spring when the wildflowers are blooming profusely. Dirt trails meander throughout. Follow the one-and-a-half-mile trail that winds uphill, under shade trees, back through the canyon along the seasonal creek and to a bridge and waterfall. Picnic tables are scattered throughout the park, so bring a sack lunch.

Hours: Open daily, sunrise - sunset.
Admission: $5 per vehicle.
Ages: All

TOPANGA STATE PARK

(818) 880-0350 or (310) 454-8212 / parks.ca.gov
1501 Will Rogers State Park Road, Pacific Palisades
(From Pacific Coast Highway [1], exit N. on Sunset Blvd., L. on Will Rogers State Park Rd. From San Diego Fwy [405], exit W. on Sunset Blvd., R. on Will Rogers State Park Rd. [TG: 631 C4])

Believe it or not, this massive state park, actually a huge natural preserve, is all contained within the Los Angeles city limits. Thirty-six miles of hiking trails goes through canyons, hills, and cliffs of the Santa Monica Mountains. The trailhead for the park is at WILL ROGERS STATE HISTORIC PARK (see pg. 124).

Hours: Open daily, 8am - sunset.
Admission: $5 per vehicle; $4 for seniors.
Ages: 5 years and up.

TOWSLEY CANYON

(661) 255-2974 / www.smmc.ca.gov
24255 The Old Road, Newhall
(Exit Golden State Fwy [5] on Calgrove and go W. back under the freeway, S. on The Old Road. Look for entrance signs. [TG: 4640 F4])

This beautiful mountain wilderness park contains some spectacular geological structures. First, visit the nature center located at Canyon View trailhead, which contains displays on the history of the park. These include old photographs, taxidermied animals, and artifacts from the days when this area was an oil boom town. A picnic area and restrooms are here, too. Hiking trails range from easy to difficult. The two-mile Canyon View loop trail is a mostly moderate hike with a few short, steep grades. The five-and-a-half-mile Towsley View loop trail has more strenuous grades. This trail, which hooks up to Wiley Canyon, parallels the creek as it goes past grassy areas, the Narrows (where there are unique rock formations), and old oil drilling grounds. Be on the lookout for seasonal wildflowers, plus valley and coastal live oak trees, and animals that share this habitat. The Wiley Canyon trail is two miles round trip and a fairly easy walk. Also see EAST AND RICE CANYONS (pg. 41), as that park is just down the road.

Hours: Open daily, sunrise - sunset.
Admission: Free
Ages: 3 years and up.

TROUTDALE

(818) 889-9993
2468 Troutdale Drive, Agoura Hills
(Exit Ventura Fwy [101] S. on Kanan Rd., L. on Troutdale Dr. [TG: 587 H3])

"Fishy, fishy in a brook/ Daddy caught him with a hook./ Mammy fried him in a pan/ And baby ate him like a man." (Childcraft, Poems and Rhymes, 1966)

Troutdale is in a woodsy setting with two small ponds to fish from - perfect for beginners. There are logs to sit on around the perimeter of the ponds. The entrance price includes a bamboo fishing pole and bait. For an extra 50¢, you can get your fish cleaned. Munch at the snack bar or bring a picnic lunch to eat while you're catching dinner. Be sure to pick up a flyer that has recipe ideas.

Hours: Open Mon. - Fri., 10am - 5pm; Sat. - Sun., 9am - 5pm. Weekend hours are extended during the summer.

Admission: $5 per person, fishing or not. Fish prices vary depending on its length. For instance, a rainbow trout that is 10" - 11" long costs $4.25.

Ages: 3 years and up.

VASQUEZ ROCKS

(661) 268-0840 / parks.co.la.ca.us
10700 W. Escondido Canyon Road, Agua Dulce
(Exit Antelope Valley Fwy [14] N. on Agua Dulce Canyon Rd., R. on Escondido Canyon Rd. Follow the signs along the way. [TG: 4373 F4])

This park became an instant favorite with my boys. The Ranger Station, housed in a barn with corralled horses outside, sets the mood for this all-natural, rustic park. Some of the huge unusual rock formations are almost triangular in shape, jutting practically straight up from the ground. They have ridges along their sides making them moderately easy to climb, although my kids also climbed much higher (to the tops!) than my heart could take. For those who don't like heights, there are several smaller rocks to conquer, and plenty of walking trails.

If you experience "deja vu" while here, it's probably because this park has been used in numerous commercials and films, such as *The Flintstones*, as well as westerns and science fiction thrillers. Tip: Call before you come because sections of the park are closed when filming is taking place.

Vasquez Rocks, named for an outlaw who hid among the rocks here, also contains Tatavian Indian sites and a seasonal stream. Be forewarned - drinking water is not available in the park. Camping for organized youth groups is allowed.

Hours: Open daily, 8am to a half-hour before sunset.

Admission: Free

Ages: 3 years and up.

VINCENT LUGO PARK

(626) 308-2875 / www.sangabrielcity.com
Wells Street, San Gabriel
(Exit San Bernardino Fwy [10] N. on Ramona St., R. on Wells St. [TG: 596 D6])

There are three great play areas immediately visible here: A small enclosed one for toddlers; one with a rocket structure to climb up and slide down; and another that is just fun. In the summertime a very small enclosed wading pool is open. A sand pit, lots of grassy running space, and picnic tables help classify this park as a good one.

According to my "park-smart" kids, however, the best part of the park is across the service road and to the south, almost hidden from sight. Children can play on the oversized cement sea creatures that have surfaced here, such as an octopus and whale. Shouts of "this is the best!" came from my kids as they slid down the sea serpent that is wrapped around a lighthouse. Another giant sea serpent is curled around a rocky hill, which has a huge shade tree growing from it, plus a slide to go down. Like a chest filled with gold on the bottom of the ocean floor, this nautical park was a treasure of a find!

Hours: Open daily, 7:30am - 10pm.

Admission: Free

Ages: All

VIRGINIA ROBINSON GARDENS

(310) 276-5367 / parks.co.la.ca.us/virginia_gardens.html
1008 Elden Way, Beverly Hills
(Exit San Diego Fwy [405] E. on Sunset Blvd., L. on Crescent, R. on Elden. [TG: 592 E6])

Once the estate of the department store magnate, Robinsons (of Robinsons-May), this house has the distinction of being one of the first homes built in Beverly Hills. A twenty-minute guided tour through the house shows off the furnishings and other collections gathered from around the world. Visitors walk through the living rooms, bedroom, kitchen, and other rooms.

Probably of more interest to older kids is the one-hour tour through the six acres of botanic gardens. The hilly gardens, which are not stroller or wheelchair friendly, feature lush tropical and subtropical plants, roses, and more. Brick pathways connect the diverse areas of foliage that are also landscaped with ponds, fountains, and an Olympic-size pool. The grounds are a gardener's delight!

Hours: Open by reservation only on Tues. - Thurs., 10am and 1pm; Fri., 10am.

Admission: $10 for adults; $5 for seniors and students; $3 for ages 4 - 11; children 3 years and under are free.

Ages: 9 years and up.

WHITTIER NARROWS RECREATION AREA

(626) 575-5526 / parks.co.la.ca.us
Rosemead Boulevard and Santa Anita Avenue, South El Monte
(There are a few different entrances - Exit Pomona Fwy [60] N. on Rosemead Blvd. to the athletic facilities; exit S. on Santa Anita Ave. to the lake and park; exit S. on Peck, R. on Durfee to the nature center. [TG: 636 J5])

Whittier Narrows will broaden your horizons with the scope of its recreational activities. This expansive 1,100-acre park offers something for every age, interest, and activity level in your family. The section of park on the northern side of the freeway is for the sports-oriented with sixteen lighted tennis courts, six soccer fields, seven baseball diamonds, an archery range, a trap and skeet shooting range, a model plane airfield, a model car track, playgrounds, bike trails, and a bicycle motocross (BMX) track - (626) 575-5521. Check out the adjacent AMERICAN HERITAGE PARK / MILITARY MUSEUM (pg. 81.)

Don't want to make waves? Visit the placid Legg Lake, which is south of the freeway. Pedal boat rentals are available here on weekends only at $15 a half hour. Kids can have a "reel" fun time fishing here, too. Model boat races usually take place on Sunday afternoons. The pretty parkland surrounding the lake has shade trees, large grass areas, and playgrounds. A very pleasant, three-plus mile, hard-packed dirt hiking/biking trail goes around the odd-shaped lake and can actually be finished, or started, at the nature center down the road, or entirely within the park.

For those who hear nature calling, the nature center is located at 1000 Durfee, (626) 575-5523. The center is small, but it has live snakes, lizards, tarantulas, and some aquatic life as well as a few taxidermied animals. We saw cardinals and blue jays at the bird feeders just outside. Ask about the center's hour-and-a-half guided school tours. Knowledgeable docents lead the kids on a hike, pointing out and explaining about the plants and animals seen along the way. Students will also listen to a ranger talk regarding the displays in the nature center building. Another tour option is taking a forty-five-minute tractor-drawn hayride around the area. The ranger talk is included in this tour, too. Bring a sack lunch to enjoy at the picnic site here. Note: Hayrides are available for individuals and families every Saturday at 10am. Inquire about other park programs.

Hours: The park is open daily, sunrise - sunset. The nature center is usually open Mon. - Sat., 9:30am - 5pm; Sun., 11am - 5pm. Closed Christmas. Call to make tour reservations.

Admission: Parking is free on weekdays; $3 on weekends and holidays. Admission and parking are free at the nature center. The hiking tour is $10 total for up to sixty students. The hayride is $50 total for up to fifty children. The Sat. hayride is $2 for adults; $1 for children.

Ages: All

WILDERNESS PRESERVE

(626) 355-5309 / www.ci.arcadia.ca.us
2240 Highland Oaks Drive, Arcadia
(Exit Foothill Fwy [210] N. on Santa Anita Ave., R. on Elkins Ave., L. on Highland Oaks. [TG: 537 E7])

This wilderness park/preserve is in the foothills of the mountains, on the same street as residential housing. A short dirt trail through the shade trees loops around a large grassy area. Plenty of picnic tables are scattered among the woods. A picnic shelter with enough picnic tables for a busload, or two, is on the grounds, next to the kitchen facility that has two sinks, a freezer, a refrigerator, and an oven. This shelter area is available for group rental and also has a fire ring with amphitheater-type seating. Call before you come to ask if the Santa Anita creek, kept in check by controlling the water from the Santa Ana dam, is flowing. If so, get at least your feet wet - so refreshing on a hot summer's day. A swimming hole at the north end of the creek usually has three or four feet of water, regardless if the dam is flowing or not.

The nature center contains quite a few glass-encased, taxidermied animals. We looked at barn owls, ravens, a gold eagle, black bear, mountain lion, coyote, raccoon, and lots more. The building also has a mounted insect collection, a few live snakes, and small waterfall and "pond." Ask about the many classes that the park offers, including merit badge classes.

Hours: Open October through April, Mon. - Fri., 8:30am - 4:30pm. Open May through September, Mon. - Fri., 8:30am - 7pm. Weekend admission is by advanced reservation only.

Admission: Free

Ages: All

WILLIAM S. HART MUSEUM AND PARK

(661) 254-4584 - museum; (661) 259-0855 - park and camping / www.hartmuseum.org

24151 San Fernando Road, Newhall

See the entry for WILLIAM S. HART MUSEUM AND PARK on page 124 for details.

-----*MALLS*-----

DEL AMO FASHION CENTER - KID'S CLUB

(310) 542-8525 / www.delamofashioncenter.com

Carson Street at Hawthorne Boulevard, Torrance

(Exit Harbor Fwy [110] W. on Carson. [TG: 763 D6])

Join in an hour of fun and frivolity every Thursday morning by the International Food Court on the second level. Top name kids' entertainers encourage your children to laugh, sing, and dance along with them as they tell stories, sing songs, juggle, perform magic tricks, and more. There are free drawings after every show and discounts offered for stores and restaurants. This mall, by the way, is the largest one in the western U.S. with over 350 stores and three food courts - talk about choices!

Hours: Every Thurs. at 10:30am.

Admission: Free

Ages: 1½ - 6 years.

THE GROVE / KIDS' THURSDAYS

(888) 315-8883 or (323) 900-8000 / www.thegrovela.com

189 The Grove Drive, Los Angeles

(Exit Santa Monica Fwy [10] N. on Fairfax Ave., R. on 3rd St.)

What a contrast in malls! The definitely upscale Grove is located just across the way from the down-to-earth, original FARMERS MARKET (see pg. 14). The Grove is an outdoor complex with walking streets that boasts of beautiful landscaping; a choreographed "dancing" fountain that moves every half hour to a variety of musical selections; a double-decker trolley with a bell-ringing conductor who conveys patrons from one end to the other; eateries and restaurants; and children's activities. On Thursdays, kids are invited to listen to storytellers, make crafts, hear and join in on songs, watch a marionette show, or something else equally entertaining.

The name retail shops here include Gap Kids, J. Crew, Nordstrom, Wentworth Gallery, Barnes and Noble, and FAO Schwartz. The latter is an incredible toy store that carries almost everything you can imagine. Pacific Theaters has fourteen screens here and, in keeping with the posh atmosphere, the theater has an elegant lobby, stadium seating, some reclining seats!, and loge seating for private parties.

If you don't find something you like at this mall, or just for a change of ambiance, walk across the way to Farmer's Market.

Hours: The stores are open daily, usually 10am - 6pm. Children's activities are available on Thursdays starting at 11am. Call for a schedule.

Admission: Free, but bring spending money. Kids' Thursdays are free. Parking in the structure is $1 for the first three hours.

Ages: 2 years and up.

LAKEWOOD CENTER MALL - KID'S NIGHT OUT

(562) 531-6707 or (562) 633-0290 / www.shoplakewoodcenter.com

200 Lakewood Center Mall, Lakewood

(Exit Artesia Fwy [91] S. on Lakewood Blvd. [TG: 766 A3])

The whole family can enjoy a kid's night out where entertainment by L.A.'s top children's performers give it their all by the Terrace Cafe's Food Court. Come join in the toe-tapping music, laugh at a comedic juggler, watch a puppet show, see and learn about reptiles during a presentation, create a holiday craft, or be amazed at a magician's slight of hand. Call for a schedule of events. Children 10 years and under (and their families) are entitled to free membership and discounts from participating mall stores.

The mall also hosts occasional special events such as live animals presentations or Civil War reenactor speakers. A carousel is here year round. Near the food court, close to Macy's, is a small, semi-enclosed soft play area designed for younger ones. Against a colorful background mural, they can play on giant padded foam pieces representing picnic food, including a spilled soda, hot dog, and fruit.

Hours: Every Tues. at 6pm.

Admission: Free

Ages: 2 - 11 years.

LOS CERRITOS CENTER - KID'S NIGHT OUT

(562) 402-SHOP (7467) / www.shoploscerritos.com

239 Los Cerritos Center, Cerritos

(Exit San Gabriel Fwy [605] E. on South St., L. into mall parking lot, around the building to Mervyn's. [TG: 766 F2])

Kids (and parents) get to hear and participate in some great performances by name entertainers at Mervyn's court. Musicians, dancers, magicians, puppet masters, animal presentations, and others enthrall young visitors for about forty-five minutes. Special prizes are raffled off each week. Members get a free gift on their birthday and store discount coupons. Membership is free. So, come for a night out!

Hours: Shows are every Wed. at 6pm.

Admission: Free

Ages: 2 - 11 years.

NORTHRIDGE FASHION CENTER - KID'S CLUB

(818) 885-9700 / www.northridgefashion.com

9301 Tampa Avenue, Northridge

(From San Diego Fwy [405], exit E. on Nordhoff St. From Ventura Fwy [101], exit N. on Tampa Avenue. It's on the corner of Nordhoff and Tampa. [TG: 500 F6])

Become a NFC kid and get in on all the fun! Forty-five-minutes of storytelling, singing, dancing, art workshops, circus acts, or puppet shows are on the morning's agenda at food court. The Club also gives its young members discounts at participating mall stores, and a free gift on their birthday.

This mall also features a soft play area with a padded foam giant starfish, surfboards, and dolphins, plus play sports cars and a backdrop scene of the Hollywood Hills. It's located on the lower level, near Macy's.

Hours: The first and third Thurs. of each month at 10:30am.

Admission: Free

Ages: 1 - 7 years.

PUENTE HILLS MALL - MOMMY AND ME CLUB

(626) 965-5875 or (626) 965-8086

449 Puente Hills Mall, City of Industry

(Exit Pomona Fwy [60] S. on Azusa Ave. Mall is immediately on L. [TG: 678 G4])

    Mommy and me arts and crafts activities are offered in the Center Court for preschoolers during the traditional school year. The craft-oriented time is enhanced by preschool curriculum, such as learning letters and sounds. Borders bookstores often then invites all participants (and whoever else would like to join in the fun) to a time of storytelling and other book-related events at 1:30pm. In the summertime and on Saturdays, the emphasis shifts to including elementary-aged kids, too, for the arts projects.

    Hours: Every Wed. from 11:30am - 1pm and on the second Sat. of each month from 1pm - 3pm.

  Admission: Free

      Ages: 2 - 6 years during the week; preschool through elementary on weekends and during the summer.

SOUTH BAY GALLERIA - KIDS CLUB

(310) 371-7546 / www.southbaygalleria.com

1815 Hawthorne Boulevard, Redondo Beach

(Exit San Diego Fwy [405] W. on Artesia Blvd., L. on Hawthorne. [TG: 763 C1])

    Once a month kids can come to the Galleria and enjoy an hour of entertainment such as stories, puppets, animal presentations, magic shows, sing-alongs, or seasonally-oriented arts and crafts activities presented on the third level near the food court. After each show, raffles or drawings are held for mall certificates. Make new friends as you and your child become regulars! Make sure you sign up to become a Kids Club member (membership is free) because a postcard is mailed out once a month listing a schedule of events and offering give-aways from retailers.

    Hours: The first Tues. of each month at 6:30pm.

  Admission: Free

      Ages: 2 - 10 years.

SOUTHBAY PAVILION - LI'L SHOPPERS CLUB

(310) 366-6629 / www.southbaypavilion.com

20700 S. Avalon Boulevard, Carson

(Exit San Diego Fwy [405] N. on Avalon Blvd. [TG: 764 E4])

    Encourage your little shoppers to join the Li'l Shoppers Club, which meets at center court. Children enjoy the forty-five-minute of club time as they participate in activities, such as making arts and crafts projects, or are entertained by singers, magicians, some real clowns, jugglers, and others.

    Hours: Every Thurs. at 6pm, February through November.

  Admission: Free

      Ages: 1½ - 10 years, depending on the agenda.

STONEWOOD CENTER - KID'S NIGHT OUT

(562) 904-1832 / www.shopstonewoodcenter.com

251 Stonewood Street, Downey

(Exit San Gabriel River Fwy [605] W. on Firestone Blvd. Mall is on the corner of Firestone and Lakewood Blvd. [TG: 706 C5])

    Kids get their own night out (but you're welcome to come, too) when they join in the hour of fun and entertainment provided for them near the Robinsons May court. Shows and activities vary, featuring singers, dancers, puppets, magicians, crafts, reptile presentations, and more. What a great family outing! Register your 10 year old or younger children for the club and they will receive a free gift on their birthday as well as discounts from participating stores.

    Hours: Every Thurs. at 6pm.

  Admission: Free

      Ages: 1½ - 10 years.

THIRD STREET PROMENADE

(310) 393-8355 - Promenade; (310) 394-1049 - Santa Monica Place / www.downtownsm.com;
www.santamonicaplace.com

3rd Street, Santa Monica

(Exit Santa Monica Fwy [10] N. on Lincoln Blvd., L. on Wilshire Blvd. Park wherever you can. [TG: 671 D2])

This three-block pedestrian walkway is a fascinating outdoor mall experience. It rates an A+ for people-watching as the international mix of people, converging here from the nearby Los Angeles International Airport, make it a cultural adventure. Nighttime and weekends bring out performers who want to show off their talents, however glorious or dubious they might be. We've seen and heard African drum playing, tap dancing, folk songs, acrobatics, men acting like robots, clowns making balloon animals, and an organ grinder monkey begging - all within the span of an hour. Benches are plentiful, so if you really enjoy some of the entertainment, sit down and watch. A plethora of artsy and unique stores and boutiques, plus movie theaters line the "street." Vendor carts are along the sidewalks. Choose from a multitude of restaurants that range from upscale to grab-a-bite, or snack at a bakery or ice cream shop. A few fountains, featuring dinosaurs spouting water, complete the eclectic ambiance at the promenade.

If you haven't gotten enough shopping in, at the other end of the promenade is Santa Monica Place, which is 140 stores and three levels of indoor shopping. Note: The Big Blue Bus, (310) 451-5444 / www.bigbluebus.com, runs a loop from Main Street to Third Street Promenade every fifteen minutes at a cost of 75¢ per person.

Hours: Most stores and restaurants are open daily, 10am - 9pm.
Admission: Free, but bring spending money.
Ages: All

VALENCIA TOWN CENTER - KIDSTOWN

(661) 287-9050 / www.valenciatowncenter.com

24201 W. Valencia Boulevard, Valencia

(Exit Golden State Fwy [5] E. on Valencia Blvd. [TG: 4550 F3])

Kidstown comes to town every other Thursday morning by the Sears court. Join in the forty-five-minute show of puppetry, song, dance, or animal presentations - it's all interactive fun for young kids. Members of Kidstown also receive merchant discounts from participating stores. (Membership is free.) This mall also features a carousel and an EDWARDS IMAX THEATRE (see pg. 145) with 2-D and 3-D movies.

Hours: Every other Thurs. morning at 10:30am, March through November.
Admission: Free
Ages: 1½ - 6 years.

WESTFIELD SHOPPINGTOWN EAGLE ROCK - KIDS CLUB

(323) 256-2147 / www.westfield.com

2700 Colorado Boulevard, Los Angeles

(Going E. on Ventura Fwy [134], exit S. on Harvey Dr., immediate L. on E. Wilson Ave., which becomes W. Broadway, which turns into Colorado. Going N. on Glendale Fwy [2], exit E. on Colorado. [TG: 564 J5])

Join in a fun one-hour show featuring comedy, juggling, puppets, live animal presentations, singers, or dancers! Call for a specific show schedule.

Hours: The first Wed. of every month at 6pm.
Admission: Free
Ages: 2 - 11 years.

WESTFIELD SHOPPINGTOWN FASHION SQUARE - ART2GO

(818) 783-0550 or (818) 501-1447 / www.westfield.com

13780 Riverside Drive, Sherman Oaks

(Exit Ventura Fwy [101] N. on Woodman Ave., L. on Riverside. [TG: 562 B4])

This large, two-story indoor shopping center is in partnership with the Los Angeles Childrens Museum to offer special ART2GO workshops for kids. Past projects here have included making modeling clay and sculpting a masterpiece; making a topographical map using all the necessary messy ingredients; planting a tree (using seeds); crafting a visor; designing a holiday card; and more. Occasionally the mall hosts performances or concerts for kids, too.

Other mall accouterments include a food court, a Discovery Channel store, and a small, glass-covered koi fish pond that visitors can walk on. In order to see the fish in the pond, which is located just outside Bloomingdale's, inquisitive guests must kneel down on the dark glass (or sprawl out on it, as younger kids are wont to do), cup the outside of your eyes, and peer through it. Bring your cameras for some interesting shots (and not of the fish!).

Hours: The workshops are offered the third Fri. of every month from 3pm - 7pm.
Admission: Free
Ages: 4 - 11 years old..

WESTFIELD SHOPPINGTOWN FOX HILLS MALL - KID'S CLUB

(310) 390-7833 or (310) 390-5073 / www.westfield.com
294 Fox Hills Mall, Culver City
(Going N. on San Diego Fwy [405], exit N.E. on Sepulveda. Going S. on 405, exit E. on Slauson Ave. Or take Marina Fwy [90] E. to the end and turn L. on Slauson. It's on the corner of Sepulveda and Slauson. [TG: 672 H6])

The third Thursday of every month features "name" entertainment, showcasing puppetry, music, juggling, and more for the whole family. All programs are about an hour in length. Dinner and shopping seem like a natural follow up! This mall also year round miniature train rides for kiddies.

Hours: The third Thurs. at 6pm.
Admission: Free
Ages: 2 - 11 years.

WESTFIELD SHOPPINGTOWN PROMENADE - KIDS CLUB

(818) 884-7090 / www.westfield.com
6100 Topanga Canyon Boulevard, Woodland Hills
(Exit Ventura Fwy [101] N. on Topanga Canyon Blvd. [TG: 530 A7])

Meet at Westie's Playtown, a soft play area for kiddies to enjoy storytime from guest authors and interactive play time with musical instruments, as well as to meet costumed characters and have more kinds of fun.

Hours: Every Sat. at 11am.
Admission: Free
Ages: 1 - 8 years.

WESTFIELD SHOPPINGTOWN SANTA ANITA - KIDS CLUB

(626) 445-3116 or (626) 445 - MALL (6255) / www.westfield.com
400 S. Baldwin Avenue, Arcadia
(Exit Foothill Fwy [210] S. on Baldwin. [TG: 567 A6])

Thematic (and just for the fun of it) arts and crafts activities are offered here such as decorating flower pots (Mother's Day), making calendars, and decorating cookies. Sometimes the Kids Club features great participatory entertainment instead. Call for a schedule.

Hours: The first Wed. of every month at 4:30pm.
Admission: Free
Ages: 2 - 11 years, depending on the agenda.

WESTFIELD SHOPPINGTOWN TOPANGA PLAZA - KIDS CLUB

(818) 594-8740 / www.westfield.com

6600 Topanga Canyon Boulevard, Canoga Park

(Exit Ventura Fwy [101] N. on Topanga Canyon Blvd. [TG: 530 A7])

Families can enjoy free shows and/or a craft time the second Thursday night near the food court. Past shows have included clowns, magicians, and dancing. Craft projects are usually themed, such as making Valentines cards near Valentine's Day. After the show shop at the more than 150 stores, but not all of them on one visit.

Hours: The second Thurs. of every month from 5pm - 7pm.

Admission: Free

Ages: 4 - 11 years.

WESTFIELD SHOPPINGTOWN WEST COVINA - KIDS CLUB

(626) 960-1881 / www.westfield.com

112 Plaza Drive, West Covina

(Going W on San Bernardino Fwy [10], exit S. on Sunset, mall is on the L. Going E. on 10, exit S. on West Covina Pkwy. The mall is on the L. [TG: 598 F7])

The hour-long kids club consists of some old-fashioned family time together while enjoying a variety of entertainment and festive events. Discounts at certain mall stores and the food court are offered to participants. Bring a friend!

Hours: The second Tues. of each month at 6pm.

Admission: Free

Ages: 2 - 11 years.

WESTSIDE PAVILION - KIDS' CLUB

(310) 474-6255 / www.westsidepavilion.com

10800 W. Pico Boulevard, Los Angeles

(Exit San Diego Fwy [405] E. on Santa Monica Blvd., R. on Westwood Blvd. The mall is on the corner of Westwood and Pico. Or, exit Santa Monica Fwy [10] N. on Overland Ave. The mall is on the corner of Overland and Blythe Ave. [TG: 632 D6])

Parents and kids can enjoy a forty-five-minute presentation together on Wednesday nights at Westside Pavilion. Shows can consist of puppetry, magicians, bubbles, musicians, and more. Free membership to the club allows kids to receive a monthly postcard promoting special offers from Pavilion retailers. Note that this mall has a BUILD-A-BEAR WORKSHOP (see pg. 129).

Hours: The first and third Wed. at 6pm.

Admission: Free

Ages: All

WHITTWOOD MALL - KIDS CLUB

(562) 947-2871 / www.whittwoodmall.com

15603 Whittier Boulevard, Whittier

(From San Gabriel River Fwy [605], exit E. on Whittier Blvd. From Santa Ana Fwy [5] or Artesia Fwy [91], exit N. on Beach Blvd. L. on Whittier. [TG: 707 H4])

This Kids Club meets once a month, sometimes for a time of entertainment, such as music, puppetry, or live animals shows, and sometimes for a time of making arts and crafts projects. The mall also presents special events or activities throughout the year. Past activities have included taking a train through a teddybear wonderland and riding in a stationary hot-air balloon.

Hours: Once a month at 4pm if it's to make a craft; at 5pm or 6pm if it's for a show. Call for the exact dates.

Admission: Free for the Kids Club. Most of the special events are free, too.

Ages: 2 -10 years.

-----*MUSEUMS*-----

ADAMSON HOUSE AND MALIBU LAGOON MUSEUM

(310) 456-8432 - museum; (310) 456-1770 - docent during museum hours;
(818) 880-0363 - lagoon tour / www.adamsonhouse.org
$$

23200 Pacific Coast Highway, Malibu

(Exit Ventura Fwy [101] S. on Las Virgenes Rd., which turns into Malibu Cyn. Rd. Go to the end, L. on P.C.H. It's on P.C.H., W. of Malibu Pier, near Serra Rd. [TG: 629 B7])

The Adamson House and its adjacent museum are on beautifully landscaped grounds just a few feet away from the Malibu Surfrider Beach and lifeguard station, and the Malibu Lagoon - definitely beach front property. The outside of the house and the fountains integrate the colorful Malibu tiles in their design. We wandered around the grounds on flagstone walkways that wove through grassy lawns, beneath shade trees, along several gardens (including a rose garden), past a pool that was once filled with salt water from the ocean, and to the chain-link fence which marks the house boundaries. Here, just a short distance from the pier, we watched surfers do their thing.

The small museum features exhibits pertaining to the history of Malibu including cattle brands, arrowheads, maps, fossilized shells, and numerous photographs. I liked the Malibu Colony of Stars' pictures of Robert Redford, Bing Crosby, Clara Bow, Joan Crawford, and others. Ask for a tour, or for explanations regarding the history of the railroad, the dam, and the movie colony.

The two-story house was built in 1929. The rooms can be seen on a one-hour, guided tour. Adults and older children will appreciate the bottle-glass windows, hand-painted murals, additional tile work (especially in the kitchen), furnishings, and unique decor.

There isn't any direct access to the lagoon (i.e. the parcel of water and land that is a haven for various bird species) from the house. You can get to this area by walking or driving over the bridge and down Cross Creek Road. We observed pelicans, herons, sandpipers, and other birds coming in for a landing before taking to the skies once again. Visit here on your own or make tour reservations to educate your kids (and yourself) about the waterfowl, ecology, the area's Chumash Indian past, and more. The lagoon programs are given by a state park ranger. Note: Although the beach is accessible by going through the museum parking lot, the waters are for surfers only. If your kids want to go swimming, head towards Malibu Pier, just up the street.

Hours: The house and museum are open Wed. - Sat., 11am - 3pm. The last house tour begins at 2pm. Closed New Year's Day, July 4th, Thanksgiving, and Christmas Day. Call for information on lagoon tours and programs.

Admission: The house and museum tour is $3 for adults; ages 17 and under are free. Parking in the county lot adjacent to the museum costs $5 per vehicle. Some free street parking is available. Lagoon tours cost $6 per vehicle for parking.

Ages: 7 years and up for the house tour and museum; 4 years and up for the lagoon tour.

ADOBE DE PALOMARES

(909) 620-0264 / www.osb.net/pomona
$

491 E. Arrow Highway, Pomona

(Exit San Bernardino Fwy [10] N. on Towne Ave., L. on Arrow Hwy. [TG: 601 A4])

This thirteen-room restored adobe was originally built in 1854. A guided tour of the house includes seeing the courtyard and authentic period furniture, as well as cooking utensils (how did they live without so many technical doohickeys?!), tools, antique clothing, canopy beds, and children's toys. The rooms look quite livable, even by today's standards. The landscaped grounds are lovely. A blacksmith shop is also on site and features saddles, ranching tools, branding irons, and a horse-drawn carriage circa 1880's. Adjacent to the adobe is Palomare Park, so bring a picnic lunch and enjoy some running around space.

Hours: Open Sun., 2pm - 5pm. Special tours are given by appointment.

Admission: $2 for adults; $1 for ages 18 and under.

Ages: 6 years and up.

AFRICAN AMERICAN FIREFIGHTER MUSEUM

(213) 744-1730 / www.lafd.org/aafm.htm
1401 S. Central Avenue, Los Angeles
(Exit Santa Monica Fwy [10] N. on Central Ave. It's on the corner of Central and 14th St. [TG: 634 F7])

This small, beautiful museum is set in a Los Angeles neighborhood. It chronicles the history of black firefighters by honoring them and their white colleagues who pushed for integration. The walls and reference books contain photographs and stories that tell of the once-segregated station. For instance, although black and white men battled fires and fought side-by-side to save lives, they couldn't cook or eat together. African Americans even slept in beds designated "black beds." Exhibits include a fire engine, uniforms, boots, fire extinguishers, badges, helmets, and other mementos.

Hours: Open every Tues. and Thurs., 10am - 2pm; and the second and fourth Sun. of each month, 1pm - 4pm. Special tours can be arranged by appointment.
Admission: Free
Ages: 5 years and up.

AIR AND SPACE GALLERY

(213) 744-7400 / www.casciencectr.org
Exposition Park, Los Angeles
(Exit Harbor Fwy [110] W. on Exposition Blvd., L. on Flower, L. on Figueroa. Or, exit Santa Monica Fwy [10] S. on Vermont, L. on Exposition, R. on Figueroa. [TG: 674 A2])

This multi-story building is actually part of the CALIFORNIA SCIENCE CENTER. It's hard to miss with a United Airlines plane out front and a jet fighter perched precariously on its side! The atmosphere is uplifting with planes, such as a replica of the 1902 Wright Glider, a real Air Force jet, and a F-20 all suspended from the ceiling in mock flight. On the second floor, climb into a real police helicopter and man (or woman) the controls. To feel air lift, put on a pair of foam wings, stand in front of the wind machine, and fly. (I guess I was too heavy to get off the ground.) Press a button to launch small parachutes. On the upper level, press a button to hear the difference in heartbeats on earth and after just returning from orbit. Which beats faster? (Come to the museum and find out.) Look at your face in a mirror and see how it looks on earth. Then, look at a special mirror to see how you look in orbit, when fluids shift toward the upper body - it's not a pretty sight. Trace a pattern while looking in a mirror (it's harder than it looks) and work your muscles on an exercise bike to test the effects of muscle atrophy from prolonged space flight.

See a full-scale model of the Cassini (the real one was sent to orbit Saturn), a full-scale prototype of the Viking Lander, a heat shield from the Gemini 11, two original space capsules, a J47 turbo engine, and more. Downstairs is small mission control room for astronauts 7 years and under. Sit at a table to read about space, put together puzzles, or "check out" (for free) a variety of discovery boxes filled with different kinds of toys and activities. One box held packages of prepacked astronaut food to look at (not appetizing); one had astronaut-type of clothes to try on; and another showed why planes have wings and included a glider plane.

Another favorite activity is putting together different types of small model planes and flying them in a specified area to determine which wing types and body shapes fly the fastest or most on course. Look at the pieces of meteorites here and/or try out the motion simulator ride. ($4.50 a ride.) School tours are offered to enable kids to glean even more information about our universe.

A wonderful way to round out your day is to have a picnic and visit one of the other attractions in this complex - CALIFORNIA AFRICAN AMERICAN MUSEUM (see pg. 84), CALIFORNIA SCIENCE CENTER (see pg. 85), EXPOSITION PARK (see pg. 44), IMAX THEATER (see pg. 148), and NATURAL HISTORY MUSEUM OF LOS ANGELES (see pg. 109).

Hours: Open Mon. - Fri., 10am - 1pm; Sat. - Sun. and holidays, 1pm - 4pm. Closed New Year's Day, Thanksgiving, and Christmas.
Admission: Free. Parking is $6.
Ages: 3 years and up.

AMERICAN HERITAGE PARK / MILITARY MUSEUM

(626) 442-1776 / www.members.aol.com/tankland/museum.htm $$
1918 N. Rosemead Boulevard, South El Monte

(Exit Pomona Fwy [60] N. at Rosemead Blvd. The entrance is on the R. side of the street, at the northern part of Whittier Narrows Recreation Area. [TG: 636 J3])

Attention! Over 170 pieces of equipment, representing all branches of the United States Military, can be found at this outside museum. The collection contains vehicles and weapons from World War I through Desert Storm. It includes Jeeps, amphibious trucks, ambulances, helicopters, cannons, gun turrets, and thirty-ton Sherman tanks. The vehicles can be looked at, but not sat on or touched.

To the untrained eye it looks like a random compilation of old military equipment. And it is. However, some pieces are in the process of being restored, and some have been used in movies and T.V. shows. The volunteers are knowledgeable and know many of the "inside" stories about the vehicles. Tip: This is an ideal setting if your kids are studying any of the wars and want to make a video.

Hours: Open Fri. - Sun., 10am - 4:30pm. Open at other times for group tours by appointment only. Closed on rainy days.

Admission: $4 for adults; $3 for seniors and military; $2 for ages 10 - 16; 50¢ for ages 5 - 9; children 4 and under, and weekday groups, are free.

Ages: 4 years and up.

ANGELS ATTIC

(310) 394-8331 / www.internetimpact.com/angelsattic $$
516 Colorado Avenue, Santa Monica

(Exit Santa Monica Fwy [10] N. on 5th St., R.. on Colorado [TG: 671 E2])

Picture a quaint Victorian house filled with beautiful collectable doll houses and dolls. Now, add a warm inviting atmosphere and you've got Angels Attic. The two-story1895 Queen Anne-style house/museum has antique toys, dolls, and numerous doll houses. The doll houses are complete with furnishings, wall paper, chandeliers, tiny pieces of silverware, and more. The house in the design of a shoe is particularly clever. Can't get to France? See the Versailles here, in miniature. There are several one-room themed dioramas that hold miniatures, too, such as a bakery that's filled with tiny pastries that look good enough to eat (almost!). Although little hands may not touch, little eyes will enjoy looking, especially since most exhibits are at eye level.

If all this makes you long for a Lilliputian lifestyle, check out the small gift shop. Purchase doll house accessories and books and magazines related to collecting miniatures and dolls. Tea time, with homemade cake, cookies, and lemonade is available here on the enclosed porch with advanced reservations and an additional $7.50 per person.

At Christmas time, the outside of Angels Attic is decorated and so is every doll house - truly a mini extravaganza. Don't miss Santa's Workshop in miniature, with reindeer, Santa and Mrs. Claus, and over 100 elves completing the festive scene.

Hours: Open Thurs. - Sun., 12:30pm - 4:30pm. Closed most major holidays.

Admission: $6.50 for adults; $4 for seniors; $3.50 for children 11 years and under.

Ages: 5 years and up.

ANTELOPE VALLEY INDIAN MUSEUM

(661) 942-0662 - state park; (661) 946-3055 - museum / www.calparksmojave.com $
15800 Avenue 'M', Lancaster

(Exit Antelope Valley Fwy [14] E. on Ave. 'K', R. on 150th St. East, L. on Ave. 'M'. Or, exit Pearblossom Hwy [138] N. on 165th St. East, which turns into 170th St., L. on Ave. 'M'. [TG: 4109 E4])

Built into and around rock formations of the Mojave Desert, the outside of this Indian museum looks incongruously like a Swiss Chalet. The inside is just as unique. Once the home of artist Howard Edward, portions of the interior (e.g. walls, ceilings, and flooring) are composed of boulders. My kids' reaction was simply "WOW!" The large main room is lined with Kachina dolls on the upper shelves and painted panels of the dolls on the ceiling. (The Hopi people believed that Kachina dolls brought rain.) The unusual furniture and the support beams are made from Joshua trees. A connecting room has several glass-cased displays of pottery shards that were once used for money and jewelry; cradle-boards; baskets; and various items made from plants, such as yucca fiber sandals.

Kids love climbing up the narrow stony steps into a large display room, which is carved out of rock. Exhibits here include arrowheads, whale bone tools, shells, whale ribs, harpoons, and weapons. Go back down a few of the steps. Stop. Look up. You'll see Indian dioramas and re-created cave paintings.

Outside, you'll pass by a series of small cottages that were once used as guest houses. Your destination is Joshua Cottage, a place that has some hands-on activities for kids. They can grind corn with stone mortars and pestles, try their hand at using a pump drill to drill holes, and "saw" with a bow drill to create smoke. Kids can even learn how to make a pine needle whisk broom. (The brooms may not have much practical use now-a-days, but it's a fun and educational project.) Docents will gladly explain the use of various seeds and other plant parts. The small adjacent room is a gallery that's also used for educational programs.

The museum is part of the California Department of Parks and Recreation. Enjoy an easy half-mile nature walk on the trails through the buttes and desert just behind the Indian Museum. A guidebook (50¢) explains the fourteen Native American symbols on the posts along the trail.

> **Hours:** Open mid- September through mid- June, Sat. - Sun., 11am - 4pm. Closed in the summer. Tours are available Tues., Wed., and Thurs. by appointment.
>
> **Admission:** $2 for adults; ages 16 and under are free.
>
> **Ages:** 5 years and up.

AUTRY MUSEUM OF WESTERN HERITAGE

(323) 667-2000 / www.autry-museum.org
4700 Western Heritage Way, in Griffith Park, Los Angeles
(Going N. on Golden State Fwy [5] or W. on Ventura Fwy [134], exit at Zoo Dr. and follow the signs. Going E. on 134, exit S. on Victory Blvd., L. on Zoo Dr. Going S. on 5, exit S. on Western, L. on Victory Blvd. to Zoo Dr. The museum is across the parking lot from the L. A. Zoo. [TG: 564 B4])

The cowboy lifestyle lassos our imagination. Bryce, my middle son, wants to become a cowboy missionary (yes, he is special), so this museum really spurred on his interest, at least regarding the cowboy part of his career choice. It will also delight fans of the Old West with its complete array of paintings, clothing, tools, weapons (one of Annie Oakley's guns!), and interesting artifacts. Movie clips, videos, and movie posters throughout the museum highlight specific areas of this romanticized period. In the Spirit of Imagination Hall, a big hit is sitting on a saddle and making riding motions to become part of an old western movie showing on a screen behind the rider. My kids particularly enjoyed the hands-on children's Discovery Gallery, set up like the home and workplace of the Sees, a Chinese American family. Visit their parlor and read some books, or listen to an old-fashioned radio. Pretend to prepare a meal in the realistic mini kitchen. Visit the Sees' antique store; pretend to cook up some Chinese food at a re-created portion of the real restaurant, Dragon's Den; and try on Chinese clothing.

The entire museum is interesting and wheelchair/stroller-friendly, but you do have to keep your kids corralled, as most of the exhibits are not touchable ones. Saturday programs, for ages 6 to 12, are more interactive with storytelling, games, and even sing alongs. Ask about the museum's weekly summer history classes for kids. Autry Museum also offers numerous outstanding programs throughout the year, such as sleepovers. A cafe is on the grounds, as is a wonderful, large, grassy picnic area.

> **Hours:** Open Tues. - Sun. (and certain Mon. holidays), 10am - 5pm; open Thurs. until 8pm. Closed most Mon., Thanksgiving, and Christmas.
>
> **Admission:** $7.50 for adults; $5 for seniors and ages 13 - 18; $3 for children 2 - 12. Certain discounts available through AAA. Admission is free on the second Tues. and on Thurs. from 4pm - 8pm. (See C.E.E. L.A. for membership savings, page 86.)
>
> **Ages:** 4 years and up.

BANNING RESIDENCE MUSEUM AND PARK

(310) 548-7777 / www.banningmuseum.org

401 E. M Street, Wilmington

(Exit Harbor Fwy [110] E. on Pacific Coast Highway, R. on Avalon Blvd., L. on M St. [TG: 794 F5])

This huge Victorian museum, where the founder of Wilmington once lived, is reflective of the Banning family lifestyle in the 1800's. The hour guided tours are best suited for older children as there is much to see, but not to touch. First, walk through the photo gallery, past a display of brilliant cut glass, and into the house where each of the seventeen rooms are beautifully decorated with period furniture and eclectic art work. (Note: The house is completely decked out at Christmas time and looks particularly splendid.) Check out the hoof inkwell in the General's office. Get the kids involved with the tour by asking them questions like, "What's missing from this office that modern offices have?" (Answer - a computer, a fax machine, etc. Surprisingly, a copy machine *is* here.) The parlor doubled as a music room and contains a piano, violin, and small organ as well as an unusual-looking chair made out of buffalo hide and horns. Other rooms of interest are the children's nursery; the bedrooms - one has a unique hat rack made of antlers, while another has a stepping stool that is actually a commode; and the kitchen with its pot-bellied stove and all of its gadgets. (Obviously some things never change.) Request to see the Stagecoach Barn, a fully-outfitted, nineteenth-century working barn with real stagecoaches. Ask your children if they can figure out how some of the tools were used.

School groups are given two-hour tours, geared for fourth graders, that include attending class in the one-room schoolhouse which has old-fashioned desks, slates, and McGuffy primers. Kids don an apron or ascot, get a math or English lesson from that time period, and go out for recess to play games of yesteryear. Ask about Heritage Week in May, when special school programs and a free public weekend event encourages visitors to partake in activities from the 1880's.

The museum is situated in the middle of a pretty, twenty-acre park that has a small playground, a few picnic tables, a rose garden, eucalyptus trees, giant bamboo trees, and grassy areas.

Hours: Tours are given Tues. - Thurs. at 12:30pm, 1:30pm, and 2:30pm; Sat. - Sun. at 12:30pm, 1:30pm, 2:30pm, and 3:30pm.

Admission: $3 per adult; children 12 and under are free.

Ages: 7 years and up.

BLACKBIRD AIRPARK / HERITAGE AIRPARK

(661) 277-3510 - Blackbird; (661) 267-5100 - Heritage / www.edwards.af.mil; www.cityofpalmdale.org

2001 Avenue P and 25th Street East, Palmdale

(Exit Antelope Valley Fwy [14] E. on Avenue P. They're at the Flight Test Installation at Plant 42. [TG: 4196 E4])

Three historic, sleek-looking planes are on display at the Blackbird Airpark - the Lockheed SR-71A, the A-12, and the once top-secret D-21 drone. The A-12 is perhaps the best known because it is the first Blackbird ever built and flown. The inscribed, inlaid tiles recognize record setters and program participants. The park is an annex of, and maintained by, the Air Force Flight Test Center Museum at Edwards Air Force Base. In this area so steeped in aeronautical heritage, Blackbird Airpark is one of many interesting stops for aviation buffs.

Separated from Blackbird by a chain link fence is Heritage Airpark. It has numerous planes and reduced scale model planes that pertain to aircraft built, tested, or flown at Plant 42. You see a B-52 at the entrance, plus a F-4 Phantom, F-100 Super Sabre, F-104 Starfighter, and more. This park is still in the process of being completed at the time of this writing.

Hours: Open Fri. - Sun., 11am - 4pm.

Admission: Free

Ages: 7 years and up.

BORAX VISITOR CENTER

(760) 762-7588 or (760) 762-7432 / www.borax.com

Borax Road, Boron

(Exit Highway 58 N. on Borax Rd. This facility is E. of Edwards Air Force Base.)

Borax isn't something that my family normally spends a lot of time thinking about. However, visiting this center made us realize how widely this mineral is used. As you drive past the active mine (and past the sign that states the speed limit as 37½ m.p.h.), you'll see what appears to be a little city, complete with buildings, trucks, and Goliath-type machines used to extract and process the borax. This area supplies nearly half the global need for the mineral!

Up the hill is a state-of-the-art visitors' center. Outside are original twenty mule team wagons, with harnessed mule statues, that were once used to haul the ore over 165 miles through desert and rocky terrain. Inside is a large sample of kernite, a type of borate ore, plus a pictorial timeline of the Borax company, and an exhibit that shows the process of ore being transformed (crushed, actually) into fine dust. The "Borax at Home" display shows the mining and geology processing of raw ore into everyday finished products such glass, ceramic glazes, detergent, shaving creams, and plant fertilizer. For products closer to a child's heart, the display features footballs, Play Doh™, and nail polish. Borax is also added to commodities to make them sparkle, including toothpaste and fireworks.

An adjacent room shows continuously running videos of Borax commercials starring Ronald Reagan, Dale Robertson, Clint Eastwood, and others. A fifteen-minute video titled *The World of Borax* gives a history of the mining process. An all-glass wall shows an unobstructed panorama of the entire open pit mine. High-powered microscopes are available for closer inspection of borax and other in-house crystals. Free, organized school tours of the center are given and fun supplemental materials are available to aid learning. Don't forget to stop off at the TWENTY MULE TEAM MUSEUM (see pg. 121) and the adjacent SAXON AEROSPACE MUSEUM (see pg. 117), which are just down the road.

> **Hours:** Open daily, 9am - 5pm, excluding major holidays and during inclement weather.
> **Admission:** $2 per vehicle.
> **Ages:** 4 years and up.

CALIFORNIA AFRICAN AMERICAN MUSEUM

(213) 744-7432 / www.caam.ca.gov   *$$*

600 State Drive, at Exposition Park, Los Angeles

(Exit the Harbor Fwy [110] W. on Exposition Blvd., L. on Flower, L. on Figueroa. Or, exit Santa Monica Fwy [10] S. on Vermont, L. on Exposition, R. on Figueroa. Parking is available the first driveway on the R. [TG: 674 A2])

This museum portrays the works of African American artists documenting the African American experience in this country. The two large permanent galleries contain an array of wood-carved masks and headdresses (one looks like a baby crocodile), plus statues, a room showcasing famous African Americans, and more works of art. We particularly enjoyed the lenticular pictures in the heritage section which change images as you walk by. The exhibits in the rotating galleries are equally interesting to people of all races. See the nearby AIR AND SPACE GALLERY (pg. 80), CALIFORNIA SCIENCE CENTER (pg. 85), EXPOSITION PARK (pg. 44), IMAX THEATER (pg. 148), and NATURAL HISTORY MUSEUM OF LOS ANGELES (pg. 109).

> **Hours:** Open Wed. - Sat., 10am - 4pm. Closed New Year's Day, Memorial Day, Thanksgiving, and Christmas.
> **Admission:** Free. Parking costs $6.
> **Ages:** 5 years and up.

CALIFORNIA HERITAGE MUSEUM

(310) 392-8537 / www.californiaheritagemuseum.org   *$*

2612 Main Street, Santa Monica

(Take Santa Monica Fwy [10] W. almost to the end, exit S. on 4th St., R. on Pico, L. on Main. [TG: 671 F4])

Inside this two-story house/museum, the downstairs living room is cozy and rustic-looking. The dining room atmosphere is more elegant as the table is set with fine china. The restored kitchen is the one Merle Norman originally used to cook-up her cosmetic recipes. (From such humble beginnings . . .)

The upstairs is redecorated each time a new exhibit is installed. Often the exhibits are aimed at appealing to the younger generation. Past themes have focused on cowboys, guitars from all over the world, children's books and illustrations, and model trains. Call for information on the current display. A grassy lawn welcomes picnickers. Note that a Farmer's Market is held here on Sundays.

  Hours: Open Wed. - Sun., 11am - 4pm.
 Admission: $3 for adults; $2 for seniors and students; children 12 and under are free.
   Ages: 5 years and up.

CALIFORNIA SCIENCE CENTER   ☼
(323) SCIENCE (724-3623) / www.casciencectr.org   *$$*
700 State Drive, Exposition Park, Los Angeles
(Exit Harbor Fwy [110] W. on Exposition Blvd., L. on Flower St., L. on Figueroa. Or, exit Santa Monica Fwy [10] S. on Vermont, L. on Exposition, R. on Figueroa. Parking is available in the second driveway on the R. [TG: 674 A2])

  Hanging from a very high ceiling that connects the IMAX Theater to the Science Center are hundreds of various-sized gold balls dangling on wires: an intriguing mobile. Inside, the lobby is dominated by another science-oriented piece of art - a fifty-foot, kinetic folding and unfolding structure, suspended by cables and designed by an artist-engineer. The first floor contains the museum store, which has an extensive selection of science experiments, kits, books, and lots more. It also has a McDonald's (which gets <u>extremely</u> busy during lunch hours), and the less-crowded MegaBites eatery.

  The second floor was our favorite. The west wing, titled World of Life, is packed with exhibits that pertain to human and animal lives. Look closely at cells via a microscope and a video. Crank a knob to watch how a model's digestive system unravels to stretch over eighteen feet. Watch a movie of an actual heart transplant as it is laser-beamed onto a statue patient. Drive a simulator car to experience the difference in driving sober and driving drunk. See preserved fetuses in jars ranging from a few weeks old to nine months. View a movie on conception (suitable for older children). Sit on a clear, no-butts-about-it chair filled with over 200 cigarettes and watch a movie on lung cancer. Press buttons to match recorded heartbeats to real hearts that are on display, from the huge elephant's to the medium-sized cow's to the tiny mouse's. Look at the real brains of a human, monkey, and a rat. Learn about the basic needs of plants and animals through other interactive displays. Tess, the reclining, fifty-foot human figure, comes to "life" in a well-done, fifteen-minute presentation in the BodyWorks room. A large movie screen above her head stars a cartoon character who helps Tess explain how her body parts work together to keep her system in balance (i.e. homeostasis). Periodically, her muscles, organs, and circulatory system are illuminated by fiber optics. An adjacent Discovery Room allows younger children to put on puppet shows and look at small live animals such as frogs and mice.

  The east wing, or Creative World, features communication exhibits. Inside the large Creative World room, visitors can play virtual volleyball; whisper into a parabolic dish and have someone across the room hear them; type in telephone or television messages that are then relayed by satellite; play air drums and digitize the sound; construct buildings using scale model parts and then subject them to the shake, rattle, and roll of an earthquake via a shake table; build archways using Styrofoam blocks to learn about the strength of compression; and more. There are several large and small screen videos in both the east and west wings that offer enticing and entertaining visual bits of information, although they are often not accompanied by written or verbal data.

  Part of the third floor is a continuation of Creative World, focusing on transportation. Fans blow wind to move model sailboats and a solar-paneled car in a few of the exhibits here. The Discovery Room has a play house and game activities that enable younger children to learn more about the displays throughout the center. The west room, the Weingart Gallery, features wonderful, usually hands-on, special rotating exhibits. It was a geography room when we visited. Kids learned about people, customs, plants, and unique geological formations from all over the world, via interactive displays.

  Ever want to join the circus and try the high-wire act? Here's your chance. For $3, you can pedal a weighted bike across a cable wire that is forty feet above the ground. Although you're strapped in and safety netting is in place, it is still a slightly scary venture, especially when the staff person tilts the bike before pushing it across the cable wire!

  Ask about the numerous special classes and programs offered for children and adults. For instance, audience-participatory shows, including Science Comes Alive, are presented for various age groups. Call the education department at (213) 744-7444 for a schedule of other programs and for more information. Check the museum's calendar for special exhibits that might have a cost. The Titanic exhibit was outstanding!

Tips: 1) School kids come in busloads on weekday mornings, so several exhibits require waiting in line to view or use during these peak hours. Therefore, consider either arriving early to watch an IMAX movie and explore the grounds and other nearby museums first, or come here in the early afternoon. 2) Avoid restaurant lunch lines by packing a lunch. There are several shaded grassy areas for picnicking. 3) Locker rentals are available on the first floor. Note: The Center is stroller/wheelchair accessible. Check out the nearby AIR AND SPACE GALLERY (pg. 80), which is actually part of the Science Center, CALIFORNIA AFRICAN AMERICAN MUSEUM (pg. 84), IMAX THEATER (pg. 148), and NATURAL HISTORY MUSEUM OF LOS ANGELES (pg. 109).

Hours: Open daily, 10am - 5pm. Closed New Year's Day, Thanksgiving, and Christmas.
Admission: Free. Parking is $6 per vehicle. Membership here is a great deal and reciprocal with the DISCOVERY SCIENCE CENTER in Santa Ana and REUBEN H. FLEET SCIENCE CENTER in San Diego.
Ages: 3 years and up.

C.E.E. L.A.

(818) 957-9400 / www.cee-la.com

You can $ee L.A. or you can ¢.E.E. L.A.! The Cultural Entertainment Events card (C.E.E. L.A.) is an incredible way to explore fifteen top museums, including AUTRY MUSEUM OF WESTERN HERITAGE, HOLLYWOOD ENTERTAINMENT MUSEUM, JAPANESE AMERICAN NATIONAL MUSEUM, BOWERS KIDSEUM, RICHARD NIXON PRESIDENTIAL LIBRARY AND BIRTHPLACE, RONALD REAGAN PRESIDENTIAL LIBRARY AND MUSEUM, SOUTHWEST MUSEUM, U.C.L.A. HAMMER MUSEUM, and more for only $43.95 (plus $3.95 in shipping and handling) a year for you and your family! This card also offers 50% off of some major sporting events, and some theater and concert venues. If you mention this book, *Fun and Educational Places to go With Kids and Adults in Southern California*, you pay only $40 for the card (plus shipping and handling).

THE DOCTORS' HOUSE MUSEUM

(818) 242-4290 / www.glendalehistorical.org/doctors.html
1601 W. Mountain Street, Glendale
(Exit Golden State Fwy [5] N. on Western Ave., R. on Mountain. It's in Brand Park. [TG: 534 B7])

Tour through this delightfully restored Queen Anne Eastlake-style home that was once owned by three doctors. (Hence the name.) Docents point out and discuss the doctors' office with its instruments and vials, period furniture from the early 1900's, clothing, and other artifacts from the Victorian time period. One-hour, free school tours, for third graders and above, are given during the week. In addition to the house tour, students also play outdoor Victorian games. Ask about special functions throughout the year, such as the candlelight tour in December.

Just outside the house is an expansive green lawn and a gazebo. A Japanese tea garden, complete with a waterfall, koi fish, and a Japanese tea house to peek into is also on the grounds. The Doctors' House Museum and the adjacent beautiful Glendale Library are located in BRAND PARK (see pg. 35).

Hours: Open Sun., 2pm - 4pm, except major holidays, inclement weather, and the month of July.
Admission: The museum is $1 for adults; ages 16 and under are free.
Ages: 6 years and up.

THE DRUM BARRACKS CIVIL WAR MUSEUM

(310) 548-7509 / www.drumbarracks.org
1052 Banning Boulevard, Wilmington
(Exit Harbor Fwy [110] E. on Pacific Coast Highway, R. on Avalon Blvd., L. on 'L' St., R. on Banning Blvd. [TG: 794 F6])

The year is 1861 and the Civil War has broken out. Although most of the fighting was done in the east, troops from Camp Drum, California, fought on the Union side. Your forty-five-minute tour of the medium-sized barracks/house/museum starts in the library research room. The first video is six minutes long and tells the history of Camp Drum through reenactments, with a costumed character narrating. Do your kids enjoy a good mystery? The second video features the Drum Barracks in an episode of *Unsolved Mysteries*. Apparently, a few good ghosts from the Civil War still hang out here. Needless to say, my kids heard "ghostly" noises throughout the rest of our visit.

The parlor room is where the officers entertained. Besides period furniture, it also has a stereoscope, which is an early Viewmaster™, to look through. Q: Why didn't people smile for photographs back then? A: Many people had bad teeth, plus it took a long time to actually take a picture.

The hallway shows a picture of the Camel Corps. which was a regiment that actually rode camels. It also has a flag from an 1863 battlefield - have your kids count the stars (states). Upstairs, the armory room has a few original weapons, like a musket and some swords. A rotating exhibit up here has displayed a hospital room with beds, old medical instruments, and a lifelike mannequin of a wounded soldier; a quarter master's quarters; and more. The officer's bedroom has furniture, personal effects, and old-fashioned clothing. Q: Why did women usually wear brown wedding dresses? A: You'll have to take the tour to find out!

Hours: Tours are given Tues. - Thurs. on the hour between 10am - 1pm; Sat. - Sun, 11:30am - 2:30pm.
Admission: $3 for adults; students and children 12 and under are free.
Ages: 5 years and up.

EL MONTE HISTORICAL MUSEUM

(626) 580-2232
3150 N. Tyler Avenue, El Monte
(Exit San Bernardino Fwy [10] S. on Santa Anita, L. on Mildred St., L. on N. Tyler Ave. It's on the corner, next to El Monte School. [TG: 637 C1])

A visit to this adobe-style museum offers fascinating glimpses into the history of the United States, as well as the history of the pioneers of El Monte. There is plenty to see and learn to keep young people's interest peaked, even though no touching is allowed. Items in the numerous glass displays are labeled, making it easy to self-tour. However, I highly recommend taking a guided tour, given for groups of ten or more people, so your family, or school group, doesn't miss out on the many details and explanations of the exhibits.

My kids were captivated by the hallway showcasing Gay's Lion Farm, which was a local training ground in the 1920's for lions used in motion pictures. The photos depict the large cats interacting with people in various circus-type acts. There are also several adorable shots of lion cubs. A lion's tail and teeth are on display, too. The Heritage Room, toward the back, looks like an old-fashioned living room with antique furniture and a piano, plus cases of glassware, ladies' boots, and clothing. The walls are lined with pictures of walnut growers and other first-residents of El Monte.

The Pioneer Room has wonderful collections of typewriters, lamps/lanterns, dolls, toys, books, bells, quilts, army medals, and Bibles. It also contains ornate swords, a flag (with two bullet holes in it) from the battlefield at Gettysburg, a piece of the Berlin wall, George Washington's lantern, and an actual letter written by the Father of our Country who, by the way, had nice handwriting! The Frontier Room is equally interesting with early-day policeman and fireman hats, police badges and guns, a 1911 Model T, a wall of old tools, early Native American artifacts, and a re-created old-time law enforcement office.

The huge Lexington Room is sub-divided into smaller, themed "rooms" such as a turn-of-the-century schoolroom with desks, maps, and schoolwork; an old-time general store filled with shelves of merchandise; a barber shop with a chair; a music shop with ukuleles, violins, a Victrola, and more; and a dressmaker's shop with beautiful dresses, sewing machines, elegant hair combs, and beaded handbags. Most of the rooms also have period-dressed mannequins. This section of the museum also contains re-created rooms that would have been found in a house of the early 1900's such as a parlor, bedroom, kitchen, and library. Each room is fully furnished and complete to the smallest detail. The El Monte Historic Museum, with a plaque that commemorates it as "the end of the Santa Fe Trail," offers a window to the world!

For further study, or just for the joy of reading, the El Monte Public Library is only a few buildings down.

Directly across the street from the museum is a park. This pleasant corner park offers plenty of picnic tables and shady oak trees, plus a few slides and some metal transportation vehicles to climb on.

Hours: Open Tues. - Fri., 10am - 4pm; Sun., 1pm - 3pm. Open on Sat. by appointment and during the week for school tours.

Admission: Free

Ages: 5 years and up.

FORT MACARTHUR MUSEUM

(310) 548-2631- museum; (310) 548-7705 - Angels Gate Park / www.ftmac.org

3601 S. Gaffey Street, San Pedro

(Exit Harbor Fwy [110] S. on Gaffey St. Drive almost to the end of Gaffey, then R. through the gates on Leavenworth Dr., past Angels Gate Park. [TG: 854 B2])

This concrete World War II coastal defense battery building really fires up kids' imaginations as they walk the grounds and tour rooms filled with big artillery guns, cannons, mines, uniforms, pictures, and other war memorabilia. Military history is important to learn, but my boys really loved walking through some of the underground corridors, which can only be seen on a guided tour.

A sixteen-minute video shows recoil guns shooting as well as the history of this museum. In the small Decontamination Room my kids pretended they had come in contact with poisonous gas and stepped on an air pump to blow it off, just like the soldiers of old. Only then could they enter the Communications Room, which has fascinating old radios and transmitters behind glass. Store Room 2 has riveting pictures of battleships being blown up. The pictures also tell stories of soldiers' bravery and hardships. The Barracks Display shows the inside of a soldier's (small) room and typical army articles.

Talking through the elaborate speaking tube system keeps kids busy for a long time, as someone speaks through one end while someone else tries to find the receiving end. Don't forget to take the steps up to the top of the defense building where one of the hideouts, used by lookouts with guns to watch for incoming, attacking ships, is still open to spy from. Note: Check the Calendar entry for Old Fort MacArthur Days war reenactments (see pg. 591) and ask about other events, such as "living history" days. Ask to take a guided tour is you're interested in learning more about this site.

Just east of the museum, on a hill in Angels Gate Park, sits the seventeen-ton Korean Friendship Bell set in a traditional, Korean-style pagoda. Let the kids run loose to enjoy the grassy knolls. There are a few pieces of climbing apparatus and a basketball court, too. Since it's a fairly treeless area, it's also ideal for kite flying. On a clear day the coastal view is gorgeous, and you can see Catalina Island.

Hours: Open Tues, Thurs., Sat. - Sun., noon - 5pm. Docent tours are offered by appointment. The park is open daily, sunrise - 6pm.

Admission: Free. Suggested donations for a guided tour are $3 for adults; $1 for ages 12 and under.

Ages: 3 years and up.

THE GAMBLE HOUSE

(626) 793-3334 / www.gamblehouse.org

4 Westmoreland Place, Pasadena

(Exit Foothill Fwy [210], near where it intersects with the Ventura Fwy [134], W. on N. Orange Grove Blvd., turn R. into the Gamble House. [TG: 565 G4])

Wood, and the way various types are crafted and blended, is the primary focus of the Gamble House. Teak, maple, cedar, redwood, and oak were used in the furniture, cabinetry, paneling, carvings, and exterior walls in a way that represents the best of the Arts and Crafts movement from the turn-of-the-century. Not that kids care about these details, but they are impressed by the natural beauty of the rooms, original furnishings, and terraces. A one-hour guided tour explains the history of the house, the era in which it was built, and the architecture's harmonious use of wood and natural light in the home in accord with its environmental surroundings. Highlights, besides the use of wood, include the appealing open porches (used as sleeping porches), and the Tiffany glass throughout. Note: Only the first floor of the house is stroller/wheelchair accessible.

The outside grounds are classy looking, with beautiful landscaping, rolling green lawns, and a brick walkway and driveway.

Hours: Open Thurs. - Sun., noon - 3pm. It's closed on major holidays.

Admission: $8 for adults; $5 for seniors and students with ID; children 11 and under are free.

Ages: 6 years and up.

GEORGE C. PAGE MUSEUM / LA BREA TAR PITS

(323) 857-6311 / www.tarpits.org

5801 Wilshire Boulevard, Los Angeles

(Exit Santa Monica Fwy [10] N. on Fairfax, R. on Wilshire Blvd., L. on Curson St. [TG: 633 C2])

$$$

Kids boning up on becoming paleontologists will really dig this place. First, take them to see the fifteen-minute movie, *Treasures of the Tar Pits*. It gives an interesting overview and explains that the fossils they'll see in the museum have been excavated from the pits, just outside.

The George C. Page Museum has over thirty different exhibits including saber-tooth cats, an imperial mammoth, dire wolves, mastodons, bison, giant ground sloths, and a variety of birds and plants. (Forewarn your kids that dinosaurs had been extinct for many years before the tar pit entrapments occurred, so the only thing here on dinosaurs is a short film.) The exhibits are comprised of fossils, skeletons, and lifelike murals, plus an animated model of a young mammoth. Kids can pit their strength against the force of asphalt by pulling on glass enclosed cylinders stuck in the sticky stuff. The futility of this effort makes it easier to understand why animals, of any size, couldn't escape the tar pits.

Other highlights include the La Brea Woman, whose image changes via optical illusion, from a skeleton to a fleshed-out figure; the wall display of over 400 dire wolf skulls; and watching, through the huge windows of a working paleontologist's laboratory, the on-going process of cleaning, studying, and cataloging newly excavated fossils. Kellan, my oldest son, wanted to become a *bone*afide paleontologist until he saw how tedious the work can be. I'm encouraging him to keep an open mind. Toward the exit is a room devoted to the theory of evolution.

Outside, enjoy a walk around the twenty-three acres of beautifully landscaped Hancock Park, otherwise known as the La Brea Tar Pits. The pits are comprised of asphalt that has seeped to the surface to form sticky pools in which the animals got trapped and died. There are several active tar pits in the park, with hundreds more having been dug out and filled in. For two months during the summer, you can see real excavation work going on at Pit 91. The park, with its outdoor amphitheater and picnic facilities, is also a backyard, and has connecting walkways, to the LOS ANGELES COUNTY MUSEUM OF ART (see pg. 103). Note: If all else fails, kids will have a great time rolling down the hills outside the museum and climbing on the statues!

Hours: Open Mon. - Fri., 9:30am - 5pm; Sat. - Sun., 10am - 5pm. Closed New Year's Day, July 4th, Thanksgiving, and Christmas.

Admission: $6 for adults; $3.50 for seniors and students with ID; $2 for ages 5 - 12; children 4 and under are free. The museum is free to everyone on the first Tues. of the month. Parking in the lot behind the museum is $8; $6 with validation, or try parking on 6th Street directly behind the museum, for free.

Ages: 3½ years and up.

THE GETTY CENTER / J. PAUL GETTY MUSEUM

(310) 440-7300 / www.getty.edu

1200 Getty Center Drive, Los Angeles

(Exit San Diego Fwy [405] W. on Getty Center Dr. It is just N. of I-10. [TG: 631 G1])

$

Everything you've heard about the Getty Museum is true! Your adventure begins with a four-and-a-half-minute tram ride up a winding track that seemingly hugs the edge of the road. You may also hike up the 1.9 mile road, but you'll get enough exercise walking around the Getty.

The architecture of the museum is stunning - it elicited several exclamations of admiration from my kids. The all-white marble structures can also be blinding, so bring sunglasses. Once inside the lobby, make your first stop at one of two theaters that show a ten-minute orientation movie regarding the Center. Next, invest $3 for an audio guide that suggests special stops for families, and describes over 250 works in a total of nine hours (which is longer than you'll be here, I know). Simply press the number on your tape machine that corresponds to the number near the work of art to hear commentary and interviews regarding that specific piece. Note: Guided tours and special classes are available for school groups.

Stroll down the courtyard toward the boulder fountain as you aim for your next destination, the Family Room. This small room contains several child-oriented art books, a computer for finding out more art information, and five costumes for children to try on that are originally depicted in paintings found in the Getty. Note: Kids will find these particular paintings in the museum and think it's cool that they dressed up like that, too! You can check out art cards from the Family Room that enables your kids to go from mere observers to interactive participants in the galleries. Make up your own activities, too, such as having your children imitate portrait poses, or encourage them to be on the lookout for paintings with bridges or dogs or the color red. Note: The museum offers family workshops for ages 5 through 13 years old, usually on Saturdays and Sundays, that include a guided tour and related art activity.

The four Art Information rooms, staffed with knowledgeable volunteers, are worthy of your time. One shows step-by-step depictions of how bronze statues are made using wax moldings. It also has samples of crushed rocks, plants, insects, charred human bones, and copper corrosion that were used for color in illuminated manuscripts. Another room has easels, paper, colored pencils, and still life objects for aspiring artists to use for drawing their own masterpiece. As pictures can be displayed here for the day, you can truthfully boast that your child had a picture hanging at the Getty.

Now it's time to actually see the world-renown art. Forgive me for not going into detail here about the works - they are too numerous and grand. Suffice to say that the five, multi-level galleries feature paintings, sculptures, drawings, photography, and decorative arts (e.g. elegant gold-gilded furniture, tapestries, vases, and more) in natural-light conditions, which enhance the beauty of the work. My boys were fascinated with the overhead sun panels that automatically adjust to let in the right amount of light. Many of the works have stories about the pieces printed alongside them, making them more interesting than just another pretty picture. A separate, darkened room features medieval, illuminated (i.e. hand-painted) manuscripts with still-vivid colors painted on vellum (i.e. sheep skin). From Van Gogh to Rembrandt to Renoir, the Getty has something to please every *palette.*

Hardwood floors and elevators make the Center stroller/wheelchair accessible, although the doors that connect the galleries are heavy to push and pull open. As the Getty is on a hill, the several terraces offer magnificent vistas from Mt. Baldy to Catalina to the surrounding Beverly Hills area. We particularly liked the cactus garden on top of a building outside the South Pavilion. Another outside attraction is the tiered, maze-like, central garden which you may walk in and around.

Hungry visitors have several options. Two cafeterias have both indoor and outdoor seating, and serve a variety of prepacked cold or hot lunch and dinner items for an average of $7. The on-site restaurant is an elegant, sit-down dining experience, and entrees range from $12 to $38. You may also bring a lunch to enjoy at the large picnic area by the base of the tram ride. It has grassy green lawns and numerous covered picnic tables. This last choice entails taking the electric tram down to the parking lot and then back up to the museum.

Here are a few tips to make your day more memorable: 1) Consider pre-purchasing (through the Getty bookstore or elsewhere) *A is for Artist*, a Getty Museum pictural alphabet book that inspires children to be on the lookout for certain works of art. (Familiarity, in this case, breeds pleasurable recognition.) Or, buy *Going to the Getty* by J. otto Seibold and Vivian Walsh, a book that gives a solid and fun overview of the museum, as well as a look at a few pieces in particular. 2) Look for fossils embedded in the Getty walls, particularly at the plaza where the tram arrives. 3) Pre-warn your children to stand 6" to 12" away from the art. There are no ropes in front of the pieces, and while the security guards are friendly, they are also insistent. 4) A free coat/bag check is available in the entrance hall. 5) Going outside, just to another building, is almost unavoidable, so if it's raining bring an umbrella. 6) Wear comfortable walking shoes! 7) Parking reservations are required on weekdays only up until 4pm. You may arrive here, however, without reservations, by bike, taxi, or bus.

Our eyes were glazed over when we left the Getty, but our minds and hearts were filled with wondrous works of art.

Hours: Open Tues. - Thurs. and Sun., 10am - 6pm; Fri. - Sat., 10am - 9pm. Closed Mon. and major holidays. Parking reservations are needed up to 4pm on weekdays.

Admission: The museum is free. Parking is $5 per vehicle.

Ages: 3 years and up.

GORDON R. HOWARD MUSEUM / MENTZER HOUSE

(818) 841-6333 - museum; (818) 846-0857 - tours

1015 W. Olive Avenue, Burbank

(Exit Ventura Fwy [134] N. on Victory Blvd., L. on Olive Ave. Or, exit Golden State Fwy [5] W. on Olive Ave. The Museum is located at 115 N. Lomita St. and the Mentzer House is connected to the museum by a walkway. [TG: 563 G1])

Make sure to save a Sunday afternoon to come and explore the Gordon Howard Museum. The hallway has old toys and dishes on display, plus a drawing room and a music room. The salon contains wedding dresses, old dresses (that are now back in style), and a stunning 1898 dress with beads and lace, plus ladies boots, jeweled hat pins, and dolls.

The Historical Room is large and filled with interesting slices from Burbank's past. Along one wall are glass-enclosed rooms, each one complete with furniture and period-dressed mannequins. Look into the rooms, pick up an old-fashioned telephone receiver, press a button, and listen to stories about Dr. Burbank (does that name ring a bell?), a family-owned winery, a 1920's hotel lobby (when $1 paid for a room!), a country store, and the *Jazz Singer*, Al Jolson. Other exhibits in this room include military uniforms, flags, and other war memorabilia; a display devoted to Lockheed, comprised of numerous pictures and model airplanes; a tribute to Disney featuring animation cells, photographs, and posters; and an ornate desk used by Spanish noblemen.

The Vehicle Room is packed with lots of antique "stuff," such as an old switchboard, tools, parking meters, a huge Gramophone, a hotel telephone booth, and fire hats. It also showcases classic cars in mint condition, and several vintage vehicles including a 1922 Moreland Bus, a 1909 Ford horseless carriage with a crank, and a 1949 fire engine with a huge target net that my kids thought was a trampoline. The small upstairs gallery has pictures and paintings as well as a complete collection of old cameras. A video on the history of Lockheed is shown at 1:10pm and again at 2:30pm.

Follow the walkway from the museum courtyard to the reconstructed Mentzer House, which was originally built in 1887. On your walk-through tour you'll see two bedrooms, a dining room, and a living room containing period furniture, plus old-fashioned items such as a phonograph, an old telephone, and a vacuum cleaner. The kitchen has a beautiful coal stove, china dishes, and cooking gadgets. Adult and children tours are given during the week for groups of ten or more by reservation.

Right next door is the Olive Recreation Center, easily identified by the model F-104 Starfighter in the front. The park has picnic tables and a playground, plus tennis and basketball courts.

Hours: Open Sun., 1pm - 4pm.

Admission: $1 donation per person is requested.

Ages: 5 years and up.

GRIER MUSSER MUSEUM

(213) 413-1814 / www.griermusser.losangeles.museum

403 S. Bonnie Brae Street, Los Angeles

(Exit Harbor Fwy [110] W. on 3rd St., L. on Bonnie Brae. The house/museum is in a L.A. neighborhood, with parking behind the building. [TG: 634 C2])

This thirteen-room, two-story, green and rust-colored Queen Anne-style house/museum was built in 1898. It was the Grier Musser family home. Since the tour guides are family relatives, they know and share the history and interesting stories of the memorabilia. The house is literally packed with personal ~~stuff~~ treasures accumulated over the years. The front parlor contains an original chandelier, Delph plates, a grandfather's clock, and other antiques. The family room has a 1950's television set, a piano, and a fainting couch for women who did just that. The dining room's fireplace is decorated with ornate tiles and beautifully carved wood work. The kitchen has a wood-burning stove, a gas stove, a beaded chandelier from the 1915 Exposition Fair, dishes from the Depression era, a collection of cookie jars, kitchen gadgets, and china cabinets filled with original boxes of Ivory Soap, Morton's Salt, and more. At the foot of the stairs is a red velvet chaperone's seat. While a gentleman courted his lady love, a chaperone would sit out of the way, but within eyesight.

An upstairs study contains a desk, grandma's diploma from high school, and a pictorial history of the Red Cross, plus a closet full of nursing uniforms from WWII. The master bedroom and adjoining bedroom have maple furniture, and closets full of hats, dresses, and boots. The children's bedroom is filled with toys, stuffed animals, dolls, and dollhouses. The dresser displays old bottles and hairbrushes as well as a more unique sign of the past - a container of leg makeup from WWII. Women would put this makeup on their legs to make it look like they were wearing nylons - seams and all. The sundeck is a favorite room for kids because of the numerous games and toys, and extensive Disney collection. Open the printer drawers to see even more treasures, such as jewelry.

Using the maid's stairway, go down to the basement to see pictures of the family and the Los Angeles area, and an extensive postcard collection from around the world. A visit here makes you wonder if maybe you should have kept that bottle cap collection, or at least your great grandfather's fishing pole as a potential museum piece.

Hours: Open Wed. - Sat., noon - 4pm. Call for a reservation for any size group.

Admission: $6 for adults; $5 for seniors and students; $4 for ages 5 - 12; children 4 and under are free.

Ages: 5 years and up.

GRIFFITH OBSERVATORY AND PLANETARIUM

(323) 664-1191 / www.griffithobservatory.org

2800 E. Observatory Road, in Griffith Park, Los Angeles - permanent observatory; Zoo Drive, Los Angeles - temporary satellite.

(Exit Golden State Fwy [5] W. on Los Feliz Blvd., take Hillhurst Ave. N. past the Greek Theater to the Observatory - permanent observatory. For the temporary satellite observatory - going N. on Golden State Fwy [5] or W. on Ventura Fwy [134], exit at Zoo Dr. and follow the signs. Going E. on 134, exit S. on Victory Blvd., L. on Zoo Dr. Going S. on 5, exit S. on Western, L. on Victory Blvd. to Zoo Dr. [TG: 593 J2])

This world-famous observatory is undergoing a major renovation that is expected to be completed in late 2005. In the interim there is an observatory satellite near the "real" one at 4800 Western Heritage Way, just south of the LOS ANGELES ZOO (see pg. 183) parking lot. The viewing is definitely not as good, but they offer many good programs, a few astronomy exhibits, a telescope to safely view sunspots and look at the nighttime stars, and even a planetarium show. The exhibits include meteorites, visuals of Mars, a mural of the Pathfinder landing site, a scale model of Hubble Space Telescope, and a six-foot moon globe. Grades 4 through 6 are welcome for hour-long, interactive school field trips.

The remodeled observatory will continue to be one of the best places to get an overview of the city on a cloudless day, and to view the city lights and stars on a clear night. Coin-operated telescopes will enable kids to get that "closer" look they insist they need. The largest public telescope in California will be available again to use (for free) every clear evening in the summer from dusk to 9:45pm. It will be available the rest of the year Tuesday to Sunday from 7pm to 9:45pm. Call the Sky Report, (323) 663-8171, for twenty-four-hour recorded information.

The Astronomers Monument on the front lawn of the observatory is an almost forty-foot tall statue featuring Copernicus, Hipparchus, Galileo, Kepler, Newton and Herschel. The original grandeur of the observatory will be restored with its shining copper domes and architecture. Look up as you'll enter the rotunda to see heavenly murals. The seamless projection dome will be huge at seventy-seven feet across and make the fiber optic planetarium shows seem even more vibrant and real than before. The existing upstairs Hall of Science will retain its classic look. Some favorite exhibits are scheduled to remain such as the Tesla coil (watch the sparks jump!), the huge Foucault pendulum that knocks big pegs over to illustrate the rotation of the earth, and the scales - step on one to see how much you'd weigh on Mars or Jupiter. (The moon scale is my personal favorite.) New exhibits may include a giant astrolabe, a series of large dioramas or "habitats" of moon observers from different cultures and ages, a steerable camera obscura, and a life-size replica of the Farnese Atlas.

A whole new 35,000 square foot underground space will hold numerous stellar exhibits that focus on the exploration of space, a 200-seat Leonard Nimoy (yes, the Vulcan) Event Horizon lecture hall and theater, a bookstore, and a cafeteria-style cafe. A sun clock, a simple astronomical tool that uses the sun to mark noon each day, will be next to the cafe. Take an elevator between floors, or travel through a "wormhole" - a corridor that will connect the upper story to the lower. The mezzanine level will also hold more displays.

Look up AUTRY MUSEUM OF WESTERN HERITAGE (pg. 82), GRIFFITH PARK (pg. 48), LOS ANGELES ZOO (pg. 183), and TRAVEL TOWN (pg. 121) for close-by attractions. Note: The Greek Theater, a nationally-renown venue for concerts and other events, is also just down the road.

Hours: The satellite observatory is open Tues. - Fri., 1pm - 10pm; Sat. - Sun., 10am - 10pm. Closed Mon., Tues., and some holidays. Call for planetarium show hours. Call for observatory hours when it reopens.

Admission: Free for the observatory. Call for prices on the planetarium shows.

Ages: 4 years and up.

GUINNESS WORLD OF RECORDS MUSEUM

(323) 463-6433

6764 Hollywood Boulevard, Hollywood

(Exit Hollywood Fwy [101] W. on Hollywood Blvd. [TG: 593 E4])

There are over 3,000 facts, feats, and world records told about and shown at this very Hollywood museum, so there is something to astound all ages. See life-size models, pictures, videos, and special effects of the tallest, smallest, most tattooed, most anything and everything. (The kids should be great at Trivial Pursuit after this visit.) We were enthralled with the domino exhibit, which shows a video of an incredible domino run.

Prep your children before their visit: Q: Do you know who holds a record for the most fan mail in one day? A: Mickey Mouse. He received 800,000 letters one day in 1933. Q: What animal had the smallest brain in proportion to his body? A: Stegosaurus. Q: What was the longest length a human neck was stretched using copper coils? And why? A: Fifteen and three-quarter inches. I don't know why, though. Watch some fascinating footage of intriguing and bizarre facts about our world and the people and animals in it: *The Human World*, *The Animal World*, *Planet Earth*, *Structures and Machines*, *Sports World*, and a salute to *The World of Hollywood*.

Hours: Open daily, 10am - midnight.

Admission: $10.95 for adults; $8.50 for seniors; $6.95 for ages 6 - 12; children 5 and under are free. Combination tickets with HOLLYWOOD WAX MUSEUM (see pg. 96) are $15.95 for adults; $13.95 for seniors; $8.95 for ages 6 - 12.

Ages: 4½ years and up.

HACIENDA HEIGHTS YOUTH SCIENCE CENTER

(626) 854-9825 / www.youth.net/ysc

16949 Wedgeworth Drive, Hacienda Heights

(Exit Pomona Fwy [60] S. on Azusa, R. on Pepper Brook, R. on Wedgeworth. It's located in classroom 8 at the Wedgeworth Elementary School. [TG: 678 F4])

The Youth Science Center functions as a museum and a classroom. Actually, the museum is in a classroom that's decorated with colorful, informative posters, at Wedgeworth Elementary School. Although it's not state-of-the-art, a lot of science is contained in this room. A sand pendulum creates patterns depending on how you swing it; a heat-sensitive, liquid crystal display leaves colored impressions when touched; a Jacob's ladder of electricity is on display; a case of fossils and drawers of butterflies and other insects can be examined; and a tank with fish in it shares shelf space with a few other live critters like snakes, frogs, tortoises, a tarantula, and a scorpion. Also here are computer stations with game cartridges, Geo Safaris, puzzles, books, construction toys, and numerous scientific videos to borrow. The retail store area is a small space packed with rocks, shells, science books, and experiments.

For a minimal fee, children can attend classes like "The Great Paper Airplane Race," where they'll learn about aerodynamics and wind, while making and flying paper airplanes. Several field trips, such as nature hikes and tours, are offered throughout the school year. A terrific array of science-related classes, from model rocket-building to hands-on, physical science, are available during the summer. Call for a schedule.

Hours: Open in the summer, Mon. - Fri., 8am - noon. Open during the school year, Tues. and Fri., noon - 3:45pm; Sat., 10am - 2pm.

Admission: Free

Ages: 4 years and up.

HERITAGE JUNCTION HISTORIC PARK

(661) 254-1275 / www.scvhs.org

24101 San Fernando Road, Santa Clarita

(Take Golden State Fwy [5] to Antelope Valley Fwy [14], exit N.W. on San Fernando Rd. The museum shares the grounds with the Saugus train station. [TG: 4641 A2])

A steam locomotive is on the tracks out in front of this restored, late 1800's train station/museum. Inside the museum are photographs, information, and artifacts that show and tell the history of this valley, including the Spanish era, the petroleum and mining areas, and its rich film history. Five building that have been restored and several other buildings, in various stages of restoration, comprise the rest of the junction. You can walk back and peek in through the windows of the little red school house, the Ramona chapel, and the Edison house. On the first Sunday of the month, you may take a tour through the small Kingsbury house that contains nineteenth-century furniture and some of the other buildings. We weren't here long, but it was an interesting, historical stop. Note: The junction park is right next to the WILLIAM S. HART MUSEUM AND PARK (see pg. 124).

Hours: Open daily just to walk the grounds. The buildings are open Sat. - Sun., 1pm - 4pm. Open for school tours during the week by appointment.

Admission: Free

Ages: 6 years and up.

HERITAGE PARK (Santa Fe Springs)

(562) 946-6476 / www.santafesprings.org/hpark.htm

12100 Mora Drive, Santa Fe Springs

(Exit San Gabriel River Fwy [605] E. on Telegraph Rd., past Pioneer, R. on Heritage Park Dr. to the end. [TG: 706 H5])

Heritage Park is like a breath of fresh air among the historical parks. Its six acres of beautifully landscaped grounds make any length visit here a pleasure. The high-ceiling, wood Carriage Barn, which holds turn-of-the-century exhibits, is a must-see. Two carriages from horse and buggy days take the center floor. Behind glass is a large display of period clothing, including a wedding dress, plus dolls, toys, and books. The small touch and play area has clothing to try on, an old telephone to dial (it's not a touch tone or cell phone), and a few other articles to play with. Inventing a Better Life display features old phonographs, typewriters, bikes, roller skates (not in-line skates), plus cameras and other equipment. It's interesting to see how the inventions of yesteryear benefit us today.

A thirty-two-foot dome-shaped dwelling is the centerpiece of a recreated Native American (Tongva) village. A small creek, a granary, and a sweatlodge are also featured. This area often showcases storytellers, a craft time, demonstrations, and "Journeys to the Past" presentations.

Grab a bite to eat at The Kitchen, an outside, full-service snack bar. It's open Monday through Friday from 8am to 3pm. The average cost of a sandwich or salad is $4. Or, bring your own lunch, and enjoy the garden setting with beautiful old shade trees and wooden picnic tables. A walk-through aviary has parakeets, canaries, and a few other birds. A small window to an archeological pit shows excavated trash such as cattle bones and pottery. There are remain sites marking original fireplace and basement foundations, but kids cannot go down in them to explore. A hedge around the beautiful formal gardens gives way to an old fig tree with huge roots that are irresistible for kids to climb on. An immaculate wood-paneled tank house, once used to store water, is at the far end of the park. On a school tour, kids can go inside the tank house and walk up the crisscross stairs to the top, then go outside, and take in the view.

I can't emphasize the beauty of this park enough. It's clean, green, and the walkways throughout make every area accessible. Ask about the park's special programs throughout the year, including a Pow Wow in November (pg. 611).

Just outside the park gates are three restored railroad cars on a track. Take a tour of the engine car and ring the bell, then go through the caboose and see where coal was stored. Exceptional, two-hour, school tours of Heritage Park include lots of historical information, presented in a kid-friendly way, plus hands-on activities. Tours are free.

Hours: The park is open daily, 7am - 10pm. Railroad exhibit and Carriage Barn hours are Tues. - Sun., noon - 4pm. Closed Mon. and some holidays. Guided tours are offered Wed. and Thurs. Call for a reservation.

Admission: Free

Ages: All

HERITAGE SQUARE MUSEUM

(626) 449-0193 - recorded info; (626) 796-2898 / www.heritagesquare.org

3800 Homer Street, Montecito Heights

(Exit Pasadena Fwy [110] S.E. on Avenue 43. Take an immediate R. on Homer St. [TG: 595 B5])

$$

This little "town" behind a gate at the end of a residential street has five houses, plus a carriage barn (used for storage), a church building, and a train depot. The elegant Victorian homes, originally built between 1865 to 1914, have been relocated here and are in various stages of restoration. Each one has a different architectural style. One is white with columns, almost colonial-looking, while another is green, gingerbreadish in style, and has a brick chimney. The octagon-shaped house is the most unique-looking house here. Its unusual configuration makes it interesting to look at as well as walk through.

Only on the one-hour guided tours can you go through some of the homes. The Queen Anne house on the tour is the only one completely furnished and restored. The grassy grounds are ideal for picnicking. Two-hour school tours are offered Tuesday through Thursday and include a tour with a period-dressed docent, a craft from the era, and a short play involving the students. Tours are geared for either third through fifth graders or older students who are studying architecture.

Hours: Open most of the year, Fri. - Sun., noon - 4pm. Open in the summer, Fri. - Sun., noon - 5pm. Open some holiday Mon.

Admission: Admission is $6 for adults; $5 for seniors; $3 for ages 6 - 12; children 5 and under are free. Tours are a minimum of $75.

Ages: 6 years and up.

HOLLYWOOD BOWL MUSEUM

(323) 850-2058 / www.hollywoodbowl.org

2301 N. Highland, Hollywood

(Exit Hollywood Fwy [101] at Highland and follow signs to Hollywood Bowl. [TG: 593 E3])

!

While at the Hollywood Bowl for a concert, or if you're in the area, stop by the Hollywood Bowl Museum. This 3,000 square-foot museum offers a history of the Bowl via displays of musical instruments and pictures of performers and conductors. Video displays show concerts featured at the Bowl. The second story has rotating exhibits focusing on various aspects of music. A music education program is offered for school groups where kids learn about music, as well as try their hands at playing some instruments. The program specifics change from season to season.

Hours: Open during the summer, Tues. - Sat., 10am - 8:30pm. Open the rest of the year, Tues. - Sat., 10am - 4:30pm. It's also open during intermission on concert evenings.

Admission: Free. Parking is free.

Ages: 7 years and up.

HOLLYWOOD ENTERTAINMENT MUSEUM

◐

$$$

(323) 465-7900 / www.hollywoodmuseum.com

7021 Hollywood Boulevard, Hollywood

(Exit Ventura Fwy [101] W. on Hollywood Blvd. [TG: 593 D4])

The main room in this entertaining museum is done up dramatically in true Hollywood style with movie posters, old movie cameras, microphones, lighting equipment, a Hollywood timeline, and video screens that show the history and background information of particular exhibits. Listen to Walt Disney talk about animation, or see Buster Keaton in action. Other exhibits include the armor, sword, and helmet from *Ben Hur*; a gown worn by Marilyn Monroe; a Max Factor display showing stars at their most glamourous; and the opportunity to become a Star Trek character, via a mirrored reflection. A central screen intermittently shows a montage of film clips and/or a mini-documentary. The stage below the screen has a model of the town of Hollywood built into the floor and covered with plexiglass so you can walk on it. Note: Flash photography is not allowed in the museum.

Take the behind-the-scenes tours which are included in your admission price. One enables you to see a prop room filled with masks, desks, stuffed animals, clocks, sports equipment, musical instruments, and lots more, plus closets stuffed with costumes and outfits categorized by color and season. *Star Trek* fans (and others) can beam aboard the Enterprise's bridge, sit in the captain's chair, and watch clips from the original and *Next Generation* series. Picard's ready room is also here. Look closely at the diagrams and technical jargon on the display panel in the hallway. You'll see a hamster on a wheel, "slippery when wet" signs, and sayings such as, "In space no one can hear you scream." The cameras never shot close enough to catch these details! Another room follows, this time it contains the set from *X-Files*, namely Agent Mulder's office. For a change of scenery, walk through the entire original *Cheers* bar, where everybody knows your name.

The second tour is the fascinating Foley Sound Stage. Station one shows how sound effects bring life to motion pictures. Horses clopping, kissing, even putting on a leather jacket are all sounds later incorporated into a film using a variety of creative props, such as trash can lids. Kids (and adults) can try out their new-found knowledge at station two where a silent clip is shown once, and then again. The second time, the audience is invited to add dialogue and use the provided props of a doorbell, typewriter, telephone, and more, at the proper spots. The clip is played for a third time with the (hilarious) results recorded.

Students (and field trip organizers) take note: The museum offers several options for learning more about the entertainment industry. Ninety-minute field trips at the museum can be tailored to fit the groups requirements. Outreach programs and presentations are also available. After-school programs and workshops provide a variety of hands-on, industry-related projects such as working with and on editing film, music videos, sound effects, animation segments, and much more.

The museum is located in a complex with a theater and several shops and restaurants. It is also in the heart of Hollywood's Walk of Fame, so look down to see the stars' names adorning the sidewalks. Just a few blocks down is Disney's EL CAPITAN THEATER (see pg. 145), the famous GRAUMAN'S CHINESE THEATER (see pg. 147), plus other Hollywood museums and activities.

Hours: Open Thurs. - Tues., 11am - 6pm. Closed Wed., New Year's Day, Thanksgiving, and Christmas. Open daily in the summer the same hours.

Admission: $8.75 for adults; $5.50 for seniors; $4.50 for students; $4 for ages 5 - 12; children 4 and under are free. Metered parking is available wherever you can find it, or park for $2 around the corner on Sycamore Street. (See C.E.E. L.A. for membership savings, page 86.)

Ages: 6 years and up.

HOLLYWOOD WAX MUSEUM

◐

$$$

▥

(323) 462-5991 / www.hollywoodwax.com

6767 Hollywood Boulevard, Hollywood

(Exit Hollywood Fwy [101] W. on Hollywood Blvd. [TG: 593 E4])

Hundreds of celebrities from the world of television, movies, sports, politics, and religion are presented in waxy lifelikeness, surrounded by appropriate and realistic settings. Kids will enjoy "seeing" their favorite stars like Sylvester Stallone as Rambo, Clint Eastwood dressed in his "make my day" attire, Dorothy and her companions in the *Wizard of Oz*, Kareem Abdul Jabbar, Elvis, and hundreds more. A permanent exhibit here includes over 100 original movie costumes such as Christopher Reeve's *Superman*, Esther Williams' bathing suit, and more. A word of caution: There is a House of Horrors which might frighten younger children, though thankfully it has a separate walking loop.

Hours: Open Sun. - Thurs., 10am - midnight; Fri. - Sat., 10am - 1am.

Admission: $10.95 for adults; $8.50 for seniors; $6.95 for ages 6 - 12; children 5 and under are free. Combination tickets with GUINNESS WORLD OF RECORDS MUSEUM (pg. 93) are $15.95 for adults; $13.95 for seniors; $8.95 for ages 6 - 12.

Ages: 4 years and up.

HOLYLAND EXHIBITION

(323) 664-3162

2215 Lake View and Allesandro Way, Los Angeles

(Going S. on Golden State Fwy [5], exit R. on Fletcher Dr., make a quick L. on Riverside Dr., R. on Allesandro St., R. on Oak Glen Pl. [across a bridge], R. on Allesandro Way. The house is on the corner of Lake View and Allesandro. Going N. on [5], exit at Stadium Way, make a quick L. on Riverside Dr., L. on Allesandro St., then follow the above directions. [TG: 594 E5])

I could take this tour at least three more times and still not see and learn everything this museum has to offer! The Holyland Exhibition is an inconspicuous two-story corner house that was built in the late 1920's. It contains an incredible collection of priceless Egyptian and biblical items. Most of the two-hour tour is not hands on. It does involve a lot of listening and learning. An incredibly well-informed costumed docent will take you first to the tapestry-rich Bethlehem/Egyptian room which, like all the rooms, is not large, but packed with artifacts. You'll feel transported to a different time and country. Some of the items explained in depth are the 2,600-year-old mummy case; the hand-made brass art pieces and plates; papyrus; shoes made of camel hide and ram skin; headdresses; and a lunch bag made of goat skin. Each item is presented with its history and its biblical connection. You'll also see jewelry, engraved leather goods, a 2,000-year-old lamp, and much more.

The Bible Art and Archaeology Room has stones, shells, pottery, spices, and more from Nazareth, Bethlehem, the Jordan River, and surrounding areas. You'll view the type of large thorns used in Christ's crown of thorns; a big chunk of salt called Madame Lot; a very comprehensive family tree detailing lineage from Adam to Jesus; the kind of stones crushed and used for pitch on Noah's ark; a picture of Mt. Ararat where *ark*eologists believe the ark landed; and a re-created Ark of the Covenant. Make sure your tour guide explains how Mr. Futterer, the museum founder, went on an expedition to find the ark and how this was the basis for the movie *Raiders of the Lost Ark*. (This will definitely spark your children's interest.) Again, amazing amounts of Bible references are given with the presentation of each article.

The Damascus Room has an intricate game table inlaid with mother-of-pearl that took fifty man-years to make - kids may not play games on it! The room also contains beaded lamps, musical instruments, a camel saddle, animal skin (to write on), and many unique pieces of furniture. In another room, enjoy a taste of Israel while sitting on oriental rugs around low tables, as you're served small samples of Holy Land refreshments. The Jerusalem Bazaar is a gift shop with souvenirs (and great teaching aids) made of olive wood, mother-of-pearl, and other materials, at bargain prices. With all that I've just written, I've barely scratched the surface of what this museum features. So, come, take a trip to the middle east, via the Holyland Exhibition, and learn about its peoples and customs. The interdenominational museum is frequented by Christians, Jews, Muslims, and people of various other faiths.

Hours: The museum is open to tour seven days a week, including holidays and evenings. Call at least a week ahead of time, and choose the most convenient time for your family or group.

Admission: $2.50 for adults; $2 for ages 3 - 16; children 2 and under are free.

Ages: 6 years and up.

THE HOMESTEAD MUSEUM   ☼

(626) 968-8492 / www.homesteadmuseum.org   !
15415 E. Don Julian Road, City of Industry
(Exit Pomona Fwy [60] N. on Hacienda Blvd., L. on Don Julian Rd. [TG: 678 C1])

The Homestead Museum resides on six acres of land. A major portion of the property is an open, grassy area between the main group of buildings and the old mausoleum. A shady picnic area is here, too. A one-hour guided tour, starting at the water tower, will take you behind the gates. Kids will see and learn about the history of the United States, and about California in particular. They'll learn, for instance, that our state was once Mexican territory, and how that influence has factored in the development of our culture. They will also learn about the art and architecture of the 1830's through the 1930's.

The tour goes into the two residences on the premises. The Workman adobe home has no furniture inside, but outside are a few artifacts that kids can touch. La Casa Nueva house is spacious with twenty-six rooms, mostly furnished in 1920's decor. Kids will also get information about the on-site pump house, tepee, mausoleum, and cemetery. Ask about the many events that go on year round.

Hours: Open Wed. - Sun., 1pm - 4pm. Tours are given on the hour. Open for tour groups, minimum ten people, at other times throughout the week. Call for a reservation. Closed major holidays.

Admission: Free

Ages: 6 years and up.

HUNTINGTON LIBRARY, ART COLLECTIONS AND BOTANICAL GARDENS ☼

(626) 405-2141 / www.huntington.org   *$$$*
1151 Oxford Road, San Marino
(Exit Foothill Fwy [210] S. on Sierra Madre Blvd., R. on California, L. on Allen Ave., straight ahead into park. [TG: 566 D7])

The Library houses one of the world's greatest collections of rare books, manuscripts, and documents including a Gutenberg Bible; Ellesmere Chaucer's *The Canterbury Tales*; Benjamin Franklin's autobiography, in his own handwriting; original works by Whitman and Dickens; and letters written by George Washington, Thomas Jefferson, and Abraham Lincoln.

The Huntington Art Gallery is the epitome of opulence. This mansion contains sculptures, rare tapestries, miniatures, period furniture, and famous paintings, including Gainsborough's *Blue Boy*. Watch the interesting, thirteen-minute video about this painting first, then see if you can find some of the hidden elements in the painting. Get kids involved with observing the paintings by pointing out the ones with children and ones with different styles of dress. Tell them stories about the subjects. For instance, sweet-faced *Pinkie*, by Sir Thomas Lawrence, died soon after her portrait was finished, and the boy in *Lavina, Countess Spencer and her son Viscount Althorp* was one of Princess Diana's great great (great, etc.,) grandparents. This is a gentle way to introduce children to some truly great works of art. There are three other outstanding galleries on the grounds, all worthy of a look through.

The botanical gardens are comprised of twelve separate, amazing gardens that cover 150 acres of the 200-acre estate. As Lisa Blackburn, a museum associate says, "The gardens . . . have wide open spaces and vast rolling lawns; great for running, somersaulting, cartwheeling, shrieking, and releasing all that boundless energy that is sometimes stifled in traditional museum settings." There are waterfalls, lily ponds, koi, ducks, turtles, and frogs to capture kids' attention - almost more than can be seen in one day. The Desert Garden has, again to quote Lisa, "twelve acres of some of the most bizarre, colorful, creepy-crawly plants that a child could imagine." The Shakespeare Garden features plants mentioned in the bards' plays, accompanied by placards of pertinent poetry phrases. Another favorite garden is the Japanese garden, which is a quarter-mile west of the main entrance. This has a traditionally furnished Japanese house, stone ornaments, an old temple bell, a moon bridge, and a bonsai court. My little Tarzans said the best part of coming to the Huntington, though, is hiding in the bamboo groves in the Jungle Garden.

Discovery Carts can be found at three locations on Saturdays only. The carts contain a variety of small projects for children. For example, water samples collected from the pond can be examined under a microscope.

The year 2004 brings great changes to the Huntington. A striking-looking building, the Conservancy for

Botanical Science, opens its doors, with an educational center that focuses on kids 9 to 12 years old. Some features will nclude interactive learning stations and four different environments - tropical forest, cloud forest, carnivorous plants, and a field lab. A Children's Garden, behind the conservancy, is aimed toward younger children. Fragrant and colorful plant life will be interspersed with tunnels, bridges, stepping stones, and kinetic sculptures. An adjacent Teaching Greenhouse will offer youngsters an opportunity to get their hands dirty at the potting benches and provides a place for horticultural and botany programs for young people and adults. Think Ming Dynasty and you'll get the picture for the largest classical Chinese Garden outside China that's being built here, too. A one-acre lake, a tea house serving refreshments, a pavilion, and a few bridges, plus acres of plants native to China is all in the works.

Picnicking is not allowed on the grounds at the Huntington. However, a special treat for you and your daughter, as it's not really a boy's cup of tea, is to dress up and sip English tea in the Rose Garden Tea Room, (626) 683-8131, which overlooks three acres of roses. The all-you-can-eat buffet includes a variety of finger sandwiches, tea, scones, cheese and crackers, seasonal fruit, and delightful English desserts and miniature pastries. The cost is $12.95 for adults, $6.50 for children 6 years and under. Reservations are required. A cafe serving hamburgers, hot dogs, and quesadillas ($8 to $11 for an average meal) and offering a children's menu is on the grounds, too. Ask about the numerous special classes and programs, including the Kid's Nature Crafts, which is offered the first Saturday of every month.

Hours: Open in the summer, Tues. - Sun., 10:30am - 4:30pm. Open the rest of the year, Tues. - Fri., noon - 4:30pm; Sat. - Sun., 10:30am - 4:30pm. Self-guiding tour brochures are available. Closed Mon. and major holidays (except Easter Sunday). The tea buffet is served Tues. - Fri., noon - 3:30pm; Sat. - Sun., 10:45am - 3:30pm.

Admission: $10 for adults; $8.50 for seniors; $7 for ages 12 - 18; $4 for ages 5 - 11; children 4 years and under are free. Admission is free the first Thurs. of every month.

Ages: 4 years and up.

INTERNATIONAL PRINTING MUSEUM

(714) 529-1832 / www.printmuseum.org

315 Torrance Boulevard, Carson

(Exit Harbor Fwy [110] E. on Torrance Blvd. [TG: 764 C5])

$$$

A visit to this museum helps kids to understand the history and importance of the printed word, and how printing presses changed the world of reading. Visitors see a working wooden press from 1750, a replica of Gutenberg's first press, several other presses, numerous printing artifacts, and demonstrations of bookbinding and papermaking. They also have the opportunity to fold their own book as a keepsake. The tour is informative, interactive, and presented in an interesting and fun manner for all ages. General tours are offered for the public and specific tours are offered for groups of up to seventy people. As a parent and a readaholic, I appreciate all that this fine museum has to offer, especially the presentations that encourage kids to realize the joy of reading.

Two, two-hour group tours, which also include a general museum tour, are The Pages of Invention: The Communication Tour, and The Pages of Freedom: The Constitutional Convention. The first tour, Pages of Invention, is a fascinating journey that begins thousands of years ago when the Chinese first invented paper and "wrote" on it using carved blocks of wood. Children continue traveling to the period when Egyptian scrolls were written on papyrus, then on to the time of Gutenberg's invaluable contribution of the printing press. Students learn about the tools of the trade while listening to anecdotes and information on bookbinding. They also learn how long it took to make a hand-written book (three to five years); the price of a book; the increase in availability of books to the common people because of the press; and a lot more. A costumed appearance by Benjamin Franklin - well, not the real one, but one who is a dead ringer - then follows. Utilizing slides and equipment, Ben explains his numerous inventions and discoveries, such as electricity, an unsteady chair (i.e. rocking chair), markers called milestones, and more. Eager audience members participate in experiments that demonstrate static electricity and electricity generated through a replica 1750 electro static generator. He regales listeners about his life in Colonial America and encourages children to get educated by reading.

The Pages of Freedom Tour is a reenactment of the Constitutional Convention. Divided into thirteen groups (colonies), students use pre-written cards to debate foundational issues such as representation taxation, election of the president, and slavery. Ben Franklin presides over the meeting which ends with the colony deputies signing the Constitution. This is an outstanding, experiential history lesson/tour!

If your group comprises more than fifty students, reserve a two-hour History in Motion: A Museum on Wheels presentation, where a component of the museum comes to your site. This is similar to the Pages of Inventions tour. The traveling van carries a working Colonial printing press. Kids are enthralled as they learn the history of print and "help" Ben Franklin with his experiments. Again, I can't recommend this museum and its tours highly enough.

Hours: Open to the public, Sat., 10am - 4pm. Open for groups and other individuals by appointment.

Admission: $8 for adults; $6 for seniors and ages 5 - 18; children 4 and under are free. In-house group educational tours are $150 for up to 25 people; $6 per person over that number. The traveling tours, for up to 150 students, are a flat fee of $500 for the two-hour presentation; $350 for the Inventive Dr. Franklin Show.

Ages: 6 years and up.

JAPANESE AMERICAN NATIONAL MUSEUM

(213) 625-0414 / www.janm.org

$$$

369 E. 1st Street, Los Angeles

(Exit Harbor Fwy [110] E. on 1st St. Or, exit Hollywood Fwy [101] S. on Alameda, R. on 1st St. It's on the corner of 1st St. and Central Ave. in Little Tokyo. Park in the lot across the street for $2 or $3 for the day. [TG: 634 G4])

During World War II more than 120,000 people of Japanese ancestry, most of whom were American citizens, were incarcerated in American relocation/concentration camps from 1941 to 1946. This museum is dedicated to preserving the memory of that time period, and learning from it. The glass building is nicely laid out and has seven gallery rooms, plus a research library, classrooms, and a theater room. The exhibit rooms holds rotating displays, varying from art exhibits, to the history of Japanese Americans, to athletes of Japanese ancestry. Permanent displays include authentic wooden barracks from an internment camp in Wyoming and a gallery reminiscent of an Ellis Island tribute with suitcases and immigrants' belongings, such as clothing (i.e. wedding dresses, uniforms, and everyday clothing), personal articles, board games, and numerous photographs. Articles on discrimination in the 1920's and on the loss of citizens' rights during WWII offer both shameful and fascinating information. Videos in several galleries complete the museums' offerings.

The museum anchors the east end of Little Tokyo Historic District which is comprised of ethnic shops and restaurants. Try an unusual flavor of ice cream here, such as green tea or red bean.

Hours: Open Tues. - Sun., 10am - 5pm (open Thurs. until 8pm). Closed New Year's Day, Thanksgiving, and Christmas.

Admission: $6 for adults; $5 for seniors; $3 for ages 6 - 17; children 5 and under are free. Admission is free every Thurs. from 5pm - 8pm, and all day on the third Thurs. of every month. (See C.E.E. L.A. for membership savings, page 86.)

Ages: 7 years and up.

JUSTICE BROTHERS RACING CAR MUSEUM

(626) 359-9174 / www.justicebrothers.com

!

2734 E. Huntington Drive, Duarte

(Exit San Gabriel Fwy [605] E. on Huntington Dr. It's just past Las Lomas St. [TG: 568 D5])

Justice Brothers is an established name in car care products. In the main lobby of their headquarters office building is a slick exhibit of their collection containing thirteen-plus cars and a few motorcycles. Featured models include gleaming and colorful vintage Kurtis midget and sprint cars dating back to the 1930's, a 1968 Ford GT-40 LeMans, a Ford Model T, and a classic Corvette and Thunderbird. Other memorabilia includes numerous gasoline pumps, a great display of lights from the top of old gasoline pumps, models, photographs, engines, and even a biplane "flying" overhead. The winner for most unique motorcycle goes to an ice motorcycle, or "icycle," with its steel spikes on the tires to grip ice in Russia and a few other cold countries.

There are two other, smaller display areas in adjacent buildings that showcase a few more race cars and a Chevy truck.

> **Hours:** Open Mon. - Fri., 8am - 5pm.
> **Admission:** Free
> **Ages:** 6 years and up. Visitors under 18 must be accompanied by an adult.

KENNETH G. FISKE MUSICAL INSTRUMENT MUSEUM

(909) 621-8307 / www.cuc.claremont.edu/fiske
747 N. Dartmouth Avenue, Claremont College, Claremont
(Exit San Bernardino Fwy [10] N. on Indian Hill Blvd., R. on 4th St. The College is at the corner of 4th St. and College Way. The museum is on the lower level of the Bridges auditorium. [TG: 601 D3])

This museum is like music to your ears. The gallery contains a comprehensive collection of 450 rare, historic, and ethnic musical instruments. The instruments in display cases and lining the wall, range from the 1600's to the twentieth century. They include exotic drums, a Russian bassoon with a dragon's head, an armonica (i.e. a set of musical glasses invented by Benjamin Franklin), a walking cane violin, mandolins, Civil War bugles, a seven-foot trumpet, square pianos, player pianos, and lots more. On the half-hour tour, the curator explains the various instruments and even plays a few of them. This museum can be instrumental in teaching your kids about music! Tip: To continue your musical adventure, check out the nearby Folk Music Center shop, (909) 624-2928, at 220 Yale Avenue, which has an array of interesting folk instruments.

> **Hours:** Call for an appointment.
> **Admission:** Free; donations accepted.
> **Ages:** 7 years and up.

KIDSPACE CHILDREN'S MUSEUM

(626) 449-9143 / www.kidspacemuseum.org
Brookside Park, Arroyo Seco, Pasadena

Slated to reopen in 2004 at its new location in Brookside Park, this terrific children's museum will feature three, large barn-like buildings with over thirty hands-on activities and exhibits, a large garden area with different environments, a 300-seat theater, a cafe, and bookstore. Keep posted by contacting the website.

> **Hours:** Call for details.
> **Admission:** Call for details.
> **Ages:** 1½ - 11 years old.

LANCASTER MUSEUM and ART GALLERY

(661) 723-6250 / www.cityoflancasterca.org/Parks/museumgallery.htm
44801 North Sierra Highway, Lancaster
(Exit Antelope Valley Fwy [14] E. on Ave. J, L. on Sierra Hwy. [TG: 4015 H5])

This lovely museum has rotating exhibits featuring a wide range of interests from Egyptian mummies, space suits, and mammoth bones, to artwork by Picasso, Renoir, and da Vinci. Themes vary and include 3-D art, photography, paintings, sculpture, and other art forms. The permanent collection tends to reflect the history of Lancaster represented by furniture, musical instruments, antique clothing, mining tools, and more, plus a display on prehistoric wonders (*really* early history!). Note that the museum closes for a few weeks between exhibitions, so call first.

> **Hours:** Open Tues. - Sat., 11am - 4pm; Sun., 1pm - 4pm. Closed Mon. and some holidays. Ask about
> the Late Friday Nights program.
> **Admission:** Free
> **Ages:** 5 years and up, depending on the current exhibit.

THE LEONIS ADOBE

(818) 222-6511 / www.leonisadobemuseum.org   *$*
23537 Calabasas Road, Calabasas
(Exit Ventura Fwy [101] S. on Valley Circle Blvd./Mulholland Dr., take a quick R. onto Calabasas Rd. [TG: 559 F4])

Step back over 100 years in time when you visit the Leonis Adobe. The restored buildings help kids to picture the wealthy ranchero as it once was. The rustic grounds, complete with grape arbors, old farm equipment, windmills, and a corral containing longhorn cattle, horses, sheep, and goats, enhance the yesteryear atmosphere. Officially Los Angeles' Historic Cultural Monument No. 1, the adobe was once owned by Miguel Leonis, a Basque who led a very colorful life, and Espiritu, his Native American wife. Both the museum and its owners have a rich and fascinating history that kids will enjoy hearing.

The Visitor's Center is actually the re-located Victorian-style Plummer House, the oldest house "in" Hollywood. It contains a few glass-cased displays of mannequins dressed in period clothing and a gift shop. Outside, a huge, 600-year-old oak tree dominates the grounds. You are welcome to explore the barn, complete with wagons and buggies; a blacksmith's shop that is outfitted with saddles and tools; and the adobe. The bottom story of the adobe has a kitchen with a wood-burning stove and other old-fashioned kitchen implements; a pantry for preserving and drying food (kids like the hanging cow with fake blood); and a dining room with adobe floors. Upstairs is the Leonis' elegant bedroom that has a red velvet bedspread over the canopy bed, plus ladies' boots, and leather trunks. You'll notice that the hallway floor tilts at a downward angle, slanting away from the house. It was built like that to ensure that rains would run away from the walls, not seep into them. The Juan Menendez (bed) Room has a ghost story associated with it. (Every good historical home has at least one such story!) Also up here is an office, complete with desk, ledger, and guitar. Elsewhere on the ranch grounds are penned turkeys, ducks, and chickens; a covered beehive oven which was used for baking bread; and steps leading up to the tank house, or worker's bedroom. The Leonis Adobe is a classy reminder of the relatively brief, but pivotal Mexican/California era.

Ask about the terrific year-round school programs offered here, where kids immerse themselves in this time period.

Just a short walk eastward, past the Sagebrush Cantina restaurant, is the small, but beautiful Calabasas Creek Park. It offers a pleasant picnic area and respite with a rose garden out front, wrought-iron benches throughout, massive shade trees, and bridges over the duck pond. The only drawback to this serene scene is the ever-present freeway noise.

Hours: The Leonis Adobe is open Wed. - Fri. and Sun., 1pm - 4pm; Sat., 10am - 4pm.
Admission: $4 for adults; 50¢ for children 12 and under.
Ages: 4 years and up.

LOMITA RAILROAD MUSEUM

(310) 326-6255 / www.lomita-rr.org   *$*
250th Street and Woodward Avenue, Lomita
(Exit Harbor Fwy [110] W. on Pacific Coast Hwy., R. on Narbonne, R. on 250th St. [TG: 793 H4])

Stop, look, and listen! This small, re-created, turn-of-the century train depot is as charming to look at - with its decorative wrought iron, gingerbread molding, and brick patio - as it is to tour. Inside the depot museum/souvenir shop, visitors will see various train memorabilia such as an old-time station agent ticket office, scale model train cars, telegraph equipment, locomotive whistles, marker lights, an exhibit of railroad ties, and glass cases filled with photographs, and more artifacts. Hanging from the ceiling and the walls is a collection of hand-lanterns.

Outside, on real train tracks, are two railcars: An all-wood, 1910 Union Pacific "bobber" (i.e. caboose) to look around in and a 1902 Southern Pacific Steam locomotive with a cab that the kids can climb in and let their imaginations go full steam ahead. Note that the valves and handles are labeled with explanations for their use, but they are not for touching.

The museum annex park is just across the street. This pretty little grassy spot, with one picnic table under shade trees, boasts a real wood box car and a 1923 Union Oil tank car that are for display purposes only.

Hours: Open Wed. - Sun., 10am - 5pm. Closed Thanksgiving and Christmas.
Admission: $2 for adults; $1 for children 11 and under.
Ages: 1½ years and up.

LONG BEACH MUSEUM OF ART

(562) 439-2119 / www.lbma.org

2300 E. Ocean Boulevard, Long Beach

(Take Long Beach Fwy [710] S. to the end, exit E. on Shoreline Dr., R. on Ocean. [TG: 825 G1])

This two-story art venue by the beach (what a view!) contains a permanent collection of paintings, drawings, sculptures, decorative furnishings, and more. The rotating exhibits vary in medium and content, so call to see what's currently showing to see if it has kid-appeal. Grab a bite to eat at the on-site cafe.

Note that on the second Sunday of every month, at 2pm, a family artmaking workshop is hosted for ages 5 and up. The museum also offers Summer Art Adventures (i.e. day camps) for kids to learn how to draw and paint, as well as education programs, music programs, and other special events.

Hours: Open Tues. - Sun., 11am - 5pm. Closed Mon. and holidays.
Admission: $5 for adults; $4 for seniors and students; children 11 and under are free.
Ages: 7 years and up.

LOS ANGELES COUNTY MUSEUM OF ART and L.A.C.M.A. WEST

(323) 857-6000 / www.lacma.org

5905 Wilshire Boulevard, Los Angeles

(From Santa Monica Fwy [10], exit N. on Fairfax Ave., R. on Wilshire Blvd. From San Diego Fwy [405], exit E. on Wilshire Blvd. [TG: 633 B2])

Art, according to Webster, is: "The use of the imagination to make things of aesthetic significance; the technique involved; the theory involved." This leaves the interpretation of what constitutes art wide open! The Los Angeles County Museum of Art is composed of a grouping of buildings, plus the Bing Center of theater and movies for older audiences. Each building features a different style of art.

The Anderson building is a favorite with its modern and contemporary art, which translates as "anything goes." We started in the "Garage" (our title for the exhibit). Open the door to this walk-through exhibit, and it's like being in your grandfather's garage. It's crammed with old, rusted tools hanging up on the walls, other storage-type incidentals, and a car that needs more work than it will ever get. (I can now tell my husband that our garage is not a mess - it's art.) Throughout the Anderson building, kids are attracted to and puzzled by the larger-than-life sculptures, abstract paintings on gigantic canvases, and common objects that express artistic creativity, like a kitchen sink, or an arrangement of cereal boxes.

In contrast, the Ahmanson Building has more traditional works of art from Medieval European, the Romantic, and the Renaissance periods. Classic paintings and portraits hang in various galleries throughout the stately, three-story building. Gilbert gold and silver pieces, such as elaborate bowls and candelabras, are on display here, as are incredibly detailed, inlaid stone pictures. Other works of art on view include Korean, Chinese, Islamic, and American art.

The Pavilion for Japanese Art is architecturally unique, inside and out. It houses mostly paintings and a few sculptures in a serene, natural-light setting. The Samurai warrior statue, dressed in eighteenth-century black chain mail armor, gets our vote for the most interesting piece here. The ramp spirals downward, toward the small waterfall and pond on the lowest level. The Hammer Building specializes in photography, impressionism, and prints. The permanent and temporary exhibits here portray another medium of artistic endeavor.

Although many docents are on hand to insure that nothing is touched, the atmosphere is not stifling. Contact the museum about their great art classes, school tours, and family programs offered throughout the year. For instance, our school group took the free sculpture tour where we went on a guided tour of the sculptures here and then went to the on-site classroom to make sculptures out of the provided clay. Family Fun Days are held every Sunday and include art workshops, live performances, and a family gallery tour. For your information a cafe serving reasonably priced food and a more formal sit-down restaurant are in the courtyard. Enjoy walking around the museum's spacious backyard, Hancock Park. The parks hosts concerts and presentations at the amphitheater, has picnic tables, grassy areas, trees, and is home to the La Brea Tar Pits and adjacent to the GEORGE C. PAGE MUSEUM (see pg. 89). Note that the NEXGEN ARTS program gives free museum membership to youths 18 and under, which includes that youth and one adult.

The L.A.C.M.A. West is a satellite building of the huge main museum and is on the corner of Fairfax and Wilshire, just down the street from L.A.C.M.A. (One admission fee pays for entry to both museums.) This building is home to the museum's vast Latin American art collection and pieces are shown on a rotating basis. Boone Children's Gallery is the most interesting one for kids here as family members enjoy changing hands-on themed exhibits, corresponding games, crafts, and perhaps some computer activities.

Hours: Open Mon., Tues., and Thurs., noon - 8pm; Fri., noon - 9pm; Sat. - Sun., 11am - 8pm. Closed Wed., Thanksgiving, and Christmas. School tours are often given in the morning hours.

Admission: $7 for adults; $5 for seniors and students; $1 for ages 6 - 17; children 5 and under are free. Admission is free on the second Tues. of each month, except for ticketed events. Parking costs $5 in the lot at the S.E. corner of Wilshire Blvd. and Spaulding, or at Hancock Park at Sixth St. and Curson Ave.

Ages: 6 years and up.

LOS ANGELES MARITIME MUSEUM

(310) 548-7618 / www.lamaritimemuseum.org

Berth 84, San Pedro

(Take Harbor Fwy [110] to the end. It turns into Gaffey St. Turn L. on 9th, L. on Harbor Blvd. It's at the foot of 6th St. [TG: 824 C5])

If you have older children who dream of sailing the oceans blue, they will enjoy walking through the six galleries of changing exhibits in this maritime museum, which is housed in an old ferry building. There are hundreds of ship models to look at, ranging from real boats to ones inside a bottle. (How do they do that?) An impressive twenty-one-foot scale model of the Poseidon and two cut-away models, of the Titanic and Lusitania, give your kids the inside scoop on ocean liners.

A highlight is the Amateur Radio Station where your child might be able to talk to someone on the other side of the world.

Hours: Open Tues. - Sun., 10am - 4:30pm. Closed New Year's Day, Thanksgiving, and Christmas.

Admission: $1 per person.

Ages: 5 years and up.

LOS ANGELES MUSEUM OF THE HOLOCAUST MARTYRS MEMORIAL

(323) 761-8170

6006 Wilshire Boulevard, Los Angeles

(From Santa Monica Fwy [10], exit N. on Fairfax Ave., R. on Wilshire Blvd., R. on Ogden Drive. Museum is at SW corner of Ogden and Wilshire. From San Diego Fwy [405], exit E. on Wilshire Blvd. It's located on Museum Row diagonally across from LACMA. Free parking at rear of museum or metered parking nearby. [TG: 633 B2])

The first story of this building is the museum, which consists mainly of photographs and information panels on the walls, artifacts, a part of a (human) cargo train car to walk through, and a model layout of the Sobibor death camp. Touch screens throughout show newsreels from WWII Germany and interviews with survivors. Note: Several of the photographs are necessarily graphic (i.e. piles of naked bodies). A few display cases exhibit typical family belongings, religious items, and cultural arts memorabilia. Guided school/group tours can be arranged. The museum can provide speakers, docents, and survivors who address classrooms on Jewish history by incorporating art, music, and/or writing.

Hours: Mon. - Thurs., 10m - 5pm; Fri., 10am - 2pm; Sun., noon - 4pm. Closed Sat.

Admission: Free. Ask about tour information.

Ages: 4th graders and up.

MISSION SAN FERNANDO REY DE ESPAÑA

(818) 361-0186

$$

15151 San Fernando Mission Boulevard, Mission Hills

(From San Fernando Valley Fwy [118], exit N. on Sepulveda Blvd., R. on San Fernando Mission Blvd. Going N. on San Diego Fwy [405], exit E. on San Fernando Mission Blvd. Going S. on 405, exit E. on Rinaldi St., R. on Sepulveda Blvd., L. on San Fernando Mission Blvd. [TG: 501 H2])

What was life like in the early days of California? Take a self-guided tour of one of my family's favorite missions to find out. Mission San Fernando Rey, founded in 1797, was the seventeenth mission in the chain of outposts along the coast of California. It has a beautiful, large courtyard, with a small sundial at the north entrance, and west gardens that are surrounded by numerous rooms. These rooms lead to small, alcove rooms - what delightful exploration! The Museum Room is a good place to begin as it's filled with old photos (including one of a bathroom that looks like a small indoor pool), statues, bows and arrows, peace pipes, a bell collection, and several more artifacts. The Madonna Room is fascinating as it contains over 100 representations of the Madonna, each depicted by different nationalities and cultures. From simplistic versions to ornate ones, there are Chinese, African, and Indian Madonnas, plus one that looks like a prairie woman, another like an Eskimo, and more.

Other rooms and items of interest we saw include a hospice that held beds made with rope supports (pre-box springs); simply furnished bedrooms; plain wooden tables and chairs; the Convent, where meat was hung to dry; mission vestments; a library containing shelves of very old books including a colorful, hand-illuminated liturgical book with large Gothic lettering; brick ovens; and pipe organs. The workshop and weaving rooms are interesting because they hold, respectively, blacksmith tools, saddles, and scythes, and a large wooden loom with cowhide chairs. The church, which still holds regular worship services, has adobe walls and an ornately decorated altar with gold-leaf overlay. A small cemetery behind the church opens into a huge, neighboring cemetery. In the midst of all this history, my boys loved seeing the many peacocks that wandered the grounds. They even "discovered" a few roosters that were tame enough to pet.

Brand Park, once a part of the mission, is just across the street. This grassy park has lots of shade trees, plenty of picnic tables, and running around space, but no playground. It also has vats where mission wines were once produced.

Hours: Open daily, 9am - 4:30pm. Closed Thanksgiving and Christmas.

Admission: $4 for adults; $3 for seniors and ages 7 - 15; children 6 and under are free. Admission to Brand Park is free.

Ages: 5 years and up.

MISSION SAN GABRIEL ARCHANGEL

(626) 457-3048 / www.sangabrielmission.org

$$

428 S. Mission Drive, San Gabriel

(Exit San Bernardino Fwy [10] N. on Del Mar Ave., L. on Mission Rd. [TG: 596 D4])

Located in the Mission District, California's fourth mission is aptly nicknamed "Queen of the Missions." The graceful buildings and pleasant grounds transport you back to 1771, when the mission was founded. They also offer a wonderfully visual way to learn about California's Spanish/Mexican heritage.

In the midst of the cactus garden are tanning vats, with a placard describing the tanning process. Walk up a few stone steps to see four large holes in the ground, which were once the soap and tallow vats. The San Gabriel Mission supplied soap and candles to most of the other missions. There is one fountain and several statues distributed throughout the mission gardens. In the cemetery, for instance, is a life-size crucifix - a memorial to the 6,000 Indians buried on the grounds.

The Mission Church is still in use. The wall behind the altar is eye-catching as it is ornately decorated. The small baptismal room is equally impressive. Next to the church, the small and somewhat dark museum contains only a few articles that were of interest my kids - big, old books covered in sheepskin dating from 1489 and 1588, and a Spanish bedroom set. Knowing that the museum was once a series of rooms, such as sleeping quarters, weaving rooms, and carpenter shops, made it a bit more interesting.

Located in the center of the mission is the Court of the Missions. Models of each of California's twenty-one missions, varying in size and layout, but similar in style, are on display here. Vaya con Dios! (Go with God!)

Hours: Open daily, 9am - 4:30pm. Closed New Year's Day, Easter, July 4th, Thanksgiving, and Christmas.

Admission: $5 for adults; $4 for seniors; $2 for ages 6 - 12; children 5 and under are free.

Ages: 5 years and up.

MONTEREY PARK HISTORICAL MUSEUM / GARVEY RANCH PARK

(626) 307-1267

781 S. Orange Avenue, Monterey Park

(Exit San Bernardino Fwy [10] S. on Garfield Ave., L. on Graves Ave., R. on Orange Ave. The museum is situated in Garvey Ranch Park. [TG: 636 D3])

This small museum's claim to fame is its twenty-one scale models of the California missions. The adobe-like museum has three reconstructed rooms that also house Indian artifacts, household items (such as toys and a phonograph), tools, period clothing, photographs, and a corner dedicated to Laura Scudder (who lived in Monterey Park).

Adjacent to the museum is a small observatory, operated by the L.A. Astronomical Society, that is open for public viewing on Wednesdays at about 7pm. The next-door Garvey Ranch Park is a nice park with grassy areas, trees, a few covered picnic areas, paved pathways, two lighted baseball diamonds with stadium seating, basketball courts, playgrounds, and two tennis courts just up the hill.

Hours: The museum is open Sat. - Sun., 2pm - 4pm. The park is open daily, sunrise - sunset.

Admission: Free

Ages: 5 years and up.

MUSEUM OF CONTEMPORARY ART / GEFFEN CONTEMPORARY / PACIFIC DESIGN CENTER

$$$

(213) 626-6222 / www.moca.org

250 S. Grand Avenue, Los Angeles

(Going W. on Hollywood Fwy [101], exit S. on Grand Ave. Going E. on 101, exit E. on Temple St., R. on Grand Ave. From Harbor Fwy [110], exit E. on 4th St., L. on Broadway, L. on 1st St. L. on Grand. [TG: 634 F3])

The elegant Museum of Contemporary Art (MOCA), located on top of a plaza, presents rotating exhibits of eclectic art work - paintings, sculptures, photos, and more. This type of museum is a fun one to bring kids to as an introduction to art because the pieces are unusual, imaginative, and sometimes puzzling. Idea: After visiting the museum, have the kids come home and create their own contemporary or abstract piece of art. As we looked at the huge paintings on canvas, my boys and I took the liberty of renaming several pieces. (I think some of their title choices were more apropos than the ones the artists chose.) This involved the kids in studying the art and therefore enhanced our visit here. Downstairs in the museum is a reading room with several books, many geared for children, that pertain to the art and artists currently featured at the MOCA.

One satellite building of MOCA, the Geffen Contemporary, is located one mile away at 152 N. Central Avenue in Little Tokyo, across the plaza from the JAPANESE AMERICAN NATIONAL MUSEUM (see pg. 100). Another satellite is the Pacific Design Center (PDC) at 8687 Melrose Avenue in West Hollywood. The Center features rotating exhibits of architecture, design, and selections from MOCA's permanent collection. The Museum of Contemporary Art, then, is actually one museum in three buildings!

Hours: Open Tues. - Sun., 11am - 5pm (Thurs. until 8pm). Free public tours are given at noon, 1pm, and 2pm. Closed New Year's Day, July 4th, Thanksgiving, and Christmas.

Admission: $8 for adults; $5 for seniors and students with ID; children 11 and under are free. Paid admission is good for all locations of the museum - the MOCA and Geffen if visited on the same day, and the PDC if visited within 30 days. Admission to just Geffen and PDC is $3 for adults; children 11 and under are free. Admission is free on Thurs. to all locations. Parking in the plaza costs about $7.

Ages: 6 years and up.

MUSEUM OF LATIN AMERICAN ART
$

(562) 437-1689 / www.molaa.com

628 Alamitos Avenue, Long Beach

(Exit Long Beach Fwy [710] E. on Anaheim St., R. on Alamitos. [TG: 795 F7])

    This museum has a nicely laid out main gallery and surrounding gallery rooms. Rotating exhibits feature art, sculpture, and paintings by Latin American artists. The museum regularly hosts hands-on art workshops on Sundays for children, usually geared for ages 6 and up, that tie in with the present exhibit. Explore Latin American culture and heritage while experiencing its art. Note: The gift shop is filled with wonderful, cultural items to purchase.

    Hours: Open Tues. - Fri., 11:30am - 7pm; Sat., 11am - 7pm; Sun.,11am - 6pm. Closed Mon., New Year's Day, Thanksgiving, and Christmas.

    Admission: $5 for adults; $3 for seniors and students; children 11 and under are free. Admission is free on Fri.

    Ages: 6 years and up.

MUSEUM OF NEON ART
$

(213) 489-9918 / www.neonmona.org

501 W. Olympic, Los Angeles

(Exit Harbor Fwy [110] E. on 9ᵗʰ St., R. on Grand Ave., R. on Olympic. It's on the corner of Olympic and Hope, with the entrance on Hope. Free underground parking is available at the Renaissance Tower on Grand Ave., just N. of Olympic Blvd. [TG: 634 E5])

    For an enlightening experience, bring your kids to the Museum of Neon Art. Only here can you see Mona Lisa's smile really light up. Walk through the rainbow arch and into the warehouse-like rooms that display rotating exhibits of artists who use kinetic and electric art as an outlet for their creative endeavors. In other words, there are some funky-looking, 3-D reliefs and sculptures in here! Most of the pieces are fragile, but some of them have buttons to push that make parts light up or move around. For "neonophytes," the museum offers a three-hour monthly tour that focuses on the neon signs around the L.A. area. Participants, mostly adults, start at the museum and tour the city on a roofless double decker bus. Bring a jacket. Learn about the history of the city and the buildings as you pass by the neon signs flashing their advertisements.

    Just outside the museum is Hope Grant Park, which is the front lawn to the Fashion Institute of Design and Merchandise. This haven of greenery in the middle of downtown Los Angeles is a welcome respite. It has a small playground, a few picnic tables, a mosaic clock tower, colorful mosaic art forms, and a large fountain with steps around its perimeter that kids love to climb.

    Hours: The museum is open Wed. - Sat., 11am - 5pm; Sun., noon - 5pm. On the second Thurs. of each month, the museum is open until 8pm. The park is open daily, 7am - 6pm. Neon bus tours are given April through October. Call for dates.

    Admission: $5 for adults; $3.50 for seniors and students; children 12 and under are free. Admission is free on the second Thurs. of every month from 5pm - 8pm. The bus tour is $45 per person. The park is free.

    Ages: 4 years and up.

THE MUSEUM OF TELEVISION & RADIO
$$$

(310) 786-1000 / www.mtr.org

465 N. Beverly Drive, Beverly Hills

(Exit Santa Monica Fwy [10] N. on Robertson, L. on Wilshire, R. on Beverly Dr. Or, exit San Diego Fwy [405] E. on Santa Monica Blvd., R. on Beverly Dr. Two hours of free valet parking, with validation, is available under the museum, just off Little Santa Monica Blvd. [TG: 632 F1])

    Tune in to the Museum of Television & Radio, which houses the ultimate collection of broadcasting programs. Inside the upscale, contemporary-looking building are various rooms to watch and listen to shows, with just the touch of a button. The lobby has rotating exhibits of art, mementos, storyboards, costumes, sets, and more. The Radio Listening Room is just what its name implies. The room is quiet as visitors use headphones to choose from five preset radio channels. A sampling of the rotating selections can include comedy, rock 'n roll, history of radio, witness to history (e.g. historic speeches), etc. There is also a fully-equipped radio station in here to do live broadcasts. Next door, watch a pre-selected show in the fifty-seat Screening Room, or watch a film or program in the 150-seat Theater Room. Call to see what's playing.

Use the upstairs computer library to select your choice of radio or television show. For example, key your television selection into the computer, then view it in the adjacent Console Room. This room has individual monitors as well as family consoles which accommodate up to four people. Your child is in couch potato heaven here, able to choose his own television programs from literally thousands of titles available.

Some of the benefits of this museum include viewing (and listening to) historic shows both for school-aged children and for researchers. Ready access to programs is also great if you just want to choose a favorite show. Call for information on special children's events. Hot tip: On most Saturdays from 10am to noon kids 9 to 14 years old are invited to partake in an old-time radio workshop called Re-creating Radio. Participants use scripts, sound effects, and music to produce a broadcast, and they even get a copy of the tape to keep. (It's sent in the mail.) The cost is $5 and reservations are required. What a fun (and unique) birthday party idea!

Hours:	Open Wed. - Sun., noon - 5pm. Closed Mon., Tues., New Year's Day, July 4th, Thanksgiving, and Christmas.
Admission:	Admission is free, however suggested donations are $10 for adults; $8 for seniors and students; $5 for children 14 and under.
Ages:	6 years and up.

MUSEUM OF TOLERANCE / SIMON WEISENTHAL CENTER   ☼

(800) 900-9036 or (310) 553-8403 / www.wiesenthal.com   *$$$*
9786 W. Pico Boulevard, Los Angeles
(Exit San Diego Fwy [405] E. on Santa Monica Blvd., R. on Westwood Blvd., L. on Pico. [TG: 632 F4])

The Simon Wiesenthal Center's Beit Hashoah Museum of Tolerance is unique in its format of numerous technologically advanced, interactive major exhibits, and in its focus on personal prejudice, group intolerance, the struggle for civil rights in America, and the Holocaust. After orientation, enter through the door marked Prejudiced or the one marked Unprejudiced to begin your journey in the American Experience/Tolerancenter. A computer exhibit of the L.A. riots asks visitors for a personal profile - age, gender, ethnicity - then asks thought-provoking questions about social justice and responsibility. In a mock 50's diner, called Point of View, visitors use jukebox monitors to watch various scenarios and answer a menu of questions about personal responsibility regarding drinking, drugs, hate speeches, and other issues. Enter the Millennium Machine room, which looks like the set of a futuristic game show, where participants add their input by answering questions about global crimes, human rights abuse, and the threat of terrorism. You'll be riveted and affected by the sixteen-screen video Civil Rights Wall and an interactive U.S. map that discloses 250 hate groups in America.

The Holocaust "tour" begins as you print out a child's passport. You then witness a series of chronological vignettes, while listening to narration that explains the events leading up to the Holocaust. This factual and emotional forty-five-minute tour is one of the most informative and visual ways to begin to understand what happened. After walking through a replica of the gates of Auschwitz, your tour culminates in the Hall of Testimony, where you'll discover the fate of the child whose passport you hold.

The second floor of the museum contains a multimedia learning center with over thirty work stations. Numerous films - on Anne Frank, Harriet Tubman, Helen Keller, and others - are available for viewing. Also housed here are letters of Anne Frank, a bunkbed from a concentration camp, and medical instruments. One of the most powerful experiences at the museum is listening to Holocaust survivors share their testimonies. They speak here Sundays through Thursdays at 1pm, 2pm, and 3pm. The third floor displays rotating exhibits. Call for a current schedule. The fourth floor has a cafeteria that serves light snacks and refreshments. Note: Cameras are not allowed in the museum.

Hours: Open year round, Mon. - Thurs., 11:30am - 6:30pm; Sun., 11:30am - 7:30pm. The museum is open November through March, Fri., 11:30am - 3pm and April through October, Fri., 11:30am - 5pm. Visitors will not be admitted into the museum about two-and-a-half hours before closing time, because it won't give them enough time to see it all. Closed Sat., New Year's Day, Thanksgiving, Christmas, and Jewish holidays. School tours for twenty or more students are offered as early as 8:30am.

Admission: $10 for adults; $8 for seniors; $6 for ages 12 - 18. Free validated underground parking is available on Pico Blvd.

Ages: 10 years and up - it's too intense for most younger children.

NATIONAL HOT ROD ASSOCIATION MOTORSPORTS MUSEUM

(909) 622-2133 / www.nhra.com/museum/index.html *$$*

1101 W. McKinley Avenue, Pomona

(Going E. on San Bernardino Fwy [10], exit N. on White Ave., L. on McKinley. Going W. on 10, exit S. on Orange Grove Ave., R. on McKinley. It's adjacent to Pomona Raceway, near Gate 1. [TG: 600 G5])

To see some really hot wheels, visit this stylish hot rod museum that showcases over eighty very cool cars in mint condition. The cars chronicle the colorful history of drag racing, from its days as an illegal street activity to its current status as a major spectator event. Some of the legendary cars on display include Kenny Bernstein's 1992 Budweiser King Top Fuel Dragster, the first car to break the 300mph barrier in NHRA competition; Warren Johnson's 1997 GM Goodwrench Pontiac Firebird, the first Pro Stock machine to break the 200 mph barrier; and John Athans '29 Highboy, once driven by Elvis Presley; plus Indy roadsters, midgets, and much more. With all of this inspiration, what kid (or man) wouldn't dream of being behind the wheel of any one of these cars and racing towards the finish line?! Glass cases that run almost the length of the museum contain trophies, photographs, helmets, driving uniforms, and more. Murals and paintings decorate the other walls.

Want to do some cruising of your own? The first Wednesday of each month, April through December, from 4pm to 8pm, join in on the Twilight Cruise. Over 300 of the finest early rods, customs, muscle cars, and classics fill the parking lot outside the museum. Cruise around on your own two legs to check out the autos and/or purchase some food and drink. This event is free and gives you $2 off entry to the museum. So, don't be a drag; race to this museum. Note: GANESHA PARK (see pg. 46) is just east on McKinley Avenue. It offers picnic tables, grassy areas to run around, basketball courts, and a community swimming pool.

Hours: Open Wed. - Sun., 10am - 5pm. Closed Mon. and Tues., Easter, Thanksgiving, and Christmas.

Admission: $5 for adults; $3 for seniors and ages 6 - 15; children 5 and under are free.

Ages: 3 years and up.

NATURAL HISTORY MUSEUM OF LOS ANGELES COUNTY

(213) 763-3466 / www.nhm.org. *$$$*

900 Exposition Boulevard, Los Angeles

(Exit the Harbor Fwy [110] W. on Exposition Blvd., L. on Flower, L. on Figueroa. Or, exit Santa Monica Fwy [10] S. on Vermont, L. on Exposition, R. on Figueroa. Metered parking is available on the street across from U.S.C., or park in the lot on Menlo Blvd. [TG: 674 B1])

This museum has a lot of a little bit of everything. In the foyer are complete skeletons of a T. rex and triceratops engaged in battle with each other. Catch the sights, sounds, and even smells of a fire's importance in the chaparral ecosystem via a multi-media presentation. A few long halls showcase numerous North American, African, and exotic mammals mounted in a backdrop of their natural habitat (i.e. huge dioramas). The gigantic walrus, buffalo, and elephant are the most impressive. Take a walk through time in the American and California history rooms. They contain early vehicles, such as tractors, stagecoaches, and a streetcar; mannequins dressed in period clothing; early weapons; and numerous other pioneer artifacts. In the adjacent Gem and Mineral Hall the over 2,000 outstanding rocks and minerals include fluorescent minerals (that shine neon colors under black light); rocks that are so brilliant in color or so oddly shaped that they look unreal; a touch area with a meteorite, a giant slab of jadeite, and more; 300 pounds of natural gold, plus mining artifacts; and a vault to walk through which contains cut rubies, emeralds, sapphires, and topaz. Some of our favorite exhibits at the museum are the dinosaurs in life-like poses. Some of the massive animals are in skeletal form, while others are fleshed out, so to speak. Other exhibits on this floor include a real mummy; a preserved, unusually long, and flat-looking fish - the oarfish; a Megamouth shark; and a room devoted to pre-Columbian archaeology. Just some of the extensive Native American artifacts on display include baskets, beadwork, pottery, jewelry, and a replica of a Pueblo cliff dwelling. An audiovisual presentation tells the story of L.A.'s Native American community. Also, check out the collection of Zuni Fetishes, which are small animals carved out of stone and shell.

The second floor has an entire wing devoted to our fine feathered friends. There are taxidermied penguins, vultures, ostriches, ducks, turquoise cotingas (guess what color they are?), and more. Pull out the drawers of the cabinets in the hallway to see a variety of feathers and bird eggs. A large part of the ornithology (study of birds) exhibit is interactive. Turn a disk to get a magnified view of wings, feathers, and bones. Step on a scale to see how much just your bones weigh - they make up 17% of your body weight. (Although I'm sure my bones weigh more than that.) Walk through a dark, two-story rain forest habitat that resounds with bird noises and has a waterfall. Another room upstairs presents an in-depth look at marine life via murals, mounted animals, and information.

"Hands-on" is the motto at the wonderful Discovery Center. This includes putting on puppet shows; making rubbings (you'll take home a lot of these papers); playing on computers; going for a fossil dig at the small sandpit; looking under a microscope at various items; and touching rocks, shells, bones, and skulls of an alligator and polar bear. Kids can also touch (or wrap themselves in) skins of deer, fox, skunk, opossum, sheep, and other animals. There are live animals in here, too, such as iguanas, toads, a python (he gets fed once a week), and fish. Forty different Discovery Boxes offer different activities with varying degrees of difficulty: Sharks simply has shark teeth and fossil vertebrae to look at and study, plus books on sharks to read. Native Games gives directions and materials to play with walnut shells, dice, and Indian darts. Listen Up is a game where the same objects that are in clear jars are also in black jars. Shake them, listen, and then match the sounds and the jars.

Just up the stairs is the Insect Zoo, which has cases swarming with live insects! Show no fear (or disgust) in front of your kids - some of the little buggers are quite interesting. You'll see scorpions, millipedes, tarantulas, beetles, and more (than you've ever wanted!).

The museum also features wonderful rotating exhibits, usually downstairs, such as "Cats, Mild to Wild," which featured house cats to lions in dramatic pictures, interactive animated figures, and more. Call to see what is currently showing. Also, ask about the museum's numerous, in-depth field trips for various age groups, as well as their special events held on site. In particular, look at the Calendar entry for details about the Bug Fair (see pg. 577).

From late April through August walk into the Pavilion of Wings, an enclosed outdoor butterfly garden. Watch as butterflies that are every color of the rainbow alight on the plants and on you. The entrance cost just for the pavilion is $3 for adults; $2 for seniors and students; $1 for ages 5 - 12; children 4 and under are free.

Picnic tables and lots of grassy areas surround the museum. Also see the nearby AIR AND SPACE GALLERY (pg. 80), CALIFORNIA AFRICAN AMERICAN MUSEUM (pg. 84), CALIFORNIA SCIENCE CENTER (pg. 85), EXPOSITION PARK (pg. 44), and IMAX THEATER (pg. 148).

Hours: Open daily, 10am - 5pm. Closed New Year's Day, Thanksgiving, and Christmas.

Admission: $8 for adults; $5.50 for seniors and students; $2 for ages 5 - 12; children 4 and under are free. Certain discounts are available through AAA. Special exhibits raise the admission price a few dollars. The first Tues. of every month is free admission day. Entrance to the butterfly pavilion is an additional $3 for adults; $2 for ages 5 - 12; children 4 and under are free. Parking in the lot costs $6.

Ages: 2½ years and up.

NETHERCUTT COLLECTION / NETHERCUTT MUSEUM

(818) 367- 2251 or (818) 364-6464 / www.nethercuttcollection.org

15200 Bledsoe Street, Sylmar

(Exit Golden State Fwy [5] N.E. on Roxford St., R. on San Fernando Rd., L. on Bledsoe St. [TG: 481 H4])

There are two buildings that hold an impressive array of vintage automobiles, as well as hood ornaments, mechanical musical instruments, and time pieces collected by J. B. Nethercutt, the co-founder of Merle Norman Cosmetics. The Nethercutt Collection, housed in a five-story box-like building, offers two-hour guided tours. The inside is opulently decorated with marble floors and columns in the Grand Salon room, plus chandeliers, elegant wood paneling, and spiral staircases elsewhere. The Salon features more than two dozen classic American and European luxury cars in pristine condition, including a 1934 Packard Dietrich Convertible Sedan, a one-of-a-kind 1933 Dusenberg Arlington Torpedo Sedan, and a few Rolls Royces and Cadillacs. The Louis XV-style dining room has a chandelier similar to the one in Versailles, a stunning grandfather clock, and collection of musical pocket watches. The third floor mezzanine showcases over 1,000 "mascots" (i.e. hood ornaments), including some made out of crystal, and ornate eighteenth-century French furniture (both originals and reproductions). The spacious fourth floor displays mechanical musical instruments such as music boxes, reproducing (i.e. player) pianos, nickelodeons, and the crown jewel - the Mighty Wurlitzer Theater Pipe Organ. The tour guide describes the mechanical system of each instrument and also plays a few of them. Visitors are asked to dress appropriately (i.e. befitting the atmosphere) for a tour - no jeans or shorts.

The Nethercutt Museum is another huge building, across the street, that displays over 175 more antique and immaculate automobiles, described as "rolling works of art." Let me whet your appetite for this stunning collection by mentioning just a few makes and models on display here: Dusenberg, Packard, Pierce Arrow, Rolls Royce, an 1898 Eisenach Runabout, a 1967 Ferrari 365, and a classic 1913 steam pumper fire truck. Again, the cars are displayed in beautiful surroundings. A fully-staffed automotive restoration facility, where classic cars are striped to the bare "bone" and then painstakingly rebuilt according to original specifications, is also on the premises. Outside are an immaculately restored 1937 Royal Hudson steam locomotive and a Pullman private rail car on tracks.

Hours: The Collection is open for guided tours only, Tues. - Sat., at 10 and 1:30. Reservations are required, usually about 6 weeks in advance. The Museum is open Tues. - Sat., 9am - 4:30pm - peruse at will. Closed Sun., Mon., and holidays.

Admission: Both buildings have free admission.

Ages: Must be at least 12 years old for a tour of the Collection; ages 8 years and up will enjoy the Museum.

NORTON SIMON MUSEUM

(626) 449-6840 / www.nortonsimon.org

411 W. Colorado Boulevard, Pasadena

(Exit Foothill Fwy [210] (just south of the Ventura Fwy [134]) W. on Colorado. It's on the R. [TG: 565 G5])

The museum brochure describes some of the masterpieces as "highly important works" and "glorious compositions," which lets astute readers know that this is not a hands-on museum for younger children. A visit to the museum and observing the numerous museum employees/security guards confirms this impression.

The Norton Simon is, however, a treasure for art connoisseurs as the pieces are truly outstanding and tastefully displayed in an atmosphere of quiet elegance. The permanent collection of this thirty-eight gallery, two-story, fine arts museum consists of seven centuries of European art, from the Renaissance to the twentieth century. A sampling of the featured artists includes Raphael, Botticelli, Rembrandt, Renoir, Monet, van Gogh, Goya, Picasso, and Matisse. Western art and Asian sculpture are also well represented. A special exhibits section presents more of the permanent collection on a rotating basis. Tip: Ask for a free family guide to get the kids more involved with the paintings and sculptures. Another way to get children (and other family members) interested in the pieces is to rent one of two self-guided audio tours. One is geared for adults, covering eighty work; the other, for children and families, covering thirty-six works. The "tours" are $3 per.

Beginning at 12:30pm and running alternately throughout the day, the museum theater presents two films: A thirty-minute orientation documentary movie on the life and collections of Norton Simon called the *Art of Norton Simon*, and another film hosted by the "art nun," called *Sister Wendy at the Norton Simon*. The theater room is also a venue for concerts and lectures.

$$

Educational tours, and accompanying study guides with activity sheets, are available by reservation for students. Personally, I benefit greatly from the "insider" information and explanations.

Hours: Open Mon., Wed. - Sun., noon - 6pm. Open Fri. until 9pm. Closed Tues., New Year's Day, Thanksgiving, and Christmas.

Admission: $6 for adults; $3 for seniors; free for ages 18 and under.

Ages: 10 years and up.

PASADENA MUSEUM OF HISTORY

(626) 577-1660 / www.pasadenahistory.org $$

470 W. Walnut Street, Pasadena

(Exit Foothill Fwy [210], near where it turns into Ventura Fwy [134], W. on W. Walnut St., L. on N. Orange Grove Blvd., and turn L. into the first driveway past the mansion on the corner. [TG: 565 G4])

Pasadena's stately heritage landmark Fenyes mansion showcases gracious living at the turn-of-the-century. A one-hour guided tour through the house allows visitors to see original (now antique) furnishings which came from all over the world. The stories about the artifacts are intriguing, especially the legend of flying carpets, which is thought to come from prayer rugs supposedly endowed with magical powers. A prayer rug is located in the studio. Some of the highlights include the wood-paneled study; the elegant living room with its exquisite furniture and period-dressed mannequins; a grandfather clock in the foyer that has rotating, colored-glass slides of early Pasadena; old-fashioned utensils in the kitchen (my boys needed an explanation about the rug beater); china in the butler's pantry; numerous volumes of books in the hallway and office; the solarium; fine wooden tables and chairs; and chests in the living room and studio ornately finished with tortoise shell, ivory, and mother-of-pearl. The elegantly-decorated master bedroom and a child's bedroom are upstairs.   A few small rooms downstairs hold old tools, a piano, a collection of old cameras, and several military uniforms.

Another component the Pasadena Museum of History is the museum with two galleries that display changing exhibits. A recent exhibit was one of children's toys, quilts, and clothing from 1850 to 1950. It showed how life was before video games (was there life before video games?) and how things change over time, at least in design, with displays of dolls, trucks, stuffed animals, books, games, clothing, and more. The Finnish Folk Art Museum, just next door, is a homey three-room replica of a Finnish farmhouse that contains handmade furniture, plus utensils and folk costumes.

Educational tours are offered to adult's and children's groups, as are special programs. The grounds are beautifully landscaped with plants, trees, a pond, and a rose garden. The well-stocked gift shop carries some unique items. Pasadena is a city steeped in rich cultural history that is well represented by the mansion and museums.

Hours: Mansion tours are offered Wed. - Sun. at 1:30pm and 3pm. The museum is open Wed. - Sun., noon - 5pm. The Finnish museum is open Thurs. - Sun., 1pm - 4pm.

Admission: Mansion tours are $3 for adults. Museum admission (for the galleries and Finnish museum) is $5 for adults; $4 for seniors. A combo package is $7 for adults; $6 for seniors. There is no admission cost for children 11 and under at any of the buildings.

Ages: 6 years and up.

PETERSEN AUTOMOTIVE MUSEUM

(323) 930-CARS (2277) / www.petersen.org $$$

6060 Wilshire Boulevard, Los Angeles

(Exit Santa Monica Fwy [10] N. on Fairfax, R. on Wilshire. [TG: 633 B2])

The driving force behind this 300,000 square foot, state-of-the-art museum is dedication to the art, culture, and history of the automobile. Streetscape, on the first floor, takes you on a chronological walk through time via cars, from horse and buggy, vintage automobiles, and an exhibit of gas pumps, to prototypes, solar-powered, and other, futuristic-type cars. Each car is displayed in its own walk-through, diorama-like setting, complete with asphalt, manholes, sidewalks, fake plants - whatever cultural surroundings fit the car - as well as mannequins dressed in period outfits. Sounds, like birds chirping where a Model T is "Stuck in the Mud," help children enter into the spirit of the lifestyles represented here. Kids can climb aboard the trolley car used in old Laurel and Hardy movies, although other cars on this floor are not hands-on.

The second floor has six galleries, including a terrific collection of hot rods, roadsters, race cars, and classics in prime condition. A glitzy Hollywood Gallery stars cars that were featured in movies and television shows, and/or that were owned by celebrities. Check out the changing exhibits here because they are consistently fabulous and always appeal to car aficionados. Biking enthusiasts will appreciate the adjacent Otis Chandler Motorcycle Gallery. However, the ultimate in kid-cool is putting on a helmet and getting behind the wheel of a real Indianapolis 500 race car!

The third floor, the Discovery Center, will really get kids revved up with its 6,500 square feet of motor vehicle interaction! They can ride on a real Highway Patrol motorcycle, complete with sirens blaring and flashing lights. Learn how sound travels via the Doppler Effect by triggering infra red detectors (the ones in the display only, please!) to hear dogs barking or a squeal of tires. Have your children dress up in a motoring duster, cap, and scarves and "drive" a Model T. (Bring your camera.) A Sparklett's water truck contains plastic jugs filled with a variety of games, puzzles, costumes, and construction toys all pertaining to the car motif. A play area is set up for toddlers to race mini-cars around on tracks and play mats. Another large room is for the mechanically minded. It has a giant dashboard; a display that traces the route an engine takes to come to life from ignition to the voltage regulator; photos and information panels and gear shifts that coordinate together to learn about fuel and conservation; and other learning stations. Our favorite "feet-on" exhibit consists of sitting on a car seat, that's really part of a giant combustion engine on huge wheels, and becoming a human spark plug. Move the engine across the room when you (and some strong-legged friends) push down on oversized pistons that pop up at regular intervals. (Fun, but tiring.) A few other highlights include holding a spinning bicycle wheel at a tilt while sitting on a chair to feel angular motion; watching billiard balls clack their way down a giant maze of tracks to explore motion and gravity; and racing wheels down a track to learn about inertia (or just to see who wins). The Discovery Center hosts fun activities the first Saturday of every month from 2pm to 4pm.

Take a pencil Treasure Hunt and/or ask about the other special activities and classes. Hour-long school tours are offered during the week for all ages at $1 per person. Know that a visit here will definitely accelerate your child's interest in cars!

Hours: Open Tues. - Sun., 10am - 6pm. The Discovery Center closes at 4pm, Tues. - Fri. and at 5pm on Sat. The museum is closed Mon. (except some holiday Mon.), plus New Year's Day, Thanksgiving, and Christmas.

Admission: $10 for adults; $5 for seniors; $3 ages 5 - 12; children 4 and under are free. Enter the museum parking structure from Fairfax - $6 for all-day parking.

Ages: 5 years and up.

PETTERSON MUSEUM

(909) 621-9581 / www.pilgrimplace.org

660 Avery Road, Claremont

(Exit San Bernardino Fwy [10] N. on Indian Hill Rd., L. on Harrison Ave., R. on Mayflower Rd., L. on Avery. It's at Pilgrim Place. [TG: 601 C3])

This small, intra-cultural museum is housed on the grounds of a community of retired pastors, missionaries, and other church professionals. Those who shared the gospel in far corners of the globe often return with significant mementos of their host culture and crafts, covering many centuries of human history. Some of the exotic artifacts in display cases include costumes, textiles, masks, statues, dolls, shells, and pottery. The docent-guided tours give insight into the exhibits. Note: Check the Calendar entry for the annual Pilgrim Place Festival (see pg. 610).

Hours: Open to the public, Fri. - Sun., 2pm - 4pm. Call to make a reservation to take a tour at another time.

Admission: Free

Ages: 6 years and up.

POINT VINCENTE INTERPRETIVE CENTER AND PARK

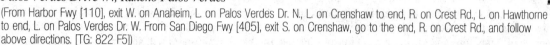

(310) 544-5260

Palos Verdes Drive W., Rancho Palos Verdes

(From Harbor Fwy [110], exit W. on Anaheim, L. on Palos Verdes Dr. N., L. on Crenshaw to end, R. on Crest Rd., L. on Hawthorne to end, L. on Palos Verdes Dr. W. From San Diego Fwy [405], exit S. on Crenshaw, go to the end, R. on Crest Rd., and follow above directions. [TG: 822 F5])

Note: This interpretive center is planning on re-opening mid-2004. This small museum has a variety of natural wonders on display, such as fossils of ocean animals, a side-by-side comparison of fossilized shells with recent shells of the same type, and taxidermied animals such as the great horned owl, a gray fox, and a peacock.

Whales are the main focus here as this is a prime site for whale watching. The museum has an overhead model of a gray whale, a continuously running video on whales, and a telephone so kids can literally listen to the call of the whales. There is a small enclosed area upstairs and an outside area that are good spots to either watch the whales as they migrate, January through March, or just to see a terrific view of the coastline. The Point Vincente Lighthouse is close by and on foggy days, you'll hear the horn blast its warning signal.

A quarter-mile paved trail winds around the Interpretive Center and the few picnic tables that are here. If your family is in a hiking or biking mood, there is a three-mile, or so, narrow dirt trail leading from the Center and looping back around. This main pathway and its offshoots are alternately flat and hilly, so be prepared for some real exercise! Have a whale of a time at this small museum and at the park.

Hours: Call for hours.

Admission: Call for prices. There is no admission for the surrounding park and trails.

Ages: 2½ years and up.

QUEEN MARY

(562) 435-3511 / www.queenmary.com

Pier J, Long Beach

(Take Long Beach Fwy [710] S. to the end, R. on Queen's Way Bridge and follow signs. [TG: 825 E3])

Cruise over to Long Beach Harbor to see the Queen, *Queen Mary* I mean - one of the largest luxury passenger liners ever built. Take a one-hour guided Behind-the-Scenes tour and learn about the ship's fascinating history. Only on this tour can you see the dining room/ballroom, boiler room, and an original first class suite. Younger children will get antsy. We thoroughly enjoyed our self-guided Shipwalk tour. Starting on the lower decks, we watched a video called *The Queen Mary Story* about its construction, maiden voyage, and service during WWII. The Hall of Maritime Heritage, a small museum, displays navigating instruments, ship models, and pictures and stories of famous doomed ships, including the *Titanic*. Everything in the engine room is clearly marked, making it easy to explain the machinery's function to youngsters. The last remaining propeller on the ship is in an open-top, propellor box in water. It looks like a shark fin at first. Tell your kids that the life-size diver in the water is just a model. We toured the bridge, the wheel house where officers were quartered, and the state room exhibits. A highlight for my boys was playing on the gun turrets on the bow of the ship, as they fought off invisible enemies.

Did you see that? It looked just like a . . . ghost! Capitalizing on the numerous ghost reports, the half-hour guided Ghosts and Legends attraction takes visitors through lower decks including the forward work areas, six-story boiler room, and swimming pool (which is empty) area. Special effects designed to make the paranormal experiences come alive, so to speak, include changes in temperature in certain rooms, ghostly images against ceilings and walls, electrostatic charges, and the finale - a shudder like two ships colliding and a deluge of water that seemingly bursts through the hull of the *Queen Mary*.

The wooden upper decks are great for strolling around. Note: As an older ship, there are many narrow staircases, but not many ramps on board. Elevators enable those using strollers or wheelchairs to get from deck to deck.

Queen Mary's Seaport, adjacent to the ship's berth, has the Queen's Marketplace for your shopping and dining pleasures. There are also several fine shops and restaurants on the ship that run the gamut from the very elegant and expensive Sir Winston's, open daily, 5:30pm to 10pm; to Chelsea, open Wednesday through Sunday from 5:30pm to 10pm; to a more family-style and family-priced eatery, Promenade Cafe, which is open daily, 6am to 10pm. Inquire about the buffet-style champagne Sunday brunch in the Grand Salon of the ballroom. Here's a good deal: If you have a reservation at either Sir Winston's or Chelsea, where entrees average between $20 to $30, you don't pay the ship's admission fee although you're free to then tour it, and your parking is validated.

Other tips: 1) For a ~~cheap~~ inexpensive family date, come on board after 6pm when there isn't an admission charge, only a parking fee. Although the stores and many parts of the ship are not open then, some restaurants are open, so you can indulge in a dessert. Plus, it's fun for kids to walk around, and the sunsets are beautiful. Don't miss the ship! 2) Remember, that you can sleep on board the *Queen Mary*, as it functions as a floating hotel, too. 3) Look up SCORPION (pg. 117), SHORELINE VILLAGE (pg. 127), and AQUARIUM OF THE PACIFIC (pg. 178) for information on these nearby attractions. Also catch the AQUALINK (pg. 168) for a cruise around the harbor.

Hours: Open most of the year daily, 10am - 6pm.

Admission: General admission, which includes the self-guided tour and Ghosts and Legends tour, is $24.95 for adults; $22.95 for seniors; $12.95 for ages 5 - 11; children 4 and under are free. (Ask about AAA discounts.) The Behind-the-Scenes guided tour and a World War II tour are each an additional $5 for adults and seniors; $3 for ages 5 - 11. Parking is $8 per vehicle. Beat parking prices by catching the free Passport shuttle that runs from downtown Long Beach to the *Queen Mary*.

Ages: 3 years and up.

RANCHO LOS ALAMITOS

(562) 431-3541 / www.lbparks.org

6400 E. Bixby Hill Road, Long Beach

(Exit San Diego Fwy [405] S. on Palo Verde Ave. to the end. Go through the gated entrance [tell the gate employee you are going to the museum], L. on Bixby Hill. [TG: 796 E6])

This beautiful, historic ranch appeals to kids of all ages. The barn has several horse stalls, a few of which have been converted into small rooms, or self-contained history lessons. They display photographs, animal pelts, branding irons, and (our favorite) a suspended horse harness, showing how a horse was hooked up to help plow. Other buildings of particular interest, in this area, contain a blacksmith shop filled with old tools, and a room with lots of saddles and branding irons. A ranch is not complete without animals, so goats, sheep, chickens, ducks, and Shire horses are in outside pens.

An hour-and-a-half long tour includes going inside the adobe ranch house. It's always fun to try to guess the name and use of gadgets in old kitchens. The bedroom, library, music, and billiards rooms are interesting to older children.

The front of the house has a garden and two, 150-year-old Moreton Bay fig trees with huge roots. An Artifacts Room is open at certain times so kids can touch - that's right - artifacts! Most of the site is wheelchair/stroller accessible. Ask about the rancho's terrific school tours.

Hours: Open Wed. - Sun., 1pm - 5pm. Tours are offered on the half hour. School tours are given at various times throughout the week. Call to make reservations. The rancho is closed on holidays.

Admission: Free; donations appreciated.

Ages: 3 years and up for the outside grounds; 6 years and up for a tour of the house.

RANCHO LOS CERRITOS

(562) 570-1755 / www.lbparks.org

4600 Virginia Road, Long Beach

(Exit San Diego Fwy [405] N. on Long Beach Blvd., L. on Roosevelt, then make a quick R. on Virginia Rd. [TG: 675 D5])

This picturesque historic rancho is situated almost at the end of Virginia Road. The visitors center has a clever exhibit of big puzzle pieces representing different eras with pictures and information on them, that attempt to fit together pieces of our past. The information is interesting and some of the window-type "pieces" offer glimpses into the past by displaying old pottery, equipment, and other artifacts.

The perimeter gardens are beautifully landscaped around a grassy center area. There is also a huge old Moreton Bay fig tree with tremendous roots. A one-hour tour takes you through the house which is furnished as it was in the late 1870's. This is a terrific way to see and learn about our Mexican-California heritage. Kids can more easily relate to the bigger picture of state history when they explore a small part of it. Ask for a Kids' Activity Treasure Hunt, where young visitors use pencil and paper as they look for particular items throughout the museum - it makes a visit here that much more interesting. Bring a sack lunch as there are picnic tables on the grounds. Ask for a schedule of the Rancho's special family events - they are great. See the Calendar entry for Mud Mania (pg. 595).

School group tours include hands-on fun, such as candle-dipping and playing old-fashioned games. Students also have the opportunity to do chores, such as butter churning and washing clothes, the way they were done years ago.

Hours: Open Wed. - Sun., 1pm - 5pm. Guided tours are given on the weekends only, on the hour. School tours are given on Wed. and Thurs., 9:30am - noon.

Admission: Free; donations appreciated.

Ages: 7 years and up.

RAYMOND M. ALF MUSEUM

(909) 624-2798 / www.alfmuseum.org

1175 W. Baseline Road, Claremont

(Exit the San Bernardino Fwy [10] N. on Towne Ave., L. on Baseline Rd., R. up the hill. It is part of the Webb Schools. [TG: 571 A7])

Make no bones about it, this unique, circular museum displays dinosaur skeletons, trackways, fossils, and archaeological finds from all over the world. See the complete (and very large) skeletal cast of the Allosaurus fragilis (how do you measure up?), the skull of a T. rex, a giant fossil alligator skull, dinosaur eggs, and more. A kid's area has computer games, books, dinosaur puzzles, and a small sandpit for archaeologists-in-training to "dig" for fossils (and they are guaranteed to find them - not quite like being out in the field). The touch table has mastodon tusks, vertebrae, rocks, and a fossilized turtle shell, which is surprisingly heavy.

The downstairs room consists mainly of trackways, which are rock slabs with castings of dinosaur, camel, horse, and bear-dog footprints. The trackways are displayed on the walls, and around the room, under glass-encased coffee tables (albeit, priceless ones). Footprints in the Sands of Time is an unusually large rock slab containing numerous reptile footprints that is reportedly 250 million years old. Video and exhibits describe how trackways are formed and studied, including field research and curation. Visitors can also view behind-the-scenes via windows cut into the fossil preparation lab and through to the center storage area, where students work on specimens.

Good-sized rock and mineral specimens, like geodes and petrified wood, abound, as do fossils such as mammoth molars, and fern imbedded in rock. Have your kids look at the rocks and ask them if they know the difference between a fossil and a mineral.

This museum is great for older kids who are interested in paleontology, or for younger ones to just see the sheer size of some of the animals from long ago. Hour-and-a-half long school/group tours are offered Monday through Thursday at 9:30am, with reservations, for second graders and up. Travel presentations are also available. Second through fourth graders can attend after school, junior paleontology classes. Day-long family fossil digs enable participants to prospect and collect fossils. Month-long research expeditions, which combine fossil collecting and camping, are available for high school students during the summer.

Hours: The museum is open Mon. - Fri., 8am - noon and 1pm - 4pm; Sat., noon - 3pm. It's closed July 4th, Sat., June through August, Thanksgiving weekend, and between Christmas Eve and New Year's day.

Admission: $3 for ages 5 and up; children 4 and under are free. Admission is free every Wed. Tours are $20 for up to 35 students.

Ages: 4 years and up.

RIPLEY'S BELIEVE IT OR NOT! MUSEUM (Hollywood)

(323) 466-6335 / www.ripleys.com

6780 Hollywood Boulevard, Hollywood

(Exit Hollywood Fwy [101] W. on Hollywood Blvd. [TG: 593 E4])

$$$

See the entry for RIPLEY'S BELIEVE IT OR NOT! MUSEUM (Buena Park) on page 247 for details. This museum displays nearly 300 unusual and amazing items and facts collected from around the world.

Hours: Open Sun. - Thurs., 10am - 10pm; Fri. - Sat., 10am - 11:30pm.

Admission: $10.95 for adults; $9.95 for seniors; $7.95 for ages 6 - 12; children 5 and under are free. Certain discounts are available through AAA.

Ages: 5 years and up.

SAXON AEROSPACE MUSEUM

(760) 762-6600 / www.rnrs.com/20MuleTeam

26922 Twenty Mule Team Road, Boron

(Exit Highway 58 S. on Boron Ave., R. on Twenty Mule Team Rd. The city of Boron is N.E. of Edwards Air Force Base.)

The F-4 fighter outside lets you know you've reached the right destination. The museum was built to look like a hangar and the artifacts inside all reflect aviation interests. There are several models, some experimental aircraft, a replica of the Voyager, a few computers with aeronautic programs, uniforms, lots of pictures, and other interesting exhibits to look at and learn about. Come for a tour or to explore it on your own. Just across the street is a small park with a roadside display that includes an antique fire engine. Make sure to visit the adjacent BORAX VISITOR CENTER, listed in the above entry.

Hours: Open daily, 10am - 4pm. Closed on some major holidays.

Admission: Free; donations appreciated.

Ages: 4 years and up.

SCORPION

(562) 435-3511 / www.queenmary.com

1126 Queens Highway, Long Beach

(Take Long Beach Fwy [710] S. to the end, R. on Queen's Way Bridge and follow the signs to the *Queen Mary*, as it is docked adjacent to the famous ship. [TG: 825 D3])

$$$$

Do your kids like to play spy? The 300-foot-long *Scorpion*, technically known as the Povodnaya Lodka B-427, is a Soviet-built, Foxtrot-class submarine that is docked here. In service for twenty-two years, it was once equipped with low-yield nuclear torpedoes. (That information alone makes it interesting to kids.) It was assigned mainly to gather intelligence on Allied naval activities. Now a tourist attraction, the *Scorpion* inspires spy game ideas, at least with my kids, as well as being a vessel of education and intrigue. Note: You may view the submarine, topside, without going on a tour.

Before you board, go into a holding room that contains labeled artifacts from the sub, such as an emergency escapes suit, flags, pressure gauges, manuals in Russian, and more. Get your feet wet, so to speak, by watching a thirteen-minute reenactment video on the history of the submarine and its "warriors beneath the waves."

Your actual tour inside the *Scorpion* is self-guiding, with a Russian-accented narration piped into each compartment. Begin by going down a narrow staircase to the forward torpedo room. The room contains six torpedo tubes and replicas of the warheads once loaded inside them. Then, think thin and squeeze through several porthole-style hatches, walk down narrow hallways, and look into (through glass-covered doorways) very small sleeping quarters, a control room, a dining room, the galley, and various other rooms. The tour has its own momentum as there is not a lot of room for the people behind you to pass. Visitors can peer through a periscope to the outside world, push the numerous buttons, and turn the wheels on board. My boys would have liked to stay down here for hours. Down another staircase is the engine room filled with gadgets that helped churn the water to power the sub. The last stop on your tour is the aft torpedo room which held four torpedoes. It is a relatively short tour for your money, but it is historic and fascinating.

Note that strollers aren't allowed on the *Scorpion*, nor may you carry children on the tour. If you get claustrophobic, this isn't the place to be. Ladies, stepping up through hatch openings and down narrow ladders doesn't lend itself to wearing dresses or heels.

See the entry for AQUARIUM OF THE PACIFIC (pg. 178), QUEEN MARY (pg. 114), SHORELINE VILLAGE (pg. 127), and AQUALINK (pg. 168) for attractions in the immediate vicinity.

Hours: Open daily, 10am - 6pm. Open in the summer daily, 10am - 9pm.

Admission: $10 for adults; $8 for seniors and military personnel; $9 for ages 3 - 11; children 2 and under are free. Parking is $3 for the first half hour, then it jumps to $8 for the day. Take a free Passport shuttle from downtown Long Beach to save on parking fees.

Ages: 4 years and up.

SHERIFFS MUSEUM

(562) 946-7081

11515 S. Colima Road, Whittier

(Going N. on Santa Ana Fwy [5], exit N. on Carmenita Rd., R. on Leffingwell, L. on Colima. Going S. on 5, exit E. on Imperial Hwy., L. on Colima. [TG: 707 E6])

This 5,000 square foot museum depicts the history of the Los Angeles County Sheriffs Department from 1850 through the present day. A classic 1938 Studebaker police car can not be touched, but kids can "ride" on the police motorcycle next to it and push a button to make the red lights flash. (I hope this won't bring back any bad memories!)

A western-style jail has a replica of a nineteenth-century sheriff's office, complete with a model sheriff and a prisoner behind bars. The Vice Exhibit showcases how different carnival-type games can be rip-offs, as well as illegal. The back room, which can be bypassed, contains a gun case, a display of gang weapons, and graphic scenes of some infamous cases. Other displays include items from and about the riot squad, the reserve forces, and regarding women in the department.

Another room contains an entire helicopter. It also has the side of a Search and Rescue helicopter mounted on a wall, with a dangling child mannequin being air-lifted in a basket. The live-video footage shows the awesome job that Search and Rescue teams perform. Ask about information on school tours, which are recommended for third grade and up.

Outside, a wall too filled with plaques memorializes officers killed in the line of duty. For your information, every May a memorial ceremony is held here that commemorates the lives of peace officers who have died in the line of duty in L.A. County in the past year. This moving ceremony, attended by numerous officers, families of slain officers, and government officials, is also open to the public.

Hours: Open Mon. - Fri., 9am - 4pm. Closed on major holidays.

Admission: Free

Ages: 5 years and up.

SKIRBALL CULTURAL CENTER

(310) 440-4500 / www.skirball.org

2701 N. Sepulveda Boulevard, Los Angeles

(Exit San Diego Fwy [405] W. on Skirball Center Dr. [TG: 591 F1])

This Cultural Center tells the story of the Jewish people, from post-biblical days and journeys, to present day life in America. The core exhibit, Visions and Values, features objects from the museum's permanent collection and traces the history, accomplishments, and values of the Jewish people over 4,000 years. Exhibits include ancient and modern artifacts, photographs, art, film, and video screenings all housed in a building beautifully designed with archways and high-ceilings. The variety of the unique Torah mantles and Hanukkah lamps on display is outstanding. One of our favorite menorahs has each of its eight branches fashioned like the Statute of Liberty.

The Liberty Gallery features a reproduction of the hand and torch of the Statue of Liberty at seventy percent of full scale. It's huge! This room also contains documents from past United States Presidents that supported non-discrimination. The Lincoln display has a lifemask of his face (i.e. a mold of his actual face), which is one of only six ever made.

Check out a free exploration kit, geared for ages 4 to 8, which contains games, books, related objects, and activity cards that motivate children to investigate the items in the galleries.

In the Discovery Center, geared for ages 8 and up, kids can uncover the wonders of the archaeological world. Upstairs is a re-creation of a dig site, a hands-on tool area, and a great computer game called "Dig It." The stairway is lined with lamps behind glass displays. The downstairs has a reproduction of a tomb in a rock; displays that show the new condition of an animal or object, and then its remains after years have gone by; and over twenty "discovery" game boxes containing great activities that reinforce the concepts presented. Kids can also learn about the history of writing and try different forms of it at the rubbing table. Students on school tours will gain a tremendous amount of insight into the archaeological world as docents teach and guide them through the Discovery Center. They'll also go outside where they can excavate roads, walls, an alter, and more, at a small mock dig site. Note that a new hall, an amphitheater, and a large children's area known as Noah's pArk are currently under construction.

Zeidler's is a full-service restaurant within the center that offers reasonable prices for lunch or afternoon coffee. Menu choices include pizza, pasta, sandwiches, omelettes, salads, fish, house-baked breads, and chocolate desserts.

As you enter and exit the Skirball Center you'll see, etched in stone, words fit for everyone - "Go forth . . . and be a blessing to the world." (Genesis 12: 1 - 3)

Hours: Open Tues. - Sat., noon - 5pm, Sun., 11am -5pm. Closed Mon.

Admission: $8 for adults; $6 for seniors and students; children 11 and under are free.

Ages: 7 years and up.

SOUTHWEST MUSEUM

(323) 221-2164 / www.southwestmuseum.org

234 Museum Drive, Highland Park

(Exit Pasadena Fwy [110] N.E. on Avenue 43, R. on Figueroa St., L. on Ave. 45, R. on Marmion Way, L. on Museum Dr. [TG: 595 B4])

There are three ways to enter this museum on a hill: One is an unadventurous walk up the driveway; another is walking up the steep Hopi trail, which is a stone stairway. Catch your breath at the top, and take a look at the view of the city and beyond. Up the hill a bit further is an archeological dig site. The third is walking (running) through a 250-foot tunnel - which echos every footstep and shout - burrowed into the museum hillside. It's lined with twenty dioramas depicting Indian life. From here, take the elevator up into the museum.

The Southwest Museum's vast collection represents Native American cultures from Alaska to South America. The two-story building has displays of Indian clothing, some of which are decorated with elk's teeth or bone; costumes; boots; beautifully beaded moccasins; an extensive collection of baskets; rabbit-skin blankets; weapons; turquoise and silver craft jewelry; early baby snugglies (cradleboards); musical instruments such as a flute, drum, and rattle; and Kachina dolls, which are supposedly rain-bringing spiritual beings. The exhibits are mostly behind glass. One room in the museum has an eighteen-foot Cheyenne tepee (just to look at), and a big rock with reproduced pictographs. Kids can crawl through a doorway (think dog door) that has photographs on the other side. Also on display in this room are headbands, arrowheads, bows, and rattles made of cocoons and rattlesnakes.

Rotating exhibits change once a year and focus on a particular part of the collection. We saw, for example, Spirit Horses, where the entrance of the exhibit was a simulated cave, with horses painted on its walls. The room contained statues of horses, paintings of horses, a mural of horses, beautiful saddles, and more - it embodied the American Indian legend that the horse is a spiritual gift of the gods.

How do you learn more about Native Americans? An extensive research library on the museum grounds is open to the public Wednesday through Saturday, 1pm to 5pm. If you're looking for a place to picnic, just drive north on Figueroa Street to Highland Park.

Hours: Open Tues. - Sun., 10am - 5pm. Closed Mon. and major holidays.

Admission: $6 for adults; $4 for seniors and students; $3 for ages 7 - 17; children 6 and under are free. (See C.E.E. L.A. for membership savings, page 86.)

Ages: 5 years and up.

S. S. LANE VICTORY

(310) 519-9545 / www.lanevictoryship.com

Berth 94, San Pedro

(Exit Harbor Fwy [110] or Vincent Thomas Bridge on Harbor Blvd. Cross Harbor Blvd. onto Swinford St. and follow signs to Berth 94. [TG: 824 D4])

This almost sixty-year-old ship served as a cargo ship during World War II, the Korean War, and the Vietnam War. The large Victory ship is not only seaworthy, but it is also a museum, with one-hour-plus tours given by retired merchant marines. We sensed adventure, though, and decided to explore the ship unaccompanied. (Small groups or individuals may do this.)

You and your kids will get ship-shape by climbing up and down ladders from the bridge and crew's quarters to the radio room, and into the huge engine room. The multi-level engine room is a bit spooky, with the noises and bulky machinery, but this added to the excitement of being on our own.

Guns and superstructures make the decks interesting to investigate. (Tell your kids that they are on a poop deck - it will make your outing a big hit!) Below deck, the ship's museum room features memorabilia such as flags, whistles, photographs, and cannons. The Gift Shoppe sells wonderful nautical items from clothing to medals to model ship kits. Batten down the hatches and be sure to wear tennis shoes for your ship-to-shore adventure.

Six times during the summer the S.S. Lane Victory hosts an all-day cruise to Catalina where a "Nazi spy" is discovered on board. Nazi fighters are soon attacking the ship, but American aircraft come to the rescue. The mock aerial dogfight uses blanks, but the World War II planes are real. This is more exciting than any Hollywood movie! The cruise also includes continental breakfast, live music, and a buffet luncheon. The cost is $100 for adults; $60 for kids 15 years and under.

Hours: Open daily, 9am - 4pm.

Admission: $3 for adults; $1 for ages 5 - 15; children 4 and under are free. Parking is free for the first hour.

Ages: 5 years and up.

TOURNAMENT HOUSE / THE WRIGLEY GARDENS

(626) 449-4100 / www.tournamentofroses.com

391 S. Orange Grove Boulevard, Pasadena

(Take Pasadena Fwy [110] N. to the end, where it turns into Arroyo Pkwy., L. on California, R. on Orange Grove. Going W. on Foothill Fwy [210], exit S. on Fair Oaks, R. on Colorado, L. on Orange Grove. Going E. on Ventura Fwy [134], exit E. on Colorado, R. on Orange Grove. [TG: 565 G5])

The Tournament House, more aptly referred to as a mansion, is used throughout the year as the meeting headquarters for committees, float sponsors, and practically everything else associated with the annual Tournament of Roses Parade. Once owned by Wrigley, of the chewing gum fame, each room is simply, but elegantly furnished. The downstairs contains a spacious living room, a library, meeting rooms, and the Eisenhower bathroom - so named because when the president was Grand Marshall, he got stuck in here and no one knew where he was, not even the Secret Service agents.

The second floor is interesting to kids who have some knowledge and interest in the Rose parade and Rose Bowl games. Each former bedroom is dedicated to various elements of Tournament of Roses' traditions. The Rose Bowl Room showcases pennants and football helmets from Rose Bowl teams, plus photographs, trophies, and other memorabilia dating back to the first game in 1902. The Queen and Court Room is femininely decorated to allow the reigning Queen and her Court, who attend over 100 events a year, a place to recuperate. A display case in here features past winners' crowns, tiaras, and jewelry. The Grand Marshall's Room shows photographs of past Grand Marshals like Bob Hope, Shirley Temple Black (do your kids know who she is?), Hank Aaron, Walt Disney, Charles Schultz, and others. Out in the hallway is an impressive 240-pound sterling silver saddle - heigh ho, Silver, away! The President's Room has pictures and other mementos of past presidents of the Rose Parade, plus models of the current year's winning floats. You are also invited to watch an interesting fifteen-minute behind-the-scenes film on how the floats and parade are put together.

The beautifully-landscaped grounds have a fountain surrounded by one of the rose gardens. Another huge rose garden at the north end also blooms seasonally.

Hours: Tours of the house are given February through August, on Thurs., 2pm - 4pm.

Admission: Free

Ages: 7 years and up.

TRAVEL TOWN

(323) 662-5874 / www.lacity.org

5200 W. Zoo Drive, Los Angeles

(Going N. on Golden State Fwy [5] or W. on Ventura Fwy [134], exit at Zoo Dr. and follow the signs. Going E. on 134, exit at Forest Lawn Dr., L. on Zoo Dr. Going S. on 5, exit S. on Western, L. on Victory Blvd. to Zoo Dr. It's north of the L. A. Zoo. [TG: 563 J4])

"All aboarrrrrd!" This wonderful outdoor "town" has a "trainriffic" atmosphere. There are real boxcars, a few cabooses, and some steam locomotives to climb into (but not on top of). A few of the trains, still on tracks, are located in an open pavilion for preservation purposes. Grassy areas invite you to rest (one can always hope), play, and/or picnic. A scaled model train takes you for a ride around the small town - $2 for adults; $1.50 for seniors; free for ages 18 months and under. Note that the museum is in the process of building train tracks from Travel Town to meet up with the Los Angeles Zoo.

Inside the buildings are old-fashioned carriages, wagons, and some period automobiles. It's tempting to touch the vehicles, but don't give in to temptation. Note: Live Steamers, located just west of Travel Town, offers free, twelve-minute rides through a part of Griffith Park on most Sundays from 11am to 3pm. Call (323) 662-8050 or (323) 661-8958 / www.lals.org for more information.

For a listing of other things to do in this area see AUTRY MUSEUM OF WESTERN HERITAGE (pg. 82), GRIFFITH PARK (pg. 48), GRIFFITH OBSERVATORY (pg. 92), and LOS ANGELES ZOO (pg. 183).

Hours: Open most of the year, Mon. - Fri., 10am - 4pm; Sat. - Sun. and holidays, 10am - 5pm. It's open one hour later in the summer. Closed Christmas.

Admission: Free; donations appreciated.

Ages: 2 years and up.

TWENTY MULE TEAM MUSEUM

(760) 762-5810 / www.rnrs.com/20MuleTeam

26962 Twenty Mule Team Road, Boron

(Exit Highway 58 S. on Boron Ave., R. on Twenty Mule Team Rd. The city of Boron is N.E. of Edwards Air Force Base.)

This small-town museum is built around its claim to fame - the Twenty Mule Team wagons. Beginning in 1883, these wagons were used for five years to haul borate ore 165 miles through the desert and rocky outcroppings, from Death Valley to the Mojave railhead. The museum displays the history of the surrounding area from the late nineteenth century up to the present day via enlarged photographs, a continuously running video, and four small rooms that contain artifacts. Some of the items on exhibit include samples of kernite and borate ore (components of Borax); mining equipment, such as replica scale mine cars, and caps that held candlesticks and lamps; models of planes tested at Edwards Air Force Base; clothing worn during the turn-of-the-century; and handcuffs and prison garb from the nearby federal prison.

Stroll around outside to see more exhibits, such as rusty agricultural and mining equipment, a large granite boulder with holes (because it was used for drilling contests), water pumps, an ore bucket, a surrey, and a miner's shack. There is also a shade area with a few picnic tables. Just across the street is a small park with a roadside display that includes an antique fire engine. Make sure to visit the adjacent SAXON AEROSPACE MUSEUM (see pg. 117) and the nearby BORAX VISITOR CENTER (pg. 83) listed in the above entry.

Hours: Open daily, 10am - 4pm. Closed on some major holidays.

Admission: Free; donations appreciated.

Ages: 4 years and up.

U.C.L.A. HAMMER MUSEUM

(310) 443-7000 / www.hammer.ucla.edu
10899 Wilshire Boulevard, Westwood
(Exit San Diego Fwy [405] E. on Wilshire. Park under the museum. [TG: 632 B3])

The fairly large Hammer art museum features an interesting array of paintings, sculpture, photographs, lithography, and graphic arts in its permanent and rotating exhibits. Impressionist and Post-Impressionist works include paintings by Monet, Pissarro, Cassatt, and Van Gogh. Samples from European old masters to more modern American artists are creatively displayed on the walls and sometimes, on the floors. Modern art is definitely intriguing, if somewhat baffling, to kids. Ask about guided tours and/or the variety of educational programs.

> **Hours:** Open Tues. - Wed., 11am - 7pm; Thurs., 11am - 9pm; Fri. - Sat., 11am - 7pm; Sun., 11am - 5pm. Closed Mon. and many major holidays.
> **Admission:** $5 for adults; $3 for seniors; ages 17 and under are free. Thursday is free admission day. Parking is $2.75 for the first three hours.
> **Ages:** 8 years and up.

VISTA DEL LAGO VISITORS CENTER

(661) 294-0219
Vista del Lago Road, Gorman
(Exit Golden State Fwy [5] on Vista del Lago. It is 20 miles north of Santa Clarita Valley and 12 miles S. of Gorman.)

Overlooking Pyramid Lake is a hexagon-shaped building showcasing California's liquid gold - water. This surprisingly interesting museum features many educational and interactive exhibits that show the State Water Project's water supply and delivery systems throughout California. Step on special scales in the first room and find out how much of your body is comprised of water (60%), and how much you actually weigh. Visual displays show the amount of water needed daily to grow and process food, manufacture household items, do laundry, and so on. Video presentations and information panels point out that although water is abundant in the north, most of the population is in the south, so we need ways to transport it down. Learn how water is treated before it is delivered to homes and how it is tested for quality. Thirsty yet? Go with the flow by playing the computer games and using the touch screens in each of the three display rooms. The theater room shows several short films, ranging from five to seventeen minutes, that present various aspects of water, for instance *Water for Farming*, *Save Water*, and *A Visit to the Feather River Fish Hatchery*. Educators take note: Not only can the videos be rented, but there is a lot of information given here on a field trip. Pamphlets, comic book-style booklets, teacher's guides, and lots more add to a guided tour of the facility.

The Visitors Center is a great place to quench your child's desire to learn about irrigation, flood control, and water conservation. Tip: After your visit here, enjoy the rest of the day at PYRAMID LAKE (see pg. 62), where you can boat, fish, swim, picnic, hike, and even camp.

> **Hours:** Open daily, 9am - 5pm. Closed New Year's Day, Thanksgiving, and Christmas.
> **Admission:** Free
> **Ages:** 4 years and up.

WELLS FARGO HISTORY MUSEUM

(213) 253-7166 / www.wellsfargohistory.com
Wells Fargo Center, 333 S. Grand Avenue, Los Angeles
(From Harbor Fwy [110], exit E. on 4th St., L. on Olive St., L. on 3rd St., R. on Grand. Going N. on Hollywood Fwy [101], exit S. on Grand. Going S. on 101, exit E. on Temple, R. on Grand. [TG: 634 F4])

Discover the Old West in the middle of downtown Los Angeles. The history and development of the West (and of Wells Fargo) is laid out like booty in this museum. Highlights include a 107-year old stagecoach, which kids may not climb on; a replica stagecoach, that they are welcome to climb in; a replica of an 1850's agent's office; a mining display with yes, real gold; a gold miner's rocker; a telegraph machine to try out; photographs; and a fifteen-minute film that depicts the hardships of a journey taken in 1852 from Omaha to San Francisco.

Buy a pan and some gold here so kids can try their hand at working a claim in their own backyard!

Hours: Open Mon. - Fri., 9am - 5pm. Closed bank holidays. Tours are available with advanced reservations and a minimum of fifteen people..

Admission: Free. Parking starts at $6 on Hope and 3rd Sts.

Ages: 4 years and up.

THE WESTERN HOTEL / MUSEUM

(661) 723-6260 / www.cityoflancasterca.org/visitors.htm

557 W. Lancaster Boulevard, Lancaster

(Going N. on Antelope Valley Fwy [14], exit N. on 20th St. West, R. on Ave. 'J', L. on 10th St. W., R. on Lancaster Blvd. Going S. on 14, exit E. on Ave. 'J', L. on 10th St. W., R. on Lancaster Blvd. [TG: 4015 H5])

This small, quaint Western Hotel/Museum has been restored to look like it did when it was originally built in the late 1800's, when room rentals were only $1 a day. The downstairs has a few bedrooms and a parlor that contains old furniture, a wheelchair, and a phonograph that belonged to the last owner, Myrtie Webber. Kids are interested in hearing some of the stories about her, and are impressed that she lived until she was 110 years old! (She doesn't look a day over 70 in her photographs.)

Upstairs is a room with antique clothing; one with a re-created turn-of-the-century schoolroom; another featuring Native American artifacts; and one that is Myrtie's bedroom, which displays some of her clothing and hats, along with her bedroom furniture. The highlight for my boys was seeing the vivid black-and-white pictures of jack rabbit hunts. The rabbits were hunted, corralled, and then clubbed to death. Although it is not a pretty sight, it is an interesting slice of Lancaster history.

Hours: Open Fri. - Sat., noon - 4pm.

Admission: Free

Ages: 4 years and up.

WESTERN MUSEUM OF FLIGHT

(310) 332-6228 / www.wmof.com

12016 S. Prairie Avenue, Hawthorne

(From the San Diego Fwy [405], exit E. on El Segundo, L. on Prairie. From the Glenn Anderson Fwy [105], exit S. on Prairie. It's in the Hawthorne airport, on the corner of Prairie and 120th. [TG: 733 D1])

A rendition of "Off we go, into the wild blue yonder, flying high into the sky. . ." goes through one's mind when visiting this museum. The Western Museum of Flight "houses" between twelve to fifteen rare planes like the YF23A, YF17, a Freedom Fighter, and an exact replica of the first controlled aircraft, an 1883 glider. Most of the planes are outside, braving the elements, although several are inside the hangar. The ones inside are in the process of being restored, so kids have the opportunity to see this process. Also in the hangar, which resembles a somewhat of a workshop, are displays of engines, model planes, medals, leather helmets and jackets, and other memorabilia from WWI and WWII. This museum is for the more serious students of flight. For those interested in doing aeronautical research, a library is available. Call for more details.

Hours: Open Tues. - Sat., 10am - 3pm.

Admission: $3 for adults; children 11 and under are free.

Ages: 6 years and up.

THE WHITTIER MUSEUM

(562) 945-3871 / www.whittiermuseum.org

6755 Newlin Avenue, Whittier

(Exit San Gabriel River Fwy [605] E. on Whittier Blvd., L. on Philadelphia, L. on Newlin. It's on the corner of Philadelphia and Newlin. [TG: 677 C6])

Journey back in time to the early days of Whittier, circa 1900. Stroll along a wonderfully re-created, full-size Main Street. The Victorian style is predominate in both the store and home fronts, and in the fully-furnished, walk-through rooms. A stereoscope and an old-fashioned stove and bathtub are some of our favorite items. Authentically-dressed mannequins all around make the visitors feel a part of this era.

The next few rooms feature an outhouse, a water pump that kids can actually try, photos, murals depicting early Whittier as a farming community, a tractor, old farm tools, and a model of an oil derrick. Sitting on old church pews, kids can watch a video that shows the history of Whittier. The transportation room has photos and an encased display of old medical instruments and medicine vials, plus a doctor's buggy, a racing plane, and a replicated front end of the historic Red Car. Walk up through the Red Car into the children's room filled with hands-on delights, such as old typewriters, adding machines, telephones, and a switchboard. There are also old-fashioned toys to play with and clothes for dressing up. The Library Room is an archival room housing documents on the history of Whittier. Upstairs is a large gallery room with changing exhibits. Call to see what's currently showing. Kids enjoy walking through history at this museum.

Hours: Open Sat. - Sun., 1pm - 4pm. Group tours are also given Tues. - Fri., by appointment.
Admission: Free
Ages: 4 years and up.

WILLIAM S. HART MUSEUM AND PARK

(661) 254-4584 - museum; (661) 259-0855 - park and camping / www.hartmuseum.org
24151 San Fernando Road, Newhall
(Take Golden State Fwy [5] N. to Antelope Valley Fwy [Hwy 14], exit W. on San Fernando Rd., approximately 1½ miles to the park, after the railroad tracks. [TG: 4640 J2])

William S. Hart was a famous western star of the silent films - a bit before my time. His Spanish, colonial-style home is now a museum. It is a short, but tough hike up a winding trail to reach the house/museum on the hill. Note: Seniors and physically disabled people can get a pass from the park ranger to drive up the side street to the house. The half-hour guided tour of his home is quite interesting, as the house is filled with western and Native American art and furnishings. Kids can look at, but not touch, the saddles, guns and other weapons, forty-pound buffalo coat, bear skin rug, stuffed buffalo head, paintings, and western movie memorabilia.

The park covers over 265 acres, with almost 110 acres set aside for wilderness area. A herd of American bison roam the grounds (which definitely adds to the Old West ambiance), within an enormous fenced-in enclosure. Many deer consider this area home, too. Hiking and nature trails through chaparral and woodland start behind the museum, and loop back around. Primitive camping is available here, too.

At the bottom of the hill, a large picnic area is located next to a grouping of bunk houses which contain period artifacts. A smaller picnic area is behind the on-site "farm." Purchase some animal feed to entice the barnyard animals - sheep, ducks, horses, burros, and cows - to come within petting distance. Note: See the adjacent HERITAGE JUNCTION HISTORIC PARK (pg. 94).

Hours: Hart park is open daily, 7am - sunset. The museum is open in the summer, Wed. - Sun., 11am - 3:30pm. It's open the rest of the year, Wed. - Fri., 10am - 12:30pm; Sat. - Sun., 11am - 3:30pm. Docent-led tours are given every half hour. The museum is closed New Year's Day, July 4th, Thanksgiving, and Christmas.
Admission: Free
Ages: All

WILL ROGERS STATE HISTORIC PARK

(310) 454-8212 / parks.ca.gov
1501 Will Rogers State Park Road, Pacific Palisades
(From Pacific Coast Highway [1], exit N. on Sunset Blvd., L. on Will Rogers State Park Rd. From San Diego Fwy [405], exit W. on Sunset Blvd., R. on Will Rogers State Park Rd. [TG: 631 C4])

"I never met a man I didn't like." These famous words were spoken by the "cowboy philosopher," actor, columnist, humorist, and philanthropist - Will Rogers. His ranch house was deeded to the state, and is now a museum. It has been left virtually unchanged from when he lived here in the late 1920's. The rustic, wood-beamed living room features many Indian blankets and rugs, saddles, animal skins, a longhorn steer head over the fireplace, a wagon wheel "chandelier," Western statues, Will's boots, and furniture. You'll also see his library/drawing room, upstairs bedrooms, and an office, which are all simply and comfortably furnished, and decorated with a western flair, of course.

The Visitors Center shows a free, continuously playing twelve-minute film on Will Rogers, featuring some of his rope tricks. Also available at no cost is an audio wand tour. Borrow a wand and place it at the several designated locations throughout the park, and it will tell you information about that area.

Picnic tables are plentiful at the park. The huge grassy area is actually a polo field. Games are held on weekends April through September. So come, have fun, learn a little history about a fascinating man, and if you feel like horsing around, watch a polo match.

There are several trails leading through the park that connect with its "backyard" neighbor, the huge TOPANGA STATE PARK (see pg. 70). One of the most popular hikes is the almost two-mile loop trail to Inspiration Point which, on a clear day, gives an inspirational, breathtaking view.

Hours: The park is open daily, 8am - sunset. Tours of the house are available every hour on the half hour from 10:30am - 4:30pm, staff and weather permitting. Note that the house is undergoing renovation and will re-open late 2004.

Admission: $5 per vehicle; $4 for seniors. House tours and polo matches are free.

Ages: 5 years and up.

ZIMMER CHILDREN'S MUSEUM

(323) 761-8989 / www.zimmermuseum.org
6505 Wilshire Boulevard, suite 100, Los Angeles
(From Santa Monica Fwy [10], exit N. on Fairfax Ave., L. on Wilshire Blvd. From San Diego Fwy [405], exit E. on Wilshire Blvd. It's on the ground floor of the Jewish Federation Building. [TG: 633 A2])

Shalom and welcome to this colorful, two-story, completely hands-on museum, developed for kids to have fun while learning about Jewish history, customs, values, holidays, folklore, traditions, heros, and music, as well as Shabbat, Israel, and the Hebrew language. Oy!

At the entrance is a giant, neo-lit Tzedakah pinball game. Children are given a choice of disks to insert symbolizing giving money, time, or of oneself (the latter disk is mirrored). Flick the puck up to the second floor and watch it come down pinball style. A Piper aircraft, with real cockpit controls and headsets where passengers can watch a video of a flight to and around Israel, and an airport waiting room are in the lobby. Some of the exhibits and things to do in the museum include a theater, complete with a dressing area, costumes, makeup tables and a blue screen backdrop so the video camera can superimpose children over a variety of locales; a mini version of the Jerusalem wall; a Geodesic dome that simulates outer space with a high-tech mock mission control center and astronaut costumes (see how well the kids can actually move in these!); a full-size ambulance parked outside the mini-hospital emergency room, which is complete with machinery and doctor's uniforms; and a main street with a kid-size home, synagogue, bookstore, cafe, park, puppet theater, and toddler play area.

A variety of family programs and workshops are offered throughout the year. School and group tours are welcome. The museum is wheelchair/stroller friendly.

Hours: Open Tues - Thurs., 12:30pm - 4pm; Sun., 12:30pm - 5pm. Closed Mon., Fri., Sat., national holidays, and Jewish holidays. Group tours are scheduled between 10am - 12pm on days when the museum is open.

Admission: $5 for adults; $3 for ages 3 - 12; children 2 and under are free. Grandparents are free when accompanied by a grandchild. Free parking is available on the west side of the building.

Ages: 2 - 12 years.

-----PIERS AND SEAPORTS-----

FISHERMAN'S VILLAGE

(310) 823-5411
13755 Fiji Way, Marina Del Rey
(Take Marina Fwy [90] to the end where it turns into the Marina Exwy, L. on Mindanao Wy., L. on Lincoln, R. on Fiji Wy. [TG: 702 B1])

This turn-of-the-century, New England-themed shopping, restaurant, and boating complex is located on the main channel of the Marina Del Rey harbor. It offers pier fishing and boat rentals. (See MARINA BOAT RENTALS on page 173.)

I still say the best things in life are free, or at least relatively inexpensive. It's fun just walking along the pier, looking at the boats, maybe grabbing a snack, and feeling the ocean breeze.

Hours: The Village is open Sun. - Thurs., 9am - 9pm; Fri. - Sat., 9am - 10pm.
Admission: Free. Two-hours of free parking with validation.
Ages: All

PORTS O' CALL VILLAGE

(310) 732-7696 / www.sanpedrochamber.com/champint/portcall.htm
Berth 77, San Pedro
(Exit Harbor Fwy [110] S. on Harbor Blvd. and follow the signs. [TG: 824 D6])

This picturesque, New England-style seaside village has over sixty shops and restaurants, something to please everyone. The meandering cobblestone pathways making it an interesting stroll (and bumpy stroller ride). Take a narrated tour of the L.A. Harbor, the busiest cargo terminal in the U.S. See the Transportation section for cruises that depart from Ports O' Call. Tip: The electric, green trolley has several stops in San Pedro and Ports O' Call is one of them. Take the trolley to LOS ANGELES MARITIME MUSEUM (see pg. 104), S. S. LANE VICTORY (see pg. 120), or around town. At 50¢, this is a fun, mini adventure. Another old-time mini adventure can be had by taking the replicated and the restored Red Cars, circa 1920 and 1940, up and down the boulevard. $1 per person allows unlimited boarding and reboarding throughout the day, and is good for riding the trolley, too.

Hours: Most shops are open daily, 11am - 6pm. Restaurants are open later in the evenings. Shops and restaurants are open longer in the summer. Closed Christmas.
Admission: Free, but bring spending money.
Ages: All

REDONDO BEACH INTERNATIONAL BOARDWALK / KING HARBOR / BEACH

(310) 374-3481 - marina; (310) 374-2171 - visitor's center / www.redondo.org; www.rbmarina.com
Where Torrance Boulevard meets the sea, Redondo Beach
(From San Diego Fwy [405], exit S. on Western, R. on 190th St., which turns into Anita St., L on Pacific Coast Highway, R. on Torrance. From Harbor Fwy [110], exit W. on Torrance. [TG: 762 H5])

This is no ordinary pier, but a fascinating place to explore with your family! Starting at the north end of the harbor, come hungry because enticing food smells waft through the air. Choose from egg rolls, gyros, hamburgers, or pizza as the international restaurants run the gamut from grab-a-bite to elegant. We munched as we watched the ducks and boats in the water, and soaked up the ambiance.

Stop off at Quality Seafood - it's like a mini sea-zoo with tanks of live crabs, lobsters, shrimp, and shellfish. You cannot entirely avoid the Fun Factory, which is a huge, under-the-boardwalk, amusement center. It is open daily and has over 200 video, arcade, and carnival-style games, plus kiddie rides, tilt-a-whirl, and other rides for all ages. All this adds up to a lot of noisy stimulus. Call (310) 379-8510 for more information. Come up for a breather and take a boat ride. See the Transportation section for information on cruises and watercraft rentals.

Back on the cement, horse-shoe shaped pier, have your kids look down at the various sea etchings, including blue whales and sting rays. Try your luck at fishing off the pier. The gift shops on the older, wooden boardwalk offer a variety of merchandise for sale. Check out the store Shark Attack. Not only does it sell shark teeth, sea shells, and more, but for an additional $1.50 for adults, $1 for kids 10 years and under, you can go past the curtain and see a sixteen-and-a-half foot, taxidermied, great white shark.

Last, but not least, there are rock jetties here. Deeming them fairly safe for the kids to walk on, my husband and I won the coveted, "You guys are the greatest!" award from our children. Ah, the simple pleasures.

This boardwalk and harbor area really extends outside of this immediate area. For instance, there are numerous restaurants to choose from, both in the marina confines and next "door" or within walking distance. Check out RUBY'S, a 40's diner (pg. 21), or Captain Kidd's, a fresh seafood waterfront restaurant with a "kidd's menu," plus Sea Gull Cafe, Tony's On the Pier, Chart House, Tasty Pastry Cafe, and many more. A two-mile stretch of beach, with fine sand, is adjacent to the pier and harbor. Veteran's Park, located just south of the pier on Catalina Avenue and Torrance Boulevard is a large, grassy park with plenty of trees, some picnic tables, and a great view of the ocean. Look for the nearby Whaling Wall. This incredible mural of the California gray whale, painted by marine artist, Wyland, decorates the massive wall of the Redondo Generating Station building located on Harbor Drive at Herondo Street. It's worth a drive by, or a stop and stare. And check out THE SEA LABORATORY (pg. 186) for a hands-on learning experience with an assortment of sea life.

Hours: Most restaurants are open daily for breakfast, lunch, and dinner. Most of the stores and attractions are open daily, 10am - 6pm; open later in the summer.

Admission: Parking is always 50¢ for each 20 minutes. During the summer, it's $5 maximum on weekdays; $7 maximum on weekends. During the rest of the year, it's $3 maximum on weekdays; $5 on weekends.

Ages: All

SANTA MONICA PIER

(310) 458-8900 / www.santamonicapier.org

$$

Foot of Colorado Boulevard, Santa Monica

(Exit Santa Monica Fwy [10] N. on 4th St., L. on Colorado Blvd. It dead-ends at the pier. Park on the pier or just around the corner at 1550 Pacific Coast Highway. [TG: 671 E3])

This renowned wooden pier offers a lot to do, including just soaking up the beach atmosphere. There are food stands, restaurants, and great shops that carry a little bit of everything. Peek in the fresh fish store as it has tanks of live lobsters, crabs, and other shellfish. Or, go fishing off the pier to catch your own fresh meal. Rent a pole for about $3 an hour at the bait and tackle shop at the end of the pier.

A major kid-attraction on the pier is PACIFIC PARK (see pg. 2). A food court is near the amusement park to service your tummy. A carousel is open Thursday through Sunday 11am to 5pm during the school year and open daily in the summer. Rides are $1 for adults; children 4 and under are free. The Playland Arcade draws kids like a magnet with its video and arcade games. A friendly warning: Weekends in the summer can be almost overwhelmingly crowded here.

Discover a place where touchable tidepool life is teeming under the boardwalk at the OCEAN DISCOVERY CENTER (pg. 184). Santa Monica beach offers plenty of long stretches of beach, great surf, and several playgrounds.

Feel like going for a ride? A twenty-mile bike path goes through Santa Monica; from the north at Wills Rogers State Beach to the south at Torrance Beach. If you forget your wheels, call Sea Mist Rentals at (310) 395-7076. They also have in-line skates and boogie boards for rent.

Hours: The stores are usually open year round, 10am - 6pm and open extended hours in the summer.

Admission: Free to the pier. Parking can be hard to find. Parking on the pier during the winter, "off season," is $3 for the first two hours, maximum $6. Parking during peak season is a $7 - $8 flat rate. Parking on P.C.H. is $6 Mon. - Fri.; $7 on the weekends.

Ages: 2 years and up.

SHORELINE VILLAGE

(562) 435-2668 / www.shorelinevillage.com

$

419 Shoreline Village Drive, Long Beach

(Take Long Beach Fwy [710] to the end, E. on Shoreline Dr., R. on Shoreline Village Dr. [TG: 852 D2])

This turn-of-the-century coastal "village" has specialty shops and places to eat, including Parker's Lighthouse Restaurant, which is a multi-story landmark lighthouse building on the water's edge. There are also the all-important candy stores and an ice cream shop. Catch a narrated harbor cruise via SPIRIT CRUISES - Long Beach (pg. 175) or rent a jet ski or kayak at OFFSHORE WATER SPORTS (pg. 174). Weekday mornings are a great time to enjoy serenity here. Stroll along the walkways and/or take the cement pathway all the way to the AQUARIUM OF THE PACIFIC (pg. 178), and even beyond to a grassy park. Catch a water taxi, or AQUALINK (see pg. 168), to the Aquarium, the QUEEN MARY (pg. 114), or SCORPION (pg. 117).

Hours: The stores are open daily, usually 10am - 9pm. Open extended hours in the summer.
Admission: Free. Parking is free for the first two hours with validation and a minimum $3 purchase. It is $1 for every half hour after that; $6 maximum.
Ages: 2 years and up.

-----POTPOURRI-----

ALLIED MODEL TRAINS
!/$

(310) 313-9353 / www.alliedmodeltrains.com
4411 S. Sepulveda Boulevard, Culver City

(Going S. on San Diego Fwy [405], exit on Washington Blvd., turn L. at the end of the off ramp, L. on Culver Blvd., R. on Sepulveda. Going N. on 405, exit N on Sawtelle Blvd., R. on Braddock Dr. It's on the corner of Sepulveda and Braddock. [TG: 672 F4])

Chug on over to the world's largest model railroad store to pick up anything one could possibly use or need for trains, tracks, villages, and other accessories. Allied caters to the casual hobbyist, the diehards, and everyone in between. Their stock includes ¼-inch-tall Z-gauge people, Thomas the Tank pieces, and collector's items costing thousands of dollars. We like to gaze at the multitude of marvelous displays. Streets, towns, even entire worlds (well, not quite) are on exhibit with working trains, lights, and animated scenes. Young kids may need to be lifted up to see some of them. If you aren't enamored with trains when you first come through the doors, I bet you'll at least be tempted to buy a layout by the time you leave.

Hours: Open Mon. - Thurs. and Sat., 10am - 6pm; Fri., 10am - 7pm. Closed Sun., except during Christmas when it's open noon - 5pm.
Admission: Technically, free.
Ages: 3 years and up.

BLUES SCHOOLHOUSE (Hollywood)

!/$$

(323) 769-4671 or (323) 848-5100 / www.hob.com/foundation
8430 Sunset Boulevard at the House of Blues, Hollywood

(From the Hollywood Fwy [101], exit W. on Sunset Blvd. From the Santa Monica Fwy [10], exit N. on La Cienega, R. on Sunset. [TG: 593 A5])

Three days a week this renown House of Blues music clubhouse is transformed into a Blues Schoolhouse. (For a description of the building, see GOSPEL BRUNCH (Hollywood) on page 16.) The three-hour class covers the history and evolution of the blues in a unique manner. The class begins on the third floor, with a description and look at the paintings out of mud, sculptures, stained glass, ceiling from a castle in England, carvings, collages using beads, murals, and other folk art that decorates the inside of this "house."

Next, at the main stage downstairs, two to three actresses present dramatic vignettes as they tell stories of the history of blues and incorporate music influenced by the blues. They act out, talk, and play music that has to do with the history of Africa; spirituals; the slave trade, from kidnaping to selling to emancipation, including work and freedom songs; the Jazz Age; and causes (and cures) for racism. We were immersed in the events. Kids then get in the act with miming inventions created by African Americans, such as the roller coaster and ticket dispensers.

The last hour concludes with a live band performance. The band plays samples of all the music that has been influenced by the blues including jazz, rock 'n' roll, rap, hip-hop, call and response, rhythm and blues, and even country. Toe-tapping, hip-hopping, interactive and educational fun - what a great way to learn!

Notes: Call in the spring to book for the fall; call in the fall to book for the spring. Curriculum guides are available. School assemblies are a project in the works. You may stay for lunch at the restaurant which is open daily, 11:30am to 4:30pm, for the cost of lunch. This mid-day meal menu includes seafood gumbo ($4.25 a bowl), Cobb salad ($8.95), blackened chicken sandwich ($7.50), burger ($6.95), and Cajun catfish tortilla wrap

($7.50), plus a variety of desserts. Note: Another Blues Schoolhouse / House of Blues location is in Anaheim.

Hours: Offered August through June (not during the summer), Tues., Wed., and Thurs., 9am to noon.

Admission: Free to public school students and non-profit youth organizations. The cost for a private group is $700 for up to 100 students.

Ages: 5th through 12th graders.

BUILD-A-BEAR WORKSHOP (Glendale)

(818) 545-9842 - local; (877) 789-BEAR (2327) - national / www.buildabear.com

2225 Glendale Galleria, Glendale

(Exit Golden State Fwy [5] E. on Colorado St. Galleria is on Colorado and Central Ave. The shop is on lower level, next to Nordstrom. [TG: 564 D5])

See the entry for BUILD-A-BEAR WORKSHOP (Newport Beach) on page 250 for details.

Hours: Open Mon. - Fri., 10am - 9pm; Sat., 10am - 8pm; Sun., 11am - 7pm.

BUILD-A-BEAR WORKSHOP (Hollywood)

(323) 461-6105 - local; (877) 789-BEAR (2327) - national / www.buildabear.com

6801 Hollywood Boulevard, suite 200, Hollywood

(Going N. on Ventura Fwy [101], exit W. on Hollywood. Going S. on 101, exit S. on Highland Ave. [170], R. on Hollywood. In Hollywood and Highland, on the 2nd level. [TG: 593 E4])

See the entry for BUILD-A-BEAR WORKSHOP (Newport Beach) on page 250 for details.

Hours: Open Sun. - Thurs., 10am - 7pm; Fri. - Sat., 10am - 10pm.

BUILD-A-BEAR WORKSHOP (Los Angeles)

(310) 446-3290 - local; (877) 789-BEAR (2327) - national / www.buildabear.com

10800 W. Pico Boulevard at Westside Pavilion, Los Angeles

(Exit San Diego Fwy [405] E. on Santa Monica Blvd., R. on Westwood Blvd. The mall is on corner of Westwood and Pico. Or, exit Santa Monica Fwy [10] N. on Overland Ave. The mall is on corner of Overland and Blythe Ave. The workshop is on the 2nd level near the security desk. [TG: 632 D6])

See the entry for BUILD-A-BEAR WORKSHOP (Newport Beach) on page 250 for details.

Hours: Open Mon. - Fri., 10am - 9pm; Sat., 10am - 8pm; Sun., 11am - 6pm.

CAMERA OBSCURA

(310) 458-8644

1450 Ocean Avenue at Palisades Park, Santa Monica

(Exit Santa Monica Fwy [10] N. on 4th St., L. on Colorado Blvd., R. on Ocean. It's on the corner of Broadway, in front of the Santa Monica Pier. Metered street parking. The entrance to the Camera Obscura is through the Senior Recreation Center. (You'll need to leave a form of ID to use the key to the camera room.) [TG: 671 E2])

A visit to the Camera Obscura takes just a little longer than it takes to snap a picture, but not much. The Camera's building design involves a revolving metal turret that pokes through the roof of the building with a mirror inside the turret angled at forty-five degrees. The outside surrounding city street and beach scene is reflected through a convex lens down onto a large circular table screen. Artists and drafts people have used this type of camera in years past to sketch landscapes. The bottom line is that kids can see a 360-degree view of the outside world and learn how a camera operates by (kind of) being inside one. Tips: 1) Come on a sunny day as the Camera Obscura depends on sunlight to work effectively, and 2) turn off the light in the small viewing room!

Palisades Park is a long, grassy park above the beach, with a paved pathway that parallels the beach. The park is popular with both joggers and transients.

Hours: Open Mon., 9am - 2pm; Tues. - Fri., 9am - 3pm; Sat. - Sun., 11am - 3pm.

Admission: Free

Ages: 6 years and up.

CATALINA ISLAND
(310) 510-1520 - Visitors Bureau / www.catalina.com
Across the water!
([TG: 5923 H4])

    ☼
    $$$$

Catalina Island is a resort in the truest sense of the word. It's twenty-one miles long, eight miles wide, 85% natural (meaning development is only allowed on 15% of the land), only twenty-two miles from the mainland, and packed with all sorts of things to see and do. The city of Avalon has an abundance of shops and restaurants along the beach and harbor, and all within walking distance of each other. (It's a only one-square mile.) Come to Catalina to fish in the deep blue sea; take a glass bottom boat ride; go horse-back riding, hiking, or camping on the untamed side of the island; take an Island safari, where kids thrill at seeing real buffalo; or just enjoy the beach and all the water activities, such as swimming, snorkeling, and canoeing. There are two main beaches in Avalon - the long strip in front of the main harbor, and Descanso Beach Club, which is a short walk away on the other side of the Casino. The latter beach costs $1 per person admission. Kayak rentals are available here. Catalina has a quaint ambiance and is a wonderful family day trip or weekend excursion. I highly recommend ordering the Visitors Guide as it has all the information you could possibly want about Catalina. (Contact the Visitors Bureau at the above number to order it.) The following information covers many of the main attractions and a few of the minor ones:

How much time you have in Catalina will dictate what you should do. Consider taking a tour or two as you'll see more of the island. Both Catalina Adventure Tours, (310) 510-2888 / www.catalinaadventuretours.com and Discovery Tours, (800) 322-3434 / www.scico.com, offer numerous and diverse tours at comparable prices. The following prices are quoted from Adventure Tours, unless otherwise stated. Get acquainted with Catalina by taking a forty-five-minute, narrated **city tour** to see the Wrigley estate, the city streets, and an unparalleled view of the harbor while hearing about Catalina's history - $11 for adults; $10 for seniors; $6 for children ages 2 to 11. Note: Children's admission prices are for ages 2 to 11, unless otherwise stated. A longer city tour includes a stop at the **Botanical Garden and Wrigley Memorial** - a nice spot to walk along the pathways - $26 for adults; $23 for seniors; $13 for children. During the **two-hour inner island bus tour** you'll see canyons to coastlines, plus wild bison and maybe wild turkeys and foxes. A stop at Airport-in-the-Sky is good for stretching your legs, watching small planes land and take-off, trying a buffalo burger at the Buffalo Springs Station, and visiting the (free) Nature Center, (310) 510-0954. This tour costs $26 for adults; $23 for seniors; $13 for children. One of my favorite Discovery Tour options is the **four-hour Inland Motor narrated bus tour**, which includes seeing the inner island, wild bison, and a visit to the Airport-in-the-Sky (all of the two-hour tour listings), plus a stop at the Pacific side of Catalina (a beach overlook), and at El Rancho Escondido, where refreshments and an Arabian horse performance are part of the deal - $44.50 for adults; $40 for seniors; $22.50 for kids.

There are several cruise and water taxi options, at about $4 per person, if you want to see Catalina from the water. The two tour companies also offer forty-minute, narrated **glass-bottom boat rides**, which are *clearly* one of the best ways to see the many varieties of fish and underwater gardens off the coast of Catalina. Aboard the Sea View, via Adventure Tours, you can even feed fish through specially designed tubes and watch the feeding frenzy. (It's just like the dinner table at home!) Night excursions are also available. Prices for the Sea View glass-bottom boat tour are $10 for adults; $9 for seniors; and $6 for children. The Nautilus is a forty-five minute **semi-submersible sub** ride offered by Adventure tours where visitors use the fish food torpedoes as entertainment and education. A sub ride is $30 for adults; $27 for seniors; and $15 for children. Both companies also have forty-five-minute boat rides out to **Seal Rock**, where seals sunbath, bark, and are just plain fun to watch. Admission is $12 for adults; $11 for seniors; $6 for children. Don't miss the amazing Discovery Tours **nighttime flying fish tour**, where yes, the fish really do "fly" across the water as the light from the boats hits and scares them. Excursions cost $19.50 for adults; $17.50 for seniors; $9.75 for children. Combo tour packages are available for all of the above. Our absolute favorite combo is the **Sundown Isthmus Cruise** with Discovery Tours. The four-hour trip combines a cruise out to Two Harbors, which is on the other side of the island, with an hour stop over at the beach. You may walk the beach or eat dinner at the restaurant or eat a picnic dinner that you packed. The Flying Fish "tour" happens on the way back! The cost is $47.25 for adults; $42.50 for seniors;

and $23.75 for children.

There are a myriad of other water activities to choose from, too, besides the obvious choice of swimming. Ocean Rafting Trips, (800) 990-RAFT (7238) / www.catalinaoceanrafting.com, offers numerous **half-day and full-day voyages** to explore coves, beaches, and sea caves. A half-day voyage, which includes snorkeling, is $89 per person. Take a **guided kayak excursion** with Catalina Island Expeditions, (310) 510-1226 / www.kayakcatalinaisland.com. For instance, a two-hour guided tour, which is really a natural history field trip, is two-plus miles of kayaking - $35 for adults; $26.25 for children 11 years and under. There is an abundance of other options, including classes for kids and kayak trips that include snorkeling. **Parasailing**, (310) 510-1777 / www.parasailingcatalina.com, offers the thrill of flying - ten minutes air time - for $59 per person. The flying and boat ride take about an hour total. Additional, non-flying passengers in the boat are $10 each. The ultimate experience for staying dry while in the water is the **Seamobile Submarine**, available June through October. This two-person submarine has a bubble-like top for a 360 view underwater. A diver, outside the vessel, narrates and steers the sub, although riders can maneuver somewhat, too, with a joystick. The hour-long voyage includes a half hour actually under the water. Two people must go on each ride and the cost is about $125 per person. Call (877) 252-6262 or (909) 626-6262 / www.seamagine.com for more information.

Dryer, land activities are fun, too! Go on a guided **horseback ride** via Catalina Stables, (310) 510-0478, through the mountains to see the unspoiled countryside, and a great view of Avalon. Children must be at least 8 years old. A one-hour-and-fifteen-minute ride is $52. Get it in gear and rent a **bike** at Brown's Bikes, (310) 510-0986, to explore the island. Take an open **jeep tour** of the rugged inland with Jeep Eco-Tours, (310) 510-2595, starting at $98 per person for a three-hour ride, minimum two people per ride. Play a beautiful and challenging **miniature golf** course at Golf Gardens, (310) 510-1200 - $6.50 for adults; $4 for children 7 years and under. There are two other noteworthy short stops: The small **Catalina Island Interpretive Center**, (310) 510-2514, which has mostly pictorial and informational displays, plus rocks that were found on the island. A marine mural contains buttons to push to listen to whale sounds and a large kelp mural has text. The Center is open Tuesday through Sunday, 10am to 4pm, and admission is free. The **Catalina Island Museum**, (310) 510-2414, is located in the famous Casino building. (If you take a tour of the building, admission to the museum is included). The museum has a wall with trophy fish such as Marlin, a few models of ships, old switchboards, and informational and photographic displays of the island's history. It's open Friday through Wednesday (closed Thursday) 10am to 4pm. Admission is $2.50 for adults; $1.50 for seniors; $1 for children 5 to 11 years old.

To really get away from it all, explore Catalina by **hiking** and/or **camping**. Off-season camping, mid-November through March, is $6 per person at all the campgrounds. On-season camping, April through mid-November is $12 for adults; $6 for ages 2 to 11 per night at all the campgrounds. A two-three night stay is required on certain weekends and holidays. Cabins that sleep up to six people are available at Two Harbors Campground and at Hermit Gulch in Avalon. Cabins are $40 a night. Refreshing seaside camping is available at Two Harbors Campground, which is a quarter-mile from the small town of Two Harbors. The town is at the isthmus, down the coast quite a bit from Avalon. It's like being in another part of the world. This is a popular camping site because of its accessibility and water activities, such as kayaking and snorkeling. Two Harbors also has a snack bar, general store, and restaurant; an eleven-room B&B in an historic building (call [310] 510-2800 for information); and the Wrigley Marine Science Center ([310] 510-0811). The center is a marine lab open on weekends for tours. It includes visits to touch tanks and demonstrations of the staff feeding moray eels. Ask about snorkeling in the cove here. For your information, a two-hour bus drive from Avalon to Two Harbors is $20 one way for adults; $14 for children. Parson's Landing Campground is remote, located at the complete opposite end of the island from Avalon. An optional extra $9 is charged for firewood and water. It is beautiful, and suitable for older kids who like to backpack. Little Harbor Campground is on the other side of the island from Avalon. The campground is near two sandy beaches under small, but somewhat shady, palm trees. It is accessible by taking a shuttle bus. Blackjack Campground is situated among a grove of pine trees, away from the water toward the interior of the island. It's for hardy campers. The surrounding area is great for hiking. Hermit Gulch Campground is the only campground in the city of Avalon. This is getting-away-from-it-all camping, but not too far away. Reservations are always recommended, and are necessary in July and August. For more information regarding campgrounds, for reservations, and to inquire about equipment rental (i.e. tents and such), call Santa Catalina Island Company at (888) 510-7979 / www.scico.com/camping.

Another way to visit Catalina is via a five-day **Volunteer Vacation**, where campers participate in the ecological restoration of the island and enjoy its beauty. Large tents, padded bunks, hot showers, dinner, and an outdoor kitchen are provided. Ages 12 years and up may participate when accompanied by a parent. The cost is $115 per person. Call (310) 510-2595 for more information.

Note: Catalina's busiest season is the summer. September, however, provides balmy weather and travel discounts.

Channel crossing time takes anywhere from one to two hours, depending on the point of departure and type of boat. Some numbers to call for cruise information, with various points of departure, are: *Catalina Express*, (800) 315-7925 or (800) 9201 / www.catalinaexpress.com - departing from Dana Point for an hour-and-a-half cruise has admission of $44.50 for adults, $40.50 for seniors; $34 for ages 2 to 11; $3 for infants under 2. Departing from Long Beach or San Pedro Harbor for an hour cruise, admission is $42 for adults; $38 for seniors; $32.50 for ages 2 to 11; $3 for infants under 2. All-day parking is $7 - $9. *Catalina Passenger Service*, (949) 673-5245 / www.catalinainfo.com, departs from Balboa in Newport Beach. The hour-and-fifteen-minute cruise costs $37 for adults; $34 for seniors; $21 for ages 3 to 12; $3 for children 2 years and under. All-day parking is $7. *Catalina Explorer*, (877) 432-6276 or (949) 5308 / www.catalinaexplorerco.com departs from Dana Point or Long Beach for $38 for adults; $34.50 for seniors; $28 for ages 3 - 11; $5 for children 2 years and under. Parking is about $7 for the day. The Explorer also goes to Two Harbors on Catalina. If time is of the essence, take a fifteen-minute helicopter ride with *Island Express Helicopter Service*, (310) 510-2525 / www.islandexpress.com, which departs from Long Beach or San Pedro - $68.86 one way for all ages; children under 2 ride free on a parent's lap. Once on the island, you'll need to walk fifteen minutes to get to town, or take a taxi which costs about $6.50 for two people.

Admission: Prices given above.
Ages: All

CERRITOS LIBRARY
(562) 916-1350 / www.ci.cerritos.ca.us
18025 Bloomfield Avenue, Cerritos
(Exit San Gabriel River Fwy [605] E. on South St., L. on Bloomfield. [TG: 767 A1])

This is one of the coolest libraries in Southern California. From the titanium exterior to the fanciful fountains outside - enhanced by oversized fake flowers and a dolphin that looks ready to swim away - to the "extras" inside, this is the place to read, learn, and let imaginations soar.

Inside the library is a large wall aquarium filled with colorful tropical saltwater fish, and sharks! Ask when a scuba diver will next be inside the tank to clean it. The diver is usually wearing an underwater microphone so he can communicate with spectators. Enter into the amazing children's library through enormous model books placed over the archway. There are over 80,000 kids' books and rows of computer cubicles. Special reading nooks are decorated with large fake rocks and plants. One nook has a lighthouse and a little wooden pier. Other intriguing elements in this huge room include constellations on a dome-shaped ceiling; a life-size T-Rex skeleton on a rock watching over a puzzle table (ever feel like someone is looking over your shoulder?); a scale model of a NASA space shuttle; and a large (fake) Banyan tree that's accompanied by piped in rain-forest sounds. Towards the back is an art area has ready-to-do art projects and a geology wall with 3-D layers of rock formations. A corner theater has walls that contain three portholes showing fish videos. Learning should always be this entertaining! Pick up a brochure or ask about the numerous programs that the library offers including reading programs, performances, arts and crafts classes, and tours.

The rest of the multi-story library is almost equally exciting. There is a multimedia presentation room; a circulation desk built to resemble a time machine; a small, elegant reading room across from the children's library with a holographic fire; a very small local history museum; and a gift shop - and that's just the first floor. Upstairs are computer stations, reading rooms, and more books.

Hours: Open Mon. - Fri., 10am - 9pm; Sat., 9am - 5pm; Sun., 1pm - 5pm. Closed most major holidays.
Admission: Free. Residents can check out books for free; non-residents must pay $100 for a library card.
Ages: 3 years and up.

CHALLENGER LEARNING CENTER (Carson)

(310) 243-2627 / www.csudh.edu/clc/info.htm; www.challenger.org

1000 E. Victoria Street, at California State University Dominguez Hills, Carson

(Exit Artesia Fwy [91] S. on Avalon Blvd., L. on Victoria St. [TG: 764 E2])

What did you want to be when you grew up? I'm sure that you, or someone you knew, wanted to be an astronaut, at least once while deciding on a career. The Challenger Center, established in memory of the Challenger crew and sponsored by NASA, allows students the opportunity to live out this dream, while stationed on earth, of course.

Participants solve problems and make decisions at the realistic, mock space station via real computer consoles, communication headsets, continuous messages on the loud speakers, electronic messages, teammates they can sometimes only see on video monitors, and emergency sounds and flashing lights. Working together, the mission specialists (that's their official name) become a part of one of eight teams, critical to the running of a successful mission. Some of the teams are navigation, which uses star charts to locate celestial objects in the star fields and control lunar landings; probe, which gathers data via a probe to relay data for analysis; isolation, which uses robots to handle "hazardous" chemicals and conduct tests, and workers who wear gloves to reach into the glass dome "box" to maneuver and pick up objects; life support, which monitors and repairs spacecraft's water, air, and electricity; and data team, which transmits diagrams and info through a computer link.

There are several ways to participate in a mission. Families can call for information on weekend missions. Simulations are offered for birthday parties and for school groups. For the latter, the center provides several weeks worth of curriculum, including a mandatory day-long teacher workshop, that culminates in a two-hour, hands-on, simulated space mission inside a "spacecraft" and Mission Control room. The center also offers *challeng*ing, week-long summer camps. Let your space pioneer help explore the final frontier! Note: Also see CHALLENGER LEARNING CENTER (San Diego) (pg. 440) for another Southern California location.

Hours: Call to make a reservation. Missions are offered Mon. - Fri., for school groups; weekends for all others.

Admission: $500 per class of 24 - 36 students. Ask for prices for other missions.

Ages: 6th - 12th graders.

CHINATOWN

N. Broadway Street, Los Angeles

(Going N.W. on Hollywood Fwy [101], exit N. on Alameda, L. on Alpine, R. on Broadway. Going S.E. on 101, exit N. on Broadway. [TG: 634 G2])

Instead of digging a hole to China, hop in the car and drive to Chinatown. Walk along North Broadway to meander through the red and gold decorated stores here (faux palace architecture), or immerse yourself in this Far East experience by entering the pedestrian plaza through a large Chinese-style gate with a sign that announces "Chinatown." (This entrance is just past College Street.) Take along a few coins to toss at the wishing well inside that has signs directing you to throw your money at appropriate desires: love, health, wealth, etc. (And may all your wishes come true!)

Among the open air booths, small stores tucked away, and stores with neon signs, your kids will see touristy stuff as well as authentic Chinese items. You'll find Chinese-style silk dresses, fortune cookies (which did not originate in China), whole barbecued ducks hanging in windows, robes with beautiful embroidery, chopsticks, jewelry, dragon statues, toys, and lots, lots more. The herb shops are fascinating, and many people swear by the concoctions. The bakeries are tantalizing. Hungry for something more substantial? Give your taste buds (and stomach) a surprise by trying ostrich, fried large intestines, or other unusual fare. Or, stop in at the GOURMET CAROUSEL RESTAURANT (pg. 16). Enjoy your cultural adventure!

Hours: Most stores are open daily, 10am - 6pm, or so.

Admission: Free, but bring spending money.

Ages: All

CIRCUS VARGAS

(760) 248-6801 / www.circusvargas.com

The circus is in town! Appearing at a city near you throughout the year is Circus Vargas, a predominantly California circus. With all the bells and whistles and clowns and animals associated with the excitement of a Big Top, this two-hour show produces terrific family entertainment. See an elephant, tigers, cats, and dogs perform tricks. Watch incredible acrobats, jugglers, daring trapeze artists, and clever and silly clowns in the extravaganza. Join 2,000 other guests around one ring (that's the European style) to laugh and to be in awe. Other activities include a petting zoo, pony rides, and on opening day, a free backstage tour for kids.

Hours: Call for dates and times.

Admission: Tickets run from $13 - $30 for adults; $6 - $17 for ages 2 - 11; children under 2 are free. Note: Check on-line for discount coupons.

Ages: 1 year and up.

EL PUEBLO DE LOS ANGELES HISTORICAL MONUMENT / OLVERA STREET

$$$

(213) 628-1274 / www.cityofla.org/elp

125 Paseo de la Plaza #400, Los Angeles

(Going N.W. on Hollywood Fwy [101], exit N. on Alameda, L. on Paseo de la Plaza. Going S.E. on 101, exit N. on Los Angeles St., which turns into Paseo de la Plaza. [TG: 634 G3])

This attraction is not a single monument, but the oldest part of the city of Los Angeles. It contains twenty-seven historic buildings, eleven of which are open to the public, and four of those are restored as museums. A traditional Mexican-style plaza and Olvera Street are also here. Tip: Read up a little on the history of this area, as it will make your visit here more meaningful.

The circular plaza is the central hub and has some interesting statues to look at. Usually a docent is on hand giving out maps and other information. Across the way is the **Firehouse Museum**. Inside is a restored, old fire engine that was once hooked up to a horse and a few other pieces of fire-fighting paraphernalia. The walls are decorated with different fire hats.

Olvera Street is one of the oldest streets in Los Angeles. In 1930 it was closed to through traffic and reborn as a Mexican marketplace. It is very commercial and a definite tourist attraction, but it still conveys the flavor of old Mexico. Enjoy a walk down the brick-paved "street" to look at the colorful displays, watch a glassblower at work, see candles being dipped, hear strolling mariachi bands, and munch on bakery goods. There are inexpensive and expensive Mexican handicrafts to purchase both inside the stores and at the center stalls. Note: Kids love the variety of candy that is conveniently placed at their grabbing level.

Olvera Street offers four full-service restaurants. A favorite one is La Luz del Dia, located toward the entrance, because the food is good and kids can climb the ornately tiled steps and peer into the kitchen to see tortillas being made by hand.

The Sepulveda House is a few doors down from the entrance on the west side of Olvera Street. You can also enter it from Main Street. It has an encased display of Mrs. Sepulveda's bedroom, and her kitchen as it appeared in the late 1800's. Inside a curtained room is an eighteen-minute film, *Pueblo of Promise* about the early history of Los Angeles. (My kids actually watched and enjoyed the movie.) It contains books, a small gallery around the corner with some interesting artifacts from the area, and a mural by a renown Latino artist.

The Avila Adobe is located almost directly across from the Sepulveda House. This is the city's oldest building, constructed in 1818. It has rooms to walk through that reflect the style of a wealthy ranch owner in the 1840's. Some of the more interesting items include a child's bed that used rope and cowhide instead of box springs, a wooden bathtub, and a Chinese shawl that was used as a bedspread. The Courtyard, a packed-dirt patio, was used as a kitchen because most of the cooking was done outside. We enjoyed the side trip here, and learned a little along the way.

The Visitors Center, located on Olvera Street, offers two types of tours. One is a free, one-hour guided walking tour of the highlights of El Pueblo Monument. Best suited for ages 10 years and up, it is offered Tuesday through Saturday at 10am, 11am, and noon. Reservations are required for groups, but not for individuals. The second tour is a four-hour guided bus tour, for a minimum of fifteen people, maximum of fifty. For $10 per person, and a very comfortable bus, the tour covers the central city and points of historic interest. Stops along the way depend on the docent giving the tour. It starts at 10am on the first and third Wednesdays of each month. Reservations are required.

As you walk around this historic area, enjoy soaking up the atmosphere of a different country while so close to home! Tip: Consider taking the train from your area to Union Station, which isn't too far away from Olvera Street.

Hours: Olvera Street is open daily in the summer, 10am - 10pm. Open the rest of the year, 10am - 7pm. The Sepulveda House is open Mon. - Sat., 10am - 3pm. The Avila Adobe is open daily, 9am - 5pm. The Firehouse Museum is open Tues. - Sun., 10am - 3pm.

Admission: The entrance to everything is free. Parking is available at a number of lots that charge between $5 - $10 for the day. The one on Main St., between Hope and Arcadia, charges $8 for the day. Some of them are quite a walk to the plaza.

Ages: 3 years and up in general; 7 years and up for the tours.

FOREST LAWN MEMORIAL PARK (Glendale)

(800) 204-3131 or (323) 254-3131 / www.forestlawn.com
1712 S. Glendale Avenue, Glendale
(Exit Golden State Fwy [5] N. on Glendale Ave., which turns into Brand Blvd., R. on San Fernando Rd., L. on Glendale Ave. [TG: 594 E1])

Most of the Forest Lawn Memorial parks have outstanding works of art, including beautiful works of stained glass. Tip: Pick up a map at the entrance. The Great Mausoleum at this park contains Leonardo da Vinci's Last Supper re-created in stained glass, as well as replicas of Michelangelo's La Pieta and Moses. Please note that many of the statues are naked. The larger-than-life replica of David is on the grounds, as are other statues and a huge mosaic titled, Signing of the Declaration of Independence.

Make sure to visit the Hall of Crucifixion/Resurrection. A twenty-two-minute "show" features an audio presentation of Christ's last days on earth, complete with various voices, sound effects, and a narrator. As the dramatic story is told, a spot light shines on parts of one of the largest religious oil paintings ever created, a 45-foot by 190-foot painting titled *Crucifixion*. At the end, the picture is seen in its entirety. The *Resurrection* painting, a close runner up in size and impact at 51-foot by 70-foot, is also highlighted in the same manner during the re-telling.

Next door, an on-site museum contains stained glass pictures, coins mentioned in the Bible, statues, medieval armor, and an art gallery with exhibits that rotate every three months. Through the Adventures in Art Program, a variety of educational and artistic films, hands-on workshops, and sometimes interactive storytelling accompany each of the art exhibits. Did you ever think there could be so much history and art at a mortuary? Also, ask about the audio art tours where you borrow a cassette (for free) and take a self-guided tour around the park to learn about the art and architecture. Note: See the Calendar entry for Visit with Michelangelo and Leonardo Da Vinci (pg. 571), Forest Lawn's terrific, free History Comes Alive programs.

Hours: The museum is open daily, 10am - 5pm. The Crucifixion/Resurrection paintings and show can be seen daily on the hour, 10am - 4pm. The curtain covering The Last Supper stained glass is raised on the half-hour.

Admission: Free, although $1 donation per adult is requested for the Crucifixion/Resurrection "show."

Ages: 7 years and up.

FOREST LAWN MEMORIAL PARK (Hollywood Hills)

(800) 204-3131 or (818) 241-4151 / www.forestlawn.com
6300 Forest Lawn Drive, Los Angeles
(Exit Ventura Fwy [134] S. on Forest Lawn Dr. It's W. of Griffith Park. [TG: 563 E5])

A cemetery might seem like an odd addition to this book, but this Forest Lawn has several impressive art pieces and tributes to American history. There is a huge memorial and statue of George Washington, as well as larger-than-life commemorations of Abraham Lincoln and Thomas Jefferson. A 30-foot by 165-foot tiled mosaic graces the outside of the Hall of Liberty building. The colorful, chronological, mosaic scenes of freedom depict the surrender of General Cornwallis, the crossing of the Delaware, Betsy Ross making the flag, and the signing of the Declaration of Independence.

Inside the hall is a replica of the Liberty Bell, models of famous early Americans in period costumes, and a continuously running film regarding the founding of our country called *The Birth of Liberty*. A small Museum of Mexican History is adjacent to the Hall of Liberty. It contains pictures, statues, models, clothing, and artifacts from Mayan, Aztec, and other Indian and Mexican cultures. See the Calendar entries for Visit with Montezuma (pg. 582) and Visit with Washington and Lincoln (pg. 566), for Forest Lawn's fantastic, free History Comes Alive educational programs.

Hours: Open daily, 9am - 6pm. Closed during private services.
Admission: Free
Ages: 6 years and up.

FRY'S ELECTRONIC (Los Angeles County)

Burbank - (818) 526-8100; City of Industry - (562); Manhattan Beach - (310); Woodland Hills - (818)   *!*
227-1000 / www.frys.com
Burbank - 2311 North Hollywood Way; City of Industry - 13401 Crossroads Parkway North; Manhattan Beach - 3600 Sepulveda Boulevard; Woodland Hills - 6100 Canoga Avenue

I know this is an odd addition (another one!) to the book, but some of these stores are so fancifully themed in their decor that I had to at least mention them. My husband and boys love to look around in here, and as much as I love to shop, electronics (over 50,000 per store!) doesn't do it for me. I do, however, like looking at the imaginative "decorations." The store in Woodland Hills, for instance, is themed after Lewis Carroll's *Alice in Wonderland*. Rose bushes, with white and red roses, and other huge topiaries, as well as gigantic cards "flying" overhead comprise an eye-catching entryway. Other objects throughout the store include a flying dragon, a large "thatched" roof house, and oversized (ten to fifteen foot high) figures representing characters from the book. Very fun.

The other stores are equally well done: Fountain Valley - hails the ruins of ancient Rome, complete with a flowing aqueduct. Manhattan Beach - re-creates Tahiti with sculpted lava Tiki heads and its own rain forest. Anaheim - features a replica of the NASA flight deck for the Endeavor Space Shuttle, complete with launches on big screen TV's, and other space ships in flight. Burbank - time travels back to the 1950's with a retro space theme from Hollywood, complete with a Martian-style robot. The City of Industry - has a factory setting that is a salute to the Industrial Revolution, complete with oversized gears and cogs. San Marcos - is reminiscent of the lost city of Atlantis, with its aquariums, exotic fish, and waterfalls. The stores are worth a stop and peek if you're in the neighborhood.

Hours: Call for store hours.
Admission: Technically, free.
Ages: 5 years and up.

LOS ANGELES CENTRAL LIBRARY
(213) 228-7000 - Children's Literature Department;   *$*
(213) 228-7040 - cultural and educational activities / www.lapl.org
630 W. 5ᵗʰ Street, Los Angeles
(Exit Harbor Fwy [110] E. on 6ᵗʰ St., L. on Grand, L. on 5ᵗʰ. It's at Hope and 5ᵗʰ St. [TG: 634 E4])

This 125-year old library is a classic. From the unique architecture to the millions of books to the areas and exhibitions that focus on special interests, it is an oasis to researchers and readers of all ages who can easily spend hours here. The Language Learning Center offers audio tapes and instruction manuals in twenty-eight languages. What a unique adventure for your children's ears. Over 250 newspapers and periodicals are offered in numerous languages. The children's section is a haven for young book lovers with its comfy furniture and shelves of books that open their imagination to new worlds.

On the second floor, in the Children's Literacy Department, the KLOS Story Theater presents a free, one-hour show on Saturdays at 2pm. Various past shows have featured magic tricks, instructions on how to make a book (followed by actually making one), and storytelling with puppets. On Sundays at 2pm a free, one-hour children's video is shown. At least once a month, on the first floor of the library, at the Mark Taper Auditorium (which seats 225), a free, one-hour, usually culturally-themed performance, such as folk-dancing, is given. Call for specific themes and shows. Also note that the Mark Taper contains galleries of rotating exhibits. (The one on the pop-ups books was wonderful!) One-hour school tours are given Mondays, Thursdays, and Fridays for kindergarten to fifth graders at 10am and 11am. Tours consist of a half-hour tour of the library and a half hour of story time or making a craft. Call (213) 228-7055 to make a reservation.

Hours: The library is open Mon., Thurs. - Sat., 10am - 5:30pm; Tues. - Wed., noon - 8pm; Sun., 1pm - 5pm. Closed most major holidays.

Admission: Free. Enter the parking structure under the library on 524 S. Flower St. - $1 for the first hour, $2.20 for the second hour - with validation for library card holders.

Ages: 3 years and up.

MOUNT WILSON OBSERVATORY and SKYLINE PARK

(626) 793-3100 / www.mwoa.org

Angeles Crest Highway, Los Angeles

(From Foothill Fwy [210] in La Canada - Flintridge, exit N. Angeles Crest Hwy (Hwy 2) about 7 miles - don't turn L. onto Palmdale Rd., but go straight another 7 miles. Turn R. at "Mount Wilson" sign. It's another 5 miles to the top of the mountain, through a gate. Walk a ¼ mile to reach observatory and museum. [TG: 506 J7])

Observant kids will enjoy the incredible view from atop the world, above the clouds, and also seeing the observatory, which was founded in 1904. Hike around the grounds on the aptly named Skyline Park and/or come for a free, two-hour, guided tour. Besides walking the area, the tour takes visitors to the U.C.L.A. 150-foot solar tower within a tower telescope where oftentimes access is allowed inside to see current images of the sun. You also see the visitor's gallery of the 100-inch Hooker telescope where you can gawk at the large instrument through a big window, and you go to the astronomical museum. Inside the museum are numerous photographs taken of the skies accompanied by information about the photographed objects, a scale model of the observatory, and a few star searching tools. Special guided tours, where visitors go inside more of the Observatory facilities, are available upon request.

If you come to visit this area during the week, or when guided tours are usually available, take a free copy of the Self Guided Tour Brochure available at the museum. Note the elevation of Mt. Wilson is 5,800 feet and it is often cold, or at least cool, up here. There is frequently snow on the ground in the winter.

Hours: The grounds and museum are open daily, 10am - 4pm. Guided tours are usually offered Sat. and Sun. at 1pm, weather permitting.

Admission: Free

Ages: 7 years and up.

MRS. NELSON'S TOY AND BOOK SHOP

(909) 599-4558 / www.mrsnelsons.com

1030 Bonita Avenue, La Verne

(Going N. on Foothill Fwy [210], exit E. on Bonita. Going S. on 210, exit E. on Arrow Hwy, L. on Bonita. [TG: 600 E2])

Mrs. Nelson has a delightful selection of books, educational toys, games, puzzles, tapes, and arts and craft supplies. Storytelling, followed by a related craft, is offered on Tuesdays at 10am, and again on Saturdays at 11am, unless a special program is being offered. A few times a year, you are invited to bring your picnic blankets and enjoy a free sing-along or dance-along concert. Sign up to receive a quarterly newsletter that gives dates and times for these activities as well as workshop information, author book signings, character appearances, and more.

Hours: Open Mon. - Thurs. and Sat., 9am - 6pm; Fri., 9am - 7pm; Sun., 11am - 5pm.

Ages: 2 years and up.

NATURALIZATION CEREMONY

(213) 741-1151 / www.lacclink.com

1201 S. Figueroa Street, Los Angeles Convention Center, Los Angeles

(Going N. on Harbor Fwy [110], exit E. on Pico Blvd., L. on Figueroa. Going S. on 110, exit at Olympic Blvd., turn L. at end of off ramp on Blaine St., L. on 11th St., R. on Figueroa. [TG: 634 D5])

Naturalized citizens must meet three requirements: be lawful permanent residents of the United States; have lived here for at least five years; and pass a written citizenship test. Many applicants study our history so intensely that they know it better than those of us who have lived here all our lives.

The naturalization ceremony usually takes place once a month, and as several hundred people can be inducted at one time, it can take a few hours. After green cards are turned in and the applicants seated, each one is given a congratulatory letter from the White House and a small American flag to wave after the swearing in. A district judge pounds the gavel and administers the Oath of Citizenship in which the almost-new citizens renounce any foreign allegiance and promise to uphold the Constitution. Next on the agenda, an INS representative gives a short speech, a patriotic song is sung (with not many dry eyes in the audience), and a short video shows a sweeping overview of America. Ta da - new American citizens have been born! Finally, Certificates of Citizenship are handed out.

I mention this ceremony as an outing because I think older kids who are studying the Constitution or immigration might be interested in seeing this process and perhaps even catch a little national fever. Note that the public is welcome, but they must sit or stand near the back of the huge hall.

Hours:　Call for dates.

Admission:　$10 for parking

Ages:　10 years and up.

OXMAN'S SURPLUS, INC.

(562) 921-1106 / www.oxmans-surplus.com

14128 East Rosecrans Avenue, Santa Fe Springs

(Exit Santa Ana Fwy [5] E. on Rosecrans. [TG: 737 D3])

This unique army surplus store offers an eclectic mix of items and activities. The store carries everything camouflage, plus camping gear, knives, boots, tarps, tools, swords, clothing, and more. Packed into one area is a very small "museum" (i.e. a collection of various memorabilia). Most of the articles are labeled. The museum features helmets, patches, a Devil fish skeleton, a 15th century suit of armor, a few surface-to-air missiles, a WWII oxygen breathing tank, Hitler's bayonet, a permanent hair wave machine, and a sighting station for a B-26 bomber. Visitors can sit in the B-17 cockpit on display.

A small gallery for paint ball target practice is also located inside Oxman's. The short range has targets that light up and offer a few sound effects. The cost for fifty rounds, or two minutes, is $4. Players must be 18 years old or be accompanied by an adult.

Just outside the building is a fenced-off area containing a B-29 engine, a Bull Pup missile, a jet engine, and a few other odds-and-ends artifacts. This area is only to groups taking a tour. The short, but interesting, tour, available only to small groups, also includes a description of and insight into the articles in the museum and some of the miscellaneous items in the store. Hint - Boy Scouts love this sort of place! Note: There is a McDonald's just around the corner from the store and a park just down the street.

Hours:　Open Mon. - Sat., 9am - 6pm. Closed Sun. Tours are given by appointment.

Admission:　Free

Ages:　6 years and up.

ROSE HILLS MEMORIAL PARK

(562) 699-0921 / www.rosehills.com

3900 S. Workman Mill Road, Whittier

(Exit San Gabriel River Fwy [605] E. on Rose Hills Rd., L. on Workman Mill Rd. to the East Park. [TG: 677 C1])

This is one of the world's largest memorial parks. The east park features a three-and-a-half-acre rose garden with more than 750 varieties. We enjoyed their fragrance as well as their names: Iceberg, The Doctor, Las Vegas, Confetti, Mister Lincoln, Summer Fashion, etc. The west park has a small, traditional Japanese garden with a meditation house, lake, and a bridge that add to the serene beauty. Again, as with FOREST LAWN (see previous entries in this section), perhaps this is an odd addition to this book, but can be an enjoyable (and obviously different) place to go.

Hours: Open daily, 8am - 5pm. Open extended hours in the summer.

Admission: Free

Ages: 4 years and up.

STORYOPOLIS

(310) 358-2500 / www.storyopolis.com

116 N. Robertson Boulevard, Plaza A, Los Angeles

(From Santa Monica Fwy [10], exit N. on Robertson. From Hollywood Fwy [101], exit E. on Silver Lake Blvd., which turns into Beverly Blvd., L. on Robertson. Storyopolis is on the E. side of the street, in the Plaza, just N. of 3rd St. [TG: 632 H1])

This unique store offers a perfect way to introduce children to art and to encourage a love of reading. Half of Storyopolis has rotating, book-related exhibits. We saw original art work by illustrators of children's books. The art was displayed at kids' eye level. Each book, from which the illustrations were inspired, was on a stand in front of its appropriate picture(s). My middle son, a budding artist, and I first read excerpts from the book and then matched the framed art work to illustrations in the book. He remarked that it gave him the idea to write and illustrate his own book so that "maybe people can see my work here, too."

The other half of this medium-sized store has a cozy reading area and a terrific selection of children's books, with an emphasis on the arts. Storyopolis regularly hosts themed craft and story hours, author-signings, super-sized workshops for ages 6 to 12 (such as an architecture workshop and making animation flip books), and special presentations. Call for a schedule of events. Storyopolis also offers storybook-inspired birthday parties.

Hours: Open Mon. - Sat., 10am - 6pm; Sun., 11am - 4pm.

Admission: Free. Some of the events and workshops cost.

Ages: 4 years and up.

U.C.L.A.

(310) 825-4321 / www.ucla.edu

U.C.L.A. Campus, Westwood

(Exit San Diego Fwy [405] E. on Wilshire Blvd., L. on Westwood Blvd. to the information kiosk. Make sure you ask for a map. Parking lot 9 is the closest to the garden. [TG: 632 A2])

University of California at Los Angeles is a classic campus with huge old brick buildings and stately trees. I hope our visit here planted some dreams in my children's mind of going to college. If, in fact, you have a college-bound high schooler, take the free two-hour walking tour of the campus which highlights housing, academics, financial aid, and, most importantly, social activities. Tours are given Monday through Friday at 10:15am and 12:15pm, and Saturday at 10:15am. The following are some of our "discoveries" as we walked the campus on our own. Tip: There are several places on campus to eat lunch or grab a snack, and since you've paid for parking, you might as well make a day of it!

Mathias Botanical Garden, located on the lower part of the campus, gave us the feeling of being in a secret garden, with its stony pathways through a lush "forest" and a hidden dirt path along a small creek. Trails crisscross through cactus and various other plant sections, all of which are as interesting to study as they are beautiful. The gardens are open Monday through Friday, 8am to 5pm; Saturday and Sunday, 8am to 4pm. Admission is free. Call (310) 825-3620 or (310) 825-1260 / www.botgard.ucla.edu for more information.

We took a free shuttle to the north end of the campus to the Murphy Sculpture Garden, which has over sixty sculptures scattered around an open grassy area. My 11-year old summed it up best from a kid's perspective; "I thought this was supposed to be great art. How come it's just a bunch of naked people?"

The U.C.L.A. **Fowler Museum of Cultural History**, (310) 825-4361 / www.fmch.ucla.edu, is also on the north end of campus. The majority of the exhibits are sophisticated, with a focus on anthropology. Older kids might enjoy them. Call for a current schedule of exhibits showing in the gallery rooms. Inquire about their children's programs and family workshops. The museum is open Wednesday through Sunday, noon to 5pm; open Thursday until 8pm. Admission is $5 for adults; $3 for seniors; ages 17 and under are free. Admission is free every Thursday. For information on the planetarium, look up DONALD E. BIANCHI PLANETARIUM (pg. 145).

X Cape, (310) 206-0829, in Ackerman Union building, Level A, is a game room with video and virtual reality games, and a very high noise level. It's open daily from 9am to 10pm. Admission is $6, which pays for unlimited game play. For the last hour, admission is only $3. A small food court and even a gift shop are also in this building.

The **Athletic Hall of Fame**, (310) 206-6662, is a showplace for U.C.L.A. athletes. It houses photos, trophies, and a few pieces of equipment used by Bruin athletes who have excelled at tennis, basketball, football, volleyball, and other sports. A small theater shows a short film of the athletes in action. The hall is open Monday through Friday from 8am to 5pm. Admission is free.

U.C.L.A. abounds with other forms of entertainment, too. Check out the U.C.L.A. CENTER FOR PERFORMING ARTS (pg. 156) for first-rate theater productions.

Just across the street from the campus, at 10619 Bellaglo Road, is the U.C.L.A. **Hannah Carter Center**, (310) 825-4574 / www.japanesegarden.ucla.edu. This two-acre, almost hidden, beautiful Japanese garden has a teahouse, a shrine, bridges, a pond with koi fish and lily pads, and a "jade rock" brought here from Japan, along with other rocks and boulders. Guided group tours can be arranged, but enjoy it on your own Tuesday, Wednesday, and Friday and on the first Sunday of the month from 10am to 3pm. It is not stroller/wheelchair accessible. Admission is free. Reservations are required simply because there are only two parking spaces.

Hours: The campus is usually open daily, 8am - 5pm. Attractions are usually closed on University holidays.

Admission: Parking is $7 for the day.

UNIVERSAL CITYWALK   ☼

(818) 622-4455 or (818) 622-9841 / www.citywalkhollywood.com   *$$$*
Universal Center Drive, Universal City
(Going N.W. on Hollywood Fwy [101], exit N. at Universal Center Dr. Going SE on 101, exit at Lankershim Blvd., L. on Cahuenga, L. on Universal Center Dr. It's right next to Universal Studios Hollywood. [TG: 563 C6])

CityWalk is an outdoor, multi-level mall built in theme-park style with fantastic stores, unique restaurants, and unusual entertainment. Everything here, from the larger-than-life neon signs to the oversized, Disneylandish-decorated storefronts is done with spectacular Hollywood flair, and that's just the outside of the buildings! On weekend nights, live entertainment, such as jugglers, magicians, musicians, and puppeteers, add to the carnival-like atmosphere.

Here are just a few of the major attractions along the walkway: **Jillian's Hi Life Lanes** has a games room downstairs featuring video games and virtual bowling using real balls. Upstairs, ten real bowling lanes have monitors above, showing mostly rock videos. Glow-in-the-dark balls and pins are standard equipment at nighttime and weekends during Cosmic bowl. The **Awesome Atoms** store offers a fine selection of scientific and educational games and toys. Outside the **Hard Rock Cafe** is a gigantic neon guitar. Inside this restaurant, dedicated to the preservation of rock 'n roll, guitars, costumes, posters, and personal items from famed musicians decorate the walls. (See HARD ROCK CAFE on page 17 for details.) Across the way from the Cafe is an eighteen-screen movie theater, (818) 508-0588, and a **3-D IMAX** Theater, (818) 760-8100, that shows both 3-D and 2-D movies on a screen six stories high. 3-D tickets are $9 for adults; $6 for seniors and ages 3 to 11. Shake, rattle, and roll your way through a five-minute simulator ride in the **Imaginator**. It is open Sunday through Thursday 10am to 8pm, and Friday through Saturday 10am to 1am. Kids must be at least 42" tall to ride. Each ride costs $5. **NASCAR Silicon Motor Speedway**, (818) 763-7959 / www.smsonline.com, offers virtual racing in an almost life-sized stock car. Race against the clock or other competitors for $9 for a six-minute ride. **Sam Goody** has a giant neon gorilla (think King-Kong) hanging on its sign. Inside, kids like the constant music, the enormous wall posters, going up the grated stairs to the Coffee Cafe, and walking over the bridge to check out the mini-museum that has signed Beatles photos, a Judy Garland letter, record plaques, and costumes of famous performers. Look out for the **water fountain** in the center circle of CityWalk, where water spouts up at unexpected times in hot weather. You could have a glow about you if you visit **Glow,** a store that sells an assortment of glow-in-the-dark products. Feeling all wound up? **Wound and Wound Toy Co.** has a great selection of wind-up toys. Two terrific kids' bookstores, **Upstart Crows Nest** and **Golden Showcase**, are decorated as I dream a really large children's room should look like. **Hollywood Freeway** lures people in with Hagen-Daz ice cream. Its entrance sign has the upside down front end of a '57 Chevy crashed through it. On the storefront of **Things From Another World** the back half of a spaceship, which is still emitting smoke, is all that remains from a crash landing. Whew - the extravagant gimmicks alone are worth the price of parking! An outdoor ice-skating rink is here November through February. During other months, concerts and other special events are offered.

Restaurants on the walk aim to please any taste bud, as the wide-ranging food selections indicate. Eat Chinese (including Dim Sun), Mexican, Italian, Cuban, sushi, hamburgers, steaks, or order deli. At **Cafe Tu Tu Tango** watch painters and sculptors at work while eating from an all-appetizer menu. UNIVERSAL STUDIOS HOLLYWOOD (see pg. 4) is at one end this pedestrian thoroughfare. You can experience practically all of Hollywood at CityWalk - all at one time! Note: Weekend nights, especially, with the crowds, activities, music piped in everywhere, and rock videos playing on a large screen outside the movie theaters, are a bit too stimulating for younger children (and sometimes adults!).

Hours:	Most stores and restaurants are open Mon. - Thurs., 11am - 9pm; Fri. - Sat., 11am - midnight; Sun., 11am - 10pm.
Admission:	Free. Parking, in a lot also shared by Universal Studios Hollywood, is $8. Valet parking is $5 for the first two hours with validation; $2.50 for each half hour after that.
Ages:	2 years and up.

WAYFARERS CHAPEL

(310) 377-1650 / www.wayfarerschapel.org
5755 Palos Verdes Drive South, Palos Verdes
(Exit San Diego Fwy [405] S. on Crenshaw Blvd. and stay on this street into the city of Palos Verdes; turn R. on Crest Rd., L. on Hawthorne to the end, L. on Palos Verdes Dr. It's about 2 miles on the L. [TG: 823 A4])

This unique, relatively small church, is nicknamed the "Glass Church" because it's built almost entirely of glass, and some stone. It is nestled in a few overgrown trees and looks to be almost a part of them. It was designed by Lloyd Wright, son of Frank Lloyd Wright. The church is built on a bluff overlooking the Pacific Ocean, surrounded by redwoods and gardens. The chapel is unique and charming, and the landscaping is beautiful. This is a short stop off, so look up ABALONE COVE (pg. 34), REDONDO BEACH INTERNATIONAL BOARDWALK (pg. 126), or SOUTH COAST BOTANICAL GARDENS (pg. 68) for other things to do in this area.

Hours:	Open daily, 7am - 5pm. Church functions take precedence over public accessibility.
Admission:	Free
Ages:	5 years and up.

-----*SHOWS AND THEATERS*-----

AHMANSON THEATER
(213) 628-2772 or (213) 972-7211 / www.musiccenter.org
135 N. Grand Avenue at the Music Center of Los Angeles, Los Angeles

See the MUSIC CENTER OF LOS ANGELES entry on page 151 for details.

ALEX THEATRE

(800) 233-3123; (818) 243-2611 - box office / www.alextheatre.org

216 N. Brand Boulevard, Glendale

(Going E. on Ventura Fwy [134], exit Central/Brand Blvds. and go straight over Central, R. on Brand. Going W. on 134, exit Central/Brand Blvds. and go L. on Brand. [TG: 564 E4])

The gorgeous Alex Theatre seats 1,450 and offers a wide variety of performances and programs, for both professional and community performing arts groups. These include Peking Acrobats, folk dance ensembles, holiday shows, music theater (such as *The Music Man* and *Ain't Misbehavin'*), and even family-oriented and classic films. Special kid's presentations given on Sunday afternoons at 2pm and 5pm, have featured *Parachute Express, Beakman's World, Gizmo Guys*, and more.

Free public tours are given so visitors can learn the history of the seventy-five-year-old theater, including its architecture and artwork. Seeing the dressing rooms, green room, lobby, and back stage are all part of the tour, too. Ask about educational outreach programs for students and special school presentations and matinees.

Hours: Call for a complete schedule.

Admission: Prices vary depending on the show. Sun. afternoon kid's shows are $14 per person.

Ages: 4 years and up, depending on the show.

BEN BOLLINGER'S CANDLELIGHT PAVILION

(909) 626-1254 / www.candlelightpavilion.com

455 W. Foothill Boulevard, Claremont

(Exit San Bernardino Fwy [10] N. on Indian Peak Rd., L. on Foothill Blvd. [TG: 601 C2])

This family-owned, elegant dinner theater serves gourmet cuisine along with its ninety-minute, professional musical productions. Families dress up in their Sunday best, and sit down in padded booths with linen tablecloths, or larger groups may sit at equally nice, long tables. Tiered seating is available on the main floor, or choose terrace seats. Candlelight wall chandeliers and candles on the table add to the ambiance. (My oldest son liked the draped stage curtains, too.)

Dinner is served for almost two hours before the show begins. (If kids get antsy, wander outside on the cement pathways, near the fish pond.) Entrees differ with each show but usually include variations of tri tip, chicken, fish (we had grilled salmon with shrimp mousse strudel), or a vegetarian dish. Meals come with vegetables and delicious hot rolls. The children's menu changes, offering macaroni and cheese, chicken strips with french fries, or something equally tasty. Full waiter service makes dining here a real treat. The dessert selection includes cheesecake, honey orange ice cream in an almond phyllo nest, and (my personal favorite) chocolate strawberry euphoria - brownies topped with ice cream, fresh strawberries, chocolate mousse, and chocolate. Note: The show and dinner are included in the admission price, but appetizers, beverages, and desserts are extra. Champagne brunches are served Sundays at the matinee seating. A performance is included with the brunch.

The eight, yearly musical productions are first rate, and most of them are suitable for children. Past shows have included *Secret Garden, Joseph and the Amazing Technicolor Dreamcoat, Ben Bollinger's Broadway, The Sound of Music*, and the annual *Wonderful World of Christmas*. Reservations are required for all shows. Appropriate attire is requested.

Hours: Dinner seatings are Thurs. - Sat., 6pm; Sun., 5pm. Enjoy brunch on Sat. and Sun. at 11am. Shows begin at 8:15pm, 7:15pm, and 12:45pm, respectively.

Admission: $33 - $67 per person, depending on where you sit (the terrace is the most expensive) and your entree selection. Children's rates for Fri. evenings and Sat. matinees are $22 in section A and the main floor, only. Children must be 12 or under to order a children's entree. (If a child's entree is desired at another show time, you must call ahead of time.)

Ages: 6 years and up.

BIOLA YOUTH ARTS

(562) 906-4574 / www.biola.edu/academics/community

$$$

13800 Biola Avenue, La Mirada

(Going N.W. on Santa Ana Fwy [5], exit N. on Valley View Ave., R. on Rosecrans Ave., L. on Biola. Going S.E. on 5, exit E. on Rosecrans, L. on Biola. It's in Biola University. [TG: 737 F2])

Young children and teens present one full-length, popular musical or theater production each semester. Past productions have included *Oliver*, *Anne of Green Gables*, and *The Lion, the Witch, and the Wardrobe*. Two different casts perform; a home school cast and an after-school cast. Maybe your child will enjoy the performance so much that he/she will want to audition for the next production!

Hours: Call for a schedule of performances.

Admission: $8 for adults; $5 for students. Daytime school presentations are less expensive.

Ages: 5 years and up.

BOB BAKER MARIONETTE THEATER

(213) 250-9995 / www.bobbakermarionettes.com

$$$

1345 W. 1ˢᵗ Street, Los Angeles

(From Hollywood Fwy [101], exit S. on Glendale, L. on 1ˢᵗ St., which is just before the bridge. From Harbor Fwy [110], exit E. on 3ʳᵈ St., R. on Lucas, R. on 1ˢᵗ. [TG: 634 E2])

The Bob Baker Marionette Theater has been around since 1961, proving its staying power in this ever-changing world. Interactive marionette performances are given while children sit on a horseshoe-shaped carpet around the stage, and parents sit in chairs behind them.

The musical revues feature marionettes, and some stuffed animals, that range in size from very small to the size of a two-year-old. They "sing" and "dance" their way right into your child's heart. The puppeteers, dressed in black, become invisible to the audience as the kids get swept away in the magic of the show. The performance is done within touching distance of the kids, and sometimes the marionettes even sit in their laps! This is a great way to keep short attention spans riveted. If the story line seems a little thin to you and your attention drifts, watch the puppeteers manipulate the strings - it's a good show in itself. If it's your child's birthday, for an additional $6, he/she will get special recognition with a crown, a song just for him/her, and a little present.

After the hour-long show, chat with the puppeteers and enjoy a sack lunch (that you supply) at the picnic tables in the lobby - no strings attached. Note that there are puppets and marionettes for sale here, too. Reservations are required for all shows. Ask about touring puppet shows that come to you.

Hours: Performances are given Tues. - Fri. at 10:30am; Sat. - Sun. at 2:30pm. There are additional shows given during the month of December.

Admission: $10 for ages 2 and up; $8 for seniors; children under 2 (lap sitters) are free. Free parking next to the theater.

Ages: 2½ - 11 years.

THE BRIDGE: CINEMA DE LUX

(310) 568-9950 / www.thebridgecinema.com

$/$$$

6081 Center Drive in the Promenade at Howard Hughes Center, Los Angeles

(Going N. on San Diego Fwy [405], E. at Howard Hughes Pkwy, R. on Center. Going S. on 405, exit E. on Howard Hughes, L. on Center. [TG: 672 H7])

The Bridge is a classy movie theater located in an upscale outdoor mall. It features a lounge, appetizers, a bar, a coffee bar, and indoor/outdoor seating for the cafe. The theater seats can be classified as a cut above. But you don't have to spend big bucks to see a movie here. Once a month the Silver Screen Classics program shows a classic film from the 30's on up through the 80's on the big screen. Your admission price of $1 covers not only the movie, but popcorn and a soft drink, too - what a deal! Arrive early - numerous movie fans like this deal, as well.

Another fun option, is watching a movie in the IMAX theater here. This over-sized screen shows movies in both the 2-D and 3-D format. 3-D movies are a visual and sensory experience as the images seem to come out of the screen and right into the theater. The show titles change so there is always something new to see.

Hours: Call for show times. The Silver Screen Classics are usually shown on the third Tuesday of every month.

Admission: Admission prices change depending on the movies being shown. 3-D is generally $9 for adults; $8 for seniors; $7 for ages 3 - 11.

Ages: 6 years and up for the classics; 4 years and up for 3-D movies.

CARPENTER PERFORMING ARTS CENTER

(562) 985-7000 / www.carpenterarts.org

6200 Atherton Street, on the campus of California State University of Long Beach, Long Beach

(From San Diego Fwy [405], exit S. on Palo Verde Ave. Follow CSULB signs, R. on Atherton St. From San Gabriel River Fwy [605], exit W. on 7ᵗʰ Street [22], R. on Bellflower Blvd., R. on Atherton St. Enter the Carpenter Center parking lot on your L. [TG: 796 D5])

$$$$

Lovers of musical theater, dance, dramatic theater, juggling, concerts, and children's performances will enjoy shows given at this center. One-hour-plus family matinees are also given four to six times during the season. Troupes have entertained youngsters with magic, comedy, circus-type acts, dance, storytelling, ballet, and more. Ask about their annual, Wide-Screen Film Festival (where classic and popular films are shown), usually held in October. Come join the fun!

Hours: Family matinees are given on selected weekends at 2pm. Call for other show dates and times.

Admission: Prices range in price depending on your seat location, the date, and show.

Ages: Some shows are for ages 5 and up; some shows are recommended for older kids.

CERRITOS CENTER FOR THE PERFORMING ARTS

(800) 300-4345 / www.cerritoscenter.com

12700 Center Court Drive, Cerritos

(Going W. on Artesia Fwy [91], exit W. on Artesia Blvd., L. on Bloomfield. Going E. on 91, exit S. on Bloomfield. From Bloomfield, turn L. on Town Center Dr., R. on Center Court Dr. [TG: 767 A1])

$$$$$

Every season this absolutely beautiful Center (with grounds that are equally lovely) features four or five top-rate performances specifically for families, such as puppetry, dance, circus acts, or dramatic theater. Cerritos also features star-studded headliners such as Bill Cosby; Peter, Paul, and Mary; the Moscow Ballet; and numerous others. Check the Calendar entry for the annual Family Arts Festival (pg. 584). Educators, ask about the free or minimal cost professional performances given especially for students throughout the year.

Hours: Call for a schedule.

Admission: Show prices usually start at $35.

Ages: 5 years and up.

DEAF WEST THEATER

(818) 762-2998 - voice; (818) 762-2782 - TTY / www.deafwest.org

5112 Lankershim Boulevard, Hollywood

(Exit the Hollywood Fwy [170], E. on Magnolia, R. on Lankershim. [TG: 562 J3])

$$$$

This unique theater puts on adaptations of classic, contemporary, children's, and original plays featuring deaf and/or hard of hearing actors, directors, costume designers, and others. A children's play is performed at least once a season. Hour-and-a-half shows are performed in American Sign Language, while a spoken version can be heard through headsets. Under-the-seat subwoofers enable deaf patrons to actually feel the music and the sound effects. Past shows include *Cinderella*, *A Christmas Carol*, and *Aladdin and the Wonderful Lamp*. Older patrons have enjoyed *Romeo and Juliet*, *Oliver*, and *Saint Joan*, among other productions. What a great opportunity for both hearing-impaired and hearing guests to enjoy a show together! Inquire about one-hour children's workshops that are free and open to the public, where children hear a story and then help create characters on stage.

Hours: Call for show times.

Admission: Prices range, depending on the show, from $15 for dramas to $25 for musical.

Ages: 6 years and up.

DONALD E. BIANCHI PLANETARIUM

(818) 677-2488 / www.csun.edu/physicsandastronomy/Miscellaneous/planetarium_page.htm *$$*

1811 Nordhoff Street at California State University of Northridge, Northridge

(Exit San Diego Fwy [405] E. on Nordhoff, R. on Lindley. Park at Lot G4 on Zelzah Ave. [TG: 501, A7])

It's written in the stars, or so it seems when you visit this 105-seat planetarium. The show titles might change, but all explore different aspects of our universe. Current shows include *Sky Tour* that lights up the nighttime sky with seasonal constellations; *Voyager Encounter*, which is narrated by Patrick Stewart and talks about the history of the outer planets of the Solar System; and *Search for Life in the Universe*, narrated by Leonard Nimoy, that ponders the possibility of life elsewhere. Live narrators present other elements of space and astronomy in their programs. Two shows are given each night; one ticket pays for both viewings. Be on time as latecomers will not be admitted. Weather permitting, come look through the telescopes after the shows.

Hours: Shows are usually given the first and third Sat. at 7pm and 8pm, during the traditional school year.

Admission: $5 for adults; $3 for seniors and ages 17 and under.

Ages: 8 years and up.

DOROTHY CHANDLER PAVILION

(213) 972-7211 / www.musiccenter.org

135 N. Grand Avenue at the Music Center of Los Angeles, Los Angeles

See the MUSIC CENTER OF LOS ANGELES entry on page 151 for details.

EDWARDS IMAX THEATER (Valencia)

(661) 287-1740 / www.edwardscinemas.com *$$$*

24435 Town Center Drive, Valencia

(Exit Golden State Fwy [5] E. on Valencia Blvd. [TG: 4550 F3])

Come see a film that's larger than life, or at least larger than a film is on a normal movie screen. The towering IMAX screen shows films in both 2-D and 3-D format. The 3-D is a favorite because the images being shown seem to jump out at you, making them more realistic. The titles, as with any movie, change all the time so you'll want to come back more than once.

Hours: Call for movie titles and times.

Admission: $10 for adults; $8 for seniors and children.

Ages: 4 years and up.

EL CAPITAN THEATER

(800) DISNEY6 (347-6396) or (818) 845-3110 / www.elcapitantickets.com *$$$$*

6838 Hollywood Boulevard, Hollywood

(Exit Hollywood Fwy [101] W. on Hollywood Blvd. [TG: 593 E4])

This Disney-owned tiered theater is lavishly decorated, reminiscent of the late 1920's with ornate edifices and a sense of grandeur. New Disney releases such as *Monsters, Inc., Holes, Piglet's Big Movie,* and *Finding Nemo* are shown here with state-of-the-art technology. First, though, a live stage show is performed, starring familiar Disney characters in song and dance. Then, comes the feature presentation. Sometimes characters from the movie are on hand to greet visitors and have their pictures taken. In the interim between new movies releases, the theater shows Disney classics often with an added audience participation activity or two.

Hours: Call for show dates.

Admission: Ticket prices vary according what is playing. The first-run movies with all the activities usually cost $14 for ages 12 and up; $12 for seniors and ages 3 - 11; children 2 and under are free. Group rates are discounted.

Ages: 4 years and up.

FALCON THEATRE

(818) 955-8101 / www.falcontheatre.com

$$$

4252 Riverside Drive, Burbank

(Going E. on Ventura Fwy [134], exit S. on Pass Ave, R. on Alameda, which turns into Riverside. Going W on 134, exit at Hollywood Way, at the bottom of the off ramp, go L. on Alameda, which turns into Riverside. [TG: 563 D4])

This professional theater produces at least four shows a year aimed at high-school kids and adults; another four are geared for kindergartners through middle schoolers. Just a few of the past productions have included *Rumpelstiltskin, Hansel and Gretel,* and *The Lion, the Witch and the Wardrobe.*

Hours: Adult productions usually run Thurs. - Sun. at 8pm, with matinees on weekends. Children's programs generally run on Sat., 1pm and 3pm; Sun. at 1pm. Call for a complete schedule.

Admission: Tickets range between $10 (for the children's show) up to $37.50 for more mature-themed shows.

Ages: K and up - depending on the show.

FAMILY SATURDAY SERIES - PILLOW THEATRE

(213) 972-8000 / www.musiccenter.org

$$$$

135 N. Grand Avenue at the Music Center of Los Angeles, Los Angeles

(From Harbor Fwy [110], exit E. on 4th St., L. on Olive St., go to end, L. on 1st St., R. on Grand. Going N. on Hollywood Fwy [101], exit S. on Grand. Going S. on 101, exit E. on Temple, R. on Grand. Parking is available on Grand Ave. and, on the evening and weekends only, at the Dept. of Water and Power on Hope St. [TG: 634 F3])

Saturday Family Series, or Pillow Theatre, is comprised of hour-long shows geared for young children. Held at the Dorothy Chandler Pavilion, classics from *Mother Goose* and other favorite tales come to life via stories, songs, and family participation. The shows are perfect for little ones to get familiar with and begin to love live theater.

Hours: Selected Saturdays at 11am.

Admission: $10 per person. Parking is about $8.

Ages: 3 - 6 years.

GLENDALE CENTRE THEATRE

(818) 244-8481 / www.glendalecentretheatre.com

$$$$

324 N. Orange Street, Glendale

(Going E. on Ventura Fwy [134], exit S. on N. Central Ave., L. on Lexington Dr., R. on Orange St. Going W. on 134, exit S. on N. Brand Blvd., R. on Lexington Dr., L. on Orange St. [TG: 564 E4])

Many block-buster musicals and comedies suitable for the family are performed here throughout the year. This theater puts on terrific, one-and-a-half-hour shows for children. Past productions have included *The Little Mermaid, Sleeping Beauty, Hansel and Gretel,* and *Jack and the Beanstalk.* The season begins in March and ends in November.

Check out the theater's Shakespearience outreach school programs for junior and senior high. It includes select interactive performances from the Bard, workshops, and study materials.

Hours: Children's shows are usually performed Sat. at 11am. Call for other show times.

Admission: Children's show prices are usually $12.50 for adults; $10.50 for children 12 and under. Other show prices usually range from $14 - $20.

Ages: Depends on the show.

GOURMET CAROUSEL RESTAURANT / OCEAN SEA FOOD

(323) 721-0774; (323) 721-0763 - Chinatown Center event planner / www.chinatowncenter.com

911 N. Broadway / 747 N. Broadway, Los Angeles

See the entry for GOURMET CAROUSEL RESTAURANT / OCEAN SEA FOOD on page 16 for details.

GRAUMAN'S CHINESE THEATRE

(323) 461-3331 / www.manntheatres.com; www.seeing-stars.com/landmarks

!/$$$

6925 Hollywood Boulevard, Hollywood

(Going N. on Ventura Fwy [101], exit W. on Hollywood. Going S. on 101, exit S. on Highland Ave. [170], R. on Hollywood. Limited parking is available on the streets, but there are several pay lots in the area ranging from $2 - $7. [TG: 593 E4])

The classic Grauman's theater looks like a giant Chinese pagoda, with a huge dragon snaking across the front and two stone lion-dogs guarding the entrance. However, the big tourist draw is not just the architecture, but the *concrete* evidence of star's shoe and hand sizes, and how well they write their name. Over 200 past and present stars have left their imprints - shoe prints, hand prints, and autographs - in the cement front courtyard. Step into and see if you can fill John Wayne's shoeprints, or Marilyn Monroe's. Harrison Ford, Tom Cruise, Jimmy Stewart, Jack Nicholson, Shirley Temple, Julie Andrews, Tom Hanks, Arnold Schwarzenegger and Darth Vader are just a few other immortalized stars.

Inside the exotic theater, the lobby is rich with Asian motif murals. The actual theater continues along the same theme with more, although subtle, murals and friezes. 2,200 seats, under a Hollywood-esque, star-burst chandelier, face the screen that plays first-run movies.

Half-hour tours of the theater are given that explain the varied history of the theater and of the stars who left their imprints. The tour is $5 for adults; ages 4 years and under are free. Call for tour hours.

Hours: Open daily. Call for show times.

Admission: Free to the front courtyard. Call for movie ticket information.

Ages: 6 years and up.

HARRIET AND CHARLES LUCKMAN FINE ARTS COMPLEX

(323) 343-6600 or (323) 343-6100 / www.luckmanfineartscomplex.org

$$$$

5151 State University Drive, on the California State Los Angeles campus, Los Angeles

(Exit San Bernardino Fwy [10] N. on Eastern Ave., stay to the R. on Paseo Rancho Castilla, then immediate R. on State University Dr. [TG: 635 F2])

The modern-looking buildings of the Luckman Fine Arts Complex consist of a 1,125-seat theater, which is the main presentation arena for modern dance, ballet, opera, and other musical performances; a modular 250-seat theater, a more intimate setting for solo artists; a contemporary art exhibits gallery where interactive workshops are offered for kids to intertwine a hands-on art experience with a specific performance; and a small amphitheater for concerts and Street of the Arts presentations.

Hours: Call for show dates and times.

Admission: Prices vary greatly depending on the show. Parking is about $5.

Ages: Depends on the show.

HERMOSA BEACH PLAYHOUSE

(310) 372-4477 / www.hermosabeachplayhouse.com; www.civiclightopera.com

$$$$$

710 Pier Avenue, Hermosa Beach

(Exit San Diego Fwy [405], W on Artesia Blvd., L. on Aviation Blvd., R. on Pacific Coast Hwy. It's on the corner of Pacific Coast Hwy. and Pier Ave. [TG: 762 H2])

The 500-seat playhouse is a division of the Civic Light Opera of South Bay Cities. (Please see the REDONDO BEACH PERFORMING ARTS CENTER, on page 154, for more details on the light opera.) This intimate theater contains an even more intimate theater room, just down the hall, for smaller, but still worthy, productions. Past productions have included *Late Nite Catechism* and *Always... Patsy Cline*.

Hours: Call for show times.

Admission: $35 - $40 per person.

Ages: 9 years and up.

IMAX THEATER

(213) 744-2014 / www.casciencectr.org

$$$

700 State Drive, Exposition Park, Los Angeles

(Exit the Harbor Fwy [110] W. on Exposition Blvd., L. on Flower, L. on Figueroa. Or, exit Santa Monica Fwy [10] S. on Vermont, L. on Exposition, R. on Figueroa. It's adjacent to the California Science Center. Parking is available the first driveway on the R. [TG: 674 B1])

Moviegoers can enjoy both traditional 2-D and newer 3-D film formats at this large screen IMAX Theater. In the 3-D format, the use of polarized glasses, a surround sound system, and the seven-story high, ninety-foot-wide screen shows films take you and your child on wonderful adventures. You'll explore the depths of the ocean and swim with fish (watch out for the sharks!); river raft through the Grand Canyon; enter the world of outer space; and more. In other words, you'll feel like you actually experience whatever is on the screen, without ever leaving your seat. "Edutainment" is what this theater all about! Look up the following attractions as they are all in the same complex: AIR AND SPACE GALLERY (pg. 80), CALIFORNIA AFRICAN AMERICAN MUSEUM (pg. 84), CALIFORNIA SCIENCE CENTER (pg. 85), EXPOSITION PARK (pg. 44), and NATURAL HISTORY MUSEUM OF LOS ANGELES COUNTY (pg. 109).

Hours: Call for show titles and show times. Shows run Mon. - Fri., 10am - 6pm; Sat. - Sun., 10am - 8pm.

Admission: Most movies are $7.50 for adults; $5.50 for seniors and students; $4.50 for ages 4 - 12; children 3 years and under are free. Prices might fluctuate depending on the film. Parking is $6.

Ages: 3 years and up.

JOHN DRESCHER PLANETARIUM

(310) 434-4223 or (310) 434-3000 / www.smc.edu/planetarium

$$$

1900 Pico Boulevard, Santa Monica

(Going W. on Santa Monica Fwy [10], exit S. on Cloverfield, R. on Pico. Going E. on 10, exit S. on 20th St., R. on Pico. It's in room 223 of Drescher Hall on the campus of Santa Monica College. [TG: 671 H2])

Do your kids have stars in their eyes? Bring them to the planetarium, then lean back, look up at the nighttime sky, and watch some of the mysteries of the heavens unfold. The first presentation, titled *Night Sky Show* is a weekly interactive update on the night sky, highlighting the latest news in space exploration and astronomy. There is a time to ask questions at this show, too. The second show, a lecture and changing fifty-minute presentation, has titles such as *Alien Skies*, *Cosmic Collisions*, or *Visualizing the Earth in 3D*. These shows focus on different aspects of astronomy, and the possibility of extra-terrestrials. The December show, *Star of Wonder*, resets the nighttime sky to the time of Jesus' birth. Explore the possibilities of the origin of the Star of Bethlehem as the astronomer/lecturer incorporates Bible passages and the research known to astronomers from that time period.

The planetarium is available for special showings for school or other groups during the week. The cost is $60 for up to twenty people, or $3 per person after the minimum is met.

Hours: Shows are most Fri. nights at 7pm and 8pm. (The latter time is the feature presentation.) Note: There are no shows in August.

Admission: $5 for adults for a single show, $8 for both shows; $4 for seniors for a single show, $7 for both; $3 for ages 12 and under for a single show, $5 for both.

Ages: 6 years and up.

L. A. CONNECTION COMEDY THEATER

(818) 710-1320 / www.laconnectioncomedy.com

$$$

13442 Ventura Boulevard, Sherman Oaks

(Exit Ventura Fwy [101] S. on Woodman, L. on Ventura Blvd. [TG: 562 C5])

The Comedy Theater produces numerous shows appropriate for adults, however, you can also tickle your children's funnybones by bringing them here for special comedy improv performances by kids, for kids. The almost hour-long improvisational show is given in a small room with tiered, theater-type seating. The performers consist of one adult and usually six kids that are between 7 to 14 years old. The kids are members of the Comedy Improv for Kids and are trained in the L.A. Connection's Improv Workshops.

Audience participation is mandatory as the actors ask for help in creating characters, or supplying ideas to use in a skit. Your children love to see their suggestions acted out. Remember, the performers are kids, so there is a lot of kid-type humor. As with any improv show, the success of a skit depends on the improvisationalists and the audience. The L.A. Connection really connected with my kids! If your child thinks the whole world is a stage, then maybe he should be on it. Sign him up for comedy improv classes and the next performance you see could be his.

Hours:	Performances are Sun. at 3:30pm.
Admission:	$7 per person.
Ages:	5 years and up - younger ones won't get the humor.

LA MIRADA THEATER FOR THE PERFORMING ARTS

$$$

(562) 944-9801 / www.cityoflamirada.org
14900 La Mirada Boulevard, La Mirada
(Exit Artesia Fwy [91] or Santa Ana Fwy [5] N. on Valley View, R. on Rosecrans, R. on La Mirada. [TG: 737 G4])

Golden State Children and Programs for Young Audiences are two production companies that present children's programs here three to five times a year. The theater also hosts several productions a year appropriate for families, such as comedies, musical, dramas, and concerts. Past shows include *Seussical the Musical* and *The Diary of Anne Frank*.

Hours:	Call for show dates and times.
Admission:	Tickets are usually $8 per person for the children's programs. Other tickets depend on the show, date, and time.
Ages:	5 years and up.

LANCASTER PERFORMING ARTS CENTER

$$$

(661) 723-5950 / www.lpac.org
750 W. Lancaster Boulevard, Lancaster
(Exit Antelope Valley Fwy [14] E. on Ave. 'J', N. on 10th St. West, R. on Lancaster. [TG: 4015 G5])

The theater productions here run the gamut of Broadway musicals, classical ballet and other dance, jazz or big band music, comedies, and dramas. Past performers and shows include Earth, Wind and Fire; B.B. King; *Hansel and Gretel*; Cirque Eloize; Barry Manilow, Marcel Marceau; and *Jack and the Beanstalk*. The Arts for Youth program usually stages five plays a year. Past productions have included *Rumpelstiltskin, Nutcracker, Sleeping Beauty*, and *Revenge of the Space Pandas*. If you're interested in taking a behind-the-scenes tour of the theater, call (661) 723-5876 for information.

Hours:	Call for show dates and times.
Admission:	The Arts for Youth program are usually $12 for adults; $5 for children. Other performances range from $5 - $75 per person, depending on the show, date, and time.
Ages:	3 years and up, depending on the production.

LOS ANGELES CENTRAL LIBRARY

(213) 228-7000 - Children's Literature Department;
(213) 228-7040 - cultural and educational activities / www.lapl.org
630 W. 5th Street, Los Angeles

See the entry for LOS ANGELES CENTRAL LIBRARY on page 136 for details.

MAGICOPOLIS

$$$$

(310) 451-2241 / www.magicopolis.com
1418 4th Street, Santa Monica
(Exit Santa Monica Fwy [10] N. on Lincoln Blvd., L. on Wilshire, L. on 4th St. [TG: 671 E2])

Abracadabra - make a magical place appear. Poof! Magicopolis, meaning "City of Magic," was actually created by veteran magician, Steve Spill, to make first-class magic shows available for the whole family. He has succeeded wonderfully. Penn and Teller have even given their blessings to Magicopolis by having their hands and feet cast in cement inside the lobby. While waiting for the shows to begin, watch what a resident magician has up his sleeve, and/or grab a bite to eat from the inside cafe that serves muffins, coffee, and juice.

The magic is executed in two main rooms. In the Hocus Pocus room, an intimate setting of thirty-four seats, three different magicians perform in a ninety-minute show integrating quicker-than-the-eye and "mind-reading" acts. Being close-up to the performers, however, does not insure that audience members will "get" the trick; at least it usually doesn't in my case. The Abracadabra room has 150 theater-style seats and a comfortable atmosphere. Professional, featured magicians perform in ninety-minute shows that entertain and mystify visitors with larger-scale illusions. Comedy and sleight-of-hand acts are often part of the show, too. My kids and I sat watching with mouths opened and asked, "How did he do that?" Each show incorporates some audience participation, adding to the overall enjoyment. For those who want to try a little magic of their own, check out the in-house retail shop.

Hours: Performance schedules vary, although shows are usually given in the Hocus Pocus room on Fri. at 8pm and in the Abracadabra room Sat., 2pm and 8pm; Sun., 2pm. Call for a complete schedule.

Admission: $20 per person for an evening performance; $15 for a matinee.

Ages: 6 years and up.

MARK TAPER FORUM
(213) 628-2772 or (213) 972-7211 / www.musiccenter.org
135 N. Grand Avenue at the Music Center of Los Angeles, Los Angeles

See the MUSIC CENTER OF LOS ANGELES entry on page 151 for details.

METROPOLITAN EDUCATIONAL THEATRE NETWORK (Northridge)
(877) 536-4519 / www.met2.org   *$$$$*
18111 Nordhoff Street, at the California State University of Northridge, Northridge
(From San Diego Fwy [405], exit E. on Nordhoff. From Ronald Regan Fwy [118], exit S. on Reseda Blvd., L. on Nordhoff. From Ventura Fwy [101], exit N. on Reseda, R. on Nordhoff. [TG: 501 A7])

See the entry for METROPOLITAN EDUCATIONAL THEATRE NETWORK (San Diego) on page 447 for details.

METROPOLITAN EDUCATIONAL THEATRE NETWORK (Torrance)
(877) 536-4519 / www.met2.org   *$$$$*
3330 Civic Center Drive, James Armstrong Theatre at the Torrance Cultural Arts Center, Torrance
(From Harbor Fwy [110], exit W. on Carson St., R. on Madrona Ave., R. on Civic Center Dr. From San Diego Fwy [405], exit E. on Artesia, L. on Prairie Ave., which turns into Madrona Ave., L. on Civic Center Dr. [TG: 763 E5])

See the entry for METROPOLITAN EDUCATIONAL THEATRE NETWORK (San Diego) on page 447 for details. This theater also offers numerous other family-oriented, as well as adult, productions.

MORGAN-WIXSON THEATRE
(310) 828-7519 / www.morgan-wixson.org   *$$$$*
2627 Pico Boulevard, Santa Monica
(Going W. on Santa Monica Fwy [10], exit S. on Cloverfield, L. on Pico. Going E. on 10, exit S. on 20th St, L. on Pico. [TG: 671 J1])

Several times a year the Rainbow Factory, a teenage resident children's theater company, produce show specifically for young audiences. Past shows have included *Frog Prince, The Emperor's New Clothes, Midsummer Night's Dream,* and *Rumpelstiltskin.* There are other theater shows for the whole family, as well as comedies, musicals, and dramas for older audiences. Some of these titles are *Sherlock's Last Case, Oliver,* and *Fiddler on the Roof.*

Hours: Call for shows hours.
Admission: General admission is usually $15 for adults; $12 for seniors; $10 for children, but prices
fluctuate according to show, date, and time. Call first.
Ages: Depends on the show.

MUSIC CENTER OF LOS ANGELES

(213) 972-7211 - general info; (213) 972-7483 - tours / www.musiccenter.org

$$$$$

135 N. Grand Avenue, Los Angeles

(From Harbor Fwy [110], exit E. on 4th St., L. on Olive St., go to end, L. on 1st St., R. on Grand. Going N. on Hollywood Fwy [101],
exit S. on Grand. Going S. on 101, exit E. on Temple, R. on Grand. Parking is available on Grand Ave. and, on the evening and
weekends only, at the Dept. of Water and Power on Hope St. [TG: 634 F3])

The Music Center is the crown jewel of the Los Angeles cultural scene. This sprawling, two-city block Los
Angeles complex features four powerhouse entertainment venues, each with a resident company. The
Ahmanson Theater, (213) 628-2772 or (213) 972-7200, seats about 1,700 and puts on world-class, big-name,
mainstream and Tony-award winning musical productions, many of which are terrific for the whole family. Past
productions have included *Phantom of the Opera* and *Thoroughly Modern Millie*. The **Dorothy Chandler
Pavilion**, which seats almost 3,200, is home the Los Angeles Opera, as well as numerous kid-friendly programs.
The fabulous **Walt Disney Concert Hall** is home to the Los Angeles Philharmonic and the Los Angeles Master
Chorale. There are several other performance and education facilities associated with the Disney Hall, too.
Wow! The 2,265-seat, acoustically-sophisticated, state-of-the-art concert hall is gorgeous. The fantastic-looking
pipe organ in the back is eye-catching, too. The hall also has two outdoor amphitheaters; a 300-seat one for
children's programs and a 120-seat venue for pre-concert events. Note: Just down the road at 2nd and Hope
streets is the Roy and Edna Disney/CalArts Theater (REDCAT) that seats up to 266 patrons. The 750-seat
Mark Taper Forum, (213) 628-2772, produces spectacular theater such as *Big River* and *Bring in 'Da Noise,
Bring in Da' Funk*. Note: Free guided tours of all the buildings, for third graders and up, are offered during the
week. Call for tour dates and times.

Call, or check the website, for the numerous family and educational events, some of which are free. One of
my favorite April events is Spotlight, where the stars of tomorrow (i.e. incredibly talented high schoolers)
compete in six categories in a variety show format. See FAMILY SATURDAY SERIES - PILLOW THEATRE
on page 146 for a description of a program for young children. The Young Arts series is for ages 7 to 12 and
held at Zipper Concert Hall (just down the street) on selected Saturdays at 10am for $6 per person.

Hours: Call for show dates and times.
Admission: Varies, depending on the show. Parking is about $8.
Ages: 5 years and up, depending on the show.

NORRIS CENTER

(310) 544-0403 / www.norristheatre.org

$$$$

27570 Crossfield Drive, Rolling Hills Estates

(Exit San Diego Fwy [405] S. on Hawthorne Blvd. Drive about 8 miles and turn L. on Indian Peak Rd., L. on Crossfield Dr. [TG: 793
A7])

Ballet, big band, off-Broadway shows, Chinese acrobats, storytelling, puppetry, and comedy are just a few
examples of the assortment of programs and shows put on at the Norris theater. Past productions specifically for
kids, collectively titled the Children's Series, include *Carnival of the Animals, Ramona Quimby, Ugly Duckling,
Heidi*, and the *Nutcracker*. There are usually four children's shows in the spring and four in the fall.

Hours: Call for show dates and times. Children's productions are on certain Sun. at 1pm and 4pm.
Admission: Various shows cost different prices. Tickets for the Children's Series are usually $12 per person.
Ages: 2 years and up, depending on the show.

OLD TOWN MUSIC HALL, INC.
(310) 322-2592

140 Richmond Street, El Segundo

(Exit San Diego Fwy [405] W. on the Century Fwy [105] to the end, where it turns into Imperial Hwy, turn L. on Main St., R. on Grand, L. on Richmond. [TG: 732 E2])

$$$

Step back in time, to the golden era of film where silent movies and "talkies" dominated the screens. The rich red drapes, chandeliers, intimate seating, and the sound of the mighty Wurlitzer pipe organ, which is like a one-man band, create an atmosphere of yesteryear. The proprietors, two older gentlemen who have been in business together here for over thirty years, share organ duty and run the movies. The audience gets warmed up with four or five sing-alongs while on-screen slides provide lyrics and hokey cartoons. The Wurlitzer is played at every showing and accompanies silent epic and comedy films. Past films have included *The General*, *Wings*, *Phantom of the Opera*, and the original *Ben Hur*. Talkies have included *The Firefly* with Jeanette MacDonald, *Donkey Serenade*, *Roaring Twenties* starring James Cagney and Humphrey Bogart, and *The Little Princess* with Shirley Temple. Grand pianos are on hand for ragtime and jazz concerts. What a great this-it-the-way-it-was experience for kids (and adults!).

Hours: Show times are Fri., 8:15pm; Sat., 2:30pm and 8:15pm; Sun., 2:30pm. Call to see what's playing and when the concerts are given.

Admission: $6 per person for a matinee; $7 for a nighttime show. Concerts are $20 per person.

PALMDALE PLAYHOUSE
(661) 267 - ARTS (2787) or (661) 267-5685 / www.cityofpalmdale.org/events/playhouse.html

38334 10th Street E., at the Antelope Valley Community Arts Center, Palmdale

(Exit the Antelope Valley Fwy [14] E. on Palmdale Blvd., R. on 10th St. E. [TG: 4286 B1])

$$$$

Comedy, drama, country music, jazz, magic, improv, ballet, community theater, and more is yours to experience throughout the year at the 350-seat Playhouse. Past performances have included a smorgasbord of shows from *A Victorian Holiday* to *1776* to *The Lion, the Witch, and the Wardrobe*. Annual festivals include the Shakespeare Festival and the Children's Festival, the latter of which is a day of arts, crafts, and storytelling.

Hours: Call for show hours.

Admission: Prices vary according to the show.

Ages: It depends on the show.

PANTAGES THEATER
(323) 468-1770 / www.nederlander.com/pantages.html

6233 Hollywood Boulevard, Hollywood

(Going N. on Hollywood Fwy [101], exit W. on Hollywood Blvd. Going S. on 101, exit S. on Vine St., L. on Hollywood. [TG: 593 F4])

$$$$$

The finest in Broadway musicals, as well as dramas and hot comedies, are performed at this classic venue. Theater doesn't get much better than this. A few of our favorite past productions include *Peter Pan*, which starred Cathy Rigby, and *Phantom of the Opera*. Call for a current schedule.

Hours: Call for show dates and times.

Admission: Varies, depending on the show, but ranges from $33 - $250.

Ages: 5 years and up.

PASADENA PLAYHOUSE
(626) 356-7529 / www.pasadenaplayhouse.org

39 S. El Molino Avenue, Pasadena

(Exit Foothill Fwy [210] S. on Lake Ave., R. on Colorado Blvd., L. on El Molino. [TG: 566 A5])

$$$

The Playhouse has two areas of interest for kids. The first is the plays themselves. The Playhouse does not have a family series, but often the plays are appropriate for middle-school-aged children and older. The best bargain for students are matinees, offered during the week to school groups or other children. After the play, join in a post-play discussion with some of the actors. The second area of interest is a one-hour tour. See

PASADENA PLAYHOUSE (tour), on page 165, for details.

Hours: Call for dates and times of shows.

Admission: Show prices vary according to show, date, and time. Matinees are less expensive and student rush tickets, available about 20 minutes before curtain time, are usually about $10. (Must show student ID)

Ages: 4th graders and up.

PASADENA SYMPHONY MUSICAL CIRCUS

(626) 793-7172 / www.pasadenasymphony.org

300 E. Green Street, at the Pasadena Civic Auditorium, Pasadena

(Exit Pasadena Fwy [110] N. on Fair Oaks Ave., R. on Green. [TG: 565 J5])

Eight, one-and-a-half-hour interactive and educational presentations of the Musical Circus are given October through May. This is a wonderful introduction to various types of music. The first half hour is spent in the lobby of the auditorium for the "Petting Zoo," where children are invited to try out the various instruments - clarinets, flutes, trumpets, violins, and cellos - and ask questions of the musicians. During the next hour, a soloist or a small group of musicians give a mini concert, and this is sometimes followed by a final rehearsal of the Pasadena Symphony. I bet this show will strike a chord with some of your children! Of course, the symphony also puts on concerts for older kids and adults, too.

Hours: Presentations are given on selected Sat. starting at 8:30am.

Admission: Free

Ages: 2 - 10 years.

PEPPERDINE CENTER FOR THE ARTS

(310) 506-4000 or (310) 506-4522 / www.pepperdine.edu/cfa

24255 Pacific Coast Highway, Malibu

(Exit Ventura Fwy [101] S. on Las Virgenes Rd., which turns into Malibu Cyn. Rd. Go to the end, R. on Pacific Coast Hwy. [TG: 628 G7])

Pepperdine offers a variety of programs including orchestral, choral concerts, guitar competitions, musicals, and plays. The Family Fun Series (great title!) at the Smother's Theatre presents magic, acrobatic, puppetry, song, dance, and other entertaining shows for kids. Show titles in this series have included *Jungle Book*, *Treasure Island*, and *Ugly Duckling*.

The Weisman Museum of Art, adjacent to the theater, is open one hour prior to most performances and through intermission, besides its regular operating hours. The museum features rotating temporary exhibits of historic and contemporary art. Call (310) 506-4851 for more details.

Hours: The Family Fun Series is presented one Sat. a month at 11am and at 1pm, usually in the months of October, January, February, March, and April. Call for other show dates and times.

Admission: $17.50 per person for the Family Fun Series. Inquire about prices for other shows.

Ages: 3 years and up.

PLANETARIUM SHOW

(909) 594-5611, ext. 4794 / www.mtsac.edu

1100 N. Grand Avenue at Mount San Antonio College, Walnut

(Exit Pomona Fwy [60] N. on Grand Ave., R. on Temple Ave., L. on Bonita Dr. The entrance is on Bonita. [TG: 639 H3])

Students can take a one-hour journey through the solar system to learn about constellations in the night sky, our moon, comets, meteors, and about our sun. The 100-seat planetarium holds shows for first graders through sixth graders.

Hours: Shows are offered October through May, Mon. and Wed. at 10:45am. Reservations are necessary and show spots fill up fast!

Admission: $2.50 per person.

Ages: 1st through 6th graders.

REDONDO BEACH PERFORMING ARTS CENTER

$$$$$

(310) 937-6607; (310) 372-4477 - Civic Light Opera box office /
www.redondo.org/depts/recreation/facilities/rbpac/default.asp; www.civiclightopera.com
1935 Manhattan Beach Boulevard, Redondo Beach
(Exit San Diego Fwy [405] S. on Inglewood, R. on Manhattan Beach Blvd. It's on the corner of Aviation and Manhattan Beach. [TG: 733 A5])

Home to the professional Civic Light Opera of South Bay Cities, this lovely theater, which seats about 1,450 patrons, puts on musicals that are often enthralling for the whole family. Past productions have included *The Music Man*, *Ragtime*, *West Side Story*, *Forever Plaid*, and *Funny Girl*. The center is also host to numerous other prestigious productions, including ballets, dance troupes, folk ensembles such as Aman, magicians, jazz musicians such as David Benoit, country and rock and roll musicians, distinguished speakers such as David McCullough and Robert Kennedy Jr., comedians, national athletic championships such as California Bodybuilding Championship, and much more.

Hours: Call for a schedule of events.
Admission: Prices range depending on the show, date, and seating.
Ages: 5 years and up, depending on the show.

SANTA MONICA PLAYHOUSE

$$$

(310) 394-9779 / www.santamonicaplayhouse.com
1211 4ᵗʰ Street, Santa Monica
(Exit Santa Monica Fwy [10] N. on Lincoln Blvd., L. on Wilshire, L. on 4ᵗʰ St. [TG: 671 D2])

This ninety-two seat Playhouse offers original, one-hour, family-style musicals every weekend. Most of the productions are based on well-known characters and have titles like *Alice's Wonderful Teapot* and *Captain Jack and the Beanstalk*. There is a cookies and punch intermission. Young and old will enjoy this theater experience. Ask about their special classes and workshops for acting.

Hours: Every Sat. (and some Sun.) at 12:30pm and 3pm.
Admission: $10 for adults; $9 for ages 12 and under.
Ages: 3 years and up.

SANTA MONICA PUPPETRY CENTER

$$$

(310) 656-0483 / www.puppetmagic.com
1255 2ⁿᵈ Street, Santa Monica
(Exit Santa Monica Fwy [10] N. on Lincoln Blvd., L. on Arizona, R. on 2ⁿᵈ St. Parking is on the R. The center is near the Third Street Promenade. [TG: 671 D2])

What do you get when you mix Harry Houdini with Edgar Bergen? Steve Meltzer! Steve puts on forty-five minute, musical, one-man puppet/ventriloquist/magic shows that intrigue youngsters, confound older kids, and entertain everyone. The theater, tastefully decorated with pictures and posters of magic and puppeteer greats, seats up to forty-five people in comfortable theater-style chairs. The first half of the show consists of puppets and marionettes that speak, sing, tell jokes, and even dance, with Steve's help, of course. (Remember that only person is doing this show, so it may lag a bit in places.) This former elementary school teacher has a delightful range of voices and "personalities." My kids were amazed at the magic tricks and kept trying to figure out how he did them, usually to no avail. Audience interaction throughout the show is an added highlight. Tip: This is a great place for a birthday party!

After the performance, you'll get the opportunity to see (with your eyes, not your hands) Steve's hundreds of puppets. You may also peek into his puppet workshop where you might see one of his creations in process. A small Magic Shop is here, too where puppets and magic tricks are for sale. Puppetry classes are available, too. Note: The Center is near the THIRD STREET PROMENADE (see pg. 76).

Hours: Shows are usually performed Wed. at 1pm and Sat. - Sun., 1pm and 3pm. Call first. Call, also, for Magic Shop hours and for special performance times.
Admission: $6.50 per person.
Ages: 2 to 12 years.

SILENT MOVIE THEATRE

(323) 655-2520 / www.silentmovietheatre.com

611 N. Fairfax Avenue, Los Angeles

(Going S. on Ventura Fwy [101], exit S. on Highland Ave., R. on Melrose Ave., L. on Fairfax. Going N. on 101, exit E. on Melrose, L. on Fairfax. From the Santa Monica Fwy [10], exit N. on Fairfax. From the San Diego Fwy [405], exit E. on Santa Monica Blvd., R. on Melrose, R. on Fairfax. [TG: 593 B7])

Douglas Fairbanks, Clara Bow, the Little Rascals, Alfred Hitchcock, Boris Karloff, Lillian Gish, Mary Pickford, Charlie Chaplin, and Fred Astaire - these once-household names are back in vogue again at the vintage, art deco Silent Movie Theatre. Come to enjoy two hours of old-time dramas, or for comedies, with the likes of Laurel and Hardy, The Marx Brothers, or Buster Keaton. Sunday matinees, in particular, are aimed toward the younger generation. And yes, kids laugh uproariously at clean, classic comedy - even if it's in black and white. Live organ music usually accompanies the feature presentation in this 224-seat theater. Shorts or cartoons precede the feature film classic.

Upstairs is a lounge, a cafe that sells beverages and snacks, and a silent movie stars' photo gallery to use during intermission or for a birthday party. Come here not to just watch a movie, but to experience the Hollywood of old.

Hours: Movies are shown Fri. - Sat. at 8pm (doors and box office open at 6pm); Sun. at 1pm. Call first as hours fluctuate.

Admission: $15 for adults; $10 for seniors, students, and children 11 and younger.

Ages: 7 years and up.

STORYBOOK THEATER AT THEATRE WEST

(818) 761-2203 / www.theatrewest.org

3333 Cahuenga Boulevard West, Los Angeles

(Going S. Hollywood Fwy [101], exit at Lankershim Blvd., S. on Cahuenga. Going N. on 101, exit E. on Lankershim, L. on Cahuenga. [TG: 563 C7])

Every Saturday, Storybook Theater presents a fun, musical, audience-participatory play geared for 3 to 9 year olds. Classics are re-done to appeal even more to children (with all the violence eliminated), like *Little Red Riding Hood* and *Jack In The Beanstalk*. There is an apple juice intermission in this hour-long show. Afterward, the cast stays around to talk with the kids. What a wonderful "first theater" experience! Call to find out what's playing. Ask, too, about on-site school field trips.

Hours: Sat. at 1pm.

Admission: $10 for adults; $8 for ages 12 and under.

Ages: 3 - 9 years.

SYMPHONY IN THE GLEN

(800) 440-4536 or (213) 955-6976 / www.symphonyintheglen.org

Griffith Park, Los Angeles

(Going N. on Golden State Fwy [5] or W. on Ventura Fwy [134], exit at Zoo Dr. Going E. on 134, exit S. on Victory Blvd., L. on Zoo Dr. Going S. on 5 Fwy, exit S. on Western, L. on Victory Blvd. to Zoo Dr. It's at the Old Zoo picnic area, S. of the L.A. Zoo. [TG: 564 B5])

Three or four times a year between June and October, families tote a blanket, picnic lunch/dinner, and sunscreen to the park's grassy expanse to listen to an hour-and-a-half of classical music. Past performances have included *Peter and the Wolf, Birds and Beasts,* and *Divine Mortals* featuring Beethoven's Fifth. Make sure you come for one of two pre-concert activities, offered on alternating dates. One activity is the Jr. Maestro conducting class where children and parents learn the basics of tempo and how to conduct an orchestra. Six youngsters are chosen to help lead the forty-piece orchestra. The other activity allows audiences to learn and identify how different instruments sound - flutes, violins, French horns, trumpets, etc. - and perhaps play one or two of them. Note: You have to walk the equivalent of two city blocks to reach this site. Remind your children gently that although they're at a park, this is time to sit down and soak in the ambiance of beautiful music played in a natural, outdoor setting, not run around screaming.

Hours: Pre-concert activities usually begin at 1:30pm. Concerts usually start at 3:15pm

Admission: Free. Canned good donations are requested.

Ages: 4 years and up.

TORRANCE CULTURAL ARTS CENTER / JAMES ARMSTRONG THEATRE

(310) 781-7171 - general info; (310) 781-7171 - theatre box office / www.tcac.torrnet.com

3330 Civic Center Drive, at the Torrance Cultural Arts Center, Torrance

(From Harbor Fwy [110], exit W. on Carson St., R. on Madrona Ave., R. on Civic Center Dr. From San Diego Fwy [405], exit E. on Artesia, L. on Prairie Ave., which turns into Madrona Ave., L. on Civic Center Dr. [TG: 763 E5])

The center is composed of several buildings that serve the community in various capacities. The Armstrong Theatre has a 500+ seat theater with plush seats. It's host to a variety of professional and community productions, as well as film screenings. Five special programs featuring professional performers, titled the Peanut Gallery Theatre Series, are given for youngsters and their parents usually in the months of January, February, September, November, and December. The programs feature dance, music, drama, comedy, or any combination thereof. Past shows have included *Jim Gamble Puppets*, *Sleeping Beauty*, *Dan Crow* (zany music and comedy), the *Ugly Duckling* (musical theater), and children's concerts. Check the schedule to see who and what is playing.

The Joslyn Fine Arts Gallery has three galleries usually showcasing local artists's work. Call (310) 618-6340 for more information. A music room; a performing arts studio, utilized mainly for classes and as a dance and exercise studio; and two outdoor plazas complete the complex. A small, traditional Japanese garden in the plaza area is a lovely way to connect all the buildings. It has a waterfall, koi pond, stone pathways, and something not so traditional - a redwood amphitheater.

Hours: Call for show times and dates. Peanut Gallery series' shows are given Sat. at 10am.

Admission: Prices vary for each show. Peanut Gallery shows are $8 per person

Ages: 3 to 8 years old.

TOYOTA SYMPHONIES FOR YOUTH SERIES

(323) 850-2000 / www.laphil.org

First and Grand Avenue, at the Disney Concert Hall in the Music Center, Los Angeles

(From Harbor Fwy [110], exit E. on 4th St., L. on Olive St., go to end, L. on 1st St., R. on Grand. Going N. on Hollywood Fwy [101], exit S. on Grand. Going S. on 101, exit E. on Temple, R. on Grand. [TG: 634 F3])

Five times a year the Los Angeles Philharmonic offers one-hour concerts under the collective title of Toyota Symphonies for Youth. They are designed to excite kids, particularly between the ages of 5 to 12, about the wonderful world of orchestral music. First enjoy a variety of pre-concert activities. Different stations can include arts and crafts, storytellers, dance, and/or meeting with musicians who will demonstrate their instruments. All the activities help to introduce (and reinforce) the morning's concert theme. Then, onto the concert. Past concerts include *Magical Melodies*, *Fun with Bach*, and *Peter and the Wolf*. See MUSIC CENTER (tour), on page 164, for details about taking a tour of this gorgeous facility.

Hours: Pre-concert workshop activities begin at 10am. Concerts begin at 11am on selected Sat., usually in the months of November, December, February, April, and May.

Admission: $11- $13 per person, depending on your seat. Parking is available in the Music Center Garage for $7 or at the Department of Water and Power on Hope St. for $5.

Ages: 5 to 12 years.

U.C.L.A. CENTER FOR PERFORMING ARTS

(310) 825-2101 / www.performingarts.ucla.edu; www.tickets.ucla.edu

University of California in Los Angeles, Los Angeles

(Exit San Diego Fwy [405] E. on Wilshire Blvd., L. on Westwood Blvd. to the information kiosk. Make sure you ask for a map. [TG: 632 B2])

Name it, and it plays at U.C.L.A. There are several different concert and theater venues here - the huge, 1,800-seat Royce Hall, the 580-seat Freud Playhouse, the 500-seat Schoenberg Hall, and a smaller theater that seats 200. Over 200 performances, combined in all the theaters, are featured here annually including a wide variety of musicals, classical music, chamber music, ballet, dance, circus-type of performances, Broadway's best, theater, concerts, and for-the-family shows, including family film festivals. If U.C.L.A. doesn't have it - does it exist? One of our favorites was *Stomp,* a high-energy show where performers created rhythm and music using brooms, trash can lids, and other unusual "instruments."

Hours: Call for a schedule of current shows.
Admission: Prices vary depending on the show, date, and time. Parking is $7.
Ages: It depends on the show.

U.C.L.A. PLANETARIUM

(310) 825-4434 / www.astro.ucla.edu/planetarium

$$

U.C.L.A. Campus, Westwood

(Exit San Diego Fwy [405] E. on Wilshire Blvd., L. on Westwood Blvd. to the information kiosk. It's located in the Math and Science building. Make sure you ask for a map. [TG: 632 A2])

The planetarium offers a free almost hour-long presentation every Wednesday night during the school year. The show, which is used as a teaching tool for astronomy students, but open to the public, displays and discusses the night sky in both hemispheres and the configuration of the galaxies. The show's contents varies with the presenters. Afterward, view the real sky, weather permitting, through three rooftop telescopes.

Hours: Wed. at 7pm during the school year.
Admission: Free. Parking is $7.
Ages: 8 years and up.

UNIVERSAL CITYWALK IMAX 3-D THEATER

(818) 760-8100 / www.citywalkhollywood.com

$$$

100 Universal City Plaza, Universal City

(Going N.W. on Hollywood Fwy [101], exit N. at Universal Center Dr. Going SE on 101, exit at Lankershim Blvd., L. on Cahuenga, L. on Universal Center Dr. It's right next to Universal Studios Hollywood. [TG: 563 C6])

This theater shows both 3-D and 2-D movies on a screen six stories high. The 3-D films bring a sense of involvement to the viewers as the images on screen seem to physically appear in front of the audience. While you're here, don't forget to explore the rest of UNIVERSAL CITYWALK (see pg. 140), as well as UNIVERSAL STUDIOS HOLLYWOOD (see pg. 4).

Hours: Call for a show schedule.
Admission: 3-D tickets are $9 for adults; $6 for seniors and ages 3 to 11. 2-D tickets are $12 for adults; $11 for seniors; $10 for ages 3 - 11. Parking, shared with Universal Studios Hollywood, is $8.
Ages: 4 years and up.

WALT DISNEY CONCERT HALL

(213) 972-7211 / www.musiccenter.org

135 N. Grand Avenue at the Music Center of Los Angeles, Los Angeles

See the MUSIC CENTER OF LOS ANGELES entry on page 151 for details.

WILL GEER THEATRICUM BOTANICUM

(310) 455-3723 - box office; (310) 455-2322 - more info / www.theatricum.com

$$$

1419 N. Topanga Canyon Boulevard, Topanga

(From the Ventura Fwy [101], exit S. on Topanga Canyon. Go about 5½ miles and it's on the R. From Pacific Coast Highway, go N. on Topanga Canyon Blvd. about 6 miles. It's on the L. [TG: 590 C3])

A professional, resident acting company uses repertory to perform several classics, including at least one Shakespeare play, during its season at this 300-seat outdoor amphitheater. Past productions have included

Taming of the Shrew, Our Town, A Midsummer Night's Dream, and *Harold and Maude.* During the summer, Family Fundays Kid's Shows are also presented. They feature stories and plays such as the *Velveteen Rabbit* and *Legend of King Arthur*, or performers such as Joanie Bartels and Parachute Express. Dress warmly for evening shows, bring a blanket, and pack a picnic lunch/dinner. You may also purchase food from the cafe which offers tuna salad, grilled chicken breast, Greek salad, pastries, cold drinks, and snacks.

Besides on-going classes for both children and adults and a summer youth drama camp, the Botanicum presents two other theater options for children. One option is the School Days Educational Program offered in May. Students receive a Shakespeare resource packet and an in-class visit by an actor/teacher who explains the language and the story. Once at the theater, students meet costumed actors such as Queen Elizabeth I and William Shakespeare, or President and Mrs. Lincoln, depending on the time period being studied. Some students rehearse for the play while others participate in workshops which include Stage Illusion, Mime, and Elizabethan Dance. After lunch, students watch the play. The second option is the Classroom Enrichment series. An actor/teacher will visit the classroom several times to direct students (in song, dance, stage combat, or acting) in a play to be performed before the school. Or, invite an actor/teacher to simply perform excerpts from great plays or novels by William Shakespeare, Mark Twain, Victor Hugo, or F. Scott Fitzgerald.

Hours: Call or check the website for a schedule. The Fundays are usually performed on Sundays.

Admission: Prices for the plays range from $13 - $20 for adults; $9 - $14 for students, depending on the seats; ages 6 - 12 are always $7; children 5 and under are free. The Fundays are usually $7 per person. The School Days Educational Program is $13 per student for the full day and all the preliminaries; $6 per student for most of the program and the play. Call about other program offerings.

Ages: Plays - 8 years and up. Programs can be adapted for K - 12 graders.

-----*TOURS*-----

AIR FORCE FLIGHT TEST CENTER

(661) 277-3517 / www.edwards.af.mil

Edwards Air Force Base

(Exit Golden State Fwy [5] N. on Antelope Valley Fwy [14], E. on Edwards/Rosamond and drive for a few miles. [TG: 3835 H4])

Your ninety-minute tour starts off with about a half hour or so at the Air Force Flight Test Center Museum where you'll see a short film on the history of flight testing called *First Flights*. The museum has over twenty aircraft on display outside such as a B-52D, T-33, F-104A, YA-7D, UC-45, and F-86. Inside are several grounded airplanes while others are suspended in air. You'll see an F-16, NA-37, AQM-34 Firebee drone, the X-25B concept demonstrator, and a full-scale replica of the Bell X-1. The museum is packed with memorabilia fitting for the birthplace of supersonic flight. One section is dedicated to "Mach Busters," the men who broke sound barriers, including, of course, Chuck Yeager. It shows and tells how planes (and men) were tested for this significant breakthrough. The "First Flights Wall" is a model display of the more than 100 aircraft that completed their first flight at Edwards AFB. Other items on exhibit include aircraft propulsion systems, rocket engines, life support equipment, photographs, fine art, flight jackets, personal memorabilia, and the geology, or history, of the formation of the lakebeds.

The second part of the tour consists of riding a bus along the flight line to see test planes taking off, several unmanned vehicles, and whatever else is on the base that particular day. You'll learn about the missions and the history of this center, too. The tour is comprehensive and if coupled with a tour of the NASA DRYDEN FLIGHT RESEARCH CENTER (pg. 164), you'll have a thorough overview of aeronautics and flight testing. The tour is only for groups of fifteen to forty people; fourth graders and older. Advanced reservations are required.

Hours: Call to schedule a tour date.

Admission: Free

Ages: 10 years old and up.

BIOTREK

(909) 869-6701 / www.csupomona.edu/~biotrek

$/$$

3801 W. Temple Avenue at California State Polytechnic University, Pomona

(Going E. on San Bernardino Fwy [10], exit S. on Kellogg Dr. Going N. on Orange Fwy [57], exit W. on Temple, R. on S. Campus Dr., L. on Kellogg Dr., R. on Eucalyptus, R. on University Dr. Park. Biotrek is housed in building 4 on Camphor Ln. [TG: 640 B2])

"It sure is hot in here!" is a comment from kids as they enter the humid jungle atmosphere of the rain forest. Biotrek is a three-building learning facility that features the rainforest, an ethnobotany area, and an aquatic biology center, all designed for visitors to learn about environmental preservation.

Enter the huge greenhouse, the rainforest environment, replete with 100 species of tropical plants. The tour guide explains the global impact and importance of the rainforest; and its vegetation and animals. He also talks about the different plants and their use - some are used to make spices, some for food, and some for other functions. The animals in here include a spectacled caiman, which is related to the crocodile; the odd-looking matamata "snorkeling" turtles; stick insects, which visitors can hold; and Madagascar hissing cockroaches. The building also has houses a museum of sorts, showcasing the five bionomes of Southern California in a diorama style; the impact man has had on the rainforest via mining and logging; and artifacts and exhibits that pertain to the Tongva/Gabrielino Indian tribes.

Outside, adjacent to the rainforest green house, is the ethnobotany learning center garden. (Ethnobotany means the study of how different cultures use plants). Native plants of indigenous people and other "wild" vegetation are landscaped around a pathway, running brook, and a pond. Visitors learn fascinating facts about the relationship between the Tongva and plants. They also can try their hand at grinding acorns with stones and a few other activities.

The aquatic biology component of this tour is in another adjacent building that holds a few large aquarium tanks, as well as several smaller ones. Set up by habitat, the facility includes a flood zone, representing when the Amazon River floods the rainforest and fish feed off treetops. One of the fish here is a lungfish, which adapts to search for food in muddy water. The mangrove habitat holds scat and puffer fish. Colorful, tropical fish can be seen in the coral reef tank, such as the clownfish, foxface, and even an eel. The kelp forest contains bass, sting rays, a horned shark, and sculpin fish. Other intriguing creatures include fish that make loud sounds and ones that generate electricity. A table sink allows visitors to see tidal animals up close.

Tours of Biotrek last about ninety minutes and require a minimum of sixteen people, and not more than ninety. At certain times the facility is open to the public and although the tours are not guided then, per se, a staff members are available to answer questions. Note: There is a grassy area to enjoy a picnic lunch or go to the on-campus Taco Bell or Carl's Jr.

Hours: Open September through mid-June. Call to schedule a tour. It is open to the public one day a week - call for hours.

Admission: Tours are $6 per student; adults are free. Admission for the general public is a $2 donation.

Ages: 5 years and up.

CALIFORNIA INSTITUTE OF TECHNOLOGY - SEISMOLOGY TOUR

(626) 395-6327 or (626) 395-6811 / www.gps.caltech.edu/seismo/seismo.page.html

1200 E. California Boulevard, Pasadena

(Exit Foothill Fwy [210] S. on S. Lake Ave., L. on California Blvd. It is on the Caltech campus in the Mudd Building, on the N.E. corner of Wilson Ave. and California Blvd. [TG: 566 B6])

Too often in Southern California there is a whole lot of shakin' going on. What causes this? Find out by taking a seismology tour. Much of the information is technical, but older children can appreciate it. The one-hour tour starts in the lobby, which has a timeline that shows how information comes into the lab. The lobby also has a computer that shows recent earthquake activity around the world and a computer with a touch screen that shows (with sound and animation) information on the Northridge quake and others. From here you go through the seismology lab to see giant drums where seismic data are recorded, and learn how to read the seismographs. You also go through the media center, where press conferences are held after a quake. Note: This is not a hands-on tour.

Tours are given for school groups of at least ten people, maximum twenty-five. If your group has less than ten, you will be assimilated in with another group, if possible. Students must be at least 12 years old or in the sixth grade. All tours must book the date at least one month in advance so participants have time to receive and review the provided educational materials before coming. Note: It is a requirement that all tour participants be familiar with the materials prior to taking a tour as this outing is meant to supplement, not introduce, knowledge of seismology.

Hours: Tour are offered on the first Tues. and first Thurs. of the month at 10am, 11am, 1:30pm, and 2:30pm. They are not offered during the months of January, July, August, or September.

Admission: Free

Ages: At least 12 years old or 6th grade and up.

CHINATOWN TOURS

323) 721-0774 - Chinatown Center event planner / www.chinatowncenter.com $$$$

911 N. Broadway at the Gourmet Carousel Restaurant, Los Angeles

(Going N.W. on Hollywood Fwy [101], exit N. on Alameda, L. on Alpine, R. on Broadway. Going S.E. on 101, exit N. on Broadway. [TG: 634 G2])

This tour combines a walk around Chinatown with lunch at a Chinese restaurant and cultural entertainment. The guided walking tours begin around 10am. (Large groups will be split into smaller ones.) As we walked, our guide pointed out buildings of interest, so we learned the hows and whys of the colorful architecture throughout Chinatown, as well as a history of the Chinese people, particularly the ones in this vicinity, and a history of this area. It depends on the tour guide exactly what you will see and learn about. We visited a local school, a bank, a temple, and a few other places.

Lunch is served around 11:30 at the restaurant. After a full Chinese meal in a room upstairs we were entertained by the traditional lion dance; a brief fashion show of Chinese costumes, using audience participation; and the highlight, the acrobats. Their feats are amazing! Our "tour" was done around 1pm, so we went shopping! Look up CHINATOWN (pg. 133) for details on the nearby stores and venues.

Hours: Weekdays at 10am, by reservation only.

Admission: $25 for adults; $15 for students.

Ages: 8 years and up.

FEDERAL RESERVE BANK OF SAN FRANCISCO

(213) 683-2900 / www.frbsf.org $

950 S. Grand Avenue, Los Angeles

(Exit Harbor Fwy [110] on 9th St., R. on Grand. Look for public parking close by or park at a lot at the corner of Olympic Blvd. and Olive St. [TG: 634 E5])

What actually happens to our money once it's deposited in a bank? Find out by taking a tour of the Los Angeles branch of the Federal Reserve Bank. The ninety-minute tour starts with a fifteen-minute video that describes the bank and the role of the Federal Reserve System in the U.S. economy. The rest of the tour focuses on the cash and check processing operations. You'll see how coin, currency, and checks are processed by high speed machines. You may also peruse the World of Economics exhibit in the lobby of the bank. The exhibit attempts to simplify the complex ideas of American economics by using a timeline, computer games, videotapes, and colorful murals. Over 100 free publications are available to render further aid.

Rules are enforced at the bank as a matter of security. Visitors must wear badges at all times, pass through a metal detector, and stay with the tour. No cameras are allowed. Tours need a minimum of eight participants, a maximum of thirty, and must be arranged in advance.

Hours: Tours are given Tues., Wed., and Thurs. at 10am and 1pm. The lobby is open to the public Mon. - Fri., 8am - 5pm.

Admission: Free. Parking costs about $3.

Ages: 9th graders and up.

GOODWILL INDUSTRIES (Long Beach)

(562) 435-3411 / www.goodwill.org
800 W. Pacific Coast Highway, Long Beach
(Exit Long Beach Fwy [710] E. on Pacific Coast Hwy. [TG: 795 C5])

See the entry for GOODWILL INDUSTRIES (Santa Ana) on page 265 for details. The minimum number for the tour is ten people and reservations are needed.

Hours: Tours are offered Mon. - Fri., 9am - 2pm.
Admission: Free
Ages: At least 8 years old.

GOODWILL INDUSTRIES (Los Angeles)

(323) 223-1211 / www.lagoodwill.org
342 North San Fernando Road, Los Angeles
(From the Golden State Fwy [5], exit E. on Broadway/Spring, R. on Ave 20, which turns into San Fernando. Going N. on Pasadena Fwy [110], exit W. on Figueroa, L. on San Fernando. Going S. on 110, exit N. on Ave 26, L. on Figueroa, L. on San Fernando. [TG: 594 J7])

See the entry for GOODWILL INDUSTRIES (Santa Ana) on page 265 for details.

Hours: Tours are offered Mon. - Fri., 9am - 3pm.
Admission: Free
Ages: Preferably 5th graders and up.

GUIDE DOGS OF AMERICA

(818) 362-5834 / www.guidedogsofamerica.org
13445 Glenoaks Boulevard, Sylmar
(From Golden State Fwy [5], exit N. on Roxford St., R. on Glenoaks Blvd. From Foothill Fwy [210], exit S. on Roxford St., L. on Glenoaks Blvd. [TG: 481 H3])

Guide Dogs of America is a center that breeds, raises, and trains Labrador retrievers, golden retrievers, and German shepherds for the blind. It is also a school that teaches blind men and women how to use guide dogs. These services are offered free of charge. Free tours, which last about an hour and a half, are given of the facility.

First you'll watch a twenty-minute video that shows puppies frolicking, plus students getting to know their dogs and testimonies on their lives being changed by being mobile. The film tugs at your heart. You'll walk past the administrative offices and hallways lined with photos of graduates and tour the dormitories where students stay for a month while receiving training. Note: If students are in residence, this part of the tour is bypassed. The best part, according to kids, is seeing the kennels and whelping bays of future guide dogs. Tip: Call first to see if there is a puppy litter because seeing them makes the field trips extra special. Tours are offered for groups of ten or more people with an advance registration of thirty days. Walk-in tours, or individuals, may join in on an on-going tour if one is scheduled.

Have you ever thought about being a foster parent - for a dog? Guide puppies, or future guide dogs, need temporary homes for the first eighteen months of their life. If you are willing to teach them basic obedience, love them, and encourage them to be well socialized (sort of like raising children), call for more information. The heartbreak of separation from your pup comes in the knowledge that your family enabled a blind person to be mobile and independent. You're invited to attend the graduation ceremony of your dog and the student you've helped.

Hours: Group tours are given Tues., Wed., and Thurs. at 10am and 2pm, by reservation only.
Admission: Free
Ages: Geared for fourth graders and up.

IN-N-OUT BURGER

(800) 786-1000 - locations; (626) 813-7376 - tour / www.in-n-out.com

13800 Francisquito Avenue, Baldwin Park

(Going E. on San Bernardino Fwy [10], exit at Francisquito Ave., R. onto Francisquito. Going W. the 10, exit at Francisquito Ave., L. onto Garvey at the bottom of the off ramp, follow Garvey to Francisquito. [TG: 638 B1])

Come learn the ins-n-outs of this scrumptious burger chain. Forty-five-minute tours can be given at most local fast food restaurant locations, or take a tour of the headquarters and "university" in Baldwin Park. In fact, the first In-N-Out was started in Baldwin Park in 1948. On any tour, students learn about the fresh ingredients that go into making a burger. They also might help cut up some produce, including onions, learning the proper and safe way to do so. A tour through the kitchen is insightful and so is learning about career opportunities for older kids. A meal is included in your time here - ya-hoo! A minimum of fifteen people is needed for a tour with a maximum of twenty-five students. The minimum age is kindergarten and each student must have a signed release form.

Hours: Call to make a tour reservation, which must be taken in the morning around 8:30am or 9am.
Admission: Free
Ages: Must be kindergarten and up.

JET PROPULSION LABORATORIES

(818) 354-9314 / www.jpl.nasa.gov

4800 Oak Grove Drive, Pasadena

(Going N.W. on Foothill Fwy [210], exit S.E. on Foothill Blvd., go to end and turn L. on Oak Grove Dr. Going S.E. on 210, exit S. on Gould Ave., L. on Foothill Blvd., go to end and turn L. on Oak Grove Dr. [TG: 435 E5])

"Space, the final frontier." JPL is a leading research and development center for NASA, with 160 buildings on 177 acres of land. Its mission is to observe earth, explore new worlds (via unmanned, robotic spacecraft), send back pictures, and ultimately, find the answer to the question, "Are we alone?" A twenty-minute film, *Welcome to Outer Space,* shows spectacular pictures of stars, moons, and various planet surfaces. It made my family aware of the incomprehensible vastness of our universe. My boys were awed by this realization - I just felt very small and insignificant. (Did you know that one light year translates as six trillion miles?)

Trekking over to another building, we watched Mission Control in action. The viewing room allows visitors to see the Operations Chief and others tracking and (maybe) communicating with spacecraft - it depends on what's going on. While here the docent explains all about the current space programs, hopeful future ones, and how transmission is accomplished. The next stop is the huge assembly area, or clean area, where, again, depending on what is in process, you might see actual spacecraft being assembled. Maybe you'll see a piece of history in the making!

The last stop, the museum, contains vivid photographs of star fields and pillars of gas; replica models of the Voyagers; and a Voyager gold record made for other intelligent life forms to listen to and learn about planet earth. Press the display button and listen to a sampling of the recording. The actual recording contains greetings in fifty-five languages as well as photographs of our culture, and sounds of music, the rain forest, a heartbeat, and much more. We watched a short "animated" movie about the Mars Rover, too. There are also replicas of early and modern space craft including the 1958 Explorer, the Mars Pathfinder, a full-scale model of the Galileo, and the Cassini. Our tour guide talked extensively about the models and their actual missions. Although some of it was a bit too technical for my kids (and me - I guess I'm no rocket scientist), we learned a lot.

JPL facilities can only be seen on a two-hour walking tour, which involves covering a bit of ground and going up and down several flights of stairs. You are welcome to take pictures. Reservations are required. Individuals should make reservations at least five weeks in advance. Groups need to make reservations about five months in advance. Bring your space cadets here and have a blast! Note: See the Calendar entry for details about JPL's annual Open House (pg. 580).

Hours: Tours are offered for individual or family members comprising less than 9 people, on alternating Mon., Wed., and Fri., usually at 1pm. Tours are offered to groups comprising 10 to 40 people Mon. - Fri., 10am - noon and 1pm - 3pm. Reservations are required for all tours.

Admission: Free
Ages: 7 years and up.

LONG BEACH AIRPORT TOUR

(562) 570-2679 or (562) 570-2611 / www.lgb.org
4100 Donald Douglas Drive, Long Beach
(Exit San Diego Fwy [405] N. on Lakewood Blvd., L. on Donald Douglas Dr. [TG: 796 A1])

Invite your kindergartners (and older kids) to come to the airport and take a pretend trip. A minimum of ten is required. A customized, forty-five to seventy-five-minute tour answers all their questions about what goes on here. They'll see lots of different things, depending on the busyness of the airport. Kids can talk to skycaps, go to the boarding lounges, and walk through the screening area where monitors show items going through the conveyor. Be prepared to answer questions like, "How does it take pictures of the insides of things?" and "Why?" Visitors also learn about the artwork in and architecture of this facility.

The Observation Deck is great for, well, observing planes landing and taking off. Your trip might also include a visit to the baggage area - you just never know what your child might find interesting. Kids might even get to see an Airport Fire and Rescue truck with all of its heavy-duty equipment. They will board a mock wooden aircraft and watch a video that simulates a flight. Afterwards, the kids are given little souvenirs of their "trip." Flexibility is a key for this high-flying tour.

Hours: Tours are available at your convenience, but preferably given Mon. - Fri. Three week reservations are needed.
Admission: Free
Ages: 6 years old and up.

LOS ANGELES TIMES

(213) 237-5757
202 W. 1st Street, Los Angeles
(Exit Harbor Fwy [110] E. on 4th St., L. on Main St., L. on 1st St. Or, exit Hollywood Fwy [101] S. on Alameda, R. on 1st St., L. on Spring to park at 213 S. Spring, the "employee" parking garage. To reach the Olympic plant from the 101, continue S. on Alameda St. and turn L. on 8th St. [TG: 674 B2])

Children who are at least 10 years old, or in the fifth grade, with journalistic tendencies enjoy seeing how a newspaper is put together. The beautiful, historic building with marble flooring has a lobby that contains old printing artifacts, as well as an informational and visual timeline which chronicles the inception of the Times through present day. The forty-five-minute tour goes through the editorial offices, where news from all over the world is gathered, written, and edited; the composing room, where news stories and advertisements are put together in page format and computer-generated graphics are used; and the Sports area. Visitors can look into the library, the photography department, and the test kitchen, where recipes are tested and photographed for the Food Section.

Groups may also go down the street to 2000 E. 8th Street and take a one-hour tour through the aptly-named Olympic plant, the enormous warehouse facility where over half a million copies of the newspaper are made each evening and temporarily stored. Pass through a pressroom, which is twice the size of a football field; the newsprint storage area, where robot-like automated vehicles carry rolls of newsprint weighing 2,500 pounds; the plate-making area, where newspaper pages go from photographic negatives to aluminum printing plates; and the mail room, where an automated distribution system takes newspapers from presses to the delivery trucks. Depending on the day of your visit, you might view the presses actually running, from the lobby.

Tip: Our group took both tours and found plenty to see and do in between tour times. From the Times, walk through the GRAND CENTRAL MARKET (pg. 17), walk to the LOS ANGELES CENTRAL LIBRARY (pg. 136), and/or shop downtown L.A.!

Kids (and adults) rarely realize what it takes, on a daily basis, to put together the internationally acclaimed newspaper that gets read with a cup of coffee every morning. Individuals and groups, which must consist of ten to twenty people, need to make reservations for either tour at least a week in advance. Also see LOS ANGELES

TIMES, ORANGE COUNTY (pg. 266), for a tour of the Orange County edition.

Hours: Tours of the Times building are offered to individuals Tues. and Thurs. at 1:30pm. Individuals may tour the Olympic plant Mon. - Fri., 11am, and on selected days at 9:30am and 1:30pm. Tours for groups are offered at both facilities Mon., Wed., and Fri. at 9:30am and 1:30pm; Tues. and Thurs., 9:30am. No tours are given on major holidays. Reservations are required for all tours!

Admission: Free. Parking is free at the Times garage.

Ages: Children must be at least 10 years or older.

MUSIC CENTER (tour)

(213) 972-7483 - tours / www.musiccenter.org

135 N. Grand Avenue at the Music Center of Los Angeles, Los Angeles

(From Harbor Fwy [110], exit E. on 4th St., L. on Olive St., go to end, L. on 1st St., R. on Grand. Going N. on Hollywood Fwy [101], exit S. on Grand. Going S. on 101, exit E. on Temple, R. on Grand. Parking is available on Grand Ave. and, on the evening and weekends only, at the Dept. of Water and Power on Hope St. [TG: 634 F3])

This two-city block Los Angeles complex features powerhouse entertainment venues - the Ahmanson Theater, Dorothy Chandler Pavilion, Walt Disney Concert Hall, and Mark Taper Forum. Free guided tours of all the buildings, for third graders and up, are offered during the week. Call for tour dates and times. See MUSIC CENTER (pg. 151) for details about the buildings.

Hours: Call for tour dates and times.

Admission: Free. Parking can cost up to $8.

Ages: 2nd graders and up.

NASA DRYDEN FLIGHT RESEARCH CENTER

(661) 276-3446 / www.dfrc.nasa.gov

Lilly Avenue, Edwards Air Force Base

(Exit Golden State Fwy [5] N. on Antelope Valley Fwy [14], E. on Edwards/Rosamond, R. on Lilly Ave., almost to Hwy 58. [TG: 3835 H4])

A mural of twenty aircraft that reflects the aeronautical heritage of NASA Dryden is in the lobby of the Visitors' Center. This is the primary research and test center for flight research and the space shuttle program, as well as a backup landing site. The tour begins with a fifteen-minute, somewhat technical film that gives insight as to the importance and accomplishments of the space program. During your ninety-minute guided walking tour, you'll go into a large hangar to see and learn about past research aircraft, particularly the 'X' series of experimental aircraft; some of the current planes being tested; and the massive dry lake bed used for a runway and NASA landing site. We saw a lunar aircraft (LLRV), too, that helped train Apollo astronauts how to land on the moon. Note: Neil Armstrong was a research pilot here before joining the space program. Admittedly, my children also like seeing the doors to the office building because it was a shot frequently used in the TV show, *I Dream of Jeannie*.

Much of the information on the tour is technical, so I was a little surprised how much my boys (as they range in ages) enjoyed it. Any and all questions (and my kids had a lot) are fully answered, and the knowledge that does sink in help make this a memorable tour. Outside, next to the parking lot are several more test planes to look at. The tour is only open for groups of fifteen people to a maximum of sixty-five. Docents try to adjust the tour to make it age appropriate. Reservations for tours are necessary, so please call at least three weeks before you'd like to visit. Combine your visit here, if possible, with a trip down the street at the AIR FORCE FLIGHT TEST CENTER. (See page 158.)

Hours: Tours are offered Mon. - Fri. at 10:15am and 1:15pm by reservation only.

Admission: Free

Ages: 8 years and up.

NBC STUDIO TOUR

(818) 840-4444

3000 W. Alameda Avenue, Burbank

(Going E. on Ventura Fwy [134], exit S. on Pass Ave., L. on Alameda. Going W. on 134, exit at Hollywood Way, R. on Alameda. [TG: 563 E3])

Start your seventy-minute walking tour of the NBC Studios by, fittingly enough, watching TV. A six-minute film depicts the history of NBC, including clips of classic shows. Then, walk through huge warehouses filled with props from past and present shows. It helps to be a fan of either *Days of Our Lives* or *The Tonight Show* since the tour emphasizes these particular shows. You might see, depending on availability, *The Tonight Show* set, the wardrobe department, a video demonstration of make-up, an NBC Sports Presentation, set construction, production studios, and maybe even a star or two. It's all contingent on what is going on at the studio that day, but the tour gives at least a glimpse of behind the scenes of a working television studio. In the last room, a few visitors are asked to stand against a blue background. Via screen magic, on the video monitor they look like they are flying. Note: Free tickets for *The Tonight Show,* for ages 18 years and older, are available at the studio, so you can combine a behind-the-scenes tour with watching a live show all in the same day. Be forewarned that the tickets go fast.

Bring a sack lunch and go to the JOHNNY CARSON PARK (see pg. 51), right across the street from the studio.

Hours:	Tours are given Mon. - Fri., 9am - 3pm, every hour on the hour. Tours are also given Sat., 10am - 2pm during the summer.
Admission:	$7.50 for adults; $4 for ages 5 - 12; children 4 and under are free.
Ages:	6 years and up.

NORWALK DAIRY

(562) 921-5712

13101 E. Rosecrans, Santa Fe Springs

(Going N.W. on Santa Ana Fwy [5], exit N. on Carmenita Rd., L. on Rosecrans Ave. Going S.E. on 5, exit E. on Rosecrans. [TG: 737 B3])

California once boasted of numerous dairies, but they've become more rare with urbanization. This family-owned and operated working dairy shows city slickers how their over 200 cows are cared for, fed, and milked. Visitors also see the processing room for the milk, the homogenizer, and how milk is bottled and cartoned. Norwalk Dairy produces and bottles their own brand of milk - homogenized, whole, low-fat, and most important, chocolate. The forty-five-minute tour needs a minimum group of fifteen. No tours are given for a while after it rains.

Hours:	Call to schedule a tour.
Admission:	Free
Ages:	4 years and up.

PASADENA PLAYHOUSE (tour)

(626) 356-7529 / www.pasadenaplayhouse.org

39 S. El Molino Avenue, Pasadena

(Exit Foothill Fwy [210] S. on Lake Ave., R. on Colorado Blvd., L. on El Molino. [TG: 566 A5])

The renowned Playhouse offers one-hour tours. Visitors see first hand what the audience normally doesn't see - behind-the-scenes. The tour may include seeing the green room, dressing rooms, and other rooms of interest, while hearing the history of the theater as well as this particular area. A minimum of five people is necessary. See PASADENA PLAYHOUSE (pg. 152) for details about the shows presented here.

Hours:	Call to book a tour.
Admission:	Free
Ages:	4th graders and up.

SANITATION DISTRICTS OF LOS ANGELES COUNTY TOURS

(562) 699-7411 / www.lacsd.org

1955 Workman Mill Road, Whittier

(Going N. on San Gabriel River Fwy [605], exit at Peck Rd., turn L. at bottom of off ramp on Pellissier which turns into Workman Mill. Going S. on 605, exit S. on Peck R., L. on Workman Mill. [TG: 637 E6])

Do your kids run after trash trucks? Mine did when they were little. Now it's a struggle to get them to take out the trash. The sanitation department offers two different tours regarding trash and sewage treatment. The ninety-minute landfill tour takes visitors into and kind of through one of the largest landfills in the country. (Don't breathe in too deeply.) There are several stops along the way including the station where trucks are weighed; the disposal yard where trash is sorted and separated by category such as recyclables, appliances, yard waste, etc; and an area where biogases, namely methane, are converted to electricity and clean-burning automobile fuel. Students learn about ecology and what happens when a landfill closes. Note that for this tour, only one vehicle (i.e. a bus) is allowed on the premises.

The one-hour walking tour of the water treatment plant can be taken in conjunction with the landfill tour, or separately. Students walk through the control room of the plant and see tanks of water where solids have settled. They'll learn how water is cycled, about water quality, conservation, and see pictures and samples of treated water. The minimum number of participants on each tour is fifteen; the maximum is seventy. If you can't come to the plant, staff members will come to your facility to talk about wastewater treatment, solid waste management, and even environmental careers. Various resources are available for teachers.

Hours: Call to schedule a tour given Mon. - Fri. between 8am - 3pm.

Admission: Free

Ages: 5th graders and up.

SONY PICTURE STUDIOS TOUR

(323) 520-TOUR (8687)

$$$$

10202 W. Washington Boulevard, Culver City

(Exit Santa Monica Fwy [10] S. on Overland Ave., L. on Washington Blvd., R. on Madison Ave. Park under the Sony Plaza on the L. [TG: 672 G1])

Catch a glimpse of great moments in movie and television history that have been made on this forty-four-acre lot. The two-hour-plus walking tour begins in the lobby of the architecturally gorgeous Sony Plaza building. Some of the costumes we saw on display behind glass here included Captain Hook's pirate outfit, Tinkerbell's dress, and dresses (and furniture and a stagecoach) from the 1994 version of *Little Women*.

First watch a twenty-minute movie on the history of Columbia/Tristar/Sony, including some classic film footage. Then, walk across the street to the main cluster of buildings. In a park-like setting, visit the Thalberg building which houses two original Oscars, as well as several others made for the studios, for "Best Picture" awards. The tour continues past numerous buildings that were once dressing rooms to stars and are now less-glamorous editing or business offices. You'll hear a little bit about Louis B. Mayer, Judy Garland, Joan Crawford, and other famous alumni.

Because this is a real working studio, what you see next differs from tour to tour, depending on the day, the time of day, and what shows are being filmed. We saw the scoring stage, with chairs and microphones ready for musicians to record; the wardrobe department, where seamstresses were busy at work and where the clothes "closet" was almost as big as my house; and we walked through many of the sound stages, including the one housing the Jeopardy set. The huge sound stages, which have padded walls that block out 98% of sound, are in a constant state of flux - either under construction, being torn down, or containing sets of shows currently on the air. Not to take away from the magic of Hollywood, but we saw a lot of equipment, free-standing doorways, stairs that led nowhere, props of all kinds, and lots of stuff (i.e. nails, trash, and boards) just left around. Watch your step! Our tour guide pointed out the sound stage where the yellow brick road once wound through Munchkinland, the one where agents from *Men in Black* battled outlaw aliens from outer space, and another one that holds a pool (i.e. tank) where Ethel Merman swam. Tip: Call ahead to get a schedule of shows being filmed to combine a tour with the possibility of being part of a studio audience. Finish your time here by shopping on

Main Street, which is the only place picture-taking is allowed. The "street" is comprised of a row of stores, including an emporium stocked with Sony products, and a few places to grab a bite to eat.

> **Hours:** Tours depart Mon. - Fri., at 9:30am, 11am, noon, and 2:30pm. Reservations are required.
> **Admission:** $20 per person.
> **Ages:** 12 years and up only.

VAN NUYS AIRPORT TOUR

(818) 785-8838 / www.lawa.org

Roscoe Boulevard, Van Nuys

(Exit the San Diego Fwy [405] W. on Roscoe Blvd. The actual address is on Sherman Way, but this is where visitors meet for a tour. [TG: 531 D2])

Here's a way to stay grounded while touring an airport - take the ninety-minute bus tour of the Van Nuys airport. Groups must provide their own bus, or ask if the airport has one available. There are several stops along the way, depending on what's available on the day of your visit. You cruise along the service road and runway, and look inside hangars. Stops could include seeing the fire station and the radar facilities. Visit "Vinny," the airport's kid-friendly educational airplane. As the children watch planes land and take off, they'll learn the history of the airport and gain some high-flying knowledge. Bring a sack lunch and eat at the observation site while watching the planes in flight.

> **Hours:** Tours are offered for groups of fifteen or more people, Mon. - Fri., 9:30am and 11am.
> Reservations are required.
> **Admission:** Free
> **Ages:** Must be at least in the 1st grade, and up.

WARNER BROS. VIP STUDIO TOUR

$$$$$

(818) 972-TOUR (8687) / wbsf.warnerbros.com

4000 W. Warner Boulevard, Burbank

(Going E. on Ventura Fwy [134], exit S. on Pass Ave., L. on Olive/Warner. Going W. on 134, exit at Hollywood Way, L. on Alameda., L. on Hollywood Way to Warner. [TG: 563 D4])

Kids must be at least 8 years old to participate in this two-hour, part walking, part cart tour that gives an intimate, historical, and educational look at how a studio works. The waiting room has props from *Casablanca* and *Batman*. First you'll watch a short film that offers highlights of shows created by Warner Bros., just to get you in the mood. Board a cart to the museum, a fantastic archive of rows and rows and rows of costumes, plus props, original scripts, and more. See what you recognize from your favorite flicks.

Whatever else you see on the day of your visit depends on what is happening that day at the studio. You'll see numerous backlots and exterior sets from classic to current movies and television shows; sound stages and interior sets from *Friends* and *Norm* (the sets rotate, depending on what is currently being filmed here); and you might even see a set being constructed at the craft/production shop. You could see a celebrity or the filming of a current show. There might be the opportunity to enter the Foley stage to see how sound is recorded. No matter what you see and do, this tour affords visitors a great opportunity to see what actually goes go on behind the scenes. It will also either take some of the romance out of picture-making, or make your child want to be involved in the process! Reservations are required. Adults need photo a I.D. No video or tape recording is allowed.

> **Hours:** Tours, for no more than 12 people at a time, leave every half hour Mon. - Fri., 9am - 3pm.
> **Admission:** $32 per person.
> **Ages:** 8 years and up.

WILDLIFE SANCTUARY TOUR

(909) 594-5611, ext. 4794 / www.mtsac.edu

1100 N. Grand Avenue, Mount San Antonio College, Walnut

(Exit Pomona Fwy [60] N. on Grand Ave., R. on Temple Ave., L. on Bonita Dr. The entrance is on Bonita. [TG: 639 H3])

A forty-five-minute guided tour of this wildlife environment includes walking the dirt footpath, which is not stroller-friendly, to see and learn about the plants and animals and their eco systems. Look for the turtles in the pond and the variety of birds that visit. There are no caged animals here, but free roaming lizards, squirrels, raccoons, and other critters. A guide from the college explains why the plants and animals need protection and what visitors can do to help. The minimum number of students is ten; the maximum, thirty. Also see FARM TOUR (pg. 181) for another tour given by Mount San Antonio College.

      Hours: Tours are offered Tues. and Thurs. at 9am, 10am, 11am, 2pm, 3pm, and 4pm. Reservations are required.
  Admission: Free, but donations are appreciated.
      Ages: Elementary-school age kids.

-----TRANSPORTATION-----

ALFREDO'S
(562) 434-6121

Alfredo's has seventeen concessions throughout Southern California, along the beach and in many parks. They rent kayaks - $5 an hour for single, $15 an hour for double; pedal boats - $15 a half hour; as well as bikes, skates, and boogie boards. The boat rentals are available usually daily in the summer, and on weekends only the rest of the year. Call for their locations.

AMERICAN HERITAGE MARINE INSTITUTE
(714) 970-8800 / www.americanpride.org
Rainbow Harbor off Shoreline Drive, Long Beach
(Heading S. on the Long Beach Fwy [710] follow the signs to Downtown Long Beach and the Aquarium of the Pacific, R. on Aquarium Way into the parking structure. The ship is at Dock #3. [TG: 825 D2])

$$$$

Isn't she a beauty? This three-mast "tallship," originally built in 1941, now serves as a historic nautical educational tool for students and adults. Several programs, both at dock and at sea, are offered throughout the year. For instance, a four-hour at-dock program includes getting the galley ready for a pretend voyage. This entails swabbing the decks, singing sea chanteys, hoisting barrels, and talking with the in-costume characters/sailors about their life and their duties on board ship. The cost is $20 per student. A six-hour program, part sailing and part at dock, includes reliving the life of a 19th-century sailor - learning history by living it. The cost is $48 per student. Other programs include sleeping overnight on the ship, sailing to Catalina, and even three-day journeys. Whale-watching tours are given in season - December through April - with a marine biologist on board. Participants look for whales as well as help raise the sails, dissect fish, and learn elementary navigation skills. The cost for whale watching starts at $14 per person.

      Hours: Call for a schedule of events or to book a tour.
  Admission: Prices are listed above.
      Ages: Most programs are geared for 3rd graders and up.

AMTRAK
(800) USA RAIL (872-7245) / www.dot.ca.gov/hq/rail; www.amtrak.com

Ride the rails! See page xi (in the front) for more information.

AQUALINK
(562) 591-2301 / www.lbtransit.com/aqualink.html
Shoreline Drive, Long Beach
(Exit San Diego Fwy [405] S. on Long Beach Fwy [710] to the end of the Downtown exit, which turns into Shoreline Dr., R. on Aquarium Way. This stop is in front of the Long Beach Aquarium. [TG: 825-D1])

$

"Taxi!" The AquaLink, or water taxi, is a fun and inexpensive way to see a part of the Long Beach Harbor. The seventy-five seat catamaran cruises by the *Queen Mary*, past charter fishing boats, and past the working port in the fifth largest city in California. A snack shop is available. One-way fare covers departing from the AQUARIUM OF THE PACIFIC (pg. 178) and arriving at Alamitos Bay Landing (towards Seal Beach), or vice versa, with a stop over at the QUEEN MARY (pg. 114). Note that if you de-board at the *Queen Mary*, you'll have to pay another one-way fare if you want to resume your cruise. A round-trip ride takes ninety minutes.

Hours: Open daily in the summer; open the rest of the year, Fri. - Sun. Call for a schedule of departure/arrival times.

Admission: $1 per person each way; $2 round trip.

Ages: All

BEVERLY HILLS TROLLEY

$$

(310) 285-2438 or (310) 285-2551 / www.beverlyhills.org
Departs from the corner of Rodeo Drive and Dayton Way, Beverly Hills
(Exit San Diego Fwy [405] E. on Santa Monica Blvd., R. on Dayton Wy. There is parking just past Rodeo Dr. on the R. [TG: 632 F2])

This is the best bargain in Beverly Hills! If you're in the area and want to give your kids a taste of the posh lifestyle, at an affordable price to you, hop on board a trolley for your choice of mini-adventures. A forty-minute Sites and Scenes narrated tour shows riders some of the most famous sights in Beverly Hills, including a few celebrity homes, film locations, some of the high-priced boutiques, and the elegant hotels. The ninety-minute Art and Architecture tour points out some of the most significant art and architectural locations around town, including City Hall, galleries, Creative Artists Agency, Museum of Television & Radio, and more. Note: Parking in the structure on the corner is free for the first two hours, so after your ride, spend some time window shopping on Rodeo Drive!

Hours: The Sites tour runs May through June, and September through November on Sat. only on the hour, noon - 4pm. It also runs July through Labor Day and the latter part of December, Tues. - Sat. every hour, noon - 5pm. The Art tour is offered July through New Year's on Sat. at 10:30am. All tours are canceled if it is raining.

Admission: $5 for adults per tour; $1 for children 11 and under. Tickets are available from the trolley driver on a first come, first serve basis.

Ages: 5 years and up.

BIKE MAPS (Los Angeles County)

The web site www.labikepaths.com is a fantastic resource. It actually covers all of Southern California, not just L.A., with links to specific counties for maps, bikeways, and other cycling information. Another helpful contact website and phone number is for the State of California Caltrans Office of Bicycle Facilities: (916) 653-0036; www.dot.ca.gov/hq/tpp/offices/bike/contracts.htm. Also try the Los Angeles County Metropolitan Transportation Authority at (213) 922-3068 or Los Angeles County Public Works at (626) 458-3941.

BIKE TRAIL: LONG BEACH SHORELINE

!/$

Bay Shore Avenue to Shoreline Village, Long Beach
(Take San Diego Fwy [405] or San Gabriel River Fwy [605] to 22 Fwy W. Exit S. on Studebaker, R. on Westminster, which turns into 2nd St, L. on Bay Shore Ave.[TG: 826 B3]; Or, start at the other end by exiting the Long Beach Fwy [710] E. on Shoreline Dr. and into Shoreline Village. [TG: 825 D2])

This 3.1 mile (one-way) easy, paved riding path follows along the Pacific Ocean. An ocean breeze and practically no hills makes it a delightful ride for the family. Stop and shop at SHORELINE VILLAGE (see pg. 127) with its nice array of quaint-looking restaurants and stores. Also, check out other places nearby - AQUARIUM OF THE PACIFIC (see pg. 178), QUEEN MARY (see pg. 114), and SCORPION (see pg. 117).

Hours: Open daily, dawn - dusk.

Admission: Free, although parking at Shoreline Village costs up to $6 maximum.

Ages: 5 years and up.

BIKE TRAIL: LOS ANGELES RIVER TRAIL

(323) 913-4688 or (323) 913-7390 - Griffith Park; (213) 381-3570 - Friends of the L.A. River

Griffith Park, Los Angeles

(Going N. on Golden State Fwy [5] or W. on Ventura Fwy [134], exit at Zoo Dr. and follow the signs. Going E. on 134, exit S. on Victory Blvd., L. on Zoo Dr. Going S. on 5 Fwy, exit S. on Western, L. on Victory Blvd. to Zoo Dr. The bike trail extends from Victory Blvd. in Burbank to Fletcher Drive at Atwater Village. The best place to park is inside Griffith Park, near the bike trail entrance where Zoo Drive meets Riverside Dr./Victory Blvd. [TG: 564 B4])

The first five miles of this urban bikeway are not always quiet, as some of it parallels the Golden State Freeway. The paved bike trail is, however, entirely off-road. Although the riverbed is up against concrete slopes, there are now trees, flocks of birds, and even a few ponds along the way, plus portions of it are lit at night. The next forty-seven miles are still in the planning and making-it-work stage, although the next three-mile stretch, heading through Elysian Valley towards downtown L.A., has already begun. Eventually, the pathway will stretch from the mountains all the way to sea along the Los Angeles River. For now, the bike path goes along GRIFFITH PARK (see pg. 48), so enjoy a side trip into the park. (See this entry for more details about the park, its zoo, and its museums.)

    Hours: Open daily, sunrise - sunset.

Admission: Free

     Ages: 6 years and up.

BIKE TRAIL: SAN GABRIEL RIVER TRAIL

Lakewood, Long Beach, Seal Beach

(Exit San Gabriel Fwy [605] W. on South St. (by Cerritos Mall), L. on Studebaker, turn R. into Liberty Park to park. [TG: 766 F2])

This two-way, concrete river trail, a right-of-way for bicyclers and skaters, actually travels almost the whole length of the San Gabriel River (i.e. flood control waterway). It begins (or ends, depending on how you look at it) in Seal Beach at Marina Drive, just west of 1st Street, and ends (or begins) in Azusa at San Gabriel Canyon Road, north of Sierra Madre. The pathway has several access points along the way. The route sometimes follows along main streets, although it just as often veers completely away from them. Depending on where you catch the trail, it passes under bridges; goes through some scenic areas that are a delight to behold; past parks; past people's backyards; and even through sections that don't feel as safe as I'd like.

One of our favorite stretches starts at LIBERTY PARK (Cerritos) (see pg. 53) and goes all the way to SEAL BEACH (see pg. 199). Along the way, we sometimes stop off at Rynerson Park, which has playgrounds and paved pathways throughout; the Long Beach Town, which has restaurants, fast food places, a movie theater, Barnes and Noble, Sam's Club, and lots more stores; and EL DORADO NATURE CENTER (see pg. 43) and EL DORADO PARK (see pg. 43). The latter park is beautiful and there is no admission fee from the bike path. Sometimes we actually make it to Seal Beach! We then ride to the ocean's edge and go along Main Street into the quaint town of Seal Beach, where there are plenty of shops and a RUBY'S restaurant (see pg. 206) at the end of the pier. (We also cheat sometimes and invite my husband to meet us for lunch or dinner, and then have him drive us all home in the van!) Non-stop from Liberty Park to Seal Beach takes my older children and I about an hour. This section of the riverbank route is also great for birdwatching. We've seen numerous herons, egrets, and pelicans.

    Hours: Open daily, dawn - dusk.

Admission: Free

     Ages: 4 years and up.

BIKE TRAIL: SOUTH BAY

Torrance County Beach to Pacific Palisades

(Torrance Beach: Exit Harbor Fwy [110] W. on Pacific Coast Hwy., L. on Ave I when P.C.H. turns north, R. on Esplanade Ave. Find an entrance to the beach and start pedaling. [TG: 792 H1]; Pacific Palisades: Take Santa Monica Fwy [10] W. to the end and go N. on Palisades Beach Rd. [1], which turns into P.C.H. The north end of Will Rogers State Beach is located by the intersection of P.C.H. and Sunset Blvd. [TG: 630 H6])

Life's a beach and this twenty-mile, two-lane, relatively flat concrete bike trail emphasizes that by cruising mostly right along the sandy shores of California's beaches. It passes through Venice beach, the Santa Monica Pier, and other state treasures. There are many stores and eateries (and restrooms!) to stop off at along the strand. Of course weekends, especially in the summer, are very crowded. Don't forget your sunscreen.

Hours: Open daily, sunrise - sunset.
Admission: Free
Ages: 4 years and up.

CALIFORNIA AQUATICS

$$$

(562) 431-6866 - office; (562) 434-0999 - beach
Bay Shore Avenue and 2nd Street, Long Beach
(Take San Diego Fwy [405] or San Gabriel River Fwy [605] to 22 Fwy W., exit S. on Studebaker Rd., R. on Westminster which turns into 2nd St. Bay Shore is just over the second bridge. [TG: 826 B2])

Kayak rentals are $5 to $7 an hour here. California Aquatics also offers weekend water field trips for the family. Another option is to sign up to become a member of the Snorkeling By Kayak Club. The $35 membership fee is good for four years for high school students only, entitling the card bearer and immediate family members (best suited for junior high schoolers and up) to rent kayaks, wetsuits, and skin-diving equipment for only $10 per day! This organization will also come to your school (a facility with a pool is preferable) and teach a series of classes on snorkeling and kayaking. Note that there is another Aquatics location on Appian Way, by Mother's Beach.

Hours: Open weekends only in the winter. Call for all hours.
Ages: 5 years and up.

GONDOLA AMORE

$$$$$

(310) 376-6977 / www.gondolaamore.com
260 Portofino Way at the Portofino Hotel and Yacht Club, Redondo Beach
(From San Diego Fwy [405], exit S. on Western, R. on 190th St., which turns into Anita St., L. on Pacific Coast Hwy. From Harbor Fwy [110], exit W. on Torrance, R. on Pacific Coast Hwy. From P.C.H., turn W. on Beryl, which turns into Portofino Way. Your gondolier will meet you in the lobby. [TG: 762 H4])

O solo mio! This one-hour gondola cruise is a unique way to see the Redondo harbor and shoreline. During the day you'll also see Catalina Island (on a clear day), sailboats, waterfowl, and maybe a few seals. Nighttime rides bring about their own magic (and romance). The two gondolas, operated by the owner and by lifeguards, seat up to four people, have canopies for privacy, and small twinkling lights around the boat and canopies. Amore provides blankets, as the ocean air can get chilly even on a summer night, cups for your drinks, fresh fruit, and bread and cheese. Your list of things to bring includes jackets, a music cassette, beverages, and your camera. Tips: Before or after your cruise, check out the nearby Cheesecake Factory for scrumptious food and/or walk around the pier. (Look up REDONDO BEACH INTERNATIONAL BOARDWALK on page 126 for details.)

Hours: Open daily, noon - 9pm. Reservations are required. Note: Holiday seasons book quickly.
Admission: $75 for two people; $10 for each additional person. Note: AAA members receive a discount.
Ages: 4 years and up.

GONDOLA GETAWAY

$$$$$

(562) 433-9595 / www.gondolagetawayinc.com
5437 E. Ocean Boulevard, Long Beach
(Exit San Diego Fwy [405] S. on Cherry Ave., L. on Ocean Blvd. [TG: 762 H4])

Long Beach, California is transformed into Venice, Italy when you go on this gondola ride. I know this attraction is thought of as a romantic excursion, and it is. It is also a wonderful treat for your child. Step into a Venetian gondola and for one hour, gently slip in and out through the waterways and canals of Naples. Your gondolier will serenade you with Italian music, regale you with interesting tales, or quietly leave you alone. After our kids plied my husband and I with questions about the possibility of sharks and whales, they settled down to enjoy the ride and look at the incredible homes along the waterfront. Christmas time is particularly spectacular, as many of the houses are decked out with lights, animated figures, etc. Make reservations for this time period far in advance.

Bread, cheese, salami, and a bucket of ice are provided, as is a blanket for the colder nights. Bring your own liquid refreshment. Your child will now be dreaming of visiting a tiny little town far away in a boot-shaped country. Ciao!

Hours: Open daily for cruises, 11am - 11pm. Suggested reservations are two weeks in advance.

Admission: Gondolas carry two to six people - $65 for the first two passengers; $15 for each additional person. The Carolina carries eight to fourteen people - $20 per person. Fleet cruises carries twenty to fifty-six people - $18 per person.

Ages: 4 years and up.

LONG BEACH MARINE INSTITUTE

(714) 540-5751 / www.longbeachmarineinst.com

5857 Appian Way, Long Beach

(Take San Diego Fwy [405] or San Gabriel River Fwy [605] to 22 Fwy W. Exit S. on Studebaker, R. on Westminster, which turns into 2nd St., R. on Appian Way, near the bridge, first L. in the Marina lot parking, on the Sea Explorer Base. [TG: 826 D2])

"The Long Beach Marine Institute, formerly the Newport Institute of Oceanography, is an association of researchers and educators dedicated to bringing marine field research into the classroom and the classroom into the field." (A quote from the institute's brochure.) L.B.M.I. offers a myriad of different programs to encourage hands-on learning about marine life and their habitats. Most programs are offered for groups of twenty-five or more. If your group number is smaller, the L.B.M.I. workers will hook you up with another group. Besides going on the guided kayak tours, snorkeling excursions, and guided tidepool tours, being on board the *Conqueror* is a main attraction. This ninety-foot, ship-shape vessel is the host and means of transportation for several field trips.

The three-hour Sea Creature Trawl is a popular expedition. After a slide presentation and boat orientation, set sail for adventure. Organisms from the sea floor are gathered (by use of a trawl) on board to be inspected and sorted through. Kids love being able to put their hands in this fascinating pile of gunk to find "treasures." They can also examine their findings under a microscope. Combine the Sea Creature Trawl with the Marine Mammal Safari (more than just a whale-watching cruise) for only a few dollars more. Another special outing combines a sleep-over on the boat with the Sea Creature Trawl, and a morning kayak trip in the back bay.

Hours: Call for times for various excursions.

Admission: Prices range from $6 per person for a tidepool tour to $18 for a Sea Creature Trawl to $73 for the sleep over, and so on.

Ages: 4 years and up, depending on the activity.

LONG BEACH SPORT FISHING

(562) 432-8993

555 Pico Avenue, Long Beach

(Exit Long Beach Fwy [710] W. on Anaheim, L. on Santa Fe Ave., L. on 9th St., which turns into Pico. [TG: 825 C2])

Fishing and whale-watching cruises (January through March) are offered here.

Admission: $13 for adults for the two-and-a-half hour whale-watching cruise; $10 for children 12 and under.

Ages: 6 years and up.

LOS ANGELES COUNTY RACEWAY

(661) 533-2224 / www.lacr.net

6850 East Avenue T, Palmdale

(Exit Antelope Valley Fwy [14] on Pearblossom, which turns into East Avenue T when it crosses Hwy 138. [TG: 4287 E5])

The raceway is home to the National Hot Rod Association Championship Drag Strip (i.e. a legal place for drivers to "street" race) and International MOTO Cross Track. Spectators can watch a variety of cars and motorcycles compete in speed contests.

    Hours: Call for a schedule.

    Admission: $5 - $10 per person, depending on the date and type of race.

    Ages: 6 years and up.

LOS ANGELES SIGHTSEEING CRUISES

(310) 831-0996 / www.lasightseeingcruises.com

Berth 78, Ports O' Call Village, San Pedro

(Exit Harbor Fwy [110] S. on Harbor Blvd. and follow the signs. [TG: 824 D6])

    Enjoy a one-hour cruise of the inner and outer harbor, past supertankers, cruise ships, a Coast Guard station, Terminal Island, a Federal Prison, and Angels Gate Lighthouse. Two-hour coastline cruises along the Palos Verdes Peninsula, and whale-watching cruises are also available. Two-and-a-half hours cruises go all the way to Long Beach, past the *Queen Mary* and *Scorpion*, under bridges and through canals.

    Hours: One-hour cruises depart from the Village Boat House on the hour, Mon. - Fri., noon - 4pm; Sat. - Sun. and holidays, noon - 5pm. Two-hour cruises (and longer) depart on the weekends at 11:30am, 1:30pm, and 3:30pm. Closed Thanksgiving and Christmas.

    Admission: One-hour cruises are $8 for adults; $4 for ages 6 - 12; children 5 and under are free. Two-hour cruises are $12 for adults; $6 for ages 6 - 12. Two-and-a-half hour cruises are $15 for adults; $8 for ages 6 - 12.

    Ages: 4 years and up.

MARINA BOAT RENTALS

(310) 574-2822 / www.boats4rent.com

13719 Fiji Way, Marina Del Rey

(Take Marina Fwy [90] to the end where it turns into the Marina Exwy, L. on Mindanao Wy., L. on Lincoln, R. on Fiji Wy. [TG: 702 B1])

    Located in FISHERMAN'S VILLAGE (see pg. 125), Marina Boat Rentals includes kayaks - $12 per hour for a single, $20 an hour for a double; pedal boats - $15 an hour; sailboats - $30 an hour for a fourteen footer; motorboats - $40 an hour for a six-passenger boat that doesn't leave the harbor, and $75 an hour for a six-passenger boat that does; electric boats - $60 an hour; and wave runners - $90 an hour.

    Hours: Open in the summer daily, 9am - 9pm. Open the rest of the year daily, 10am - 5pm or so, depending on the weather.

    Admission: Prices listed above.

    Ages: 4 years and up.

METROLINK (Los Angeles County)

(800) 371-5465 / www.metrolinktrains.com

    Metrolink offers a fairly hassle-free mode of transportation that links the counties of Ventura, Los Angeles (mostly in Antelope Valley), San Bernardino, Riverside, and Orange.

    Hours: All trains run Monday through Friday; some run on weekends, too. Trains do not run on major holidays.

    Admission: One-way tickets start at about $4.25; round trip, $6.75. Kids 5 and under ride for free.

    Ages: All.

METRO RAIL

(213) 626-4455 / www.mta.net

Los Angeles

    This rail mode of transportation is a work-in-progress, but the rail lines that are complete make going to a destination an adventure. The Blue Line runs north and south between Long Beach and downtown Los Angeles. Trains run every ten minutes. The Green Line runs east and west, connecting Norwalk, so far, to El Segundo and Redondo Beach. Trains run alongside, but separate from, the 105 freeway. The Red Line runs two lines from Union Station in downtown Los Angeles; one to Wilshire Boulevard and one to North Hollywood. The advantages of riding the rails are numerous, such as it's inexpensive, you don't have to fight traffic, you don't have to try to find a parking spot, and kids consider it a treat. Pick up a map of the route at Union Station or ask for a copy to be mailed directly to you.

Hours: Trains usually run daily, 6am - 11pm.
Admission: About $1.35 for adults, plus 25¢ for a transfer; children 4 and under are free.
Ages: All

OCEAN ADVENTURES

$$$

(310) 374-3481 / www.rbmarina.com
Harbor Drive where Torrance Boulevard meets the sea at Redondo Beach Pier, Redondo Beach
(From San Diego Fwy [405], exit S. on Western, R. on 190th St., which turns into Anita St., L on Pacific Coast Highway, R. on Torrance. From Harbor Fwy [110], exit W. on Torrance. [TG: 762 H5])

The *Ocean Racer* is a high-speed racer that seats 149 passengers. Ride high and fast on a half-hour tour of the harbor (and beyond). See REDONDO BEACH INTERNATIONAL BOARDWALK (pg. 126) for adjacent activities.

Hours: Open on the weekends and holidays year round, weather permitting, noon - sunset.
Admission: $10 for adults; $5 for ages 9 and under.
Ages: 2 years and up.

OFFSHORE WATER SPORTS

$$$

(562) 436-1996 / www.kayaks4rent.com
Shoreline Village Drive, Long Beach
(Take Long Beach Fwy [710] to the end, E. on Shoreline Dr., R. on Shoreline Village Dr. Look for the Jet Ski and Boat Rental sign [TG: 852 D2])

Rent a kayak ($10 an hour), wave runner ($79 an hour), and a few other types of watersport vehicles at this facility. Look up SHORELINE VILLAGE (see pg. 127) for more information on what to do in the immediate area.

Hours: Open during the summer. Call for hours.
Admission: See above prices.
Ages: 6 years and up, depending on the craft.

REDONDO SPORTFISHING

$$$

(310) 372-2111 - cruise info; (310) 374-3481 - marina / www.rbmarina.com
233 N. Harbor Drive, where Torrance Boulevard meets the sea at Redondo Beach Pier, Redondo Beach
(From San Diego Fwy [405], exit S. on Western, R. on 190th St., which turns into Anita St., L on Pacific Coast Highway, R. on Torrance. From Harbor Fwy [110], exit W. on Torrance. [TG: 762 H5])

The *Voyager* is a double deck wooden boat ideal for those who like viewing the ocean at a slower pace and ideal for younger ones as the excursions can be as short as a half-hour long. Be on the lookout for the colony of sea lions that usually hangs around. Three-hour whale-watching cruises are offered the day after Christmas through March. See REDONDO BEACH INTERNATIONAL BOARDWALK (pg. 126) for adjacent activities.

Hours: The half-hour cruises are available during the summer on weekends and holidays only, from noon - sunset (or so). Whale-watching cruises operate seasonally daily, usually 10am and 1:30pm.
Admission: Half-hour cruises are $6 for adults; $4 for ages 1 - 12 . Whale-watching cruises on the weekends are $14 for adults; $10 for ages 1 - 12. During the week, admission is $12 for adults; $8 for kids. Parking at the pier is always 50¢ for each 20 minutes. During the summer, it's $5 maximum on weekdays; $7 maximum on weekends. During the rest of the year, it's $3 maximum on weekdays; $5 on weekends.
Ages: 2 years and up for the short cruise; 6 years and up for whale watching.

SPIRIT CRUISES (Long Beach)　　　

(562) 495-5884 / www.spiritmarine.com　　　　　　　　$$$
401 E. Shoreline Drive, Long Beach
(Take Long Beach Fwy [710] to the end, E. on Shoreline Dr. [TG: 825 E1])

Enjoy a forty-five-minute narrated cruise through Queen's Way Bay, past the QUEEN MARY (pg. 114), SCORPION (pg. 117), and AQUARIUM OF THE PACIFIC (pg. 178), or take an hour-and-a-half narrated cruise to learn about and see more of the harbor and beyond, including Terminal Island and tankers and cargo ships. You go under four bridges, too. Narrated whale-watching cruises, usually about two hours in length, are available the end of December through March. Dinner cruises are also available with Spirit Cruises. Reservations for all cruises are always recommended.

Hours:　Summertime departures are daily at 1pm, 2pm, 3pm, and 4pm. Wintertime departures are usually weekends only.

Admission:　$8 for adults for the forty-five-minute harbor cruise; $4 for ages 3 - 12. $12 for adults for the longer cruise; $8 for children. $15 for adults for whale-watching; $8 for children.

Ages:　5 years and up.

SPIRIT CRUISES (San Pedro)　　　

(310) 548-8080 / www.spiritmarine.com　　　　　　　　$$$
Berth 77, Ports O' Call Village, San Pedro
(Exit Harbor Fwy [110] S. on Harbor Blvd. and follow the signs. [TG: 824 D6])

Cruise through the main channels and see the sights! Reservations are suggested. See the above SPIRIT CRUISES for a complete description.

VOYAGES OF REDISCOVERY (Los Angeles County)　　　

(800) 401-7835 or (415) 331-3214 / www.hawaiianchieftain.com; www.ladywashington.org　　　$$/$$$$$
Long Beach, Marina Del Rey, and San Pedro,

The *Lady Washington* is a faithful replica of the first American square-rigged ship to round Cape Horn and come to the Pacific Northwest. The *Hawaiian Chieftain* is an authentic replica of a typical European merchant trade ship, similar to those used by Spanish explorers in the late eighteenth century. Both ships set sail from their base in northern California and travel together to our southern harbors for a few months in the winter. They dock periodically in Santa Barbara, Oxnard, Marina Del Rey, San Pedro, Long Beach, Newport Beach, and San Diego, during the winter months. Boarding the ship, students experience first hand the life of sailors, coastal explorers, traders, missionaries, and Native Americans. This is accomplished by a dockside tour or a sailing expedition, which is fantastic! In preparation for either tour, Voyages sends the school group a packet of suggested pre-trip activities and a bibliography. Costumed docent educators are the instructors on the tours, both of which are geared specifically for fourth and fifth graders.

At the one-hour dockside tour, students visit each of three learning stations. The first one teaches line handling and the life of a sailor; the second, navigation and the work of officers; and the third, the history of the many cultures along the coast from more than 200 years ago. The three-hour tour (that's right - a three-hour tour) incorporates the same kind of "classes" as in the dockside tour, as well as actually setting and trimming the sails, steering the ship, and using traditional navigation tools. Kids learn mathematics, cartography, astronomy, and other sciences, and most of all, how to work together as a team. (We also learned another meaning of the phrase, "heave ho.")

Programs run rain or shine, just like sailors of old, who sailed (almost) no matter what the weather conditions were like. Each tour must have a minimum of thirty participants (this number includes chaperones and teachers) for either ship, with a maximum of forty-five. Smaller groups may be able to share their tour with another group.

Individuals and families wishing to explore the ships may do so in two ways. One is by going sailing on a three-hour battle reenactment led by period-dressed crew members. The passengers are spectators as the two ships try to out maneuver each other by sailing furiously. A highlight is the firing of the cannons. (The cannons don't use real ammunition, but there is lots of noise and smoke.) The second way is to explore the ships when they are docked. A formal tour is not given, but docents are on hand to answer questions. Whatever you choose to do, come sail the high seas of adventure!

Hours: All tours take place from the above-mentioned ports during the months of December through February. Dockside tours for school groups are given Mon. - Fri. at 9am, 10am, and 11am. Sailing expeditions for groups are offered once a day, Mon. - Fri. from 12:30pm - 3:30pm. Battle reenactments are conducted Sat. from 2pm - 5pm; Sun. from 10am - 1pm and 2pm - 5pm. Dockside exploration for individuals and families is available Mon. - Fri. between 3pm - 6pm; Sat. between 10am - 1pm.

Admission: Dockside tours for groups are $5 per participant. Sailing expeditions are $30 per participant. Battle reenactments are $40 for adults; $20 for children 12 and under. Dockside exploration for individuals is $3 for adults; $2 for seniors and students; $1 for children 12 and under. Or, pay $7 for a family (i.e. immediate family members). This tour is free on arrival day.

Ages: 4th and 5th graders for tours; 6 years and up for battle reenactments; 3 years and up for dockside exploration for families.

WILLOW SPRINGS INTERNATIONAL MOTORSPORTS PARK

(661) 256-6666 / www.willowspringsraceway.com $$$
3500 75th Street West, Rosamond
(Exit Antelope Valley Fwy [14] W. on Rosamond Blvd. and go about 6 miles. It starts on corner of Rosamond and 75th.)

This sprawling 600-acre complex has enough vroooom for six very different race tracks, ranging from clay oval, paved oval, a kart track, a lighted speedway, a road course, and the original 2.5 miles, nine-turn raceway built in 1953. Call or check the website for the complete schedule to make sure you're seeing the cars, karts, and motorcycle races that you want. General admission also allows you access to the pit area as long as kids are supervised by parents or other adults.

Hours: Call for a schedule.
Admission: Usually $10 for adults; children 8 and under are free with a paying adult.
Ages: 5 years and up.

YOUNG EAGLES PROGRAM (Lancaster)

(661) 940-1709 / www.youngeagles.com
4555 W. Avenue G, Fox Field, Lancaster
(Exit Antelope Valley Fwy [14] W. on Ave. 'G' and drive for about 3 miles. This program alternately uses the Cal City airport in Mojave and Rosamond airport. [TG: 3924 H7])

See the entry for YOUNG EAGLES PROGRAM (Pacoima) below for a description.

Hours: Usually offered on the second Sat. of the month, starting at 8am.
Admission: Free
Ages: 8 - 17 years.

YOUNG EAGLES PROGRAM (Long Beach)

(562) 570-2679 - airport / www.youngeagles.com
4100 Donald Douglas Drive, Long Beach
(Exit San Diego Fwy [405] N. on Lakewood Blvd., L. on Donald Douglas Dr. [TG: 796 A1])

See the entry for YOUNG EAGLES PROGRAM (Pacoima) below for details.

Hours: Usually offered every other month on the Sat. following the second Thurs. (honest!) at about The chapter alternates with the Fullerton Airport.
Admission: Free
Ages: 8 - 17 years.

YOUNG EAGLES PROGRAM (Pacoima)

(818) 725-4AIR (4247) - Pacoima; (800) 843-3612 - national number / www.youngeagles.com

12653 Osborne Street, Whiteman Airport, Pacoima

(Exit the Golden State Fwy [5] N.E. on Osborne, past San Fernando Rd., turn L. [TG: 502 E4])

"They will soar on wings like eagles." (Isaiah 40:31) I think all kids (and adults) dream of flying, and the Young Eagles Program helps those dreams become a reality. Young Eagles is a national program sponsored by the EAA (Experimental Aircraft Association), who desire to introduce children to the joy of aviation. There are several Young Eagle chapters throughout Southern California who offer aviation camps, educational programs, and more, as well as an opportunity to actually fly (for free!) in a two- or four-seater airplane. Kids, between the ages of 8 and 17 years, are invited to participate, one time only, in this unique flying experience. Please remember that everyone here is volunteering their time, including pilots, so be patient with a process that might take a few hours. Although the following information is fairly standard, call the particular program you're interested in for specific dates, times, and other details. Reservations are necessary at most of the airports. A signed consent form by a parent or legal guardian is required for each child.

At the airport, after your child registers, he/she will (in no particular order):
• Participate in a preflight inspection training, which means looking over an airplane to make sure it's mechanically sound while learning some technical aspects of how to fly a plane. • Fly! The flight is usually twenty minutes round trip. What a thrill! If it becomes too thrilling for your child, airsick bags are provided. • Take a tour of the control tower if available. Kids will need to keep their voices low so they don't disturb the tower operators. Two more wonderful freebies are a certificate upon completion of the flight, and a magazine called *Sport Aviation for Kids* that comes later in the mail. Plan on bringing something to munch on as many airports have picnic tables available. Kids who are grounded will enjoy watching the planes take off and land. Blue skies and tail winds to you!

At the Pacoima airport, kids will fly over Magic Mountain, which makes their flight extra special.

Hours: One Sat. a month, starting at 10:30am. Call for specific dates.
Admission: Free
Ages: 8 - 17 years old.

YOUNG EAGLES PROGRAM (Santa Monica)

(310) 458-8591 - airport; (310) 202-8727 - program / www.youngeagles.com

3200 Airport Avenue, Santa Monica Airport, Santa Monica

(Exit Santa Monica Fwy [10] S. on Bundy Dr., R. on Airport Ave. [TG: 672 A2])

See the entry for YOUNG EAGLES PROGRAM (Pacoima) on page 177 for details. Ask about this chapter's other Young Eagle events and educational programs.

Hours: Three or four selected Sat. throughout the year.
Admission: Free
Ages: 8 - 17 years.

YOUNG EAGLES PROGRAM (South Bay)

(310) 374-4812 / www.youngeagles.com

Compton Airport, Hawthorne, and Torrance Airport

See the entry for YOUNG EAGLES PROGRAM (Pacoima) on page 177 for details. Most pilots at this program try to let the kids have a turn at the controls, for just a short period of time. They fly out of the above airports when they have a group of thirty, or so, young pilot wannabes.

Hours: Offered about eight times a year on selected Sat., starting at noon.
Admission: Free
Ages: 8 - 17 years.

-----ZOOS AND ANIMALS-----

ANIMAL ADVENTURES and EXOTIC ANIMAL TRAINING SCHOOL ☼
(323) 665-9500 / www.animalschool.net $$$$$
Canyon Country, Santa Clarita
(It's near Magic Mountain. The exact address is given when you sign up for a class or adventure.)

Have you ever wanted to go on a safari to Africa? An Animal Adventure in Southern California might be the next best thing. There are eighteen lions, seven Bengal tigers, an elephant (who paints and exhibits over 300 other behaviors), a zebra, a few grizzly bears, a black bear, and monkeys and chimps that consider the compound home. The school's primary focuses are to educate the public on animal preservation and to give formal training for people who are interested in careers as animal caretakers and trainers. The owner is a veteran Hollywood animal trainer and many of the animals here have been featured in movies and on television. The school is not a zoo, park, or college, but a working professional studio animal company. However, if intensive training is not what you are looking for, the school offers other options as well.

Animal Encounters, for instance, allows one-on-one time between you and the animal, or animals, of your choice, and as much physical contact as is safe. Get to know the animals by working with them, feeding them, stroking them, and photographing them. Or, sign up for a group seminar where you get a behind-the-scenes look at the film business (and hear anecdotes about the animals and actors), learn training methods, kiss a grizzly, bottle feed a tiger cub, pet a panther, play with a monkey, and more. What a wild opportunity!

Hours: Call for a class or encounter schedule. Seminars are from 10am - 3pm on selected dates.
Admission: $495 per person for the encounter; $100 per person, or $180 for two people, for the group
               seminar. Ask about fees for other classes.
Ages: 10 years and up.

AQUARIUM OF THE PACIFIC ☼
(562) 590-3100 / www.aquariumofpacific.org $$$$
100 Aquarium Way, Long Beach
(Exit San Diego Fwy [405] S. on the Long Beach Fwy [710] to the end of the Downtown exit, which turns into Shoreline Dr., R. on Aquarium Way. [TG: 825 D1])

Something fishy's going on at one of the largest aquariums in the United States. The first stop in this multi-level aquarium is the spacious entryway where your attention is immediately riveted by a life-size, eighty-eight-foot blue whale (no way can a creature be so large!) hanging overhead with her calf "swimming" beside her. This hall also contains preview tanks of the main exhibit regions. Watch a sea-related film in the theater or even a 3-D special presentation movie. Information and breath-taking footage on the audio/video screens throughout the aquarium answer many of the questions visitors have about the animals here. Note that almost everything in the tanks, besides the fish, is man-made, although it is incredibly realistic looking. Note, too, that small Discovery Labs are located in each area of the main areas and staffed with docents to answer questions, give demonstrations, and allow you to touch selected sea creatures. All exhibits are handicapped accessible. There area four main exhibit areas to view: California/Baja, Northern Pacific, Tropical Pacific, and Explorer's Cove.

The natural flow of the aquarium leads visitors toward the back of the building, to the **California/Baja** area. Watch the enthralling moon jellies and other exotic drifters float gracefully around in their tanks. Peek at the Swell Shark egg cases where baby sharks are getting ready to be born. A kelp display shows those of us who aren't marine biologists that kelp is used as an ingredient in lipstick, Jell-O, toothpaste, and other household items. Catch an underwater look at the seals and sea lions splashing around. (Ask about feeding times, when divers often interact with the animals.) Walk up the stairs and outside to see these mammals sun themselves on the surface of the rocky "shoreline." Tiered cement seating allows good viewing for everyone. This outdoor plaza also features sea turtles, shore birds (who are unable to fly away), and a touch tank that holds stingrays and batrays. They feel like rubber. The Discovery Lab here contains sea urchins, anemones, sea stars, and crabs to gently touch. Back inside, on the second floor of the gallery, you'll see aptly-named garden eels and a rocky reef that holds unusual looking fish, particularly the Lookdowns, which are a vertically flattened fish.

For a change in venue and temperature, enter the **Northern Pacific** gallery. The most popular attraction here are the playful sea otters in a tank with underwater and above-water viewing. Ample information is given about their fur (for which they've been voraciously hunted), their food, their habitats, and more. Other draws include the tank of anchovies (no pizza!), diving puffins (seabirds), monstrous-looking Giant Japanese Spider Crabs, and a Giant Pacific Octopus, which is not menacing, but so shy that you might not even see him.

The **Tropical Pacific** is one of the most colorful sections here. It's set up so you'll "travel" through the reef and into deeper waters as you venture deeper into this gallery. The coral lagoon showcases brilliantly-colored fish - electric blue, canary yellow, jade green, and vivid purple. The largest tank, containing a tropical reef and its 1,000 inhabitants, offers various levels of viewing which is interesting because of the diversity of life shown in here. You'll see clown fish, zebra sharks, giant groupers, and more. At feeding time the divers are equipped with aquaphones to answer any questions. A partial water tunnel allows visitors to see sharks, and every parent knows that an aquarium visit is not complete without seeing sharks. Other outstanding exhibits in this gallery include deadly sea snakes; sea horses; the strange-looking leafy sea dragons and weedy sea dragons; upside-down jellies, who were created to live like this; orange-spined unicorn fish; sex reversal fish (mainly wrasses) who change from females to males as they mature or undergo stress - go figure; and beautiful, but venomous or poisonous fish, such as the lionfish.

Explorer's Cove has a favorite area - the shark lagoon. It contains 150 sharks. Roll up your sleeves and touch sharks in the shallow "petting" tanks. Try to come by at feeding time to see a frenzy of activity. A few other interactive exhibits regarding sharks here highlight their size, teeth, and other characteristics. The canopied-covered marine life theater has presentations daily, depending on the weather. Walk through a lorikeet aviary and purchase a small cup of nectar ($1) to feed these colorful birds. Take pictures of your astonished kids as the birds land on their head and arms.

Cafe Scuba has good food and indoor tables, plus outdoor tables that overlook the seal and sea lion exhibit and Rainbow Harbor. And yes, fish is on the menu.

Ask about the multitude of special events and programs offered to families and school groups including sleep overs (which are so fun to do with your child), one-hour behind-the-scenes tours, and studies of a particular animal or species. Two classrooms in the educational wing are fully stocked with lab equipment, live systems (touch-tank animals), terrestrial aquariums, craft projects, and other good stuff. An educator's room, available for teachers, contains computers, books, arts and crafts resources, and more.

Note: Weekend and holidays are peak attendance times, which translates as lots of people and waiting in line to get in. You can purchase pre-sell tickets and at least avoid the wait in line.

The aquarium is adjacent to Rainbow Harbor. In between the aquarium and harbor is an esplanade and a large green lawn. Feel free to bring a blanket and a picnic lunch. Head out on the esplanade (i.e. cement walkway) to the colorful-looking buildings of SHORELINE VILLAGE (see pg. 127), a shopping and eating complex. Head the other way around the harbor toward a quasi park (i.e. an expanse of green lawn with a few picnic tables) where you can view the QUEEN MARY (see pg. 114) and SCORPION (see pg. 117) just across the waters. Take an aquabus around - see AQUALINK (pg. 168) for details.

Hours:	Open daily, 9am - 6pm. Closed Christmas and the weekend of the Grand Prix in April.
Admission:	$18.95 for adults; $14.95 for seniors; $9.95 for ages 3 - 11; children 2 and under are free. Parking is $6. Catch a free ride to the aquarium on a bright red Long Beach Passport shuttle bus that cruises Pine Ave., Shoreline Dr., and Ocean Blvd. in the downtown area, and connects to the Metro Blue Line at the Transit Mall on First Street. Passport buses will also deliver you to the *Queen Mary* and *Scorpion*.
Ages:	All

CABRILLO MARINE AQUARIUM

(310) 548-7562 / www.cabrilloaq.org

3720 Stephen M White Drive, San Pedro

(Take Harbor Fwy [110] to the end, L. on Gaffey St., L. on 9th St., R. on Pacific Ave. almost to the end, L. on 36th St. which turns into Stephen M White. [TG: 854 C2])

Explore the underwater treasures of Los Angeles Harbor without ever getting wet! Cabrillo Marine Aquarium specializes in the marine life of Southern California. It features quite a few tanks, mostly at kids' eye-level, filled with a wide variety of sea life.

The front courtyard has full-size killer whale, shark, and dolphin models, plus a full-grown gray whale outlined on the cement. Kids are welcome to touch the whale bones in the adjacent Whale Graveyard.

The exhibit halls have tanks filled with live jellies (usually referred to as jellyfish), crustaceans, octopuses, fish, leopard sharks, moray eels, and other sea animals. There are numerous displays of preserved animals, such as seals and sea lions; bones, skeletons, jaws, and teeth of sharks and whales; pictures; and other models of sea life. My boys liked pushing the button to hear the recording of a whale singing, although their renditions of it were more grating than musical. We also watched a shark blend into the sandy ocean floor; touched a sample of shark skin and compared it to a sample of sandpaper; and saw a slide presentation at the auditorium. Call to see what's currently showing.

As most kids have this inherent need to explore the world with their hands and not just their eyes, a definite favorite is the tidepool touch tank. Here kids can gently touch sea anemones, sea stars, and sea slugs.

The Cabrillo Aquarium offers seasonal events such as whale watching (January through April) and grunion hunting (March through July), plus various workshops and programs, such as Sleep With the Fishes. At low tide - call for particular times and seasons - tidepool tours are given at the beach in an area called Pt. Fermin Marine Life Refuge. A paved, wheelchair-accessible trail runs from the parking lot to the aquarium, across the beach, and to the water's edge at the tidepools. You are welcome to explore this area on your own, too.

Don't forget to pack your swimsuits and beach towels as CABRILLO BEACH (see pg. 8) is right outside the aquarium. Wonderful sandy stretches and a play area await your children. For more adventuresome kids (or whosoever's parents will let them), there are rock jetties to explore. Enjoy your day playing by the ocean, and learning more about it.

Hours: The Aquarium is open Tues. - Fri., noon - 5pm; Sat. - Sun., 10am - 5pm. Closed Mon., Thanksgiving, and Christmas. The touch tank doors open for twenty minutes at a time Tues. - Fri. at 1:30pm, 2:30pm, and 3:30pm; Sat. - Sun. at 11:30am, 1:30pm, 2:30pm, and 3:30pm. Slide shows are presented Tues. - Sun. at 11am and 2pm. The beach is open daily, 6am - 10pm.

Admission: The aquarium is free; suggested donations are $5 for adults, $1 for ages 12 and under. Parking is $7 per vehicle in the summer; the rest of the year, Mon. - Fri., $4.50; Sat.- Sun., $5.50. If you get here early enough, you can park on the street and just walk through the beach/aquarium entrance gate.

Ages: All

EXOTIC FELINE BREEDING COMPOUND

(661) 256-3793 / www.cathouse-fcc.org

Rhyolite Avenue, Rosamond

(Exit Antelope Valley Fwy [14] W. on Rosamond Blvd. [to the E. is Edwards Air Force Base], R. on Mojave-Tropico Rd., L. on Rhyolite Ave.)

This place is the cat's meow! There are fifty exotic wild cats living here, representing over fifteen different species. Since it is a breeding compound, you're almost guaranteed to see a few kittens, too. Unlike traditional zoos, the safety fences keep you only a few feet (not yards) away from the caged animals. This allows for plenty of up-close viewing and photo opportunities.

Stroll along the cement pathways to see jaguars, panthers, pumas, lynxes, fluffy Amur leopards, regal-looking servals, weasel-like jaguarundi, and lots of Chinese leopards. Ask for a guided tour to learn about the animals - what they eat, how much they weigh, their life span, and more - and about the importance of this breeding compound. Three huge Siberian tigers live in the back (in cages) and will be back on exhibit when their homes are rebuilt.

The gift shop has a few displays showing some of the reasons these cats are facing extinction - one fur coat was made from fifteen bobcats, and another was made from over fifty leopards. Tip: Late afternoon and cooler months are the best times to visit the compound as this is when the felines are more active. Special Twilight

Tours are offered three times a year for ages 18 and older. See areas not open to the daytime public and have your picture taken with a cat (if one is cooperating). Please call if you want to schedule a tour for ten or more people. Educational outreach programs are also available.

Hours: Open Thurs. - Tues., 10am - 4pm. Closed Wed., Thanksgiving, and Christmas.
Admission: $3 for adults; $1.50 ages 3 - 18. Twilight tours are $15 per person.
Ages: 4 years and up.

THE FARM

(818) 341-6805 - recording; (818) 885-6321 - The Farm on weekends.
8101 Tampa Avenue, Reseda
(Exit Ventura Fwy [101] N. on Tampa. [TG: 530 G2])

This Farm reminds me of Old MacDonald's place in that song with all those vowels. There are over 100 animals to pet, and even a few to hold. The llamas, cows, chickens, bunnies, turkeys, sheep, ducks, pigs, peacocks, and goats are readily accessible to pet through the fence pens. If you come at the right time of year, you'll also see baby animals and have the opportunity to cuddle lambs and kids (i.e. baby goats). Animal feed is available for purchase. Old tractors, bales of hay, and the aroma of farm animals add to the barnyard atmosphere. Riding lessons ($15) and/or pony rides around a track ($3) are available, too. And yes, The Farm does birthday parties.

Hours: Open Sat. - Sun. and holidays, 10am - 5pm, weather permitting. Open in the summer one hour later. Open weekdays for groups with reservations.
Admission: $5 for ages 1 and up; $2 for seniors.
Ages: All

FARM TOUR

(909) 594-5611, ext. 4794 / www.mtsac.edu
1100 N. Grand Avenue, Mount San Antonio College, Walnut
(Exit Pomona Fwy [60] N. on Grand Ave., R. on Temple Ave., L. on Bonita Dr. The entrance is on Bonita. [TG: 639 H3])

Take a forty-five-minute guided tour of the farm animals on this college campus. You'll see cows, horses, goats, and sheep, and depending on your guide, learn about what the animals eat, how to take care of them, and more. The tour is geared for younger children and is simply a fun introduction to farm animals. Note that it is not a petting zoo. Pack a sack lunch to enjoy at a picnic area under nearby shade trees, adjacent to a hilly, grassy field. The minimum number of students is ten; the maximum is seventy. Check out WILDLIFE SANCTUARY TOUR (on pg. 167) for another tour offered by the college.

Hours: Tours are given Mon. - Thurs., 9am, 10am, and 11am. Reservations are required.
Admission: Free, but donations are appreciated.
Ages: 3 - 10 years.

HOLLYWOOD PARK

(310) 419-1500 / www.hollywoodpark.com
1050 S. Prairie Avenue, Inglewood
(Exit San Diego Fwy [405] E. on Century, L. on Prairie. Or, exit Century Fwy [105] N. on Prairie. [TG: 703 D4])

Do your kids like horsing around? At Hollywood Park they can see thoroughbred horses and enjoy a children's play area located at the north end of the park. The play area has a grassy lawn for picnicking as well as some playground equipment. Arcade games are also available here. The landscaping of the park, with its lagoons and tropical trees, is pleasing to the eye.

Hours: The season goes from mid-April through mid-July, and November through mid-December. Call for racing information and times.
Admission: $7 for adults (which includes parking and a program); ages 17 and under are free with a paid adult.
Ages: 4 years and up.

INTERNATIONAL CENTER FOR GIBBON STUDIES

(661) 296-2737 / www.gibboncenter.org

$$$

Esquerra Road, Santa Clarita

(Exit Golden State Fwy [5] E. on Valencia Blvd., L. on Bouquet Canyon [about 5½ miles], R. on Esquerra Rd., which is a dirt road on the right-hand side that is easy to miss - it is before you enter the Angeles National Forest. Go through the stream bed (hard to cross if it's raining), a quick R. on Galton (the middle of 3 dirt roads), L. on the first dirt road to the L. Park outside the six-foot high chain-link fence. [TG: 4461 G3])

What's the difference between a monkey and an ape? If you answered, "Monkeys have tails," you are correct. Next question: Are gibbons monkeys or apes? Hint - they have no tails. A one-hour, or so, guided tour of this outdoor facility takes you past sixteen enclosures that hold over thirty-five gibbons in their natural family groupings. The enclosures are sizable chain-link cages, scattered over the hard-packed dirt grounds and under shade trees. The tours are informative, entertaining, and vary according to the interests and ages of the participants in the group. Note: To ensure the safety of the gibbons, visitors must be in good health, not have had any recent contact with a person or animal with an infectious disease, and stay a minimum of five feet away from all enclosures.

Gibbons are arboreal apes - they swing from tree to tree - and are found in the rain forests of Southeast Asia. This research facility, which has six out of the eleven species, studies their behavior and helps to increase their endangered gene pool, which means you could see babies on your visit here. Gibbons are the only non-human primates to walk upright and they have earned the name of loudest land mammal. Every species has a different way of singing (that's the technical name - I call it screaming) to each other, usually in the morning hours. They can project their voices a distance of up to two miles. We heard them. I believe it. The kids loved it. Siamangs have vocal sacs that inflate to the size of a large grapefruit (reminiscent of a bullfrog) when they sing. This is fascinating to listen to and watch. Males and females in certain species are born one color and change colors as they mature. (Is this the same thing as humans "going gray"?) We also learned about gibbons' nutrition, why they are dying off, preventative medical care, and more. My boys went ape over this center!

Hours: Open by appointment for groups of twenty or more people, or minimum $100, with tours starting in the morning. Individuals may call to see if they can join an already scheduled tour.

Admission: $9 for adults; $8 for seniors and students; $7 for ages 3 - 12; children 2 and under are free.

Ages: 4 years and up.

KELLOGG ARABIAN HORSE CENTER

(909) 869-2224 / www.csupomona.edu/~equine/Kellogg.htm

$

Kellogg Drive, California State Polytechnic University, Pomona

(Going E. on San Bernardino Fwy [10], exit S. on Kellogg Dr. Going N. on Orange Fwy [57], exit W. on Temple, R. on S. Campus Dr., L. on Kellogg Dr. Parking is on the R. in the campus parking lot. Cross the street to the university farm. [TG: 640 B2])

The Kellogg Arabian Horse Center at Cal Poly houses over one hundred thirty purebred Arabian horses. The center's thirty-eight scenic acres are set in the hills and encompass a huge pasture, three barns, foaling stalls, a breeding area, a veterinary clinic, a farrier shop, an arena, and a covered grandstand that seats 900.

Staff members and students of horse husbandry and equine sciences present hour-long shows that put the horses through their various paces. Guests see demonstrations of English and western riding, with riders in appropriate costumes, as well as drill team and precision maneuvers, and horses jumping over small fences. Riders in silver and gold flowing Arabian dress are crowd pleasers as their horses, decorated in jewel-toned brocade and tassels, prance around the ring. Our favorite act was the horse that performed several tricks, including walking a baby carriage and rocking a cradle.

After the show, children can ride a horse around a path for $3; watch a thirty-minute video on the history of Kellogg's center (note that the small video room contains a horse skeleton); and walk around the stables. Families can pet the beautiful horses, watch them being bathed and groomed, and simply enjoy the ambiance. Springtime is the best time to visit as there are newborn colts to see.

Hours: Shows are offered October through June on the first Sun. of each month at 2pm. Shows are also offered several Thurs. in both the spring and fall at 10:30am for elementary students. Reservations are required.

Admission: Sun. shows are $3 for adults; $2 for seniors and ages 6 - 17; children 5 and under are free. Thurs. shows are $1 per person.

Ages: 3 years and up.

LOS ANGELES ZOO

(323) 644-4200 / www.lazoo.org

$$$

5333 Zoo Drive, Los Angeles

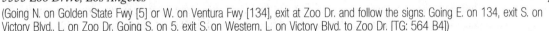

(Going N. on Golden State Fwy [5] or W. on Ventura Fwy [134], exit at Zoo Dr. and follow the signs. Going E. on 134, exit S. on Victory Blvd., L. on Zoo Dr. Going S. on 5, exit S. on Western, L. on Victory Blvd. to Zoo Dr. [TG: 564 B4])

All the big-name animals star at the evolving Los Angeles Zoo - elephants, tigers, mountain lions, giraffes, bears, kangaroos, polar bears, and rhinoceros. Our favorites are the gorillas, apes, orangutans, chimps, and other primates - they provide entertainment that tops television any day! The chimps have their own play area as do the orangutans. An aquatic area features otters and seals. The hippos are getting an underwater pool with glass walls so visitors can view below the waterline activities. The darkened Koala House has koalas in their nighttime environment, since they are supposed to be more active at that time. Don't forget to sssssstop by the Reptile House to see the snakes and lizards, and especially the Komodo dragons. A playground is located at the far end of the zoo, too. You'll want to catch the sea lion training in the aquatics section and the animal encounters "show."

If you get tired of walking around this huge and hilly zoo, purchase an all-day shuttle pass for $3.50 for adults, $1 for seniors, $1.50 for ages 2 to 12. The shuttle goes around the perimeter of the zoo, and will drop you off or pick you up at various stops along the way.

Enter the children's zoo to pet goats, sheep, alpacas, rabbits, pot-bellied pigs, donkeys, and a miniature horse. Watch a twenty-minute animal encounter on stage to see, maybe touch, and definitely learn about an assortment of critters in an intimate setting. At the Adventure Theater, the shows include game show themes and dressing up young ones in costumes. Young spelunkers can explore a man-made cave, which offers tunnels to crawl through, exhibits on cave creature dwellers to look at, and (pretend) stalactites and stalagmites to see. One cave features Desert Trail, a tunnel exhibit showcasing tortoises, bearded lizards, scorpions, and tarantulas. An indoor Kid's Korner offers storytelling, books, arts and crafts, puppet shows, and up-close encounters with live animals such as ferrets and chickens. The Family Care Center (i.e. nursery) houses small mammals, birds, and newborns that need special care.

At the prairie dog exhibit kids can pop their heads up from underneath the ground into a plexiglass dome while real prairie dogs are looking at them! This is a fun photo opportunity. Look - it's a bird, it's a plane, it's Superman! No, it's a bird! The World of Birds shows feature free-flying birds - a ~~flight~~ sight not to miss.

In the summer months, join in a Sundown Safari where your family can join numerous others and sleep in tents on the zoo grounds. Enjoy a delicious dinner, campfire snack, and breakfast, plus enjoy special nighttime and early morning behind-the-scenes tours of the animals. What a great experience! Ask about their numerous other special programs and events, including free guided tours given to mid and upper elementary school-aged kids.

Hours: Open daily, 10am - 5pm. Closed Christmas. Call for show times.

Admission: $8.25 for adults; $5.25 for seniors; $3.25 for ages 2 - 12. Certain discounts are available through AAA. Sundown Safari costs $75 per adult; $50 per child.

Ages: All

MARINE MAMMAL CARE CENTER AT FORT MACARTHUR

(310) 548-5677 - center; (310) 547-9888 - tours / www.mar3ine.org

!

3601 S. Gaffey Street, San Pedro

(Exit the Harbor Fwy [110] S. on Gaffey St. Go almost to the end of Gaffey, turn R. through the gates on Leavenworth Dr., just past the Fort MacArthur Museum. [TG: 854 B2])

Injured or sick marine mammals, like sea lions and seals, are brought here, doctored, and taken care of until they can be released back into the wild. Rehabilitation can take one to three months, depending on the case. We saw one seal that was severely underweight and another that had numerous shark bites. This small facility houses between five to ninety marine mammals outside in chain link fence pens, depending on the season. Stormy weather and pupping season (February through July) bring in more injured or abandoned animals. However, the staff has more time to spend during non-busy times. Your children have an opportunity to learn more about these animals as knowledgeable volunteers are on hand to answer any questions kids might ask. And they do ask!

A variety of educational tours and classes are offered for all ages that incorporate a visit with the animals, a video, reinforcement activities, and pre- and post-visit materials. Fourth graders and up may also utilize the laboratory inside the adjacent building, operating the microscopes and computers and looking at the aquarium. Tours are an hour for pre-schoolers through kindergartners, and two hours for older children, with an emphasis on the academics. Inquire about the International Day of the Seal festival in April. Look up FORT MACARTHUR MUSEUM (see pg. 88), as it is located just across the street.

Hours: Open daily, 8am - 4pm.
Admission: Free. The educational tours and classes cost $25 for curriculum materials for up to 60 people.
Ages: All - younger ones will just enjoy seeing the animals, while older ones can learn about them and appreciate what the Center does.

MONTEBELLO BARNYARD ZOO / GRANT REA PARK

(323) 887-4595 - park; (323) 727-0269 - pony and horse rides
600 Rea Drive, Montebello
(Exit San Gabriel River Fwy [605] E. on Beverly Blvd., R. on Rea Dr. [TG: 676 F1])

A small Barnyard Zoo is at one corner of the Grant Rea Park. It has a small pond for ducks, an aviary with doves and peacocks, and pens holding goats, pigs, a cow, llamas, horses, and sheep that kids can pet through the fences. Visiting this "zoo" makes a stop at the park a little more special. Other activities include a short train ride around the "track" - $2 per person; a merry-go-round - $2 per person; and pony rides for younger children, twice around the walking track - $2. A snack bar is open here on the weekends with hot dogs, churros, beverages, and more. Forty-five-minute guided tours, minimum ten kids, include visiting with each of the animals, plus a train, pony, and merry-go-round ride.

The surrounding, nice-sized park is pretty. It has baseball diamonds, batting cages (open at certain times), picnic tables under shade trees, barbeques, a playground, and bike trails along the river bed.

Hours: The park is open daily, 7am - dusk. The zoo is open Mon. - Fri., 10am - 4pm; Sat. - Sun., 10am - 6pm. Specialty rides are usually available during zoo hours. Tours are offered daily. Call first.
Admission: Free to the park and zoo. Prices for rides are given above. Tours are $7 per child.
Ages: 1 - 10 years.

OCEAN DISCOVERY CENTER

(310) 393-6149 / www.odc.ucla.edu; www.healthebay.org
1600 Ocean Front Walk, Santa Monica
(Exit Santa Monica Fwy [10] N. on 4th St., L. on Colorado Ave. It is at the foot of the Santa Monica Pier. [TG: 671 E3])

Discover what really lives in the Santa Monica Bay at the Ocean Discovery Center, located under the Santa Monica Pier. This small, but fascinating center has several tanks of live sea creatures to look at and touch. The changing exhibit is the open ocean tank. We saw moon jellies that were mesmerizing to watch as their milky white bodies floated gracefully around in their tank. Another large aquarium holds crabs, sea stars, and various fish. Use the provided flashlight to see tiny Swell Sharks developing inside their hanging egg cases. Mature Swell Sharks (which aren't necessarily wonderful sharks, it's just the name of that shark species), sand crabs, sand dollars, leopard sharks, and batrays are too fragile for fingers, but they are easily seen in shallow tanks placed at a child's eye level. Kids can, however, gently touch tidepool life such as sea stars, sea anemones, and sea slugs. A touch table displays a shark's jaw and individual teeth. It also has a microscope for closeup look at scales, shells, etc.

Another prime attraction in the center is the numerous Discovery boxes that are filled with age-appropriate activities, games, and/or books. Choose from Diving Deep, Knot Relay, Ocean Life Puzzles, Beach Bingo, and more. Computer terminals offer software featuring the marine environment. On weekends a variety of short, ocean-related films are shown throughout the day. The beautiful, marine-muraled classroom was designed for the instructional use of the school programs that are offered here. These informative, wonderful, and interactive one-hour-plus programs are offered year round.

Make a day of your visit to the Discovery Center by taking a walk on the pier (see SANTA MONICA PIER on page 127), enjoying some rides at PACIFIC PARK (see pg. 2), or just playing at the beach!

Hours: Open Mon. - Fri., 2pm - 6pm; Sat. - Sun., 12:30pm - 6:30pm. Call first as hours sometimes fluctuate. School programs are offered Mon. - Fri. Call to make a reservation.

Admission: $3 for adults; children 2 and under are free. School programs are $120 for up to sixty students.

Ages: 3 years and up.

ROUNDHOUSE AQUARIUM
!/$

(310) 379-8117

Manhattan Beach Boulevard, at the end of Manhattan Beach Pier, Manhattan Beach

(Exit San Diego Fwy [405] W. on Rosecrans Ave., L. on Pacific Coast Highway. Take the next R. on Valley Dr., R. on Manhattan Beach Blvd. [TG: 732 E6])

Come see the stars of Manhattan; sea stars that is. The Roundhouse Aquarium is a very small marine learning center, but packed with information and exhibits. The shark tank (always a favorite!) contain four species of sharks common to this area, plus moray eels, and some fish. A lobster and crab tank hold a California spiny lobster, giant spider crabs, and more. The nursery tank shows off just-hatched babies of the sea and a petting pool contains several types of rays to gently stroke. A tidepool touch tank containing mostly sea stars, a surge tank, and a few other aquariums with tropical fish and local invertebrates round out the collection at Roundhouse Aquarium. There are also whale bones and shark's teeth to examine. Upstairs is a play and study center, that is complete with sea animal puppets, books, and videos. Note: It gets crowded quickly inside the aquarium.

The aquarium offers many marine science programs, field trips for students, and fun family activities. For example, the one-hour Ocean Discovery class, for at least eight or more people of any age, includes learning about the marine environment and teaching time by the touch tanks. The cost is $4 per person. A three-hour class, given for kindergartners through twelfth graders, includes a lot of fa*sea*nating information, as well as hands-on fun such as touching sea stars and even petting a shark. The cost is $205 for thirty students. Sleeping with the Sharks is an overnight field trip that includes a pizza party (i.e. similar to a shark feeding frenzy), touching sharks and shark teeth, dissecting parts of a shark, and more. The cost is $50 per person. Join in on arts and crafts and/or storytelling on Sunday mornings.

On your way out to the aquarium, which is located at the end of a concrete pier, check out all the beach activity - sand volleyball, surfing, swimming, and of course, sun bathing. You can also, ironically, fish from the pier. Sidewalk shops are just down the street.

Hours: Open Mon. - Fri., 3pm - sunset; Sat. - Sun., 10am - sunset. Call for tour and program times.

Admission: Free entrance to the aquarium; donations of $2 per person are encouraged. Tour prices are given above. Metered parking is available on Manhattan Beach Blvd. by the stores, or wherever you can find it!

Ages: 2 years and up.

SANTA ANITA PARK
!/$$

(626) 574-7223 / www.santaanita.com

285 W. Huntington Drive, Arcadia

(Exit Foothill Fwy [210] S. on Baldwin Ave., L. into the parking lot for Gate 8. The park is located next to a shopping mall. [TG: 567 A5])

Hold your horses! One of the most famous thoroughbred horse racing parks in the United States is surprisingly family-friendly. Watch the horses being put through their paces during their morning workouts from 5am (this is a little too early for me!) to 10am. Grab a bite to eat at Clocker's Corner Cafe breakfast counter which offers inexpensive items that can be eaten at the outside patio area overlooking the track. On Saturdays and Sundays, weather permitting, between 8am and 9:30am take a free, fifteen-minute, behind-the-scenes, narrated tram ride. Catch the tram near the cafe in the parking lot near the west side of the grandstands. You'll ride along dirt "roads," through a hub of horse activity, and past rows of stables where walkers, trainers, and jockeys are exercising, bathing, and grooming horses. Tip: Call first as the tram ride is not offered on days of major races.

Walk in the beautifully landscaped Paddock Gardens, located just inside the admission gate, to look at the flowers, statues, and equine-themed topiary plants. In the gardens, twenty minutes prior to post time, there is a brief "show" as jockeys, in their colorful silks, walk and ride their mounts around the walking ring before going on to the race track. Note: The first race on Monday usually begins at 1pm while races Wednesday through Sunday begin at 12:30pm. Weekends bring special events such as mariachi bands and dancers, costumed park mascots strolling about, and more. Ask for a schedule of their numerous, family-oriented events, such as Family Fun Days and the annual Irish Faire.

Go through a paved tunnel from the gardens to the infield (i.e. interior of the racetrack) to reach a playground. Kids can horse around on the large play structure with slides, monkey bars, a merry-go-round, and swings. One end of the playground is best suited for toddlers and the other for slightly older kids. The infield also features large grassy areas for running around and picnicking, so pack a lunch. Family Fun Days are held once a month on the infield which include a bounce house, face-painting, pony rides ($2 per), and other fun things to do. Note: You may stay in the infield during races.

From the time the starting gates (which are portable) and jockeys are in position, to the finish line, enthusiasm runs rampant through the crowd. The actual races, although over quickly, are thrilling, even for non-betters. (The numerous manned windows and wagering machines receive a lot of frantic activity.) My boys "scientifically" deduced who to root for - according to the horse's name and/or the color of the jockey's silks. Tip: Sitting in grandstand seats is the best way to see the action as the slanted cement standing area in front of the seats fills up quickly with people who are always taller than you. Note: It is almost a half an hour between races.

Lunchtime food can be purchased at snack bars, the cafeteria, the casual, but nice Turf Club, or the posh Club House, where appropriate dress is required. Prices vary according to venue.

I wager your kids will have a good time watching the "Sport of Kings."

Hours: The season runs October to mid-November, and the end of December through April.

Admission: Free admission before 9:30am includes watching the daily horse workouts and, on weekends, going on the tram ride. If you arrive after gates open, general admission is $5 for adults; free for kids 17 and under when accompanied by an adult. Parking is $4 after 9:30am.

Ages: 4 years and up.

THE SEA LABORATORY

(310) 318-7438 / www.sealaboratory.org

1021 N. Harbor Drive, Redondo Beach

(Going N.E. on San Diego Fwy [405], exit S. on Western Ave., R. on 190th St. which turns into Anita St. and then Herondo St., L. on Harbor. Going S.W. on 405, exit W. on Artesia Blvd., L. on Aviation Blvd., L. on Pacific Coast Hwy., R. on Herondo St., L. on Harbor. [TG: 762 H4])

"Under the boardwalk, down by the sea. . . " is the Sea Laboratory, although it's not really under a boardwalk. Inside the building is a display on a storm drain vs. sewage, and the subsequent effects that trash has on the oceans and sea animals. The ocean supermarket exhibit showcases products on a shelf, like at a supermarket. When visitors use a scanner on a product, it reveals how much of what ocean element is used in

that particular everyday item. There are also a few tanks in here that hold a variety of sea creatures such as octopus, eels, Garibaldi, and moonjellies.

Outside is a fairly large tidepool touch tank with sea stars, sea anemones, and more. Beyond the gate, and open to the public with a guide, are several large tanks, that look like small pools, containing an assortment of sea life. There are lobsters, large halibuts (sorry, no fishing allowed) that are part of the halibut hatchery, giant sea bass, bat rays, sea stars, and more. Most of these creatures have arrived at this destination via the storm drains. Three big "selling points" for a visit to the lab are that kids can ask as many questions as they want and they can see and touch almost all of the animals here. The staff will even take the lobsters and sea stars out of the tanks for a closer look and touch. A native plant nursery at the facility is also a butterfly habitat.

Coming here is a fun family outing. There are oceans of opportunity for school field trips, too. Free, three-hour, age-appropriate classes cover a gamut of topics that not only meet the state science standard, but are engaging. Time is spent at the lab, learning about the animals, and seeing and touching them. A portion of the time is also spent at the big lab, the beach. One project that the kids do is look at the water from a different perspective, through a microscope, and test for water quality. After expending some energy and gaining more knowledge about aquatic life, it's back to the building for a related craft or hands-on activity. Can't come to the Sea Lab? Then they'll come to you. Note: If you have a teen who is 14 years or older inquire about the volunteer program.

Hours: Open to the public most of the year, Sat., 8am - 2pm. Open Sat. in the summer, 8am - 5pm. Call to schedule a field trip.

Admission: Free

Ages: 4 years and up.

STAR ECO STATION

(310) 842-8060 / www.theecostation.org
10101 W. Jefferson Boulevard, Culver City
(Exit San Diego Fwy [405] E. on Jefferson Blvd., L. on Sepulveda Blvd., and go straight as Sepulveda then turns into another Jefferson Blvd. [TG: 672 H2])

You can't miss the building - or maybe you can, since there is camouflage netting all around it. Done in the style of a lost Mayan temple, complete with archways, wall friezes, floor tiles with "fossils," (fake) greenery all around, and murals, the ECO Station's message of teaching kids the importance of preserving the environment and protecting wildlife comes across in an inviting manner. This place is, in fact, a designated wildlife sanctuary and works with the Department of Fish and Game. Illegal articles, seized from people trying to smuggle them into the country via airports, seaports, and over the border, are displayed here for show and tell.

Hour-and-a-half guided tours are given to see all the rooms and their inhabitants. Colorful birds line the hallway in their cages. You'll be greeted with loud "caw"s inside the large bird room, filled with green-cheeked Amazons, toucans, cockatoos, African gray parrots, Macaws, and others. An adjacent Environmental Village room contains booths with information regarding saving the environment and wildlife. It also features Chumash and Hope artifacts, such as drums, tools, and headdresses. The reptile room houses chameleons, numerous iguanas, geckos, bearded dragons, Burmese pythons (one weighs over 200 pounds!), boas, a small crocodile, and several tortoises. Your guide will tell you how the reptiles were rescued and brought here. Sometimes kids (and adults) are invited to touch the chameleons and/or wrap the pythons around themselves, or for the more squeamish, to merely stroke them (or not). The mammal rescue center room provides temporary homes for various animals, depending on which creatures are in need of the Eco Station facilities. We saw bobcats and servals. Again, the guide tells the story of how and why the animals are here and emphasizes why not to keep wild animals as pets. Whale bones and other display allows visitors to see animal parts up close.

Confiscated goods in the next room include boots made out of rattlesnakes; a purse made out of an alligator, including its head and paws; animal pelts such as tiger, zebra, and cheetah; an elephant foot stool; and more. Visitors will be educated about endangered species. Walk through a faux kelp forest that simulates scuba diving, while learning about the food chain and how to keep the ocean healthy, free from litter that comes through storm drains. Aquariums here contain a tropical reef tank, newts, colorful angelfish, blue tangs, jellyfish, Picasso fish, coral that's been harvested, lionfish, and pufferfish, and other aquatic creatures taken from people attempting to bring them into the U.S. Other marine-oriented containers hold turtles and a touch tank with horseshoe crabs, sea stars, and sea slugs.

Outside the building is a covered picnic area for individuals or groups. Two-hour school or group tours are offered during the week.

Hours: Open to the public Sat., 10am - 4pm. Open for school/group tours, minimum 40 students and maximum 80, Mon. - Fri., 9am - 3pm.

Admission: $7 for adults; $6 for seniors; $5 for ages 2 - 12; children under 2 are free. The cost for a school/group tour is $3.50 per child; $5 for adults, with one adult free for every ten children.

Ages: 2 years and up.

ORANGE COUNTY

Upwardly mobile urbanites live in this county designed to meet the needs of growing families. It boasts a great number of parks and playgrounds, including the most famous one of all - Disneyland Park. The intimate San Juan Capistrano, the upscale Laguna Beach, the natural preserves of Coto de Caza, the bustling Anaheim, the hills of Mission Viejo, and every city in between comprise a county that offers numerous places to sightsee. From Knott's Berry Farm to Huntington Beach to Medieval Times to Rainforest Café to Richard Nixon Library to Dana Harbor to Fullerton Arboretum - "orange" you glad you came to visit?

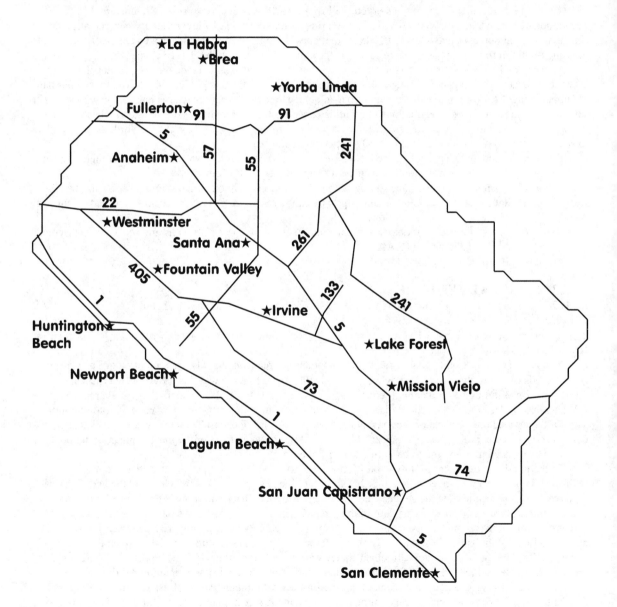

-----AMUSEMENT PARKS-----

ADVENTURE CITY
(714) 827-7469 / www.adventure-city.com
10120 S. Beach Boulevard, Anaheim
(Exit Artesia Fwy [91] S. on Beach Blvd. It's 2 miles S. of Knott's Berry Farm on the L. in the Hobby City complex. [TG: 797 J1])

My family travels a lot and one of our favorite cities to visit is Adventure City. This clean, two-acre little theme park, located in the HOBBY CITY complex (see pg. 252), is perfect for younger children. The colorful city scene facades throughout resemble storybook illustrations. The twelve or so rides, designed to accommodate parents, too, include a wonderful train ride around the "city," a few roller coasters, an airplane ride, a hot-air balloon ride, and a bus with wheels that goes 'round and 'round. Kids can have a really hot time dressing up in full fireman apparel before (or after) they "drive" around on the 9-1-1 vehicle ride.

Adventure City also offers do-it-yourself face painting, a few video and arcade games, plus terrific interactive, educational puppet and magic shows at the theater. After the show, kids are allowed to try their hand at puppeteering. Classes in puppeteering are also available. Thomas the Tank play area has a huge wooden train set that encourages toddlers' imaginations to go full steam ahead. A small petting zoo has goats, sheep, chickens, bunnies, and a llama. Mount Adventure is a rock climbing wall just the right size for kids (and adults) to scale. It's twenty-five-feet high and cost $3 per person to climb.

The food is good and reasonably priced. Note: You may not bring your own food inside, but there is a small picnic area just outside the gates. Come and spend a delightful day in this city!

Hours: Open in the summer and during school break, Mon. - Thurs., 10am - 5pm; Fri., 10am - 8pm; Sat., 11am - 9pm; Sun., 11am - 8pm. Open the rest of the year, Fri., 10am - 5pm; Sat. - Sun., 11am - 7pm. Call for holiday hours.

Admission: $11.95 for ages 1 and up; $8.95 for seniors; children under 12 months are free. Certain discounts are available through AAA.

Ages: 1 - 10 years.

CALIFORNIA ADVENTURE
(714) 781-4565 - recorded information; (714) 781-7290 - operator / www.disneyland.com
1313 Harbor Boulevard, Anaheim
(Going S. on Santa Ana Fwy [5], exit R. on Disney Way. Going N. on the 5, exit L. on Disneyland Dr. Follow the signs. Trams go from the parking lots to California Adventure. [TG: 798 H2])

This is Disney's version of California, which is sometimes realistic, and always entertaining. The California Adventure is one-third the size of Disneyland, which is directly across the way, with twenty-two rides and attractions. Enter through 11.5 feet high letters that spell out "CALIFORNIA," under a large scale replica of the Golden Gate Bridge, and to the central plaza, which features a landmark fifty-foot sun made of gold titanium. The park is divided into four major sections. Note: Make use of the "Fastpass" system, which means that computer-assigned boarding passes (dispensed from ticket machines in front of the most popular attractions) reserve a designated time for you to be in line to board the ride.

To the left of the entrance is **Hollywood Pictures Backlot**, which describes exactly what it looks like. The main road looks like a real street with a huge backdrop of blue sky and a few white clouds at the end. Famous Hollywood movie facades line the streets. The ten-minute Muppet Vision 3D show is great for Muppet fans. Watch out for objects that come flying "out of the screen." The Muppet preshow, shown on several large screens in a dressing room with lots of costumes and props, is equally entertaining. The Superstar Limo ride is similar to Roger Rabbits ride in Disney's Toontown. Stars (i.e. guests) sit in limos and are driven through Beverly Hills, kind of, as signs and cartoonish characters pop out along the way. The Hyperion Theater, which seats 2,000, presents outstanding professional musicals and shows. The Disney Animation building is a main attraction. It offers two different shows and three small rooms with interactive exhibits. The shows, Drawn to Animation and the Art of Animation, use animated figures on the screen that interact with live Disney staff to show the creative process of animation - inception to the final product. A small adjacent "museum" shows this process via sketches and sculpture of several famous Disney characters. In the Sorcerer's Workshop, which is decorated in a dark dungeon-style tone, draw your own Zoetrope (i.e. an early animation strip); enter the Beast's Library, which looks like a set from *Beauty and the Beast*, to match up your personality traits with a Disney character by having your picture taken and pressing buttons on a "magic" book; and, relive (as well as rewrite) Disney scenes in Ursula's Grotto by replacing the real voices with your speaking or singing voice, matched to an on-screen scene. On a set that looks and feels like the real thing, come play *Who Wants to be a Millionaire?* and win some Disney prizes. Debuting in 2004 is the Twilight Zone Tower of Terror, where visitors will hurtle down a run-away elevator in a haunted hotel.

Behind and to the right of the huge sun in the plaza is **Golden State.** To the immediate right is the highly touted, and rightly so, Soarin' Over California ride. Walk through its hangar and sit in a chair, with your feet dangling over the edge, in front of a giant screen that will immerse you in a virtual hang gliding adventure over California. Swoop over San Francisco, seemingly dip your feet into the Pacific Ocean, barely avoid treetops - watch riders lift their feet! - and literally smell orange blossoms and pine trees. You will get wet on the next ride, Grizzly River Run, an eight-passenger raft ride that goes down mountain sides, through caverns, and down a river onto a spouting geyser. At the outdoor play area, Redwood Creek Challenge Trail, kids let off steam by running around, scaling a short rock climbing wall, going up fire towers, down slides, and across cargo nets, zip lines, and swaying bridges. Nearby, the twenty-two-minute film, *Golden Dreams*, is narrated by Whoopie Goldberg, who plays Queen Califa, the essence of the state of California. It shows and tells the history of California through present day via various immigrant's eyes.

A **Bug's Land** is themed around the animated film, *A Bug's Life*. Walk back to Flik's Fun Fair where four kiddie rides, and the scenery, are oversized, supposedly reducing visitors to a bug's size. The rides include Heimlich's Chew Chew train, very slow bumper cars (with a minimum height requirement of 42" to ride; 48" to drive alone), spinning teacups, and pretend hot-air balloons. There is also a water play area with a few water fountains that spurt up at unexpected times. (Bring a change of clothing.) A Bug's Land also features "It's Tough to be a Bug" 3-D animation show - not for those with arachnophobia. The show features bugs of all kinds, such as termites, huge tarantulas that seemingly come out of the screen, stinkbugs (with an olfactory emission), an angry hoard of hornets that buzz loudly in a blackened room as a "stinger" pokes through the back of your chair. Also, experience the sensation of bugs crawling over you. O.K. - it wasn't my favorite attraction! Another small water playground and plots of California-based crops complete this area. Right next door, you can walk through an on-site tortilla factory and a sourdough bread factory and enjoy fresh samples. The adjacent restaurant is a great spot for lunch as salad or soup comes in a freshly-made bread bowl. Watch a seven-minute film on the making of wine at Wine Terrace. Wine sampling is available for adults.

On to **Paradise Pier**, which is like a boardwalk carnival, filled with old-fashioned rides and carnival-type games. The "E-ticket" ride here is California Screamin', a colossus roller coaster that earns its name with steep hills, high speed drops, and a loop-de-loop around a huge Mickey Mouse face. The giant Ferris wheel is another heart-stopper. Cages swing independently of each other, so passengers go around and around, <u>and</u> around and around! Other rides here include a swing ride, inside a large orange; a carousel; the Jumpin' Jellyfish parachute ride; old-fashioned-looking spinning rockets; a smaller roller coaster; and the Maliboomer, which catapults riders up in two seconds, and brings them down bungee style. Younger children enjoy a small ship that's really a play area. They can climb on deck, hang-ten on a stationary surfboard, turn the ship's wheels, and squirt each other with fireboat hoses.

Eureka, the Spirit of California, is a multi-cultural parade with participants in colorful costumes, plus live drummers, other music, skate and bike performers on-board floats, larger-than-life puppets, and street performers. Plan on seeing the long-standing favorite evening show - Electrical Main Street Parade.

There is a lot of "eye candy" at the park. Buildings, like Dinosaur Jack's Sunglass Shack is in the shape of an enormous, friendly-looking dinosaur wearing shades. Note: There are traditionally fewer crowds here on Mondays and Tuesdays. Tip: We often pack a meal to save money. For $6 a day, we rent a large-size locker. The lockers and picnic area are almost concealed, encircled by trees on the walkway between the two Disneys. See DISNEYLAND, on page 192, which is just across the walkway from California Adventure, and DOWNTOWN DISNEY, on page 251, a huge pedestrian "street" adjacent to both amusement parks that offers unique shopping and dining experiences.

Hours: Open daily in the summer, 8am - 1am. Open the rest of the year, Mon. - Thurs., 9:30am - 6pm; Fri. - Sat., 9am - midnight; Sun., 10am - 10pm. Hours fluctuate, so call before you visit.

Admission: $47 for adults; $45 for seniors; $37 for ages 3 - 9; children 2 and under are free. Parking costs $8. Ask about 2 or 3 day passes. Several times throughout the year Southern California residents are offered a substantial discount on admission.

Ages: 6 years and up.

DISNEYLAND

(714) 781-4565 - recorded information; (714) 781-7290 - operator / www.disneyland.com $$$$$

1313 Harbor Boulevard, Anaheim

(Going S. on Santa Ana Fwy [5], exit R. on Disney Way. Going N. on the 5, exit L. on Disneyland Dr. Follow the signs. Trams go from the parking lot to Disneyland. [TG: 798 H1])

The world-famous "happiest place on earth" amusement park has so many things to do, see, and ride on, that entire books are written about it. The following description is a brief overview along with some tips. Note that Disney has a "Fastpass" system, which means that computer-assigned boarding passes (dispensed from ticket machines in front of the most popular attractions) reserve a designated time for you to be in line to board the ride.

The park is "divided" into different sections and each section favors a particular theme. The following attractions are just *some* of the highlights in these various areas. **Fantasyland** is located mostly inside the castle "walls." Rides include Mr. Toad's Wild Ride, Alice in Wonderland (where the ride vehicle is shaped liked a caterpillar), a carousel, and more. This area is definitely geared for the younger set, although some of the images on the rides may be scary for them. Storybook Land is a boat ride through canals lined with miniature buildings that are from Disney's classic tales. Fantasyland also features Matterhorn Bobsled (a roller coaster), and "it's a small world," where a slow moving boat takes you past animated children from all over the world dressed in their culture's attire and singing the theme song in their native language. (If you didn't know the song at the beginning of the ride, you will never forget it afterward.) Just down the road is Fantasyland Theater where "fantasytastic" musical productions appeal to youngsters. **Mickey's Toontown** is put together at crazy, cartoonish angles. Meet Mickey and Minnie in "person" at each of their houses and get your picture taken with him/her. Kids enjoy Goofy's Bounce House, the scaled-down roller coaster ride, simply sitting in cars that look like they are straight out of a cartoon, and just running all around this toddler-friendly "town." Roger Rabbit is the most popular ride here as riders sit in a car that they can actually spin around. **Frontierland** features Big Thunder Mountain Railroad (a roller coaster), Mark Twain River boat (which looks authentic), and Tom Sawyer's Island. On the island, kids can climb on (fake) rocks, go through secret passages in the rocks, and play at the frontier fort. **New Orleans Square** boasts the classic Pirates of the Caribbean. Yo ho, yo ho, with its catchy music and cannons "blasting" under a nighttime setting, it's a pirate's life for me. The Haunted Mansion is a ride through, well, a haunted mansion, that showcases various ghosts. **Critter Country** features everyone's favorite bear, Winnie the Pooh. Take a "hunny" of a ride through the Hundred Acre Wood, a very popular attraction with the younger set, and enjoy the rest of the similarly-themed area. This country also has Splash Mountain, a wet roller coaster ride, with entertaining characters on the sidelines. **Adventureland** has the thrilling (and jolting) Indiana Jones roller coaster ride. You'll encounter snakes, skeletons, a huge boulder rolling toward your jeep, and other dangers. Height restrictions apply as younger children will most likely be frightened by the content. Tip: This ride offers a single rider pass. That means if your family members or friends are willing to go on the ride by themselves, each one can get a ticket from the attendant, bypass everyone else waiting in line (by going through the exit line), and wait in a very short line to be a "filler" on the ride. **Tomorrowland**, with its sixty-four-foot mobile of gold, spinning planets, at the entrance ushers in a new era. Zoom through the darkness of outer space in Space Mountain, one of the fastest roller coaster rides at Disneyland. Bump along through Star Tours, a motion simulator ride. *Honey, I Shrunk the Audience* is an exciting 3-D movie experience where objects seemingly come out at you from the screen. Warning: If you do not like mice, keep your feet off the floor. Bring a bathing suit (or change of clothing) in the summertime if you want to get wet running through the huge fountain in Tomorrowland. The water shoots up in some sort of pattern, but my kids usually just got wet, pretty much on purpose, I think. The rotating Innoventions building features educational and entertaining computer and video games on the first floor. The second level has more of the same, including virtual reality games and trying to step to the beat in a dance game. Drivers 52" and taller can rev up the engines and drive the Autopia course. And yes, the monorail is still here to offer a (low flying) bird's eye view of the park.

The daily (and nightly) themed parades and shows are truly memorable. They are usually based on Disney's latest animated films. *Fantasmic* is usually shown daily in the summer, and on the weekends only the rest of the year. This twenty-five-minute show, presented near Tom Sawyer's Island, centers around Mickey Mouse's imagination battling evil forces. Fountains of water create a misty "screen" for laser-projected images from *The Sorcerer's Apprentice*, *Dumbo*, and other films. Lighted boats cruise by with costumed characters on board acting out scenes from Disney movies. Fire flashes on the water, fireworks explode, and the finale is played with a thunderous symphony of music. Arrive early to get a good viewing spot. Weekend evenings throughout most of the year and every night during the summer (at 9:30pm) comes Believe, a choreographed fireworks extravaganza accompanied by a music and story-telling soundtrack. You have to see it to Believe it! Call for a complete list of show information and times.

Main Street, U.S.A. is perfect for all your mini (and Mickey) shopping needs. It also features restaurants and ice cream eateries. One of our favorite stops is the Candy Palace, where you can watch delicious confections being made before your eyes. (No free samples, though - sigh.) At Christmas, the candy makers create candy canes - a fascinating process. Also inside this palace are penny arcades and nickel games. Put a penny in a slot and peer through the viewer to see short, old-time "movies." Play games for just 5¢. Don't miss "Great Moments With Mr. Lincoln." This theater show uses headphones for advanced audio technology to tell the story of President Lincoln meeting a young soldier. The buzzing fly and hair-clipping shears sound so real! An animatronic Lincoln recites a stirring rendition of the Gettysburg Address for the finale. You can get something for nothing (really!) at the Bank of Main Street, just inside the entrance gate. Come inside to make your own souvenir pressed penny - in fact, the bank will give you a shiny new penny to press. Your child's favorite Disney characters are strolling all around the park, so keep your eyes open and your camera ready. Quite a few of the characters are gathered at Town Square when Disneyland opens in the morning. If you want to have more knowledge than the average tourist, take a guided tour of the park, for an additional fee. Whatever you decide, come spend at least a day at the "Magic Kingdom." Note: There are traditionally fewer crowds here on Mondays and Tuesdays. Tip: We often pack a meal to save money. For $6 a day, we rent a large-size locker. The lockers and picnic area are almost concealed, encircled by trees on the walkway between the two Disneys. See CALIFORNIA ADVENTURE (pg. 190), which is another Disney theme park adjacent to Disneyland, and DOWNTOWN DISNEY (pg. 251), a huge pedestrian "street" adjacent to both amusement parks that offers unique shopping and dining experiences.

Hours: Open daily in the summer, 8am - 1am. Open the rest of the year, Mon. - Thurs., 9:30am - 6pm; Fri. - Sat., 9am - midnight; Sun., 10am - 10pm. Hours fluctuate, so call before you visit.

Admission: $47 for adults; $45 for seniors; $37 for ages 3 - 9; children 2 and under are free. Parking costs $8. Ask about 2 or 3 day passes. Several times throughout the year Southern California residents are offered a substantial discount on admission.

Ages: All

KNOTT'S BERRY FARM

(714) 220-5200 / www.knotts.com
8039 Beach Boulevard, Buena Park
(Exit Artesia Fwy [91] S. on Beach Blvd. [TG: 767 H3])

$$$$$

The atmosphere of the Old West is re-created throughout most of California's original theme park. Knott's version of an Old West **Ghost Town** has a humorous Wild West Stunt Show, an old-fashioned stagecoach ride, steam engine train rides, a roller coaster ride through a mine, the log ride (on which you will get splashed, if not soaked), and lots of stores with a Western motif, including a real working blacksmith shop, and several arts and crafts stores. There are quite a few old looking, authentic buildings here that represent Anytown Main Street in the Old West. Find the small jail and go back to visit the criminal behind bars because this mannequin "talks" to visitors. (I won't tell the secret.) Catch a professionally-acted play at the Bird Cage Theater. A huge, relatively long, wooden-trestle roller coaster named Ghost Rider is a fast, bone-rattling, high-*spirited* thrill ride. (Part of the time I was lifted out of my seat!) The adjacent **Indian Trails** section has tepees to go in, Indian crafts to see, and terrific shows featuring Native American storytellers and dancers. The hoop dance is our favorite.

Fiesta Village's rides and shops have a Mexican theme, for the most part. Enter Jaguar, a roller coaster, through a Mayan-styled pyramid temple and experience ancient wonders (and a fun ride!). A pendulum-type swing ride, a merry-go-round, the hat dance (similar to a spinning teacup ride, only with hats), and Montezuma's Revenge roller coaster are all here. The **Boardwalk** has some of the most exciting rides. Go straight up about 250 feet and take a free fall, dropping at faster than 50 m.p.h. in the appropriately named Supreme Scream. And this is fun? My boys responded to that question with a resounding, "YES!" Go down Perilous Plunge at your own peril since it's one of the tallest water rides in the world (at least for now). Boats go over the edge at an almost vertical angle - you will get drenched. Your heart rate will accelerate on the Xcelerator, a 50's-themed roller coaster that both rocks and rolls. Boomerang zooms riders forward through six loops, and then does it all again, in reverse. The bumper cars, however, are my kind of ride. One of the most popular rides here is Kingdom of the Dinosaur, though it's a bit dark and scary for younger kids.

Beware - at **Wild Water Wilderness** the Roaring Rapids raft ride <u>will</u> get you completely wet. A"hidden" part to Knott's is a small, but terrific, Ranger Station in front of the rapids ride. Inside, kids can see and hold a variety of insects and arachnids such as a giant millipede and a hissing cockroach. They can also pet a snake and touch animal pelts. The Mystery Lodge hosts the image of mystical Native American storyteller narrating his tales.

Kids 2 to 8 years old can spend almost the whole day in **Camp Snoopy** with its numerous rides and attractions. Many of Snoopy's friends, such as Peppermint Patty, Lucy, and Charlie Brown, are on hand dispensing hugs, along with Snoopy himself. This "camp" has a kiddie roller coaster, pedal cars, Red Baron airplane ride, speedway, mini-scrambler, scaled-down steam train ride, hot-air balloon ride, Ferris wheel, kid-size Supreme Scream (making it a pre-teen scream), a walk-through fun house, and several other attractions geared just for young Peanut's fans. A favorite ride is Joe Cool's GR8 SK8 where guests slide back and forth (forty-feet up in the air) on a giant skateboard. The Camp Snoopy Theater features the Peanuts Gang in musical performances throughout the day.

A lot can be learned about the Old West and Native American life styles by talking to some of the costumed employees and using some of the stores as mini-museums in the Ghost Town and Indian Trails areas. There are also many terrific educational tours available through Knott's education department. Become knowledgeable about our early American heritage, pan for real gold, see a blacksmith at work, explore Indian Trails with an Indian guide, go on a natural history adventure, and much more! Knott's even provides educational assemblies that come to your school. Call (714) 220-5244 for information on their over twenty field trips.

In addition to Knott's Berry Farm's rides and attractions, there are twenty-six shops; delicious restaurants, including the famous Mrs. Knott's Chicken Dinner Restaurant; and the Charles M. Schulz Theatre, where major entertainers, including Snoopy, perform in extravaganzas. Acros the street is a full-size reproduction of INDEPENDENCE HALL (see pg. 253) and a water park, KNOTT'S SOAK CITY U.S.A. (See the below entry.) Knott's goes all-out for major holidays in decor and special events. Note: Mondays and Tuesdays are the best days to come here as it's usually less crowded.

Hours:	Open in the summer, Sun. - Thurs., 9am - 11pm; Fri. - Sat., 9am - midnight. Open the rest of the year, Mon. - Fri., 10am - 6pm; Sat., 10am - 10pm; Sun., 10am - 7pm. Hours may vary. Closed Christmas.
Admission:	$42 for adults; $32 for seniors and ages 3 - 11; children 2 and under are free. Certain discounts available through AAA. After 4pm admission is $15 per person for all ages. Parking is $8. Knott's offers numerous special admission deals throughout the year, including some for California residents only.
Ages:	All

KNOTT'S SOAK CITY U.S.A. (Buena Park)

(714) 827-1776 / www.soakcityusa.com

8039 Beach Boulevard, Buena Park

(Exit Artesia Fwy [91] S. on Beach Blvd. It's across the street from Knott's Berry Farm. [TG: 767 H3])

Hang ten at this thirteen-acre water park with a 1950's and early 1960's Southern California beach cities theme. Long boards and surf woodies dot the landscape and surf music plays in the background. The numerous intense rides and attractions include six high-speed slides - lie on your back and let 'er rip; tube rides that range from a little thrilling to hair raising; a relaxing tube ride that circles around a portion of the park in two-and-a-half feet of water; Tidal Wave Bay, where a series of waves roll out into a good-sized "bay" every few minutes; a racing slide (six people side by side) that utilizes mats; and two activity areas for kids. The Beach "House" is four stories of hands-on water fun with squirt guns, slides, and a huge bucket that periodically unloads hundreds of gallons of water to deluge everyone below. For younger children, the colorful Gremmie (surfer lingo for "young surfer wannabe") Lagoon is a pint-sized playground with gadgets to squirt, sprinkle, and soak fellow playmates. Climb aboard a submarine in the middle of the lagoon which is covered by an octopus with slides for tentacles. A few grassy areas and plenty of lounge chairs round out this way cool water park. Full-service food and snack stations abound, of course. Tip: Bring a picnic lunch to enjoy on the grounds of INDEPENDENCE HALL (see pg. 253), located just outside the gates. Hot tip: Wear water shoes or sandals as the walkways get very hot.

Hours: Open mid-April through mid-May weekends only and mid-May to the end of June daily, 10am - 6pm. Open July 1 through Labor Day daily, 10am - 8pm; weekends in September, noon - 8pm.

Admission: $22.95 for adults; $16.95 for ages 3 - 11; children 2 and under are free. After 3pm, admission is $13.95 for all ages. Parking is $8.

Ages: 1½ years and up.

WILD RIVERS WATERPARK

(949) 768-WILD (9453) / www.wildrivers.com

8770 Irvine Center Drive, Irvine

(Exit San Diego Fwy [405] S. on Irvine Center Dr. [TG: 891 A3])

This park's all wet with twenty acres of over forty water rides and attractions! The mild to wild rides include a relaxing river raft ride, wave pools (one has "real-size" waves), completely enclosed slides (i.e. dark and scary), and vertical drops. My boys also enjoyed shooting the rapids, and the opportunity to go belly-sliding down Surf Hill.

Younger kids have their own terrific water play area at Pygmy Pond. It has a climbing structure that shoots out water, a gorilla swing, just-their-size slides, and kiddie tube rides. Tunnel Town offers both wet and dry fun with twisting and turning tunnels to crawl through.

Two pools just for swimming are also here. One pool is three-and-a-half-feet deep, while the other is a bit deeper and has a water basketball area. All of this, and plenty of sun-bathing opportunities, makes Wild Rivers a fantastic beach alternative.

Picnic areas are available outside the park, as no outside food may be brought in. Locker rentals are between $5 to $8, depending on the size. Additional tube rentals are available for $5. Hot tip: Wear water shoes or sandals as the cement walkways get very hot.

Hours: Open mid-May through mid-June and mid-September through the beginning of October on weekends only, 11am - 5pm. Open mid-June through mid-September daily, 10am - 8pm.

Admission: $26 for 48" and taller; $18 for 47" and under; children 2 and under and seniors are free. Parking is $6. After 4pm, admission is only $14 for ages 3 and up. Ask about Monday Carloads, offered June through Labor Day, when admission is discounted.

Ages: 1½ years and up.

-----ARTS AND CRAFTS-----

COLOR ME MINE (Orange County)

(877) COLOR ME (265-6763) - for a listing of all locations. Brea - (714) 671-2808; Chino - (909) 628-7533; Costa Mesa - (949) 515-8612; (714) 241-8072; Huntington Beach - (714) 960-3834; Mission Viejo - (949) 367-9757; and Tustin - (714) 505-3975 / www.colormemine.com

$$$$

See the entry for COLOR ME MINE (Los Angeles County) on page 6 for details.

"CREATE IT" CERAMIC STUDIO

(714) 641-8124

$$$$

801 Baker Street, Costa Mesa

(From San Diego Fwy [405], exit S. on Fairview Rd., L. on Baker. From Costa Mesa Fwy [55], exit W. on Baker. [TG: 859 C5])

Create your own work of art at this paint-it-yourself ceramic studio. Choose from bisque, plaster, and greenware to decorate plates, mugs, figurines, vases, and other objects. All of the supplies to use are on hand, plus paints, brushes, and glazes are available for purchase as well. Ask about the specialty classes offered such as painting on glass, on gourds, and air brushing.

Hours: Open Tues., 10am - 9pm; Wed., 1pm - 5pm; Thurs., 10am - 9pm; Fri., 1pm - 6pm; Sat., 10am - 4pm. Closed Sun. and Mon.

Admission: The cost of the piece, plus half the cost of the piece as a materials fee, plus $6 for studio time.

Ages: 4 years and up.

OUR WAY CERAMIC

(562) 690-7306

$$$$

2351 W. Whittier Boulevard, La Habra

(Exit Riverside Fwy [91] N. on Beach Blvd., which dead-ends on Whittier after about 5 miles. Go L. and into the second driveway. [TG: 708 B4])

Is there a special gift-giving holiday coming up? This is the place to create that one-of-a-kind present. Choose a ready-to-paint ceramic piece, created on the premises, and enjoy the artistic endeavors that flow out of your paint brush, or just look around at finished products for inspiration. A definite plus to this ceramic place - there is no hourly painting fee! The cost of the item includes paints, brushes, and other necessary materials. This store also carries raw clay and other crafting supplies.

Hours: Open Mon., Wed., Fri., 10am - 5pm; Tues. and Thurs., 10am - 9pm; Sat., 10am - 3pm. Closed Sun.

Admission: The cost of an item starts at $10.

Ages: 4 years and up.

-----BEACHES-----

ALISO BEACH

(949) 661-7013 / www.ocparks.com

$

31131 Pacific Coast Highway, Laguna Beach

(Exit San Diego Fwy [5] S. on Laguna Fwy, which turns into Laguna Cyn., L. on Pacific Coast Highway. Or, exit San Diego Fwy [5], S. on Crown Valley Pkwy., R. on P.C.H. [TG: 951 B7])

This beautiful, cove-like beach has a small playground, plus barbecues, and picnic tables.

Hours: Open daily, 7am - 10pm.

Admission: Metered parking is 75¢ an hour (or a parking pass).

Ages: All

BOLSA CHICA STATE BEACH

(714) 846-3460 / parks.ca.gov

Pacific Coast Highway, Huntington Beach

(Exit Garden Grove Fwy [22] S. on Bolsa Chica Rd., R. on Warner Ave., L. on Pacific Coast Highway. Going N. on San Diego Fwy [405], exit E. on Warner Ave., L. on P.C.H. [TG: 857 C3])

There are six miles of beach here that are ideal for families because of the picnic areas (campfires are allowed), outdoor showers, five snack bars, and beach rentals. Year-round camping in self-contained vehicles is allowed, but there are no hook ups. No tent camping is permitted.

Hours: Open daily, 6am - 9pm.

Admission: $5 per vehicle. Camping is $18 a night.

Ages: All

CORONA DEL MAR STATE BEACH and TIDEPOOL TOURS

(949) 644-3044 / parks.ca.gov

On Poppy Avenue and Ocean Avenue, Corona Del Mar

(Take the San Diego Fwy [405] or the Costa Mesa Fwy [55] to the Corona Del Mar Fwy [73], which turns into MacArthur Blvd., S. on E. Coast Highway, R. on Poppy Ave. [TG: 919 E3])

Come for a few hours to explore some of the best tidepools in Southern California, then spend the rest of the day playing at the adjacent beach. Tidepools are a rich natural resource and a fascinating way for kids to learn about marine life. You are welcome to investigate the tidepools on your own, or sign up for a guided tour. After giving a short lecture, tour guides are helpful in pointing out interesting animal and plant life.

Just a short drive away, off Ocean Boulevard, is the big beach of Corona Del Mar. Besides sand and water, Big Corona provides fire rings, picnic tables, volleyball courts, and a snack bar.

Hours: Open daily, sunrise - sunset. Tidepool tours are given by reservations only.

Admission: $5 per vehicle for day use. Tours are $25 per group, up to thirty people, which includes parking fees.

Ages: 3 years and up.

CRYSTAL COVE STATE PARK BEACH

(949) 494-3539 or (800) 444-7275 / parks.ca.gov

E. Coast Highway, between Laguna Beach and Newport Beach, Laguna Beach

See the entry for CRYSTAL COVE STATE PARK on page 221 for details.

DANA COVE PARK, "BABY BEACH," and TIDEPOOLS

www.danapoint.org

Dana Point Harbor Drive, Dana Point

(Going S. on San Diego Fwy [5], exit on Pacific Coast Highway/Camino Las Ramblas and bear R. onto P.C.H. [Hwy 1] northbound, L. on Dana Point Harbor Dr./Del Obispo St. Go all the way to the end of road near Cove Rd. Heading N. on 5, exit on Beach Cities/Camino Las Ramblas into the L. lane to continue N. on Pacific Coast Highway [Hwy 1], L. on Dana Point Harbor Dr./Del Obispo St. [TG: 971 G7])

The protected harbor of "Baby Beach" (called so because of its waveless waters) offers picnic tables on the bluffs, plus barbecues, free parking, showers, and lifeguards. A good tidepool area is just around the "corner." See DANA POINT HARBOR (pg. 249), DOHENY STATE BEACH PARK (pg. 198), and the OCEAN INSTITUTE (pg. 244) for more details about the surrounding area.

Hours: Open daily, sunrise - sunset.

Admission: Free

Ages: All

DOHENY STATE BEACH PARK

(949) 496-6172 / www.dohenystatebeach.org

25300 Dana Point Harbor Drive, Dana Point

(Going S. on San Diego Fwy [5], exit on Pacific Coast Highway/Camino Las Ramblas and bear R. onto P.C.H. [Hwy 1] northbound, L. on Dana Point Harbor Dr./Del Obispo St. Going N. on 5, exit on Beach Cities/Camino Las Ramblas into the left lane to continue N. on Pacific Coast Highway [Hwy 1], L. on Dana Point Harbor Dr./Del Obispo St. [TG: 972 A6])

Doheny State Beach Park is big and absolutely gorgeous. The park is divided into three parts. The northern area, also accessible by metered parking off Puerto Place, is for day use. It is five acres of grassy, landscaped picnic area, with barbecue grills and fire rings along the beach. The rocky area is ideal for tidepool exploration during low tide. Since DANA POINT HARBOR (see pg. 249) is right next door, this is also a perfect spot to watch the boats sail in and out.

The central section, south of the San Juan Creek, is a campground with 121 sites. Farther south is another day use area with fire rings, beach volleyball, and showers. Throughout the entire stretch of the park there are sandy beaches and beckoning ocean waves!

A small Interpretative Center is to your left as you go through the entrance gates. It contains five fish tanks and a simulated tidepool (not a touch tank) with sea stars and leopard sharks. The mural-covered wall has wood shells that pose questions such as, "Do all sharks kill?" Lift the shell tab for the answer. There are also taxidermied animals, including twenty-five mounted birds, plus fossils and skeletons of a fox, raptor, and whale. Want to learn more about oceanography? Check out the nearby OCEAN INSTITUTE. (See page 244.)

Hours: The park is open daily, 6am - 8pm. Summer hours are daily, 6am - 10pm. The Interpretative Center is open Sat. - Sun., 10am - 4pm. Call for weekday hours.

Admission: $5 per vehicle for day use; $4 for seniors. Admission to the Interpretative Center is free. Camping prices are $16 - $20 a night depending on location and time of year.

Ages: All

HUNTINGTON BEACH

(714) 969-3492

Pacific Coast Highway, Huntington Beach

(Going N. on San Diego Fwy [405], exit S. on Euclid. Euclid turns into Ellis Ave and heads W., bear L. on Main St and go to the end. Going S. on 405, exit S. on Goldenwest St., L. on Garfield, R. on Main. Directions are to the pier, the beach is on either side. Look for street parking. [TG: 887 H2])

The surfing capital of California, Huntington Beach has waves, eight-and-a-half miles of sandy beach, and one of the longest concrete piers in California, plus several shops and restaurants in the immediate area. Tip: Check the water quality first.

Ages: All

MAIN BEACH / HEISLER PARK

(949) 497-0716 or (949) 497-0706

Cliff Drive and Myrtle Street at Pacific Coast Highway, Laguna Beach

(Exit San Diego Fwy [5] S. on Laguna Canyon Rd. [133], to the end. Turn R. on P.C.H. [1] for Main Beach. Heisler Park is just N. of the beach. [TG: 950 F3/G3])

I mention this park and beach together because they are on either side of Highway 133. Both are incredibly popular (i.e. crowded) and noted for their unparalleled views of the ocean. The water is clear, and the horizon seems to go on forever.

Some activities available at Heisler Park are lawn bowling, shuffleboard, and biking or skating on the paved paths. Main Beach offers a grass play area along with basketball courts, volleyball courts, and a small playground. This is a terrific place for beaching it and for swimming. Good luck finding a parking spot, though! Across the street from Main Beach are a variety of restaurants and shops.

Hours: Both are open daily, sunrise - sunset.

Admission: Free. Most parking is metered, at 25¢ per 15 minutes.

Ages: All

NEWPORT DUNES RESORT MARINA

☼
$$
🔥

(949) 729-3863 / www.newportdunes.com
1131 Backbay Drive, Newport Beach
(Take Newport Fwy [55] S.W. to the end, which turns into Newport Blvd., L. on W. Coast Hwy., L. on Jamboree Rd., L. on Backbay Dr. Or, from Corona Del Mar Fwy [73], exit S.W. on Jamboree Rd., R. on Backbay Dr. before E. Coast Hwy. [TG: 889 D6])

Toddlers to teens enjoy the enclosed acres of clean beach here, along with a waveless lagoon and a myriad of boating activities. There is a large fiberglass, stationary whale, nicknamed Moe B. Dunes, in the water for kids to swim out to, and one on the beach. The playground equipment includes a pirate ship to climb aboard - ahoy mateys!

Remember the joys of collecting seashells? Newport Dunes is one of the rare beaches around that still has shells. Note: Shellmaker Island and UPPER NEWPORT BAY ECOLOGICAL RESERVE (see pg. 233) are adjacent to the resort marina.

If you forget to bring food, have no fear of a growling tummy as a grocery store and cafe are inside the gates, just around the corner from the beach. Two outdoor showers are also available. RESORT WATERSPORTS (see pg. 271) rentals is located in the park for your kayaking, pedalboat, and windsurfing needs.

Overnight camping is available here and there are plenty of RV hook-ups. Free-standing (i.e. no stakes) tent camping is allowed, too. The surroundings are pretty; activities for campers, such as crafts, ice cream socials, and special movie showings are offered; and the Dunes has a swimming pool, indoor showers, and laundry facilities. What more could you want out of life? This local resort is my kind of "roughing it" vacation!

Hours: Open daily, 8am - 10pm.
Admission: $8 per vehicle for day use. Camping prices start at $32 a night, depending on location and camping equipment.
Ages: All

SEAL BEACH

☼
!/$
🔥

(562) 430-2613 - lifeguard station / www.ci.seal-beach.ca.us
Main Street, Seal Beach
(Exit San Diego Fwy [405] S. on Seal Beach Blvd., R. on Pacific Coast Highway, L. on Main St. [TG: 826 E4])

This beach has lifeguards, a pier, great swimming, and a playground. My kids love to gather the crabs crawling along the pier wall and put them in buckets. (We let them go before we go home.) Take a walk on the pier as the coastline view is terrific. No license is required for fishing off the pier and bait is available to purchase. There is also a RUBY'S diner (see pg. 206) at the end of the pier. Directly across the street from the beach is Main Street, which is lined with unique shops and restaurants (and a few ice cream stores).

Hours: Open daily, sunrise - sunset.
Admission: Park along the street or in a nearby lot for free for a few hours, or pay a $5 entrance fee for the day at the parking lot at the beach.
Ages: All

-----*EDIBLE ADVENTURES*-----

ALICE'S BREAKFAST IN THE PARK

◐
$$$
🔥

(714) 848-0690
6622 Lakeview Drive in Huntington Central Park, Huntington Beach
(Exit the San Diego Fwy [405] W. on Warner Ave., L. on Edwards St., L. on Central Park Dr. It's the red building at the end of the parking lot in Huntington Central Park. [TG: 857 G3])

Since breakfast is the most important meal of the day, why not start your day at Alice's Breakfast in the Park?! The red, barn-like building has a dining room that seats fifty. It's packed with antiques and Alice's varied collections, giving it a homey atmosphere. We also enjoy eating outside at the patio tables by the lake's edge. This is a delightful treat, especially for kids who don't always like to sit down throughout a meal. Watch out for the ducks, geese, and other birds that are usually waddling around, hoping for a handout.

Mmmmm - fresh baked bread or buns are served at all of Alice's breakfasts and lunches. Try an "outrageously delicious" cinnamon roll; at $2.75, it's (almost) big enough for a meal. Breakfast averages $5.95 for two eggs, home fries, and fruit. The menu offers a wonderful variety of other breakfast favorites, too, as well as fresh-squeezed orange juice. The lunch menu includes large sandwiches (average $5.25), salads, burgers, chili, and more. Breakfast and lunch kids' meals range from $1.95 to $3.95 and include a choice of grilled cheese sandwich, cheese omelet and fruit, hamburger, or fish sticks. Fries are included.

The restaurant is located in HUNTINGTON CENTRAL PARK (see pg. 225), so after your meal - go play!

Hours: Open daily, 7am - 2pm.
Admission: Prices are listed above.
Ages: All

ANGELO'S AND VINCI'S RISTORANTE

(714) 879-4022 / www.angelosandvincis.com
550 N. Harbor Boulevard, Fullerton
(Exit Riverside Fwy [91] N. on Harbor Blvd. [TG: 738 H6])

$$$

Attenzione - this ristorante and full bar not only bears the names of two of Italy's finest artists, but the cuisine and atmosphere is sure to please any *palette*. The dimly-lit restaurant creates a cozy ambiance by its eclectic decor packed around a main square room and upstairs mezzanine. Look up to see re-created Italian marketplace stalls along the walls. The fruit store, meat market, wine shop, etc., display realistic-looking fruit, hanging sausages, jars of pasta, hanging grapes and grapevines, and more, all with toddler-sized dolls dressed as merchants. There are also small knights in shining armor, framed art work, angel mannequins, signs, posters of the Mona Lisa, banners, a doll-sized stage, and bottles of wine all around, as well as trapeze figures and white Christmas lights suspended from the ceiling - always something to keep one's attention. A chapel wall holds statues, including a replica of the David, and old family photographs. There are a few uniquely-decorated banquet rooms at the restaurant. Take a quick peek, if you want, at the small basement/dungeon with its display of monsters, such as Dracula and Frankenstein.

Menu specialties include Old World-tasting pizza with a huge variety of toppings ($16.95 to $22.95 for a medium), extra large calzone ($17.25), spaghetti (average $7.50), tortellini ($13.75), and linguini and clams ($14.25), plus chicken, shrimp, salads, and more. There isn't a children's menu, but young ones can easily share a meal. The all-you-can-eat buffet lunch is $5.95 during the week for chicken wings, pasta Alfredo, chicken cacciatore, spaghetti, lasagna, salad, soup, breads, and more. The brunch buffet on Sunday is $8.95 and includes all the aforementioned food choices, plus champagne.

Hours: Open Sun. - Thurs., 11am - 9:30pm; Fri. - Sat., 11am - midnight. Closed Thanksgiving and Christmas.
Ages: All

BENIHANA OF TOKYO (Orange County)

Anaheim - (714) 774-4940; Newport Beach - (949) 955-0822 / www.benihana.com
Anaheim - 2100 E. Ball Road; Newport Beach - 4250 Birch Street
(Anaheim: Exit Orange Fwy [57] E. on Ball Rd. [TG: 769 C7]; Newport Beach: Exit San Diego Fwy [405], S. on MacArthur Blvd. R. on Birch. [TG: 859 F7])

$$$$

See the entry for BENIHANA OF TOKYO (Los Angeles County) on page 11 for details.

BREAKFAST WITH CHIP AND DALE

(714) 956-6755 / www.disneyland.com
1600 Disneyland Drive at Storytellers Cafe in the Grand Californian Hotel, Anaheim
(Going S. on Santa Ana Fwy [5], exit R. on Disney Way. Going N. on the 5, exit L. on Disneyland Dr. Follow the signs. [TG: 798 H2])

$$$$

Which one is Chip and which one is Dale? Only kids know for sure. The two chipmunks, often accompanied by Pluto or another Disney character, walk around to greet each guest at this special breakfast, sign autographs, and hug (or high five) little guests. Order the buffet, which consists of egg dishes, fresh bakery items, fruit, and juice, or order a la cart. Menu choices include a two-eggs any style served with country potatoes, ham, and toast - $9.50; eggs Benedict - $11; Mickey-shaped waffles - $8.50. A Farmer's Market buffet comes with fruit, an omelet, home-style breakfast, and bakery goods - $18.95.

The restaurant is done up in turn-of-the-century style and decorated with storytelling murals. Ask your server to tell you a few of the stories. Visit the adjacent DISNEYLAND HOTEL (see pg. 250) and DOWNTOWN DISNEY (see pg. 251) for more fun things to do and see. DISNEYLAND (see pg. 192) and CALIFORNIA ADVENTURE (see pg. 190) are just next door.

Hours: Open daily, 6:30am - 11:30am
Admission: The buffet is $18.95 for adults; $9.95 for ages 3 - 11; children 2 and under eat for free. Other menu items are available.
Ages: All

BREAKFAST WITH MINNIE AND FRIENDS

(714) 956-6755 / www.disneyland.com $$$$
1717 Disneyland Drive at the Paradise Pier Hotel, Anaheim
(Going S. on Santa Ana Fwy [5], exit R. on Disney Way. Going N. on the 5, exit L. on Disneyland Dr. Follow the signs. [TG: 798 H2])

This breakfast is described as "character dining." I'm still not sure if the "character" reference refers to Disney characters or to my children! The colorful, art-deco-styled restaurant offers a breakfast buffet with an array of delicious foods: omelets made any way you like 'em (my boys considered watching the cook make omelets part of the entertainment), cereal, yogurt, fresh fruit, hash browns, Danish (hungry yet?), mouse-shaped waffles, and smoked salmon. You may also order a la carte from the menu. A traditional Japanese breakfast is also available.

Minnie Mouse makes an appearance, dispensing hugs to all the kids. She, along with Daisy and Max, get guests involved with doing the limbo (how low can you go?) and the Conga line. Join in the fun and don't forget to bring your camera!

Take some time, before or after your meal, to ride the glass elevator in the lobby to the top of the hotel. It's not much of a view, but the ride was a thrill for my kids. Sometimes, it's the simple things in life that are the most pleasurable. Visit the adjacent DISNEYLAND HOTEL (see pg. 250) and DOWNTOWN DISNEY (see pg. 251) for more fun things to do and see. DISNEYLAND (see pg. 192) and CALIFORNIA ADVENTURE (see pg. 190) are just next door.

Hours: Open daily, 6:30am - 11am.
Admission: The buffet costs $18.95 for adults; $9.95 for ages 3 - 11; children 2 and under eat for free. A la carte menu prices range from $7 to about $11. Parking is free for first three hours.
Ages: All

CHUCK E. CHEESE

See the entry for CHUCK E. CHEESE on page 12 for details.

ELIZABETH HOWARD'S CURTAIN CALL DINNER THEATER

(714) 838-1540 / www.curtaincalltheater.com
690 El Camino Real, Tustin

See the entry for ELIZABETH HOWARD'S CURTAIN CALL DINNER THEATER on page 257 for details.

ESPN ZONE

(714) 300-ESPN(2776) / www.espn.go.com $$$$
1545 Disneyland Drive at Downtown Disney, Anaheim
(Going S. on Santa Ana Fwy [5], exit R. on Disney Way. Going N. on the 5, exit L. on Disneyland Dr. Follow the signs to Downtown Disney. [TG: 798 H1])

I took my kids to the ESPN Zone so now I got game. This place is a must for sports fans of all ages. Live radio broadcasts that visitors are welcome to watch (and maybe become part of) happen frequently in the studio inside the entrance. This is one of the many features that makes ESPN Zone unique. The majority of the downstairs is a restaurant. One side features a sixteen-foot digital television screen that dominates a wall, surrounded by twelve other screens showing various sporting events. The booths in here have their own screen on the table with capabilities to change channels (sports channels only) and volume. The sound is heard through a system that wraps around the inside of the booth. Recliner chair occupants get front-row viewing with their own personal sound system. There is a full bar in this section. Check out the wall sculpture of an athlete made from sand.

The other restaurant side features more television screens, of course. Note: There are over sixty-five throughout the Zone, including in the bathrooms, so you don't miss a moment of action! This section also features slightly elevated newscasting areas, where actual broadcasts take place. You could be part of the local affiliate audience. Call for a schedule. The food, which is very tasty American grill, got two thumbs up from my kids - they cleaned their plates. The menu includes buffalo wings ($8.99), cheese fries, grilled chicken salad ($10.99), baby back back back ribs ($19.99), salmon ($15.99), hamburgers ($8.99), pasta ($10.99), steak sandwich, and filet of beef ($15.99). The children's menu offers a choice of hot dog, burger, chicken tenders, or pasta, plus fries and a beverage for $5.99. Ordering over the din of the televisions is a fun challenge - talk about kids getting distracted! But it's worth it. Note that it gets very crowded and lively here during any play off or major sporting event.

Upstairs is the sports center, or games area, which you are welcome to visit without eating at the restaurant. Purchase a "credit card" in any monetary increment worth a certain amount of points. Slide it into whatever game you want to play and that game's point value will be deducted. For instance, air hockey "costs" eight points; bowling, sixteen points; wave runners are eight points, and so on. All the games are sports themed. Knock down pins at the two forty-five-feet bowling lanes using heavy mini balls. The score is kept electronically for you. Test your slapshot in a small enclosed hockey area where you shoot pucks at a life-size metal goalie that moves back and forth. Another player (i.e. a friend) can pay and stand outside, behind you, and make the goalie move by pulling on a lever. Throw a football through metal receivers with holes for arms (which seems just like a real receivers sometimes!) as they move back and forth. For twenty-four points, climb aboard a real Formula One race car and speed up to 200 m.p.h. to drive your way to victory against a computer-generated race track. Use a pole and reel in an on-screen marlin or another big one in a specially designed fishing chair. Shoot some hoops (ten points). Put up your dukes and MoCap Box with a virtual opponent by jabbing the air towards him and by physically moving to dodge punches. A motion capture system guides you in your endeavors to become the champ. Other interactive games, and most incorporate "playing" against a screen, involve shooting at targets, becoming a jockey on a mechanical horse (this is funny to watch), skateboarding, swinging a golf club, Daytona racing, and more. A big attraction is climbing the thirty-foot Xtreme Glacier, a rock climbing wall. Get harnessed and get ready for various climbing routes - from beginner to advanced. (This attraction is twenty-four points.) And once, again, you are never far from the TV action in the sports center. Note that not all of the games are open in the daytime.

The Zone has an attached gift shop. It also offers shuttle service to and from the Ducks and Angels games. After or before your visit, take some time to walk around DOWNTOWN DISNEY (see pg. 251).

Hours: Open Sun. - Thurs., 11:30am - 11:30pm; Fri. - Sat., 11:30am - 12:30am.
Admission: Prices for food are listed above. Cards for the sports center cost, for instance, $20 for ninety points.
Ages: 5 years and up.

FARMER'S MARKETS
See the entry for FARMER'S MARKETS on page 14 for details.

THE GARDEN COTTAGE & TEA ROOM

(714) 990-4TEA (4832) / www.gardencottageandtea.com $$$$

518 E. Imperial Highway, Brea

(Exit Orange Fwy [57] W. on Imperial Hwy [90]. [TG: 739 B1])

This cozy little tea house is big on ambiance. The windows have flowers painted on them and white picket fences. The white lattice inside is interlaced with vines and ivy. Walls are painted in soft colors with memorable sayings penned on them. Soft music plays in the background. Tables are covered with glass that holds down old pictures, notes, and newspaper clippings. Shelves are filled with tasteful bric-a-brac. A few gift items are for sale here, too. A couple of tables are just outside the door, facing the main highway.

Oh yes - the food and beverage! The Queen Anne's Tea includes a pot of tea (and there are twenty-five different flavors), scones, cream and jam, spinach quiche, two tea sandwiches, three petite desserts, and one hot dessert for $16.95. The Lady and Duchess teas offer equally delicious fare. Children 9 years and under will enjoy the Princess Tea of tea, scones, cream and jam, and one hot dessert for $7.95. As they say at the cottage - "Tea ya later!"

Hours: Open Tues. - Fri., 10am - 4pm; Sat., 10am - 5pm. Closed Sun. and Mon.

Admission: Menu prices are listed above.

Ages: 4 years and up.

GOOFY'S KITCHEN

(714) 956-6755 / www.disneyland.com $$$$

1150 Magic Way at the Disneyland Hotel, Anaheim

(Going S. on Santa Ana Fwy [5], exit R. on Disney Way. Going N. on the 5, exit L. on Disneyland Dr. Follow the signs. Trams go from the parking lot to Disneyland. [TG: 798 H2])

For a special, Disney-style meal, come to Goofy's Kitchen for an all-you-can-eat brunch or dinner buffet. Your children's favorite characters come by the tables for a hug. We were visited by Pluto, Minnie Mouse, Chip (or was it Dale?), John Smith, Miko and, of course, Goofy. Kids even eat a bite or two in between hopping up to touch the costumed characters. Remember to bring your camera (and your autograph book)!

We stuffed ourselves at the dinner buffet with prime rib, ham, chicken, seafood, fruit, salad, and scrumptious desserts. (The way my family suffers just to be able to share with you!) The kids have their own food bar that offers familiar favorites like macaroni and cheese, mini-hotdogs, spaghetti, breaded shrimp, and chicken strips. The brunch buffet consists of salads, fruit, vegetables, pastas, chicken, barbecue beef ribs, Mickey-shaped waffles, pancakes, home fries, cereal, oatmeal, and omelets.

Goofy's Kitchen offers good food in a fun, family atmosphere. Make your outing even more of a treat by coming early, or staying after mealtime, to walk around and enjoy the hotel grounds. Visit the adjacent DISNEYLAND HOTEL (see pg. 250) and DOWNTOWN DISNEY (see pg. 251) for more fun things to do and see. DISNEYLAND (see pg. 192) and CALIFORNIA ADVENTURE (see pg. 190) are just next door.

Hours: Open Mon. - Fri., 7am - 1pm. Open Sat. - Sun., 7am - 2pm. Open daily for dinner, 5pm - 9pm.

Admission: Brunch buffet is $18.95 for adults; the dinner buffet is $26.95 for adults. Both buffets are $9.95 for ages 3 - 11; children 2 and under eat for free. Parking is free for the first three hours, with validation.

Ages: 1½ years and up.

GOSPEL BRUNCH (Anaheim)

(714) 778-2583 / www.hob.com $$$$$

1530 S. Disneyland Drive at the House of Blues at Downtown Disney, Anaheim

(Going S. on Santa Ana Fwy [5], exit R. on Disney Way. Going N. on the 5, exit L. on Disneyland Dr. Follow the signs. It's in the Downtown Disney venue. [TG: 798 H1])

See the entry for GOSPEL BRUNCH (Hollywood) on page 16 for details. This location's building doesn't resemble a shack and it is located in DOWNTOWN DISNEY. (See pg. 251.)

HARD ROCK CAFE (Newport Beach)
(949) 640-8844 / www.hardrock.com
451 Newport Center Drive, Newport Beach
(Exit San Diego Fwy [405] S. on Jamboree Rd., L. on Santa Barbara, L. on Newport Center Dr. It's near Fashion Island mall. [TG: 889 E7])

$$$

    See the entry for HARD ROCK CAFE (Los Angeles County) on page 17 for details.

JOE'S CRAB SHACK (Orange County)
Garden Grove - (714) 703-0505; Newport Beach - (949) 650-1818 / www.joescrabshack.com
Garden Grove - 12011 Harbor Boulevard; Newport Beach - 2607 W. Coast Highway
(Garden Grove: From Garden Grove Fwy [22], exit N. on Harbor. From Santa Ana Fwy [5], exit W. on Chapman Ave., L. on Harbor. [TG: 798 J4]; Newport Beach: Take Costa Mesa Fwy [55] to end, where it turns into Newport Blvd., L. on Coast Hwy. [TG: 888 J7])

$$$

    See the entry for JOE'S CRAB SHACK (Los Angeles County) on page 18 for details.

JOHNNY REB'S SOUTHERN SMOKEHOUSE (Orange)
(714) 633-3369
2940 E. Chapman Avenue, Orange
(Exit Costa Mesa Fwy [55] E. on Chapman. [TG: 800 B4])

$$$

    See the entry for JOHNNY REB'S SOUTHERN SMOKEHOUSE (Los Angeles County) on page 18 for details. The Orange County location is large, the wall hangin's are more orderly than the mish mash decor of the other locations, and it has a tin roof porch for outside seating.

MCDONALD'S (with a train theme)
(714) 521-2303 / www.mcdonalds.com
7861 Beach Boulevard, Buena Park
(Exit Artesia Fwy [91] S. on Beach Blvd. It's just N. of Knott's Berry Farm. [TG: 767 H3])

$$

    We've nicknamed this "Train McDonald's" because the center of the eating area has a large model train exhibit with seating available all around it. Kids (and adults) are enthralled as the train goes around the mountains, through the tunnels, and past villages. Tracks and a train also run overhead. And yes, there are all the normal McDonald's foods.

      Hours: Open daily, 5am - midnight.
      Ages: All

MEDIEVAL TIMES
(714) 521-4740 / www.medievaltimes.com
7662 Beach Boulevard, Buena Park

    See the entry for MEDIEVAL TIMES on page 259 for details.

THE OLD SPAGHETTI FACTORY (Orange County)
Fullerton - (714) 526-6801; Newport Beach - (949) 675-8654 / www.osf.com
Fullerton - 110 E. Santa Fe Avenue; Newport Beach - 2110 Newport Boulevard
(Fullerton: From Orange Fwy [57], exit W. on E. Chapman Ave., L. on Harbor Blvd., L. on Santa Fe. From Riverside Fwy [91], exit N. on Harbor, R. on Santa Fe. [TG: 738 H7]; Newport Beach: Take Costa Mesa Fwy [55] S. to the end, continue on Newport Blvd about 2 miles. [TG: 918 H1])

$$$

    See the entry for THE OLD SPAGHETTI FACTORY (Los Angeles County) on page 19 for details.

PLAZA GARIBALDI DINNER THEATER
(714) 758-9014
1490 S. Anaheim Boulevard, Anaheim

    See the entry for PLAZA GARIBALDI DINNER THEATER on page 261 for details.

POFOLKS

(714) 521-8955 / www.pofolks.com

7701 Beach Boulevard, Buena Park

(Exit Artesia Fwy [91] S. on Beach Blvd. [TG: 767 H3])

$$$

PoFolks is a great place to come for home-style cooking and a nice, family atmosphere. The walls are decorated with pictures, toll-paintings, and other things that make it look homey. A model train is running on tracks overhead and there are a few table games to keep kids entertained. Menu choices include soup ($3.99), salads - chicken, shrimp, tuna, or chef's ($6.99), country ham steak ($8.99), home-style dinners like pot roast ($8.99), plus chicken, ribs, and fish. Kids' meal choices include chicken, fish, a burger, a corn dog, or a grilled cheese sandwich for $3.45. Beverages are extra. Tip: McDonald's, just a bit south down the street, has a free magazine called "Welcome" that usually contains discount coupons for PoFolks.

Hours: Open Sun. - Thurs., 7am - 9pm; Fri. - Sat., 7am - 10pm.

Ages: All

RAINFOREST CAFE (Orange County)

Anaheim - (714) 772-0413; Costa Mesa - (714) 424-9200 / www.rainforestcafe.com

$$$

Anaheim - 1515 S. Disney Drive at Downtown Disney; Costa Mesa - 3333 Bristol Street in South Coast Plaza

(Anaheim: Going S. on Santa Ana Fwy [5], exit R. on Disney Way. Going N. on the 5, exit L. on Disneyland Dr. Follow the Downtown Disney signs. [TG: 798 H1]; Cost Mesa: Exit San Diego Fwy [405] N. on Bristol. [TG: 859 D3])

Deep in the heart of the Rainforest Cafe, realistic-looking animatronic beasts come to life - gorillas beat their chests, elephants trumpet, and parrots squawk. Periodic thunder and lightening "storms" explode through the restaurant. This is not a quiet place to eat. Cascading waterfalls, fake dense foliage, and "rock" walls add to the atmosphere, as do the jaguars and cheetahs that are partially hidden in the banyan trees. Rain drizzles down from the ceiling around the perimeter of the cafe, ending in troughs of misty waters. You'll enter the cafe under a 6,000 gallon fish tank archway that holds a colorful array of saltwater fish. Two more aquariums are inside the cafe and one contains beautiful, but poisonous, lionfish. There is always something to grab your attention here!

Savor your meal at a table, or on a bar stool that is painted to look like a giraffe, zebra, frog, or another animal. The delectable menu offers everything from salmon, flatbread pizza, Oriental chicken salad, and Jamaica Me Crazy! porkchops to hamburgers, meatloaf, and lasagna. Prices start at $9.99 for hamburgers and go up to $29.99 for steak and fish. Portions are large. Children's meals average $5.99 for a choice of a grilled cheese sandwich, catfish, chicken nuggets, hamburger, pasta linguine, or pizza, and include a drink with a souvenir cup. Desserts are deliciously unique. My favorite was Monkey Business - coconut bread pudding with bits of apricots, topped with shaved chocolate and whipped cream.

The adjacent Rainforest Cafe Retail Village (i.e. store) is themed with equal attention to detail. In the front of the store a (pretend) life-size crocodile resides in a small swamp. He moves around and roars every few minutes. Live macaws and cockatoos are on perches just above the crocodile. A knowledgeable animal care specialist will tell your inquisitive little ones all about the birds. Ask about educational programs that take students on a half-hour safari through the restaurant to learn about endangered species, conservation, and the environment. Tours include lunch and a lesson plan. Catch jungle fever and experience the Rainforest Cafe! Note: The location in Anaheim is in DOWNTOWN DISNEY (see pg. 251), is multi-level, and doesn't have a crocodile. This location, does, however, have a short bird presentation every half hour until 6pm. There is another location in ONTARIO MILLS MALL. (See pg. 334.)

Hours: Open Mon. - Thurs., 11am - 9:30pm; Fri., 11am - 10pm; Sat., 11am - 10pm; Sun., 11am - 8pm.
            (The Anaheim location is open Sun. - Thurs., 8am - 10:30pm; Fri. - Sat., 8am - midnight.)

Ages: All

RITZ-CARLTON HOTEL TEA

(949) 240-2000 / www.ritzcarlton.com

1 Ritz-Carlton Drive, Dana Point

$$$$$

(Going S. on San Diego Fwy [5], exit on Pacific Coast Highway/Camino Las Ramblas and bear R. onto P.C.H. [Hwy 1] northbound, L. at Ritz-Carlton Dr. Going N. on 5, exit on Beach Cities/Camino Las Ramblas into the left lane to continue N. on Pacific Coast Highway [Hwy 1], L. at Ritz-Carlton Dr. [TG: 971 F4])

The Ritz-Carlton is an incredibly classy hotel. Celebrate your child with a special afternoon of tea in an elegant room that overlooks the ocean. The Traditional Tea offers a delectable variety of pastries, scrumptious finger sandwiches, a fruit platter, and tea (of course) for $30 per person. Get the royal treatment with the Royal Tea, which comes with champagne or a non-alcoholic cocktail, a choice of teas, finger sandwiches, pastries, and strawberries and cream, all for $35 per person. Come early or stay a bit afterwards to explore the gracious hotel and beautiful grounds. Teddy Bear Teas, for families, are offered on selected days in December and include a marionette show. Call for times and details.

Hours: Seatings for tea are Thurs. - Sun., every half hour between 2pm - 4pm. Reservations are required for all teas. There are special seatings during the Christmas holiday season.
Admission: Prices are quoted above.
Ages: 5 years and up.

RIVERBOAT RESTAURANT

$$$

(949) 673-3425 / www.riverboatrestaurant.com
151 E. Coast Highway, Newport Beach
(Take Costa Mesa Fwy [55] to end, where it turns into Newport Blvd., L. on E. 17th St., R. at end on Dover Dr., L. on E. Coast Hwy. It's on Newport Bay. [TG: 889 B7])

Dine Mark Twainish style in an intimate room on board a Mississippi riverboat. The view of the harbor is nice and the food is a cut above. Dinner selections range from $10 to $50 and include prime rib, filet mignon, chicken specialties, a selection of fish, jumbo prawns, and more. Come early for the sundown specials. Enjoy live entertainment, via a pianist and vocalist, on Friday and Saturday evenings.

The luncheon fare is equally delicious. Kid's meals are $6.95 for a burger, chicken fingers, or pasta, plus fries and a beverage. Brunch is served only on Sundays. Note: The restaurant shares the boat with the NEWPORT HARBOR NAUTICAL MUSEUM (see pg. 243).

Hours: Lunch is served Tues. - Sat., 11am - 3pm. Brunch is Sun., 10am - 3pm. Dinner is served Sun., Tues. - Thurs., 4:30pm - 9pm; Fri. - Sat., 4:30pm - 10pm. Closed Mon. and some holidays.
Admission: See menu prices above.
Ages: All

RUBY'S (Orange County)

$$$

(800) HEY RUBY (439-7829) / www.rubys.com
There are over 15 locations in Orange County - I'm sure you'll find one close to you!

These 1940's-style diners offer good food and have a terrific atmosphere for kids. They've readily become one of our favorite places to eat. Old-fashioned-looking jukeboxes that play favorite oldies; red vinyl booths and bar stools; decorations that match the time period ambiance; and the kind of attentive service that all but disappeared years ago, are some of Ruby's trademarks. Since the restaurants are franchised, each one is slightly different in decor (some have trains going around on tracks overhead), and in their choice of menu items. Most breakfast choices include omelettes (about $5), waffles (about $4), etc. Lunch and dinner foods include a wide selection of burgers (beef, turkey, veggie, or chicken), for an average cost of $7. Salads, sandwiches, and soups are available, too. The delicious concoctions from the soda fountain, including flavored sodas and old-fashioned ice cream desserts, keep us coming back for more. Kids' meals average $3.50 for a choice of a grilled cheese sandwich, corn dog, hamburger, or chicken fingers. Their meals come with fries, a kid-size ice cream cone, and a toy. Drinks are extra. Note: You'll find Ruby's at the end of several Southern California piers, kind of like a pot of gold at the end of a rainbow.

Hours: Open daily for breakfast, lunch, and dinner.
Ages: All

SAM'S SEAFOOD "POLYNESIAN SPECTACULAR"

(562) 592-1321 / www.samsseafood.com

16278 Pacific Coast Highway, Huntington Beach

(Exit San Diego Fwy [405] S. on Seal Beach Blvd., L. on Pacific Coast Highway. [TG: 826 J6])

$$$$

Aloha! Imagine a balmy evening where Hawaiian music plays softly in the background while you're savoring delicious seafood. Welcome to . . . not Hawaii, but Sam's! This tropically-themed restaurant offers all this, plus beautiful South Seas murals, a waterfall decorated with flowers and real volcanic rocks, carved wood totem poles, and (padded) bamboo furniture. Dining here is a treat for the senses and palate. Lunch choices include fried clam strips ($4.95), fried jumbo shrimp ($6.50), broiled salmon ($15.95), swordfish steak ($15.95), shrimp Louie ($9.95), steak sandwich ($6.95), or hamburger ($4.95 each). Dinner selections include calamari ($13.95), steamed clams ($8.95) prime rib ($16.95), lobster tail ($23.95), and teriyaki steak or barbeque ribs ($13.95 each). The childrens' menu is the same for both lunch and dinner. It includes fish 'n chips, fried chicken, a grilled cheese sandwich, or a burger, plus fries, for $4.95. Beverages are extra.

If you want to spend more time vacationing at the Pacific islands (via Sam's), come to the three-hour Polynesian Spectacular offered in a "hidden" room just off the main dining area. Seating begins at 7pm, with each party being seated at individual tables. Live music accompanies your meal - feel free to sway along. Although the traditional music is good, two hours of this pre-show fare, including songs sung in native languages, can make a younger child antsy. Dinner selections include prime rib, salmon, baby back barbecue ribs, Snow Crab legs, teriyaki shrimp, or Hawaiian-style chicken, accompanied by salad, rice, and dessert. Beverages are served with little paper parasols.

The featured one-hour-and-fifteen-minute show starts at 9pm on a stage that has a waterfall surrounded by rocks and flowers. The singers, dancers, and musicians have Polynesian roots. The variety of performers' costumes include colorful print shirts and dresses, grass skirts, bandeau tops, and feather headdresses. The costumes authentically reflect the islands represented throughout the show - Hawaii, Tahiti, Samoa, and New Zealand. Highlights include the Samoan body slap dance (ouch!), graceful hula dances, belly dances (how do they move like that?), and fierce-looking Maori warriors, complete with face paint and spears, who stomp around and stick out their tongues.

Tip: If you're celebrating a birthday, anniversary, or other special event, tell your waiter upon arrival so that the emcee can include it during her announcements. Also, hang loose and go native by wearing a tropical outfit!

Hours: Sam's is open Sun. - Thurs., 11:30am - 9:30pm; Fri. - Sat., 11:30am - 10:30pm. The Polynesian Spectacular is offered Fri. nights April through November, 7pm - 10:15pm.

Admission: Meal prices are listed above. The Polynesian Spectacular is $31.95 for adults; $26.95 for ages 4 - 10; children 3 and under are free.

Ages: 5 years and up.

SPAGHETTI STATION

(714) 956-3250 / www.spaghetti-station.com

999 W. Ball Road, Anaheim

(Going S. on Santa Ana Fwy [5], exit Ball Rd. It's on the corner of the off ramp and Ball Rd. Going N. on 5, exit N. on Harbor Blvd., L. on Ball Rd. [TG: 768 H7])

$$$

For a taste of the Old West, come eat at Spaghetti Station. The lobby area has a stuffed mountain lion and deer, Butch Cassidy's saddle (yes, it really belonged to him), wooden Indians, and cowboy statues. Either before or after your meal take a "tour" through the rustic restaurant. Lots of terrific Western memorabilia is displayed in glass cases in the rooms, such as lanterns, cowboy boots, woman's lace-up shoes, saddles, musical instruments, guns, arrowheads, tomahawks, and arrows, plus statues of bulls, cowboys, and stagecoaches. Upstairs is a small game room with a billiard table.

Each room has a stone fireplace in a house-like setting. The menu has fun facts about the gold rush and other important Western dates and happenings. Food choices include spaghetti, fixed with a wide variety of sauces, plus ribs, chicken, pizza, salad, and more. Prices range from $7.95 to $15.95. The kids' menu offers pizza, spaghetti, cheese ravioli, or chicken tenders for $5.95 to $6.95. Beverages are $1.85. Although there is a bar toward the front, the rest of the restaurant is great for your little cowhands.

Hours: Open Sun. - Wed., 4pm - 10pm; Thurs. - Sat., 4pm - 11pm.
Admission: Menu prices are listed above.
Ages: 2 years and up.

TEA HOUSE ON LOS RIOS

(949) 443-3914 / www.theteahouseonlosrios.com   *$$$$*

31731 Los Rios Street, San Juan Capistrano

(Exit San Diego Fwy [5], W. on Ortega Hwy., L. on Del Obispo St., R. on Los Rios. [TG: 972 C1])

Take a sip of tea and just relax. The ambiance of this historic district flows with Old World charm, as does this Tea House which is in a restored 1911 cottage. The garden has a profusion of flowering plants. The white picket fence, trellis, and covered veranda add to the cultivated atmosphere. Inside are intimate rooms decorated with plates, tea cups, other tea time paraphernalia, and fresh flowers. Fine china and linens are used at the tables.

A variety of teas are offered here, ranging from Cottage Tea, with scones, cream, and preserves, and a selection of tea for $13.75 to Victorian Tea, with scones et. al, and tea, plus soup and salad, assorted finger sandwiches, fruit with heavy cream, dessert, and champagne for $29.95. A la carte brunch and lunch entrees include a cup of soup, ($3.50), Mediterranean salad ($13.95), Shepards Pie ($12.95), island-style rice with chicken breast ($13.95) and prime rib ($19.95). Children 9 years and under will especially enjoy the Tree House Tea which consists of a peanut butter and jam sandwich, fruit, scones, and a soft drink or juice for $12.75. Before or after your tea time, take a stroll around San Juan Capistrano and enjoy the rest of what this quaint city has to offer.

Hours: Open Wed. - Fri., 11am - 5pm; Sat. - Sun., 10am - 5pm. Closed Mon., Tues., and some holidays.
Admission: Prices are listed above. Note that there is a $7 per person minimum.
Ages: 4 years and up.

TIBBIE'S MUSIC HALL

(888) 4TIBBIES (484-2243) / www.tibbiesmusichall.com

7530 Orangethorpe Avenue, Buena Park

See the entry for TIBBIE'S MUSIC HALL on page 262 for details.

VICTORIAN MANOR TEA ROOM

(714) 771-4044 / www.victorianmanor.com   *$$$$*

204 N. Olive Street, Old Towne, Orange

(Exit Costa Mesa Fwy [55] W. on Chapman Ave., R. on Olive. [TG: 799 G4])

Simply enchanting! This turn-of-the-century Queen Anne Victorian home, including a charming garden, has been lovingly restored and embellished. Each of the five intimate tea rooms are painted a different color. Every one is uniquely decorated (to the hilt!) with old-fashioned women's hats, tea pots and cups, antique boots, period clothing, stencils, and/or an amazing assortment of knickknacks, some of which are available to purchase. The tablecloths are lacy, checkered, or velvety; the centerpieces are traditional (flowers) or whimsical (ornamental teapots); and individual chairs are artistically painted with clouds, a garden scene, polka dots, and other designs. Soothing music plays in the background in each room.

Besides a wide variety of teas, such as apricot, vanilla cream spice, jasmine flower, raspberry cream pecan, and Earl Grey, the Manor offers a menu with sandwiches, soups, and Chef, Ceasar, or chicken salads, as well as scones and confections. Your choice of sandwich - tuna salad, egg salad, turkey, ham and cheese, BLT, roast beef or club - is $8.98, and includes potato salad, fruit, apple sauce or pudding. Side orders of scones (and cream and jam) or dessert are also available. High teas are a highlight. The Lady Barbara Tea, for instance, consists of a pot of tea, scones with cream and jam, soup of the day, tea sandwiches, vegetables, fruit, cookies, and other confections for $17.98. Children, up to 12 years old, can partake of teas, too (or tea for two?) such as the Victorian Tinkerbell Tea, comprised of tea, pink lemonade, or hot chocolate; scones with cream and jam; four tea sandwiches of peanut butter and jelly, egg salad, cheese, and tuna (or ask the waitress for other choices); and the dessert of the day all for $12.98. Special teas are also available. What a *tea*licious stop!

Hours: Open Tues. - Fri., 10am - 5pm. Open Sat. - Sun., 10am - 6pm. Closed Father's Day, Thanksgiving, and Christmas.

Admission: Prices are mentioned above.

Ages: 4 years and up.

WATSON DRUGS AND SODA FOUNTAIN

$$$

(714) 633-1050 - restaurant; (714) 532-6315 - pharmacy / www.watsondrug.com

116 E. Chapman Avenue, Orange

(Exit Costa Mesa Fwy [55] W. on Chapman Ave. It's just E. of the shopping center circle. [TG: 799 G4])

Watson Drugs and Soda Fountain, built in 1899, has the distinction of being the oldest drugstore in Orange County. Located in the wonderful shopping center of Old Town, it is a great place to stop for a meal, or just a treat. Part of Watson Drugs is a pharmacy/gift shop. Look up at the eclectic, old-fashioned items on the overhead shelves. The old-fashioned candy selection is fun, too.

The other half is a retro 40's diner, with a big jukebox, red vinyl seats, and lots of memorabilia, including old license plates that decorate the walls. Breakfast, such as omelets, pancakes, or french toast, costs about $6. Lunch, like chicken salad, roast beef, burgers, or tuna melts, costs about $6. Dinner, such as steak, fish, or chicken, costs, on the average, $8. The kids' menu includes a choice of a hot dog, tuna fish sandwich, or a grilled cheese sandwich for $3.95. Fries are included in the kids' meals, but drinks are extra. Let's not forget the most important food item - dessert! Ice cream floats, sundaes, shakes, and more, are yours for the asking (and the paying). Eat inside and enjoy the ambiance, or choose one of the tables outside, and watch the world go by.

Hours: Open Mon. - Sat., 6am - 9pm; Sun., 8am - 6pm. Closed Christmas.

Ages: 2 years and up.

WILD BILL'S WILD WEST DINNER EXTRAVAGANZA

(800) 883-1546 or (714) 522-6414

7600 Beach Boulevard, Buena Park

See the entry for WILD BILL'S WILD WEST DINNER EXTRAVAGANZA on page 263 for details.

-----FAMILY PAY AND PLAY-----

BALBOA FUN ZONE

$

(949) 673-0408 / www.thebalboafunzone.com

600 E Bay Avenue, Newport Beach

(Take Costa Mesa Fwy [55] to the end, which turns into Newport Blvd., which turns into Balboa Blvd., L. on Main St. Park and walk. [TG: 919 B2])

This strip called the Fun Zone is across the road from the pier. (See BALBOA PIER on page 249 for details.) The carousel, Ferris wheel, bumper cars, and Scary Dark Ride (that's its real name) are the main attractions here. Rides require one to two tickets, and tickets are $1.75 each. Arcade games, a clown bounce for younger children ($1 for a few minutes of bouncy fun), and an indoor nine-hole miniature golf course ($4) are also here. Craft activities in the Zone include making spin art pictures and other fun projects.

Kids also enjoy walking around, shopping, or eating a famous Balboa Bar which is an ice-cream bar with various toppings. If you're looking for physical activity, bike rentals are available at Bayside Sun and Sport on Palm Street. Rentals are $6 for the first hour for children's bikes, and $14 for tandems. They also have in-line skates and more. Parasailing, (949) 673-3372, is between $55 to $75 for ten minutes of air time and an hour boat trip. Call for hours of operation. See the Transportation section for harbor cruises launched from this immediate area.

Take the historic Balboa ferry which runs Monday through Friday from 6am to midnight (longer on the weekends) to Balboa Island. At only 50¢ per person one way, free for children 4 years and under, or $1.25 for car and driver - the ferry is a fun, affordable way to get to the island and kids love this mini-adventure. Once on the man-made island, there is not a lot for kids to do. Enjoy a walk on the paved pathway along the beach or perhaps head east toward the main shopping street. Note: The Island can also be reached by exiting Pacific Coast Highway [1] S. on Jamboree Road, where it turns into Marine Ave.

Hours: Stores and attractions along the Balboa Fun Zone are open most of the year, Mon. - Thurs., 11am - 8pm; Fri. - Sat., 11am - 10pm; Sun., 11am - 8pm. Summer hours are Mon. - Thurs., 11am - 11pm; Fri., 11am - 11pm; Sat., 10am - 11pm; Sun., 10am - 10pm. Most parking along the street is metered.

Admission: Attractions are individually priced above.

Ages: All

BOOMERS! (Anaheim)

(714) 630-7212 / www.boomersparks.com

1041 N. Shepard, Anaheim

(Exit Artesia Fwy [91] N. on Kraemer/Glassell, R. on La Palma, R. on Shepard. It's next door to Camelot, miniature golf. [TG: 769 G2])

This is a fun center, but bring your money because fun costs. The many attractions include **bumper boats** - $4.50 for 45" and taller, $2 for passengers 44" and under; **batting cages**; **go-karts** - $6 for a five-minute ride and children must be at least 58" tall to drive; **Naskarts** - $5 a drive (height restrictions apply); **rookie go-karts** - $4.50 for drivers at least 42" tall; a **rock climbing wall** - $3.50 for a few tries to the top; and **Big Top Fun Zone**, with six carnival rides, including a carousel, bounce house, and some kiddie rides. Rides are $3.75 each or purchase an unlimited rides pass. Lots of arcade games and a full-service snack bar are available, here, too.

Hours: Open Mon. - Thurs., 11am - 9pm; Fri., 11am - 11pm; Sat., 10am - 11pm; Sun., 10am - 10pm. Open extended hours in the summer.

Admission: Attractions are individually priced above. An unlimited pass available on weekends only is $22.95 for 58" and taller; $14.95 for 54" and under. Ask about other specials.

Ages: 2 years and up.

BOOMERS! (Fountain Valley)

(714) 842-1011 / www.boomersparks.com

16800 Magnolia Street, Fountain Valley

(Exit San Diego Fwy [405] S. on Magnolia. [TG: 828 C7])

Boomers is fun for the whole family. The attractions here include **miniature golf** - $7 for adults, $5.50 for seniors and kids 12 years and under; **bumper boats** - $5 for a six-minute ride, and kids must be at least 44" tall to ride by themselves (children under 40" can ride with an adult for $2); **batting cages** - eighteen pitches for $1; and **go karts** - $6 for a five-minute ride, and kids must be at least 58" tall to drive by themselves, $2 for additional passengers who must be at least 40" tall. The **Kiddie Big Top** has carnival rides, geared for ages 7 and under, such as a Ferris wheel, a roller coaster, train ride, and balloon ride, plus a short rock climbing wall. Each ride, or attraction, takes five tickets: Twenty-four tickets are $7, forty-four tickets are $12. Kidopolis is a multi-level soft play area with tubes to crawl through and ball pits. Admission is $2 per child. A full-service Boomer's Cafe is on-site, too.

Admission: Attractions are individually priced above, or pay $20.95 for 58" and taller; $14.95 for 57" and under.

Ages: 2 years and up.

BOOMERS! (Irvine)

(949) 559-8336 / www.boomersparks.com

3405 Michelson Drive, Irvine

(Exit San Diego Fwy [405] S. on Culver Dr., R. on Michelson. Or, exit San Diego Fwy [405] S. on Jamboree, L. on Michelson. [TG: 859 J6])

This purple palace, which can be seen from the freeway, is definitely a kids' kingdom. There is an almost overwhelming amount of video and arcade games, or, to quote my boys, "Wow!" There is also a ticket redemption center and an Express McDonald's Restaurant. Also inside the castle walls are activities for the younger set, such as kiddie arcade games and **Palace Playland**, which is a two-tiered, soft play area with soft-play mazes, ball pits, tunnels, and slides - $3.50 for all-day play for kids 48" and under.

Outside, are three, terrific, themed **miniature golf** courses with windmills, castles, houses, and other buildings - $7 a round for adults, children 5 years and under are free. **Rock climbing** is $6 for two climbs up the wall. Splash Island **bumper boats** are $5 a ride, $2 for additional riders who must be over 42" tall. I allowed my 11-year old to steer the boat and he did so gleefully - right under the fountain's waters. Oh, the joy of spending time together! **Go-carts,** where drivers must be a minimum of 58" tall, are $7 per ride, $2 for additional riders who must be at least 42" tall. Younger speedsters, at least 44" tall, can drive their own cars at **Kiddie Go-karts** for $3.75 a ride. **Batting cages** are here, too. In **Laser Storm**, you and your at least 5-year-old child (personal recommendation) enter a darkened, maze-like room with walls that are three-feet high and lit by fluorescent markings. For about five minutes you'll engage in laser tag, which entails alternately safeguarding your base while shooting at the players on the opposing team. It's a blast. The cost is $6.50 per game.

Last, but not least, for skaters and BMX riders, is the **Gravity Games Skate Park**, a 21,000 square-foot outdoor skate park with several wooden ramps, quarter pipes, a half pipe, grinding boxes, and other street skate features, plus some skating (or biking) room, all on a base of smooth concrete. Two-hour sessions cost between $5 to $10 for members; $9 to $12 for non-members, depending on the day and time. Helmet, elbow, and knee pads are required and can be rented for $5 for everything. Participants under 18 must have a waiver signed by a parent or legal guardian.

If the urge strikes, next door is the Irvine Recreation Center with plenty of bowling lanes.

Hours: Open Mon. - Thurs., 11am - 10pm; Fri., 11am - midnight; Sat., 10am - midnight, Sun., 10am - 10pm. Hours may fluctuate.

Admission: Attractions are individually priced above or purchase a park pass, which includes everything but the skate park and batting cages, for $23.95 for 58" and taller; $16.95 for 57" and under.

Ages: 2 years and up.

CAMELOT

(714) 630-3340 / www.golfland-sunsplash.com/camelot

3200 Carpenter Avenue, Anaheim

(Exit Riverside Fwy [91] N. on Kraemer/Glassell, R. on La Palma, R. on Shepard, L. on Carpenter. It's next door to Boomers! (Anaheim). [TG: 769 G3])

In short, there's simply not a more congenial spot for happy ever aftering than here in Camelot! This huge castle has dragons, knights in shining armor, and anything else your prince or princess might consider fun decor. Choose from five exciting **miniature golf** courses - $7 for adults, $6 for seniors and ages 5 to 11, children 4 years and under are free with a paid adult (all replays are only $2); **Lazer Joust**, which is an exciting game of tag using laser guns - $5 for the first game Monday through Thursday, $6 for the first game Friday through Sunday, with all replay games costing $3; five **waterslides** (usually open from May to September) - $4 for ten rides, $6 for twenty rides, and $8 for an all-day rides pass; over 300 video and arcade games (ask about arcade mania pricing - if you want); and a full-service snack bar, serving pizza, sandwiches, and Dryer's ice cream.

Hours: Most of Camelot is open in the summer, Sun. - Thurs., 10am - midnight; Fri. - Sat., 10am - 1am. The rest of the year it's open Sun. - Thurs., 10am - 11pm; Fri - Sat., 9:30am - midnight. The water slide is open seasonally, daily from 11am - 6pm.

Admission: Attractions are individually priced above.

Ages: 2½ years and up.

CHUCK E. CHEESE

See the entry for CHUCK E. CHEESE on page 12 for details.

CLIMBX

(714) 843-9919

18411 Gothard Street, Unit I, Huntington Beach

(Exit San Diego Fwy [405] W. on Talbert Ave., L. on Gothard. It's in an industrial section. [TG: 857 J3])

$$$$

        This indoor rock climbing facility is not as large as others we've found, but it has all the essential ingredients - several contoured wall structures built at angles that look and climb like real rock; colorful hand and foot holds that mark a variety of "trails"; a small bouldering cave; twenty-six top ropes; and enough challenges for seasoned climbers, along with lots of encouragement and easier routes for beginners. It's encouraging to know that athletic prowess is not necessary when learning how to climb. This is a sport that teaches balance and thinking while instilling a sense of confidence. Climbers are in a safety harness which is attached to a belayer, so even if one should misjudge a hand or foot hold (which my kids sometimes did on purpose), the climber will not fall, but merely swing in the air. ClimbX marks the spot for indoor fun! Note: This facility has a separate party room.

Hours: Open Mon. and Fri., 11am - 8pm; Tues. - Thurs., 11am - 10pm; Sat. - Sun., 11am - 6pm.

Admission: An all-day pass is $13 per person. Shoe or harness rentals are $3 each, per person, or $5 for both. Introductory classes are $65 for two hours.

Ages: 5 years and up.

DROMO 1

(714) 744-4779 / www.dromo1.com

1431 N. Main Street, Orange

(Exit the Orange Fwy [57] E. on Katella Ave., L. on Main. [TG: 799 F1])

$$$$

        Put the pedal to the metal at this 45,000 square-feet indoor karting facility. Enjoy challenging, high performance racing with up to seven other drivers in a safe, controlled environment. Each session is about twenty laps or twelve minutes. Drivers must be over five feet tall and are supplied with a driving suit, helmets with fullface goggles, and a neck brace. Please wear close-toed shoes. Participants under 18 years old must be accompanied by their parent, who must sign a liability waiver. If you're wondering what to do while waiting for your turn to race, you can pick up a game of air hockey or pool.

Hours: Open Mon. - Fri., 1pm - 10pm; Fri. - Sat., 1pm - 11pm; Sun., 1pm - 9pm.

Admission: $20 - $25 per session, depending on the time of day.

Ages: At least 5 feet tall.

ESPN ZONE

(714) 300-ESPN(2776) / www.espn.go.com

1545 Disneyland Drive at Downtown Disney, Anaheim

        See the entry for ESPN ZONE on page 201 for details.

FLIGHTLINE

(949) 253-9JET (9538) / www.flightlineusa.com

17831 Sky Park Circle - B, Irvine

(Exit San Diego Fwy [405] N. on MacArthur Blvd., L. on Sky Park E., R. on Sky Park Circle. [TG: 829 G4])

$$$$

        For older kids aiming to be Top Guns, these six flight simulators are the next best thing to actually being airborne. Five of the simulators, which are lined up side-by-side in this small room, have dual seats, with separate controls. After suiting up in flight gear, you'll receive a fifteen-minute briefing and in-flight instruction on the basics of flying (for novices) and the particulars of your cockpit. The pilot (that's you!) can choose to fly a F16 Fighting Falcon, A-10 Warthog, the F4 Phantom, or other planes. Cockpits are realistic with fully functional avionic control panels, heads-up display, and hands-on stick and throttle controls. During your forty-minute flight you are in constant contact with the control tower instructors. Compete in dog fights against computer-generated opponents or against a buddy in the next plane. Being a part of a military combat squadron is another option. Squadron members learn advance piloting skills such as air combat maneuvering, precision bombing, and navigation. Ask about the education programs that are offered here, too.

For those who remain grounded, go upstairs to the small room called the "Officer's Club", or watch the action on monitors from the observation deck that show exactly what each pilot is experiencing.

Hours: Usually open Wed. - Fri., 1pm - 7pm; Sat. - Sun., 10am - 8pm. Closed Mon. and Tues. Call to schedule a flight.

Admission: $35 per person. Special programs have different fees.

Ages: Must be at least 9 years old.

LASER QUEST

(714) 449-0555 / www.laserquest.com

229 E. Orangethorpe Avenue, Fullerton

(Exit Riverside Fwy [91] N. on Harbor Blvd., R. on Orangethorpe Ave. [TG: 768 H1])

$$$

This large arena, with gothic decor, sets the stage for an exciting game of laser tag. Armed with laser guns, and vests with target lights, enter the multi-level maze. Amid the strobe lights, ramps, catwalks, partitions, fog, and pulse-pounding music (which covered up my heavy breathing from being out of shape), race against the clock to "tag" the opposing team members with laser shots, and score. The fifteen-minute games are fast-paced, and leave you either tired or fired up to play another round! The lounge has video games and there is a separate party room.

Hours: Open Tues. - Thurs., 6pm - 10pm; Fri., 4pm - midnight; Sat., noon - midnight; Sun., noon - 8pm. Open on holiday Mon. Open extended hours in the summer.

Admission: $7.50 per game.

Ages: 6 years and up.

PHARSIDE

(949) 574-9966

1644 Superior Avenue, Costa Mesa

(Take Costa Mesa Fwy [55] S. to the end. Proceed to Newport Blvd., R. on 18th St. L. on Superior Ave. It's near 16th St. There is no parking on the lot. During the week, park at "Public" parking places. On weekends only, you may use the Model Glass's lot, across the street. [TG: 888 H4])

$$

This is a place for after school and weekend skateboarders, in-line skaters, and BMX riders to practice and hang out. There are a few ramps inside toward the back, through the pro shop, such as a six-foot spine connected to a nine-foot half pipe and a four-foot half pipe. Outside on the asphalt is a six-foot half pipe and a grind box. (Your kids will understand this terminology if you don't.) It isn't anything fancy, but skaters and bikers just want a place to do their thing. A small snack shop is available. Helmet, knee pads, and elbow pads are required and so is a parent-signed waiver.

Hours: Open Mon. - Fri., 11am - 6pm; Sat., 10am - 6pm; Sun., 11am - 5pm. There are specific times for skateboarding, blading, and for BMX riding. (All BMX riders must be at least 16 years old.)

Admission: $10 for non-members for the day; $5 for members. Ask about specials for any given day. Equipment rents for $2 per item, or $5 for the set.

Ages: 8 years and up.

ROCKCITY

(714) 777-4884 / www.rockcityclimbing.com

5100 E. La Palma, suite 108, Anaheim

(Going E. on the Riverside Fwy [91], exit N. on Lakeview, R. on La Palma, R. on Kellogg to park. Going W. on 91, exit N. on Imperial Hwy., L. on La Palma, L. on Kellogg. [TG: 770 C1])

$$$$

I'm gonna rock 'n roll all night! Well, I'll at least rock for a good portion of the day. This large indoor rock climbing gym is very family oriented. It has thirteen top ropes, numerous lead routes on variously-angled walls, a bouldering wall, and a bouldering cave. Perfect for first time climbers and still very challenging for experts, RockCity offers the best of both worlds. Parents, learn to belay your kids or just relax (remember, they *are* wearing harnesses) and watch them go at it during kid's climbs when the staff does all the work. Remember that classes are available for all skill levels, too.

For a different kind of challenge, try the outdoor high ropes challenge course constructed with telephone poles, steel cables, and rope. With two zip lines, over 175 feet in length, thirty-five-feet high, and twelve different routes, the emphasis here is not on speed, but on attempting and doing. The course is operated by RockCity, but located down the road at 24001 Santa Ana Canyon Road in Anaheim Hills at Featherly Park. It is geared for groups of ten or more, although there are days that individuals can come. Note that signed waiver and liability forms, available on-line, are required by all rock and challenge course climbers.

Hours: Open Mon. - Fri., noon -10pm; Sat., 10am - 6pm; Sun., noon - 6pm. Kids are welcome to climb anytime, but times especially for them are Thurs., 6pm - 8pm; Sun., 1pm - 3pm.

Admission: $12 for an adult day pass; $10 for a day pass for 14 years and under. The harness and shoes are an additional $5 per person. Kid's climb is $20 for two hours, which includes the rental equipment and a belayer. The challenge course is $20 for the day.

Ages: 5 years and up.

ROCKREATION (Costa Mesa)

(714) 556-ROCK (7625) / www.rockreation.com $$$$

1300 Logan Avenue, Costa Mesa

(Exit San Diego Fwy [405] S. on Fairview Rd., R. on Baker St., L. on McClintock Wy., R. on Logan Ave. [TG: 859 A5])

Get the kids geared up - it's time to *rock* out at Rockreation! This huge indoor warehouse/rock climbing gym is a great place for beginners to learn climbing techniques in a safe and controlled environment. It also provides enough rocky terrain for serious climbers to train. The multi-colored rocks of various shapes and sizes jut out from the twenty-seven-foot geometrical walls for handholds and footholds, offering over 150 different climbing routes. Some of the walls are straight up and down, others have slight inclines, while still others have very challenging angles and overhangs. Belayers, those who hold the rope so if you slip you don't fall, are provided during specific Climb Time hours, for ages 6 and up. Even if you were to hit rock bottom (which you won't), it's "carpeted" with black foam padding. Kids warm up using a short practice wall. Although my boys were a bit intimidated at first, by the end of our time here, they were really climbing the walls - all the way to the top. Enroll your child in a summer camp or one of the year-round classes offered for various levels and ages. Hang out with your kids here, or better yet, tell them to go climb a rock! Also look up ROCKREATION (Los Angeles) on pages31.

Hours: The gym is open Mon. - Thurs., noon - 10pm; Fri., noon - 9pm; Sat. - Sun., 10am - 6pm. Climb Time, for kids 6 and older, is offered Tues. and Thurs., 6pm - 8pm; Sat. - Sun., noon - 3pm.

Admission: $15 per person for an all-day pass. Equipment rental - shoes, harness, and chalk - is an additional $5.

Ages: Depending on your child's agility - 5 years and up.

SCOOTERS JUNGLE

(714) 223-5730 / www.scootersjungle.com $$$$

921 Via Rodeo, Placentia

(Exit Riverside Fwy [91] N. on Lakeview Ave., L. on Mira Loma Ave., take the second R. on Via Rodeo (it's a horshoe shape so there are two connections to Via Rodeo, the second one is closer to Scooters). [TG: 770 B1])

Grab a vine and swing on over to Scooters Jungle. The small lobby has a few toys and some fun-house mirrors to keep kids occupied before they enter the main play room. In the play room palm tree murals add to the tropical theme ambiance. Your little monkeys will go bananas! There are two huge inflatable bounce structures in here; one is a twenty-foot-high slide and the other is hard to explain. The second huge bounce forms a v-shape in its middle. Kids (or adults) climb up the small inflatable steps on either side to slide down in the middle, or (and this is the popular choice) grab the rope and just swing back and forth over the chasm until they drop. The ratings for this bounce go off the scale! There is a smaller bounce for younger kids. Note: Socks are required for all bounces. Another fun and unique feature is the small super ball room. Participants don helmets and goggles and just go into the room and throw super balls all around. Sounds simple, but they love it. The play room also has an air hockey table, foosball table, and ping pong.

An adjacent party room has long tables and chairs and a throne for the birthday child. Catch jungle fever and visit Scooters Jungle!

Hours: Open mostly for private parties. Call about occassion open-to-the-public dates.

Admission: $205 for up to twenty-two kids and twenty adults for two-and-a-half-hours of time, including an hour of party room time, Mon. - Fri. until 2:30pm. $240 for the same as the previous, except from Fri. after 2:30pm - Sun. The last option is $150 for up to fourteen kids and sixteen adults for one-hour-and-forty-five-minutes of play time, Mon. - Fri. until 2:30pm. Children under 2 are not included in the kid count. Call for open-play prices and dates, and prices for drop-off summer camps.

Ages: 4 years and up.

SEAL BEACH SKATEBOARD PARK

(562) 431-2527 / sbrecreation.tripod.com

12th St. and Landing, Seal Beach

(Exit San Diego Fwy [405] S. on Seal Beach Blvd., R. on Landing (just past Pacific Coast Hwy.), enter at the gate near Zoeter Field park. Adjacent to a child care center. [TG: 826 F4])

This local, outdoor skate park just has a few wooden quarter-pipes, a funbox, and a half pipe all on asphalt. It's just for the fun of it! Safety equipment - helmet and knee and elbow pads - must be worn. A parental waiver must be on file for skaters under 18 years old.

Hours: Open traditional school days, Wed. - Fri., 4pm - 6pm; Sat. - Sun., noon - 6pm. Open in the summer and holidays, Wed. - Sun., noon - 6pm.

Admission: $1 an hour.

Ages: 7 years old and up.

SOLID ROCK GYM (Lake Forest)

(949) 588-6205 / www.solidrockgym.com

26784 Vista Terrace, Lake Forest

(Exit San Diego Fwy [5] N.E. on Lake Forest Dr., R. on Vista Terrace, R. into the industrial park and follow the signs. [TG: 862 B7])

See the entry for SOLID ROCK GYM (San Diego) on page 381 for details.

Hours: Open Mon. - Fri., 11am - 7pm; Sat., 9am - 9pm; Sun., 11am - 7pm.

Admission: An all-day pass Mon. - Fri. is $12 for any age; weekend prices are $15 for adults; $13 for ages 16 and under. Harness and equipment costs are an additional $6.

Ages: 5 years and up.

VANS SKATEPARK (Orange)

(714) 769-3800 / www.vans.com

20 The City Boulevard West, Orange

(Exit Garden Grove Fwy [22] N. at The City Drive, near the intersection of I-5. It's in The Block at Orange mall. [TG: 799 C5])

Wow! Awesome! Incredible! And these were just the first few words out of my boys' mouths. This part-indoor, part-outdoor skate park at The Block mall has 46,000 square feet of wooden ramps, concrete bowls, a Combi pool, half pipes, pro and outdoor street courses, mini and vert ramps, and more, all at a mega mall. Rollerbladers and skateboarders, and cyclists can all use the park at various times. It is a training "camp" for competitors as well as a practice place for enthusiasts of all levels. Beginners have certain areas that are recommended just for them. Observers can sit anywhere on the multi-level stadium seats that semi-surround the main skate area. Our first few times here we just watched before my older boys actually ventured out on the ramps, and then they were off! Participants under 18 must have a waiver signed by a parent or legal guardian. Waivers are available on-line. An attached pro-shop hawks Vans brand merchandise and everything that a skateboarder needs and wants. It also provides rentals of helmets, knee pads, and elbow pads, all of which are mandatory.

You might have to go more than once around "The Block" to see all the unique stores and fun restaurants here. A huge Borders (we love bookstores), Ben & Jerry's, Dave & Buster's (restaurant and games place), Cafe Tu Tu Tango (an art-themed restaurant often with artists painting here), AMC Theaters, and the all-important Krispy Kreme are just few of the places to visit.

Hours: Open daily, 10am - 11pm.

Admission: Free to observers. Sessions are two hours long and cost between $5 - $14, depending on the time of day and if you are a member or not. Gear rentals are $2 per item or $5 for all of it, per session.

Ages: 3 years and up to watch; 7 years and up to participate.

-----GREAT OUTDOORS-----

ADVENTURE PLAYGROUND / UNIVERSITY COMMUNITY PARK

(949) 724-6818 / www.ci.irvine.ca.us

1 Beech Tree Lane, Irvine

(Exit San Diego Fwy [405] S. on Jeffrey, which turns into University Dr., R. on Beech Tree. It's in the University Community Park. [TG: 890 C1])

This park is a dream come true for children, as they are actually encouraged to play in the mud! In warm weather, they can go down a waterslide (i.e. a tarp-covered hill with a hose) into the mud, and ooze their way through an obstacle course. Tip: Call to make sure that the water is being turned on the day you plan to come - no water, no mud. Bring a change of clothes for the kids (and you). There is an outdoor shower (i.e. spray off with a hose).

Drier play equipment includes kid-size buildings and a big wooden climbing structure. Kids 6 years and older can add on to the little shanty town here. After completing a safety course (yea!) they are free to use the wood, hammer, and nails provided by the park to build onto existing forts, clubhouses, and castles - whatever they imagine the structures to be.

Some of the special classes offered (for a small fee) include Woodworking, Crafts, Campfire Cooking, and many different others.

Shade is scarce in Adventure Playground, but fun isn't. Bring a picnic lunch to enjoy either in here or just outside the gates at University Community Park. This spacious grassy park has non-muddy playgrounds, a Frisbee golf course, basketball courts, sand volleyball courts, tennis courts, a baseball diamond, playgrounds, and open areas for field sports.

Note: Close-toed shoes are required at Adventure Playground. The best times to come are on Saturdays or during the week after 2pm as day campers often ~~invade~~ visit this unique play area. Call to confirm these "best times" hours. Note: See the Calendar entry for details on the Adventure Playground in Huntington Beach (pg. 582). It is only open, however, for five weeks in the summer.

Hours: Open in the summer, Tues. - Sat., 10am - 5pm. Open the rest of the year, Fri., 2:30pm - 5pm; Sat., 10am - 5pm.

Admission: Free. Groups must call for reservations, and more than nine kids are charged a fee.

Ages: 5 - 14 years. Note: Kids under 6 years must be accompanied by an adult at every activity.

ALISO AND WOOD CANYONS WILDERNESS PARK

(949) 923-2200 or (949) 923-2201 / www.ocparks.com

28373 Alicia Parkway, Laguna Niguel

(Going N. on San Diego Fwy [5], exit W. on Crown Valley Pkwy., R. on La Paz Rd., L. on Aliso Creek Rd., L. on Alicia. Going S. on 5, exit S.W. on Alicia. The entrance is 500 ft. S. of Alicia Pkwy. and Aliso Creek Rd. [TG: 951 F1])

This regional park has 3,400 acres of wilderness sanctuary to explore by hiking or biking. You and your child will see everything that patience allows - coastal sage, chaparral, oak woodlands, open grassland meadows, canyons, and creeks, plus wildlife such as deer, possums, coyotes, bobcats, and lizards.

This huge park is like life, offering many paths to choose from. Take a trail from here into the adjacent Laguna Niguel Regional Park; ride the twelve-mile Aliso Creek Bikeway, which basically follows along Alicia Parkway; or choose from several other paths inside the park. We walked the Aliso Trail. The first part is paved and rather bland, scenically speaking. As we reached the dirt pathway and went into the hills, the terrain and scenery became much more interesting. (Strollers and bikes can go here, but it does get a bit bumpy.) Just down the road a bit is the Nature Center which houses Indian artifacts, taxidermied animals, photographs of wild flowers in blooms, and maps.

There are numerous caves, or overhangs, throughout the park. A few are open to the public. Past the Nature Center, or Gate 2, is Cave Rock. Kids enjoy climbing up into Cave Rock, and sliding back down. Further back on the trail, is Dripping Cave, also called - and this has much more kid-appeal - Robbers Cave. Legend has it that bandits used this cave as a hideout after a robbery! At one time the holes inside supposedly had wooden pegs to hold their saddle bags, and bags of booty. Tell this to your kids and let their imaginations take over. If you have the time and energy, keep on going to Coyote Run, deeper into the heart of the park. Tip: Bring water!

Look up the ORANGE COUNTY NATURAL HISTORY MUSEUM (pg. 246) for information on this museum that's located at the trailhead of the park.

Hours: The park is open daily, 7am - sunset. The Nature Center is open Wed. - Sun., 11am - 5pm.
Admission: $2 per vehicle.
Ages: 2 years and up.

AROVISTA PARK / SKATE PARK

(714) 990-7100 / www.ci.brea.ca.us
Elm Street and Sievers Avenue, Brea
(Exit Orange Fwy [57] W. on Imperial Hwy., L. on Brea Blvd., R. on Elm. [TG: 739 A1])

The park has baseball diamonds, two lighted basketball courts, sand volleyball courts, an amphitheater, a playground, and open grassy areas with picnic tables and barbecues. The 10,000 square-foot cement skate park has a kidney pool, pyramid, table top, quarter pipes, rails, and street section. Skateboarders and rollerbladers only - no bikes allowed! Spectators are welcome to gather 'round and watch the show! Wearing a helmet and knee and elbow pads is strictly enforced.

Hours: The skate park is open daily, 7am - dusk. The park is open daily, 7am - 10pm.
Admission: Free
Ages: All

ATLANTIS PLAY CENTER

(714) 892-6015
9301 Atlantis Way, Garden Grove
(Exit the Garden Grove Fwy [22] S. on Magnolia, L. on minster, L. on Atlantis Way. It's N. of the Garden Grove Park. [TG: 828 C1])

This "lost island" park is quite a find. Atlantis Play Center is a wonderful, large, enclosed play area for kids of all ages. Several different playgrounds are scattered around the park that feature slides, tubes, swings, sand pits, grassy expanses, and big, concrete aquatic creatures to play on. The sea serpent slide is a favorite. The green rolling hills are perfect for picnicking. Numerous shade trees make the park surprisingly cool, even in the heat of the summer. A full-service snack bar is open daily during the summer, and usually on the weekends the rest of the year.

One of my boys' favorite things to do is to play in and amongst the bushes that go around the perimeter of the park. The bushes become hideouts, forts, a pirate's landing, or whatever - a little imagination goes a long way!

Just outside Atlantis is the Garden Grove Park, with more play equipment and wide open grassy areas.

Hours: Open in the summer, Tues. - Sat., 10am - 4pm; Sun., noon - 4pm. Open the rest of the year, Tues. - Fri., 10am - 2pm; Sat., 10am - 4pm; Sun., noon - 4pm. Closed Easter, Thanksgiving, and Christmas week.
Admission: $1 for ages 2 and older; children under 2 are free. Adults are not admitted without a child.
Ages: 1½ - 12 years.

BEEBE PARK / MISSION VIEJO SKATE PARK

(949) 470-3061 / www.ci.mission-viejo.ca.us
24190 Olympiad Road, Mission Viejo
(Exit San Diego Fwy [5] N.E. on La Paz Rd., go to end and turn L. on Olympiad. [TG: 892 F7])

    This 9.8 acre sports park also sports the "latest" in sports - a skateboard park. The 9,000 square foot unsupervised concrete park has bowls, a vert wall, bauer box, rails, spine, pyramid, hips, steps, and ramps. Helmet and elbow and knee pads are required. Other park amenities include a lighted soccer/football field, lighted baseball diamond, sand volleyball court, playgrounds, short walking trails, and picnic tables.

    Hours: Open daily, 7am - dusk.
Admission: Free
     Ages: All

BOLSA CHICA ECOLOGICAL RESERVE

(714) 846-1114 - interpretative center; (714) 840-1575 - tour info / www.bolsachica.org
17851 Pacific Coast Highway, Huntington Beach
(Exit San Diego Fwy [405] S. on Bolsa Chica Rd., R. on Warner Ave., L. on Pacific Coast Highway. The reserve is opposite Bolsa Chica State Beach. [TG: 857 B2])

    This 300-acre, saltwater wetland reserve is home to a variety of plant and waterfowl such as avocets, egrets, plovers, sand pipers, ducks, and terns. We also saw herons, and a few brown pelicans that swooped down to scoop up fish. Bird lovers should bring binoculars. The nesting and breeding islands are protected by a chain link fence. You may, however, cross over the wooden bridge to walk along an easy and stroller-friendly, mile-and-a-half trail that loops through the reserve, and partially along the highway. No bikes or dogs are allowed. My little explorers especially liked walking down to inspect the water and its inhabitants, a little closer than I felt comfortable with. Free, guided tours are given the first Saturday of every month beginning at 9am.

    A small Interpretative Center is housed in a trailer on the corner of the reserve, at 3842 Warner Avenue and Pacific Coast Highway. Inside are local ecology displays such as pictures of birds in the area, a rattlesnake skin, a preserved stingray and leopard shark, a touch table, a salt water fish tank with native species, and information panels on the value of wetlands. Interested in helping take care of this area? Clean-up Saturday, where volunteers pick up trash and remove non-native plants, is held the last Saturday of each month. Note: For more fun in the sun, BOLSA CHICA STATE BEACH (see pg. 197) is directly across the street from the reserve.

    Hours: The Reserve is open daily, 8am - sunset. The Center is usually open Tues. - Fri., 10am - 4pm;
                   Sat. 9am - noon; Sun., noon - 3pm.
Admission: Free
     Ages: All

BOYSEN PARK / ANAHEIM TENNIS CENTER

(714) 991-9090 - tennis center
975 S. State College Boulevard, Anaheim
(Exit Artesia Fwy [91] S. on State College Blvd. The park is at the intersection of State College Blvd. and Wagner. [TG: 769 C6])

    Take off to this park whose main attraction is a large gray cement airplane. The wings are tipped just enough so kids can climb up on them (wingwalkers!) and into the instrumentless cockpit. Other park amenities include picnic tables, a playground, baseball fields, and sand volleyball courts. The adjacent schoolyard, available to use when school is not in session, has basketball courts, a few scattered playgrounds, and more baseball diamonds. The park wraps around the Anaheim Tennis Center. Get in the swing of things by playing on one of the Center's twelve lighted courts and/or the ball-machine court.

    Hours: The park is open daily. The Tennis Center is open Mon. - Thurs., 8am - 10pm; Fri., 8am - 9pm;
                   Sat. - Sun., 8am - 5pm.
Admission: The park is free. Tennis costs vary from $3 an hour for adults to $7 an hour, depending on the
                   time of day. Children 11 and under are $1.50 an hour.
     Ages: All for the park.

BROOKHURST COMMUNITY PARK

(714) 765-5263
2271 W. Crescent Avenue, Anaheim
(Going S. on Santa Ana Fwy [5], exit S. on Brookhurst St., R. on Crescent. Going N. on 5, exit W. on La Palma Ave., L. on Brookhurst, R. on Crescent. From Crescent, turn R. on Ventura, which turns into Greenacre. The park is right there. [TG: 768 D4])

Baseball diamonds, basketball courts, a supervised skatepark (a helmet and pads are required), a few picnic tables, and barbecue pits are here, but more importantly, your kids can come to this park and walk on the moon! "Crater Park," our nickname for it, resembles the surface of the moon with play equipment inside crater-shaped areas. There are slides, swings, climbing structures, a rocket ship (for blasting off to parts unknown), and a big white cement walkway that interconnects the play areas. Being here almost eclipses playing at other parks.

Hours: The park is open daily, sunrise - sunset. The skate park is open daily, 10am - dusk.
Admission: Free
Ages: 2 years and up.

CARBON CANYON REGIONAL PARK

(714) 996-5252 / www.ocparks.com
4442 Carbon Canyon Road, Brea
(Exit Riverside Fwy [91] N. on Imperial Hwy., R. on Valencia Ave., R. on Carbon Canyon Rd. [TG: 709 J7])

Talk about recreational opportunities! Carbon Canyon is 124 acres big and offers everything for the sports-minded and fun-loving family. There are tennis courts, volleyball courts, horseshoe pits, softball fields, a huge open field for whatever other sport you feel like playing, and five great playgrounds scattered throughout the park.

Other activities include taking a hike to the ten-acre Redwood Grove, cycling on the one-and-a-half-mile paved trail, or riding the equestrian trail that accesses Chino Hills State Park. The beautiful four-acre lake in the middle of the park has two fishing piers, but it is not stocked. Bring suntan lotion and food, and have a great day.

Hours: Open November through March daily, 7am - 6pm. Open April through October, 7am - 9pm.
Admission: $2 vehicle entrance Mon. - Fri.; $4 on Sat. - Sun.; $5 on holidays.
Ages: All

CARL THORNTON PARK

(714) 571-4200 / www.goodtime.net/sfsan.htm
1801 W. Segerstrom Avenue, Santa Ana
(Going E. on San Diego Fwy [405], exit N. on Fairview Rd., R. on Segerstrom Ave. Going S. on Costa Mesa Fwy [55], exit E. on Dyer Rd., which turns into Segerstrom Ave. [TG: 859 C1])

The front part of this park is a huge open area, great for kite flying because the trees are short (at least right now). A small creek runs through this area, ending in a big pond that attracts a lot of ducks, geese, and sea gulls. (Don't get goosed by the geese!) For your sporting pleasure, there are also two baseball diamonds.

At the northeast corner of the park, accessible by paved pathways, is an enclosed "barrier free" playground. This means that it has special apparatus designed for disabled children. One of the swings can hold a wheelchair-bound child. A sand play area, with water fountains to make sand castles, is elevated for kids in wheelchairs. Other play areas are great for all kinds of kids, as there are slides, tunnels, and things to climb. Stone turrets give the playground a castle-like setting. A large grassy area is inside the enclosure for safe, run-around play.

Hours: Open daily, 6am - 10pm.
Admission: Free
Ages: All

CEDAR GROVE PARK

(714) 573-3325 / www.tustinca.org/parksrec
11385 Pioneer Road, Tustin
(Exit Santa Ana Fwy [5] N. on Jamboree Rd., L. on Tustin Ranch Rd., R. on Pioneer Way. It's located at the intersection of Pioneer Way and Pioneer Rd. [TG: 830 H2])

This park is unique in that it has play equipment for all ages, including two and a half (that's right!) basketball courts, and two grassy volleyball courts. Starting at the parking lot, follow the winding pathway (reminiscent of a snake's trail), back to three interconnecting playgrounds which are geared for ages 2 to 5, 6 to 10, and 10 years and up, respectively. The toddler playground, built in the sand, has a wooden train to board, a castle play structure (complete with a drawbridge), a heavy-duty sand digger, and an area that has a few water spigots for making wet sand creations. Tip: Bring a change of pants for your child. Go over or under a wooden bridge to reach the next play area which is padded with dense foam. Kids can pretend to sail the seas on the wooden Adventure Ship, as well as play on the swings, wavy slides, monkey bars, rings, climbing structure, and cargo net. Older kids have their own small play area. It has several colorful metal ladders and geometric shapes for kids to climb on or across. (Being practical minded, I wondered if the shapes had a particular function or purpose, but my imaginative kids had a great time just playing on them.) Other fun things here include trying to balance yourself on a rope ladder without it twisting you around and holding on to S-shaped poles as their bases spin around. Plenty of picnic tables line the playground's pathway.

The huge, adjacent grassy area has numerous cedar trees around its perimeters, and a pathway all the way around. Next to this is a grove of shady pine trees with picnic tables nestled underneath.

Hours: Open daily, sunrise - sunset.
Admission: Free
Ages: All

CRAIG REGIONAL PARK

(714) 990-0271 / www.ocparks.com
3300 N. State College Boulevard, Fullerton
(Exit Orange Fwy [57] W. on Imperial, L. on State College. [TG: 739 C2])

124 acres and three separate playgrounds make this an ideal park for all ages. The upper area is hilly and woodsy, blessed with lots of pine trees. The lower slopes flatten out, with alder and willow trees. One of the playgrounds meets the ADA (Americans with Disabilities Act) Standards; one is geared towards little ones; and another is designed for slightly older kids, as it has steeper slides.

There are picnic gazebos, baseball diamonds, volleyball courts, tennis courts, racquetball courts, and a lake. Fishing is allowed in the lake, but it isn't stocked so bring your wiggliest worms. The Nature Center has dioramas depicting the changing environment of animals in Craig Park and the surrounding areas.

Hours: Open April through October daily, 7am - 9pm. Open November through March daily, 7am - 6pm. The Nature Center is open Sat. - Sun., 10am - 3pm.
Admission: $2 per vehicle Mon. - Fri., $4 Sat. - Sun.; $5 on holidays.
Ages: All

CROWN VALLEY COMMUNITY PARK

(949) 425-5100 / www.ci.laguna-niguel.ca.us
29751 Crown Valley Parkway, Laguna Niguel
(Exit San Diego Fwy [5] W. on Crown Valley Pkwy. The park is W. of La Paz Rd. [TG: 951 G4])

This delightful park has something that will appeal to each member of your family. Several short trails wind through the eighteen-acre hillside botanical garden. Some of the trails are cement, and therefore stroller-friendly (although uphill), and some are dirt paths with wooden steps. Hike up to the picturesque viewpoint and enjoy beautiful landscaping along the way. A playground at the base of the hill has swings, slides, and a wooden ship to climb aboard. Picnic tables are scattered throughout the park. Summer concerts are given on an outdoor stage with tiered seating on a grassy hill. At the top of another hill is a soccer field and baseball field.

Between the park office and the adjacent Y.M.C.A. is a regulation-size swimming pool that is open year round to the public and for swim meets. Diving competitions also take place on the two low diving boards, two high dives, and a (really high) diving platform. Cement stadium seats are on one side of the pool. The canopied-covered wading pool is great for your little tadpoles. Finally, a three-quarter-mile bike path here connects to Laguna Niguel Regional Park. This park is a *crown* jewel in Laguna Niguel.

Hours: The park is open daily, 6am - 10pm. The pool is open for public swim sessions year round, Mon. - Fri., 1pm - 4pm; Sat. - Sun., noon - 4pm. It's open in the summer for an additional session Mon. - Fri., 9am - noon.

Admission: Free to the park. Swim sessions are $2 for adults; $1.50 for seniors and children 2 - 12.

Ages: All

CRYSTAL COVE STATE PARK

(949) 494-3539 / parks.ca.gov

E. Coast Highway, between Laguna Beach and Newport Beach, Laguna Beach

(Take the San Diego Fwy [405] or the Costa Mesa Fwy [55] to the Corona Del Mar Fwy [73], which turns into MacArthur Blvd. Exit MacArthur Blvd. S. on E. Coast Highway. A gated entrance is just opposite Newport Coast Dr. The visitor center and ranger station are farther down on Coast Hwy., on the L. [TG: 920 C7])

This 2,800-acre, largely undeveloped state park encompasses everything from coastal and canyon areas on one side of the freeway, to three-and-a-half miles of sandy beach on the other side. The size of the park allows a variety of programs and fun things to do, such as guided tidepool tours (when the tide is low), whale watching, fishing, hiking, and camping, or just enjoying the beach! An eighteen-mile round trip, moderate mountain bike trail winds through the park also. Bikers share the back country hills with deer, roadrunners, and other wildlife. Ask for a trail map.

Environmental camping - meaning whatever you backpack in you take out - is an adventure in the "back country" of the park. The closest campsite is a two-and-half-mile hike. No open fires are allowed. With twenty miles of trails on relatively untouched land, hiking and/or camping here is a real opportunity to commune with nature! Pick up a map at the headquarters.

If you get hungry, the Crystal Cove Shake Shop, serving shakes and sandwiches, is across the way at 7408 Pacific Coast Highway, (949) 497-9666. This little "shack" has a tasty array of homemade shakes, including monkey flip, papaya, and their signature creamy date shake. A few benches and tables are here, too, overlooking the ocean for a vista of the shoreline and beyond. It's open daily, 11am to 4pm.

Hours: Open daily, sunrise - sunset.

Admission: $3 per vehicle. Camping is $7 a night.

Ages: All

DOWNTOWN SKATE ZONE

(714) 765-4501

225 S. Philadelphia Street, Anaheim

(Exit Santa Ana Fwy [5] E. on Lincoln Ave., R. on Anaheim Blvd., L. on Center, R. on Philadelphia. [TG: 768 J5])

Skaters must be members of the Downtown Youth Center and go through the gym in order to reach the skate park. The 6,000-square feet of skater's turf features ramps, pipes, ledges, and more for in-line skaters and skateboarders. A parental waiver must be on file for ages 17 and under and helmet and pads are required. The gym has basketball courts and a gymnasium for working out.

Hours: Open daily, 10am - dusk.

Admission: Gym membership ranges from $10 - $15 for the year.

Ages: 7 years and up.

EDISON COMMUNITY CENTER

(714) 960-8870 or (714) 536-5486 / www.surfcity-hb.org

21377 Magnolia Street, Huntington Beach

(Exit San Diego Fwy [405] S. on Magnolia. [TG: 888 C2])

Although the park is not outstandingly pretty to look at, it is packed with fun things to do. Within its forty acres it has four lighted tennis courts, open to play on a first-come, first-*serve*d basis; six racquetball courts; four full basketball courts and several half courts, with lights; two baseball diamonds; lots of open space; a paved trail throughout; a covered picnic area with barbeque pits; a community center building; sand and grass volleyball courts; horseshoes pits (bring your own horseshoes); and a large, sand-based play area complete with slides, swings, tot swings, climbing apparatus, and a section boasting a ship motif.

Hours: The park is open daily, dawn - dusk. The community center is open Mon. - Fri., 9am - 9:30pm; Sat., 9am - 5pm.

Admission: Free. Tennis costs only when you want to make a reservation. Reservations are taken beginning at 5pm nightly and are $2 an hour.

Ages: All

EISENHOWER PARK

(714) 744-2225

2864 N. Tustin Avenue, Orange

(Exit Costa Mesa Fwy [55] W. on Lincoln, R. on Oceanview, R. at Main to the park. The actual address does you no good in finding the park! [TG: 769 J4])

Driving down Lincoln Boulevard, it's easy to miss Eisenhower Park, but it's worth looking for. This park has a stream running through it with almost irresistible stepping stones. You may fish in the lake, although it is not stocked. There are two small play areas for slightly older kids. One area is especially "cool" with a rocket ship play structure, wavy slides, swings, and a big sand area. This big park offers plenty of green rolling hills, plus a few scattered picnic tables and barbecue pits to make your day picnic perfect. Cement pathways make the entire park stroller accessible.

Hours: Open daily, sunrise - sunset.

Admission: Free

Ages: All

ENVIRONMENTAL NATURE CENTER

(949) 645-8489 / www.encenter.org

1601 16th Street, Newport Beach

(Take Costa Mesa Fwy [55] S.W. to the end, continue on Newport Blvd., L. on 17th, R. on Irvine Ave., L. on 16th. [TG: 889 A6])

This three-and-a-half acre nature center is an almost hidden gem that has been here for more than twenty-five years! Walking back to the trailhead, notice the rocks along the path containing imbedded fossilized shells. Although buildings are around the perimeters of this wooded area, you'll still feel like you're in the midst of nature while walking along the various crisscrossing trails. You'll see a cactus garden, pine trees, woodland trees, and a small rock-lined stream. You can purchase a pamphlet (25¢) at the center to help identify the various plants and animals found here.

The small nature center building has shelves and tables that contain rocks, shells, animals skins, turtle shells, skulls, feathers, and bird's nests, plus many nature-inspired craft ideas. My boys also liked seeing the live snakes, crickets, and lizards in here.

Hours: Open Mon. - Fri., 8am - 4pm; Sat., 8am - 3pm. Closed Sun. and school holidays.

Admission: Free

Ages: 2½ years and up.

FAIRVIEW PARK

(949) 548-7246 - engineers; (714) 962-5052 - b-day party info for the train /
www.livesteamclubs.com/Ocme/Ocme.html

2525 Placentia Avenue, Costa Mesa

(Going S.E. on San Diego Fwy [405], exit S. on Brookhurst St., L. on Adams Ave., R. on Placentia. Going N.W. on 405, exit S. on Harbor Blvd., R. on Adams, L. on Placentia. [TG: 888 G1])

Fairview Park has two main attractions - dirt trails and model train rides. There are miles and miles of dirt trails, which are great for jogging, but kid-wise, they are ideal for riding bikes. Up and down, over hill and dale, and to the outer edge of the park, which is lined with coastal shrubs, the trails are just plain fun. The large size of the park, slight wind factor, and layout also lends itself to flying kites. Just across the road is a station that hosts one of the largest model layouts of its kind in Southern California. The Orange County Model Engineers run two miles of track and offer rides for free to park-goers. Bring a picnic, a bike, a kite, and make a day of it.

Hours: The park is open daily, dawn - dusk. The train is here on the third weekend of each month, 10am - 3:30pm.

Admission: Free

Ages: All

FRONTIER PARK

(714) 573-3325 or 3000 / www.tustinca.org/parksrec
1400 Mitchell Avenue, Tustin

(From Santa Ana Fwy [5], exit S.W. on Red Hill Ave., R. on Mitchell. Going N. on Costa Mesa Fwy [55], exit N.E. on Newport Ave., R. on Mitchell. [TG: 830 B5])

This park features a plastic playground in sand with a fort-like theme. It has many slides, some bridges, and a rope wall to climb. Other key components are a frisbee golf course with chain baskets and two lighted handball courts, plus picnic tables, shade trees, and grassy area to run around.

Hours: Open daily, 7:30am - 5:30pm.

Admission: Free

Ages: All

FULLERTON ARBORETUM

(714) 278-3579 - arboretum; (714) 278-2843 - house/museum / www.arboretum.fullerton.edu
1900 Associated Road, Fullerton

(Exit Orange Fwy [57] W. on Yorba Linda, L. on Associated Rd. [or Campus Dr.] onto California State Fullerton campus. [TG: 739 C4])

This twenty-six-acre botanical garden is divided into four main sections. The cultivated garden section is a favorite because it is a delightful, verdant refuge, with flower-lined pathways, a pond, a stream, and a few bridges. It's also big enough to let the kids run loose a little. Take a whiff - the air is perfumed with the scent of roses, mint, and citrus, from the rose garden, herb garden, and fruit grove and deciduous orchard, respectively. Garden benches here offer a picturesque resting spot, underneath shade trees in the midst of the plants and flowers. Idea: Have your kids dress up and bring your camera for some potentially great shots in a garden setting.

The woodland section features redwoods, rainforest plants, a meadow, and a colorful subtropical garden with a small pool. The Mediterranean showcases chaparral and shrubs, while the desert section grows a variety of cactus.

An 1894 Victorian Heritage House, once the home and office of the first physician in Orange County, is also on the grounds. Older kids will appreciate a tour through the house that has turn-of-the-century furnishings.

There are many special events going on at Fullerton Arboretum throughout the year, including Science Adventure programs, volunteering opportunities, and much more. Please call for details.

Hours: The Arboretum is open daily, 8am - 4:45pm. Closed New Year's Day, Thanksgiving, and Christmas. The house is open for tours Sat., 11am - 1pm; Sun., 2pm - 4pm. Call to make an appointment for other days and hours. The house is closed for tours in January and August.

Admission: The Arboretum has a donation box by the entrance gate. The house tour is a $2 for adults; $1 per child.

Ages: All

HART PARK

(714) 744-7272
701 S. Glassell Street, Orange
(Exit Garden Grove Fwy [22] N. on Glassell. [TG: 799 G6])

Stone walls add to the beauty of this spacious park. The northern section has <u>lots</u> of picnic tables and barbecue pits, a playground, trees to climb, a few tennis courts (although kids were roller skating on them when we visited), horseshoe pits, a sand volleyball court (or, for younger kids, a sandbox with a net), and a swimming pool.

The southern section has a large open grassy area lined with trees, plus soccer fields and a few baseball diamonds. One of the diamonds has stadium seating and lights.

Hours:	The park is open daily, 8am - 10pm. The pool is open in the summer daily, with one-hour-and fifteen-minute swim sessions, Mon. and Wed., 2:30pm - 8:15pm; Tues., Thurs. - Sun., 1pm - 5:15pm.
Admission:	The park is free. Each swim session costs $2 for adults; $1.50 for ages 17 and under.
Ages:	All

HARVARD COMMUNITY ATHLETIC PARK

(949) 551-0601 / www.ci.irvine.ca.us
14701 Harvard Avenue, Irvine
(Exit Santa Ana Fwy [5] S.W. on Jamboree Rd., L. on Walnut Ave., R. on Harvard. [TG: 860 E1])

This expansive park has three soccer fields, six lighted baseball/softball fields, picnic tables, barbecue grills, and open play areas. The big attraction for skateboarders is the concrete corner skate park which has a pool, ramps, verts, grind boxes, grinding poles, and other standard skate street equipment. Safety equipment - helmet and knee and elbow pads - is required.

Hours:	The park is open daily, dawn - dusk. The skate park is open during school hours, Mon. - Fri., 2pm - 8pm; Sat., 10am - 9pm; Sun., noon - 8pm. During the summer and on school breaks, it is open daily, 10am - 9pm.
Admission:	Free
Ages:	All

HERITAGE PARK (Irvine)

(949) 724-6750 - youth services center; (949) 559-0472 - Aquatics Complex;
(949) 552-8218 - athletic field / www.ci.irvine.ca.us
14301 Yale Avenue, Irvine
(Going S. on Santa Ana Fwy [5], exit S.W. on Culver Dr., L. on Walnut Ave., L. on Yale Ave. Going N. on 5, exit S.W. on Jeffrey Rd., R. on Walnut Ave., R. on Yale Ave. [TG: 860 G2])

Heritage Park is large community park with the emphasis on community. The park has a wooden water tower slide that is almost as tall as a real water tower - whoosh on down!! There are two terrific playgrounds here. One has a pirate ship with bridges, slides, and a ropes obstacle course - kid heaven! Several buildings line the perimeter. The center area has a beautiful small lake (with numerous ducks) to skate or stroller around, and lots of grassy, gently rolling hills to play on. There are also basketball courts, twelve lighted tennis courts, and four lighted fields for organized sports play.

Several buildings line the perimeter of the park, such as the youth services center, which has a few billiard tables and other games; the library; and the Irvine Fine Art Center, which has a small art gallery and offers art classes. The Heritage Park Aquatics Complex is just around the corner on Walnut Avenue. Two of their pools are open for recreational swim in the summer.

Hours:	The park is open daily. The pools are open daily in the summer, Mon. - Fri., 1pm - 3pm; Sat. - Sun., 1pm - 4pm.
Admission:	The park is free. Swimming costs $2 for adults; $1 for ages 17 and under.
Ages:	All

HILLCREST PARK

Brea Boulevard, Fullerton

(Exit the Riverside Fwy [91] N. on Harbor Blvd., R. on Brea Blvd., R. into the park. [TG: 738 H5])

For some Fullerton fun, try Hillcrest Park. This huge hilly park has a winding road throughout, with parking lots in several different spots along the way. We saw some creative kids using cardboard to slide down a hill, which probably isn't great for the grass, but it looked like fun. Hillcrest has a few woodland areas with dirt paths for hiking. There are also some play areas, picnic tables, and barbecue pits. The wooden structure at the base of the hill, on Lemon Street, is in the shape of a ship.

Hours: Open daily.

Admission: Free

Ages: All

HUNTINGTON CENTRAL PARK

(714) 536-5486 / www.ci.huntington-beach.ca.us/CityDepartments

Goldenwest Street, Huntington Beach

(Exit San Diego Fwy [405] S. on Goldenwest St. There are entrances from Goldenwest, Slater, Ellis, and Gothard sts. [TG: 857 H2])

This gigantic park offers many options for all kinds of fun. Fish at the un-stocked lake, which is tucked in the corner. Let the kids go wild on the four playgrounds. Ride bikes along the six miles of cement pathways that crisscross all over. Walk on the several other miles of dirt trails. Enjoy the expansive green lawns. Retreat under shade trees. Play on the sports fields. Use the Frisbee golf course on the west side of Goldenwest Street, which offers instructions, maps and an opportunity to purchase your own disc. See a weekend polo match or horse show at the Equestrian Center (call [714] 848-6565 for details). Check out books from the huge library off Talbert Street (see HUNTINGTON BEACH CENTRAL LIBRARY on page 252). Play at Adventure Playground (see page 582) for summertime fun. If you'd like to have breakfast or lunch in the park, eat at ALICE'S BREAKFAST IN THE PARK (see page 199).

Hours: The park is open daily, sunrise - sunset.

Admission: Free

Ages: All

IRVINE LAKE

(714) 649-9111 / www.irvinelake.net

4621 Santiago Canyon Road, Orange

(Exit Costa Mesa Fwy [55] E. on Chapman, which turns into Santiago Canyon Rd. [TG: 801 E6])

Casting around for fun places to go with your little fisherman? Irvine Lake is a large lake stocked seasonally with a variety of fish such as bass, trout, catfish, crappie, and bluegill. There is a five fish limit per person. (I wish I had this problem!) A five-acre kid's lagoon is cordoned off just for youngsters to fish. If there are dryer areas of the lake bed, depending on the season, it's a terrific place to bird watch. We saw herons, pelicans, cranes, and at least a half dozen other birds I feel like I should be able to identify.

Towards the entrance is a small playground, a grassy area, a horseshoe pit, a volleyball court, a few picnic tables under shade trees, a cafe, and a very small, almost-guarantee-you'll-catch-something Catch Out Pond stocked with trout. Conveniently, a bait and tackle shop, and even a breakfast and sandwich cafe counter, are also on the grounds. No fishing license is needed. Overnight camping is $15 for tent or RV (for up to six people), plus a mandatory per person entrance fee.

Boat rentals are available. Motorboats are $30 on weekdays (Monday through Thursday), $45 weekends (Friday through Sunday) or holidays; rowboats - $20 on weekdays, $25 on weekends and holidays; and pontoons - $85 on weekdays, $100 on weekends and holidays.

Hours: Open daily, 6am - 4pm. Open in the summer additionally, Fri. - Sat. until 11pm.

Admission: Fishing is $16 for adults; $9 for ages 4 - 12; children 3 and under are free. Rates include the entrance fee and up to five fish. The Catch Out Pond is $3 for the gate entry and $4 per pound of each fish that your catch. Rental rods are $6.

Ages: 4 years and up.

IRVINE REGIONAL PARK

(714) 633-8074 / www.ocparks.com
1 Irvine Park Road, Orange
(Exit Costa Mesa Fwy [55] E. on Chapman, N. on Jamboree, which ends at Irvine Regional Park. [TG: 800 J3])

Entire days can be spent exploring all there is to see and do at this 477-acre regional park. The middle area is "carved out," with lots of grass for picnic areas, playgrounds, and baseball diamonds. Toddlers through about 8 years old can ride ponies around a track that is open weekdays 11am to 4pm and weekends 10am to 4:30pm. Rides are about $3 each. Kids 8 years and older can take a guided horseback ride inside the park past coastal live oaks, sycamore trees, and chaparral. Rides are available Tuesday through Sunday for $25 an hour by reservation only. Call Country Trails at (714) 538-5860 /www.ctriding.com for further horseback riding rental information. More fun can be had with pedal boat rentals, which are available weekends 10am to 5pm at $9 per half hour. Bike rentals are available weekends 10am to 5pm at $12 per hour for side-by-sides. Ten-minute, one-third-scale model train rides around the park are available daily, 10am to 5pm at $3 per person. This is a fun little trip! Call (714) 997-3968 / www.irvineparkrr.com for more information.

The Interpretive Center, (714) 289-9616, has taxidermied animals to look at; skulls, furs, and animal pelts to touch; a grinding rock to try out; plus displays and information about the wilderness part of the park. Biking, hiking, and equestrian trails are plentiful in Irvine Regional Park with creeks, sagebrush, and animals throughout. Rangers are available for school and scout tours. Also, look up ORANGE COUNTY ZOO (see pg. 274), as it's located inside the park.

Hours: Irvine Park is open April through October daily, 7am - 9pm. It's open the rest of the year daily, 7am - 6pm. The Nature Center is usually open Sat. - Sun., 11am - 3:45pm.

Admission: $2 per vehicle, Mon. - Fri., $4 on Sat. - Sun; $5 on holidays.

Ages: All

LAGUNA HILLS SKATE PARK

(949) 707-2600 / www.skateboardparks.com/california/lagunahills
25555 Alicia Parkway, Laguna Hills
(Exit San Diego Fwy [5], S.W. on Alicia Pkwy. [TG: 921 H3])

The skate park is part of a community parks and sports center. Skateboarders and bladers can skate at the lighted, 10,000 square-foot cement park that features a pyramid, cones, steps, grinding rails, volcano, and ramps. All participants must wear helmet and knee and elbow pads.

Hours: Open daily, 8am - 10pm.

Admission: Free

Ages: 7 years and up.

LAGUNA LAKE PARK

Lakeview Drive and Euclid, Fullerton
(Exit Riverside Fwy [91] N. on Euclid, R. on Lakeview Dr. [TG: 738 F2])

Leaping frogs! This lake is literally covered with large lily pads. In contrast to my earlier thinking, I now know that parks don't require a playground to make it "good." It simply must have kid-appeal, and this one does. The dirt path around the long lake is bike and stroller friendly. The marshy reeds are a great place for dragonfly hunting. Bring bread for the ducks, bait for your fishing pole, and enjoy this unusual park. Barbecue pits and picnic tables are here, too.

Hours: Open daily, sunrise - sunset.

Admission: Free

Ages: All

LAGUNA NIGUEL REGIONAL PARK

(949) 831-2791 - park; (949) 362-3885 - fishing / www.ocparks.com; www.lagunaniguellake.com
28241 La Paz Road, Laguna Niguel

(Exit San Diego Fwy [5] W. on Crown Valley Pkwy., R. on La Paz. [TG: 951 G1])

This park is 236 acres of adventures waiting to be had. It offers volleyball courts, horseshoe pits, tennis courts, bike trails, an area for flying remote-controlled airplanes, toddler-friendly playgrounds, open grass areas, barbecue pits, and picnic shelters, plus a forty-four-acre lake for fishing and boating. No fishing license is required, but day use permits are. The lake is seasonally stocked with catfish and bluegill, with a limit of five fish per person, per day. Bass are strictly catch and release. Fish from the floating docks or rent a boat at $8 an hour. A bait and tackle shop are conveniently located on the park grounds. The shop rents poles for $6 a day. The park tends to get crowded on weekends and holidays, so get an early start!

Hours: Open April through October daily, 6am - 9pm. Open November through March daily, 6am - 6pm.

Admission: $2 per vehicle Mon. - Fri.; $4 on Sat. - Sun.; $5 on holidays. Fishing permits cost $15 for adults; $12 for ages 16 and younger.

Ages: All

LAGUNA NIGUEL SKATE & SOCCER PARK

(949) 425-5100 / www.ci.laguna-niguel.ca.us

27745 Alicia Parkway, Laguna Niguel

(Going N. on San Diego Fwy [5], exit W. on Crown Valley Pkwy., R. on La Paz Rd., L. on Aliso Creek Rd., L. on Alicia. Going S. on 5, exit S.W. on Alicia. [TG: 921 F7])

The 22,000 square-foot concrete lighted skatepark has all the features both intermediate and advanced skaters look for; bowls, rails, funbox, a street course, and more. It is a supervised park and requires a parental waiver on file for ages 17 and under. Skaters must wear helmet and pads. The adjacent soccer park's playing field is synthetic grass. The field has lights for night play.

Hours: The skate park is open during the school year, Mon. - Fri., noon - 9:30pm; Sat. - Sun., 9am - 9:30pm. Holidays and summer time hours are daily, 9am - 9:30pm.

Admission: $10 per person for the skate park per day, or purchase an annual pass for $20 for residents; $30 for non-residents.

Ages: 7 years and up.

LIBERTY PARK (Westminster)

(714) 895-2860

13900 Monroe Street, Westminster

(Exit Garden Grove Fwy [22] S. on Beach Blvd., L. on Westminster, L. on Monroe. [TG: 828 A1])

The park is a typical, medium-sized park with open grassy areas, a few trees, a few picnic tables, a basketball court, and a playground. The real draw, I think, is for skateboarders and bladers. Their play area is a mid-size cement skate park which has a mini-pool, kidney pool, stair-rail plaza, funbox, and a street course. Wearing safety gear - a helmet, knee and elbow pads - is enforced!

Hours: The park and skate park is open daily, sunrise - sunset.

Admission: Free

Ages: 7 years and up for the skate park.

MILE SQUARE PARK

(714) 962-5549 - park; (562) 431-6866 - Surrey Cycle Rentals / www.ocparks.com

16801 Euclid Street, Fountain Valley

(Exit San Diego Fwy [405] N. on Euclid St. [TG: 828 F7])

Mile Square Park has everything you need for a full day of family fun, so be there or be *square*. Besides the three regulation golf courses, there are picnic areas with barbecue grills, bike trails, two soccer fields, baseball fields, an archery range (bring your own equipment), and four playgrounds. One of the playgrounds is on an island in one of the lakes. Kids can take the bridge across and have fun climbing up and down the tower. You may fish in the two man-made lakes - no license is needed unless your child is over 16 years old. Ask about the fishing derby. An adjacent area also has basketball courts, more play areas, and tennis courts. Bike ride through the park or head to nearby concrete paths that cover hundreds of acres.

Get physical on the weekends with various pleasure rentals - surrey bikes are between $12 (for two adults and two small children) to $22 (for a limo - up to eight people) an hour; funcycles or tandems are $8 an hour; and paddle boats are $12 an hour. All rentals are usually available on weekends, 11am to 7pm.

Hours: Open daily in the summer, 7am - 9pm. Open daily the rest of the year, 7am - 6pm.

Admission: $2 per vehicle Mon. - Fri; $4 on Sat. - Sun.; $5 on holidays. Some free street parking is available on Warner Ave.

Ages: All

NORTHWOOD COMMUNITY PARK

(949) 724-6728 / www.ci.irvine.ca.us

4531 Bryan Avenue, Irvine

(Exit Santa Ana Fwy [5] N. on Culver, R. on Bryan. [TG: 860 H1])

The focal point of this park is the big, fortress-like structure which is great for climbing on and around. It has a slide, steps, and a rocky wall that completes the fortress image. The playground also has tire swings, a balance beam, slides, a wooden and cement pirate ship, and sand boxes.

The surrounding park has soccer fields, tennis courts, racquetball courts, fitness course, a basketball court, shuffleboard, a handball court, and baseball diamonds, plus a paved pathway around the fields. You can check out play equipment, free of charge, at the information building.

Hours: The park and information building are open Mon. - Fri., 9am - 9pm; Sat. - Sun., 9am - 6pm.

Admission: Free

Ages: All

OAK CANYON NATURE CENTER

(714) 998-8380 / www.anaheim.net

6700 Walnut Canyon Road, Anaheim

(Exit Riverside Fwy [91] S. on Imperial Hwy, L. on Nohl Ranch Rd., L. on Walnut Canyon. It's next to the Anaheim Hills Golf Course. [TG: 770 J4])

This rustic Nature Center is a fifty-eight-acre natural park nestled in Anaheim Hills. Surrounded by such beauty, it doesn't seem possible that there is a city nearby. Take a delightful, easy hike along the wide pathways along the stream and through the woods that boast of huge oak and other shade tress. Or, opt for more strenuous hiking on the six miles of trails offered here. No bikes or picnicking are allowed so that the animals and plants that consider this canyon their home can continue to live here unharmed.

The good-sized, Nature Center building houses live critters, plus several trays of mounted butterflies and other insects. The small stage area is great for putting on shows using the animal puppets.

The Nature Center offers many different programs. One-hour programs for preschoolers, like Feed the Critters or Mudpies and Stone Soup, include a guided nature walk and related activities and perhaps a craft. The fee is $3 per child. Every Saturday morning a family program is offered that incorporates learning about nature with doing a craft together. This program is usually free. On Wednesday evenings throughout the summer, Nature Nights for families begin at 7pm with a twilight walk through the canyon. A formal presentation is given at 7:30pm at the outdoor amphitheater. Ask about their summer day camps.

Hours: Open daily, 9am - 5pm.

Admission: Free

Ages: All

O'NEILL REGIONAL PARK / ARROYO TRABUCO

(949) 858-9365 - O'Neill; (714) 858-9365 - Arroyo / www.ocparks.com

30892 Trabuco Canyon Road, Trabuco Canyon

(Exit Santa Ana Fwy [5] N.E. on El Toro Rd., R. on Live Oak Canyon Rd., which turns into Trabuco Canyon Rd. [TG: 863 B7])

As we explored parts of this over 2,000-acre park, I kept thinking of how absolutely gorgeous it is. O'Neill Park is a canyon bottom and so filled with trees, it's like being in a forest. A creek runs throughout, creating lush greenery. The abundant nature trails (about eighteen miles!) are mostly hilly dirt trails, though a few are paved "roads."

The playground has a log cabin-like building with slides and swings and such around it. Inside the small Nature Center are taxidermied animals around the perimeter of the room. A few tables in the middle display skulls, furs, and rocks to touch. Join in a morning, ranger-led hike to learn how to identify animal tracks and find out other facts about the park's inhabitants. The park also has beautiful campgrounds.

Arroyo Trabuco is a more than 900-acre parcel of pristine wilderness preserve adjacent to O'Neill park area. Hiking, mountain biking, and wildlife observation are the main recreational activities available here. This entire park area is nature at its finest.

Hours: The park is open daily, 7am - sunset. The Nature Center is usually open Sat. - Sun., 2pm - 4pm; (Open Sat. - Sun., 11am - 1pm if staff is available.)

Admission: $2 per vehicle on Mon. - Fri.; $4 on Sat. - Sun; $5 on holidays. Camping starts at $12 a night.

Ages: All

PETERS CANYON REGIONAL PARK

(714) 227-1780 / www.ocparks.com

Canyon View Avenue & Jamboree Road, Orange

(Exit Costa Mesa Fwy [55] E. on Chapman., R. on Jamboree, R. on Canyon View. [TG: 800 J4])

My boys and I have decided that this huge, 354-acre undeveloped park is for rugged hikers. The lake by the parking lot is one of the most scenic spots here. The narrow dirt trails are lined with sage scrub, grassland areas, and willow and sycamore trees. The upper Lake View Trail guides you through the reservoir, while the lower East Ridge Trail provides a panoramic view of the canyon and the surrounding area. The park, and its seven miles of trails, are closed for two or three days after a rain.

Hours: Open daily, 7am - sunset.

Admission: Free

Ages: 5 years and up.

RALPH B. CLARK REGIONAL PARK

(714) 670-8045 / www.ocparks.com

8800 Rosecrans Avenue, Buena Park

(Exit Santa Ana Fwy [5] N. on Beach Blvd., R. on Rosecrans. [TG: 738 A4])

This sixty-five-acre park is one of the most aesthetically pleasing parks we've seen. It has all the things that make a park great - a lake to fish in, ducks to feed, tennis courts, horseshoe pits, three softball fields, a baseball diamond, volleyball courts, and a few small playgrounds. Take a short hike around Camel Hill, or let the kids climb on the small, therefore ironically named, Elephant Hill. A paved bicycle trail goes all around the perimeter of the park.

The Interpretative Center has a working paleontology lab where kids can look through a big window and observe the detailed work being done. The Center also houses a twenty-six-foot Baleen whale fossil; a skeletal saber-tooth cat "attacking" a skeletal horse; fossils of a ground sloth and a mammoth; shells; and more.

Kids really dig the marine fossil site across the street where a *bone*afide paleontologist conducts "Family Fossil Day" four times a year, usually in February, May, September, and December. This three-hour class is geared for youngsters 6 years and up. They can practice their fossil-finding skills by looking for fossilized shells at the marine site, then study and classify fossils back at the lab at the Interpretive Center. They'll also make a craft related to that day's theme. The price for the field trip is simply the price of admission to the park.

Hours: The park is open November through March daily, 7am - 6pm; April through October daily, 7am - 9pm. The Interpretative Center is usually open Tues. - Fri., 12:30pm - 5pm; Sat. - Sun., 10am - 4:30pm. Call first to make sure staff is available.

Admission: $2 vehicle entrance Mon. - Fri.; $4 on Sat. - Sun.; $5 on holidays.

Ages: All

RANCHO MISSION VIEJO LAND CONSERVANCY

(949) 489-9778 / www.theconservancy.org

!/$$

Off Ortega Highway, San Juan Capistrano

(Exit San Diego Fwy [5] E. on Ortega Hwy. [74]. It's about 5.1 miles. Look for signs for Rancho Mission Viejo on the R. [TG: 973 E1])

The Land Conservancy manages a 1,200 acre wilderness reserve in the coastal foothills. They offer an incredible array of special programs to the general public and to school groups that give intimate glimpses into the wilderness of Orange County. Programs include guided nature walks, bird watching (and finding), wildlife workshops, astronomy nights, owl outings, bat walks, butterfly classes, butterfly counting (for research purposes), trail maintenance, and much more. The programs are given by trained docents, or professionals in that field of study. What a wonderful opportunity for kids to become aware of wildlife, and what they can do to help protect it. Also see RONALD W. CASPERS WILDERNESS PARK (pg. 230) which is just down the road.

Hours: Call for program hours or to receive a calendar of events.

Admission: Depending on the program, the fees range from free to $8.

Ages: Varies, depending on the program.

RICHARD T. STEED MEMORIAL PARK / RALPH'S SKATE PARK

(949) 361-8264 / ci.san-clemente.ca.us

!

247 Avenida La Pata, San Clemente

(Exit San Diego Fwy [405], E. on Avenida Pico, R. on Avenida La Pata. [TG: 973 B7])

The memorial park has several ball fields and is home to many tournaments - it even has a concession stand. There are also batting cages, a playground, picnic areas, volleyball courts, and a skate park. The unsupervised 14,000 square-foot, concrete skate park features bowls, ramps, stairs, rails, and pyramids. It has lights, too. A helmet and knee and elbows pads must be worn for safety's sake and because the patrolling police will cite offenders.

Hours: Both are open daily, dawn - dusk.

Admission: Free

Ages: All

RONALD W. CASPERS WILDERNESS PARK

(949) 728-0235 / www.ocparks.com

$

33401 Ortega Highway, San Juan Capistrano

(Exit San Diego Fwy [5] E. on Ortega Hwy. It's about 7 miles. [TG: 953 G3])

Orange County's largest park is massive, and consists mostly of canyon wilderness such as seasonally verdant valleys, groves of live oak and sycamore trees, meadows, and running streams. We saw mule deer and jackrabbits scampering through the woods and quail walking/running alongside the dirt road. The over thirty miles of hiking trails range from easy walks to strenuous, mountain-man hikes. The moderate, four-mile Bell Canyon loop is a nice jaunt. Start on the nature trail loop, go through oak trees, left on the Oak Trail cutoff that heads north along a streambed then onto a fire road. Your best bet is to pick up a trail map at the front entrance. Give kids the freedom to hike, but beware that mountain lions sometimes roam this area, too. Mountain bike usage is permitted on designated roads only. Visitors can also enjoy a barbecue under shade trees; play on the large wooden playground with swings and slides, surrounded by trees; and check out the Nature Center that has a few taxidermied animals and hands-on activities.

The numerous camp sites are picturesque, wonderful for enjoying nature. Campsites have picnic tables, charcoal-burning stoves, fire rings, and a nearby water source. Also see RANCHO MISSION VIEJO LAND CONSERVANCY (pg. 230) which is just down the road.

Hours: Open daily, 7am - sunset. Call for extended hours.

Admission: $2 per vehicle Mon. - Fri.; $4 Sat. - Sun; $5 on holidays. Camping is $12 a night; $10 for seniors and handicapped.

Ages: All

SAN JOAQUIN WILDLIFE SANCTUARY / SEA & SAGE AUDUBON

(949) 261-7963 / www.seaandsageaudubon.org

Riparian View, Irvine

(Exit San Diego Fwy [405] S. Jamboree, L. on Michelson, R. on Riparian View. Go until you come to the end of the road, which is past the first sign that states San Joaquin Wildlife Sanctuary and past the Irvine Ranch Water District plant. [TG: 829-J7])

Who would have imagined that there would be this beautiful, peaceful bird sanctuary smack in the midst of the Irvine business district? Park at the grouping of six buildings, one of which is the Audubon center. The center contains a collection of taxidermy birds and is a great place to pick up information, maps, and even purchase something from the small gift shop. Binoculars and birding guides are available for loan here, too. The nicely-landscaped grounds have an open green lawn, a few picnic tables, and restroom facilities. Note: Across the road from the center is the San Diego Creek, which offers more and diverse wildlife (and a walking trail alongside).

There are twelve miles of fairly level, dirt walking trails through the almost 300 acres of the sanctuary, as well as five large ponds (and several smaller ones), nesting islands, and riparian habitat. What a delight! This area is home to 223 species of birds, as well as rabbits (of which we saw several), raccoons, coyotes, lizards, dragonflies (by the marshy areas), and bats. Come to look for Canada geese, snowy egrets, peregrine falcons, great blue herons, black-necked stilts, and more birds, or just come to enjoy being in nature.

Explore the sanctuary on your own or join in any number of programs, such as the free monthly bird walks offered on the second Sunday; workshops for teachers and students, including classroom kits on owls, songbirds, butterflies, and more; nature camps; and two-hour hands-on field trips on wetland birds and pond life. If you're *pond*ering what to do, come here let your imagination take flight!

Hours: Trails are open daily, dawn - dusk. The center is open daily, 8am - 4pm.

Admission: Free

Ages: All

SANTIAGO OAKS REGIONAL PARK

(714) 538-4400 / www.ocparks.com

2145 N. Windes Drive, Orange

(Exit Costa Mesa Fwy [55] E. on Katella, which turns into Villa Park, then into Santiago Canyon Rd., L. on Windes, to the end. [TG: 770 G6])

Get back to nature at this 350-acre park that has beautiful hiking and equestrian trails that connect to the Anaheim Hills trail system. Take a short path along the creek leading to a waterfall at the dam, or travel more rugged terrain into the heart of the park. Be on the lookout for animals such as lizards, squirrels, deer, and birds. Mountain lions have been seen on rare occasion, too.

A favorite activity here is cooking breakfast over the charcoal barbecues early in the morning, while it's still quiet and cool. A small playground and a few horseshoe pits round out the facilities under a canopy of oak trees. The small Nature Center has taxidermied animals, pictures, and a few hands-on activities. Free, ranger-led tours are given on the weekends beginning at 10am by reservation only.

Hours: The park is open daily, 7am - sunset. The nature center is open daily, 8am - 4pm.

Admission: $2 per vehicle Mon. - Fri., $4 Sat. - Sun.; $5 on holidays.

Ages: All

SANTIAGO PARK

(714) 571-4200 / www.ci.santa-ana.ca.us

2535 N. Main Street, Santa Ana

(From S. of Santa Ana, exit the San Diego Fwy [5] N. at Main St./Broadway, R. on Main St. From N. of Santa Ana, exit San Diego Fwy [5] S. at Main St./Broadway (look for signs to Discovery Science Center), L. on Santa Clara, L. at Main St., then an immediate R. Or, go a street further and turn R. on Memory Lane for another entrance. It's directly across from the Discovery Science Center. Tip: Park here and walk through the underpass to the Center, saving a $3 parking fee. [TG: 799 F6])

You can literally stroll along Memory Lane here, simply because that's the name of the street adjacent to the park. This long park, located directly across the street from the DISCOVERY SCIENCE CENTER (see pg. 238), has several areas with play equipment, plus scattered picnic tables, shade trees, grassy patches, and barbecue pits. We usually spend most of our time at the first play area, with its slides, swings, sand area, wooden bridges, tunnels, and a green, wooden fort-like structure. A little further east is a slightly sunken grassy area (perfect for a group party), a lawn bowling center, a baseball diamond, an archery range, tennis courts, and more play equipment. A rocky riverbed path follows along one side of the park. The pathway actually leads all the way to HART PARK (see pg. 224), although it is a half hour, non-stroller friendly walk to get there.

    Hours: Open daily, sunrise - sunset.
Admission: Free
     Ages: All

TEWINKLE MEMORIAL PARK

(714) 754-5300 / www.ci.costa-mesa.ca.us
970 Arlington Drive, Costa Mesa
(Going E on the San Diego Fwy [405], exit S. on Fairview Rd., L. on Arlington. Going W. on 405, exit S. on Bristol St. R. on Newport Blvd., R. on Arlington. Going N. on the Costa Mesa Fwy [55], exit N.W. on Del Mar Ave., R. on Newport, L. on Arlington. [TG: 859 B7])

    This fifty-acre park has something for everyone. There is a play area with a big tire to climb on, volleyball courts, baseball fields, tennis courts, a utility field, and plenty of picnic tables.

    I think nature-loving kids will enjoy this park most. A stream goes around a good portion of it, with ducks and geese having a swimmingly good time. They also populate the small lake. A hike up the hill yields the treasure of a pond in a small, forest-like setting. This park is cool, even on a hot day.

    Hours: Open daily, dawn - dusk.
Admission: Free
     Ages: All

THOMAS F. RILEY WILDERNESS PARK

(949) 459-1687 / www.ocparks.com
30952 Oso Parkway, Coto De Caza
(Exit San Diego Fwy [5] E. on Oso Pkwy. It's 6½ miles off the freeway right before Oso dead-ends at Coto De Caza Dr. There are also entrances to the park on Coto De Caza. [TG: 923 B5])

    This hilly wilderness preserve is a sanctuary for native wildlife - coyotes, mountain lions, raccoons, mule deer, a multitude of birds, and lots more. It's comprised of hills with protected sagebrush, oak trees, and other plant life, plus a pond and seasonal creek. Five miles of rugged dirt trails (stroller occupants would have a bumpy ride) loop throughout the park and visitors are asked not to stray from them. Although housing developments border part of the park, miles of undeveloped canyons, tree groves, and Santa Ana Mountain peaks can still be seen from the viewpoints.

    Take a self-guiding nature hike, or sign up for a guided walk or program. The park makes a wonderful outdoor "classroom" and offers students of all ages firsthand knowledge about the environment. Some of the programs offered include merit badge classes, which could include a topical game and craft; Bat Habits, which includes a slide show and short hike into bat country; Star Watch, designed for viewing and learning about the stars and moon; Jr. Rangers, which is a six-week, springtime class; special classes for toddlers; and more. Most of the programs have a minimal fee.

    The small nature center contains a few taxidermy animals and a game that kids can take on the trail to help them identify objects they find along the way. A few picnic tables are under shade trees in front of the nature center. A butterfly garden is here, too. Note: The rangers are very friendly and dedicated to enabling children to learn more about the wilds of Orange County.

    Hours: Open daily, 7am - sunset. Call for seasonal hours.
Admission: $2 parking fee.
     Ages: 4 years and up.

TURTLE ROCK PARK / IRVINE OPEN SPACE NATURE TRAIL

(949) 854-8144 - park; (949) 724-6738 - nature trail / www.ci.irvine.ca.us; www.irvineopenspace.org

1 Sunnyhill Drive, Irvine

(Exit Corona Del Mar Fwy [73] S. on Jamboree, L. on University Dr., R. on Culver Dr., L. on Bonita Cyn., L. on Sunnyhill. [TG: 890 D4])

Irvine Open Space operates a nature center building that is the entrance way to a small, five-acre nature preserve. The preserve has both a desert habitat and pine trees, so that the stroller-friendly trail is partially in the sun and partially in the shade. A ranger here said that going around a little pond, over a few bridges, and looping back around takes "ten minutes if you don't see anything, thirty minutes if you follow the trail guide. The longer you're here, the more you'll learn." Guided tours of the trail are offered by reservation, as are tours for scouts earning badges.

The surrounding Turtle Rock Park has lighted tennis courts, a basketball court, sand volleyball courts, and a playground, plus a nature trail that goes over a creek.

Hours: The nature trail is usually open daily - call for hours. The park is open daily, 9am - 9pm.

Admission: Free to the park and to walk the nature trail on your own. Guided tours are $1 per person; scout tours are $5 per scout.

Ages: 2 - 13 years.

UPPER NEWPORT BAY ECOLOGICAL RESERVE / PETER AND MARY MUTH INTERPRETIVE CENTER

!/$$

(714) 973-6820 - interpretive center; (949) 640-6746 - reserve;

(949) 640-9960 - marine studies center / www.newportbay.org; www.ocparks.com

2301 University Drive, Newport Beach

(Ecological Reserve: Take Costa Mesa Fwy [55] S.W. to end, which turns into Newport Blvd., L. on W. Coast Hwy., L. on Jamboree Rd., L. on Backbay Dr. to Shellmaker. [TG: 889 C6]; Interpretive Center: Exit San Diego Fwy [405] S. on Bristol St., R. on Santa Ana Ave., L. on University. [TG: 889 D2])

The impressive-looking Peter and Mary Muth Interpretive Center is at the northern part of the ecological reserve, which also spans quite a few miles southward. The Center offers a few hands-on activities for kids, such as lifting panels to find answers to questions such as "Why does mud stink?', and walking through a short tunnel of (fake) mud to see what lives there. The center also has numerous information panels and displays around the inside perimeters; an exhibit on what comprises an estuary, accompanied by a real fish tank; taxidermied animals; a cut away to show life above and below the waterline; and a theater room with several TV screens to view films. Look for butterflies in the small butterfly garden planted just outside the building. The center is not visible from above as it's tucked under the observation bluff overlooking the northern portion of the reserve.

A short, somewhat stroller-friendly dirt hiking trail in this immediate area takes visitors to vistas overlooking the bay and reserve. A three-and-a-half mile paved biking/walking trail goes around the reserve, mostly along the one-way street, Backbay Drive, where cars can only go fifteen miles an hour. This is a great way to explore the estuary. Note: You will frequently hear planes flying overhead from the nearby John Wayne Airport.

This ecological reserve, a remnant of a once-extensive wetland, is part of an endeavor to conserve wildlife in the Upper Bay. Although surrounded by urban development and ringed by roads, the bay and small islands are home to sea critters, a variety of plants, and hundreds of waterfowl as it's a stopover for migrating birds on the Pacific Flyway. Introduce your children to the valuable natural resources that God originally put on the earth by involving kids in the wide variety of interactive and interpretive programs offered here. As you "Kayak the Back Bay" (an outstanding "tour") with a naturalist, you'll see and learn about herons, egrets, and numerous other birds and animals. Join in on a free walking tour, or participate in an educational kayak tour, youth fishing programs, clean-up day, or shark study - mere samplings of what is offered here. Special tours are offered for students, scouts, and interested adults. Programs and tours are offered at the interpretive center, outdoors at Shellmaker Island (just down the road), and for high-schoolers and beyond, at the California Department of Fish and Game Marine Studies Center, next to Shellmaker Island. Curriculum aids are available. For swimming, camping, and more water-sport fun, look under the NEWPORT DUNES RESORT (see pg. 199), which is at the southern end of the bay.

Hours: The center is open Tues. - Sun., 10am - 4pm. Closed Mon. and major holidays. The reserve is open daily, sunrise - sunset.

Admission: Free to the center. Program prices vary.

Ages: 5 years and up.

WHITING RANCH WILDERNESS PARK

(949) 589-4729 / www.ocparks.com

Santiago Canyon Road, Portola Hills

(Exit San Diego Fwy [5] E. on Lake Forest, go 5 miles and turn L. on Portola Pkwy., R. on Market, first driveway on the left. Or, from Lake Forest, turn R. on Portola Pkwy., L. on Glenn Rd. and into the large dirt parking area. This section leads into Serrano Canyon. [TG: 862 C5])

"Real" hikers can explore the hills of Trabuco Canyon via Whiting Ranch Wilderness Park. Follow the trails through forested canyons, along streams, and past huge boulders. A moderate hike starts at the Borrego Trail and leads to the Red Rock Canyon trail, which is five miles round trip and loops back around. Note: This trail is more easily reached from the Market Street entrance. The scenery is outstanding. The size and beauty of this park offers the opportunity to enjoy some good, back-to-nature time with your kids. I'm not trying to give contrary information, but also remember that this is a wilderness area and wild animals, including mountain lions and rattlesnakes, inhabit this place.

Hours: Open daily, 7am - sunset.

Admission: $2 per vehicle.

Ages: 5 years and up.

WILLIAM R. MASON REGIONAL PARK

(949) 854-2490 / www.ocparks.com

18712 University Drive, Irvine

(Exit San Diego Fwy [405] S. on Culver Dr., R. on University Dr. [TG: 890 A1])

This 350-acre park is serene (even with kids!) and beautiful. The picturesque lake is a central feature. Fishing, with a license, is allowed, but be forewarned - the lake isn't stocked. Honking gaggles of geese will vie for your attention (and bread crumbs). There are four different playgrounds with modular plastic equipment such as tunnels, slides, swings, forts, etc. The park also boasts of volleyball courts, a ball field, horseshoe pits, a disc golf course, picnic shelters, open grassy expanses, large shade trees, and two miles of lovely paved walking/biking trails that crisscross throughout.

Hours: Open November through March daily, 7am - 6pm. Open April through October daily, 7am - 9pm.

Admission: $2 per vehicle Mon. - Fri.; $4 Sat. - Sun.; $5 on holidays.

Ages: All

YORBA REGIONAL PARK

(714) 970-1460 / www.ocparks.com

7600 E. La Palma Avenue, Anaheim

(Exit Riverside Fwy [91] N. on Imperial Hwy, R. on La Palma. [TG: 740 G7])

This pleasant, 166-acre elongated park follows along the Santa Ana River. It offers a myriad of activities including trails for bike riding (along the river bank), hiking, and horseback riding; four softball fields and a lighted baseball diamond; an exercise course; lakes for fishing, with a valid fishing license for fishermen over 16 years; a lake for operating model boats; paddle boat rentals at $10 a half hour (usually available on the weekends only); a few playgrounds; horseshoe pits; and several volleyball courts.

Hours: Open April through October daily, 7am - 9pm; November through March daily, 7am - 6pm.

Admission: $2 per vehicle during the week; $4 on weekends; $5 on holidays.
Ages: All

-----MALLS-----

IRVINE SPECTRUM CENTER

(949) 789-9180 / www.irvinespectrumcenter.com

!/$

At the junction of the 405 and 5 Fwy, Irvine

(Going S. on Santa Ana Fwy [5], exit at Alton Pkwy. At the end of the off ramp, go straight into the Spectrum. Going N. on 5, exit W. on Alton Pkwy, L. on Gateway Blvd. Going S. on San Diego Fwy [405], exit N. on Irvine Center Dr., R. on Pacifica. [TG: 891 B2])

Just some of our favorite stores in this outside mall include a gigantic Barnes and Noble Bookstore; Houdini's Magic Shop, a small shop that sells magic tricks; Glow, where every item glows in the dark; and Dapy which sells odd articles and Hollywood icon memorabilia. The center also has a Dave & Busters, an eatery/arcade/virtual game play place for adults, and an array of other fun stops. Hungry? Eat at the food court or choose from numerous restaurants including P. F. Chang's China Bistro; the 50's style diner, Johnny Rockets; Cheesecake Factory; Creperiede Paris; Thaifoon - Taste of Asia; and Wolfgang Puck. Ben and Jerry's, Cold Stone Creamery, and a sweet shop can help you in the dessert area.

As usual, kids enjoy the simple pleasures, like playing (and getting wet) on the turtle statues in the fountain outside the food court. They also enjoy riding the 108-foot Giant Wheel ($2 per person), found at one end of the spectrum and/or the carousel ($1 per person). See EDWARDS IMAX 3-D THEATER, on page 257, for information on the large screen and 3-D format theater here. Note that there is an Improv Comedy Theater here, too - for adults. Call (949) 854-5455 / www.improv.com for dinner and show information.

Hours: Open daily, 11am - 11pm.
Admission: Technically free.
Ages: All

WESTFIELD SHOPPINGTOWN MAINPLACE - KIDS CLUB

(714) 547-7000 / www.westfield.com

!

2800 East Main Street, Santa Ana

(Going W. on the Garden Grove Fwy [22], exit at Main St., L. on LaVeta, L. on Main St. Going E. on 22 exit at Main St., R. on Town & Country to MainPlace. Going N. on Santa Ana Fwy [5], exit N. on Main St. Going S. on 5, go E. on the 22 and follow the above directions. [TG: 769 E6])

Monthly entertainment for kids is a great reason for coming to the mall. The Kids Club meets near the customer service center. This mall also features a TEDDYCRAFTERS. (See pg. 255.)

Hours: The third Fri. from 5pm to 7pm.
Admission: Free
Ages: 2 - 11 years.

WESTMINSTER MALL

(714) 898-2550 / www.shopsimon.com

!

Bolsa Avenue and Goldenwest Street, Westminster

(Exit San Diego Fwy [405] S. on Goldenwest St. [TG: 827 G3])

One fairly standard, but still fun-for-kids feature, is the carousel. Special exhibits are presented here at various times throughout the year. For instance, in celebration of Project Earth, giant sea creatures (up to forty feet long!) came alive via Dinamation - they roared and thrashed their tails. Other exhibits in conjunction with this theme included a display from SeaWorld's wild arctic, weekend stage shows, and a rivers and oceans wetlands exhibit. Who knew that malls could be so fun and educational?!

Hours: Call for a schedule of special events.
Admission: Free
Ages: All

-----*MUSEUMS*-----

ANAHEIM MUSEUM

(714) 778-3301

241 S. Anaheim Boulevard, Anaheim

(Exit Santa Ana Fwy [5] E. on Lincoln Ave., R. on Anaheim Blvd. [TG: 768 J5])

This small museum is housed in Anaheim's restored 1908 Carnegie Library building. The upstairs room displays show the growth of Orange County's oldest city from an orange grove and grapevine-producing society to the opening of Disneyland in 1955 to the present. There are photos, a model of Disneyland, and a display of old tools and machines, as well as orange crate labels.

Downstairs is a small, children's gallery that features rotating, hands-on exhibits such as puppets, toys, musical instruments, and games. It reminds me of a culturally-aware kindergarten classroom, but there are also workshops for older kids.

Hours: Open Wed. - Fri., 10am - 4pm; Sat., noon - 4pm.
Admission: $2 for adults; children 15 and under are free.
Ages: 2 years and up.

AUTOMOTIVE ROAD OF DREAMS

(949) 723-6663 / www.ocmarketplace.com

88 Fair Drive at the Orange County Fairgrounds, Costa Mesa

(Exit Costa Mesa Fwy [55] S.W. on Newport Blvd., R. on Fair Dr. It's on the Orange County Fairgrounds. [TG: 859 B7])

About thirty-five antique, classic, and celebrity-owned automobiles grace this museum. They range from 1904 (a Cadillac) up to the 1980's. Some "famous" cars include a 1929 Pierce Arrow that belonged to Charlie Chaplin, Reggie Jackson' Ragster, O.J. Simpson's Bentley, and Cornelius Vanderbilt's Stutz. The cars are in staged settings from seven different time periods. This means that they are surrounded by a mural, buildings, plants, and/or some memorabilia that defines that particular vehicle and time period. The themes include a farm, citrus packing facility, drive-in theater, lovers lane, used-car lot, and speedway racing arena. At the museum entrance are photos of old Orange County. Note that the Road of Dreams is adjacent to, and open about the same hours as, the huge Orange County Marketplace (i.e. swap meet). Note, too, that museum is host to several car shows and other special events throughout the year.

Hours: Open Sat. - Sun., 9am - 3pm.
Admission: $2 for adults; children 11 and under are free. This includes entrance into the Marketplace.
Ages: 6 years and up.

BOWERS KIDSEUM

(714) 480-1520 / www.bowers.org

1802 N. Main Street, Santa Ana

(Going S. on Santa Ana Fwy [5], exit S. on Main St. Going N. on 5, exit W. on E. 17th St., R. on Main St. It's located on the corner of Main and 18th St., just S. of the Bowers Museum of Cultural Art. And yes, the building was a bank at one time. [TG: 829 F1])

Kidseum is a hands-on, cultural museum designed to assist kids, ages 6 to 12, develop an appreciation of art and the ways of life in cultures from around the world. Cross over the short (symbolic) bridge from the lobby into the main gallery. Your kids will love trying on unusual masks from around the world; playing unique musical instruments, like deer hoof shakers, African drums, and string instruments; and dressing up in a wide variety of ethnic costumes in the theater area.

The Time Vault, which was an actual bank vault, has an incredible mural on the wall. Kids can "saddle up" on the workbench horses in here or grind pretend corn with a stone mortar and pestle. Playing games from foreign lands; working on geography puzzles; doing rubbings; and putting on your own puppet show at the small theater - all this is available at Kidseum, too!

Weekends at the museum is a time for telling tales, storytelling tales, that is. The storytelling room also brings to life Asian tales in January, in celebration of the Chinese New Year; African tales in February to celebrate Black History Month; and so on. Stop by the Art Lab, where kids can paint, color, learn how to make Indian rain sticks, experiment with sand art, and more at different times throughout the year. Most activities are included in the price of admission. School tours here are my favorite combination of hands-on fun and learning. Kidseum proves that learning about other cultures can be exciting!

Note: The Bowers Museum, located just down the street at 2002 N. Main Street, is the parent museum of Kidseum. It contains carvings, pictures, and other art work from African, Asian, and Native American cultures. Older kids might appreciate a walk through the galleries. As admission is reciprocal with Kidseum when visited on the same day, why not visit both?!

Hours: Open in the summer and during school breaks, Tues. - Fri., noon - 4pm; Sat. - Sun., 11am - 4pm. Closed Mon. Open the rest of the year, Sat. - Sun., 10am - 4pm. Call to make a reservation to take a group tour during the week.

Admission: $5 for ages 3 and up. There is reciprocal admission with the Bowers Museum if both are visited on the same day. (See C.E.E. L.A. for membership savings, page 86.)

Ages: 3 - 13 years. Young children will enjoy the hands-on quality of this museum, though signs do ask for a gentle touch.

C.E.E. L.A.

(818) 957-9400 / www.cee-la.com

See the entry for C.E.E. L.A. on page 86.

CENTENNIAL HERITAGE MUSEUM

(714) 540-0404 / www.discoverymuseumoc.org

3101 W. Harvard Street, Santa Ana

(Exit San Diego Fwy [405] N.E. on Warner Ave., L. on Fairview, L. on Harvard. [TG: 829 A7])

Travel back to Victorian times as you visit the Kellogg House (i.e. the Centennial Heritage Museum), built in 1898. Take a few moments to walk around the truly lovely grounds. Tours begin in the parlor where kids can play a pump organ, crank an old telephone, listen to music played on an Edison talking machine, and look through a stereoscope - an early version of the modern-day View Master™. The kitchen has wonderful gadgets that kids can learn about as well as touch. The wood dining room is oval-shaped with cabinets specially made to bend with the curves, like the inside of a ship. The twisted, wooden staircase got "cool" raves from all the kids. Upstairs, children play a game that teaches them the parts of a Victorian house. The master bedroom is now a room to dress up in authentic Victorian clothing, with beautiful dresses for the girls and dapper coats and vests for the boys. The hats are great, too. The children's room has old-fashioned toys to play with. Kids may sit at the one-room schoolhouse desks and write with chalk on the slate boards.

Outside, on the back porch, children can practice *real* chores like "washing" clothes on a scrub board and drying them with the clothes wringer. Sometimes visitors are invited to make their own butter or learn how to play Victorian-era games. Make sure you take a look into the working blacksmith's shop. Demonstrations, such as crafting candlesticks out of iron or creating a horseshoe, are given here periodically. After the official tour, kids are welcome to go back and explore their favorite rooms, with parental supervision, of course.

Enjoy a picnic lunch in the Gazebo area. Throughout the year the museum offers special events, such as American Indian Day; themed teas where kids are invited to make crafts and participate in topical projects; and family activities, such as storytelling, a craft, blacksmith demonstrations, or a nature hike. Call for a schedule and for pricing. School groups, with a minimum of ten students, should inquire about their wide array of programs including gardening, a pirate's treasure hunt (focusing on math, map-making, compass-reading, and other skills), ecology themes, and more. Two-hour classes start at $7 per student. Children 12 years and up can even become volunteer youth naturalists.

Of all the historical homes we've toured, and we've been through quite a few, this one has earned one of the highest ratings from my boys. Most houses, while beautiful and worthy of a tour, are understandably hands off. The Discovery Museum has hands-on activities, plus the docents gear the tour towards youngsters, both in the tour length and the way the information is presented. Come here and let your kids touch history!

Hours: Open Wed. - Fri., 1pm - 5pm; Sun., 11am - 3pm. Open Sat. for special events only. Closed Mon. and Tues. Call to book a school tour or scout outing during the week.

Admission: $5 for ages 3 and up; $4 for seniors; children 2 and under are free.

Ages: 3 years and up.

CHILDREN'S MUSEUM AT LA HABRA

(562) 905-9793 / www.lhcm.org

301 S. Euclid Street, La Habra

(Exit Artesia Fwy [91] N. on Euclid. [TG: 708 E6])

This museum, housed in a renovated Union Pacific Railroad Depot, has a child's interest at heart. Out front are dinosaur print trackways of a tyrannosaurus, sauropod, and theropod; a sand bed where visitors can make their own tracks; and a replica nest containing unhatched "dino" eggs.

Inside, a small Science Station encourages hands-on exploration with a Dino Dig (i.e. digging in sand for "fossils"), a few science experiments, and even a gas pump to fill 'er up. The adjoining room has a carousel to ride, a mini-market for kids to shop like grown ups (without the grown up bills), a shadow wall that takes a temporarily picture, and the front end of an Orange County Transit bus to practice driving skills. The next room has wonderful, interactive, changing exhibits. Past themes have included "Cowboys and the Wild West," which featured western gear to try on, a wooden horse with a saddle, and a guitar to strum on the range; and "Would You Look At That?" which featured fun with lenses, light, and optical equipment. This room is always enlightening! Do you hear trains chugging, clanging, and whistling as they come around the mountain? A connecting room contains a large model train layout. The train room then leads to the nature room. Listen to the sounds of nature (e.g. birds chirping) as you look at the taxidermied wildlife, such as bears, mountain lions, a raccoon, and a wart hog. Hanging on the wall are stuffed animal heads of deer, moose, and buffalo. A touch table in here has fur, bird's nests, and skulls. A bee observatory gets the kids all a-buzz.

Quiet on the set! The dress-up area, with its stage, numerous costumes (including several fireman uniforms), and even prepared scripts, inspires future actors and actresses. The lighting booth, with all of its working buttons, is perfect for aspiring directors. The adjoining playroom, for children 5 years and under only, has a fake tree to climb, a little puppet theater, and a play castle. Just outside the museum is a train caboose that is open to walk through at certain times.

On Saturdays, the museum hosts special programs such as craft projects, storytelling, or shows for kids to enjoy and participate in. Call for a schedule of events. Note that the LA HABRA DEPOT THEATRE (see pg. 258) is adjacent to the museum.

The museum is situated in Portola Park. The remaining part of the park, in the back of the museum, is open daily and features a playground, baseball fields, tennis courts, picnic tables, and barbecue grills.

Hours: Open Mon. - Sat., 10am - 5pm; Sun., 1pm - 5pm. Closed major holidays.

Admission: $5 for ages 2 and up; children under 2 are free.

Ages: 1½ - 10 years.

DISCOVERY SCIENCE CENTER

(714) 542-CUBE (2823) / www.discoverycube.org

2500 N. Main Street., Santa Ana

(From S. of Santa Ana, exit the San Diego Fwy [5] N. at Main St./Broadway, R. on Main St., across the intersection. It's on the left. From N. of Santa Ana, exit San Diego Fwy [5] S. at Main St./Broadway (look for signs), L. on Santa Clara, L. at Main St. The distinctive ten-story-high cube, which tilts precariously on top of the building, is visible from the freeway. [TG: 799 F7])

This two-story, high-caliber science center has over 100 hands-on exhibits and displays throughout its eight major exhibits areas: Perception, Quake Zone, Dynamic Earth, Principles of Flight, Human Performance, Space Exploration, Exploration Station, and KidStation. The bed of nails, a favorite because it's unusual, is a large wooden table with 3500 sharp steel nails embedded in it. Visitors can lie down on the on the bed and not get hurt, due to the equal distribution of body mass. (May your kids never complain about an uncomfortable mattress again!) Press your flesh against a wall of pinheads to create a 3-D impression (and some mighty odd poses). See yourself in a "new light" inside a room with a camera that takes real time pictures of your movements. Watch your image reflected on a screen in vivid colors and lights. If you can't get enough of the real California quakes, enter the Shake Shack, a room with a platform that simulates major and minor quakes. Or, use a seismograph and construct a model building to see if it's up to earthquake code. Walk through an eight-foot-tall artificially generated tornado and even redirect its pattern. Speak through a tube that changes your voice from normal to sound like you're underwater, in an opera, an alien, and more. Use wind to blow sand into dunes or other formations. The stream and silt table allows kids to form dams or create erosion, or just get their hands dirty. Create a cloudy day (inside!) by pushing on large rings around a cloud machine which then form various-sized clouds. Fly a model airplane into the wind using a throttle. Experience what you would weigh on the moon or on Mars by hoisting yourself up on a properly weighted pulley system. Test your hand-eye coordination and reaction time. See what speed you get clocked at when you pitch a ball. Balance yourself on a board resembling a see-saw. (This is much harder than it looks!) Take apart certain machines (with screwdrivers, not hammers) at designated times at the tool area. Jump around to the beat (and on the beat) of a musical floor. Create an animated movie (we spent an hour just doing this!), participate in live science shows, climb a rock wall, log on to the several computer terminals to play educational games, and so much more. Don't forget to catch a twenty-minute show at the 3-D Laser Theater!

In the space-themed KidStation, designed for children five years and younger, kids can suit up as an astronaut, turn and "repair" gears at the Gear Wall, fingerpaint electronically (a lot less messy than the real thing), build things using large foam blocks, construct bridges using wooden blocks, play with space-age toys, and read books about the stars and planets.

The Showcase Gallery features traveling exhibits that titillate your senses. Past exhibits here include the Physics of Fun (starring a real life juggler, plus activities and experiments) and Whodunit? The Science of Solving Crime. Ask about the packed calendar of events offering special in-house programs; a series of science-based workshops that includes an experiment or demonstration and a make-and-take project; science camps; scout programs; youth group sleepovers with exciting experiments; school outreach programs, including a portable planetarium; off-site classes for students (these are outstanding!); and more. The Discovery Science Center unites education with entertainment in an appealing format for all generations.

Note: An on-site Taco Bell and Pizza Hut have an indoor and outdoor eating area. Also, see SANTIAGO PARK (pg. 231), which is across the road, but accessible by an underpass. Parking at the park is free.

Hours: Open daily, 10am - 5pm. Closed New Year's Day, Thanksgiving, and Christmas.

Admission: $11 for adults; $8.50 for seniors and ages 3 - 17; children 2 and under are free. Free admission to Santa Ana residents (bring a valid photo ID with your Santa Ana address) and up to three additional guests is offered on the first Mon. of every month. Shows at the 3-D Laser Theater are an additional $1 per person. Parking is $3 per vehicle. Note: Membership here is reciprocated at the CALIFORNIA SCIENCE CENTER in Los Angeles and the REUBEN H. FLEET SCIENCE CENTER in San Diego. Call around for the best membership deal.

Ages: 2 years and up.

DOLL AND TOY MUSEUM

(714) 527-2323
1238 S. Beach Boulevard, Anaheim
(Exit Artesia Fwy [91] S. on Beach Blvd. Or, exit Garden Grove Fwy [22] N. on Beach. The museum is in Hobby City, 2 miles S. of Knott's Berry Farm. [TG: 797 J1])

Take a walk down memory lane as you go through this museum. It contains a personal collection of the owner's over five thousand rare and antique dolls from around the world, all housed in a half-scale model of the White House (making the museum easy to spot). Some of the more kid-recognizable dolls include Cupie dolls, Star Wars figures, and an extensive Barbie collection. This small museum is for the special child who can resist the touching urge. The attached shop buys, sells, and repairs old and modern dolls. They also carry a line of doll clothes, shoes, wigs, hats, and books. Look up the adjacent attractions - HOBBY CITY on page 252 and ADVENTURE CITY on page 190.

Hours:	Open daily, 10am - 5:30pm. Closed major holidays.
Admission:	$2 for adults; $1 for ages 12 and under.
Ages:	3 years and up.

FULLERTON MUSEUM CENTER

(714) 738-6545 - museum; (714) 738-3136 - tour info / www.ci.fullerton.ca.us/museum

301 N. Pomona Avenue, Fullerton

(Exit Riverside Fwy [91] N. on Harbor Blvd., R. on Commonwealth, L. on Pomona. It's on the corner of Wilshire and Pomona. [TG: 738 H7])

This small cultural museum has two galleries with rotating exhibits that often have kid-appeal, plus a video that explains more about what is currently showing. Past exhibits have included The Nature of Collecting, which featured different collections ranging from *I Love Lucy* paraphernalia to pencil sharpeners and old radios; Touchable Sculptures, with over seventy touchable, lifecast sculptures of contemporary and historic figures such as George Bush, Clint Eastwood, and Dizzy Gillespie; and Anne Frank, a re-creation of the life and times of Anne Frank through photographs and facsimiles of her diary, plus commentary.

One-and-a-half-hour school tours are given that include an in-depth tour of the museum and a hands-on activity that correlates to the current exhibit.

Super Saturdays are year-round family workshops, held on one Saturday a month from 1pm to 3pm. The art activity is geared for kids ages 5 through 10. Super Tuesdays are held on most Tuesdays during the summer from 9:30am to 11am. The activities are geared for kids ages 8 to 12 years. These culturally-themed and/or art workshops, like Secrets of Pharaoh, Papermaking, International Christmas Tree Ornaments, or Day of the Dead, include an interesting lesson followed by a related craft. Reservations are needed. Also inquire about the summer art camps.

Hours:	The museum is open Tues. - Sun., noon - 4pm; open Thurs. until 8pm. Closed Mon. and most major holidays.
Admission:	$4 for adults; $3 for seniors and students; $1 for ages 6 - 12; children 5 and under are free. The first Thurs. of every month from 6pm - 8pm admission is $1. Super Saturdays are $16 per parent/child.
Ages:	5 years and up.

GEORGE KEY RANCH HISTORIC SITE

(714) 973-3190 / www.ocparks.com/keyranch   *!/$*

625 W. Bastanchury Road, Placentia

(Exit Orange Fwy [57] E. on Yorba Linda Blvd., L. on Placentia Ave., L. on Bastanchury. Parking is not permitted on the grounds, but on the adjacent streets of Gilman Circle or Key Drive. [TG: 739 D3])

Orange groves, originally planted in 1893, once covered most of the George Key Ranch. On your guided tour here you can still see the remaining acre of producing orange trees and the verse garden. Tours begin with a brief history about the Key family. The two-story house contains furnishings dating from the 1800's that came from local ranch houses; old photographs; the kitchen with a 1908 wood-burning stove and a gas stove; one of Mrs. Key's dress dating from 1866; and artifacts related to ranch life, such as a squirrel and gopher smoker, an avocado picker, an alfalfa/grass chopper, and implements used in picking and packaging oranges; and carpentry and blacksmith tools. Walk the Old Farm Trail with its old farm equipment and machinery such as plows, harrows, spreaders, seeders, orchard heaters, a citrus spray rig, and even wagons from the early 1900's.

Guided tours for groups are given by advanced reservation. Come during public hours to see the first story of the house and enjoy a stroll along the brick-lined garden and grounds. Bring a sack lunch to enjoy at the picnic tables. Ask about the ranch's special programs.

Hours:	Open Tues. - Fri., and the first Sat. of every month, 11:30am - 4:30pm. Call to schedule a guided tour.
Admission:	Free. A guided tour is $2 per person.
Ages:	6 years and up.

HERITAGE HILL HISTORICAL PARK

(949) 855-2028 / www.ocparks.com/heritagehill

25151 Serrano Road, Lake Forest

(Exit San Diego Fwy [5] N.E. on Lake Forest Dr., L. on Serrano. It's on the corner. Parking is available in the adjacent shopping center. [TG: 891 J2])

Heritage Hill consists of several restored historical buildings in a beautiful gated setting. Four buildings are open to tour that reflect part of Orange County's heritage. The Serrano Adobe dates from 1863 and has furniture from the late nineteenth century. The Bennet Ranch House, built in 1908, reflects a ranching family's lifestyle from the early twentieth century. St. George's Episcopal Mission, built in 1891, has many of its original interior furnishings. El Toro Grammar School was built in 1890. It is a favorite with kids because it has school books from that era, as well as desks and other school-related items. The Historical Park has a few picnic tables on the grounds.

Two school tours are offered. The third grade tour is called "Hands On." It is one-and-a-half hours long, costs $2 per person, and is designed for ten to sixty students. Groups go through each house and do an activity in each, such as grinding corn in the adobe. In the school house, they participate in a mini school session. The fourth grade tour is called "Living History." It is two hours long and cost $3 per person. Seventeen to thirty-five students participate in hands-on lessons in the school house. Learning was never so interesting! Reservations for tours are required.

If your kids need more running around space, visit Serrano Creek Park, just behind Heritage Hill. Serrano is a long, narrow, wooded park with a paved walkway and a creek running through it. The big wooden play structure, which looks like a clubhouse, has a bridge, slides, and some huge tires to climb on.

Hours: Heritage Hill is open Wed. - Sun., 9am - 5pm. Guided tours are the only way to see the interior of the buildings. Tours for the general public are given Wed. - Fri. at 2pm; Sat. - Sun. at 11am and 2pm. School groups can make reservations for tours at other times throughout the week. Closed major holidays.

Admission: Donations.

Ages: 6 years and up.

HUNTINGTON BEACH INTERNATIONAL SURFING MUSEUM

(714) 960-3483 / www.surfingmuseum.org

411 Olive Avenue, Huntington Beach

(Going N. on San Diego Fwy [405], exit E. on Ellis Ave., veer L. past Beach onto Main St. Going S on 405, exit S. on Beach, R. on Main. From Main, go R. on Olive near end of Main. [TG: 887 J1])

Surf's up at this small museum that celebrates surfing and surf culture, from its roots in Hawaii to the present day. Get in the mood with beach music playing in the background. Feel like catching a wave? Check out some of the famous and unique surfboards here, like the Batman board and a surfboard made in three pieces. There are also trophies, clothes, and photographs to look at. A wall completely covered with skateboards is popular with kids. Look at early examples of slalom and vertical to current long boards and motorized boards. Clothing, posters and movies featuring skateboards complete the display. A skin diving exhibit features early face masks, fins, spear guns, and other diving gear, as well as photos and information panels. Note that the Surfer's Walk of Fame, honoring eleven people, is just down the street.

Hours: Open June through Labor Day daily, noon - 5pm. Open the rest of the year, Wed. - Sun., noon - 5pm.

Admission: $2 for adults; $1 for kids; children 6 and under are free.

Ages: 6 years and up.

MARCONI AUTOMOTIVE MUSEUM

(714) 258-3001 / www.marconimuseum.org

1302 Industrial Drive, Tustin

(Exit Cost Mesa Fwy [55] E. on Edinger Ave., R. on Red Hill Ave., R. on Industrial Dr. [TG: 830 A6])

The museum's main purpose is to raise money to donate to children's charities by showing automobiles from Dick Marconi's private collection, and renting out the facility. That said, the public, too, can come and look. The front hallway of this classy museum is lined with gleaming motorcycles. Inside are over fifty cars (specific ones sometimes rotate) housed here and kept in mint condition. They vary in style, shape, and color. His collection includes a 1929 Ford Model 'A' Cabriolet, 1937 Ahrens-Fox Fire Engine, 1954 green Chevrolet, 1973 canary-yellow convertible Ferrari Daytona Spider (once owned by Cher), restored 1964 Corvette Sting Ray, and a jet-black 1989 Lamborghini Countach, plus seventeen racing Ferraris, an assortment of motorcycles, and a few kid-size cars. Marconi's prized possession is the last car Mario Andretti drove to victory at the 1993 Phoenix International Raceway. It is signed by Andretti. My boys' favorite was the rather colorful car completely decoupaged with magazine covers featuring boxing champions. Racing flags, trophies, drivers' jumpsuits and helmets, and a huge, shining silver horse constructed out of old car bumpers complete this museum.

Hours: Open Mon. - Fri., 9am - 4pm by appointment only. You may call as little as a few hours before you would like to visit.

Admission: $5 for adults; children 12 and under are free.

Ages: 8 years and up.

MISSION SAN JUAN CAPISTRANO

(949) 234-1300 / www.missionsjc.com

Camino Capistrano and Ortega Highway, San Juan Capistrano

(Exit San Diego Fwy [5] W. on Ortega Hwy. [74]. It's on the corner of Ortega Hwy and Camino Capistrano. [TG: 972 C1])

$$

The Mission, founded in 1776, is the oldest building in California. It is ten acres of historic stone buildings and beautifully landscaped gardens, courtyards, and walkways. It's easy to see why the San Juan Mission was considered the "Jewel of the Missions." There are many "parts" to the Mission, so there is something to interest almost any age child. It's a history treat for school kids as they visit and "experience" the early Native American, Spanish, and Mexican lifestyles, depicted in separate rooms. Walk through rooms that contain murals such as Indians hunting, and artifacts such as bone weapons. The Soldiers' Barracks room looks "lived in," just as it did many years ago. It contains life-size models of soldiers and their (few) possessions. Note: Outside, behind the barracks, are some picnic tables.

The extensive grounds are a maze of pathways. The Central Courtyard, the cemetery, the areas of archaeological excavation, and the industrial center are all interesting. For instance, tanning vats in the industrial center were used to turn animal skin into sellable leather, while the ovens were used to turn animal fat into candles, soap, and ointments.

The Mission has two churches. One is the Serra Chapel, the oldest building in California, where mass is still regularly performed. The glittery baroque altar, made of gold leaf overlay, is eye-catching. The other church, the Great Stone Church, was once a magnificent cathedral. Some of it was destroyed by an earthquake in 1812. Today, the ruins are being preserved.

Mission San Juan Capistrano offers several special, educational activities such as Saturday at the Mission. A series of four programs, offered on a rotating basis, are given during the traditional school year on the first and third Saturday of the month from 9am to 11:30am. The programs are geared for kids ages 6 to 12. A topic is introduced and then reinforced with a related, take-home craft, and by playing games, or even by participating in a mission activity. Living History Day occurs on the second Saturday of each month from 11am to 3pm. Authentically costumed docents become living historians. Talk with them to find out about mission life "firsthand."

If you're looking for somewhere fun to eat, RUBY'S (see pg. 206) is across the street and up the stairs at the shopping district. This 1940's diner has a train going around overhead, red vinyl seats, and kids' meals that are served in a forties-style, cardboard car. Afterwards, take a walk around Camino Capistrano, which is a street with many interesting stores with truly unique merchandise. For example, the Moonrose store sells candles, and visitors can even make their own. Idea: Take a train into town and really make a day of your visit here! The train depot is only two blocks away from the Mission. (Look up JONES FAMILY MINI FARM, on page 273, for a fun, close-by adventure.) Check the Calendar entry for the Fiesta de las Golondrinas (see pg. 568) held at the mission.

Hours: Open daily, 8:30am - 5pm. Closed Good Friday afternoon, Thanksgiving, and Christmas.

Admission: $6 for adults; $5 for seniors; $4 for ages 3 - 11; children 2 and under are free. Saturday at the Mission is $15 per participant.

Ages: 5 years and up.

MODJESKA HISTORIC HOUSE & GARDEN

(949) 855-2028 / www.ocparks.com/modjeskahouse *$$*

Modjeska Canyon Road, Modjeska Canyon

(Exit Costa Mesa Fwy [55] E. on Chapman, which turns into Santiago Canyon Rd., L. on Modjeska Canyon and go about 1.5 miles. [TG: 832 G7])

This picturesque old cottage and surrounding gardens have withstood the test of time in a gracious manner. Once owned by a renowned Shakespearean actress, the public is now invited to tour through the residence to admire the furnishings and the architecture. The porches and gables are reminiscent of a more romantic era.

The wooded area around the house is alive with oak trees, a grove of redwoods, palms, and other plants. Walk along the rock lined pathway through the Forest of Arden, so named from Shakespeare's play "As You Like It." A guided tour is the only way to see Modjeska and the docent explains the history of the home and the theatrical lifestyle of the original owners.

Hours: Open for guided tour four times a month, by advanced reservation only. No walk-ins allowed.

Admission: $5 per person.

Ages: 9 years and up.

MOVIELAND WAX MUSEUM

(714) 522-1154 / www.movielandwaxmuseum.com *$$$*

7711 Beach Boulevard, Buena Park

(Exit Artesia Fwy [91] S. on Beach Blvd. It's 1 block N. of Knott's Berry Farm. [TG: 767 H3])

Over 400 movie and television celebrities are immortalized in wax, posed in the settings that made them famous. To insure authenticity, almost every measurement and picture angle imaginable is taken of the star before the sculptor begins his work. Often times the costumes and props adorning the wax figure, and its surrounding settings, are personally donated by the stars.

Kids who are film buffs will probably get more out of this museum, but almost any age child enjoys "seeing" Dorothy and the whole *Wizard of Oz* gang; Robin Williams as Mrs. Doubtfire; and Michael Jackson dressed from his video *Bad*; Keanu Reeves in a scene from the *Matrix*; Jim Carey as the *Ace Pet Detective*, as well as Whoopi Goldberg, *Star Trek* crew members, Superman, the Little Rascals, Julia Roberts, Ricky Martin, and many more. Special lighting, sound effects, and animation are also used throughout the museum to enhance the realism of the exhibits. Halfway through the museum, you are routed through a gift and candy shop and small arcade area. Here you have the choice of whether to go through the Chamber of Horrors or bypass it. (The Chamber of Horrors, which holds scary and sometimes gross figures, could frighten younger children.)

Hours: Open Mon. - Fri., 10am - 6pm; Sat. - Sun., 9am - 7pm.

Admission: $12.95 for adults; $10.55 for seniors; $6.95 for ages 4 - 11; children 3 and under are free. Certain discounts available through AAA. Combo prices with RIPLEY'S BELIEVE IT OR NOT! MUSEUM (see pg. 247), which is just across the street, are $16.90 for adults; $13.95 for seniors; $9.75 for ages 4 - 11.

Ages: 4 years and up.

NEWPORT HARBOR NAUTICAL MUSEUM

(949) 673-7863 / www.nhnm.org *!*

151 E. Coast Highway, Newport Beach

(Take Costa Mesa Fwy [55] to end, where it turns into Newport Blvd., L. on E. 17th St., R., at end, on Dover Dr., L on Coast Hwy., on Newport Bay. [TG: 889 B7])

This beautiful paddlewheel riverboat, now harbored in Newport Bay, looks like it just came down the Mississippi River. Our visit here wasn't long, but it was interesting. An upstairs room is devoted to glass-enclosed model ships. Touch screen kiosks and short movies and narrations regarding certain models are also here. The huge (for a scale model) *Fort Victoria* is displayed in the center. The *U.S.S. Missouri* model, built in remembrance of the men who served on her and for the WWII peace treaty which was signed on board, is complete with men and little cannons, plus waves under the bow and stern. Other outstanding models were crafted from sterling silver, intricately-carved wood, and bone. Elegantly displayed exhibits in the other upstairs room consist of artifacts from early California. My boys particularly liked the bowl made from whale vertebrae and the necklace made from fish bones. Downstairs is a changing exhibit - we saw a display of ships in a bottle and a collection of seashells. You can also watch a short, grainy, homemade video taken during a real hurricane in Newport Beach in 1939.

If you've worked up an appetite, dine at the classy RIVERBOAT RESTAURANT (pg. 206), located on board.

Hours: The museum is open Tues. - Sun., 10am - 5pm. Closed Mon.

Admission: Free

Ages: 6 years and up.

NEWPORT SPORTS MUSEUM

(949) 721-9333 / www.newportsportsmuseum.org

100 Newport Center Drive, suite 100, Newport Beach

(Exit San Diego Fwy [405] S. on Jamboree Rd., L. on Santa Barbara, L. on Newport Center Dr. It's near Fashion Island mall. [TG: 889 E7])

Name a sport, any sport. Almost any one that you can think of is represented in this 6,000 square-foot sports museum filled with signed memorabilia. The hundreds of game-used and game-worn equipment and clothing on display include jerseys, shoes, helmets, rows and rows of hockey sticks, basketballs, golf clubs, a multitude of footballs, baseballs, bats, and more. Included in this collection is the ball Babe Ruth hit for his last home-run, George Kelly's 1920 first baseman's mitt, and other baseball items signed by Cal Ripken, Joe DiMaggio, Nolan Ryan, Jackie Robinson, and lots more. The downstairs room contains numerous baseball keepsakes and has stadium seats facing a mural of a baseball field. One room upstairs is devoted to baseball, especially Angels' memorabilia from 1940 to present day, including a ball signed by the entire winning team. Several other small rooms display boxing gloves honoring Mohammad Ali, hockey items that belonged to Wayne Gretzsky, a football signed by John Elway, and pictures of or equipment used in water polo, tennis, horse racing, etc. An Olympic section contains Olympic memorabilia and paraphernalia. Every living baseball hall of fame inductee, every Heisman trophy winner, and every Cy Young award winner is represented at the museum.

The Newport Sports Collection Foundation is the non-profit organization who own and operate this facility. It also puts on programs where athletes come in and speak to kids about staying in school and staying off drugs. Call for more information about this program, but come by and see the sports collection any time.

Hours: Open Mon. - Fri., 9am - 6pm; Sat., 10am - 3pm.

Admission: Free

Ages: 6 years and up.

OCEAN INSTITUTE

$$

(949) 496-2274 / www.ocean-institute.org

24200 Dana Point Harbor Drive, Dana Point

(Going S. on San Diego Fwy [5], exit on Pacific Coast Highway/Camino Las Ramblas and bear R. onto P.C.H. [Hwy 1] northbound, L. on Dana Point Harbor Dr./Del Obispo St. Go all the way to the end of the street. Heading N. on 5, exit on Beach Cities/Camino Las Ramblas into the left lane to continue N. on Pacific Coast Highway [Hwy 1], L. on Dana Point Harbor Dr./Del Obispo St. [TG: 971 G7])

The Ocean Institute's series of buildings are a research center and classroom setting designed to teach maritime history and teach about the marine environment to kindergartners through highschoolers, and beyond. Students and teachers are here in force during the week, while the public can enjoy the facilities on the weekends. The lobby has displays of and on underwater archeology, pirate cannonballs, and a magnetometer that visitors can maneuver to understand how divers find metal artifacts buried on the ocean floor.

The lecture hall is interesting to peek into because of the whale skeleton hanging from the ceiling. The ecology learning center contains several learning stations complete with wet tables, hydrophones, microscopes, and magnification cameras for up-close viewing. Some of the tanks in here have large bubbles where kids can stick their heads up "inside" and get a fish-eye view. The tanks hold octopus, crabs, squid, flatfish, and perch. The adjoining theater is used for virtual underwater experiences, interactive shows, puppet shows, or other presentations.

The two-story surf science building has a wave tank downstairs, plus a small skate and ray pool and a research station to study the physical sciences of the surf zone. Upstairs, with a balcony and a great view of the surf, is a room decorated with netting, surfboards, and surfboard sleeping mats. Students can spend the night and learn what makes a perfect wave while they track storms at sea in the National Weather Service-certified observation station.

A favorite stop is the last one because of the tank farms which contain moon jellies, small sharks, huge lobsters, sea bass, sea stars, and bottom-dwelling creatures.

Just one of the many cruises the Institute offers is the Bio-Luminescence cruise. This two-and-a-half-hour night cruise highlights glowing worms, glow fish, and plankton. The cost is $22 for adults, $19 for seniors and ages 4 to 12. Children must be at least 4 years old for this cruise. Check out the Marine Wildlife Cruise where nets are hauled in filled with sea life. Sort through the creatures (and sediment) to study certain specimens via microscopes. Of course, you'll get the bigger picture by looking at the waters, too, for dolphins and whales, in season. The cost is $22 for adults; $19 for seniors and kids. Numerous other cruise options, including an overnight Catalina Island Ecology Safari, a four-hour Advanced Floating Lab for high-schoolers through college age ($24), and a one-hour Dana Harbor Cruise for everyone ($11 for adults, $8 for children) are available.

A 130-square-foot replica of the historic Tallship *Pilgrim,* rigging and all, is moored in front of the building and open to walk through most Sundays. (See the Calendar entry for the terrific annual Tallships Festival on page 601 for details.) Want to swab the decks, matey? *Pilgrim* offers one to eighteen-hour on-board programs which recreate the austere life of a sailor in the early nineteenth century. Students learn sea chanteys, how to raise the sails, load cargo, and other period related activities.

The Institute offers a full range of outstanding classes for all ages, incorporating literature, social sciences, and history with the maritime theme. Ask about guided tidepool hikes, too.

Behind the Institute is a small park overlooking the harbor, with rock jetties, a few picnic tables, and tidepools. (See DANA POINT HARBOR on page 249 for details.)

Hours: The Institute is open daily, 10am - 4:30pm. The touch tank is open Sat. - Sun., 10am - 4:30pm. The *Pilgrim* is open most Sun., 10am - 2:30pm. Call for school group tours. Everything is closed on major holidays.

Admission: Call for class fees. Weekend admission is $5 for adults; $3 for ages 5 - 12; children 4 and under are free.

Ages: 3 years and up.

OLD COURTHOUSE MUSEUM

(714) 834-3703 or (714) 834-4691 / www.ocparks.com/oldcourthouse
211 W. Santa Ana Boulevard, Santa Ana
(Going S. on Santa Ana Fwy [5], exit S. on Main St., R. on Civic Center Dr. Going N. on 5, exit W. on 1ˢᵗ St. R. on Main St., L. on Civic Center Dr. Although the address is on Santa Ana Blvd., metered parking is on Civic Center Dr. [TG: 829 F2])

Order in the court! Older kids interested in the history of our legal system, or in seeing what an actual courtroom looks like, will enjoy visiting the oldest courtroom in Southern California. Built in 1901, this huge, red sandstone building contains three floors of Orange County history. The bottom floor has glass cases of archaeological artifacts, such as fossils and bones. The second floor, which is the entrance, has two displays containing information about the museum, the history of the courthouse, and the court of law.

The third floor is your ultimate, and most interesting, destination. It features a turn-of-the century courtroom, jury room, and judge's chambers, plus a court reporter's room that has original transcribing machines, a candlestick telephone, and an old roll-top desk. My boys and I role-played a bit here so they could get a feel for how the court system is set up. The museum, which is a room of changing exhibits, is across the way from the Superior Courtroom. Past exhibits have included displays of sheriff's badges, war posters, a mock-up of a 1940's living room, and World War II artifacts from Orange County. A visit to the Old Courthouse Museum is a good beginning for future lawyers. I rest my case.

Hours: Open Mon. - Fri., 9am - 5pm. Forty-five-minute guided tours are available by appointment.
Admission: Free
Ages: 6 years and up.

ORANGE COUNTY DENTAL SOCIETY MUSEUM

(714) 634-8944 / www.ocds.org
295 S. Flower Street, Orange
(Exit Orange Fwy [57] E. on Chapman Ave., R. on Flower St. [TG: 799 D5])

This small museum doesn't floss over America's early dental period. It contains several old dental chairs, including an 1855 wooden chair with a straight back and a spittoon - no running water on this device; an 1876 velvet, rose-colored chair with fringe and a spittoon; and a modern-day chair with all the amenities. The glass-enclosed display shelves are lined with old dental tools that made me wince just to look at them, such as extraction forceps, clamps for separating teeth, and small saws. My youngest son commented, "I'm going to brush my teeth ten times a day from now on!" We also saw a lot of false teeth, porcelain shade guides (used to match teeth for bridge work or capping), metal swagging sets (for making gold crowns), a buffalo horn mallet (used before plastic), and numerous steel instruments - some made with ivory and some with mother-of-pearl handles. The crowning jewel here is in a silver trinket box - a partial denture of four of George Washington's ivory teeth! You are welcome to explore the museum on your own, as everything is labeled, or ask for further explanations across the hall at the Dental Society. This museum is something you can really sink your teeth into!

Hours: Open Mon. - Thurs., 8am - 3pm; Fri., 8am - 1pm.
Admission: Free
Ages: 4 years and up.

ORANGE COUNTY NATURAL HISTORY MUSEUM

(949) 831-3287 / www.ocnha.mus.ca.us
28373 Alicia Parkway, Laguna Niguel
(Exit San Diego Fwy [5] S.W. on Alicia Pkwy, cross Aliso Creek Rd., R. on Awma. It is located in a spacious trailer by Gate One at Aliso and Wood Canyons Regional Park. [TG: 951 E1])

This terrific trailer museum has exhibits of fossils and seashells, and an extensive butterfly and moth collection. It also has a skeleton of a dolphin, the tooth of a great white shark, whale bones, and the remains of Waldo, a walrus or sea lion. Children may touch the animals bones and pelts. Many taxidermied birds are on display - some in flight and others lying down - including owls, hummingbirds, quail, a scrubjay, and a warbling. Other stuffed native animals are a coyote, raccoon, opossum, badger, and more. Make tracks of the wildlife by using life-size paw print stamps in a box of dirt. Live lizards, toads, and several kinds of snakes, including a huge rattlesnake, take up residence here in glass cases. Look for fossils in the pile of rocks here, and look at some of the shells recently gathered from Shellmaker Island and surrounding areas. Kids can take a pencil safari where they are given a list of things to find and check off. Picnic tables are just outside the trailer under a few shade trees. See ALISO AND WOOD CANYONS WILDERNESS PARK (pg. 216) for details on exploring the adjacent wilderness park.

Micropals is one of the many programs offered and sponsored through this museum. It is taught by a geologist and allows kids to extract specimens, process samples, and go on field trips while learning about the world of micropaleontology. Call for more information about this and other programs.

Hours: Open Wed. - Sun., 11am- 5pm. Closed Mon., Tues., and holidays.

Admission: $2 for adults; $1 for seniors and children 12 and under; $5 for a family of four or more. Parking is $2.

Ages: 3 years and up.

RICHARD NIXON PRESIDENTIAL LIBRARY AND BIRTHPLACE

$$

(714) 993-3393 / www.nixonlibrary.org

18001 Yorba Linda Boulevard, Yorba Linda

(Exit Orange Fwy [57] E. on Yorba Linda. Or, exit Riverside Fwy [91] N. on Imperial Hwy [90], L. on Yorba Linda. [TG: 740 B4])

This museum/library/grave site/rose garden features nine acres of galleries and gardens, plus the restored birthplace of - here's a quiz - what number president? (The answer is at the end of this description.) Bring a pencil and request a Children's Treasure Hunt to encourage your kids to become more involved with the exhibits in the museum. They'll search for objects like the Presidential Seal, the Woody Station Wagon Nixon used for campaigning, and the piano he practiced on in his younger years.

The theater presents a half-hour movie, documenting Richard Nixon's political career. It's a great introduction to who he was, both personally and presidentially. There are several videos and touch screens throughout the museum showing different aspects of his life, including the Kennedy/Nixon debates, footage from his speeches, a tribute to Pat Nixon, and a presidential forum with over 300 questions to choose from. I was surprised at how interested my kids were in all of this. The Area 37 exhibit contains an astronaut suit, moon rock, lots of photographs, the recording between the president and Apollo 11 astronauts when they landed on the moon, and other space-age artifacts.

The exhibit of ten, life-size statues of world leaders (some of whom were very short) is impressive. Touch screens offer comments and biographical summaries on the leaders. Gifts of State are unique treasures to look at. My oldest son, however, thought the pistol from Elvis Presley was the coolest gift. The Structure of Peace gallery features presentations about Nixon's strategy for peace regarding Peoples Republic of China, the Soviet Union, and Vietnam. A twelve-foot high chunk of the Berlin Wall is also in this gallery. Other pieces of history include the presidential limo that at various times held Johnson, Ford, Carter, and Nixon; a fully-furnished re-creation of the White House's Lincoln Sitting Room; numerous photographs; Nixon's daughters' wedding dresses; and Nixon's private study from his New Jersey home, complete with hand-written letters and speech notes. In the Watergate Room excerpts of the "smoking gun" tape can be heard through headsets. A pictorial and descriptive timeline of this historic event takes up an entire wall. Tip: At the very least, know how to explain the term "impeach" to your kids. Note: A replica of the White House East Room is targeted to debut a the library in late 2004.

Walk outside, through the First Lady's beautiful rose gardens (which look prettier in bloom), to the home where Nixon was born. A tour of the small house only takes fifteen minutes. Richard Nixon was, by the way, our thirty-seventh President.

Ask about the numerous special programs offered here. Two-hour-plus, free tours are given Monday through Friday for fifth through twelfth graders, with advanced reservations. Throughout the tour, docents are placed at certain locations to pose questions and to answer them.

Hours: Open Mon. - Sat., 10am - 5pm; Sun., 11am - 5pm. Closed Thanksgiving and Christmas.

Admission: $5.95 for adults; $3.95 for seniors and students; $2 for ages 8 - 11; children 7 and under are free. Certain discounts are available through AAA. (See C.E.E. L.A. for membership savings, page 86.)

Ages: 6 years and up.

RIPLEY'S BELIEVE IT OR NOT! MUSEUM (Buena Park)

$$$

(714) 522-7045 / www.ripleys.com

7850 Beach Boulevard, Buena Park

(Exit Artesia Fwy [91] S. on Beach Blvd. It's just N. of Knott's Berry Farm. [TG: 767 H3])

As a reporter, Robert Ripley traveled all over the world visiting over 200 countries and meeting with Kings and Queens, Cannibal Chieftains, and tribesmen to collect interesting, humorous, and bizarre items and facts. There are hundreds of pictures, life-size models, special effects, statues, and assorted odd artifacts throughout the museum. My son, Bryce, summed up the exhibits best by saying, "They're kind of cool and kind of gross."

The "native" section is a little eerie and includes a real shrunken head. The Asian section contains a model of a Chinese man who had two sets of pupils in each eye, and a man who held a real burning candle *in* his head, among others exhibits. (Truth can definitely be stranger than fiction.)

The next section has unusual, rather than weird, displays, such as a sculpture of Michael Jackson made from over a quarter of a million "real" dollars (that will make your child's mouth drop open); a miniature violin, which is only five-and-a-half inches long, yet can actually be played; and a complete landscape scene painted on a potato chip. Two of my favorite exhibits here are a rendition of the Last Supper done with 260 pieces of toast (varying from barely toasted to burnt), and the huge portrait made out of dyed clothes dryer lint. How do people think of doing these things, and why?

Videos show amazing feats such as unusual body contortions, swallowing razor blades, and more. (Don't try these activities at home.) Trivia buffs can really study up here. Toward the end of the museum are a few graphic "bloody" exhibits in the Chamber of Horror. Word of warning: If you take an inquisitive child who can't read the explanations, be prepared to read a lot of information and answer a lot of questions!

Hours: Open most of the year, Mon. - Fri., 11am - 5pm; Sat. - Sun., 10am - 6pm. Open in the summer, Mon. - Fri., 11am - 5pm; Sat. - Sun., 10am - 8pm.

Admission: $8.95 for adults; $6.95 for seniors; $5.25 for ages 4 - 11; children 3 and under are free. Certain discounts available through AAA. Combo prices with MOVIELAND WAX MUSEUM (see pg. 243), which is just across the street, are $16.90 for adults; $13.95 for seniors; $9.75 for ages 4 - 11.

Ages: 5 years and up.

WESTMINSTER MUSEUM / HISTORICAL PARK

(714) 891-2597

8612 Westminster Boulevard, Westminster

(Exit Garden Grove Fwy [22] S. on Magnolia St., R. on Westminster. It's the gated historic park on the S. side of the street. [TG: 828 B1])

Like many other cities who want to preserve their roots for future generations, the city of Westminster has a historical museum. It houses displays from its founding in 1870, to the present day. The museum building, which looks like a converted auditorium, has exhibits, mostly in glass cases, set up in chronological groups. Each grouping has a number that corresponds to an information sheet which explains the memorabilia, thus making for an easy self-guided tour. If you prefer, a docent will explain articles more fully and allow children to touch just a few items - this is a mostly "eyes-on" (as opposed to hands-on) museum. Some of the more interesting items to see include a very small 1897 child's bed; an old stove, washboard, butter churn and other kitchen implements; an antique, wind-up phonograph that still works; old-fashioned ladies' hats and clothing; a collection of dolls from around the world; war posters; and the head of a water buffalo.

Four other small buildings are on the park's grounds. A California Crazy, or Shutter Shack, is a little, picture-perfect "store" that looks like a camera. (It was once used for dropping off and picking up film.) A docent will take you through the other buildings. The small, restored McCoy-Hare House was the community's first drugstore as well as a home. The front room contains a pump organ, plus shelves filled with jars of medicine, bolts of fabric, and sundries. The adjacent living room has some period furniture and clothing. Next, walk through the Warne Family Farmhouse to see the parlor, which holds a 1749 grandfather's clock and a piano; a dining room, with its table set with china; the bedroom that contains a bed (people were much shorter back then!) and a ceramic pot (i.e. port-a-potty); and the kitchen with its stove and old-time telephone. A sink wasn't necessary as water and garbage were simply thrown out the back door to feed the plants and the chickens, respectively. The adjacent large barn contains saddles, large farm equipment, a wooden sugar beet wagon, and tools. Everything is well-labeled. Walk into the part of the barn that has two fire engines and an antique paramedic "van." Kids may climb into the cab of the 1959 white fire engine and "drive" around.

A few grassy areas and a picnic table on the premise complete this park.

Hours: Open to the public the first Sun. of each month, 1pm - 4pm. School groups may call to book a tour during the week.

Admission: Free

Ages: 5 years and up.

-----PIERS AND SEAPORTS-----

BALBOA PIER

Main Street, Newport Beach

(Take Costa Mesa Fwy [55] to the end, which turns into Newport Blvd., which turns into Balboa Blvd., R. on Main St. to the end of the pier. [TG: 991 B2])

Enjoy the miles of sandy beach for sunning and surfing; fish from the pier just for the fun of it; or grab a bite to eat at the small RUBY'S Diner (see pg. 206) at the end of the pier. Peninsula Park is on the east side of the pier. This grassy park, shaded only by palm trees, has barbecues, picnic tables, and even a small playground. See BALBOA FUN ZONE (pg. 209), located just across the road, and combine both attractions for a full day of fun.

Hours: Open daily.

Admission: Free. Parking in the lot costs about $3.

Ages: All

DANA POINT HARBOR

(949) 496-1094 / www.danapointharbor.com; www.danapointharbor.com

34675 Street of the Golden Lantern, Dana Point

(Going S. on San Diego Fwy [5], exit on Pacific Coast Highway/Camino Las Ramblas and bear R. onto P.C.H. [Hwy 1] northbound, L. on Dana Point Harbor Dr./Del Obispo St. Going N. on 5, exit on Beach Cities/Camino Las Ramblas into the left lane to continue N. on Pacific Coast Highway [Hwy 1], L. on Dana Point Harbor Dr./Del Obispo St. [TG: 971 J7])

Dana Point Harbor has beaches, tidepools, a seaside shopping village, boat rentals, picnic areas, and more. The shopping village offers many specialty stores, from Indian jewelry to seafaring items. Food choices range from the elegant to the quick bite, plus ice cream and candy shops, of course. Your young sailor can watch boats of all sizes, shapes, and colors sail in and out of the harbor and up and down the coast. See the Transportation section for details about cruises and whale watching.

At the western end of the harbor, next to the Ocean Institute, is Dana Cove Park, or "Baby Beach." There are a few picnic tables here overlooking the bluffs, a long rock jetty to climb out on, a waveless beach, and a youth group facility which holds classes for water sports. On the other side of the Institute is a rocky patch of beach and tidepools of the marine preserve, which you can explore on your own or call for a guided tour. Tip: Wear shoes with good tread.

Enjoy the day with your family day at Dana Point, whatever you choose to do! (See DOHENY STATE BEACH PARK, on page 198, and OCEAN INSTITUTE, on page 244, for other things to do here.)

Hours: Most shops are open daily, 10am - 6pm. Open extended hours in the summer.

Admission: Parking is free.

Ages: All

-----POTPOURRI-----

BLUES SCHOOLHOUSE (Anaheim)

(714) 778-2583

1530 S. Disneyland Drive at the House of Blues in Downtown Disney, Anaheim

(Going S. on Santa Ana Fwy [5], exit R. on Disney Way. Going N. on the 5, exit L. on Disneyland Dr. Follow the signs. It's in the Downtown Disney venue. [TG: 798 H1])

See the entry for BLUES SCHOOLHOUSE (Hollywood) below for details. Note that this House of Blues is in DOWNTOWN DISNEY, so see this entry on page 251 for details.

BUILD-A-BEAR WORKSHOP (Anaheim)

(714) 776-5980 - local; (877) 789-BEAR (2327) - national / www.buildabear.com $$$
1540 S. Disneyland Drive, suite 104, in Downtown Disney, Anaheim

(Going S. on Santa Ana Fwy [5], exit R. on Disney Way. Going N. on the 5, exit L. on Disneyland Dr. Follow the signs. It's in the Downtown Disney venue. [TG: 798 H1])

See the entry for BUILD-A-BEAR WORKSHOP (Newport Beach) on page 250 for details. For other things to do here, see the entry for DOWNTOWN DISNEY (pg. 251).

Hours: Open Sun. - Thurs., 10am - 10pm; Fri. - Sat., 10am - 11pm.

BUILD-A-BEAR WORKSHOP (Mission Viejo)

(949) 347-6992 - local; (877) 789-BEAR (2327) - national / www.buildabear.com $$$
310 The Shops, Mission Viejo

(Exit San Diego Fwy [5] N. at Crown Valley Pkwy, turn R. into The Shops mall. It's on the lower level near Robinsons May. [TG: 922 B7])

See the below entry for BUILD-A-BEAR WORKSHOP (Newport Beach) for details.

Hours: Open Mon. - Fri., 10am - 9pm; Sat., 10am - 7pm; Sun., 11am - 6pm.

BUILD-A-BEAR WORKSHOP (Newport Beach)

(949) 640-0865 - local; (877) 789-BEAR (2327) - national / www.buildabear.com $$$
925 Newport Center Drive at Fashion Island, Newport Beach

(Exit San Diego Fwy [405] S. on Jamboree Rd., L. on San Joaquin Hills Rd., R. on Santa Cruz Dr., to Newport Center Dr. and follow the signs to the Fashion Island mall. The store is located between Macy's and Bloomingdale. [TG: 889 E7])

Make your own new best friend at the Build-A-Bear store. First choose a furry bear, frog, cow, monkey, kitty, or dog body. Add a sound or record your own message to put inside the critter. Then, help stuff it by pressing on a pedal that (gently!) shoots stuffing into your animal, fluffing him/her until he/she is just right. After putting a little heart inside your new buddy, have the last few stitches sewn up, and choose a name to put on a personalized birth certificate or inside of a storybook. The store also offers over 200 outfits and accessories to dress up your furry friend. What a fun excursion or *bear*thday party idea! Note that there are several workshops throughout Southern California; many of them located inside malls.

Hours: Open Mon. - Fri., 10am - 9pm; Sat., 10am - 7pm; Sun., 11am - 6pm.
Admission: The "bear" minimum prices are $10 - $25, depending on the size of the bear. Clothing, accessories, and storybooks are extra.
Ages: 2 years and up.

CIRCUS VARGAS

See the entry for CIRCUS VARGAS on page 134 for details.

DISNEYLAND HOTEL

(714) 956-6592 or (714) 778-6600 / www.disneyland.com $$
1150 Magic Way, Anaheim

(Going S. on Santa Ana Fwy [5], exit R. on Disney Way. Going N. on the 5, exit L. on Disneyland Dr. Follow the signs. [TG: 798 H1])

If a day at the "Magic Kingdom" doesn't fit into your budget or energy level, come spend an hour or two at the magic hotel. One section of the lobby contains a collection of Disney memorabilia, while around the corner is a huge wall collage displaying trinkets from Disneyland's past. (Remember 'E' ride tickets?)

Walk down the eastern part of the hotel complex that connects with Downtown Disney, which is a pedestrian street filled with unique shops and restaurants. See DOWNTOWN DISNEY on page 251 for more details. Both DISNEYLAND (see pg. 192) and CALIFORNIA ADVENTURE (see pg. 190), the two Disney amusement parks, are just at the end of the "street." Treat your kids to a meal with some real characters at GOOFY'S KITCHEN (see pg. 203), BREAKFAST WITH MINNIE AND FRIENDS (see pg. 201), and BREAKFAST WITH CHIP AND DALE (see pg. 200).

Disney delights in the back courtyard include the waterfalls, water show, and more. Your kids will thrill at walking down the stony steps (this part is not stroller accessible), and going behind the waterfalls. It does get loud down here for younger ones because of the roar of the waterfall, and it is a little wet, as it's real water (not animated) that spritzes the pathways. After sunset, the underwater lights turn the waterfalls into a rainbow of cascading colors. Back on the surface, check out the koi pond. Call the hotel to find out what time the koi feedings are. For $2 per "ride," you can pilot remote-control boats that are replicas of Disney's Jungle Cruise on a mini safari. A small arcade area is tucked away under the crystal shop here. Want to indulge in the sweeter pleasures of life? Stop for an ice-cream cone at Croc's Bits and Bites for $2.50 a single scoop.

Three or four times a night on the hour, usually starting at 7pm, experience the highlight of a nocturnal visit to the hotel - a free, twenty-minute, Fantasy Waters show, in an area near the koi pond. The dramatically-lit water-jet fountains dance, sway, and pulsate to classic and rock versions of Disney tunes. From this same spot every summer night and Friday and Saturday nights the rest of the year, at 9:30pm, look between the hotel buildings to see a dazzling fireworks display put on by Disneyland Park; a terrific way to end your evening with a bang!

From the end of November through the beginning of January celebrate the ho-ho-holidays with lavish decorations, strolling carolers in Dickens-style dress, and a visit with Santa Claus.

Hours: The hotel is open daily.

Admission: Parking is $8 a day. Parking at the nearby Downtown Disney is free for the first three hours.

Ages: All

DOWNTOWN DISNEY

(714) 300-7800 / www.downtowndisney.com

Disneyland Drive/Disneyland Way, Anaheim

(Going S. on Santa Ana Fwy [5], exit R. on Disney Way. Going N. on the 5, exit L. on Disneyland Dr. Follow the signs. There are 2 self-parking lots for Downtown Disney. The N. on is located just W. of Disneyland Dr. at Magic Way and Downtown Dr. The S. lot is N. of Katella, just W. of Disneyland Dr. [TG: 798 H1])

Downtown Disney has an uptown feel. It is a wide, non-gated, beautifully landscaped pedestrian walkway, lined with unique restaurants, shops, nightclubs, and a movie theater.

Top restaurants picks include the Inca temple-styled RAINFOREST CAFE (see pg. 205); Ralph Brennan's Jazz Kitchen, an upscale French Quarter-look building with Cajun cuisine, a kid's menu, and usually live Dixieland music at night; Naples Ristorante e Pizzeria, serving Italian cuisine, using a wood burning oven, in an elegant, Mediterranean atmosphere; and the ESPN ZONE (see pg. 201), done in a red-bricked, brewery architectural design, that combines American grill food, live sports telecasts from around the world showing on numerous monitors all around, and competitive sports games. Of course, sometimes it's just as much fun to come downtown for a scoop (or two) of ice cream at Haagen-Dazs.

Favorite stores in this eclectic mixture, include the massive World of Disney, which is one of the world's largest collections of exclusive Disney merchandise. If you can't find it here, they don't make it! Lego Imagination Center carries a huge variety of Lego products. See BUILD-A-BEAR WORKSHOP (pg. 250) for a *beary* good treat for kids. An independent book store, candle shop, surfer's shop, traveler's aide stores, AMC Theaters, and more round out this area.

Downtown Disney is located in between DISNEYLAND (see pg. 192) and CALIFORNIA ADVENTURE (see pg. 190), and connects with the DISNEYLAND HOTEL (see pg. 250) and the Grand Californian Hotel. The latter gigantic (and expensive) hotel is done in the Arts and Crafts design with a woodsy yet understated elegant theme. Take a walk through and gawk at the high, high beam ceiling and the lobby fireplace that dominates the room because of its size and timber trusses that look like a castle gate door. The hotel does offer free tours and free storytelling in the lobby on most Saturdays. It also has two on-site restaurants; the comfortable, Storyteller's Cafe (see BREAKFAST WITH CHIP AND DALE on page 200) and the more refined Napa Rose, which has three hosts for every table, incredible food fixed in a theater-type of kitchen (the "show" makes it great "eatertainment"), and even a children's menu.

Hours: The "street" is open daily, 7am - 2am. Most of the stores and restaurants open at 9am. Closing times vary.

Admission: Free. Parking is free for the first 3 hours. Validate an additional 2 hours from a full-service restaurant or at the movie theaters.

Ages: All

FRY'S ELECTRONIC (Orange County)

Anaheim - (714) 688-3000; Fountain Valley - (714) 378-4400 / www.frys.com

Anaheim - 3370 East La Palma; Fountain Valley - 10800 Kalama River Avenue;

(Anaheim: Exit Riverside Fwy [91] N. on Kraemer Blvd., R. on La Palma. [TG: 769 G2]; Fountain Valley: Exit San Diego Fwy [405] N. on Ellis Ave., L. on Kalama River. [TG: 858 G2])

See the entry for FRY'S ELECTRONIC (Los Angeles County) on page 136 for details.

HOBBY CITY

(714) 527-2323

1238 S. Beach Boulevard, Anaheim

(Exit Artesia Fwy [91] S. on Beach Blvd. Or, exit Garden Grove Fwy [22] N. on Beach Blvd. It's 2 miles S. of Knott's Berry Farm. [TG: 797 J1])

What did you collect when you were a kid? Hobby City offers seventeen different hobby, craft, and collector's shops to get your youngster started (or add to) his/her hobby habit. Some of the more kid-oriented shops include The Bear Tree (in the shape of a tree trunk), the enormous Prestige Hobbies & Models (airplanes, ships, cars, trains, and more), the American Indian Store, Baseball Card Shop, Stamps, Coins, Gem and Jewelry, and My Favorite Things, which has a doll shop and offers porcelain and bisque doll-making classes. A few other fun shops have reptiles and sea shells. One large store contains over 150 vendors that sell hand-crafted items. Happy hobbying!

The "city" also has a doll museum (see DOLL AND TOY MUSEUM on page 239) and an amusement park just for younger children (see ADVENTURE CITY on page 190). Hobby City is very kid-friendly - it even has a small picnic area.

Hours: Most stores are open daily, 10am - 6pm.

Ages: 3 years and up.

HUNTINGTON BEACH CENTRAL LIBRARY and CULTURAL CENTER

(714) 842-4481 / www.hbpl.org

7111 Talbert Avenue, Huntington Beach

(Going N. on San Diego Fwy [405], exit N. on Euclid St., L. on Talbert Ave. Going S. on 405, exit S. on Beach Blvd., R. on Talbert Ave. [TG: 857 H2])

When is a library more than just a place to peruse books? When it is the Huntington Beach Central Library! This multi-level facility is delightful to visit. Kids are captivated by the huge center fountain inside and the spiraling paved walkway that encircles it. The fountain is loud, especially on the lower level, in contrast to the normal quiet tones associated with a library. The bottom floor has vending machines and tables and chairs for eating, reading, and/or studying. Look up and see returned books being transferred to be re-shelved via a metal conveyor belt. (Only kids notice this sort of thing.)

One side of the main floor has an incredible number of books organized on several levels within the library. A map is available to help you find your topic of interest. There are even a few small art galleries in this wing.

Just outside the Children's Room is a circular aquarium - look for the eel. The Children's Room has a large selection of books. It also contains a reading area, a toddlers' section, a wooden frame of a boat for tots to play in, and a big screen monitor that intermittently shows children's films. The adjacent Tabby Storytime Theater, which is used for storytelling events, and a media/computer room make this library complete. Pick up a calendar listing of children's events, or call (714) 375-5107 for children's programing information.

The Huntington Beach Playhouse is located on the lower level. Several, mostly adult-oriented performances, are given throughout the year. Children's productions are occasionally offered here, although usually given in the upstair theater room. These can include marionette and puppet shows, musicals, and so on.

HUNTINGTON CENTRAL PARK (see pg. 225) surrounds the library. Directly behind the library is a trail leading down to a pond. Acres of trails, rolling green hills, shade trees, and picnic areas are all here to enhance your visit. For summertime fun, check out Adventure Playground (pg. 582), just up the hill from the library.

Hours: The library is open Mon., 1pm - 9pm; Tues. - Thurs., 9am - 9pm; Fri - Sat., 9am - 5pm; Sun., 1pm - 5pm. Call for hours for special events, and for the shows.

Admission: Free to the library, although it is $25 a year if you are a non-resident and want to check books out.

Ages: All

INDEPENDENCE HALL

(714) 220-5244 - Knott's Berry Farm education department /
www.knotts.com/group/sales/education/index.shtml
Beach Boulevard, Buena Park
(Exit Artesia Fwy [91] S. on Beach Blvd. It's right across the street from Knott's Berry Farm (pg. 193) and adjacent to Knott's Soak City U.S.A. (pg. 310) [TG: 767 J4])

This full-size reproduction of Independence Hall houses, among other things, a replica of the Liberty Bell. Press a button to hear a prerecorded history message about the bell. See the re-created room where the Declaration of Independence was signed. Every half hour, a twenty-minute "show," called *Storm in Philadelphia*, is presented. It consists of sitting in the darkened room while candle lights flicker and a "storm" rages outside, and listening to voices debate the ratification of the Declaration of Independence. It is very well done and stirs up patriotism in an American's heart. The gift shop here has patriotic memorabilia to purchase at good prices. Tip: Bring a dime to put in the machine to watch the miniaturized Spirit of '76 army march around. It also has period-dressed mannequins and artifacts, such as a cannon. Tip: Purchase a copy of the self-guided tour brochure ($1) before you bring a group here, just to acquaint yourself with all the hall has to offer.

The education department with Knott's Berry Farm provides over twenty-nine guided tours for all grade levels incorporating the amusement park and/or Independence Hall. For instance, the two-hour Our Early American Heritage tour at the hall has a costumed docent explain the history of our revolutionary times, and then students meet with and listen to Benjamin Franklin and Patrick Henry. Before you visit Independence Hall, you might want to call first and see if a tour will be in progress.

The surrounding park area has a pond with ducks, shade trees, and grass - perfect for picnicking.

Hours: Open daily, 10am - 4pm.

Admission: Free. $8 for parking, or park at the by-the-hour parking for cheaper rates.

Ages: 5 years and up.

ROGER'S GARDENS

(800) 647-2356 or (949) 640-5800 / www.rogersgardens.com
2301 San Joaquin Hills Road, Corona Del Mar
(Exit San Diego Fwy [405] S. on MacArthur Blvd., L. on San Joaquin Hills Rd. [TG: 889 F7])

Enter the world of gardening fantasy; a fantasy for me as I have a black thumb. Roger's Gardens sells an enormous variety of plants and shrubs in a beautifully landscaped, garden-like setting. Walk the two-tiered paved trails and fill your eyes with an explosion of color. My kids loved the unusual plants as well as seeing ones that could supposedly bloomed in our garden, too. The front patch of grass has a model train set that goes over hill and dale. There are a few good-sized gift shop rooms that sell gardening tools, books, dried flower arrangements, specialty soaps, cards, and other paraphernalia. At Christmas time, one room is completely adorned with decorated Christmas trees.

Hours: Open daily, 9am - 6pm.
Admission: Free
Ages: All

SAN JUAN CAPISTRANO RESEARCH INSTITUTE

(949) 240-2010 / www.psi.edu/sji/ed/ed.html
31882 Camino Capistrano, suite 102, San Juan Capistrano
(Exit San Diego Fwy [5] W. on Ortega Hwy., L. on El Camino Real to the Playhouse, which is where the classes are held. [TG: 972 C1])

Funded in part by NASA, this two-and-a-half-hour interactive class gives students a good overview of the solar system, gases, and a few scientific principles, as well as a basic introduction to physics and chemistry. The presiding science teacher lays the foundation in the first forty-five minutes by explaining various gases, the solar spectrum, the order and substance of planets, phases of the moon, and giving information about objects in space. Kids get to hold a piece of a meteor at this point. Students follow along with the lecture by filling out a workbook that is included with the class. A documentary video, *Toys in Space,* shows the difference in playing with toys on earth and in space.

The second part of the class involves smaller groups rotating to different stations. Accompanying parents and teachers help direct the activities with the aid of worksheets. Students are supposed to learn a particular scientific principle at each station, try the corresponding experiment, and again, fill out their workbooks. The experiments include looking through a telescope at sunspots; making vibrating waves with a string and vibrator; playing with magnets; viewing primary colors of lights via a television screen; changing frequencies on a machine to see and hear voice and sound vibrations; looking at a computer with 3-D glasses; and more.

The last segment is comprised of demonstrations, such as adding dry ice to colored water (the mad scientist effect) and attaching a balloon with baking soda onto a bottle containing vinegar (the balloon expands). Overall, although a few more cohesive explanations would have helped me to understand some of the principles better, the kids certainly added to their knowledge about our universe and how it works. Tip: Bring a picnic lunch to enjoy at the adjacent park.

Hours: Classes are offered Tues. and Thurs. at 9am or 9:30am.
Admission: Minimum $250 for a group of up to 50 students; an additional $5 for each additional student.
Ages: 3rd - 6th graders.

SOUTH COAST STORYTELLERS GUILD

(949) 496-1960 / www.storyguild.com
2845 Mesa Verde Drive East, Costa Mesa
(Exit San Diego Fwy [405] S. on Harbor Blvd., R. on Adams, R. on Mesa Verde. It's at the Piecemakers Village. [TG: 858 J5])

"It is an ancient art, yet it is ever new." (Heinrich Heine) What marvels have been passed down from generation to generation through the ancient art of storytelling! For parents and other educators, as well as students, who aspire to become better storytellers, help is at hand. The Guild offers a wealth of information via meetings (held the third Thursday evening of each month), workshops, story swaps, special classes for kids, and children's storytelling teas and crafts (often held at KIDSEUM, see page 236). The best advice given to me for obtaining terrific (and inexpensive) selections of stories was, "Look up section 398.2 at your local library for folk tales, fables, and fairy tales." Ask the Guild for their complete set of guidelines, available at a nominal fee, for starting an ImagUtelling Club or Tellabration festival at your local school or church, or for a group of your children's friends. For more storytelling helps, call the National Storytelling Network at (800) 525-4514, which produces *Storytelling Magazine.*

There are about sixty Guild members. Several of them perform at various locations around the Southland, such as bookstores, museums, schools, children's shelters, and libraries. They also sponsor the annual Southern California Story Swapping Festival. Call for the date and time. So many tales to tell, so little time!

Hours: Call for a schedule of activities.

Admission: Call for cost on activities.
      Ages: 8 years and up.

TEDDYCRAFTERS (Santa Ana)

(714) 479-0045 / www.teddycrafters.com
2800 N. Main Street, suite 308, in the Main Place Mall, Santa Ana
(Going W. on the Garden Grove Fwy [22], exit at Main Street, L. on La Veta, L. on Main St. Going E. on 22, exit at Main St., R. on Town & Country to MainPlace. Going N. on Santa Ana Fwy [5], exit N. on Main St. Going S. on 5, go E. on the 22 and follow the above directions. Lower level near Macy's. [TG: 799 E6])

   See the entry for TEDDYCRAFTERS (Escondido) on page 443 for details.
   Hours: Open Mon. - Fri., 9am - 9pm; Sat., 10am - 7pm; Sun., 11am - 6pm.

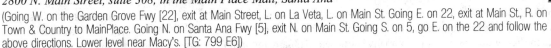

-----SHOWS AND THEATERS-----

BALLET PACIFICA

(949) 851-9930 / www.balletpacifica.org
650 Laguna Canyon Road, Festival of Arts Forum Theater, Laguna Beach
(Exit San Diego Fwy [405] or Santa Ana Fwy [5] S. on Laguna Canyon Rd. [Hwy 133]. It's on the R., on the Festival of the Arts grounds. [TG: 950 G2])

   Ballet Pacifica has a Children's Series, consisting of four productions a year, at the Forum Theater. The ballet productions are held in September or October, February, March, and April. Past performances include *The Emperor's New Clothes, Winnie-the-Pooh,* and *Puss in Boots.* Note: The *Nutcracker* is performed over fifteen times in December. Each show is a winner for the whole family, especially your blossoming ballerina. Check for time and location, as the company performs contemporary ballet pieces here and also at other locations, such as the IRVINE BARCLAY THEATER. (See page 258.)

   Hours: Call for a schedule.
Admission: Tickets for the Children's Series are $17 for adults; $12 for seniors and ages 12 and under. Other performances usually cost $29 for adults; $25 for seniors; $14.50 for students.
      Ages: 5 years and up.

BROADWAY ON TOUR CHILDREN'S THEATER

(714) 542-6939 / www.broadwayontour.org
625 French Street at the Ebell Theater, Santa Ana
(Going N. on the Santa Ana Fwy [5], exit S. on Grand Ave., R. on Santa Ana Blvd., R. on French St., R. on Civic Center Dr., R. into parking lot. Going S. on 5, exit S. on Main St., L. at Civic Center, past French St., R. into the parking lot. [TG: 828 F2])

   At this 300-seat theater, kids 10 to 18 years old put on presentations for younger children who delight in seeing just slightly older versions of themselves on stage. The one-hour musicals are usually based on classic fairytales, and they run for six weeks. Come early for cookies, tea, and pink lemonade with the cast before the show. Reservations are required for the tea.

   Longer, full-length Broadway musicals, still performed by kids, are offered for the whole family. Broadway on Tour's motto is, "Children bringing theatre to children." Call for show information and to find out how your child could become a performer.

   Hours: One-hour shows are usually performed on Sat., 11am and 1pm; Sun., 2pm. "Tea" is served at an hour before show time. The full-length musicals are usually performed on Fri. evening, and Sat. - Sun. afternoons. Call for hours.
Admission: The one-hour shows are $7 per person; $10 for the tea and show. The full-length productions are $9 for adults; $6 for seniors and children.
      Ages: 4 - 12 years.

BROWN BAG PLAYERS

(949) 581-5402 / www.childrenstheatreworkshop.org
21801 Winding Way, Lake Forest
(Exit San Diego Fwy [5] N.E. on Lake Forest Dr., L. on Serrano Rd., L. on Winding Way. It's held across the street from Heritage Park at Rancho Canada School. [TG: 891 H2])

The Brown Bag Players are a division of the Children's Theater Workshop. The Workshop teaches theater to children ages 7 to 16, who then put on a production. Other Brown Bag Players are seasoned actors whose goal is to make theater accessible to children via interaction. Kids are invited to bring their own brown bag lunch (hence the name of the company) between 11:30am and noon to eat while watching the actors prepare for the performance. As the actors put on their make-up, children are invited to join in by putting on make-up (or face paint). During the show, kids are intermittently invited on stage to help tell the story. Afterward, the actors answer questions about scenes, scenery, costumes, technical equipment, or other things kids wonder about. What a great way to encourage kids to be involved with theater! Past one-hour presentations have included *Aladdin, Jungle Book,* and *Treasure Island.* Ask about kid's series of workshops, too, that culminate with a production.

Hours: Each of the three yearly productions are put on for three consecutive weekends. The doors for lunch are open at 11:30am; the play starts at 12:15pm.
Admission: $6 per person.
Ages: 2 - 12 years.

CALIFORNIA STATE FULLERTON PERFORMING ARTS

(714) 278-3371 / www.arts.fullerton.edu/events
800 N. State College, Fullerton
(Exit Orange Fwy [57] W. on Nutwood. The college is on the corner of Nutwood and State College. [TG: 739 C6])

Undergrads put on numerous major theater and dance productions here annually, and many of them are fun for the family. The Kaleidoscope Players put on special presentations every February, just for kids. In the spring, groups come to elementary schools to give special performances.

Hours: Call for show date and time.
Admission: Call for prices.
Ages: 5 years and up.

CURTIS THEATER / CITY OF BREA GALLERY

(714) 990-7722 - theater; (714) 990-7730 - gallery / www.curtistheatre.org
1 Civic Center Circle, Brea
(Exit Orange Fwy [57] W. on Imperial, R. on Randolf, R. on Birch, R. on Civic Center Circle. [TG: 709 C7])

Curtis Theater boasts Brea's Youth Theater and Kids Culture Club. The Youth Theater is comprised of a talented cast of young actors and actresses (i.e. kids) who put on two musical extravaganzas a year in the summer and in the winter. Past productions include *Peter Pan* and *Joseph and the Amazing Technicolor Dreamcoat.* Call for information about signing your kids up to be in a future production. The terrific Culture Club is comprised of a wide variety of eight professional productions a year from October through May. Previous year's forty-five-minute headliners have included a music and laser show, a magic show, the *Nutcracker Suite,* a cowboy trick roper, the Highland fling, and Jim Gamble's puppets. Call for a current schedule.

Across from the theater, the Civic Center also has a small gallery called City of Brea Gallery where exhibits change periodically. The gallery also has a Children's Art Space where young visitors may create their own masterpiece that is related to the current exhibit. The Brea Gallery is usually open on performance nights and gives kids something to look at while waiting for the theater doors to open.

Hours: Youth Theater productions are usually in July and January. Culture Club programs are once a month on Sun. at 2pm. The gallery is open Wed. - Sun., noon - 5pm (open Thurs. and Fri. until 8pm). The Children's Art Space is open Wed. - Thurs., 3:30pm - 4:30pm; Sat. - Sun., 2:30pm - 3:30pm.

Admission: Tickets for the Youth Theater usually run $9.50 for adults; $7.50 for children 12 and under. Tickets for the Culture Club are $6 per person. The gallery is $1 for adults; free to youth 17 and under.

Ages: 5 years and up.

EDWARDS IMAX THEATER (Irvine)

$$$

(949) 450-4900 / www.edwardscinemas.com

At the junction of the 405 and 5 Fwy., at the Irvine Spectrum Center, Irvine

(Going S. on Santa Ana Fwy [5], exit at Alton Pkwy. At the end of the off ramp, go straight into the Spectrum. Going N. on 5, exit W. on Alton Pkwy, L. on Gateway Blvd. Going S. on San Diego Fwy [405], exit N. on Irvine Center Dr., R. on Pacifica. [TG: 891 B2])

For your viewing pleasure, Edwards Theater has a twenty-one screen theater complex in the heart of the Irvine Spectrum entertainment center. The crown jewel of this Hollywood-looking building is a 3-D IMAX theater. The giant screen is six stories high and ninety-feet wide. The lightweight headsets, which look like heavy duty sunglasses, help create three-dimensional images that look incredibly real. You become part of the forty-five-minute movie as you swim with fish, fly in an airplane, etc. You feel like you're really living the adventure! Watch your kids reach out to try to touch objects that seemingly jump right off the screen. The movies can be a terrific educational tool, too. If you make reservations to come on a class field trip, request a Teacher's Resource Guide for the group. The theater also shows wonderful 2-D movies on the huge screen. See IRVINE SPECTRUM CENTER (pg. 235) for information on the rest of the mall.

Hours: The first show starts daily at 10am.

Admission: The 3-D IMAX is $10.50 for adults; $8 for seniors and ages 3 - 12. 2-D prices are $11 for adults; $10 for seniors; $9 for ages 3 - 12. Call first as prices do fluctuate according to the show.

Ages: 4 years and up.

ELIZABETH HOWARD'S CURTAIN CALL DINNER THEATER

$$$$$

(714) 838-1540 / www.curtaincalltheater.com

690 El Camino Real, Tustin

(Going S.E. on Santa Ana Fwy [5], exit N.E. on Newport Ave., L. on El Camino Real. Going N.W. on 5, exit N.E. on Red Hill Ave., L. on El Camino Real. [TG: 830 B4])

Prepare for an evening of fine dining and a terrific Broadway musical when you come to this dinner theater. The restaurant/theater holds up to 300 people, and tiered seating insures that every seat has a good view of the stage. Seating for your three-course meal begins two hours prior to show time, although younger kids will get antsy if you actually arrive this early. The main entree selections include roast chicken, baked ham, or New York roast. A vegetarian lasagna, may be pre-ordered. Soup, salad, a potato, and vegetables come with the meal, while desserts and beverages cost extra. Savor the food and enjoy the service! (It's just like the kind of meals we have at my house. Oh, never mind, that's Martha Stewart's house I'm thinking of.)

The ninety-minute musicals are enthralling, especially for children who appreciate the opportunity of seeing live theater. Most of the shows are suitable for the family, but call first and ask to see what is currently playing. Five different shows are performed each year. Past titles include *Camelot*, *Sound of Music*, and *The King and I*.

Hours: Meal seating begins Tues. - Sat. at 6:15pm; Sun. at 11:15am and at 5:15pm. No performances are given on Mon.

Admission: $29.95 - $40.95 per person, depending on the night you visit. (Tues. is the least expensive.)

Ages: 6 years and up.

FULLERTON CIVIC LIGHT OPERA
(714) 879-1732 or (714) 526-3832 / www.fclo.com   *$$$$$*
218 W. Commonwealth Avenue, Fullerton
(Going E. on the Riverside Fwy [91], exit N. on Harbor Blvd., L. on Commonwealth. Going W. on the 91, exit Lemon/Harbor to the second signal, R. on Harbor, L. on Commonwealth. From the Orange Fwy [57], exit W. on Nutwood/Chapman through Nutwood Ave. to Chapman and turn R. Turn L. on Harbor, R. on Commonwealth. [TG: 738 G7])

Now in the thirtieth season, the Fullerton Civic Light Opera produces five top-notch Broadway musical productions each year, many of them perfect for the family. Past shows include *Ragtime*, *The Best of Andrew Lloyd Weber*, *Joseph and the Amazing Technicolor Dreamcoat*, and *Singin' in the Rain*. The theater is an ideal way to spend a night of enjoyable entertainment together.

Hours: Shows are usually performed Thurs. - Sun. evenings, with an occasional Sat. matinee.
Admission: $19 (Thurs. night, upper balcony) - $42 (Sat. night, front orchestra).
Ages: 7 years and up.

IRVINE BARCLAY THEATER
(949) 854-4646 / www.thebarclay.org   *$$$*
4242 Campus Drive, Irvine
(Exit San Diego Fwy [405] S. on Culver Dr., R. on Campus Dr. [TG: 889 J2])

This theater offers four to five family-oriented shows a year, plus several touring shows geared for kids, and for adults. The various types of shows include circus acts, folk singers, Indian dancers, ballet, chorus music, modern dance, ensembles, youth orchestras, acrobats, and specifically, the *Nutcracker Suite*. Applause, applause - not a seat in the house is more than sixty feet away from the stage.

Hours: Call for show dates and times.
Admission: Tickets range from $5 - $50.
Ages: 5 years and up.

THE LAGUNA PLAYHOUSE
(800) 946-5556 or (949) 497-9244 / www.lagunaplayhouse.com   *$$$$*
606 Laguna Canyon Road, Laguna Beach
(Exit San Diego Fwy [405] or Santa Ana Fwy [5] S. on Laguna Canyon Rd. [Hwy 133]. It's on the R., in the Laguna Moulton Theater, on the Festival of the Arts grounds. [TG: 950 G2])

"Orange County's Award-Winning Theater for Young People and the Young at Heart!" The playhouse offers a main stage season, a youth theater showcase where youth acting companies perform, and Theatrereach - an ensemble that comes to schools for on-site performances. Four, great-for-the-kids plays are presented here each year. Past productions include *Wind in the Willows*, *Wizard of Oz*, and *The Best Christmas Pageant Ever*.

Hours: Call for show dates and times.
Admission: Tickets by the youth companies are usually $5. Other tickets usually run between $14 - $17.
Ages: 5 years and up.

LA HABRA DEPOT THEATRE
(562) 905-9626 / www.lahabrabiz.com/non_profit/depot   *$$$$*
311 South Euclid Street
(Exit Artesia Fwy [91] N. on Euclid. [TG: 708 E6])

For about twenty-five years, the community Depot Theatre has been entertaining young and old theater-goers alike. Most performances are family-oriented. Past shows have included *Oklahoma*, *Pinocchio*, and *Peter Pan*. Come see what's playing. Note that the theatre is adjacent to the CHILDREN'S MUSEUM AT LA HABRA. (See pg. 238.)

Hours: Call for complete schedule.
Admission: Most shows are $12 for adults; $10 for seniors and students.
Ages: 4 years and up, depending on the show.

MEDIEVAL TIMES

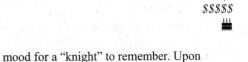

(800) 899-6600 or (714) 521-4740 / www.medievaltimes.com
7662 Beach Boulevard, Buena Park
(Exit Artesia Fwy [91] S. on Beach Blvd. [TG: 767 H3])

"Joust" the sight of this eleventh-century-style castle sets the mood for a "knight" to remember. Upon entering the castle hall, wear the crowns to given ye, good Lords and Ladies, as the color designates which one of the six knights you'll cheer for. The Lord of the castle has invited you, and hundreds of your closest friends, neighbors, and foes to a two-hour royal tournament. Bring your camera to take pictures with the knights in shining armor all around the castle. Note: The Museum of Torture is open before the show. This unusual museum displays over thirty reproductions of instruments of torture and ridicule used during the Middle Ages, like the Rack, and the Stock and Pillories. Each instrument is explicitly labeled as to its use. Personally, I wouldn't go through the museum again. Admission is $2 for adults, $1 for kids 12 years and under.

Tiered spectator seating encircles the dirt floor arena where fog starts to rise up and the music swells - the story and show begin. Hear and become part of the tale where the king, the princess, a master of arms, a druid priest, and six knights and their squires first celebrate a victory, and then discovery a treachery.

As dinner commences, the invited guests (that's you and your family) are entertained by silky-maned horses that prance, high-step, and even jump. These elegant displays of horsemanship delight horse fans young and old. As the story continues to unfold (and you continue to eat) the main event is held - an authentic jousting tournament, which the castle Lord presides over. Six knights on horseback compete against one another as they perform feats of real skill in several medieval games before a wildly cheering crowd. (Yelling is encouraged !) After every game, the winning knight throws flowers out to his rooting section. As the show progresses, the knights engage in choreographed battle by pairs, with their swords actually sparking as they strike each other. The knights fight on horseback and on foot until there is just one victor. The traitor is subsequently revealed, beaten in battle, and vanquished to the dungeon.

Throughout the evening serfs and wenches serve a four-course feast, eaten without utensils, of course. The finger-licking delicious meal consists of vegetable soup, a half of roasted chicken, bread, spare ribs, potatoes, a pastry, and drink. We enjoyed the food and were riveted by the action. After the show, the gift shop selling medieval memorabilia is open, or dance at the in-house Knight Club.

Student Matinees are offered during the week, year round, on selected dates from 11am to 1pm for grades kindergarten through twelfth. A medieval history lesson is given by a Master of Ceremonies on horseback, in place of some of the pageantry of the nighttime show. Kids still see, though, the knights engaging in period games, sword fights, and all the good stuff. This educational "tour" includes a lunch of chicken, potato, apples, cookies, and a drink. The cost is $22.50 per person. Teachers take note: The tour also includes a 100-page educational resource packet that meets the California state standards. The packet emphasizes reading, writing, and social studies in a story that revolves around the famous Spanish knight, El Cid.

One-hour, educational Castle Tours are offered for a minimum of twenty students. Kids are guided by a costumed Master of Ceremonies through the decorated halls. Life in the Middle Ages is explained as they look at authentic medieval artifacts, and learn about chivalry and knighthood. The highlights are meeting a "real" knight, and seeing demonstrations of horsemanship and actual medieval weapons. Tours are given Monday through Thursday, at 10am and 11:30am. Call to make a reservation. The cost is $5 per person. The castle is also usually open during the day, except on matinee days, for those who want to simply come in and look at the horses and the arena, and shop.

Hours: Call for times for the knightly performances.

Admission: The price, including dinner, show, and tax, is $43.95 for adults; $30.95 for ages 12 and under. Reservations are required. Certain discounts available through AAA, but not on Sat. Note: A person gets in free during the month of his/her birthday with three other adults paying the full amount, and with proof that it really is his/her birthday.

Ages: 3 years and up.

MERLIN'S MAGIC DINNER SHOW
(714) 744-9288 / www.ribtrader.com
2710 E. Chapman Avenue at the Rib Trader (restaurant), Orange
(Exit Costa Mesa Fwy [55] E. on Chapman Ave. [TG: 800 E4])

$$$$

It's no illusion, Merlin's Magic Dinner Show is very entertaining. Located in a room that seats about 100 people, guests are invited to sit at long tables for two-hours of down-home magic, comedy, and food. Medieval music plays in the background. Home-made soup is served as Merlin opens with jokes and sleight of hand tricks. Then comes more delicious food, served by wenches. The adults are given baby back ribs, barbecued chicken, honey-baked corn bread, beans, and coleslaw. Kids receive chicken fingers, fries, and fresh fruit. Appetizers, beverages, and desserts are extra. Merlin periodically appears on stage for interludes of more magic and comedy.

After dinner, he performs the bulk of his show, which includes a lot of audience participation. He confounds guests with his cards, ropes, and rings tricks, as well as numerous other magical feats. There were several times after he finished a trick that no one clapped immediately, only because we were trying to figure out how he did it. (In fact, we're *still* trying to figure out how he did it!) Most of the comedy is kid appropriate. Reservations are required. Note: The adjacent, small Rib Trader restaurant is jungle-themed with bamboo decor and (fake) animal heads on the walls, such as zebra, rhino, lion, and more. The food is great.

Hours: Shows are performed Fri., 8pm; Sat., 5pm and 8pm; Sun., 5pm.

Admission: Admission includes the show and dinner, but not tax and tip: $24.95 for adults; $14.95 for ages 12 and under.

Ages: 4 years and up.

ORANGE COUNTY PERFORMING ARTS CENTER / MERVYN'S MUSICAL MORNINGS
$$$$

(714) 556-2787 - performing arts center; (714) 755-5799 - symphony (Mervyn's mornings) /
www.ocpac.org; www.pacificsymphony.org
600 Town Center Drive, Costa Mesa
(Exit San Diego Fwy [405] N. on Bristol St., R. on Town Center. [TG: 859 D3])

On selected Saturdays, the almost 300-seat Center hosts family-oriented musical performances - seats are on a first-come, first-served basis. Of course, the Center also offers first-class performances geared for adults, too. Productions include Broadway plays and musicals, cabaret, jazz, ballet, concerts, symphony performances, and much more. Past special events have included *Oklahoma, Lord of the Dance, Blues Clues! Live, Forever Plaid*, and a sing-a-long *Sound of Music*. Note: One hour prior to each performance in the Dance, Jazz, and Chamber Music Series, a noted expert gives a free informative talk, open to all ticket holders, to share insights about the performance. See ORANGE COUNTY PERFORMING ARTS CENTER (tour), on page 266, for information on taking a tour of this center.

Six Saturdays a year, Pacific Symphony Orchestra puts on Mervyn's Musical Mornings, which are concerts designed for kids. The performances vary in content, but aim to be pieces that children are familiar with, such as music from *Nutcracker Suite,* or even from cartoons. They are always fun for kids, as well as interactive. Activities can include a musical treasure hunt through the lobby, a "petting zoo" (touch, and perhaps play, a few instruments), a computer center, and participation in a dance or theater number.

Hours: Call for a show schedule. Mervyn's mornings and other family shows are offered on select Sat. at 10am and 11:30am.

Admission: Performance prices vary according to show, date, and time. Saturday family programs are usually $9 per person. Mervyn's mornings prices, depending on your seat, range between $14 - $16 for adults; $12 - $22 for children 12 and under.

Ages: 4 years and up, depending on the show..

PLAZA GARIBALDI DINNER THEATER

$$$$

(714) 758-9014 / www.plaza-garibaldi.com

500 N. Brookhurst Street, Anaheim

(Going S.E. on Santa Ana Fwy [5], exit S. on Brookhurst. Going N.W. on 5, exit W. on La Palma, L. on Brookhurst. [TG: 799 A1])

Experience the finest Mexican entertainment and cuisine this side of the border. Your almost two-hour dinner/show features a variety of acts such as Mariachis, singers, folkloric dancers with colorful costumes and sombreros, cowboy ropers (this is a highlight!), tango dancers, and more. The fiesta atmosphere, traditional costumes, and authentic decor enhance your visit here.

The stage area seats 320 patrons in both booths and a long tables (make some new friends). Note that there is a separate room for those who just want to come eat, but not watch the show. Adults can choose from numerous entrees of Mexican fare that come with all the side fixings including tacos, fajitas, chicken salad, wet burritos, quesadillas, chili verde, and more. Kids can choose from chicken tenders with fries, carne asada with rice and beans, or a burrito. Beverages are extra. Sunday brunches are all-you-can-eat buffets that come with champagne. Ole!

    Hours: Shows are given Fri. - Sun., at 7:30pm, 9:30pm, and 11:30pm. Sunday brunches are at 12:30pm and 2:30pm.

Admission: $16.95 - $27.50 (for a fiesta platter) for adults depending on the meal choice; $12 for ages 5 - 12 who are ordering from the kid's menu; children 4 and under are free. The price includes dinner and the show.

     Ages: 4 years and up.

SAM'S SEAFOOD "POLYNESIAN SPECTACULAR"

(562) 592-1321 / www.menusunlimited.com/samsseafood

16278 Pacific Coast Highway, Huntington Beach

See the entry for SAM'S SEAFOOD "POLYNESIAN SPECTACULAR" on page 207 for details.

SOUTH COAST REPERTORY

$$$

(714) 708-5555 or (714) 708-5577 / www.scr.org

655 Town Center Drive, Costa Mesa

(Exit San Diego Fwy [405] N. on Bristol, R. on Town Center Dr. [TG: 859 D3])

Come to these acclaimed theaters for year-round professional productions. Note that most plays are geared for older children and adults. There are three family productions a year that run for about three weeks. Productions have included *The Emperor's New Clothes* and *Wind in the Willows*. Kids can also sign up to be in a production that, after months of rehearsals, culminate in performances given for the public.

Or, or invite the theater to come to your child's school as the repertory has fantastic educational outreach programs. Musicals and dramatic presentations correlate with school curriculum on a variety of subjects, including multi cultural themes, dealing with relationships, and even Shakespeare. Call for a schedule and pricing information.

    Hours: Call for show dates and times.

Admission: Varies, depending on the show.

     Ages: 10 years and up, depending on the show.

TESSMANN PLANETARIUM AT SANTA ANA COLLEGE

$$

(714) 564-6356 / www.sac.edu

1530 W. 17ᵗʰ Street, Santa Ana

(Exit Santa Ana Fwy [5] W. on 17ᵗʰ St., L. on Bristol and enter at the south side of the campus. Park in lots 7, 8, or 9. Parking is $1. It is a brisk, at least 5-minute walk through campus to the north end to the planetarium. [TG: 829 C1])

Twinkle, twinkle little star, how I wonder what you are? Your kids can begin to find the answers to this question, and many more, at shows in the ninety-seat planetarium. Several hour-long programs, such as *A Tour of the Solar System, Adventures in Astronomy,* or *How Far is Up?*, are wonderful trips around the galaxy, as you see and learn about planets, constellations, our solar system, comets, and more. All the shows have live narrations given by an astronomer. Various programs appeal to guests 5 to 95 years old. There is time after the presentation for questions and answers. If you have a group of fifty or more, ask about reserving the auditorium for your group. Dates depend on availability and reservations are required. See the Calendar entry for more information on the wonderful Christmas show, *The Star of Bethlehem* (pg. 617).

Hours: Shows are presented on selected dates year round, Mon - Fri., at 9:30am. A second show is offered Tues. and Thurs. at 11am. Reservations are needed. School, or other groups, are welcome to make reservations, too, and large groups can book the planetarium at other times.

Admission: $3 per person.

Ages: 5 years and up.

TIBBIE'S GREAT AMERICAN CABARET

(888) 4TIBBIES (484-2243) / www.tibbiescabaret.com

505 N. Sycamore Street at the Santa Ana Performing Arts and Events Center, Santa Ana

(Exit Golden State Fwy [5] W. on 17th St., L. on Broadway, L. on 5th St., L. on Sycamore.)

$$$$$

More than just dinner, and more than just a show - Tibbie's is a wonderful two-hour, dinner, musical song and dance revue in an upscale atmosphere. The eight waiters and waitresses are also the entertainers. They start the show by singing as they bring in the Caesar salad, and they entertain all the way through dessert. They perform on the stage, as well as all around you. Their high energy, beautiful voices, numerous costumes changes, and well-choreographed dance moves make any show here a delight. Past show titles have included *From Stage to Screen* (favorite Broadway show tunes and movie music), *Solid Gold* (songs from the 70's), and the fantastic, annual Christmas show, *Holiday Follies*. Audience participation and other surprises throughout the evening add to your family's enjoyment.

The delicious dinner selections for adults include prime rib, salmon, a chicken entree, or chef's pasta special. All meals come with twice-baked potatoes, fresh bread, veggies, and dessert. The topsoil (i.e. chocolate cookie crumbs) and dirt (i.e. vanilla ice cream) served in a pot with a silk flower isn't your garden variety dessert; it's much tastier. Children are offered penne pasta or chicken strips with fries, plus a beverage and the special dessert. If your child or another member of your party is celebrating a birthday, graduation, or other special occasion, be sure you tell Tibbie's beforehand so they will mention it sometime during the show. Enjoy your night out on the town where the food is good and the entertainment is clean and fun. One to two week reservations are suggested. Five or six different shows are presented throughout the year, so call for particular show titles.

Hours: Shows are Fri. at 7:30pm; Sat. at 7pm; and selected Sun. at 2pm. Ask about their expanded holiday hours.

Admission: The show, dinner, and dessert are $44.95 for adults; $28.95 for children 12 and under.

Ages: 6 years and up.

TRINITY CHRISTIAN CITY INTERNATIONAL

(714) 708-5405 / www.tbn.org

3150 Bear Street, Costa Mesa

(Exit San Diego Fwy [405] S. on Bristol St., R. on Paularino Ave., R. on Bear St. [TG: 859 C4])

A lavish fountain outside, surrounded by beautiful landscaping and white archways, enhances the serene garden setting. The lobby of T.C.C.I.'s international headquarters is opulently decorated in whites and golds, along with beveled mirrors on the walls and around the columns. (I kept wishing for my own bottle of Windex™, so my children's visit here wouldn't be *so* obvious, although they were never looked at disparagingly. I've rarely encountered friendlier staff.) A powerful-looking angel at the top of the ornate central staircase immediately draws your attention. He is made out of white marble, brandishes a real sword, and is stepping upon a representation of Satan. The ceiling of the rotunda, just over his head, depicts heavenly scenes painted in a Victorian style.

Take the stairs, or a glass-enclosed elevator, to the second floor where you'll see a non-traditional church setting and a broadcasting room. Check out all the lighting and camera equipment! You are invited to attend free broadcasts and tapings of the Trinity Broadcast Network programs that air from either room. Call for dates and times.

After my boys and I stopped gaping, we went back downstairs into a small theater room. Tip: Just before you enter, note the "mirror room" where you look through several sets of beveled mirrors, seemingly into infinity. A fifteen-minute preview, hosted by Paul Crouch, president and founder of T.B.N., presents the history and Christian heritage of Orange County and T.B.N. Afterward, as the screen and curtain rise, you are invited to walk along an excellent re-creation of Via Dolorosa, the cobblestone street in the city of old Jerusalem where Jesus carried his cross to Calvary. The street ends at the entrance of another theater.

Four, one-hour-long movies are shown in this forty-nine seat Virtual Reality Theater. (Virtual Reality, or "surround" sound, means that you literally feel the rumblings of earthquakes and thunder, and that the loud noises and music are amplified.) Three of the movies are outstanding reenactments that vividly bring Biblical events to life. Each film, shot on location in Israel, is presented at least once a day. Call for the schedule. Note that the films powerfully and realistically portray their subject, so certain scenes are necessarily graphic and thereby intense for younger children. *The Revolutionary* shows the life of Christ, from His birth to His resurrection. Graphic scenes include a demon being cast out and Christ being nailed on the cross. *The Revolutionary II* is about the miracles of Jesus' ministry. Graphic scenes include a demon being cast out and Christ being nailed to the cross. (I know that last part sounded familiar.) *The Emissary* depicts the Apostle Paul's life, his conversion, his subsequent new life of faith, and his struggles. Graphic scenes include the stoning of Stephen, beatings, and a shipwreck. The fourth movie, the *Omega Code,* is more modern. It deals with Bible prophecy and end times. It's definitely geared for older kids as the storyline is somewhat complex and there is on-screen violence.

A beautiful, fully-stocked gift shop is also on the premises. See TRINITY BROADCASTING NETWORK (pg. 267) for an associated attraction. Tip: Pack a sack lunch because Shiffer Park is just across the street. The park has a few playgrounds, large grassy areas, shade trees, and picnic tables.

Hours: The building is open Mon. - Thurs., 10am - 6pm; Fri. - Sat., 10am - 7pm; Sun., 1pm - 6pm. Movies, beginning on the half hour, run Mon. - Thurs., 10:30am - 4:30pm; Fri. - Sat., 10:30am - 7:30pm; Sun., 1:30pm - 5:30pm. Call for a program schedule.

Admission: Free

Ages: 6 years and up.

WILD BILL'S WILD WEST DINNER EXTRAVAGANZA

$$$$$

(800) 883-1546 or (714) 522-6414 / www.wildbillscalifornia.com

7600 Beach Boulevard, Buena Park

(Exit Artesia Fwy [91] S. on Beach Blvd. [TG: 767 H3])

Put on your best cowboy or cowgirl duds and see how the West was fun. Stagecoaches are outside, while posters, a saloon-door entrance (great for picture taking), a few stuffed buffalos, and steer's horns decorate the inside.

The two-hour, non-stop, high-energy show features Wild Bill as the host, who also sings and plays guitar; Miss Annie, Bill's co-host, who also sings and dances; dancing girls; Indian dancers; and specialty acts. The Native American dancers in full regalia, especially the one who usually perform the always-captivating hoop dance, are incredible. Another favorite is Bonnie, a trick rope artist, who twirls ropes, cracks whips, and spins guns like you've never seen - what a show! One of the specialty acts that we saw, and these rotate, was a hilarious and talented comedic magician. The music, dancing, costume changes, and special effects, are wonderful, and the audience participation is a lot of fun. (How often are your kids encouraged to yell at the top of their lungs in public?!) On a personal note, Wild Bill and Miss Annie have a very flirtatious relationship, with numerous nuances. Also, Miss Annie's outfits and the dancing girl's costumes are saloon-style, as in very pleasing for cowboys.

A four-course, finger-lickin', all-American meal is served throughout the performance. The food includes delicious chicken, ribs, salad, biscuits, baked potato, corn on the cob, apple pie a la mode, and a beverage.

Terrific, two-hour educational programs, for preschoolers through sixth graders, are offered several times throughout the year, and almost weekly in the summer. Another two-hour program is offered for junior highschoolers during the tradition school year. In both presentations, albeit geared differently for ages of the audience, Wild Bill welcomes the guests, sings a little, and teaches the history of the Old West, as well as explains the artifacts in the banquet hall. An Indian dancer, dressed in full costume, explains his heritage and performs some intricate dances. Bonnie performs her lariat-twirling, whip-cracking (always a hit), and gun-slinging. Again, kids are encourage to hoot and holler. The younger kids help put on a Wild Bill Show at the end and it is a highlight. For the older kids, a comedic magician puts on a funny and spellbinding show. Lunch is fried chicken legs, potato chips, corn on the cob or fruit, ice cream, and soda.

Hours: Shows for the general public are performed Sun. - Thurs., 7pm; Fri., 7:30pm; Sat., 5pm and 8pm. School programs are given at 11am on selected days.

Admission: $41.95 for adults; $26.95 for ages 3 - 11. Younger kid's school programs are $11.95 per person; jr. high programs are $16.95. Both school presentations include tax and gratuity.

Ages: 4 years and up.

-----*TOURS*-----

BODEGA FUDGE AND CHOCOLATES   ☀

(714) 429-1057 - store; (714) 432-0708 - tour / www.bodegachocolates.com   !

3198-A Airport Loop Drive, Costa Mesa

(Exit San Diego Fwy [405] S. on Bristol St., L. on Paularino Ave., L. on Red Hill Ave., R. on Airport Loop. [TG: 859 F4])

My middle son has never met a chocolate he didn't like, so he *really* loved Bodega. This family-owned and operated business has received numerous awards for their fudge truffle confectionary concoctions. Groups of ten or more preschoolers through elementary-school-aged children are invited, along with their parents, to take a half-hour tour of the Bodega "factory," which is really like a large kitchen. (Tours are also offered for senior citizens.) Visitors will learn how the chocolates are made, what makes the products kosher, how the machines run, and how quality control is maintained by making small batches at a time. Best of all, samples are given out. (You know how vital it is to taste test.)

Please visit their retail store (the tour facility is in a different location) in South Coast Plaza on Bristol Avenue to purchase several different flavors of truffle bars, including rocky road and butter vanilla, plus chocolate truffle sauce and traditional English toffee. How sweet it is! Another store location is at The Grove in Los Angeles.

Hours: The store is open Mon. - Sat., 9am - 5pm. Tours are given by appointment February through June.

Admission: Free

Ages: 4 years old to 6th graders, and senior citizens.

CRYSTAL CATHEDRAL OF THE REFORMED CHURCH IN AMERICA   ☀

(714) 971-4013 / www.crystalcathedral.org   !

4201 Chapman Avenue, Garden Grove

(Exit Santa Ana Fwy [5] W. on Chapman Ave. [TG: 799 B4])

This spectacular sanctuary, enclosed by 10,000 mirrored windows, is an impressive place to see. The windows are panes of glass that overlay a massive amount of steel trestled framework. Kids (and adults) look up and around in amazement at this church. Tour on your own, or take a forty-minute guided tour which goes through the church and around the other facilities. The tour guide will explain how and why the cathedral was built, as well as offer information about the different ministries going on here. Look down at the concrete floor panels to read various Bible verses. The grounds are beautiful, with a fountain between the office buildings, a sunken garden, and a food court. A museum on the second level of the building titled International Center for Possibility Thinking, shows and tells Robert Schuller's story. The tower of the Cathedral contains a fifty-two bell carillon that rings every fifteen minutes. Look for details on the spectacular shows, *Glory of Christmas* (pg. 614) in December, and *Glory of Easter* (pg. 568) in March.

Hours: Tours are given Mon. - Sat., 9am - 3:30pm. (Church functions affect tour times.) Closed major holidays.

Admission: Donations are accepted.

Ages: 6 years and up.

FULLERTON MUNICIPAL AIRPORT

(562) 691-6280 or (714) 738-6323 / www.ci.fullerton.ca.us/airport

4011 W. Commonwealth, Fullerton

(Exit Artesia Fwy [91] or Santa Ana Fwy [5] N. on Magnolia to end, L. on Commonwealth, 1 block to the Tower. [TG: 738 A7])

Help navigate your kindergartner or older child on this one-hour walking tour. A docent, who is a member of the Fullerton's Pilot Association, will show your group, of at least five people, around the airport.

Tours are modified to fit your particular children's interests and questions. A highlight is sitting in a small Cessna plane and in a helicopter owned by the Fire Department. Small groups of older kids may visit the Control Tower - depending on how busy the air traffic is. They'll get a bird's eye view of planes landing and taking off, and see how radar works. The tour ends on a high note as souvenirs, like plastic wings for future pilots, are given out.

Hours: Hours and days are flexible, although Mon. - Fri. is preferred.

Admission: Free

Ages: 5 years and up.

GOODWILL INDUSTRIES (Santa Ana)

(714) 547-6308 / www.ocgoodwill.org

410 N. Fairview Street, Santa Ana

(Going E. on Garden Grove Fwy [22], exit S. on Fairview St. Going W. on 22, exit S. on Haster St., L. on Garden Grove Blvd., R. on Fairview St. From the Santa Ana Fwy [5], exit W. on 1st St., R. on Fairview St. [TG: 829 A3])

Learn how to spread goodwill as you accompany your kids on a forty-minute tour of this facility. You'll get an overview of what Goodwill Industries does by observing people, including many disabled people, being trained to work in several different areas. Watching assembly lines are interesting, as things are put together and packages are shrink wrapped. Kids will also see recycling in action, as old stuffed animals and toys get fixed up for someone else to play with and love. Check out the receiving dock where the donations are piled. Idea: Clean out your closets and have your kids bring their old toys and clothes to Goodwill on your tour date. Tip: Next door to this facility is a thrift store and an "as is" store where kids can hunt for treasure amidst the junk. (I think we bought as much as we brought!) There is no minimum number of people required for a tour, but a week's notice is requested. There are several other GOODWILL INDUSTRIES in other counties.

Hours: Tours are given Tues. and Thurs., 10am - 2pm.

Admission: Free

Ages: At least 7 years old.

JOHN WAYNE AIRPORT TOUR

(949) 252-5168 or (949) 252-5219 / www.ocair.com

3151 Airway Avenue, Costa Mesa

(Exit San Diego Fwy [405] S. on Bristol St., L. on Paularino, R. on Airway. [TG: 859 E5])

This terrific, one-hour tour is tailored toward the participants' ages. It shows how the airport is similar to a small city, with different people doing different jobs, each one making a contribution to the community. The knowledgeable docents are retired pilots. Kids see the public access places while learning about the history of the airport and some basic information on aviation. The tour goes all around the terminal to see the various activities. There are huge windows all along the field, and a V-shape one jutting into it that offers a wonderful view of the planes landing and taking off, planes being serviced, and baggage being loaded and unloaded. A fun remembrance, such as an airplane coloring book, is given out at the end of the tour. Happy landings! A minimum of ten people and maximum of twenty-five are needed for a tour.

Hours: Tours are available Mon. - Sat., 10:30am - 3:30pm. Reservations are required. No tours are given in August.

Admission: Free; parking is $1 per hour.

Ages: 6 years and up.

KOCE-TV

(714) 895-5623 / www.koce.org

15751 Gothard Street, at Golden West College, Huntington Beach

(Going S. on San Diego Fwy [405], exit S. on Goldenwest St., L. on Edinger Ave., L. on Gothard. Going N. on 405, exit S. on Beach Blvd., R. on Edinger, R. on Gothard. Park in the lot advertising KOCE. [TG: 827 H5])

At KOCE, Southern Californians have the opportunity to look at the behind-the-scenes workings of a television station, not just what viewers see on air. Orange County's first television station and Public Broadcasting System member produces the "Real Orange" news show as well as several other shows. The first stop on the one-hour guided tour is the actual studio set, with sound absorbing walls and lots of lights, camera equipment, and Teleprompters. The tour goes at a relaxed pace, so we saw and learned about the consoles, master control room, make up room, newsroom, editing room, and post production office, and asked questions along the way. We dubbed the tour "insightful." Well, I dubbed it insightful and the kids learned a new word. Groups between ten to fifteen people are welcome. Reservations are required.

Hours: Tours are offered Mon. - Fri., 9am - 3pm.

Admission: Free

Ages: 8 years and up.

LOS ANGELES TIMES, ORANGE COUNTY

(714) 966-5960 / www.latimes.com

1375 Sunflower Avenue, Costa Mesa

(Exit San Diego Fwy [405] N. on Fairview Ave., L. on Sunflower. [TG: 858 J3])

Walk through the photo, graphic, sports, and features departments and hear a representative from each (depending on the day and circumstances) explain a little about his or her work and the function of that particular department. Learn how the paper is laid out, the plates are made, the actual printing is done, and how the paper is distributed. It's a thrill for any news buff to see how this working facility puts together the front page, sports, comics, and even the classifieds. Note: Although morning and afternoon tours are basically the same, the presses (which are incredibly loud!) usually run in the afternoon. The one-hour tour is open for groups only, consisting of ten to twenty people. Children must be at least 10 years old.

Hours: Tours are given Mon. - Fri., 10am - 4pm by appointment only.

Admission: Free

Ages: 10 years and up.

ORANGE COUNTY PERFORMING ARTS CENTER (tour)

(714) 556-2787 / www.ocpac.org

600 Town Center Drive, Costa Mesa

(Exit San Diego Fwy [405] N. on Bristol St., R. on Town Center. [TG: 859 D3])

All the world's a stage! Get a behind-the-scenes look at the 3,000-seat Segerstrom Hall, a beautiful facility, where major symphony concerts, operas, ballets, and Broadway musicals are presented. Take an hour-and-fifteen-minute tour, beginning at the ticket box office, through the theater, to the star's dressing rooms and wardrobe area, and finishing up backstage. Tour routes may vary due to rehearsal and performance schedules and backstage construction. Visitors will also see and learn about the architecture, sculptures, and other art objects that grace the interior and exterior of the Center. For show information, please see ORANGE COUNTY PERFORMING ARTS CENTER (pg. 260).

Hours: Guided tours are offered Wed., and Sat. at 10:30am. Reservations are required for a group of 10 or more people. Closed on some holidays.

Admission: Free

Ages: 10 years and up.

ORANGE COUNTY SANITATION DISTRICT

(714) 962-2411 or (714) 593-7108 / www.ocsd.com

10844 Ellis Avenue, Fountain Valley

(Going S. on San Diego Fwy [405], exit at Euclid Ave., go straight through signal. Going N. on 405, exit at Euclid Ave., turn R., immediately after underpass turn left at signal. Enter main gate and turn R. [TG: 858 G3])

The seventy-five minute education program is geared for high schoolers and up. A fifteen-minute video explains how water is treated. The rest of the program is spent hearing about and seeing the different levels of water treatment. Students learning about microbiology, for example, will look at various water particles under a microscope and identify what they see. Visitors also learn why it's important to conserve. The minimum number for a tour is five; the maximum, twenty-five.

Hours: Tours can be scheduled Mon. - Fri. between 9am - 3pm.

Admission: Free

Ages: Geared for high schoolers and up.

TRINITY BROADCASTING NETWORK

(714) 832-2950 / www.tbn.org

14131 Chambers Road, Tustin

(Exit Santa Ana Fwy [5] S. on Tustin Ranch Rd., L. on Walnut Ave., L. on Franklin Ave., L. on Michelle Dr., L. on Chambers. Trinity owns several buildings in this section, but the tour starts in the main lobby. [TG: 830 D6])

This forty-minute walking tour starts in the plush lobby of T.B.N. The docent takes visitors to the prayer room on the third floor, a room that has cushioned benches around the perimeters and ornately-painted Biblical scenes on the ceilings and walls. In another building across the street, you'll see another prayer room with more of the colorful scenes from the Old and New Testament. The tour guide explains the scenes as well as the work that T.B.N. does. Walk down a hallway lined with photos of Paul and Jan Crouch - hosts of the *Praise the Lord!* program and co-founders of T.B.N. - along with many of their celebrity guests. The studio contains a beautiful living room set for programs that are sometimes filmed before a live audience. The tour ends back across the street in the attractive T.B.N. library where oak shelves are filled with books that the public is welcome to use, but not check out. Tip: See TRINITY CHRISTIAN CITY INTERNATIONAL (pg. 262) for their other, much larger facility which features four of their production movies.

Hours: Tours are offered Mon. - Fri. at 11am or 3pm.

Admission: Free

Ages: 6 years and up.

-----*TRANSPORTATION*-----

ADVENTURES AT SEA YACHT CHARTERS

(800) 229-2412 or (949) 645-BOAT (2628) / www.gondola.com   *$$$$*

3101 W. Coast Highway, suite 209, Newport Beach

(Take Costa Mesa Fwy [55] S. to end where it turns into Newport Blvd. After about 2 miles take right lane which exits to Coast Hwy [1]. Don't go over the bridge, but turn L. on W. Coast Hwy. Adventures at Sea is about 250 yards down on the right. [TG: 672 A2])

These luxurious, electric gondolas are made out of mahogany, have leather seats, a canopy, and are operated by gondoliers either dressed in a tuxedo (depending on the occasion), or in the traditional, Venetian outfit. Take a peaceful cruise along the waterways of Newport Beach Harbor and Newport isle to view the boats and waterfront homes. The gondoliers will begin your cruise from the harbor office, or pick you up at one of several harbor-side restaurants. Adventures at Sea provides a chilled bottle of Martinellis and Godiva chocolates, or it can provide a complete dinner served on china. This is definitely an upscale adventure!

Hours: Open daily, call for reservations.

Admission: $125 for two people, $20 each additional person.

Ages: 4 years and up.

AIR COMBAT USA, INC.

(800) 522-7590 / www.aircombat.com

230 N. Dale Place, Fullerton

(Exit Artesia Fwy [91] or N. Santa Ana Fwy [5] N. on Magnolia, L. on Commonwealth, R. on Dale St., veer right for Dale Pl. Or, exit S. on the Santa Ana Fwy [5], E. on Artesia, R. on Dale Pl. (just after Dale St.). It's at Beach/Aviation, on the N. side of airport. [TG: 738 A7])

$$$$$

If being a Top Gun is your top dream, here's the opportunity to make it a reality. You, perhaps being an unlicenced pilot and leading an otherwise normal life, will actually fly and fight air-to-air combat. "The SIAI Marchetti SF260 is a current production, Italian-built, fighter aircraft. It has 260 horsepower, can fly at 270 MPH, FAA certified to +6 to -3 G's and can perform unlimited aerobatics. It was originally designed to transition student pilots to jet fighters. It is maneuvered by the stick grip complete with gun trigger, identical to the F4 Phantom. The pilot and guest pilot sit side-by-side with dual controls." (Excerpted from Air Combat's brochure.) If all this has your adrenaline pumping, go for it!

You'll be prepped for your flight in a one-hour ground school, which covers the basics, with emphasis on tactical maneuvers. After being fitted with a flight suit, helmet, and parachute, you'll soar for one hour with the birds over Catalina waters. You're actually in control of the aircraft 90% of the time, while receiving constant instruction on how to get the "enemy." After practicing maneuvers, you'll engage in six "g-pulling" (i.e. gut wrenching) dogfights against a real opponent (e.g. friend, spouse, etc.) A direct hit registers through an electronic tracking system, complete with sound effects and smoke trailing from the other aircraft. This is as close to the real thing as you can possible get without being in the military. I will confess that after a few high/low yo-yos and roll overs, I used that special white bag and became part of the 10% that share in this ritual.

After you've landed, and come down from your high, you can view the videos, complete with sound, that were simultaneously recorded from each aircraft. Relive your flight and your "hits" again and again on the copy you receive to take home. This is an unforgettable experience!

Hours: Four classes/flights that accommodate two people each, are offered every day. Class/flight times are usually 7am, 9:30am, noon, and 2:30pm. Call for a specific schedule.

Admission: $995 a flight. Ask about specials, such as discounts for two people, or ready/alert, which means you'll be called to come over A.S.A.P. if there is a cancellation.

Ages: 8 years old and up - large enough to wear a parachute and in good health.

ALFREDO'S

(562) 434-6121

See the entry for ALFREDO'S on page 168.

AMTRAK

(800) USA RAIL (872-7245) / www.dot.ca.gov/hq/rail; www.amtrak.com

Ride the rails! See page xi (in the front) for more information.

BALBOA BOAT RENTALS

(949) 673-7200 / www.boats4rent.com

510 E. Edgewater, Newport Beach

(Take Costa Mesa Fwy [55] to the end, which turns into Newport Blvd., which turns into Balboa Blvd., L. on Island Ave, R. on Edgewater. [TG: 919 B1])

$$$

Rentals includes kayaks - $12 per hour for a single, $20 an hour for a double; pedal boats - $15 an hour; sailboats - $30 an hour for a fourteen footer; motorboats - $40 an hour for a six-passenger boat that doesn't leave the harbor, and $75 an hour for a six-passenger boat that does; electric boats - $60 an hour; and wave runners - $90 an hour.

Hours: Open daily in the summer, 9am - 9pm. Open the rest of the year daily, 10am - 5pm. Call first.

Admission: Prices listed above.

BIKE MAPS (Orange County)

The web site www.labikepaths.com is a fantastic resource. It actually covers all of Southern California, not just L.A., with links to specific counties for maps, bikeways, and other cycling information. Another helpful contact website and phone number is for the State of California Caltrans Office of Bicycle Facilities: (916) 653-0036; www.dot.ca.gov/hq/tpp/offices/bike/contracts.htm. Also try the Orange County Transportation Authority at (800) 636-RIDE (7433) or (714) 636 - RIDE (7433) / www.octa.net. Many Orange County buses are equipped with bike racks. To inquire about trail closures and detours on county-operated off-road trails (i.e. mountain biking), call the EMA - Harbors, Beaches, and Parks Operation at (714) 567-6222 or (714) 834-2400.

BIKE TRAIL: SANTA ANA RIVER

7600 E. La Palma Avenue in Yorba Regional Park, Anaheim to Pacific Coast Highway, Sunset County Beach, Huntington Beach

(Anaheim: Exit Riverside Fwy [91] N. on Imperial Hwy, R. on La Palma. Huntington Beach: Exit San Diego Fwy [405], S.E. on Warner, go to the end and turn R. on P.C.H. [TG: 740 G7 - 826 J7])

The twenty-three mile, mostly easy-riding trail extends from beautiful Yorba Linda Regional Park to a premiere beach, Huntington Beach. Starting at the park, the first few miles are park-scenic, then meander through an adjacent wilderness area with shade trees and flocks of birds. A good stopping point (and maybe turning around area?) is the ten-mile mark, just before the Arrowhead Pond, where a pocket park has the necessary amenities. (Bring your own snacks, though.) Hearty bikers - bike on!

Hours: Open daily, sunrise - sunset.

Admission: Free

Ages: 5 years and up.

CAPTAIN DAVE'S DOLPHIN SAFARI

$$$$$

(949) 488-2828 / www.dolphinsafari.com

34675 Golden Lantern, Dana Point

(Going S. on San Diego Fwy [5], exit on Pacific Coast Highway/Camino Las Ramblas and bear R. onto P.C.H. [Hwy 1] northbound, L. on Dana Point Harbor Dr./Del Obispo St. L. on Golden Lantern. The office is located inside the Dana Wharf Sportfishing building. Going N. on 5, exit on Beach Cities/Camino Las Ramblas into the left lane to continue N. on Pacific Coast Highway [Hwy 1], L. on Dana Point Harbor Dr./Del Obispo St. [TG: 971 J7])

Captain Dave is a marine naturalist who is passionate about dolphins and whales. On board his thirty-five-foot catamaran is an underwater camera, speakers, and a hydrophone for listening to the mammals and playing music to them. The two-and-a-half hour safaris are a time of learning about and observing the dolphins, whales (in season), sea lions, and other sea life in the wild aquarium; the ocean. Models of dolphins and whales, plus whale vertebrae and baleen are also on the vessel. Bring some munchies and a jacket or windbreaker, and set sail.

Hours: Open year round - cruises usually depart at 9am and 11:30am. Call first.

Admission: $40 for adults; $35 for ages 12 and under.

Ages: 6 years and up.

DANA WHARF SPORTFISHING, CHARTERS, AND WHALE WATCHING

$$$$

(949) 496-5794 / www.danawharfsportfishing.com

34675 Golden Lantern, Dana Point

(Going S. on San Diego Fwy [5], exit on Pacific Coast Highway/Camino Las Ramblas and bear R. onto P.C.H. [Hwy 1] northbound, L. on Dana Point Harbor Dr./Del Obispo St., L. on Golden Lantern. Going N. on 5, exit on Beach Cities/Camino Las Ramblas into the left lane to continue N. on Pacific Coast Highway [Hwy 1], L. on Dana Point Harbor Dr./Del Obispo St. [TG: 971 J7])

Cruise the coastal waters in the lovely ninety-five-foot vessel, *Dana Pride*. Ninety-minute cruises are offered for the family on Saturday evenings at sunset and include free appetizers (with a cash bar), and (usually) live music. Two-hour whale-watching cruises are offered in season - the end of November through March. Sportfishing is available as well.

Hours: Cruises are Sat. at sunset year round and on Fri. at sunset in the summer. Call for other cruise hours and options.

Admission: Sunset cruises are $20 for adults; $9 for ages 3 - 12; children 2 years and under are free. Whale watching cruises are $15 for adults; $9 for ages 3 - 12; children 2 years and under are free.

Ages: 6 years and up.

DAVEY'S LOCKER

(949) 673-1434 / www.daveyslocker.com   *$$$$*

400 Main Street, Newport Beach

(Take Costa Mesa Fwy [55] to the end, which turns into Newport Blvd., which turns into Balboa Blvd., L. on Main St. [TG: 919 C2])

Skiff rentals, fishing, and whale-watching cruises (the end of December through March) are offered here.

Admission: $15 for adults for the two-and-a-half whale-watching cruise; $10 for ages 4 - 12. $47 for a half day for skiffs.

FUN ZONE BOAT COMPANY

(949) 673-0240 / www.funzoneboats.com   *$$*

600 E. Edgewater Avenue, Newport Beach

(Take Costa Mesa Fwy [55] to the end, which turns into Newport Blvd., which turns into Balboa Blvd., L. on Island Ave, R. on Edgewater. [TG: 919 B1])

Board the *Pavilion Queen* or *Pavilion Belle* for a forty-five-minute cruise that is perfect for kids as they'll go around Balboa Island and, hopefully, see some sea lions. On the other forty-five-minute cruise see several star's homes and hear the history of Balboa Island Peninsula. The ninety-minute cruise is a combination of both cruises - the best of both worlds. One-hour sunset cruises and whale-watching cruises (December through March) are also available. Special sightseeing tours are available in December during the Parade of Lights - what a view!

Hours: Summer tours depart daily every half hour from 11am - 7pm. Sunset cruises leave at 7pm. The rest of the year, tours departure every hour from 11am - 4pm.

Admission: $6 for adults for the forty-five-minute cruise; $2 for ages 5 - 11; children 4 and under are free. $9 for adults for the ninety-minute cruise; $2 for ages 5 - 11; children 4 and under are free. Sunset cruises are $7 for adults; $2 for kids. Whale-watching cruises are $14 for adults; $8 for kids. Closed December 24 - 25.

Ages: 4 years and up.

METROLINK (Orange County)

See the entry for METROLINK (Los Angeles County) on page 173 for details.

NEWPORT HARBOR TOUR, BALBOA PAVILION

(949) 673-5245   *$$*

400 Main Street, Newport Beach

(Take Costa Mesa Fwy [55] to the end, which turns into Newport Blvd., which turns into Balboa Blvd., L. on Main St. [TG: 919 C2])

Forty-five and ninety-minute cruises are available here. Depending on the length of your cruise, you'll see stars' homes such as George Burns and John Wayne; Pirate's Cove, where Gilligan's Island was filmed; and tour around six of the eight islands in the immediate area.

Hours: Daily departures are 11am - 7pm in the summer; 11am - 4pm the rest of the year. Closed Christmas.

Admission: $6 for adults for the forty-five-minute cruise; $4 for seniors; $1 for ages 5 - 12; children 4 and under are free. $8 for adults for the ninety-minute cruise; $4 for seniors; $1 for ages 5 - 12; children 4 and under are free. Certain discounts available through AAA.

Ages: 4 years and up.

NEWPORT LANDING SPORTFISHING

(949) 675-0550 $$$$

309 Palm, suite F, Newport Beach

(Take Costa Mesa Fwy [55] to the end, which turns into Newport Blvd., which turns into Balboa Blvd., L. on Palm. [TG: 919 B2])

Two-and-a-half hour whale-watching cruises are available here the end of December through mid-April.

Hours: The boats departs during the season Mon. - Fri. at 10am and 1pm; Sat. - Sun., 9am, noon, and 2:30pm.

Admission: $14 for adults; $10 for seniors and children 12 and under.

OCEAN INSTITUTE

(949) 496-2274 / www.ocean-institute.org

24200 Dana Point Harbor Drive, Dana Point

See the entry for OCEAN INSTITUTE, on page 244, for details about boat outings.

PADDLEPOWER

(949) 675-1215 / www.paddlepowerkayaks.com $$$

500 W. Balboa Boulevard, Newport Beach

(Take Costa Mesa Fwy [55] to the end, which turns into Newport Blvd., which turns into Balboa Blvd. [TG: 919 B2])

Kayak rentals are available here, at a store dedicated to ocean sports, particularly kayaking.

Hours: Open Mon., Wed. - Fri., 10am - 5pm; Sat., 9am - 5pm; Sun., 10am - 5pm. Closed Tues. Usually open an hour later in the summer.

Admission: Prices start at $12 an hour for a single, $18 an hour for a double.

RESORT WATERSPORTS

(800) 585-0747 or (949) 729-1150 $$$$

1131 Backbay Drive, Newport Dunes Resort, Newport Beach

(Take Newport Fwy [55] S.W. to end, which turns into Newport Blvd., L. on W. Coast Hwy., L. on Jamboree Rd., L. on Backbay Dr. Or, from Corona Del Mar Fwy [73], exit S.W. on Jamboree Rd., R. on Backbay Dr. before E. Coast Hwy. [TG: 889 D6])

Located in NEWPORT DUNES RESORT (see pg. 199), this rental facility has everything you need to make your day at the beach more exciting. Going rates are: $20 an hour for pedal boats, $65 for electric-powered boats, $18 an hour for windsurfers, $17 an hour for sail boats, $13 an hour for single kayaks, and $16 an hour for double kayaks. Bike rentals, skate rentals, and California chariots (a cross between a skateboard and scooter) start at $6 an hour. They also offer guided kayak tours of an adjacent wildlife estuary reserve every Sunday at 10am, weather permitting. In the estuary, you can see crabs, blue herons, snowy egrets, and other birds and animals in their natural habitat. We took this tour and learned why this reserve is becoming endangered, as well as some of the clean up projects that we can get involved with. A two-hour tour is $20 per person; $15 for ages 12 years and under. What a work-out for those of us not physically fit! But it is also a fun and educational way to spend some family time together.

Hours: Open in the summer daily, 9am - 8pm. Open year round on the weekends, usually from 10am - 5pm. Call for other hours of operation.

Admission: Prices are stated above, plus a $8 per vehicle entrance fee.

VOYAGES OF REDISCOVERY (Orange County)

(800) 401-7835 or (415) 331-3214 $$/$$$$$
Newport Beach

See VOYAGES OF REDISCOVERY (pg. 175) for details.

YOUNG EAGLES PROGRAM (Fullerton)

(562) 570-2679 / www.youngeagles.com
N. Dale Place, Fullerton

(Exit Artesia Fwy [91] or N. Santa Ana Fwy [5] N. on Magnolia, L. on Commonwealth, R. on Dale St., veer right for Dale Pl. Or, exit S. on the Santa Ana Fwy [5], E. on Artesia, R. on Dale Pl. (just after Dale St.). It's at Beach/Aviation, on the N. side of airport. [TG: 738 A7])

See the entry for YOUNG EAGLES PROGRAM (Pacoima) on page 177 for details.

Hours: Usually offered every other month on the Sat. following the second Thurs. (honest!) at about The chapter alternates with the Long Beach Airport.

Admission: Free

Ages: 8 - 17 years.

-----ZOOS AND ANIMALS-----

CENTENNIAL FARM

(714) 708-1618 / www.ocfair.com/ocfec/centennialfarm/home_farm.asp
88 Fair Drive, Costa Mesa

(Exit Costa Mesa Fwy [55] S.W. on Newport Blvd., R. on Fair Dr., through Gate #1. It's on the Orange County Fair Grounds. [TG: 859 B7])

This outdoor working farm has pigs, chickens, sheep, bunnies, ducks, Clydesdale horses, llamas, and a buffalo. During the springtime, in particular, be on the lookout for the many animal babies that are born here. The bee observatory is fascinating and with their nonstop motion, it's easy to see where the term "~~busy boys~~" oops, I mean "busy bees," came from.

Walk around the grounds to learn about other aspects of farming. Younger kids will probably be amazed to see vegetables such as carrots, zucchini, lettuce, and corn being grown, not already picked and packaged as in the grocery stores. (Please do not pick the vegetables or feed the animals.) The Millennium Barn has horse stalls, a tack room, a small museum area, and a milking parlor. Volunteers are usually posted at stations to answer questions. A few picnic tables are here at the farm too, so pack a sack lunch. The huge parking lot is usually empty at this time, so bring skates or bikes.

A ninety-minute tour of the farm is available for grades kindergarten and up, for groups of ten or more students. One day a month is reserved for preschoolers. The tour includes walking all around the farm, milking a cow, going into the main building and seeing chicks hatch in the incubator, planting a seed (and then taking it home), and learning about the food groups. Reservations are required. The four-hour "Agademics" tour, for fourth through sixth graders, is a more in-depth look at farming and includes more hands-on activities. Students attending this tour need to bring a lunch. We have enjoyed all of their tours.

Hours: The farm is open to the public August through May, Mon. - Fri., 1pm - 4pm; Sat. - Sun., 9am - 4pm. Tours for kindergartners and up are given mid-September through May, Mon. - Fri. at 9am and 11am. Agademics is offered Mon. - Fri. at 9am. The farm is closed to the public in June. It's open in July only with paid admission to the Orange County Fair (see pg. 592). Access may be limited on some weekends due to special events.

Admission: Free. All tours are also free.

Ages: 2 years and up during public hours; K - 6th graders for most tours; Pre-K for their twice-a-month tour.

FRIENDS OF THE SEA LION MARINE MAMMAL CENTER

(949) 494-3050 / www.fslmmc.org

20612 Laguna Canyon Road, Laguna Beach

(Exit San Diego Fwy [405] or Santa Ana Fwy [5] S. on Laguna Canyon Rd. [Hwy 133]. It's just S. of El Toro Rd. [TG: 920 J5])

This Center is a small safe harbor for sea lions and harbor seals that are abandoned, ailing, or in need of medical attention. The animals are kept outside in small outdoor pools until they are ready to be released back into the wild. This is a good opportunity for kids to see these animals up-close, while learning more about them and the effect that we have on our oceans (i.e. their habitats). The volunteers are great at answering the numerous (and sometimes off-the-wall) questions kids ask.

Feeding time, usually around 3pm, is lively as the sea lions go wild, barking in anticipation of a meal. (It sounds like mealtime at our house.) There are usually between five to twelve mammals here, but lots more arrive toward the end of pupping season, which is the end of February through July. One-hour educational programs that feature a slide presentation and a guided tour are $20 plus $3 per person; children 4 and under are free. Ask about summer day camp and after-school programs. (Also see LAGUNA KOI PONDS, on page 273, located just north of the center.)

Hours: Open daily, 10am - 4pm.
Admission: Free; donations gladly accepted.
Ages: 3 years and up.

JONES FAMILY MINI FARM / LOS RIOS DISTRICT

(949) 831-6550 / www.sanjuancapistrano.net/JonesFarm

31791 Los Rios Street, San Juan Capistrano

(Exit the San Diego Fwy [5] W. on Ortega Hwy [74], L. on Del Obispo, over the railroad tracks, R. on Paseo Adelanto, which is the backside of the farm. [TG: 972 C1])

This working "mini-farm" will become a favorite stopping place whenever you visit San Juan Capistrano. Inside the barn is a small petting pen with goats, sheep, rabbits, and guinea pigs. The farm also has a few other animals to pet through the fence pens, such as horses, sheep, and a pot-bellied pig. Chickens, geese, and a few cats roam the grounds. Feed is available to purchase for the animals for $1. Starting at 8 months old, kids up to eighty pounds can ride a pony around a track. Scale model train rides around the farm and hay rides around historic Los Rios street are also available. For a birthday party with a real farm, or western flavor, rent the large outside picnic area for $100 for two hours.

In front of the farm is the 100-year-old Olivares Home, and next door is the O'Neill Historic Museum, (949) 493-8444. Older kids might enjoy a walk through these Victorian homes to see antique furniture and clothing. You can park your car at MISSION SAN JUAN CAPISTRANO (see pg. 242), which is just down the street. Note that the Amtrak depot is just a block away, if you're interested in taking a train to this city. Either way, enjoy a short walk to the farm and around this quaint, historic area.

Hours: The Farm is open Wed. - Sun., 11am - 4pm. Closed rainy days, Thanksgiving, and Christmas. O'Neill Historic Museum is open Tues. - Fri., 9am - noon and 1pm - 4pm; Sun., noon - 3pm.
Admission: Free to walk around outside of the farm. $1 entrance to go inside the petting farm; children under 2 are free. Pony rides are $2 for one lap around the track. Train rides are $2 per person. O'Neill Museum is free; donations of $1 per person are appreciated.
Ages: All

LAGUNA KOI PONDS

(949) 494-5107 / www.lagunakoi.com

20452 Laguna Canyon Road, Laguna Beach

(Exit San Diego Fwy [405] or Santa Ana Fwy [5] S. on Laguna Canyon Rd. [Hwy 133]. It's just S. of El Toro Rd. [TG: 920 J5])

This fun little stop off has several cement tanks filled with Koi fish and a store carrying fish supplies. We enjoy just looking at these colorful fish with their beautiful patterns. Who knows, you may want to purchase a few to raise at home. You may also feed them at certain times - 25¢ for a handful of pellets. It's fun to watch their large mouths open quickly and bite at the food. Combine a trip here with a visit to the FRIENDS OF THE SEA LION MARINE MAMMAL CENTER (see pg. 273), which is located just south of the ponds.

Hours: Open Mon. - Sat., 9am - 5pm; Sun., 11am - 5pm

Admission: Free

Ages: All

LOS ALAMITOS RACE COURSE

(714) 995-1234 / www.losalamitos.com

4961 E. Katella Avenue, Los Alamitos

(From San Gabriel River Fwy [605], exit E. on Willow/Katella. From San Diego Fwy [405] or Garden Grove Fwy [22], exit N. on Valley View, L. on Katella. [TG: 797 C3])

Thoroughbreds, quarter horses, Arabian horses, and harness racing are the attractions here. Have your child cheer for his favorites! Call for schedule information.

Hours: Open year round - call for specific races and hours.

Admission: $3 for adults, or $5 for the clubhouse; kids 15 and under are free. Free parking.

Ages: 4 years and up.

MAGNOLIA BIRD FARM (Anaheim)

(714) 527-3387

8990 Cerritos, Anaheim

(Going N. on Santa Ana Fwy [5], exit W. on Ball Rd., L. on Magnolia, R. on Cerritos. Going S. on 5 or E. on Artesia Fwy [91], exit S. on Magnolia, R. on Cerritos. It's on the corner of Cerritos and Magnolia. [TG: 798 B1])

Take your flock of kids to visit their fine feathered friends at the Magnolia Bird Farm pet shop. Birds here range from common doves and canaries to more exotic cockatoos and macaws. A small-bird aviary is located just outside the main building.

The Bird Farm has bird accessories, including a wide assortment of bird cages. Here's a craft idea: Buy a simple wooden cage for your kids to paint and decorate, then fill it with bird seed, and hang it up in your backyard. While you're here, have your kids take the bird challenge - see if they can get one of the talking birds to actually speak to them! (Also see MAGNOLIA BIRD FARM (Riverside) on page 301.)

Hours: Open Tues. - Sat., 9am - 5pm.

Admission: Free

Ages: All

ORANGE COUNTY ZOO

(714) 633-2022 or (714) 973-6847 / www.ocparks.com/oczoo

1 Irvine Park Road, Orange

(Exit Newport Fwy [55] E. on Chapman, N. on Jamboree, which ends at Irvine Regional Park. [TG: 800 J3])

Take a trip to the zoo while you're in the park! Tucked away in the massive IRVINE REGIONAL PARK (see pg. 226) is the eight-acre Orange County Zoo. The zoo has barnyard animals such as sheep, goats, and pigs to pet through fence pens. Food dispensers are here, too. The main section of the zoo features animals native to the southwestern United States, such as mountain lions, bobcats, deer, beaver, coyotes, an Island fox, two black bears, porcupines, and a variety of birds, including a bald eagle and golden eagle.

Hours: Open daily, 10am - 3:30pm. Closed New Year's Day and Christmas.

Admission: $1 for ages 6 and up; children 5 and under are free. This admission is in addition to the vehicle entrance fee to the park.

Ages: All

SANTA ANA ZOO

(714) 835-7484 / www.santaanazoo.org

1801 E. Chestnut Avenue, Santa Ana

(Going S. on Santa Ana Fwy [5], exit at 4th St. go straight on Mabury St., which turns into Elk Ln., L. on Chestnut. Going N. on 5, exit W. on 1st St., L. on Elk Ln., L. on Chestnut. It's at Prentice Park. [TG: 829 H3])

Lions and tigers and bears - not here! This small zoo, however, is perfect for young children. They can easily walk around it, see all the animals, and still have of time to play on the playground, all within just a few hours. The Santa Ana Zoo houses llamas; cavies; small mammals, such as porcupines; birds, including bald eagles; fruit bats; sloths; and a wide variety of monkeys - our personal favorites. The cages and animals are not far off in the distance, but right along the pathways, so you can see (and hear) all the antics. Walk through the wonderful aviary where you can observe beautiful and exotic birds close up. The Children's Zoo has pigs, goats, and sheep to pet through pens, plus reptiles and amphibians to look at. Note that a new children's zoo area is under construction. It will have a large red barn as an education center with classrooms, labs, and a hatchery for chicks (to look at and to hold newborns). There will be more run-around space and fun displays and activities, like crawling inside a huge turtle shell, hearing the world through rabbit ears, riding a carousel, and pony rides.

Kids can ride a real elephant once round a small trail between 11am to 3pm on most weekends, and holiday Mondays, October through May for $3 per person. Scale model train rides around part of the zoo are available Friday through Sunday from 11am to 3pm for $1 per person. The on-site playground has a small climbing hut, slides, and turtle statues. The gift shop has a wonderful variety of animal-oriented merchandise. Purchase lunch at the snack bar, which is usually open, or enjoy a sack lunch right outside the zoo gates at the adjoining Prentice Park which offers picnic tables, grassy areas, and shade trees.

Breakfast with the Beasts, offered a few times a year, is a Saturday morning program offered for ages 3 and older. It includes a light breakfast, a guided tour, and a chance to feed some animals in the Children's Zoo. The fee is $8 per person. Looking for a different kind of sleepover this summer? Enjoy the Roar and Snore at the zoo where nocturnal visits with the animals, dissecting an owl pellet, a continental breakfast, and making fast friends is all included in the time and price. A variety of other educational and interactive programs for kids are also offered throughout the year.

Hours: Open Mon. - Sun., 10am - 4pm. (The grounds close at 5pm) Closed rainy days, New Year's Day, the fourth Sat. in August, and Christmas.

Admission: $5 for adults; $3 for seniors and ages 3 - 12; children 2 and under and the physically impaired are free. AAA discounts are available.

Ages: All

RIVERSIDE COUNTY

Once a grove of orange trees that spawned a thriving citrus industry, the southern Inland Empire is now very diverse. It claims the city of Temecula, a fast-growing community that still maintains its small-town feel; historic downtown Riverside with its famous Mission Inn; and Palm Springs (and the surrounding desert cities) - an oasis that's no mirage. With all of the county's attractions and small cities, Riverside still has plenty of open spaces left to explore.

Note: Since the Palm Springs area is often a multi-day destination, its attractions are listed in a separate section in the back of this county starting at page 301.

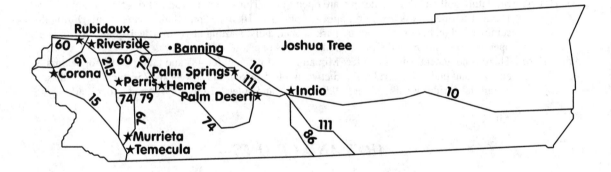

-----*AMUSEMENT PARKS*-----

CASTLE PARK
(909) 785-3000 or (909) 785-3031 / www.castlepark.com
3500 Polk Street, Riverside
(Exit Riverside Fwy [91] N. on La Sierra Ave., R. on Diana St., L. on Polk St. It's between the Galleria at Tyler and La Sierra Ave., and visible from the freeway. [TG: 744 F1])

Castle Park has a lot of action packed into its twenty-five acres. The compactness of the park makes it easy to walk all around. It has four scenic and challenging eighteen-hole miniature golf courses, complete with waterfalls, a miniature Big Ben, Dutch windmill, and western fort. The three-level arcade has over 200 video games and games of skill, plus a redemption center. Check out the Ghost Blaster ride within the arcade where riders shoot ghosts with their laser "Boo Blaster" to receive redemption point.

The rest of the park contains over thirty rides and attractions. The rides include the log ride (which will get you wet), a huge carousel, roller coasters, a swing ride, airplane ride, a free fall, the sea dragon ride, a Ferris wheel, two train rides, and lots more. There are plenty of "big kids" rides, as well as delightful kiddie rides. The atmosphere here reminds me of Coney Island in that the flashy rides are interspersed with carnival-type games. Check out the reproduction of the Liberty Bell, proclaiming liberty through all the park. Special events and package deals are on-going at Castle Park, so call for a schedule and more information.

The massive BIG TOP FOOD 'N' FUN RESTAURANT (see pg. 279) looks like a circus Big Top, and serves pizza and other food.

Hours: Miniature golf and the arcade area are open Sun. - Thurs.,10am - 10pm; Fri. - Sat., 10am - 11pm. The ride park is open Fri., 5pm - 10pm; Sat., 10am - 10pm; Sun., 10am - 8pm. During the summer and on holidays the entire park is open daily, starting at 10am. Big Top Restaurant is open the same hours as the ride park, but closes one hour earlier.

Admission: There is no general admission fee. Miniature golf is $5.99 for 48" and taller; $4.99 for seniors and 47" and under. Each ride takes between 3 to 5 tickets and tickets are 75¢ each, or purchase an unlimited rides wristband for $19.99 for 48" and taller; $14.99 for 47" and under. Parking is $5.

Ages: All

-----*ARTS AND CRAFTS*-----

COLOR ME MINE (Riverside)
(909) 684-2645; (877) COLOR ME (265-6763) - for a listing of all locations. / www.colormemine.com
5225 Canyon Crest Drive, #3, Riverside
(Going N. on Moreno Valley Fwy [215], exit E. at Martin Luther King Blvd., go straight on El Cerrito Dr., L. on Canyon Crest. Going S. on 215, exit W. on Martin Luther King Blvd., immediate L. on Canyon Crest. [TG: 686 D7])

See the entry for COLOR ME MINE (Los Angeles County) on page 6 for details.

PAINTED EARTH
(909) 676-2447
27493 Ynez Road, Temecula
(Exit Temecula Valley Fwy [15] E. on Rancho California Rd., L. on Ynez Rd. [TG: 958 H6])

Paint your own ceramic masterpiece at Painted Earth. Choose from decorative figurines to microwavable plates and mugs. All the paints, brushes, and glazes are included in the studio fee, so feel free to express yourself and enjoy a lasting, hand-crafted treasure.

Hours: Open Mon. - Thurs., 11am -9pm; Fri. - Sat., 11am - 10pm; Sun., 11am - 6pm.

Admission: The price of the item - for example $4 for figurines, $10 a bowl or coffee mug, or $12 a dish - and a $6 all-day studio fee, which includes the price of glazing.

Ages: 4 years and up.

-----EDIBLE ADVENTURES-----

BIG TOP FOOD 'N' FUN RESTAURANT
(909) 785-3090 or (909) 785-3000 / www.castlepark.com

3500 Polk Street, Riverside

(Exit Riverside Fwy [91] N. on La Sierra Ave., R. on Magnolia Ave., R. on Polk St. It's adjacent to CASTLE PARK. [TG: 744 F1])

For big time fun, come eat at Big Top Restaurant! The good-sized restaurant resembles a circus big top, complete with a lifelike statue of a circus elephant outside. The inside feels like a circus, too. (Then again, meal times at our house always feel like a circus what with balancing plates of food, kids acting clownish, etc.) Red and white are the predominant colors. Overhead are stuffed animals in acrobatic poses.

The food is good, with pizza being the featured item - $16 for a medium, two-topping pizza. A salad bar, burgers, hot dogs, chicken nuggets, and sandwiches are also available. Kids love to be entertained at meal time (any time!), so the Big Top bear mascot occasionally appears on stage for a short show. There are a few kiddie rides, and a small arcade room with "G-rated" games, plus a redemption center. See CASTLE PARK (pg. 278) for a description of the adjacent park.

Hours: Open in the summer daily, 10am - 9pm. Open the rest of the year, Fri., 5pm - 9pm; Sat., 10am - 9pm; Sun., 10am - 8pm.

Ages: 2 years and up.

CHUCK E. CHEESE
See the entry for CHUCK E. CHEESE on page 12 for details.

FARMER'S MARKETS
See the entry for FARMER'S MARKETS on page 14 for details.

THE OLD SPAGHETTI FACTORY (Riverside)
(909) 784-4417 / www.osf.com

3191 Mission Inn Avenue, Riverside

(Going N. on Riverside Fwy [91], exit E. on University Ave., L. on Vine St., R. on Mission Inn. Going S. on 91, exit at University, go E. on Mission Inn. [TG: 685 H4])

See the entry for THE OLD SPAGHETTI FACTORY (Los Angeles County) on page 19 for details.

RUBY'S (Palm Springs)
(760) 406-RUBY; All locations - (800) HEY RUBY (439-7829) / www.rubys.com

155 S. Palm Canyon Drive, Palm Springs

(Exit Interstate 10 S. on Indian Canyon Dr., R. on Tahquitz Canyon Wy., L. on Palm Canyon Dr. [Hwy 111]. [TG: 786 D2])

See the entry for RUBY'S (Orange County) on page 206 for details.

RUBY'S (Riverside County)
(909) 359-RUBY; All locations - (800) HEY RUBY (439-7829) / www.rubys.com

1298 Galleria at Tyler, # G19, Riverside

(Exit Riverside Fwy [91] N. on Tyler St. It's in the mall. [TG: 714 G7])

See the entry for RUBY'S (Orange County) on page 206 for details.

TOM'S FARMS
(909) 277- 9992 or (909) 277-4422 - general info; (909) 277-4103 - Tom's Hamburgers; (909) 277-2857 - Senor Toms' Mexican Restaurant / www.tomsfarms.com

23900 Temescal Canyon Road, Corona

(Exit Corona Fwy [15] S. on Temescal Canyon Rd., past the fast food restaurants at the corner. [TG: 804 D5])

Tom's Farms consists of several separate buildings, each one selling different products. The front building has farm fresh produce, dried fruit, nuts, and candies. This is a delicious stop. The adjacent Bird's Nest is unusual with its various live birds and related bird items for sale. Senor Tom's Mexican Restaurant offers breakfast, lunch, and dinner - the whole enchilada. Menu items include breakfast burritos ($4.49 - $5.25), chimichangas ($5.49), plus tacos, salads, quesadillas, and more either in a combo plate or a la carte. Kid's meals are $3.29 for a choice of burrito, quesadilla, taco, or taquitos. If you prefer American-style food, the small restaurant, Tom's Hamburgers, offers large portions of food. Tasty hamburgers start at $3.20. Kids have their choice of a corn dog, grilled cheese sandwich, chicken strips, or a burger, plus fries and a drink for an average of $3. An outside eating area is set up around a small pond that has ducks. Beyond the pond are a few penned farm animals to pet. A wine and cheese store also offers baked goods and a gourmet deli. On weekends only, the farm takes on the feel of a small "old tyme" country fair with craft booths, face painting, and shaved ice, as well as carousel rides, a Ferris wheel, and train rides through ten acres of countryside and under a bridge. The train is a reproduction of an 1800's steamer. (Some of the rides might be open during the week, too - call first.) Come grab a snack or eat a meal at this "farm" with a folksy ambiance.

Hours: Open daily, 8am - 8pm. The weekend fair happens March through December.
Admission: Free
Ages: All

-----FAMILY PAY AND PLAY-----

ADAMS KART TRACK
(800) 350-3826 / www.adamskarttrack.net $$$$
5292 24th Street, Riverside
(Exit Pomona Fwy [60] N. on Market St. It's on the corner of 24th St. and Market. [TG: 645 F7])

The main track, which is six-tenths of a mile of turns, twists, and straight track, is a great introduction to real racing. This race track school offers classes for kart racing, available for kids 5 years and up. Call for a class schedule.

Hours: The track is open Mon. - Tues., Thurs. - Fri., 10am - 5pm; Sat. - Sun., noon - 5pm. Closed Wed.
Admission: Bring your own kart for the main track - $25 a day for non-members; $20 for members; $20 for an extra passenger; $8 for pit person/spectator. Classes start at $75 for two hours of instruction and racing.
Ages: 5 years and up.

ADRENALINE GAMES
(909) 461-8932 / www.adrenalinepaintball.com $$$$$
41185 Golden Gate Circle, Murrieta
(Exit Temecula Valley Fwy [15] S.W. on Murrieta Hot Springs, L. on Madison, L. on Golden Gate. It's located in the old Edge Sports Park. [TG: 958 E2])

An innovative company converted two outdoor lighted hockey rinks into two paintball fields, complete with a sand base and perimeter fences. Inflatable obstacles are strategically placed and used as cover to sneak up on an "enemy," who is probably laying in wait, ready to ambush. Playing paintball, day or night, certainly gives participants an adrenaline rush. Don't forget to wear protective clothing and face gear. A parental waiver, available on-line, must be signed for participants ages 17 and under. Thursday night is for "Young Guns" only, ages 10 to 16.

Hours: Open Wed. - Fri., 6pm - 11pm; Sat., 9am - 4pm and 6pm - 11pm; Sun., 9am - 4pm.
Admission: $15 for walk ons with their own gear; $30 for those who need to rent all the equipment - gun, goggles, first tank of CO_2. Paintballs are an additional $5 for 100.
Ages: Must be 10 years or older.

CHUCK E. CHEESE
See the entry for CHUCK E. CHEESE on page 12 for details.

JUNGLE-ISLAND

(800) 5JUNGLE (558-6453) or (909) 461-8932 / www.jungle-island.com

14881 Temescal Canyon Road, Corona

(Exit the Corona Fwy [15] S. on Lake St, R. on Temescal. [TG: 835 F4])

$$$$$

It's a jungle out there! Actually, there are twelve different, themed playing fields on fifty-six acres and the jungle is only one of them. The Tank field has mock tanks, a maze, and a real military "crashed" helicopter. Valley field has a mock battle field with a camouflage truck, ambulance, defensive hill, foxholes, and more. Pipes field has countless cement pipes. Volcano field looks like there was an eruption. City field looks like an inner city with vehicles and buildings. There is also Amazon field, Island field, and more. Games last about twenty minutes.

A snack bar serving pizza and beverages is on the premises. A picnic table is out front. Wear appropriate attire - old, long sleeve shirts, jeans, and running boots. A parental waiver, available on-line, is necessary for ages 17 and under.

     Hours: Open Fri., 6pm - 11pm; Sat., 9am - 4pm and 6pm - 11pm; Sun., 9am - 4pm.

Admission: $20 for walk ons with their own equipment. Package deals, which include all the necessary gear, start at $35. Paintballs are additional $5 for 100.

     Ages: Must be 10 years or older.

LASER TAG FAMILY FUN CENTER

(909) 737-1211

400 N. Main Street, Corona

(Exit Riverside Fwy [91] N. on Main St. [TG: 743 D4])

$$

This casual fun center offers a large central room with some arcade games, air hockey, foosball, a pool table, a dart board, and other games to play. The games aren't jam-packed in here so the atmosphere isn't as frenzied as some other arcade-oriented places. A good-sized darkened room contains a laser tag arena which has neon-lit obstacles to hide behind and plot strategy. Players are vested and armed as they aim and shoot other players with laser guns to accumulate points.

     Hours: Open Sun. - Thurs., 10am - 10pm; Fri. - Sat., 10am - midnight.

Admission: Free admission. Laser tag is $4.75 per game. Other games cost about 50¢, on average.

     Ages: 6 years and up.

S.C. VILLAGE PAINTBALL PARK

(949) 489-9000 / www.scvillage.com

Hellman Road & River Road, Corona

(From Riverside Fwy [91], exit N. on Lincoln Blvd., L. on River Rd. From Ontario Fwy [15], exit E. on 6th, which turns into Norco Dr., which turns into Corydon Ave., R. on River Rd. From River Rd., make sure to stay L. on River Rd. as the main road turns into Archibald Ave. [TG: 712 J5])

$$$$$

Rambos, Terminators, Xenas, and people from all other walks of life are invited to play paintball on this massive, sixty-acre playing field with twenty different settings. Battle it out in desert terrain, jungle tracts, or even in the city of Beirut. Each field has special props which may include a downed helicopter, ambulance, tents, tanks, radar towers, huts, bridges, tunnels, swamp, camouflage netting, and acres of woods or brush. In this updated version of Capture the Flag, paintball guns and non-toxic gelatin capsules (i.e. paintballs) are used. Two teams compete against each other using the props to run around and hide behind. The object of the game is to somehow capture your opponents' flag and return it to your team's flag station. However, if you are hit with a paintball (which can sting), you are out of the game. Games last between twenty to thirty minutes. All games have referees to insure safe and fair play. There are two levels of play - beginner and advanced. Come by yourself or with a group of friends. All amenities, including a food concession, equipment, and supplies are on-site. Participants under 18 must have a waiver signed by a parent or guardian.

Hours: Open to the public, Sat. - Sun., 7:30am - 4pm. Weekday games are by appointment only.

Admission: General admission is $20 per person for half day; $25 for all day. Rental equipment varies in price according to what you want. Goggles/face masks (mandatory) are $5; jumpsuits are $7; guns range from $10 - $15; and paintballs start at $11 for 200 rounds. Package deals are available. For instance, a $45 starter package includes half-day admission, full mask, pump rifle, 200 rounds of paintball, and initial tank of CO_2 air. For an additional $5, play all day.

Ages: At least 10 years old.

TOMBSTONE PAINTBALL PARK

(909) 737-0899 / members.cox.net/tombstonepaintball/home.htm

Auto Center Drive, Corona

$$$$$

(Exit Riverside Fwy [91] N. on Auto Center/Serfas Club. Club house is less than ½ mile from fwy. [TG: 642 G4])

On my tombstone I want written, "She painted the town before going down." I don't really want that on my tombstone, but paintball is a fun and somewhat intense game. The eleven fields include a Civil War theme with stacked logs as obstacles and hiding places; Sup' Airball which uses large inflatable shaped objects as obstacles; and Urban Chaos with wood framed buildings and a few cars. An on-site clubhouse offers a respite from the game and cold drinks. A parental waiver, available on-line, must be signed for ages 17 and under.

Hours: Open Sat. - Sun. and holidays, 8am - 4pm.

Admission: $20 with your own equipment; $40 for a full package deal (i.e. guns, air, and mask), plus $7 for 100 paintballs.

Ages: Must be 10 years and up.

-----GREAT OUTDOORS-----

ALLIANCE SKATE PARK / MCVICKER CANYON PARK

(909) 674-9000 / www.skateparkofelsinore.com

29335 Grand Avenue, Lake Elsinore

$$$

(Going S. on Corona Fwy [15], exit S. on Lake St which turns into Grand. Going N. on 15, exit E. on Hwy 74, stay on 74 as it turns R. then L., turn R. on Grand Ave. when 74 turns L. again. [TG: 865 F5])

This large, lighted, supervised skate park is on a concrete slab with ramps made of skatelite surface. The street course has grind rails, a mini half pipe, a half pyramid, and several planters and ledges. All the elements are spaced out so there is plenty of room to skate, maneuver, and gain speed. BMX riders are allowed on the course at certain times. Sessions are three hours long and skaters and bikers must wear safety gear (rentals are available), and have a signed parental waiver, if 17 or younger. The rest of the park consists of baseball fields, a small playground, and some picnic tables.

Hours: Open Mon. - Fri., 3pm - 9pm; Sat. - Sun., 11am -9pm.

Admission: $15 a year membership.

Ages: 7 years and up for the skate park.

ARLINGTON PARK

(909) 826-2000 / www.ci.riverside.ca.us/park_rec

3860 Van Buren Boulevard, Riverside

!

(Exit Riverside Fwy [91] N. on Van Buren Blvd. It's just past Magnolia, on the W. side of the street. [TG: 714 H6])

This nice corner park has an older style playground and well-used shuffleboard courts. It also has basketball courts, tennis courts, barbecue pits, and a swimming pool.

Hours: The park is open daily. The pool is open in the summer, Mon. - Sat., 1pm - 5pm; plus Tues. and Thurs., 6pm - 8pm.

Admission: Free to the park. Swim sessions are $2.25 for adults; $1 for ages 6 - 17; 75¢ for children 5 and under.

Ages: All

CALIFORNIA CITRUS STATE HISTORIC PARK

(909) 780-6222 / parks.ca.gov

Van Buren Boulevard and Dufferin Avenue, Riverside

(Exit the Riverside Fwy [91] S. on Van Buren Blvd., L. on Dufferin Ave., R. into the park. [TG: 745 B2])

The park, with its acres of citrus groves, captures the spirit of Riverside's slogan, "The land of citrus and sunshine." The main section is beautifully landscaped, has a big, grassy area for running around and for picnicking, a small visitor's center, and a gift shop / museum in a restored home. The museum features mostly historical photographs with narrative.

There are two, mile-long hiking trails. The Arroyo Trail goes through a wooded area and creek bed, up towards the dam. The Knolls Trail takes the high, non-shady road, past Grower's Mansion (a restaurant) towards the dam. Neither trail is very strenuous; just good, short nature hikes. Don't forget to stop and smell the oranges along the way!

Hours: The park is open in the summer daily, 8am - 7pm; open the rest of the year, 8am - 5pm. The nature center is open weekends, 11am - 3pm.

Admission: Free

Ages: 2 years and up.

DIAMOND VALLEY LAKE

(800) 273-3430 - recorded info; (800) 211-9863 - visitors center / www.mwd.dst.ca.us

300 Newport Road or Domenigoni Parkway, Hemet

(To get to the overlook: Going S. on Escondido Expressway [215], exit E. on Hwy 74, S. on Hwy 79/Winchester Rd., L. on Domenigoni/Construction Rd. Going N. on Temecula Valley Fwy [15], exit N. on Hwy 79/Winchester Rd., R. on Domenigoni/Construction. To get to the visitors center: Exit 74 S. on State St., R. on Newport Rd. From San Diego, after turning R. on Domenigoni, R. on State St., R. on Newport. [TG: 870 H1])

In the somewhat long process of being completed, this enormous, man-made lake (i.e. reservoir) will hold 260 billion gallons of water - enough to secure a six month supply in case of an earthquake emergency. I knew you wanted to know that. With its twenty-six miles of shoreline, this premium lake will eventually have two marinas that can be home to 500 boats; fresh water fishing - perch, catfish, bass, and trout; sailing and other boating opportunities; two large dams to contain the water, one on the west end of the lake, aand one on the east, plus a small one on the north side; and two large community parks under the dam areas. Much more is in the works for this lake area, too.

The visitor's center, on Newport Road, contains information as well as a few exhibits, such as the fossils uncovered during the excavation, including a sloth and mammoth, and displays on water conservation. Educational programs for school groups offer in-depth information and hands-on activities to do with water preservation, water quality, and dams.

Hours: The visitors center is open Fri. - Mon., 10am - 4:30pm. The overlook is open Mon. - Fri., 7:30am - 3:30pm; Sat. - Sun., 9am - 4:30pm.

Admission: Free, right now.

Ages: All

FAIRMOUNT PARK

(909) 826-2000 - park; (909) 715-3406 - boathouse / www.ci.riverside.ca.us

2624 Fairmount Boulevard, Riverside

(Exit Pomona Fwy [60] S. on Market St. The park is on the immediate R. [TG: 685 H2])

This lush park has a lot to offer. The huge playground has swings, slides, bridges, and lots of other fun things. The surrounding grassy area is large, with plenty of shade trees and picnic tables. With all this, plus tennis courts, basketball courts, and horseshoe pits, kids can play here all day. The park's rose garden is located at the corner of Redwood and Dexter drives.

Take a very windy drive around the lakes, and watch out for the ducks - they're everywhere. Don't forget your fishing poles as you can stop almost anywhere to fish, including from a small, horseshoe-shaped pier. A fishing permit is required. Pedal boat and rowboat rentals are available seasonally.

The Information Center is open Monday through Friday, 8am to 5pm and on the weekends, 10am to 5pm. It has exhibits of local history and environmental projects. You'll have a better than fair day at Fairmount Park!

Hours: The park is open daily, sunrise - 10pm. The boathouse is open weekends only, 10am - 3m. Call for other hours.

Admission: Free. Boat rentals are $5 per half hour.

Ages: All

HIDDEN VALLEY WILDLIFE AREA

(909) 785-7452 / www.riversidecountyparks.org

Near end of Arlington Avenue, Riverside

(Exit Riverside Fwy [91] N. at La Sierra, keeping L. as it turns into Arlington. The wildlife area is on the R. before Arlington turns into North Ave. [TG: 714 A1])

Aptly named, this 1,300-acre wildlife area is indeed off the beaten path. There are several options to see at least parts of this "park": Drive along the ridge to see vast expanses of treeless stretches that are close to the road, and wooded areas that are further back into the park; hike along the numerous trails and view the wildlife closer up; or horseback ride, which is obviously a popular option judging from the number of horse trailers we observed.

As Hidden Valley is located along the Santa Ana River, much of the wildlife encouraged and seen here are migratory birds. There are many ponds, too, as you'll discover if you hike into this sprawling park. A small Nature Center is up the road a bit.

Hours: Open daily, 7am - 4:30pm. The Nature Center is open Tues. - Fri. by appointment, and open to the public Sat., 10am - 4pm.

Admission: $4 per vehicle.

Ages: 4 years and up.

HUNTER PARK

(909) 779-9024 - Live Steamers train rides / www.ci.riverside.ca.us

1400 Iowa Avenue, Riverside

(Exit Riverside Fwy [215] E. on Columbia Ave. It's just N. of 91/60/215 Jct., on the corner of Iowa and Columbia. [TG: 686 B1])

Hunter Park is comprised mostly of grassy playing fields. Its best feature occurs on the second and fourth Sunday of each month when scale model train rides are offered. Kids love taking a ride on the track that encircles the park.

Hours: Steam train rides are on the second and fourth Sun., 10am - 3pm.

Admission: Free

Ages: All

HUNT PARK

(909) 826-2000

4015 Jackson Street, Riverside

(Going E. on Riverside Fwy [91], exit N. on Van Buren Blvd., R. on Magnolia Ave., L. on Jackson. Going W. on 91, exit N. on Adams St., L. on Magnolia, R. on Jackson. [TG: 714 J5])

This park has several family-fun amenities such as a softball field (with lights), basketball court (with lights), volleyball court, playground, run around space, picnic facilities, soccer field, swimming pool, and a medium-sized lighted skate park with a cement bowl and other features. Helmet and pads are required for skateboarding.

Hours: The park is open daily, sunrise - sunset. The skatepark is open daily, 10am - dusk; closed on holidays. The pool is open seasonally. Call for hours.

Admission: Free. Admission to the pool is $2.25 for adults; $1.75 for ages 17 and under.

Ages: All

LAKE PERRIS STATE RECREATION AREA

(909) 940-5603 - general info; (909) 657-2179 - marina;
(800) 444-7275 - camping reservations. / parks.ca.gov

17801 Lake Perris Drive, Perris

(Exit Escondido Fwy [215] E. on Cajalco Expressway/Ramona Expressway, L. on Lake Perris Dr. [TG: 748 A6])

Come for at least a day of play at the popular Lake Perris! This gigantic (8,800 acres!), man-made lake supports a multitude of water activities. (It's hot out here in the summer, so you'll need them.) For your boating pleasure, choose from four- or six-seat passenger boats, ranging from $29 for two hours during the week up to $69 on the weekend; or pontoon boats, ranging from $50 to $180 a day. Waterskiing is available, if you bring your own boat. A cove is also here for non-motorized boats, such as sail boats and kayaks. Fish at the lake and catch a big one, or at least try to. A license and day permit is required for those over 16 years. There is a swim beach here with a playground, grassy areas, and barbecue pits.

Drier activities include listening to a concert at the amphitheater, picnicking, hiking, biking (a ten-mile fairly level, mostly paved trail goes around the lake), and rock climbing (outside - you're on your own), What more could nature-loving kids want?! Camping! There is so much to do at Lake Perris, that you'll want to spend a night, or two, here. Ask about their summer programs, such as campfire times held on Saturday evenings and the Jr. Ranger program for ages 7 to 12.

Hours: The recreation area is open in the summer, 6am - 10pm. Open the rest of the year, 6am - 8pm. The marina is open 6am - 8pm year round.

Admission: $5 per vehicle. Tent camping is $10 a night; RV camping is $16 with hook-ups - prices include vehicle admission, but not the $7.50 camping reservation fee.

Ages: All

LAKE SKINNER COUNTY PARK

(909) 926-1505 - recorded info.; (909) 926-1541 - park ranger;
(800) 234-7275 -camping reservations. / www.riversidecountyparks.org

37701 Warren Road, Winchester

(Exit Temecula Valley Fwy [15] N.E. on Rancho California Rd. About 12 miles from the Fwy, turn R. on Warren Rd at the second big bend. There are signs for Lake Skinner. [TG: 930 D3])

Here's the skinny on Lake Skinner. The main attraction is fishing, either from a boat ($55 for all day), or from the shore. A California state license is required for ages 16 and up. Day permits are $5 for adults; $4 for children 12 years and under. The well-equipped marina offers all sorts of fishing supplies as well as a cafe/restaurant for those who didn't have much luck catching their own meal.

Other activities include hiking, picnicking, playing on the small playground, and swimming in the half-acre lagoon pool that is surrounded by a sandy beach. Overnight camping is available here as well.

Hours: The park is open daily, 6am - dusk. Fishing is available daily, 6am - dark. The pool is open Memorial Day through Labor Day daily, 11am - 6pm.

Admission: $2 for adults; $1 for children 12 and under. The pool is an additional $1 per person. Tent camping is $13 a night during the week; $15 on weekends. RV camping is $16 during the week; $18 on weekends.

Ages: All

LOUIS ROBIDOUX NATURE CENTER

(909) 683-4880 / www.riversidecountyparks.org

5370 Riverview Drive, Riverside

(Exit the Pomona Fwy [60] S. on Rubidoux Blvd., R. on Mission St., L. on Riverview Dr. As Riverview turns into Limonite Ave., turn L., staying on Riverview. [TG: 685 A4])

This nature park is wonderful for kids who have an adventuresome spirit. A grouping of big rocks in front of the nature center is fun for climbers. A pond is at the trailhead of Willow Creek Trail, which is an easy half-mile loop to walk around. Other pathways veer off in all directions, allowing some real hiking excursions. Walk along a tree-lined creek; explore the woodlands and water wildlife along the Santa Ana River; or go farther into the Regional Park system along the horse trail that has extensive chaparral. No biking is allowed, and only off-road strollers will make it. Pick up a self-guided trail map, which also has nature questions for kids to answer.

The main building, or Interpretive Center, houses live animals such as snakes, taxidermied animals, and an extensive butterfly and insect collection. Kids are welcome to touch the various animals pelts; use the discovery boxes that contain skulls, seeds, or feathers; or just play with the puzzles. As with most nature centers, special programs are offered throughout the year. Note: The trail by the parking lot leads into RANCHO JURUPA REGIONAL PARK (see pg. 287).

Hours: The park and trails are open daily, sunrise - sunset. The Interpretive Center is open to the public on Sat., 10am - 4pm. With advanced reservations it's open Tues. - Fri. for school groups and other large groups.

Admission: Free

Ages: All

MOUNT RUBIDOUX

(909) 826-2000 / www.ci.riverside.ca.us/park_rec

Off Buena Vista Drive, Riverside

(Exit Riverside Fwy [91] W. on University Ave., R. on Redwood Dr., L. on Buena Vista Dr. Just S. of the Santa Ana River, turn in where you see a small green picnic area and park at the base of the mountain. [TG: 685 F3])

For kids who enjoy a somewhat rugged hike, climbing Mount Rubidoux is a great adventure. The steep, two-and-a-half-mile trail winds around the hill that is barren except for boulders and cacti. "The trail is two miles up and one mile down." Reaching the top is a climax. At the top is a cross and a flag. There are also rocks to climb on, and on a clear day, the panoramic view of the San Gabriel and San Bernardino Mountains is beautiful. On the western slope of the hill, watch vintage planes take off and land at Rubidoux's Flabob Airport. (A paved trail is down this side of the hill.) Hiking here in the summer gets hot, so bring a water bottle. Plan on about an hour-and-a-half round trip. Next door, along the river, is the Mount Rubidoux Park. The bike trail at the base of the mountain goes a few miles back to Martha McClean/Anza Narrow Park and beyond.

Hours: Open daily, sunrise - sunset.

Admission: Free

Ages: It depends how far up you want to hike!

PALM DESERT CIVIC CENTER PARK / SKATE PARK

(760) 568-9697 - park;

(760) 346-0611 - skate park / www.cityofpalmdesert.org; www.palmdesertart.com

Fred Waring Drive and San Pablo Avenue, Palm Desert

(Exit Interstate 10 S. on Cook St, R. on Fred Waring Dr. [TG: 818 F7])

The park, bordered by the civic center and the sheriff's station, encompasses a good portion of land and offers a wide variety of things to do and see. There are four baseball fields, six tennis courts, a dog park, nine volleyball courts, three basketball courts, a YMCA building, a tot lot, an amphitheater for concerts and special events, jogging paths, a small lake, a rose garden, acres of wildflowers, artwork, and a skate park. There are about twenty-five works of art, mostly bronze sculptures and some memorials, scattered throughout the park land. Favorite pieces include the large abstract baseball catcher titled "Today"; the two-piece "The Dreamer," who reposes on the grass with his stomach being part of the lawn; and the figures of children.

15,000 square feet of the skate park is designed for the advanced skater. It has two connected bowls - a four-foot and six-foot one - boxes, pyramids, rails, drop ins, and stairs. The other 5,000 square feet are geared for beginners with a shorter pyramid, box, drop in, and rails. The skate park is lighted, fenced, and monitored. Skaters must wear a helmet and pads, have a signed parental waiver for ages 17 and under, and have a registration card which costs $5 a year. Consider it your civic duty (and a lot of fun!) to visit the Civic Center Park.

Hours: The park is open daily, sunrise - sunset. The skate park is open daily, 6am - 10pm.

Admission: Free
Ages: All

RANCHO CALIFORNIA SPORTS PARK AND COMMUNITY RECREATION CENTER / TEMECULA SKATE PARK ☼ 1/$

(909) 694-6410 - park; (909) 695-1409 - skate park / www.ci.temecula.ca.us
30875 Rancho Vista, Temecula
(Exit Temecula Fwy [15] E. on Rancho California Rd., S. on Ynez Rd., L. on Rancho Vista. [TG: 959 C6])

Have a ball at this terrific sports park! It has twelve ball fields, seven soccer fields, lots of open grassy areas for running around, two great playgrounds, shade trees, picnic shelters, and barbecue grills. The roller hockey rink has some open time, although it is used mostly by leagues. Bring your Tony Hawk wannabes (i.e. Tony Hawk is a pro skateboarder) to practice at the gated, one-acre, outdoor cement skate park which is equipped with all the "necessary" features. The sixty-foot diameter bowl has ramp entry which also leads to an upper bowl with a street plaza that consists of a pyramid, fun box, curbs, ramps, stairs, and a hand rail. All participants must have a signed waiver form prior to park entry. Proper safety equipment is mandatory - helmet, elbow pads, and knee pads - and may be rented on site.

The indoor gym offers basketball, but it can be set up for volleyball, too. Keep your cool in the twenty-five-meter outdoor swimming pool that has a diving board and a waterslide. There is also a shallow pool just for tots. The Teen Center is a great place for 12 to 18 year olds to hang out. It offers pool, air hockey, Carom, Nintendo, and more. This park offers everything active kids need - my boys would be very happy living there!

Hours: The park is open daily, sunrise - 10pm. During the school year the skateboard park is open Mon. - Fri., 4pm - 9:30pm; Sat., 10am - 9:30pm; Sun., 1pm - 6:30pm. It's open during the summer, Mon. - Sat., 10am - 9:30pm; Sun., 1pm - 6:30pm. Sessions last for 2½ hours. The roller hockey rink is usually available for open play Mon. - Fri. before 4pm. After 4pm and on most weekends, it's booked for league play. The pool is open weekends only in April, May, September, and October, 1pm - 5pm. During summer it's open Mon., Wed., Fri., 2pm - 5pm; Sat. - Sun., 1pm - 5pm. The Teen Center is open Mon. - Fri., 2pm - 8:45pm during school hours. Weekends and off-school hours, it's open noon - 8:45pm.
Admission: The park is free. Skateboard sessions are $2 for residents; $5 for non-residents. Bring your own equipment, or rent everything needed for $5. Pool rates are $1 per person for residents; $3 per person for non-residents. The Teen Center asks that a resident card be purchased - $1 for a year's membership.
Ages: All ages for the park. Skateboarders under 7 years must be accompanied by an adult. Kids must be between 12 - 18 years to hang out inside the Teen Center.

RANCHO JURUPA REGIONAL PARK ☼ $

(909) 684-7032 / www.ci.riverside.ca.us/park_rec
4800 Crestmore Road, Riverside
(Exit Pomona Fwy [60] S. on Rubidoux Blvd., L. on Mission Blvd., R. on Crestmore Rd., about 1 mile. [TG: 685 D4])

This huge mountain-wilderness park, which is part of the even bigger Santa Ana River Regional Park system, provides a delightful escape from the city. The two small lakes are stocked with trout in the cooler months and catfish in the summertime. Fishermen (and women) 16 years and older must have a state fishing license. Near the lake is a big wooden play structure with slides, swings, and monkey bars. Enjoy a day (or two or three) here by camping in one of the eighty camp sites that are slotted in a big open space near one end of the lake. Horseshoe pits are located over here, too.

On the other side of the main lake are a few smaller lakes, big grassy open spaces for baseball or whatever, plenty of picnic tables, and barbecue pits. Enjoy an easy hike along the river trail to the adjoining LOUIS ROBIDOUX NATURE CENTER (see pg. 285), where more trails, an Interpretive Center, and rocks to climb on await your kids.

Hours: Open Sun. - Thurs., 7am - 5pm; Fri. - Sat., 7am - 10pm. Call for extended summer hours.

Admission: $2 per person for ages 13 and up; $1 per person for children 12 and under. Dogs are $2 each. Fishing is $5 for ages 16 and older; $4 for ages 6 - 15; children 5 and under fish for free with a paid adult. A campsite with one vehicle and two people costs $16. Each additional person is $1; up to six people allowed in one campsite. Group rates are available.

Ages: All

REAL RIDE SKATEPARK

(909) 943-5744 or (909) 657-4221 / www.farmersfair.com/skatepark.html
18700 Lake Perris Drive, Gate D, at the Lake Perris Fairgrounds, Perris
(Exit Escondido Fwy [215] E. on Cajalco Expressway/Ramona Expressway, L. on Lake Perris Dr. [TG: 778 A1])

This truly is an extreme park with 100,000 (!) square feet of lighted blacktop on which to use your skateboard, in-line blades, bike, or scooter. Here's a slightly scary fact - all of these modes of transportation can be used at the same time: They say it's safe. There are various sections covered with awnings and large portions of the park out in the elements. All of the ramps, grinding poles, stairs, pyramids, and other street course features are moveable. There are also dirt jumps and a twenty-five by twenty-five-foot foam pit for roll-ins (i.e. doing tricks without landing on a hard surface). A parental waiver must be signed for all participants 17 years and under. A helmet and pads are necessary. Sessions are three hours long.

Hours: Open Tues. - Fri., 3:30pm - 10pm, Sat. - Sun., noon - 10pm. Closed Mon. Ask about extended summer and holiday hours.
Admission: $8 per session or $10 for the day.
Ages: 7 years and up.

SANTA ROSA PLATEAU ECOLOGICAL RESERVE

(909) 677-6951 / www.santarosaplateau.org
22115 Tenaja Road, Murrieta
(Exit Temecula Valley Fwy [15] W. on Clinton Keith Rd. and go about 6 miles to the trailhead. You'll see entrance signs. Another trailhead is located further down the road, where Clinton Keith/Tenaja Rd. turns into Via Volcano. [TG: 957 C3])

From riparian stream sides to basalt-capped mesas, this gigantic 8,300-acre reserve covers the gamut of topography. The thirty-plus trails range from one mile to five miles round trip. Depending on which one you choose, you'll hike through oak woodlands, acres of grasslands, chaparral, up the Santa Ana mountains, and down to creek beds. Look for treefrogs and turtles in the water, and ground squirrels, woodpeckers, hawks, and horned lizards along the wooded pathways. There is a picnic spot at the vernal pools, which is a four-mile round-trip hike. Pick up a trail map from the visitors center at 39400 Clinton Keith Road. Guided hikes are offered Saturdays at 9:30am.

Hours: Open daily, sunrise - sunset. The visitor's center is open Sat. - Sun., 9am - 5pm.
Admission: $2 for adults; $1 for children 2 - 12.
Ages: 3 years and up.

UNIVERSITY OF CALIFORNIA AT RIVERSIDE BOTANIC GARDENS

(909) 787- 4650 / www.gardens.ucr.edu
Campus Drive, University of California, Riverside
(Exit Moreno Valley Fwy [215]/State Highway 60 E. on Martin Luther King Blvd., R. at Canyon Crest Ave into the campus, follow signs to parking lot 13. [TG: 686 E5])

Riverside's climate ranges from subtropical to desert to mountains, all within forty acres and five miles of hilly trails! A gently sloping walkway provides access to the gardens main areas for wheelchairs and strollers. Explore the botanic gardens to see rose gardens, fruit orchards, an herb garden, saguaros, barrel cacti, pine trees, giant sequoias, and so much more.

Besides the diverse plant life, numerous animals share this habitat. Be on the lookout for bunnies, lizards, squirrels, snakes, coyotes, and numerous bird species. A main trail loops around, and is walkable in forty-five minutes. At the far end of the trail is a pond supporting more wildlife such as frogs, turtles, dragonflies, and koi.

A dome-shaped building made of cedar that houses a "living fossils" collection and a greenhouse are more discoveries you'll make along the way.

Come with your kids to enjoy the beauty of the gardens, and/or come for an educational field trip. Ask for a self-guiding tour booklet, such as *Outdoor Classroom* or *Deserts of the Southwest*, which will greatly enrich your day of exploring and learning.

Hours: Open daily, 8am - 5pm. Closed New Year's Day, July 4th, Thanksgiving, and Christmas.
Admission: Free.
Ages: All

<h2 style="text-align:center">-----MALLS-----</h2>

GALLERIA - KID'S CLUB

(909) 351-3110 / www.galleriatyler.com
1299 Galleria at Tyler, Riverside
(Exit Riverside Fwy [91] N. on Tyler. [TG: 714 G7])

Kids between 3 to 12 years old enjoy a new craft project every month, while supplies last, near the lower level of Macy's Court. All the materials are provided and the crafts are often holiday themed. Ask about the Galleria's occasional special exhibits, too.

Hours: The first Wed. of every month from 4pm - 7pm.
Admission: Free
Ages: 3 - 12 years.

<h2 style="text-align:center">-----MUSEUMS-----</h2>

CALIFORNIA MUSEUM OF PHOTOGRAPHY

(909) 784-FOTO (3686) / www.cmp.ucr.edu
3824 Main Street, Riverside
(Exit Riverside Fwy [91] W. on University Ave. and park near Main St. The museum in on the pedestrian walkway. [TG: 685 H4])

Expose your kids to the photographic arts at the unique, three-story California Museum of Photography. The main level has rotating photo exhibits, with an emphasis on various photography styles or photographers, such as Ansel Adams. The back area houses a collection of cameras, including working miniature cameras (my boys refer to them as "spy" cameras), old-fashioned cameras with the drape cloth, a Spiderman camera, and one that is part of a radio-controlled car!

Take the spiral stairs up to the mezzanine terrace, which is a catwalk-like hallway gallery. The top floor often focuses on kids with its small, interactive gallery with rotating exhibits. When we were visited, children used the Zoetropes to draw pictures and spin them around in a drum, creating moving images - early animation! We also learned that not all shadows are black as the images shadowed here produced a rainbow of colors. The next display visually explained how the aperture of a camera is similar to the pupils in eyes. We looked into a light and watched in the mirror as our pupils enlarged or contracted, according to the amount of light entering in. The Shadows Room temporarily imprinted body outlines on the photosensitive wall when a light flashed. Camera Obscura is a small, dark room with a tiny hole of light that projects an upside down image of the outside scene on its wall. This is a visual demonstration of how a camera lens works. Kids will get a wide angle view of photography at this Museum! Note: Guided school tours are available for 7th through 12th graders.

Hours: The museum is open Tues. - Sun., 11am - 5pm.
Admission: Free
Ages: 3 years and up just to look at things; ages 5 and up will begin to really appreciate it.

FENDER MUSEUM OF MUSIC AND THE ARTS

(909) 735-2440 / www.fendermuseum.com

365 N. Main Street, Corona

(Exit Riverside Fwy [91] N. on Main St. [TG: 743 D4])

Tune in to the Fender Museum which offers an array of things to see and do. Enter under an artsy metallic sculpture and look at information and picture panels that show the timeline of the Fender guitar, from humble beginnings to an acclaimed instrument. On display are some classic Fender guitars including a 1951 "no caster" guitar, a Stratocaster, and a 1956 Jaguar guitar in beach surroundings of a Tiki hut and sand. A few guitars are showcased in a set that looks like a back stage dressing room. An area resembling a workshop shows wood guitars at various stages of completion. Two favorites of ours include the Celtic guitar, inlaid with mother of pearl, and the Star Trek Stratocaster.

A large side room, the Visual Arts Gallery, features an art gallery with rotating exhibits. We saw a few music-related paintings and unusual sculptures. This room also has a stage and seating for performances. Concerts are often given at the outside 500-seat amphitheater, too. Call for a schedule. The lobby is especially fun because there are instruments to play - all with attached headphones, thank goodness! Electric drums, guitars, bass, and keyboards allow visitors to compose impromptu, albeit quiet, music.

Fender also offers one-hour-plus school field trips for a minimum of twenty-five students. Tours start with an interactive demonstration with a musician, then a self-guided walk through the museum. A scavenger hunt is offered upon request. The company has two other note-worthy offerings: Studio FM, a 48-track digital recording studio, and a program called Kids Rock Free. The program offers free or low-cost music lessons to kids 7 to 17 years. Call for information, and rock on.

Hours: The museum is open Wed. - Sun., 11am - 4pm (open until 8pm on Thurs).

Admission: $3 for adults; $2 for seniors and students; children 12 and under are free with a paying adult.

Ages: 7 years and up.

GILMAN HISTORIC RANCH AND WAGON MUSEUM

(909) 922-9200 / www.riversidecountyparks.org

On Wilson Street and 16th Street, Banning

(Exit San Bernardino Fwy [10] N. on 22nd Ave., R. on Sunrise Ave., R on Wilson. [TG: 721 J2])

Wagons, ho! Take the dirt road back to the Gilman Historic Ranch and Wagon Museum, and explore life as it was over 150 years ago. The exhibits are set up in a chronological order. Over fifteen wagons from yesteryear are inside the museum including chuck wagons, stagecoaches, and prairie schooners. Some of the wagons are hitched to large wooden horses. Learn how our pioneer ancestors traveled across the country, and hear about the hardships that they endured. Also on exhibit are photographs, saddles, a bedroom set with a ladies' riding habit and surrey, a blacksmith's shop, and Indian artifacts.

The adjacent section of the ranch has a few historic buildings, shaded picnic grounds, and hiking trails. Some of the trails go across the creek and to the upper reservoir, while others go deeper into the canyons. Be on the lookout for rabbits, deer, and other wildlife.

School groups, with a minimum of twenty students, can take outstanding and informative two-hour tours, which include a tour of the museum and grounds, a nature hike, and hands-on activities. The activity choices include creating a brand (out of a rubber stamp), panning for real gold flakes in sluices set in the woods (you may keep whatever you pan), and grinding corn meal as part of the Native American program. Scout groups may use the campfire sites and fire rings and choose badge-earning activities. Enjoy your day reliving the past! Teachers, ask about the Mountain Men Days in the April (see pg. 574) and Wild West Days in September put on just for students - they are wonderful.

Hours: The museum and grounds are open to the public March through November on Sat., 10am - 4pm. Tours for school groups are offered throughout the week by reservation.

Admission: $2 for adults; $1 for children 11 and under. Tour prices range between $4 - $5.50 per participant, depending on the activities involved.

Ages: 5 years and up.

HERITAGE HOUSE

(909) 689-1333 / www.ci.riverside.ca.us

8193 Magnolia Street, Riverside

(Exit Riverside Fwy [91] N. on Adams St., R. on Magnolia St. It's on the N. side of the street. [TG: 715 B4])

Heritage House is a beautiful Victorian house built in 1892. It is fully restored and filled with elaborate, turn-of-the-century furniture. Adding to its charm is the wrought iron fence in front, the well-kept grounds, the backyard windmill, and the barn complete with clucking chickens.

Your older children will appreciate the half-hour guided tour as they see and learn about a different era and style of living. Kids can look through the stereo-optic, which is an early version of today's View Master™ and view a unique, old music box. Explaining the Edison phonograph is a lot harder now that record players are also a thing of the past! The formal oak stairway leads upstairs to the master bedroom. You'll also find the office/library with trophy animal heads and a bearskin rug, and the servant's quarters up here. Heritage House graciously displays the life of an affluent citrus grower.

The second Sunday of every month is Living History Day, when the past comes to life in the present. Docents dress up as from the late 1900's owner and have (pretend) party preparations. Talk to the hostess, maid, cook, and guests to learn about customs from this time period. Call about the House's other special events. Forty-five-minute group tours, for a minimum of twenty people, are offered by appointment.

Hours: Open Thurs - Fri., noon - 3pm; Sun., noon - 3:30pm. Closed July through Labor Day.

Admission: Suggested donations are $1 for adults; 50¢ for kids.

Ages: 7 years old and up.

JENSEN-ALVARADO RANCH HISTORIC PARK

(909) 369-6055 / www.co.riverside.ca.us

4307 Briggs Street, Riverside

(Exit Pomona Fwy [60] S. on Rubidoux Blvd., R. on Mission St., L. on Riverview Dr., L on 42nd St., R. on Briggs St. [TG: 685 C3])

This historic site brings the history of the 1880's to life. The front part of the park is a large area with picnic tables. Rusty old farm equipment lines the main pathway. The corral and animal pens, with a few horses, sheep, chicken, and other ranch animals, are located next to the Jensen-Alvarado Ranch House. Behind the house was a winery; it's now a small museum. Inside is period furniture, plus wine-making presses, barrels, and other equipment.

A two-and-a-half-hour school tour includes seeing all of the above, plus hearing a living history presentation from a costumed docent; participating in hands-on demonstrations such as making ice cream, butter, or tortillas; and maybe, feeding the animals. Ask about special events such as the 4th of July picnic, and the summer history camp. Note: Check the Calendar entry for Ranch Days (see pg. 611).

Hours: Open to the public Sat., 10am - 4pm. Open September 15 through June 30, Mon. - Fri. for school and large groups only, by reservation.

Admission: Sat. admission is $3 for adults; $1.50 for ages 3 - 12; children 2 and under are free. School tours are $5 per person.

Ages: 6 years and up.

JURUPA MOUNTAINS CULTURAL CENTER / EARTH SCIENCE MUSEUM

(909) 685-5818 / www.the-jmcc.org

7621 Granite Hill Drive, Riverside

(Exit Pomona Fwy [60] S. on Pedley Rd., L. on Mission Blvd., L. on Camino Real, under the freeway. [TG: 744 H7])

This center is a rock hound's paradise where kids can either start or add to their rock collection. The main building is a gigantic warehouse with an incredible array of rocks, minerals, dinosaur skeletons, and fossils of all sizes and quality, for display and purchase.

The adjacent Earth Science Museum has outstanding rocks, minerals, fossils, and Indian artifacts displayed according to classification. The large crystals, geodes, carbons, etc., are worthy of a few "oohs" and "aahs." The collection of ancient and modern Native American artifacts includes tools, weapons, a wonderful arrowhead exhibit, an 1100 year-old corn cob, and costumes, in particular, a beautiful fringed and beaded wedding dress. Products, like Borax, are shown in their commercial form next to their original mineral form. Other unique exhibits are the florescent exhibit, which literally highlights rocks with luminescent characteristics; the space exhibit, which includes moon rocks; and the ivory exhibit, which has examples of intricately carved scrimshaw. Note: The outside of the building is comprised of petrified wood and fossils.

If your kids want to take home their own, hand-picked treasures, go Rock Collecting at the Dinosaurs on Saturdays. This drop-in, family field trip starts at the magnetic rock, proceeds to the small petrified wood "forest," and has several other stops along the way, with kid-appropriate explanations about the fascinating plants and rocks you see. (I finally understand that fossil simply means, "something that was once living.") The destination, dinosaur mesa, has eight, giant, kid-made dinosaurs. The highlight of the excursion is sorting through the huge spread of rocks and rock chips strewn at the dino's feet, and picking out twelve to take home! Crystals, jasper, malachite, petrified wood, amethyst, chrysocolla, and sulphur, are some examples of what can be found here. Egg cartons are provided. Back at the warehouse/store, you can label each of your treasures, with a geologist's help if needed.

Another great drop-in field trip is Kids' Fossil Shack, geared for ages 6 and up. Kids learn about fossils, and then clean and prepare one to take home. This is, obviously, a more sit-down activity, but another great way to combine hands-on education with fun.

The Jurupa Cultural Center offers a wide variety of terrific school group and scout programs, such as gold panning, lapidary workshops, creating an Indian pictograph, archaeology, and lots more. The Center also comes to schools for on-site classes. Call for information on their periodic Pow Wows and Renaissance Fairs, as well as week-long classes of Nature School in the summer that range from hiking and survival, to dinosaurs and fossils.

Hours: The warehouse store is open Tues. - Sat., 8am - 4:30pm. The Earth Science Museum is open Tues. and Thurs., noon - 4pm, Sat., 8am - 4pm. Both are closed on national holidays. Rock Collecting at the Dinosaurs is held every Sat., 9am - 10:30am and 1:30pm - 3pm, weather permitting. During inclement weather, inquire about other Sat. outings. Kids' Fossil Shack is held Sat., 10:30am - noon. Once-a-month public classes include worm composting, gold panning, Indian pictograph, Jr. lapidary, and more.

Admission: Entrance to the warehouse store is free. The Earth Science Museum admission is by donation. Rock Collecting at the Dinosaurs and Kids' Fossil Shack are $5 per person, each event. No reservations are needed. School tours start at $5 per participant. Call for specific information and a class schedule.

Ages: 3 years and up.

KIDZONE YOUTH MUSEUM

(9090 765-1223 / www.kidzone.org

123 S. Carmalita Street, Hemet

(Exit Escondido Fwy [215] E. on Ethanac Rd. [74] which turns into the Pinacate Rd. which turns into Florida Ave., R. on Carmalita. [TG: 811 A7])

Kids need a place to call their own and KidZone is it! The huge, rectangular room is divided into colorful sections with various interactive machines, games, and exhibits. Each one emphasizes a particular educational aspect. Note: Some exhibits do rotate.

Does the ground you're standing on feel a little shaky? It's not your *fault*; you've just entered the Shakezone. The ground doesn't really shake in the exhibit, but guests learn where and why it does by using maps, free-standing models, and shake tables to test building structures. Information on retrofitting your home (along with a sample gas meter), the importance of earthquake preparedness, and how to make a survival kit, complete this zone. Pump it up - the water, that is. Pump water to see the water cycle in action as it courses through pipes and ducts. This shows the process of water being filtered at a re-created treatment plant, from rain to reservoir, and it shows how much water is used during various activities.

A toddler area has soft play toys as well as a small wooden row boat with a life vest and fishing pole, and a child-sized kitchen in which to prepare a meal. Uncover bones at a paleontology sand pit. Climb aboard a mock fire engine. Spin around and around and around on a momentum machine (but don't get sick). Use a computer to morph your face into different animals. Play a game of wheelchair basketball, which is much harder than it looks. Put on a helmet and hop on a police motorcycle complete with a radio and working lights. Practice rescuing techniques in a fully-equipped ambulance with lights and a two-way radio that is connected to the police motorcycle and to the nearby kid-sized medical office. The office has white lab coats for visiting "doctors" as well as a stethoscope, skeleton, crutches, an examining table, X-Ray machine, scales, and more. Besides the doctor's office and the police station, with it's jail and official belt holsters, a few other mini city-themed rooms are lined up against one wall. These include a school room with puzzles, books, and tessellations (i.e. geometric shapes), and a TV station. Future anchormen and women dress up, sit behind the newscaster's desk, and watch themselves on a TV monitor. (All those funny faces they're making also show on a screen at the entrance to the museum!)

Towards the back of the museum is an art and crafts room; a bank with a teller's desk, office equipment, and play money; and the front end of a bus for "driving" around town. A Fender guitar exhibit shows the various stages of how a guitar is made. There is also a finished product to strum.

Ninety-minute school tours are offered that focus on a particular theme and include plenty of just play time. Special workshops and events are offered for families throughout the year. The museum brochure says it all: "KidZone is not a 'museum', it's a 'do-seum' and doing is what learning is all about." Tip: Just around the corner from the museum is the MINOR ZOO. (See pg. 301.)

Hours: Open Wed. - Sat., 10am - 3pm. Closed Sun., Mon., Tues., and some holidays.
Admission: $5 per person; $4 for seniors; children under 2 are free.
Ages: 1 - 12 years.

MARCH FIELD AIR MUSEUM

(909) 697-6600 / www.marchfield.org
16222 Interstate 215, March Air Force Base
(Exit Moreno Valley Fwy [215] E. on Van Buren Blvd. [TG: 747 B3])

A P-40 Warhawk stands guard at the entrance of March Field Museum, which is the proud home to one of the most extensive collection of military aircraft and aviation artifacts in the United States. The walkway is lined with airplane engines, plus a jeep that kids can get into and "drive" around. Outside, over sixty historic airplanes are on display, from the smaller F-84 to the massive B-52 to the sleek Blackbird SR-71. Kids are welcome to look at the planes, but not to climb in them.

Inside, the huge hangar displays everything possible pertaining to the Air Force. Airplanes, such as a biplane trainer, have landed in here, as have exhibits of flight uniforms, a "war dog" memorial, photographs, model planes, engines, medals, weapons, and equipment from both World Wars, Korea, Viet Nam, the Cold War, and Desert Storm. This museum defines the word "comprehensive!"

The March Field Story and other informative films are available for viewing with prior notice. A three-minute jolting simulator ride can be taken for $5. Although the only touchable activity for kids is to strap themselves into a flight training chair, they really enjoy the museum, especially your pilots-in-training.

Hours: Open daily, 9am - 4pm. Closed New Year's Day, Easter, Thanksgiving, and Christmas.
Admission: $5 for adults; $3 for ages 5 - 11; children 4 and under are free.
Ages: 3 years and up.

MISSION INN / MISSION INN MUSEUM

(909) 784-0300 - Inn; (909) 788-9556 - museum / www.missioninn.com
3649 Mission Inn Avenue, Riverside
(Going N. on Riverside Fwy [91], exit W. on University Ave., R. on Orange St., L. on Mission Inn. Going S. on 91, exit at University, go W. on Mission Inn. [TG: 685 H4])

Is it a European castle? Not quite, but this elegant, old, sprawling Inn is beautiful to look at and tour. The hour-plus tour shows much of its eclectic architecture and furnishings. Mediterranean style, emphasized in the colorful tiles, spiral columns, and bells, is incorporated with an Oriental influence, such as a hotel kitchen chimney in the shape of a pagoda, plus other unique touches. Only through the tour can you see all four wings of the hotel with highlights including the gilded eighteenth-century altar in the wedding chapel; the music room; the Court of Birds (there are no actual birds still here, but the stories about them give wings to the imagination); the Taft Chair, that seats up to five kids at one time; and the open-air, five-story spiral staircase in the rotunda, which is quite grand looking. If your kids are interested in architecture or hearing about the Inn's history, they will enjoy the tour. If not, at least take a quick walk through the grounds.

A small museum is located on the pedestrian walkway, next to the Inn's gift shop. Frank Miller, the Inn's builder, had an international collection that reflected his tastes. Housed in the museum are a scale model of a pagoda, encased figurines, artifacts, and photos. The most appealing exhibit to kids has old-time barber shop chairs (not to sit in) with mirrors and hair cutting instruments.

Hours: The Inn is a functioning Inn so it is open daily. Tours are given daily at certain intervals throughout the day. The museum is open daily, 9:30am - 4pm.

Admission: You can walk around the hotel at no charge. The tour costs $8 for adults; children 11 and under are free. The museum is $2 per person.

Ages: 8 years and up.

ORANGE EMPIRE RAILWAY MUSEUM
(909) 657-2605 / www.oerm.org
2201 S. 'A' Street, Perris

See the entry for ORANGE EMPIRE RAILWAY MUSEUM on page 300 for details.

RIVERSIDE MUNICIPAL MUSEUM   ☼
(909) 826-5273 - museum; (909) 788-2747 - educational tours / www.ci.riverside.ca.us   !
3580 Mission Inn Avenue, Riverside
(Going N. on Riverside Fwy [91], exit W. on University Ave., R. on Orange St., L. on Mission Inn. Going S. on 91, exit at University, go W. on Mission Inn. [TG: 685 H4])

This museum contains a wealth of information and fun for both kids and adults. The natural history exhibits are a natural place to start. Push a button and the taxidermied mountain lion crouched on the ledge "roars." Other stuffed animals are also posed in animated positions. For instance, a baby bobcat is batting at the air and a skunk is doing a handstand on its front paws. The geology area has a nice display of rocks and minerals, plus a section on earthquakes. The paleontology exhibits have a saber-tooth cat skeleton, some fossilized elephant tusks (they are huge!), and a few dinosaur bones. The anthropology section has displays of Indian clothing, musical instruments, hunting weapons, and a few dioramas. The local history display features missions, cowboys, tools, and guns, plus machinery and crate labels of citrus growers.

Upstairs we saw exhibits that emphasized Mexican heritage via ethnic costumes, and artifacts. The hallway is lined with small botanical dioramas. A favorite room is the small Nature Laboratory. Kids can inspect shells and bugs under a microscope. They can also dissect owl pellets. There is a small sea display with preserved sea horses, and a few live reptiles in here, too - snakes, lizards, and turtles.

The entire museum rates high on kid-interest! In a program called "First Sunday," free arts and crafts activities are offered on the first Sunday of each month, October through May, 1pm to 4pm. Other museums in Riverside offer free admission and/or arts and crafts on this Sunday, too. Inquire about the after-school science adventure programs - no pre-sign ups necessary.

Hours: The museum is open Tues. - Fri., 9am - 5pm; Sat., 10am - 5pm; Sun., 11pm - 5pm. The Nature Laboratory is open Tues. - Sat., 1:30pm - 4:30pm, although it's sometimes closed on Wed.

Admission: Free

Ages: 2 years and up.

TEMECULA VALLEY MUSEUM / TEMECULA - OLD TOWN

☼
!/$

(909) 694-6480 / www.cityoftemecula.org

28314 Mercedes Street, Temecula

(Exit Temecula Valley Fwy [15] W. on Rancho California Rd., L. on Front St. to Old Town, or L. on Moreno St. to the museum at Sam Hicks Park. [TG: 958 H7])

Mosey on over to Old Town Temecula and enjoy an hour or so shopping along Main Street. This western strip of town looks and feels authentic, right down to its wooden sidewalks. The over 100 antique and specialty shops offer many unique gift items for sale, making it an alluring place to shop, even with children.

The museum is located on a corner park - Sam Hicks Park - that has a small playground, and a large rock inscribed with the names of pioneers. The small museum is an interesting glimpse into Temecula's past. On the first floor a few tools, household goods, guns, saddles, and army equipment portray life on the local ranches and frontier towns. There are also some Native American artifacts, plus memorabilia from Erle Stanley Gardner, the author of the Perry Mason stories and a one-time resident of Temecula. At the more interactive second-floor room, there are rotating exhibits. When we visited, my boys became a part of the Old West mostly by dressing up in vintage clothing and sitting on a pretend horse (I brought my camera!), plus looking at facades that depicted a frontier town.

Hours: Open Tues. - Sat., 10am - 5pm; Sun., 1pm - 5pm. Closed Mon. and holidays. Main Street shopping is usually open daily, 10am - 6pm.

Admission: Suggested donation of $2 for adults.

Ages: 5 years and up.

WORLD MUSEUM OF NATURAL HISTORY

☼
!

(909) 785-2209 / www.lasierra.edu/wmnh

4700 Pierce Street in Cossentine Hall on the campus of La Sierra University, Riverside

(Exit Riverside Fwy [91] S.W. on Magnolia, R. on Pierce. Go L. on Campus Dr. at the intersection of Pierce St. and Sierra Vista Ave. Park at the end of Campus Dr. in parking lot F on weekends. If you've made arrangements for a special tour, ask the curator to get a parking permit for you. [TG: 714 B7])

This quality museum is tremendous in its comprehensive scope of minerals and freeze-dried animals. Full-grown and young animals are displayed according to species. The old and new world primates - or monkeys, gorillas, and chimps - all look so life like! The size and variety of the Crocodiles of the World is impressive. We had not heard of at least half the ones featured here. The Indian Gavial is especially unique with a snout that resembles a long, thin saw blade. The numerous types of turtles were similarly astounding. They range from the very small to the gigantic alligator snapping turtle. Snakes of the World boasts another record-breaking variety, ranging from boas, pythons, and common garters, to venomous snakes and even a two-headed snake. Other reptiles, including the world's largest Komodo dragon (365 pounds at time of death!), are also on display. Birds from all over the world are represented here, such as pelicans, flamingoes, penguins, an imperial eagle, and a blue-hued hunting green magpie. Some of the more unusual animals on display are the flat-headed cat (which, not surprisingly, has a very flat head), bats (one is just the size of a pin), an armadillo, a kangaroo, and an Indian rhino.

An outstanding collection of rocks and minerals are grouped, in one section, according to color. These include large specimens of amethyst, malachite, etc. Other groupings include meteorites, fluorescent minerals, geodes, and huge slabs of petrified wood. There is also a large display of sphere balls or, in kidspeak, "cool-looking bowling balls." Part of this display shows the progression of a chunk of raw rock to a cube and then to the finished, sphere product. A fine display of Indian artifacts, such as arrowheads and headdresses, is also noteworthy. The World Museum of Natural History is a gem of a place!

Hours: Open Sat., 2pm - 5pm, or weekdays by appointment. Tour groups are welcome - Wed. is the best day.

Admission: Free; donations gladly accepted.

Ages: 2 years and up.

-----POTPOURRI-----

CIRCUS VARGAS
See the entry for CIRCUS VARGAS on page 134 for details.

-----SHOWS AND THEATERS-----

RIVERSIDE COMMUNITY COLLEGE PLANETARIUM
(909) 222-8090 / www.academic.rccd.cc.ca.us/academic/astronomy/planetarium.htm
4800 Magnolia Avenue, Riverside
(Exit Riverside Fwy [91] W. on 14th St., L. on Market St./Magnolia Ave. [TG: 685 G5])

Come see a truly star-studded show at the college planetarium! The theater seats sixty people and each presentation has a live narrator. Different shows study various aspects of astronomy such as constellations, revolutions (the earth's, not a country's), galaxies and measuring distances between them, lunar eclipses, and what makes the sun shine.

School groups, or other groups, of up to sixty people can schedule a time to rent out the theater for $75 to see fifty-minute shows such as *Sun's Family*, or *Finding Your Way in the Sky*, or others. These shows are geared specifically for elementary-aged kids. There are several shows and programs geared for secondary grade levels, too. *Christmas Star* is offered only in the month of December. It explores the possible origins of the Star of Bethlehem utilizing Biblical passages and astronomer's technology and understanding of the heavens.

Hours: Public shows are offered once or twice a month on Fri. nights at 7pm. Groups can see shows Mon. - Thurs. at noon. Reservations are required.

Admission: Public shows are $3 for adults; $2.50 for students; $1.50 for children 11 and under.

Ages: 6 years and up.

-----TOURS-----

BRAILLE INSTITUTE (Rancho Mirage)
(760) 321-111 / www.brailleinstitute.org
70-251 Ramon Road, Rancho Mirage
(Exit Interstate 10 S. on Date Palm, L. on Ramon. [TG: 787 H2])

Kids, as well as adults, often have preconceived ideas on what visually-impaired people can and cannot do. A one-hour tour through this institute enables visitors to see, firsthand, how well blind people can function. A tour guide, who is legally blind, takes your family or group (up to thirty people) around the campus and classrooms to look at the computers, art room, cooking facility, garden, and any other area that teaches life skills. Visitors are encouraged to ask questions - it's the best way to learn! You can also arrange to watch a film on being visually impaired and/or to have a special speaker, and you may be able to stand on a talking scale, something I personally opted out of doing. Visitors receive a card with the Braille alphabet - try it and see if you can discern the difference in letters.

Hours: Call to schedule a tour.

Admission: Free

Ages: 8 years old and up only.

QUALITY WEST WING
(909) 808-1661 / www.qualitywestwing.com
1705 W. Sixth Street, Corona
(Going E., exit Riverside Fwy [91] S. on Maple St. exit and turn R. on Maple/Sixth St. You are actually turning R. on Sixth St. Going W., exit the 91 S. on Maple/Sixth St., L. on Sixth St. Just after Paseo Grande, take a quick L. into the R. side of the Thrifty Gas Station, go thru the chain link fence gate and park at the Quality Toyota dealership. [TG: 743 J5])

"I, name, do solemnly swear (or affirm) that I will faithfully execute the office of the President of the United States . . ." If a trip to Washington D.C. is not in the foreseeable future, students can travel instead to Corona and see miniature replicas of important government institutions and a full-size re-creation of the Oval Office, via a sixty-minute-plus interactive tour.

Bud Gordon, president of this Quality Toyota dealership where the West Wing was built, has a vision - for students to know their government by bringing America's history to life. He made an executive decision and created Quality West Wing. The tour begins with a twenty-five-minute Charlie Brown video called *Birth of the Constitution*, which recaps the delegates and founding fathers debating how to best establish our government. Students can begin to fill out the worksheets that include word searches and crossword puzzles. Next, they walk down the halls and get a short oral biography on the presidents whose portraits hang here, as well as lots of fascinating presidential facts and trivia. Q: How many consecutive years can a person serve as president? A: (Look at the bottom of this entry.)

Visitors "tour" the detailed scale model of Capitol Hill, which includes all the famous monuments. 3-D replicas also depict the interiors of the House, Senate, and Supreme Court buildings in session. The highlight is a visit to the Oval Office. What an impressive office, even in replica. The tour guide explains how the decor changes with each president, how the president signs a bill into office, and other life-altering functions that take place here. Bring your camera and take a picture with a cardboard cut-out of the current President of the United States.

The last part of the visit consists of researching answers to the scavenger hunt questions on the computer terminals (using a tailor-made game) and by looking around at the documents and political pictures on the walls. As an introduction to American government and as a reinforcement for those who have studied the topic more in depth, the Quality West Wing tour wins by a landslide. A minimum of ten students and maximum of fourteen are allowed per tour. (Groups of more than fourteen will be split into two groups.) Note that the tour includes fun and educational freebies such as t-shirts for students and curriculum aids. This outstanding tour certainly has my vote! The answer to the above question, by the way, is ten years.

Hours: Tours are offered Mon. - Fri., 9am - 2pm. Reservations are required.

Admission: Free

Ages: 4th - 12th graders.

RIVERSIDE PRESS-ENTERPRISE

(909) 368-9780 / www.press-enterprise.com/nie

3512 14th Street, Riverside

(Exit Riverside Fwy [91] E. on 14th St. [TG: 685 G5])

School, scout, or other groups interested in the workings of a newsroom and how a newspaper is put together can get a behind-the-scenes look on this one-hour tour of the Enterprise. The tour begins with the history of this paper. The group then walks through the various departments, seeing and learning how each one functions along the way. The departments include advertising, the newsroom, editing, production or composing, the color lab, plate making, inserts and packaging, and the pressroom. The latter is more interesting when the presses are actually running, although it does get loud. Lots of interesting facts about newspapers are given and students will be surprised at how much paper is used for just one edition. Tours are open to a minimum of ten students and maximum of twenty; groups over twenty will be divided into smaller groups. Ask about their Newspaper In Education program.

Hours: Tours are offered year-round on Tues. and Fri. during normal business hours. Call to make a reservation.

Admission: Free

Ages: 3rd grade or above.

UNCLE BUD'S CAR MUSEUM

(909) 808-1661 / www.qualitywestwing.com

1705 W. Sixth Street

(Going E., exit Riverside Fwy [91] S. on Maple St. exit and turn R. on Maple/Sixth St. You are actually turning R. on Sixth St. Going W., exit the 91 S. on Maple/Sixth St., L. on Sixth St. Just after Paseo Grande, take a quick L. into the R. side of the Thrifty Gas Station, go thru the chain link fence gate and park at the Quality Toyota dealership. [TG: 743 J5])

Bud Gordon, president of this Quality Toyota dealership where the museum and QUALITY WEST WING (see pg. 296) is located, has a vision for kids in junior and senior high school, or older, who are looking for a technical future in the automotive industry. He wants to motivate them and enable them. In fact, the museum is currently only open to this type of program which is designed for kids.

The relatively small car museum is incredibly well put together. Students get their engines revved up as they enter and see the dozen or so vehicles here displayed in chronological order, starting with horse and buggy. Behind each "car" is a colorful and realistic mural depicting that time period, bringing the settings to life. Most cars, and there is at least one per decade, are also accompanied by another piece of history from that era, as well as information panels. Follow the carpet that looks like a road - yellow lines and all - around the curve to a complete 50's diner called Rosie's. Look into it and see the jukebox, red vinyl booths, and a soda fountain. Keep going around the horseshoe-shaped pathway to the race cars and more modern vehicles. An important element of this museum is the hands-on activities, such as the cut away to a car engine - see if the engine works; cranking the differential gears; seeing the entire electrical system to a Lexus; and so much more. There is also a fake gas station, depicted by a gas pump, murals, and lots of traffic signs covering the walls.

Hours: Call to schedule a tour.
Admission: Free
Ages: 14 years and up.

WINCHESTER CHEESE CO.

(909) 926-4239 / www.winchestercheese.com

32605 Holland Road, Winchester

(Going S. on Escondido Fwy [215], exit E. on Hwy 74, S. on Winchester Rd. [79], R. on Holland. A sign says Wesselink Dairy on the corner. Going N. on Temecula Valley Fwy [15], exit N.E. on Winchester Rd. [79], L. on Holland. [TG: 685 G5])

Smile and say "cheese"! The Winchester Cheese Co. is a family-owned dairy that produces fresh Gouda cheese in trailers located on this large tract of farm land. During the almost two-hour outdoor tour, visitors learn a lot about the dairy process and about the 400-plus cows here. They learn what cows eat and how often, when they are milked, and ultimately, how cheese is made from the raw milk. Visitors see the feed; walk around the pens to pet and even bottle feed newborn calves; peek into the windows to see the cheese being made; and go into the trailer to look at how and where the cheese and cheese wheels are kept refrigerated for future consumption. A wonderful amount of information is dispensed and, for us city folk who rarely see a real dairy "in action," the hands-on, eyes-on activities strengthens the retention. (I hope!) The last activity is also the tastiest - sampling a variety of cheese with flavors that range from sharp to mild to spicy hot. Snack time is complete with apples wedges, crackers, pretzels, and a beverage that is all provided. Feel free to bring a picnic lunch, too. Tip: Bring extra money to purchase some cheese to take home!

Hours: Tours are given Wed. and Thurs., 9:30am - 11:30am by reservation only. Groups must constitute a minimum of 30 people or $75; $3 per person is charged after 30 people and the maximum number is 40.
Admission: $3 per person.
Ages: 5 years and up.

-----TRANSPORTATION-----

AMTRAK

(800) USA RAIL (872-7245) / www.dot.ca.gov/hq/rail; www.amtrak.com

Ride the rails! See page xi (in the front) for more information.

BIKE MAPS (Riverside County)

The web site www.labikepaths.com is a fantastic resource. It actually covers all of Southern California, not just L.A., with links to specific counties for maps, bikeways, and other cycling information. Another helpful contact website and phone number is for the State of California Caltrans Office of Bicycle Facilities: (916) 653-0036; www.dot.ca.gov/hq/tpp/offices/bike/contracts.htm.

THE CARRIAGE HOUSE

(909) 781-0780

Mission Inn District, Riverside

$$$$

Take a ride in a beautiful horse-drawn carriage through the historic Mission Inn district. The carriage holds four adults comfortably or two adults, three kids. With horses named Cinderella and Belle, children feel like they are living out a storybook fantasy, if only for a short ride.

Tea parties are a perfect occasion to incorporate a carriage ride. Or, rent the wagon, which seats up to sixteen people, for a cowboy party. At Christmas time, even though there isn't any snow to glisten, the carriage sleigh bells ring if you're listenin', plus Christmas lights are even more dazzling when seen from this old-fashioned vantage point. Note: Take a ride around the block with Santa Claus for only $3 per person at Christmas time, weather permitting.

Hours: Carriages can often be found along the Mission Inn district, but calling for a reservation is your best bet.

Admission: A twenty-minute ride is $35, inclusive, for everyone in the entire carriage; an hour ride is $70.

Ages: All

CARRIAGES BY MARGARET

(909) 789-1620

Riverside

$$$$

What Cinderella or Prince Charming child hasn't dreamed of riding in a horse-drawn carriage, if only because of fairy tales? Take a ride in an immaculate white or black carriage pulled by a beautiful silky horse that is gentle enough to pet. The carriages seat up to six people, four adults comfortably. If you have a party, reserve a formal, horse-drawn trolley, or reserve a hay wagon. Choose your own route for a ride or call to use the carriage for special events

Hours: Call to make a reservation.

Admission: Prices vary, depending on the length of the ride and the destination.

Ages: All

LAKE PERRIS BMX

(909) 657-4917 / www.perrisbmx.com

18700 Lake Perris Drive at the Lake Perris Fairgrounds, Perris

(Exit Escondido Fwy [215] E. on Cajalco Expressway/Ramona Expressway, L. on Lake Perris Dr. [TG: 778 A1])

$$

Good clean fun can be had at this dirt race track. The BMX sport is for young and old as long as participants are wearing a helmet, long pants, and long sleeve shirts. The professional track is best described as "tight" (i.e. meaning very cool). Bikers under 17 years old must have a signed parental waiver on file.

Hours: Practices only are held Mon., 5:30pm - 8:30pm. Practice and races are held Wed., Fri., and Sun. evenings. Call for times.

Admission: $5 for just the practice; $10 for the practice and the race.

Ages: 4 years and up.

LAKE PERRIS REMOTE CONTROL RACE PARK

(877) 299-5777 or (909) 657-7884 / www.lprp.com

18700 Lake Perris Drive at the Lake Perris Fairgrounds, Perris

(Exit Escondido Fwy [215] E. on Cajalco Expressway/Ramona Expressway, L. on Lake Perris Dr. [TG: 778 A1])

$$$

Are you a driver who likes to be in control? Then head to the remote control race park and join up to twenty-five other cars that are racing around this large covered dirt track. Electric cars and cars that run on nitro hit the tracks here daily for practices and for races. Call to see what eventis on the current schedule. A hobby shop with workshop space is on the premises where you may fix a broken part or rent a car for the duration.

Hours: Open Mon. - Fri., noon - 9pm; Sat. - Sun., 9am - 9pm. Ask about extended holiday hours.

Admission: $5 if you bring your own car; $10 to rent a car/truck that comes with three batteries or two tanks of gas - enough for about an hour. You may purchase a vehicle here, too - $159 up to $450.

Ages: 5 years and up.

METROLINK (Riverside County)

See the entry for METROLINK (Los Angeles County) on page 173 for details.

ORANGE EMPIRE RAILWAY MUSEUM

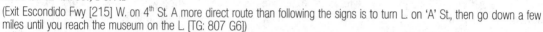

(909) 657-2605- recording; (909) 943-3020 - live person / www.oerm.org   !/$$$

2201 S. 'A' Street, Perris

(Exit Escondido Fwy [215] W. on 4ᵗʰ St. A more direct route than following the signs is to turn L. on 'A' St., then go down a few miles until you reach the museum on the L. [TG: 807 G6])

If you love trains, make tracks to the Orange Empire Railway Museum where you can really go full steam ahead! This sixty-five-acre, unique, outdoor museum is best described as a work-in-progress. Railcars from all over the country, in various states of disrepair, find their way here. Some are being restored while others are just stationed here. Walk around to see which railcars the volunteers are working on.

The museum is open daily, but weekends are the prime time to visit as this is the only time when train and trolley rides are available. Purchase an all-day ride ticket, which is good for rides on a locomotive, electric trolley, streetcar, freight car, and/or passenger car. (Three types of cars are usually running.) Each ride lasts about fifteen minutes and a conductor explains the history of the vehicles and the museum, and the impact of train transportation in Southern California. The train's whistle, the clickety-clack of its wheels, and the clanging of streetcar bells add excitement to your adventure.

Walk through the several car houses (i.e. buildings that house railcars) to see historic Yellow Cars (which my kids thought looked like school buses); a San Francisco cable car; electric railway streetcars and locomotives dating from 1900; steam engines; and wood passenger cars. The car houses are usually open on weekends. They are open during the week whenever volunteer staff is available.

Check out the Middleton Collection that includes old toy and scale model railroad cars, and others. There is an ongoing video that shows how tracks are laid. We got derailed at the gift shop, which offers videos, books, and all sorts of train paraphernalia. There are also a few picnic tables and grassy areas on site.

Hours: The grounds are open daily, 9am - 5pm. Train and trolley rides are available only on weekends and major holidays, 11 - 5pm. Closed Thanksgiving and Christmas.

Admission: The museum is free. All-day ride passes are $8 for adults; $6 for ages 5 - 11; children 4 and under ride free.

Ages: All

PERRIS AUTO SPEEDWAY

(800) 976-RACE (7223) or (909) 940-0134 / www.perrisautospeedway.com $$

18700 Lake Perris Drive at the Lake Perris Fairgrounds, Perris

(Exit Escondido Fwy [215] E. on Cajalco Expressway/Ramona Expressway, L. on Lake Perris Dr. [TG: 778 A1])

Get up to speed and race to this premier half-mile oval dirt race track. Competitions include super stocks, street stocks, champ trucks, dwarfs, sprint cars, cruisers, and more. Join in on the dance contest before the race begins. A sound system in the 8,000-seat grandstand is hooked up to speakers so the audience can hear, even over the roar of the engines.

Hours: Call for a schedule of events.

Admission: Tickets start as low as $5.

Ages: 6 years and up.

YOUNG EAGLES PROGRAM (Riverside)

(909) 683-2309 / www.youngeagles.com

4130 Mennes Street at Flabob Airport, Riverside

(Exit Pomona Fwy [60] S. on Rubidoux (not the Valleyview/Rubidoux exit), go to the end, turn L. and a quick R. through the airport gates. [TG: 685 C3])

See the entry for YOUNG EAGLES PROGRAM (Pacoima) on page 177 for details. This particular airport also features a half-hour ground school and preflight instructions, plus a snack bar and small souvenir store, and perhaps a chance at the controls while in the air. Reservations are required.

Hours: The second Sat. of the month, except August and December, starting at 7:45am.

Admission: Free

Ages: 8 - 17 years old.

-----ZOOS AND ANIMALS-----

MAGNOLIA BIRD FARM (Riverside)

(909) 278-0878

12200 Magnolia Avenue, Riverside

(Going N.E. on Riverside Fwy [91], exit S.E. on Pierce, R. on Magnolia. Going S.W. on 91, exit S.W. on Magnolia. [TG: 744 C3])

See the entry for MAGNOLIA BIRD FARM (Anaheim) on page 274 for details. The main difference between the two is size, with this location being almost three times as large. The aviary here includes parakeets, love birds, finches, and quail, as well as doves and pigeons.

As springtime brings the birth of new baby birds, kids can sometimes see them being hand fed through the glass walls. Tour groups, of at least ten or more people, will learn about seed, such as which kind is best for what species; see and study a (live) white dove; and more.

Hours: Open Tues. - Sat., 9am - 5pm. Closed Sun., Mon., and some holidays. Reservations are needed for the free, half-hour tour.

Admission: Free

Ages: All

MINOR ZOO

4080/4090 Park Avenue, Hemet

(Exit Escondido Fwy [215] E. on Ethanac Rd. [74] which turns into the Pinacate Rd. which turns into Florida Ave., L. on N. Stanford St., R. on Park Ave. [TG: 811 E6])

This zoo is the personal collection of the Minor family. It is not so much a destination in and of itself, but a stop and stare. There are several domestic animals, such as horses and goats, and several exotic animals such as zebras, camels, gazelles, a buffalo, and peacocks. Just pull over to the side of the road and admire them all. Tip: The KIDZONE (see pg. 292) is down the road a bit and a terrific "real" destination.

Hours: Open daily, sunrise - sunset.

Admission: Free

Ages: All

-----PALM SPRINGS-----

PALM SPRINGS (and the surrounding desert cities)

I know that Palm Springs, and the surrounding area, is officially part of San Bernardino County, but it seems like (and is referred to most frequently) as a destination in and of itself, so I've listed it as such. Creative liberties? (Or just thinking like a tourist!)

A collage of words and images used to come to mind when I thought about Palm Springs - desert; hot; resort; homes of the rich and famous; golf; and shopping mecca. Now that my family has thoroughly explored it, I can add to this list - kid-friendly; fun; beautiful; great hiking opportunities; and educational treasures.

AGUA CALIENTE CULTURAL MUSEUM

(760) 323-0151 / www.accmuseum.org

219 S. Palm Canyon Drive, Palm Springs

(Exit Interstate 10 S. on Indian Canyon Dr., R. on Alejo, L. on Palm Canyon Dr. [Hwy 111]. [TG: 786 D2])

This small tribal museum relates the history and culture of the Agua Caliente Band of Cahuilla Indians via changing exhibits. School tours feature an explanation of the exhibits, demonstrations, and a video presentation. The museum also offers classroom visits and field trips.

Hours: Open Memorial Day through Labor Day, Wed. - Sat., 10am - 5pm; Sun., noon - 5pm. Open Labor Day through Memorial Day, Fri. - Sat., 10am - 5pm; Sun., noon - 5pm. Closed New Year's Day, Thanksgiving, and Christmas.

Admission: Free

Ages: 7 years and up.

BIG MORONGO CANYON PRESERVE

(760) 363-7190 / www.bigmorongo.org

11055 East Drive, Morongo Valley

(Exit Interstate 10 N. on Route 62, R. on East Dr. [TG: 615 J6])

The quietness of this peaceful preserve was broken only by shouts from my kids whenever they spotted a lizard, bunny, roadrunner, or other animals. The trails are relatively easy to walk, and many of them go in and through the canyon and trees. There are several short looping boardwalk trails as well as a longer hike of five-and-a-half miles along the Canyon Trail, which extends the length of the canyon. Fresh water marshes and a variety of trees and plants add to the otherwise more traditional desert landscape. Wildlife here includes Bighorn sheep, raccoons, coyotes, and so many species of birds that people come just to observe them. Bring binoculars! Note that preserve's terrific website offers a great trail map and detailed description of the trails.

Hours: Open daily, 7:30am - sunset. No dogs or pets allowed.

Admission: Free

Ages: 3 years and up.

BOOMERS! (Cathedral City)

(760) 770-7522 / www.boomersparks.com

67700 E. Palm Canyon Drive [111], Cathedral City

(Exit Interstate 10 S. on Palm Drive/Gene Autry Tr., L. on E. Palm Canyon Dr. [Hwy 111]. [TG: 787 C7])

This huge family fun center (the first castle off Highway 111), offers a variety of entertainment for everyone. Choose from three themed **miniature golf** courses - $7 per round for ages 6 and up, children 5 and under are free with a paid adult admission; **go carts** - $5.25 a ride for drivers, $1.50 for passengers; **bumper boats** (avoid the shooting fountain waters or get refreshed) - $5 a ride for drivers, $2 for passengers; a **simulator** ride with different "experiences" - $5; a **rock climbing wall** - $6 for a two climbs; **batting cages**; and over 200 video and sport games, plus a prize redemption center. Note that height restrictions apply on some rides.

Hours: Open Mon. - Thurs., 11am - 10pm; Fri., 11am - 11pm; Sat., 10am - 11pm; Sun., 10am - 10pm.

Admission: Attractions are individually priced above, or purchase one of the super saver packages.

Ages: 4 years and up.

CABOTS PUEBLO MUSEUM

(760) 329-7610 / www.cabotsmuseum.org

67616 Desert View Avenue, Desert Hot Springs

(Exit Interstate 10 N. on Palm Dr., R. on Hacienda., L. on Miracle Hill, R. on Desert View. [TG: 697 B4])

This four-story, thirty-five room, Hopi-style pueblo with sixty-five doors and 150 windows, was built out of the side of a mountain. Cabot, the owner and builder, believed in mysticism and an Indian belief that symmetry retains an evil spirt, so he constructed the abode with slanted doorways and floors, uneven walls, windows with odd shapes, and small, narrow doorframes and staircases. (It looks like our house before remodeling.)

On the first floor is a cave-like bedroom (raised off the floor to avoid rattlesnakes), a living room with a dirt floor, a "Kiva" (i.e. prayer room), a small art gallery, a smaller Alaskan room, and a kitchen. Some of the artifacts in these rooms include ceremonial Indian costumes, headdresses, drums, carvings, pottery, baskets, and a rock collection. The forty-five-minute tour includes the fascinating history of Cabot and his pueblo. The upstairs, which is not yet open to the public, is a bathroom and a series of other rooms displaying "finds" from Cabot's travels. The outside grounds are almost as eclectic as the inside house, with an enormous Indian statute carved from a giant Sequoia, old signs, and some rusted tools and equipment. There is also a small picnic facility.

Hours: Open Sat., 10am - 4pm; Sun., noon - 4pm. Closed during the summer and on major holidays.
Admission: $6 for adults; $5 for seniors; $4 for ages 6 - 16; children 5 and under are free.
Ages: 7 years and up.

CHILDREN'S DISCOVERY MUSEUM OF THE DESERT

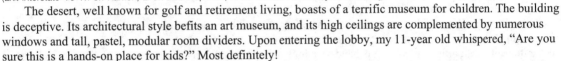

(760) 321-0602 / www.cdmod.org $$
71701 Gerald Ford Drive, Rancho Mirage
(Exit Interstate 10 W. on Ramon, L. on Bob Hope Dr., R. on Gerald Ford Dr. [TG: 788 B6])

The desert, well known for golf and retirement living, boasts of a terrific museum for children. The building is deceptive. Its architectural style befits an art museum, and its high ceilings are complemented by numerous windows and tall, pastel, modular room dividers. Upon entering the lobby, my 11-year old whispered, "Are you sure this is a hands-on place for kids?" Most definitely!

The exhibits flow easily from one to another. Note that no strollers are permitted. Some of the scientific exhibits in the front include a music machine of sorts, where a touch on a metal sculpture produces a jazz or percussion musical sound, and a stroboscope, which is a display where kids can draw their own design, attach it to the fan, and watch it "dance" in the strobe light. Follow any one of three colored ropes through a kid-size, spider-web-looking rope maze. A reading corner has several books, tables and chairs, and colorful wooden pattern pieces. Indigenous rock and flora displays add local color to one section. Put together a life-size skeleton in another area. Get properly suited up with a safari hat, goggles, and gloves and use the tools provided to find faux artifacts in a simulated dig. Climb a (fake) rock wall, complete with hand and foot holds. The relatively large Make-It-Take-It work area is a real treat for kids who like to take apart radios, computer components, and other household gadgets. They can even use the screwdrivers, glue, pieces of wood, and recycled materials to make a new creation to take home. Design a home with drafting boards and a magnetic wall that utilizes stick-on furniture. Painting a car is not normally allowed, but the VW Beetle here is a much-decorated canvas on wheels. Smocks, paints, and brushes are supplied. The Art Corner has paper, markers, a computer with art programs, and even a giant loom for young weavers. Toward the back of the museum is a well-stocked pretend grocery store with mini-carts and a checkout counter. Pizza, every child's favorite food, can be made to order just next door. This pizzeria has all the ingredients (made from cloth) to make pizzas, as well as aprons, hats, and a pretend brick oven, plus tables and chairs for "customers." An enclosed toddlers' play area and a real CHP motorcycle are also located in this wing.

Walk up the snake-like, winding ramp to the second story to Grandma's Attic Room. This area is decorated with old trunks, hat boxes, fishing poles, pictures, and adding machines and telephones. One of the best features is the quality costumes in which to play dress up. They range from princess dresses with sequins to military uniforms to suits and everything in between. Lots of hats, an assortment of shoes and boots, plus boas and ties are some of the accessories.

The above merely lists the highlights of the museum! Parental supervision is required at all times but, as each activity was so much fun, I was delighted to comply. Both the adjacent Dinah Shore theater and the outdoor amphitheater put on a variety of performances year round. Ask about numerous special programs and classes offered for children, such as art classes, ballet lessons, manners classes, and lots more.

Hours: Open January through April, Mon. - Sat., 10am - 5pm; Sun., noon - 5pm. Open the rest of the year, Tues. - Sat., 10am - 5pm; Sun., noon - 5pm. School field trips here are offered Tues. - Fri. at 9:30am - 11:30am and 12:30pm - 2pm. Closed New Year's Day, Easter, Labor Day, and Christmas.

Admission: $5 per person; children under 2 are free. Yearly membership is a great deal at $15 per person. School groups, consisting of a minimum of ten students, are $3.50 per student; teachers and chaperones are free.

Ages: 2 - 11 years.

COACHELLA VALLEY MUSEUM & CULTURAL CENTER

(760) 342-6651 / www.coachellavalleymuseum.org

82616 Miles Avenue, Indio

(Exit Interstate 10 S. on Monroe, L. on Miles Ave. [TG: 5410 F7])

Each city desires to preserve its history and make it available for future generations. The Coachella Valley Museum has displays inside the small 1928 adobe home that reflect Indian and pioneer heritage. Some of the permanent displays include Indian pottery and arrowheads; dioramas of date picking, and an interesting thirteen-minute video about growing dates; old-fashioned clothing; original kitchen appliances; and a large panel displaying various fire alarms.

Outside, on the beautiful grounds, are lots of old agricultural tools and machinery. Peek inside the blacksmith shop to see forges, anvils, tongs, and other tools. Take a guided tour to learn background information on the items here or, although nothing is hands-on, look around by yourself to get a rich, visual sampling of history.

Hours: Open mid-September - mid-June, Wed. - Sat., 10am - 4pm; Sun., 1pm - 4pm. Closed all major holidays.

Admission: $2 for adults; $1 for seniors and ages 5 -1 4; children 4 and under are free.

Ages: 5 years and up.

COACHELLA VALLEY PRESERVE

(760) 343-1234 / www.cnlm.org/coachella.html

29200 Thousand Palms Canyon Road, Coachella

(Exit Interstate 10 E. on Ramon Rd., L. on Thousand Palms Canyon Rd. [TG: 759 D5])

This 18,000-acre preserve is not only immense, but it is diverse in topography and wildlife. The preserve straddles Indio Hills and the infamous San Andreas Fault. Thousand Palms Oasis (yes, it contains at least this many palm trees) is at the heart of the Coachella Valley Preserve. The oasis is supported by water constantly seeping along the fault line.

Kids begin to appreciate the many faces of the desert as they hike through here. It is sandy, dry, and rocky, and these elements create sand dunes, bluffs, and mesas. It is also mountainous and interspersed with dense palm trees, cacti, and various other vegetation. Some of the trails are as short as one-quarter mile, while others are longer at one-and-a-half miles, and more.

Start at the rustic Visitors Center that has natural history exhibits behind glass. The displays include arrowheads, mounted insects, birds' nests, and eggs. Bring a water bottle and/or a picnic lunch and have a delightful time exploring desert wilderness at its finest.

Hours: Open daily, sunset - sunrise. Closed July - September.

Admission: Free

Ages: 4 years and up.

COACHELLA VALLEY WILD BIRD CENTER

(760) 347-2647

46500 Van Buren Street, Indio

(Exit Interstate 10 S. E. on Golf Center Pkwy and turn R. at the off ramp, L. on Ave. 45 and go 1 mile. The center is off the road to the L. [TG: 5470 J1])

This center offers a wonderful opportunity to learn about native wild birds in a variety of ways. The small inside exhibit room has taxidermied animals, literature, and a few other displays, as well as several iguanas and live snakes such as rosy boas, racers, and king snakes. Outside are enclosures that hold birds that have been injured, imprinted, or abused. Some are releasable; some are not. The enclosures hold hawks, geese, great horned owls, and others. Docents talk about the birds - why they are here, what they eat, why they are not good to have as pets, and lots more good information. Beyond this area are fenced-in wetlands with reeds, a few ponds, and more life-sustaining elements. Sandpipers, mallards, pelicans, and other waterfowl nest here, or at least drop in for a visit. Bring binoculars. Bring a sack lunch to take advantage of the on-site picnic area. Tours are given by reservation. Call beforehand and ask what supplies you can bring to help out the center, such as trash bags, paper towels, film, etc.

Hours: Open daily, 10am - 5pm. The wetlands area is open earlier by appointment.

Admission: Free; donations are appreciated.

Ages: 4 years and up.

COVERED WAGON TOURS

$$$$$

(800) 367-2161 or (760) 347-2161 / www.coveredwagontours.com

Washington Street, Thousand Palms

(Going E. on Interstate 10, exit E. on Ramon Rd., which turns into Washington at Thousand Palms Cyn Rd. Going W. on 10, exit N. on Washington St. The tour begins off a dirt road about ½ mile E. of Thousand Palms Cyn. A sign is there when the tour is open. [TG: 390 C8])

Travel in a mule-drawn, covered wagon for a two-hour narrated tour of the Coachella Valley Preserve. You travel along the San Andreas fault and see three oases and lots of wildlife. Occasionally you get out along the way. The wagons are not the primitive ones your pioneer ancestors used, as these have padded seats, springs, tires, and other amenities, although part of the fun is the bumpiness of the ride. Take just the tour, or add on a chuck wagon cookout dinner and one-man Western Cowboy show for the full western experience.

Hours: Call for tour times.

Admission: Tours are $36 for adults; $18 for ages 7 - 16; children 6 and under are free. Tour and dinner costs $60 for adults; $30 for ages 7 - 16; children 6 and under are free.

Ages: 5 years and up.

DESERT ADVENTURES

$$$$$

(888) 440-JEEP (5337) or (760) 324-5337 / www.red-jeep.com

67555 E. Palm Canyon Drive, Cathedral City

(Exit Interstate 10 S. on Palm Drive/Gene Autry Tr., L. on E. Palm Canyon Dr. [Hwy. 111] It's In Canyon Plaza. [TG: 787 C6])

Explore the natural wonders of the desert by choosing from several different excursions or adventures via a two- to four-hour, seven-passenger jeep ride. All the guides are knowledgeable in history, geology, animals, Native American heritage, and more. The Indian Cultural Adventure takes you through archaeology sites; an authentically re-created Cahuilla Indian village; a hidden, lush oasis; and a stream, all the while learning about the history of Cahuilla Indians and the Palm Springs area. Lost Legends of the Wild West Adventure is for cowboys and cowgirls as passengers explore a replica of an old Wild West Mining Camp, complete with a walk-through mine and the necessary equipment. Through no fault of their own, visitors may also straddle the San Andreas Fault line, as well as inspect a fossil bed and look at the great geography. The Mystery Canyon Adventure is a great combination of an off-road adventure and a naturalist tour. Travel through a rich agricultural area to steep-walled canyons and ravines, fantastic and colorful rock formations, and cross the San Andreas Fault. The Sunset - Nightwatch Adventure is special, and there really are millions of stars in the sky (at least out here in the desert!). See God's masterpiece sunsets on an original canvas.

Some of the tours involve hiking around the area. Bighorn sheep, coyotes, and other wildlife are abundant along the back roads, so keep your eyes open. Bring your camera! Dress appropriately with closed-toed shoes and a hat, and bring sun block, sunglasses, and a water bottle.

Hours: Open year-round, weather permitting. Call first to make a reservation.

Admission: Two-hour tours are $59 for adults; three-hour tours are $79; four-hour tours are $99. Seniors and ages 6 - 12 are $5 off. Sunset tours are $79 per person.

Ages: 6 years and up.

DESERT IMAX THEATER

(760) 324-7333 / www.desertimax.com

$$$

68510 E. Palm Canyon Drive, Cathedral City

(Going E. on Interstate 10, exit S. on Date Palm Dr., R. on Palm Canyon [Hwy111]. Going W. on 10, exit W. on Ramon Rd., L. on Date Palm, R. on Palm Canyon. [TG: 787 E7])

Larger than life! That's the images shown on the huge IMAX screen, which features several films on any given day. Some of the films are entertaining and some are educational. I am personally partial to the 3-D format, also available here, as viewers get more involved with the on-screen action. Ask about double feature specials and school group discounts.

Hours: Movies are shows daily, noon - 8:45pm.

Admission: 2-D movie tickets are $7.50 for adults; $6.50 for seniors; $5.50 for ages 3 - 12. 3-D movies are $8.50 for adults; $7.50 for seniors; $6.50 for ages 3 - 12. Matinee prices are cheaper.

Ages: 3 years and up.

DINOSAURS / WHEEL INN RESTAURANT

(909) 849-8309 - dinos; (909) 849-7012 - restaurant

!/$

50900 Seminole Drive, Cabazon

(Exit Interstate 10 N. on Main St., R. on Seminole. It's E. of Hadleys, about 20 minutes N.W. of Palm Springs. [TG: 723 E3])

While cruising down the desert highway, looking out the window, your kids see the usual things, such as big trucks, cactus, and dinosaurs. Screech go the brakes! The gigantic (150-feet long) Apatosaurus, with fiery eyes, is almost triple the size of the actual dinosaur that roamed the earth long ago. The same goes for the Tyrannosaurus behind him. Enter the steel and concrete Apatosaurus through its tail. Along the cave-like stairway are a few fossils and rocks behind glass displays, plus information and explanations regarding these two huge time travelers. Up in the Apatosaurus' belly is a gift shop, specializing in everything dinosaur. The fun for a child is just being inside here. The T-Rex, however, can only be looked at.

Wheel Inn Restaurant is a folksy truck-stop cafe with merchandise for sale, such as gift items and sculptures, which are also displayed throughout. Retail pictures on the walls range from Disney to the Southwest. (Note: There are pictures of scantily-clad women toward the back.) Note: A Burger King is also at this stop, kind of in front of the dinosaurs. All in all, though, it's a *dino*-mite little stop!

Hours: The dinosaur gift shop is open October through April daily, 9:30am - 5:30pm; May through September daily, 8am - 7pm. The restaurant is open twenty-four hours.

Admission: Free to look and walk around the dinosaurs.

Ages: All

EL DORADO POLO CLUB

(760) 342-2223 / www.eldoradopolo.com

!/$$

50950 Madison Street, Indio

(Exit Interstate 10 S. on Monroe St., R. on 50th, L. on Madison. [TG: 5470 C6])

This huge club features thirteen polo fields (and just one is really big!), a stick and ball field, an exercise track, and stabling for up to 1,200 horses. Visitors are invited to come and watch an exciting game of polo, where the thundering hooves and "whack" of the mallet keep eyes riveted on horses and riders. Practice matches are generally held during the week. On weekends, especially on Sundays, top players often compete in tournament matches that last about an hour. An announcer is brought in for Sunday's games. Bring a picnic lunch to enjoy on the grass or have a tailgate party.

Hours: Games are usually played Sun. (and sometimes on Fri. and Sat.), November through April, at 10am, noon, and 2pm. Call for a schedule as there are other times to come watch, too. Closed New Year's Day, Thanksgiving, and Christmas.

Admission: Free for practices matches and Fri. and Sat. games; Sun. games are $5 per person for clubhouse seating.

Ages: 3 years and up.

GENERAL PATTON MEMORIAL MUSEUM

(760) 227-3483

6250 Chiriaco Road, Chiriaco Summit

(Exit Interstate 10 at Chiriaco Summit. The museum is right off the freeway, 30 miles east of Indio. [TG: 5477 A6])

Any study of World War II includes at least one lesson on war hero, General George Patton. Even if kids don't know who he is yet, they will like all the "war stuff" at the museum. Outside the memorial building are over a dozen tanks. Kids can't climb on them, but they can run around and play army.

Inside, the front room is dominated by a five-ton relief map depicting the Colorado River Aqueduct route and surrounding area. The large back room is filled with General Patton's personal effects, and lots of WWII memorabilia such as uniforms, weapons, flags, artillery, and more. Our favorite exhibits include a jeep, a lifelike statue of General Patton (who looks amazingly like George C. Scott), and rounds of machine gun bullets. Special displays showcase Nazi items taken from fallen Nazi soldiers; a small, but powerful pictorial Holocaust display; and items found on the battlefield of Gettysburg.

Over one million servicemen and women were trained at this huge Desert Training Center site during WWII. If your child is especially interested in this period of military history, take him to the remnants of the training camps, accessible by four-wheel vehicles. Call the museum for directions and more details.

Hours: Open daily, 9:30am - 4:30pm. Closed Thanksgiving and Christmas.

Admission: $4 for adults; $3.50 for seniors; children 11 and under are free.

Ages: 3 years and up.

GUIDE DOGS OF THE DESERT

(760) 329-6257 / www.guidedogsofthedesert.com

60740 Dillon Road, Whitewater

(Exit Interstate 10 N. on Highway 62 [Twenty-Nine Palms], go about ¼ of a mile, L. on Dillon Rd. [TG: 725 F2])

Thirty or so dogs consider this place their temporary home as they are trained to become guide dogs for their blind owners. Visitors learn about the program which takes pups, places them in loving homes for eighteen months or so, then brings them back for serious training as guide dogs, and matches them with a new master or mistress. Explore the kennels where the puppies are raised (call first to see if any puppies are currently here); tour the dormitories (if they are unoccupied) where owners stay for their orientation; watch dogs being trained; learn how to treat guide dogs (i.e. when it's acceptable to touch them and when it's not); and learn how to put a harness on the dogs. Tours can last a half hour up to an hour and a half, depending on the interest of the visitors.

Hours: Tours are given by reservation, Mon. - Fri., 9am - 3pm; Sat., 10am - 1pm.

Admission: Free; donations appreciated.

Ages: 3 years and up.

HI-DESERT NATURE MUSEUM

(760) 369-7212 / www.yucca-valley.org/services/museum.html

57116 Twentynine Palms Highway, Yucca Valley

(Exit Twentynine Palms Highway [62] N. on Dumosa, just E. of Sage Ave. [TG: 4957 J2])

I *highly* recommend the Hi-Desert Nature Museum. It offers lots of activity, and has fascinating exhibits on wildlife, geology, culture, and science.

Just some of the rotating exhibits in the front room have included Wild on Wildflowers; Shake, Rattle & Roll - Living With Earthquakes; and Holiday Traditions from around the world. We saw Black Widow.

Arachnophobia aside, the fantastic photographs, video, and information combined with live and dead specimens made learning about this feared insect interesting. The far wall in this room contains encased displays of Indian baskets, arrowheads, pottery, and Kachina dolls.

Another room has taxidermied waterfowl plus animals that are unique to the desert such as mule deer, quail, roadrunners, jack rabbits, and coyotes. A touch corner in here has skulls and soft fur to match to the stuffed animals.

Fossils and a wonderful rock and mineral collection comprise the earth science room. The petrified logs are unusual, as are the sphere balls. Rocks such as amethyst and malachite are shown in their rough, natural state, and also in a polished version. Raw minerals are shown next to their commercial counterpart such as fluorspar next to toothpaste, and talc next to baby powder. This helps kids to make connections and understand that man-made products were first God-created resources.

A mini-zoo has live squirrels, lizards, snakes, and a tarantula. A docent is often on hand to assist your child in holding one of the animals. I'm proud to write that after recovering from my cold sweat, I held the (large!) tarantula.

The Kids' Corner is action packed. There is a small sand pit (I mean archaeological dig); animal puppets; a butterfly and insect collection; stone mortar and pestles with corn kernels to grind; animal tracks to match with animals; a touch table with whale bones, rocks, and shells; books; and containers of construction toys. The Hi-Desert Nature Museum also offers themed traveling classroom programs on insects, wildflowers, a particular animal, and more.

The community center/park just behind the museum is equally fine. It has four basketball courts, a baseball field, a skateboard park with cement ramps and steps, a sand volleyball court, a covered picnic area, grassy areas, and three playgrounds complete with slides, climbing apparatus, and swings. All this and a few shade trees are against the backdrop of Joshua trees and the desert mountains.

Opening an oyster and finding a pearl that's been created by a grain of sand, is like opening the doors to this museum and finding a part of the sandy desert that has been transformed to a treasure of great worth.

Hours: Open Tues. - Sun., 10am - 5pm. Closed Mon. and major holidays.
Admission: Free
Ages: 1 year and up.

INDIAN CANYONS

(800) 790-3398 or (760) 325-3400 / www.indian-canyons.com
S. Palm Canyon Drive, Palm Springs
(Exit Interstate 10 S. on Indian Canyon Dr., which turns into Palm Canyon Dr. [Hwy 111], keep going S. for a few miles. [TG: 816 F3])

Vast, spectacular, and awesome are three words that come to mind when exploring Indian Canyons. Long ago, ancestors of the Agua Caliente Cahuilla Indians made their homes in these canyons and the surrounding area. Today, a large number of Indians still reside on the reservation here. The Tribal Council has opened the canyons for the public to explore.

A mile or so past the entrance gate is the trading post. Kids enjoy looking at the trinkets, jewelry, and Indian art work. Beyond the store are picnic grounds, and hiking and horse trails.

Palm Canyon is fifteen miles long and abundant with palm trees; a stark contrast to the surrounding rocky hills. The moderately-graded, paved walkway into this valley leads you along a stream, and to a picnic oasis. The scenery almost makes you forget that you're hiking! Andreas Canyon is unexpectedly lush with fan palms and more than 150 species of plants, all within a half-mile radius. Walk along a stream and see unusual rock formations. Challenge your kids to look for shapes or people in the rocks. There are also Indian caves back in the canyon and old grinding stones.

Hike to Murray Canyon from Andreas Canyon. Murray is smaller and less accessible, but no less beautiful. There are caves here also, which always sparks a child's imagination. Tahquitz Canyon, at 500 W. Mesquite, has a visitor's center and is only open for two-hour guided walking tours at $12.50 for adults; $6 for ages 11 and under. Call (760) 416-7044 to make reservations. Hiking in Indian Canyons is a wonderful opportunity to explore the desert wilderness surrounded by the stunning backdrop of the rocky mountains.

Hours: Open daily, 8am - 5pm. Summer schedule may vary.

Admission: $6 for adults; $4.50 for seniors, military, and students; $2 for ages 6 - 12; children 5 and under are free.

Ages: All, but older kids for real hiking.

JOSHUA TREE AND SOUTHERN RAILROAD MUSEUM

(760) 366-8503 / www.jtsrr.org

8901 Willow Lane, Joshua Tree

(Exit Highway 62 S. on Park Blvd., which turns into Quail Springs Rd., R. on Rincon, immediate L. on Willow Lane. [TG: 4959 D6])

This site is great for those who are *loco* about trains! Both the Live Steam Club and the railroad museum are located here. Model railroad enthusiasts can not only work on their hobby, but some have engineered it so that they live here, too. The trains range from two-and-a-half-inch scale models to full-size rail cars. If it's running, you're invited to ride on a model train which covers about a mile of track, over bridges and through desert terrain. Take a tour of the full-size cars including a diner, with its old-fashioned stove and icebox; a mail car, with small pigeonholes that are labeled with city names; a Pullman sleeping car, which always makes sleeping on a train seem romantic; and the grand finale - a caboose.

Inside the museum are model steam engines and lots of railroad memorabilia from Francis Moseley's collection. Ask to watch the video which shows how a model train operates.

Hours: Open to the public by appointment. Call to reserve a tour.

Admission: Free; donations appreciated.

Ages: 3 years and up.

JOSHUA TREE NATIONAL PARK

(760) 367-5500 / www.nps.gov/jotr

Joshua Tree

(South entrance: Exit Interstate 10 N. on Pinto Basin Rd. to the Cottonwood Springs Visitor Center, 25 miles east of Indio [TG: 390 K10]; North entrance: Exit Twentynine Palms Highway [62], S. on Utah Trail, in the town of Twentynine Palms [TG: 4962 H6]; West entrance: Exit Twentynine Palms Highway [62], in the town of Joshua Tree, S. on Park Blvd., which turns into Quail Springs Rd. [TG: 4959 H5]. This is the best way to reach Keys View and Hidden Valley.)

This over 900,000-acre park gets its name from the unique Joshua trees that Mormon visitors likened to the biblical Joshua reaching up to God. Explore the riches of this national treasure by car, by foot, and/or by camping.

Entire books are written on Joshua Tree National Park, so consider the following information a very condensed version. Just a few phrases attributed to this enormous park are "wind-sculpted boulders"; "massive granite monoliths"; "five fan palm oases dotting the park"; "wildflowers and wildlife"; "mountainous"; and "rugged." Start your visit at the main headquarters/Visitors Center in Oasis of Mara, located off the north entrance. You can get a map here, look at the botanical displays, and watch a slide show that gives a good overview of the park. One destination worth mentioning in particular is Desert Queen Ranch, a gold mine turned ranch. Guided tours, for $5 per person, are offered October through May. Explore and learn about the ranch and its colorful owners, and see the numerous vestiges of the people that once lived here. Against a backdrop of boulders, the ranch grounds are strewn with old rusty equipment and cars.

If you are automobile adventurers, which is a good way to get a lay of the land, there are many roads to travel. Keys View is the most popular destination because of its breathtaking view of the valley, mountains, and deserts. (Bring a panoramic camera.) If you don't mind a few bumps along the way, and kids usually don't, there are many dirt roads accessible only by four-wheel drive. Particularly outstanding is the eighteen-mile Geology Tour Road, which showcases some of the most incredible landscape the park offers.

Hiking runs the gamut from easy, one-tenth-of-a-mile trails, to strenuous, over thirteen-mile long trails. Three of the trails that offer fascinating terrain also lead to special destinations. The first one is the one-mile loop, Hidden Valley, with trails winding through massive boulders. It leads to and through legendary cattle rustlers' hideouts. The second is Barker Dam, which was built almost 100 years ago and is now a reservoir that many desert animals frequent. Approach it in whispers, if possible, so as not to scare away any critters. Encourage your children to look for some of the "hidden" wildlife in the water. The third is Lost Horse Mine, which is a rugged one-and-a-half-mile hike. This mine was used for prospecting and gold mining. Maybe there still is gold in them thar hills! **Bring water** no matter which trail you take because it is not supplied in the park.

Rock climbing is a very popular sport here. Even if your kids are too young to participate, they'll get a vicarious thrill at watching more experienced climbers. Boulder hopping is also fun, and that can be done by kids of all ages.

Camping is primitive at most of the 500 sites in Joshua Tree. Many campsites are located in the shelter of rocks, while others, at higher elevations, offer spots of shade. It is hot during the day, much cooler at night (even cold), and at times quite windy, but kids revel in it all. Water is only provided at Cottonwood and Black Rock Canyon campgrounds, so other sites are really back to basics.

National parks are sometimes called "universities of the outdoors." Joshua Tree National Park is an outstanding university to attend. Everyone will go home with a special memory, and a different reason for wanting to come back.

Hours: Open daily. Most of the visitors centers are open daily, 8am - 5pm.

Admission: $10 per vehicle, which is good for 7 day's admittance. Family campgrounds are $10 a night.

Ages: All

KNOTT'S SOAK CITY U.S.A. (Palm Springs)

(760) 325 - SURF (7873) or (760) 327-0499 / www.soakcityusa.com

1500 Gene Autry Trail, Palm Springs

$$$$$

(Exit Interstate 10 S. on Palm Drive/Gene Autry Trail. Or exit 10 W. on Ramon Rd., L. on Gene Autry. [TG: 787 B4])

This twenty-two-acre waterpark is truly an oasis in the desert. Built in and on top of a rocky hill, with an adjoining resort health club, the surroundings are luxurious. Eight waterslides for big kids range from mild uncovered slides, to enclosed forty-m.p.h. slides, to a seventy-foot free-fall slide. Cowabunga - the four-story interactive water playground is really rad with water squirting everyone and slides and everything fun. Get carried away in the gentle, three-foot-deep circular Lazy River inner tube ride. Catch a wave, dude, in the wave pool where kids can body or board surf. Younger children can take the plunge in their own small water play area that has a mushroom showering water, and a slide. Soak City also offers locker rentals ($8), private cabana rentals, full-service snack bars, and an indoor restaurant for all your creature comforts. Note: You cannot bring your own food inside the park. And yes, there is a video arcade here, too. Bring water shoes or flip flops because the cement gets really hot.

Tip: For a rocky mountain high in the desert, try your hand (and foot) at the UPRISING ROCK CLIMBING CENTER (see pg. 316), which is located right next door.

Hours: Open the end of March through Labor Day daily, usually 10am - 6pm. Open the rest of September through mid-October weekends only, usually 10am - 6pm. Call for hours as they fluctuate.

Admission: $22.95 for adults; $16.95 for ages 3 - 11; children 2 and under are free. After 3pm admission is $14.50 per person. Parking is $6.

Ages: All

LAKE CAHUILLA

(760) 564-4712 - lake; (800) 234-PARK (7275) - camping reservations

58075 Jefferson, La Quinta

$

(Exit Interstate 10 S. on Monroe St., R. on Avenue 58. [TG: 5530 A7])

Escape from the heat at Lake Cahuilla recreation park. The gigantic, stocked lake is a prime spot for fisherboys and girls to reel in the catch of the day. Kids 16 years and up need a state fishing license. Night fishing is open Friday and Saturday during the summer. Although swimming in the lake is prohibited, there is a pool open for your aquatic pleasure. A playground is located behind the pool - youngsters always have energy to play, no matter what temperature it is!

The park is not abundantly blessed with shade trees, but there are large grassy areas and palm trees to enhance its beauty. Hiking trails traverse the park, so make sure you've got plenty of sunscreen and water. Over 150 campsites are available here, complete with barbecues and other amenities. Come escape the city life, if just for a day or night.

Hours: The park is open mid-October through April daily, sunrise - sunset. It's open May through mid-October, Fri. - Mon., sunrise - sunset. Call for pool hours.

Admission: $2 for adults; $1 for ages 2 - 12. The swimming pool is an extra $1 per person. Primitive camping (space and a table - no shade trees) is $12 a site; an upgraded site is $16 a night. The camping reservation fee is $7.50. Fishing is $5 for ages 16 and up; $4 for ages 6 - 15; children 5 and under are free.

Ages: All

THE LIVING DESERT WILDLIFE AND BOTANICAL GARDEN PARK   ☼

(760) 346-5694 / www.livingdesert.org $$$

47900 Portola Avenue, Palm Desert

(Exit Interstate 10 S. on Monterey Ave., L. on Palm Canyon [Hwy 111], R. on Portola. [TG: 848 G4])

Kids can experience a lot of living in the 1,200-acre Living Desert! Choose one of three areas of interest - botanical gardens, wildlife, or hiking - or partake in some of each.

The nocturnal (this can be your child's new word for the day) animals exhibit is to your immediate left through the entrance gate. Bats are always a highlight in here. Behind this exhibit is the good-sized Discovery Room. Children can get a real "feel" for desert life as they touch live snakes, turtles, and a big hairy tarantula, plus feathers, bones, rocks, and fur. They can also put together puzzles.

The northern section of this "like a zoo, only better" park is mostly botanical. The pathways weave in and out amongst an incredible variety of desert floral including saguaros, yuccas, and towering palm trees. Caged bird life is abundant along the walkways, too. We took the time to really watch our feathered friends' activities and learned quite a bit.

Eagle Canyon houses twenty desert animal species living in their natural element. Powerful mountain lions, Mexican wolves, and the small fennec foxes dwell in their own craggy retreats that are easily viewed through glass. Don't miss the tree-climbing coyote! The three-acre African Village, Wa Tu Tu, has hyenas, camels, leopards, and a petting zoo (but not with the aforementioned animals!).

A trail system lies to the east, traversing through some of the 1,000-acre wilderness section of the park. Three loops offer something for every level hiker: An easy three-quarter mile hike; a moderate one-and-a-half-mile hike; and a strenuous five-mile, round-trip hike to the base of Eisenhower Mountain. Don't get me wrong, however, the walk around the park is a hike in itself. If you get tired, take the fifty-minute, narrated tram tour that goes all around the park. A pick up and drop off shuttle is available for $6 per person. (This service is also included in the tram price.)

Animals in the Living Desert dwell in outdoor enclosures that resemble their natural habitat. A rocky mountain is home to the Bighorn sheep. Look for them leaping among the boulders. Other exotic animals include Arabian oryx, aardwolves, zebras, cheetahs, small African mammals, giraffes, and birds. We saw several other animals in the wild, too, such as a snake slithering across our path and the ever-speedy roadrunner darting out of the bushes. Seeing them authenticated the unique setting of this park. Want to see more animals, more up close? See Wildlife Wonders, a live animal presentation at the outdoor theater, featuring your favorite desert critters. Also check the schedule for "Meet the Keeper," where the animal keepers visit the enclosures and talk about five different critters each day, such as cheetahs, hyenas, big horn sheep, and more.

Visit here during the spring when the desert flowers and trees explode in a profusion of colors, or come in the winter to see Wildlights (see pg. 618). Anytime you choose to visit the Living Desert will be a time of wonder, relaxation, and education.

Hours: Open September through mid-June daily, 9am - 5pm. Open mid-June through August daily, 8am - 1:30pm. Closed Christmas. The Children's Discovery Room is open daily, 10am - 4pm, but closed the first Tues. of the month. The weekend Wildlife Wonders show is usually given at 11am and 2pm most of the year; at 10am in the summer.

Admission: $9.95 for adults; $8.50 for seniors; $5.25 for ages 3 - 12; children 2 and under are free. The tram tour is $5 a person. School groups, with reservations, are free, however spaces fill up fast so make your reservation soon.

Ages: All

MCCALLUM THEATRE

(760) 340-ARTS (2787) / www.mccallumtheatre.org $$$$
73000 Fred Waring Drive, Palm Desert
(Exit Interstate 10 S. on Palm Desert/Monterey, L. on Fred Waring Dr. It's in the Bob Hope Cultural Center. [TG: 818 E7])

This beautiful theater seats over a thousand people and has three levels of seating, including box seats. First class productions include *Sound of Music*, *Riverdance*, *Cats*, and *The Nutcracker Suite*, as well as famous individual artists. Several one-hour, just-for-kids plays and musicals are put on throughout the year, too. Past titles include *Romana Quimby*, *Pippi Longstocking*, and *Pinocchio*. There are also several productions that are enjoyable for the entire family. Ask about the Field Trip Series in which slightly abbreviated dance and theater performances are given for free for students and educators. Art is important! Tours often focus on the stage and technical aspects of the facility. Contact the McCallum for more information.

Hours: Call for a program schedule.

Admission: Tickets for the kids' shows range between $5 - $15 per person, depending on the seat. Tickets for other performances range from $40 - $100 per.

Ages: 4 years and up.

MOORTEN BOTANICAL GARDEN

(760) 327-6555 $
1701 S. Palm Canyon Drive, Palm Springs
(Exit Interstate 10 S. on Indian Canyon Dr., which turns into Palm Canyon Dr. [Hwy111]. When the main road turns L. and becomes E. Palm Canyon Dr., make sure to stay R. on S. Palm Canyon. The garden will be on your R. [TG: 786 E5])

This place has plenty of prickly plants along pleasurable pathways. In other words, this compact botanical garden, specializing in cacti, is a delightful stroll and an interesting way to study desert plant life. There are over 3,000 varieties of cacti, trees, succulents, and flowers, plus lots of birds! You'll see giant saguaros, ocotillos, and grizzly bear cactus, and you may walk through a greenhouse (or cactarium). Toward the entrance are petrified logs, and a few, small desert animals in cages. Enjoy this spot of greenery in the midst of the sandy, brown desert.

Hours: Open Mon. - Tues., Thurs. - Sat., 9am - 4:30pm; Sun., 10am - 4pm. Closed Wed., Thanksgiving, and Christmas.

Admission: $2.50 for adults; $1 for ages 5 - 15; children 4 and under are free.

Ages: All

OFFROAD RENTALS

(760) 325-0376 / www.offroadrentals.com $$$$$
59511 US Highway 111, Palm Springs
(Exit Interstate 10 S.W. on White Water, which turns into Tipton Rd., go L. at the intersection of Wendy Rd. to stay on Tipton, then L. on Hwy. 111. It's 4 miles N. of the Palm Springs Aerial Tramway. The office is in a white train caboose. [TG: 725 D6])

Come ride the sand dunes in Palm Springs! After watching a ten-minute video on safety in a cave-like setting, put on helmet and goggles (provided by Offroad), hop on your single-seater, four-wheel ATV, and go for an exhilarating ride. An expansive, flat area immediately in front of the rental facility is great for beginners, and it is the only place children may ride. The "course" has tire obstacles, too. More experienced riders (i.e.

older) can venture out on the large sand hills beyond this area. Machines are suited to the age and size of the rider, and speed limits are built into the vehicles. (Yea!) For instance, children 6 to 10 years, or so, are assigned vehicles that can't exceed four m.p.h. The ride here was a highlight for all of us. A beverage is included in your admission price, but bring your own sun block. Riders must wear long pants and closed-toed shoes. Ask about their two-hour educational dune buggy tours.

Hours: Open daily, 10am - sunset. Hours might vary during the summer.
Admission: Forty-five-minute rides start at $35 per person.
Ages: 6 years and up.

THE OLD SCHOOLHOUSE MUSEUM

(760) 367-2366 / www.virtual29.com/hsociety
6760 National Park Drive, Twentynine Palms
(Exit Interstate 10 E. to Twentynine Palms Hwy [62]. Go approximately 42 miles to the town of Twentynine Palms. Once in town, look for National Park Dr. - one block east of Adobe Rd. (1st stop light), turn R. [TG: 4892 F6])

Originally built in 1927, the old schoolhouse now houses historical exhibits of the early settlers, mostly via pictures and written information. The books on display are on Native Americans, gold miners, cowboys, and homesteaders. A re-created schoolroom, complete with wood desks, a flag, and a blackboard, is now a small research library. The gift shop carries pamphlets on the history of this area as well as cards and gift items. Call if you would like information on a school field trip.

Hours: Open Wed. - Sun., 1pm - 4pm.
Admission: Free
Ages: 7 years and up.

PALM SPRINGS AERIAL TRAMWAY

(760) 325-1391 / www.pstramway.com
1 Tramway Road, Palm Springs
(Exit Interstate 10 S. on Palm Canyon Dr. [Hwy.111], R. on Tramway Rd., 3½ miles up the hill. [TG: 755 F7])

Ten minutes an eighty-passenger, rotating, enclosed car, carries you seemingly straight up the side of Mount San Jacinto. The scenery change in this short amount of time is almost unbelievable - from cactus and desert sand below, to the evergreen trees and cool air up above. (Call ahead to see if there is snow.) The altitude up at Mount San Jacinto State Park is 8,516 feet.

The Mountain Station at the top has a game room, a gift shop, and observation areas where you can see a panoramic view of the entire valley, including the Salton Sea which is forty-five miles away. The Top of the Tram Restaurant, which is open 11am to 9pm, serves lunch, averaging $5 to $12 per entree, and a buffet dinner which is $13.50 for adults, $7 for children. There is also a snack bar here. The bottom floor of the Station has a few taxidermied animals and an interesting twenty-minute film on the history of the tramway.

Behind and down the Mountain Station building is Mount San Jacinto Wilderness State Park, with fifty-four miles of great hiking trails, campgrounds, and a ranger station. Call (909) 659-2607 for camping information. Though we just walked along the easier trails, the mountain scenery anywhere up here is unbeatable! Just remember that the trail you go down from the peak Mountain Station, you must also come back up to catch the tram. Horse rentals, (909) 763-2473, are available at certain times for a guided tour. Snow equipment rentals are available in the winter, November 15 through April 15, conditions permitting. There are plenty of areas to go sledding, snow-shoeing, snow-tubing, and cross country skiing. Guided nature walks are offered weekends during the summer. Tip: Always bring jackets for everyone and wear closed-toed shoes - it **really** does get cold up here!

Hours: Cars go up every half hour Mon. - Fri., starting at 10am; Sat. - Sun., starting at 8am. The last car goes up at 8pm, and the last car comes down at 9:45pm.
Admission: $20.80 for adults; $18.80 for seniors; $13.80 for ages 3 - 12; children 2 and under are free. Discounts are offered to AAA members and military personnel. Tickets after 3pm are $17.80 for adults; $10.80 for kids.
Ages: 3 years and up.

PALM SPRINGS AIR MUSEUM

(760) 778-6262 / www.palmspringsairmuseum.org

745 N. Gene Autry Trail, Palm Springs

(Exit Interstate 10 S. on Palm Drive/Gene Autry Trail. [TG: 787 B3])

$$$

Enjoy happy landings at this classy air museum, conveniently located next to the Palm Springs Airport. Inside the three hangars and outside on the grounds are usually twenty-six vintage WWII aircraft; some come and go on a rotating basis. Most of the planes are in flight-ready condition and some are being restored. The collection can include a Grumman F4F Wildcat, Grumman 56F Hellcat, Grumman F7F Tigercat, Grumman A6 Intruder, P-40 Warhawk, B-17, and many more. The planes are not cordoned off, making it easier to look at them close up, although touching is not allowed. Walk under and look up into the belly of an A-26 Invader attack bomber. My kids were thrilled to see the places where it actually held real bombs!

The hangars are designated Army/European, Navy/Pacific, and B17. The planes are fascinating for the part they've played in history, and visually exciting for kids because most have decorative emblems painted on their sides. In the Navy/Pacific hangar climb aboard a Grumman Goose cockpit and pretend to pilot it. Bunkers and displays around the perimeter of the airy hangars honor different eras of flight by featuring various uniforms, flight jackets, combat photographs, patches, model planes, combat cameras, murals, and more. Other exhibits include gleaming antique cars from the 20's and 30's, maps of missions, touch screens, and five ten-foot-long replicated warships. Tour the inside of a B-17 for a donation of $3 per person, or just admire it from the outside.

Starting at 10am, the Wings Theater continuously shows war movies, combat videos, or interviews with war heroes. Kids always enjoy watching small planes land and take off at the adjacent runway. In the library use a computer and joystick to engage in a simulated dogfight for $2 per person. For more entertainment with an altitude, every other Saturday hear a special guest speaker in a program that almost always concludes with a fly-over. Ask about their almost two hour school (minimum age is 8 years old) and group tours offered throughout the week. If you'd like to hear the complete history of all the planes at the museum, rent an audio TourMate for $5. This museum also offers a plethora of other programs and events and all of them are exceptionally well done.

Hours: Open in the summer daily, 9am - 4pm. Open the rest of the year daily, 10am - 5pm. Closed Thanksgiving and Christmas.

Admission: $8 for adults; $6.50 for seniors and military with ID; $3.50 for ages 6 - 12; children 5 and under are free.

Ages: 4 years and up.

PALM SPRINGS DESERT MUSEUM

(760) 325-7186 or (760) 325-0189 / www.psmuseum.org

101 Museum Drive, Palm Springs

(Exit Interstate 10 S. on Indian Canyon Dr., which turns into Palm Canyon Dr. [Hwy 111], R. on Tahquitz Canyon Way, R. on Museum Dr. [TG: 786 D2])

$$$

There are many facets of this museum jewel. One area features exhibits on the Cahuilla Indians, including life-size dioramas and mannequins, and a replica of one of their dwellings that visitors can actually walk through. Listen - you can hear the Cahuillans speaking in their native tongue. The Ice Age Mammal gallery showcases entire casts of a giant ground sloth and a large sabertooth tiger. Skulls of other predators, such as an American lion, cave bear, and dire wolf reside here, too. Desert Life: Night and Day gallery has realistic-looking wall murals, plus taxidermied desert animals. Use the lighted interpretative panels to test your knowledge about the desert. A rock "wall" with windows allows visitors to see live animals such as a variety of snakes (e.g. sidewinders and kings), gila monsters, scorpions, and kangaroo rats.

The left wing is a fine arts gallery with changing exhibits of paintings, sculptures, and other forms of art. As the gallery is not overwhelmingly large, exploring the art world is a feasible journey for youngsters. My middle son has an artistic temperament, so I'm hoping art exposure will develop the talents, too!

Further back on the main floor are a few rooms devoted to Western and Native American art. One room consists mainly of paintings, blankets, and numerous baskets. Another, called the George Montgomery

Collection, features the western star's movie posters, plus furniture, paintings, and bronze sculptures of cowboys and Indians that Montgomery designed. The William Holden Collection offers some of Holden's prized art pieces. Also in this area is a miniature collection displaying twelve perfectly proportioned dioramas inset in the walls. A small gallery contains art from ancient Latin American civilizations.

The upper level room and mezzanine level have over 100 rotating exhibits of twentieth century art, which means expect the unexpected. I love seeing what's new up here.

The downstairs Annenberg Theater presents shows mostly for adult audiences, such as plays, ballets, operas, and concerts. Even if you don't eat here, take a stroll through the Gallery Cafe to check out its colorful mobiles and funky decor. Outside, all-age visitors will enjoy the small, twentieth-century sculpture garden.

Inquire about the variety of free, guided, on-site adult and one-hour school tours, the summer camps, family programs, and student workshops. The two-hour Eyes On/Hands On is a favorite with kids because it combines a museum tour with a related craft project. The classy Palm Springs Desert Museum is an interesting way to learn about natural history and different art styles, plus it's a respite from the heat!

Hours: Open Tues. - Sat., 10am - 5pm; Sun., noon - 5pm. Closed Mon. and major holidays. Docent guided tours are conducted each day at 2pm.

Admission: $7.50 for adults; $6.50 for seniors; $3.50 for ages 6 - 17; children 5 and under are free. The first Fri. of each month is free admission day.

Ages: 4 years and up.

PALM SPRINGS VILLAGEFEST

!/$

(760) 320-3781 or (760) 325-1577 / www.pschamber.org

Palm Canyon Drive, Palm Springs

(Exit Interstate 10 S. on Indian Canyon Dr., which turns into Hwy 111. It's between Barristo Rd. and Amado Rd. [TG: 786 D2])

It's Thursday night and you're in Palm Springs with the kids, wondering what to do. You pick up this terrific book called *Fun and Educational Places to go With Kids and Adults* and read about VillageFest - problem solved! The VillageFest, or international old-time street fair, is held along several blocks on Palm Canyon Drive in the heart of Palm Springs. There is food, arts and crafts vendors, boutiques, cafes, and entertainment, such as live music. For kids, various attractions could include pony rides, magic shows, a party bouncer, a gyroscope, school band competitions, and a stage for children's productions.

Hours: Thurs. nights, usually 6pm - 10pm. Closed Thanksgiving.

Admission: Free entrance.

Ages: 4 years and up.

SUNRISE PARK / PALM SPRINGS SWIM CENTER

!/$$

(760) 323-8278 or (760) 323-8278 / www.ci.palm-springs.ca.us

405 South Pavilion Way, Palm Springs

(Exit Interstate 10 S. on Indian Canyon Dr., which turns into Hwy 111, L. on Ramon Rd., L. on Sunrise Way. [TG: 786 G3])

This park has activities that will keep your family busy and refreshed from sunrise to sunset. Besides the wonderful grassy areas and big playground with bridges, slides, and swings, the most important feature here is the Olympic-size swimming pool. (It has a shallow end for younger kids to cool off.) Bring your own lawn chairs. There is an adjacent baseball stadium which has lights.

Hours: The park is open daily, sunrise - sunset. The pool is open year-round, Mon., Wed., and Fri., 11am - 5pm; Tues., Thurs., Sat. - Sun., 11am - 3pm for recreational swim. Call for lap swim hours. Night swimming is available in the summer.

Admission: The park is free. Swim sessions are $3.25 for adults; $2.25 for ages 4 - 12; children 3 and under are free with a paid adult. Such a deal - pay a $20 one-time fee for membership and then pay an additional $25 for a card worth twenty-five swims!

Ages: All

UPRISING ROCK CLIMBING CENTER

(888) CLIMB ON (254-6266) or (760) 320-6630 / www.uprising.com

1500 S. Gene Autry Trail, Palm Springs

(Exit Interstate 10 S. on Palm Drive/Gene Autry Trail. Or exit 10 W. on Ramon Rd., L. on Gene Autry. It's in the same complex as Knott's Soak City. [TG: 787 B4])

$$$$

Do your kids have you climbing the walls? Then you'll feel right at home at Uprising Rock Climbing Center. The three, outdoor climbing structures have micro mists systems and are covered with an awning to block out direct sunlight. Kids can test their rock climbing skills here and train to reach new heights. The tallest wall is forty feet high while another, connected structure, has a thirty-foot repelling tower. There are thirty-four top ropes in all. All climbers are belayed and wear harnesses, although lead climbing for advanced climbers is available. The twenty-foot "teaching" wall might not look that high, but it seemed tall to me when I was at the top! It's a great spot for beginners to get a grip on this sport. A small bouldering area (i.e. no ropes needed) is also here.

Rental gear is available, or you can bring your own. Climb a few times during your visit, or make it an all-day workout. Ask about climbing excursions to Joshua Tree, Idyllwild, and out-of-state sites.

Hours: Usually open Mon. - Fri., 10am - 8pm; Sat. - Sun., 9am - 5pm. Call for hours. Closed Thanksgiving and Christmas.

Admission: Prices vary greatly, depending on your skill level, if you bring any people with you, and how long you plan on being here. For instance, an "opener" class includes one hour of climbing, equipment rental, and a belayer for $25. Harness, shoes, helmet, and chalk bag are available to rent.

Ages: At least 6 years, and up.

WESTFIELD SHOPPINGTOWN PALM DESERT - KIDS CLUB

(760) 568-0248 or (760) 346-2121 / www.westfield.com

72840 Highway 111, Palm Desert

(Exit Interstate 10 S. on Monterey. It's on the corner of Monterey and Hwy 111. [TG: 848 D1])

Calling all kids! The kids club offers a variety of activities and programs. Sometime the club hosts craft activities, such as designing calendars, picture frames, aprons, and more; sometimes an educational presentation; sometimes a guest speaker, like a fire fighter; and sometimes a storytime or other entertainment. Club members (and membership is free) receive discount coupons from participating retailers. A free Playtown area, near JCPenney, allows little ones to climb on hard foam animals and play on a big tic-tac-toe wall hanging.

Hours: The club runs the second Fri. of each month, except December, 5pm - 7pm.

Admission: Free

Ages: 3 - 10 years.

WHITEWATER TROUT CO. / RAINBOW RANCHO TROUT FISHING

(760) 325-5570

9160 Whitewater Canyon Road, Whitewater

(Exit Interstate 10 N. on Whitewater Canyon Rd, along the Whitewater Cut Off. Across from the Whitewater Rock Supply Company, L. (N.) on Whitewater Canyon Rd. It's located 5 miles back. [TG: 654 G5])

$$$

Grilled, baked, and fried are just a few savory suggestions as to how you can fix the trout lunch or dinner that you're almost sure to catch. In fact, you can rent a picnic table in the barbecue area, fix your fish, and eat 'em right there. A state license is not necessary. Two stone-lined ponds with benches around them, shade trees, and a grassy expanse offer a visual and physical respite from the desert surroundings. Tip: Bring your own cooler for your fish. For the non-fish eaters in the family, a cafe is on the grounds, serving hamburgers and hot dogs. Camp on the pleasant grounds here via a tent or RV, or rent a cabin. (It is about 10 degrees cooler here than in Palm Springs.) And take a peek at the adjacent fish hatchery while you're visiting. It's been at this location since 1939.

Hours: Open, Wed. - Sun., 10am - 5pm. Closed Mon., Tues., New Year's Day, Thanksgiving, and Christmas.

Admission: $1 per person for those who don't fish; 50¢ for those who do. The $3 per person fishing fee includes a pole, bait, and tackle. (You may not use your own equipment.) Fish start at $3.28 per pound. It's 25¢ (per fish) for cleaning. Rent a picnic table for $20 a table. Camping is $22 a night. The cabins are $30 and come with bunk beds.

Ages: 3 years and up.

WIND MILL TOURS

(760) 320-1365 or (760) 320-1365 / www.windmilltours.com; www.bestofthebesttours.com

$$$$

20th Avenue, Palm Springs

(Exit Interstate 10 N. on Indian Avenue., L. on the frontage road of 20th Ave. 1¼ mile to the trailer buildings. [TG: 726 B4])

If you like learning about alternative energy sources and are fascinated by the power that wind can generate, you'll be (literally) blown away by this tour. To state the obvious, it is usually very windy out here. Why? Because cool coastal air comes inland and pushes the hot air through the narrow mountainous San Gorgonio Pass.

The ninety-minute tour of one of several wind farms in the world, takes place via a bus. Driving around on the grounds you'll hear the thumping noise created by the huge pinwheels in motion. At selected stops you'll have the opportunity to inspect components (e.g. blades and nacelle [battery covers]) up close. Blades, by the way, can span more than half the length of a football field. You'll see the older-style wind turbines and new, sleeker, more efficient ones. And, yes, you'll finally find out if these wind mills are simply tax shelters or actually producing usable, affordable energy! A lot of technical information is given, but even I understand a bit more now about electricity, sources of clean energy, and what comprises a kilowatt hour. Although the tour got a little long winded for my boys, they particularly liked hearing about the wind smiths, those brave people who climb up the 150-foot tower ladders to do maintenance work.

Hours: Tours are usually offered Tues., Thurs., and Sat. at 9am and sometimes at 2pm. Reservations are suggested. Call first.

Admission: $23 for adults; $20 for seniors; $10 for ages 11 and under. Call for group tour prices.

Ages: 9 years and up.

318

SAN BERNARDINO COUNTY

Originally settled by the Serrano Indians, the land has changed hands many times over the years and today incorporates a flavor from all of its past inhabitants. Tour through a restored rancho in Rancho Cucamonga. See a once-working silver mine in the revitalized ghost town of Calico. Take a walk in the deserts of Barstow (but not in the summertime). Enjoy the mountainous woodlands of Big Bear Lake. Pick apples in Oak Glen. Shop at Ontario Mills Mall. Visit an airplane museum in Chino. This Inland Empire has something to cater to every interest.

Note: Since Big Bear is often considered a resort destination, you'll find its attractions listed in a separate section in the back of this county starting at page 349.

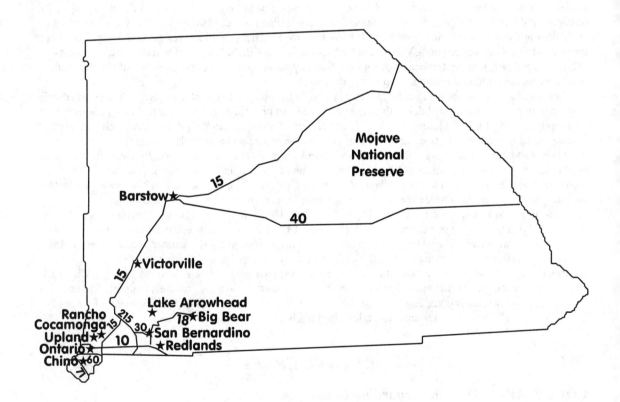

-----AMUSEMENT PARKS-----

PHARAOH'S LOST KINGDOM

(909) 335- PARK (7275) / www.pharaohslostkingdom.com

1101 N. California Street, Redlands

(Exit San Bernardino Fwy [10] N. on California St. It's the first pyramid off the fwy. [TG: 607 F6])

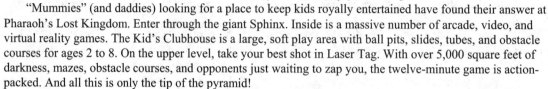

"Mummies" (and daddies) looking for a place to keep kids royally entertained have found their answer at Pharaoh's Lost Kingdom. Enter through the giant Sphinx. Inside is a massive number of arcade, video, and virtual reality games. The Kid's Clubhouse is a large, soft play area with ball pits, slides, tubes, and obstacle courses for ages 2 to 8. On the upper level, take your best shot in Laser Tag. With over 5,000 square feet of darkness, mazes, obstacle courses, and opponents just waiting to zap you, the twelve-minute game is action-packed. And all this is only the tip of the pyramid!

Outside, the Race Car Complex offers three different tracks - kiddie, Grand Prix, and a banked Indy speed track; some height and age restrictions apply. Bumper boats are another great family attraction. Travel to ancient and exotic lands via the four, nine-hole miniature golf courses. The holes don't have a lot of challenging obstacles, but they are intriguingly embellished. For an adrenaline rush, dare to try Sky Coaster, a harnessed "ride" that lets you fly and swing from over 100-feet high for $15; height and age restrictions apply. The sixteen amusement rides, geared for young kids and older kids (i.e. adults), include a Ferris wheel, carousel, Tilt-A-Whirl, bumper cars, mini motorboats, a Screaming Mummy roller coaster, and more. Note that children under two years are not permitted on the amusement park rides.

We found a lot of fun at the Lost Kingdom water park. Climb up the central tower to go down the six slides that range from enclosed body slides with a sheer drop, to open tube rides that hurl riders down. (The Wrath of Ra is aptly named.) Enjoy a blissful raft ride in three feet of water on the Endless River, a large circular river encompassing the water park. Body or board surf with the wave machine at Riptide. Younger children have their own wading pool with a big water play structure and slides. Another activity pool, for elementary-school-aged kids, has a few short slides, a water volleyball area, and a challenging ropes course over hard foam mummies and tiles. A beach and sand volleyball court are also here. King Tut never had it so good! Just outside the water park are two full-service snack bars and a picnic area so you can bring in your cooler.

Hours: Open Sun. - Thurs., 10am - 10pm; Fri. - Sat., 10am - midnight. The amusement rides and laser tag usually open in the early afternoon until 10pm during the week, and 11am - 10pm on weekends. The water park is open April - May and September - October, weekends only. The end of May through Labor Day, it's open daily, 10am - 7pm. Call for its "off season" hours.

Admission: Call for individual attraction prices and combo packages. Admission to the water park is $19.99 for ages 11 and up; $13.99 for ages 2 - 10; children 1 and under are free. Unlimited amusement rides, attractions, and usage of the water park is $24.99 for ages 11 and up; $19.99 for ages 2 - 10. Season passes are a great deal. Parking is $5.

Ages: 1½ years and up.

-----ARTS AND CRAFTS-----

COLOR ME MINE (San Bernardino County)

(877) COLOR ME (265-6763) - for a listing of all locations. Chino - (909) 628-7533; Ontario - (909) 481-0662. / www.colormemine.com

Chino - 4005 Grand Avenue, Suite B; Ontario - 980 North Ontario Mills Drive, Unit C

(Chino: Exit Chino Valley Fwy [71], E. on Grand. [TG: 681 D2]; Ontario: Going N. on Ontario Fwy [15], exit W. on 4th St, L. on Ontario Mills Dr. Going S. exit 15 at 4th and conitue straight on Ontario Mills Dr. [TG: 603 E6])

See the entry for COLOR ME MINE (Los Angeles County) on page 6 for details.

-----EDIBLE ADVENTURES-----

BARSTOW STATION

(760) 256-0366 / www.barstowstation.com
$$

1611 E. Main Street, Barstow
(Exit Mojave Fwy [15] E. on Main St. [TG: 3680 B3])

Several retired railroad cars are grouped together to form a unique, albeit brief, shopping and eating experience. Eating McDonald's food in an old train car might taste the same as eating it elsewhere, but the atmosphere here makes it fun. Other rail cars offer bakery goods, ice cream, candy (these are all the important things in life!), souvenirs, and knickknacks. The Station fulfills its goal of being an interesting edible adventure.

Hours: Open Mon. - Thurs., 7:30am - 7:30pm; Fri. - Sun., 7:30am - 9:30pm. McDonald's is open Sun. - Thurs., 6am - 10pm; Fri. - Sat., 6am - 11pm.
Admission: Free to enter; bring spending money.
Ages: All

BENIHANA OF TOKYO (San Bernardino County)
(909) 483-0937 / www.benihana.com
$$$$

3760 E. Inland Empire Boulevard, Ontario
(Exit San Bernardino Fwy [10] N. on N. Haven Ave., R. on Inland Empire. [TG: 603 C7])

See the entry for BENIHANA OF TOKYO (Los Angeles County) on page 11 for details.

CHUCK E. CHEESE

See the entry for CHUCK E. CHEESE on page 12 for details.

FARMER'S MARKETS

See the entry for FARMER'S MARKETS on page 14 for details.

GAMEWORKS
(909) 987-4263 / www.gameworks.com
$$$
4541 Mills Circle, Ontario

See the entry for GAMEWORKS on page 326 for details.

MILL CREEK CATTLE CO.
(909) 389-0706 / www.millcreekcattleco.com
$$$
1874 Mentone Boulevard, Mentone
(Exit San Bernardino Fwy [10] N. on Orange Ave., R. on Lugonia Ave., which turns into Mentone. [TG: 608 H5])

From the outside, this very unique restaurant looks like building fronts along Main Street in an Old West town. Wooden facades are labeled saloon, hotel (complete with balconies), barbershop, and U.S. Marshall's office, with a painted silhouette of a cowboy marshal. Bales of hay, cactus, antlers, and travel trunks complete the ambiance.

Enter through the restaurant doors for inside and inside/outside seating. The lobby continues an Old West theme with saddles hanging on the walls, old lanterns, old-time photographs, steer skulls, and an old-fashioned furnace. Eat inside the bar area, decorated with bits, bridles, a fireplace, a bear head over the piano, swords, and a flag that is half Confederate and half Union, plus pictures of Robert E. Lee and Ulyses S. Grant.

The other dining area is really quirky. It is inside the restaurant walls, but the roof is only camouflage netting. (Tip: Find an alternative place to eat on a rainy day.) The decor is an eclectic mix of more Old West building fronts, highlighted with neon signs, plus a corner waterfall enhanced by fake rocks and colorful fake flowers. Two real, tall palm trees shoot up through the "ceiling," surrounded at their base by an odd combination of more fake flowers and real cactus. The room also has heat lamps, old posters, and mounted deer and wild boar's head.

Amid the unusual atmosphere of the Cattle Co., enjoy great food. Appetizers include jalapeno peppers stuffed with cream cheese ($6.75), spicy buffalo wings ($5.95), and quesadillas ($7.95). Meal menu items include chili ($3.95), Greek salads ($8.95), liver and onions ($9.95), burgers ($5.95), smoked tri-tip sandwiches ($6.95), baby back ribs ($17.95), spicy sausage links ($9.95), and ham steaks ($10.95), plus a choice of pastas and seafood. Kids' meals are $3.25 for either chicken tenders, grilled cheese, hamburger, barbecue ribs, barbecue chicken, or spaghetti. Drinks are extra. Breakfast, with cowboy beans, biscuits and gravy, and apple coffee cake, is also available.

While here, visit the adjacent MB's Gift Shop and General Store. It stocks all sorts of country store goodies, collectibles, antiques, dolls, and more.

Hours: Open Sun. - Thurs., 11am - 9pm; Fri. - Sat., 11am - 10pm.
Admission: Menu prices are listed above.
Ages: 3 years and up.

OAK GLEN / APPLE PICKING & TOURS

(909) 797-6833 / www.oakglen.net
Oak Glen Road, Oak Glen

(From the San Bernardino Fwy [10], exit N.E., on Yucaipa Blvd., L. onto Oak Glen Rd. In about 6 miles, you'll see the sign, "Welcome to Scenic Oak Glen." Orchards and shops dot the long and winding road. From the 60 Fwy exit N. on Beaumont, which turns into Oak Glen Rd. after quite a few miles. This entry names the attractions in order, via exiting the 10 Fwy. [TG: 610 J7])

Your *delicious* journey into Oak Glen takes you through a town that is *ripe* with fun things to do. Several orchards offer U-Pic, which means you pick your own apples, raspberries, blackberries, pears, and pumpkins, all in season, of course. Apple varieties range from the exotic, such as Ida Red and Pearmain, to the more familiar ones of Jonathon, Granny Smith, Pippin, Braeburn, and Red Delicious. Most orchards also have wonderful country stores with all sorts of apple concoctions and apple-related items for sale. Although berry-picking season starts in late July and apple season runs from September through the middle of November, there are many year-round reasons to visit Oak Glen. Tips: Although weekends (especially in October) can be crowded, some orchards will only let you pick apples then, so get an early start on your day's adventure. Call the orchards to find out when your favorite type of apple will be ripe. Buy an apple-recipe book, as kids get a little carried away with the joy of picking apples! Here are a few of our favorites stops:

Parrish Pioneer Ranch, 38561 Oak Glen Road, (909) 797-1753 / www.parrishranch.com: The Ranch has a picnic area, pre-picked apples for sale, a few gift shops, and a restaurant. Goats, emus, a donkey, miniature horse, a bull, sheep, and a cow are in pens by the parking lot. Harvest season entertainment includes Johnny Appleseed (Sundays in October) and Yodeling Merle, who sings cowboy songs (April through December). At the half-hour Stunt Masters of the Old West shows (April through November) performances always include a talk on firearm safety, followed by stunts, a melodrama, or a farce on life in the 1800's. The shows take place at the outside theater at 1pm, 2:30pm, and 4pm on weekends, weather permitting. Call first. Admission is $2 for adults; $1 for seniors and ages 7 to 15; children 6 years and under are free. The shops are open daily, 10am to 6pm.

Oak Tree Village, (909) 797-4020 / www.oaktree-village.com: Located in the center of Oak Glen is the Village, a wonderful place to shop, play, and eat. Kids enjoy walking on the hilly trail through the good-sized animal and nature park. Penned deer, sheep, llamas, goats, and birds are in here, plus a lot of squirrels that are running around freely. Admission is $3 per person; children 1 year and under are free. On the weekends year round, the Village offers pony rides ($3); scale model train rides ($2); panning for (and keeping) real gold ($2 per pan); and fishing at the small trout ponds inside the animal park. Fishing costs the $3 entrance fee into the nature park plus the price per inch of whatever fish you catch. Poles and bait are available for rent for $2. Up the walkway is Mountain Town, a store with a small cave-like museum that displays taxidermied wildlife as well as a few live reptiles. Entrance is $1 per person. Along the perimeter of the museum are mini-stores that display merchandise tempting to shoppers young and old.

Snow Line Orchard, 39400 Oak Glen Road, (909) 797-3415 / www.snow-line.com: This short drive up the road offers rows and rows of U-Pic raspberries in season. (We pick basketfuls and freeze them.) In the store, purchase fresh apples and tasty blends of raspberry/apple cider and cherry/apple cider. Tip: On weekends watch the doughnut machine at work providing sweet concoctions. The orchard is open September through mid-December daily from 9am to 5pm.

Two-hour tours are offered for a minimum of twenty-five students (or adults) and a maximum of 125 at $4.50 per person. The tours include learning about this orchard that's been here for more than a century and seeing how it operates, plus making cider and packing and grading fruit. For school tours, teachers receive a bag of apples and the children get an apple and a cup of cider (and a lot of knowledge). Tours are offered Wednesday through Friday mornings.

Los Rios Rancho, 39610 Oak Glen Road, (909) 797-1005: This working apple ranch has acres of orchards, a store, a delicious bakery, U-Pic fruit, wonderful nature walking trails, and two picnic areas. One picnic area is the large, grassy front lawn that has picnic tables. The other is a pretty, wooded area, with picnic tables, located behind the store.

Los Rios offers hour-long tours during harvest season (mid-August through mid-November) for groups of ten or more. This informative tour includes taste testing and comparing the different types of apples, walking through the packing house/cider mill, hearing the history of local families, and going into the apple orchards to learn about agriculture, particularly the organic aspects of farming. Tours are $3.50 per person. Add on a tour or activity, too, such as an hour nature walk where participants learn about the plants, how the local Indians used them, animal tracks, and more (we really enjoyed this tour) - $1.50 per person; pressing (and sampling) cider - $15 per half gallon; or picking apples from the trees - $12 for an eight pound bag. U-Pic raspberries are available mid-August through September, or so. The Rancho is open January through August, Wednesday through Friday from 10am to 5pm, and Saturday and Sunday from 10am to 5pm. It's open September through December daily from 9am to 5pm.

Wildlands Conservancy, 39611 Oak Glen Road, (909) 797-8507 / www.wildlandsconservancy.org: The conservancy shares and operates the land with the above-mentioned Los Rios Rancho. An almost two-mile dirt nature trail, with several off shoots and dead-ends, loops around on one section of the ranch land. It leads alongside a stream, through chaparral, and past two ponds where ducks flock when the pond water is not being used to irrigate the apple orchard. One trail branch, the California tree trail, even has a few redwoods and Giant Sequoias along the route. The trails are open to the general public on weekends and holidays Mondays from 9am to 4:30pm, and for tour groups during the week.

Oak Glen School House Museum (see separate entry on page 339 for details.)

Riley's Log Cabin Farm and Orchard, 12201 S. Oak Glen Road, (909) 797-4061: This orchard looks like it is set in the same time period as *Little House on the Prairie* and has a delightful store that offers old-fashioned toys, books, and other items. On weekends in July and August come pick berries, some apples, and a few other types of fruit. In the fall, thirteen different varieties of apples, plus pumpkins, are ripe for visitors to harvest.

A bountiful crop of fall tours includes a colonial or farm Bible study; participating in frontier skills such as chopping wood, washing clothes through a wringer, writing with a quill pen, starting a fire with flint and steel, pumping water, and gardening and harvesting crops; building a log cabin; learning old-fashioned dances such as the minuet and/or square dancing; grinding corn and baking Johnny cakes; taking an etiquette class; listening to a cowboy explain life on the range; archery; tomahawk throwing; and pressing apple cider. Tours begin Labor Day weekend until the end of November and are offered Tuesday through Friday, usually between 10am to 2pm, to groups with a minimum of thirty people or $240. Tour options range from two to six hours and cost between $8 and $12 per person. Rope making, kazoo making, a nature walk, crafting a corn husk doll, and creating a water carrier are the other activities offered. Bring a sack lunch to enjoy by the pond picnic area. Two-hour weekend tours are offered to groups of at least twenty people for $8 per person and include some of the above activities. Advanced reservations are needed for all tours.

Riley's is also open on weekends during the fall from 10am to 4pm for families and individuals. Visitors are welcome to pick their own apples or partake in some activities such as pressing cider at $10 a gallon, practicing archery for $1 for four arrows, tomahawk throwing for $1 for six throws, and eating hot-dipped caramel apples for $2.50. Saturday entertainment includes "Johnny Appleseed" playing his fiddle. The farm also hosts occasional musical programs and hoedowns. Riley's is closed December through July.

Riley's Frontier Events, 12211 S. Oak Glen Road, (909) 790-2364 or (909) 790-5435 / www.rileysfrontier.com: Neighboring in-laws own this Riley's farm. This orchard also has U-Pic apples and berries, and a trading post store that sells colonial-times toys and games, hand-made soaps, candles, and more modern purchases. Pears, blackberries, and raspberries ripen in late summer. Apples are ready to be picked, baked, sauced, and pressed in the fall. If you don't feel like doing the work, make sure you purchase an absolutely scrumptious, fresh-baked, eight-pound apple pie here.

Gather around the Conestoga pioneer wagon to start your two-hour fall tour. The tours are offered September through November, Tuesday through Friday at 9am and 11:30am and on weekends at 9am, for a minimum of twenty-five people. Activities include a taking a horse-drawn hayride, making cider (a fascinating process), drinking cider (an even better process), eating hot-dipped caramel apples (a personal favorite), and your choice of buttermaking, candlemaking, doing farm chores, tin smithing, making a small wooden toy, or gaining access to the petting farm. $6.50 per person for this tour is a great deal! Bring a picnic lunch. The farm is open to the general public on weekends from 10am to 5pm. Families and individuals are invited to participate in picking apples (of course) as well as going on a hayride, making candles, and pressing a gallon of cider to take home.

Spring tours are given mid-March through June during the week at 10am. These tours don't include the apple-related activities, but they do include the other fun and educational things to do and experience. Reservations are required for all tours.

Colonial Chesterfield / Riley's Farm, 12253 S. Oak Glen Road / www.rileysfarm.com: This part of the Riley conglomeration has two different phone numbers and focuses for edible adventures.

Pluck, pick, press, squeeze, and savor a myriad of fruit here from the end of June through November. Crops include cherries, ollalieberries, raspberries, pears, peaches, and apples. Call to find out when the fruit is ripe. You can pick your pumpkins here in the fall, too. Some picking is done by appointment only. During the fall, U-Pic hours are Monday through Saturday, 9am to 5pm. Call (909) 797-5145 for more information. This the number for the Civil War Reenactments, too.

Seasonal fruit picking tours, a cider pressing tour, and an early morning or evening milking tour (yes, participants do milk a cow) are offered at this location, too. Call (909) 797-7534 for more information. That number is also the one to call for information on their outstanding participatory Living History Adventure tours - both the Colonial Farm and the Revolutionary War. (See COLONIAL CHESTERFIELD (pg. 344.)

Apple-picking season is September through mid-November, with most U-Pics open on the weekends only. Stores, tours, and many other activities are usually open year round.

Hours: Pay for U-Pic fruit by the pound. See Los Rios, Snow Line, and both Riley's for tour prices and hours.

Ages: All ages for most activities; 5 years and up for the educational tours.

THE OLD SPAGHETTI FACTORY (Rancho Cucamonga)
(909) 980-3585 / www.osf.com
11896 Foothill Boulevard; Riverside, Rancho Cucamonga
(Exit Ontario Fwy [15] W. on Foothill. [TG: 603 E1])

See the entry for THE OLD SPAGHETTI FACTORY (Los Angeles County) on page 19 for details.

PEGGY SUE'S 50's DINER (Victorville)
(760) 951-5001 / www.peggysuesdiner.com
16885 Frontage Road, Victorville
(Exit Mojave Fwy [15] N.W. on Stoddard Wells Road. [TG: 4296 F2])

See the entry for PEGGY SUE'S 50's DINER (Yermo) on page 325 for details. This location's building, however, is much smaller and is not as extensively decorated.

Hours: Open Mon. - Thurs., Sat. - Sun., 7am - 8pm; Fri., 7am - 9pm. Open and hour later in the summer. Closed Thanksgiving afternoon and Christmas.

PEGGY SUE'S 50's DINER (Yermo)

(760) 254-3370 / www.peggysuesdiner.com

35654 Yermo Road, Yermo

(Exit Mojave Fwy [15] S. on Ghost Town Rd/Daggett - Yermo Rd., L. on Yermo Rd. [TG: 3681 F2])

$$$

If your cruisin' for good food served in a really happening place, head over to Peggy Sue's. This original roadside diner has several rooms, including small ones packed with booths and a larger room with chairs and tables. The walls feature an impressive and eclectic array of movie and television personality memorabilia, including Lucille Ball, Ricky Ricardo, Cary Grant, Marilyn Monroe, Elvis, James Dean, Buddy Holly, Laurel and Hardy, and the gang from the Wizard of Oz, all portrayed in pictures, posters, masks, dolls, and paintings. Gaudy decor (i.e. paintings on black velvet and cheesy trinkets) is interspersed with nicer mementos (i.e. fine portraits of celebrities and expensive-looking memorabilia). An occasional mannequin dressed in period clothing adds to the kitschyness. The jukebox plays 50's music every night except Friday nights when live music is performed. The diner also features a full pizza parlor towards the back, an arcade, a soda fountain with old-fashioned drinks and dessert, an ice cream parlor, and a very small outdoor park with a pond for ducks, fountains, grass, koi pond, and a few shade trees. An attached 5 and Dime Store sells touristy television and movie souvenirs and older-style toys from a simpler time, as well as a number of collector items. Look at the thirteen-foot Marlin here and life-size model of Betty Boop. Note that CALICO GHOST TOWN (pg. 343) is just down the road.

Breakfast options include three eggs any style with ham ($6.89) or pancakes ($4.49). Lunch fare includes a burger ($5.69), club sandwich ($7.49), or meatloaf ($5.99). For dinner, try a New York steak ($10.49), ham steak ($8.99), Southern fried chicken ($9.39), or chef salad ($7.29). Desserts include Green River or cherry phosphates ($1.59), malts or shakes ($3.19), berry pie ($2.49) or cheesecake ($3.29). Kid's menu choices for breakfast include an egg with toast ($1.99); one egg, two strips of bacon or sausage and hash browns ($3.29); french toast and two strips of bacon or sausage ($2.69); or a hot cake with bacon or sausage ($2.69). Lunch and dinner selections, which all include french fries, range from grilled cheese sandwich or chicken nuggets to a hot dog or a hamburger. Each meal is $2.99 and drinks are an additional 99¢.

Hours: Open daily, 6am - 10pm. Closed Christmas.
Admission: Prices are listed above.
Ages: All

RAINFOREST CAFE (Ontario)

(909) 941-7979 / www.rainforestcafe.com

4810 Mills Circle in Ontario Mills Mall, Ontario

(From San Bernardino Fwy [10], exit N. on Milliken Ave., R. on Mall Dr. From Ontario Fwy [15], exit W. on 4th St., L. on Franklin Ave. [TG: 603 E6])

$$$

See the entry for RAINFOREST CAFE (Orange County) on page 205 for details.

-----FAMILY PAY AND PLAY-----

BOOMERS! (Upland)

(909) 981-5251 / www.boomersparks.com

1500 W. 7th Street, Upland

(Exit San Bernardino Fwy [10] N. on Mountain, L. on 7th. [TG: 601 H4])

$$$

Upland Boomers fun center offers fun for everyone in your family! This giant fun center has four, themed **miniature golf** courses with all the whimsical decorations that make each hole fun. Two of the courses, the Old West and Storybook Land, are indoors so rainy days won't put a damper on your swing. Numerous arcade games are also inside the building. Golf prices are $7 a round for adults; ages 6 and under are free. Take a spin on a **go kart** at $6 a ride (no sandals allowed) - drivers must be over 58" tall. An additional passenger under this height is $2. **Bumperboats** are always fun - $5 for kids over 44" tall, $2 for riders under this height. There are six **kiddie rides** here, including a Ferris wheel, roller coaster, and mini-airplanes. Each ride or attraction costs three to five tickets. Twenty-four tickets are $7 or forty-four tickets are $12. The rock climbing wall is $6 for two climbs for people weighing forty pounds or more. Kids can also practice for the big league at the **batting cages,** or play at the over 100 video and arcade games.

If you've worked up an appetite, Boomers Cafe is right next door. Your choice of hamburgers, pizza, or chicken is served in a fun atmosphere, where there are more arcade games to play. (There is no escape from them.)

Hours:	Open most of the year, Sun. - Thurs., 11am - 10pm; Fri., 11am - midnight; Sat., 10am - midnight. Open in the summer daily, 10am - midnight.
Admission:	Attractions are individually priced above, or purchase an all-day pass which includes unlimited use of everything, except the arcade games; $22.95 for 58" and taller; $14.95 for 57" and under.
Ages:	3 years and up.

CHUCK E. CHEESE
See the entry for CHUCK E. CHEESE on page 12 for details.

FIESTA VILLAGE

(909) 824-1111 / www.fiestavillage.com
1405 E. Washington Street, Colton
(Exit Riverside Fwy [215] E. on Washington. [TG: 646 F2])

Come party at Fiesta Village! There are two, Western-motif **miniature golf** courses - $5 for adults, $4.50 for children 12 years and under; **go karts**, where drivers must be at least 53" tall - $4.95 for a five-minute ride; **batting cages**; and three rides - a giant slide, a super swing, and dizzy dragon (like a teacup ride) - 2 tickets each and tickets are 6 for $5. The three **waterslides** with a lounging area for spectators, is open seasonally - $7.95 for an all-day pass for ages 4 years and up; $2 for a spectator. Note: You can't swim around in the landing pool. Video arcades are in the lobby.

A full snack bar with pizza, hot dogs, corn dogs, chips, popcorn, and candy, is adjacent to Fiesta Village. If you're in the mood to play, there are video and arcade games, air hockey, and a pool table in here, too.

Hours:	The dry land activities are open Sun. - Thurs., noon - 9pm; Fri. - Sat., noon - 10pm. Open extended hours in the summer. The waterslides are open in May and September on weekends only, 11am - 5pm, and in the summer daily, noon - 6pm.
Admission:	Attractions priced above, or buy an unlimited day pass for $14.95 per person.
Ages:	4 years and up.

GAMEWORKS

(909) 987-4263 / www.gameworks.com
4541 Mills Circle, Ontario
(From San Bernardino Fwy [10], exit N. on Milliken Ave., R. on Mall Dr. From Ontario Fwy [15], exit W. on 4th St., L. on Franklin Ave. It's in Ontario Mills Mall. [TG: 603 E6])

GameWorks is a high-tech entertainment venue dedicated to the latest (and greatest) interactive virtual reality and video games, many of them sports oriented, plus motion simulator rides. The rides allow participants to be at the controls and interact with the screen to move all around. Vertical Reality employs movable seats in front of a twenty-four-foot screen and simulates a three-story free fall, as well as navigating around obstacles - you ride the game. At the Indy 500, hop in a full-size race car and zoom around the curves shown on the screen. Experience a hair-raising ride through a virtual obstacle course in Monster trucks. Sounds like a lot of virtual fun. Other motion simulator games include Top Skater and Wave Runner. Play the "classic" games, too, such as Pac-Man, air hockey, and pool.

The full-service grill serves appetizers (Tex Mex rolls, coconut shrimp, buffalo wings, and more); soups (try the chicken tortilla); salads; pizzas; burgers; sandwiches (club, French dip, barbecue pork, and more); tri tip steak; ribs; chicken breast; and grilled meatloaf. Note that there is a bar here, too.

Hours: Open Sun. - Thurs., 11am - midnight; Fri., 11am - 1am; Sat., 10am - 1am. Only patrons 18 years and older are allowed inside after10pm.

Admission: Free. A debit-style game card costs about $25 for 2 hours of play. The Vertical Reality, Monster Truck, and Indy 500 rides cost extra.

Ages: 7 years and up.

HANGAR 18 INDOOR ROCK CLIMBING

(909) 931-5991 / www.climbhangar18.com

256 Stowell Street, suite A, Upland

(Exit San Bernardino Fwy [10] N. on Euclid Ave., R. on Stowell (just after 8th St.). It's on the R. [TG: 602 C3])

Love a good cliffhanger? Hangar 18 boasts of 10,000 square feet of overhangs, two large lead caves, and textured climbing walls dotted with numerous multi-colored stones that represent different routes. Both lead climbing and the bouldering area gives seasoned climbers, as well as beginners, the opportunity to practice their bouldering technique. Come with a friend (i.e. a fellow belayer) or call beforehand to see if a belayer will be at the gym. Classes in belaying are also available for ages 10 and up. This fun and safe activity builds confidence and stamina. A party room is available. In the after school programs, offered for students in 4th through 12th grades, children learn basic rock climbing technique, knot tying, and belaying. The program includes rental equipment, supervision, and instruction.

Hours: Open Mon. - Thurs., 10am - 10pm; Fri., 10am - 8pm; Sat. - Sun., 10am - 7pm.

Admission: Day passes are $14 for adults; $9 for children 14 and under. Rental equipment - shoes and a harness - is $5. Kids that need a belayer are $15 per hour, $25 for 2 hours.

Ages: 5 years and up.

MULLIGAN FAMILY FUN CENTER (Murrieta)

(909) 696-9696 / www.mulliganfun.com

24950 Madison Avenue, Murrieta

(Exit Temecula Valley Fwy [15] S.W. on Murrieta Hot Springs Rd., R. on Madison Ave. [TG: 928 B6])

Calling all ranch hands: Git along to Mulligan Family Fun Center for some family fun! Take a look at all the fun props outside, like cowboy mannequins literally hanging around. This western-themed miniature golf center has two impressive **miniature golf** courses, with water hazards and sand traps. (Note: You can see the red rock boulders, small western buildings, and stagecoaches from the freeway, when you're heading southbound on the I-15.) A round of golf costs $6 for ages 13 and up; $5 for seniors and children 12 and under. Other attractions include **batting cages**; **bumper blaster boats** which almost ensure you will get wet, if not from the bumping, then from the blasting of water through the guns - $4.25 for the driver, $2 for passengers (height restrictions apply); **go-karts** - $4.75 for drivers, $2 for passengers (height restrictions apply); **mini go-karts** in a police and fire engine cart for kids 43" and under - $3; **laser tag** in a 3,500 square-foot arena which is a lot of running around and shooting space - $5; and a twenty-one-foot high **rock climbing wall** - $4 for two tries. There are three **kiddie rides** here, too - tea cups - $2; train ride - $2; and kangaroo jump - $2. Complete your day (or night) on the town by coming in the spacious "town hall," which is done up right fine with a jail and kids' saloon (cafe). The cafe serves salads, pizza, hot dogs, chicken strips, and other food essentials. There are also plenty of modern-day shoot-out games (i.e. arcade and video games).

Hours: Open Mon. - Thurs., 11:30am - 9pm; Fri., 11:30am - 11pm; Sat., 10am - midnight; Sun., 10am - 10pm. Closed Thanksgiving and Christmas.

Admission: Attractions are individually priced above. Unlimited all-day passes are available Fri. after 4pm and all day Sat. - Sun., $19.95 for 56" and taller; $16.95 for 55" and under.

Ages: 3 years and up.

SCANDIA AMUSEMENT PARK

(909) 390-3092 / www.scandiafun.com

1155 S. Wanamaker Avenue, Ontario

(Exit Ontario Fwy [15] W. on Jurupa, R. on Rockefeller, R. on Wanamaker. [TG: 643 E2])

Vikings might have come to this country just to play at this amusement park! Well, maybe not, but it is a lot of fun and very well kept up. Attractions include two Scandinavian-themed **miniature golf** courses with unlimited play at $7.95 for 54" and taller; $5.95 for 53" and under; 35" and under are free with a paying adult. The sixteen **amusement rides** include some for big kids such as a roller coaster, bumper boats, Tilt-A-Whirl, go-karts, Thor's Hammer, and scrambler; and some for little kids such as a small semi-truck ride around a track, a carousel, a mini coaster, train ride, and a slide. Tickets cost $1 each or $17.95 for twenty. Children's rides require one to three tickets; big kids' (or adult) rides require three to six tickets. There are also **batting cages**, arcade games, and a full-service snack bar here, too.

   Hours: Open in the summer, Sun. - Thurs., 10am - 11pm; Fri. - Sat. 10am - 1am. Open the rest of the
       year, Sun. - Thurs., 10am - 10pm; Fri. - Sat., 10am - midnight.
 Admission: Attractions are individually priced above, or purchase an unlimited pass (excluding arcade
       games) - $19.95 for 54" and taller; $15.95 for 53" to 36"; $9.95 for kids 35" and under. Inquire
       about weekday specials.
   Ages: 3 years and up.

SCANDIA FAMILY FUN CENTER

(760) 241-4007
12627 Mariposa Road, Victorville
(Exit Mojave Fwy [15] E. on Bear Valley Rd., L. on Mariposa. [TG: 4386 A5])

Enjoy some high desert fun at Scandia Family Fun Center. There are two Scandinavian-themed **miniature golf** courses, with castles, bridges, and other small buildings that add interest - $6.95 for 54" and taller; $5.50 for 53" - 36" tall; children 35" and shorter play for free. **Go-karts** and **bumper boats** are $4.95 per ride - height restrictions apply. **Batting cages**, a full-service snack bar, arcade and video games, and prize redemption center are also here for your enjoyment.

   Hours: Open Sun. - Thurs., 10am - 10pm; Fri. - Sat., 10am - 11pm.
 Admission: Attractions are individually priced above, or buy a pass for $12.95 per person that allows you to
       play on each attraction once, as well as receive 5 tokens. An unlimited pass is $17.95 per person.
       Ask about specials, particularly Monday night deals.
   Ages: 4 years and up.

VANS SKATEPARK (Ontario)

(909) 476-5914 / www.vans.com
4758 E. Mills Circle, Ontario
(From San Bernardino Fwy [10], exit N. on Milliken Ave., R. on Mall Dr. From Ontario Fwy [15], exit W. on 4th St., L. on Franklin Ave. It's in Ontario Mills Mall. [TG: 603 E6])

See the entry for VANS SKATEPARK (Orange) on page 215 for details. This location features an Xbox lounge, meaning that visitors who are hanging out in the lobby can play video games against each other on-line. While at the skatepark, don't forget to visit some of the great shops and restaurants, plus the food court and movie theaters and other fun places at the ONTARIO MILLS MALL (pg. 334).

-----GREAT OUTDOORS-----

AFTON CANYON

(760) 252-6000 / www.ca.blm.gov
Afton Rd., Afton
(Exit Mojave Fwy [I-15] S. on Afton and travel 3 miles to campsite. It's 36 miles NE of Barstow. [TG: 350 B6])

Referred to as the "Grand Canyon of the Mojave," the canyon is at the site where the river surfaces after being underground for more than fifty miles. Since this is one of the few places in the desert where water is available, several wildlife species consider the canyon home, including bighorn sheep, migratory birds, and birds of prey. There are a few established roads through the multi-colored canyon as well as hiking and equestrian trails. Washes and dry stream beds make for good hiking trails, too, although not during a flash flood. Hobby rock collecting is permitted. Primitive camp sites are available with a picnic table and single tap. Bring your own firewood and water.

Hours: Open daily, 7:45am - 4:30pm.

Admission: Free to the park. $6 to camp.

Ages: 6 years and up.

AMBOY CRATER

(760) 326-7000 / www.ca.blm.gov

National Trails Highway (Old Route 66), Amboy

(Going E. [from Barstow] on the Needles Fwy [40], exit S.E. on National Trails Hwy [just past Ludlow]. Going W. on 40, exit S. on Kelbaker Rd. and drive for 11 miles, R. on National Trails Hwy. It's located about 1 hour between Barstow and Needles just W. of the town of Amboy. [TG: 370 J4])

What do volcanoes look like? Well, instead of seeing one erupt (which would be thrilling, but potentially deadly), you can see the aftermath by hiking around this cinder cone. The surrounding lava flows surface is black with specks of green-colored, olivine crystals. The surface texture is alternately rough like jutting rocks or smooth like glass. There are twelve, bowl-shaped depressions that add even more variety to the volcanic features.

The Bureau of Land Management suggests a minimum of three hours hiking time to hike around the entire crater rim. The cone is about one mile from the parking lot and it is one mile in circumference. If you follow the trail to the right of the cinder cone, you'll head up to its wide opening where an eruption breached the crater wall. From here the climb to the top is only an eighty-foot incline. There are a few, scattered picnic tables and some informational kiosks, but no restrooms. A favorite time to visit is between March and May when the desert flowers are blooming and the sunrises and sunsets are often pink and purple hued. Tips: Carry water! Wear tough boots or tennis shoes as the lava rock can cut bottoms of shoes. Winters can be really cold here, and summer is blazing hot. Note that the town of Amboy is only five miles to the east of the crater.

Hours: Open daily, 7:30am - 4pm.

Admission: Free

Ages: 7 years and up.

CALICO EARLY MAN ARCHAEOLOGICAL SITE

(760) 252-6000 or (760) 254-2248 / www.ca.blm.gov

Minneola Road, Calico

(Exit Mojave Fwy [I-15] N on Minneola Rd., follow the signs and drive 2½ miles along graded dirt road to the site. It's about 15 miles from Barstow, and 6 miles east of Calico Ghost Town. [TG: 393 A2])

At this brief natural pit stop, visitors hike a half-mile to look into this "in-place museum" of Pleistocene archaeology. In other words, look down into excavated pits to see artifacts on the walls and floors made by early man. There are two master pits where most of the findings have been made, one training trench, and four test pits. On your guided tour, which is the only way to see the pit, you'll learn about the area's geography and history. A very small museum shows some of the pottery shards and other artifacts that have been excavated.

Hours: Tours are offered Wed. at 1:30pm and 3:30pm; Thurs. - Sun. at 9:30am, 11:30am; 1:30pm and 3:30pm.

Admission: $5 for the first 2 adults in your group, $2.50 for each adult thereafter; $2 for seniors; $1 for ages 12 and under.

Ages: 7 years and up.

CUCAMONGA-GUASTI REGIONAL PARK

(909) 481-4205 / www.county-parks.com
800 N. Archibald Avenue, Ontario
(Exit San Bernardino Fwy [10] N. on Archibald Ave. [TG: 602 J6])

Guasti Regional Park offers seasonal catfish and trout fishing at its nice-sized lakes. Pedal boat rentals are available in the summer. The playground has a tire swing, monkey bars, and cement tubes with holes to climb through, plus open grassy areas for running around.

During the summer have some wet fun by going down the two waterslides and/or swimming in the pool. You can also just beach it on the sandy area around the pool and grassy area beyond that. A snack bar, open seasonally also, sells hot dogs, burritos, chips, and ice cream, and is located next to the bait shop - make sure you choose the right food place for yourself!

Hours: The park is open Fri. - Wed., 7:30am - 5pm. Closed on Thurs. Call for extended summer hours.
Admission: $5 per vehicle. Pedestrians are $2. Fishing permits are $5 for ages 8 and older; $2 for 7 and under. Pedal boat rentals are $5 a half hour, and available in the summertime only. Swimming is $2 weekdays for ages 4 and up, plus the entrance fee; $3 on weekends. An all-day swim and waterslide pass costs $8, plus the entrance fee.
Ages: All

GLEN HELEN REGIONAL PARK

(909) 887-7540 / www.county-parks.com
2555 Glen Helen Parkway, San Bernardino
(Going W. on San Bernardino Fwy [215], exit S. on Devore Rd., which turns into Glen Helen Pkwy. Going E. on 215, exit E. on Cajon Blvd. (just after 15 jct.), R. on Devore. From Ontario Fwy [15], exit N.E. on Glen Helen Pkwy. [TG: 545 C1])

This scenic 1,340-acre park, nestled in the mountains, is worth the drive. It offers an assortment of year-round fun, such as catfish and trout fishing in the sizeable lake (a license is needed for those over 16 years old), volleyball courts, a baseball diamond, horseshoe pits, wide open grassy areas, playgrounds, and lots of trails for hiking up and down the mountain. Favorite summer activities include renting pedal boats, swimming in the pool, slip-sliding down the two waterslides that end in a small pool, and sunbathing on the surrounding beach area. Replenish your energy at the nearby snack bar. Many special events occur at the huge pavilion including concerts and other programs. Note: See the Calendar entry for details about the annual Renaissance Pleasure Faire (pg. 575) held here.

Camping is available just across the road. The close-together camping sites are just off the freeway and are comprised mostly of dirt and very few trees, but it is a place to stay.

Hours: Open daily in the summer, 6:30am - 8pm; open the rest of the year daily, 6:30am - 5:30pm. Water activities are open Memorial Day through Labor Day, Wed. - Sun. from 10am - 5pm.
Admission: $5 per vehicle, or $2 for pedestrians. All-day swimming and use of the water slides is $4 per person in addition to the entrance fee. Pedal boat rentals are $5 for a half hour and are available on weekends only. Camping starts at $10 a night for 4 people, $3 extra per person.
Ages: All

JACK BULIK PARK / FONTANA SKATE PARK

(909) 428-8360 / www.fontana.org
16581 Filbert, Fontana
(Exit San Bernardino Fwy [10], N. on Sierra Ave., L. on San Bernardino Ave., R. on Juniper Ave. It's on the corner of Juniper and Filbert. [TG: 604 H4])

Wahoo - this 25,000 square-foot skate park is fantastic for both beginners and advanced skaters. It has four cement bowls, from one- to three-feet up to seven- to nine-feet; street elements with fun boxes, rails, and stairs; a meandering sidewalk around the perimeters; and shade trees. Safety equipment - a helmet and pads - must be worn as police officers will cite offenders. Lights are here for nighttime fun.

The surrounding park has plenty of other things to do besides skate. There are several ball fields, picnic facilities, covered basketball courts, a covered roller-hockey rink, a playground, and more.

Hours: The park is open daily, sunrise - 10pm. The skate park is open Mon. - Wed., 9am - 10pm; Thurs., noon - 9pm; Fri. - Sun., 9am - 10pm.

Admission: Free

Ages: All

JURUPA HILLS REGIONAL PARK / MARTIN TUDOR

(909) 428-8360

11660 Sierra, Fontana

(Exit San Bernardino Fwy [10] S. on Sierra Ave. [TG: 644 J3])

Jurupa Hills is another good park nestled into a rocky mountainside. It has a great wooden playground for slightly older kids, with wavy slides, a big spiral slide, swaying bridges, and swings. The playground is just outside the water play area. A 418-foot long, gently winding waterslide helps cool off sweaty bodies during the hot summer months. There is also a pool with a small slide. The lower level of the park has a grassy picnic area, along with a baseball diamond, and a few swings. Look up the MARY VAGLE MUSEUM AND NATURE CENTER (pg. 332) because it is just around the corner. In fact, a hiking/biking trail at the south end of the park goes around the base of the hill to the nature center. Another trail, behind the pool, goes up and over the hill.

Hours: The park is open daily, dawn - dusk. The pool and slide are open Memorial Day through mid-June weekends only, noon - 6pm; open in the summer through Labor Day daily, 11am - 6pm.

Admission: $2 per vehicle is charged on weekends only during the summer. An additional $5 per person includes admittance to all the water activities (groups of ten or more are $4 per person); kids 39" and under are free.

Ages: All

LAKE GREGORY

(909) 338-2233 / www.co.san-bernardino.ca.us/parks

24171 Lake Drive, Crestline

(From Rim of the World Hwy [18], go N. on Hwy 138, stay straight on Lake Drive when 138 forks left and follow signs to Lake Gregory. It's about 7 miles off the hwy. [TG: 516 J3])

Crestline is a little mountain town that crowds usually just pass through on their way to stay at Lake Arrowhead or Big Bear Lake. Lake Gregory, toward the east end of Crestline, is a large beautiful lake with clear blue water and a stretch of white sandy beach. It's nestled in the San Bernardino mountains and surrounded by pine and oak trees. During the summer months, a four-acre section of the waveless water is roped off for swimmers and paddle boarders, and is patrolled by lifeguards. The long, thin paddle boards rent for $2 a half hour and must be handled with some degree of finesse if you want to stay topside. Another fun aquatic option is a 300-foot-long, twisting waterslide that ends in a small pool. Barbecue pits and picnic tables are available at the swim beach, as are two sand volleyball courts. You may bring in ice chests, but no glass containers or alcohol. Two snack bars are here, too.

The rest of the lake is open year round for boating and fishing. The on-site bait and tackle shop rents poles. Rowboat rentals are available for $5 an hour, with a $10 minimum, plus a $25 deposit. Seasonal boat rentals include canoes, kayaks, and windsurfers. Pedal boats, which seat four people, and Aqua Cycles (i.e. big-wheel-type water cycles that seat two people) both use pedal power and rent for $6 a half hour, each. They are available daily in the summer, and on weekends through October.

Hours: The lake is open daily sunup to sundown for fishing. The swim beach and waterslide, and most boating activity is open Memorial Day through Labor Day daily, 10am - 5pm.

Admission: $3 for ages 4 and up for the swim beach; children 3 and under are free. In addition to the entrance fee, an all-day waterslide pass is $6; five rides on the slide is $4. A permit is needed for fishing for ages 16 and up - $11.05. A California state license is not necessary.

Ages: All

MARY VAGLE MUSEUM AND NATURE CENTER

(909) 428-8386 / www.fontana.org/main/parks_rec/vagle.htm

11501 Cypress Avenue, Fontana

(Exit San Bernardino Fwy [10], S. on Sierra Ave., R. on Jurupa Ave., L. on Cypress. [TG: 644 H3])

This delightful nature center is at the foothills of a rock-covered hill which is great for climbing and hiking on trails. One such trail leads up to petroglyphs. A windy bike trail goes around the base of the hill to connect to the JURUPA HILLS REGIONAL PARK / MARTIN TUDOR (see pg. 331) on the other side.

The front of the nature center has a pond and acres of land for wildlife. Inside the building are live animals such as snakes, tarantulas, a rabbit, a chinchilla, lizards, and a tortoise. A small touch tidepool tank has sea stars and sea anemones. Microscopes, books and videos on nature, and touch tables are also available here. Join the staff of the museum/center in an array of family programs and classes, topical crafts on Saturday afternoons, guided nature walks, and seasonal events. Teachers, inquire about the three-hour school field trips here which incorporate lots of hands-on learning in the great outdoors. Field trips require a minimum of twenty-five students for grade K through 6th and cost $3 per pupil.

Hours: The museum/center is open Wed. - Fri., 2pm - 5pm; Sat., 11am - 5pm; Sun., noon - 5pm. Call for extended summer hours. The grounds are open daily, sunrise - sunset.

Admission: Free. The crafts are $3.

Ages: All

MOJAVE NARROWS REGIONAL PARK

(760) 245-2226 - park;

(760) 244-1644 - horse rentals / www.county-parks.com

18000 Yates Road, Victorville

(Exit Mojave Fwy [I-15] E. on Bear Valley, N. on Ridgecrest Rd., which turns into Yates. [TG: 4386 H1])

This delightful park hosts the annual Huck Finn Jubilee in June and, indeed, it looks like it belongs in Huck Finn country. There are two lakes. The larger one, Horseshoe Lake, is great for fishin' (no license needed for ages 15 years and under), has a bait shop near the entrance, and an island in the middle of it. A stream runs through part of the park which boasts of wide open grassy spaces; lots of trees, including willow thickets and patches of cottonwoods; some hiking and riding trails; and pasture land for the numerous horses boarded at the on-site stables. Decent tent and full hookup camp sites (with showers), an equestrian campground, a few playgrounds, pedal and row boat rentals, an archery range, hay rides, and picnic shelters complete the park.

Hours: Open daily, 7am - dusk. Horse rentals are available during the summer, Tues. - Sun., 9am - 6pm; during the rest of the year, weekends and holidays only, 9am - 5pm. All boat rentals are available year round on weekends only.

Admission: $5 per car. Camping is $10 a night without hookup. Horseback riding is $20 an hour for ages 6 and up. Pedal boat rentals and row boats are each $5 a half hour. Fishing costs $5 for ages 8 and up; $2 for children 7 and under.

Ages: All

MOUNT BALDY TROUT PONDS

(909) 982-4246

Mount Baldy Road, Mount Baldy Village

(Exit San Bernardino Fwy [10] N. on Monte Vista Ave., which turns into Padua Ave., R. on Mount Baldy Rd. It's about 11 miles past Montclair, just N. of Mt Baldy Village. [TG: 512 B4])

No waders are needed to catch fish at this delightful fishing spot up in the mountains. The clear, spring water ponds are surrounded by shady oak trees. The first pond stocks fish 13" through 18"; the second holds smaller fish, 9" through 13". The fish are abundant here, so chances are your young fisherboy/girl will make at least one catch of the day! All fish caught must be kept and paid for. After you've caught your fill, or the kids need more action, take a hike through the woods on the surrounding trails. During the summertime, enjoy a refreshing dip in the nearby stream; during dryer month, hike or play in the riverbed. Mount Baldy Village, which has a few shops and places to eat, and the ranger station, where you can pick up a map of the area hiking trails and a wilderness permit, are both just down the road from the trout pond.

Hours: The ponds are open Sat., Sun., and holidays (including week-long school holiday breaks) 9am - 4:30pm. Additionally, they are open July through August, Tues. - Sun., 10am - 4pm. Note: You must be here at least a half hour before closing time. Closed Thanksgiving and Christmas.

Admission: $1 if you bring your own pole; $2 to rent a pole. Price includes bait, cleaning, and packing fish in ice. You may share poles. Fish prices range from $2.15 for 9" to $16.45 for 18".

Ages: 3 years and up.

PRADO REGIONAL PARK

(909) 597-4260 - park information; (909) 597-5757 - horse rentals. / www.co.san-bernardino.ca.us/parks

16700 S. Euclid Avenue, Chino

(From Chino Valley Fwy, exit N.E. on Euclid. From Pomona Fwy [60], exit S. on Euclid. [TG: 712 C2])

This is another, has-it-all regional park! Besides the three softball diamonds, two soccer fields for tournament games or family fun, and year-round fishing at the huge lake (over 16 years old needs a license), there are four playground areas. One playground has assorted cement shapes to climb up and through, while the others have newer equipment with more traditional activities.

For those of you with delicate noses, you have correctly detected the nearby presence of horses, cattle, and sheep, as this is farm country. There are herds and ranches all up and down Euclid Street. The Prado Equestrian Center is located at the northern end of the park. Children 7 years old and up can take a one-hour, or more, ride on a trail through the park and to the basin. Rides are $20 for the first hour; $10 for the second. Kids 2 to 7 years can be led inside the arena for a minimal charge.

Get physical on the weekends in the summer by renting a row boat, pedal boat, or aqua cycle. There is a special area for radio-controlled boats, too. A snack bar is also open in the summer. The paved street that winds all around the park will have to suffice for most skating or hiking desires. Across Euclid Street, the park also has trap and skeet fields.

If you like it here so much that you don't want to go home, stay and camp. The campgrounds are at the far end of the park and are nice-looking. While a few of the sites have small shade trees, the majority of the campsites are near barren, gently sloping hills.

Hours: The park is open daily, 7:30am - 5pm; open extended hours during the summer. Boat rentals are available in the summer only. Horseback riding is available Tues. - Sun., 8am - 5pm.

Admission: $5 per vehicle. Pedestrians are $2. Boat launches are $2. Fishing, ages 7 and older, is $5 a person; $2 for children 6 and under. Pedal boats rentals are $6 for half an hour. Aqua boats are $7 for half an hour. Rowboats are $5 an hour, with minimum rental hours required. Camping is $10 a night for tents; $16 for RVs.

Ages: All

RAINBOW BASIN

(760) 252-6000 / www.ca.blm.gov

Fossil Canyon Loop Road, 8 miles N. of Barstow

(Exit Mojave Fwy [15] N. on Barstow Rd., L. on Main St., R. on First St., L. on Fort Irwin Rd. Go about 6 miles, turn L. on Fossil Bed Rd. and go about 2 miles, R. toward Owl Canyon Campground. The 4 mile, narrow, bumpy, one-way dirt road loops around. [TG: 349 B6])

ROY G BIV (red, orange, yellow, green, blue, indigo, and violet) and all the in between, somewhat muted, colors of the rainbow are represented at the aptly named Rainbow Basin. Note: Although the dirt roads are a bit bumpy, the destination is worth the jolting. (Four-wheel drive vehicles are recommended, but our van made it without any problems.) Tip: Bring water! The colorful sedimentary rock formations are eye catching. We stopped the car several times to get out and look more closely at the variety of rocks and to hike among the formations, even though there are no developed trails. We didn't find any, but we read that this area is rich with mammal fossil remains as mastodons, pronghorns, "dog-bears," and horses have been found here. Collecting fossils, however, is forbidden.

The adjacent Owl Canyon Campground has thirty-one fairly primitive sites. Facilities include fire rings, grills, and vault toilets. Bring your own firewood and water. Remember that, as with any desert area, extreme temperatures occur.

Hours: Open daily, dawn - dusk.
Admission: Free. Camping is $6 a night.
Ages: 4 years and up.

YUCAIPA REGIONAL PARK

(909) 790-3127 / www.co.san-bernardino.ca.us/parks
33900 Oak Glen Road, Yucaipa
(Going E. on San Bernardino Fwy [10], exit N.E. on Yucaipa Blvd., L. on Oak Glen Rd. Going W. on 10, exit N. on Live Oak Canyon/Oak Glen. It's W. of the Oak Glen apple orchards. [TG: 649 J1])

Nestled in the rocky San Bernardino Mountains is this huge, beautiful oasis of a park offering year-round fun. Fish in any one of the three, very large, picturesque lakes to catch seasonal bass, trout, or catfish. A fishing license is required.

During the summer months, get in the swim of things in the one-acre swim lagoon, and/or go for the two long waterslides. White sandy beaches frame the water's edge, with grassy areas just beyond them. A few steps away is a full-service snack bar, plus pedal boat and aqua cycle rentals. A wonderful playground is right outside the swim area. Another playground, designed specifically for disabled children, is across the way.

RV and tent camping is available for those who really want to get away from it all for a weekend or so. The grassy areas, trees, and mountains are a scenic setting for the camp sites. There are plenty of picnic tables and shelters, as well as barbecue pits. Hiking is encouraged on either paved trails or along the few dirt pathways. (See OAK GLEN / APPLE PICKING & TOURS, on page 322, for nearby places to go.)

Hours: The park is open most of the year daily, 7:30am - 5pm; open in the summer daily, 7:30am - 6pm. Swimming is available in the summer, Tues. - Sun.,10am - 5pm.
Admission: $5 per vehicle. Pedestrians are $2. A fishing license is needed for those over 16 - available here for $10.75. Fishing is $5 a day for ages 8 and older; $2 for ages 7 and under, plus park admission. Entrance to the swim lagoon on Tues. - Fri. is park admission plus $2 per person for kids 4 and up; $3 on Sat. - Sun. An all-day waterslide and swim pass is park admission plus $8 per person. Pedal boat and aqua cycle rentals are $6 for a half hour. Camping prices range from $11 to $18 per night, for up to six people.
Ages: All

-----*MALLS*-----

ONTARIO MILLS MALL

(909) 484-8300 / www.ontariomillsmall.com
One Mills Circle, Ontario
(From San Bernardino Fwy [10], exit N. on Milliken Ave., R. on Mall Dr. From Ontario Fwy [15], exit W. on 4th St., L. on Franklin Ave. [TG: 603 E6])

Ontario Mills is California's largest outlet mall with over 200 outlet, speciality, and off-price retail stores. The mall also offers various forms of "shoppertainment." AMC features thirty movie screens and Edwards has the EDWARDS IMAX 3-D movie theater (see pg. 346) which offers both 2-D and 3-D shows. Other entertainment offered at the mega mall includes GAMEWORKS (see pg. 326); Dave & Buster's, a combination restaurant/bar and game/arcade center geared for adults; Improv Comedy Theater for adults (909) 484-5411 / www.improv.com; and VANS SKATEPARK (see pg. 328). Kids will love making their own teddy bears here at BUILD-A-BEAR WORKSHOP. (See pg. 342.)

The food court is fancifully decorated with large, colorful, inflatable foods. Other tantalizing eating experiences in unique surroundings are Wolfgang Puck's Cafe and RAINFOREST CAFE (see pg. 325). Krispy

Kreme Doughnuts (a personal favorite!) is located just outside the mall.

Hours: The mall and most attractions are open Mon. - Sat., 10am - 9:30pm; Sun., 10am - 8pm.
Admission: Technically, free.
Ages: All

-----*MUSEUMS*-----

THE AIR MUSEUM "PLANES OF FAME"
(909) 597-3722 / www.planesoffame.org
7000 Merrill Avenue, Chino
(Exit Riverside Fwy [91] N. on the 71, N. on Euclid [or the 83]. Exit Hwy 83 R. on Merrill Ave., R. on Cal Aero Dr., past the National Air Race Museum. [TG: 682 D5])

For some *plane* old fun, come see over 100 vintage aircraft (some of which are flyable) that have landed here, including one of the only air-worthy Japanese Zeros in the world. Many of the planes are touchable without any formal barriers to keep visitors away, making it a comfortable place to take children.

Planes, parts of planes and helicopters, and military vehicles are stationed outside the north hangar. The hangar is dedicated to Japanese and German aircraft from WWII, some of which are "flying" around overhead, while others are grounded. My boys were drawn to the "Wild Grinning Face of the Green Dragon Unit" - a nose of a plane that has machine guns and is decorated with a fire-breathing dragon painted on its side. The "Betty" bomber is displayed looking like it has crashed landed in a jungle, complete with an overgrowth of plants, plus dirt and a background mural. This building also displays airplane engines and small models of Japanese army aircraft, plus news clippings regarding Pearl Harbor. The two south hangars hold numerous other colorful and historic aircraft. The Enterprise hangar is dedicated to Navy planes and currently has ten planes on display. Take the catwalk around part of the building and look into the built-in exhibit windows that hold various artifacts.

Another hangar is part restoration work area, part model aircraft display, and part hands-on Aviation Center. Visitors are welcome to watch the restoration, but may not touch anything. The model aircraft collection is one of the largest we've ever seen in one place. Kids who are aeronautically inclined will be in their element at the Aviation Center. They can climb into three experimental planes and play pilot; practice their mechanical skills by "using" rivet guns, drills, and control sticks; and take apart (and put together) parts of an engine. This hangar also displays gun turrets, instrument panels, cutaways of aircraft engine, and uniforms.

A B-17 Bomber is available on weekends, only, to walk through or sit down in and "fly." The first Saturday of every month features a particular plane, or type of planes, plus a seminar at 10am with panelists or veteran pilots who were directly associated with that plane. Whenever possible, this event concludes with a flight demonstration.

It's a short drive around the corner to the Fighter Jets Museum and Space Exhibit. The Bell X-1 was used in the movie, *The Right Stuff* and was the first plane to break the sound barrier. Other planes here, including the red "Stinger" Formula One Racer, have descriptions that are equally informative, though some are a bit technical. The Space Exhibit has a full-size model of the Apollo 13 capsule, a test pilot's suit, and a Mercury spacecraft mock up, along with posters, photos of astronauts, and rockets blasting off - all underneath a ceiling painted to look like a starry, nighttime sky.

The Air Museum is in the Chino airport, so kids can experience the thrill of seeing planes take off and land. Don't miss the annual Air Show in May! (See pg. 576.) If you get hungry, pilot your way to Flo's Cafe, which is also on airport grounds.

Hours: Open daily, 9am - 5pm. Closed Thanksgiving and Christmas.
Admission: $8.95 for adults; $1.95 for ages 5 - 11; children 4 and under are free.
Ages: 3 years and up.

A SPECIAL PLACE
(909) 881-1201
1003 E. Highland Avenue, San Bernardino

(Exit Hwy 30 S. on Waterman, L. on Highland, L. on Harrison St. to park. [TG: 577 A3])

A Special Place is ideal for younger children who delight in hands-on activities. (That should include all of the younger population!) Outside, a small covered cement patio enhances disability awareness via a wheelchair; a swing for kids in wheelchairs; braces to try on; crutches to use; and even prostheses to touch. Your children will get a feel for what it's like to be mobile in different ways. Also out here is western gear, such as boots, cowboy hats, and a few saddles so kids can ride the range.

Inside, two rooms are divided into sections. The drama area has face painting and costumes. It's a hot time in the old town when kids dress up as firefighters. The schoolroom area has a few old-fashioned school desks and a thirteen star flag. (See if your kids notice this and know how many stars are on our flag today.) There is also a working traffic light here to play the game Red Light, Green Light.

Along the back wall is a wonderful aquatic mural, plus fish and turtle aquariums, and a cage of birds. Kids can turn a handle at an Edison display to try to generate enough electricity to power a light bulb. At the puppet theater, children make the puppets come to life.

Another section is set-up like a mini-Kaiser clinic, with an X-ray machine, infant incubator, and blood pressure machine. Prepare your child to go to the doctor or to become one! The Shadow Room is always fun. When the light flashes, kids love posing to leave a temporary shadow of their body on the photo-sensitive wall.

The museum is small, but it has a great variety of interactive things to do, making it a special place, indeed.

Hours: Open Mon., 1pm - 5pm; Tues. - Fri., 9am - 5pm; Sat., 11am - 3pm. Closed Sun.

Admission: $2 per person; children 2 and under are free. The first Sat. of each month is free for grandparents who are accompanied by a paying child.

Ages: 6 months to 10 years.

CHINO YOUTH MUSEUM

$$

(909) 464-0499 / www.chinoyouthmuseum.org
13191 6th Street, Chino
(Exit the Pomona Fwy [60] S. on Central Ave., R. on D St., R. on 6th St. [TG: 641 G7])

This children's museum has a main room with several smaller rooms that branch off from it. Each room is themed around a particular function or career choice found within city limits. The themes are enhanced with a mural or building facade, and a prop or two. For instance, kids can try on firemen clothes, slide down a pole, and sit on a real police motorcycle as they become civil servants for a day; "shop" in a grocery store; work at a bank behind the teller's window; use a judge's costume and gavel to send little criminals to the little jail; and even catch magnetic fish (with a special pole) in a water conservation area. Ah, to be young again and just have to pretend at working a job! The museum also has a room just for arts and crafts.

Hours: Open Wed., 8am - noon and 2pm - 6pm; Thurs. - Fri., 2pm - 6pm; Sat., 10am - 4pm.

Admission: $4 for adults; $2 for seniors and ages 2 - 18.

Ages: 2 - 8 years.

EDWARD-DEAN MUSEUM AND GARDENS

$

(909) 845-2626 / www.edward-deanmuseum.org
9401 Oak Glen Road, Cherry Valley
(Exit Moreno Valley Fwy [60] N. on Beaumont Ave., which turns into Oak Glen Rd. Look for signs to the museum. [TG: 690 J2])

This elegant, medium-sized fine arts museum seems almost out of place in the rural town of Cherry Valley. It is situated on beautifully landscaped grounds with formal gardens, accompanied by grassy lawns and a small pond with lily pads. Just outside the museum is a fountain surrounded by a rose garden.

The two-story museum has several galleries that specialize in art from the late 16th to early 19th centuries. The left wing gallery has rotating exhibits. We saw "Art in Miniature" which showcased buildings, artwork, and scenes in miniature. The permanent upstairs galleries are situated in a home-like atmosphere. They feature furniture, china, a Buddha exhibit in a room with ornate wood wall carvings, silk tapestries, portraits, a beautiful oriental robe, statues, and a music room with a piano and a harp. Downstairs is a small reference library, plus a wing displaying a pope's wooden traveling desk and few other items. The docents we encountered were friendly and readily explained many of the exhibit pieces. Note that the museum is just down the road from all the fun at OAK GLEN. (See pg. 322.)

Hours: Open Fri. - Sun., 10am - 5pm. Open during the week for free hour-long school tours. Transportation is included.

Admission: $3 for adults; $2 for seniors and students; children 12 and under are free.

Ages: 7 years and up.

GRABER OLIVE HOUSE
(909) 983-1761 / www.graberolives.com

315 E. Fourth Street, Ontario

(Going E. on San Bernardino Fwy [10], exit S. on Euclid, L. on Fourth St. Going W. on 10, exit W. on 4ᵗʰ St. [TG: 602 C6])

This is an unusual pit stop for kids. On the grounds are a small museum, an olive processing plant, a gift shop, and the owner's house. The one-room museum shows a pictorial history of olive processing. It also has an eclectic mix of antiques such as a big wooden olive grader, a Singer sewing machine, a sausage stuffer, and more.

Take a short tour around the working olive plant. The "on-season" is mid-October through December, when the machinery and workers are in full production. This, then, is the best time to take a tour. Walk into the grading room, where olives are sorted by size and quality, and peer into the enormous olive vats. The boiler room, where olives are sterilized, the canning machine, and the labeling machine are all interesting to look at. A ten-minute video, that shows the history of the packing plant, is also available to watch.

The gift shop is very classy with etiquette videos, stationery, delicious jams, and elegant candies. (The chocolate-covered cherries are to die for!) Kids can sample a Graber olive, which might mean more to them after a tour. Family tours are given whenever someone is available. Twenty-minute school or scout tours are given only by the teacher or leader, respectively, and only after he/she has first taken a guided tour.

Hours: Open Mon. - Sat., 9am - 5:30pm; Sun., 9:30am - 6pm.

Admission: Free

Ages: 5 years and up.

JOHN RAINS HOUSE - CASA DE RANCHO CUCAMONGA
(909) 989-4970 / www.co.san-bernardino.ca.us/museum/rains.htm

8810 Hemlock Street, Rancho Cucamonga

(Exit San Bernardino Fwy [10] N. on Vineyard. It's 2 blocks N. of Foothills Blvd., on the corner of Vineyard and Hemlock, in a residential area. [TG: 602 G1])

Built with bricks in 1860, this restored rancho residence is a lovely example of a house from this era. Tours are given through the historical home to see period furniture in the bedrooms, living rooms, and other rooms, and around the beautiful grounds, complete with green lawns, trees, picnic tables in the backyard, and the central courtyard. Docents recount stories about the people who once lived here. Their lives were like soap operas, complete with affairs, murders, buried treasure, and more sordid happenings - kids love this! (And they are learning history.) Ask about school and group tours and the special events that the Rancho hosts, such as Old Rancho Days. Note: The house is exquisitely decked out at Christmas time.

Hours: Open Wed. - Sat., 10am - 4pm; Sun., 1pm - 4pm. Tours are given every forty-five minutes. Closed New Year's Day, Thanksgiving, and Christmas.

Admission: Suggested donation of $2 for adults; $1 for children 11 and under.

Ages: 6 years and up.

KIMBERLY CREST HOUSE AND GARDENS
(909) 792-2111 / www.kimberlycrest.org

1325 Prospect Drive, Redlands

(Exit San Bernardino Fwy [10] S.W. on Ford St., R. on Redlands Blvd., L. on Highland Ave., L. on Prospect. [TG: 648 D3])

This three-story, rather large, light lime green and gray French chateau, with yellow trim, was originally built in 1897. The turrets add to its eye-catching appeal, as do the formal Italian-style gardens and grounds, complete with lotus blossoms and koi in the lily ponds, plus the gazebo and surrounding orange groves.

The period (replicated) furniture and decor is as grand as the outside with gilt furniture and silk damask wall coverings. Tour the French parlor, library, living room, dining rooms (set with crystal), bedrooms, and other beautifully accessorized rooms. The gift shop is located in a one-hundred-year-old carriage house.

The Crest house is nestled in one end of the lush, Prospect Park. After your tour, enjoy a walk on the dirt trails through the park.

Hours: Tours are given Thurs. - Sun., 1pm - 4pm, with the last tour at 3:30pm. Closed holidays and August. The surrounding park is open daily, 9am - 5pm.

Admission: $6 for adults; $5 for students; children 11 and under are free.

Ages: 6 years and up.

LINCOLN MEMORIAL SHRINE

(909) 798-7636 - Shrine;

(909) 798-7632 - Heritage Room at the Smiley Public Library / www.akspl.org/lincoln.html

125 W. Vine Street, Redlands

(Exit San Bernardino Fwy [10] S. on Hwy 38 [or Orange St.], R. on Citrus Ave., L. on Eureka St. [TG: 608 B7])

"Fourscore and seven years ago. . ." begins the Gettysburg Address. If your older children are studying our revered sixteenth president, but can't make it to Washington D.C., bring them to the Lincoln Memorial Shrine in Redlands. The central, octagon-shaped building also has two wings, all devoted to Abraham Lincoln and Civil War memorabilia. The building contains research books; surgical instruments; letters and documents written from and about Abraham Lincoln, Robert E. Lee, and Stonewall Jackson; Civil War photographs; bullets found on battlefields; officers' uniforms; medals; and a lifemask (i.e. an exact likeness of a person via a mold) and handcast of Abraham Lincoln. Mementos from his assassination include his cuff links, a strand of his hair, mourning bands, and the wreath that laid on his casket. The shrine also displays other Civil War artifacts such as swords, an 1863 Springfield rifle, hardtack, documents, models, and pictures of Abraham Lincoln, Robert E. Lee, and Ulysses S. Grant.

Come view the materials here on your own. Better yet, take a guided tour and benefit from knowledgeable docents who explain the exhibits in more detail. Exhibits at the memorial rotate because the small shrine cannot contain the 3,000-plus manuscripts and other items in the archives. The outside of the building is inscribed with excerpts from Lincoln's inaugural addresses and various other speeches.

The shrine is located behind the Smiley Public Library, with an expanse of green lawn in between. The multi-level library, established in 1894, is an architectural and book-lovers delight.

Hours: Open Tues. - Sun., 1pm - 5pm. Closed holidays except for Lincoln's birthday. Small group tours can be arranged for morning hours.

Admission: Free

Ages: 7 years and up.

MCDONALD'S Museum

(909) 885-6324 / www.route-66.com/mcdonalds

1398 North 'E' Street, San Bernardino

(Exit Riverside Fwy [215] at Base Line exit and go E. on 13th St., L. on 'E' St. [TG: 576 G5])

"We love to see you smile!" is just one McSlogan touted at this "museum." The building is on the site of the first McDonald's Restaurant, which was established in 1948. Inside, half of the space is used for the administration offices of Juan Pollo Restaurants, the company that now owns the building.

The other half is a tribute to McDonald's and a refuge for all of its merchandising paraphernalia - that's a lot of Happy Meal toys! (Kind of makes you wish you hadn't thrown out all of those toys; kind of.) Besides the toys, display cases hold old menus, to-go bags, and cups; a 1940's milk shake machine; a 1950's potato press (to make French fries); and lots of photographs and articles on McDonald's, including the ones detailing the feud between the McDonald's brothers and Ray Kroc. There are also a few pieces of Playland equipment, a character costume or two, and an array of promotional products.

In the back of the museum (for lack of a better word), are some artifacts, memorabilia, and information panels from and about historic Route 66.

Hours: Open daily, 10am - 5pm.
Admission: Free
Ages: 5 years and up.

MOJAVE RIVER VALLEY MUSEUM / DANA PARK

(760) 256-5452 - museum; (760) 256-5661 - park
270 E. Virginia Way, Barstow
(Exit Mojave Fwy [15] N. on Barstow Rd. [TG: 3679 H4])

This little museum is full of interesting artifacts and displays. My boys, for instance, liked hearing the story and seeing the bones of a headless horseman, found astride his horse. The rock and minerals on display include nice specimens of arrowheads, quartz, calate, and black and gold forms of chalocopyrite, plus fluorescent minerals that glow neon colors under black light. Other glass-encased exhibits are an eclectic mixture, such as lanterns, irons, rug beaters, pottery, clothing, a collection of glass insulators used by telegraph companies, and more. Kids can try their hand at grinding corn with stone mortar and pestle. They can also touch various animal skins, a turtle shell, bones, pinecones, rocks, and cotton. Short nature films are available to watch upon request. Call to arrange a field trip, and students will not only learn a lot about local history, but they can pan for real gold (and keep it!). Classes are usually taught by Mr. Walker, an archaeology instructor at the college.

The outside of the museum has large mining equipment around its perimeters - ore carts, picks, and other tools. Check out the "Tracks Through Time," where animal tracks, now in concrete, from around the Barstow area date back to the Jurassic period. Across the street is the small Centennial Park, which is actually an extension of the museum. It has a caboose, an army tank, and a mining display, which are representative of the three industries that helped formed Barstow. Dana Park is just across Virginia Way. It has picnic shelters, some grassy hills to roll down, and a playground.

Hours: The museum is open daily, 11am - 4pm.
Admission: Free to the museum, though donations are appreciated.
Ages: 3 years and up.

MUSEUM OF HISTORY AND ART, ONTARIO

(909) 983-3198 / www.ci.ontario.ca.us
225 S. Euclid Avenue, Ontario
(Exit the San Bernardino Fwy [10] S. on Euclid, L. on Transit. It's on the corner. [TG: 642 C1])

The Museum of History and Art captures the flavor of historic Ontario. The small museum's galleries feature artifacts regarding early inhabitants, from Native Americans and California Rancheros to early twentieth century settlers and, in particular, the founder of Ontario. Displays represent home and community life, and exhibits from the agricultural heritage, citrus groves, and industry and social life. Another section focuses on locally famous roads, such as Euclid Avenue and Route 66. The north wing presents changing exhibits every two months or so. Ask about docent guided gallery tours and family workshops that include a hands-on, theme-related projects, or the classroom outreach programs. Set in a Mediterranean-style building with a big fountain out front, the museum is a pleasant way to learn more about local roots.

Hours: The museum is open Wed. - Sun., noon - 4pm.
Admission: Free
Ages: 6 years and up.

OAK GLEN SCHOOL HOUSE MUSEUM

(909) 797-1691
11911 S. Oak Glen Road, Yucaipa
(Exit San Bernardino Fwy [10] N. on Beaumont Ave., which turns into Oak Glen Rd. It's N. of Riley's Cabin. [TG: 651 C2])

This small, one-room school house museum was originally built in 1927. The stone exterior encompasses a room containing old-fashioned desks facing a black board, a pot-belly stove, a phonograph, a stereoscope, newspaper clippings, apple crate labels from ranches, and old pictures. Tours are offered to the public upon request. School groups can take the basic fifteen-minute tour and then add on additional activities, such as making a candle by rolling up a sheet of beeswax, dipping pen in an ink bottle and writing, and taking a short nature walk. Teachers are welcome to bring their own curriculum to teach, too.

The adjacent, picturesque small park has grassy lawns, shade trees, picnic tables, and some play equipment.

Hours: Open to the public Sat., noon - 4pm; Sun., 1pm - 5pm, weather permitting. Call to make a reservation for a school tour and for extended hours during apple-picking season (September through November).

Admission: $1 for adults; 50¢ for children. School tours cost 50¢ per student, per activity.

Ages: 4 years old and up.

SAN BERNARDINO COUNTY MUSEUM

(909) 307-2669 / www.sbcountymuseum.org
2024 Orange Tree Lane, Redlands
(Exit San Bernardino Fwy [10] N. on California St., R. on Orange Tree Ln. [TG: 607 G6])

Spend a day at the incredible San Bernardino County Museum where the hallway exhibits are just as fine as the ones in the exhibit rooms! The distinctive half-dome attached to the main building is the Fisk Gallery of Fine Arts. The Hall of History and Anthropology is down the ramp from the main level. Here you'll find a covered wagon and a Wells Fargo stage coach, along with period clothing. The Anthropology section has Indian artifacts, such as arrowheads and painted rock art.

The hallway going to the Upper Level is lined with exhibits such as old-time medicine bottles, fossilized mammoth tusks, the bones of a ground sloth, and a saber-tooth cat skull. The other side of the hallway is a wonderful prelude to the Upper Level, displaying taxidermied birds and bird eggs. The eggs, in this substantial collection, vary in size from very large elephant bird eggs to very small hummingbird eggs.

If your kids show any interest in ornithology, the study of birds (calling each other bird brain doesn't count), they will be fascinated by the entire Upper Level. The Hall of Water Birds takes you on flights of fancy, although with taxidermied birds you won't get very far. See if your kids can correctly match the birds to their eggs, which are also on display throughout the room. The next wing, Hall of Land Birds, displays birds and eggs according to regional habitat. Look for the "awww, so cute" hatchling exhibit. I have never seen so many birds flocked together.

A large stuffed California Condor guards the entrance to the Upper Dome Gallery. This gallery has rotating exhibits of art work.

An absolutely dazzling display of rocks, minerals, and gemstones line the hallway toward the Lower Level. The doors in the hallway lead out to the Exploration Station, but we'll come back to that. Continue down the ramp into the Hall of Mammals. The walls in here are lined with fossilized animal bones, horns, and teeth. Bug collectors will be bug-eyed at the comprehensive collection of mounted insects of all sizes, shapes, and colors. Also along the walls are dioramas of smaller taxidermied animals and reptiles, such as spotted skunks, possums, and turtles. The Hall of Mammals is unique in that it also has exhibits of larger taxidermied animals, such as a polar bear, an Alaskan brown bear, a mountain lion, a bison, and a gigantic moose. My kids were really impressed by the sheer size of some of the animals.

Outside, between the main building and the Exploration Station, is a patio area designed just for kids. The displays include a mining car carrying "explosives" on track toward a tunnel and a full-size caboose and steam engine. Picnic tables are here for snack attacks.

The Exploration Station is a learning center that has small, live mammals, such as bunnies and bats, and reptiles, such as iguanas, a boa, and other snakes. Kids can touch fossils, animal furs, and casts of bones and dinosaur fossils. The room also has aquariums.

The Special Exhibit Hall has terrific, changing, usually interactive displays. A past exhibit was rather batty - Masters of the Night - The True Story of Bats. It included entering through the portals of a gothic castle, seeing videos, touching models of bats, and literally hanging around in a bat cave.

Family Activity Day is usually offered once a month and designed to educate the entire family about a particular topic or animal in a fun, hands-on manner. The programs are free with general museum admission. Ask about special events, classes, and tours.

Hours: Open Tues. - Sun., 9am - 5pm. The Exploration Station is open Tues. - Thurs., 10am - 1pm; Fri., 10am - 4pm; Sat. - Sun., 1pm - 4pm. The museum is closed Mon., New Year's Day, Thanksgiving, and Christmas.

Admission: $4 for adults; $3 for seniors and students; $2 for ages 5 - 12; children 4 and under are free.

Ages: 2 years and up.

SAN BERNARDINO RANCHO ASISTENCIA

(909) 793-5402 / www.co.san-bernardino.ca.us/museum/asist.htm
26930 Barton Road, Redlands
(Exit San Bernardino Fwy [10] S. on California Ave., L. on Barton Rd. [TG: 647 G1])

This lovely restored set of buildings was once an outpost as part of Mission San Gabriel's Rancho. A grassy courtyard, surrounded by a few small adobe buildings, a bell tower, a fountain, and a grist mill complete this picturesque asistencia. Explore a part of the ranchero history as you walk through the main structure. The tour guide helps bring the past to life, explaining the people that once lived here and their way of life. School groups are welcome; just call to make a reservation.

Hours: Open Tues. - Sat., 10am - 4pm. Closed Sun. and Mon.

Admission: $2 for adults; $1 for ages 12 and under.

Ages: 6 years and up.

VICTOR VALLEY MUSEUM

(760) 240-2111 / www.vvmuseum.com
11873 Apple Valley Road, Apple Valley
(Exit Mojave Fwy [I-15 to Hesperia] E. on Bear Valley Rd., go 7 miles, turn R. on Apple Valley Rd. [TG: 4387 C6])

This classy, off-the-beaten-track museum is like an oasis in the desert. A landmark two-ton giant tortoise sculpture resides outside the building. An art wing with rotating exhibits of local and regional art is to the left of the lobby.

The museum contains taxidermied animals in life-like poses such as a cougar, buffalo, muskox, and grizzly bear. A wall of mounted heads showcases a pronghorn, buffalo, moose, caribou, and goat. The "Old West" section contains twelve saddles, horseshoes, rope, bronze cowboy sculptures, a stagecoach, farm tools, and great-great-grandma's kitchen and household utensils, such as a butter churn and candle mold. An adjacent workroom contains drills, wrenches, hammers, axes, saws, and more, hanging on the wall. A living room section contains a phonograph, pump organ, radio, an early TV, and various other items. There are also collections of telephones, cameras, pictures (people back then didn't smile because they had to hold absolutely still for an entire minute or so), and real monies from the Bible (i.e. thirty pieces of silver and a widow's mite). The Native American section features baskets, arrowheads, and more. A doctor's buggy circa 1890's and a replica of the Old Woman meteorite are also found here.

A children's room, the Imagination Station, features hands-on fun such as an old-fashioned switchboard, a stone mortar and pestle, face painting, panning for gold, a small school "room," some games and puzzles, and a hospital room with an X-Ray machine, an IV set-up and clothing for doctors and patients. Other dress-up clothing in the Station includes policemen and firemen uniforms, sailor outfits, and lots more. The room also contains air plane models, dolls and toys from around the world, snake skins, and taxidermied snakes and gila monsters.

A self-guided tour is good, but a guided tour, as usual, is much better. We learned about heros, such as Indians - how they made and did so much with seemingly so little - and Earl Bascom, a local rodeo star. As we inspected Native American baskets we learned how the weaving was so tightly done that the baskets could hold water. And we gained more knowledge about the rocks, minerals, and numerous other artifacts on display. Pre and post-visit lesson packets are available for classrooms.

Hours: Open Wed. - Sat., 10am - 4pm; Sun., noon - 4 p.m.

Admission: The museum is $3 for adults; $2 for seniors and ages 12 - 21; children 11 and under are free. Entrance to the Imagination Station room is $1 for ages 11 and under with a paid adult.

Ages: 6 years and up.

YORBA-SLAUGHTER ADOBE

(909) 597-8332 / www.co.san-bernardino.ca.us/museum/yorba.htm

17127 Pomona Rincon Road, Chino

(Exit Chino Valley Fwy [71] N.E. on Euclid, take a quick L. on Pomona Rincon Rd. [TG: 712 A4])

Just for the record, the name "Slaughter" refers to a family that once lived here - not the slaughtering of animals. The adobe was built in 1852 and therefore receives the distinction of being the oldest standing residence in San Bernardino. A tour through the adobe, which is fairly well kept up, allows visitors to see its low beam ceilings; a dining room, with a table set for company; a living room and music room with period furniture and artifacts that include a piano, sewing machine, dolls, and a pot-bellied stove; a kitchen; a bedroom; and a few, simply furnished rooms upstairs.

There are a few other buildings on the grounds that are also original, but very weathered in appearance. A shed with a stone chimney, a winery building, a one-ton solid copper pot (used for tallow), a grist mill, and a few pieces of old farming equipment complete the homestead. Note: Group and school tours are given by appointment.

Hours: Open to the public Wed. - Sat., 10am - 4pm; Sun., 1pm - 4pm. Closed Mon., Tues., New Year's Day, Thanksgiving, and Christmas.

Admission: $2 for adults; $1 for ages 12 and under.

Ages: 7 years and up.

-----POTPOURRI-----

BUILD-A-BEAR WORKSHOP (Ontario)

(909) 484-8300 - mall; (877) 789-BEAR (2327) - national / www.buildabear.com

One Mills Circle in Ontario Mills Mall, Ontario

(From San Bernardino Fwy [10], exit N. on Milliken Ave., R. on Mall Dr. From Ontario Fwy [15], exit W. on 4th St., L. on Franklin Ave. [TG: 603 E6])

See the entry for BUILD-A-BEAR WORKSHOP (Newport Beach) on page 250 for details.

Hours: Open Mon. - Sat., 10am - 9:30pm; Sun., 10am - 8pm.

CAL-EARTH

(760) 244-0614 or (760) 956-7533 / www.calearth.org

10177 Baldy Lane, Hesperia

(Exit Mojave Fwy [15] E. on Main St., L. on Topaz, L. on Live Oak, R. on Baldy Ln. [TG: 4475 H4])

Nestled among Joshua trees, the California Institute of Earth Art and Architecture (aka Cal-Earth) has an educational facility that emphasizes building structures utilizing the four basic elements - earth, water, air, and fire. Domed, igloo-like structures made out of superadobe bricks, which look like sand bags, are on the grounds; prototypes for future buildings. The structure uses archways instead of the typical, box-like corners and doorframes. Both the United Nations and NASA have expressed interest in the designs and environment-friendly building materials.

The general public is invited to come, learn, and tour around. A minimum group of fifteen students are offered three-hour or full-day workshops. In the "class," they learn how (by hearing about and by physically working) to build homes with arches and vaults using the earth (i.e. dirt); how to build emergency housing that is flood and fire-proof; teamwork; and how to live in harmony with the environment, using solar energy for glazing buildings and for cooling them. Deforestation is examined as alternative choices are shown and worked with. Prepare the kids for some hard labor and for out-of-the-box thinking. Note: A museum and nature center are in the process of being built using these methods. They are located a short drive away at the end of Main Street, by Hesperia Lake. This lake offers picnic tables, fishing, a children's play area, and camping.

Hours: Open May through October the first Sat., 9am - 1pm; 4pm - 7pm. Open November through April the first Sat., 10am - 3pm. Call first. Tours are given by appointment Sat. after 2pm or for school groups during the week.

Admission: Free on the first Sat. School tours cost between $5 - $15 per person, depending on the length of time and activities.

Ages: 8 years and up.

CALICO GHOST TOWN

(800) TO CALICO (862-2542) / www.calicotown.com

36600 Ghost Town Road, Yermo

(Exit Mojave Fwy [15] N. on Ghost Town Rd. It's about 10 miles E. of Barstow. [TG: 3591 H2])

Once upon a time, a rich vein of silver was found in a mine underneath some multi-colored mountains. Word about the strike spread like wildfire, and pretty soon there were 5,000 people, of twenty different nationalities, living in and around this mining town. The town was called Calico because the varied minerals that created the different colors of the mountains were "as purty as a gal's Calico skirt." Between 1882 and 1907, the 500 mine claims produced eighty-six million dollars worth of silver and forty-five million dollars worth of borax. Then, the price of silver dropped. And the boom town went bust. Thankfully, the story doesn't end here.

Nowadays, this authentic western town has twenty-three unique shops and restaurants (including an ice cream parlor) on both sides of the wide, dirt, main road that snakes up the mountain - put your walking shoes on. Some of the current shops are even housed in original buildings. Topping our list of favorite shops are the rock and fossil shop, the leather works, and an 1890's general store. School tours are offered to educate students on the history of the town and this era. Tours include a free education packet and a discount on entrance and attraction fees.

There are several other attractions here. Gun fights break out daily every hour on the half hour starting at 10:30am. Visit the re-created schoolhouse at the end of the road where an authentically-dressed schoolmarm will gladly teach your kids what going to school was like in the olden days. There is a sturdy wooden teeter-totter and swing outside the schoolhouse. Don't be a fool when you pan for gold 'cause it's only fool's gold. The Mystery Shack is a small house of optical illusions where water rolls uphill, a broom stands up at an angle without falling over, and more. Before you walk through Maggie Mine, a real silver mine, look at the mining tools on display, such as a stamp mill, ore cart, re-created assay office, and more. Just inside the mine is a display of rocks and minerals mined from these parts, including fluorescent ones that glow in neon colors when the lights are turned off. Take the short walk through the mine, which has mannequin miners in action and audio explanations of the mining process. The Odessa Railroad is simply an eight-minute train ride on a narrow-gauge railcar. It takes you around part of a mountain where you'll see small cave-like openings that were front doors to miners' homes. On your ride you'll learn that the huge pile of "tailing" from the Silver King Mine still contains six million dollars worth of silver ore, but it would cost nine million dollars to process. Oh well! Sharpshooters can test their skill at the shooting gallery. Look at and into the house made of bottles - it's the ultimate in recycling.

Call for a schedule of special events or check the Calendar section for information on a Civil War Reenactment (pg. 564) on President's Day Weekend or Calico Days (pg. 602) on Columbus Day Weekend. Oh, and do explain to your kids that the term, "ghost town" doesn't mean that there are ghosts here, but just that the town went from being inhabited to being deserted.

Tent, RV, or cabin camping (which sleeps four) is available just below the town, as is a bunkhouse, which sleeps between twelve to twenty people. The sites are small, but the surrounding area makes it especially attractive for kids because there are (small) caves all over. In fact, seeing and even going into a few caves, was one of the things my children liked best about Calico. If you have a four-wheel drive vehicle, turn left after leaving Calico and head for the hills to explore some of the hiking trails (and mineral deposits) in this area.

Hours: Open daily, 9am - 5pm. Closed Christmas.

Admission: Entrance is $6 for adults; $3 for ages 6 - 15; children 5 and under are free. The Mystery Shack is $2 for adults; $1 for ages 6 - 15; children 5 and under are free. Train rides are each $2.50 for adults; $1.25 for kids. A walk through Maggie's Mine is $1 per person. Gold panning is $1. (This attraction is only open in warm weather.) The Shooting Gallery is $1 for 20 shots. The schoolhouse, shootouts, guided tours, and tram ride up the hill from the parking lot, are free. Tent camping is $18 a night; the cabin is $28; the bunkhouse starts at $60.

Ages: All

CIRCUS VARGAS

See the entry for CIRCUS VARGAS on page 134 for details.

COLONIAL CHESTERFIELD / RILEY'S FARM - Living History   ☼

(909) 797-7534 - Colonial Farm Life, Revolutionary War, (and fruit tours); (909) 797-5145 - Civil War $$$
(and U-Pic fruit); (909) 790-5852 - Gold Rush and Old Joe Homestead. / www.rileysfarm.com

12261 S. Oak Glen Road, Oak Glen

(Going E. on San Bernardino Fwy [10], exit N. on the Yucaipa exit, L. onto Oak Glen Rd. In about 6 miles you'll reach the "Welcome to Oak Glen" sign. This farm is at the end of the windy road. From the 60 and 10 intersection, go N. on Beaumont Blvd. which turns into Oak Glen Rd., drive up a few miles. [TG: 651 C3])

The year is 1775. The Revolutionary War is imminent. Students can learn first hand how it felt to be involved with this radical war by participating in a four-hour reenactment. Upon arrival, students are broken into "townships" and each group then visits various stations to experience life in this era. Some of the activities they participate in include visiting a blacksmith, witnessing Colonel Fenton's attempt to bribe Sam Adams, encountering British soldiers, learning about the Stamp Act, going through a court trial, grinding wheat, churning butter, learning etiquette of the times, and in a grand finale - marching across the orchard lands with arms (i.e. sticks and fake gun stocks) in a battle re-creation. Kids become a part of the history - living it and learning it. A typical fare of lunch rations is also served: a hunk of bread, slice of cheese, piece of fruit, and beef jerky. Tip: Bring some of your own lunch! The tour begins at 10am and cost $12 per student. Ask about minimum and maximum number of tour participants. The Revolutionary War Overnight combines the above reenactment with more of the same - sentry duty against the redcoats, period dancing, skirmishes, sleeping on rope bunk beds, and eating! The cost is $95 per person with a thirty-five person minimum.

If kids are studying the Civil War, Riley's also has a reenactment for this pivotal time period that is just as engrossing and just as authentic as the Revolutionary War. These tours were a favorite for my troops! The Civil War requires prep work as students have drama assignments, costume guides, vocabulary helps, etiquette information, and more for this re-creation.

The similar, learn-it-by-living-it two-hour Colonial Farm Life tour offers a choice of activities including playing 18th century games, making cheese and butter, pressing cider, weaving, baking bread, learning etiquette, making candles, stamping, and eating a hot-dipped caramel apple. This tour is $8.75 per person with a thirty person minimum. The four-hour Gold Rush field trip offers gold panning in a sluice box, panning for gold, dry mining, digging in a mine shaft, looking inside a miner's cabin, etiquette and manners "class," a rope climbing challenge, and tomahawk throwing, as well as a lesson in California economics and a drama involving a gold theft. The price is $12 per person for a minimum of twenty-five guests. A period lunch, more of a ration, is served. Tip: Bring your own lunch here, too. During the two-hour Old Joe Homestead tour, you'll learn about and partake in the care and training of farm animals, plus beat rugs, wash clothes by hand, dip candles, take a horse-drawn hayride, do farm chores, press cider, square dance, and eat a hot-dipped caramel apple. The tour is $9 per person for a minimum of twenty-five people.

Riley's Farm, set in the hills of Oak Glen, has a naturally rural ambiance with running streams, apple orchards, and dirt trails. If your group is too small to meet the minimum number for a reenactment, ask about joining up with another group. See OAK GLEN / APPLE PICKING & TOURS on page 322 for more on fruit picking and other things to do in this immediate area.

Hours: Tours are offered February through mid-June and September through mid-December by reservation.

Admission: See above for prices.

Ages: 3rd graders through high schoolers, but not all grades combined for one field trip.

MOUNTAIN SKIES ASTRONOMICAL SOCIETY ASTRONOMY VILLAGE

(909) 336-1699 / www.mountain-skies.org/astro-village.html

2001 Observatory Way, Lake Arrowhead

(Exit San Bernardino Fwy [10] N. on 215 Fwy, follow "Mountain Resorts" sign, stay R. on the 30 Fwy, N. at Waterman/Hwy 18 for 16 miles [past Blue Jay turnoff], L. on Observatory Way to upper parking lot.)

$$$

Observe the universe, or parts of it, at the astronomy village which is comprised of a research facility, library, gift shop, and observatory that houses a 16" F/10 Schmidt Cassegrain with a top mount of a 4" refractor. The facility is open daily during the day to take a look around and purchase a piece of space. The gift shop sells asteroid pieces, blue smoke, and rare space shuttle memorabilia. The library has displays of meteors, Mars rocks, Apollo display models, signed astronaut photographs, and more.

The best time to visit, though, is on a Saturday night for the Sky Quest Program. This two-and-a-half hour program starts off with a lecture, discussion, and question and answer time. A half-hour slide show follows. A powerful laser pointer is used to point out constellations, specific stars, and other cosmic happenings outside. Finally, guests have the opportunity to look through the telescope. Ask about school education programs, including great teacher resource equipment, and their other special events.

Hours: Open daily, 10am - 4pm. Sky Quest Programs for the public are offered on selected Sat. evenings.

Admission: Free to walk around and visit. Sky Quest Programs are $7 for adults; $5 for ages 17 and under. Pre-purchase tickets or pay $2 more at the door.

Ages: 6 years and up.

-----SHOWS AND THEATERS-----

AT THE GROVE

(909) 920-4343 / www.culturalcenter.org/orgs/grove.htm

276 E. 9th Street, Upland

(Exit San Bernardino Fwy [10] N. on Euclid, R. on 9th. [TG: 602 C3])

$$$$

Fine, professional, dramatic live theater is performed at the grove, along with comedies, concerts, six musicals per season, and children's workshops. Past shows have included *My Fair Lady, Fiddler on the Roof,* and *Barnum.*

Hours: Call for show dates and times.

Admission: Varies, depending on the show.

Ages: Varies, depending on the show.

BEATTIE PLANETARIUM

(909) 384-4400 / sbvc.sbccd.cc.ca.us/events/planetarium.htm

701 S. Mount Vernon Avenue at San Bernardino City College, San Bernardino

(From the Riverside Fwy [215], exit E. on Mill St., L. on Mount Vernon. From San Bernardino Fwy [10], exit N. on Mt. Vernon. [TG: 606, E3])

$

Join in a gathering of the stars, the celestial stars that is. The sixty-seat planetarium shows the night sky and a live narrator discusses what the heavens are up to. Hour-long show topics change frequently so you can come back more than once.

Hours: Shows are presented September through May, twice a month on Fri. at 7pm. No late arrivals.

Admission: $3 for adults; $2 for seniors and students; $1 for ages 10 and under.
Ages: 6 years and up.

EDWARDS IMAX THEATER (Ontario)

(909) 476-1525 or (909) 941-4487 / www.edwardscinemas.com

$$$

4900 E. 4th Street, Ontario

(From Ontario Fwy [15], exit W. on 4th St. From San Bernardino Fwy [10], exit N. on Milliken, R. on 4th St. It is just outside Ontario Mills Mall. [TG: 603 E5])

Going to the movies is a lot more fun if you are part of the action, not just watching it happen. Besides the twenty regular movie screens, this Edwards allows you to "experience" a 3-D movie on the giant IMAX screen by using lightweight headsets that create three-dimensional images. Objects will jump out at you, float around you, and seemingly become a part of your immediate surroundings. (Watch your kids try to reach out and touch the objects.) Live whatever adventure you see on the screen, whether it's underwater with fish, in the sky with birds, etc. Use your visit as an educational tool if you come with a group of students, and request a Teacher's Resource Guide, which are very well put together. Note that the theater sometimes also offers 2-D movies on its huge screen. See ONTARIO MILLS MALL (pg. 334) for other nearby attractions.

Hours: The first show starts at 10am.
Admission: $8 - $10 for adults; $6 - $8 for seniors and ages 12 and under. Prices vary according to film.
Ages: 4 years and up.

MILLIKEN PLANETARIUM

(909) 941-2758 / www.chaffey.edu/planet

$$

5885 Haven Avenue at Chaffey College, Rancho Cucamonga

(Exit San Bernardino Fwy [10] N. on Haven, turn into the college at Amber Ln., and park in the lot just after Myrtle Dr. The Planetarium is across the lot from Amber Ln. [TG: 573 B3])

A forty-five-minute up to ninety-minute introduction to celestial bodies is given most Friday nights here at the seventy-four-seat college planetarium. See and learn about our solar system and other galaxies as you gather under the indoor nighttime stars. Some of the show titles to choose from include *Our Solar System*, *Finding Your Way in the Sky*, and *Eclipses*. School groups coming during the week can choose from a variety of shows geared for particular age groups. Shows conclude with a ten-minute demonstration of the tools of the planetarium. Advanced reservations are necessary.

Hours: Shows for the general public are given most Fri. nights at 7pm. Call to book a weekday school tour.
Admission: $4 for adults; $3 for Chaffey students; $2 for ages 6 - 10. (Most shows aren't geared for younger children.) School groups are $60 for up to seventy-six people.
Ages: 7 years and up.

-----*TOURS*-----

GOODWILL INDUSTRIES (San Bernardino)

(909) 885-3831

!

8120 Palm Lane, San Bernardino

(Exit 215 Fwy E. on 6th St., R. on E St., L. on 5th St., R. on Waterman Ave., L. on 3rd St., L. on Palm Ln. [TG: 607 A1])

See the entry for GOODWILL INDUSTRIES (Santa Ana) on page 265 for details. This location is a main donation center, where goods get consolidated and processed. It also has manual production lines and the work activity area, plus a retail store next door.

Hours: Tours are offered Mon. - Fri., 8am - 4pm by reservation.
Admission: Free
Ages: 7 years and up.

OAK GLEN / APPLE PICKING & TOURS
www.oakglen.net
Oak Glen Road, Oak Glen

    See the entry for OAK GLEN / APPLE PICKING & TOURS on page 322 for details.

-----TRANSPORTATION-----

AMTRAK
(800) USA RAIL (872-7245) / www.dot.ca.gov/hq/rail; www.amtrak.com

    Ride the rails! See page xi (in the front) for more information.

BIKE MAPS (San Bernardino County)
    The web site www.labikepaths.com is a fantastic resource. It actually covers all of Southern California, not just L.A., with links to specific counties for maps, bikeways, and other cycling information. Another helpful contact website and phone number is for the State of California Caltrans Office of Bicycle Facilities: (916) 653-0036; www.dot.ca.gov/hq/tpp/offices/bike/contracts.htm.

CALIFORNIA SPEEDWAY
$$$$$

(800) 944-RACE (7223) / www.californiaspeedway.com
9300 N. Cherry Avenue, Fontana
(Exit San Bernardino Fwy [10] N. on Cherry Ave. [TG: 604 C4])

    The best in NASCAR racing roars to life in Southern California! Located on over 525 acres, this state-of-the-art speedway features a two-mile, D-shaped oval super speedway with a 1.3 mile infield road course. The track can accommodate three to four cars side by side. (Racers clock average speeds of up to 200mph!) The two major race weekends occur in April for the NASCAR Winston Cup series and October/November, for the CART Series. The stadium seats allow great views of the races. Gigantic screens and hundreds of smaller monitors show the action to spectators, too. Thirteen huge message boards, an incredible speaker system, a car-themed children's play area, sometimes live entertainment, and "real" food (including lobster), as well as standby's of hot dogs and hamburgers, all aid in making this a very fan-friendly speedway.

    Hours: Major races occur in April and October/November. Call for a race schedule.

Admission: Fri. practices are $10; Sat. assigned seating is $35 - $45 (AAA members are given certain discounts); Sun. assigned seating is $39 - $105. Pay an additional $45, in addition to a grandstand pass, for a pit pass (only for those 18 and older).

      Ages: 5 years and up.

METROLINK (San Bernardino County)
    See the entry for METROLINK (Los Angeles County) on page 173 for details.

YOUNG EAGLES PROGRAM (Chino)
(909) 393-8802 / www.youngeagles.com
Merrill Avenue, Chino Airport, Chino
(From Riverside Fwy [91], exit N. on the 71, N. on Euclid, R. on Merrill, R. on Airport Way. From Pomona Fwy [60], exit S. on Euclid, L. on Merrill, R. on Airport. It is near hangar #3, by the Fighter Jets Museum part of the Air Museum. [TG: 682 D5])

    See the entry for YOUNG EAGLES PROGRAM (Pacoima) on page 177 for details. This program allows kids the opportunity to control the aircraft - for a short period of time! Each young pilot gets a Polaroid picture taken of himself/herself, too. The program gives Boy Scouts half of what they need for their aviation merit badge. Since you are here, check out the adjacent AIR MUSEUM "PLANES OF FAME" (pg. 335).

    Hours: Offered four times a year on selected Sat., starting at 10am.

Admission: Free

    Ages: 8 - 17 years.

YOUNG EAGLES PROGRAM (Redlands)

(909) 798-3933 / www.youngeagles.com

1745 Sessums Drive, Redlands Airport, Redlands

(Going E. on San Bernardino Fwy [10], exit N. on University Ave., R. on Colton Ave., L. on Wabash Ave. Going W. on 10, exit N. on Wabash. Wabash dead-ends into the airport. [TG: 608 G3])

See the entry for YOUNG EAGLES PROGRAM (Pacoima) on page 177 for details. Reservations are needed.

Hours: Offered four or five times a year on selected Sat., starting at 9am.
Admission: Free
Ages: 8 - 17 years.

YOUNG EAGLES PROGRAM (Upland)

(909) 982-8048 / www.youngeagles.com

1749 W. 13ᵗʰ Street, Cable Airport, Upland

(Exit San Bernardino Fwy [10] N. on Central, R. on Foothill, L. on Benson, L. on 13ᵗʰ into the airport. [TG: 601 H1])

See the entry for YOUNG EAGLES PROGRAM (Pacoima) on page 177 for details. At this location, a forty-minute video is viewed that shows the history and goals of EAA (Experimental Aircraft Association). Reservations are required for this program; please call at least a week ahead of time.

Hours: Offered on the Sat. following the second Fri. of each month, except January and December. Be here by 8am.
Admission: Free
Ages: 8 - 17 years.

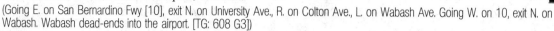

-----ZOOS AND ANIMALS-----

AMY'S FARM TOURS

(909) 393-2936 / www.amysfarm.com

7698 Eucalyptus Avenue, Chino

(From Chino Valley Fwy [71], exit N.E. on Euclid Ave., R. on Eucalyptus. From Pomona Fwy [60], exit S. on Euclid, L. on Eucalyptus. [TG: 682 D4])

For a really mooooving tour, visit Amy's Farm, which is really a family-run, working ten-acre calf ranch. Other animals that consider the farm home besides the 150 baby calves include ducks, bunnies, chickens, geese, a water buffalo, sheep, goats, pigs, and a pony. A ninety-minute tour includes learning all about the animals; the story of milk - from cow to grocery store; petting goats and sheep; feeding the pigs; perhaps harvesting crops from the vegetable garden; and feeding bottles to baby calves - this is a highlight! A visit here is an awesome way to gain first-hand introductory knowledge and experience with a farm. Note that although the tour involves walking around, it is also set up for special needs groups. A picnic area is on the grounds. A minimum of ten paying guests are required to schedule a visit and tours are age-appropriate. See the Calendar entry for information about the pumpkin tours (pg. 601). Ask about other seasonal events, such as summer camps.

Hours: Tours are offered Mon. - Sat.; call for a specific date and time.
Admission: $5 per person; one adult free with every 10 kids.
Ages: 2 years and up.

BRACKEN BIRD FARM

(909) 792-5735 / www.brackenbird.com

10797 New Jersey Street, Redlands

(Exit San Bernardino Fwy [10] S. on California St., L. on Redlands Blvd., R. on New Jersey. [TG: 607 G7])

This store is for the birds, and for people, too. The wide variety of birds for sale here include canaries, doves, parrots, finches of all kinds, cockatoos, macaws, and even toucans. Their colors range from drab brown to a rainbow of hues. We walked by the cages indoors and strolled by the ones in the outside aviary. The aviary has a small pond with goldfish and a few free-flying birds.

Adjacent to the bird farm are animals in enclosures. We saw a longhorn steer, a camel, a horse, a few pot-belly pigs, goats, ostriches, emus, and turkeys. Ducks and swans were swimming in the small pond.

Hours: Open Wed. - Mon., 9am - 5pm. Closed Tues., New Year's Day, July 4th, Thanksgiving, and Christmas.
Admission: Free
Ages: All

MOJAVE STATE FISH HATCHERY

(760) 245-9981
12550 Jacaranda Avenue, Victorville
(Exit Mojave Fwy [15] E. on Bear Valley Rd., about 6 miles, L. on Mojave Fish Hatchery Rd. [TG: 4387 A5])

This facility is the largest trout producing hatchery in California. Six raceways (i.e. holding tanks for the fish) at 1,000 feet long each, hold six strains of rainbow trout that supplies seven counties. Tempting though it may be, you may not bring your fishing pole.

Hours: Open daily, 7am - 3:30pm.
Admission: Free
Ages: 2 years and up.

WOLF MOUNTAIN SANCTUARY

(760) 248-7818 / www.wolfmountain.com
7520 Fairlane Road, Lucerne Valley
(Exit Mojave Fwy [15] E. on Bear Valley Rd. At the first Y stay R. and continue on Hwy 18. At the next Y (intersection of 18 and Hwy 247), stay R. and go about 6 miles. You will see a white picket fence on your R., turn L. on Fairlane. The Sanctuary is the first house you come to on your left. Call first. [TG: 4571 J2])

Fifteen, or so, wolves that have been discarded from movie makers or put out to pasture by wolf breeders now roam the enclosures here. Visitors are invited to first watch a video to understand the ways of wolves, listen to a talk about the owner's first hand experiences, and then visit the magnificent-looking creatures. Some of them are friendly enough to allow guests to pet them. According to the owner, many people also come for the healing powers attributed to wolves. The types of wolves here include British Columbia Black, McKenzie Timber, Alaskan Tundra, and Alaskan Grey.

Hours: Call in the morning or evening to schedule a tour.
Admission: $10 per person.
Ages: 3 years and up.

-----BIG BEAR-----

BIG BEAR LAKE (and the surrounding area)

I know that Big Bear is really in San Bernardino County, but I think most people think of the area as a destination in and of itself, so I've taken the liberty to list it as such.

This four-season mountain resort is close enough to escape to for a day or a weekend, although it offers enough activities for at least a week's vacation. The pine trees and fresh air that beckon city-weary folks, plus all the things to do, make it an ideal family get-away. November through March (or so) the mountains become a winter wonderland with lot of opportunities for snow play and skiing. This section, however, also covers a broader base of activities because Big Bear Lake is great any time of year! For specific information on events held during the time you plan to visit, call (909) 866-5753 - chamber of commerce or www.BigBeartodaymag.com. For lodging information call (800) 4BIG BEAR (424-4232) / www.bigbearinfo.com

General directions to Big Bear Lake are as follows: Head E. on the Riverside Fwy [91] or San Bernardino Fwy [10], N. on the 215 Fwy, E. on Hwy 30, N. on 330 to Hwy 18.

ALPINE SLIDE at MAGIC MOUNTAIN

(909) 866-4626 / www.alpineslideatmagicmountain.com

Big Bear Boulevard, Magic Mountain Recreation Area, Big Bear Lake

(¼ mile W. of Big Bear Lake Village. [TG: 4811 D2])

Alpine Slide lifts family fun to new heights! Take the chairlift up the mountain. Then, you and your child sit on heavy-duty plastic toboggans and rip down the quarter-mile, cement, contoured slide that resembles a bobsled track. Control your speed by pushing or pulling on the lever. We were cautious only on our first ride. Your child can go down by himself if he's at least 7 years old.

If you don't succumb to motion sickness, take a whirl on the Orbitron. You'll be harnessed to the inside of this big sphere and spun around in all directions. Doesn't that sound like fun? The miniature golf course, Putt 'N Around, has just a few frills, but kids still enjoy puttin' around on it. Go karts are available here, too. Inside the main building are a few video games, of course, and a snack bar. That delicious food you smell is a burger ($2.50) or hot dog ($1.50) being barbecued right outside, or maybe a bowl of soup or chili served in a bread bowl.

Summer play is enhanced by two zippy waterslides. You'll end with a splash in the three-and-a-half-feet deep pool, but it's not for swimming in. Winter allows you and the kids a chance to cultivate the fine art of throwing snowballs or to inner tube down the snowplay hill on four, side-by-side runs that resemble a snake's trail. Instead of trudging back up the hill, with tube in hand, take the Magic Carpet, which is similar to a moving conveyor belt. You'll have mountains of fun any season you come to Alpine Slide at Magic Mountain.

Hours: The Alpine Slide, Orbitron, miniature golf, and go karts are open mid-June through mid-September and November through Easter daily, 10am - 5pm (weather permitting). In the summer, these attractions are often open later on weekends. The rest of the year they are open the same hours, but on weekends only. The waterslide is open mid-June to mid-September daily, 10am - 6pm. The snow play area is open as long as snow is available daily, 10am - 4pm.

Admission: Alpine ride - $4 for one ride; $18 for a five-ride book. Orbitron - $4 a ride. Miniature golf - $4 a round for adults; $3 for kids. Go karts - $3.50 a single car; $5.50 a double car. Waterslide - $1 for one ride; $7 for a ten-ride book; $12 for an unlimited day pass. Snow play - $18 for an unlimited day-pass with a tube (you may not bring your own tube). Fri., Sat., and holiday night tubing sessions, 5pm - 9pm, are $12 per person. Children 2 - 6 are free with a paying adult on the Alpine slide, waterslide, and snow play area, as long as they are accompanied by a paying adult.

Ages: 3 years and up.

ALPINE TROUT LAKE

(909) 866-4532

440 Catalina Road, Big Bear Lake

(Exit Big Bear Blvd. S.E. on Catalina, just N.E. of Moonridge Rd. [TG: 4811 J1])

Tall pine trees line the perimeters of this small stocked lake, making it a beautiful place to fish. And catching a fish is (almost) guaranteed, which is great for kids (and adults) who get discouraged easily, like the author of this book! Two-pounders are quite common. Make a day of your time here as picnic tables and barbecue pits are also on the grounds, so catch your meal and eat it, too. In fact, the owners also sell fixings for the trout as well as barbecue coals. You are also welcome to bring in your own food and beverages. This is a private lake, so a fishing license is not required. Tip: Bring a cooler in case you want to take some fish home.

Hours: Open May through September daily, 10am - 5pm. Open the rest of the year, Mon. - Tues. and Thurs. - Fri., noon - 4:30pm; Sat. - Sun., 10am - 5pm. Closed Wed.

Admission: $5 for a family or group of up to 6 people. Rod rentals, reel, and bait are an additional $4 per person. Fish cost $5.15 per pound.

Ages: 3 years and up.

BALDWIN LAKE STABLES

(909) 585-6482 / www.baldwinlakestables.com

$$$$$

E. Shay Road, Big Bear Lake

(Go E. on Big Bear Blvd., past the Hwy 38 turnoff, and follow it as it turns into Shay Rd., then watch for sign on the R. The stables are right where Shay Rd. turns into Baldwin Lake Rd. [TG: 4743 A5])

Leave the city behind and horseback ride through the scenic national forest. The breathtaking mountain views, and sore bottoms for those unused to trotting, are all included in your ride price. Enjoy a one- to- four-hour ride along the Pacific Crest Trail, or see things in a different light by taking a sunset ride! Ask about the over night camp ride, which includes a ride, a traditional western dinner, sleeping in a tent, and a hearty campfire breakfast. Hand-led pony rides for young bronchos are $5 per child for three laps around the track. A petting zoo here has bales of hay all around and a barn-like small building. For $3 per person, enter the pen to pet and/or feed llamas, bunnies, goats, sheep, and ducks.

Hours: Open daily most of the year, weather permitting, 9am - 5pm. Winter hours are daily, 10am - 4pm. Call before you come.

Admission: $25 an hour per person. Sunset rides are $45 per person - no children allowed.

Ages: At least 7 years old and 4' tall.

BEAR VALLEY BIKES

(909) 866-8000 / www.bearvalleybikes.net

$$$

40298 Big Bear Boulevard, across Magic Mountain Recreation Area, Big Bear Lake

(It's ¼ mile W. of Big Bear Lake Village, on top of Red Ant Hill, across from the Alpine Slide at Magic Mountain. [TG: 4811 D2])

Pedal your way around town or sign up for a guided tour. Bear Valley has mountain bikes, tandems cycles, BMX bikes, trailers for children, toddler bikes, and even helmets.

Hours: Open daily, 10am - 5pm. Call for winter hours.

Admission: Mountain bikes are $7 an hour; tandems are $12 an hour; BMX bikes are $5 an hour.

Ages: All

BIG BEAR BIKES

(909) 866-2224 / www.burrobikes.com

$$$

41810 Big Bear Boulevard, Big Bear Lake

(On Big Bear Blvd., near Snow Summit Blvd. [TG: 4811 H1])

Need some wheels to get around town? Big Bear Bikes offers, fittingly enough, mountain bikes and suggests trying out the beautiful North Shore bike path. This bike shop also rents snowshoes (in season!) and can suggest numerous destinations for putting them to good use. Snowboard packages are available here, too.

Hours: Open in the summer daily, 9am - 5pm. Open the rest of the year, Mon. - Fri., 8am - 5pm; Sat. - Sun., 8am - 10pm, weather permitting

Admission: Bike rentals start at $6 per hour. Tandems are $10 an hour. Snowshoe rentals begin at $10 a day.

Ages: All for bikes; 6 years and up for snowshoes.

BIG BEAR DISCOVERY CENTER

(909) 866-3437 or (909) 866-2611 / www.bigbeardiscoverycenter.com

!/$

40971 N. Shore Drive, Highway 38, Big Bear Lake

(Between Fawnskin and Stansfield Cutoff, at the Ranger Station. [TG: 4741 G5])

This ranger station is the best place to call or visit for trail maps, camp sites, and special program information. The center has informational and pictorial panels, plus other exhibits regarding the forest and the lake and their inhabitants. One of their special programs focuses on Native American lifestyles and includes arts, crafts, and demonstrations such as drum making, working with clay, and gourd painting. Hour-long Nature Nights presentations, held every Thursday night during the summer and every other Friday in other seasons, cover a variety of topics. Other programs and activities include weekend campfire programs, snowshoe rentals, and more.

Pick up your free *Eagle Discovery Guide and Games* booklet at the center. The guide will help you find eagles on your own, plus it offers fun ways to learn about eagles and their habitats. Another option to "hunt" for eagles during their winter season in the mountains is to board the Eagle Discovery Tour twelve-passenger bus for a two-hour-plus journey through Big Bear. There are several stops along the way. A professional naturalist will aid you in identifying eagle habitats and the surrounding eco system, while informally teaching interesting facts about our national symbol. You'll receive the use of binoculars and a spotting scope. A light snack is included, too.

During the summer join on a three-and-a-half hour naturalist-led mountain mining adventure tour where participants travel in a van to a limestone quarry to see equipment blasting; sit on a giant tractor here; learn the history of the Gold Rush in this area; and visit the site of the Gold Mountain Mine. On two-and-a-half hour guided canoe tours of Grout Bay, you paddle along the bay while learning about gold mining and the history of the lake, and looking for beavers, great blue herons, and ducklings. Bottled water and snacks are included.

Pick up an Adventure Pass at the center, too. An Adventure Pass is required for all vehicles parking on National Forest property for recreational purposes.

Hours: Open daily in the summer, 8am - 6pm. Open in the winter, 9am - 4:30pm. Closed New Year's Day, Thanksgiving, and Christmas. Eagle tours are given December through March on Sat. and daily during holiday periods. The mountain mining tour is offered in the summer on Fri. at 10am. Canoe tours are available May through August, Fri., Sat., and Sun. at 4:30pm; September through October at 4pm. Reservations are required for all tours.

Admission: The Adventure pass is $5 per day or $30 for an annual pass. The eagle discovery and mountain mining tours are each $30 for adults; $20 for ages 3- 16. The canoe tour is $20 for adults; $12 for ages 3 - 12.

Ages: All

BIG BEAR HISTORICAL MUSEUM

(909) 585-8100 / www.bigbearinfo.com/mpcspmuseum.html
600 Greenway Drive, Big Bear Lake
(Exit W. Big Bear Blvd. N. on Greenway. The museum is in the N.E. portion of the Big Bear City Park, E. of the airport. [TG: 4742 D5])

The past is definitely present at the Eleanor Abbott Big Bear Valley Historical Museum. The buildings that comprise the museum are very old (and old looking). The small main building contains a good assortment of taxidermied animals such as a golden eagle, skunk, red fox, badger, and others, displayed mostly behind glass in "natural" settings. Other exhibits include birds' nests, eggs, arrowheads, rocks, fossils, unique leather carvings, old photographs of old Big Bear, Native American artifacts, and old-fashioned toys. Outside on the porch are turn-of-the-century post office boxes, plus mining equipment and mining artifacts.

An on-site, furnished, 1875 one-room log cabin offers a real look into the pioneer lifestyle. The docents in here are wonderful at explaining to kids how pioneer families lived, and the uses of some of the household items. My boys couldn't believe that chamber pots were really used as portable potties. It finally dawned on them that entire families lived together in this one room; sleeping, cooking, eating, and playing together. I hope they'll be more thankful about their own living arrangements!

The blacksmith foundry puts on demonstrations of metal work - call for dates and times. One log structure here is actually a mule barn used to house mules. A stamp mill to crush gold bearing ore and hard rock to recover gold, and lots of old, rusted agriculture equipment are also on the grounds.

An adjacent park has a few pieces of play equipment and some old tennis courts. The park is good mostly for visitors to just run around in its overgrown fields. Shade is scarce, but there are a few picnic tables here.

Hours: Open Memorial Day to the second Sun. in October on Wed., Sat., and Sun. (and holiday Mon.), 10am - 4pm.

Admission: $1 per person donation.

Ages: 3 years and up.

BIG BEAR LAKE PERFORMING ARTS CENTER

☼
$$$$

(909) 866-4970 / www.bigbearpac.com
39707 Big Bear Boulevard, Big Bear Lake
([TG: 4811 C2])

This center is a catch-all for almost any kind of stage performance in the Big Bear area. Shows run the gamut from professional productions of *Oklahoma*, comedy acts, magicians from the Magic Castle in Hollywood, Barbershop Sweet Adelines, and master chorale groups, to high school and middle school performances, dance recitals, and dog shows. Check the schedule to see who or what is playing.

Hours: Depends on performance.
Admission: Depends on performance.

BIG BEAR MARINA

☼
$$$$

(909) 866-3218 / www.bigbearmarina.com
500 Paine Road, Big Bear Lake
(Exit Big Bear Blvd. N. on Paine Rd. [TG: 4811 E1])

The Marina offers a boatload of fun for the family. Five passenger motorized fishing boats start at $45 for two hours. Pedal boats, kayaks, and canoes rent for $20 an hour per. Two-seater wave runners are $75 an hour. Rent a small pontoon, a flat-bottomed boat that is almost seasick proof, for $55 an hour. It seats up to eight people. A larger pontoon, which seats up to twelve people, is $65 an hour. Take an hour-and-a-half, narrated tour around Big Bear Lake on the *Big Bear Queen*. Tours are given daily, in season, always at 2pm, and sometimes at 10am, noon and 4pm, if at least fifteen people are signed up. Prices are $11 for adults; $10 for seniors and ages 3 to 12; children 2 years and under are free.

Where can your family go for dinner that is a fun, kid-friendly treat (and I don't mean McDonald's)? Somewhere that is exotic, yet cost efficient? Different, but agreeable to all? The answer to all these questions is - on a pontoon sunset dinner cruise! *Big Bear Queen* offers dinner cruises in the summer on Tuesday and Thursday nights starting at about 7pm for $16.50 per person, which includes a guided tour and a dinner of chicken (on Tuesdays) and enchiladas (on Thursdays). Reservations and prepayment are required.

Hours: Open daily, seasonally, usually spring through October, 7am - 7pm.
Admission: Prices are listed above.
Ages: 3 years and up.

BIG BEAR PARASAIL

☽
$$$$$

(909) 866-IFLY (4359) / www.pineknotlanding.com
At the north end of Pine Knot Boulevard, Big Bear Lake
(Exit Big Bear Blvd. N. on Pine Knot Blvd. [TG: 4811 F1])

Ever had dreams where you can fly? Parasailing is the next best thing. Start off on dry land, attached by a harness to the parasail and by a tow rope to the boat. As the boat pulls away, you are lifted into the air for ten minutes of flight. You can stay dry if you want, and if all goes well, or take a quick dip (more like a toe touch) in the lake before being airborne again. This is a thrill-seeking experience for kids and adults.

Hours: Seasonal only - late spring through early fall - Mon. - Fri., 9am - 5pm; Sat. - Sun., 8am - 6pm.
Admission: Single - $40 weekdays; $45 weekends. Tandem - $70 weekday; $80 weekends.
Ages: 90 pounds and up.

BIG BEAR SOLAR OBSERVATORY

☽
$

(909) 866-5791 / www.bbso.njit.edu
40386 North Shore Lane, Big Bear Lake
(Exit North Shore Dr. on North Shore Ln. It's past Fawnskin. [TG: 4741 D6])

The small, thirty-foot dome solar observatory offers a unique way to study the often sunny skies in Big Bear. Three telescopes monitor and record images of the sun, which are then displayed on video monitors. Cameras can show sharper details than the unaided eye can see. Take a forty-five-minute tour to get the hot facts

about the sun.
Hours: Open July 4th through Labor Day, Sat., 4pm - 6pm.
Admission: $2 for adults; $1 for children.
Ages: 8 years and up.

CHILDREN'S FOREST

(909) 337-5156 or (909) 884-6634 / www.sbnfa.org
On Highway 18, between Running Springs and Arrow Bear Lake
(On Highway 18, by Keller Peak Rd. [TG: 519 D7])

The Children's Forest Visitor Information Center is at the gateway to the Children's Forest, which is a spread of 3,400 acres within the San Bernardino National Forest. The center, staffed primarily by youths, offers information on recreation opportunities in the forest, education programs, the opportunity to purchase the Adventure Pass, themed workshops, and more. There are displays of local flora and fauna, a nature table, and other hands-on exhibits.

The information center and forest's main purpose is to encourage children to develop a passion for the environment by training youth naturalists and offering opportunities for kids to take a hike. There are several outstanding educational programs offered through this center, both to the public and to school groups. A sampling includes Forest Ecology - learning how plants and animals depend on each other for survival; Finding the Wild Things - learning how animals adapt to the environments, where they live, what they eat, and how to read the signs of their presence; Soil Erosion - physically working to prevent soil erosion; and Charting Your Course - learning map and compass reading techniques. Seasonal snowshoe field trips are available to aid in learning about winter ecology. Get a workout while following animal tracks! School exploration programs are offered Monday through Friday, year round. Each program is four hours long. The majority of the time is spent in the forest, plus there are games and hands-on activities.

Drive on Keller Peak Road or hike it if you're brave (about four miles) to the Children's Forest Interpretive Trail. Use a self-guided brochure to walk the only established trail here, a three-quarter-mile paved trail. Find engraved animals on the signs and rub them onto a piece of paper. Among the pine trees and along the mountain stream be on the lookout for wildlife such as birds, deer, squirrels, unusual insects, etc. Don't forget to pack lunch, water, sunscreen, and binoculars.

Keller Peak Lookout is a mile above the trail. It is staffed and open to the public daily in the summer and during fire season from 9am to 5pm - what a view! On a clear day you can see all the way to the ocean. When the lookout is open, you may drive out to it or hike to it. With all that it offers and set in such beautiful surroundings, I'm glad the Children's Forest is open to adults, too!
Hours: The paved trail and the forest are open in the spring, summer, and fall daily, sunrise - sunset. Program times vary - call for a schedule or to make an appointment.
Admission: $5 per vehicle per day to stop anywhere in the forest. Call for various program prices.
Ages: All for the paved trail and walking around; other age requirements depend on the program.

COWBOY EXPRESS STEAK HOUSE

(909) 866-1486 / www.cowboyexpress.com
40433 Lake View Drive, Big Bear Lake
(Exit Big Bear Blvd. N. on Lake View. It's 3 blocks W. of the village. [TG: 4811 D1])

Rustle up some good lunch or dinner grub in this rustic, cowboy-themed restaurant. Some enticing entrees include T-bone steaks, $16.95; chicken steak, $11.95; beef back ribs, $14.95; hamburgers, $7.50; buffalo burgers, $8.95. Children can choose chicken strips, cheeseburger, corn dog or pork ribs for $6.95. Steak or shrimp is $7.95. All kids' meals come with fries, a drink, and a small sundae.
Hours: Open daily, 11am - 9pm. Closed Easter, Thanksgiving, and Christmas.
Admission: Prices mentioned above.
Ages: All

HIKING

(909) 866-3437 / www.sbnfa.org

There are many, *many* places to go hiking in the Big Bear area. See BIG BEAR DISCOVERY CENTER (pg. 351) for information on the ranger station, where you can obtain trail maps. Note: Anywhere you park in the national forest for recreational reasons, you must pay for an Adventure Pass. Just two of the places my family has enjoyed trekking include:

CASTLE ROCK:

(FROM HIGHWAY 18, THE TRAILHEAD IS ABOUT ONE MILE EAST PAST THE DAM.)

The trail is only eight-tenths of a mile, but it is an uphill walk over some rocky terrain. The destination is Castle Rock, a large rock that kids love to climb on. Its name gives lead to a lot of imaginative play time here. All of my kids wanted to be king - what a surprise! If everyone still has the energy, keep hiking back to the waterfalls, and/ or to Devil's woodpile. The scenery along the way is spectacular.

WOODLAND TRAIL:

(ON HIGHWAY 38, PARKING IS ALMOST DIRECTLY ACROSS THE STREET FROM M.D. BOAT RAMP, JUST WEST OF THE STANFIELD CUTOFF ROAD.)

This one-and-a-half-mile loop is an easy walk, as the dirt trail follows more along the side of the mountain, rather than into the mountain. Although you can hear the traffic from certain sections of the trail, the changing landscape, from pine trees to coastal shrub to cactus, still offers the sense of being immersed in nature. An interpretative trail guide is available through the Ranger Station. Make it an educational field trip as well as a nice walk!

Hours: Open daily.

Admission: $5 a day for an Adventure Pass.

Ages: 4 years and up.

HOLLOWAY'S MARINA and RV PARK

(800) 448-5335 / www.bigbearboating.com

398 Edgemoor Road, Big Bear Lake

(Exit Big Bear Blvd., N. on Edgemoor, about 1½ miles E. of the village. [TG: 4811 C1])

Holloway's rents almost anything that is water worthy. For instance, two-seater or four-seater paddle boats are $14 an hour. Eight- to ten-people flat bottom pontoons are $50 an hour, $80 for two hours. Twelve- to fourteen-people pontoons are $60 an hour. Aluminum motorized fishing boats are $21 an hour. Kayaks and canoes are $25 per hour. Wave runners, sailboats, and even fishing poles are also available for rent. See THE TIME BANDIT (pg. 359) for information on a cool-looking pirate ship. The RV park is adjacent to the marina and has all the amenities, including a playground, horseshoe pits, basketball court, small convenience store, showers, and place to do laundry.

Hours: Open April through October, 6am - sunset, weather permitting.

Admission: Prices are mentioned above. RV camping is $25 - $40 a night.

Ages: 2 years and up, depending.

THE HOT SHOT MINIATURE GOLF COURSE

corner of Catalina and Big Bear Boulevard, Big Bear Lake

(On Big Bear Blvd., just N. of Moonridge. [TG: 4811 J1])

Putt around under shady pine trees at this basic, but fun miniature golf course. Encourage your kids to be hot shots here!

Hours: Open daily seasonally, weather permitting, 10am - 6pm. Closed during the winter.

Admission: $5 for adults; $4 for ages 12 and under. Replays are $1 per person.

Ages: 3 years and up.

LAKE ARROWHEAD CHILDREN'S MUSEUM

(909) 336-3093 / www.mountaininfo.com/kids

28200 Highway 189, in the Village Shopping Center, Lake Arrowhead

(Exit San Bernardino Fwy [10] N. on the 215, E. on the 30. Take the Waterman Ave. [Hwy 18] exit 'up the hill' to Lake Arrowhead. The museum is located in the lower level of the Village, at the end of the peninsula, just past Jockey's Sportswear. [TG: 518 A1])

In the Lake Arrowhead Village shopping center, kids now have a place of their own to "shop" for fun. This museum is comprised of a large room, decorated with beautiful nature murals, divided into interactive exhibit areas. At the Ant Wall, children are the ants, climbing up and down carpeted ramps and tunnels. Recyclable "trash" is crafted into take-home treasure at Inventor's Workshop. Blow bubbles up to kid-size or get creative with face paint at another section. The toddlers' room features several toys, and Peter Pan's ship to climb aboard and sail off to Never Land. The scientifically oriented can experiment with magnets, hand batteries, and more. Technologically-minded children enjoy playing educational games on the computers. The space section has glow-in-the-dark chalk and a chalkboard, black lighting, and control panels of a space ship. Have a ball in the ball pits. Does your child have a talent for playing musical instruments? Try the accordion, xylophone, and/or melody harp. A forestry exhibit has animal pelts to touch and information on forestry conservation. The Village Merchants set up has playhouse-size "stores" such as a fire station, post office, bank, Vet's office with lots of stuffed animals, and a mini-mart with cash registers, carts, and pay food. Check out the imaginative temporary exhibits here, too. There is always something fun to do at this children's museum!

Hours: Open in the summer daily, 10am - 6pm. Open the rest of the year daily, 10am - 5pm. Closed Thanksgiving and Christmas.

Admission: $4 for adults; $5 for ages 2 - 12; children under 2 are free.

Ages: 2 - 11 years.

MCDILL SWIM BEACH / MEADOW PARK

(909) 866-9700

Park Avenue, Big Bear Lake

(Exit Big Bear Blvd. N. on Knight St. to the end. [TG: 4811 F1])

This waveless lagoon, with a lifeguard on duty, offers a refreshing respite during the hot summer months. Kids can play in the water, or build castles on the sandy beach. Swimmers enjoy going beyond the roped area, out to the floating dock that they can lay out on or dive off. A small playground, a volleyball court, and a snack bar round out the facilities at this beach. And the view of the mountains is spectacular! Children 10 years and under must be supervised by an adult.

Meadow Park is just outside the Swim Beach gates. This large, grassy park has a small playground, nice tennis courts, volleyball courts, baseball diamonds, and horseshoe pits. Bring a picnic dinner to cook at the barbecue pits, and enjoy the sunset.

Hours: The swim beach is open seasonally on weekends, noon - 6pm, and daily in the summer, noon - 6pm. The park is open sunrise - sunset.

Admission: The swim beach is $3 for adults; $2 for seniors and ages 4 - 12; children 3 and under are free. The park is free.

Ages: All

MOONRIDGE ANIMAL PARK

(909) 584-1171 or (909) 866-0183 / www.bigbearzoo.com

43285 Goldmine Drive, Big Bear Lake

(Exit Big Bear Blvd. S.E. on Moonridge Rd. The Animal Park is at the end of the road, on Goldmine Dr. [TG: 4812 C3])

Get a little wild up in the mountains! Animals from the surrounding mountains that need extra care, whether they are orphaned or hurt, find sanctuary in this small animal park. Grizzly bears, snow leopards, black bears, wolves, bison, coyotes, bobcats, raccoons, deer, and birds of prey such as eagles, hawks, owls and other birds and animals now consider the animal park their home. It's just the right size for kids to walk around easily, and since the enclosures are not too large, it's easy to see the animals up close. Walk through a flight enclosure that holds shore and other aquatic birds. And don't missss the walk-through reptile housssse!

Special daily events include animal presentations at noon, where an animal is brought out and talked about, and a feeding tour. The forty-five-minute educational feeding tour is given at 3pm daily (except on Wednesdays) most of the year and on weekends only in the winter. It takes place at each cage. As the animals are fed (mush, dead chicks, and other stuff) a staff member explains why the animal is here, its habits, and more. We've always found the docents and trainers willing, even eager, to answer our kids' questions, so it makes our visit here more memorable. The Animal Park also offers seasonal special programs, such as flashlight tours, tasty ice cream safaris, and day camps. Traveling exhibits are offered to school groups. Call (909) 584-1299 for more information.

A small grassy picnic area inside the zoo has a few picnic tables. A small education center in the lobby has a few nature exhibits such as bird eggs and nests, fossils, and animal jawbones.

Hours: Open May through September daily, 10am - 5pm. Open October through April daily, Mon. - Fri., 10am - 4pm; Sat. - Sun., 10am - 5pm, weather permitting.

Admission: $4 for adults; $3 for seniors and ages 3 - 10; children 2 and under are free.

Ages: All

PINE KNOT LANDING

$$$$

(909) 866-BOAT (2628) / www.pineknotlanding.com
439 Pine Knot Avenue, Big Bear Lake
(Exit Big Bear Blvd. N. on Pine Knot Blvd. [TG: 4811 F1])

Boat rentals here are "knot" a problem! Come on board the double decker *Sierra Belle* paddle wheel boat for a one-and-a-half-hour narrated excursion. Learn the history of the lake, famous people who have or still live here, and general information about Big Bear Valley. Sunset cruises are another special way to tour the lake. Cruise around on your own via an eight-passenger pontoon boats at $50 an hour, or a twelve-passenger pontoon at $60 an hour. Motorized fishing boats start at $15 an hour for four passengers. One and two-passenger kayaks and canoes are $10 for one hour. Jet skis are $75 an hour. Go parasailing for $45 for a ten-minute flight; tandems are $80. This rental facility also offers water-ski tows.

Hours: Open April through October, Mon. - Fri., 6am - 7pm; Sat., Sun., and holidays, 6am - 8pm. Always call first! The *Sierra Belle* tour is available daily, if there is a minimum of fifteen passengers. Note that reservations are necessary for most outings.

Admission: The narrated tour is $10 for adults; $8.50 for seniors; $6 for ages 4 - 12; children 3 and under are free. Other prices are listed above.

Ages: 4 years and up.

ROCKING "K" RIDING STABLES

$$$$$

(909) 878-4677
At the top of Lassen Drive, Big Bear Lake
(Exit Big Bear Blvd. S.E. at Moonridge Rd. Go to the end of Moonridge and turn L. on Lassen Dr. It's at the foot of Bear Mountain Ski Resort. [TG: 4812 C4])

There is only so much you can see of Big Bear from the car! A horseback ride is an ideal way to experience the beauty of the mountains. Children 7 years and up can take a one- or two-hour guided horseback ride through the pine trees and over mountain ridges. At the stables, younger children can take pony rides around the track.

Hours: Open May through September daily, 10am - 5pm, during good weather. Call first, just in case.

Admission: $30 per hour per person for horseback riding. $7 for three laps around the track on a pony.

Ages: 1 - 6 years for pony rides; 7 years and up for horseback rides.

SCENIC SKY CHAIR

$$$

(909) 866-5766 / www.bigbearmountainresorts.com
880 Snow Summit Boulevard, at Snow Summit ski area, Big Bear Lake
(Exit Big Bear Blvd., S. on Summit Blvd. [TG: 4811 H2])

Do your kids appreciate the awesome scenery of mountains, trees, and Big Bear Lake, plus breathing clean air? If not, they'll still enjoy the mile-long, thirteen-minute (each way) chair ride up the mountaintop. At the top, there is a picnic and barbecue area, so bring your own food, or purchase a burger, chicken sandwich, etc., from the snack bar. As there are over forty miles of trails through the forest and wilderness areas, hikers and biking enthusiasts are in their element up here. The terrain varies, meaning that trails range from easy, wide, forest service roads to arduous, single-track, dirt trails. What better way to spend a day than up here in a place readily described as "God's country."

Bike rentals are available at the base of Snow Summit at Team Big Bear Mountain Bikes, (909) 866-4565 / www.teambigbear.com. Mountain bikes are the recommended cycle, and helmets are required for all riders. The store has maps for all the Big Bear trails.

Hours: The sky chair operates May through mid-June and mid-September through October (or the beginning of ski season) on weekends only, 9am - 4pm. It's open daily, mid-June through mid-September, Mon. - Fri., 9am - 4pm; Sat., 8am - 5pm; Sun., 8am - 4pm, weather permitting.

Admission: One-way ride (no bike) - $7 for adults; $4 for ages 7 - 12; children 6 and under are free when accompanied by a paying adult. One-way ride with a bike or a scenic round trip (no bike) - $10 for adults; $5 for ages 7 - 12. An all-day pass with a bike - $20 for adults; $9 for kids. Ask about half-day prices.

Ages: 3 years and up.

SKIING and SNOW PLAY

☼

$$$$$

The following is a list and quick bites of information on ski slopes and snow play areas in and around the Big Bear area. I found the website: www.onthesnow.com/skireport/SouthernCalifornia.html, helpful for up-to-the-minute ski conditions. Ask each resort about beginner specials, other special promos, half-day tickets, and even a free lift ticket on your birthday:

Bear Mountain: 43101 Goldmine Drive - from Hwy 18 to Big Bear Lake, R. on Moonridge Rd. and follow the signs - (909) 585-2519 or (909) 866-5766; (800)BEARMTN (232-7686) - ski conditions / www.bigbearmountainresorts.com. Bear Mountain has 12 lifts and 32 runs on 200 acres, with the longest run being 2 miles. Top elevation is 8,800 feet. Non-holiday rates are $43 for adults; $35 for ages 13 - 19; $14 for ages 7 - 12; children 6 and under are free. Holiday rates are $50 for ages 13 and up; $21 for ages 7 - 12.

Mountain High: 24510 Hwy 2 in Wrightwood - (760) 249-5808; (888) 754-7878 (ski conditions) / www.mthigh.com. Mt. High has 13 chairs and 47 runs on 220 acres. The elevation is 8,200 feet. Ski both east and west mountains with free shuttles going in between. Lift tickets are $43 for adults; $15 for children ages 7 - 12; ages 6 and under are free with a paying adult. Night skiing, 5pm - 10pm, is available.

Mount Baldy: from 10 Fwy, exit N. on Mountain Ave. and go N. on Mt. Baldy Rd. - (909) 981-3344 or (909) 982-0800 / www.mtbaldy.com. Mt. Baldy has 4 lifts and 26 runs. The elevation is 8,600 ft. Lift tickets are $40 for adults; $20 for seniors; $25 for ages 10 - 16; $10 for ages 9 and under.

Mount Waterman: exit 210 Freeway N. on 2 Fwy; it's E. of Wrightwood - (626) 440-1041 or (818) 790-2002 / www.rideacr.com. Waterman has 3 lifts and 23 runs on 150 acres. It does not have a snow-making machine. The top elevation is a little more than 8,000 feet. Skiers can also go "tree skiing," meaning they can venture off the marked runs and go through the forest. Lift tickets are $35 for adults; $20 for ages 7 - 12; free for children 6 and under with a paying adult.

Ski Sunrise: off Hwy 2, N. on Table Mt. Rd. in Wrightwood - (760) 249-6150 / www.skisunrise.com. Sunrise has 4 chairs and 16 runs on 100 acres. The elevation is 7,600 feet. Admission is $35 per person on weekends and holidays; $25 per person during the week.

Snow Summit: 880 Summit Road - exit Big Bear Blvd. R. on Summit Blvd. in Big Bear Lake - (909) 866-5766 or (909) 866-5841; (888) summit-1 (for ski conditions) / www.bigbearmountainresorts.com. Summit has 12 chairs and 32 runs on 230 acres. The elevation is 8,000 feet. Non-holiday rates are $43 for adults; $35 for ages 13 - 19; $14 for ages 7 - 12; children 6 and under are free. Holiday rates are $50 for ages 13 and up; $21 for ages 7 - 12. Night skiing is available on Friday, Saturday, and holidays, 3pm - 9:30pm.

Snow Valley: on Hwy 18, 5 miles E. of Running Springs - (909) 867-2751 or (909) 867-5151; (800) 680-

SNOW (7669) (ski conditions) / www.snow-valley.com. Snow Valley has 11 lifts and 27 runs on 240 acres. The elevation is 7,440 feet. Snow Valley also has an adjacent snow play area. Lift tickets are $40 for adults; $20 for seniors; $13 for ages 6 - 12; children 5 and under are free with a paying adult. Night skiing is available on Friday nights, 4pm - 9pm.

SUGARLOAF CORDWOOD CO.

(909) 866-2220

42193 Big Bear Boulevard, Big Bear Lake

(At the corner of Big Bear Blvd. and Stanfield Cut-off. [TG: 4741 J7])

The gigantic, wooden, chain-saw carvings of bears, Indians, and other figures, will attract your attention as you drive along Big Bear Boulevard. This unique store is worth a stop. Take a walk through the lot and inside the rooms to see smaller carvings and other unusual, artistic, gift items.

Hours: Open most of the year, Mon. - Fri., 10am - 5pm; Sat. - Sun., 9am - 6pm. In the winter, the store is open daily, 10am - 5pm.

Admission: Free

Ages: 3 years and up.

SUGARLOAF PARK

Baldwin Lane and Maple Lane, Big Bear Lake

(Exit Big Bear Blvd. [38] S. on Maple Ln., L. on Baldwin. [TG: 4742 F7])

It is a beautiful drive to this well-worn park, but where up here isn't the scenery beautiful? Sugarloaf Park has a softball field, a few tennis courts, a sand volleyball court, a basketball court, and older metal playground equipment, plus picnic shelters and barbecue pits. It also has a small grouping of short trees that could feel like a mini forest to younger kids.

Hours: Open daily, sunrise - sunset.

Admission: Free

Ages: All

THE TIME BANDIT

(909) 878-4040 / www.bigbearboating.com

398 Edgemoor Road at Holloway's Marina, Big Bear Lake

(Exit Big Bear Blvd., N. on Edgemoor About 1½ miles E. of the village. [TG: 4811 C1])

If it's adventure you're seekin' matey, then climb aboard and hoist the sails! This jet black, one-third-scale replica of a 16th century pirate ship comes complete with its own crew of pirates, well at least a captain. Sail across Big Bear Lake (it's kind of like sailing the seven seas, just a shorter trip) on a ninety-minute narrated cruise and stop by the Discovery Center and Whaler's Pointe restaurant. *The Time Bandit*, named after the 1981 movie in which it was featured, often offers live entertainment at night. Overnight charters are available as the ship is equipped with a stateroom and bed, and bunk beds for kids.

Hours: Usually open June through October, with tours leaving daily at 2pm. If enough people are signed up (the ship holds 25), tours also depart at 10am, noon, 4pm, and 6pm.

Admission: $12.50 for adults; $11.50 for seniors; $9.50 for ages 12 and under. Infants or lap-sitting toddlers are free.

Ages: All

VICTORIA PARK CARRIAGES, LTD / BEAR VALLEY STAGE LINES

(909) 584-2277 / www.buggies.com; www.stagelines.com

Big Bear Lake

There is no more elegant, storybook way to explore Big Bear than by horse and carriage. Take ride through the Village, and down to the lake. Carriages seat between four to seven people. Or, go for a whole different feel by taking on the west - ride a stagecoach! Coaches seat up to twelve people.

Hours: Call to make a reservation for carriage and stagecoach.

Admission: Carriage prices are about $130 for an hour. Prices fluctuate depending on date, time of day, and type of carriage. Stagecoach rides are $8 for adults; $4 for ages 2 - 11.

Ages: 2 years and up.

SAN DIEGO COUNTY

San Diego is the site of the first permanent European settlement on the California coast - the West Coast equivalent of the East Coast's Jamestown. From coastal cities to beaches that are the epitome of California dreaming, the county is also home to Legoland, the amusement park built largely with a favorite toy; the extensive military base of Camp Pendleton and other San Diego bases; the enchanting town of Julian; Old Town San Diego, which is steeped in early California heritage; several missions founded by Father Junipero Serra; the resort town of La Jolla; and vast acres of trails to hike. A visit to this county probably wouldn't be complete without seeing the world-class San Diego Zoo and/or San Diego Wild Animal park and some of the first-class museums all located in the massive Balboa Park. Drive just to the south and go over the border to Mexico - into a whole other world.

Tip: Contact the San Diego Convention and Visitors Bureau at (619) 230-7084 or (619) 236-1212 / www.sandiego.org. because it offers discount coupons on attractions, tours, harbor cruises, trolley rides, restaurants, hotels, and more.

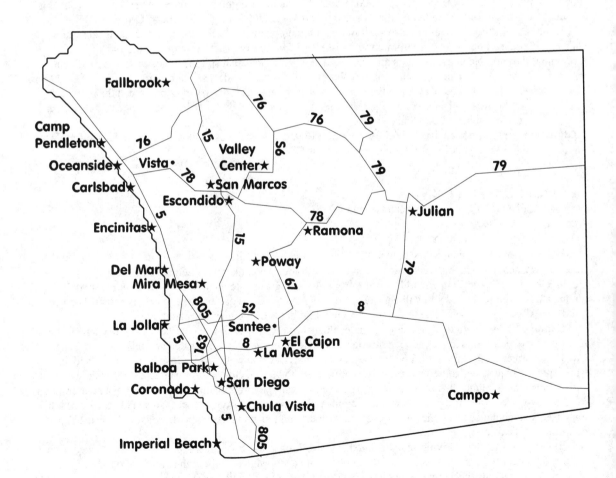

-----AMUSEMENT PARKS-----

KNOTT'S SOAK CITY U.S.A. (Chula Vista)
(619) 661-7373 / www.soakcityusa.com
2052 Entertainment Circle, Chula Vista
(Exit Jacob Dekema Fwy [805] L. on Main St./Auto Park Dr., turn R. on Entertainment Circle. [TG: 1331 A6])

☼
$$$$$
🎂

Welcome to Southern California circa 1950! San Diego's liquid gold attraction is colorful, beach-themed, fun, and most important, very wet. The park is spread over thirty-three acres with a large, centrally located grassy area. The kids come here in hordes to plunge down the sixteen water slides lined up side by side: six inner-tube slides, six body slides, and four speed slides.

Rip the curl in the wave pool, where waves can reach up to three-and-a-half-feet high. Don't wipe out! This huge pool can hold hundreds of swimmers and surfer wannabes at one time. A four-story, interactive kid's water play structure has water cannons to shoot, cargo nets to crawl and climb on, and a floating lily-pad bridge across the pool. Going across on the "lily pads" is more challenging than it looks. A large toddler play area has mini slides, splash pools with waterfalls, and a climbing structure in shallow waters. Sunset River is a restful inner tube ride inviting you to float along a continuous river that encircles a good portion of the park. Take your Big Kahuna, Gidget, and rest of the family for an exciting raft adventure down the Coronado Express slide.

Knott's Soak City also features a softball field, sand volleyball courts, a game arcade area, lockers, and showers. If you get hungry, choose from three, full-service eateries, or snack from one of the "stands" scattered throughout the park. No outside food is allowed inside the park. So splish splash, forget about your bath, and come and put your swimming suits on. Hot tip: Wear water shoes or sandals as the cement pathways can get hot.

Hours: Open the end of April to the end of May on weekends only, 10am - 6pm. Open the month of June daily, 10am - 6pm. Open July through Labor Day daily, 10am - 8pm. Open weekends in September, noon - 8pm.

Admission: $22.95 for adults; $18.95 for seniors; $16.95 for ages 3 - 11; children 2 and under are free. After 3pm, admission is discounted. Parking is $6.

Ages: 1½ years and up.

LEGOLAND CALIFORNIA
(760) 438-LEGO (5346) / www.legolandca.com
1 Lego Drive, Carlsbad
(Exit San Diego Fwy [5] E. on Cannon Rd., R. on Lego Dr. [TG: 1126 J2])

☼
$$$$$
🎂

Lego mania reaches an all-time high at the 128-acre Legoland California which features over fifty family rides, shows, and interactive attractions, as well as areas to build and play with Legos™, and restaurants. (There are three other Legolands in the world.) Over thirty *million* Legos create the models used in and around this unique amusement park (and you will get tired of reading the word "Lego" by the end of this entry). The Lego builders really are incredible! The following are some highlights of the main attraction areas:

Explore Village has a boat ride through an enchanted forest, past animated classic fairy tale characters and settings. Take a short ride in a Lego jeep through a "jungle" that has ninety animated animals made of Legos. Choo choo around the railroad track on the Legoland Express. At the waterworks area turn a handle and aim water spray at objects and at pretend animals to bring them to "life." Kids can get wet here, too, as they play in and amongst the fountains that spurt up at unexpected intervals. (Bring a change of clothing.) Younger children can happily while away the day creating and playing at the Duplo playground. It has a maze to crawl through, a train ride, an ambulance and police motorcycle to "drive," and lots more. A magic demonstration is usually performed at the theater here.

Fun Town offers two driving schools, one for young kids, one for younger kids - no adults allowed. Drive Lego-looking electric cars (not on a track!), complete with a stop signs, traffic lights, turns, and traffic jams. (There is a reason kids this young do not have licenses.) At the Sky Tower, sit in outward-facing seats and pull yourself up a thirty-foot tower, then experience a controlled "free fall" down. For another perspective, pedal the Sky Cycle around an elevated circular track. Other attractions and activities in this area include piloting a kid-size helicopter up and down via a joystick; maneuvering a bumper boat around buoys (and other boats); taking a walk through Adventures' Club building to see ancient lands, the Arctic, and more all depicted in Legos; touring a small-scale Lego factory to see how the bricks are made and packaged; and eating an ice cream at the Club House where a Lego Robot Band performs. Kids (and adults) will belly-laugh at the funny Big Test show where acrobatic/clownish fire firefighters try to teach safety tips. Don't miss the ventriloquist/bird show - this guy is amazing! This town also offers a shop with bins where kids can pick out the color and shape of the Lego bricks they want to create their own specialty masterpiece. The bricks are sold by weight. Get a picture perfect present at the Lego Clubhouse: After a digital photo is taken, you receive all the bricks needed to make the portrait in 3-D. Tip: The Marketplace offers fresh cooked, good, non-fast food.

Past the rocks that sing "we will rock you" is the medieval-themed **Castle Hill**. A highlight here is the roller coaster that takes all-age riders through a castle and into a cave past a fire-breathing dragon. Another coaster keeps riders in suspension, as it is floorless. Kids (only) can also mount a "horse" and take part in a simulated joust ride. Everyone can have adventures at a huge, multi-level playground that has rope ladders, cargo nets, and slides. Visitors can also pan for "gold" to be exchanged for a Lego medallion and take a nature walk past models of native animals.

Miniland re-creates five areas of the U.S. constructed in 1:20 scale. Each area has fourteen to thirty-three animations and some interactivity: *New England Harbor* has farmlands, a traditional harbor and a shipyard, and underwater divers exploring a sunken ship. *Washington, D.C.* is impressive with its Lincoln Memorial, Washington Monument, White House, a presidential motorcade, baseball games, and more capital activities. *New York City* showcases the Manhattan and Brooklyn bridges, Central Park (i.e. joggers, the zoo, etc.), Times Square complete with police cars with lights and sirens, and the Statue of Liberty. *California Coast* combines beaches and mansions in Beverly Hills with cable cars and Ghiradelli Square. *New Orleans* offers paddle steamers on the river front, plantation houses, Mardi Gras, and the sound of jazz.

The mostly hands-on **Imagination Zone** offers both free-play opportunities and structured workshops and contests for all ages. Inspiration is all around such as a Technic T-Rex, and a fifteen-foot Einstein. A learning center here also features computers with Lego software for Mindstorms robots. Tip: If you're interested in taking a class sign up early in the day. The Imagination Zone theater shows a twelve-minute 4-D film on a giant screen, called *Lego Racers*. As music and other sounds pulsate, viewers are immersed in the sensations of a car race through different landscapes while actually feeling the wind, snow, water, and tire smoke. Ride the Technic Coaster for a fun and fairly fast (for Legoland standards) trip on the switchback tracks. Take a spin around (and around and around!) on the Bionicle Blaster - individual cars that spin around as much as you want them to. Imposing giant Bionicles stand guard here. Aquazone participants circle around in power ski-like water vehicles as spectators press buttons that control blasts of water directed towards them. You're an all-star in the Lego Sports Center. Shoot real hoops under the watchful eyes of life-size NBA players (made out of Legos). Young athletes can also kick soccer balls towards goals and throw footballs through a moving target, plus climb a wall (literally). Let them get their energy out! Enjoy a meal at the Sport Diner, here, too, or at the nearby pizza place where a whole pizza, drinks, and salad is only $19.95 (at the time of this writing).

Another picturesque part of Legoland is a large lake, where families can take a cruise and see - what else - more Lego animals and characters!! Lastly, note that the Legoland store is the largest one in the U.S. It carries everything Lego, including hard-to-find pieces and kits. The store gets mobbed towards the end of the day, so shop early.

Hours: Open most of the year, Mon., Thurs. - Sun., 10am - 5pm. (Often closed on Tues. and Wed.) Open daily in the summertime, 10am - 8pm.

Admission: $41.95 for adults; $34.95 for seniors and ages 3 - 12; children 2 and under are free. Certain discounts available through AAA. Parking is $7. Two-day passes, to be used within a 5-day period, are $49.95 for adults; $42.95 for seniors and ages 3 - 12.

Ages: Most of the rides and shows are geared for ages 2 - 11, but you are never too old to play with Legos.

THE WAVE
(760) 940-WAVE (9283) or (760) 726-1340 / www.wave-waterpark.com
161 Recreation Drive, Vista
(Exit 78 Fwy N. on Vista Village Dr., R. on Recreation Dr. [TG: 1087 H6])

Catch a wave at The Wave on the Flow Rider wave machine. Swoosh on down the four water slides here - two are enclosed, and two are convertible-style (no tops). Some height restrictions apply. Slip 'n slide down the fifth slide, which is short, slopes gently, and ends into Crazy River, a large ring of water that encircles the slide and lounge area. For those 48" and under, there is also a small, children's water play area with climbing apparatus that has water spouting out and a few slides. The large rectangular pool, usually used for lessons and the swim team, is open to the public during Wave hours. There are a limited number of picnic tables here, as well as a few grassy areas for picnicking or sunbathing. You may bring in your own lounge chairs. Lockers, double inner tubes, and shade pavilions are all available for a small fee. Use of single inner tubes and body boards are included in your admission price. Outside food is not allowed in, but there is a full-service snack bar here that sells food at very reasonable prices. Have big time fun at this small water park!

Hours: Open the end of May through the beginning of June, and the month of September on weekends and holidays, 11am - 5pm. Open the beginning of June through Labor Day daily, 10:30am - 5:30pm.
Admission: $12 for 42" and taller; $9 for seniors and 41" and under; children 2 and under are free.
Ages: 1½ years and up.

-----ARTS AND CRAFTS-----

BAUBLES ETC.
(619) 448-2422
1363 N. Cuyamaca, El Cajon
(Exit San Vincente Fwy [67] W. on Fletcher Pkwy / Broadway, R. on N. Cuyamaca. [TG: 1251 D3])

This small storefront ceramic studio has a good selection of ceramic, greenware, and bisque. Besides the normal fun of painting your own ceramic piece, children's classes are offered that include firing and casting demos. Come here to make something more special than just a bauble.

Hours: Open Mon. - Fri., 10am - 5pm (Tues. until 9pm); Sat., 9am - 2pm
Admission: The price of the item, plus $5 studio time for the first hour, $2.50 for each hour after that. Studio time prices include paints, brushes, stencils, and other materials.
Ages: 4 years and up.

CERAMICAFE (Del Mar)
(858) 259-9958 / www.ceramicafe.com
12921 El Camino Real, Del Mar
(Exit San Diego Fwy [5] E. on Del Mar Heights, R. on El Camino Real and into Del Mar Heights Town Center. Ceramicafe is toward the N. end. [TG: 1188 A6])

This well-lit, paint-your-own ceramics store has a great array of objects to choose from. We painted dragon figurines, deep mugs, a vase, and a heart-shaped tile. (We were busy!) I used the stencils and stamps, while my boys free-formed it. All the artistic aids, paints, and brushes are included in the price. Finished masterpieces are ready for pick up in about three days. Ceramicafe also offers after-school activities where kids can learn painting techniques, creating with clay, mosaics, and more.

Hours: Open daily, 10am -10pm.
Admission: There is no per-hour studio fee. Mugs range from $15 - $18, bud vases are $15, 4 x 4 tiles are four for $20, etc.
Ages: 4 years and up.

CERAMICAFE (La Mesa)

(619) 466-4800 / www.ceramicafe.com
5500 Grossmont Center Drive, La Mesa

(Exit Mission Valley Fwy [8] N. on Jackson Dr., R. on Fletcher Pkwy, R. on Grossmont Center Dr. It's in a shopping center. [TG: 1271 A1])

See the above entry for CERAMICAFE (Del Mar) for details.

Hours: Open Mon. - Thurs., 10am - 9pm; Fri. - Sat., 10am - 10pm; Sun., 10am - 6pm.

CLAY 'N LATTE

(858) 487-9293 / www.claynlatte.com
10175 Rancho Carmel Drive, San Diego

(Exit Escondido Fwy [15] E. on Ted Williams Pkwy., L. on Rancho Carmel. [TG: 1189 J3])

A ceramic piece, some paint, and a little latte goes a long way in making a ceramic masterpiece to take home. Choose from a wide selection of items (over 1,000!), such as plates, bowls, flower pots, goblets, salt and pepper shakers, animal figurines, and more. Kids will have a field day picking out colors (over 100 to choose from) and thinking of ways to design their chosen piece. Warning: This recreational activity can become habit forming! Paints, paintbrushes, and stencils are all provided - you simply provide the artistic creativity (and the money).

Hours: Open Mon. - Thurs., 10am - 8pm; Fri. - Sat., 10am - 9pm; Sun., noon - 6pm.

Admission: Price of item, plus an $8 studio fee for adults, $6 for children 12 and under. Ask about specials.

Ages: 4 years and up

-----*BEACHES*-----

CORONADO MUNICIPAL BEACH

www.coronadovisitors.com
Ocean Boulevard, Coronado

(Exit San Diego Fwy [5] onto the Coronado Bridge. Continue straight off the bridge as the street turns into 4th St., L. on Orange Ave., R. on Isabella Ave., straight onto Ocean Blvd. [TG: 1288 G7])

This beach offers a long stretch of sand, plus a lifeguard station, volleyball courts, a few sand dunes, and a view of Navy vessels who use this waterway. If you walk toward the south, you'll end up in front of the famous Hotel Del Coronado.

Hours: Open daily, sunrise - sunset.

Admission: Free

Ages: All

LA JOLLA SHORES BEACH

(619) 221-8899 / www.sannet.gov/lifeguards/beaches
8200 Camino del Oro, La Jolla

(Going S. on San Diego Fwy [5] exit W. on La Jolla Village Dr., L. on Torrey Pines Rd., R. on La Jolla Shores, L. on Avenida De La Playa, R. on Camino del Oro. Going N. on 5 exit N. to Ardath Rd., which turns into Torrey Pines Rd., and follow above directions. [TG: 1227 H4])

This beach comes fully loaded for a full day of fun! The one-mile-plus stretch of beach, which is adjacent to the Underwater Ecological Reserve, has a separate area for surfers and for swimmers. Year-round lifeguard service, rest rooms, showers (a parent's essential), and a few playgrounds for the kids, complete with swing sets and climbing apparatus, add up to make this a fun place to go with kids. A temporary rubber walkway allows limited access to the beach for wheelchairs and strollers. A beach wheelchair is available, on a first-come, first-served basis, near the main lifeguard station. Kellogg Park, the grassy area behind the main lifeguard station offers another way to enjoy this length of coastline. A cement boardwalk parallels a portion of the beach between the park and the sand. Incorporate a drive around picturesque La Jolla with a visit to the beach. See

SCRIPPS PARK (pg. 400) for other places to visit in the immediate area.

    Hours: Open daily, sunrise - sunset.

  Admission: Free - good luck with parking!

     Ages: All

MISSION BAY PARK

(619) 221-8901 / www.sannet.gov/park-and-recreation/centers

2581 Quivira Court, San Diego

See the entry for MISSION BAY PARK on page 395 for details.

TIDE BEACH PARK

(858) 793-2564 / www.ci.solana-beach.ca.us

302 Solana Vista Drive, Solana Beach

(From San Diego Fwy [5], exit W. on Lomas Santa Fe, R. on N. Coast Hwy [101], L. on Solana Vista Dr. to the end. Street park where ever possible. It's right next to Cardiff State Beach. [TG: 1167 E6])

This is a beach for tidepool explorers and rock collectors. The beach is accessible by stairs and is part of cliff overhangs that create small caves or nooks and crannies along the shoreline. Don't hang out here during high tide! The tidepools are not the best I've seen for observing marine life, but they are fun nonetheless. We did see lots and lots of limpets, plus muscles, sea anemones, and some small crabs.

Just north of the tidepools is Cardiff State Beach, which we promptly nicknamed "Rocky Beach." There isn't a lot of uncovered sand towards the southern end of the beach, but there are literally tons of multi-colored, round, smooth rocks here. Bathrooms are available and lifeguards are on duty here, too.

    Hours: Open daily, sunrise - sunset.

  Admission: Free

     Ages: 2 years and up.

-----*EDIBLE ADVENTURES*-----

94th AERO SQUADRON

(858) 560-6771 / www.94thaerosquadron.signonsandiego.com

$$$$

8885 Balboa Avenue, San Diego

(Exit Cabrillo Fwy [163] E. on Balboa. [TG: 1249 D2])

The ivy-covered brick restaurant is a replica of a French WWI-era farmhouse. Outside, cannons are in a semi-circle around sandbags. Bales of hay are suspended over wooden carts that look like they're falling apart. A bi-plane, trees, and a wooden fence are also out front. Listen to swing and other older-style music being piped outside.

Inside the ambiance is just as rustic and charming. Dark wood beam ceilings, huge brick fireplaces with large kettles, and walls and ceiling tastefully lined with helmets, war posters, photos, medals, plane parts, vests, farm implements, and even sandbags add to the romantic atmosphere. There are even a few pocket booths that contain headphones so diners can listen to the FAA control tower on the adjacent Montgomery Field Airport. Out back, tables on a grassy embankment overlook the airfield, bunkers with camouflage netting, more grounded airplanes, an army jeep, and a duck pond.

The lunch menu includes escargot in mushroom caps ($7.95), fried calamari ($5.95), Cobb salad ($8.95), hamburger ($6.95), French dip sandwich ($8.95), hot crab and artichoke sandwich ($8.95), grilled salmon ($10.95), London broil ($9.95), and pastas. The dinner menu includes some of the aforementioned foods plus filet mignon ($19.95), lobster tail (market price), rack of lamb ($22.95), and more. The Sunday buffet brunch has an incredible assortment of delectable foods - blintzes, carved roast beef, crab legs, an omelette bar, a fajita bar, waffles, muffins, crepes, cheesecake, eclairs, and more. Catch the next flight to the 94th Aero Squadron.

    Hours: Open Mon. - Thurs., 11am - 10pm; Fri., 11am - 11pm; Sat., 4;30pm - 11pm; Sun., 9am - 3pm - brunch; 4pm - 10pm - dinner.

Admission: Prices are listed above. Brunch is $17.95 for adults; $8.95 for ages 4 - 10; children 3 and under are free.
Ages: 4 years and up.

ANTHONY'S FISH GROTTO
(619) 463-0368 / www.gofishanthonys.com
9530 Murray Drive, La Mesa
(Exit Mission Valley Fwy [8] N. on Severin/Fuerte, R. on Murray Dr. [TG: 1251 C7])

Shell I tell you about this restaurant that resembles an underwater sea cave? It's a pearl of a place. Enter through a giant clam shell. Fish are "swimming" around on the ceiling. Octopus-covered lamps are at the front desk and a fish mosaic covers the wall here. The booths are upholstered with fish designs. Waist-high coral barriers separate the restaurant into sections. (Look for eel and other creatures peeking out from the coral rocks.) The bar is in a cave-like setting. Even the restrooms maintain the theme!

Dining is available inside, or outside under shade trees on patio tables and chairs. Both seating arrangements allow guests to overlook the grotto's small lake. Duck feed is available from the restaurant. A dry-docked boat on the lawn houses a small video arcade.

The Fish Grotto specializes in a wide variety of fresh fish and shellfish, of course, although it also offers chicken and steak as well. Here's a sampling of the menu: Crab stuffed mushrooms ($7.95); clam chowder ($4.50 a pint); shrimp, scallop and swordfish kabobs ($10.50); hand-battered oysters ($11.95); coconut fried shrimp ($15.95); and Alaskan King crab legs ($26.95). The kid's menu offers fish dippers ($3.50), grilled cheese ($2.50), pasta ($3.50), cod ($4.95), and chicken ($4.95). Drinks are extra. Note: Take some of Anthony's fish home as this location also has a retail market.

Although this is the only Anthony's so wonderfully themed, other Anthony's locations have the same great food and most have some sort of view. Other locations are San Diego Bay at 1360 N. Harbor Drive at Ash Street - (619) 232-5103 - a waterfront restaurant overlooking the San Diego Bay, and Chula Vista at 215 W. Bay Boulevard off Hwy 5 at 'E' Street - (619) 425-4200 - an open and airy atmosphere with a fish aquarium, fish sand castings, and more.
Hours: Open Sun. - Thurs., 11am - 9pm; Fri. - Sat., 11am - 10pm. Closed all major holidays.
Admission: See menu prices above.
Ages: All

AVIARA FOUR SEASONS RESORT
(760) 603-6800 / www.fourseasons.com/aviara
7100 Four Seasons Point, Carlsbad
(Exit San Diego Fwy [5] E. on Poinsettia Ln., R. on Aviara Pkwy., R. on Four Seasons Point. [TG: 1127 C6])

All dressed up and nowhere to go? Indulge in an elegant repast of tea time at this fine resort hotel. Tables in the Tea Lounge are covered with white linen, sprinkled with rose petals, and set with fine china. A three-tiered silver cake plate bears scrumptious edibles of finger sandwiches; scones with rose petal jelly, lemon curd, and Devonshire cream; and petit fours. Sip your choice of teas, including herbal and fruit infusions.
Hours: Tea is served Wed. - Sun., 2pm - 4:30pm.
Admission: $19.50 per person (with champagne - $26.50). Valet parking is complementary, with the tea.
Ages: 4 years and up.

BENIHANA OF TOKYO (San Diego)
(619) 298-4666 / www.benihana.com
477 Camino Del Rio S., San Diego
(From Mission Valley Fwy [8], take the exit towards Mission Center Rd/Auto Circle, L. on Camino Del Rio N., L. Mission Center Rd., R. Camino Del Rio S. [TG: 1269 A4])

See the entry for BENIHANA OF TOKYO (Los Angeles County) on page 11 for details.

CHUCK E. CHEESE

See the entry for CHUCK E. CHEESE on page 12 for details.

CORVETTE DINER

(619) 542-1476 / www.cohnrestaurants.com

3946 5th Avenue, Hillcrest, San Diego

(Going S. on Cabrillo Fwy [163], exit W. on Washington St., L. on 4th Ave., L. on University St., L. on 5th Ave., which is a one way street. Going N. 163, exit E. on Robinson Ave., L. on Vermont St., L. on University St., R. on 5th Ave. Valet park or circle around the block for self parking. [TG: 1269 A5])

This 50's-style diner is a really bebopping place to eat! The music played from the deejay's booth; the license plates, neon signs, and hub cabs that decorate the walls; the old gas pumps; the Bazooka bubble gum displays; and the red Corvette (parked inside) all add to the atmosphere of the restaurant. The rest of the decor incorporates black and white checked tiles with blue marbleized vinyl booths. Waiting for a table here can be more fun than usual as you sit on a bench made from the back seat and the fins of an old Cadillac. On Tuesday and Wednesday evenings, from 6:30pm to 9:30pm, be entertained by a magician who plies his tricks of the trade and his jokes at your table. On Friday and Saturday evenings, from 6pm to 9pm, balloon artists use more than hot air to entertain customers. Most evenings after 6pm a live DJ plays 50's and 60's music and takes requests.

The food here is great! A Hawaii 5-O burger (burger with pineapple) or a Philly steak sandwich is about $8. Other food choices include grilled Reubens, ribs, meatloaf, blackened chicken pasta, salads, and more. Desserts are delectable. They range from Green Rivers to peppermint smoothies to Whopper Malt cheesecake to Death by Chocolate Cake. Kids' meals are $5.95 for their choice of spaghetti, burger, corn dog, grilled cheese sandwich, or chicken fingers, plus fries, a soft drink, and an ice cream bar. Was life really this good in the fifties?!

Hours: Open Sun. - Thurs., 11am - 10pm; Fri. - Sat., 11am - midnight.

Admission: Prices are listed above.

Ages: All

FAIROUZ RESTAURANT AND GALLERY

(619) 225-0308 / www.alnashashibi.com

3166 Midway Drive, #102, San Diego

(Exit Ocean Beach Fwy [8] S. on Mission Bay Dr., which turns into Midway. It's in a small shopping center. [TG: 1268 D5])

The aroma of Greek and Lebanese cuisine tantalizes your tastebuds the moment you step into this small, storefront restaurant. Ethnic music plays in the background. The booths and tables are surrounded by murals, paintings, and other artwork adorning the walls, as well as clothing items for sale. There is even a small library of books to peruse while eating. Food choices include Greek salad ($4.25), lamb kafta sandwiches ($5.75), falafels ($4.25), moussaka ($9.99), stuffed grape leaves ($6.99), and lots more. The ambiance, the food, the art - it's all Greek to me!

Hours: Open Sun. - Thurs., 11am - 9pm; Fri. - Sat., 11am - 10pm. Closed New Year's Day and Christmas.

Admission: Prices are listed above.

Ages: 5 years and up.

FARMER'S MARKETS

See the entry for FARMER'S MARKETS on page 14 for details.

FARRELL'S ICE CREAM PARLOUR

(858) 578-9895 / www.partyinsandiego.com

10606 Camino Ruiz #10, Mira Mesa

(From Jacob Dekema Fwy [805], exit E. on Mira Mesa Blvd. From Escondido Fwy [15], exit W. on Mira Mesa. It's on the corner of Mira Mesa and Camino Ruiz, in the Target shopping center. [TG: 1209 B4])

Remember Farrell's from your high school days? Nostalgia is slightly updated with a few video arcade games and kiddie rides, but there are still rows of candy to tempt children, an old-fashioned player piano, and the ice-cream specialty desserts. Try the Zoo - a five-flavor, myriad topping, ice-cream extravaganza carried to you on its own litter, accompanied by sirens and bells - $39.99; the Volcano with thirty (count 'em, thirty!) scoops of vanilla ice-cream and hot fudge overflowing down the sides, brought out while it's still erupting (bring a friend, or ten, to help you eat this) - $39.99; or the Trough, which is two banana splits piled high with goodies, eaten from a trough as the waiter exclaims, "This person made a pig of himself at Farrell's" and awards the consumer a ribbon - $10.99. There are, of course, numerous other, single-serving choices, such as a Tin Roof, mudslide (coffee ice cream on devil's food cake drenched in hot fudge and Oreo cookie crumbles), and malts.

This very family-oriented restaurant serves all-American food in a fun atmosphere. Hamburgers start at $6.25; patty melt, $7.29; tuna salad, $7.90; and chicken club sandwich, $7.75. Kid's meals, for ages 10 and under, which average $3.95, offer a choice of grilled cheese, hamburger, hot dog, peanut butter and jelly sandwich, or chicken nuggets, and come with fries. Save room for a clown sundae. Ask about weekday specials, such as paying for one adult, and getting one child's meal for 99¢. Lunch time can be quiet here, so I actually prefer the rowdier, dinner hour. Note: The birthday party prices are very reasonable. If you don't have a party here, show proof it's your birthday and you receive a free sundae.

Hours: Open Mon. - Thurs., 11:30am - 10:30pm; Fri., 11:30am - midnight; Sat., 11am - midnight; Sun., 11am - 10:30pm. Closed Thanksgiving, Christmas Eve, and Christmas.

Admission: Menu prices noted above.

Ages: All

HARD ROCK CAFE (San Diego County)

La Jolla - (858) 456-7625; San Diego - (619) 615-7625 / www.hardrock.com

La Jolla - 909 Prospect Street; San Diego - 801 4th Avenue, near Horton Plaza in the Gaslamp Quarter

(La Jolla: Exit San Diego Fwy [5] W. on La Jolla Village Dr., L. on Torrey Pines Rd., R. on Prospect Pl., which turns into Prospect St. [TG: 1227 E6]; San Diego: Going S. on San Diego Fwy [5], exit S. on Front St., L. on Broadway, R. on 4th. Going N. on the 5, exit S. on 6th Ave. R. on Broadway, L. on 4th. [TG: 1289 A3])

See the entry for HARD ROCK CAFE (Los Angeles County) on page 17 for details.

HORTON GRAND HOTEL / IDA BAILEY'S RESTAURANT

(619) 544-1886 / www.hortongrand.com

311 Island Avenue, San Diego

(Going S. on San Diego Fwy [5], exit W. on Imperial Ave., R. on 12th Ave., L. on Island Ave. Going N. on 5, exit at 'J' St., continue straight off the off ramp and turn L. at Island. [TG: 1289 A4])

Put on the lace gloves, extend your pinky, and enjoy a delicious afternoon tea at this Victorian-style hotel. Afternoon Tea consist of petit fours, finger sandwiches, scrumptious scones, cake, and an assortment of teas. High Tea is a bit more formal and also includes sherry (not for the kids!), a sausage roll, and truffle. Brunch includes a buffet of anyway-you-like-them omelettes, waffles with various toppings, breakfast potatoes, steak, ham, salads, pastas, and desserts.

As this hotel is in the heart of the historic Gaslamp District, take a stroll around before or after your tea to soak in the district's ambiance. There are many unique stores, so both window shoppers and "real" shoppers will be appeased.

Hours: Teas are served Sat., 2pm - 5pm; Sun. brunch is 10am - 2pm.

Admission: $13.95 per person for Afternoon Tea; $15.95 for High Tea; $21.95 for adults for brunch; $12.95 for ages 11 and under.

Ages: 5 years and up.

HOTEL DEL CORONADO - TEA TIME
(619) 435-6611 / www.hoteldel.com
1500 Orange Avenue, Coronado
(Exit San Diego Fwy [5] W. on 75 and cross over the Coronado Bridge, L. on Orange Ave. [TG: 1308 J1])

$$$$$

This hotel is the creme-de-la-creme of hotels (personal opinion), and tea time served on the Palm Court is a true taste of elegance. (Note: You must make some time before or after your tea to explore this incredible hotel and its grounds!) Teas consist of grilled squash and herb toast, egg salad, caviar (it's amazing what kids will try in an etiquettely-correct atmosphere), creme fraiche, smoked salmon, shrimp, duck, smoked ham salad, watercress, cranberry scone, scones and Devonshire cream, seasonal berry tart, and a variety of teas, of course.

Hours: Tea is served every Sun., noon - 4pm; daily during the Christmas holiday season.
Admission: $22.95 per person. Parking in the hotel lot costs $3 for 3 hours with validation, $4 an hour without it. Street parking, which is limited, is free.
Ages: 5 years and up.

JOE'S CRAB SHACK (San Diego County)
Pacific Beach - (858) 274-3473; San Diego - (619) 260-1111;
San Diego - (619) 233-7391 / www.joescrabshack.com
Pacific Beach - 4325 Ocean Boulevard; San Diego - 7610 Hazard Center Drive, #703; San Diego - 525 E. Harbor Drive

$$$

See the entry for JOE'S CRAB SHACK (Los Angeles County) on page 18 for details.

JULIAN TEA & COTTAGE ARTS
(760) 765-OTEA (0832) / www.juliantea.com
2124 3rd Street, Julian
(From Hwy 78, which turns into Main St., go N.E. on Washington St., R. on 3rd. [TG: 1136 B7])

$$$$

This quaint (what in Julian isn't quaint?), 100-year-old house is a *tea*lightful place to take your daughter for an afternoon of one-on-one time. The traditional and popular Afternoon Tea ($12.50) includes finger sandwiches, scones with jam and whipped cream, desert, and, of course, a pot of tea. Add a cup of homemade soup or a salad for just a $1.95 per item. Another option is Cream Tea ($6.50), with two scones with whipped cream, jam, and a pot of tea. More filling teas that include lunch (yea!) include the Drew Bailey Tea ($10.95) that comes with a sandwich, cup of soup or a salad, dessert, and tea, and the Ploughman's Lunch ($10.95) with green salad, cheese wedges, fruit, bread or cheese scone, cookie, and of course, tea. Or, just come for dessert. Holiday teas, such as ones offered for Valentines' Day and Mother's Day, are always extra special.

Although tea is served in the tea room and the front porch, the cottage also has a few other rooms which contain items for sale - china, tea pots, baby gifts, bridal gifts, books on teas, cards, teas, and cottage arts such as weaving. Each room is decorated with a variety of tea paraphernalia. The upstairs room, which is decorated to resemble a garden, is reserved for private parties.

Hours: The shop is open Mon. - Sat., 10am - 5pm; Sun., 11am - 5pm. Lunch is served 11am - 2pm; tea until 4pm. Closed Thanksgiving and Christmas.
Admission: Prices vary depending on the tea.
Ages: 4 years and up.

NIEDERFRANK'S ICE CREAM SHOP/FACTORY
(619) 477-0828
726 A Avenue, National City
(Going S. on San Diego Fwy [5], exit E. on 8th Street, L. on A Ave. Going N. on 5, exit E. on Plaza Blvd., L. on A. [TG: 1309 H1])

$

I am mentioning this particular family-owned ice cream shop because it dishes up delectable, all-natural, home-made ice cream that tastes incredibly smooth and creamy. The mouth-watering flavors, besides the usual ones, are all handmade on the premises and include Washington Red Peach, Lemon Custard, Brownies and Cream, Coconut Almond Joy, and more.

Hours: Retail hours are Mon. - Fri., 11:30am - 5:30pm; Sat. - Sun., noon - 5pm.
Admission: A single scoop costs $1.90.
Ages: All

THE OLD SPAGHETTI FACTORY (San Diego County)

(619) 233-4323 / www.osf.com
275 5th Avenue, San Diego

(Going S. on San Diego Fwy [5], exit at Sassafras/Airport., go straight on Kettner Blvd., L. on L. on W. Harbor Dr., L. on 5th. Going N. on 5, exit S. on 6th Ave. R. on Market St., L. on 5th. [TG: 1289 A4])

See the entry for THE OLD SPAGHETTI FACTORY (Los Angeles County) on page 19 for details.

PETER PIPER PIZZA (San Diego County)

El Cajon - (619) 670-5197; National City - (619) 477-1788 / www.peterpiperpizza.com
El Cajon - 2983 Jamacha Road; National City - 3007 Highland Avenue

(El Cajon: Take Fwy [94] E. to the end and continue on Campo R., L. on Jamacha. [TG: 1271 J6]; National City: Exit 54 Fwy N. on Highland. [TG: 1310 A3])

See the entry for PETER PIPER PIZZA (Los Angeles County) on page 20 for details.

REUBEN E. LEE RIVERBOAT

(619) 291-1880
880 E. Harbor Island Drive, San Diego

(Going S. on San Diego Fwy [5], exit W. on Sassafras, L. on Pacific Hwy., R. on Laurel St. Going N. on 5, exit N. on Brant, L. on Laurel. From Laurel, go R. on Harbor Dr., L. onto Harbor Island, L. on Harbor Island Dr. Park. [TG: 1288 G2])

Harken back to the days of river boats along the Mississippi. Nowadays, you can still enjoy the ambiance of a riverboat (but in Southern California!) aboard the Reuben E. Lee. The elegant rooms in this permanently anchored, multi-deck, replica paddle-wheeler overlook the picturesque San Diego Bay.

Half of the boat operates under the name Jared's and specializes in steak. Menu selections include filet mignon, $31.95; rib eye steak, $29.95; lamb t-bones, $27.95; and appetizers of exotic mushroom strudel, $8 and a five onion tart for $7.25. The Reuben E. Lee side of the boat offers some steak and chicken, but specializes in seafood. Menu selections include salmon, $21; swordfish, $23; and tuna, Mahi-mahi, and catfish at various prices. Appetizers include crab cakes or oysters for $12 and deep fried clams for $10. The children's menu, only available at Reuben's, offers fish 'n chips, hamburger, cheeseburger, or fried shrimp for $7.50 per entree.

Hours: Open Wed. - Sat., 5pm - 10pm; Sun., noon - 9pm.
Admission: Prices are listed above.
Ages: 3 years and up.

RUBY'S (San Diego County)

(800) HEY RUBY (439-7829); Carlsbad - (760) 931-RUBY; Oceanside - (760) 433-RUBY;
San Diego - (619) 294-RUBY / www.rubys.com
Carlsbad - 5630 Paseo Del Norte, suite 130; Oceanside - 1 Pierview Way; San Diego - 1640 Camino Del Rio N., suite 360P

See the entry for RUBY'S (Orange County) on page 206 for details.

SEAU'S, THE RESTAURANT

(619) 291-SEAU (7328) / www.seau.com
1640 Camino Del Rio North, #1376, in the Mission Valley Shopping Center, San Diego

(Exit Mission Valley Fwy [8] N. on Auto Circle/Mission Center Rd., R. on Camino Del Rio Rd. It's next to Robinsons-May, towards the east end of the mall. [TG: 1269 C2])

San Diego Charger's All-Pro linebacker, Junior Seau, has a two-story restaurant for the good sports in your family to enjoy. Notice how the outside of the restaurant resembles a coliseum. The inside decor is equally eye-catching with a huge mural of Junior Seau, model sports figures in action poses, and signed sports paraphernalia all around such as surfboards, football helmets, baseballs, bats, jerseys, hockey sticks, and lots more. Suspended T.V. monitors show sporting events, and the huge main screen shows the sports channel. (What a surprise!)

The black table tops have sports plays drawn on them. Don't try to erase them, however, because even though it looks like they were done in chalk - they weren't. (We saw others try to do this, too.) Our kids enjoyed watching the pizza-maker toss pizzas, and then cook them in the wood-burning stove. The simplest entertainment is sometimes the best kind.

The food goes the whole nine yards - everything we ate was scrumptious. Menu choices run the gamut from burgers ($7.95) and pizza ($9.95) to rib-eyed steak ($16.95) and lobster ravioli ($14.95). The generously-portioned kids' meals range from $3.95 (choice of hot dog or cheese quesadilla) to $4.05 (pizza or burger) to $6.95 (jr. shrimp). Meals come with fries and a beverage in a small take home sports bottle. For an extra $1, they can get a scoop of Haagen Dazs ice cream. Ah, to be 12 years old (or younger) again!

Hours: Open Sun. - Thurs., 11am - 10pm; Fri. - Sat., 11am - 11pm. Closed Thanksgiving and Christmas.

Ages: All

U.S. GRANT HOTEL

(619) 232-3121 / www.wyndham.com

326 Broadway, San Diego

(Going S. on San Diego Fwy [5] exit S. on Front St., L. on Broadway. Going N. on the 5, exit S. on 6th Ave. R. on Broadway. [TG: 1289 A3])

Old-time elegance permeates tea time in the Grant Hotel lobby. Amid crystal chandeliers, polished mahogany furniture, and beautiful floral arrangements, little girls and boys transform into young ladies and gentlemen, respectively. Savor an assortment of finger sandwiches, scones with fresh cream and preserves, crumpets and pastries, and a fine selection of teas. What a delightful treat! Note: If your children don't care for tea, just request hot chocolate, or juice, for them. Reservations are required.

Hours: Tea is served Tues. - Sat., 3pm - 6pm.

Admission: $16.95 per person.

Ages: 5 years and up.

WESTGATE HOTEL

(619) 557-3650 / www.westgatehotel.com

1055 2nd Avenue, San Diego

(Going S. on San Diego Fwy [5] exit S. on Front St., L. on Broadway. Going N. on the 5, exit S. on 6th Ave. R. on Broadway. From Broadway, go N. on 1st Ave, R. on C St., R. on 2nd. [TG: 1289 A3])

Fashioned after an anteroom at Versailles, children will feel like royalty as they sip their tea and nibble on fancy finger sandwiches, truffles, petit fours, strawberries and cream, and scones topped with preserves, honey, seasonal berries, or Grand Marnier cream. (I wanted to write that the food is lip-smacking good, but the refined atmosphere here dictates a more decorous choice of words.) Reservations are requested. A Teddy Bear Tea is offered during the Christmas seasons. The luxurious surroundings include a Steinway piano, rich tapestries, gilded mirrors, and crystal chandeliers.

Hours: Tea is served Mon. - Sat., 2:30pm - 5pm. Harp music starts at 2:30pm.

Admission: $18 for adults; $13 for ages 3 - 11 from the above set menu. You may also order items a la cart.

Ages: 5 years and up.

WHOLESOME HERITAGE FARM

(760) 746-8822

14305 San Pasqual Valley Road, Escondido

See this entry on page 470 for details.

-----*FAMILY PAY AND PLAY*-----

AHA MINI GOLF / MISSION BAY GOLF COURSE
(858) 490-3370
2702 N. Mission Bay Drive, Mission Bay
(Exit San Diego Fwy [5] W. on Clairmont Blvd., R. on Mission Bay Dr. and follow it around the bend. The mini golf course is adjacent to the regular golf course and driving range. [TG: 1248 C6])

The Aha miniature golf course is different than other mini golf courses we've played. It's not fancy in the way that most other courses have small buildings and decorated objects adorning each hole. This one is situated in a garden-like, and sometimes even forest-like, setting and has a subtle Native American/missions theme. Some of the holes are incredibly challenging and unique, such as the multi-layered hole, the one with the spinning wheel, and a few others that bend and curve almost wickedly. A nice restaurant adjacent to the real golf course (which has lights) is also on the grounds.

    Hours: Open daily, 9am - sunset.
Admission: $4 for adults; $2 for ages 10 and under.
     Ages: 4 years and up.

BELMONT PARK
(858) 488-1549 - amusement rides; (858) 488-3110 - The Plunge / www.giantdipper.com
3146 Mission Boulevard, San Diego
(Exit San Diego Fwy [5] W. on Sea World Dr. and follow the signs to W. Mission Bay Dr. Take Mission Bay Dr. to end. [TG: 1267 J2])

Shops and restaurants encircle the ten or so amusement rides at Belmont Park. In the center, is the Giant Dipper Roller Coaster ($4) which doesn't have any loops, but has plenty of ups and downs! A replica of the Looff Liberty wooden carousel ($2) has horses as well as an ostrich, giraffe, and tiger to ride on. Other amusement rides include bumper cars ($3) that spin around (drivers must be at least 52" tall), a Tilt-A-Whirl ($3), Vertical Plunge ($3), and four kiddie rides such as Baja Buggies ($2), Thunder Boats ($2), Submarines ($2), and the Sea Serpent ($2). Jumpstart your heart with Trampoline Bungee, where you can safely do flips because you're harnessed in - $6 per jumping session. PIRATE'S COVE (see pg. 379), an indoor play area for younger children, is adjacent to the park.

While at Belmont Park, take a plunge at The Plunge. This large indoor swimming pool, located on the other side of the movie theater, boasts a beautiful underwater/whale mural, painted by renown marine artist, Wyland. The enclosed pool, kept at 83 degrees, is surrounded by huge windows looking out on palm trees, suggesting a tropical atmosphere. Swim sessions are $3.50 for adults; $2.25 for seniors and children 6 months to 17 years.

Too nice a day to go swimming inside? Go for a dip outside, as the ocean is just a few steps away. The surf and sand, and bike trail on the beach are "shore" to help make your day at the park a good one!

    Hours: The stores and restaurants are open daily, usually 10am - 7pm. In the summer, the rides are open Sun. - Thurs., 11am - 10pm; Fri. - Sat., 11am - 11pm. The rest of the year the rides are open Mon. - Thurs., 11am - 6pm; Fri. - Sun., 11am - 10pm. Call first as hours fluctuate. The Plunge is open Mon. - Fri., 5:30am - 8am and noon - 8pm; Sat. - Sun., 8am - 4pm.
Admission: Attractions are priced above. An unlimited rides pass is $13.95 for 50" and taller; $9.95 for 49" and under. Tuesday nights during the summer, beginning at 4pm, most rides at the amusement park are 75¢ each. Ask about a special deal offered during the week for unlimited kiddie rides plus entrance to Pirate's Cove.
     Ages: All

BOARDWALK
(619) 449-7800 / www.boardwalk-parkway.com
1286 Fletcher Parkway, El Cajon

(Going E. on Mission Valley Fwy [8], exit N. on Johnson Ave., L. on Fletcher Pkwy. Going W. on 8, go N. on San Vicente Fwy [67] and then immediately exit W. on Broadway, which turns into Fletcher Pkwy. Going S. on 67, exit W. on Fletcher Pkwy. [TG: 1251 D4])

This Boardwalk is not made of boards, nor is it by the seaside; it is, however, a large indoor amusement center for kids. It's clean with brightly-colored games and rides that elicited several, "This is FUN!" comments from my kids. Each token costs 25¢. The main attractions are the **carousel** (three tokens), **castle bounce** (three tokens), **bumper cars** (six tokens), **barrel of fun**, which is similar to the teacups ride (three tokens), **frog hopper** (six tokens), **Himalaya** (six tokens) and **soft play gym** (eight tokens). This two-story soft play gym area, for kids 60" and under, has balls pits, a mini zip line, slides, and obstacle courses, plus tubes to crawl through. There are numerous arcade and video games here. The full-service snack bar offers salads, pizza, pasta, and more, and weekly family deals. Kids meals are $2.75 for a choice of corn dog, chicken nuggets, or pizza, plus fries and a drink. If you feel like scoring more fun, strike out to PARKWAY BOWL (see pg. 378), the connecting bowling alley which has laser tag and other attractions.

Hours: Open Sun. - Thurs., 11am - 10:30pm; Fri. - Sat., 11am - midnight.
Admission: Attractions are individually priced above. An unlimited play pass is $5.75 Mon. - Thurs., and $6.75 Fri. - Sun. and holidays.
Ages: 1½ years - 12.

BOOMERS! (El Cajon)

(619) 593-1155 / www.boomersparks.com
1155 Graves Avenue, El Cajon
(Going N. on San Vicente Fwy [67], exit at Broadway/Fletcher Pkwy, at the end of off ramp, turn L. on Graves. Going S. on 67, exit E. on Fletcher Pkwy, go under fwy. and make immediate L. on Graves. [TG: 1251 F3])

Come to this family fun center to play for just an hour, or have fun all day. Green fees pay for two rounds at any of the three, nine-hole themed **miniature golf** courses. Choose Memory Lane (fairy tale motif), Iron Horse (western), and/or Lost Crusade (Egyptian) - $7 for adults; $5 for seniors and kids 12 years and under. Other attractions include **bumper boats** - $5 for adults, $2 for passengers (height restrictions apply); **go-karts** - $6.50 for drivers who must be at least 58" tall, $2 for passengers who must be at least 40" tall; **batting cages**; and the **Kids' County Fair**. The latter is comprised of four rides for young children, 36" to 52" tall, - a roller coaster, train ride, Ferris wheel, and mini-planes. Each ride costs $2.50, or purchase a book of twenty-four tickets for $6.50 or forty-four tickets for $10. **Kidopolis** is a multi-level, soft play area with ball pits, slides, and climbing ladders. It's for kids 44" and under and it's free! Socks are required. A **rock wall** cost $6 for two climbs - make the most of them. The two-story arcade and video game building is attractively set up. A full snack bar/restaurant is also at this fun center. Food and fun - what more could you want?!

Hours: Kids' County Fair is open Mon. - Fri., noon - 8pm; Sat. - Sun., 10am - 8pm. Other attractions are open Mon. - Thurs., 11am - 9pm; Fri., 11am - 11pm; Sat., 10am - 11pm; Sun., 10am - 9pm. Hours fluctuate, so please call before you come.
Admission: Attractions are individually priced above, or purchase an unlimited use pass for $24.95 for 58" and taller; $14.95 for 57" and under. Ask about specials.
Ages: 2½ years and up.

BOOMERS! (Escondido)

(760) 741-1326 / www.boomersparks.com
830 Dan Way, Escondido
(Going E. on Hwy 78 Fwy, exit S. on Centre City Pkwy., R. on W. Mission Ave., R. on Dan. Going W. on Hwy 78, turn L. on W. Mission, R. on Dan. [TG: 1129 G2])

This Boomers, just one in a chain of several, is packed with fun activities. The three **miniature golf** courses offer interesting embellishments such as a double-headed dragon, a castle, a windmill, fountains, and miniature housing structures - $6.50 a round for adults; $5 for seniors and ages 6 - 12 years; children 5 and under are free. The four rides in **Kid's County Fair** include a kiddie swing, train, mini-roller coaster, and mini airplanes. An unlimited pass for just these rides is $8. Other attractions here are the **batting cages**; **go-karts** - $6 per (drivers must be at least 58" tall), $2 for passengers under 36"; **bumper boats** - $5 (drivers must be at least 44" tall), $2 for passengers under 44"; and video and arcade games. A full-service snack bar is available to take care of the inevitable hunger pangs. If you haven't had enough of kids running around, Chuck E. Cheese is right next door!

Hours: Open most of the year, Mon. - Thurs., 11am - 9pm; Fri., 11am - 11pm; Sat., 10am - 11pm; Sun., 10am - 10pm. Open in the summer, Sun. - Thurs., 10am - 10pm; Fri. - Sat., 10am - 11pm.

Admission: Attractions are individually priced above. All day/all play passes (not including batting cages and video and arcade games) are $20.95 for 58" and taller; $14.95 for 57" and under.

Ages: 2 years and up for Kiddieland; 4 years and up for most of the other attractions.

BOOMERS! (San Diego)

(858) 560-4212 / www.boomersparks.com

6999 Clairemont Mesa Boulevard, San Diego

(Exit Jacob Dekema Fwy [805] E. on Clairemont Mesa Blvd. [TG: 1248 J1])

So much fun can be had at just one place! Choose from two, themed **miniature golf** courses: Storybook Land with a castle, Cinderella's pumpkin, the shoe from the old woman who lived in one, and more, or Western Town, with a bank, jail, storefront facades, a livery stable, and wagons - $7 a round for adults; children 5 and under are free with a paying adult. Other attractions include **go karts** - $6.50 for a five-minute ride (drivers must be at least 58" tall), $2 for a passenger; **bumper boats** - $5 per driver, who must be at least 44" tall, $2 per passenger; **batting cages**; and **Lazer Runner**. This last game is laser tag played inside an inflated, spaceship-looking big bounce. With six to eight players, it's every kid (or adult) for himself/herself. Although this game is played with the usual laser tag equipment of a vest with flashing lights and a laser gun, running around inside a bounce (with obstacles, even!), adds a whole new element of fun. Five minutes of sweaty fun costs $5 per person, and players must be at least 5 years old. The **Fun Zone** has seven rides, including teacups, a Ferris wheel, a train ride, a swing, and a fire engine that goes in the air and around and around. Rides cost $2.50 each or purchase and all-day rides pass for $8. Of course there is a video and arcade game area and a prize redemption center. There is also a separate section for less violent kiddie video games. For those making every nickel count, a special video arcade area has games to play for only 5¢. A Boomer's Cafe serving pizza and other necessary foods is on-site here, too.

Hours: Open Mon. - Thurs., 11am - 10pm; Fri., 11am - midnight; Sat., 10am - midnight; Sun., 10am - 10pm. Open extended hours in the summer. The Fun Zone shuts down earlier than the rest of the attractions.

Admission: Attractions are individually priced above or buy an all-play pass for $24.95 for 58" and over; $14.95 for 57" and under.

Ages: 2 years and up.

BOOMERS! (Vista)

(760) 945-9474 / www.boomersparks.com

1525 W. Vista Way, Vista

(Exit 78 Fwy N. on Emerald Ave., R. on W. Vista Way. [TG: 1107 D1])

This family fun center really has it all! If you're in a mutinous mood, play the **miniature golf** course with a pirate ship and fountains. If you're feeling rather noble, play King Arthur's course with its huge (relatively speaking) castles and dungeons, and a bridge over water. Golf prices are $7 for adults; $5 for seniors and kids 12 years and under. **Laser Runner** is an every man/woman/child for himself laser tag game played inside an inflatable battleship bounce. There are soft obstacles to hide behind (or jump on) and even small rooms to run around in. The game is action-packed, sweaty, and fun. The cost is $5 for a five-minute game, and children must be 5 years old to play. A **Motion simulator** ride is $5 per adventure. **Kidopolis** is a huge, four-story soft-play area with slides, obstacle courses, ball pits, tubes and tunnels. This major gerbil run was a major hit with my boys. The cost is $3 for kids, who must be under 50" and wear socks. Other attractions here include **batting cages**; **go karts** - $6.50 for drivers, who must be at least 58" tall, $2 for passengers, who must be at least 40" tall; and **bumper boats** - $5 a driver, who must be at least 44" tall, $2 for passengers.

The noisy, but attractive, main two-story building houses numerous video and arcade games. A nickel arcade section is upstairs. Boomers Cafe is a full-service restaurant where pizza and other tasty family fare is served along with a fun atmosphere.

Hours:	Open most of the year, Mon. - Thurs., 10am - 10pm; Fri., 11am - midnight; Sat., 10am - 11pm; Sun., 10am - 11pm. Open extended hours in the summer.
Admission:	Attractions are individually priced above, or purchase an unlimited pass for $22.95 for 58" and taller; $14.95 for 57" and under.
Ages:	2 years and up.

CHUCK E. CHEESE

See the entry for CHUCK E. CHEESE on page 12 for details.

FUN-4-ALL

(619) 427-1473

950 Industrial Boulevard, Chula Vista

(Going S. on San Diego Fwy [5], exit E. on J St., R. on Colorado Ave., R. on L St., L on Industrial. Going N. on 5, exit at L. St. [TG: 1330 A3])

This small, family amusement park has an older, well-used, **miniature golf** course with a nautical theme - $5.50 a round for adults, $4.25 for kids 12 years and under; a fun **bumper boat** ride around a few islands - $4 for drivers and $1.75 for passengers; **go-karts** - $4.50 for drivers and $1.75 for passengers (height restrictions apply); and **batting cages.** There are also several video and arcade games inside the main building, and a full-service snack bar.

Hours:	Open in the summer daily, 9am - midnight. Open the rest of the year daily, 9am - 10pm.
Admission:	Attractions are individually priced above, or play one of every attraction, plus receive a soda, for $18 per person.
Ages:	4 years and up.

FUN FARM GO-KARTS AND ARCADE

(619) 423-0793

408 Hollister Street, Otay

(Exit San Diego Fwy [5] E. on Main St., R. on Hollister. It's near Otay Valley Regional Park. [TG: 1330 B6])

Like the title suggests - the Fun Farm is for go-karting and arcading. Drivers must be 54" tall.

Hours:	Open Sun., Tues. - Thurs., noon - 9pm; Fri. - Sat., noon - 11pm. Closed Mon.
Admission:	$4 per six-minute ride in a go-kart.
Ages:	54" tall and up.

IMPERIAL BEACH SKATE PARK / CURB BONEZ SKATE PARK

(619) 423-8615 / www.ci.imperial-beach.ca.us

425 Imperial Beach Boulevard at the Sports Park Recreational Complex, Imperial Beach

(Exit San Diego Fwy [5] W. on Corona Ave, which turns into Imperial Beach Blvd. [TG: 1349 F1])

This community building has been taken over by skaters and bikers. The indoor facility has a few wooden ramps, fun boxes, and a slider bar. Helmet, knee pads, and elbow pads are required, as is a parent/guardian signed permission slip and liability waiver. An adjacent room has an air hockey machine and a few couches for lounging around. There is also a pro shop/food area selling snacks, beverages, and ice cream cones. This is a good place for neighborhood kids to hang out. The outside park has a playground, baseball field, picnic tables, and open grassy areas.

Hours:	The park is open daily, sunrise - sunset. The skate park is open Mon. - Fri., 2pm - 6pm; Sat. - Sun., 11am - 6pm. Hours are extended during the summer and on holidays. Each session is two-hours.

Admission: The park is free. The skate park is $5 per session for non-members. Annual membership is $10, and then admission is $3 per session. Rental gear is $4 for everything.

Ages: Must be at least 7 years old.

LASER STORM

(760) 721-3907

1401 S. Coast Highway, Oceanside

(Exit San Diego Fwy [5] W. on Oceanside Blvd., L. on Coast Hwy. [TG: 1106 B2])

This 1,200 square-foot laser tag arena is black lit, with fog adding to the "storm" ambiance. Tip: Wear dark-colored clothing to blend in with the background. Point, aim, and fire your laser gun at opponents and at targets, but realize that both opponents and targets can fire back. Players can work up a sweat as they walk fast, strategize, and duck for cover. If the mood strikes, go just outside Laser Storm and go bowling! The adjacent Surf Bowl has several lanes plus a snack bar.

Hours: Laser tag is open Fri., 6pm - midnight; Sat., noon - midnight. Reservations are recommended.

Admission: $3.75 a game or $12 for 3 hours of play time.

Ages: 6 years and up.

MAGDALENA YMCA ECKE FAMILY SKATE PARK

(760) 942-9622 / ecke.ymca.org

200 Saxony Road, Encinitas

(Exit San Diego Fwy [5] E. on Encinitas Blvd., L. on Saxony Rd. [TG: 1147 C6])

This YMCA really knows how to reach active kids. A great, outdoor, 32,000-square foot skate park at the Y features an eleven-foot-high vert bowl ramp and six-foot-high double-bowled and double-hipped ramp, plus a full street course with a handrail station, quarter pipes, bank ramps, pyramids, roll-in's, and slider station. Street course ramps are layered in Masonite and half pipes are layered in steel. The course is challenging for experienced skaters, yet allows less-experienced ones the opportunity to try some more difficult maneuvers. Younger (or beginning) skaters have a separate, gated area with lower ramps so they can build confidence as they attempt trickier moves.

Behind the skatepark is a good-sized BMX course, a dirt playground with jumps, roll-ins, and banks. Practices and games (and lots of fun!) are held here throughout the year. Both parks require full safety gear to be supplied by the skaters and bikers and a parent waiver consent form must be signed, on-site, for participants 17 years and under. Sessions are two-and-a-half hours long.

Hours: Both parks are open December through February, Mon. - Fri., 2:30pm - 5pm; Sat. - Sun., 9am - 5pm. Open March through mid-June and September through November, Mon. - Fri., 3:30pm - 6pm. The weekend schedule is the same as above. Open mid-June through August, Mon. - Fri., 3:15pm - 8pm. There are camps in the morning hours in the summer. Closed all major holidays.

Admission: Weekday sessions are $4 for members, $10 for non-members. Weekend sessions are $6 for members, $10 for non-members. Membership is $30 a year and comes with a t-shirt and photo ID card.

Ages: 7 years and up.

MR. PAINTBALL FIELD U.S.A.

(760) 737-8870 - office; (760) 751-2931 - field / www.mrpaintballusa.com

25320 Lake Wohlford Road, Escondido

(Going N. on Escondido Fwy [15], exit E. on Via Rancho Pkwy which turns into Bear Valley Rd., then Valley Rd., R. on Lake Wohlford Rd. about 2.2 miles. The field is on the L. Heading S. on 15 Fwy, exit E. on Hwy 78 to the freeway end, straight ahead on Lincoln, R. on Citrus, L. on Washington, L. on Valley Rd., R. on Lake Wohlford. [TG: 1110 H3])

Armed with semi-automatic paint guns and dressed in goggles, mask, and layers of clothing (to reduce the somewhat painful impact of the paintballs), you are now ready to play the wildly exhilarating and intense game of paintball. Eighteen different fields on 100 acres of land are the outside playing area where hills, valleys, trees, props, man-made huts and spools, villages, natural obstacles, trenches are used for both offensive and defensive tactical maneuvers. Try to zap your opponents with paintballs, without getting hit yourself. Games last between fifteen to thirty minutes. A Subway sandwich or Chinese food is provided in your cost. Bring running shoes, a water bottle, and most of - stamina. Note: Participants 17 and under must have a signed parental waiver.

Hours: Open Sat. - Sun. and some holidays, 8am - 4pm.

Admission: $19 per player if you come self equipped. $29 per person for the basics includes all day play, camouflage clothing, face mask, a Stingray marker, air, and lunch. Ask about other prices All players must purchase 500 rounds of paintball at the field for $18.

Ages: 10 years and up.

PARKWAY BOWL / LAZER TAG

(619) 448-4111 / www.parkwaybowl.com

1280 Fletcher Parkway, El Cajon

(Going E. on 8 Fwy, exit N. on Johnson Ave., L. on Fletcher Pkwy. Going W. on 8, go N. on San Vicente Fwy [67] and then immediately exit W. on Broadway, which turns into Fletcher Pkwy. Going S. on 67, exit W. on Fletcher Pkwy. [TG: 1251 D4])

$$

If you can *spare* some time for family fun, this place will *bowl* you over. Sixty-two lanes for regular bowling and thirty-six lanes that use automatic bumpers (no more gutter balls!) are just the beginning. Imagine flashing lights and loud music, all while you're trying to concentrate on bowling - that's Cosmic bowling and it is really out of this world. Another pocket of fun is the family billiards center with thirteen tables to rent by the hour and four coin-operated tables to pay per game. There are also nine TV screens in this room all tuned to various sporting events. Zap your opponents as you try to dodge their laser shots in an exhilarating game or two of lazer tag. The arena joins the bowling alley to yet another family fun venue, BOARDWALK (see pg. 373). The bowling alley also has a full-service Mexican restaurant, a pizzeria, arcade and video games, and a redemption center for prizes.

Hours: Cosmic bowling is played in two-hour increments starting Fri. at 8:30pm and 11pm; Sat., 6:30pm, 9pm, and 11:30pm. Register an hour or so beforehand. Billiard tables are available Mon. - Thurs., 4pm - 11:30pm; Fri., 4pm - 2am; Sat., noon - 2am; Sun., noon - 11:30pm. Lazer tag is open Mon. - Thurs., 5pm - 10:30pm; Fri., 5pm- midnight; Sat., 11am - midnight; Sun., 11am - 10:30pm.

Admission: Cosmic bowling is $8.95 per person or $39.95 per lane rental for up to 6 people. Shoe rentals are extra. Billiards is $6 per table for an hour before 6pm; $8 - $8.95 after 6pm. Coin operated tables are 75¢ a game. Ask about specials. Lazer tag is $4 per person for the first game; $3 for replays. Ask about specials.

Ages: 4 years and up for bowling. 10 years and up for billiards. 6 years and up for lazer tag.

PENDLETON PAINTBALL PARK

(800) 899-9957 / www.cppaintball.com

Camp Pendleton, Oceanside

$$$$$

(Exit San Diego Fwy [5] W. on Camp Pendleton/Ocean Harbor Drive. Go to the main gate and show the MP guard your license, registration, and car insurance. Drive about 7.5 miles and look for the sign. [TG: 1085 J6])

I think I would be at a definite disadvantage playing paintball against marines! Actually although the paintball park is on in the marine base, anyone can play. The park is seventy-five acres big with seven tournament-size fields that boast of bunkers, buildings, trenches, big trees, and sandbag fortifications to keep play interesting and challenging. Capture the Flag is the most common game played although alternatives include Center Flag, where two teams go for just one flag, and Elimination, where the winning team must annihilate (figuratively speaking) all members of the opposing team. Wear a long sleeve shirt and long pants even on summer days. Protective gear is included with the price. Note: Gatorade and candy bars are available to purchase and a McDonald's is only a mile down the road. You are welcome to bring in your own food. Participants under 18 must have a waiver signed by a parent or guardian.

Hours: Open Sat. - Sun., 9am - 4:30pm. Call ahead to check on gear availability.

Admission: $12 per person if you have your own equipment, although you must purchase paintballs here - $4 for 100; $44 per person with rental equipment (goggles, semi-automatic paint gun, CO2 refills, and 500 paintballs) included.

Ages: 10 years and up.

PIRATE'S COVE

(858) 539-7474 / www.giantdipper.com

3106 W. Mission Boulevard / W. Mission Bay Drive, San Diego

(Exit San Diego Fwy [5] W. on Sea World Dr. and follow the signs to W. Mission Bay Dr. [TG: 1267 J2])

At one end of BELMONT PARK (see pg. 373) there are two buildings with wonderful pirate murals that comprise an indoor family playland called Pirate's Cove. One building has air hockey, a few video games, and kiddie rides. Downstairs, is an underground cave-like tunnel that connects the two Cove buildings. This second building, with costumed pirate mannequins, is where most of the swashbuckling action takes place. Here are the ball pits, soft play areas, obstacle courses, and big plastic tunnels and tubes that your mateys dream of! There is also a separate area for younger buccaneers to pillage, I mean play on. Note: Socks are required at Pirate's Cove.

Hours: Open in the summer, Sun. - Thurs., 10am - 9pm; Fri. - Sat., 10am - 10pm. Open the rest of the year, Mon. - Thurs., 10am - 7pm; Fri. - Sun., 10am - 9pm. Call first as hours fluctuate.

Admission: $6.50 for ages 3 to 12; $4.50 for children 2 and under; two parents can play for free for each paying child. Note: If you come play here for just the last hour, admission is $3 per child. Ask about combo prices for Pirate's Cove and the kiddie rides at Belmont Park.

Ages: 6 months - 12 years.

POWAY FUN BOWL

(858) 748-9110 / www.powaybowl.com

12941 Poway Road, Poway

(Exit Escondido Fwy [15] E. on Poway Rd. [TG: 1190 D4])

If you have some time to spare, score some fun at this thirty-lane bowling alley. It also features bumper bowling for younger children and Rock-n-Roll Bowl, where bowling balls, pins, and lanes light up with bright neon colors while rock music plays in the background. The latter is usually offered after 9pm on weekdays and on certain weekends. Have a blast in the laser tag room which has tall partitions covered in futuristic-looking neon splatterings. The sharp angles of the partitions and the occasional ramp make the ten-minute game more challenging - the chase is on! A full-service snack bar is at the bowling alley, too.

Hours: Call for open bowling times. Laser tag is open daily, 6pm - 10pm.

Admission: Rock-n-Roll Bowl is $15 per hour per lane or $3.50 per person per game after 6pm. Laser tag is $5 per game.

Ages: 3 years and up for bumper bowling; 6 years and up for laser tag.

ROLLERSKATELAND AND LASER STORM

(619) 562-3791 / www.rollerskatelandlaserstorm.com

9365 Mission Gorge Road, Santee

(Going N. on San Vicente Fwy [67], exit W. on Prospect Ave., R. on Cuyamaca St., L. on Mission Gorge Rd. Going S. on 67, exit W. on Woodside Ave., which turns into Mission Gorge Rd. Going E. on Fwy 52, go to the end, E. on Mission Gorge Rd. It's behind Jack-in-the-Box. [TG: 1231 B6])

Take two opposing teams, arm them with laser phasers and vests, let them loose in a darkened arena with neon-colored partitions, and let the games begin! A dividing line separates the teams. When you shoot the "enemy," you deactivate his phaser. He has to go to the energy pod and reactivate it to get back into the game. Of course, if you get hit, you must do the same thing. A scoreboard keeps track of which team is ahead, and which team ultimately wins. Each exciting game lasts for about ten minutes. But just like potato chips, it's hard to stop at just one (game). Roller skating is a separate activity from laser tag. Call for skate sessions.

Hours: Laser Storm is open Thurs., 7:30pm - 10pm; Fri., 6:30pm - 11pm; Sat., 10am - 4; 6:30pm - 11pm; Sun., 1:30pm - 5:30. Call for extended summer hours. The arena can be reserved at other times for groups. Call for skate sessions.

Admission: Laser Storm costs $3.50 for the first game; $2.50 for additional games. Skate sessions vary in cost depending on the date and time. In-line skate rentals are an additional $3.

Ages: 6 years and up.

SALVATION ARMY RAY AND JOAN KROC CORPS COMMUNITY CENTER ☼
(619) 287-5762 / www.kroccenter.org $$
6845 University Avenue, San Diego   ♨
(Exit I-8 S. on 70th St., R. on University Ave. The facility is located between 69th St. and Aragon St. [TG: 1270 E4])

Oh my gosh - this facility is amazing! This long series of buildings contains so many wonderful activities and programs that if it's not offered here, it must not be fun. (That might be a slight exaggeration, but only a slight one.)

The indoor skate park has great ramps, some grinding poles, and other skater favorites. Pads, a helmet, and a parental waiver form for ages 17 and under are required. Check out the recreation field for soccer, flag football, and lacrosse. The field also has a walking track. Feeling challenged? Try the adjacent outdoor challenge course which offers both high-and low-rope elements and a thirty-foot tall climbing tower. This is where you can actually go climb a rock! A parental waiver must be signed for kids 17 years and under.

Join in and play a game of basketball, volleyball, and badminton in the gym. Adults are welcome to use the fitness area for aerobics, weight training, kickboxing, and other exercise equipment and classes. Babysitting is available for members only. Just hang out in the recreation room or pick up a game of air hockey, billiards, table tennis, foosball, and/or play a board game. Swim a couple of laps in the twenty-five meter competition pool or just splash around on a hot summer's day. The ice arena is open for general skating sessions, skating lessons, and for hockey leagues. Non-participants can watch from ringside seats. (Brrrring a jacket!)

The performing arts center boasts a 600-seat theater where family-appropriate shows are presented. The center also has a dance studio, band and orchestra room, large multi-purpose room, art workshop rooms, and vocal practice room. A fireside reading room, computer lab, classrooms, church classes, and an abundance of programs (i.e. day camps, after-school programs, etc.) for all ages and interests complete this center. Also note that this is the Salvation Army's food and toy distribution center during the holidays. Whew!

Each activity has its own hours, prices, skill levels, and age requirements, so please call first. Note that all sessions require a minimum number of participants for the session to proceed. The following is information on some of the more popular features.

Hours: The skate park is open daily. Beginners, intermediates, and advanced skaters each have their own assigned time. Each session is two hours long. Call for a specific schedule. General ice skating sessions are two hours long and available daily. Call for a schedule. Rock climbing is open Mon. and Wed., 2:30pm - 5:30pm; Sat., 1pm - 4pm. The Challenge course is open Sat., 1pm - 4pm. The pool is open Mon. - Fri., 1pm - 5pm; Sat. - Sun., noon - 6pm. The recreation center is open daily.

Admission: Note that with most sessions, members pay $1 less than the non-member prices I've listed. Tip: Ask about multi-use passes and membership rates. Skateboarding is $4 per session. Ice skating is $6. Skate rentals are $2.50. Rock climbing is $5. The challenge course is $5. Swimming and gymnasium combo is $5 for adults; $4 for seniors; $3 for kids 6 - 17. The recreation center is $2 for all day play.

Ages: Skateboarders and challenge course users must be at least 6 years old. Swimmers 6 and under must be accompanied by an adult.

SOLID ROCK GYM (Poway)   ☼
(619) 299-1124 / www.solidrockgym.com $$$$
13026 Stowe Drive, Poway   ♨

(Exit Escondido Fwy [15] E. on Poway Rd., R. on Pomerado Rd., L. on Stowe. [TG: 1190 E6])

See the entry for SOLID ROCK GYM (San Diego) below for details.

SOLID ROCK GYM (San Diego)

(619) 299-1124 / www.solidrockgym.com

2074 Hancock Street, San Diego

(Going S. on San Diego Fwy [5], exit at Old Town Ave. off the off ramp onto Hancock St. Going N. on 5, exit at Moore St., L. on Old Town Ave, L. on Hancock St. [TG: 1268 G6])

Experience the thrill and physical challenge (i.e. you'll get sweaty) of rock climbing in a safe, indoor, controlled atmosphere. Novice climbers can learn the basic skills and importance of a well-placed foot and/or hand, while experienced climbers will enjoy the opportunity to continue training by sharpening their skills. This is a great sport to introduce kids to because it builds confidence, physical fitness, and strategic thinking. (All this just by rock climbing - and we thought school was important!) Staff members are experienced climbers and are always around to instruct and encourage, although everyone must bring their own belayer.

Multi-colored stones mark various routes on the walls, overhangs, and the bouldering cave. Although a child may be tentative at the beginning, by the end of the first time, he/she is usually literally climbing the walls, and having a great time doing it. So, if you're looking for a creative way to channel your child's excess energy, turn off the cartoons and come *rock* and roll on Saturday mornings! Note: A party room is on the premises. Lessons and membership are available.

Hours: Open Mon. - Fri., 11am - 7pm; Sat., 9am - 9pm; Sun., 11am - 7pm.

Admission: An all-day pass Mon. - Fri. is $12 for any age; weekend prices are $15 for adults; $13 for ages 16 and under. Harness and equipment costs are an additional $6.

Ages: 5 years and up.

SOLID ROCK GYM (San Marcos)

(619) 299-1124 / www.solidrockgym.com

992 Rancheros Drive, San Marcos

(Going W. on 78 Fwy, exit at Woodland Pkwy., R. on Rancheros at end of off ramp. Going E. on 78, exit E. on Barham Dr., L. on Woodland (under the fwy.), R. on Rancheros. [TG: 1109 B7])

See the entry for SOLID ROCK GYM (San Diego) above for details.

SURF AND TURF

(858) 481-0363 / www.surfandturfgolf.com

15555 Jimmy Durante Boulevard, Del Mar

(Exit San Diego Fwy [5] W. on Via de la Valle, L. on Jimmy Durante Blvd. [TG: 1187 G2])

Next to this driving range are two, eighteen-hole, miniature golf courses. The courses have the mandatory embellishments of small structures and other objects to putt through and around, plus plenty of twists and turns to keep the holes interesting and fun. Note: Older kids might want to try out a bigger back swing at the driving range.

Hours: Open daily, 8am - dark.

Admission: $5 per person - for as many rounds as you want to play.

Ages: 4 years and up.

ULTRAZONE (San Diego)

(619) 221-0100 / www.ultrazonesandiego.com

3146 Sports Arena Boulevard, San Diego

(Going W. on Ocean Beach Fwy [8], exit before the end of the freeway S. on Midway Dr./Mission Bay Dr., L. on Sports Arena Blvd. [TG: 1268 E5])

Come play laser tag - the tag of the future! Put on your vest, pick up your laser gun, and for fifteen minutes you'll play hard and fast. Laser tag is action-packed, and the thrill of the chase really gets your adrenaline pumping! This Ultrazone, with its dark, cave-like setting, is themed "Underground City." The multi-level city, or playing arena, is huge. Run up and down ramps; seek cover behind floor-to-ceiling walls; duck into partly-hidden doorways; and zap your opponents. Tip: The best time for younger kids to play is weekday afternoons and early evenings, or during the day on weekends. Older kids come out here in hordes at nighttime.

Hours: Open Mon. - Thurs., 4pm - 11pm; Fri., 2pm - 2am; Sat., 10am - 2am; Sun., 10am - 11pm. Summer hours vary.

Admission: $7 a game. Sat. and Sun. from opening until 2pm is Kids Zone, where kids 10 and under pay $5.50 per game - games must be completed by 2pm.

Ages: Must be at least 7 years old.

VERTICAL HOLD SPORT CLIMBING CENTER, INC.

(858) 586-7572 / www.verticalhold.com

9580 Distribution Avenue, San Diego

(Exit Jacob Dekema Fwy [805] E. on Miramar Rd., L. on Distribution Ave. Or, exit Escondido Fwy [15] W. on Pomerado Rd./Miramar Rd., R. on Distribution Ave. [TG: 1228 J1])

Indoor rock climbing is rapidly becoming one of the fastest growing indoor sports in America. This physically challenging and mentally stimulating activity is a great way to redirect a child growing up in our couch potato/video game society. Vertical Hold has over 200 routes that are changed every few months. Climb vertical walls (of course!), overhangs, and chimney routes, or try your hand (and feet) at bouldering. You need to bring your own belayer (i.e. the person who stays on the ground attached to your rope so if you should slip or fall, you won't fall far). If you, as an adult, don't know how to belay, an instructor can show you the ropes. Don't just crawl out from under a rock - go climb it! Note: A party area is available here.

Hours: Open Mon. - Fri., 11:30am - 10pm; Sat., 10am - 9pm; Sun., 10am - 8pm. Kids are welcome to climb at any time with a belayer.

Admission: Adults (or children) with their own equipment - $13 a day; $95 for 10 visits; or $6 per visit at lunchtime (between 11:30am - 1:30pm). Otherwise, it's $18 a day with equipment rental of a harness, rope, shoes, and chalk included in this price. Sat. - Sun. prices are $12 per child, 15 years and under, which includes equipment.

Ages: 5 years and up.

VISTA ENTERTAINMENT CENTER / LASER STORM

(760) 941-1032

435 W. Vista Way, Vista

(Exit 78 Fwy N. on Melrose Dr., R. on W. Vista Wy. [TG: 1087 G7])

(Laser) lights! Action! Laser Storm is a quick, action-packed game of laser tag. The arena is designed with cardboard hanging partitions painted with neon-colored "gak" splats. There are no solid walls to hide behind, so you need to be constantly on your guard and ready to fire. The ten-minute games, played nearly in the dark, are played by shooting laser guns at the opposite team members' vests and/or at their base, to score points. When you are hit - not "if" because you will get hit - you'll be unable to shoot for just a few seconds while your gun is being recharged. Laser Storm might not be as elaborately set-up as other laser tag places, but it is less expensive and a lot of fun!

Score more fun when you bowl in the lanes just outside the Laser Storm doors. The Entertainment Center has a large bowling alley, a small video games room, a full-service snack bar, and a nice-sized nursery/childcare room.

Hours: Laser Storm is open Mon. - Thurs., 6pm - 10pm; Fri., 6pm - midnight; Sat., noon - midnight; Sun., noon - 8pm. Hours do fluctuate. Call for open bowling times.

Admission: Laser Storm is $3 per game Mon. - Thurs.; $3 Fri. - Sun. Ask about specials.

Ages: 6 years and up.

WEEKEND WARRIORS

(619) 445-1217 / www.paintballfield.com

25 Browns Road on the Viejas Indian Reservation, Alpine

(Exit Interstate 8 N. on Willows, R. on Browns Rd. [TG: 1235 A5])

$$$$$

True to its name, you look like (and probably feel like) a warrior in this game of paintball. Suited up with a full, wrap-around face shield and a paint ball gun (and maybe even some camouflage clothing), you are ready to play a combination of Tag, Hide-and-Go-Seek, and Capture the Flag, at one of eighteen outdoor "battlefields." Moving stealthily through the trees, using rocks as covers, you spy an opponent, then pull the trigger, and splat - he/she has been tagged (ouch!) with a paint ball and is out of the game. (Realize that this can happen to you, also.) Each game lasts about fifteen minutes. Strategizing and staying focused are key elements. (Oh yea, and having fun, too.) Your admission fee includes all-day play, which is about fifteen games, and one tank of CO_2. Wear dark clothing that you don't care much about, and expect it to get very dirty. Ask about kids-only events. Participants under 18 must have a waiver signed by a parent or guardian. Tip: Paint ball is a great way to burn calories! Note: Next to the field is a full-service grocery store, two restaurants, and an RV park and campground with a pool, showers, and Jacuzzi.

Hours: Open Sat. - Sun. and certain school holidays, 8am - 4pm.

Admission: $25 includes field entrance, semi-auto gun rental, all day air, goggles, and a face shield. $35 includes all of the above plus 200 paintballs, a camo jacket, pods, and a belt. Prepaid groups of ten or more save a lot of money on entrance and rental equipment. Parents play free with a paying child, although parents must purchase their paintballs here.

Ages: As young as 10 years old with a parent; 12 years and up on their own.

-----GREAT OUTDOORS-----

AGUA CALIENTE SPRINGS COUNTY PARK

(858) 694-3049 - park; (619) 565-3600 - reservation / www.co.san-diego.ca.us/parks

39555 Great Southern Overland Stage Route of 1849, Agua Caliente Hot Springs

(From 8 Fwy head E. to Ocotillo, N. on Imperial Hwy [S2]. It's about 25 miles to the park. From Route 78 head E. through Julian, S. on S2. [TG: 430 D3])

$

For a more therapeutic take on life, come visit Agua Caliente Springs County Park. It features a big, glass-enclosed pool with water temperature maintained at 102 degrees as it is fed by underground hot mineral springs. Ahhhh - feels so good! However, only kids 56" and up and adults may use the indoor pool. The fifteen-foot by thirty-foot shallow outdoor pool is fun for children to use, though.

The park also has a general store, shuffleboard courts, horseshoe pits, play areas, hiking trails and over 140 campsites. There are several trails to choose from, including a half-mile loop called Ocotillo Ridge Nature Trail and a more arduous two-and-a-half-mile trail called Moonlight Canyon Trail. The park is pretty and parts of it are lush with lots of plants and trees fed by the natural springs running throughout. Look for the many species of birds, and other wildlife, that call it home.

Hours: The park is open Labor Day through Memorial Day, Mon. - Thurs., 9:30am - 6pm; Fri. - Sun., 9:30am - 9pm. The indoor pool is open daily for day use and over night campers, 10am - 5:30pm. It is open just for adults at other times. The outdoor pool is open March through May daily, 9:30am - 5pm; September through February daily, 9:30am - sunset. The park is closed for the summer.

Admission: $2 per vehicle for day use. Use of the pools are included in this fee. Camping costs between $10 (tents) - $16 (full hook-ups) a night. There is an additional $3 fee for camping reservations.

Ages: 3 years and up.

ANZA BORREGO STATE PARK

(760) 767-5311 - state park; (760) 767-4205 - visitor center; (760) 767-4684 - wildflower hotline; (800) 444-7275 - camping reservations. / www.anzaborrego.statepark.org

$

200 Palm Canyon Drive, Borrego Springs

(From San Diego: Exit 8 Fwy N. on Cuyamaca Hwy [79], through Julian, go E. on San Felipe Rd [S-2] about 4.5 miles, L. on Montezuma Valley Rd. [S-22] into Borrego Springs, L. at first stop sign, Palm Cyn. Dr., which dead-ends into the Visitors Center. Look for the flagpole as the Visitors Center building is hidden. From Escondido Fwy [15], exit E. Rt.79 through Warner Springs, S. on S-2, then look at the directions from San Diego for the park entrance. From San Diego Fwy [5], exit E. on 78 Fwy to Julian. Take 78 E. out of Julian, N. on Yaqui Pass Rd. [S-3], L. on Borrego Springs Rd., L. on Palm Cyn. Dr. [S-22], stay on Palm Canyon to the end. [TG: 410 B8])

This massive state park is over 600,000 acres of living desert, which includes palm trees, flowers, oases, bighorn sheep, and lizards, plus sand, rocks, mountains, and much more. The following description merely touches on a few of the activities and places that this park has to offer. Remember that this is a desert and the temperatures can reach over 125 degrees during the summer - always bring water!!! Nighttime temperatures can drop drastically, no matter what time of year, so be prepared for anything!

As with any major park, your best bet is to start at the Visitors Center. Get familiar with the park by watching the slide show that is presented upon request, and looking at the exhibits such as taxidermied animals and photographs. Be sure to pick up trail guides and a map.

Anza Borrego has some of the most incredible scenery in Southern California and although much of it can be seen by driving through the park, the really awe-inspiring vistas and landscape can only be seen by hiking. Within the park, take your choice of hiking trails which range from easy loops to arduous "mountain man" trails. One of the most popular hikes is a one-and-a-half-mile nature trail from the Borrego Palm Canyon campground up through Borrego Palm Canyon. The end of the trail is a sight for sore eyes (and hot bodies) - a refreshing waterfall with a pool! Parking is available near the trail entrance for $5 per vehicle.

There are several campsites available in this gigantic park, including one for campers with horses. Tip: Try to choose a site that has some shelter from the desert winds that blow in seemingly at random. For more information call the park office at the number above.

See the previous entry, AGUA CALIENTE SPRINGS COUNTY PARK, as it located at the southern part of Anza Borrego park, as well as OCOTILLO WELLS STATE VEHICULAR RECREATION AREA (see pg. 458).

Hours: The park is open 24 hours a day, 365 days a year. The Visitor's Center is open October through May daily, 9am - 5pm. It's open June through September on weekends and holidays only, 9am - 5pm.

Admission: Free. Day use in a camping spot is $5. Overnight camping prices range from $7 - $19 a night, depending on location and facility. Camping reservations are an additional $7.50.

Ages: 3 years and up.

BALBOA PARK
(619) 239-0512 / www.balboapark.org
Balboa Park, San Diego

See the entry for BALBOA PARK on page 408 for details.

BATIQUITOS LAGOON ECOLOGICAL RESERVE
(760) 943-7583; (760) 845-3501 - Fri. - Sun., 10am - 2pm. / www.batiquitosfoundation.org
E. Batiquitos Drive, Carlsbad

(Going N. on San Diego Fwy [5], exit E. on La Costa Ave., L. on El Camino Real [S-11], L. on Aviara Pkwy, L. on Batiquitos Dr. Going S. on 5, exit E. on Poinsettia Ln, R. on Batiquitos. From Batiquitos, follow lagoon and look for parking. [TG: 1127 D7])

Although we parked at an overlook point, this pretty walking trail (no bikes allowed) is mostly a fairly level hard dirt pathway. The trail is sandwiched between a golf course on one side (that boasts a beautiful waterfall) and the lagoon on the other. There is even a branch of the trail that goes closer to the water for a short ways. Bring binoculars for a more up-close look at the wide variety of birds that flock here. Along the almost two-mile, non-looping trail, are trees, benches, and interpretative signs that describe the critters that call this salt marsh their home.

A nature center, housed in a trailer at the end of Gabbiano Lane, has birds, rocks, trail guides, and some reference materials. Stop by here if you get a chance.

Hours: The lagoon is open daily, dawn - dusk. The nature center is usually open Wed., Thurs., and Sat., 10am - 2pm.

Admission: Free

Ages: All; strollers/wheelchairs are O.K. for a good part of the path.

BELL GARDENS

(760) 749-6297 / www.bellgardensfarm.com

30841 Cole Grade Road, Valley Center

(Going S. on Escondido Fwy [15], exit E. on Gopher Canyon Rd. (near Escondido) and cross the freeway. Turn R. onto Champagne Blvd., L. on Old Castle Rd. until it joins with Lilac Rd. Continue S.E. on Lilac Rd., L. on Valley Center Rd., L. on Cole Grade Rd. and look for entrance on R. Going N. on 15, exit E. on Valley Pkwy and follow it through Escondido until it becomes Valley Center Rd., L. on Cole Grade Rd. [TG: 1070 F3])

What Mexican fast food restaurant rings a bell with your kids? Yes - Taco Bell! Glen Bell, founder of Taco Bell, is also the founder of this delightful garden. This agricultural learning center is also a real working farm that encompasses 115 acres of cultivated fields, a greenhouse, a creek bed, walking trails that are stroller/wheelchair friendly, lawns for picnicking and play (you are welcome to bring your own food), a tractor-drawn hay wagon ride, and a quarter-scale train ride with two-and-a-half miles of tracks. Your rides, depending on the season, take you past cornfields, tomato plants, various other vegetables, and a pumpkin patch, plus a small lake (stocked with catfish - no fishing allowed), and through an oak grove. The on-site produce stand sells fresh-picked, seasonal fruits and veggies, such as artichokes, beans, carrots, garlic, Indian corn, melons, peas, rhubarb, spinach, and strawberries, plus some newer food combos such as yellow seedless watermelon and lemon cucumbers. You may pick some of the produce yourself, too. For instance, pick a half of flat of strawberries for $7. Gourds and dried flower arrangements are also available for purchase.

Bell Gardens also offers seasonal events and activities, guided tour programs for groups of twenty or more during the week, and farm-related classes and workshops. For instance, the general farm tour, which is offered year round, consists of a veggies show-and-tell, samples to taste, and a walk through and to the demonstration gardens for a visit - $3 per person. The Strawberry Pick, offered April through June, lets visitors learn all about the crop and then pick a basket full of berries - $5 per child. A walk through a corn maze and exploration of the pumpkin patch is offered in October. Most of the tours also include the hay ride and train ride. Note: For your information, you'll pass an Arabian Horse Farm on the way into Bell Gardens.

Hours: Open daily, 11am - 5pm. Call for summertime hours. The train and hay rides are open weekends only from 11am - 3pm. Tours are offered during the week for groups of twenty or more. Closed Thanksgiving, December, January, and February, and during inclement weather.

Admission: Free general admission to the gardens. $3 includes both a ride on the train and a hayride for ages 3 and up; children 2 and under are free.

Ages: All

BLUE SKY ECOLOGICAL RESERVE

(858) 679-5469 / tchester.org/sd/places/bs/blue_sky.html

Espola Road & Green Valley, Poway

(Exit Escondido Fwy [15] E. on Rancho Bernardo Rd., which turns into Espola. [TG: 1170 G3])

Head for the hills! From the parking lot, that is your only option. The large, mostly hard-packed dirt fire road follows along a seasonal creek into the hills. The main trail, leading to 700 acres of nature, is surrounded by tall, leafy oak and sycamore trees, and shrubs. One trail branches off to hook up at the neighboring LAKE POWAY (see pg. 393). Bring your own water. No bikes allowed. Guided groups hikes, such as Owl Prowl and Star Party, are offered several times throughout the year.

Hours: Open daily, sunrise - sunset.

Admission: Free

Ages: 4 years and up.

BRENGLE TERRACE PARK

(760) 726-1340 / www.ci.vista.ca.us

1200 Vale Terrace Drive, Vista

(Exit 78 Fwy N.E. on Escondido, R. on E. Vista Way, R. on Vale Terrace. [TG: 1088 A5])

Lighted ball fields, multi-purpose fields, and basketball courts are here as well as tennis courts, volleyball courts, picnic tables, a tot lot play area, horseshoe pits, a gym, and an amphitheater. Come play! See Musicals Under the Stars (pg. 585) for information on the programs at Moonlight Amphitheater.

Hours: Open daily, sunrise - sunset.
Admission: Free
Ages: All

CABRILLO NATIONAL MONUMENT

(619) 557-5450 / www.nps.gov/cabr

Cabrillo Memorial Drive, at the southern end of Point Loma, San Diego

(Take Ocean Beach Fwy [8] to the end, L. on Sunset Cliffs Blvd., L. on Nimitz Blvd., S. on 209. Follow the signs. [TG: 1308 A2])

In 1542 Juan Rodriguez Cabrillo sailed into San Diego Bay and claimed it for Spain. A huge statue of Cabrillo, commemorating his epic voyage along the western coast of the U.S., resides on the tip of the peninsula at this national park. Press the button near the monument to hear the history of Cabrillo and the bay area.

Older kids will appreciate the exhibit hall in the building behind the monument. Displays include maps and drawings of the areas Cabrillo and other explorers "discovered"; lots of written information; examples of food eaten on board ship, like dried fish and hardtack; and models of ships. The adjacent Visitors' Center offers pamphlets, film programs, and guided walks of this area, plus a book shop and an incredible view.

Before walking out to Point Loma Lighthouse, which was used from 1855 to 1891, listen to its history by pressing an outside storyboard button. We listened to it in Japanese and German [as well as English] - just for the fun of it. Kids think it's great to actually climb up the spiral staircase inside the refurbished lighthouse. The odd-shaped bedrooms are fully furnished with period furniture and knickknacks, as is the small living room, kitchen, and dining room. The entrance to the top floor is closed by a grate, but you can look through it and see the huge light that was a beacon to so many sailors.

Take the Bayside Trail, about two miles round trip, to walk further out to the point. Along the way look for remnants of a coastal artillery system used during both world wars. The trail goes down through a coastal sage scrub "forest." Topside of the trail, behind plexiglass, is a whale overlook. From late December through March, catch a glimpse of the gray whales during their annual migration. Audio information is, again, available at the touch of a button. (This time we listened to explanations in French and English.) Even if you don't see a whale, the view is spectacular.

From this viewpoint, look down to see the rocky marine environment of the tidepools. A driveable road from the monument leads down to them. Check with a park ranger for dates and times of low tides. Exploring tidepools is always a wondrous adventure for my kids. See and touch (but don't bring home) sea stars, anemones, and limpets, and be on the lookout for crabs and even octopus. Tip: Be sure to bring your camera, wear rubber-soled shoes (the rocks get slippery), and keep a close eye on your little ones! Ask about free, ranger-guided school tours for third to fifth graders for the tidepools, monument, and surrounding parkland.

Hours: Open daily, 9am - 5:15pm.
Admission: $5 per vehicle (which is valid for up to 7 days); $2 for walk-ins; seniors are free.
Ages: 3 years and up.

CACTUS SPORTS COUNTY PARK

(619) 390-6017 or (619) 448-2718 / www.lakesideca.com/parks

10567 Ashwood, Moreno

(Exit San Vicente Fwy [67] E. on Mapleview, L. on Ashwood. It's next to El Capitan highschool. [TG: 1232 B2])

Cactus County Park has a few memorable features. On the west side of the road this dirt park has baseball fields with stadium seating and a rugged BMX track. Practices are held on Fridays and Saturdays. Racing is done on Monday and Thursday evenings, and Saturday mornings. Call for more information. On the east side of the road is a model airplane runway and work station. Bring your own airplane or just come to watch them soar above the surrounding hillsides.

Hours: Open daily, dawn - dusk.
Admission: Free. Call for BMX prices.

CARLSBAD SKATE PARK

(760) 434-2851
25600 Orion Way, Carlsbad
(Exit San Diego Fwy [5] E. on Palomar Airport Rd., L. on El Camino Real, R. on Faraday, L. on Orion Way. [TG: 1127 E1])

This good-sized, non-supervised lighted skate park features cement bowls and other fun street elements, plus a beginner's area. The park is located between the police and fire departments. Wearing safety gear is enforced by the policemen that drive by. A small circle of grass is across the way and a baseball diamond is just down hillside.

Hours: Open daily, 8am - 10pm.
Admission: Free
Ages: 8 years and up.

CHOLLAS LAKE

(619) 527-7683 / www.sannet.gov/park-and-recreation/centers
6350 College Grove Drive, San Diego
(Exit Martin Luther King Jr Fwy [94], N.W. on Broadway/College Ave., L. on College Grove Dr. [TG: 1270 D7])

This sixteen-acre reservoir lake, surrounded by trees, is a designated fishing lake just for youth, ages 15 and under only. How great to be a kid! A short dirt path that goes partially around the lake is popular with bicyclists and joggers. There are picnic tables with barbecue grills, a play area, and a small basketball court. Ask about the fishing clinics and ranger-guided nature walks.

Hours: Open daily, 6:30am - a half hour before sunset. Closed New Year's Day, Thanksgiving, and Christmas.
Admission: Free
Ages: All

CIVIC CENTER PARK / VISTA SKATE PARK

(760) 726-1340 / www.ci.vista.ca.us
600 Eucalyptus Avenue, Vista
(Going W. on 78 Fwy, exit N. on Escondido Ave., R. on Eucalyptus. Going E. on 78, exit N. on Vista Village Dr., R. on Escondido, L. on Eucalyptus. [TG: 1087 J6])

This outdoor, 9,000 square foot cement skate park has curbs, small ramps, stairs, rails, platforms, all in bowl-shaped sides. Spectators watch from a slightly elevated standpoint. All participants must wear a helmet and knee and elbow pads, especially as the park is located near a police station. Picnic tables and a playground are also on the grounds. The surrounding park also has a grassy area and a playground.

Hours: Open Mon. - Fri. for bikes from 2:30pm - 4pm; skaters from 4pm - dusk. Open Sat. - Sun. for skaters from 10am - 2:30pm; bikes from 2:30pm - dusk.
Admission: Free
Ages: 7 years and up for the skate park.

CUYAMACA RANCHO STATE PARK / LAKE CUYAMACA

(760) 765-0755 - park; (800) 444-7275 - camping reservations / parks.ca.gov
12551 Cuyamaca Highway [79], Descanso, San Diego County
(Exit 8 Fwy N. on Hwy. 79, about 9½ miles up; or exit Hwy 78 [from Julian] S. on Hwy. 79. [TG: 1196 G6])

Retreat from the buildings, noise, and general busyness of city life to this outstanding state park with its

25,000 acres of pristine wilderness - a balm to the mind and soul. Take in the forests, grassy meadows, streams, peaks, and valleys that this park has to offer. There are over 120 miles of hiking trails and forty miles of biking trails along the fire roads and access roads. As the terrain varies, hiking trails vary in their degree of difficulty. Be on the lookout for birds, mule deer, lizards, coyotes, and other critters. Pick up a trail map (50¢) at the park headquarters, or call for one to be sent to you. While at the headquarters, go through the adjacent museum, which features Native American artifacts, and other exhibits regarding the history and the plant and animal life of this area.

Seasonal changes at this altitude of 4,000 feet are often drastic and beautiful: Autumn bursts on the scene with its rich colors of gold, red, and orange; winter brings a white blanket of snow; spring explodes with a profusion of brilliant wildflowers; and summer offers refreshment, by sitting near a stream, under a canopy of trees.

Want to go horseback riding through the mountainside, but don't own a horse? Call Adventure on Horseback riding stables, (619) 445-3997 / www.holidaysonhorseback.com, and enjoy a one-and-a-half-hour ($40 per person) or two-hour ($50 per person) excursion. Riders must be at least 7 years old. Ask about the half-day, lunch-included, ride, too. Reservations are needed for all rides - no walk-ins.

Campgrounds in the park, and some near rivers, are available for families at either Paso Picacho or Green Valley. You can hike to waterfalls from the latter campground. The campsites have picnic tables, fire rings, and heated showers (50¢). Paso Picacho also has a few one-room cabins available, too. You can even camp with your horse at specific campgrounds. Note that there are some great trails heading out directly from the campgrounds. We hiked up to the peak, which was arduous, but worth it.

Fishing or boating at Lake Cuyamaca, (760) 765-0515 / www.lakecuyamaca.org, is another way to enjoy this area. Motorboat rentals are $28 a day *or* rent a row boat at $14 a day. Canoes are $9 an hour. Fishing permits are $5 for adults; $2.50 for kids 8 to 15 years; children 7 years and under are free with a licensed adult. A California license is also required for ages 16 and up for $11.05. Depending on the season (and your luck), you can catch trout, catfish, bass, bluegill, and crappie. The lake is at the northern end of the park and a bait and tackle shop are located here, also. There is also a full-service restaurant at the lake - in case you don't catch your own meal! Camping at the lake is $14 for tent camping and $20 for RV.

Hours: The park is open daily, sunrise - sunset. The gift shop and museum are open Fri. - Mon., 10am - 4pm. Fishing and boat rentals are open daily, 6:30am - sunset. Call for extended summer hours.

Admission: There are several designated scenic turn-outs along Hwy. 79 that offer picnic tables and hiking trails; parking here is free. Parking for day use of a campground is $4 per vehicle. Camping is $12 a night off season; $15 from May to September. The camping reservation fee is $7.50. 12 X 12 cabins are $27 a night.

Ages: 2 years and up.

DALEY RANCH   ☼
                                                                                             !
(760) 741-4680 or (760) 839-6266 / www.ci.escondido.ca.us/visitors
3024 La Honda Drive, Escondido
(Exit Escondido Fwy [15] E. on El Norte Pkwy., L. on La Honda Dr. It's next to Dixon Lake. [TG: 1110 C3])

This 3,058-acre ranch is a hiking/mountain biking wilderness habitat preserve that offers a variety of terrain, from meadows to open grasslands to hills with rugged boulders. Twenty miles of main trails and offshoots traverse the property and range from wide, easy paved fire roads to narrow, up and down, dirt trails. We hiked the somewhat steep East Ridge route (1.6 miles) and reached two decent-sized ponds. Boulder Loop Trail (2.5 miles) offers a great view and rock "gardens." The wide Ranch House Loop Trail (2.5 miles) passes the site of Daley's original (unrestored) log cabin. The ranch house, built in 1927, will eventually become an interpretative center. On Sunday, a free shuttle service that runs every half hour, takes visitors from the parking area up a dirt road to the ranch house. Note: DIXON LAKE, see the below entry, is just "next door."

Hours: Open daily, dawn - dusk.

Admission: Free

Ages: 5 years and up.

DIXON LAKE

(760) 741-3328 or (760) 839-4680 / www.dixonlake.com
1700 N. La Honda Drive, Escondido
(Exit Escondido Fwy [15] E. at El Norte Pkwy, L. at La Honda Drive. Dixon Lake is to the R.; Daley Ranch is to the L. [TG: 1110 C3])

This beautiful get-away offers year-round fishing with promising areas of the reservoir titled Trout Cove, Catfish Cove, and Bass Point. Fish off the shoreline, off the piers, or rent a motorboat or row boat to try your luck. Paddle boat rentals are also available. The lake is cradled in pines, poplars and other vegetation along the surrounding hillsides. There are a few short walking trails along the lake. (For longer hikes, go "next door" to DALEY RANCH; see the above entry.) One picnic area, with a small playground and a patch of grass, is at the entrance of the park. Another, larger one, with some picnic shelters and more play equipment, is farther in. A concession stand is open seasonally.

Camping spots are up on the mountain ridge and overlook the valley on one side, the lake on the other. Some of the sites are a very short hike down from the parking area and therefore a bit more private than other sites. All in all - Dixon Lake is scenic and peaceful. Note: No swimming or biking is allowed.

Hours: Open daily, 6am - dusk.
Admission: $1 per vehicle. Camping is $12 a night, plus an advance registration fee of $5. Fishing is $5 for ages 16 and up; $4 for seniors; $3 for ages 8 - 15; children 7 and under are free. A fishing license is also required. Night fishing is available during summer months. Row boat rentals are $8 for half a day; $10 a full day. Motorboats are $14 for half a day; $18 a full day. Paddle boats are $6 a half hour for up to 4 people.
Ages: All

DOS PICOS REGIONAL PARK

(858) 694-3049 / www.co.san-diego.ca.us/parks
17953 Dos Picos Park Road, Ramona
(Exit Hwy 67 S. on Mussey Grade Rd., R on Dos Picos Rd. [TG: 1171 H5])

This is my kind of "secluded" wilderness - close to a small town, yet seventy-eight acres that are mostly al natural. Huge boulders dot the hillsides and a trail leads up amongst them. The valley of the park is filled numerous oak trees that provide wonderful shade, as well as open grasslands and chaparral. The park also provides a pond (those over 16 years old need a fishing license), play area, horseshoe pit, picnic area, exercise course, open play areas, and tent and RV camping. Ask about the programs offered here, such as the junior ranger program and the campfires that incorporate some old-fashioned family fun. There are other wilderness attractions (such as LAKE POWAY) not far away, and the town of Ramona is just around the bend.

Hours: Open daily, 9am - sunset. Closed Christmas.
Admission: $2 per vehicle per day. Tent camping is $12 a night; RV, $16.
Ages: All

FELICITA PARK

(760) 745-4379 or (619) 644-3366 / www.co.san-diego.ca.us/parks
742 Clarence Lane, Escondido
(Exit Escondido Fwy [15], E. on Citracado Pkwy., L. on Felicita Rd., R. on Clarence at the park entrance. [TG: 1149 J1])

This spacious, truly lovely woodland park beckons guests to play, hike, picnic, and climb on boulders. A large grassy area for running around and several playgrounds help make the park younger-child friendly. Older kids will enjoy the ball fields, horseshoe pits, and volleyball courts. Walk on trails through huge shady oak groves or near the rock-lined seasonal creek. Join in on the many ranger programs offered here that specialize in local and Native American history. For instance, take a tour to the Indian grinding holes and learn about the village life of the local Indian tribes, learn the brutal history of "treeing" a thief, or learn about backcountry safety. This park is also home to the Renaissance Faire (see pg. 573).

Hours: Open daily, 9:30am - sunset. Closed Christmas.
Admission: $2 per vehicle.
Ages: All

IMPERIAL SAND DUNES

(760) 337-4400 / www.ca.blm.gov

On Highway 78, Glamis

(Exit State 78, between Highway 111 and Highway S34, near the city of Glamis, which is near the borders of Mexico and Arizona. North of the 78 is the dunes wilderness; south is open for off-road vehicles. [TG: 431 H1])

The expansive Imperial Sand Dunes, also referred to as the Algodones Dunes, extend for over forty miles - almost as far as the eye can see. They change in appearance from smooth surfaces to rippling waves, depending on the prevailing winds. They conjure up images of science fiction flicks, or of a lone sunburnt person clothed in rags crawling across them desperately crying out, "Water, water!" Tip: Bring your own water.

Stop off first at the Osborne Overlook, located two miles east of Gecko Road along SR78. Here you'll see a great view of the dunes and the surrounding Imperial Valley. The appropriately named "wilderness" area is north of the 78, between Ted Kipf Road and the Coachella lands. A viewing area is two miles north of Glamis along Ted Kipf Road. Awe-inspiring dunes are towards the west side, while the east side has mostly smaller dunes and washes. The region is open for you to walk, run, jump, and roll down the dunes. Horseback riding is also allowed. Note that summer temperatures can rise to 110 degrees, so the most favorable months to visit are between October and May. Bring your sunglasses, camera, and a bucket and shovel.

The area south of the highway is open for tent and RV camping, off-highway vehicles (OHVs), and all-terrain vehicles (ATVs). Dune buggies are not readily available for rent, so you must bring your own vehicle. Camping is primitive, and trash must be packed out. For more information and an area map, call the BLM (i.e. Bureau of Land Management) at the above number.

Hours: Open daily, sunrise - sunset.

Admission: $10 for a week pass.

Ages: It depends on how far you want to hike, or if you are content with just playing in the sand.

JACK'S POND

(760) 744-9000 / www.ci.san-marcos.ca.us/cs/facility/jackpond/jackpond.htm

986 La Moree Road, San Marcos

(Going E. on Hwy 78, take Barham Dr/Woodland Pkwy, bear R. on Rancheros Dr , R. on Woodland Pky, L. Barham Dr. R. La Moree. Going W. on 78, exit S. on Barham, R. on La Moree. [TG: 1129 B1])

This clean, small park with two barn-like structures offers a tot play area, a fenced-in grassy area, a pond, short hiking trails, a youth center building, and a Wildlife Discovery Center. This little discovery center has some fun hands-on exhibits, activities, and programs. It contains rocks, live bunnies, sand tables with models to make animals tracks, and more. Fishing is allowed at the pond. Children 16 years and under do not need a fishing license. A trail is in the works that will go around most of the pond.

Hours: The park is open daily, sunrise - sunset. The discovery center is open Sat., 9am - noon.

Admission: Free

Ages: 10 years and under.

KIT CARSON PARK / ESCONDIDO SPORTS CENTER

(760) 839-4691 - park; (760) 839-5425 - sports center / www.ci.escondido.ca.us/sportscenter; www.ci.escondido.ca.us/visitors/parks/kit

3333 Bear Valley Parkway, Escondido

(Exit Escondido Fwy [15] E. on Via Ranch Pkwy which turns into Bear Valley Pkwy. [TG: 1150 B2])

Come to where the action is! A "state-of-the-art" outdoor sports center is located in the heart of Kit Carson Park. It has an arena soccer field with bleachers, a roller hockey arena, a 20,000 square-foot skate park, and a pro shop and concession stand. The fully-lighted skate park is complete with variously-sized ramps, a full street course with rails, spine, pyramids, quarter pipes, a bowl, and more - impressive! At times the skate park is open for bikers as well as skaters. Bring your own safety equipment because it is mandatory. A parental waiver is required for participants 17 and under. Sign up for leagues, camps, and/or skate sessions, or just come to watch the action. A pond is located across the way from the Sports Center.

Just north of the center is the Humane Society and the rest of Kit Carson Park with its 185 undeveloped acres and 100 developed acres. It's very family-friendly with pretty landscaping, bridges over a creek, plenty of picnic tables, barbecue pits, green grassy areas for running around, nine ball fields (some with stadium seating), tennis courts, soccer fields, an amphitheater, a fitness course, a fitness trail with markers, hiking trails, a few playgrounds (plus one just for tots). Whew! The playgrounds feature a gigantic multi-arched cement snake, a Paul Bunyan-sized wagon tilted to slide down, a few climbing tree, and some paved pathways. This park handily accommodates all of your family's different activities.

Hours: The park is open daily, dawn - 10pm. Call for hours on the various sporting center activities. The skate park is open during the school year, Mon. - Fri., 4pm - 9:30pm; Sat. - Sun., 9am - 9:30pm. It's open for an additional session in the summer, Mon. - Fri., 9am - 11:30am. The first session on Wed. and Sat. is for kids 6 - 12 years only. The second session on Wed. and the last session on Sun. is for bikers only.

Admission: The park is free. Skate/bike sessions are $10 per two-a-half-hour session. Year memberships are available at $15 per person, which brings the cost of each session down to $4 during the week, $6 on weekends.

Ages: All

KRAUSE FAMILY SKATE PARK

(619) 279-9254 - skate park; (619) 298-3576 - Y.M.C.A. / missionvalley.ymca.org/facilities/skate.html $$
3401 Clairemont Drive, Clairemont
(Exit San Diego Fwy [5] E. on Clairemont.)

Skateboarders and roller bladers flip (not literally) for this huge (53,000 square feet!), gated outdoor skate park that's associated with the Mission Valley Y.M.C.A. It has numerous and variously-sized ramps and half pipes, plus grinding boxes, rails, and other street skate elements, as well as areas to simply skate. An large in-ground bowl has a maximum ten-foot depth - a favorite feature. There is also a good-sized beginner area. Sessions are three hours long. The park is supervised and all skaters must wear elbow and knee pads and a helmet. There are no rentals available. Bikes are allowed on certain days. Skaters and bikers 17 and under must have a waiver signed by a parent in person, or notarized, for their first session.

Hours: Open Mon. - Fri., 2pm - 5pm, 5pm - 8pm; Sat. - Sun., 11am - 2pm, 2pm - 5pm, 5pm - 8pm. Check on holidays hours.

Admission: $10 per session; or $20 for a membership, then $4 per session.

Ages: 7 years and up.

LA JOLLA INDIAN RESERVATION CAMPGROUND / TUBING ON SAN LUIS REY RIVER

$$$

(760) 742-1297 or (760) 742-3771 / www.lajollaindians.com
22000 Highway 76, on the La Jolla Indian Reservation, Pauma Valley
(Going S. on Escondido Fwy [15], exit E. on Rt. 76 and up about 28 mountain miles. Going N. on 15, exit N.E. on Valley Pkwy., which turns into Valley Center., R. on 76 and go about 8 miles. It's 100 yards N. of Segnme Oaks Rd., R. at the Texaco Gas Station. [TG: 409 G7])

Come to the campground just for the day, or spend a night or two here in the lush, semi-wilderness of the foothills of the beautiful Palomar Mountains. Hike amongst the beautiful foliage along the San Luis Rey River; climb the rocks on the river banks; try your luck at fishing; or wade in the river waters.

For more wet thrills, go inner tubing down the river along a two mile stretch, which takes about an hour. Hike back up to go again, or better yet, come here with a friend who drives and leave one car at each end. Parts of the river are idyllic, while other parts are a bit more exciting (and bumpy). Be prepared for this adventure by wearing a hat, tee shirt, sunscreen, and sneakers (for painlessly stepping on the rocks on the river bottom). B.Y.O.T. (Bring Your Own Tube) or rent an inner tube here for $6. Tip: Tie your inner tube to your child's so you can stay together!

Almost all of the camping sites are located right by the river. (The water can be soothing or loud, depending on how you interpret its sound.) If you are coming for the day, you are advised to bring your own table, chairs, and barbecues as those items are limited in number in the camp. Chemical toilets are scattered throughout the camp, and hot showers are available at designated places. Campfires are allowed. Firewood, tackle, supplies, and food are available at the small Trading Post on the grounds. Note that Sengme Oaks Water Park (see pg. 401) is just down the road.

Hours: Open March through November, sunrise - sunset. Tubing is usually available daily the end of April through September, 8am - 6pm. Call first.

Admission: $12 per vehicle for day use for up to four people; additional passengers are $2 per person. River tubing is included in this price. Tube rentals are $6. Camping is $18 per vehicle for tent campers for up to four people; $25 for RVs. No pet allowed.

Ages: 4 years and up.

LAKE JENNINGS COUNTY PARK   ☼

(619) 466-0585 or (858) 565-3600; (858) 565-3600 - camping; $
(619) 667-6293 - boating / www.co.san-diego.ca.us/parks
10108 Bass Road, Lakeside
(Exit San Vicente Fwy [67] E. on Mapleview St., which turns into Lake Jennings Park Rd., L. on Bass Dr. [TG: 1232 E4])

Fishing is the main draw here with trout, catfish, bass, and bluegill yours for the catching, depending on the time of year (and your luck). Fish from the shore seven days a week at the various coves, or venture out on the sprawling lake via boat on Fridays and Sundays only. Row boat rentals are $15 per a day; $30 a day for a motorized boat. The concession stand also sells bait. A daily permit and a California fishing license for those 16 years old and over are required. Permits are $4.75 for adults; $4.50 for seniors; $2.75 for ages 8 to 16; children 7 and under are free with a paying adult. Picnic tables overlook the lake. Miles of hiking across the chaparral-covered hills is another reason to visit Lake Jennings. And don't forget about tent and RV camping. There are some walk-back tent sites, too, which offer a bit more seclusion. Ask about the Saturday programs offered here. They can include making bird feeders, taking a nature walk, seeing and learning about snakes, and more.

Hours: The park is open daily, 9am - sunset. Fishing is allowed Mon. - Sat., 6am - dusk.

Admission: $2 per vehicle. Camping starts at $14 a night, plus a $3 reservation fee.

Ages: All

LAKE MORENA   ☼

(858) 694-3049 - general info; (858) 565-3600 - reservations; $
(619) 478-5473 - fishing info / www.co.san-diego.ca.us/parks
2550 Lake Morena Drive, Campo
(Exit Mission Valley Fwy [8] S. on Buckman Springs Rd., R. on Oak Dr., R. on Lake Morena. [TG: 1297 D5])

This large, remote reservoir/lake is surrounded by over 3,000 acres of wilderness. The landscape includes chaparral, oak woodlands, marshy grass areas, and more. The land really belongs to the wildlife - bald eagles, mountain lions, mule deer, migratory waterfowl, and others that roam (or fly over) the backcountry. Fishermen are lured to the lake in hopes of catching the big one, or at least, one. Fish from the boulder-lined shore or rent a boat. Hook trout in the winter and bass starting in the spring. Sometimes the fish are tagged so the anglers who catch them win a prize.

Hikers have a field day here. Explore the well-known Pacific Crest Trail, but don't try to reach the end as the trail terminates in Canada. Overnight tent and RV camping is available. The eighty-five sites are largely located under huge oak trees. Primitive cabins (i.e. no electricity and no water) sleep up to eight people. The lakeside view from the cabins is my kind of roughing it. There is a youth area campground also.

Hours: Open ½ hour before sunrise to ½ hour after sunset. Closed Christmas.

Admission: $2 per vehicle for day use. Camping is $12 - $16 a night; cabins are $25. Boat rentals are $8 - $30 a day. Fishing is $3.50 a day for adults; $2 for seniors and ages 8 - 15; children 7 and under are free.

Ages: 5 years and up.

LAKE POWAY RECREATION AREA

(858) 679-4393 - general info; (858) 679-5465 - lake info;
(858) 486-1234 - concession stand / www.ci.poway.ca.us
14164 Lake Poway Road, Poway
(Exit Escondido Fwy [15] E. on Rancho Bernardo Rd., which turns into Espola, L. on Lake Poway. [TG: 1170 H4])

Nestled between mountains, this pretty park features green grassy rolling hills, two playground areas, thirteen exercise stations, ball fields (one that is lighted), a sand volleyball court, picnic tables overlooking the lake, horseshoe pits, an archery range, and miles of dirt pathways and hiking trails. One trail, great for hardy hikers and mountain bikers, is a scenic, three-mile rocky trail that goes a good distance around the lake. More rugged trails include the two-and-a-half-mile hike up to Mt. Woodson, and trails leading into the adjacent BLUE SKY ECOLOGICAL RESERVE (see pg. 385). Be on the lookout for wildlife such as red-tail hawks, raccoons, and even deer.

The large Lake Poway is seasonally stocked with trout or catfish. Bait, fishing permits, and fishing licenses (for ages 16 years and up) can be purchased at the concession stand. Looking for something fun to tackle on summer nights? Try night fishing any Thursday, Friday, and/or Saturday night from 4pm to 11pm, Memorial Day through Labor Day. Boats rentals are available here: Rowboats - $10 a day; motorboats - $15 a day; paddle boats - $8 an hour; and canoes - $8 an hour.

Hours: Open daily, 7am - dusk. The lake is open for fishing and boating Wed. - Sun., sunrise - sunset.
Admission: Free for Poway residents; $4 per car for non-residents is charged April through October on weekends and holiday Mon. (It's free the rest of the year.) Fishing permits are $4.50 for adults; $2 for ages 8 - 15; free for ages 7 and under.
Ages: All

LAKEVIEW PARK and DISCOVERY LAKE

(760) 744-9000 / www.ci.san-marcos.ca.us/cs/facility/lakeview/lakeview.html
Foxhall and Poppy streets, San Marcos
(Exit Highway 78 S.W. on San Marcos Blvd., L. on S. Bent Ave., which turns in to Craven, R. on Foxhall. [TG: 1128 G3])

This attractive park has a small, younger children's play area by the parking lot with two wooden trains to climb on, a grassy area, and a covered picnic pavilion. An eight-acre lake is ringed by a ¾ mile smooth trail; half of which is paved in asphalt, the other half is hard-packed dirt. The pathway makes for a nice stroll or bike ride. A two-and-a-half mile trail branches off and leads up to the ridgeline (1,000 foot gain of elevation) for a wonderful view. Another trail, one mile long, follows along Discovery Creek.

Fishing is allowed in the lake, although one has to be fairly optimistic or incredibly lucky to catch anything as the lake is not stocked.

Hours: Open daily, dawn - dusk.
Admission: Free
Ages: All

LAS POSAS AQUATIC CENTER

(760) 599-9783 or (760) 744-9000 / www.san-marcos.net
N. Las Posas and W. Borden Roads, San Marcos
(Exit Hwy 78 N. on Rancho Santa Fe Rd., R. on Mission Rd., L. on Las Posas Rd. [TG: 1108 E5])

The park has two tennis courts, a huge treeless field, a soccer field, and a baseball diamond. The main attraction here is summertime fun in the heated pool that has a shallow water area for children and handicapped access ramp. A small water play "sprayground" on the deck adjacent to pool adds to the fun for younger children and a water play area for slighter older kids aids them in having a "cool" time. Restrooms and showers are here, too.

Hours: The park is open daily, dawn - dusk. The pool and sprayground are open seasonally, May to mid-September.
Admission: The park is free. Admission is $2 per person to the pool.
Ages: All

LIVE OAK PARK (Fallbrook)

(760) 723-8780 / www.co.san-diego.ca.us/parks
2746 Reche Road, Fallbrook
(Exit Escondido Fwy [15] E. on E. Mission Rd., L. on Live Oak Park Rd., L. on Reche at the park entrance. [TG: 1028 C5])

Ah - the pause that refreshes. As its name implies, this inviting park has a bounty of huge, old shady oak trees. Scattered picnic tables, a few play areas, softball fields, sand volleyball courts, and a few hiking trails also make this park a worthwhile place to visit. There is also a small botanic garden to meander through, plus a seasonal creek with bridges over it, stroller-friendly pathways, and exercise areas.

Hours: Open daily, 9:30am - sunset. Closed Christmas.
Admission: $2 per vehicle
Ages: All

LOS PENASQUITOS CANYON PRESERVE / CANYONSIDE RECREATION CENTER COMMUNITY PARK

(858) 538-8066 - preserve; (858) 484-7504 - ranch house;
(858) 484-3219 - friends of the preserve / hike schedule;
(858) 538-8105 - community park / www.sannet.gov/park-and-recreation/parks; www.penasquitos.org
12020 Black Mountain Road / 12350 Black Mountain Road, San Diego
(Exit Escondido Fwy [15] W. on Scripps Poway Pkwy/Mercy Rd. which ends at Black Mountain. [TG: 1189 D7])

This is a great "combo" destination meaning it has a combination of elements that appeal to various ages and interests. One part is the Canyonside Recreation Center which has a small playground, ten lighted tennis courts ($3 for non-members to play), picnic tables, grassy areas, seven baseball fields, and a community building. Another aspect of the park/preserve grounds is the 1824 adobe Rancho Santa Maria de los Penasquitos on Canyonside Drive. Forty-five-minute guided tours are offered on weekends of this second oldest standing residence in San Diego. Check out the three-foot thick walls of the adobe, and the Mexican and Indian artifacts as you tour through the kitchen, bedrooms, office, and mock schoolroom. A natural year round spring is on this site, too.

The largest portion of this attraction is the thousands of acres and six miles of Canyon Preserve. Hike through chaparral, wildflowers, sage, and riparian woodlands with oaks, sycamores, willows, and cottonwoods. Walk along a year round creek, among dense canyon vegetation, and past several ponds populated by fish, crayfish, and frogs (and tadpoles in season) to reach the year round waterfall. The boulder-lined waterfall carves through bedrock. It is reached by hiking inland about three miles or approximately half the length of the preserve. Coming from the western route, it is also reached by going through a few creek crossings. Bring a water bottle. The wildlife at the preserve is as rich and diverse as the plant life. Be on the lookout for mule deer, small mammals, lizards, birds, and, specifically, waterfowl. The crisscrossing trails are frequented by hikers, mountain bikers, and horseback riders. Ask about the numerous naturalist programs such as the geology hike, tracker walks (learn how to track animals), and ecology scavenger hunts.

Hours: The reserve is open daily, dawn - dusk. The ranch is open for guided tour Sat., 11am and Sun., 1pm. Call to reserve a school group tour during the week. The community park is open daily.
Admission: The preserve is free or $1 per vehicle, depending on where you park. Tours of the ranch house are $3 for adults; children 10 and under are free. The community park is free.
Ages: All

LOUIS A. STELZER PARK

(619) 561-0580 - park; (619) 390-7998 - Discovery Kit Program / www.lakesideca.com/parks
11470 Wild Cat Canyon Road, Lakeside
(Exit San Vincente Fwy [67] E. on Mapleview, L. on Ashwood, which turns into Wild Cat Canyon, drive up a few miles. [TG: 1212 C7])

What a delightful respite! The 314-acre back country park has two playgrounds and several clusters of picnic tables, with barbecues, under sprawling oak and sycamore trees. (My boys also found a few good climbing trees, of course.) The park is disabled-friendly with a wheelchair exercise par course, incorporating specially designed and standard play equipment, and pathways that are wheelchair/stroller accessible. A series of short hiking trails almost form a full loop. The .7 mile Riparian Trail begins near the ranger/visitor center and goes over a series of bridges as it follows along the seasonal creek. It connects to the Wooten Loop and then you have a choice. Go left onto the .6 mile Stelzer Ridge Trail, which meanders through oak groves, or go straight, which is a relatively quick climb up to the summit and promontory point.

The small visitor center has a few taxidermied animals and a Discovery Kit Program. Each kit features pre and post visit materials for teachers and involves hands-on, interactive learning for elementary-aged children to learn about Native Americans, geology, birding, or general ecology.

Hours: Open daily, sunrise - sunset.
Admission: $2 per car; bring quarters.
Ages: All

MAST PARK

(619) 258-4100 / www.ci.santee.ca.us/csd/index.htm
9125 Carlton Hills Boulevard, Santee
(Going N. on San Vicente Fwy [67], exit W. on Prospect Ave., R. on Cuyamaca St., L. on Mission Gorge Rd. Going S. on 67, exit W. on Woodside Ave., which turns into Mission Gorge. Going E. on Fwy 52, exit E. on Mission Gorge Rd. From Mission Gorge, go N. on Carlton Hills. [TG: 1231 B6])

This attractive park, that's located along a bank of the San Diego River, can get very populated. The front of the park is the play area, with a half basketball court, an exercise course, and a small playground in sand foundation. The large plastic boat-like shape here is fun for climbing into. Shade trees, picnic tables, and barbecues add to the family-friendly ambiance. There are two looping paved trails that go around the wooded back side of the park; a shorter trail and a slightly more extensive one. We came in autumn as the trees were losing their leaves and crunched underfoot as we walked the pathway.

Hours: Open daily, sunrise - sunset.
Admission: Free
Ages: All

MIRAMAR RESERVOIR

(619) 668-2050; (619) 390-0223 concessionaire / www.sannet.gov/water/recreation/miramar.shtml
Scripps Lake Drive, San Diego
(Exit Escondido Fwy [15] E. on Mira Mesa Blvd., R. on Scripps Ranch Blvd., L. on Scripps Lake Dr. [TG: 1209 G4])

Take a gander at all the geese and ducks waiting for a hand out at the reservoir. B.Y.O.B. (Bring Your Own Bread!) This lovely lake offers paddle boat and rowboat rentals, fishing, and lakeside picnic tables and barbecue areas. An almost seven-mile paved trail loops around the lake and, judging by the number of people we saw, it's ideal for walking, biking, rollerblading, and skateboarding. November through September families can enjoy fishing and boating. Fishermen 16 years and older need a fishing license and a permit which are available to purchase here. Rowboat rentals are $12 a day or $8 for just the afternoon. Two-seater paddle boats rent for $8 an hour; four-seaters are $10 an hour.

Hours: The park and perimeter trail is open daily, sunrise - sunset. The lake is open for fishing and boating Sat. - Tues., sunrise - sunset. The lake is closed for the month of October.
Admission: Free. Fishing permits are $5 for adults; $2.50 for ages 8 - 15; children 7 and under don't need a permit.
Ages: All

MISSION BAY PARK

www.sannet.gov/park-and-recreation/parks/missbay.shtml
2581 Quivira Court, San Diego

(Exit San Diego Fwy [5] W. on Clairemont Dr. to drive the Mission Bay loop - go S. on E. Mission Bay Dr. to Sea World Dr. to Mission Bay Dr. [or N. on Ingraham St.] to Grand Ave. [TG: 1268 A4])

Mission Bay Park is not a singular bay or park like the name implies - it is thousands of acres of incredibly beautiful vistas, and of beaches, water, pathways, playgrounds, grassy areas, and various attractions. Generic things to do include jogging, cycling, in-line skating, swimming (there are nineteen miles of beaches here!), picnicking, fishing, kayaking, sailing, paddle boating, and camping. Park at any one of the scenic spots you see along Mission Bay Drive, or Ingraham Street, and enjoy. Hot spots include: **Pacific Beach**, just north of Mission Beach on Mission Boulevard - a favorite hang out for surfers, swimmers, joggers, and others; **Fiesta Island**, just northeast of SeaWorld, and **Vacation Isle**, on Ingraham Street north of Sea World Drive - both have numerous biking trails, delightful picnic areas, and a few playgrounds; **South Mission Beach** and **North Mission Beach**, both along Mission Boulevard - popular beaches for swimming and laying out; and **De Anza Cove**, on E. Mission Bay Drive - a nice area for swimming.

A few helpful names and phone numbers in the Mission Bay area include: Campland on the Bay, (800) 4BAY-FUN (422-9386), for camping, with over 650 sites; Mission Beach Club, which is a building shaped like a castle, (858) 488-5050, for rentals of bikes, skates, boogie boards, and more; Mission Bay Sportcenter (858) 488-1004 / www.missionbaysportcenter.com, for rentals of Waverunners ($75 an hour), single kayaks ($13 an hour), double kayaks ($18 an hour), and more; and Windsport Kayak & Windsurfing Center, (858) 488-4642 / www.windsport.net, for single kayak ($15 an hour), double kayak ($20 an hour), and other rentals.

Attractions listed separately in Mission Bay Park are: BELMONT PARK (see pg. 373), PIRATE'S COVE (see pg. 379), SAN DIEGO VISITOR INFORMATION CENTER (see pg. 442), SEAWORLD (see pg. 469), and TECOLOTE SHORES PLAY AREA (see pg. 402). Check the website for a lot more information on this park.

> **Hours:** Open daily.
> **Admission:** Free
> **Ages:** All

MISSION TRAILS REGIONAL PARK

(619) 668-3275 / www.mtrp.org

One Father Junipero Serra Trail, San Diego

(There are several entrances to the park. From Mission Valley Fwy [8], exit N. on Mission Gorge/Fairmount and go 4 miles N. on Mission Gorge Rd. The Visitor and Interpretive Center entrance is on the L. between Jackson Dr. and Golfcrest Dr., on Father Junipero Serra Trail. From Route 52, exit S. when it ends on Mission Gorge Rd. If visiting the Old Mission Dam area, the Old Mission Dam entrance is about ½ mile down Mission Gorge Rd. The Visitor and Interpretive Center is about 2 miles further down Mission Gorge Rd. See directions from Fwy 8. [TG: 1250 D2])

This massive, almost 6,000-acre recreational area is comprised of several major areas and points of interest and fifty miles of trails. **The Visitor and Interpretive Center** - This architecturally beautiful building blends in with the natural rock setting of the park, and is a great starting place for an adventure. Every thirty minutes the small theater presents a film on the park. Pick up trail guides, program information, and/or enjoy some interactive exhibits inside. Kids gravitate to the Indian faces carved from "rocks." Several touch screens offer information about the park - where to go, and all about the plants and animals. Walk to the upper story of the center amid bird and animal sounds. See ancient volcanic rock and a great view of your surroundings. Outside the center is a small stage and rocks that are almost irresistible for kids to climb. The kids sweated (I glowed) as we hiked on the moderate looping trail around the Visitors Center, which took us a good hour. Our mission, should we decide to accept it, is to come back to Mission Trails and experience more of what it has to offer! **Lake Murray** (619) 668-2050 / www.sannet.gov/water/recreation/index.shtml - At the southern part of the park this beautiful, stocked lake allows fishing and boating activities from sunrise to sunset on Wednesdays, Saturdays, and Sundays between November and Labor Day. A paved trail goes partly around the lake. Picnic tables are also available. **Cowles Mountain** - Hiking is the main sport here. For an outstanding 360 degree view of the city, take the one-and-a-half-mile trail (about two hours) to the top of the mountain. **Old Mission Dam Historic Area** - This is a starting point for several hikes. Picnic tables are here, too. People of all abilities can go on a self-guided paved pathway from the parking lot to the footbridge across the San Diego River, lush with

foliage. Further along is the gorge with rock cliffs. Press buttons along the trail to listen to explanations of the area. Take a longer hike, too. So many trails - so little time! **East Fortuna Mountain** - This area offers some of the most diverse environments of the park. Check out some of the canyons! The smallish Kumeyaay Lake, accessible from Father Junipero Serra Trail, is fun for shoreline fishing. A relatively flat one-and-a-half-mile trail goes around the lake. Campers enjoy primitive camping here and the numerous programs offered for families. Call (619) 668-2748 for reservations and more information. **West Fortuna Mountain** - You can hike or mountain bike up plateaus and series of canyons.

Hours: The trails and park are open daily, sunrise - sunset, although the car entry gates are open 9am - 5pm. The Center is open daily, 9am - 5pm. Closed on Christmas.

Admission: Free

Ages: 3 years and up.

OCEAN BEACH ATHLETIC AREA / ROBB FIELD SKATEBOARD PARK

(619) 531-1527 - athletic area;
(619) 525-8486 - skate park / www.sannet.gov/park-and-recreation/centers
2525 Bacon Street, Ocean Beach
(Exit Ocean Beach Fwy [8] S. on Sunset Cliffs, R. on W. Point Loma, R. on Bacon. [TG: 1267 J5])

This huge park has something for every athlete in the family. It boasts eight baseball diamonds, soccer fields, racquetball courts, several tennis courts, a football field, lots of grass areas, picnic tables, a bike path that follows along the adjacent San Diego River, and a terrific skate park at the east end.

In front of the skate park are a few very shallow cement pools (more like a toe dip area than pool) and cement area. This area is free and a good place for young skaters to practice. The gated, outdoor, smooth concrete-surface skate park has numerous pools of varying depths along with ramps, steps, a split fun box, ledges, blocks, an octagon volcano, and pump bump, plus a few flat areas and a pathway around the perimeters. Benches are just outside for ~~anxious~~, I mean, observing parents. Vending machines carry snacks and beverages. Note: All participants must have a liability release form on file signed by a parent or guardian for skateboarders under 18 years old. Helmet, elbow and knee pads are required (and available here to use at no extra charge). Parents who drop off kids take note: If a green flag is flying, the session is open. If a red flag is flying, the session is closed.

Across the street, Dusty Rhodes Park offers more picnic and run around area, plus a playground. To the west is Dog Beach, where furry visitors from all over come to romp and play frisbee on this stretch of beach. Tip: Watch where you walk.

Hours: The park is open daily, sunrise - sunset. The skate park is usually open Mon. - Fri., 10am - sunset; Sat. - Sun., 9am - sunset. Call first as hours fluctuate. Sessions are 2½ hours each.

Admission: The park is free. The skate park is $5 per session (or all day if it's not busy); $30 for an annual pass.

Ages: All

OCEANSIDE SKATEPARK

(760) 435-5233
Northeast corner of Myers Street & Pier View Avenue, Oceanside
(Exit the San Diego Fwy [5] W. on Mission Ave., R. on Myers. [TG: 1086 A7])

This skate park is up the road from Oceanside Pier, just south of the railroad tracks. Skateboarders and in-line bladers enjoy the "portable" ramps and rails on this blacktop base. There are stadium seats for parents and other spectators. A parental waiver must be signed for participants 17 years and under. Wearing a helmet and elbow and knees pads are required. They have some free equipment to loan out.

Hours: Open daily noon - 6pm.

Admission: Free

Ages: 7 years and up.

OLD POWAY PARK

(858) 679-4313 / www.ci.poway.ca.us; www.powaymidlandrr.org
14134 Midland Road, Poway

See the entry for OLD POWAY PARK on page 441 for details.

OTAY LAKE COUNTY PARK

(619) 482-7361 - park; (619) 668-2050 - lake / www.sannet.gov/water/recreation
Wueste Road, Chula Vista

(Exit Jacob Dekema Fwy [805] E. on Telegraph Canyon Rd., which turns into Otay Lakes Rd., R. on Wueste Rd., L. at the fork in the road where the sign says Eastlake. If you continue straight, you'll end up at the Arco Olympic Training Center. [TG: 1332 B3])

The view from atop this small park is beautiful as it overlooks lower Otay Lake. The playground has slides, swings, and climbing equipment, plus talking tubes and a mini zip line. A grassy area, picnic tables, and three short hiking trails up the hillside complete this scenic park. Enjoy motor or row boating and fishing in the lake that is stocked once a year with catfish. Note: Visit the nearby ARCO OLYMPIC TRAINING CENTER (see pg. 439) on your way to or from the park.

Hours: The park is open Mon. - Fri., 9:30am - 5pm; Sat. - Sun., 9:30am - sunset. Fishing and boating are available February through September, Wed., Sat., and Sun., sunrise - sunset. No fishing or boating is allowed October through January. (It's duck season.)

Admission: $2 per vehicle to the park. Fishing is $5 for adults, plus a fishing license; $2.50 for ages 8 - 15 (no license necessary); children 7 and under are free. Row boats are $13 for the day; motorboats are $40 for the day.

Ages: All

PALOMAR MOUNTAIN STATE PARK / PALOMAR OBSERVATORY

(760) 742-2119 - observatory; (760) 742-3462 - state park;
(800) 444-7275 - camping reservations. / parks.ca.gov; www.astro.caltech.edu/palomarpublic
S6, Palomar Mountain

(Exit Escondido Fwy [15] E. on Pala Rd. [Route 76], L. [N.E.] on S6 about 26 miles up the mountain to the observatory. [TG: 409 G6])

Up in the Palomar Mountains, at the end of a long and winding road, is the Palomar Observatory. A short hike up to the observatory allows you to see the famed 200" Hale telescope. But forewarn your children - you can only look <u>at</u> the telescope which is housed behind glass panes; you cannot look through it. The telescope is magnificent in size and scope and seeing it is almost worth the drive here! The small one-room museum displays outstanding photos of star clusters, galaxies, and clouds of glowing gas. It also shows a continuously running video about the workings of the telescope and about our universe.

Just a few miles down the road is Palomar Mountain State Park. If you're planning on coming to the observatory, I suggest making the park a destination, too, as just walking around the observatory and museum took us only half an hour. Palomar Mountain General Store, (760) 742-3496, is at the junction of S7 and S6, making it a natural stopping place before going on to the park. The store has a bit of everything, including fossils, gems, Indian jewelry, and artifacts.

Continue about three miles on S7 to reach the park. At 2,000 acres, this Sierra Nevada-like park is incredibly beautiful. It also can get snow in the winter. You'll find several hiking trails through the scenic mountainside. The Boucher Hill Lookout trail, for instance, is a looping four-mile hike with marvelous vistas. Fishing is available at Doane Pond, which is stocked with trout regularly. There is a five fish limit per day, and those 16 years old and older need a California state license. The park also provides areas for picnicking and overnight camping. Each of the thirty-one family campsites have fire rings and picnic tables, plus community coin-operated hot showers. Call the ranger station (park office) for more information.

Hours: The museum and the observatory are open daily, 9am - 4pm. Closed Christmas Eve and Christmas Day. The state park is open daily, 8am - sunset.

Admission: Free to the observatory and museum. A $4 vehicle entrance fee is charged for day use of the park. Overnight camping is $15 a night, plus a $7.50 camping reservation fee.

Ages: 8 years and up for the observatory and the museum; ages 3 and up for the park.

QUAIL BOTANICAL GARDENS

(760) 436-3036 / www.qbgardens.com
230 Quail Gardens Drive, Encinitas
(Exit San Diego Fwy [5] E. on Encinitas Blvd., L. on Quail Gardens Dr. There are signs along the way. [TG: 1147 D6])

We didn't see any quail on our visit to the Quail Botanical Gardens, but we did see (and hear) woodpeckers plus a variety of other birds such as wrens, finches, scrub jays, and hermit thrushes. The thirty landscaped acres here include desert, exotic tropical, palm, bamboo, and native California plants. The lush foliage; the incredible array of flowers; the meandering trails (some dirt, some paved); the beautiful waterfall; and the benches under shade trees, all invoked the sensation of visiting a secret garden. Some of our highlights included seeing the Sausage Tree, with its large and very heavy pods that really do resemble sausages; walking up to the Overlook Pavilion for a 360-degree view of the gardens, mountains, ocean, and surrounding community; and taking pictures of the unique flowers. Our favorite flowers were the white and yellow upside-down bellflowers. Make sure you look at the fanciful topiary figures and the waterfall by the gift shop.

The Native Plants/Native People section is unique and reminiscent of the landscape hundreds of years ago with its coastal sage, a pond, and a Native American (Kumeyaay) dwelling. South of the parking lot, kids have their own little separate garden called Seeds of Wonder. It has a few topiary figures, a hand water pump, animal sculptures, a small hidden garden, a grassy hill to roll down, and some scale size structures such as a bamboo gazebo, a barn (look through the windows), and an Alice in Wonderland house with a whimsical backyard. Ask about guided tours, family programs such as art in the garden or the insect fair, and other listings in the packed calendar of events.

Hours: Open daily, 9am - 5pm. Closed New Year's Day, Thanksgiving, and Christmas.

Admission: $8 for adults; $5 for seniors; $3 for ages 3 -12; children 2 and under are free.

Ages: 2 years and up.

RANCHO BERNARDO COMMUNITY PARK & RECREATION CENTER

(858) 538-8129 - park; (858) 487-9698 - tennis club / www.sannet.gov/park-and-recreation/centers
18448 W. Bernardo Drive, Rancho Bernardo
(Exit Escondido Fwy [15] S.W. on W. Rancho Bernardo Dr./Pomerado Rd. [TG: 1150 A6])

This community park has a playground, six baseball diamonds, basketballs courts, the Bernardo Tennis Center, picnic tables, barbecue pits, and lots of grassy areas and paved pathways throughout for all kinds of wheels. All of this is nice, but what makes this park stand out is the adjoining open area with some fairly easy dirt hiking trails. The area has hard-to-resist-climbing-on large rocks scattered throughout, gentle hills, and a trail that leads to Lake Hodges, a lake within visual range from the park.

Hours: The park is open daily, sunrise - sunset. Play tennis daily, 7am - 9pm. (Of course you'd be tired if you played that often.)

Admission: Free. Tennis is $5 per hour and a half.

Ages: All

SAN PASQUAL BATTLEFIELD STATE HISTORIC PARK

(760) 737-2201 / parks.ca.gov
15808 San Pasqual Valley Road (SR78), San Pasqual
(Going S. on San Diego Fwy [5], or Escondido Fwy [15], exit E. on Hwy 78, which turns into San Pasqual Valley Rd. Going N. on 15, exit E. on Via Rancho Pkwy., which turns into Bear Valley Rd., R. on San Pasqual Rd., which turns into Via Rancho Pkwy., go to end, R. on San Pasqual Valley Rd. It is just E. of San Diego Wild Animal Park. [TG: 1131 B7])

This is the site of the worst (i.e. bloodiest) battles in California during the Mexican-American War. Kids need to know this fact for its historical significance, and because it will make their visit here more exciting. The grounds have picnic tables and a quarter-mile, looping trail. The visitors center overlooks the battlefield, which is actually across the highway, on private land. The small center has interpretive panels, a few uniforms, weapons, and a ten-minute video entitled *Mr. Polk's War*. Living History Days are held the first Sunday of each month from 11am to 2pm., but not during the summer. Docents are dressed in period costume and do old-fashioned chores, crafts, and other activities. Periodically, you can also see a cannon being fired. Note: The battle is reenacted in December. See the Calendar entry, on page 617, for details.

Hours: The park is open Sat. - Sun., 10am - 5pm. Guided school tours are given during the week, by appointment.

Admission: Free

Ages: 6 years and up.

SANTEE LAKES REGIONAL PARK AND CAMPGROUND

(619) 596-3141; (619) 596-3141 reservations / www.padredam.org/santee.htm

9040 Carlton Oaks Drive, Santee

(Take the 52 Fwy E. to the end, go E. on Mission Gorge Rd., L. on Carlton Hills Blvd., L. on Carlton Oaks Dr. Going N. on San Vicente Fwy [67], exit W. on Prospect Ave., R. on Cuyamaca St., L. on Mission Gorge Rd., R. on Carlton Hills Blvd., L. on Carlton Oaks Dr. Going S. on 67, exit W. on Woodside Ave., which turns into Mission Gorge Rd., R. on Carlton Hills Blvd., L. on Carlton Oaks Dr. [TG: 1231 A6])

This regional park is made up primarily of a series of lakes that are seasonally stocked with trout, catfish, bluegill, and bass. A permit is required and available for purchase at the park entrance. No swimming is allowed. Boating and paddle boat rentals are available. The park also contains playgrounds, campgrounds, hiking and biking trails, a swimming pool (for campers only), a general store, laundry facilities, and a recreation center. Full hook-up campgrounds start at $29 a night. Primitive campgrounds, open Friday and Saturday only, are available for $20 a night. Each campsite has a picnic table and barbecue pit.

Hours: The park and fishing are open Mon. - Thurs., 8am - sunset; Fri. - Sun., 6am - sunset. The pool is open seasonally.

Admission: $2 per vehicle during the week; $3 per vehicle on the weekends. Fishing permits are $7 for adults; $4 for ages 7 - 15; children 6 and under are free. Camping prices are listed above.

Ages: 2 years and up.

SCRIPPS PARK / LA JOLLA COASTLINE

www.sandiegocity.org/lifeguards/beaches

1180 Coast Boulevard, La Jolla

(Going S. on San Diego Fwy [5] exit W. on La Jolla Village Dr., L. on Torrey Pines Rd., R. on Prospect St., look for signs and bear R. on Coast Blvd. Going N. on 5 exit N. to Ardath Rd., which turns into Torrey Pines Rd., and follow above directions. Good luck parking! [TG: 1227 F6])

This delightful grassy park overlooks a gorgeous stretch of the California coastline and the Pacific Ocean. The park itself has few amenities - picnic tables, a few palm and cypress trees, and a covered overlook. It's an ideal place for flying a kite and to catch a concert on Sunday afternoons in the summer. Take a walk on the cement sidewalk that follows up and down along the coast and revel in the breathtaking scenery and in the variety of landscape.

Just to the north of the park is tiny Shell Beach (good for collecting seashells) and La Jolla Cove, a patch of beach with palm trees swaying in the wind on top of the adjoining sandstone cliffs. The cove's water visibility can sometimes exceed thirty feet, making this a favorite spot for snorkelers and scuba divers. (Think Hawaiian waters, kind of.) The cove is part of the San Diego La Jolla Underwater Park Ecological Reserve which safeguards marine life in the area.

Further north is the LA JOLLA SHORES BEACH (see pg. 365). Heading just south of the park, with easy walking distance, is the SEAL ROCK MARINE MAMMAL RESERVE (see pg. 469). Continue on to small South Casa Beach and Wipeout Beach (hard to tell where one stops and the other begins), which has a semi-circular portion of sand (embraced by rocks), sea caves, and rocks - large, flat rocks to climb on and jump off (at least the shorter ones). My boys loved this aspect of the beach. Tidepooling is a great activity to do at certain nooks along the coastline.

Note that parking anywhere around this area in the summer time is slightly insane, but worth it. Go "off season" and enjoy all the same benefits. Look up the LA JOLLA CAVE AND CRESCENT CAFE on page 440 for information on another nearby attraction.

Hours: Open daily.
Admission: Free
Ages: All

SENGME OAKS WATER PARK

(760) 742-1921 / www.lajollaindians.com

22000 Highway 76 and Sengme Road, on the La Jolla Indian Reservation, Pauma Valley

(Going S. on Escondido Fwy [15], exit E. on Rt. 76 and up about 28 mountain miles. Going N. on 15, exit N.E. on Valley Pkwy, which turns into Valley Center., R. on 76 and go about 8 miles, turn on Sengme Rd. Look for signs. [TG: 409 G7])

This small water park, located at the foothills of Palomar Mountains on the Indian reservation, is a fun place to enjoy some family time. The mountain scenery is always a welcome sight. There are five slides here - including a few speed slides, serpentine slides, and a rampage slide. A good-sized kiddie pool has water play structures and a large umbrella that showers down water over its sides. The large swimming pool is another way to cool off during the hot summer days. A few shade trees, barbecues, picnic tables (bring your own chairs), volleyball courts, and a full-service snack bar are also on the grounds. You are welcome to bring in your own cooler of food. Overnight camping inside the water park boundaries is available, too. See LA JOLLA INDIAN RESERVATION CAMPGROUND / TUBING ON SAN LUIS REY RIVER (pg. 391) for another attraction just down the street.

Hours: Open Memorial Day through Labor Day, Fri. - Sat., 11am - 7pm; Sun., 11am - 6pm
Admission: $5 per person. Camping is $35 per night for two people.
Ages: All

SOUTH CLAIREMONT RECREATION CENTER / POOL

(858) 581-9924 - recreation center;
(858) 581-9923 - pool / www.sannet.gov/park-and-recreation/centers/index.shtml

3605 Clairemont Drive, Clairemont

(Going N on San Diego Fwy [5], exit E. on Balboa Ave., R. on Clairemont. Going S. on 5, exit S. on Mission Bay Dr., L. on Garnet Ave., which turns into Balboa Ave., R. on Clairemont. [TG: 1248 E5])

This large community park offers various activities for families to enjoy. Green grassy areas and scattered picnic tables provide a picnic atmosphere, while the older-style playground, complete with hopscotch, slides, swings, and climbing apparatus, provides the fun. Check at the community center building for special classes, programs, and events. There are also two tennis courts and a good-sized, outdoor swimming pool that is open year round. During the week, only half of the pool is open for public use because the swim team uses the other half. On weekends, the whole pool is open for the public to use.

Hours: The park is open daily, sunrise - sunset. The pool is open Mon. - Fri., 10am - 3:45pm (shallow end only); Sat. - Sun., 11am - 3pm (whole pool). Call for hours as they do fluctuate.
Admission: The park is free. Swimming sessions cost $2 for adults; $1.50 for seniors and ages 15 and under.
Ages: All

SWEETWATER REGIONAL PARK / ROHR PARK

(619) 691-5071 - park; (619) 422-3175 - Chula Vista Live Steamers, Inc.;
(858) 565-3600 - camping / www.co.san-diego.ca.us/parks

4548 Sweetwater Road, Bonita

(Exit Jacob Dekema Fwy [805] E. on Bonita Rd., L. on Willow, R. on Sweetwater Rd. [TG: 1310 H2])

Sweetwater Regional Park is a long stretch of land that runs between Sweetwater Road and Bonita Road.

Fred Rohr Park is a nice oblong park, within Sweetwater Park, that parallels a golf course. The lake here is home to numerous ducks. Picnic tables are scattered throughout the park along with a few barbecue pits. Entertainment is provided by using swing sets, jungle gyms, volleyball courts, softball fields, basketball courts, grassy areas, shade trees, and cement bike and blade paths. A monthly highlight is a ride on a scale model steam locomotive around the park. The Live Steamers, who run the locomotive, also operate 1/8-scale diesel and electric trains.

Over fifty campsites accommodate RV or tent camping at the summit site of the park that overlook the reservoir. There are fifteen miles of hiking trails in the area.

Hours: The park is open daily, sunrise - sunset. The trains run on the second full weekend of each month (except September) between noon and 3pm.

Admission: Free to the park. Train rides are 25¢ per person. Camping is $16 a night, plus a $3 reservation fee.

Ages: All

TECOLOTE SHORES PLAY AREA

1600 E. Mission Bay Drive, San Diego

(Exit San Diego Fwy [5] W. on Clairemont Dr., L. on E. Mission Bay Dr., past the Hilton. [TG: 1268 D2])

Head for some big time fun at the large Tecolote Shores Play Area. This wonderful playground has a great combination of old and new equipment. In the main area, with its sand-covered grounds, there are slides, swings, and cement turtles to climb on (and under). Other sections include aquatic cement creatures, a pirate ship, mini-obstacle ropes course, bridges, and various other climbing apparatus. There are plenty of picnic tables and grassy areas here, too. As the playground is right on the bay, the view is beautiful. Tip: There aren't many tall trees here, at least right now, so this is a great place to fly a kite.

Hours: Open daily, sunrise - sunset.

Admission: Free

Ages: All

TIDELANDS PARK

(619) 686-6225 - park; (619) 522-7342 - skate park / www.coronado.ca.us

Glorietta Boulevard, Coronado

(Exit San Diego Fwy [5] onto Coronado Bridge, first R. onto Glorietta. You'll see the park from the bridge. [TG: 1289 A6])

This delightful, large, corner park offers a spectacular view of San Diego across the bay, plus pathways, a bike path, playgrounds, a fitness course, picnic tables, ball fields, grassy areas, and a sandy beach for swimming (no lifeguards). A good-sized, gated skate park near the beach has several concrete pools along with steps and grinding boxes. Fun tip: Check out the Marriot Hotel next to the park as it has real flamingos outside in its front fountain.

Hours: The park is open 6:30am - 10:30pm. The skate park is open Mon. - Fri., 1pm - dusk; Sat. - Sun., 9am - dusk. Call for extended summer hours.

Admission: The park is free. The skate park is an annual fee of $10 (which includes your first session), then $3 per session Mon. - Fri., $5 per session Sat. - Sun.

Ages: All

TIJUANA ESTUARY and VISITORS CENTER / BORDER FIELD STATE PARK

(619) 575-3613 - Estuary and Visitors Center / www.tijuanaestuary.com

301 Caspian Way, Imperial Beach

(Exit San Diego Fwy [5] W. on Coronado Ave., which turns into Imperial Beach Blvd., L. on 4th St., R. on Caspian Wy. [TG: 1349 F1])

First things first - an estuary is: "The wide part of a river where it flows near the sea; where fresh water and salt water mix." (That's why this book is called "Fun and *Educational* . . .") The Visitors Center has several wonderful interactive exhibits. One of our favorite displays are ordinary-looking, black and white sketched pictures of habitats that magically reveal brightly colored birds, insects, fish, and other animals when viewed through a polarized filter. The touch table contains snake skin, nests, skulls, and a dead sea turtle. The food chain is portrayed through pictures and graphs. Beneath the Sand exhibit entails pressing the bill of bird puppet heads into holes in various levels of "sand." A light on the side panel displays what birds with shorter beaks, that reach only shallow levels, eat (insects and plant seed), compared to what birds with longer beaks, that can reach deeper levels, eat (crabs and worms). Upon request, a small theater shows films such as *Timeless River* and *Tide of the Heron.*

Eight miles of walking trails are interspersed throughout the reserve. Ask for a map at the center, as there are different entrance points. Some of the trails follow along the streets, while others go deeper into the coastal dunes and near the Tijuana River. Be on the lookout for terns, egrets, herons, curlews, and other birds and wildlife. On a very short loop around the center, my boys and I saw interesting plants and birds, plus thirteen bunnies! Take a guided walking tour to learn more about the flora and fauna at the estuary, or sign the kids up for one of the numerous programs available. The Jr. Ranger Program, for students 7 to 11 years old, is offered every Thursday from 3:15pm to 4:45pm. During the program kids will enjoy a walk, earn patches or buttons, and/or make a craft - all free of charge!

Just south of the estuary is Border Field State Park, which borders Mexico. A marker shows the United States-Mexico boundary. The cliffs provide an awesome view of the ocean, and of the whales during whale-watching season, which is January through March. You can even see some of Tijuana from here, including a bullfighting ring. Picnic tables, grassy areas for running around, and pathways for hiking into parts of the estuary are all parts of the park.

An exciting way to see more of the park is by taking a horseback ride on the beach. Wear long pants, a windbreaker, and close-toed shoes before saddling up for a one- to three-hour adventure. Call Sandy's Rental Stables, located at 2060 Hollister Street (go east on Coronado Avenue, right on Hollister), at (619) 424-3124 / www.sandysrentalstable.com. The stables offers other rides too, such as going on the wildlife trail in the estuary, or mounting up for a Chuckwagon Meal Ride. Children 7 years and up may join in a horseback ride; younger children may take a parent-led pony ride around the arena.

Hours: Border park is open daily, sunrise - sunset. The Visitors Center is open daily, 10am - 5pm. Closed Thanksgiving and Christmas. The stables are open daily, 9am - 5pm.

Admission: Free to the Visitors Center. Horseback riding is $30 an hour; $60 for a three-hour trail and beach ride; $15 for a half-hour pony ride.

Ages: 3 years and up.

TORREY PINES STATE RESERVE

(858) 755-2063 / www.torreypine.org

Torrey Pines Park Road, La Jolla

(Exit San Diego Fwy [5] W. on Del Mar Heights Rd., L. on Camino Del Mar, turns into N. Torrey Pines Rd., R. on Torrey Pines Park Rd. past the beach and up the hill. [TG: 1207 H3])

The Torrey pine tree grows only in this and one other reserve (that's also in Southern California) in the whole world! My kids were impressed with this fact and by the beauty of the park. Our favorite trail was the Guy Fleming Trail. It's an easy loop, only two-thirds of a mile, and incredibly scenic through the trees out to a cliff overlooking the ocean. Tip: Hold on to younger children! Other trails include the half-mile Parry Grove looping trail; the two-thirds-of-a-mile Razor Point Trail with dramatic views of gorges; the steep, three-quarters-of-a-mile (one way) Beach Trail which ends at the San Diego - La Jolla Underwater Park; and the two, demanding, Broken Hill Trails.

The Visitors Center shows a short film that gives an overview of the reserve - just ask to see it. The exhibits here offer good visual information regarding the plants and animal wildlife of the reserve. On display are taxidermied raccoons, skunks, and birds; a pine cone display; a pine needle display; and more. We appreciated Torrey Pines Reserve for its glorious nature trails and its breath of fresh air! A lifeguarded Torrey Pines City Beach is right below the reserve for those who are into sand and surf. Note that the north side of the beach, the state beach also known as Black's Beach, allows nude bathing.

Hours: The reserve is open daily, sunrise - sunset. The visitors center is open daily, 9am - 5pm.

Admission: $4 per vehicle. Walk-ins are free.
Ages: 3 years and up.

VOLCAN MOUNTAIN NATURE PRESERVE

(760)765-4098 / www.co.san-diego.ca.us/parks
Near the intersection of Wynola and Farmer Roads, Julian
(On Hwy 78, just N. of town, take Main St., which becomes Farmers Rd., turn R. at the 4-way intersection with Wynola, then take an immediate L. The entrance is on your R. [TG: 1136 B3])

This preserve has God's fingerprints all over it with its spectacular wilderness scenery. Hikers can go halfway up the mountain, about a mile-and-a-half one way, to the gate, passing through meadows, high chaparral, and forests of oak and pine. If you want to hike to the summit for a 360 degree panoramic view of the surrounding area, including the Salton Sea, you'll need to join a guided ranger hike given on selected Saturdays.

Hours: Open daily, sunrise - sunset.
Admission: Free
Ages: 3 years and up.

WILLIAM HEISE COUNTY PARK

(760) 765-0650 / www.co.san-diego.ca.us/parks
4945 Heise Park Road, Julian
(From Hwy 78, take Pine Hills Rd. S. for 2 miles, head E. on Frisius R. for another 2 miles, R. on Heise. [TG: 1156 C5])

Consider this forest-like park a family destination. With eight miles of hiking and equestrian trails to choose from, there is bound to be a trail, or two, suitable for each member of the family. Select an easy pathway that leads through a mountain meadow and a cedar forest, a moderate trail that goes through canyon live oak, or choose a rugged trail for more experienced hiker, such as the 5.75-mile Kelly Ditch Trail which leads to Lake Cuyamaca. Two shaded picnic areas, a horseshoe pit, a playground, and a pond are all available here, too.

Over forty tent sites, sixty RV sites, and two cabins with electricity and a few furnishings, provide overnight camping in this beautiful area. The campgrounds have piped-in water, showers, barbecues, and fire rings. The one-room cabins each have a fireplace and sleep up to six people. Bring your own bedding and know that reservations usually need to made at least three months ahead of your arrival date.

Hours: Open daily, 9am - 5pm.
Admission: $2 per vehicle. Camping Sun. - Thurs. is $12 for tents; $14 for RVs; Fri. - Sat., $14 for tents; $16 for RVs. The cabins are $35 a night.
Ages: All

WOODGLEN VISTA PARK AND SKATE POCKET

(619) 258-4100 / www.ci.santee.ca.us/csd/index.htm
10250 Woodglen Vista Drive, Santee
(Going N. on San Vicente Fwy [67], exit W. on Prospect Ave., R. on Cuyamaca St., L. on Mission Gorge Rd. Going S. on 67, exit W. on Woodside Ave., which turns into Mission Gorge. Going E. on Fwy 52, exit E. on Mission Gorge Rd. From Mission Gorge, go N. on Magnolia Ave., L. on Woodglen Vista. [TG: 1231 D2])

Woodglen has a little something for everyone. The nice-sized playground with wood chips "flooring" has swings, slides, and big plastic animals to ride. A ball field, tennis court, basketball court, and small skatepark motivate the sports enthusiast to get moving. The cement skate park, aptly named a "pocket," has a half pyramid, grinding wall, rails, spine, steps, and four-foot-high half bowl. Skaters must wear safety equipment. A large grassy area and picnic tables round out this neighborhood park.

Hours: Open daily, sunrise - sunset.
Admission: Free
Ages: All

WOODLAND PARK AND AQUATIC CENTER

(760) 746-2028 - pool complex; (760) 744-9000 - community services / www.san-marcos.net

672 Woodland Parkway, San Marcos

(Going E. on Hwy 78, exit E. on Barham, L. on Woodland Pkwy. Going W. on 78, exit E. on Rancheros Dr. L. on Woodland Pkwy. [TG: 1109 C6])

A large, picturesque fountain and a small, man-made rock-lined pond decorate the corner section of this park. A short paved walkway winds around the pond and up through the park inviting strollers to use it. A children's play area and a long grassy area, plus picnic tables and barbecue pits, make the park a fun outing. Up the small hill from the park are three pools, one of which is a wading pool. The swimming pool has a fifty-foot curvy waterslide and the diving pool has a high dive and low diving board - fun features. Showers are available here, too.

Hours: The park is open daily, dawn - dusk. The pool is open mid-May through mid-September.

Admission: Free for park facilities. $2.50 per person for pool usage.

Ages: All

WOODS VALLEY KAMPGROUND

(760) 749-2905 / www.woodsvalley.com

15236 Woods Valley Road, Valley Center

(Exit Escondido Fwy [15] E. on Old Castle Rd., which turns into Lilac Rd., R. on Valley Center Rd., L. on Woods Valley Rd. about 3 miles on a gently winding country road. [TG: 1090 H5])

Kamp (or camp) in pretty, back woods country, seemingly far removed from city life. Eighty-nine camp sites are available for either tent or RV use. The campground contains fun amenities such as a swimming pool, a kid's fishing catch and release pond, a playground, a recreational hall, a general store, and nearby (not in the campground) hiking trails. Woods Valley is not open for day use. Look up BATES NUT FARM (see pg. 439) for a fun nearby place to visit.

Admission: Tent camping is $29 during the week; $35 on the weekend. RV camping is $32 during the week; $35 on the weekend. Camping prices are for up to four people; additional campers are $3 per person.

Ages: All

-----*MALLS*-----

HORTON PLAZA

(619) 238-1596 - plaza; (619) 236-1212 - San Diego Visitor's Bureau / www.westfield.com

324 Horton Plaza, San Diego

(Going S. on San Diego Fwy [5] exit S. on Front St., L. on Broadway. It's on the corner of 4th and Broadway. Going N. on the 5, exit S. on 6th Ave. R. on Broadway. [TG: 1289 A3])

This outdoor mall is seven city blocks of shopping, dining, and entertainment. Colorful and unique architecture, with buildings designed at various, odd angles, contain over 125 places to shop. Favorite kid-friendly stopping places include FAO Schwarz (a gigantic toy store), the Nature Company, and the Disney Store. Other attractions are the numerous movie theaters and over twenty places to dine. Stop by the visitor's bureau to pick up a coupon booklet, information, and/or maps on the area. Horton Plaza is also home to the San Diego Visitors Bureau.

Hours: Open Mon. - Fri., 10am - 9pm; Sat., 10am - 7pm; Sun., 11am - 6pm.

Admission: Technically, free.

Ages: All

VIEJAS OUTLET CENTER

(619) 659-2070 / www.shopviejas.com

5005 Willows Road, Alpine

(Going W. on 8 Fwy, exit N.E. on Willows. Going E. on 8, exit at Alpine Blvd., go L. on the end of the off ramp on Via La Mancha, R. on Willows. The mall is directly across from the Viejas Casino. [TG: 1234 J5])

This factory outlet outdoor mall is located on an Indian reservation and has a Native American theme. Adobe-style stores decorated with wooden beams and large boulders border the walkways. A small stream runs through one section while a grassy expanse of lawn, the Viejas Park, is integrated at the east end of the mall. The stores include Gap Outlet, Liz Claiborne, London Fog, Tommy Hilfiger, Vans, Paper Outlet, and many more, plus a few eateries, such as Rubio's and McDonalds. There is a large fountain that shoots up water from its ground holes in some sort of pattern (although I couldn't figure it out). Kids love getting wet here in warmer weather.

Although the shopping is great and the aesthetics of the center is pleasant, I've really included this entry because the mall offers two nightly shows, weather permitting, at the outside show court near the fountain. Rows of chairs encircle the large water fountain to allow guests just to watch the "dancing" waters that move to the beat of music and pulsating lights. It's quite mesmerizing. Although the second feature changes three times a year, each of the twenty-minute shows incorporate music, lasers, lights, videos on the huge screens above the audience's seats, and pyrotechnics - it's a mini spectacular. One show, usually running February through April, is called "Splashtrack - A Musical Journey" which used the fountain while presenting a rock and roll review of music from the 40's through the 90's. We saw "Spirit of Nightfire," a tale of Native American heritage starring a costumed dancer in the fountains, and several special effects. It is shown May through October. "Legend of the Ice Princess," running November through January, again incorporates a live performer with a flashy show. The shows might not be a main destination, but if you're in the neighborhood, they are a worthwhile addition to your itinerary.

Hours: Mall hours are Mon. - Sat., 10am - 9pm; Sun., 10am - 7pm. The dancing waters "show" usually starts at 7:30pm in the fall and winter; 9pm in the spring and summer. The main presentation starts a half hour later. Call for hours.

Admission: Free

Ages: All

WESTFIELD SHOPPINGTOWN NORTH COUNTY - FAMILY NIGHT

(760) 489-0631 / www.westfield.com

272 E. Via Rancho Parkway, Escondido

(Exit the Escondido Fwy [15] E. on Via Rancho Pkwy. It's near Beethoven Rd. [TG: 1150 B3])

Come and join the fun at center court for an hour of craft time or wonderful entertainment such as storytelling, song and dance, puppetry, animal presentations, and more. The mall also has 180 stores and restaurants, including a McDonalds with a play center, and a TEDDYCRAFTERS (see pg. 443).

Hours: The first Wed. at 6:30am.

Admission: Free

Ages: 2 - 10 years

WESTFIELD SHOPPINGTOWN PARKWAY - FAMILY NIGHT

(619) 579-9932 / www.westfield.com

415 Parkway Plaza, El Cajon

(Going E. on 8 Fwy, exit N. on N. Johnson Ave. It's on the corner of Fletcher Pkwy and Johnson. Going W. on 8, exit N. on Mollison Ave., L. on Broadway, which turns in to Fletcher. Going S. on San Vicente Fwy [67], exit W. on Fletcher. [TG: 1251 F4])

Have fun with bubbles, puppets, magicians, musical groups, or other programs and presentations for about an hour at center court. This could be the highlight of you child's month! Merchants offer various discount coupons for kids (and adults) who attend the family night. This mall also has year-round miniature train rides ($1.50 per ride) and a free Playtown just for young 'uns located near JCPenney.

Hours: The first Mon. at 6pm

Admission: Free

Ages: 2 - 10 years.

WESTFIELD SHOPPINGTOWN PLAZA BONITA - FAMILY NIGHT

(619) 267-2850 / www.shoppingtowns.com

3030 Plaza Bonita Road, National City

(Exit Jacob Dekema Fwy [805] E. on Bonita Rd., L. on Plaza Bonita Rd. From the 54 Fwy, exit S. on Reo Dr., which turns into Plaza Bonita Center Wy., R. on Sweetwater Rd. [TG: 1310 D4])

Have some fun while making new friends at the Family Night at Plaza Bonita. Free, hour-long, weekly entertainment could include puppet shows, toe-tapping music, storytelling, and/or singing. Meet in the center court near J. C. Penney. This mall also hosts other events throughout the year such as Circus Vargas and, of course, visits from the Easter Bunny and Santa Claus.

  Hours: The first Thurs. of every month at 6:30pm.

  Admission: Free

  Ages: 2 -10 years.

WESTFIELD SHOPPINGTOWN PLAZA CAMINO REAL - FAMILY NIGHT

(760) 729-7927 / www.westfield.com

2525 El Camino Real, Carlsbad

(Exit 78 Fwy S. on El Camino Real. [TG: 1106 G3])

Bring the family and come join in the fun at the center court, lower level. Free, forty-five-minute monthly entertainment can include laughing with kids' comedians, dancing, singing, storytelling, and general silliness.

  Hours: The first Tues. of every month at 6:30pm.

  Admission: Free

  Ages: 2 - 10 years.

WESTFIELD SHOPPINGTOWN U.T.C. - FAMILY NIGHT

(858) 453-2930 / www.westfield.com

4545 La Jolla Village Drive, San Diego

(From Jacob Dekema Fwy [805], exit W. on La Jolla Village/Miramar Rd. From San Diego Fwy [5], exit E. on La Jolla Village. [TG: 1228 D2])

This outdoor mall offers family nights the first week of each month by the children's play area. Past activities have included arts and crafts, educational plays, musicals, live animal presentations, and more. Call for a specific event schedule. Know that store discounts and meal deals are also offered on these nights.

  Hours: The first Mon. - Fri. evening of each month at 6:30pm.

  Admission: Free

  Ages: 2 - 10 years.

-----*MUSEUMS*-----

ANTIQUE GAS & STEAM ENGINE MUSEUM, INC.

(800) 5-TRACTOR (587-2286) or (760) 941-1791 / www.agsem.com

2040 N. Santa Fe Avenue, Vista

(From San Diego Fwy [5], exit N.E. on San Luis Rey Mission Exwy [76]. From Escondido Fwy [15], exit W. on Pala Rd [76]. From 76. go S. on N. Santa Fe Ave. From 78 Fwy, exit N. on Melrose Dr., R. on W. Bobier Ave., L. on Santa Fe Ave. [TG: 1087 F2])

California has a museum for almost any interest. This one answers the age-old question, "Where do engines go when they run out of gas (or steam)?" The forty-acre, mostly outdoor museum, has hundreds of tractors, combines, gas and steam engines (that's a given from the name of the museum), horse-drawn carriages, and equipment used in mining, oil drilling, construction, agriculture, and more. The machines have been (or are in the process of being) restored to working condition. In fact, some of the equipment is used to help farm the adjacent lands. Walk around on your own or make a reservation for a tour, which is offered for pre-schoolers through college internship students. Kids will see many of the machines in action and learn a lot about the history of agriculture via harvesting and grounding flour, baking bread in a wood stove, and more. Another option is to visit here on the third and fourth weekends of June and October during Threshing Bees and Antique Engine & Tractor Shows. Watch or take part in planting, harvesting, household chores, early American crafts, blacksmithing, log sawing, parades, and square dancing. It's a good ol' time! See the Calendar entry, on page 588, for more details.

Some of the museum's collection is housed in structures that collectively resemble a small town. Featured buildings include a huge (and complete) blacksmith and wheelwright shop, a farm house with parlor, a sawmill, a one-third scale train with a telegrapher's office, and a barn. A (non-working) gas station is also on the premises. There are picnic tables here and even a small playground with two small, stationary tractors to climb on. The museum is interesting to visit anytime, but it's especially exciting to visit at exhibition time!

Hours: Open daily, 10am - 4pm.
Admission: $3 for adults; $2 ages 6 - 12; children 5 and under are free.
Ages: 4 years and up.

BALBOA PARK   ☼

(619) 239-0512 - Visitors Center; (619) 692-4919 - Morely Field Sports Complex / www.balboapark.org   !
Balboa Park, San Diego

(Going S. on San Diego Fwy [5], exit at Sassafras/Airport, go straight on Kettner Blvd. L. on Laurel St., which turns into El Prado. Going N. on 5, exit N. on Pershing Dr., L. on Florida Dr., L. on Zoo PL., L. on Park Blvd. Going S. on Cabrillo Fwy [163], exit N. on Park Blvd. (near end). The museums are W. on Park Blvd. [TG: 1289 C1])

This massive 1,158-acre park is the cultural and recreational heart of San Diego. An incredible number of programs and seasonal events are held here so see the Calendar section in the back of the book, call for a schedule of events, or pick up a copy of the bi-monthly events guide. The park has shade trees, grassy areas, several gardens, and picnic areas. The playgrounds are located at Pepper Grove Picnic Area on Park Boulevard, south of the San Diego Zoo (this park is ADA accessible), and at the north end of Balboa Drive. Morley Field Sports Complex, located off Morely Field Drive in the northeastern section, has twenty-five public tennis courts available for all-day use at $5 per person for adults; $3 for seniors; $2 for ages 17 and under. Call the Balboa Tennis Club at (619) 295-9278 for reservations. It also has a fitness course; boccie ball, which is an Italian sport similar to lawn bowling; a velodrome that hosts races and offers classes; an archery range; baseball diamonds; a frisbee golf course; lawn bowling for adults; playgrounds; picnic areas; a frisbee golf course; and a swimming pool that is open year round - call for hours. Swim sessions cost $2 for adults, $1.50 for seniors and children. Call (619) 692-4920 for more pool information.

Balboa Park is home to a majority of the city's best museums, as well as the world famous SAN DIEGO ZOO (see pg. 468). Individual museum entries are found under this section, listed by their official titles: MINGEI INTERNATIONAL FOLK ART MUSEUM, MUSEUM OF PHOTOGRAPHIC ARTS, MUSEUM OF SAN DIEGO HISTORY, REUBEN H. FLEET SCIENCE CENTER, SAN DIEGO AEROSPACE MUSEUM, SAN DIEGO ART INSTITUTE, SAN DIEGO AUTOMOTIVE MUSEUM, SAN DIEGO HALL OF CHAMPIONS SPORTS MUSEUM, SAN DIEGO MODEL RAILROAD MUSEUM, SAN DIEGO MUSEUM OF ART, SAN DIEGO MUSEUM OF MAN, and SAN DIEGO NATURAL HISTORY MUSEUM. VETERANS MEMORIAL CENTER AND MUSEUM is across the street. Passports can be purchased to visit the twelve museums plus the Japanese Gardens (so really thirteen museums) for $30 for adults. (Children's admissions are already discounted or free.) Passes can be bought at the Visitors Information Center and are good for one week from the date of purchase. Below is a list of which museums are free on particular Tuesdays: First Tuesday: S.D. Natural History (permanent exhibits only), Reuben H. Fleet Science Center, and S.D. Model Railroad; Second Tuesday: Museum of Photographic Arts and Museum of S.D. History; Third Tuesday: Japanese Friendship Garden, Mingei International Folk Art Museum, S.D. Museum of Art (permanent exhibits only), S. D. Art Institute, and S.D. Museum of Man; Fourth Tuesday: S. D. Hall of Champions Sports, S.D. Aerospace Museum, S.D. Automotive Museum, and Cottages and House of Pacific Relations International whose Hall of Nations films, such as *Children Around the World* show at 11am to 3pm.

The park also offers many other attractions that are worthy of mention. The beautiful, latticed **Botanical Building** is located at the north end of the lily pond next to the San Diego Museum of Art. It has (labeled) tropical and subtropical plants on display. It is open Friday through Wednesday 10am to 4pm. Admission is free. The **Timken Museum of Art** is located next to the Visitors Center. Housed here are collections of works by European Old Masters, eighteenth- and nineteenth-century American paintings, and Russian icons. It is open Tuesday through Saturday, 10am to 4:30pm; Sunday, 1:30pm to 4:30pm. Admission is free. The **Japanese Friendship Garden** is a Japanese-style house with a main room that has a traditional table set with (fake) Japanese food. Children must stay on the short path leading to the small garden and koi pond. If you are interested in seeing this room and garden, come here when admission is free, on the third Tuesday of the month, as admission is otherwise $3 per person. Free outdoor concerts are given on the famous **Spreckels Pipe Organ** year round on Sundays 2pm to 3pm, plus Mondays, 8pm to 9:30pm during July and August. The organ is located at an architecturally beautiful building set in a huge half circle. My kids think the steps here are a great place for picnicking. The **Spanish Village Art Center**, (619) 233-9050, is just north of the San Diego Natural History Museum. The "village" has retained its old-world charm with its Spanish architecture and colorful courtyard tiles and flowers. The thirty-five art studios and galleries include woodcarvings, sculptures, and gems and minerals, for show and sale. Oftentimes, the artisans demonstrate their craft which makes the Spanish Village Center an intriguing stop for slightly older kids. The **House of Pacific Relations**, (619) 234-0739, is located behind the United Nations Building, across from the Spreckels Organ. The "House" is comprised of seventeen cottages that are home to thirty different nationalities. Exhibits in each cottage pertain to specific ethnic groups. Special lawn programs of music and dance are held on Sundays 2pm to 3pm from February through mid-November. Nations are represented on a rotating basis. The cottages are open Sundays 12:30pm to 4:30pm and on the fourth Tuesday from noon to 3pm. Admission is free. Three other kid-friendly attractions are the **miniature train ride, carousel,** and **kiddie rides**. All of the attractions are open daily in the summer from about 11am to 6pm, and on Saturdays, Sundays, and school holidays, 11am to 5pm, the rest of the year. The kiddie rides, located just in the entrance of Zoo Place, are comprised of an airplane and butterfly ride for ages 5 and under. Located south of the Zoo and north of the Spanish Village Center are the three-minute train ride, (619) 231-1515, and an old-fashioned carousel, (619) 460-9000, that, along with horses and other animals to ride on, even offers a chance to grab at the brass ring. Each attraction is $1.50 per person. There are a few restaurants and cafes scattered throughout Balboa Park, although we usually bring a picnic lunch, and a few theaters such as MARIE HITCHCOCK PUPPET THEATER (see pg. 447), GLOBE THEATRE (see pg. 448), and SAN DIEGO JUNIOR THEATRE (see pg. 448).

At any time during your visit to the park, you are welcome to hop aboard the Balboa Park Tram. This free, intra-park transportation system can take you from Presidents Way and Park Boulevard, up to the carousel, through where the museums are, and up north to 6th Street and the MARSTON HOUSE (pg. 418). It makes several stops along the way, so you can catch it coming or going. It operates daily from 9am to 6:15pm, with extended hours in the summer. Plan to visit Balboa Park many times, as you obviously cannot see it all in one, two, or even three days!

Hours: The park is open daily. The Visitors Center is open daily, 9am - 4pm. Individual attractions are listed in separate entries.

Admission: Entrance to the park itself is free. Individual attractions are listed in separate entries.

Ages: All ages for the park.

BANCROFT RANCH HOUSE MUSEUM

(619) 469-1480 / www.sandiegohistory.org/societies/springvalley
9050 Memory Lane, Spring Valley
(Exit Martin Luther King Jr. Fwy [94] S. on Bancroft Dr., L. on Memory Ln. [TG: 1271 B5])

I love visiting old house/museums because I always learn some history about the original owners and the time period that they lived there. With every new tidbit learned, it's like fitting in another piece of a huge historical puzzle. For instance, in the early 1900's Howe Bancroft, one-time owner of this adobe ranch house, was a renowned historian who wrote and compiled thirty-nine books describing the civilization of the Old West.

A truth window, where visitors here can see the layers of original adobe - mostly mud and hay - is one of the first things the guide points out. One small room contains a few display cases of Native American artifacts such as grinding stones, arrowheads, and baskets. Another room contains a straw bed, Bancroft's history books, and few period household goods. A connecting room has an old school desk and a map. The last room holds display cases of boots, clothing, tools, kitchen implements, and most exciting of all because kids can hold them - ship to shore cannon balls, and tumbler balls used to crush rocks. School groups are encouraged to visit.

There are a few picnic tables under shade trees out front of the house and an indigenous garden. An adjacent parcel of land will hopefully be turned into a park. When we saw it, it had a large grouping of very old palm trees, and the surface run off from an underground spring. Although the surrounding area is a bit rundown and the museum grounds are a work in progress, seeing and hearing a potion of history makes the Bancroft Museum a worthwhile visit.

Hours: Open Fri. - Sun., 1pm- 4pm. Closed Easter and Christmas.
Admission: Free, but donations are appreciated.
Ages: 8 years and up.

BARONA CULTURAL CENTER AND MUSEUM

(619) 443-7003 / www.angelfire.com/falcon/bccm
1095 Barona Road, Lakeside
(Exit San Vicente Fwy [67] E. on Willow Rd., L. on Wildcat Canyon which becomes Barona Rd.. It's about 6 miles from Willow, just past the Barona Casino on the L. in the community center. Or exit Hwy 78, S. on San Vicente Rd., S. on Wildcat Canyon/Barona Rd. [TG: 1192 J6])

What a classy little museum! A large rock in the lobby features numerous re-created Indian pictographs, and the logo of the tribe. The display case contains items from Barona war veterans, such as their uniforms, medals, and personal effects.

Press the buttons located near several of the displays to hear the history and other information about the artifacts. We especially liked hearing the voices of the Bird Singers who sang ceremonial songs, accompanied by gourd rattles. Other exhibits in this area include a small roundish house made of willows; metates and manos (i.e. grind stones) that visitors can actually try out; and baskets. Another section showcases grunion, how to track the sun with stone markers, and how to make paint with natural products. A timeline with informational panels and photos depicts the ceremonies and background of Native Americans in San Diego. A short video describes how the museum was created. The small back room has a stuffed diamondback snake and a few changing displays.

Free, guided half-hour tours are available for up to thirty students. The tour encompasses the museum and more insight into the Barona / Kumeyaay people's heritage. Note that there are picnic facilities south of the museum at Stelzer County Park.

Hours: The museum is open Tues. - Sun., noon - 5pm. Closed Mon. and holidays. Tours are offered by appointment.
Admission: Free
Ages: 7 years and up.

BIRCH AQUARIUM

(619) 534-FISH (3474) / www.aquarium.ucsd.edu
2300 Expedition Drive, San Diego
See the entry for BIRCH AQUARIUM on page 462 for details.

BUENA VISTA AUDUBON NATURE CENTER

(760) 439-BIRD (2473) / www.bvaudubon.org
2202 S. Coast Highway, Oceanside
(Exit San Diego Fwy [5] W. on Vista Way, L. on S. Coast Highway. It is just N. of the Buena Vista Lagoon. [TG: 1106 D4])

This museum is not just for the birds! The exhibits inside this small building consist mainly of taxidermied birds (some in flight) such as a pelican, a great blue heron, a red-tailed hawk, a colorful yellow western tanager, and more. A stuffed owl has a mouse in its beak and a pellet at its feet that contains partially digested animal parts. Other mounted animals on display include a bobcat, red fox, possum, and more. The touch table has a raccoon skin, petrified wood, and whale bones, among other things. Look through a kid-level porthole on the central display to see fish "swimming" underneath. Spread your arms against a wall to measure your "wing span" up to a variety of bird's span. A book corner for children has a nice selection of nature books to read. Other items of interest are the fish tank with catfish (it's easy to see where they got their name), a small rock and mineral display, and a live tarantula.

Outside, take a walk through the marshy reeds out to the lagoon. This area is home to a wide variety of birds. Guided field trips are one of the best ways to really learn about the abundant wildlife at Buena Vista. Migrate over to the picnic tables which are available to make your day just ducky!

Free, one-hours tours are offered for kindergartners through 4th graders that cover a variety of topics such as what makes a bird a bird, birds of prey, and migration.

Hours: Open Tues. - Sat., 10am - 4pm; Sun., 1pm - 4pm.
Admission: Free
Ages: 3 years and up.

CABRILLO NATIONAL MONUMENT
(619) 557-5450
Cabrillo Memorial Drive, at the southern end of Point Loma, San Diego

See the entry for CABRILLO NATIONAL MONUMENT on page 386 for details.

CALIFORNIA SURF MUSEUM
(760) 721-6876 / www.surfmuseum.org
223 N. Coast Highway, Oceanside
(Exit San Diego Fwy [5] W. on Mission Ave., R. on N. Coast Hwy. [TG: 1086 A7])

Surfing is the heart of the Southern California beach culture. This small museum aims to preserve the history and lifestyle of surfing so it won't be wiped out. It displays a diverse selection and variety of surfboards. To the inexperienced eye, some might look simply like thick boards, but I'm learning that there is more to the board than meets the eye. A Hawaiian hut made of palm leaves pays homage to surfing's roots, as do the many photographs and information regarding surfing. Exhibits rotate yearly and have included a tabletop wave and California surfriders from 1900 to 1940.

Hours: Open Thurs. - Mon., 10am - 4pm. Closed Tues., Wed., and holidays.
Admission: Free; donations gladly accepted.
Ages: Surfer dudes 8 years and up.

CAMP PENDLETON
(760) 725-5569 - general information / pendleton.usmc.mil
Oceanside
(Exit San Diego Fwy [5] at Oceanside Harbor/Camp Pendleton exit onto the base. You'll need to show your driver's license and vehicle registration at the main gate. [TG: 1085 J6])

Driving on I-5 between Orange County and Oceanside, it's hard to miss the sprawling Camp Pendleton. At the gate, ask for a newspaper that gives self-driving directions, the camp's history, and information on the buildings. This military training camp is one of the largest, especially for amphibious training. My boys like the thought of being on a real marine base, so taking a "windshield tour" (i.e. driving around in here) was a treat for them. We saw the Marines working out, many military vehicles, and even the helicopter landing pad. Camp Pendleton is also on an historical site where early Spanish explorers traveled. For a more detailed understanding of this time period, tour the on-site Rancho Las Flores and the nineteenth-century Santa Margarita adobe ranch house, with a minimum group of twenty people. The houses retain the essence of yesteryear in both landscaping and interior furnishings. Advanced registration is needed.

The one-room Amphibious Vehicle Museum, is located at the southern end of Camp Pendleton at the Del Mar basin. (Head south on Kraus Street.) It contains L.V.T.'s (Land Vehicle Tracks) - amphibious vehicles used in combat. These large relics from WWII are accompanied by war mementoes such as uniforms, weapons, and personal artifacts. You may ask to watch the video on the history of the L.V.T.'s. Note: The PENDLETON PAINTBALL PARK (see pg. 378) is also located on base.

Hours: Note: Call first to see if the base is currently open to the public. Drive through Camp Pendleton daily during daylight hours. Call for rancho and adobe house tours. The Amphibious Museum is usually open Tues. - Sat., 9am - 4pm.

Admission: Free

Ages: 6 years and up.

CHILDREN'S DISCOVERY MUSEUM OF NORTH COUNTY
(760) 720-0737 / www.museumforchildren.org   *$$*

300 Carlsbad Village Drive, #102, Carlsbad

(Exit San Diego Fwy [5] W. on Carlsbad Village Dr. [TG: 1106 D5])

Each room at this completely hands-on museum is themed, appealing to different aspects of your child's personality. Set sail for adventure and catch some pretend fish while skippering a real boat (at least the front end of one), surrounded by a wall with a sea mural. Use a cart to hold all your items while shopping at the well-stocked Kid's Marketplace. The cashier can use the real cash register, with fake money. Things are positively medieval when your kids play at the large replica castle. Girls dress up and turn into princesses (temporarily) while boys (and girls) suit up to become knights in shining (plastic) armor. My oldest son simply declared himself king and ordered everyone else around. Hear and see sound frequencies through the water at the World of Sound exhibit. Watch a wave machine in action. (Wave back!) Look at and learn about musical instruments from all over the world and even play a few of them. Step to the beat (and *on* the beat) on a musical floor pad. Every week Creative Corner provides your child with a new art project to create and take home. Aprons are available for those with messier instincts. At the science area, test a hand battery, watch a solar-powered train go around a track, and stand in the center of a bubble that's as tall as you are. There are a few computers in the museum and a toddler's corner that has toys and books.

The museum is located in Carlsbad Village Faire Shopping Centre. The fountain in the middle of the Plaza has reclining chairs around it making it a delightful place to rest, unless your child falls in the water!

Hours: Open Sun., Tues. - Thurs., noon - 5pm; Fri. - Sat., 10am - 5pm. Closed Mon. It's open in July and August daily, 10am - 5pm.

Admission: $5 for ages 2 and up.

Ages: 1½ - 11 years.

CLASSIC ROTORS - THE RARE AND VINTAGE ROTORCRAFT MUSEUM
(760) 787-9661 / www.rotors.org   *$*

Montecito Road at Airport Hangar #301 at the Ramona Airport, Ramona

(Just W. of Hwy 78, exit Hwy 67 N. on Montecito Rd. [TG: 1152 B6])

Home to ten, or so, rotorcraft, this large hangar holds a collection of some of the most unique helicopters I've ever seen. Come look at a Vertol H-21B Shawnee "Flying Banana" that looks like a Dr. Doolittle PushMe-PullYou, a Monte Copter model 15 tri-phiban, a Brantly 305, a Sikorsky S-55/H-19, and many more. Most of the rotors are flight ready, while others are in the process of being restored, so you'll probably see some being worked on. A coming star attraction is the unusual-looking Roton Rocket ATV (Atmospheric Test Vehicle) experimental aircraft. It was once used to test and validate a unique spacecraft atmospheric re-entry system using helicopter rotors. It will be a hands-on display here.

As a volunteer takes you on a tour of the aircraft, you learn the history of the machines - where they flew and why. Many times, too, visitors are welcome to climb into the helicopters and take it out for a spin; at least an imaginary spin. The museum not only houses the rotors, but it is a tribute to the pioneers of vertical flight technology.

Hours: Usually open on Sat., 10am - 5pm, or by appointment. Call for hours as the volunteers and rotors are often out attending air shows.

Admission: Call for prices.
Ages: 6 years and up.

COMMEMORATIVE AIR FORCE WORLD WAR II FLYING MUSEUM

(888) 215-7000 or (619) 448-4505 / www.cafairgroup1.org
1860 Joe Crosson Drive, El Cajon
(Exit San Vincente Fwy [67] W. on Bradley, R. on Pioneer Wy./Floyd Smith Dr., R. on Joe Crosson. The hangar is located just S. of Gillespie Airport. [TG: 1251 E2])

This small, but mighty, aviation museum has three main planes on display - an SN-J, a L-5, and A-26. A wildcat (an airplane, not a cat that's wild) occasionally flies in. There are a few other planes in various stages of restoration. The museum, operated by WWII aviation buffs, has a friendly and casual atmosphere. Kids (and other visitors) can tour a C-97 cockpit and get a feel for the instruments. A few army jeeps, equipped with (non-operative!) machine guns, are also on the premises. The art gallery showcases a mural, photographs, posters, and paintings, including examples of "nose art." The latter refers to artwork painted on the noses of aircraft, which was fairly common during WWII. Display cases around the perimeter of the hangar hold artifacts donated to the museum and include model planes; goggles; equipment; a Norden bombsight, which was once top secret; front pages of newspapers highlighting events from the war; and lots of other paraphernalia. Tours are offered by appointment, although the workers here are willing to answer questions at any time.

Visitors will also enjoy watching small planes land and take off. The Mayday Cafe is right around the corner. See the Calendar entry for the Wings Over Gillespie Air show (pg. 582).
Hours: Open Wed - Sun., 10am - 3pm.
Admission: Suggested donation of $5 for adults.
Ages: 4 years and up.

COMPUTER MUSEUM OF AMERICA

(619) 235-8222 / www.computer-museum.org
640 C Street, San Diego
(Going S. on San Diego Fwy [5], exit at Sassafras/Airport., go straight on Kettner Blvd., L. on C St. Going N. on 5, exit S. on 6th Ave., R. on Ash St., L on Kettner, L. on C St. Parking is ugly. The museum recommends taking the trolley as there is a stop just one block away. [TG: 1288 J3])

From an abacus to PCs, this two-story museum displays over a hundred products that show the evolution of computers. The machinery is nicely arranged and a self-guided tour notebook contains explanations for all of the equipment. Some of the items here include 1930's vintage Burroughs calculators, heavy steel IBM card punches, teletypes, an IBM 360 mainframe computer of the 60's, a Royal Precision computer that used 113 vacuum tubes, a German Enigma machine, and even a few typewriters. Some of the machines are cut open so visitors can see the inner workings. One exhibit focuses on machine and computer roles in cryptology and code breaking, from ancient time to present day. My younger, not-interested-in-technology child enjoyed the interactive exhibits - he played Pong (remember this one?), Space Invaders, and the original Donkey Kong.
Hours: Open Tues. - Sat., 10am - 5pm. Closed Mon. and national holidays.
Admission: $2 for adults; $1 for seniors and children 3 - 13.
Ages: 8 years and up.

ESCONDIDO CHILDREN'S MUSEUM / MUSEO PARA NINOS

(760) 233-7755 / www.escondidochildrensmuseum.org
341 N. Escondido Boulevard, Studio 1, California Center for the Arts, Escondido
(Going N. on Escondido Fwy [15], exit E. on Valley Pkwy, R. on Grand, L. on Escondido Blvd, R. on Woodward to park. It's adjacent to Grape Day Park. Going S. on I-15, exit E. on Hwy 78, S. on Broadway, R. on Woodward [for parking]. [TG: 1129 H2])

Come play! Our kids urge my husband and I to share in playing with them because it's important to them and they like to be with us. (I'm thankful!) This children's museum, opening in fall 2003, is a delightful place to do just that.

The one big room is divided into various sections with an emphasis on natural science and cultures around the world, and yes - everything is hands-on. Explore a doctor's office, one-room schoolhouse, a costume area, touch tables, and a space just for toddlers to crawl through tunnels and on ramps, plus a mini slide and a reading area. A wildlife section has a tree house to climb, a portion that focuses on birds and butterflies, plus maps and puzzles to put together, and a crawl space so kids can sense how subterranean animals feel.

The outside California Courtyard showcases native California plants, a mission-era adobe structure, a wicki-up, and more. A multi-purpose room and a gift shop complete this museum. Ask about the many programs they offer and don't forget that it's located right next to GRAPE DAY PARK (see pg. 416).

      Hours: Call for hours.

  Admission: Call for admission prices.

       Ages: 6 months to 10 years.

FIREHOUSE MUSEUM

(619) 232-3473

1572 Columbia Street, San Diego

(Going N. on San Diego Fwy [5], exit E. on Hawthorne St., L. on Columbia. Going S. on 5, exit S. on Front St., R. on Cedar. It's on the L. at Columbia St. [TG: 1289 A2])

Have a hot time in downtown San Diego by visiting the Firehouse Museum! Housed inside an old fire station, the museum features ten antique fire engines from different time periods. Also on display are several antique pieces of fire-fighting equipment such as a water pump and steamer, helmets, axes, and speaking trumpets through which chiefs would shout their orders, plus other items such as a telephone switchboard. A more recent addition is a September 11 memorial display which includes picture and World Trade Center artifacts.

      Hours: Open Thurs. - Fri., 10am - 2pm; Sat. - Sun., 10am - 4pm.

  Admission: $2 for adults; $1.50 for seniors and ages 13 - 17; children 12 and under are free. The first Thurs. of every month is free admission day.

       Ages: 4 years and up.

FLYING LEATHERNECK AVIATION MUSEUM

(858) 693-1723 / flyingleatherneck.netfirms.com

Miramar Road at U. S. Marine Corps Air Station, Miramar

(Exit Jacob Dekema Fwy [805] or Escondido Fwy [15] E. on Miramar Road. Enter the base through the North Gate. Bring a photo I.D. [TG: 1209 D6])

This Marine Corps Aviation Museum is devoted to preserving and promoting the history of the Marine Corp, and looking to its future. There are forty-one aircraft on display - a Sikorsky 53A/D cargo helicopter, McDonnell F2H-2 "Banshee," and North American FJ-3 "Fury," to name a few. The planes and copters date from World War II up to modern day. Several aircraft are undergoing restoration, a process that ranges from a complete overhaul to simply a new coat of paint. Visitors are invited to see the planes, learn their histories, and ask questions of the docents.

The display cases contain military and aviation artifacts such as uniforms, engines, equipment, historic documents, a collection of patches (2,400!), and more. A favorite item is the F4 flight simulation cockpit where kids (and adults) can climb into the cockpit to check out all the instruments, gauges, and the joystick. Don't forget to take a look through the great gift shop. Guided tours are given of the museum by appointment. For the more technically oriented, there are numerous videos, photographs, and documents in the library.

      Hours: Open Mon. - Sat., 9am - 3pm. Closed Sun. and holidays.

  Admission: Free

       Ages: 5 years and up.

GASKILL STONE STORE MUSEUM

(619) 478-5707

31330 Highway 94, Campo

(Exit 8 Fwy [45 miles from downtown San Diego] S. on Buckman Springs Rd., 10.5 miles to Hwy. 94, bear right [1.5 miles] to the store on the corner. [TG: 430 B10])

This small museum is exactly as its name implies - a museum created from an old store built with stones in 1885. The exhibits in the room consist of a stocked, old-fashioned general store; a small, turn-of-the-century kitchen; tools; appliances; and lots of photographs and documents. The back room is a man-made cave blasted from rock, once used for storing food (i.e. a really old-fashioned refrigerator) and other items. Upstairs is a military room with mannequins in uniforms, plus photographs and information about this area's military region. A stream runs in front of the museum and a woods surrounds it. Just around the corner is the PACIFIC SOUTHWEST RAILWAY MUSEUM (see pg. 458).

Hours: Open weekends and selected holidays, 11am - 5pm.

Admission: $2 for adults; children 12 and under are free.

Ages: 7 years and up.

GUY B. WOODWARD MUSEUM OF HISTORY

(760) 789-7644

645 Main Street, Ramona

(From San Diego Fwy [5] or Escondido Fwy [15], take 78 Fwy E. to Ramona, L. on Main St. [also 78]. From 8 Fwy, take San Vicente Fwy [67] N. Stay on Hwy 67 to Ramona, which turns into Main St. [TG: 1152 H5])

A complex of buildings make up this small, early western museum "town." The outside courtyard has a stage wagon - no springs made for a bumpy ride! A red barn houses an old medicine wagon (an RV prototype). The long garage contains a 1920's tractor, old buggies, an antique fire engine, fire fighting equipment, and lots of old tools, such as saws and wheat scythes, in neat rows on the walls. Just around the corner is a Honey House which contains beekeeping equipment. A narrow Millinery Shoppe features real mink stoles, outrageous feather hats, and a few beaded dresses. Other buildings here include a real jail; an outhouse; a re-created post office; a blacksmith shop complete with all the tools of the trade; a bunkhouse where cowboys used to live; a Tack Room with dusty, rusty saddles; and a Hobby Room, which is really a catch-all room filled with old typewriters, bottles, and one of the first T.V. sets. Farm machinery is displayed all around the cluster of buildings. See if your kids can recognize washing machines, butter churns, the large incubator, a cream separator, and a machine for bottling milk.

The museum contains the heritage (and furnishings) of the older citizens of Ramona. The 1886 main house has roped-off rooms to look into including a turn-of-the-century doctor's office with a mannequin nurse and a collection of early medical instruments and vials; a beautifully decorated parlor, which is a combination of living room and music room, with mannequins dressed in period clothing; a library; a bedroom; and a kitchen that is packed with irons, dishes, butter churns, and other implements. The screened in back porch is set up like a bedroom - my kids were ready to move in!

The downstairs used to be a wine cellar, and the temperature is still cool here. The conglomeration of "stuff" now stored and displayed here includes Civil War artifacts, such as uniforms and cannon balls; a collection of cameras; a turkey-feather cape; a six-foot long Red Diamond Rattlesnake skin; Native American artifacts, such as stone mortar and pestle, and pottery; a hair perming machine that looks like something out of a science fiction film; a Casey Tibbs memorial exhibit dedicated to this World Champion rodeo rider; mining equipment; and more.

This unique museum is more than a glimpse into the past - it is a good, long, and interesting look into our ancestors' way of life. Note that school group tours are given by appointment Monday through Wednesday. While you're here, enjoy a stroll around historic Old Town Ramona, located on both sides and across the street from the museum.

Hours: Open Thurs. - Sun., 1pm - 4pm. Closed the month of September.

Admission:　$3 for adults; 50¢ for children 12 and under.
　　　Ages:　5 years and up.

HERITAGE OF THE AMERICAS MUSEUM

(619) 670-5194 / www.cuyamaca.net/museum

12110 Cuyamaca College Drive West at Cuyamaca College, El Cajon

(Going W. on 8 Fwy, exit S. on 2nd St. which turns into Jamacha Rd. [Hwy 54], continue on Jamacha Rd., R. on Cuyamaca College Dr. W. Going E. on 8, exit S. on Fwy 125, exit S. on Spring St., immediately get on 94 Fwy E., continue on to end, turns into Campo Rd., L. on Jamacha Rd., L on Cuyamaca College Dr. W. It is on the Cuyamaca College campus. [TG: 1271 J5])

This museum makes learning about our heritage much more exciting than simply reading about it in a history book. Four different exhibit halls branch off diagonally from the reception desk. The **Natural History Hall** contains rocks and minerals, including a lodestone (i.e. a hunk of rock with a magnetic "personality") with nails sticking out from it. The meteorite display is out of this world. Other favorite items in this wing include a fossilized turtle shell, a T-Rex tooth, an Allosaurus claw, trilobites, a rattlesnake skin, a prehistoric bee trapped in amber, shells, coral, and seahorses. The many taxidermied animals include a leopard, deer, coyote, and the head of a cape buffalo.

The **Archaeology Hall** contains an incredible arrowhead collection, gathered from all over the world, and from different periods of time. Some of them are practical, while others are more ornamental. Other displays in the glass cases include stone artifacts, such as hoes and ax heads; Mayan treasures of stone and clay; necklaces made of jade, quartz, and amethyst; and various forms of money, such as shells and copper. Weapons, of course, are always a hit with my boys.

The **Anthropology Hall** showcases impressive Native American artifacts such as eagle feather headdresses, ceremonial costumes, and exquisitely beaded moccasins, gloves, and vests. More intriguing, however, are the elk tooth and eagle claw necklaces; beaded mountain lion paw bag; knife made from a blackfoot bear jaw; shark tooth sword that looks like a small chain saw; and rattles (used for dances) made out of turtle shells and trap door spiders' nests. This section also displays tomahawks, guns from the Old West, and a buffalo robe.

The **Art Hall** features Western art with cowboys and Indians portrayed in drawings, paintings, photographs, and sculptures. Four different pamphlets are available that give details about exhibits in each of the halls. This hilltop museum also has two small gardens with picnic tables, plus a stunning 360-degree view.

　　　Hours:　Open Tues. - Fri., 10am - 4pm; Sat., noon - 4pm. Closed Sun., Mon., and major holidays.
Admission:　$3 for adults; $2 for seniors; $1 for students with ID; children 16 and under are free.
　　　Ages:　5 years and up.

HERITAGE WALK / GRAPE DAY PARK

(760) 743-8207 / www.ci.escondido.ca.us

321 N. Broadway, Escondido

(Exit Escondido Fwy [15] E. on Fwy 78, R. on Broadway which is Hwy 78 [TG: 1129 J2])

Grape Day Park has a charming ambiance created by a rose garden, large grassy areas, shade trees, picnic tables, Victorian buildings, a restored train depot, and a unique playground. The small playground has a climbing structure that looks like giant grape vines, along with grape leaf seats and a slide resembling a bunch of grapes. (No sour grapes at this play area.) The park has horseshoe pits, too. Equipment can be checked out weekdays from 8am to 4pm. (Parental supervision is required.)

The five buildings that comprise the museum complex of Heritage Walk were relocated here in 1976, and are open to the public. They are: 1) Escondido's first library; 2) A quaint, completely furnished two-story 1890's house with a living room, parlor, and kitchen, plus four small bedrooms upstairs; 3) A 1900's barn containing a 1890's popcorn wagon, a 1935 winery truck, a working printing press, and more; 4) A blacksmith's shop that's open on Thursdays and Fridays, and on Saturdays (except during the summer) for classes and demonstrations; and 5) An 1888 Santa Fe Depot. The two-story depot building is nice-looking and interesting to explore. Some highlights include a train master's office, a working telegraph station (send a message to someone!), and a Q & A board of Escondido history. The depot also has a real train car that can be toured. It contains a model train set with an historic layout that makes tracks around realistic looking landscape.

A tank house and a small herb garden can also be seen on the short walk around Heritage Walk. The park is a fun place for kids to play, but bring them sometime to see the museum part of it, also. Call for tour information. Note that the ESCONDIDO CHILDREN'S MUSEUM/MUSEO PARA NINOS (see pg. 413) is located adjacent to this park. If you're looking for a place to cool off in the summertime, the James Stone Municipal pool is just next door. Call (760) 838-4810 for hours and prices.

Hours: The park is open daily, sunrise - sunset. The museum complex is open Thurs - Sat., 1pm - 4pm. It's closed Thanksgiving weekend, all major holidays, and during rainy weather.

Admission: Free. Donations of $3 for adults and $1 per child for the Heritage Walk are requested.

Ages: All for the park; ages 5 and up for the museum.

HISTORICAL MAGEE PARK

(760) 434-9189 / www.carlsbad.ca.us
258 Beech Avenue, Carlsbad
(Exit San Diego Fwy [405] W. on Carlsbad Village Dr., R. on Carlsbad Blvd., L. on Beech. [TG: 1106 D5])

This quaint historic park qualifies as a park with its grassy lawns, picnic tables, barbecues, and shuffleboard courts all overlooking the Pacific Ocean. The "historic" part enters the equation because of the 1926 town meeting hall on the grounds and the vintage, 1887 one-story Magee House, a small home open to tour through on the weekends. Come enjoy a slice of history.

Hours: The park is open daily, sunrise - sunset. The house is open for tours Sat. - Sun., noon - 4pm.

Admission: The park is free. Donations are requested for the Magee House.

Ages: 8 years and up.

JULIAN PIONEER MUSEUM

(760) 765-0227 / www.julianfun.com
2811 Washington Street, Julian
(From San Diego Fwy [5] or Escondido Fwy [15], take 78 Fwy E. to Julian. 78 is Washington St. in Julian. From the 8 Fwy, take 79 N. to Julian, at 78 Jct. turn left on Main St., L. on Washington St. [TG: 1136 B7])

If I were to clean out my grandparents' and great-grandparents' attics, closets, garages, etc., I would probably find many articles similar to what is inside this pioneer museum. The wide assortment of items here include carriages, guns, saddles, tools, eyeglasses, mining equipment, rocks, bottles, clothing, arrowheads, a ceremonial Indian costume, kitchen implements, a metal bathtub, a pot-bellied stove, an American flag (with forty-five stars), and lots of old, handmade lace. My favorite exhibit was a machine from a 1930's beauty shop. It was supposed to perm hair, but with the wires and rods sticking out all over the mannequin's head, it looks more like something from a science fiction film! Tip: Ask for a pencil scavenger hunt for the kids. Bring a lunch and enjoy a picnic on the tables outside this quaint museum.

Julian is a charming town with unique shops along Main Street. Your kids will enjoy a stop-off at the Julian Drugstore, located at the corner of Main Street and Washington Street, to enjoy an ice cream at its old-fashioned soda counter. Also see EAGLE MINING COMPANY (pg. 450) to take a tour of a real gold mine.

Hours: Open December - March, Sat. - Sun. and certain holidays, 10am - 4pm. Open April - November, daily, 10am - 4pm. Closed Mon., New Year's Day, Thanksgiving, and Christmas.

Admission: $2 for adults; $1 for ages 8 - 18; children 7 and under are free.

Ages: 5 years and up.

LA MESA DEPOT

(619) 465-7776 / www.sdrm.org
4650 Nebo Drive, La Mesa
(Going E. on the 8 Fwy, exit at Spring St., at end of off ramp, go straight on Nebo Dr. Going W. on 8, exit E. on El Cajon Dr., L. on Nebo. [TG: 1270 J3])

This restored train station, circa 1894, boasts of a few cars still on the tracks - an engine, and caboose. The small depot building is contains several railroad artifacts, including an antique baggage scale.

Hours: Usually open Sat., 1pm - 4pm.

Admission: Free

Ages: All

MARINE CORPS RECRUIT DEPOT COMMAND MUSEUM

(619) 524-4426 / www.usmchistory.com

In the Marine Corps Recruit Depot on Pacific Highway and Witherby Street, San Diego

(Going S. on San Diego Fwy [5], exit at Old Town Ave., go straight from off ramp onto Hancock St., R. on Witherby St. Going N. on 5, exit at Moore St., L. on Old Town Ave, L. on Hancock St., R. on Witherby St. You must show a valid driver's license to enter the base. The museum is directly across from the guard entrance. [TG: 1268 F6])

The first thing my kids noticed were the Japanese 70mm Howitzers outside the museum. Inside, the downstairs California Room displays numerous paintings of war, including battles involving Native Americans, blue coats verses grey coats, and more. The hallway has photos of movies and television shows that have featured Marines. An on-going, twenty-minute narrated film is presented in the small theater. It shows all the different phases of Marine training, from boot camp to graduation. Naturally, the "coolest" parts of it, according to my boys, were the army maneuvers where rounds and rounds of ammunition were shot, and the nighttime target practice where spots of light were seen when the guns were fired. After the movie my youngest son, with his eyes shining, declared, "I want to be a Marine!" The visitor's lounge looks like a large living room with couches and chairs. Around the perimeter of the room are exhibits such as helicopter and ship models, various military hats, and small models of physical fitness courses that make me tired just looking at them.

The upstairs rooms are filled with military memorabilia. The extensive exhibits include uniforms, swords, medals, grenades, posters, pictures, flags, mannequins dressed in camouflage, rocket launchers, jeeps, police motorcycles, a collection of knives (including machetes and bayonets), and a room devoted to guns and ammunition. The China Room focuses on American Marines in Peking. It contains a lot of documents and news articles from this time period, plus photos, traditional Chinese military dress, and a cannon.

The museum encompasses the history of the Marines from its inception 225 years ago, through WWI and WWII, and up to the present day. Always looking for "a few good men and women," the Marine Corps maintains a museum that is historically important, and that will enlist your child's attention.

Forty-four Fridays out of the year the Marine Corps holds a brief "morning colors ceremony," where the flag is raised and the *National Anthem* is played. It begins at 8am sharp. At 9:50am, a "pass and review" parade, mini band concert, and graduation ceremony commence. The public is welcome to attend one or both ceremonies. Call for specific dates.

Hours: Open Mon. - Fri., 0800 - 1600 (8am - 4pm) - open Thurs. until 6pm. Call for summer hours. Closed most federal holidays.

Admission: Free

Ages: 5 years and up.

MARSTON HOUSE

$$

(619) 298-3142 / www.sandiegohistory.org

3525 7th Avenue, San Diego

(Going S. on San Diego Fwy [5], exit at Sassafras/Airport., go straight on Kettner Blvd., L. on Laurel St., L. on 6th Ave., R. on Upas St. It's at the end of Upas St. on 7th Ave. Going N. on 5, exit N. on 6th Ave., R. on Upas St. Going S. on Cabrillo Fwy [163], exit S. on 6th Ave., L. on Upas St. [TG: 1269 B6])

This 1905 mansion was built to provide "function, simplicity and good design." (For an interesting contrast, compare its practical exterior and interior designs to the much more elaborate VILLA MONTEZUMA JESSE SHEPARD HOUSE; see page 437.) The sixteen various rooms, covering four floors, plus a basement, are decorated in American Arts and Crafts, oriental, and Native American styles. What a fun and different way to learn the many facets of American history! The forty-five-minute tours are better for older kids who can appreciate the lifestyle changes that occurred during the early twentieth century. Also enjoy touring through the five acres of landscaped grounds.

Hours: Open Fri. - Sun., 10am - 4:30pm. Tours are mostly given on the hour.

Admission: $5 for adults; $4 for seniors; $2 for ages 6 - 17; children 5 and under are free.

Ages: 9 years and up.

MINGEI INTERNATIONAL FOLK ART MUSEUM

$$

(619) 239-0003 / www.mingei.org

Plaza de Panama, Balboa Park, San Diego

(Going S. on San Diego Fwy [5], exit at Sassafras/Airport, go straight on Kettner Blvd. L. on Laurel St., which turns into El Prado. Going N. on 5, exit N. on Pershing Dr., L. on Florida Dr., L. on Zoo PL., L. on Park Blvd., R. on Village Pl. Going S. on Cabrillo Fwy [163], exit N. on Park Blvd. (near end), L. on Presidents Wy. [TG: 1289 C1])

"Min" is the Japanese word for "all people"; "gei" means "art," so mingei translates as "art of all people," or folk art. A child's enjoyment of this folk art museum depends on the current exhibits. We saw many tapestries, handcrafted furniture, and beautiful pieces of jewelry. Past exhibits have included toys and dolls from around the world, Mexican folk art, and the horse in folk art. Call first, or go on the third Tuesday of the month when admission is free. The museum's gift shop offers colorful and unique items. (See BALBOA PARK on page 408 for a listing of all the museums and attractions within walking distance.)

Hours: Open Tues. - Sun., 10am - 4pm. Closed Mon. and national holidays.

Admission: $5 for adults; $2 for ages 6 - 17; children 5 and under are free. Admission on the third Tuesday of every month is free. Passports for thirteen museums in Balboa Park are available for $30 for adults at the Visitors Center, and are good for one week from the date of purchase. (Children's admissions are already discounted or free.)

Ages: 8 years and up.

MISSION BASILICA SAN DIEGO DE ALCALA

$

(619) 281-8449 / www.missionsandiego.com

10818 San Diego Mission Road, San Diego

(Going W. on Mission Valley Fwy [8], exit N. on Mission Gorge Rd., L. on Twain Ave., which turns into San Diego Mission Rd. From Escondido Fwy [15], exit E. on Friars Rd., R. on Mission Gorge Rd., R. on Twain Ave. [TG: 1249 H7])

Father Junipero Serra came to California on a mission - to start missions. The Mission San Diego de Alcala was the first church in California, founded by the Padre in 1769. As with a visit to any of the twenty-one missions, coming here brings the past vividly back to life. The church is long and narrow and, of course, housed in an adobe structure. The gardens here are very small, but pretty. The Padre Luis Jayme Museum, named after the missionary who was killed here by an Indian attack, contains some interesting excavated artifacts such as flintlock pistols, swords, buttons, and pottery. Other exhibits here include vestments, old photos, and small dioramas of all the missions. The monastery ruins have partial walls and the outlines of where the padres living quarters, the library, and other rooms once stood. Tips: Read the pamphlet about the mission as you explore it, because knowing its history makes it much more interesting for kids. Or, use the tote-a-tape tour, which audibly explains more about this mission. The cost is $2 per tape/recorder.

Hours: Open daily, 9am - 4:45pm. Closed Easter, Thanksgiving, and Christmas.

Admission: $3 for adults; $2 for seniors and students over 12; $1 for children 11 and under.

Ages: 7 years and up.

MISSION SAN ANTONIO DE PALA

$

(760) 742-3317

Pala Mission Road, Pala

(Exit Escondido Fwy [15] E. on Pala Rd. [Route 76], go about 6 miles, then L. on 3rd St. R. on Pala Mission Rd. [TG: 1029 J4])

This mission, founded in 1816, is the only remaining Spanish California Mission to continue in its original purpose of proselytizing and serving Native Americans. The adjacent school is for Native American children and the gift shop is run by Native Americans. The small mission is located on an Indian Reservation, a fact that greatly enhanced its value in my children's eyes.

The museum part of the mission consists of two small wings. One contains arrowheads, pottery, clothing with intricate beadwork, the Padre's small quarters, and an altar. Hand-carved religious figures and the Southwestern-style painted ceilings are eye-catching. The other wing is the Mineral Room, showcasing nice specimens of jasper, petrified wood slabs, and amethyst. The room also has a marine display that includes a stuffed puffer fish, corral, huge shells, and a giant clam shell.

The small back courtyard has a nicely landscaped garden, an altar, and a fountain with Koi. The old bell tower is around the side of the mission, next to the cemetery.

Hours: Open Wed. - Sun., 10am - 5pm. Closed most major holidays.
Admission: $2 for adults; $1 for children 12 and under.
Ages: 6 years and up.

MISSION SAN LUIS REY DE FRANCA

(760) 757-3651 / www.sanluisrey.org

4050 Mission Avenue, Oceanside

(From San Diego Fwy [5], exit N. on San Luis Rey Mission Exwy [76] about 4 miles. From Escondido Fwy [15], exit W. on Pala Rd [76] about 15 miles. From 76, exit N. on Rancho del Oro Dr. [TG: 1086 H2])

Founded in 1798, this mission has been nicknamed "King of the Missions" because it is the largest of the twenty-one missions. It is also one of the most interesting. The extensive grounds cover nearly six and a half acres, though not all of it is open to the public. The first series of rooms contain several glass-encased displays that document the history of the mission. Next, is the Friar's small bedroom with a knotted rope bed, and monks' robes. (Ten Franciscan monks still live here in a separate section of the mission.) The weavery and work rooms have a loom, spinning wheel, and implements for leather tooling, respectively. The kitchen contains pots, pans, a brick oven, and glassware typical of the Mission period. The next few rooms display embroidered vestments, statues of angels and the Madonna, and other religious art work. The big Mission Church is gorgeous. Exit the church through the Madonna Chapel into the cemetery which contains a large wooden cross to commemorate the 3,000 Indians buried here.

The grounds are equally interesting to explore. Large grassy areas, with plenty of picnic tables, are outside the mission's front doors. Just past this area are ruins of soldiers' barracks. Further down, toward the street, is an ornate stone arch and a tiled stairway that lead to an old mission laundry area and large sunken garden, where Indians bathed. The garden looks like it was left over from Babylonian times; once elegantly landscaped, but now overgrown. Mission San Luis Rey de Franca is a great one to cover for those fourth grade mission reports! And of course, guided tours are available by reservation.

Hours: Open daily, 10am - 4:pm. Closed New Year's Day, Easter, Thanksgiving, and Christmas.
Admission: $4 for adults; $3 for ages 8 - 14; children 7 and under are free. $12 is the family rate.
Ages: 5 years and up.

MUSEUM OF CONTEMPORARY ART (La Jolla)

(858) 454-3541 / www.mcasd.org

700 Prospect Street, La Jolla

(Exit San Diego Fwy [5] W. on La Jolla Village Dr., L. on Torrey Pines Rd., R. on Prospect Pl., which turns into Prospect St. [TG: 1227 E7])

I admit two things about contemporary art museums: 1) I enjoy visiting them, and 2) I don't always "get" the art on exhibit. I've learned not to step on things lying on the floor or to touch anything, even things as seemingly innocuous as a pole in the center of the room - it could be an exhibit. Displays here rotate about every three months, so there are new eclectic paintings, sculptures, photos, and other pieces to figure out every few months.

Our favorite past exhibits include a room-size metal spider carrying a nest of eggs; toddler-size figures made out of wax in various stages of melting because of the heat lamps directed on them; the "Reason for the Neutron Bomb," which had 50,000 match tips glued onto nickels on the floor, each one representing a Russian tank; and a darkened room with a large church bell which, when my kids pulled on the rope, triggered a hologram of the Virgin Mary and baby Jesus to appear.

The M.C.A. offers school tours with reservations and walk-in tours daily at 2pm, plus an additional tour on Thursdays at 5:30pm. Pick up a free children's guide (pamphlet) at the reception desk about discovering contemporary art. It asks thought-provoking questions, and gives kids things to do and look for. Join in on a free kid's art afternoon on the last Sunday of every month. Don't forget that you can enjoy a light meal at the cafe, or a cappuccino. By the way, the view of the coastline from the museum is spectacular. Also see the following entry, MUSEUM OF CONTEMPORARY ART (San Diego).

Hours: Open Mon. - Tues., and Fri. - Sun., 11am - 5pm; open Thurs. 11am - 8pm. Closed Wed.

Admission: $6 for adults; $2 for seniors, military with ID, and students; children 11 and under are free. Admission is free on the first Sun. and third Tues. of every month.

Ages: 6 years and up.

MUSEUM OF CONTEMPORARY ART (San Diego)

(619) 234-1001 / www.mcasd.org

1001 Kettner Boulevard, San Diego

(Going S. on San Diego Fwy [5], exit S. on Front St., R. on Broadway. Going N. on the 5, exit S. on 6th Ave. R. on Broadway. It's at Broadway and Kettner, right by the metro. Metered parking is sometimes available on the street or in the underground structure at America Plaza, accessed from India St., between Broadway and B St. [TG: 1288 J3])

This artsy-style building sets the right mood for your visit to San Diego's contemporary art museum. What kinds of materials are used in the art that you're looking at? Traditional materials, like paint? Or nuts, bolts, wires, or other improbable materials? These are a few of the questions listed in the (free) children's guide on discovering contemporary art, which is found at the reception desk. The guide helps your child become more involved with the art, and enables him/her to understand the artist's vision in creating their work. Contemporary art is fun because it is eclectic. Some art pieces might be as unusual as a box of cereal, while other paintings, sculptures, and/or photos are a more daring combination of design, light and texture. This small museum, which has quarterly rotating exhibits, is a branch of the main M.C.A. in La Jolla. (See the above entry.)

Hours: Open Mon - Tues. and Thurs. - Sat., 10am - 5pm; Sun., noon - 5. Closed Wed. Guided tours are offered Sat. and Sun. at 2pm.

Admission: Free. Underground parking is $2 for 2 hours with validation.

Ages: 6 years and up.

MUSEUM OF CREATION AND EARTH HISTORY

(619) 448-0900 / www.icr.org

10946 Woodside Avenue North, Santee

(From 52 Fwy/125 Fwy, exit E. on Mission Gorge Rd. Just past the intersection at Magnolia, the road turns into Woodside Ave. and forks at a stop sign; go L. on Woodside. The museum is ¼ mile on the L. From San Vicente Fwy [67], exit N. on Riverford Rd., L. on Woodside. [TG: 1231 F5])

Genesis 1:1: "In the beginning, God created the heavens and the earth." This walk-through creation museum, a part of the adjacent Institute of Creation Research, is a richly visual way of seeing how the earth and its inhabitants have developed. Each phase of the earth's history is graphically represented by murals, photographs, models, or audio sounds, plus Biblical references, questions to ponder, and lots of technical information. Start at the beginning, of course, and proceed through to modern day. Day four (when the sun, moon, stars, and planets were created) is the first dramatic depiction of the unfolding wonders of our universe. This room is basically dark, with spotlights on stunning photos of the planets, constellations, and our sun. Each photograph is accompanied by factual explanations. Entering the room for days five and six is like entering a small jungle. Greenery abounds alongside a few cages of small live animals such as birds, fish, and snakes. Accompanied by Psalm 139 ("I am fearfully and wonderfully made. . .") an entire wall shows models of man, his inner workings, diagrams, and pictures of families.

Continue on, and see the fall of man, illustrated by bones, decay, and the sound of crying; a wood-paneled room with a mural depicting Noah's ark, complete with storm sounds and lightning flashing; a room with touchable walls that are layers of the earth and a replicated Mt. St. Helens' volcano that you can walk through; a blue hallway representing the Ice Age with icicles hanging overhead and models of woolly mammoths; an Egyptian room with a scale model of the enormous Tower of Babel taking center stage; the Stone Age room; the room of civilization immortalizing (so to speak) Greek and Roman cultures; and finally, the hallway of modern man, including pictures and philosophies of evolutionists and creationists. The Museum of Creation is the ultimate, interactive timeline.

Each of the rooms offers various free pamphlets that discuss the ideas and facts presented throughout the museum. Guided tours are available for groups, between fifteen to thirty people, with reservations. The tours are geared for at least first graders and up. The museum is geared for slightly older children as a lot of the information is very technical, however, the incredible visuals make quite an impact on any age.

Hours: Open Mon. - Sat., 9am - 4pm. Closed major holidays. Hour-long free tours are offered Tues. - Thurs. at 9:30am and 11am; Sat. at 10am and 2pm. Call to make a reservation.

Admission: Free

Ages: 5 - 9 years for the visual enjoyment; 10 years old and up to understand the technical information.

MUSEUM OF MAKING MUSIC

(760) 438-5996 / www.museumofmakingmusic.com   *$$*

5790 Armada Drive, Carlsbad

(Exit San Diego Fwy [5] E. on Palomar Airport Rd., L. on Armada. It's inside the NAMM (National Association of Music Merchants) building on the R. [TG: 1126 J3])

"It makes no difference if it's sweet or hot, just give that rhythm everything you got." (From *It Don't Mean A Thing* by Irving Mills and Duke Ellington.) This would be a fitting motto for this *note*-worthy museum. The museum is nicely laid out and chronologically traces the history of music from the late 1800's through present day in an audibly and visually stimulating way. Paintings and wall-sized historic photographs of musicians add to the museum's ambiance.

Each section showcases, behind glass, instruments (over 450 total!) typical for that particular era which could include trumpets, banjos, mandolins, harmonicas, guitars, electric guitars (one signed by Jimi Hendrix), keyboards, pianos (one signed by Henry Mancini), horns, and drums. The sections also have listening stations where visitors can, at the press of a button, hear samplings of popular music, sounds of specific instruments, and even some of the key innovations and inventions that changed the style of music being produced. Expose kids to the sound of ragtime, big bands, jazz, blues, hillbilly, country, and more. Rooms toward the exit emphasize music probably more familiar to them - rock and roll, heavy metal, new wave, jazz infusion, and the Latin scene. Videos, instead of just "audios," accompany the latter years of music.

End your visit on a high note by letting the kids play the instruments in the small lobby/gift shop. Children are encouraged to try out the drum set, keyboard, and electric guitars whose sound, thankfully, can only be heard through headsets. Although the gift shop doesn't sell instruments, it does have a wide variety of them on display and it does sell some unique, music-related gifts. Forty-five-minute to hour-and-a-half (depending on the size of the group and age level) guided tours for the general public and for school groups are available.

Hours: Open Tues. - Sun., 10am - 5pm. Closed Mon., New Year's Day, July 4th, Thanksgiving, and Christmas.

Admission: $5 for adults; $3 for seniors, active military, and ages 4 - 18; children 3 and under are free.

Ages: 7 years and up.

MUSEUM OF PHOTOGRAPHIC ARTS

(619) 238-7559 / www.mopa.org   *$$*

1649 El Prado, Balboa Park, San Diego

(Going S. on San Diego Fwy [5], exit at Sassafras/Airport, go straight on Kettner Blvd. L. on Laurel St., which turns into El Prado. Going N. on 5, exit N. on Pershing Dr., L. on Florida Dr., L. on Zoo Pl., L. on Park Blvd., R. on Village Pl. Going S. on Cabrillo Fwy [163], exit N. on Park Blvd. (near end), L. on Presidents Wy. [TG: 1289 C1])

Your shutterbugs will appreciate this large showroom, with five galleries, that features changing exhibits of photographic works. Some exhibits zoom in on portraiture work or the history of American photography, while others focus more on pictures taken from all over the world. We enjoy the artistry in the pictures as well as comparing styles and choice of subjects. Ask about the Visual Classroom, a student-friendly curriculum supplement. Free guided tours are given Sundays at 1pm.

A 200-seat theater shows a variety of movies such as *All Dogs Go to Heaven*, *Angels in the Outfield*, and *Heaven Can Wait*. (See BALBOA PARK on page 408 for a listing of all the museums and attractions within walking distance.)

Hours: The museum is open daily, 10am - 5pm; Thurs. until 9pm. It's closed all major holidays. The theater shows movies usually on Fri. night. Call for specific hours.

Admission: Museum admission is $6 for adults; $4 for seniors, military, and students; children 11 and under are free. Admission to the museum is free on the second Tues. of every month. Passports for thirteen museums in Balboa Park are available for $30 for adults at the Visitors Center, and are good for one week from the date of purchase. (Children's admissions are already discounted or free.) Theater admission is $5 for adults; $4.50 for seniors, students, and ages 11 and under.

Ages: 7 years and up.

NATIONAL CITY SANTA FE DEPOT

(619) 474-4400 / www.trainweb.org/sandiegorail/sdera

922 W. 23rd Street, National City

(Exit San Diego Fwy [5] W. on Bay Marina Dr., R. on Harrison. The depot sits between 24th and 23rd on Harrison Avenue [TG: 1309 G3])

This small historic depot, originally built in 1882, is restored to its original floor plan, containing ticket offices and upstairs living quarters for the station master. It is now home to the electric railway museum, too. The main attractions for little train lovers are the model train layout and the play trains for kids to push around on tracks. Across the street is a glassed-enclosed gazebo that protects the restored an 1887 passenger coach No. 1.

Hours: The museum is open Sat. - Sun., noon - 4pm.

Admission: $3 for adults; $1 for ages 5 - 15; children 4 and under are free.

Ages: All

OLD TOWN SAN DIEGO AND STATE HISTORIC PARK

(619) 220-5422 - Robinson Rose House and park ranger;

(619) 298-8687 - Old Town Market / www.sandiegohistory.org; www.historictours.com

Taylor, Juan, Twiggs, and Congress Sts., Old Town, San Diego

(Going S. on San Diego Fwy [5] [just south of Interstate 8] exit E. [across the bridge] on Old Town Ave., L. on San Diego Ave. Going N. on 5, exit on Old Town Ave., L. on San Diego Ave. or Congress St. Parking is available on the streets if you arrive early, or at several parking lots. [TG: 1268 F5])

Old Town is a six-block area, which is closed to automotive traffic and bound by Taylor, Juan, Twiggs, and Congress streets. The places mentioned below encompass this area, plus the immediate, walkable vicinity.

This wonderful conglomeration of unique shops, scrumptious places to eat, vintage houses, museums, and a Mexican bazaar, are all located along dirt "roads" and on paved sidewalks outside of "town." Old Town contains many original and restored buildings from San Diego's Mexican period before 1846, and the early California period. A day here is a combination of history lessons and fun shopping! Just a quick note about some of the stores here: Dip your own candle in an array of waxy colors for $3.95 at the Candle Shop. Through the window at the Cousin's Candy Shop come watch salt water taffy being pulled; then go inside and buy yourself a treat. Just a few favorite other stores include Miner's Gems and Minerals, Toler's Leather Depot, The Mexico Shop, and of course the ice cream shop.

Make sure to visit the Old Town Market here. This complex, by Twiggs Street and San Diego Avenue, is housed in a renovated convent building. It features the reconstructed Casa de Aguirre which now serves as a free museum. The Casa has historical displays of old San Diego, text panels, a video on this area, and artifacts found while excavating this site. The rest of the market is comprised of gift shops and of artisans who demonstrate their craft as they work, such as a silversmith, a painter, and a bonsai sculptor. The adjacent stage is used for free shows such as storytelling, concerts, magic shows, and other presentations appealing to families.

The route for the attractions listed below starts at the Robinson Rose House - the park headquarters - then proceeds east, south, and north before looping back around. Most of the attractions are open daily, 10am to 5pm; shops are usually open until 9pm in the spring and summer. Admission is free, unless otherwise noted. All historic buildings are closed on New Year's Day, Thanksgiving, and Christmas. Free maps of the area are available at the park headquarters, in many of the stores in Old Town, and in local hotel lobbies. Free walking tours that cover all of the old buildings, not just the more kid-friendly ones I've listed here, are offered daily at 11am and 2pm beginning at Robinson Rose House.

ROBINSON ROSE HOUSE is located at 4002 Wallace Street, on the other side of the parking lot from Taylor Street. This 1853 adobe structure houses the park headquarters and has walking tour maps available for purchase. It also has a few exhibits, such as photo murals and a scale model of Old Town as it appeared in the mid 1870's.

OLD TOWN PLAZA is located directly in front of the Robinson Rose House. This area is essentially a large grassy area for kids to run around, with olive, fig, cork, and eucalyptus trees providing beauty and shade. A large fountain is in the middle of this park and there are plenty of benches for weary travelers (or shoppers).

The row of stores across from the Plaza are in reconstructed buildings dating from around 1830.

COLORADO HOUSE/WELLS FARGO MUSEUM is located on San Diego Street in the heart of Old Town. This museum has the appeal of the Old West, with a Concord Stagecoach prominently displayed in the center. Other exhibits include a colorful wall display of Wells Fargo featured in comic books, trading cards, and even a board game; rocks with gold, bags of gold found in treasure boxes, and gold coins; mining tools; Old West posters; and more. Try sending a Morse code message, using the provided "how to" sheet, to someone across the room. A video shows and describes this time period and the history of Wells Fargo. A more modern feature is the ATM machine.

CASA DE MACHADO Y STEWART is located almost directly behind the Colorado House/Wells Fargo Museum. This plain-looking adobe is an exact replica of the original house, complete with a dirt walkway leading to it. The brick-floored house contains few furnishings, including a dining table, shelves with dishes and pottery, a sparsely furnished bedroom, and some tools. Just beyond the front porch is a beehive oven and open fire stoves, evidence of the outdoor cooking that pioneers once employed.

MASON STREET SCHOOL is located on Mason Street, diagonal to the Casa de Machado y Stewart. This 1865 red schoolhouse is a child's favorite historical stop in Old Town. It was the first public schoolhouse in San Diego and retains its old-fashioned ambiance with twenty school desks, a school bell, flags, a chalkboard, a wood-burning stove, the dunce's corner (and cap), and old pictures and books. It's open daily, 10am to 4pm.

THE DENTAL MUSEUM is located on San Diego Avenue in front of the schoolhouse. Kids will enjoy a quick peek at the past here as they see a dentist chair, instruments, and even some molds of teeth.

SAN DIEGO UNION BUILDING is located on San Diego Avenue. The first edition of the San Diego Union came off the presses here way back when. Now, kids can see an old Washington handpress (printing press), typeset letters and tools, and the adjacent small newspaper office.

WHALEY HOUSE - See WHALEY HOUSE (see pg. 437) for details. It's an interesting museum! Take a quick peek into the Old Town Drug Store Museum, located behind this museum. Kids can see an old-time pharmacy containing bottles, patented medicines, and a mortar and pestle.

HERITAGE PARK, (858) 565-3600, is located north of the Whaley House, on Harvey and Juan streets. This group of buildings is enchanting to simply look at. Each of the seven Victorian houses now serve other functions: The Sherman Gilbert house, our favorite, was built in 1887 and is now the Old Doll Shoppe, offering dolls, dollhouses, miniatures, and ornaments for sale and the Christian House is now a bed and breakfast. Mrs. Burton's Tea Room is a small house packed with tea products to sell, as well as woman's clothing, accessories, and intimates. Tea, scones, and more filling food is served throughout the day in small rooms painted and decorated to appeal to ladies. Children's teas are held here, too.

THE MORMON BATTALION VISITOR CENTER, (619) 298-3317, is located on Juan Street. An informative tour guide will show your family around this small center. The first thing we noticed was a statue as tall as the biblical Goliath - he *really* was tall! Kids can hold a sun-baked adobe brick and learn its historical significance. They'll also learn how people placed copper pennies in an oven (an alternative way of baking bricks) until the pennies began to melt, at 2,000 degrees. This meant the oven was hot enough to bake bricks (and lots of other things, too!)

Although the 500 men of the Mormon Battalion never fought a battle, the 1846 volunteer unit marched 2,000 miles across country to San Diego to help fight in the Mexican/American war. Their arduous trail blazing efforts and accomplishments are reenacted in an interesting fifteen-minute film. The diorama adjacent to the screen is occasionally spotlighted to emphasize portions of the movie. After the film, we were led into another room and shown huge paintings of Jesus during various times of his ministry. As our tour concluded, we were offered a Book of Mormon and asked if we could have someone call on us regarding the Mormon religion. The visitor center is open daily, 9am to 9pm. Admission is free.

SEELEY STABLES is located on Calhoun Street. This huge, reconstructed barn contains several exhibit stalls. The saddles, bells, and harnesses, plus at least ten stagecoaches and carriages, are great visual aids for picturing the past. Free slide shows are presented in the downstairs theater throughout the day, so come and rest, and learn a little history. The upstairs loft has more exhibits of the wild, wild west, such as branding irons, spurs, more saddles, a Mexican cowboy hat, and furniture including an unusual chair made out of steers' horns. A native American display features Kachina dolls, a feather headdress, and baskets. Other exhibits up here include an old-fashioned slot machine, a roller organ, an antique telephone, a case of model horses, and a child's room with toys.

The backyard of the stables is an open courtyard with early farm equipment around its perimeters, plus several more carriages and stagecoaches in glass-cased enclosures. Also back here, or accessible from Mason Street, is THE BLACK HAWK LIVERY STABLE AND BLACKSMITH. This large blacksmith workshop holds demonstrations every Wednesday and Saturday from 10am to 2pm. Kids might see the hot fires help bend pieces of metal into horseshoes or heavy chains, or they might hear a hammer clank against the anvil to create a sword or branding iron. The stable room is filled with finished pieces and tools.

GEORGE JOHNSON HOUSE is located on Calhoun Street, near Mason Street. This small building has a room to walk through - it took us five minutes, maybe. It displays archaeological findings of the area such as bottles and pottery, plus tools of the trade and pictures showing the painstaking work of excavation and cleaning.

BAZAAR DEL MUNDO, (619) 296-3161 / www.bazaardelmundo.com, is located on the corner of Juan and Wallace streets. This gaily decorated traditional Mexican courtyard is festive in appearance and atmosphere. Mariachi bands play, costumed dancers entertain occasionally, and the colorful storefronts and wares beckon shoppers of all ages. Our favorite shops here include Geppetto's, a wonderful toy store; Just Animals, for the wild (and tame) at heart; Creations and Confections, specializing in old-fashioned candies, chocolates, and party supplies; La Panaderia, serving delectable Mexican breads and pastries, including churros; and Treasures, a store that carries gifts and crafts from exotic lands. If your tummy is saying, "Tengo hambre" (that's Spanish for "I'm hungry"), sample and savor some of the culinary delights at any one of the several restaurants here. Shops here are open daily, 10am to 9pm.

Look up the SERRA MUSEUM / PRESIDIO PARK (see pg. 436), which is located just north of Old Town.

Hours: Most "attractions" open daily, 10am - 5pm.
Admission: Free, but bring spending money. See individual listings.
Ages: 4 years and up.

PACIFIC SOUTHWEST RAILWAY MUSEUM

(619) 595-3030 / www.sdrm.org
Sheridan Rd, Campo

See the entry for PACIFIC SOUTHWEST RAILWAY MUSEUM on page 458 for details.

RANCHO BUENA VISTA ADOBE / VISTA HISTORICAL MUSEUM   ☀
                                                                                                          $
(760) 639-6164 / www.ci.vista.ca.us/adobe
651 E. Vista Way, Vista
(Exit 78 Fwy N. on Escondido Ave./Sunset Dr., R. on Vista Way. Both are adjacent to Wildwood Park. [TG: 1087 J6])

Follow the signs through the park and over the footbridge to the adobe. Guided tours, the only way to see the inside of the rancho, begin just outside the gift shop in front of an eye-catching, hand-painted map of the surrounding cities. The brick-paved patio and pathways leading to the eleven-room adobe add to the old-time ambiance. The immaculately kept grounds and adobe are often used for weddings, meetings, and other functions.

The first stop is simply to check out the thickness of adobe walls. Walk into each room, all of which are furnished with items donated by area residents. The kitchen is constantly in use and it contains numerous old-fashioned implements. In one bedroom touch cowhide (which is hard) and calf hide (which is supple) draped on a bed. The bathroom has ornate tiles from the 1930's and a cool-looking bathtub. Another room contains a loom and other workman's tools of trade. A living room contains an old piano with candle holders (used before electricity was invented), a phonograph with cylinder "records," pictures, and paintings. My boys especially liked the light fixtures with wood-carved knight figures on them. Outside are a few neatly arranged washing machines and farm tools.

Listen to the fascinating history and stories of this home, from rancho to Hollywood hangout. A few samples to pique your interest: One room supposedly still contains a skeleton in the wall because when it was discovered years and years ago, it was just covered back up again. Once a bandit came to steal a horse and instead, wound up ordering his gang to protect the owner who had befriended him. A few of the rooms were originally not enclosed and used as a thoroughfare for horses. One owner slept with his prize stallion in his room. And so on.

Two-hour California history programs, offered for groups comprising of ten to thirty-three students, include a forty-minute guided tour and two activities. Choose from candle dipping, cooking, branding, roping, weaving, Native American games, and/or Native American crafts. Activities take place in the adobe or in the backyard. Teachers may request a curriculum notebook with lesson plans and worksheets.

The small park adjacent to the rancho has a grassy area, picnic tables, and a stage.

The Vista Historical Museum is next to the park and parking lot. It contains a little bit of everything such as old clothing, gloves, hats, a collection of typewriters, rock specimens, arrows, a hair curler machine that looks like it's out of a science fiction story, tools, and more. Visitors can request a viewing of the thirty-minute *History of Vista* documentary featuring interviews with residents raised in the city during its formative years.

Hours: The rancho is open Wed. - Sat., 10am - 3pm, although tours are not always given on Sat. afternoons. (Call first.) The museum is open Wed. - Sat., 10am - 3pm. The park is open daily, dawn - dusk.

Admission: The rancho is $4 for adults; $3 for seniors and Vista residents; $1 for students; 50¢ for ages 11 and under. School programs are $6.75 per student with one free adult for every 3 students. Extra adults are $3. The museum and park are free.

Ages: 7 years and up.

RANCHO GUAJOME ADOBE

(760) 724-4082 / www.historyandculture.com/guajome

2210 N. Santa Fe Avenue, Vista

(Exit Fwy 78 N. on Vista Village Dr., L. on Santa Fe Ave. [TG: 1087 G2])

This "Cadillac of adobes," built in 1853, contains twenty-two rooms and is one of the finest examples of early California hacienda architecture. (Count all the archways!) It was built for the same reason missions were built; to protect residents from intruders and maintain a small community of family and servants on the grounds.

Encircling a large inner courtyard, the rancho consists of a schoolroom, spacious family living quarters, dining room, a separate chapel, servants' quarters, the kitchen, sheds, stables, and a Victorian-style garden. It has all been beautifully restored. The furnishings, plus the buggy in the carriage courtyard and the docent's information, make the past seem vividly present.

School groups are offered guided tours that correspond with California state curriculum for third and fourth graders. One of the highlights for students is making adobe bricks. (Dress accordingly!) Note that the ANTIQUE GAS & STEAM ENGINE MUSEUM, INC. (see pg. 407) is next door, and Guajome Regional Park, for picnic and playtime, is just down the street.

Hours: Open for tours Sat. - Sun. at 11am, 12:30pm, and 2pm, except in rainy weather. Open weekdays for groups by reservation.

Admission: $3 for adults; $1 for children 12 years and under. School tours are $1 per student.

Ages: 7 years and up.

REUBEN H. FLEET SCIENCE CENTER / IMAX THEATER

(619) 238-1233 / www.rhfleet.org

1875 El Prado, Balboa Park, San Diego

(Going S. on San Diego Fwy [5], exit at Sassafras/Airport, go straight on Kettner Blvd. L. on Laurel St., which turns into El Prado. Going N. on 5, exit N. on Pershing Dr., L. on Florida Dr., L. on Zoo PL., L. on Park Blvd., R. on Village Pl. Going S. on Cabrillo Fwy [163], exit N. on Park Blvd. (near end), L. on Space Theater Wy. [TG: 1289 C1])

This huge Science Center is a fascinating place for hands-on exploration, experimentation, and discovery. There are several permanent exhibits throughout several gallery rooms, including a periscope that literally goes through the roof to view the outside world; a virtual tour through the heart in Heartflight, where the beat goes on; and Learners Lab for ages 2 to 6 featuring musical instruments, giant tinker toys, and soft play blocks. Meteor Storm is a virtual reality game that up to six people can play at a time. They "journey" through a meteor storm to save the earth. SciTours, a simulator ride, offers a jolting, thrilling eight-minute ride/show. It holds up to twenty-three people. Riders must be at least 40" tall and children under 10 must be accompanied by a parent. There are also numerous outstanding temporary exhibits here that rotate every year, or so. A past one was called Memory, featuring thirty-eight interactive exhibits about making memories, retrieving memories, and . . . I forget what else. Check the website to see what's currently at the museum. I guarantee that whatever is here, is well worth at least one visit, if not several.

The second floor hosts many changing displays as well as TechnoVation, the corporate name for numerous, technology-based exhibits. For instance, watch a film showing laser eye surgery being performed; learn the history of computers from punch card to P.C.; have a video conference with someone across the room; see technological breakthroughs; and find out where water comes from and how it gets clean - from rain water to tap water. Live science demonstrations are also given on this floor. The CHALLENGER LEARNING CENTER (see pg. 440) is also located on this floor. Registered participants take a class in the Mission Control room and use the ten computer stations to experience hands-on learning of all the stages of launching and completing a space mission.

The geodesic dome-shaped IMAX theater shows one-hour films on a screen several times the size of screens in regular movie theaters, therefore drawing you into the show's action. The shows are usually educational and are always interesting. Other stellar productions include one-hour planetarium shows given on the first Wednesday of every month at 7pm.

Tip or warning: The gift shop appeals to all ages who are even slightly scientific or hands-on oriented. *Star Trek* fans, in particular, will have a field day here. (See BALBOA PARK on page 408 for a listing of all the museums and attractions within walking distance.)

Hours: The exhibit gallery is open Sun. - Thurs., 9:30am - 5pm; Fri. - Sat., 9:30am - 9pm. It's open in the summer and on school breaks daily, 9:30am - 9pm. IMAX films are shown throughout the day.

Admission: Exhibit gallery admission is $6.50 for adults; $5.50 for seniors; $5 for ages 3 - 12; children 2 and under are free. Admission to the exhibit gallery and an IMAX show is $11 for adults; $9 for seniors; $8 for ages 3 - 12; children 2 and under are free. Planetarium shows are $5 for adults; $4 for seniors; $3 for ages 3 - 12. Membership here is reciprocal at the DISCOVERY SCIENCE CENTER in Santa Ana, the CALIFORNIA SCIENCE CENTER in Los Angeles, and several other institutions across the U.S. Admission to the exhibits, only, is free on the first Tues. of every month. Passports for thirteen museums in Balboa Park are available for $30 for adults at the Visitors Center, and are good for one week from the date of purchase. (Children's admissions are already discounted or free.)

Ages: 4 years and up.

SAN DIEGO AEROSPACE MUSEUM
(619) 234-8291 / www.aerospacemuseum.org
2001 Pan American Plaza, Balboa Park, San Diego
(Going S. on San Diego Fwy [5], exit at Sassafras/Airport, go straight on Kettner Blvd. L. on Laurel St., which turns into El Prado. Going N. on 5, exit N. on Pershing Dr., L. on Florida Dr., L. on Zoo PL., L. on Park Blvd., R. on Village Pl. Going S. on Cabrillo Fwy [163], exit N. on Park Blvd. (near the end), L. on Presidents Wy. [TG: 1289 C1])

Take to the skies in this marvelous museum that visually chronicles the history of aviation from the dawn of flight through the age of space travel. The first few rooms, formally titled the International Aerospace Hall of Fame, give homage to the aero-engineers, pilots, and aviation founders that didn't fly off course in their vision for creating aircrafts and the aerospace industry. The hall is filled with photos, plaques, and medals of these aviation heroes. Portraits of Armstrong, Aldrich, and other astronauts, especially, caught my children's eyes. An Apollo XI display features a replica of the plaque left on the moon, the box used to collect lunar samples, and more.

The next rooms are packed with exhibits of early flying machines and models of inventions such as gliders, "birdmen" who used bicycle tires, bi-planes, and the Wright Brother's flyer, plus narrated videos that show pictures of early flying attempts. Consecutive eras are also well defined and enhanced with colorful wall murals, period-dressed mannequins, and other fine details. Wood-paneled rooms, complete with sandbags and army netting, house WWI and WWII planes and other memorabilia such as helmets, goggles, and uniforms. The flying aces and the fighter planes that served them, including the Spad, the Nieuport, Spitfires, Hellcats, and Zeros, are well represented. In between wars, the U.S. Mail service was introduced. Displays here include a Curtiss JN-4 Jenny, wall posters of stamps blown up in size that commemorate aviation, and a replicated 1918 mail office. Kids love the next exhibits of barnstormers and pictures of daredevils using planes to entertain. These showmen of the air are doing headstands on wings, transferring from a plane to a speeding car, and other feats.

The next series of rooms honor women aviators, house engines and propellers, and display lots of model airplanes. Enter a pilot's ready room to watch the film *Sea Legs*. The armed forces are saluted with their contributions and a scale model of the *U.S.S. Yorktown*, and the *U.S.S. Langley* - the Navy's first carrier.

Enter the Jet Age with the F-4 Phantom, and the spy plane, the Blackbird. This exciting time period is followed by the Space Age. This last set of rooms feature bulky astronaut uniforms, capsules, modules, a moon rock, and more. An adjacent theater room showcases the history of model making.

All this is good, but how does it really feel to be a pilot? Put on a flight suit and climb into the cockpits of an A-4 Douglas "Skyhawk," a C-47 Transport, a home-built "Kitfox," or an experimental craft Bede 5. You can also listen to live transmissions from the local Lindbergh Field in the Kitfox plane. To *really* feel the motion, try the simulator ride, with aviation-themed programs. The simulator ride is $5 per person. Soar to new heights as you and your children explore the Aerospace Museum! Behind-the-scenes tours of the aircraft restoration facility are available upon request for an additional $3 per person. Note that family day activities, free with museum admission, are offered three times a day on the second Saturday of each month. Activities include take-home projects plus learning about a particular aviation topic. (See BALBOA PARK on page 408 for a listing of all the museums and attractions within walking distance.)

Hours: Open daily, 10am - 4:30pm. Open in the summer daily until 5:30pm. Closed New Year's Day, Thanksgiving, and Christmas.

Admission: $8 for adults; $6 for seniors; $3 for ages 6 - 17; active duty military and children 5 and under are free. Admission on the fourth Tues. of every month is free. Passports for thirteen museums in Balboa Park are available for $30 for adults at the Visitors Center, and are good for one week from the date of purchase. (Children's admissions are already discounted or free.)

Ages: 4 years and up.

SAN DIEGO AEROSPACE MUSEUM AT GILLESPIE

(619) 258-1221- direct line; (619) 234-8291 - Aerospace Museum in Balboa Park /
www.aerospacemuseum.org/Gillespie/Gillespie.html
335 Kenney Street, El Cajon
(Going N. on San Vincente Fwy [67], exit W. on Prospect, L. on Magnolia Ave., R. on Kenney. Going S. on 67, exit W. on Mission Gorge Rd., L. on Magnolia, R. on Kenney. It's on the N. side of Gillespie Airport. [TG: 1251 E1])

Even I couldn't miss this museum - it has an Atlas missile on the front lawn! This museum is comprised of two hangars and lots of outside space that is a depository for "work-in-progress" planes from the SAN DIEGO AEROSPACE MUSEUM in Balboa Park as numerous planes here are in the process of being restored or rebuilt. At this writing, some of the planes being worked on include the construction of a Mead Primary Glider and a World War One Sopwith Pup fighter, plus the restoration of a Convair F-102 Dagger. What a great "eyes-on" experience young aviators and engineers can gain by visiting this unique museum! There are also several other planes on display inside the hangars. A few engines and aeronautical artifacts are also housed here.

Outside, besides the missile, are an F-14A Tomcat, F-86F Sabre, and A-4C Skyhawk, plus an army helicopter and other jet fighters. Exhibits do rotate.

Hours: Open Mon., Wed., and Fri., 8am - 4pm.

Admission: Free

Ages: 5 years and up.

SAN DIEGO ART INSTITUTE

(619) 236-0011 / www.sandiego-art.org
1439 El Prado in Balboa Park, San Diego
(Going S. on San Diego Fwy [5], exit at Sassafras/Airport, go straight on Kettner Blvd. L. on Laurel St., which turns into El Prado. Going N. on 5, exit N. on Pershing Dr., L. on Florida Dr., L. on Zoo PL., L. on Park Blvd. Going S. on Cabrillo Fwy [163], exit N. on Park Blvd. (near end). [TG: 1281 C1])

New exhibits showcasing regional artists open ever four to six weeks. This small gallery features works in various mediums, depending on the selected artist, including photography, sculpture, oil, watercolor, and more. A small side gallery debuts work from local schoolchildren. (See BALBOA PARK on page 408 for a listing of all the museums and attractions within walking distance.)

Hours: Open Tues. - Sat., 10am - 4pm; Sun., noon - 4pm.

Admission: $3 for adults; $2 for seniors and students; children 12 and under are free. Admission to the museum is free on the third Tues. of every month. Passports for thirteen museums in Balboa Park are available for $30 for adults at the Visitors Center, and are good for one week from the date of purchase. (Children's admissions are already discounted or free.)

Ages: 6 years and up.

SAN DIEGO AUTOMOTIVE MUSEUM

(619) 231- AUTO (2886) / www.sdautomuseum.org   *$$*

2080 Pan American Plaza, Balboa Park, San Diego

(Going S. on San Diego Fwy [5], exit at Sassafras/Airport, go straight on Kettner Blvd. L. on Laurel St., which turns into El Prado. Going N. on 5, exit N. on Pershing Dr., L. on Florida Dr., L. on Zoo Pl., L. on Park Blvd., R. on Village Pl. Going S. on Cabrillo Fwy [163], exit N. on Park Blvd. (near end), L. on Presidents Wy. [TG: 1289 C1])

Jump start your child's interest in automobiles at this museum that has more than eighty vehicles on display. Most of the gleaming cars are in a line and readily viewable. Some of the vintage automobiles are on display in appropriate settings, such as a fifties car in front of a backdrop of a drive-through. Understand that the vehicles on display are here on a rotating basis. Classics here range from old-fashioned Model A's to futuristic-looking DeLoreans. Other favorites (that were on display when we visited) include a 1948 Tucker "Torpedo" (only fifty-one were ever built), a 1934 convertible Coupe Roadster, a 1955 Mercedes Benz (300SL Gullwing), a 1957 Chevrolet, and Packards from 1929 to 1936. Prototypes, model cars, a race car, a re-created mechanics shop complete with tools, and an engine room for those who want the inside scoop on cars, are also found at this museum. "Gentlemen, start your engines" applied to my boys as they raced over to see the over forty motorcycles on display. They were particularly elated by the Harley Davidsons, the Indian Chief, and an army cycle.

A kid's corner features a motorcycle to sit on; a frame of a car for kids to sit in and shift gears; a floor mat designed with city streets for youngsters to race around play cars; and car pictures to color. (See BALBOA PARK on page 408 for a listing of all the museums and attractions within walking distance.)

Hours: Open daily, 10am - 5pm. Closed New Year's Day, Thanksgiving, and Christmas.

Admission: $7 for adults; $6 for seniors; $3 for ages 6 - 15; children 5 and under are free. Admission on the fourth Tues. of every month is free. Passports for thirteen museums in Balboa Park are available for $30 for adults at the Visitors Center, and are good for one week from the date of purchase. (Children's admissions are already discounted or free.)

Ages: 6 years and up.

SAN DIEGO COUNTY SHERIFF'S MUSEUM

(619) 260-1850 / www.sheriffmuseum.org   *!*

2384 San Diego Avenue, San Diego

(Going S. on San Diego Fwy [5] [just south of Interstate 8] exit E. [across the bridge] on Old Town Ave., L. on San Diego Ave. Going N. on 5, exit at Moore St., R. on Old Town Ave., L. on San Diego Ave. It's just S. of Old Town. [TG: 1268 F5])

Get deputized at this two-story, innocuous-looking adobe building. The museum houses two jails, lots of weapons (all made inoperable), and a wealth of displays and information. The two jails are from different eras: one is a replicated 1850's jail with saddles, guns, an old desk, and a safe all adding ambiance; the other is a more modern-day facility. Just a few minutes behind these bars will hopefully make an impact upon kids so that they won't want to do any time anywhere else. The weapons include Winchester rifles, colt revolvers, a submachine gun, numerous pistols, a pen gun, and a cane gun, among others.

One room contains a booking area with fingerprint and picture-taking stations. Some of the displays in here include inmate art and items that inmates have created to try to escape (i.e. "rope" made from sheets). Other exhibits include billys and cuffs; a roped-off crime scene and information panels on forensics; and a crime laboratory showing target papers revealing various gunshot angles, plus pipe bombs, mortars, and more. Listen to real police scanners. Sit on the police motorcycle that has working sirens and lights.

Upstairs walk through a working metal detector and into a re-created courtroom - you be the judge. A display on gangs, narcotics paraphernalia, and confiscated toy weapons is also here, plus a mannequin in full S.W.A.T. regalia. A corner honoring Search and Rescue teams has a wounded mannequin on a stretcher and a sheriff rendering aid. One display case shows what a washed check is and how to detect counterfeit money. A gallery here is dedicated to the memory of fallen officers and another area salutes the K-9 units. A helicopter (with realistic copter sounds) is outside in the adjacent garage.

A deputy badge, a McGruff coloring book, and other information about the history of San Diego sheriffs and about prevention of crime are available here at no cost. Kids will definitely be interested in taking a tour here, so note that school tours are given that fit in with California fourth-grade curriculum. (Younger and older kids, too, will glean a lot of helpful insight and information.) Don't forget to patrol the rest of Old Town while you're here. Look up OLD TOWN SAN DIEGO AND STATE HISTORIC PARK (see pg. 423) to check out what else there is to see and do in the immediately vicinity.

    Hours: Open Tues. - Sat., 10am - 4pm.
Admission: Free
    Ages: 5 years and up.

SAN DIEGO HALL OF CHAMPIONS - SPORTS MUSEUM

(619) 234-2544 / www.sandiegosports.org $$
2131 Pan American Plaza, Balboa Park, San Diego

(Going S. on San Diego Fwy [5], exit at Sassafras/Airport, go straight on Kettner Blvd. L. on Laurel St., which turns into El Prado. Going N. on 5, exit N. on Pershing Dr., L. on Florida Dr., L. on Zoo Pl., L. on Park Blvd., R. on Village Pl. Going S. on Cabrillo Fwy [163], exit N. on Park Blvd. (near end), L. on Presidents Wy. [TG: 1289 C1])

Give your sports fans something to cheer about by taking them to the Hall of Champions. Over forty different sports are represented in this eye-catching museum, including basketball, hockey, boxing, table tennis, surfing, racing, boating, soapbox derby, and a beach game called over-the-line. Baseball and football each have their own large galleries filled with memorabilia. The exhibits showcase athletes such as Ted Williams and Bill Walton, and teams such as the Padres, all associated with San Diego - what a winning city this is! You'll see photographs, statues outfitted in sports attire, videos, trophies, and lots of sports equipment such as uniforms, balls, and even a racing boat and a motorcycle. Use touch screens to look up information on almost any athlete or team represented.

Is your child a ham? Or a sports broadcaster wannabe? He/she can test his/her skills at the media center by watching a sports video and, using the mike in a news background setting, giving a play by play. An almost 150-seat theater is used for presentations, full-length feature films, and sometimes sports films and clips, mostly bloopers, which kids love. Ask about fantasy baseball, a school education program that integrates playing simulated baseball games with mathematics. (See BALBOA PARK on page 408 for a listing of all the museums and attractions within walking distance.)

    Hours: Open daily, 10am - 4:30pm. Closed New Year's Day, Thanksgiving, and Christmas.
Admission: $6 for adults; $4 for seniors; $3 for ages 7 - 17; children 6 and under are free. Admission on the fourth Tues. of every month is free. Passports to 11 museums in Balboa Park are available for $30 for adults at the Visitors Center, and are good for one week from the date of purchase. (Children's admissions are already discounted or free.)
    Ages: 5 years and up.

SAN DIEGO HISTORICAL SOCIETY MUSEUM

(619) 232-6203 / www.sandiegohistory.org $$
1649 El Prado, Balboa Park, San Diego

(Going S. on San Diego Fwy [5], exit at Sassafras/Airport, go straight on Kettner Blvd. L. on Laurel St., which turns into El Prado. Going N. on 5, exit N. on Pershing Dr., L. on Florida Dr., L. on Zoo Pl., L. on Park Blvd., R. on Village Pl. Going S. on Cabrillo Fwy [163], exit N. on Park Blvd. (near end), L. on Presidents Wy. [TG: 1289 C1])

This museum presents the history of San Diego, from the 1850's to the present, via numerous photographs, plus maps, works of art, costumes, household goods, furniture, and other artifacts. An authentic stagecoach is the first item you'll see and it sets the mood for your visit here. We always enjoy seeing history and understanding more about our past generation's lifestyles. The 100-seat Thornton Theater hosts education programs and more. (See BALBOA PARK on page 408 for a listing of all the museums and attractions within walking distance.)

Hours: Open Tues. - Sun., 10am - 4:30pm. Open also the second Tues. of each month. Closed Mon. and major holidays.

Admission: $5 for adults; $4 for seniors; $2 for ages 6 - 17; children 5 and under are free. Admission the second Tues. of every month is free. Passports for thirteen museums in Balboa Park are available for $30 for adults at the Visitors Center, and are good for one week from the date of purchase. (Children's admissions are already discounted or free.)

Ages: 5 years and up.

SAN DIEGO MARITIME MUSEUM

(619) 234-9153 / www.sdmaritime.org

1492 N. Harbor Drive, San Diego

(Going N. on San Diego Fwy [5], exit E. on Hawthorne St., L. on Harbor. Going S. on 5, exit S. on Front St., R. on Ash. The museum is at the end of Ash St., on Harbor Drive. [TG: 1288 J2])

"I saw a ship a-sailing, a-sailing on the sea; and, oh! it was all laden with pretty things for thee!" (An old rhyme.) The five historic ships that comprise the Maritime Museum - the *Star of India*, the *Berkeley*, the *Medea*, the *Pilot*, and the *Californian* - are laden with wonderful, nautical artifacts. The 1863 *Star of India*, the flagship of the fleet, is beautiful to behold with its intricate-looking rigging, interesting figurehead, and polished wooden exterior. Inside, kids can look out the portholes; check out the very narrow bunks that once held emigrants; look at the old tools and display of knots; and marvel at the variations of ships in bottles. Not only are the ships unique, but the shapes of the bottles vary, too. Our favorite was the ship in a lightbulb. The fifteen-minute video, *Around Cape Horn* is a bit dry, though it depicts action at sea. Top board is the captain's cabin (which is small enough to give me claustrophobia), a few passengers' cabins (which passengers had to furnish themselves), a dining room, and the chart room.

The 1898 ferryboat, *Berkeley*, contains a number of fascinating model ships and yachts. A model ship construction and repair shop is on board, and we watched a builder at work. He told us a model takes an average of five years to complete! Such detailed work! One section of the Berkeley has a whaling gun on exhibit and displays of fish (mostly tuna) and fisheries. Downstairs is the engine room which you can explore on your own. The room is intriguing with its huge machinery and gears, narrow walkways, and slightly spooky ambiance. Also below deck is another room that showcases memorabilia from America's Cup. The triple expansion steam engine is put to work and demonstrated at various times throughout the day.

Cross over the bridge from the *Berkeley* to the 1904 steam yacht, *Medea*, which is a very small vessel. Peek into the elegant, Edwardian-decorated smoking room and into the galley that contains a coal-burning stove, big copper pots, and a wooden ice box.

The *Pilot*, a restored harbor pilot boat, is now used as a teaching vessel. It also sails out around and beyond the bay with students to study marine animals. The majestic tallship *Californian* has nine sails that unfurl to catch the wind just as the 1847 Revenue Cutter did, which is what the *Californian* is modeled after. It also has gun ports for fake battles. The *Californian* sails out of port and offers terrific on-board educational living history programs where participants learn maritime history, the art of sailing tallships, how shipmates must work together as a team, and various learning stations. What a unique way to study the maritime lifestyle!

Speaking (or writing) of educational opportunities, the museum offers a full array of classes and programs for kids and adults with a variety of emphases from mechanics of seafaring to elementary physics to living history. Chart your course to have a merry time at the Maritime Museum.

Hours: Open daily, 9am - 8pm. Open one hour later in the summer.

Admission: $7 for adults; $5 for seniors and ages 13 - 17; $4 for ages 6 - 12; children 5 and under are free. Ask about AAA discounts.

Ages: 5 years and up.

SAN DIEGO MODEL RAILROAD MUSEUM

(619) 696-0199 / www.sdmodelrailroadm.com

1649 El Prado, Balboa Park, San Diego

(Going S. on San Diego Fwy [5], exit at Sassafras/Airport, go straight on Kettner Blvd. L. on Laurel St., which turns into El Prado. Going N. on 5, exit N. on Pershing Dr., L. on Florida Dr., L. on Zoo Pl., L. on Park Blvd., R. on Village Pl. Going S. on Cabrillo Fwy [163], exit N. on Park Blvd. (near end), L. on Presidents Wy. [TG: 1289 C1])

You won't have to railroad your children into coming to this museum. Just one of the things I learned here was the difference between model trains and toy trains. (Hint: The way they operate and the way they look are very different.) The museum houses the largest operating model railroad exhibits in America. Kids (and short adults) can step up onto platforms to get a closer look at the several huge layouts. Watch scale model trains make tracks through and around authentically landscaped hillsides and miniature towns that are complete with scale cars, trees, and people. Some of the exhibits depicting the development of railroading in Southern California include the Tehachapi Pass, the Cabrillo and Southwestern, and a Civil War era live steam locomotive. One of our favorites is the Pacific Desert Line, which has a model train going through a town, citrus groves, and a gorge, all of which can be seen by looking through real train car windows! A huge relief map of San Diego county is accompanied by a touch screen to aid visitors in taking a virtual tour of the area.

Kids will have the most fun in the toy train gallery, which features Lionel type 3-rail trains and more. Turn knobs, push buttons, and pull back on throttles to operate trains, make signal crossers flash, windmills turn, and toy trucks haul "rocks" to a loading dock. One model train even features sounds and smoke. A wooden Brio train set for younger children completes this interactive and at*track*tive room. As the railroad museum is always in the process of re*model*ing, it is fun and different every time you visit. (See BALBOA PARK on page 408 for a listing of all the museums and attractions within walking distance.)

Hours: Open Tues. - Fri., 11am - 4pm; Sat. - Sun., 11am - 5pm. Closed Mon., Thanksgiving, and Christmas. Call for other holiday hours.

Admission: $4 for adults; $3 for seniors; $2.50 students; children 14 and under are free. Admission on the first Tues. of every month is free. Passports for thirteen museums in Balboa Park are available for $30 for adults at the Visitors Center, and are good for one week from the date of purchase. (Children's admissions are already discounted or free.)

Ages: 2 years and up.

SAN DIEGO MUSEUM OF ART

(619) 232-7931 / www.sdmart.com

1450 El Prado, Balboa Park, San Diego

(Going S. on San Diego Fwy [5], exit at Sassafras/Airport, go straight on Kettner Blvd. L. on Laurel St., which turns into El Prado. Going N. on 5, exit N. on Pershing Dr., L. on Florida Dr., L. on Zoo Pl., L. on Park Blvd., R. on Village Pl. Going S. on Cabrillo Fwy [163], exit N. on Park Blvd. (near end), L. on Presidents Wy. [TG: 1289 C1])

This ornately-edificed building primarily features European, American, Asian, and twentieth-century art. As with any art museum, my children's interest was sparked by having them look for differences in artistic styles or color, and looking at various choices of subject. Kids need to somehow participate with the art in order to enjoy it. My boys were intrigued most by the statues, especially the fighting Minotaur. The small Image Gallery room has touch screens that introduce and teach children (and adults) more about the paintings and sculptures throughout the museum. (Anything to do with computers draws this generation's interest!) Although the museum has more appeal for older children, the quarterly Family Festivals are geared for all ages. Hands-on activities that relate to a current exhibit and live entertainment, plus free admission to the museum, make this an outing to look forward to. Tip: If you're not sure your children will enjoy this museum, come on the third Tuesday of the month, when admission is free. (See BALBOA PARK on page 408 for a listing of all the museums and attractions within walking distance.)

Hours: Open Tues. - Sun., 10am - 6pm, (open Thurs. until 9pm). Closed Mon. (except Labor Day), New Year's Day, Thanksgiving, and Christmas.

Admission: $8 for adults; $6 for seniors, military, and ages 18-24; $3 for ages 6 - 17; children 5 and under are free. An additional admission fee is sometimes charged for some special exhibitions. Admission on the third Tues. of each month is free to view the permanent collection. Passports for thirteen museums in Balboa Park are available for $30 for adults at the Visitors Center, and are good for one week from the date of purchase. (Children's admissions are already discounted or free.)

Ages: 8 years and up.

SAN DIEGO MUSEUM OF MAN

(619) 239-2001 / www.museumofman.org

1350 El Prado, Balboa Park, San Diego

(Going S. on San Diego Fwy [5], exit at Sassafras/Airport, go straight on Kettner Blvd. L. on Laurel St., which turns into El Prado. Going N. on 5, exit N. on Pershing Dr., L. on Florida Dr., L. on Zoo Pl., L. on Park Blvd., R. on Village Pl. Going S. on Cabrillo Fwy [163], exit N. on Park Blvd. (near end), L. on Presidents Wy. [TG: 1289 C1])

This museum is mostly dedicated to the theory of evolution, as well as man's past and his accomplishments (making baskets, creating tools, etc.) over the years. The first floor exhibits that we saw (they do rotate) consisted of tapestry hangings, a weaving demonstration, and plaster casts of stone monuments engraved and dedicated to deities.

Upstairs, the prevalent theme is the theory of evolution displayed throughout five galleries with the collective title, Footsteps Through Time: 4 Million Years of Human Evolution. Enter through a time tunnel that chronicles 200 years of human technological breakthroughs. There are numerous visuals, such as skeletons of apes and man side by side to compare and contrast; a theoretical timeline; and life-size models depicting what some scientists believe early man looked like. Many of the models are naked (and very hairy). In the primate hall human visitors can also compare their hands and feet to apes and monkeys. One of several dioramas shows a re-creation of a Neanderthal burial; another is a replicate of the world's oldest cave painting. Video kiosks feature famous scientists discussing their finds and their work. The Human Lab section shows what the future may hold involving gene selection, cloning, and even cyborgs. One area here allows visitors to try their hand at being an archaeologist for a day by uncovering finds in a sand pit. There are numerous touchable replicas in the galleries.

Peoples of the Southwest are represented by displays of pottery, Kachina dolls, and jewelry. Hunters are represented by displays of weapons, tools, and foods. Our favorite exhibits, pertaining to this latter category, were the rabbit skin blanket, eagle feather skirt, shoes from fibers, and a quiver made out of a raccoon. Ancient Egypt is *tut*ilating with a real mummy, dating from around 330 B.C., plus coffin masks covered with symbols of Isis, and exotic jewelry.

Experience Ancient Egypt in the hands-on Children's Discovery Center by dressing up in appropriate clothing and headwear, building pyramids with blocks, trying your hand at hieroglyphics, and playing ancient games - all in a replicated noble's home. On weekends, for an additional $3 fee, your children can also participate in a themed, take-home craft. (See BALBOA PARK on page 408 for a listing of all the museums and attractions within walking distance.)

Hours: Open daily, 10am - 4:30pm.

Admission: $6 for adults; $5 for seniors; $3 for ages 6 - 17; children 5 and under are free. Admission on the third Tues. of every month is free. Passports for thirteen museums in Balboa Park are available for $30 for adults at the Visitors Center, and are good for one week from the date of purchase. (Children's admissions are already discounted or free.)

Ages: 5 years and up.

SAN DIEGO NATURAL HISTORY MUSEUM

(619) 232-3821 / www.sdnhm.org

1788 El Prado, Balboa Park, San Diego

(Going S. on San Diego Fwy [5], exit at Sassafras/Airport, go straight on Kettner Blvd. L. on Laurel St., which turns into El Prado. Going N. on 5, exit N. on Pershing Dr., L. on Florida Dr., L. on Zoo Pl., L. on Park Blvd., R. on Village Pl. Going S. on Cabrillo Fwy [163], exit N. on Park Blvd. (near end), L. on Presidents Wy. [TG: 1289 C1])

Naturally, this huge, multi-story museum is a favorite for kids to visit! Enter through the south side, across the pedestrian street from the other Balboa Park museums, or through the north side, which leads into a beautiful glass-walled atrium. This museum features first class, major, national traveling exhibits. Call or check the website to see what is current being showcased - and don't miss it! We saw a wild and woolly exhibit with elephants, woolly mammoths, and mastodons. Knowing that elephants (and their ancestors) are the largest land animals still didn't quite prepare my kids for the impact of seeing the towering life-size models. Touching re-created hair, trunk, and feet was unique, as was seeing a live Asian elephant close up (outside, in the "backyard") and learning about its anatomy. Another favorite past exhibit was on dinosaurs.

The permanent exhibits are equally wonderful. See dinosaurs through ice-age mammals via fossils, skeletons, models, multi-sensory dioramas, and other interactive exhibits that put visitors in touch with history. Walk through some re-created regional habitats, from the mountains, to the prairies, to the oceans white with foam plus the desert, Baja California, and Sea of Cortes. (Well, not these areas in their entirety, but Southern California is well represented.) Huge walk-through dioramas with caves depict the southwestern desert. Some of the taxidermied animals on display include cougars, coyotes, gold eagles, birds, and saber tooth cats. One wall has a beautiful array of butterflies - some have fantastic fluorescent colors. Dive into another area that contains models and stuffed sea creatures such as sea lions, stingrays, dolphins, sharks, and a pilot whale. Also on display are the menacing jaws of a shark, plus skeletons, a gigantic whale fin bone, and a whale skull. The Discovery Room features live animals for visitors to see and even touch; natural objects to touch and study, such as animal fur; microscopes for closer study; activity kits; and seasonal activities.

The Hall of Minerals has amazing specimens, including petrified logs, a huge jade boulder, and a gigantic amethyst geode. Walk through a re-created mine tunnel and see "holes" that showcase garnets, topaz, and other rocks and minerals. Try the crystal radio and hear how it works. Touch a meteor that is out of this world. Observe fluorescent rocks and glowing minerals. Experiment with radioactive rock. See rainbows through special crystals using a polarizing filter. Don't let the earthquake exhibit shake you up!

The giant-screen theater shows forty-minute movies throughout the day. Past titles have included *Ocean Oasis* and *Wolves*. The museum offers many classes, tours, guided nature walks, family programs, camp outs, and even camp-ins! Call for a schedule. Several lab classrooms are also available here. (See BALBOA PARK on page 408 for a listing of all the museums and attractions within walking distance.)

Hours: Open daily, 9:30am - 5:30pm. Open in the summer one hour later. Closed New Year's Day, Thanksgiving, and Christmas. During special exhibits, daily museum hours are extended - 9am - 6pm.

Admission: $7 for adults; $6 for seniors; $5 for ages 3 - 17; children 2 and under are free. Special exhibits can cause prices and hours to fluctuate, so always call first. In between special exhibits, admission is half-price for all ages. Admission is free on the first Tues. of every month to the permanent exhibits; half price to the special exhibits. Passports for thirteen museums in Balboa Park are available for $30 for adults at the Visitors Center, and are good for one week from the date of purchase. (Children's admissions are already discounted or free.)

Ages: 3 years and up.

SAN DIEGUITO HERITAGE MUSEUM

(760) 632-9711 / www.encinitas101.com/sdmuseum.htm
561 S. Vulcan Avenue, Encinitas
(Exit San Diego Fwy [5] W. on Encinitas Blvd., L. on Vulcan Ave. [TG: 1147 C7])

This very small museum is a good stop off. Built at an ex-gas station, a stagecoach is located where the gas pumps used to be - now you can fill 'er up with history! There are also a few picnic tables outside.

Inside, the room contains exhibits in chronological order. Display cases around the perimeter hold tools, a variety of barbed wire, household items, dolls, toys, a mock Indian wickiup, Mexican Ranchero costumes, and even a few surfboards. A pseudo shanty room has period-dressed mannequins and a bed. I appreciate the docent's willingness to explain the items, and the paper and pencil treasure hunt that got the kids involved with the exhibits.

Hours: Open Wed. - Sat., noon - 3pm.

Admission: Free

Ages: 5 years and up.

SERRA MUSEUM / PRESIDIO PARK

(619) 297-3258 / www.sandiegohistory.org

2727 Presidio Drive, San Diego

(Going E. on Mission Valley Fwy [8] exit S. on Taylor St., L. on Presidio Dr., and L. again to stay on Presidio Dr. Going W. on 8, exit at Hotel Circle/Taylor St. [the exit before Morena Blvd.], go straight off the off ramp and curve over fwy, R. on Taylor St., L. on Presidio Dr., and L. again to stay on Presidio Dr. [TG: 1268 F4])

Located just above OLD TOWN SAN DIEGO AND STATE HISTORIC PARK (see pg. 423), picturesque Presidio Park has green rolling hills and lots of old shade trees. Follow the signs and walk along the Old Presidio Historic Trail and you'll be walking in the footsteps of settlers from centuries ago.

On a hilltop in the park sits the mission-style Junipero Serra Museum. It was built in 1929 to commemorate the site where Father Junipero Serra and Captain Gaspar de Portola established California's very first mission and fortified settlement. Outside the museum is an old wine press. Inside, the first floor contains 400-year-old Spanish furniture, some of which is quite elegant. Second story exhibits include clothing, weapons (such as a cannon and cannon balls), art, artifacts from the outside dig site, and housewares that belonged to Native American and early Spanish/Mexican residents. There is also a room dedicated to the founder, Father Serra, that contains personal belongings and items given to him. A seven-minute video is shown throughout the day that describes San Diego's beginnings. Upstairs, in a bell-like tower, look through the windows for an unparalleled view of San Diego.

Hours: The park is open daily, sunrise - sunset. The museum is open during the summer, Tues. - Sun., 10am - 4:30pm. It's open the rest of the year, Fri. - Sun., 10am - 4:30pm. Tours for eight or more people can be given at other times. Call for a reservation.

Admission: The park is free. The museum is $5 for adults; $4 for seniors; $2 for ages 6 - 17; children 5 and under are free. AAA members receive discounts.

Ages: The museum is best suited for ages 7 and up.

VETERANS MEMORIAL CENTER & MUSEUM

(619) 239-2300 / www.sdvmc.org

2115 Park Boulevard, San Diego

(From San Diego Fwy [5], exit N. on Pershing Dr., L. on Florida Dr., L. on Zoo PL., L. on Park Blvd., R. on Village Pl. Going S. on Cabrillo Fwy [163], exit N. on Park Blvd. (near end), L. on Presidents Wy. [TG: 1289 C1])

"The nation which forgets its defenders will be itself forgotten." (Calvin Coolidge) The Veterans center is a memorial dedicated to honor all the men and women who have served in all branches of the U.S. Armed Services, including the Merchant Marines.

The small museum is located in the former chapel of the Naval Hospital, which was built in the early 1940's and still retains the original stained glass windows. Display cases contain plaques, medals, gas masks, uniforms, and more memorabilia from WWI, WWII, the Korean War, Vietnam War, and Desert Storm. Several mannequins are dressed in military attire. Multitudes of military flags hang from the ceiling, with several versions of the American flag prominently displayed. A display table has a few uniforms and hats for kids to try on, as well as some war time field phones to use. Docents who have served in the military now serve as tour guides, so the information comes from those who have been there, done that. Memorial plaques are on the back lawn of the museum. Note: BALBOA PARK (pg. 408) is just across the street.

Hours: Open Tues. - Sun., 9:30am - 3pm. Closed Mon. and most major holidays.

Admission: Free; donations are encouraged.

Ages: 7 years and up.

VILLA MONTEZUMA JESSE SHEPARD HOUSE

$$

(619) 239-2211 / www.sandiegohistory.org

1925 K Street, San Diego

(Going S. on San Diego Fwy [5], exit E. on Imperial Ave, L on 20th St., L. on K St. Going N on 5, exit E. on J St., R. on 20th St., R. on K St. [TG: 1289 C4])

Built and designed in 1887 for celebrated author, spiritualist, and musician, Jesse Shepard, this two-story house is by far one of the most interesting and ornamental Victorian houses we've ever seen. The outside is beautiful with its steep roofs, gables, turrets, and bay windows. The rooms inside are paneled with redwood and walnut, and are decorated with intricate wood carvings and moldings. The ceilings are elegantly embossed. There are numerous, gorgeous stained glass windows throughout that depict Beethoven, Mozart, a knight, the Greek poetess Sappho, and more. The furnishings are equally elaborate, and even though much of the furniture is not originally from this house, it is from the same time period. Older kids will enjoy the hour-and-a-half tour. They'll see the large music room, the drawing room, and the downstairs kitchen and laundry room which are filled with "labor saving" devices such as an early washing machine, vacuum cleaner, kitchen gadgets, and more. Upstairs are the bedrooms that, in keeping with the rest of the house, are also stylishly decorated. My 11-year old and I were fascinated by the house, but were bewildered as to why Jesse Shepard designed such a masterpiece and incurred the city's expense to construct it only to live in it for two years! Personally, I could live here for a lot longer.

Hours: Open Fri. - Sun.,10am - 4:30pm. Group tours are available Tues. - Sun. by reservation.

Admission: $5 for adults; $4 for seniors; $2 for ages 6 - 17; children 5 and under are free.

Ages: 8 years and up.

WHALEY HOUSE

$$

(619) 297-7511 / www.whaleyhouse.org

2482 San Diego Avenue, San Diego

(Going S. on San Diego Fwy [5] [just south of Interstate 8] exit E. [across the bridge] on Old Town Ave., L. on San Diego Ave. Going N. on 5, exit at Moore St., R. on Old Town Ave., L. on San Diego Ave. It's on the corner of San Diego Ave. and Harney St. [TG: 1268 F5])

Built in 1847, this two-story brick house/museum is definitely worth touring. It has served in the community as a residence, store, theater, and courthouse, and is filled with numerous early California artifacts. It is also one of two authenticated haunted houses in California. The first room you're ushered into, the courthouse room, is fascinating. As you listen to the ten-minute tape explaining the history of the house and this time period, look around. Behind the railing is an old wooden judge's desk, and chairs for the jury. Along one wall is a bookshelf given to Ulysses S. Grant on his inauguration, and an 1860 lifemask (only one of six in existence) of Abraham Lincoln. Display cases in this room feature documents, spurs, pistols, Spanish helmets and swords, clothing, and ornate hair combs and fans. An early copy machine, a letter press, a handmade U.S. flag from 1864 (how many stars does it have?), plus pictures and portraits of George Washington, Abraham Lincoln, Ulysses S. Grant, and Robert E. Lee are also here.

The kitchen, with all of its gadgets, is downstairs, as is the beautifully decorated parlor and a small music room that contains a spinet piano used in the movie, *Gone With the Wind*. There are several bedrooms upstairs that can be viewed through the protective glass in the doorframes. The bedroom behind the staircase has a decorative wreath, framed on the far wall. It is made from the Whaley girls' hair gathered from hairbrushes and then braided - something to keep the family busy on pre-television nights. The children's bedroom has dolls and toys, while the other bedrooms contain a soldier's dress uniform, mannequins clothed in elegant, ladies' dresses, a lacy quilt covering a canopy bed, and period furniture. I highly recommend taking a guided tour, so you don't miss out on any of the background information. Ask about guided school tours.

Exit through the backdoor into a small, picturesque, tree-shaded courtyard. A quick peek into the Old Town Drug Store Museum allows kids to see an old-time pharmacy containing bottles, patented medicines, and a mortar and pestle. Push a button to hear more of the building's history. See OLD TOWN SAN DIEGO AND STATE HISTORIC PARK (see pg. 423) for details about other attractions in this immediate area.

Hours: Open Wed. - Mon., 10am to 4:30pm. Closed Tues.
Admission: $5 for adults; $4 for seniors; $3 for ages 12 and under.
Ages: 7 years and up.

-----PIERS AND SEAPORTS-----

OCEANSIDE PIER AND HARBOR

(760) 435-4000 - harbor; (760) 722-0028 - boat rentals / www.oceansidechamber.com

At the end of Pier View Way at The Strand, Oceanside

(Exit San Diego Fwy [5] W. on Mission Ave., R. on Pacific St., L. on Pier View Wy. [TG: 1105 J1])

The Oceanside Pier is one of the longest piers in San Diego County, and the majority of it is made from wood planks. It stretches out over the ocean almost 2,000 feet, or twenty minutes of walking, depending on the age of your youngest child. Don't want to walk? There is a Ruby's Scooby Doo golf-cart-like shuttle available for 50¢ one way, free the other way. The spacious RUBY'S Diner (see pg. 371), at the end of the pier, is a 40's diner serving great all-American food at good prices in a very kid-friendly atmosphere. Another pier-related activity is fishing. It doesn't require a license, so reel 'em in! A bait and tackle shop has pole rentals available. During low tide, look waaay down, over the edge of the pier to see the pylons covered with hundreds of barnacles and sea stars. The other end of the pier (the land end) offers a McDonald's restaurant (open in the summer), an outdoor amphitheater (used for in-line skating when concerts aren't in session), a community center, a playground with wooden climbing structures, sand volleyball courts, and, of course, miles of surf and sand. See OCEANSIDE SKATEPARK (pg. 397) for information on the skate park just down the street.

Breeze on over to the Oceanside Harbor, just a few streets north of the pier. The Harbor offers your choice of boat rentals at BOAT RENTALS OF AMERICA (see pg. 455). A few eateries, including the Chart House restaurant and some shops make up a small "village" here. Come on in, the water's fine for swimming and surfing. On the beach are sand volleyball courts, a playground for the younger set, fire rings, and picnic areas with barbecues and covered cabanas. Wear shoes with tread to carefully walk along the tidepools and go out on the rock jetties. RV camping only is available along the beach, too.

Hours: Most restaurants are open daily, 10am - 6pm. Open extended hours in the summer.
Admission: Parking costs $3 - $5 at the beach.
Ages: All

SEAPORT VILLAGE

(619) 235-4014 / www.spvillage.com

800 W. Harbor Drive at Kettner Boulevard, San Diego

(Going S. on San Diego Fwy [5] exit S. on Front St., R. on Broadway, L. on Kettner. Going N. on the 5, exit S. on 6th Ave. R. on Broadway, L. on Kettner. [TG: 1288 J4])

This delightful harbor-side shopping area is in an expansive, beautiful, park-like setting. There are three themed plazas here representing early California, a New England fishing village, and the Victorian era. Along its boardwalk and cobblestone "streets" the Village offers almost sixty unique shops, including Magnet Max, Miner's Gems and Minerals, and Fantasy World of Toys. There are several wonderful waterfront restaurants to choose from as well as numerous places for snackers to munch. Kids will enjoy riding the 100-year-old carousel located in the West Plaza. The carousel is open daily, 10am to 9pm. Rides cost $2 per person. See CINDERELLA'S CARRIAGE (pg. 456) for another way to see the village.

Hours: Open daily, 10am - 9pm. Open in the summer one hour later.
Admission: Technically free. Parking for two hours is free with a validation of any purchase. Otherwise, it's about $1.50 an hour.
Ages: All

-----*POTPOURRI*-----

ARCO OLYMPIC TRAINING CENTER

(619) 482-6222 / www.usolympicteam.com

1750 Wueste Road, Chula Vista

(Exit Jacob Dekema Fwy [805] L. on Olympic Parkway, R. on Wueste Rd. Follow the signs. [TG: 1312 A7])

This incredibly beautiful facility is nestled in a mountain range by the blue waters of Otay Lakes. The 150-acre campus is the training grounds for future Olympians (and other athletes) as they prepare for the thrill of victory (not the agony of defeat). Throughout the day, the visitors' center shows a free six-minute video that arouses the Olympic spirit in all of us. The gift shop is first class.

Free, guided tours of the facility are offered on the hour, or just take a detailed map and stroll along the paved Olympic Path on your own. The path slices through the center of the facility. It is elevated so you get a bird's eye view of the sports being played on both sides, including soccer, field hockey, tennis, track and field, cycling, baseball, and archery. Water sports, such as rowing, canoeing, and kayaking can also be observed from this vantage point. Visitors are asked to stay on the path, which is nine-tenths of a mile each way, as it winds through the training center. Call ahead to see which athletes are currently training here because seeing them in action makes the center come alive! The facility also has athlete housing, an athlete dining area, a medical facility, and more.

Future sport venues in development are an aquatics center and a gymnasium for volleyball and basketball.

Hours: Open Mon. - Sat., 9am - 5pm; Sun., 11am - 5pm.

Admission: Free

Ages: 6 years and up.

BASIC BROWN BEAR FACTORY

$$$

(877) 234-BEAR (2327) or (800) 554-1910 / www.basicbrownbear.com/sandiego.htm

2375 San Diego Avenue, Old Town, San Diego

(Going S. on San Diego Fwy [5] [just south of Interstate 8], exit E. [across the bridge] on Old Town Ave., L. on San Diego Ave. Going N. on 5, exit at Moore St., R. on Old Town Ave., L. on San Diego Ave. [TG: 1268 F5])

This is a beary good outing! The store contains a myriad of non-stuffed, furry bear bodies - black, brown, white, and tri-colored - as well as sheep, dragons, moose, and bunnies. Kids (and adults) can purchase a bear (or whatever) body and then participate in stuffing it via a machine that swirls the stuffing around like a dryer. Choose your bear and as a worker puts it in on a pole connected to the machine, press down on a foot lever that shoots stuffing into the bear (and occasionally onto the floor). You can choose to have the bear really packed or slightly stuffed. You can also stuff the paws with beans for a more floppy feel. The bear owner (your child) must initiate the hug test to make sure his/her bear is just right. After an employee quickly sews up the seam, your child can send the bear through the "bear bath," a machine that squirts air on the bear to get off extra stuffing or threads. The store also has a wide selection of clothing for all the stuffed animals.

Tours are given for a group of eight or more that include a twenty-minute talk on the history of teddy bears (kudos to Theodore Roosevelt) and how bear patterns are designed and put together.

Hours: Open Mon. - Sat., 10am - 6pm; Sun., 11am - 6pm. Closed Thanksgiving and Christmas.

Admission: Technically free. Bears start at $12.00.

Ages: All

BATES NUT FARM

!/$

(760) 749-3333 / www.batesfarm.com

15954 Woods Valley Road, Valley Center

(Exit Escondido Fwy [15] E. on Old Castle Rd. which turns into Lilac Rd., R. on Valley Center Rd., E. on Woods Valley Rd. about 3 miles on a gently winding country road. Look under the Woods Valley Kampground (pg. 405) for a nearby place to camp. [TG: 1091 B5])

Is your family a little nutty? Then join nuts from all over the world at Bates Nut Farm. This 100-acre ranch features acres of open green grassy areas with shade trees and picnic tables. It is a welcoming and charming place to stop and relax. Nice-sized pens hold a variety of animals to feed (bring your own) and pet through the fences - sheep, goats, llamas, an emu, ducks, and ponies.

You are invited to seasonally pick your own pumpkins at the ten-acre pumpkin patch (see page 602 in the Calendar section) and weave your way through a maze. In fact, groups of fifteen or more can take a tour here in October that includes a walk through the maze, a hayride around the farm, learning all about pumpkins, and taking one home. The one-hour Nuts For You tour is offered the other months and includes learning how nuts are grown and harvested, a walk through the roasting and packaging rooms, and a hayride. Bring a picnic lunch to enjoy on the grounds.

The larger store here has rows and rows of nuts (almonds, cashews, walnuts, and more), dried fruits, and candies, plus antiques, baskets, country crafts, and more. Grind your own peanut butter from unsalted Spanish peanuts for $2 a cupful. The smaller, adjacent Farmer's Daughter gift boutique sells books, dolls, collectibles, jewelry cards, and more country crafts. Remember, you've got *nut*in' to lose by coming here for a visit!

Hours:　Open daily, 9am - 5pm.
Admission:　Admission is free. Tours begin at $4 per person.
Ages:　All

BUILD-A-BEAR WORKSHOP (San Diego)
(619) 542-1565 - local; (877) 789-BEAR (2327) - national / www.buildabear.com
$$$
7007 Friars Road in Fashion Valley Mall, Mission Valley
(Exit Cabrillo Fwy [163] W. on Friars Rd. [TG: 1268 J3])

See the entry for BUILD-A-BEAR WORKSHOP (Newport Beach) on page 250 for details.
Hours:　Open Mon. - Sat., 10am - 9pm; Sun., 11am - 7pm.

CHALLENGER LEARNING CENTER (San Diego)
(619) 238-1233 / www.rhfleet.org/site/challenger
$$$$
1875 El Prado, Balboa Park, San Diego
(Going S. on San Diego Fwy [5], exit at Sassafras/Airport, go straight on Kettner Blvd. L. on Laurel St., which turns into El Prado. Going N. on 5, exit N. on Pershing Dr., L. on Florida Dr., L. on Zoo PL., L. on Park Blvd., R. on Village Pl. Going S. on Cabrillo Fwy [163], exit N. on Park Blvd. (near the end), L. on Space Theater Wy. It's in Balboa Park, inside the Reuben H. Fleet Science Center. [TG: 1289 C1])

See the entry for CHALLENGER LEARNING CENTER (Carson) on page 133). The San Diego center also occasionally holds three-hour public missions. Advanced reservations are required. Also see REUBEN H. FLEET SCIENCE CENTER (see pg. 427) for more information about the museum.
Hours:　Call for a schedule.
Admission:　$15 per person for the public missions. Call for other prices.
Ages:　5th graders and up.

CIRCUS VARGAS
See the entry for CIRCUS VARGAS on page 134 for details.

FRY'S ELECTRONIC (San Marcos)
(760) 566-1300 / www.frys.com
!
150 Bent Avenue, San Marcos
(Exit Hwy 78 W. on San Marcos Blvd., R. on Bent. [TG: 1128 F1])

See the entry for FRY'S ELECTRONIC (Los Angeles County) on page 136 for details.

LA JOLLA CAVE AND CRESCENT CAFE
(858) 459-0746 / www.sandiego.citysearch.com/profile/249239

$
1325 Coast Boulevard, La Jolla

(Going S. on San Diego Fwy [5] exit W. on La Jolla Village Dr., L. on Torrey Pines Rd., R. on Prospect St., look for signs and bear R. on Coast Blvd. Going N. on 5 exit N. to Ardath Rd., which turns into Torrey Pines Rd., R. on Prospect St., look for signs and bear R. on Coast Blvd. [TG: 1227 F6])

Coffee, tea, and other beverages, plus a few antiques and artwork, are for sale here, but the real centerpiece, that's literally in the center of the store, is a natural sea cave called "Sunny Jim Cave." It's accessible via a 145-step downward "tunnel" dug in 1902. Once down in the small cave, the only things to see are a view of the ocean through the cave openings, and crabs crawling around on the rocks below. The trip down the steps, which get slippery toward the bottom, was the primary adventure. My boys were excited to tell everyone that they had been inside a real sea cave, though, so it was worth it.

Hours: Open daily, 9am - 5pm
Admission: Free to the store. Going down to the cave cost $3 for adults; $2 for ages 16 and under.
Ages: 3 years and up.

OBSERVER'S INN

$$$$$

(760) 765-0088 / www.observersinn.com
3535 Highway 79, Julian
(Exit Hwy 8 N. on Hwy 79 or exit Hwy 78 S. on Hwy 79. It's 1½ miles S. of the main town of Julian. [TG: 1156 D2])

Star light, star bright, first star I see tonight; I wish I may, I wish I might, have this wish I wish tonight. Fulfill a wish by visiting this unique Inn located in the mountains of Julian. Observant guests will see and appreciate the *star* attraction - the night sky displaying all its heavenly beauty. Us city folk rarely get the full picture of the vast array of celestial bodies, but in the mountains the people-manufactured lights fade away and God's lights take over in a dazzling display. A nineteen-foot by twenty-three-foot observatory with a retractable roof, houses several research grade telescopes, although visitors are invited to bring their own, also. Take a one-hour "sky tour," as the Inn's owner acts as a guide around the visible universe. (I still have trouble "seeing" the constellations, tho!) The observatory is carpeted, has heat, a stereo system, and couches, and is decorated with lots of astronomical photos. Beverages and cookies are offered in here.

This is an Inn, too, which means you may spend the night here and spend hours on the concrete observing pads just outside the observatory using your own telescope. Bring your 35MM camera to attach to a telescope for great moon pictures. Dress warmly, even during summer months, as nighttime temperatures can drop rapidly.

Single night booking is allowed on weekdays; weekend guests must stay for a two-night minimum. A detached guesthouse has two private rooms (although the rooms can be adjoining) with queen-size beds and full baths decorated with celestial photographs. Other activities include hiking on nearby trails, picnicking, resting in a hammock under oak trees (although technically, this isn't an activity), and seasonally sledding down hills. (B.Y.O.S. - Bring Your Own Sled.). An on-site gift shop is an authorized Meade dealership.

Hours: Call for hours.
Admission: $20 per person for just the sky tour. Nightly rates are $158 for double occupancy, which includes a one-hour sky tour each night and a continental breakfast each morning of your stay.
Ages: 7 years and up.

OLD POWAY PARK

(858) 679-4313 - park;
(858) 486-4575 - Hamburger Factory / www.ci.poway.ca.us; www.powaymidlandrr.org
14134 Midland Road, Poway
(Exit Escondido Fwy [15] E. on Camino del Norte, which turns into Twin Peaks Rd., R. on Community Rd., L. on Aubrey St. It's on the corner of Aubrey and Midland. [TG: 1190 F2])

This charming park is set up like a small historic western village, complete with its own train depot. The two-acre grassy park boasts of shade trees, a gazebo, picnic tables, barbecues, crisscrossing pathways, and bridges over the creek. Come during the week to simply enjoy the park. Come on a weekend, however, for some action, because that's when the "town" is open and everything comes to life! Regular weekend activities include a farmer's market on Saturday mornings, arts and crafts booths, tours through the museum and house, and train rides. The small Heritage Museum has glass-encased displays from olden times in Poway such as pictures, clothing, a guitar, glassware, and a piano. The small Nelson House contains a turn-of-the century, fully furnished kitchen, living room, music room, and bedrooms. The blacksmith's shop puts on demonstrations of its craft on the third and fourth Saturdays of each month from 11am to 4pm.. Last, but not least, take a short ride around town on a genuine steam engine train, trolley, or speeder car. Take a look into the train barn which houses the steam engine, a 1938 Fairmont Speeder, ore cars, and a 1894 Los Angeles Yellow Trolley. Don't forget to check out the many special events that go on here throughout the year, especially the Mountain Men Rendezvous! (See the Calendar section, pg. 600.) Guided tours to learn the heritage of the park for organized groups of twenty or more are offered for $2 per person.

Bring a picnic lunch, or enjoy good old American food at the on-site Hamburger Factory. The Factory has wood-paneled walls that are decorated with buffalo heads, steer skulls, and more, giving it a rustic ambiance. The restaurant is open daily for breakfast, lunch, and dinner. Kids' meal are served starting at 11:30am. Choices include hamburger, chicken nuggets, a hot dog, or a grilled cheese sandwich. Meals come with fries and a drink for an average of $4.

Hours: The park is open daily. Rail cars operate Sat., 10am - 4pm; Sun., 11am - 2pm. This section is closed the second Sun. of each month. The museum is open Sat. - Sun., 9am - 4pm. Nelson House is open Sat., 9am - 4pm; Sun., 11am - 2pm. Attractions are closed on Christmas. The restaurant is open Sun. - Thurs., 7am - 8pm; Fri. - Sat., 7am - 9pm.

Admission: The park is free. Train rides vary from $1 to $2 for adults depending on the type of rail car; children 12 and under are 50¢. Donations are requested for the museum and Nelson House.

Ages: All

SAN DIEGO VISITOR INFORMATION CENTER

(619) 276-8200 / www.infosandiego.com

!

2688 E. Mission Bay Drive, Mission Bay

(Exit San Diego Fwy [5] W. on Clairemont Dr., into the Visitor Center. [TG: 1248 D7])

I don't normally mention visitor centers as attractions, although they are always a good source for maps and brochures. This one, however, is located right on the bay so both the scenery and the actual building are picturesque. There are basketball courts just outside the center, plus picnic tables, a small playground, a snack shop, and a paved biking/walking trail. Just down the street is the TECOLOTE SHORES PLAY AREA (see pg. 402).

Inside the center you'll find a wealth of information on things to do in San Diego (actually it's all covered in this book!), plus maps, discount coupons on attractions and hotels, and a gift shop. This center carries a free coupon booklet that offers discounts on hotels, main attractions around San Diego, harbor cruises, trolley rides, restaurants, and more. Call for information on receiving it through the mail. Check out the San Diego title page in this book for a listing of two other centrally-located visitors center that offer similar services.

Hours: Open Mon. - Sat., 9am - 5pm; Sun., 9:30am - 4:30pm. Closed Thanksgiving and Christmas.

Admission: Free

Ages: All

SUMMERS PAST FARMS

(619) 390-1523 / www.summerspastfarms.com

!/$

15602 Olde Highway 80, Flinn Springs

(Exit 8 Fwy N. on Dunbar Ln., L. on Olde Hwy. 80. [TG: 1233 C3])

Experience a genteel way of life (yes, even with kids) at Summers Past Farms. Although the Farm is not large, its beautifully-landscaped gardens, blooming with a variety of flowers and herbs, almost ensure a delightful (and fragrant) *thyme* here. The plants are both for show and sale. One of the small gardens has a little creek with a bridge over it. There is a grassy area with trees, trellises, and white wrought-iron benches. The lavender field has a Provence-style facade. No farm is complete without its resident animals, such as cats, dogs, a few birds, and rabbits.

One of the retail shops, housed in a big red barn, offers potpourri, wreaths, baskets, teas, essential oils, lotions, dried and fresh flowers, and more. Craft classes are available. The other shop is Ye Old Soap Shoppe offering a wide variety of *scent*sational herbal soaps. Pick up a free sample (I chose Lavender/French Vanilla), and maybe you'll even get to see (and smell) the owner mixing essences for his soaps. You may purchase soap-making supplies, or a complete soap-making kit that includes <u>everything</u> you need to make twenty-eight aromatic bars for about $69.95.

Hours: Open Wed. - Sat., 9am - 5pm; Sun., 10am - 5pm.

Admission: Free

Ages: 5 years and up.

TEDDYCRAFTERS (Escondido)

(760) 291-1100 / www.teddycrafters.com

200 East Via Rancho Parkway, suite 361, in the North County Fair Mall, Escondido

(Exit Escondido Fwy [15] E. on Via Rancho Pkwy. It's on the second level near Sears. [TG: 1150 B2])

$$$

Kids (and adults) first choose the right furry bear form, or another type of animal, then bring it to life. Well, life as in a stuffed animal to bring home and love. Give your animal a satin heart, then step on the pedal that causes a machine to blow fiber stuffing into him. Watch him being stitched up, choose a name for him, add a voice message if you want, and give him a bear hug - he's yours! Select from an array of clothing if you'd like to dress-up your new playmate. Cele*bear*ate a birthday party here, or other special event.

Hours: Open Mon. - Fri., 10am - 9pm; Sat., 10am - 8pm; Sun., 11am - 6pm.

Admission: The cost for a bear starts at $12. Clothing is extra.

Ages: 2 years and up.

TIJUANA, MEXICO

www.tijuana.com; www.seetijuana.com

(Across the border.)

$$$

Hola! Come spend the day in a foreign country without the European price tag (or luxuries, majestic sights, etc.). There are several ways you can arrive at and enter into Mexico: 1) Drive into Mexico; 2) Take a tram from downtown San Diego to the border, and then take a taxi or walk across; or 3) Drive your own car almost to the border, park on the U.S. side, and then walk or take a shuttle across. Following are more details about the above options: Option 1 - If you drive into Mexico you must buy Mexican automobile insurance because American insurance doesn't mean anything over there. The border town of San Ysidro has several places to purchase Mexican insurance. The cost depends on the coverage you are buying and the value of your car. A few other things to take into account if you drive into Mexico: You will experience lines getting into and especially getting out of Mexico in the afternoon as it's rush hour traffic (actually this occurs no matter what mode of transportation you use); parking can be a problem (I mean challenge); and if you think that Los Angeles drivers are scary - you ain't seen nothing yet! For those who like to live life on the edge - drive into Tijuana. Option 2 - Take a trolley/bus into Mexico from downtown San Diego, which costs $2.25 one way for ages 6 and older. Trolleys run every twenty minutes, from 5am to midnight. You can pick one up at the corner of First and Broadway at the Transit Store, or call (619) 233-3004 or (619) 685-4900 for more locations and information. There is paid parking available for your car (about $7 for the day) at the downtown location; parking is free at Old Town San Diego. The trolley takes you to the border where you can walk across the bridge or take a taxi into Mexico. It's about a mile from the border to the main shopping area in Tijuana. Even if you walk into Tijuana, you might consider taking a cab or shuttle out because you'll be carrying shopping bags, and your children will be tired (and so will you!). Taxis are plentiful, but determine exactly where you are going first, and decide on a price before you get into the cab. The fare is usually $6 to Avenida Revolucion. Option 3 - This was our personal choice, and it was fairly hassle-free. We parked on this side of the border at Border Station Parking - signs off the freeway direct you to the huge parking lots - which was $8 for all-day parking, and attendants are on duty twenty-four hours. (Note: Just behind Border Parking are factory outlet stores.) Then we took a

Mexicoach shuttle ($1.50 per person), which runs every half hour, from the parking lot into the heart of the oldest Tijuana shopping district - Avenida Revolucion, which is seven blocks of tourist-shopping heaven. You may buy up to $300 of duty free goods in Tijuana.

Shopping along Avenida Revolucion is an experience. The numerous small shops, most of which are open daily, 10am to 9pm, have goods almost overflowing onto the sidewalks that practically scream at your children to buy them. Vendors are constantly hawking their wares, enticing you, begging you, to come into their store. Be tough. Tips to keep in mind when shopping: 1) Don't feel obligated to buy just because you asked the price. 2) I can almost guarantee that you will see that exact same item at least ten more times. 3) Never pay the original asking price. Bargaining is expected. As a rule of thumb, pay around half (or a little more) of the asking price. Be willing to go higher if it's something you really want or can't live without. (Decide beforehand how much the item is worth to you.) Haggle if you want it, but be prepared to walk away in order to get a better price, or if it isn't the price you want. 4) Prepare your children beforehand that they won't always get the item being bargained for, if the price is still too high, etc. 5) Lastly, and most importantly, teach your children to not say, "I love it - I must have it!" in front of the merchants.

Merchandise that appeals most to kids includes leather vests, hats, boots, purses, gold and silver jewelry, kids' guitars, gaudy ceramic figurines, watches, blankets, ponchos, and knickknacks. The more mature shopper will enjoy leather goods and jewelry, too, as well as perfumes, pharmaceutical supplies, clothing, and more. On every street corner you'll find the touristy-looking carts hooked up to donkeys (painted to look like zebras) along with gaudy sombreros available for you to wear while having your picture taken - $5 for a Polaroid, $1 with your own camera. (Our pictures turned out nice!)

There are other places to shop in Tijuana besides Avenida Revolucion. Try Avenida Constitucion, which is the next street over, and Plaza Rio Tijuana Shopping Center - near the Cultural Center - which has a few major department stores and specialty shops. The latter is a long walk, or a short drive, from Avenida Revolucion. Mercado Hidalgo is only five minutes from the border and often overlooked. It is a true Mexican marketplace where locals shop for produce and specialty items, such as spices and cookware.

We walked around downtown Tijuana, just beyond the shopping district. Tijuana has been cleaned up and renovated in certain areas, but we also saw a lot of poverty, broken sidewalks, and people setting up shop in much less healthy environments than would be allowed in the States. It was an eye-opener for my kids. And, since they couldn't read any of the signs, it gave them an understanding of how difficult it is for foreigners in America to get around. Tip: Bring your own water, still.

There are several nearby attractions in Tijuana. Note: The 011-52-664 number designates making an international phone call and the area code; the other digits are the actual phone number. **Bullfights** at Plaza Monumental de Playas, near the border, and on Agua Caliente Blvd. at the Tijuana Bullring. Fourteen fights are held May through September on Sunday afternoons. Tickets range from $16 to $40. Call (01152-664) 680-1808, (01152-664) 686-1510, or (619) 232-5049 for more info. **Centro Cultural Tijuana** at Paseo de los Heroes y Mina. The Museum of the Californias is good, although the art gallery wasn't that exciting to my kids. The Centro also has a planetarium/Omnimax theater. (The shows, of course, are in Spanish.) Call (01152-664) 687-9600 for more info. **Hipodromo Caliente** at Blvd. Agua Caliente y Tapachula. Greyhound races takes place here. There is a small zoo on the grounds, too. Call (01152-664) 681-7811 for more info. **Jai Alai** at Avenida Revolucion at Calle 7. The beautiful old building has a Jai Alai player out front, showing kids what to expect. The fast-moving court game is played with a ball and a long, curved wicker basket strapped to the player's wrist. Games are played on various days and at various times. Tickets range from $3 to $5. Call (01152-664) 685-2524 or (619) 231-1910 for more info. **Mexitlan** at Calle 2 and Avenida Ocampo. This city-block-long attraction houses about 200 scale models of Mexico's most important monuments, buildings, churches, plazas, archaeological sites, and more. This is a great way to get an overview of the country. Open May through October, Wed. - Fri., 10am - 6pm; Sat. - Sun., 9am - 9pm. Open November through April daily, 10am - 5pm. Admission is $5 for adults; children 11 years and under are free. Call (01152-664) 638-4101 or (619) 531-1112 for more info. **Mundo Divertido** (Family Entertainment Center) at 2578 Paseo de los Heroes y Jose Ma. This Family Fun Center offers the same fun, and at comparable prices, as the Boomers! fun centers in the States - miniature golf, batting cages, bumper boats, go karts, video and arcade games, and amusement rides such as a roller coaster and a kiddie train. Call (01152-664) 634-3213 for more info. Another **Mundo Divertido** is located at Mundo Divertido Plaza in La Mesa. This facility offers bowling, too. **Rodeos** at Lienzo Charro and Avenida Bravlio Maldonado. Call (01152-664) 680-4185 for dates, times, and prices. **State Park Jose Maria Morelos Y Pavon** at Blvd. Insurgentes 16000. This state park and ecological reserve has large open spaces, grassy lawns for picnicking, and a Creative Center for children that offers a lake, an open-air theater, botanical gardens, children's rides, and games. Call (01152-664) 625-2469 for more info. **Q-Zar** at Via Oriente Local #9. This indoor laser tag arena is huge and located at the shopping Mall of Puerto Amigo. Phone (01152-664) 683-6183 for more info. **Wax Museum of Tijuana** at First Street 8281 near Avenida Revolucion. This museum is home to over eighty waxy, lifelike historical figures and movie stars such as Mikhail Gorbachev, Emiliano Zapata, Elvis Presley, Marilyn Monroe, and Christopher Columbus. It's open daily from 10am - 10pm. Admission is $7 for adults; $5 for ages 6 to 12; children 5 years and under are free. Call (01152-664) 688-2478 for more information.

Hours: Most shops are open daily, 10am - 9pm.
Ages: 5 years and up.

-----SHOWS AND THEATERS-----

CALIFORNIA BALLET COMPANY
(858) 560-6741 or (858) 560-5676 / www.californiaballet.org
San Diego

    This professional ballet company tours throughout San Diego giving performances at the CALIFORNIA CENTER FOR THE ARTS (look at the next entry) and other places, including in-school performances, outreach performances, backstage tours, and Girl Scout Patch programs. They perform three to four, ninety-minute ballets a year. Past family-oriented shows, usually put on in the spring, have included *Alice in Wonderland* and *Snow White*. The associated junior ballet company, with performers between the ages of 12 and 17 years, put on a yearly show, usually in January. The company also offers dance classes of ballet, jazz, and modern dance for children 3 years and up.

Hours: Call for a schedule.
Admission: Prices depend on the theater venue.
Ages: 6 years and up.

CALIFORNIA CENTER FOR THE ARTS /
MERVYN'S THEATER FOR FAMILIES
(800) 98-TICKETS (988-4253) / www.artcenter.org
340 N. Escondido Boulevard, Escondido
(From the Escondido Fwy [15], exit E. on Valley Pkwy; take the east bound lane which turns into Grand Ave., L. on Escondido. Going E. on the 78 Fwy, exit S. on Centre City Pkwy., L. on Washington Ave., R. on Escondido. [TG: 1129 H2])

    All the world's a stage and kids are invited to come watch the world, or at least a part of it. Broadway musicals, comedies, dramas, dance troupes, and other of the finest, top-name entertainment around is performed at the center. Many productions are perfect for the entire family. Past productions have included *The Sound of Music, Joseph and the Amazing Technicolor Dreamcoat, Late Nite Catechism,* a barbershop quartet, and the singer, Loretta Lynn. Special student performances are offered throughout the year for only $5 a show. Mervyn's Theater for Families series is designed specifically for kids. Past performances include *The Magic Schoolbus, Lazer Vaudeville,* and *The Hobbit,* which was performed with large puppets. Children's performances can also include art projects, meeting the artists, and museum admission.

    The small museum at the center focuses on contemporary and twentieth-century art. Hour-long, docent-guided tours of the museum are offered for kindergartners to adults. Through the education program, tours are followed by another hour, or so, of making exhibit-related projects. The projects are geared for a maximum of thirty-five kids, at a minimal cost. Take advantage of this terrific way to *really* learn about art - what kids make, they will remember better.

Hours: Call for the names and dates of productions. Mervyn's Theater performances are Sun., 2pm. The museum is open Tues. - Sat., 10am - 5pm; Sun., noon - 5pm. The museum stays open Fri., Sat., and Sun. evening until curtain time. Museum tours and classes are offered Tues. - Fri. at 10am and 11am. Some classes are offered at other times.

Admission: Prices vary depending on the show. Mervyn's Theater tickets are $10 per person. The museum is $5 for adults; $4 for seniors; $3 for ages 13 - 18; children 12 and under are free. The museum is free on the first Wed. of every month and free to ticket holders on the day of performance.

Ages: 5 years and up.

CHILDREN'S CLASSICS
(858) 268-4494 / www.sdactorstheatre.net
1540 Camino del Mar at the L'Auberge del Mar Hotel Garden Amphitheater, Del Mar
(Exit San Diego Fwy [5] W. on Del Mar Heights Rd., R. on Camino Del Mar. [TG: 1187 F5])

$$

An entertaining, thirty-five-minute presentation of classic children's literature, such as fairy tales, Shakespeare's works, or modern adaptations of well-known stories, is performed by the San Diego Actors Theater a few times each month. Past productions of the audience participatory shows have included *The Giving Tree*, *Snow White and the Seven Dwarfs* (where kids came up on stage to help be the dwarfs), *Hansel and Gretel*, and *Goldilocks*. These theater presentations are great for the younger (and older) set! Sometimes acting workshops are offered after the shows. Workshops are geared for kids 4 to 9 years old and cost $10 per child.

Hours: Performances are given the second and fourth Sat. of each month at 11am.
Admission: $4 per person.
Ages: 3 years and up.

CHRISTIAN YOUTH THEATER
(800) 696-1929 or (619) 588-0206 / www.cctcyt.org/cyt
San Diego

$$$

Enjoy live, musical theater, performed by students 8 through 18 years, put on at seven locations throughout San Diego County. Past productions have included *Aladdin*, *Jungle Book*, *The Secret Garden*, *Tom Sawyer*, *Willy Wonka & the Chocolate Factory*, and *Alice in Wonderland*. The theater presents wholesome entertainment for the whole family!

Hours: Call for show locations, dates, and times.
Admission: Tickets usually cost about $8 for adults; $6 for ages 12 and under. At the North County Inland location, prices are $9.75 for adults; $9 for ages 12 and under.
Ages: 4 years and up.

IMAX DOME THEATER
(619) 238-1233 / www.rhfleet.org
1875 El Prado, Balboa Park, San Diego

See the entry for REUBEN H. FLEET SCIENCE CENTER on page 427 for details. The museum houses the IMAX Theater.

LAMB'S PLAYERS THEATER
(619) 437-0600 / www.lambsplayers.org
1142 Orange Avenue, Coronado
(Exit San Diego Fwy [5] on Hwy 75 [the Coronado Bridge], L. on Orange Ave. [TG: 1288 H7])

$$$$

This 350-seat theater offers five great, usually musical, productions a year and most of them are very kid-friendly. Past shows include *Joseph and the Amazing Technicolor Dreamcoat*, *You're a Good Man, Charlie Brown*, *Dracula*, and *American Rhythm*, a journey across America through music. On Forum Friday shows, the audience is invited to stay after the performance and participate in an informal discussion with cast members.

Lamb's Players also put on productions in National City, Escondido, and Horton Plaza. Inquire about immersion programs the theater offers for school groups and about summer camps for children aspiring to the stage and screen.

Hours: Call for show dates and times.

Admission: Tickets usually range from $15 - $38 for adults, depending on the date and time. Ages 5 - 17 are half price in section A, and $4 off in section B on selected shows. Children 4 and under are not admitted. Rush tickets are sometimes available.

Ages: 5 years and up.

MARIE HITCHCOCK PUPPET THEATER

(619) 685-5990 / www.balboaparkpuppets.com

Balboa Park, San Diego

(Going S. on San Diego Fwy [5], exit at Sassafras/Airport, go straight on Kettner Blvd. L. on Laurel St., which turns into El Prado. Going N. on 5, exit N. on Pershing Dr., L. on Florida Dr., L. on Zoo Pl., L. on Park Blvd., R. on Village Pl. Going S. on Cabrillo Fwy [163], exit N. on Park Blvd. (near the end), L. on Presidents Wy. [TG: 1289 C1])

This intimate theater, located behind the San Diego Automotive Museum, presents kid-approved, half-hour, puppet shows. The type of puppets vary from show to show, and can include hand puppets, marionettes, dummies (for ventriloquists), and puppets made from anything and everything found around the house. The shows themselves are similar in that they never fail to capture a child's imagination. From *Cinderella* to *The Ugly Duckling* to *The Frog Prince*, stories are told as only puppets can tell them (with a little bit of human help)! Shows change weekly so watch out - bringing the kids here can become habit forming. (See BALBOA PARK on page 408 for a listing of all the museums and attractions within walking distance.)

Hours: Performances are usually given Wed. - Sun., 11am, 1pm, and 2:30pm.

Admission: $3 for adults; $2 for ages 2 - 12; children under 2 are free.

Ages: 1½ - 10 years.

METROPOLITAN EDUCATIONAL THEATRE NETWORK (San Diego)

(877) 536-4519 / www.met2.org

Performed at Lyceum Theater at Horton Plaza, Broadway Circle & 4th Avenue, San Diego; and the Center for Performing Arts, 15498 Espola Road, Poway

(San Diego: Going S. on San Diego Fwy [5], exit S. on Front St., L. on Broadway. Going N. on the 5, exit S. on 6th Ave. R. on Broadway. [TG: 1289 A3]; Poway: Exit Escondido Fwy [15] E. on Rancho Bernardo Rd., which turns into Espola Rd. [TG: 1170 G5])

This terrific, everyone-gets-a-role, theater group is comprised of kids 4 years old through college age, as well as a few adult performers. What a great "first-theater" exposure for kids who are acting, and those in the audience. Past productions have included *The Wiz*, *Peter Pan*, *Aladdin*, and *Fiddler on the Roof*. If your child is a thespian wannabe, call about enrolling him/her for the next production. The twelve-week Saturday course costs $160, which includes rehearsal workshops, training, and productions. Participants also have the opportunity to go abroad once a year. There are two other locations of the theater network: Northridge and Torrance, in Los Angeles County.

Hours: Call for show locations, dates, and times.

Admission: Tickets are usually $15 for adults; $12 for children 4 - 12.

Ages: 4 years on up to watch or participate.

NATIONAL COMEDY THEATRE

(619) 295-4999 or (818) 953-4933 / www.nationalcomedy.com

3717 India Street, San Diego

(Exit San Diego Fwy [5] N. on Washington St., R. on India. [TG: 1268 H6])

Your belly will be bustin' from laughing so hard at this troupe who perform fast-paced, quick-witted improvisational comedy. Two teams, comprised of two to four professional comedians, "compete" in a series of scenes which are based on audience suggestions. The referee keeps everything in check, including the suggestions. The audience also judges and picks a winner. A stand-out feature in the ninety-minute shows is that material is clean, so they are appropriate for kids (and adults). An audience member or troupe who offers up an inappropriate suggestion must wear a brown paper bag over his/her head for a segment. Enjoy a hilarious outing with the family. The troupe also offers improv comedy training, high school improv leagues, summer camps, and more.

Hours: Shows are presented Fri. and Sat., 7:30pm and 9:45pm.
Admission: $12 for adults; $10 for seniors and students.
Ages: 7 years and up.

OLD GLOBE THEATRE

(619) 239-2255 / www.oldglobe.org

$$$$$

Balboa Park, San Diego

(Going S. on San Diego Fwy [5], exit at Sassafras/Airport, go straight on Kettner Blvd. L. on Laurel St., which turns into El Prado. Going N. on 5, exit N. on Pershing Dr., L. on Florida Dr., L. on Zoo Pl., L. on Park Blvd. Going S. on Cabrillo Fwy [163], exit N. on Park Blvd. (near end). [TG: 1289 C1])

Originally modeled after Shakespeare's Globe Theatre in London, this 580-seat classic theater is accompanied by two other theaters; the 225-seat Cassius Carter Centre Stage and the 612-seat outdoor Lowell Davies Festival Theatre. Combined, the theater complex puts on about fourteen productions, usually plays, a year. Many of the productions appeal mostly to adults, but the Globe's holiday musical program, *How the Grinch Stole Christmas*, is definitely family fare. It runs November through December. Call regarding other programs, tours (see OLD GLOBE THEATRE (tour), on page 452, for details), and educational opportunities.

Hours: Call for a schedule.
Admission: Prices vary depending on show, date, and time. Tickets for the Grinch are $20 - $50 for adults; $20 - $25 for ages 17 and under.
Ages: Depends on the show.

POWAY CENTER FOR THE PERFORMING ARTS

(858) 748-0505 / www.powayarts.org

$$$$

15498 Espola Road, Poway

(Exit Escondido Fwy [15] E. on Rancho Bernardo Rd., which turns into Espola Rd. [TG: 1170 G5])

This 800-seat capacity theater offers a variety of family entertainment throughout the year, as well as a few outstanding children's programs. Past productions have included Jim Gamble puppets; a troop that performed juggling, acrobatics, and comedy combined with a laser light show; the Boys Choir of Harlem; *The King and I*; *Cinderella;* and a kid-friendly opera, *The Barber of Seville*. Other performances include Broadway musicals, big band productions, comedy routines, and more.

Hours: Call for performance times.
Admission: Ticket prices vary depending on show, date, and time.
Ages: 4 years and up.

SAN DIEGO JUNIOR THEATRE

(619) 239-1311 or (619) 239-8355 / www.juniortheatre.com

$$$

1650 El Prado in Balboa Park, Casa del Prado, San Diego

(Going S. on San Diego Fwy [5], exit at Sassafras/Airport, go straight on Kettner Blvd. L. on Laurel St., which turns into El Prado. Going N. on 5, exit N. on Pershing Dr., L. on Florida Dr., L. on Zoo Pl., L. on Park Blvd., R. on Village Pl. Going S. on Cabrillo Fwy [163], exit N. on Park Blvd. (near the end), L. on Presidents Wy. [TG: 1289 C1])

The San Diego Junior Theatre is a comprehensive workshop program, for students 4 to 18 years old, that presents six family-oriented shows a year that range from Broadway classics to locally developed pieces. Past performances of the for-kids-by-kids group have included *The Miracle Worker*, *Schoolhouse Rock*, *Master Prince and the Pauper*, and *The Adventures of a Bear Named Paddington*. Ask about special performances that are interpreted for the deaf. Midweek matinees are given for schools and other large groups, and curriculum supplements are provided for classrooms.

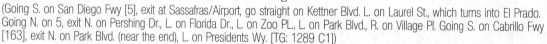

Hours: Call for show dates and times.
Admission: Prices range from $7 - $10 for adults, depending on the seat; $5 - $7 for seniors and ages 2 - 14.
Ages: 4 years and up.

VIEJAS OUTLET CENTER
(619) 659-2070 / www.viejas.com
5005 Willows Road, Alpine
See the entry for VIEJAS OUTLET CENTER on page 405 for details.

WELK RESORT THEATER
(888) 802-7469 / www.welkresort.com
8860 Lawrence Welk Drive, Escondido
(Going S. on Escondido Fwy [15], exit S. on Gopher Canyon Rd., R. on Champagne. Going N. on 15, exit E. on Mountain Meadow exit, L. on Champagne Blvd. From Champagne, go E. on Lawrence Welk Dr. [TG: 1089 B2])

$$$$$

This "wannaful" (i.e. that's the way Lawrence Welk used to say "wonderful") theater offers five different, full-production Broadway musicals a year. Audiences in the intimate 330-seat theater have seen the likes of *My Fair Lady*, *The King and I*, *Seven Brides for Seven Brothers*, *Forever Plaid*, and its annual, *Welk Musical Christmas Show*. As you can tell by the titles, many of the musicals are family-oriented.

Before or during intermission, take a short "tour" around the elegant lobby/museum. It features portions of Welk's life in chronological order via pictures, actual props, bandstands, and instruments from the Lawrence Welk Show.

Grab a bite to eat at one of the restaurants, like the pizzeria, in the Welk Village shopping area. Personally, I was glad we arrived early enough to also shop in the village. The restaurant up the hill from the theater, Mr. W's, offers a decent buffet lunch and dinner, which is always a good choice for picky eaters. Combined with a theater show, a meal here is only a few dollars more.

Hours: Matinee performances are given Tues. - Thurs., Sat. - Sun. at 1:45pm. Evening performances are given Tues., Thurs., and Sat. at 8pm. No performances are given on Fri. or Mon. The buffet lunch is served 11:15am - 1:15pm; the buffet dinner, 5:30pm - 7:30pm.
Admission: Just the show is $31 - $34, depending on the time and day, for adults; $20 for ages 3 - 12. The show and buffet meal is $42 - $48 for adults; $26 for children.
Ages: 6 years and up.

-----TOURS-----

BRAILLE INSTITUTE (San Diego)

(858) 452-1111 / www.brailleinstitute.org
4555 Executive Drive, San Diego
(Exit Jacob Dekema Fwy [805], E. on La Jolla Village/Miramar, R. on Towne Centre Dr., L. Executive. [TG: 1228 D2])

What would it be like to have limited vision, or not be able to see at all? Third graders and up are invited to take an hour-long tour of the Braille Institute campus to learn how the visually impaired can get around and learn about the tools that help them be independent. The students also get an introduction to the Braille language by feeling Braille maps and typing on a Braille typewriter. Depending on the availability and the day, visitors might also have the opportunity to talk with a librarian who reads Braille and to see the school's classrooms and computer labs.

Hours: Tours are offered Mon. - Fri. Call to make an appointment.
Admission: Free
Ages: 8 years and up.

DOWN ON THE FARM

☼

(760) 510-1606 / www.twinoaksschoolhouse.com

$$$

236 Deer Springs Road, San Marcos

(Exit Escondido Fwy [15] E. on Deer Springs Road/Mountain Meadow. The farm is on the right about 1 mile from the freeway. [TG: 1089 B7])

This field trip could easily be called "Down at the Schoolhouse" because it takes places on the lovely grounds and inside the beautifully restored one-room schoolhouse originally built in 1891. The two-and-a-half-hour "tour" consists of each group of students visiting about seven different learning stations and taking home something from several of them.

Students step into the schoolhouse and into another era. The school room has a tin ceiling, separate cloak rooms for boys and girls, desks and chairs, and a chalkboard that wraps around the front wall and spills onto the side walls. Mock school sessions, given by docents appropriately attired in late 1800's clothing, include spelling bees conducted by using slate boards. Throughout their time here students may also learn how to churn butter, dip candles, pump water, write their name with a quill pen, spin wool, make (and taste) apple fritters or popcorn, collect eggs from the chicken coop, and other turn-of-the-century tasks.

A Native American tells stories by the tepee set up outside and instructs children on how to crush corn. A nearby table has various animal hides. In the corral area kids learn about tackle and feed, and about horsemanship by brushing ponies (over the fence). Goats and lambs can also be petted over the fence. Inside the small nursery barn, you'll hopefully see piglets, chicks, and bunnies. Depending on the time of year, students can plant seedlings, or at least water them. See a restored tractor and a buggy, go into an actual gypsy wagon, and perhaps play on some playground equipment. There is also a small rose garden, plus an arbor, fountain, and stage in the large yard, along with a non-19th-century sound system throughout. After a hard morning of schooling, enjoy lunch in a picnic area that is shaded by 100-year-old eucalyptus trees. Note: The facility rents out for various functions.

Tours are geared for kindergartners through eighth graders, although there are some tours available for preschoolers, too. The minimum number needed to reserve the schoolhouse tour is forty-five; the maximum, one hundred seventy-five.

Hours: Tours are offered Tues. - Fri., at 9am or 9:30am.

Admission: $10 per student; teachers and staff are free; $5 for additional adults.

Ages: Preschool through 8th grade.

EAGLE MINING COMPANY

(760) 765-0036 / www.julianfun.com

$$$

North end of 'C' Street, Julian

(From San Diego Fwy [5] or Escondido Fwy [15], take 78 Fwy E. to Julian. From the 8 Fwy, take 79 N. to Julian. From Main St. in Julian, go N. on 'C' St. Follow the signs. [TG: 1136 B6])

Eureka! There's gold in them thar hills! Original mining equipment and a few old buildings make it look like time has stood still here. One of the buildings is a small museum/store with rock specimens, mining tools, and a glass-cased display of memorabilia from the early 1900's.

Trek through time on your one-hour, guided walking tour through two genuine gold mines that were founded in 1870: the Eagle Mine and the connecting, High Peak Mine. My kids studied about the forty-niners, but to actually go through a gold mine, walk on ore-cart tracks, see stone tunnels hand carved by picks, and learn the hardships of mining, really made a lasting impact on them. We saw the vein that the miners worked and realized, along with hundreds of other people both past and present, that gold wasn't easily obtainable. It took one ton of rock to yield a sugar-cube-size amount of gold! We went up two of the eleven levels in the mines, saw the hoist room where ore buckets were used as olden-day elevators, and experienced darkness so black that we couldn't see our hands in front of our faces. I admire the fortitude of our early engineers. It's interesting to note the difference between the earlier smooth rock tunnels that were hand drilled and the later jagged edges left from blasting with charges. Don't forget to look up at the amazing shaft tunnels (and duck your head)!

Outside, we saw the milling equipment used to crush rocks, and learned the tedious process of extracting gold. Try your hand at panning for gold (it's harder than it looks) in a "stocked" water trough on the premises, but warn kids that they can't keep the gold. And just remember: All that glitters isn't gold.

Julian is a quaint town with unique shops along Main Street. Your kids will enjoy a stop-off at the Julian Drugstore for an ice cream at its old-fashioned soda counter. The drugstore is located on the corner of Main and Washington Sts. Look up Julian under the city index for other, close-by attractions.

Hours: Open daily, 10am - 2:30pm.
Admission: $8 for adults; $4 for ages 5 - 15; $1 for children 4 and under.
Ages: 4 years and up.

GOODWILL INDUSTRIES (San Diego)

(619) 225-2200 / www.sdgoodwill.org
3663 Rosecrans Street, San Diego
(Going S. on San Diego Fwy [5] exit E. on Old Town Ave. Going N. on 5, exit at Moore St., R. on Old Town Ave. From Old Town go L. on San Diego Ave., L. on Congress St., L. on Taylor St., which turns into Rosecrans. [TG: 1268 E5])

See the entry for GOODWILL INDUSTRIES (Santa Ana) on page 265 for details. This facility does not have a shrink wrap machine.

Hours: Tours are offered Mon. - Fri., 9am - 3pm by reservation only.
Admission: Free
Ages: 15 years and up.

MCCLELLAN-PALOMAR AIRPORT

(800) 759-5667 or (760) 431-4646
2198 Palomar Airport Road, Carlsbad
(Exit San Diego Fwy [5] E. on Palomar Airport Rd., L. on Yarrow Rd. [TG: 1127 D3])

Visitors won't get airborne on this airport tour, but they can experience flight vicariously. Small airplanes are constantly landing and taking off as guides tell about the different type of aircraft here. If a grounded plane is available, children can sit inside it and check out all the controls in the cockpit. After the tour, kids are given a memento - an airplane coloring book, a Styrofoam airplane, and/or "wings."

The adjacent Airport Cafe, which is open daily, 7am to 5pm, has both indoor and outdoor seating. For those who feel the need to actually experience flight, twenty minute to hour-long biplane and cruiser rides are available. See BIPLANE, WARBIRD, AIR COMBAT ADVENTURES (pg. 454).

Hours: Tours are given by appointment.
Admission: Tours are free. Call for biplane or cruiser flights. Two hours of free parking.
Ages: 4 years and up.

NAVY SHIPS TOURS

(619) 437-2735
U.S. Navy Pier of Harbor Drive, near Broadway on the Embarcadero, San Diego
(Going N. on San Diego Fwy [5], exit E. on Hawthorne St., L. on Harbor. Going S. on 5, exit S. on Front St., R. on Ash, L. on Harbor. [TG: 1288 J3])

The Navy offers a unique opportunity for the public to tour a destroyer, frigate, amphibious cruiser, submarine, aircraft carrier, or other naval craft. A forty-five-minute or so tour is given for a minimum group of twenty, maximum of 100. Groups must sign up at least four weeks in advance. The type of ship you actually see depends on what is in the harbor on the day you plan to visit. A military tour guide will take you through the ship and answer any questions, and we all know that kids always have plenty of those. Note that the tour isn't stroller/wheelchair accessible and that there are incline ladders to climb. (Don't wear dresses or skirts, ladies!) A favorite room is the combat information center, where radar equipment is on display.

Hours: Tours are offered Tues. and Thurs., 9am - 3pm.

Admission: Free
Ages: 5 years and up.

OLD GLOBE THEATRE (tour)

(619) 239-2255 / www.oldglobe.org
Balboa Park, San Diego

(Going S. on San Diego Fwy [5], exit at Sassafras/Airport, go straight on Kettner Blvd. L. on Laurel St., which turns into El Prado. Going N. on 5, exit N. on Pershing Dr., L. on Florida Dr., L. on Zoo PL., L. on Park Blvd. Going S. on Cabrillo Fwy [163], exit N. on Park Blvd. (near end). [TG: 1289 C1])

Take a tour of the Old Globe Theatre, which was originally modeled after Shakespeare's Globe Theatre in London. You'll see behind-the-scenes of this theater and the two other ones in the complex while learning their histories, architecture, and more. Also look up OLD GLOBE THEATRE on page 448 for show information.
Hours: Tours are given on selected Sat. and Sun. at 10:30am.
Admission: $3 for adults; $1 for seniors and students.
Ages: 9 years and up.

SAN DIEGO INTERNATIONAL AIRPORT

(619) 400-2875 / www.san.org/airporttour/default.asp
Harbor Drive at Lindbergh Field, San Diego

(Going S. on San Diego Fwy [5], exit W. on Sassafras. Going N. on 5, exit W. on Hawthorne St., N. on Harbor. Follow the signs to the airport. [TG: 1288 G1])

Pilot your way to the airport for a well-organized, two-hour tour of the San Diego International Airport. Tours include a walk through a majority of the facility while learning about architecture, travel, communications, career opportunities, and the history of aviation. Hear about Charles Lindbergh while looking at a replica of the Spirit of St. Louis. See some of the works of art on display and a demonstration of what the on-site fire station does. Take a tram tour that runs parallel to the runway and wave at the various workers. Go through the baggage claim area, find out about courtesy phones, and how to use the maps on the walls. The tour enables children and adults to find out all about travel without experiencing jet lag, or the cost of a trip! Groups must consist of a minimum of twelve people and a maximum of twenty.
Hours: Tours are offered Wed. - Fri., 10am - noon.
Admission: Free
Ages: Kids must be at least 7 years and up.

SAN DIEGO UNION-TRIBUNE

(866) 291-2741 or (619) 299-3131 - general / www.signonsandiego.com
350 Camino de la Reina, San Diego

(Going W. on Mission Valley Fwy [8], exit E. at Mission Center Rd., go L. on Camino Del Rio, which turns into Camino de la Siesta, L. on Camino de la Reina. Going E. on 8, exit E. on Hotel Cir. S., R. on Camino de la Reina. [TG: 1269 A3])

A one-hour tour to see how a newspaper is put together may be just the thing to spur your child's interest in journalism. Tours may include walking through the newsroom to see reporters and editors at work, seeing the production area where composing and paste-up work is done, and learning about circulation, advertising, and numerous other newspaper components. Tours are given to groups between twenty to thirty-five students and require advance registration. If you, as an individual, would like to take the tour, you may join in with a pre-registered tour group that is usually comprised of students. The facilities are wheelchair accessible.
Hours: Tours are given Tues., 10:30am and 1:30pm; Wed. - Thurs., 10:30am.
Admission: Free. A school group may be charged a minimal fee to cover the cost of materials which are sent to the school before the visit.
Ages: Children must be 9 years and up.

ST. VINCENT DE PAUL VILLAGE

(619) 233-8500 / www.svdpv.org

1501 Imperial Avenue, San Diego

(Going S. on San Diego Fwy [5], exit W. on Imperial. Going N. on 5, exit N. on Crosby St., L. on 25th St., L. on Imperial. From Escondido Fwy [15], exit E. on Ocean View Blvd., R. on 28th St., L. on Imperial. [TG: 1289 C4])

". . . Give me your tired, your poor, your huddled masses yearning to be free. . ." (Part of a poem that is engraved on the pedestal of the Statue of Liberty.) St. Vincent's Village is a "network of residential centers providing a continuum of care to over 2,000 men, women, and children daily." This incredible, state-of-the-art, self-contained facility aids the poor and homeless in very practical ways. It offers them a new lease on life with homes, meals, life-skills programs, counseling, and medical programs.

A one-hour tour takes your group or family through most of the facility - the lobby, office, kitchen courtyard, residential buildings, food storage, and medical buildings. This is quite an operation, so a behind-the-scenes tour is eye opening. If you are seeking to instill compassion in your children and/or if they are looking for a venue to help those less fortunate, a visit to this village is a good starting point. Coming here will make an indelible mark upon hearts because the homeless are then no longer faceless or nameless, but real people with real needs.

Hours: Tours are offered Mon. - Fri. on the hour 9am - 2pm. Please call at least a week ahead of time to reserve a tour date and time.

Admission: Free

Ages: 8 years and up.

TAYLOR GUITARS

(619) 258-6957 / www.taylorguitars.com

1980 Gillespie Way, El Cajon

(Exit Interstate 8 N. on Johnson Ave., L. on Bradley, R. on Cuyamaca, L. on Gillespie Way. [TG: 1251 C1])

What do Aerosmith, Pearl Jam, President Clinton, and Garth Brooks have in common? They each own Taylor guitars. This over-an-hour-long tour is "Taylor"-made for guitar fans. Starting in the lobby, which features an informational and pictorial timeline of the guitar company, visitors see and learn how a guitar is put together, from start to glossy (or satin) finish. Cherry, Sapele mahogany, Sitka spruce, Big Leaf maple, cedar, Indian rosewood, Hawaiian koa, and walnut are just a few of the common and exotic woods used in Taylor guitars. Once the wood is cut to precise specifications, it is kept in climate controlled rooms and containers, then carved, sanded, and assembled. Specially designed (loud!) machines, such as the ones that slice grooves in the neck of the guitar, are fascinating to watch as are the workers who are involved in each step of the process. Note: It takes a week to ten days to complete just one guitar.

The tour is geared for real guitar aficionados (we had some people on ours who asked lots of "technical" questions), but kids will appreciate the different shapes, woods, colors, and sounds of the guitars. After the tour, guests are invited to purchase a wide selection of merchandise (guitar picks, jackets, etc.) imprinted with the Taylor logo. Guitars are not sold on the premises. The tour is geared for small groups, is not wheelchair friendly, and visitors must stay within specified lines and resist the temptation to touch anything in the factory warehouses. Photography is permitted.

Hours: Tours are offered at Mon. - Fri., at 1pm. Reservations are not required, but suggested. Tours are not given for a week towards the end of June, at the beginning of July, and for a week before Christmas through New Year's Day.

Admission: Free

Ages: 7 years and up.

WASTE MANAGEMENT

(619) 596-5100

1001 W. Bradley Avenue, El Cajon

(Exit San Vincente Fwy [67] W. on Bradley. [TG: 1251 D2])

Have your younger children ever stood riveted, watching the garbage men take trash from the curb and toss it into the garbage trucks? Now you can find out where the trash goes and see how it's processed. Waste Management offers interesting one-hour tours of one of its main facilities. We went through the offices; saw the huge trash trucks (and learned how expensive they are!); sat in a cab, tooted the horn, and "played" with the computer; saw the recycling area; and saw and smelled tons and tons (literally) of trash which was being scooped up and dumped onto another truck that takes the waste out to landfills. We learned how many tons make a compressed bundle, where the landfills are and how much longer they should be available, and that we should waste not, want not.

      Hours: Tours are offered Tues. and Thurs. at 9:30am for up to thirty people. Call to make a reservation.
Admission: Free
      Ages: 4 - 10 years.

WILLIAMS WORM FARM

(619) 443-1698 / www.williamswormfarm.com
14893 El Monte Road at Willows Road, Lakeside
(Exit San Vincente Fwy [67] E. on Mapleview, which turns into Lake Jennings, L. on El Monte and drive a few miles, L. at the sign that announces Van Ommering Dairy or Circle V Dairy, L. at the fork in the road. The farm is just past the dairy. [TG: 1212 J7])

"Worms are the intestines of the earth." (Aristotle) A half-hour tour of this red worm (not earthworm) farm leads credence to that visual picture. Bill, the owner, has two, 250-foot long chicken barns that now contain rows of dirt packed with worms. The worms become visible only when Bill scoops up a shovel full of earth. It takes worms thirty days to make castings (i.e. worm poop that makes great dirt). Twenty-five percent of these worms are sold for fish bait, while another portion is added to dog and cat food. A major portion of the "dirt" is sold to gardeners and composters. All this and more is yours to learn on a tour. And yes, you may even hold a handful of the wiggly critters. Note: Since the farm is next to the VAN OMMERING DAIRY (pg. 576), you may want to schedule a tour here for the same day.

      Hours: Tours are given Mon. - Fri. Call to schedule.
Admission: Free
      Ages: All

-----TRANSPORTATION-----

AMTRAK

(800) USA RAIL (872-7245) / www.dot.ca.gov/hq/rail; www.amtrak.com
Ride the rails! See page xi (in the front) for more information.

BIKE MAPS (San Diego County)

The web site www.labikepaths.com is a fantastic resource. It actually covers all of Southern California, not just L.A., with links to specific counties for maps, bikeways, and other cycling information. Another helpful contact website and phone number is for the State of California Caltrans Office of Bicycle Facilities: (916) 653-0036; www.dot.ca.gov/hq/tpp/offices/bike/contracts.htm. Also contact (619) 231-BIKE (2453) or (800) COMMUTE (266-6883) / www.sdcommute.com/bicycle.htm. Note that bike racks are available on many buses and on Coaster commuter trains.

BIPLANE, WARBIRD, AIR COMBAT ADVENTURES

$$$$$

(800) 759-5667 / www.barnstorming.com
2198 Palomar Airport Road, McClellan Palomar Airport, Carlsbad
(Exit San Diego Fwy [5] E. on Palomar Airport Rd. [TG: 1127 D3])

Flying in a restored open-cockpit biplane, wearing an old-fashioned leather helmet, goggles, and a pilot scarf reminds me of another flying ace, Snoopy, and his adventures with the Red Baron. (Yes, I do know that Snoopy isn't real.) You'll fly over the stunning San Diego coastline for twenty minutes, side-by-side with another passenger (this could be your child!), while the pilot sits behind you. It's like riding a motorcycle in the sky!

Another adventure offered here is Air Combat. After a crash course, so to speak, on general aviation and specifically, tactical maneuvers during combat, you'll suit up and take off for the wild blue yonder. When you've gotten a feel for the controls, get ready for combat with a real "enemy." You'll fly for over thirty minutes, experiencing high/low yo-yos (where the plane dips abruptly downward and zooms upward and your stomach heads in the opposite direction), and other maneuvers in a dogfight - let the fur fly! This exhilarating experience is one that you'll remember and talk about for the rest of your life.

Hours: Call to schedule a flight.

Admission: Biplane Adventures start at $59 for one person, although two people are required for twenty minutes of flight time. Air Combat starts at $249 per person, or $199 if you B.Y.O.E. (Bring Your Own Enemy). Ask about current specials. Reservations are highly recommended.

Ages: 6 years and up.

BOAT RENTALS OF AMERICA, OCEANSIDE HARBOR

$$$

(760) 722-0028 / www.boats4rent.com

Harbor Drive S., Oceanside Harbor, Oceanside

(Exit San Diego Fwy [5], W. on Harbor Dr./Vandegrift Blvd., L. on Harbor Dr. S., [TG: 1085 J6])

Rentals includes kayaks - $12 per hour for a single, $20 an hour for a double; pedal boats - $15 an hour; sailboats - $30 an hour for a fourteen footer; motorboats - $40 an hour for a six-passenger boat that doesn't leave the harbor, and $75 an hour for a six-passenger boat that does; electric boats - $60 an hour; and wave runners - $90 an hour. Make some time to shop around in the Harbor Village before or after your excursion.

Hours: Open daily in the summer, 9am - 9pm. Open the rest of the year, 10am - 6pm, weather permitting. Call first.

Admission: Prices listed above. The first two hours of parking in the village area are free.

Ages: 4 years and up.

CAJON SPEEDWAY

$$$

(619) 448-8900 / www.cajonspeedway.com

1888 Wing Avenue, El Cajon

(Exit San Vicente Fwy W. on Bradley, R. on Wing. It's adjacent to Gillespie Field [airport]. [TG: 1251 F2])

NASCAR Winston Racing Series, Coors Light Series, and stock cars - if these terms make your heart race just a little faster, you'll enjoy the races at the 3/8 mile paved oval speedway.

Hours: The season runs mid-March through mid-October.

Admission: $10 - $12 per adults; $5 for ages 6 - 12; children 5 and under are free.

Ages: 5 years and up.

CALIFORNIA WATER SPORTS AT SNUG HARBOR MARINA

$$$

(760) 434-3089 / www.californiawatersports.net

4215 Harrison Street, Carlsbad

(Exit San Diego Fwy [5] E. on Tamarack, R. on Adams, R. on Chiqueipin, L. on Harrison. You can see the marina from the freeway - follow the signs to Snug Harbor once you're on Tamarack. [TG: 1106 G7])

This is a popular place. Three marina/lagoon areas are located here for separate water activities. Wave rentals are $75 for an hour. Single kayaks are $12 an hour. Double kayaks, canoes, and pedalboats are $18 an hour each. Waterskiing is also available. You may not take the equipment out of this marina, but the area is plenty big enough. In between boating activities, lay out on the beach, eat some lunch at the picnic tables, or shop at the pro shop. Enjoy!

Hours: Open the end of May through mid-September daily, 9am - 6pm. Open the rest of the year, Fri. - Mon., 10am -5pm.

Admission: Prices are listed above.
        Ages: 6 years and up.

CINDERELLA'S CARRIAGE
(619) 239-8080 / www.cinderella-carriage.com   *$$$$$*

In front of the Harbor House Restaurant at Seaport Village, or in front of Crowces Restaurant at 5th Avenue and 'F' Street in the Gaslamp Quarter, San Diego

(Seaport Village: Going S. on San Diego Fwy [5], exit S. on Front St., R. on Broadway, L. on Kettner. Going N. on the 5, exit S. on 6th Ave. R. on Broadway, L. on Kettner. [TG: 1288 J4]; Gaslamp Quarter: Going S. on San Diego Fwy [5], exit W. on Ash St., L. on 6th Ave., R. on 'F' St. Going N. on 5, exit S. on 6th Ave., R. on 'F' St. [TG: 1289 A3])

The largest carriage company on the coast still makes every ride feel special and intimate. Enjoy the waterfront from a different vantage as you take a carriage around Seaport Village, or explore the historic and romantic Gaslamp Quarter. The one-horse powered carriages are pulled by a large draft horse (e.g. a Clydesdale or a Belgium horse). Kids (and adults) get a thrill out of clip-clopping along the streets of downtown San Diego. And don't worry, your Cinderella's carriage won't turn into a pumpkin before your ride is over.

      Hours: Carriages are available at Seaport Village daily, noon - 11pm, and at the Gaslamp District nightly, 6pm - 11pm. You may just show up, or make reservations.

Admission: A ride around Seaport Village is $25. A forty-five-minute rides is $75 for up to four people.

        Ages: All

COASTER
(619) 685-4900 - automated system for the coaster, bus, and trolley;   *$$$*

(800) 262-7837 - transit office / www.sdcommute.com

San Diego County

Coast stress-free from Oceanside to Old Town to further south in San Diego, with stops at Carlsbad, Encinitas, Solana Beach, and Sorrento Valley via the sleek transit express rail line. Pick out a destination in the above-mentioned cities, or let the ride be the adventure. Automated fare machines at the Coaster stations make obtaining a ticket a breeze, although calling to find out the schedule on the automated number can drive one a little nuts.

      Hours: It operates Mon. - Sat., except major holidays, starting at about 5:30am and ending at about 6:30pm - depending on destination.

Admission: Prices range from $3.25 - $3.75 per person one way. One child 5 and under may travel free with a paid accompanying adult.

        Ages: All

COUNTRY CARRIAGES
(760) 765-1471   *$$$$*

2134 Main Street, Julian

(From San Diego Fwy [5] or Escondido Fwy [15], take 78 Fwy E. to Julian. From the 8 Fwy, take 79 Fwy N. to Julian. 78/79 becomes Main St. in Julian. [TG: 1136 B7])

Clip clop, clip clop - a horse-drawn carriage ride through Julian fits in perfectly with the ambiance of this quaint town. Most of the tours begin in front of the Julian Drug Store, a fun place to stop for a treat at an old-fashioned soda fountain. A thirty-minute ride costs $25 per couple, or a family consisting of two adults and one to two small children; for three adults and two small children the price is $30. A one-hour ride is $55 per couple on the weekdays.

      Hours: Look for the carriage Mon. - Thurs., 11pm - 4pm; Fri. - Sun., 11am - 7pm, weather permitting. Reservations are highly recommended.

Admission: Prices are listed above.

        Ages: All

GONDOLA COMPANY

(619) 429-6317 / www.gondolacompany.com

4000 Coronado Bay Road, Coronado

(Exit San Diego Fwy [5] W. on Palm Ave. [75], stay R. to go on Silver Strand Blvd., R. on Coronado Bay. It's at Loews Coronado Bay Resort and Marina. [TG: 1309 E7])

$$$$$

This part of Coronado becomes a part of Italy via an authentic gondola cruise through the exclusive waterway of the Coronado Cays. Romantic? Yes, but it can also be a peaceful, hour-long adventure with children. The gondolier dresses in the traditional costume of striped shirt and black pants. Italian music plays in the background. The cruise includes either antipasto appetizer or chocolate-covered strawberries. An ice bucket and glasses are provided, and you supply your own choice of beverage. Each of the three gondolas can take up to six people.

Hours: Open daily, 11am - 11pm.

Admission: $60 for two people; $15 per additional person. For more of a memorable outing (and more $), enjoy a four-course meal - appetizer, salad, entree, and dessert - for $195, offered Tues. - Sun.

Ages: 4 years and up.

H & M LANDING

(619) 222-0427 / www.hmlanding.com

2803 Emerson, San Diego

(Going S. on San Diego Fwy [5], exit S. on Rosecrans St., L. on Emerson. Going N. on 5, exit at Hawthorne St., go straight on Brant St., L. on Laurel, R. on N. Harbor Dr., L. on Rosecrans St., L. on Emerson. [TG: 1288 B2])

$$$$

San Diego's oldest whale-watching expedition company offers two, three, and even five-hour cruises during whale-watching season, which is January through March. Three-hour cruises depart at 10am and 1:30pm and head to the coastal waters of Point Loma. Five-hour trips depart daily at 10am and travel to the Coronado Islands and Mexico's marine wildlife sanctuary. Be on the lookout for whales, sea lions, dolphins, and elephant seals.

Hours: Stated above.

Admission: The three-hour whale-watching excursion is $20 for adults; $17.50 for ages 13 - 17; $15 for ages 12 and under.

Ages: 6 years and up.

HORNBLOWER

(619) 725-8888 / www.hornblower.com

1066 N. Harbor Drive, San Diego

(Going S. on San Diego Fwy [5], exit S. on Front St./Civic Center, R. on Ash St., L. on Harbor Dr. Going N. on 5, exit L. on Hawthorne St./Airport., L. on Harbor Dr. Go to the Cruise Ship Terminal. [TG: 1288 J3])

$$$$

Hornblower offers one and two-hour narrated harbor cruises. You'll see numerous ships including air craft carriers and other military vessels, the *Star of India*, the Navy Seals Training base, Hotel Del Coronado, the Coronado Bay bridge, and (hopefully) lots of marine animals. The company also offers three-and-a-half-hour whale-watching cruises that include narration by the Captain; watching a documentary on whales; viewing sea lions, birds, and whales; indoor/outdoor seating; and a snack bar with hot food and drinks available. Whale sighting is guaranteed or your receive a whale check, good for another cruise. This yacht company also offers other specialty cruises, include brunch and dinner cruises, throughout the year.

Hours: Harbor cruises are offered year round, 10am - 5pm (6pm in the summer), weather permitting. Whale-watching cruises are offered the end of December through March. Tours depart daily at 9:30am and 1:30pm. Reservations aren't necessary, but call first (of course!).

Admission: One-hour harbor tours are $15 for adults; $13 for seniors and active military; $7.50 for ages 4 - 12; children 3 and under are free. Two-hour cruises are $20 for adults; $18 for seniors and military; $10 for ages 4 - 12. Whale watching is $25 for adults; $23 for seniors and military; $12.50 for ages 4 - 12.

Ages: 5 years and up, depending on the tour.

OCOTILLO WELLS STATE VEHICULAR RECREATION AREA

(760) 767-5391 / parks.ca.gov

(Take 78 E. out of Julian about 35 miles, beyond Ocotillo Wells. [TG: 1121 J2])

For a little off-roading fun, try Ocotillo Wells Recreation Area where you can go up hills, over sand dunes, and through dry washes. You must provide your own vehicles (and have them registered), but the entrance is free and so are primitive camping sites.

Hours: Open daily.
Admission: Free
Ages: 6 years and up.

OLD TOWN TROLLEY TOURS

(619) 298-8687 / www.historictours.com

4040 Twiggs Street, San Diego

(Going S. on San Diego Fwy [5] [just south of Interstate 8], exit E. [across the bridge] on Old Town Ave. Going N. on 5, exit at Moore St., R. on Old Town Ave. From Old Town Ave., go L. on San Diego Ave., R. on Twiggs St. [TG: 1268 F5])

Really get to know the city of San Diego by taking a narrated tour on board an old-fashioned looking trolley. The tour guide will tell you the history of San Diego, plus lots of fun stories. One of the best features about this tour is that you can take a continuous two-hour tour, or jump off (so to speak) and rejoin the tour at any time throughout the day. There are eight locations covered on the loop, including Old Town, Seaport Village, Horton Plaza, Hotel Del Coronado, San Diego Zoo, and Balboa Park. Appropriately nicknamed "transportainment," we enjoyed the commentary, the freedom of stopping at attractions, staying for a bit, and getting back on board when we were ready. Hassle-free parking is another plus.

The two-hour specialty Ghosts and Gravestones tour is a combination of riding the trolley and walking around to visit some "haunted" sites, such as the WHALEY HOUSE (see pg. 437), VILLA MONTEZUMA JESSE SHEPARD HOUSE (see pg. 437), a cemetery, and more. Children 7 years and under are not permitted on this tour. Ask about another specialty tour, the three-hour Navy tour where you'll see various aspects of the military in San Diego.

Hours: Trolleys run daily, 9am - 6pm. The Ghosts and Gravestones tour is given every evening except Tues. Call for hours for the Navy tour. No tours are given on Thanksgiving or Christmas.
Admission: The trolley tours is $24 for adults; $12 for ages 4 - 12; children 3 and under are free. The Ghosts tour is $28 per person.
Ages: 5 years and up.

PACIFIC SOUTHWEST RAILWAY MUSEUM

(619) 595-3030 / www.sdrm.org

Sheridan Road, Campo

(Exit 8 Fwy [45 miles from downtown San Diego] S. on Buckman Springs Rd., travel 10.5 miles to junction Hwy 94., bear R. [1.5 miles] to Old Stone Store, L. after railroad tracks on Forest Gate Rd., L. on Sheridan Rd. and follow signs to the Museum. [TG: 1318 A7])

The sound of a train whistle blowing has always been a signal for adventure! Come abooooard this train for an hour-and-a-half ride your children will never forget. You'll ride in restored classic steam or diesel locomotives, depending on what is available. My boys loved the freedom of moving about while traveling. They walked in between the cars (parents are asked to accompany minors), watched the scenic mountains and meadows roll past, saw a few cows, and played cards. Tip: We brought a picnic lunch, as only snack food is available to purchase on the train. At the halfway point, kids can view (from the windows) the engine being switched around to pull you back the way you came. The conductors were friendly and shared a lot of information about railroads and the history of the area. Two people per excursion can ride in the locomotive cab for $35 per person. Tip: Ask about the ninety-minute student appreciation train tours offered on the third Tuesday of every month at 10am by reservation. A train ride is a great "living" classroom.

Free walking tours are offered one stop before the end of the excursion. You'll see numerous old and restored rail cars such as passenger, Pullman, and freight cars; learn about the historical significance of the railways; and walk through a caboose. The forty-five-minute tour leads you back to the Campo Depot.

At the museum (depot) there are a few stationary pull carts to climb on, a Box Car Theater that shows continuously running videos about the railway system, a gift shop, and picnic tables.

Hours: The Museum hours are 10am - 5pm on weekends and holidays. Trains depart at 11am and at 2:30pm on Sat., Sun., and most holidays. Closed Thanksgiving and Christmas.

Admission: To simply come and look at the trains is free. Train rides cost $15 for adults; $12 for seniors and active military; $5 for ages 6 - 12; children 5 and under are free. The student appreciation rides are $4 per person.

Ages: 3 years and up.

POINT LOMA LANDING

(619) 223-2390 or (619) 223-1627 / www.pointlomasportfishing.com

1403 Scott Street, San Diego

(Going S. on San Diego Fwy [5], exit S. on Rosecrans St., L. on Harbor Dr., R. on Scott St. Going N. on 5, exit at Hawthorne St., go straight on Brant St., L. on Laurel, R. on N. Harbor Dr., L. on Scott St. [TG: 1288 C2])

Three-hour whale-watching cruises are offered twice daily during the whale-watching season.

Hours: Open January through March daily. Call for times.

Admission: $20 for adults; $15 for ages 5 - 15; children 4 and under are free.

Ages: 6 years and up.

SAN DIEGO BAY FERRY / OLD FERRY LANDING

(619) 234-4111 / www.sdhe.com

1050 N. Harbor Drive at the Broadway Pier in downtown San Diego, and the Ferry Landing Marketplace in Coronado

(Going S. on San Diego Fwy [5], exit S. on Front St., R. on Broadway to end. Going N. on 5, exit L. on Hawthorne St., L. on Harbor Dr. [TG: 1288 J3])

Take a fifteen-minute ride over to Coronado (and back) on the San Diego Bay Ferry. Enjoy the Ferry Landing Marketplace on the Coronado side, with its Victorian-style shopping and eating complex. Bike, blade, or walk along the waterfront paved pathways. You can also romp in the grassy lawns along the pathways, or sunbathe on the beach. A farmer's market is held on the island on Tuesdays from 2:30pm to 6pm. TIDELANDS PARK (see pg. 402) is next to the Marketplace. If you want to go to Hotel Del Coronado, take the Coronado shuttle, (619) 427-6438, from the landing. It runs approximately every hour from 9:20am to 6pm, with a few stops along the way. The shuttle is $2 a ride per person. Or, enjoy a scenic walk to the hotel (one-and-a-third miles), though it might get a little long for younger children. See SAN DIEGO HARBOR EXCURSION (pg. 459), for longer, and more scenic, boat rides.

Hours: The ferry departs from the pier every hour on the hour, Sun. - Thurs., 9am - 9pm; Fri. - Sat., 9am - 10pm. It leaves Coronado every hour on the half hour.

Admission: $2 for adults (one way); children 3 and under are free; bikes are an additional 50¢. Parking at the Broadway pier is $1 per hour; $4 maximum.

Ages: All

SAN DIEGO HARBOR EXCURSION

(800) 44CRUISE (442-7847) or (619) 234-4111 / www.sdhe.com

1050 N. Harbor Drive, Broadway Pier, San Diego

(Going S. on San Diego Fwy [5], exit S. on Front St., R. on Broadway to end. Going N. on 5, exit L. on Hawthorne St., L. on Harbor Dr. [TG: 1288 J3])

Enjoy a one or two-hour narrated harbor cruise along San Diego's coast in a nice excursion ship. A snack bar is on board. During a one-hour cruise, you'll see the *Star of India*, the Naval Air Station, and the San Diego shipyards that hold merchants' vessels, fishing boats, and more. During the two-hour cruise, you'll also travel by the Cabrillo National Monument. Three-hour whale-watching trips are given the end of December through

March. The trips are narrated by a naturalist from the Birch Aquarium. A sighting is guaranteed or you ride again for free. Tip: Bring a jacket or sweater on any journey by sea! Note that this cruise line also offers dinner and Sunday brunch cruises.

Hours: Harbor cruises depart daily, 10am to about 5pm. Seasonal three-hour whale-watching cruises depart daily at 10am and 1:15pm.

Admission: One-hour cruises cost $13 for adults; $11 for seniors and active-duty military; $6.50 for ages 4 - 12; children 3 and under are free. Two-hour cruises are $18 for adults; $16 for seniors and military; $9 for ages 4 - 12. Whale watching is $25 for adults; $21 for seniors and military; $15 for ages 4 - 12. Parking at the Broadway pier is $4 all day.

Ages: 3 years and up.

SAN DIEGO PARASAIL ADVENTURES

(619) 223-4386 / www.goparasailing.com
1641 Quivira Road, suite 101, Mission Bay

$$$$$

(Exit San Diego Fwy [5] W. on Sea World Dr. and follow the signs to W. Mission Bay Dr., turn L. on Quivira Rd. and go R. at the end on Quivira. [TG: 1268 A3])

Experience the thrill of soaring up in the air, "flying" over San Diego waters, and getting a bird's eye view of this lovely city. Rides last about eight minutes, although participants are in the boat for about an hour, to ensure that everyone gets their turn. Take off and land directly on the boat. Single or tandem flights are available.

Hours: Open April through mid-June and mid-September through October, weekends only. Open daily, mid-June through mid-September. Closed November through March. When open, the hours are 9am - 6:30pm (weather permitting).

Admission: $59.95 per person

Ages: At least 80 lbs.

SAN DIEGO TROLLEY

(619) 685-4900 - 24-hour information line; (619) 233-3004 - office;
(619) 234-5005 - for persons with hearing impairments. / www.sdcommute.com
San Diego

$$

The San Diego Trolley (and bus) line is a great way to get around San Diego. The Blue line extends from Mission San Diego all the way down to San Ysidro. From this last stop at the border, you can either walk into Mexico, or take a cab. Park for free at the Old Town Transit Center, or all day at the MTS tower garage at 12th and Imperial for $7. The Orange line goes from Santee to Seaport Village. There are several places to catch the trolley line along the routes, with many of the stops being at major attractions. Part of the fun for a child is just the ride. Also see OLD TOWN TROLLEY TOURS (pg. 458), for another way to get around San Diego.

Hours: It runs daily, 5am - 1am, with service every fifteen minutes most of the day.

Admission: One-way fares range from $1 - $4, depending on how far you go. Children 4 and under ride for free. Tickets are usually dispensed from machines.

Ages: All

SEA AND LAND ADVENTURES SEAL TOURS

(619) 298-8687 / www.sealtours.com
800 W. Harbor Drive at Kettner Boulevard, Seaport Village, San Diego

$$$$

(Going S. on San Diego Fwy [5] exit S. on Front St., R. on Broadway, L. on Kettner. Going N. on the 5, exit S. on 6th Ave. R. on Broadway, L. on Kettner. [TG: 1288 J4])

Is it a bus or a boat? Yes! The amphibious vehicle on this SEAL tour takes passengers on a narrated ride on the streets through the heart of San Diego, explaining the history of the city and highlighting points of interest. Then, splash! Drive into the waters of Mission Bay (this is an odd sensation at first). You'll spend some more time back up on land before another plunge, this time into the San Diego Bay waters where you'll cruise past (and learn about) the maritime and military history of the area. "Sail" past the sky line, Navy ships, fishing vessels (don't forget to wave), and tugboats. Be on the lookout for sea-lions and other aquatic creatures. The tour is an unforgettable way to learn about San Diego in an exciting manner. And yes, people in cars and all along the land and sea route do stare as the bus/boat is unusual looking. (Or is it the people inside who are unusual looking?!)

   Hours: The tour departs year round three to five times a day (weather permitting) - call for departure times.

Admission: $24 for adults; $12 for ages 4 - 12; children 3 and under are free, but it's not recommended for them.

    Ages: 6 years and up.

TORREY PINES GLIDER PORT

!/$$$$$

(858) 452-9858 / www.flytorrey.com
2800 Torrey Pines Scenic Drive, La Jolla
(Exit San Diego Fwy [5] W. on Genesee Ave., L. on N. Torrey Pines Rd., R. on Torrey Pines Scenic Dr., to the end onto the dirt parking lot. [TG: 1207 H7])

   Man has had dreams and aspirations to fly since the beginning of time. Hang gliding and paragliding are the closest things we'll get to it in this lifetime (and they are much better than Icarus' attempt!) Kids may participate in this uplifting sport, or come to just watch. We brought a picnic lunch, as there are tables at the cliff tops, although a full-service snack bar is here, too. Besides the exhilarating sight of gliders soaring and dipping along the coastline, there is a breathtaking view of the ocean and beach. The small planes you see flying overhead are really remote control planes that have a take-off/landing site right next "door."

   Hours: Flights are scheduled daily, although if you're coming to watch, you might want to call first to see if anyone is actually flying that day. Closed Christmas.

Admission: Free, unless you're flying! Tandem introductory lessons, starting at $150, usually take about a half hour, which includes ground school instruction and about 20 minutes of flight time. Solo lessons start at $350 for two days of lessons.

    Ages: All to come and watch; 5 years and up for tandem; at least 100 pounds for solo flights.

VOYAGES OF REDISCOVERY (San Diego County)

$$/$$$$$

(800) 401-7835 or (415) 331-3214
San Diego

   See VOYAGES OF REDISCOVERY (pg. 175) for details.

YOUNG EAGLES PROGRAM (San Diego)

!

(619) 661-6520 - airport; (619) 276-3251 / www.youngeagles.com
1409 Continental Avenue, Brown Field, San Diego
(From San Diego Fwy [5] and Jakob Dekema Fwy [805], exit E. on Route 905 (only 1½ miles from the border) and drive about 3 miles. Look for airport and EAA signs. [TG: 1351 E2])

   See the entry for YOUNG EAGLES PROGRAM (Pacoima) on page 177 for details. At this location, the flight is over the city of San Diego and over the ocean. Younger children who are grounded can ride in a simulator that has a radio, earphones, and all the instruments that are in a cockpit. The ride moves and turns as the wheel is turned. Ask about this chapter's other Young Eagle programs.

   Hours: Usually offered the second Sat. of each month at 9am.

Admission: Free

    Ages: 8 - 17 years.

-----*ZOOS AND ANIMALS*-----

BHEAU FARM

(760) 613-4211

$$$$

390 Cox Road, San Marcos

(From Escondido Fwy [15]. exit E. on Deer Springs Road/Mountain Meadow, which turns in to Twin Oaks Valley, L. on Olive, R. on Sycamore, L. on Cox. From Hwy 78, exit N. on Twin Oaks Valley, R. on La Cienega, L. on Sycamore, R. on Cox. [TG: 1109 A2])

This ranch offers a potpourri of farm-related activities for various groups. Piglets, lambs, bunnies, ducks, goats, and chickens comprise the petting farm where visitors learn how to handle, feed, and take care of farm animals. The petting zoo is portable, too, thus it is available to come to another facility.

The majority of the beautiful ranch is devoted to horses and educating the public, especially kids, on how to safely interact with horses, as well as horse care from A to Z. Participants learn, usually through a series of down-to-earth classes, how to tack, groom, and finally ride horses. Western or English riders can learn why different styles are used, what the differences are, and how each one affects horses. The clean stalls are home to Arabian stallions, Appaloosas, Shetland ponies, and miniature horses. They are also set up for crafts, Western dress up, and mini classrooms, as a few hold all the gear and necessary equestrian equipment.

A riding arena is on the grounds where riders can practice to become more competent. A horse trail system connects to the trail leading from the farm. The current trail system, by the way, is on the verge of merging with many of the local trails into one large system, the San Marcos Equestrian Park. The park system will include trails for horseback riders as well as hikers and bikers, and even a soccer field and other play areas.

Bheau Farm is perfect for small groups, individual riders, Girl Scouts, day camps, and horse lovers. Note that a few picnic tables are also on the farm grounds.

Hours: Call for a reservation.

Admission: Call for specific information as prices vary greatly according to what you want to do.

Ages: Pre-schoolers and up.

BIRCH AQUARIUM

(858) 534-FISH (3474) / www.aquarium.ucsd.edu

$$$

2300 Expedition Way, San Diego

(Exit San Diego Fwy [5] W. on La Jolla Village Dr. Stay to the R. as La Jolla Village Dr. turns into N. Torrey Pines, turn L. on Expedition - follow the signs. [TG: 1227 H3])

Visually exciting statues of leaping, large whales grace the fountain outside the entrance of the Birch Aquarium. There are also picnic tables and a snack stand out here. This outstanding, sizable, aquarium-museum has three main exhibit areas. The aquarium section contains over thirty-three large tanks filled with an incredible variety of creatures found in the Earth's oceans - from monkey face eels to sharks to flashlight fish that glow (or blink on and off) in the dark. Just some of our favorite sea animals showcased here include the almost mesmerizing moon jellies; sunflower starfish; bat rays; very large grouper fish; nurse sharks; odd-looking, longhorn cowfish; garden eels that look like hoses "standing" upright in the sand; the amazing giant octopus; and the beautiful, but venomous, striped lionfish. I also like the colorful fish at the Caribbean Reef display. The largest tank has a huge kelp forest which makes it easy to view animals that are normally hidden on ocean floors. See divers feed the fish in the forest Tuesdays and Thursdays at 12:20pm and Sundays at 10:30am. (These times may change.)

Outside, the small rocky Tidepool Plaza connects the aquarium and the museum. A wave machine gently creates natural water motion in a simulated tidepool. Kids will see up close (and can gently touch) sea stars, sea urchins, sea cucumbers, and more. Also, take in the magnificent panoramic view of the La Jolla coastline (and the world famous Scripps Institute).

The museum has several fine components. Find out everything you ever wanted to know about seahorses in the incredibly interesting and thoroughly researched Seahorse Exhibit. Did you know that seahorses adapt by changing color to blend in with their environment? See the same type of seahorse in various background settings, and therefore, various colors. Learn about threats to these creatures and how they are dried and ground up to use as medicinal aids. Watch short videos on (seahorse) dating, mating, and giving birth. Note that males give birth - this could make for some very interesting conversation. Look for the tiny baby seahorses in the nursery. And check out the utterly bizarre-looking, weedy and leafy sea dragons - cousins to the seahorse.

Another component of the museum is the oceanographic exhibit with numerous different, interactive display areas called Exploring the Blue Planet. Each area incorporates touch screens or an activity that shows and explains the integral part that oceans play in relation to how the Earth functions. Kids participate in exhibit experiments to learn about various aspects of ocean sciences such as currents, tides, and waves; earthquakes and plate tectonics; the differences between salt water and fresh water by testing solubility and electricity; and how solar heat falls on the ocean unevenly via a long wave tank. The experiments are actually quite fun! My kids also really enjoyed the Ocean Supermarket, where they used scanners on common household products to see which ingredients came from the ocean. (Did you know that ice cream uses carrageenan [i.e. red seaweed] to make it smooth and creamy?!)

The back courtyard features a fascinating destination - the shark tank. The large tank is clear so you can easily see all the angles of the many species of shark swimming around. Ask about feeding times. This area also has a simulator ride, which moves and jolts along with the action on the screen. The Birch Aquarium has a lot to offer - come "sea" it for yourself! Call about the many special activities and programs offered through the aquarium including tidepools tours, whale-watching cruises, grunion hunting, snorkeling, sleep overs, and the popular Shark Discovery Days.

> **Hours:** Open daily, 9am - 5pm. Closed New Year's Day, Thanksgiving, and Christmas.
>
> **Admission:** $9.50 for adults; $8 for seniors; $6.50 for students; $6 for ages 3 - 17; children 2 and under are free. Parking is $3. The simulator ride is $4 and participants must be 42" tall.
>
> **Ages:** 3 years and up.

CALIFORNIA WOLF CENTER

(619) 234-WOLF (9653) / www.californiawolfcenter.org
Highway 79, Julian
(Exit Highway 79, 4 miles S. of Julian at the K.Q. Ranch Campground. [TG: 1156 G5])

Who's afraid of the big bad wolf? And why? Clear up many misconceptions about North American and Alaskan Gray Wolves at the wolf center during a two-hour presentation/tour. First, gather in a room filled with wolf paraphernalia for a twenty-minute slide show. See and learn about what wolves eat; how they communicate (yes they howl, but not at the moon); the pack's pecking order, starting with an alpha (i.e. dominant) male and female; and their predators (man). Then watch a fifteen-minute portion of the video, "Return of the Wolves," shown on PBS, which showcases wolves in the wild as they hunt and capture their prey, and what happens when a new wolf tries to join an established pack. Learn the difference between a fox, a coyote, and a wolf (this being the largest of the three) via a touch table with skins, skulls, teeth, and plaster footprints. Also hold and learn about tracking collars that researchers use on wolves.

A highlight is going out to the enclosures to actually see these majestic creatures. There are currently two packs here, totaling about twenty-eight wolves. The ones used in the education programs are very curious and come close up to the fence where visitors line up - all the better to see you, my dear. Bring your camera. Take a short hike up a hill to see the other wolves who may, or may not, come over to check out the group.

The center also offers Wolf Encounters, a program for kids held either at the center or at a school. The presentation is similar to the one held here on Saturdays, except that the slide show is tailored specifically for kids and, if the encounter is at a school, two of the wolves are brought along for show and tell. Curriculum supplements are provided. Have a howling good time here!

> **Hours:** Open Sat. at 1:45pm - do not be late!! Reservations are required. Call to set up a time for group programs during the week.
>
> **Admission:** $8 per adult; $5 for seniors; $4 for children 10 and under. Wolf Encounters start at $125 for up to 35 participants, plus fuel charges if it applies.
>
> **Ages:** 7 years and up for the Sat. program; kindergartners and up for educational programs.

CHULA VISTA NATURE CENTER

(619) 409-5900 / www.chulavistanaturecenter.org
1000 Gunpowder Point Drive, Chula Vista
(Exit San Diego Fwy [5] W. on 'E' St. to park, or exit E. on 'E' St., to park at the Visitor's Center and take the free trolley into the Nature Center. [TG: 1309 J6])

Putting their hands in a pool of hungry sharks is only one of the special things that kids (and adults) are invited to do at the Chula Vista Nature Center, located in the Sweetwater Marsh National Wildlife Refuge. You'll start your visit by taking the trolley (free of charge) into the refuge as cars are not allowed. The medium-sized center is full of interactive exhibits such as using a bioscanner (i.e. a mounted camera with a zoom lens) to see anemones close up on a monitor, and poking your head up into a glassed-enclosed exhibit to watch mice run around. (Mice use the refuge to look for food.) The touch table has pelican bones, bird skulls, whale vertebrae, and fossilized shells. There are several tanks with live sea creatures, such as seahorses, halibut, the almost ethereal moon jellies, pipe fish, sea cucumbers, lobsters, and rainbow trout. Listen for the snapping sounds of the snapping shrimp as they try to frighten predators away. Like a good mystery? Then try to find the flatfish, who are hiding in plain sight.

My boys proudly boast that they've touched a shark, and lived! The outside petting pool contains leopard and horn sharks as well as batrays, stingrays, and the odd-looking shovel-nose guitarfish. (These creatures actually come within petting distance.) Join in the feeding fun, which usually takes place around 4pm.

An outside overlook affords an opportunity to observe migrating shore birds such as terns, killdeer, plovers, and more wetlands wildlife. A walk-through bird aviary features snowy egrets, sandpipers, black-necked stilts, and other water birds, well as some interactive exhibits such as rubbing tables and an oversized clapper rail nest for kids to crawl inside. Other bird enclosures contain non-releasable birds of prey, such as owls, a turkey vulture, and hawks. A hummingbird and a butterfly garden are also on the grounds. Stroller-friendly trails in front of the Center branch off in various directions and allow kids to get close to the bay to see geese, egrets, or smaller water inhabitants. Look for other wildlife along the trail such as bunnies and lizards. Visit the bird blind which raises visitors up to get a bird's eye view of, well, birds.

The Nature Center offers a variety of on-site special programs, such as Make It Take It craft workshops for ages five and up, given on Saturdays and Sundays from 1pm to 2pm for 50¢. Call to get a complete schedule. Sign up for a very informative guided group tour.

Hours: Open Tues. - Sun., 10am - 5pm. Closed most Mon., New Year's Day, Easter, Thanksgiving, and Christmas. Trolleys run approximately every twenty-five minutes or so.
Admission: $3.50 for adults; $2.50 for seniors; $1 for ages 6 - 17; children 5 and under are free.
Ages: 3 years and up.

DEL MAR FAIRGROUNDS / RACETRACK

(858) 755-1141 or (858) 793-5555 / www.delmarracing.com
Jimmy Durante Boulevard, at Del Mar Fairgrounds, Del Mar
(Exit San Diego Fwy [5] W. on Via de la Valle. [TG: 1187 G2])

Horse racing season at the famous Del Mar Fairgrounds begins in July and runs through mid-September. Kids have good horse sense - they aren't here to bet, but to enjoy the races. On most weekends, the infield is transformed to a fun zone for children with pony rides, face painting, an inflatable jump, obstacle course, and more. Admission is free for children, when accompanied by a parent. Also inquire about horse shows, rodeos, and polo games.

Hours: Gates are open July through mid-September, Mon., and Wed. - Fri. at noon; Sat. - Sun., 11:30am. Post time is usually 2pm, although it's at 4pm for the first five Fri. The track is closed on Tues.
Admission: General admission is $5 for adults for the grandstands; $10 for clubhouse seating (which is closer to the finish line); free for children 17 and under.
Ages: 5 years and up.

FREEFLIGHT

(858) 481-3148

2132 Jimmy Durante Boulevard, Del Mar

(Exit San Diego Fwy [5] W. on Via de la Valle, L. on Jimmy Durante, follow around the fairgrounds. It's located next to the Vet and Bird Hospital, just past the racetrack. Turn in at the 2126 address. [TG: 1187 G3])

This boarding house is for the birds, literally. It is also a breeding facility with baby birds available for sale. There are more than thirty perches along the short pathway in this jungle-like backyard. Look at and even gently touch some of the brilliantly-colored cockatoos, macaws, parrots, and other exotic birds. It's a good place to get some great picture of birds! Note: Loud squawking of the birds is set off by loud kids who are set off by the loud squawking, etc. Young children might be startled. Also, many of the birds have strong talons which could scare or hurt visitors, so young ones are better off simply looking at and not holding the birds. Please note that children under 13 years must be accompanied by a parent. Bring 25¢ to purchase pellets to feed the birds. Freeflight offers half-hour school tours that explain the different types of birds, their habitats, and more. Call to make a reservation. Tip: Bring a sweater because the beach weather is often cool.

      Hours: Open daily, 10am - 4pm. Closed on rainy days.
  Admission: $1 per person.
      Ages: 3 years and up.

FUND FOR ANIMALS WILDLIFE REHABILITATION CENTER

(760) 789-2324 / www.fundwildlife.org

18740 Highland Valley Road, Ramona

(Exit the Escondido Fwy [15], E. on Hwy 78. Stay on 78 into Ramona, go R. on 67. R. on Highland Valley Rd. [TG: 1172 A2])

Just off the beaten path is a rehabilitation center specializing in the rescue and medical treatment of abused and discarded exotic pets, confiscated (i.e. illegal) animals, or injured mountain lions, bobcats, coyotes, and birds of prey. If possible, when some of the animals have recovered, they are released into their original habitats. These animals are kept away from people (therefore you cannot see them) to minimize human contact. Other animals live here permanently, such as the declawed mountain lion.

A guide walks each group of people around the enclosures, explaining where the animals came from, their behaviors, and what they eat. The types of animals here rotate as many are only here on a temporary basis. We saw two llamas, mountain lions, a coyote, some goats, bobcats, lynx, a turkey vulture, a gold eagle, Arctic foxes, a hedgehog, and several old house cats. Note: There are more animals here in the spring when orphaned babies are rescued. Also note that the felines tend to be napping in the afternoon (doesn't that sound wonderful?!), thus they are not very active.

      Hours: Open Sat. - Sun. at 11am and 2pm, weather permitting.
  Admission: Free
      Ages: All

HELEN WOODWARD ANIMAL CENTER

(858) 756-4117 / www.animalcenter.org

6461 El Apajo Road, Rancho Santa Fe

(Going N. on San Diego Fwy [5], exit E. on Del Mar Height Rd., L. on El Camino Real, R. on San Dieguito Rd., L. on El Apajo. Going S. on 5, exit E. on Via De La Valle., R. on El Camino Real, L. on San Dieguito Rd., L. on El Apajo. [TG: 1168 F6])

This unique facility, whose motto is "people help animals and animals help people," is part animal shelter and part training center. It is a temporary home to cats and dogs, as well as long term homes to horses, llamas, rabbits, turtles, birds, and a few other critters. The training part of the center has many components, but all are designed for people, especially children, to experience the unconditional love and tactile benefits of animals. People with a variety of disabilities interact and ride gentle horses as they participate in the therapeutic riding program. Other programs include pet encounter therapy for abused children, seniors, and others; Camp EdVenture (day camps); family fun nights with storytelling and crafts; educational assemblies, either on-site or at a classroom; "edu-taining" birthday parties; and forty-five-minute tours of the twelve-acre campus. Most of the programs incorporate playing games and up-close animal presentations to teach animal behavior, pet responsibility, and proper pet care.

The center also contains a riding arena and stables for horses used in the programs, boarding facilities, a large and a small animal veterinary hospital, a grooming center, and classrooms.

Hours: Call for a current program schedule.

Admission: Call for prices for the activity of your choice.

Ages: Depends on the program.

LEELIN LLAMA TREKS

(800) LAMAPAK (526-2725) / www.llamatreks.com

1645 Whispering Pines Drive, Julian

(Take 78 Hwy E., from Julian. After 78 turns N., go R. on the second (not the first) Whispering Pines Dr. It's just N. of the town of Julian. [TG: 1136 C5])

Looking for an unusual outing? Sign up for a llama trek! Choose from a variety of destinations - to the lake, through the mountains, or through the town of Julian. Each member of your group leads his/her own llama that carries trekkers' lunches and other necessities. Most kids, and adults, aren't used to being around llamas, so the intrigue, as well as the scenery, makes the four to six-hour expeditions unique experiences. The animals are gentle, enjoy being pet, and by the end of the trek, your children will want to take theirs home. They can't. A deli sandwich, cold salad, cookie, and cold drink are included in your outing. The best bet for kids is the Eagle Mine Trek, which takes about five hours round trip. The trip includes a tour of the gold mine, EAGLE MINING COMPANY (see pg. 450). Children 8 and older are eligible to go on overnight trips to the Sierras. The latter excursion includes four to ten nights of camping in the mountains, hiking, and delicious, home-cooked food!

LeeLin Wikiup is a bed and breakfast, geared for couples, owned by LeeLin Llama Treks. (The llamas actually live on the grounds here.) Each room of the Wikiup, although adjacent to each other, has its own unique, completely themed decor - Native American, Victorian, or rustic.

Hours: Call for reservations. At least two people must sign up for any of the day treks.

Admission: Prices start at $90. The Eagle Mine trek is $90 for adults; $75 for children 3 - 10. Wikiup rates start at $175 per couple during the week.

Ages: 4 years and up.

THE MONARCH PROGRAM

(760) 944-7113 / www.monarchprogram.org

450 Oceanview Avenue, Encinitas

(Exit San Diego Fwy [5] W. on Encinitas Blvd., R. on Vulcan, R. on Orpheus, R. on Union, R. on Oceanview. [TG: 1147 C5])

I'm not particularly fond of most insects, so I think butterflies should be in a classification by themselves, called beautiful winged creatures, or something. This facility, located in a residential neighborhood, has two rooms devoted to our fluttery friends. The education room is in a garage that is set up like a classroom. It contains maps that show the path of butterfly migrations, books, and a few real caterpillars and chrysalides in various stages of metamorphosis. A docent is on hand to answer any questions. A video, showing the life cycle of a butterfly, can be watched upon request.

The second "room," or vivarium, is a relatively small outside enclosed area with plants, flowers, a few trees, and several butterflies flying around. Most of the butterflies in here are native to California, except the zebra butterfly. We saw a few monarchs, a swallowtail, a California dogface (which doesn't look like its namesake), and a few others. Children can hold out a piece of fruit (provided by the Monarch Program), such as a watermelon, to attract the butterflies. But, please, don't try to catch the butterflies - it could hurt them.

School/group tours are welcome during the week. A one-hour tour consists of a half-hour slide show and talk and another half hour in the vivarium. It also includes a take-home booklet that has butterfly body parts to identify and color, plus information on several species. Educators note that larva, caterpillars, and plants (for butterfly food) are available for purchase.

Bring a sack lunch to enjoy at Orpheus park, which is just down the street. The park has picnic tables,

$$$$$

$$

grassy areas, shade trees, and a playground.

Hours: Open to the public on Sat., 11am - 3pm. Open the rest of the time for school and other groups. Call to make a reservation. The program is closed November through March.

Admission: $5 for adults; $4 for seniors; $3 for ages 6 - 18; children 5 and under are free. Group tours are a flat fee of $85 for up to thirty children.

Ages: 2 years and up.

SAN DIEGO POLO CLUB

$$

(858) 481-9217 / www.sandiegopolo.com

14555 El Camino Real, Rancho Sante Fe

(Exit San Diego Fwy [5] E. on Via De La Valle. [TG: 1188 A2])

Question: Marco? Answer: Polo! Observe the fast paced, high-energy game of polo (not water polo), where eight players from junior leagues up to the pros compete on horseback. The gated playing field is on seventy-eight-acres of unobstructed, beautiful green grass. Horse and rider thunder past in an intricate game of strategy and skill. Assignment: Find out what the word chukker means. Watch the hour-long game from the tail gate of your car and bring a picnic, or bring a lawn chair field side, or sit at a table by the Player's Club, which is a restaurant and concession area. (No outside food is allowed in the Player's Club.) Admission includes entrance to the Club plus play time in the party jump that is usually on the grounds. Call for other fun, periodic "extras" like a petting zoo or even just the availability of snow cones. Arrive before the featured match to enjoy pre-game activities.

Hours: Games are played mid-June through September, Sun. at 3pm.

Admission: $5 for adults; children 12 and under are free. Parking is $5.

Ages: All

SAN DIEGO WILD ANIMAL PARK

$$$$$

(619) 234-6541 or (619) 231-1515 - general info; (760) 738-5049 - special programs; (760) 740-9383 - education programs / www.sandiegozoo.org

15500 San Pasqual Valley Road, Escondido

(Going S. on San Diego Fwy [5] or Escondido Fwy [15], exit E. on Hwy 78, which turns into San Pasqual Valley Rd. Going N. on 15, exit E. on Via Rancho Pkwy., which turns into Bear Valley Rd., R. on San Pasqual Rd., which turns into Via Rancho Pkwy., go to end, R. on San Pasqual Valley Rd. [TG: 1130 J6])

Go on a safari and see the exotic animals that live in the African veldt and Asian plains, without ever leaving Southern California. The 2,000-acre San Diego Wild Animal Park has tigers, rhinos, lions, elephants, giraffes, antelope, etc., in atypical zoo enclosures. The animals roam the grasslands freely, in settings that resemble their natural habitats which is why you don't always see them up close. The best way to see a majority of the animals is via the Wgasa Bush Line monorail, a five-mile, fifty-minute, narrated journey. Tip: Sit on the right-hand side (not the driver's side) of the monorail car as most of the animals are on this side. This fascinating ride is included in your admission price. I suggest going on the monorail first as the lines get longer later in the day.

The ride ends back at Nairobi Village, which is a great starting point for the rest of your wild animal adventure. Walk through some of the thirty acres that comprise the Heart of Africa. A paved, circuitous path in this section is three-quarters of a mile long and can take at least an hour. The trail will take you into the forest where antelope and the unusual-looking okapi roam; along a stream - look for warthogs and foxes; near waterfalls; and to a large watering hole where rhinos, waterbuck, and other animals congregate. Cross over a bridge to a small island that has a mock research station and see dart guns and lab equipment. The plains are home to wildebeest, cheetahs, and even a station, open at designated times, where visitors can hand-feed giraffes for an additional fee. Their tongues are long and black and always elicit a few "eeews" from kids.

There are numerous other attractions at the wild animal park. Watch the antics of the monkeys and gorillas. The Petting Kraal has small deer, goats, sheep, and other animals to pet and feed. Check the time for the animal shows performed (or presented) here. Our favorites include the funny and fantastic free-flying bird show and the entertaining elephant show where natural and learned behaviors are demonstrated. Hand-feeding rainbow-colored lorikeets, which look like small parrots, is a thrill. Bring your camera to capture your child's expression as the birds land on his arms or even his head. Check for feeding times and bring $1 for the food. I was enchanted by the Hidden Jungle offered in spring because a "room" in here is filled with lush green plants and colorful butterflies fluttering all around. Look through telescopes on the observation deck of Condor Ridge to see the habitats of dozens of endangered species, including, obviously, California condors. This area also has prairie dogs, roadrunners, ferrets, and big horned sheep, as well as botanical gardens. Enjoy all your travels through the animal kingdom.

Want to make your day picture perfect? The Photo Caravan (ages 8 and up) offers two photo opportunities to go on an open, flat-bed truck into some of the animal enclosures. The cost ranges from $99 to $145, depending on the length of the adventure. Your kids can feed some of the animals, take pictures of them, and learn all about them. Call (619) 718-3050 for tour dates and more information. Roar and Snore overnight tent-camping safaris include nature hikes, a campfire and food, photo opportunities, and close-up encounters with wild (and more mild) beasts! The cost is $126 for ages 12 and up; $106 ages 8 - 11 - participants must be at least 8 years old. Call (800) 934-CAMP (2267) for more information. These are just a few of the special programs offered - call for a complete schedule. Note that WHOLESOME HERITAGE FARM (see pg. 470) is just around the corner.

Hours: Open daily in the summer, 7:30am - 8pm. Open daily the rest of the year, 9am - 5pm.

Admission: $26.50 for adults; $23.85 for seniors; $19.50 for ages 3 - 11; children 2 and under are free. Certain discounts are available through AAA. Parking is $6. A combination ticket with the SAN DIEGO ZOO (to be used once at each location within five days) is $52.65 for adults; $35.35 for ages 3 - 11. Admission to the Wild Animal Park is free one day in May in celebration of Founder's Day.

Ages: All

SAN DIEGO ZOO

(619) 234-3153 or (619) 231-1515 - general info;
(619) 557-3965 - education department / www.sandiegozoo.org

2920 Zoo Drive, San Diego

(Going S. on San Diego Fwy [5], exit N. on Cabrillo Fwy [163], E. on Richmond St. (Zoo/Museums exit), follow signs. Going N. on 5, exit N. on Pershing Dr. L. on Florida Dr. L. on Zoo Place, cross Park Blvd. to parking. Zoo entrance is off Park Blvd. at Zoo Place. [TG: 1269 C7])

The world-famous San Diego Zoo is home to some of the rarest animals in captivity, and almost every animal imaginable, at least that's what it seems like. Put your walking shoes on because this zoo covers a lot of ground! In fact, you'd be hard pressed to try to see all 4,000 animals in one day, at least with young children in tow. The flamingos, just inside the entrance, are a colorful way to start your day. Tiger River, Elephant Mesa, the Horn and Hoof Mesa, Gorilla Tropics, Absolutely Apes (a personal favorite - I could watch these guys for hours and apparently, vice-versa), and the Reptile House are just a few of the exhibit areas to visit. The two-acre Ituri Forest follows a path under a canopy of trees, past a tropical jungle that houses forest buffalo, exotic okapis, monkeys, and several other species of mammals and birds. Be amazed at how enormous hippos really are and the size of polar bears in two underwater viewing exhibits - Hippo Beach and Polar Bear Plunge, respectively. Experience panda-monium and see the giant pandas that are visiting from China - what unique-looking animals! Enjoy a walk through the Rain Forest Aviary to see brilliantly colored jungle birds amidst tropical foliage; watch the antics of the bears at Sun Bear Forest; see koalas in their trees; and take the opportunity to observe kangaroos, camels, primates, and other animals in enclosures that simulate their natural habitat. If you want to find out more about particular animals and plants, and hear stories about the zoo, as well as test your zoo trivia, rent an audio guide for $4.

A forty-minute, double-decker, narrated bus tour is not only fun and informative, but it's a great way to get a good overview of most of the animals here. The bus tour is $10 for adults; $5.50 for ages 3 to 11. This bus ticket also allows visitors to use the Express bus, a vehicle that travels around the zoo enabling riders to hop on and off at five locations, as often as desired, throughout the day. The Skyfari Aerial Tram ride is another way to view a portion of the zoo at $2.50 per person, each way.

The *Sea Lion Show* and the *Wild Ones Show*, presented twice daily, are an entertaining and interesting way to see some favorite animals close up. The Children's Zoo is always a highlight as there are animals to pet; mole-rats and other unique animals to look at; and an animal baby nursery that shows off the newest zoo additions. Ask about the many special programs the zoo offers during the year, including zoo sleepovers and Close Encounters of the Zoo Kind.

Hours: Open daily in the summer, 9am - 9pm. (Grounds close at 10pm.) Open daily the rest of the year, 9am - 4pm. (Grounds close at 6pm.)

Admission: $19.50 for adults; $11.75 for ages 3 - 11; children 2 and under area free. Certain discounts are available through AAA. Ask about combo tour pricing. A combination package with the SAN DIEGO WILD ANIMAL PARK (to be used once at each location within 5 days) is $52.65 for adults; $35.35 for children. Admission is free on the first Monday of October in celebration of Founder's Day.

Ages: All

SEAL ROCK MARINE MAMMAL RESERVE

(619) 221-8901; (619) 687-3588 - docent program /
www.lajollaseals.org; www.sannet.gov/lifeguards/beaches/pool.shtml
850 Coast Boulevard, La Jolla
(Going S. exit San Diego Fwy [5] W. on La Jolla Village Dr., L. on Torrey Pines Rd., R. on Prospect St., look for signs and bear R. on Coast Blvd. Going north exit 5 N. to Ardath Rd., which turns into Torrey Pines Rd., and follow the directions above. Good luck parking! [TG: 1227 E6])

From a distance, we saw what looked like lots of lumpy rocks on the beach. As we got closer, however, we could see that they were really seals sprawling on the sand and on the nearby rocks. The seals have taken over what used to be known as Children's Pool Beach, so named because the rocks form a breakwater. My boys and I were thrilled that we were almost close enough to touch the seals, although doing so and getting too close is forbidden. (Even seals are protected by harassment laws!) Walk out on the rock jetty for more of a view. A normal family might be here for just a few minutes; we were here for an hour because we were enthralled. Warning: Seals are not sunbathing here constantly, so seeing them is a hit or miss deal. Pupping season is usually February and March.

On either side of the reserve, you'll see beaches, large rocks to climb on, and even grassy park areas. A paved sidewalk trail runs along the coastline. See SCRIPPS PARK (pg. 400) for more about this immediate area.

Hours: Open daily.
Admission: Free
Ages: All

SEAWORLD ADVENTURE PARK

(619) 226-3901 / www.seaworld.com
500 Sea World Drive, San Diego
(Exit San Diego Fwy [5] W. on Sea World Dr. [TG: 1268 B4])

SeaWorld entertains and educates people of all ages with its wide variety of sea animal exhibits. The dazzling dolphin gets top ratings. And don't miss the silly sea lion show, where the animals hilariously interact with trainers. The killer-whale show, starring Shamu and friends, is a crowd-pleaser with its thrills - a trainer riding a whale gets catapulted - and chills - those sitting in the splash-zone bleachers get drenched. Trainer For a Day is a special program that allows visitors to wade into shallow water, reach over an acrylic panel, and touch the killer whales. Real trainers also invite a few volunteers to help out and train the whales by holding targets, carrying food buckets, and rewarding the giant mammals for a behavior correctly performed. View the animals underwater at the viewing gallery. A similar program with dolphins allows visitors, who must be at least 6 years old, to put on a wet suit, wade into shallow water for about twenty minutes with the dolphins, to touch, feed, and interact with them while learning about their anatomy and personalities. The cost is $140 per person.

There are several other unique attractions, such as Shark Encounter, which culminates in a fifty-seven-foot-long enclosed people-mover tube that takes you through shark-infested waters (!). At Rocky Point Preserve kids can actually touch and feed bottlenose dolphins. They feel rubbery. If you stretch your arms far enough, you can touch bat rays and other marine animals at Forbidden Reef and the California Tide Pool. The penguin exhibit also features the penguins' cousins, the funny-looking puffins who fly through the air and sea. A theater shows special-effects laden 4-D presentations, where objects seemingly come out of the screen as in a 3-D film, but there are physical interactions, too, such as mist when the screen shows a rainy scene. A simulated helicopter ride at Wild Arctic lands you at a remote research station. (Actually, you're still at SeaWorld.) Blasts of Arctic air greet you as you view beluga whales, harbor seals, walruses, and polar bears. The year-round, high-flying bird show is terrific, as are some of their other seasonal shows.

Shamu's Happy Harbor is two acres of pure kid delight. This play area has tubes, slides, ropes, balls, a sandy beach, a moon bounce, an outdoor theater for kid-oriented entertainment, and a Funship for pretend pirates to climb aboard. For those who want (or are allowed) to get wet, there are a few water fountains to splash in, and water tubes to go through. Tip: Bring a towel or change of clothing. Another wet activity is the Shipwreck Rapids ride. A nine-passenger raft swirls past several realistic-looking shipwrecks, real sea turtles, through "rapids," and semi under a roaring waterfall. Lunch or dinner at the adjacent island cafe offers a tasty selection of food and even eater-tainment in the form of a trainer coming by with a sea lion, otter, or penguin for a brief presentation.

For an additional $2.75 per person, each attraction (or $3.75 for both), the Skytower, which offers a panoramic view, and the Bayside Skyride, which is a gondola ride over Mission Bay, are fun treats. Dine with Shamu at a pool-side buffet luncheon (dinners are only offered during the summer) where the great whale may even come out of the water to greet you. The luncheon is $30 plus tax for adults; $15 for ages 3 to 9.

SeaWorld also offers various outstanding educational tours, such as a sleep over with sharks or other animals. What fun! A sixty-minute, behind-the-scenes tour is an additional $10 for adults, $8 for seniors and ages 3 to 9. Call for information on the times, hours, and admission for other unique field trips, including sleep overs. Also ask about the monthly school days specials where admission is greatly reduced for students. Special summertime highlights at SeaWorld can include fireworks and a current favorite - Cirque de la Mer, a sister act to Cirque Du Solei. Note: Although no outside food is allowed inside, a picnic area is set up just outside the park. Spending a day (or night) here is a great way for the whole family to "sea" the world!

    Hours: Open daily in the summer, Mon. - Fri., 9am - 10pm; Sat. - Sun., 9am - 11pm. Check for seasonality. Open daily the rest of the year, 10am - 5pm.

Admission: $44.95 for adults; $34.95 for ages 3 - 9; children 2 and under are free. Certain discounts are available through AAA. A two-day package, where you may visit SeaWorld twice within a 7 day period, is a great deal at $48.95 for adults; $38.95 for ages 3 - 9. Parking is $7 per day.

    Ages: All

WHOLESOME HERITAGE FARM

(760) 746-8822 / www.bannerexotics.com

14305 San Pasqual Valley Road, Escondido

(Going S. on San Diego Fwy [5] or Escondido Fwy [15], exit E. on Hwy 78, which turns into San Pasqual Valley Rd. Going N. on 15, exit E. on Via Rancho Pkwy., which turns into Bear Valley Rd., R. on San Pasqual Rd., which turns into Via Rancho Pkwy., go to end, R. on San Pasqual Valley Rd. [TG: 1130 J6])

For some wholesome fun, visit Wholesome Heritage Farm. The petting zoo, which is easily seen from the road, has several goats, sheep, mini "baby doll" sheep, a miniature donkey, llamas, bunnies, a one hump (dromedary) and two hump camel (bactrian), tortoises, ducks, turkeys, pheasants, parrots, five ostriches, four emus, and a long-horned steer (just to look at - not to pet!).

This twenty-five acre working farm offers fresh-picked seasonal produce or U-Pic produce. Peaches, blood oranges (these are so good!), strawberries, onions, corn, squash, string beans, and much more are yours for the picking (and paying). In October, tours of the pumpkin patch are offered. See the Calendar entry, on page 608), for details. Year-round, hour-long tours are given to any age group. The tours consist of walking around the farm, learning about the animals, and also learning about animals products, like eggs and feathers. You might even see some eggs incubating. Ask about the tortoise races, too. There are also a few picnic tables to enjoy sampling your fresh food, or to eat a picnic lunch that you brought.

The on-site gift shop has unique items for sale. The huge ostrich eggs are $18. The smaller, and avocado green in color, emu eggs are $15. Other items include blown-out decorated eggs, ostrich plumes, ostrich jerky, and ostrich leather products such as wallets and hats. Check the store and the website for more shopping opportunities. Note that the farm is just down the street from the SAN DIEGO WILD ANIMAL PARK (see pg. 467).

Hours:	Open Wed. - Sun., noon - 6pm. Call to schedule a tour.
Admission:	Technically free. The petting farm is free, though donations are appreciated. Tours are $4 per person.
Ages:	All

SANTA BARBARA COUNTY

Although Chumash Indians were this county's original inhabitants, its name came from a Spanish explorer's party. Seeking shelter in the channel from a severe storm, the fleet was saved on Saint Barbara's feast day. The hub of this multi-faceted county is the compact city of Santa Barbara. The city offers a culturally rich assortment of things to do and see in a setting that is both elegant and friendly. Visitors are minutes away from the beach or the mountains. The Los Padres National Forest makes up almost half of this county! The hub's spokes, or other cities that complete the county, each have their own distinct "personality." The university town of Goleta is home to Santa Barbara's University, as well as miles of coastline. The small town of Lompoc is known for its murals. Solvang is the "Danish Capitol of America." Los Olivos, originally a stagecoach stop, is now a fine arts destination. Santa Ynez boasts of pioneer history. The far flung Santa Maria, with its farming roots, has both a quaint and lively town center, as well as the unique sand dunes.

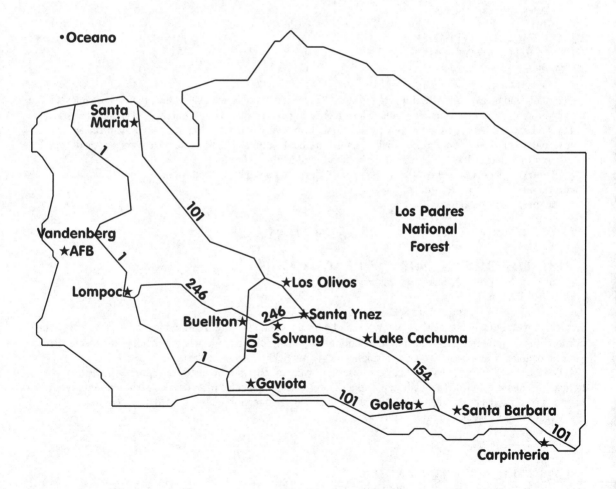

-----ARTS AND CRAFTS-----

2000 DEGREES - A CERAMIC WORKSHOP
(805) 882-1817   *$$$$*
1206 State Street, Santa Barbara
(Going S. on El Camino Real Fwy [101], exit N.E. Carillo St., L. on State St. Going N. on 101, exit N. on Garden St., L. on Anapamu. Park wherever you can near State St. [TG: 996 A3])

Whew - at 2000 degrees it sure is hot in here! Actually, it's just the pottery that gets that hot when it's fired. Painting your own ceramic piece is such a fun thing to do. This studio offers many items to choose from such as picture frames, vases, banks, plates, mugs, figurines, and much more. You can match your new masterpiece, or not, to anything in your house, or decorate it to give as a gift. The painting fee includes use of all the paints, brushes, and inspiration that you need.

> **Hours:** Open Mon. - Fri., 11:30am - 8pm; Sat., 10am - 9pm; Sun., noon - 6pm. Closed Thanksgiving and Christmas.
> **Admission:** The price of the piece plus $7 for adults (for all-day painting); $4 for ages 4 - 9.
> **Ages:** 4 years and up.

WSD CERAMIC STUDIO
(888) 736-0113 or (805) 736-0121   *$$$$*
131 South 'H' Street, Lompoc
(Exit East Ocean Ave [1] S. on 'H'. St. [TG: 916 E1])

Get all fired up at this wonderful ceramic store where all the molds are cast on the premises. Besides a large variety of items to paint, customers can take an air-brushing class, pour models, purchase clay supplies, use a potter's wheel, and choose from green ware or bisque. Prices vary depending on the size of the piece and the type of paint - glazed or non-glazed. Smaller items start at $4 an item. The $5 table fee covers most paints and all of your time here. Classes are offered for both kids and adults. What fun!

> **Hours:** Open Tues. - Fri., 10am - 8pm; Sat. - Sun., 10am - 4pm. Closed Mon.
> **Admission:** See above for prices.
> **Ages:** 4 years and up.

-----BEACHES-----

ARROYO BURRO "HENDRY'S" BEACH PARK
(805) 687-4550 - Brown Pelican / www.sbparks.org   *!*
Cliff Drive, Santa Barbara
(Exit El Camino Real Fwy [101] S. on Las Positas Rd., R. on Cliff Dr. [TG: 995 E6])

This lovely stretch of beach has plenty of sand, plus a lagoon that extends into it and bluffs that hang over a portion of it. Highlights include surfing, tidepooling, swimming, fishing, and whale watching, in season. (Bring your binoculars.) Day-use showers and a small park for picnicking complete the scene.

For those who forget to pack a lunch, or just don't want to, buy it or breakfast or dinner at the Brown Pelican restaurant which sits as the beach's edge. The Brown Pelican also offers a snack-bar window if you want to take food back onto the beach. The restaurant makes an incredible clam chowder!

> **Hours:** Open daily, sunrise - sunset.
> **Admission:** Free
> **Ages:** All

CARPINTERIA STATE BEACH
(805) 968-1033 or (805) 684-2811; (800) 444-7275 - camping reservations / www.parks.ca.gov   *$*
Palm Avenue, Carpinteria

(Exit El Camino Real Fwy [101] S. on Casitas Pass Rd., R. on Carpinteria Ave., L. on Palm Ave. Really, just follow the signs. [TG: 998 D7])

I know that it depends on the season and even the day, and that most kids don't care much about the scenery around a beach, but Carpinteria has a wonderful shoreline as well as a magnificent view from the beach of inland palm trees and the mountains beyond.

Dubbed as the "world's safest beach" because a reef helps protect the shoreline from heavy ocean swells, it features fine sand, sand dunes, some volleyball courts, lifeguards during the summer, and large rafts at swimmable distances to climb aboard. The reef to the right of the beach, that circles off from the mouth of Franklin Creek, is great for kayaking or skin diving. Kayak rentals are available at the utility building at Ash Avenue.

Across from the beach's main parking lot is Linden Field, a decent-size open grassy area that also has chin-up and sit-up bars and a few other pieces of exercise equipment. The small, adjacent Visitor's Center offers an indoor tidepool exhibit, interpretative panels, and programs, such as the Jr. Ranger's Program.

One of our favorite parts of the beach is the tidepools at the southern end, past all the camping spots, at Tar Pits Park. Parking is very limited. A short walk down the stairs and over some tar-covered rocks leads to some wonderful tidepool exploration at low tide. We have found some wonderful shells and some unusual rocks here, too. Guided tidepool walks are offered October through May. Call for more information.

Some of the camp sites are definitely better than others. Choice ones are nestled up to the beach. A majority of the other sites are literally like setting up camp in a parking lot, although each one has a fire ring and picnic table, and the camp offers coin-operated showers. RV hookups are available.

Hours: Open daily, 7am - sunset. The Visitor's Center is open Sat. - Sun., 9am - noon.

Admission: $4 for day use parking. Camping is between $16 - $26 a night. There is a $7.50 camping reservation fee.

Ages: All

EAST BEACH

(805) 564-5433 or (805) 564-5418 / www.ci.santa-barbara.ca.us/departments/parks_and_recreation

E. Cabrillo Boulevard or Waterfront, Santa Barbara

(Going S. on El Camino Real Fwy [101], exit S. on Castillo St., L. on Cabrillo. Going N. on 101, exit S. on Garden St., R. on Cabrillo. [TG: 996 E4])

Easily one of Santa Barbara's most popular beaches, East Beach stretches from the east, at ANDREE CLARK BIRD REFUGE (see pg. 481), to the west, at Stearns Wharf. On the other side of the wharf is the adjacent WEST BEACH (see pg. 477).

Miles of white sand; fourteen volleyball courts (come watch a tournament!); a playground; a grassy area; the East Beach Grill full-service restaurant, which serves breakfast and lunch; and the Pacific Ocean - what more could a body want?! At low tide, hike along the beach eastward all the way to Butterfly Beach, which is opposite the Four Seasons Hotel. Look up SANTA BARBARA HARBOR / STEARNS WHARF (pg. 507) for more details as to what else is in the immediate vicinity.

Hours: Open daily, sunrise - 10pm.

Admission: Free. Try to get free street parking, or pay $2 a day to park in the lot.

Ages: All

EL CAPITAN STATE BEACH

(805) 968-1033; (800) 444-7275 - camping reservations / www.parks.ca.gov

Refugio Beach Road, Goleta

(Exit El Camino Real Fwy [101] S. on Refugio Rd. Look for signs for the El Capitan State Beach exit. [TG: 981 J5])

The stone-lined stretch of beach offers swimming, a few tidepools towards the southern end, dune trails, and camping. The almost private camp sites off the road in El Capitan are an interesting combination of camping near the beach, yet surrounded by sycamore and oak trees, giving them a woodsy atmosphere. Note that while the upper campgrounds are nice, they are closer to the freeway and railroad tracks. Showers are available at a nominal additional cost. Other amendments include open fire pits and a seasonal snack bar. A cycling trail connects El Capitan to REFUGIO STATE BEACH (see pg. 477), which is three miles further west. Look for the Monarch butterflies that gather here October through December.

Hours: Open daily, 8am to sunset.

Admission: $4 for daily use. Camping is $16 a night March through October; $13 November through February. There is a $7.50 camping reservation fee.

Ages: All

GAVIOTA STATE PARK

(805) 968-1033 - park; (800) 444-7275 - camping reservations / www.parks.ca.gov

Refugio Beach Road, Goleta

(Off El Camino Real Fwy [101], look for signs to the beach park. It's S. of Buellton, W. of Goleta. [TG: 365 H7])

Just when you think Santa Barbara beaches and vistas can't get any better, visit Gaviota. This beach, though, is better described as a cove that's fenced in by natural rock walls. A creek from the mountains empties into the ocean, making it ideal for wading and fishing. Spend the night in this lovely countryside at any of the fifty-eight campsites which come complete with fire pits and picnic tables. The park also has a playground, grocery store, and snack bar.

Hike inland, on the other side of the road, through the huge park. One trail, across the highway, is called Trespass Road. It's about two-and-a-half miles long and leads to the hot springs in the Los Padres National Forest. Continue on up the trail, (and I mean up!) about six miles round trip to reach Gaviota Peak.

Hours: Open daily, 8am - sunset.

Admission: $4 per vehicle for day use. Camping is $11 December - February; $14 March - November. There is a $7.50 camping reservation fee.

Ages: All

GOLETA BEACH PARK

(805) 967-1300 - beach; (805) 964-7881 - Beachside Cafe / www.sbparks.com

5968 Sandspit Road, Goleta

(Exit El Camino Real Fwy [101] S. on Ward Memorial Blvd. [Hwy 217], S. on Moffet Pl. and follow the signs. It's at the east end of the University. [TG: 994 D4])

Sand, gentle surf, lifeguards, a long pier (bring your own fishing pole), a playground, a horseshoe pit, volleyball courts, picnic tables on the adjacent lawn, barbecue grills, a paved bike trail - this twenty-nine acre beach park, complete with palm trees, has it all! Bring food for a picnic lunch or eat at the Beachside Bar and Cafe, where you can sit and eat at a table while digging your toes into the sand.

Hours: Open daily, 8am - sunset.

Admission: Free

Ages: All

JALAMA BEACH

(805) 736-6316 - recorded info; (805) 736-3504 / www.sbparks.org

Star Route, Lompoc

(Exit Cabrillo Hwy [1] S. on Jalama Rd. The turn off sign is 4.5 miles S. of Lompoc. Follow it 14 miles to the coast. [TG: 365 D6])

The word "windy" has two meanings - 1) a curvy road, which is the only type of road heading to this particular beach, and 2) full of wind, which is something that Jalama boasts of quite frequently. To emphasize the latter meaning, the parks hosts the annual Heavy Wind Classic pro-am windsurfing competition.

After the windy, scenic drive, enjoy the view from a cliff-top vantage point, overlooking the crystal clear ocean waters. You'll see kelp beds, kayakers, surfers, windsurfers, a long stretch of classic California shoreline, and campsites. This isolated beach, with its fine sand and a few small sand dunes, offers all of the above as well as fishing the surf or rock outcropping, playing horseshoes or volleyball, and flying a kite. Bring your own equipment for any activity as there are no on-site rentals.

Swimming is allowed at the beach, but with waves breaking on the shore and riptides, the surf can be dangerous. There is a small lagoon and lifeguards are on duty during summer months. Rock hounds will enjoy the rocks that can be found in this area, such as agate and travertine. Also, look for grey whales as they migrate seasonally - January through March, and September through November.

110 campsites, some with RV hookup, are available on a first-come, first-served basis. Groups may reserve in advance. The few sites directly on the beach are separated by hedges on both sides. Tip: Bring tent pegs because of the wind. The other sites' boundaries aren't as clearly delineated. Hot showers, a general store, and The Grill, known for its Jalama burgers, are also located here.

Hours: Open daily, 8am to sunset.
Admission: $5 for day use. Camping fees start at $16 a night. Burgers are about $4.25.
Ages: 5 years and up.

LEADBETTER BEACH
(805) 564-5433 or (805) 564-5418; (805) 568-0064 - cafe /
www.ci.santa-barbara.ca.us/departments/parks_and_recreation
Shoreline and Loma Alta drives, Santa Barbara
(Going N. on El Camino Real Fwy [101], exit S. on Garden St., R. on Cabrillo, which turns into Shoreline Dr. Going S. on 101, exit S. on Castillo St., R. on Shoreline Dr. It's across the way from Santa Barbara City College. [TG: 996 B6])

Located between WEST BEACH (see pg. 477) and the adjacent harbor, and under the cliff-top Shoreline Park, this popular beach is noted for swimming because of moderate waves, tidepooling during low tide, beach volleyball courts, a playground, a grassy run-around area, and a picnic area underneath palm trees. At the nearby Shoreline Beach Cafe try something different and chomp on a shark taco.

Hours: Open daily, sunrise - 10pm.
Admission: Free. The first 75 min. is free parking. After that, there is a nominal fee.
Ages: All

REFUGIO STATE BEACH
(805) 968-1033; (800) 444-7275 - camping reservation / www.parks.ca.gov
10 Refugio Beach Road, Goleta
(Exit El Camino Real Fwy [101] S. on Refugio Beach Rd. Look for the exit. [TG: 981 E4])

The beach offers swimming under the watchful eyes of lifeguards during the summer (watch out for rocks on the shore), some tidepools, a basketball court, a playground, picnic tables, barbecue pits on the beach, a grocery store, a grassy area, a lagoon/marsh inlet, and a few palm trees for ambiance. There are some camp sites nearly on the beach, so be lulled to sleep by the sound of waves. If you're in the mood for pedaling, head east for about three miles on the bike trail that leads to EL CAPITAN STATE BEACH (see pg. 475).

Hours: Open daily, 8am - sunset.
Admission: $4 for day use fee. Camping is $15 a night March through November; $12 December through February. There is a $7.50 reservation fee for camping.
Ages: All

WEST BEACH
(805) 562-5433 or (805) 564-5418 / www.ci.santa-barbara.ca.us/departments/parks_and_recreation
W. Cabrillo Boulevard, Santa Barbara
(Going N. on El Camino Real Fwy [101], exit S. on Garden St., R. on Cabrillo Blvd. Going S. on El Camino Real Fwy [101] exit S. on Castillo St., L. on Cabrillo. It's between Stearns Wharf and the harbor. [TG: 996 C5])

East Beach, Stearns Wharf, West Beach, and Leadbetter Beach are all along one strip of land. (Each of these beaches has their own entry.) They are broken up by different names and by different attractions in between beaches. Eleven acres of sandy beach includes some volleyball courts, swimming in the relatively gentle waves, palm trees waving in the wind, the BIKE TRAIL: CABRILLO BEACHWAY (see pg. 516) on the beach's perimeter, watercraft large and small sailing in and out of the harbor, launching your own kayak, and a playground. Look up SANTA BARBARA HARBOR / STEARNS WHARF (see pg. 507) for details as to what to do in this immediate area.

      Hours: Open daily, sunrise - 10pm.
  Admission: Free
       Ages: All

-----EDIBLE ADVENTURES-----

AJ SPURS

(805) 686-1655   *$$$$$*
350 E. Hwy 246, Buellton
(Exit El Camino Real Fwy [101] E. on Hwy 246/Mission Rd. [TG: 919 J6])

    Hey pardner - if you mosey into town hankering for some good food and have a passion for the West, AJ Spurs is the place to go. It seems like every piece of the Old West is represented and packed into this one restaurant.

    Outside, on top of the wooden building, are a few parked stagecoaches. One is also in front, on ground level. Cactus, life-size cowboy cutouts, a small waterfall, a mill wheel, jar lanterns, wooden porch swings with ends made from wagon wheels, antlers, and scenic western murals decorate the outside of this log cabin-style eatery.

    Inside, the theme continues. Past the small coin fountain in the lobby, the wood walls and ceilings showcase more murals, mounted animals heads (both deer and buffalo), saddles, stirrups, cowboy hats, dangling horse bits, canteens, branding irons, bearskins, steer skulls, and stuffed ducks - you get the picture. There are also a few taxidermied grizzly bears lurking around corners in ferocious poses.

    A smattering of options from the bill of fare includes eight-ounce top sirloin ($17.95), a full rack of ribs ($21.95), blackened chicken ($19.95), shrimp scampi ($24.95), lobster tail (market price), Cajun chicken tortellini ($20.95), and filet mignon or grilled quail ($24.95). All meals come with vaquero soup, tequila beans, rice pilaf, salad, spuds, garlic bread, and a root beer float. Little pardners can order a meal for only $5.95, when an adult meal is ordered. Their choices include popcorn shrimp, chicken tenders, hot dog, hamburger, halibut, ribs, or top sirloin. A clean plate earns a trip to the treasure chest. (This applies just to the kids - not the adults.)

    The restaurant also offers school tours - call for information.

      Hours: Open Mon. - Fri., 5pm - 9:30pm; Sat. - Sun., 4pm - 9:30pm.
  Admission: See above menu prices.
       Ages: 3 years and up.

CIRCLE BAR B DINNER THEATER

(805) 965-9652 - dinner theater; (805) 968-3901 - horseback riding
1800 Refugio Road, Goleta

    See the entry for CIRCLE BAR B DINNER THEATER on page 511 for details.

COLD SPRING TAVERN

(805) 967-0066 / www.coldspringtavern.com   *$$$$*
5995 Stagecoach Road, Santa Barbara
(Exit San Marcos Pass/Hwy 154 S. on Stagecoach Rd. [TG: 964 E5])

    Imagine dusty, hungry, and parched travelers arriving over 100 years ago at this stagecoach stop. Not much has changed since then.

    Seemingly in the middle of nowhere, and surrounded only by woods and a seasonal stream, is a cluster of buildings with an enchantingly-rustic tavern as the centerpiece. The log cabin eatery has several small dining rooms, each with wood-beam ceilings, animals' heads mounted on the walls, and other decor that consists of old tools, jugs, and other artifacts from bygone days. The small main room has a fireplace and a bar. Outside are a few tables under shady oak trees, as well as some rough-hewn log benches.

Modern-day folk enjoy this rest stop, too, for the ambiance as well as the food. Breakfast, averaging $7.25, is served on the weekends only, with dishes of french toast, huevos rancheros with wild game chili, New York steak and eggs, and any-way-you-like-'em omelettes. Lunches, costing between $8.25 and $12.50, are offered every day and include a choice of cheeseburger, buffalo burger, French dip sandwich, grilled pork chops, and barbecue beef sandwich. Dinners, which range from $17.50 to $25, are also served daily. Entrees include Filet mignon, barbecue baby back pork ribs, rack of lamb, sauteed medallions of rabbit, stuffed pheasant breast, roast black bear, pastas, and local seafood. Don't miss out on the homemade desserts such as Granny Smith apple cobbler and cheesecake - just like grandma used to make. Note that there is usually live music on the weekends and that weekends, in general, are very crowded. Tip: Drive just around the bend to get a good view of the arch bridge.

> **Hours:** Open for breakfast Sat. and Sun., 8am - 11am. Open for lunch daily, 11am - 3pm. Open for dinner Sun. - Thurs., 5pm - 9pm; Fri. - Sat., 5pm - 10pm. Closed Christmas.
> **Admission:** See above for menu prices.
> **Ages:** 5 years and up.

FARMER'S MARKETS

See the entry for FARMER'S MARKETS on page 14 for details.

KLONDIKE PIZZA

(805) 348-3667 / www.klondikepizza.com   *$$$*
2059 S. Broadway Street, Santa Maria
(Exit El Camino Real Fwy [101] W. on Betteravia Rd., R. on Broadway. [TG: 796 H4])

Alaskan pizza? It seems to work at Klondike. The family pizzaria is decorated on the walls and on the ceiling with memorabilia from our 49th state. The adornments include a grizzly bear, elk head, Alaskan crabs, a red fox, small totem poles, advertisements about Alaska, skis, sleds, baleen from whales, and more. The sawdust on the floor and the fact that peanuts are given to hungry diners with the understanding that peanut shells are to be tossed on the ground, add to the fun atmosphere. Kids will love ordering (and eating) Road Kill pizza (i.e. all meat), or perhaps trying a pizza topped with reindeer sausage. There are numerous "normal" pizza selections with red sauce or a garlic white sauce to choose from, as well as burgers, chicken entrees, salads, and sandwiches. Of course, what good would a place be without arcade games?!

> **Hours:** Open Sun. - Thurs., 11am - 9pm; Fri. - Sat., 11am - 10pm.
> **Ages:** All

ROCK & ROLL DINER

(805) 473-2040   *$$$$*
1300 Railroad Street, Oceano
(Exit El Camino Real [101], W. on Grand Ave, L. on Pacific Blvd [1], It's parallel to Hwy 1, just S. of Pier Ave. [TG: 714 E7])

Come on, baby - let's rock & roll! Two, long, renovated railcars serve as the dining areas for this authentically 50's-themed restaurant. Twist and shout (albeit quietly) to the music on the table jukeboxes. Munch on appetizers such as fried zucchini ($4.45), jalapeno poppers ($5.95), or bacon cheese fries ($3.95). Choose from a variety of "real" foods such as a chicken fajita salad ($6.50), cheeseburger ($8.45), French dip ($7.45), meatloaf ($8.95), beef ribs ($10.95), shrimp scampi ($12.95), spaghetti ($8.95) or Greek entries like gyros ($6.45) and moussaka ($11.95). Save room for a shake. There's a whole other menu for breakfast.

Kid's meals range from $3.50 to $4.50 and include choices of spaghetti, pizza, chicken fingers, or corn dogs. Most meals come with fries. Drinks are extra. Note: I do know this diner isn't really in Santa Barbara county, but if you are visiting the OCEANO DUNES STATE VEHICULAR PARK (see pg. 485) or going out to THE GREAT AMERICAN MELODRAMA & VAUDEVILLE (see pg. 512), this is a fun place to grab a bite to eat.

> **Hours:** Open daily, 7:30am - 9pm.

Admission: Menu prices are listed above.
     Ages: All

RUBY'S (Santa Barbara County)

(805) 564-1941; All Locations - (800) HEY RUBY (439-7829) / www.rubys.com

601 Paseo Nuevo, Santa Barbara

(Going S. on El Camino Real Fwy [101], exit N.E. Carillo St., R. on Chapala St. Going N. on 101, exit N. on Garden St., L. on Ortega St. It's in the Paseo Nuevo Shopping center between the streets of Ortega, Chapala, State and Canon Perdido. [TG: 996 A4])

See the entry for RUBY'S (Orange County) on page 206 for details.

$$$

SOMETHING'S FISHY

(805) 966-6607

502 State Street, Santa Barbara

(Going S. on El Camino Real Fwy [101], exit N.E. Carillo St., R. on State St. Going N. on 101, exit N. on Garden St., L. on Cota St. Park wherever you can. [TG: 996 B4])

Ummm - delectable seafood, sushi, and hibachi-style food is served at Something's Fishy. Food cooked with the hibachi is cooked at your table - kind of like food entertainment.

Enjoy the selection of sushi, such as crab rolls at $4, California roll at $4.50, octopus at $3.25, and lots more. The lunch menu offers hibachi chicken - $8.45; New York steak - $11.95; and shrimp or scallops - $10.95. Dinner prices average about $20. The kid's menu ranges from $5 to $7.95 for lunch and $10 to $12 for dinner.

     Hours: Mon. - Fri., 11am - 3pm; 5pm - 10pm; Sat. - Sun., 11am -10pm.
Admission: See menu prices above.
     Ages: 4 years and up.

$$$$

WOODY'S BODACIOUS BARBECUE

(805) 967-3775 / www.woodysbbq.com

5112 Hollister Avenue, Goleta

(Exit El Camino Real Fwy [101] S. on Patterson, L. on Hollister. It's in a shopping complex. [TG: 994 H2])

Wowser! Woody's is a quirky mix of the Old West and everything else, plus the kitchen sink. The lobby, for lack of a better word, contains an outhouse (just for atmosphere) and an old washtub to wash your hands. Place your order at the counter and go sit at any one of the old wooden tables located in several small rooms (or go outside) where sawdust covers the floors and walls are "decorated" with pots, pans, skis, a toilet, a lantern, a deer head, etc. Most of the rooms also contain a T.V., usually showing rodeos or other sporting events. A few arcade games are scattered throughout.

Bodacious is an appropriate word to describe the savory ribs (pork, beef, and bison) and home-made barbecue sauce that has made Woody's famous. Other menu options include chili ($4.95), burgers ($6.45), half a smoked duckling ($11.45), all-you-can eat salad bar, ($5.45), chicken breast sandwich ($6.95), or prime rib ($13.95 for a roadhouse cut). Portions are large, tasty, and usually come with their special seasoned fries. Also try the nuclear waste buffalo wings if you *really* like hot food ($5.95) or jalapeno cheese nuggets ($5.45). The kid's menu offers a hot dog or burger for $3.50, ribs for $4.95, or chicken strips for $4.45. These meals come with fries and a drink. Woody's became an instant favorite with my family.

     Hours: Open Mon. - Thurs., 11am - 9pm; Fri. - Sun., 11am - 10pm.
Admission: See above menu prices.
     Ages: All

$$$

-----*FAMILY PAY AND PLAY*-----

BOOMERS! (Santa Maria)

(805) 928-4942 / www.boomersparks.com

2250 Preisker Lane, Santa Maria

(Exit El Camino Real Fwy [101] S. on Broadway/Hwy 135, R. on Preisker. [TG: 776 H3])

At this family playland try for a hole-in-one at either one of two **miniature golf** courses. Both feature fun obstacles and scale buildings such as a colorful gingerbread house, a windmill, and a castle. Bump and splash each other in **bumper boats**. Race in **go-karts**. Climb the thirty-two foot **rock wall**. Take a swing at the **batting cages**. Play over 200 video and sport games at the arcade. A snack bar here offers nachos, pizza, and drinks. Note that Boomers is across the way from PREISKER PARK (see pg. 491).

   Hours: Open Mon. - Thurs., 11am - 10pm; Fri., 11am - midnight; Sat., 10am - midnight; Sun., 10am - 10pm.

Admission: Mini golf is $7 for adults; ages 5 and under are free with a paying adult. Go karts are $5.75 and drivers must be at least 58" tall. Passengers are $2. Bumper boats are $5 and drivers must be at least 44" tall. Passengers are $2. The rock climbing wall is $6 per person for two climbs. All day, all play wristbands are $22.95 for 58" and taller; $13.95 for 57" and shorter.

   Ages: 4 years and up.

-----*GREAT OUTDOORS*-----

ALICE KECK PARK MEMORIAL GARDENS

(805) 564-5418 / www.sbparksandrecreation.com

1500 Santa Barbara Street, Santa Barbara

(Going S. on El Camino Real Fwy [101], exit N.E. Carillo St., L. on Santa Barbara St. Going N. on 101, exit N. on Garden St., L. on Micheltorenia. The garden is on the N. corner of Micheltorenia and Santa Barbara. [TG: 996 A3])

This small, 4.6-acre, botanical garden park located in a residential neighborhood, is astoundingly beautiful. Lush grassy expanses are interspersed and bordered by a rich variety of trees, plants, and flowers. The mix includes palm trees, Chinese flame trees, coastal live oaks, Ficus, pink clover blossoms, wisteria, trumpet vines, bougainvillea, camellias, morning glorys, roses, Spanish bluebells, and so much more.

A hard-packed dirt path meanders throughout the park and winds around the centerpiece pond. The pond teems with life - blooming lily pads, koi fish, turtles, ducks, and dragonflies. A few speakers are located around this area that, with the press of a button, quietly tell the history of the park and describe some of the plant life. A rock-lined stream gurgles its way around a portion of the park. Look for and test the sensory garden. Note that KIDS' WORLD / ALAMEDA PARK (see pg. 487) is just across the street.

   Hours: Open daily, sunrise - 10pm.

Admission: Free

   Ages: All

ANDREE CLARK BIRD REFUGE

(805) 564-5433

1400 E. Cabrillo Boulevard, Santa Barbara

(Going N. on El Camino Real Fwy [101], exit S. on Hot Springs/Cabrillo. Going S. on 101, exit S. on Milpas, L. on Cabrillo. [TG: 996 F4])

This forty-acre, artificial fresh-water lake and marsh pond attracts native and migratory birds that come here to rest and nest. Bring binoculars and utilize the observation platforms located on the north side of the lake. Don't forget to read the educational panels along the way.

A paved pathway encircles the lagoon and is very popular with parents with strollers as well as bicyclists, joggers, and skaters. Take the flat pathway from here, which is part of the BIKE TRAIL: CABRILLO

BEACHWAY (see pg. 516), the whole three miles to EAST BEACH (see pg. 475).

Combine an outing here with a visit to the adjacent SANTA BARBARA ZOO (see pg. 524), where you can see more exotic birds, and other animals.

Hours: Open daily, sunrise - sunset.
Admission: Free
Ages: All

BEATTIE PARK

(805) 875-8100 / www.ci.lompoc.ca.us/Parks_Rec
Olive Avenue, Lompoc
(Exit Ocean Ave. [1] S. on A St., L. on Olive. [TG: 916 F2])

Located at the southeast corner of town, this fifty-acre park offers not only a great view of the city, but kid-interesting amenities as well. Enjoy the lighted basketball courts, sunken soccer/football field, a playground with a merry-go-round and other equipment, an outdoor gym, horseshoe pits, and a picnic pavilion with grills. A small "urban forest" also offers a popular windy dirt fitness trail.

Hours: Open daily, sunrise - sunset.
Admission: Free
Ages: All

CACHUMA LAKE RECREATION AREA

(805) 686-5054 or 5055 - general recreation area; (805) 693-0691 or (805) 688-4515 - Nature Center; (805) 686-5050 - boat cruise reservation & yurt info; (805) 688-4040 - boat rentals. / www.cachuma.com
San Marcos Pass / Hwy 154, Santa Barbara
(Exit El Camino Real Fwy [101] N. on San Marcos Pass Rd/Hwy 154. Between the cities of Santa Barbara and Solvang [TG: 365 L5])

Situated in the mountain footholds, this fully-equipped recreation area offers a smorgasbord of activities including boating, fishing, hiking, and camping. The park also has playgrounds, a nature center, and a Family Fun Center. The center, open only in the summer, contains two swimming pools, bicycle rentals, a small video game center, a snack bar, and a miniature golf course. A relatively large (for a campground) general store carries all the necessary accouterments and plenty of just-for-the-fun-of-it items. Other lake amenities include a coin laundry, showers, and a gas station.

Man-made Lake Cachuma is seven miles long. Its year-round marina offers boat rentals such as outboards, rowboats, pontoons, and paddle boats, as well as launch facilities, a bait and tackle shop, and a grill that serves up a full breakfast and lunch menu. Drop a line off a pier, shoreline, or boat to catch bass, bluegill, perch, catfish, and trout. Ask about the annual fishing derbies.

Other outstanding lake features are the two-hour narrated nature cruises. On the tour given November through February, be on the lookout for migratory bald eagles, Canada geese, teals, and loons. On the Wildlife Cruise, given March through October, the on-board naturalist points out the water fowl such as osprey, great blue herons, plovers, hawks, and mallards, and even the hovering turkey vultures. Tip: Bring binoculars! You'll learn to identify the various birds by their wingspan, nests, and their habits. (We learned that turkey vultures projectile vomit as a defense mechanism.) As the boat maneuvers close to shore look for mule deer, wild turkeys, and the elusive bobcats. The naturalist guide informs listeners of the surrounding, diverse plant life along the shoreline and in the inaccessible interior land. Both tours are casual in the sense that questions are welcome. The tours are also interesting and educational.

The mostly hands-on nature center has several rooms branching off from the lobby. The lobby contains a please-touch table of rocks, fossils, feathers, and a few stuffed animals. Other exhibits include a display of arrowheads, Chumash grind stones, and discovery drawers filled with games and activities. Another room features mounted birds - a great horned owl, an eagle, a snow goose, and more. A display case holds nests and eggs. Look out the two-way mirror and (without scaring them away) observe the numerous species of birds snacking at the outside bird feeders.

A plant room showcases indigenous plants and cones, and a tree slab. (Count its rings.) The adjacent room has taxidermied animals such as coyote, mule deer, gray fox, raccoon, and mountain lion. Touch an animal fur and guess what kind of animal it is. (Lift the panel for the answer.) Other exhibits in the center include a light up board to match true statements with pictures of animals; skulls and jawbones of various animals; and rocks with geological fact sheets. Inquire about the programs here such as the junior ranger program, school field trips, guided nature walks, and summertime evening naturalist talks at the outdoor amphitheater.

There are a few short hiking trails within the park. The Sweetwater Trail, an extended 2.5 mile one-way hike, starts here and winds its way between campgrounds to the Bradbury Dam Overlook. Tequepis Trail, directly across the road from the lake, is an eight-mile hike to the Santa Ynez Mountains ridge line. There is no direct access to this trail from the recreation area and a parking permit is required.

Campers can choose from over 520 sites, many with RV hook-ups available. Some sites have trees, most have grass, and numerous have a lake view. Three yurts are on the grounds, too. Yurts are like canvas-covered cabins. They are insulated, have bunk beds with mattresses, a locking door, inside lighting and heating, and a small table with chairs - not really camping, but still in the great outdoors.

Horseback riding trail rides and lessons are available just down the road from the lake at Rancho Oso Stables. Minimum age for horseback riding is 8 years, but younger children will enjoy the pony rides. One-hour trail rides are $30 per person; pony rides are $10 a child. Call (805) 683-5110 for more information.

Hours: Most activities are open year round. Day use hours for the general park are 6am - sunset. The Nature Center is open Wed., 10am - 2pm; Fri., 1pm - 4pm; Sat., 10am - 4pm; Sun., 10am - 2pm. Eagle Cruises are offered November through February, Wed., Thurs., and Sun. at 10am; Fri. and Sat. at 10am and 2pm. Wildlife Cruises are offered March through October, Fri. at 3pm; Sat. at 10am and 3pm; Sun. at 10am. The Family Fun Center, and all of its amenities, is open Memorial Day through Labor Day.

Admission: Day use entrance is $5 per automobile. The Nature Center is free. Basic camping starts at $16. Yurts range from $35 - $55, depending on the season and number of people it holds. The swimming pool is $1 per person per hour. Cruises are $12 for adults; $5 for ages 12 and under. Boat rentals range from $14 for a four-passenger rowboat or water bike (i.e. paddle boat) to $250 for a pontoon boat accommodating 24 passengers.

Ages: All

CARPINTERIA SALT MARSH NATURE PARK

(805) 893-4127 or (805) 893-7670 / nrs.ucop.edu
Sandyland Cove Road and Avenue Del Mar, Carpinteria
(Exit El Camino Real Fwy [101] S. on Casitas Pass Rd., R. on Carpinteria Ave., L. on Linden, R. on 3rd St., L. on Ash. [TG: 998 C7])

Appearances can be deceiving. This 230-acre salt marsh reserve is not just a boring, swampy wasteland, as it might appear at first glance, but a thriving, ecological community for a variety of species. That said, kids will not find it a thrill a minute, but it is intriguing and educational.

The only way to really experience the marsh, which is bordered by houses, the freeway, and the ocean, is to join a docent-led tour offered on Saturdays. Look for the birds that consider the reserve home - herons, egrets, brown pelicans, osprey, and numerous other shore birds. Many birds also stop here during the annual migrations. Numerous plants, fish (including leopard sharks which feed at the mouth of the estuary in the summer), and other sea creatures also reside here. Remember, that CARPINTERIA STATE BEACH (see pg. 474) is just a few steps away!

Hours: Open daily, sunrise - sunset. Tours are offered Sat. at 11am.
Admission: Free.
Ages: 7 years and up.

CHANNEL ISLANDS NATIONAL PARK (from Santa Barbara)

(805) 884-1475   *$$$$$*
113 Harbor Way, Santa Barbara

(Going N. on El Camino Real Fwy [101], exit S. on Garden St., R. on Cabrillo Blvd., L. on Harbor Way. Going S. on El Camino Real Fwy [101] exit S. on Castillo St., R. on Cabrillo, L. on Harbor Way. These directions are for the Outdoors Santa Barbara Visitor Center, which has a one-room resource with maps and info on the islands. [TG: 996 B6])

For full details on the chain of islands, please see CHANNEL ISLANDS NATIONAL PARK (from Ventura), on page 533 for details. Although the park's visitors center is located in Ventura County, excursions to the islands also leave from Santa Barbara's Harbor: See TRUTH AQUATICS (pg. 520) and CONDOR CRUISES (pg. 517) for more details.

CHASE PALM PARK

(805) 564-5418 - park; (805) 963-9463 - carousel / www.sbparksandrecreation.com
323 E. Cabrillo Boulevard at Garden Street, Santa Barbara

(Going S. on El Camino Real Fwy [101] exit S. on Castillo, L. on Cabrillo. Going N. on 101, exit S. on Garden St., L. on Cabrillo. Free parking on the street is difficult to find. The adjacent beach parking lot is $2 for the day. [TG: 996 C4])

This imaginative park runs parallel to the main street of Cabrillo Boulevard, across the street from EAST BEACH (see pg. 475) and SANTA BARBARA HARBOR / STEARNS WHARF (see pg. 507). The west end of the park has a traditional carousel with wood-carved animals. Stroll along the cement and hard-packed dirt pathway as it winds the length of the park over bridges and through garden landscape, with cement picnic tables and wooden benches scattered throughout.

The east end of the park holds the treasure of a shipwreck playground, complete with sand, cement octopus tentacles, climbing structures, small bridges, slides, tubes to crawl through, and a few rocks to climb on. One area also has kid-size adobe-style walls and doors to play hide and seek. Just beyond the playground is a grassy area with gently rolling hills and a stage for outdoor concerts and events. Check out the family concerts given in the summer. A snack bar here sells hot dogs, churros, popsicles, and other necessary food items.

Hours: Open daily, sunrise - sunset.
Admission: Free. Carousel rides are $2 per person; children 1 and under are free.
Ages: 9 months to 14 years.

CHUMASH PAINTED CAVE

(805) 968-1033 / www.parks.ca.gov
Painted Cave Road, Santa Barbara

(From San Marcos Pass/Hwy 154, exit E. on Painted Cave Rd. Drive about 2 miles on a windy road, then be on the lookout for the brown sign that says "park" on the left. There is off-road parking for two cars. [TG: 964 J6])

Almost exactly two miles up a very narrow, sometimes one-lane, windy, woodland-laced road with hairpin turns, is your destination - the Painted Cave. Climb up a few boulders to peer through gratings into the cave. Its walls are covered with still-vivid paintings drawn by Chumash Indians hundreds of years ago. Yes, it's a rather precarious drive for just a few moments of sight-seeing, but to actually view such paintings can be exciting.

A trail, if one can call it that, leads up the boulder-covered hill. Be sure-footed to indulge in this short hike. We also found adventure on the opposite side of the road. A rock-lined dry creek bed (I assume the creek is seasonal!) and the surrounding woods provided my boys with a good deal of entertainment (and made the drive more justifiable).

Hours: Open daily, sunrise - sunset.
Admission: Free
Ages: 8 years and up.

COAL OIL POINT RESERVE

(805) 893-5092 / coaloilpoint.ucnrs.org
El Colegio Road & Storke Road adjacent to the UCSB campus, Isla Vista

(Exit El Camino Real Fwy [101] S. on Storke Rd. You must call the Reserve Director at the above phone number to purchase a parking permit or park on the street outside the campus and walk in. [TG: 994 D4])

This 150-acre reserve is a rich combination of undisturbed coastal dunes and estuarine habitats. The tidal lagoon area is flooded seasonally and then dries out in the summer to form salt flats and small hypersaline ponds and channels. Thousand of migratory birds, including (and most importantly), the endangered Snowy Plover, rest and nest here. A walking trail goes around the perimeters of the reserve, and one, the Pond Trail, cuts through it. The adjacent university offers several guided "tours", or field studies, for students of all ages.

The reserve has great tidepools to explore. Note that the tidepools are closed March through mid-September because they are next to the plover's seasonal nesting grounds. Just around the "corner", on West Campus Beach by the Del Playa entrance, is one of best spots for year-round tidepooling. Peak under small boulders to observe the teeming marine life. Have no *reserve*ations about coming here for an educational and fun day!

Hours: Open daily, dawn - dusk for a self-guided walk. Call to make reservation for a tour.
Admission: Free parking is on the street outside the campus, or pay $3 for on-campus parking.
Ages: 4 years and up.

COLLEGE PARK

(805) 875-8100 / www.ci.lompoc.ca.us/Parks_Rec
College Avenue and 'H' Street, Lompoc
(Exit N. 'H' St. [1] E. on College. [TG: 896 E7])

This small park's central focus is a 10,000 square-foot skate park. It has ramps and bowls and all the "extras" that make a skate park fun and challenging. Skaters - wear protective safety gear. The surrounding park has shade trees, an open grassy area, and play equipment. The park also incorporates a Y.M.C.A. and soon, an aquatic center.

Hours: Open daily, sunrise - sunset.
Admission: Free
Ages: 7 years and up.

FIGUEROA MOUNTAIN

(805) 925-9538 - U.S. Forest Service; (805) 968-6640 - Los Padres National Forest Headquarters; (800) 468-6765 - Solvang Visitors Bureau
Figueroa Mountain Road / Happy Canyon Road, Solvang
(From San Marcos Pass/Hwy 154, between Hwy 101 and Hwy 246 or the Santa Ynez/Solvang exit, turn N. on Figueroa Mountain Rd. and head about 30 miles N. from Los Olivos. [TG: 365 H4])

This over twenty miles of windy road goes through some of the most gorgeous scenery in all of Santa Barbara County. We drove a good portion of it and stopped at numerous spots along the way, sometimes at marked trails, and sometimes just where the countryside beckoned us. This mountain area offers over fifteen hiking trails and numerous unmarked "trails," with scenery that changes drastically depending on the season. In the spring, the slopes are ablaze with wild flowers, including California poppies and blue lupines. Indian summers bring fewer people and unmatched beauty. Be forewarned - oftentimes the road is closed during the rainy season. Snow can sometimes fall during the winter months. Contact the forest service for maps and more information. Fishing is available at year-round Davy Brown Creek, below the Davy Brown campground, and in Manzana Creek from March to mid-May when it's stocked with trout.

Hours: Open daily, sunrise - sunset.
Admission: Some parking areas require the $5 Adventure Pass to be posted on your windshield.
Ages: 4 years and up.

GUADALUPE-NIPOMO DUNES PRESERVE / OSO FLACO LAKE NATURAL AREA / OCEANO DUNES STATE VEHICULAR RECREATION AREA / DUNES VISITORS CENTER MUSEUM

(805) 343-2455 / www.dunescenter.org - Dunes Visitors Center Museum; (805) 473-7223/7230 / www.sbparks.com / www.ohv.parks.ca.gov - Oceano dunes; (800) 444-7275 - camping reservations at Oceano; (805) 481-9330 / www.pacificadventuretours.com - Pacific Adventure Tours (Humvee tours)

There are three entrances/addresses for the dunes: The southern entrance is West Main Street/Hwy 166 in Guadalupe; the central is Oso Flaco Lake Road in Nipomo; and the northern is Pier Avenue in Oceano. The visitors center museum is located at 1055 Guadalupe Street/Highway 1 in Guadalupe.
(Guadalupe: Exit El Camino Real Fwy [101] W. on Main St./Hwy 166 and keep on going until the end, the beach. [TG: 774 A6] Nipomo: Exit Hwy 101 in Santa Maria W. on Main St./ Hwy 166, R. on Guadalupe Hwy/Hwy 1, L. on Oso Flaco Lake Rd. [TG: 754 E3] Oceano: Exit Hwy 101 in Santa Maria W. on Main St./Hwy 166, R. on Guadalupe Hwy /Hwy 1, L. on Pier Ave. [TG: 714 D7])

Maps of the preserve, an events calendar, and helpful docents make the visitors' center (i.e. Dunes Visitors Center Museum) a good starting point for your trip to the dunes. The center also has interactive displays for kids (and adults) such as a sand pit filled with hidden treasures; skulls and other plaster bones to touch; microscopes and slides; a puppet stage and animal puppets; and award-winning computer programs written specifically to educate and fascinate visitors to the dunes. You can also choose from such video topics as birds of prey, amphibians, geology, and the making of the 1923 Cecil B. DeMille movie, *The Ten Commandments*, which was filmed here. The center has information about the movie set, which still lays buried in the area, intact, and under layers of sand. There are also a few taxidermied animals, photographs, and a small gift shop here.

There are three entrances for three very different experiences to the eighteen miles and acres and acres of sand dunes. In **Guadalupe**, the Southern-most entrance, drive past a working sand mine, through marshlands where cattle are grazing, until you almost reach the shoreline of Guadalupe Beach. Spend time exploring the rolling sandy hills, strolling along the beach, and frolicking in the water.

At **Oso Flaco**, park the car in the lot and walk along the hard-packed dirt path to a long wooden bridge and boardwalk that cross over a portion of one of the fresh-water lakes in the preserve. The pathway extends all the way to the beach (at some points the trail is almost obliterated by sand), making it a total trek of about a mile-and-a-half. Other paths branch off into the dunes. The diversity of plant and animal life here is amazing. The dunes are constantly being resculpted as the wind and water shift the sands to new depths and new heights (up to 500 feet!) We hiked to the beach, but the boys really enjoyed exploring the more dramatic dunes. We took a trail that cut to the right, before the beach, and turned right again at the fence, going "off road" to reach our play area. The kids cavorted, ran, jumped, rolled, slid, and crawled up and down the dunes. I took pictures. They were happy and tired. My pictures were great. When all is said and "dune," we had a great day.

At the northern, **Oceano** entrance, park right near the beach or take your four-wheel drive directly onto it! (Mini vans can only go so far.) You can drive quite a few miles on the beach, right up to the waves or dunes. Let the kids go wild! (Within reason, of course.) There are three-and-a-half miles of beach and 1,500 acres of sand dunes in this area available for OHV use. For those without the necessary vehicle you've got a few options. Humvee tours are quite the thrill. Zooming up and over the dunes is like riding a roller coaster. Prices start at $39 for adults; $20 for ages 14 and under. Contact Pacific Adventure Tours at the given phone number for more information. Or, rent an all-terrain vehicle - this is one of our favorite choices. The vehicles rent for about $40 for two hours for the smallest bikes (geared for 8 year olds, or so) on up to $75 for a more powerful model. The following are a few numbers to get you started on this quest: BJ's at (805) 481-5411/www.bjsatvrentals.com; Arnies at (805) 473-1610/www.pismoatvrentals.com; and Steves at (805) 474-6431/www.stevesatv.com.

Camping is also available at Oceano. Swim, surf, and/or fish in the water. This is quite a popular place to be, especially at night. It does get foggy and cold here, even in August, so grab a jacket. Bring your own wood to start a fire directly on the sand. Just outside the Oceano entrance is Pier Avenue, a short street that offers a Nature Center and a fun store stop - the Salt Water Taffy Coffee and Candy House. Delectable candies of all kinds, plus freshly-dipped caramel apples, shaved ice, firewood, and a small gift shop make up the varied selection of items. While in Oceano, check out the Pismo State Beach Campground just down the street.

There are numerous, docent-led tours of the dunes and the lakes offered for specific groups and for the general public. Learn about the eco system, history, geology, and preservation of the dunes; wildlife; habitats; and more. Note that dune access is severely limited between March 1 and September 30 because the California least tern and the western snowy plover (birds) nest in the sands. Large sections of the area are fenced off.

Hours: Guadalupe dunes are open daily, 8am - sunset. Oso Flaco Lake area is open daily, 8am - dusk. Oceano is open daily, 6am - 11pm. The visitor center is open Thurs. - Sun., noon - 4pm. Dune access is severely restricted March 1 through September 30.

Admission: Guadalupe is free. Oso Flaco is $4 per vehicle. Oceano is $4 for day use; $3 for seniors. Or find the few spaces on the street if not venturing by car out to the dunes. Camping is $6 a night; $4 for seniors.

Ages: All

HANS CHRISTIAN ANDERSEN PARK

(805) 688-PLAY (7529) / www.cityofsolvang.com/park_rec.html

Atterdag Road, Solvang

(Exit El Camino Real Fwy [101] E. on Hwy 246/Mission Dr., L. on Atterdag Rd. [TG: 920 D7])

Drive through the castle-like entrance into a delightful park. The 1.3-mile round-trip dirt trail is great for hikers and horseback riders. One picnic area has picnic tables and small barbecue pits. The playground here (with wood chip flooring) has a mini fort, several short slides, swings, a fireman's pole, climbing apparatus, and a mini zip line. We especially enjoyed the huge gnarled trees for shade and to climb on, and the seasonal creek. Another picnic area has huge charcoal pits, a nice grass area, horseshoe pits (bring your own horseshoes), and a bridge over the creek. Towards the back of the park are four tennis courts and more climbing trees. After a hard day of shopping in Solvang, give your family a storybook ending by coming to play at the park.

Hours: Open daily, 8am - sunset.

Admission: Free

Ages: All

KIDS' WORLD / ALAMEDA PARK

(805) 564-5418 / www.sbparksandrecreation.com

1400 Santa Barbara Street, Santa Barbara

(Going S. on El Camino Real Fwy [101], exit N.E. Carillo St., L. on Santa Barbara St. Going N. on 101, exit N. on Garden St., L. on Micheltorenia. Kids's World is on the E. corner of Micheltorenia and Santa Barbara. [TG: 996 A3])

Partially designed by kids, and totally designed for them, this part of the park is truly a Kid's World. A large, multi-level wooden play fort, with cupolas on top and sawdust on the floor, is the main feature and is packed with imaginative "extras." It has stairways, slides, tube bridges, maze-like crawl spaces (made for kid-size bodies!), a zip line, climbing apparatus, a rope bridge, speaking tubes, and more. In the center of the fort are benches made so that parents can chat with each other while keeping an eye on the kids. A toddler area has swings and a large tic-tac-toe board.

The fort is under a sprawling shade tree, with big roots above ground. Plenty of picnic tables are right outside the fort perimeters, as are a sizable cement beached whale and shark, and more swings.

The rest of the park is pretty and restful, comprised of lots of grassy areas and more shade trees, plus a few cement pathways. Look up ALICE KECK PARK MEMORIAL GARDENS (see pg. 481), as it is just across the street.

Hours: Open daily, sunrise - 10pm.

Admission: Free

Ages: 1 to 12 years.

LAKE LOS CARNEROS COUNTY PARK

(805) 964-4407 / www.sbparks.com

Los Carneros Road at Calle Real, Goleta

(Exit El Camino Real Fwy [101] N. on Los Carneros Rd. Hikers and bikers can also access this park from Covington Way and La Patera Ln. [TG: 994 B2])

This large park/nature reserve is also home to the STOW HOUSE MUSEUM (see pg. 506) and SOUTH COAST RAILROAD MUSEUM (see pg. 506). Depending on the season, you'll find the park to be a lush green oasis with a large pond, or very dry grass fields with a smaller pond. The ducks seem to be plentiful either way. The hard-packed dirt hiking trail cuts almost through the center of the park and is a short, easy walk for most ages. Picnic tables under shade trees are available just south of the railroad museum. At the north end of the park is Los Carneros Swim Club, which has a small pool that is open seasonally, and a picnic area. Look up STOW GROVE COUNTY PARK (pg. 493), an adjacent park just north of Los Carneros.

Hours: Open daily, 8am - sunset.
Admission: Free
Ages: All

LA PURISIMA MISSION STATE HISTORIC PARK

(805) 733-3713 / www.lapurisimamission.org
2295 Purisima Road, Lompoc
(Exit El Camino Real Fwy [101], W. on Hwy 246 about 18 miles, R. on Purisima Rd. [TG: 896 J4])

Situated on just a portion of the almost 3,000 acres of undeveloped parkland, this eleventh mission in the California chain was first founded in 1787. It is one of the most authentically restored missions as the adobe bricks, structures, mission furniture, and decor have been replicated using tools, materials, and construction methods similar to the originals. Even the types of plants in the garden and representative livestock in the corrals harken back to that era.

You're invited to peer into and/or walk through the numerous buildings sprawled over this section of rural land, and to read the informational signs. We began our self-guided visit with the visitors' center which once served as an infirmary and still contains rows of beds. Tip: Make sure to look up under the outside rafters at the birds and their mud nests. Just beyond this building is a shady picnic grove with California black walnut trees, coastal live oaks, a seasonal creek, and picnic tables.

The Tule village has three roomy huts made from tule reed. The blacksmith shop displays anvils, tools, and bellows, along with living quarters that has a bed and kitchen. A beehive oven plus kitchen, gourds, a granary, grinding mill stone, storeroom, and pottery shop are some of the components of the next series of rooms. The adjacent long building has a wine cellar; bedrooms; a large living and dining area; guest bedrooms (notice the pre-box spring ropes across the bed frames); simply furnished padres' quarters; a tanning room (not used for humans to suntan, but to cure animal hides) with several hides; a leather shop; wooden horses with saddles; and a nave with vestments behind glass. Further rooms and items of interest include the mission bell; a Mexican ox yoke; bricks to touch; a large seventeenth-century, hand-written choir book made of sheepskin parchment; a weaving room with looms and spinning wheels; a candle room with strings of hanging candles waiting to be dipped; and a cuartel - military sleeping quarters where weapons hang on the walls, over the heads of beds.

Walk through the long main church with old paintings, outside to the cemetery and on to the huge tallow vats on the "back" side of the mission. The central courtyard is comprised of beautiful gardens, a fountain, the lavanderia cistern (used for washing clothes and for bathing), and a corral. Long-horn cattle, horses, four-horn sheep, turkeys, geese, and burros dwell here.

Walking along the dusty paths between buildings gives present-time visitors a real sense of the past, as do the Mission Life Days which are held on the third Saturday of the month from 11am to 2pm. These special days feature costumed docents who re-create padres, soldiers, Indians, and other residents from the mission's heyday. Demonstrations can include wool spinning, candlemaking, and blacksmithing.

Guided tours for individuals are offered Monday through Friday at 2pm and on the weekends at 11am and 2pm. Age-appropriate guided tours for groups of school-age children and for adults are offered throughout the year, for a minimum of ten people. Ask about the special, evening candlelight tours.

Another pleasure of La Purisima is the miles and miles of hiking, biking, and equestrian trails that crisscross throughout the back country. The terrain varies from rolling hills to canyons to a pond. Trails range from the short climb of the Trail to the Landmark Cross, which does have a cross at the end of the path; to the 2.7 miles of Roadrunner Road, which is a service road forming a loop near the mission; to the miles of trails extending into the heart of the park's chaparral. Be on the lookout for all sorts of animals, especially the numerous birds that use this route for their migration. Pack your own water and/or bring a picnic lunch to enjoy on the mission grounds.

Hours: Open daily, 9am - 5pm. The buildings close at 4:30pm. Closed New Year's Day, Thanksgiving, and Christmas.

Admission: $4 per vehicle
Ages: 5 years and up.

LOS ALAMOS COUNTY PARK

(805) 934-6123 / www.sbparks.com
Drum Canyon Road, Los Alamos
(Exit El Camino Real Fwy [101] W. on Hwy 135, R. on Bell St., L. on Centennial, L. on Drum Canyon - just follow the signs. [TG: 878 G2])

   Snug up against the hills of Drum Canyon, this lovely fifty-one acre park is a refreshing place to visit and seemingly far removed from city life. Three group picnic areas encourage families to gather together for a day, or at least a meal. Each "site" has plenty of picnic tables and a huge barbecue grill - big enough to roast a pig!

   Old oak trees spread their mighty (and shady) branches, beckoning kids to climb on them. A large grass area offers run around space. Horseshoe pits (bring your own shoes), a playground with slides and swings, a ball field, two sand volleyball courts, and hills to hike up and around make this an ideal park as there is something for everyone.

Hours: Open daily, 8am - sunset.
Admission: Free
Ages: All

LOTUSLAND

(805) 969-9990 / www.lotusland.org
695 Ashley Road, Montecito
(Exit El Camino Real [101] N. on Hot Springs Rd., L. on Sycamore Canyon Rd., R. on Ashley. [TG: 986 G7])

   Plant it and they will come. This thirty-seven-acre estate boasts a botanical garden of dreams. The main pathway branches off into various themed sections, each one focused on a particular grouping or type of plant in a breathtakingly beautiful setting. A two-hour tour takes visitors through it all.

   Begin at the visitor's center, which has oddly bent cactus in the patio courtyard, as well as a small mosaic tile fountain, tile benches, and a garden shop. Enter the Australian Garden, where the plants are native to Australia. The intriguing and serene Japanese Garden features a pond with lily pads and koi fish surrounided by native trees and plants, and a wisteria arbor. The Epiphyllum Garden pathway leads visitors past shady oak trees and eucalyptus tree trunks that are decorated with blooming orchid cacti and other plants. A rock-lined streambed meanders throughout this area. The Cycad (i.e. cone bearing) Garden offers a small pond with lily pads and a little waterfall, all enhanced by encircling palm plants. Feeling blue? The plants in the Blue Garden have silver and blue-gray foliage. The Water Garden was the original swimming pool, but the only thing floating in here now are the numerous Indian lotus plants. Side ponds hold other species of lotus and water lilies.

   Cacti, bromeliads, succulents, and aloes all have their own area to call home. The aloe area also has a kidney-shaped pool with a cascading fountain made of giant clam shells. The parterre (i.e. formal planting beds) is divided into two sections by hedges: One side has a rose garden and star-shaped fountain, while the other has an intricate pebble mosaic and fanciful Neptune fountain. The Fern Garden flourishes with giant ferns hanging in baskets from trees, as well as with tree ferns and other species. The garden is bordered by another pool, a sandy "beach" with giant clam shells, and a stone wall lined with succulents. The colorful Butterfly Garden attracts garden-friendly insects, including butterflies. Look for Monarchs, or butterfly wannabes (i.e. caterpillars).

   The orchard grows citrus, such as oranges, lemons and limes, as well as deciduous trees - plums, peaches, apples, persimmons, and more. Rows of olive trees, also produced here, end abruptly at a wall fountain with a figure of a mythological horse/sea monster. Last, but not least, is the Topiary Garden which has a twenty-five-foot (in diameter) working clock as its centerpiece. I think it's a bit hard to tell the time this way. The garden also features something particularly fun for kids - a zoo of topiary plants growing in shapes of a camel, gorilla, giraffe, seal, and other animals. Reservations for this exotic plant tour must be made far in advance of when you'd like to come visit.

Hours: Open mid-February through mid-November, Wed. - Sat. at 10am and 1:30pm. Children 9 years and under may accompany adults on tours on Thurs. and the second Sat. of each month.

Admission: $15 for adults; $8 for ages 2 - 9; children under two are free.

Ages: 9 years and up.

MANNING PARK

(805) 969-0201 / www.sbparks.com

San Ysidro Road, Montecito

(Exit El Camino Real Fwy [101] N. on San Ysidro Rd. [TG: 996 J2])

There are two different facets to this park. To the west side of San Ysidro Road is a multi-level park that still feels like the estate it once was. This lush little park, with portions that could be classified as botanic gardens, has a green stretch of grass that is dotted with pine and other trees, lots of birds, a few scattered picnic tables and barbecue pits, and a really nice looking youth center building. Just up the stairs and ramp is a small playground and a few covered picnic sites. There is a tennis court on the south side of this park. No admission is charged.

On the east side of the street is a more typical park, which is accessible by walking across the street or driving to the other parking lot via Santa Rosa Lane. This medium-size park has a ball field that doubles as a grassy field, a volleyball court, a playground, large barbecue pits, and a creek that runs along one side. This park is subject to group reservations.

Hours: Open daily, 8am - sunset.

Admission: Free

Ages: All

MORETON BAY FIG TREE

Chapala and Montecito streets, Santa Barbara

(Going S. on El Camino Real Fwy [101], exit S. on Castillo St., L. on Montecito. Going N. 101, exit S. on Garden St., R. on Yanonali St., R. on Santa Barbara St., L. on Montecito. [TG: 996 B5])

This is not really an end destination, but it is an interesting natural wonder to stop off and see. This fig tree, originally a seedling brought over from Australia in 1876, now has a top that spans 160 feet which is said to have the potential to give shade to over 16,000 people. Its roots cover half a city block. The coolest fact for kids? It's listed in the Guinness Book of World Records.

Admission: Free

Ages: All

NOJOQUI FALLS

(805) 934-6123 or (805) 688-4217 / www.sbparks.com

Alisal Road, Solvang

(From Hwy 246/Mission Rd. in Solvang, go S. on Alisal Road and look for signs. From El Camino Real Fwy [101], exit E. on Old Coast Rd. to Alisal Rd. We had a hard time finding this exit going N. on the 101, so keep in mind that from the 101 turnoff to Lompoc, the park exit is another 3.8 miles N. [TG: 365 J6])

Driving the tree-lined road leading to Nojoqui Falls is like a drive in the country. The first part of the park has group picnic areas with both large and small barbecue pits, a small playground, a sand volleyball court, a large grassy area, and <u>lots</u> of trees.

One reason for this beautiful park's popularity is the ten-minute, or so, hike to the limestone cliff waterfall. Located toward the back of the park, walk the dirt-packed, stroller-friendly trail that meanders along a seasonal creek, past boulders, and over bridges to the seasonal 100-foot waterfall. (In the summer and fall, it can become a tricklefall.) The surrounding scenery, however, is admirable in any season.

Hours: Open daily, 8am - sunset.

Admission: Free
Ages: All

PREISKER PARK

(805) 925-0951 / www.santamaria.com
2301 Preisker Lane, Santa Maria
(Exit El Camino Real Fwy [101] S. on Broadway/Orcutt Exwy 135, R. on Preisker Ln. [TG: 776 H3])

Aaaah! This large circular park, located at the northern end of the city, has a plethora of mature pine and oak trees, offering shade and a peaceful ambiance. There is also plenty of open, grassy areas to run around, plus gently rolling green hills, a baseball diamond, and a good-sized playground with a sand base, dotted with big rocks, and a few pieces of play equipment. A main attraction is the wood and cement ship for little mateys to climb aboard. Located in a pond (with gangplank entrance), it's "armed" with cannon turrets. The pond has a fountain in the middle of it and is home to ducks who quack for handouts. A rock-lined stream runs through the park and flows into the pond. Picnic tables are plentiful.

Another, small play area has two wooden structures that, with some imagination, could look like forts. One has a slide and fireman's pole; the other has monkey bars. Enjoy a day in this delightful park.

Hours: Open daily, sunrise - sunset.
Admission: Free
Ages: All

ROCKY NOOK COUNTY PARK

(805) 681-5650 / www.sbparks.com
610 Mission Canyon Road, Santa Barbara
(Exit El Camino Real Fwy [101] N. on Mission St., which turns into Laguna St. - keep to the L. Go R. on Mission Canyon, past Mission Santa Barbara and as the road forks - stay to the L. [TG: 995 J1])

The park is aptly named with its rocks, seemingly strewn throughout, to climb on and jump over, and individual picnic nooks, branching off the main road. Each picnic area has its own barbecue grill.

Oak, sycamore, eucalyptus, and pine trees form a shady "ceiling" and give the park a woodsy feel. The seasonal Mission Creek is almost more fun to explore in the summer, when the water level is low and the numerous exposed rocks lining the sides and bottom practically beg kids to clamber on and around them. A small playground, a horseshoe pit, some short hiking trails, a few huge fallen logs, and two mosaic alligators near the entrance complete the park's offerings. Note: This park is near MISSION SANTA BARBARA (see pg. 498), SANTA BARBARA NATURAL HISTORY MUSEUM (see pg. 501), and SANTA BARBARA BOTANIC GARDEN (see the below entry).

Hours: Open daily, 8am - sunset.
Admission: Free
Ages: 3 years and up.

SANTA BARBARA BOTANIC GARDEN

(805) 682-4726 / www.sbbg.org
1212 Mission Canyon Road, Santa Barbara
(Exit El Camino Real Fwy [101] N. on Mission St., L. on Garden St., R. on Los Olivos past the mission (stay to the L. when the road forks), R. on Foothill Rd. [Hwy 192], L. on Mission Canyon Rd. [TG: 985 J6])

Picture walking on a hard-packed dirt trail through a natural setting of chaparral and oak woodlands, oftentimes alongside the meandering Mission Creek. Add a small desert, meadow, and manzanita section, and that sums up the mid-size Santa Barbara Botanic Garden.

The gardens do contain flowering plants, such as lilac, although trees and shrubbery make up the majority of the 1,000 species of indigenous plants. Different seasons bring a variety of wildflowers and wildlife. The 5.5 miles of trails are mostly easy walking and stroller friendly, with a few quarter-mile hiking trails being the exception. You'll find benches and a few drinking fountains along the way, plus a picnic area, so pack a lunch, or at least a snack.

Some features of particular interest include the slab of redwood at the bend in the redwood trail that shows rings dating from 1130 to 1985; the home demonstration garden with different soil amendments and mulches to touch such as coarse sand, vermiculite, peat moss, and clay; the bridge over the Mission dam and waterworks; and the display of how Native Americans used plants to create baskets, clothing, structures, and more.

A small nursery is on site if you're interested in purchasing plants. Ask about guided group and school tours. Enjoy your time here - so close to the city, but so far removed from city life.

Hours: Open Mon. - Fri., 9am - 4pm; Sat. - Sun., 9am - 5pm. Closed New Year's Day, Thanksgiving, Christmas Eve, and Christmas Day. Guided tours for individuals are offered daily at 2pm, as well as 10am on Thurs., Sat., and Sun.

Admission: $6 for adults; $4 for seniors; $3 for students and teens; $1 for ages 5 - 12 years; children 4 years and under are free.

Ages: All

SANTA YNEZ RECREATION AREA

(805) 967-3481 - USDA Forest Service / Los Padres National Forest; (805) 521-1319 or (805) 967-8766 - Rocky Mountain Recreation Company. / www.r5.fs.fed.us/lospadres; www.rmrc-recreation.com
Paradise Road, Santa Barbara
(Exit San Marcos Pass/Hwy 154 E. on Paradise Rd. [TG: 964 F1])

The Santa Ynez Recreation Area, part of the massive Los Padres National Forest, covers an extensive accessible portion of Santa Barbara County's wilderness. The above phone numbers are references for the following: Contact the Forest Service for information on field trips, education programs, and publications that enable visitors to enjoy and protect the forest. Or, contact the Los Padres Forest Association for more information at (805) 640-9060. The Rocky Mountain Company provides information on campgrounds and picnic areas, and they have a good map of the area trails. Note that trails are open for hikers, equestrians, and to hardy mountain bikers. Stop by the Los Prietos Ranger Station on Paradise Road, within the Lower Santa Ynez Recreation Area, for maps and books that show designated roads, trails, recreation facilities, and more. The ranger station is open year round Monday through Friday from 8am to 4:40pm. It's open the same hours, plus Saturdays, during the summer.

Both the Lower Santa Ynez Recreation Area and the Upper S.Y.R.A. have beautiful scenery, plus trails, camping, and picnic areas. The lower area is easily accessible by car. The upper is more remote with unpaved roads and more rustic campgrounds. Some lower S.Y.R.A. trail highlights include Aliso National Recreation Trail, which is just east of the Los Prietos Ranger Station. The trail head is at the east end of the Sage Hill campground. Pick up an interpretive brochure here (don't you just love adding to your kids' education?) and take the easy one-mile hike along the seasonal Aliso Creek. If your troops are energetic, and you've packed water, hike the entire, moderately-graded, three-and-a-half-mile loop trail.

If you continue driving east on Paradise Road, past Sage Hill, and turn left on the road past the Lower Oso picnic area up to the Upper Oso campgrounds, you'll be near the trail head for the popular Santa Cruz National Recreation Trail. This delightful trail follows along Oso Creek, through a sandstone canyon, and past nature-made pools, which are usually fairly shallow. If the kids are tired (and hungry), Nineteen Oaks Trailcamp makes a good stopping point. (You have to provide the snacks.) Past this spot, the trail ascends up three-and-a-half miles to Little Pine Mountain, and another five miles to another trailcamp.

Another popular trail, Red Rock - Gibraltar, starts at the end of Paradise Road. This area has restrooms. The trail meanders right alongside the Santa Ynez River, with the midway point at Gibralter Dam and Reservoir. Wading and swimming in the Santa Ynez River is possible at certain junctions. Fish the stocked river for rainbow trout. A license is required for ages 17 and older. Take the same trail back, which goes past steep, tall rocks and deep pools, or continue on a loop along an unmaintained dirt road to the parking area. The entire loop is seven miles long and moderately easy. The four family campgrounds at the lower S.Y.R.A. have water, barbecues, fire pits, tables, and toilets. No sites offer full-service hook-ups.

Hours: Open daily, sunrise - sunset.

Admission: $5 per automobile for a day-use pass (i.e. Adventure Pass) for stopping anywhere within the national forest. The camping fee is $15 a night.

Ages: 4 years and up.

SKATER'S POINT

(805) 564-5418

Garden Street and Cabrillo Boulevard, Santa Barbara

(Going N. on El Camino Real Fwy [101], exit S. on Garden St. Going S. on 101, exit S. on Castillo St., L. on Cabrillo Blvd. [TG: 996 C5])

This is where the skate meets the sand. This unsupervised, 12,000-foot concrete playground for skaters is just off the beach. Boarders and bladers work up a sweat on the ledges, rails, quarter-pipes, and bowls, and can then go take a swim in the ocean. Helmets and pads are required.

Hours: Open daily, 8am - sunset.

Admission: Free

Ages: 7 years and up.

STEVENS PARK

(805) 564-5418 / www.ci.santa-barbara.ca.us/departments/parks_and_recreation

258 Canon Drive, San Roque

(Exit El Camino Real Fwy [101] S. on San Roque Rd., R. on Calle Fresno, R. on Canon. [TG: 985 F7])

This slightly off-the-beaten path park is a good find. The immediately visible part of the park has shade trees, a rock-lined creek, a playground, some picnic tables, and barbecues. Discover the more hidden part of the park by taking the dirt trail that leads under the road, through San Roque Canyon, and up the hillside to the Santa Ynez mountain range, where it branches off. Either part of the park you choose makes for a fun outing.

Hours: Open daily, sunrise - 10pm.

Admission: Free

Ages: All

STOW GROVE COUNTY PARK

(805) 964-2311 / www.sbparks.com

La Patera Lane, Goleta

(Exit El Camino Real Fwy [101] N. on Los Carneros Rd., R. on Cathedral Oaks Rd., R. on La Patera. [TG: 984 C7])

This delightful park, which is just up the road from LAKE LOS CARNEROS COUNTY PARK (see pg. 487), STOW HOUSE MUSEUM (see pg. 506), and SOUTH COAST RAILROAD MUSEUM (see pg. 506), has a redwood grove encircling its picnic area. Other amenities include barbecue pits, a ball field, two volleyball courts, playgrounds, horseshoe pits (bring your own equipment), and a grassy green lawn.

Hours: Open daily, 8am - sunset.

Admission: Free

Ages: All

TORO CANYON PARK

(805) 969-3315 / www.sbparks.com

Toro Canyon Road, Summerland

(Going N. on El Camino Real Fwy [101], exit N.E. on Santa Claus Ln./Padaro, L. on Via Real, the frontage road, R. on Toro Canyon Rd. Going S. on 101, exit N. on N. Padaro, R. on Via Real, L. on Toro Canyon. From Toro Canyon, go R. on Toro Canyon Park Rd., L. at the sign that proclaims Oak Creek Canyon Equestrian Center. [TG: 997 J2])

This beautiful, remote park sports numerous old oak trees along boulder-strewn hillsides. It also has picnic tables, barbecue pits, an older-style playground with swings and slides, a horseshoe pit (bring your own equipment), and a dirt/sand volleyball court. A seasonal creek meanders throughout the park. A short hiking trail leads visitors up a hillside to an overlook gazebo. Longer hiking and equestrian trails can also be accessed through the park. Next door is the Oak Creek Equestrian Center/Therapeutic Riding Academy which leads riders into the Los Padres National Forest.

Hours: Open daily, 8am - sunset.
Admission: Free
Ages: All

WALLER PARK

(805) 934-6211 / www.sbparks.com
300 Goodwin Road, Santa Maria
(From Orcutt Exwy [135], enter the park via Goodwin Rd., or by turning onto Waller Lane and immediately onto Frontage Rd. [TG: 816 G1])

Waller Park, located at the south end of town, is 153 acres big and almost bursting with fun things to do. It has two small lakes with fountains in them (and a few rocks that my boys climbed on), several parcels of grassy lawns to run around on, shady picnic areas, a few playgrounds, basketball and volleyball courts, a frisbee disc golf course towards the main entrance, softball fields, barbecue grills, horseshoe pits, pony rides that are open weekends only, numerous picnic tables, plenty of trees, and bike trails that branch off throughout the park. We ran, ate, and played here, making a full day of it. Note that the YMCA SKATEBOARD PARK (see pg. 494), just off Skyway Drive, is right next door to Waller Park.

Woof-Pac Park, a fenced-off part of Waller Park, is a place for off-leash dogs to race around, sniff, and make new friends. This park is subdivided into enclosed sections for large dogs and a section for smaller dogs.

Hours: Open daily, 8am - sunset.
Admission: Free
Ages: All

YMCA SKATEBOARD PARK

(805) 937-8521 or (805) 937-5855 / www.smvymca.org
3400 Skyway Drive, Santa Maria
(Going S. on El Camino Real [101], exit W on Betteravia Rd., L. on Orcutt Exwy [135] R. on Skyway Dr. Going N. on 101, exit W. on Santa Maria Way, L. on Bradley Rd., R. on Lakeview Rd. which turns into Skyway. [TG: 816 G1])

Dude - this 15,000 square-foot skate park, adjacent to the YMCA and located right next to WALLER PARK, is really cool. It features ramps, including a vertical ramp, plus quarter pipes, and half pipes, as well as rails, jumps, and hills. A sound system is piped in. There is also an area just for beginners to learn the tricks of the trade. The park is supervised. A parental waiver must be on file and a helmet and pads are required.

Hours: Open Mon. - Fri., 3pm - 8pm; Sat., 10am - 7pm; Sun., 1pm - 7pm.
Admission: $10 per day.
Ages: 7 years and up.

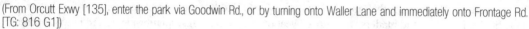

-----MUSEUMS-----

CARPINTERIA VALLEY MUSEUM OF HISTORY

(805) 684-3112
956 Maple Avenue, Carpinteria
(Exit El Camino Real Fwy [101] S. on Casitas Pass Rd., R. on Carpinteria Ave., L. on Maple. [TG: 998 D7])

In the middle of Carpinteria's "downtown" area is this surprisingly fine historical museum. One long room is separated into smaller rooms that house steamer trunks and pictures of old Carpinteria; old dolls and toys; a living room with furniture, plus a melodeon, spindle, phonograph, and sweeper broom (i.e. an early-day vacuum cleaner); Chumash arrowheads, baskets, and several stone mortar and pestles; a bedroom set; and saddles, chaps, and an adobe diorama.

One back room holds old machinery such as a collection of typewriters and cameras, plus a piano and a butterfly collection. Another small section displays an apple press, washboard, water pump, and wall murals.

Warning to the faint-hearted - if you stomp on the platform in this particular area, or clap your hands, the fake rat in the rattrap will twitch!

The museum also contains life-size cutouts of people dressed in period clothing, a stagecoach, an early Ford, and a small classroom with desks, books, slate boards, and a blackboard. A kitchen scenario holds implements such as a butter churn, dishes, and a stove. An adjacent workshop area has old tools and a walnut huller. Outside in the courtyard is an open grassy area, a few old pieces of old farm equipment, and a stagecoach. Walk around the museum on your own or ask about taking a guided tour. Ask about a calendar of events as the museum is host to numerous community events throughout the year.

Hours: Open Tues. - Sat., 1pm - 4pm
Admission: Free
Ages: 6 years and up.

THE CARRIAGE AND WESTERN ART MUSEUM

(805) 962-2353 / www.carriagemuseum.org
129 Castillo Street, Santa Barbara
(Exit El Camino Real Fwy [101] S. on Castillo St. into Pershing Park. [TG: 996 B5])

Almost hidden in a corner of the Pershing Park Ball Field are treasures from California's early golden days contained in the wood and brick building called the Carriage and Western Art Museum. Over seventy horse-drawn conveyances manufactured from 1850 to 1911 have been lovingly restored and are finely displayed. Many of the carriages, buggies, and wagons are used in August for the Old Spanish Days Parade (see pg. 591) during Santa Barbara's annual Fiesta Celebration. Some of our favorite vehicles include the Hearst carriage, a four-passenger pony runabout, the old fire wagons, surreys, and "typical" covered wagons.

The museum also displays spurs, bits, harnesses, whips, jackets, and a slew of ornately decorated saddles. Some of the more famous saddles include one that was a gift to Ronald Reagan for his 1981 inauguration; one that belonged to Clark Gable; another one owned by the Cisco kid; and another that was Will Rogers'. The room in the back also has a small stage/restaurant/bar area with western facades and neon signs.

Looking at the carriages was interesting, but taking a tour was more fascinating as we learned from the docent some of the history associated with them and with the equestrian paraphernalia.

The adjacent Pershing Park has several areas of open grassy fields, shade trees, ball fields, and eight tennis courts.

Hours: Open Mon. - Fri., 8am - 4pm to walk through on your own; Sun., 1pm - 4pm for a guided tour. Call to arrange for a group tour.
Admission: Free
Ages: 4 years and up.

CASA DE LA GUERRA

(805) 965-0093 / www.sbthp.org
15 East De La Guerra Street, Santa Barbara
(Going S. on El Camino Real [101], exit N.E. on Carillo St., R. on State St., L. on De La Guerra. Going N. on 101, exit N. on Garden St., L. on De La Guerra. [TG: 996 A4])

This historic adobe, originally built in the 1820's, is now a restored house museum. Once belonging to the commander of El Presidio, it features period rooms and special art. School tours are offered by reservation. The De la Guerra Plaza city park is in front of the Casa and plays host to many of the city festivals and events, such as Cinco de Mayo celebrations and a mercado (i.e. marketplace) during Old Spanish Days.

Hours: Open Thurs. - Sun., noon - 4pm.
Admission: Free; donations appreciated.
Ages: 6 years and up.

CASA DEL HERRERO

(805) 565-5653 / www.casadelherrero.com

1387 E. Valley Road, Montecito

(Exit El Camino Real Fwy [101] N. on San Ysidro Rd., L. on East Valley Rd. [TG: 996 J1])

Visit a bygone era when coming to this classy, Spanish-style house located in a residential neighborhood. It was completed in 1925 and shows heavy influences of Islamic and Moorish architecture. Colorful Mediterranean mosaic tiles are prevalent outside around the courtyard and inside the house as well. The foyer boasts of tapestries, ornate panels on the ceiling and walls, and church pews for seats. The house is noted for its 13th- to 18th- century Spanish furniture. The living room contains red velvet furniture, pictures, and an early stereo. Walk through the smallish kitchen, bathrooms, formal dining room, enclosed porch with a garden view, and decorative bedrooms. The children's bedrooms have beds, trunks, gold mirrors, and clocks. Look at the sculptures, wood-carved doors and furniture, fireplaces with tiles, and other fine details throughout the two-story house.

The seven acres of cultivated gardens are meticulously groomed and designed in a Moorish fashion. Go through garden gates and an archway that looks like it leads to a secret garden. Take a walk past a rose garden, a little pond, a sundial, a camellia garden, an herb garden, a Spanish patio, and even orange orchards. The tour guide explains the layout of the gardens, the types of plants, and the entertaining that was once done here.

The owner was a blacksmith and his workshop is probably one of the most intriguing stops on the tour for kids. It is filled with his tools, plus workbenches, a casting furnace, forge, and anvils. My boys' fingers were itching to try out, or at least touch, the tools.

A ninety-minute tour includes forty-five minutes inside and forty-five minutes outside in the gardens. Note that the rooms are small and groups cannot be comprised of more than ten people. Note, too, that the parking lot only holds seven cars. Reservations are required.

Hours: Tours are offered February through November, Wed. and Sat. at 10am and 2pm.

Admission: $15 per person.

Ages: Children must be at least 10 years old.

EL PRESIDIO DE SANTA BARBARA STATE HISTORIC PARK

(805) 965-0093 / www.sbthp.org

123 East Canon Perdido Street, Santa Barbara

(Going S. on El Camino Real Fwy [101], exit N.E. Carillo St., R. on De La Vina, L. on Canon Perdido. Going N. on 101, exit N. on Garden St., L. on Canon Perdido. [TG: 996 A3])

Originally built in 1792 to protect the mission, the reconstructed presidio (i.e. military fort) was the last Spanish military outpost built in North America. I appreciated the kid's info kit that the docent handed us upon arrival. Take a walk through the courtyards and the buildings and look into the sparsely furnished commander's, padre's, and lieutenant's quarters. The fort also features a decorated chapel and bell tower. Across the street is El Cuartel, the guard's house, which is the second-oldest building in California! (For the oldest building, look up page 242.) Ask about the special events and educational programs offered here throughout the year.

Hours: Open daily, 10:30am - 4:30pm. Closed major holidays.

Admission: Free

Ages: 6 years and up.

ELVERHOJ MUSEUM

(805) 686-1211 / www.elverhoj.org

1624 Elverhoy Way, Solvang

(From El Camino Real Fwy [101] exit R. on Hwy 246/Mission Drive, S. on 2nd St., R. on Elverhoy. From Santa Barbara, exit Hwy 101 N. on San Marcos Pass/Hwy 154, L. on Hwy 246/Mission Dr., L. on 2nd St., R. on Elverhoy. [TG: 940 E1])

This quaint museum is tucked away amongst residential houses near the main shopping areas of Solvang. Built in 18th-century Danish-farmhouse style, the inside displays also depict this culture and time period.

The lobby holds a traveling desk and a sample of the red Danish national costume. The country kitchen is designed with typically simple lines and folk paintings. The Early Room contains clogs, shoes made of reeds, thatch (i.e the plant used for roofs), dresses, a spinning wheel, and furniture. The parlor, or Best Room, features Danish costumes in a display case and furniture from an 1890's Danish farmhouse. Other rooms feature a children's canopy bed with a wonderful dollhouse, and clothing such as a colorful red postman's uniform and a naval officer's uniform. The other wing of the house contains a small art gallery.

On occasion, docents demonstrate a traditional craft from the old country, such as lace making or paper cutting. Guided tours are available by request.

Hours:	Open Wed. - Sun., 1pm - 4pm.
Admission:	Free; a donation of $2 per adult is suggested.
Ages:	8 years and up.

FABING-MCKAY-SPANNE HISTORICAL MUSEUM

$

(805) 735-4626 / www.store.yahoo.com/lompoc/lomhissoc.html
207 North 'L' Street, Lompoc
(Exit Ocean Ave [1] N. on 'L' St. [TG: 916 D1])

This fully-restored, two-story, wooden Victorian residence was originally built in 1875. It is furnished with items from that era and open for tours. Adjacent to the home is a carriage house, blacksmith shop, and a museum room.

Hours:	Open Mon. and Thurs., 9am - 11am; the fourth Sun., 1pm - 4pm. It's closed the month of December.
Admission:	Call for prices.
Ages:	8 years and up.

FERNALD MANSION / TRUSSELL-WINCHESTER ADOBE

$

(805) 966-1601
414 W. Montecito Street, Santa Barbara
(Exit El Camino Real Fwy [101] S. on Castillo, R. on Montecito. [TG: 996 B5])

These small, historic homes played an important role in Santa Barbara's history and are worth a look-through. The fourteen-room, Queen Anne-style house, called Fernald Mansion, was constructed in 1862 for Judge Fernald. It contains original furnishings from the nineteenth-century. Although there is not a lot of maneuverability, the forty-five-minute tour will take you through the living room, kitchen, music room with its harp at the ready, up the curved wooden staircase to the bedrooms and the bathrooms.

Next door is the adobe, built in 1854, which was constructed with timbers from a shipwreck. It contains items salvaged from a sea captain's ship and other furnishings. Note that the museum/homes are located in a residential district.

Hours:	Tours are offered Sun. at 2pm and 3pm. Closed New Year's Day and Christmas.
Admission:	$3 for adults; $1 for ages 12 and under.
Ages:	10 years and up.

HANS CHRISTIAN ANDERSEN MUSEUM / BOOK LOFT & KAFFE HUS

!

(805) 688-6010 - book store/museum; (805) 686-9970 - kaffe hus / www.bookloftsolvang.com
1680 Mission Drive, Solvang
(Exit El Camino Real Fwy [101] E. on Hwy 246/Mission Dr. [TG: 940 E1])

Fairytale favorites such as *The Steadfast Tin Soldier*, *The Ugly Duckling*, *Little Mermaid*, *Thumbelina*, *The Emperor's New Clothes*, and *The Princess and the Pea* were all penned by Hans Christian Andersen. This very small museum, located in the second story of Book Loft & Kaffe Hus, is dedicated to the Danish-born author. His books (including first and early editions), manuscripts, letters, paper cuttings (which he did for friends), a bust of Andersen, and pictures of him and of his birthplace, are on display. One glass case is dedicated entirely to the Little Mermaid. You might not be in the museum long, but it is a fun, sentimental adventure. Guided group tours are available by appointment.

The rest of the book store is a book lover's treat! The Book Loft sells both new and used books, as well as classics and rare editions. The children's section is delightful. Make sure to take a look at the small, working model of the Gutenberg Press. Adding to the charm of the store is the attached Kaffe Hus where you can sip a cup of coffee and/or enjoy a pastry.

Hours: The book store/museum is open Sun. - Mon., 9am - 6pm; Tues. - Thurs., 9am - 8pm; Fri. - Sat., 9am - 9pm. The hours might be shorter in the winter.

Admission: Free

Ages: 7 years and up.

KARPELES MANUSCRIPT LIBRARY MUSEUM

(805) 962-5322 / www.rain.org/~karpeles

21 West Anapamu, Santa Barbara

(Going S. on El Camino Real Fwy [101], exit N.E. Carillo St., L. on Chapala, R. on Anapamu. Going N. on 101, exit N. on Garden St., L. on Anapamu. [TG: 996 A4])

View actual pages of history at this museum which has millions of original documents in its archives, and several select ones on display. Each original document is enclosed in glass in a podium-like case, all artfully arranged throughout the museum. Each one also has a description of the contents, including the how, why, and when the document was written. Small busts of well-known people are also on display.

The exhibits rotate every three months. Each feature presentation on a particular person or topic focuses on about twenty-five, or so, documents. Past exhibits have included pages of Webster's dictionary; the final agreement from King Ferdinand and Queen Isabella regarding the New World and Columbus' voyage; scientific manuscripts of Galileo, Newton, and Einstein; and the surrender agreement of World War II. Most of the free pamphlets that correspond to and describe past exhibits also include an insert - a scaled down copy of an original manuscript. What a great teaching tool! One of the small permanent exhibits contains photocopied pages of sheet music from Beethoven, Handel, Mozart, Bach, and others, accompanied by that specific composer's bust. An encouraging observation for kids (and adults) is that those display manuscripts have cross outs, rewrites, or editing notes on them and that means the final, perfect-sounding draft doesn't come out perfect the first time around!

Ask about the Cultural Literacy Program for grades three up to college level, and other educational programs including on-site tours and off-site presentations. Note that there are seven other such Karpeles museums across the county.

Hours: Open daily, 10am - 4pm. Closed Christmas.

Admission: Free

Ages: 8 years and up.

LA PURISIMA MISSION STATE HISTORIC PARK

(805) 733-3713

2295 Purisima Road, Lompoc

See the entry for LA PURISIMA MISSION STATE HISTORIC PARK on page 488 for details.

MISSION SANTA BARBARA

(805) 682-4149 / www.sbmission.org

2201 Laguna Street, Santa Barbara

(Exit El Camino Real Fwy [101] N. on Mission St., which turns into Laguna St. - keep to the L. [TG: 995 J1])

Originally founded in 1786 this tenth mission, in the chain of twenty-one, is considered "Queen of the Missions" and has been occupied consistently by the Franciscan Order. The outside of the handsome mission has long been a favorite of photographers and painters, with its long front building and twin bell towers. Just outside, too, is a Moorish fountain, the basin of which was a lavanderia, used by Indian women to wash clothing.

Take a self-guided tour through the buildings that are open, where one room leads easily into the next.

Looking at glass-covered displays visitors see Chumash baskets and tools; a missionary's bedroom (with a tattered tall hat); religious portraits and sculptures; samples of weaving and candle making products; blacksmith's tools; and a kitchen with cookware and dishes. The chapel room contains an exhibit of ornate vestments and musical instruments, and offers a video about the history of the mission. Continue your tour outside through the garden courtyard and into the (still-active) mission church decorated with Mexican art. The door on the other side of the church leads to the cemetery, where early settlers and 4,000 Indians are buried. Juana Maria, the woman portrayed in the book *Island of the Blue Dolphins*, is also buried here. Guided tours of the mission are available for adult groups and school kids.

Just across the street is Mission Park, with its expanse of green grass and a good-size garden with a plethora of roses. Come for a picnic or to just relax, although that can be hard with little ones running around.

    Hours: Open daily, 9am - 5pm. Closed Easter, Thanksgiving, and Christmas.

Admission: $4 for adults; 11 years and under are free.

    Ages: 7 years and up.

MISSION SANTA INES

(805) 688-4815 / www.missionsantaines.org

1760 Mission Drive, Solvang

(Exit El Camino Real Fwy [101] E. on Hwy 246/Mission Dr. Or, exit San Marcos Pass/Hwy 154 W. on Hwy 246/Mission Dr. [TG: 940 F1])

Named in honor of Saint Agnes (the Spanish spelling is Ines), there are only a few rooms of the original mission building, which was completed in 1807, to tour through. Learn the history of the nineteenth mission (out of twenty-one) and its artifacts by pressing the seven push buttons that give a narration. The buttons are located throughout the building and the grounds.

The first room is the Vestment Room, which contains numerous ornate vestments from several centuries. Paintings adorn the walls. Walk to the second room that has a wall map of the Spanish Colonial Empire, a 19th-century confessional booth, and old mission bells. An adjoining room displays cases of old nails, candlesticks, pottery, holy implements, branding irons, Bibles, firearms, and stone mortars and pestles. Next are the Madonna Room and the adjacent church, which still holds mass on a regular basis administered by the Franciscan order. The church contains many of the original paintings and wall decorations.

The courtyard, laid out in the shape of a Celtic cross, contains a fountain and a large, lovely garden with grassy areas and a rose garden towards the back. The garden path leads to the mission's cemetery where 1,700 Indians are buried. Along a walkway on the side of the mission are the fourteen stations of the cross, each depicted by a wooden cross and picture of Christ. Note: This mission borders the quaint shopping district of Solvang, so you can combine a history lesson with a day of shopping!

    Hours: Open daily in the summer, 9am - 7pm; Open daily the rest of the year, 9am - 5:30pm. Closed Easter and Christmas.

Admission: $3 for adults; children 15 years and under are free.

    Ages: 6 years and up.

NATURAL HISTORY MUSEUM OF SANTA MARIA

(805) 614-0806

412 S. McClelland Street, Santa Maria

(Exit El Camino Real Fwy [101] W. on Main St., L. on Broadway, L. on Cook St., R. on McClelland. [TG: 796 H1])

This small museum houses a decent collection of natural history. It features copies of baleen whale bone, an eye-catching head cast of a T. Rex, a display case with a mastodon tusk and molar, some arrowheads, a mortar and pestle stone, a mounted buffalo head, and a replicated bat cave. A side room showcases a woodland diorama complete with stuffed animals such as owls, quails, a bear, fox, bobcat, and a deer head, plus the background "music" of animal sounds. The backroom contains taxidermied birds in flight overhead and a display case of sea shells, crab shells, and sea stars. The "please touch" table offers snake skin sheddings, bobcat fur, feathers, rocks, bird nests, and even a small black bear, who stands by the door. Ask about special family programs offered on selected Saturdays.

> **Hours:** Open Wed., noon - 3pm; Sat., 11am - 4pm. Tours are given by appointment.
> **Admission:** Free
> **Ages:** 3 years and up.

SANTA BARBARA HISTORICAL MUSEUM

(805) 966-1601 / www.sbthp.org
136 East De La Guerra Street, Santa Barbara
(Going S. on El Camino Real Fwy [101], exit N.E. Carillo St., R. on Anacapa, L. on De La Guerra. Going N. on 101, exit N. on Garden St., L. on De La Guerra. [TG: 996 A4])

This small, simple adobe museum complex offers a sampling of artifacts, photographs, furnishings, costumes, and fine art that represents Santa Barbara's rich multi-cultural history. One room features paintings of all twenty-one California missions. Walk through to the lovely courtyard that has a fountain and large, old pepper trees. The adjacent library contains rare literature, documents, and photographs. School and group tours are offered on request.

> **Hours:** Open Tues. - Sat., 10am - 5pm; Sun., noon - 5pm. Closed Mon. and holidays. Guided tours are
> offered on Wed., Sat., and Sun., at 1:30pm.
> **Admission:** Free
> **Ages:** 6 years and up.

SANTA BARBARA MARITIME MUSEUM

(805) 965-8864 or (805) 962-8404 / www.sbmm.org   *$$*
113 Harbor Way, Santa Barbara
(Exit El Camino Real Fwy [101] S. on Castillo St., R. on Shoreline Dr./Cabrillo Blvd., L. on Harbor Way. [TG: 996 B6])

On the waterfront, surrounded by restaurants and gift shops, is the Maritime Museum, a tribute to this area's maritime past that's worth *sea*ing. Outside the museum shop is a two-man submersible (not for those with claustrophobia) and a whaling cannon with a harpoon. Ask for a treasure map to aid the kids in hunting for certain items in the museum's collection.

Walk through the doors, under the mast head, into the two-story museum to be "greeted" by a "Jimsuit" - a one-person, incredibly heavy duty, atmospheric diving suit that looks like something from an old sci-fi movie. The first floor contains a Chumash plank canoe; an explorer's light up display to aid in learning about early explorers and their routes (great as a supplement to California studies); and displays on otter and seal hunting, and whaling. Feel otter pelts, wool, and the hides of cattle. Lift up flaps to see and smell trade spices. Other exhibits include model boats of various sizes, diving helmets, a board showing various types of knots, and several ships' parts, such as a propeller, wheel, and lantern. The kids' area has computers, craft supplies, and video monitors.

Upstairs, contained within the replicated hull of a schooner, is an eighty-six-seat theater which presents a continuous series of films regarding El Nino, yachting, octopuses, tides and currents, sea otters, and sailing around Cape Horn. Check the schedule for show times. More model boats - ranging from a royal barge from China to a Grecian fishing boat to an Inuit canoe - and a display of outboard motors share space with interactive exhibits such as lifting weights with the block and pulley system. Look through a working U.S. Navy periscope to see the ocean, beach, harbor, and houses. Learn Morse Code by operating signal lamps in a coded sequence of flashes and signal flags.

The best exhibit in this ever-expanding museum is the sportfishing chair. Sit down, grab onto the stationary fishing pole, and, from the screen, choose the type of fish you are hoping to land. (Hint - read the instructions first.) The salmon, barracuda, marlin, tuna, or bass you choose shows like a movie clip on screen as the fishing pole in your hands starts really jerking around. Reeling in the big one, tension and all, feels very real!

More interactive displays are in the works, including operating a remote-controlled submarine through a tank of water; "hard hat diving," which allows visitors a simulated diving experience; and viewing real underwater shipwrecks to conduct virtual underwater archaeology. What fun! The museum also offers activities for kids, such as singing sea chanteys and learning how to tie knots, plus classes and tours for children and adults, and outreach programs. Also see SANTA BARBARA HARBOR / STEARNS WHARF (pg. 507) for more things to do in this immediate area.

Hours: Open Memorial Day through Labor Day daily, 11am - 6pm. Open the rest of the year, Thurs. - Tues., 11am - 5pm. Closed Wed. and major holidays.

Admission: $5 for adults; $3 for seniors, students, and ages 6 - 17; $1 for ages 1 - 5 years; children under 1 year are free. The third Thurs. of every month is free admission. Parking is $2 for 3 hours.

Ages: 3 years and up.

SANTA BARBARA MUSEUM OF ART

$$$

(805) 963-4364 / www.sbmuseart.org

1130 State Street, Santa Barbara

(Going S. on El Camino Real Fwy [101], exit N.E. Carillo St., L. on State St. Going N. on 101, exit N. on Garden St., L. on Anapamu. Park wherever you can near State St. Try parking on Anacapa, the back side of the museum. [TG: 996 A3])

The colorful outside museum mural was painted by the world-renowned Mexican artist, David Alfaro Siqueiros. Degas, Matisse, Monet, Picasso, Dali, O'Keeffe, and Chagall all make appearances inside this museum of fine art, as do other masters. A diverse collection of American, 19th-century European, Latin American, and Asian artwork decorate its walls and halls. The museum also features modern art, photography exhibits, and ancient Greek, Roman, and Egyptian sculptures. Ask for a children's activity sheet upon entering the museum because the more that kids are involved with the art in whatever capacity, the more they will remember. Downstairs is a small, children's gallery featuring rotating artwork and a chance for some hands-on drawing, craft, or other activity.

Take the time to stroll the galleries on your own, or join a free, guided gallery talk usually offered at noon and at 1pm. Age-appropriate guided tours for school kids and other groups are offered by reservation. Family days, studio art classes, workshops, holiday camps, and outreach programs are just a few of the museum's other features. A cafe is also on the premises.

Hours: Open Tues. - Sat., 11am - 5pm; Fri., 11am - 9pm; Sun., noon - 5pm. Closed Mon. and major holidays.

Admission: $7 for adults; $5 for seniors; $4 for students and ages 6 - 17; children 5 years and under are free. Admission is free every Thurs. and the first Sun. of every month.

Ages: 6 years and up.

SANTA BARBARA NATURAL HISTORY MUSEUM

$$

(805) 682-4711 / www.sbnature.org

2559 Puesta del Sol Road, Santa Barbara

(Exit El Camino Real Fwy [101] N. on Mission St., which turns into Laguna St. Go R. on Mission Canyon, past Mission Santa Barbara - stay L. as the road forks. Turn L. on Las Encinas, L. on Puesta Del Sol. [TG: 995 J1])

Outside this mid-sized adobe-styled museum that's nestled into a woodland area, is a seventy-two-foot blue whale skeleton. Inside, the museum has sections devoted to geology, paleontology, native wildlife, marine life, and the culture of the Chumash Indians.

The Lizard Lounge contains small enclosures with live animals such as lizards, of course, various snakes (including rattlesnakes), and a few turtles. We liked the X-ray of the snake that swallowed light bulbs. The marine building has large dry aquariums showcasing fake fish suspended in air, plus coral, kelp, and other sea life in their "natural" habitats. Other stuffed sea creatures and models include sharks, batrays, octopus, lobsters, jellyfish, sponges, and a Japanese Giant Squid that is hanging up overhead. There is also a preserved giant squid in this room.

The paleontology/geology rooms hold skeletons of pygmy mammoths, bones of other mammoths and mastodons, a jawbone of a giant toothed whale, several fossils, and a case of rocks and minerals. The Chumash Life displays include dioramas of Indian life, baskets, and tools. The Fleischmann Hall features wonderful changing exhibits such as "Dinosaurs, the Next Generation."

Thousands of pinned butterflies, moths, bees, flies, grasshoppers, and other insects are on display at the insect and plant room. Inquisitive kids can lift panels to find answers to questions. See a termite colony, look at realistic-looking plants and flowers in diorama settings behind glass, and watch short films about ecological interactions in here also.

The mammal hall showcases taxidermied animals in natural poses. The collection includes sea lions, tule elk, bats, a grizzly bear, opossum, mountain lion, raccoon, gray wolf, and several more creatures. The bird habitats room contains numerous stuffed birds in "flight" such as a California condor with its nine-foot wingspan. Other birds in here include a barn owl with its babies, brown pelicans, orioles, cranes, a golden eagle, and several species of shore birds. An art gallery and library are also located in this section of the museum.

Towards the back of the museum is the Space Lab where visitors can test their knowledge of stars, planets, and constellations by pushing buttons to match up the picture with the name of the celestial object. Watch NASA TV that features lift-off to landing coverage of space shuttle missions, as well as frequent live coverage on board the International Space Station. Touch a meteor; observe the swinging Foucault Pendulum, which demonstrates the Earth's rotation in motion; look at a fiberoptic model of the solar system; and check out the camera obscura.

The adjacent fifty-five-seat planetarium features forty-minute, or so, programs on the evening sky, as well as specialty programs for young children. Come at a scheduled show time or book a time for a group field trip. Observe the stars for real at the Palmer Observatory. Join the astronomy club or just join them in star gazing.

The backyard of the museum, the nature center, is pretty oak woodland with the Mission Creek running through it. Climb in a replica wooden Indian boat; gaze at a few redwoods; watch out for poison oak; enjoy a presentation at the outdoor amphitheater; eat lunch or a snack at the picnic tables; and/or take a short hike on a trail that actually leaves the museum property. Ask about "discovery" backpacks filled with equipment and printed information that enable children to get the most out of understanding their environment.

A variety of one-hour thematic guided tours are available for school groups, grades K through 8, for up to thirty students. Discovery Labs, for grades 3 through 6, incorporate hands-on activities with a guided tour. Traveling astronomy and Audubon Society programs and presentations are available to come to the facility of your choice. Waves on Wheels (i.e. W.O.W. - see page 561) is another traveling program. Other programs and special exhibitions at the museum often incorporate themed activities for the family. Guided tours for the general public are offered Fridays, Saturdays, and Sundays at 2pm. Note: The museum's satellite facility is the SEA CENTER (pg. 505), located on STEARNS WHARF (pg. 507).

Hours: Open daily, 10am - 5pm. Closed New Year's Day, Thanksgiving, and Christmas. Planetarium shows are offered Wed. at 3pm; Sat., 2pm and 3pm; Sun., 1pm, 2pm, and 3pm. The *Magic Sky* show, geared for ages 4 to 7, is shown Sat. at 11am. School planetarium shows are offered October through June, Tues. through Fri. at 10am and 11am, by reservation. Star parties at the observatory, where visitors observe stars and planets through telescopes, are offered the second Sat., 8:30pm - 10pm.

Admission: $6 for adults; $5 for seniors; $4 for ages 2 - 12. Admission is free on the last Sun. of each month. Guided tours and Discovery Labs are $50 per thirty students. Planetarium admission is $3 for adults; $2 for ages 12 and under, with paid admission to the museum. Admission to the Palmer Observatory for star parties is $2 for adults; $1 for ages 12 and under.

Ages: 3 years and up.

SANTA MARIA MUSEUM OF FLIGHT

(805) 922-8758 / www.smmof.org

3015 Airpark Drive, Santa Maria

(Going S. on El Camino Real [101], exit W on Betteravia Rd, L. on Orcutt Exwy [135] R. on Skyway Dr. Going N. on 101, exit W. on Santa Maria Way, L. on Bradley Rd., R. on Lakeview Rd. which turns into Skyway. From Skyway Dr. go L. on Hangar St., R. on Airpark Dr. [TG: 796 F7])

Ready to take off to a place where the sky's the limit? This fine museum fills two hangars with small aircraft and flying memorabilia - one specializing in pre-WWII artifacts; the other from WWII to present day.

Upon entering, attention is riveted on the bright red plane, a "Hunt Special," featured in the movie *Rocketeer*. A 1931 "Great Lakes" model 2T1A was built for aerobatics. Overhead is a replica of the Wright Brothers' glider, as well as a collection of radio control planes. The hangar also contains dioramas of aviation history, a library of books and videos on aviation, model planes in display cases, a WWI gas mask, a skeleton plane that shows the inner workings of a radio control plane, and a well-stocked gift shop.

Outside, between hangars, is a Vietnam War era Huey helicopter to climb into and try your hand at "flying." Miscellaneous parts of space rockets and a missile launcher, as well as a few small planes, such as the F4 Phantom Fighter and Midway Carrier, are grounded here too. This is also a prime spot to watch small planes take off and land.

The second hangar contains a few ejection seats (that look used), a small mock up of a space ship launch, one of the few Norden bombsights still around, inert missiles, an army truck with a few non-working machine gun mounts, a 1916 Howitzer, a 1941 German trainer plane, and a working Link Trainer, which is a vintage instrument flight trainer/early simulator. The hangar also holds WWII displays, such as uniforms, and airplane pieces, such as propellers and engines.

Hour-long, guided, age-appropriate tours of the museum are offered for school-age kids. The minimum number of students needed is fifteen; the maximum, twenty-five. Note: Ask about the YOUNG EAGLES PROGRAM (Santa Maria) (see pg. 521) offered through the adjacent airport and the annual Classic Aircraft and Warbird Fly In (see pg. 598), usually held in September.

Hours: Open Fri. - Sun., 10am - 4pm.

Admission: $5 for adults; $4 for seniors; $3 for ages 12 - 18; $1 for ages 6 -11; children 5 years and under are free.

Ages: 5 years and up.

SANTA MARIA VALLEY DISCOVERY MUSEUM

(805) 928-8414 / www.discoverymuseumsantamaria.org

321 Town Center West, Santa Maria

(Exit El Camino Real Fwy [101] W. on Main St., L. on Broadway, R. into the first parking lot. It's currently near the Mervyn's shopping center. [TG: 776 G7])

There is so much for kids to discover at the hands-on Discovery Museum! The murals in this large room are wonderful and each theme or "station" has lots for young 'uns to do. My boys' favorite was the nautical area. Go up the front part of a yacht via a wooden gangplank. On board are microscopes and slides, life jackets, and maritime flag magnets with morse code apparatus. All this is enhanced by piped in sounds of waves crashing and seagulls calling. Discover the depths of the sea by crawling underneath the ship through a few "ocean tunnels" that show displays of a kelp forest and sea creatures, including sharks. Play with a bucket and shovel in the adjacent sand pit.

Gently swing a board, hanging by cables, that has attached markers over a large piece of paper to create an abstract design. Other activities include climbing on board a real tractor; transplanting your own seedling; looking at live guinea pigs, tarantulas, scorpions, iguanas, and Madagascar hissing cockroaches; peering through a microscope; putting together a puzzle; expressing oneself with a large metal board and word magnets; listening to a partner across the table talk into a microphone that delays speech (sounds like an overseas phone call); prancing in front of fun-house mirrors; creating a masterpiece at the art station; enjoying an impromptu play at the puppet theater; and much more. Sniff bottles filled with scents of cherries, peanuts, or vinegar and lifting attached flaps to see if you guessed the smells correctly. There is also a coin exhibit, a big table maze, and fun to be had with experiments. Toddlers have their own small play area with soft play toys. They also have an area set up like a pretend campfire with a tent and picnic table against a background mural of pine trees. The Discovery Museum offers classes, workshops, and school or group tours, too.

Hours: Open Tues. - Sat., 10am - 4pm; Sun., 1pm - 4pm. Closed Mon. and major holidays.

Admission: $4 per person; children 2 and under are free.

Ages: 1 - 11 years.

SANTA MARIA VALLEY HISTORICAL SOCIETY MUSEUM

(805) 922-3130

616 S. Broadway Street, Santa Maria

(Exit El Camino Real Fwy [101] W. on Main St., L. on Broadway. [TG: 796 H1])

For a small museum, this one is packed with wonderful old memorabilia! Covering Chumash Indian culture and the mission rancho and pioneer periods, some of the exhibits include baskets; a nineteenth-century buggy; a representative classroom with a desk, books, and a copy of teacher's rules; old-fashioned telephone operator's equipment; a living room set; a saddle; brands; articles of clothing; hats; a music room with a piano and a mannequin dressed in period costume; and casts of saber tooth cat fossils found in the La Brea Tar Pits. Guided tours, offered by reservation, lend precious insight into the exhibits.

Hours: Open Tues. - Sat., noon - 5pm. Closed Sun and Mon.

Admission: Free

Ages: 6 years and up.

SANTA MARIA VALLEY RAILWAY HISTORICAL MUSEUM

(805) 714-4927 / www.smvrhm.org

Town Center Mall #387, Santa Maria

(Exit El Camino Real Fwy [101] W. on Main St., L. on Broadway. It's on the 2nd floor of the mall near Robinsons-May. [TG: 776 H7])

If you're visiting the mall, this small museum is a quick stop off for railroad buffs. The window display layout has a working model train that travels past mini mountains, canyons, and a city. The back room has a few items of train paraphernalia in display cases such as Lionel O Gauge cars that date back to 1925, different size rails, and photographs depicting railroad operations in Santa Maria. A side room contains tables and tools for works in progress.

Hours: Open Sat. - Sun., 1pm - 4:30pm.

Admission: Free

Ages: 3 years and up.

SANTA YNEZ VALLEY HISTORICAL SOCIETY MUSEUM and PARKS-JANEWAY CARRIAGE HOUSE

(805) 688-7889 / www.santaynezvalleymuseum.org

3596 Sagunto Street, Santa Ynez

(Exit El Camino Real Fwy [101] E. on Hwy 246/Mission Drive, L. on Edison St., L. on Cuesta St., R. on Cuesta St. (they intersect), L. on Sagunto. [TG: 921 B5])

Go west, young man! On the main street of Santa Ynez, with its western-looking storefronts, dwells a vintage museum. Comprised of a small complex of buildings, the museum offers all that the Old West time period held dear.

The lobby contains a nice display of Native American baskets, pottery, and stone mortars and pestles, plus samples of beadwork and shell bead money. The adjacent West Room showcases wonderful collections of spurs, bridles, saddles, branding irons, chaps, barbed wire, riata (i.e. rope made of rawhide), and guns, as well as a stuffed golden eagle and a mounted boar's head.

Meander outside to the center courtyard where a fountain and a shady arbor with picnic tables invites visitors to sit and relax a spell. The next series of rooms form a u-shape around the courtyard. First stop is the Pioneer Room, which is divided into three sections - a kitchen, bedroom, and parlor-living room - all furnished with items from the late nineteenth century. Walk through to see butter molds and churns, an old-fashioned store, an 1847 sleigh bed, a crib, quilts, a treadle sewing machine, and an organ. The next room features changing displays of period clothing and accessories. We saw elegantly arranged, off-white wedding gowns, along with ornately beaded hand bags. The adjoining Valley Room's changing exhibits highlight the five small, nearby town's beginnings and early development. The exhibits include historical and cultural artifacts, and photos. Just behind the Valley Room is the Farm Annex, which boasts of farm vehicles such as horse-drawn farm machinery, a 1907 Harvester pickup truck, an early McCormick-Deering tractor, and a 1903 automobile. Forge ahead to look at the complete blacksmith shop also located back here.

Across the courtyard is the fascinating carriage house. Enter this large room and stroll down the streets of time as you admire the over thirty-five carriages parked here. Our favorites include the hunt wagons; a Goddard Buggy; a military supply wagon; the basket-style governesses' carts; surreys; stagecoaches; a still-functioning 1906 popcorn wagon; a hearse; a hitch wagon; a 1927 Model T school bus; and a fancifully-painted donkey cart from Sicily. O.K. - we like them all! There are also some saddles, bits, bridles, and other equestrian gear on display.

Guided tours that allow visitors to gain insight to the memorabilia and time period are available with advanced reservations. Note that the Santa Ynez County Park is just down the street, south on Cuesta Street. This small park offers a few pieces of play equipment, a volleyball court, a softball field, horseshoe pits, some trees, grass, and picnic tables.

Hours: Open Wed. - Sun., 12pm - 4pm.

Admission: Free; suggested donations are $3 for adults; children 15 and under free.

Ages: 6 years and up.

SEA CENTER

(805) 682-4711 / www.sbnature.org

W. Cabrillo Boulevard on Stearns Wharf, Santa Barbara

(Going N. on El Camino Real Fwy [101], exit S. on Garden St., R. on Cabrillo Blvd. Going S. on El Camino Real Fwy [101], exit S. on Castillo St., L. on Cabrillo. [TG: 996 C5])

Scheduled to reopen in summer 2004, the Sea Center, which is a satellite of Santa Barbara Natural History Museum, will really add to the *see*worthiness of the wharf. Life-sized models of a California gray whale and her calf will hang from the ceiling. With the look of a working marine laboratory and through models, aquarium tanks, and touch tanks filled with sea stars, sea anemones, and urchins, visitors will acquire a deeper understanding of local marine life. Marine biologists will be on hand to explain to individuals who visit, as well as to classes, how to study fish and ways to preserve our oceans. Look up SANTA BARBARA HARBOR / STEARNS WHARF (see pg. 507) for details of the immediate area.

Hours: Call for information.

Admission: Call for information.

Ages: 4 years and up.

SOLVANG MOTORCYCLE MUSEUM

(805) 686-9522 / www.motosolvang.com

320 Alisal Road, Solvang

(From El Camino Real Fwy [101] exit R. on Hwy 246/Mission Drive, S. on Alisal Rd. From Santa Barbara, exit Hwy 101 N. on San Marcos Pass/Hwy 154, L. on Hwy 246/Mission Dr., S. on Alisal. It's near the Royal Scandinavian Inn. [TG: 940 E1])

Over sixty vintage, rare, and classic motorcycles in excellent condition are lined up on the showroom floor, seemingly ready to roar to life. Each beautifully restored vehicle has an accompanying description of its make and history. This eclectic private collection ranges from a 1901 NSU to a 1989 custom Harley - the emphasis is on racing motorcycles.

Some of the extra special bikes include an MV Agusta, Brough Superior, 1936 Nimbus sidecar, 1960 Jawa Factory Racer, 1949 Vincent Black Lightning - Supercharged, 1950 Vincent TT Grey Flash (one of four ever made), and 1946 Indian Chief - a classic with fringe on the seat. Note that the museum rotates the bike on exhibit. The museum also has a replica of the first combustion automobile ever built.

Hours: Open Sat. - Sun., 11am - 5pm, or by appointment during the week.

Admission: $5 for adults; children 10 years and under are free when accompanied by an adult.

Ages: 6 years and up.

SOUTH COAST RAILROAD MUSEUM

(805) 964-3540 / www.goletadepot.org
300 North Los Carneros Road, Goleta
(Exit El Camino Real Fwy [101] N. on Los Carneros Rd. [TG: 994 B1])

Engineer some time for the kids to *conduct* their way to the railroad museum. Here you can walk through an old caboose still on the tracks. In a small room at the 1901 depot building watch a model train making tracks through mountains, over a cut-away bridge, and even past a mini circus. The depot waiting room features an old stove, trunks, and a motor car indicator - a signaling device that warned maintenance crews that a train was coming. You can also see a short slide show about the Goleta Depot project. Look into the ticket office which has several pieces of old equipment still in place and into the freight office with its roll-top desk, candlestick phone, and scale. Documentaries, travel films, and a for-the-fun-of-it show pertaining to the railroad are offered for free on Thursday and Sunday afternoons. Call for times.

The highlight of a child's trip here is the seven-minute train ride, of course. The miniature train chugs its way around the depot grounds, past the picnic tables and scattered trees. Riders must be at least 34" tall.

Many special events are held here throughout the year. School and youth group tours include a free ride on the train. Note that the railroad museum is located right next to the STOW HOUSE MUSEUM (see pg. 506) and is in LAKE LOS CARNEROS COUNTY PARK (see pg. 487).

  Hours: Open Wed. - Sun., 1pm - 4pm.
  Admission: Admission is free. Train rides are $1 per person; 2 rides for $1.50. Train rides are free on the first Fri. of each month, every Wed., and sometimes at other designated times - call first. Free handcar rides are offered on the third Sat. of each month.
  Ages: 3 to 14 years.

STOW HOUSE MUSEUM

(805) 964-4407 / www.goletahistory.org
304 N. Los Carneros Road, Goleta
(Exit El Camino Real Fwy [101] N. on Los Carneros Rd. [TG: 994 B1])

Woodsy surroundings and era-appropriate, landscaped grounds make this restored 1870's two-story Gothic Revival house seem as though it has never met up with modern times. I love the porch that practically encircles the huge white house. A one-hour tour through the home enables guests to see period furnishings, clothing, china, toys, kitchen gadgets, and a closer look at the architecture. Outside, notice the bench under the crossroad "street" signs made from horseshoes welded together.

The area behind Stow House is called the Sexton Museum. It is comprised of a variety of historic buildings such as a carriage house and a small maritime museum that features a few locally-found cannons. The horse stalls in this area contain farm equipment, a fire engine, a tack display, and a blacksmith shop filled with tools of the trade. On certain days there are blacksmith demonstrations, and visitors can purchase newly fashioned horseshoes (with their name engraved), wrought iron items, and more. The back farm yard contains old tractors, a variety of old-fashioned farm machinery, mining cars, and, most importantly, an outhouse.

Note that the Stow House shares land with the SOUTH COAST RAILROAD MUSEUM (see pg. 506) and LAKE LOS CARNEROS COUNTY PARK (see pg. 487). School and other groups may call to reserve tours during the week.

  Hours: Open Sat. - Sun. with tours of the house offered every half hour from 2pm to 3:30pm. The Sexton Museum is open for self-guided tours during these hours. Closed the month of January, Thanksgiving, Christmas, and rainy days.
  Admission: The Stow House is $3 for adults; ages 11 and under are free. School tours are $10 for the class. Adult tour groups pay the regular admission price.
  Ages: 6 years and up.

UNIVERSITY ART MUSEUM

(805) 893-7564 / www.uam.ucsb.edu
Ward Memorial Boulevard, Goleta
(Going S. on El Camino Real Fwy [101], exit S. at Los Carneros, L. on El Colegio, through the West Gate, R. on Ocean Rd. to parking lot 23. Going N. on 101, exit S. on Route 217/Ward Memorial Highway, through the East Gate, R. on University Rd. to parking lot 23. Follow walkway to Storke Tower - the museum is on the plaza. [TG: 994 B5])

This picturesque campus by the sea has many special features, such as Storke Tower, which is a 175-foot tower with a sixty-one bell carillon that sounds twice per hour. The campus art museum features works from the fifteenth through seventeenth centuries, Renaissance medals and plaques, and several architectural renderings. Other rotating exhibits consist of drawings and prints from Italian Masters; examples of Greek and Roman art; African sculpture; Native California baskets; and, mostly, works from the twentieth century, including photographs. Check the calendar of events as some exhibits appeal more to kids than others.

Guided tours are offered for school groups that include curriculum and, for elementary-aged children, an in-class art lesson as well. The maximum number of students is thirty-five.

Hours: Open Tues., noon - 8pm; Wed. - Sun., noon - 5pm. Closed Mon. and school holidays.
Admission: Free to the museum. Parking is $3 during the week; free after 5pm and on weekends.
Ages: 7 years and up.

WILDLING ART MUSEUM / LOS OLIVOS TOWN

(805) 688-1082 / www.wildlingmuseum.org
2329 Jonata Street, Los Olivos
(Exit El Camino Real Fwy [101] E. on Hwy 246/Mission Ave. L. on Alamo Pinata, which turns into Grand Ave., L. on Jonata. The museum is right behind Mattie's Tavern. [TG: 900 H5])

The Wildling Art Museum is a very small museum, noteworthy because it displays only art embodying America's wilderness (i.e animals, plants, topography, etc.) and because the curator (and other docents) are so willing to take visitors on a personal tour to explain each exhibit. School groups, too, benefit from learning about the background histories and artist's techniques of the rotating exhibits. Ask about classes that relate to art and nature.

The small town of Los Olivos is a haven for lovers of fine art. Many of the shops in town are art galleries, showcasing sculptures, paintings, jewelry, pottery, ceramics, and more. If your older child appreciates art, or is a budding artist, and is O.K. with not touching objects, this is an inspiring place to visit. We particularly enjoyed the outdoor sculpture garden at the Judith Hale Gallery on Grand Avenue.

Hours: The museum is open Wed. - Fri., 1pm - 5pm; Sat. - Sun., 11am - 5pm. Many of the galleries are open daily, 10am - 5pm. Some are only open Wed. - Sun., 11am - 5pm.
Admission: Free - both to the museum and the galleries.
Ages: 7 years and up.

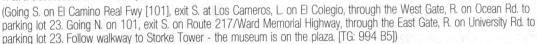

-----*PIERS AND SEAPORTS*-----

SANTA BARBARA HARBOR / STEARNS WHARF

(805) 564-5518 - Stearns Wharf; (805) 897-2683 - Harbor hotline;
(805) 966-6110 - Los Banos pool / www.stearnswharf.org; www.sbparksandrecreation.com
State Street and Cabrillo Boulevard, Santa Barbara
(Going N. on El Camino Real Fwy [101], exit S. on Garden St., R. on Cabrillo Blvd. Going S. on 101, exit S. on Castillo St., L. on Cabrillo. [TG: 996 C5])

This harbor is encompassed by long stretches of beach - from EAST BEACH (see pg. 475) to WEST BEACH (see pg. 477) to LEADBETTER BEACH (see pg. 477) - with a lot of fun in the sun in between. Walk or drive onto the wharf's creaky wooden planks. Originally built in 1872, the wharf features the SEA CENTER (see pg. 505); several restaurants - be sure to check out S.B. Shellfish Co. at the end because of its tanks of live lobsters and shellfish; and fun shops that sell shell-encrusted treasures, salt water taffy, and more. Fish from the pier, and during whale-watching seasons - late December through March for California gray whales and in the summer for the blue whales - be on the lookout for the mighty marine mammals.

Adjacent to the wharf is the harbor where yachts, commercial fishing boats, and sailboats are moored. Pick up fresh crabs and lobsters from the fishing boats on Market Day - Saturdays from 7:30am to 11:30am. More restaurants, shops, and the wonderful SANTA BARBARA MARITIME MUSEUM (see pg. 500) are also located here. This is the place to book a cruise, rent kayaks, go out whale watching on a boat, and check out other nautical excursions. See the Transportation section for specific places to contact.

Walk, skate, or bike along the waterfront paved path which extends for three miles. See BIKE TRAIL: CABRILLO BEACHWAY (pg. 516) for more information. This area is also home to a skate park (see SKATER'S POINT on page 493), art shows on the sidewalks every Sunday and on select Saturdays, a playground, and the Los Banos swimming pool. This fifty-meter municipal pool has a diving board. It is located at 401 Shoreline Drive, next door to the West Beach Wading Pool which has one-foot-deep water for kiddies. In this vicinity is the Cabrillo Pavilion Boathouse with showers, lockers, beach wheelchair rentals, and volleyball rentals. Across the street from the beach is the fabulous CHASE PALM PARK (see pg. 484).

Getting around from State Street to the wharf to the zoo is easy on the Waterfront Shuttle. It operates daily from 10:15am to 6pm and costs 25¢ for adults; children 4 years and under are free. Also look under SANTA BARBARA OLD TOWN TROLLEY (see pg. 518), as the wharf is one of the many stops along the trolley's route.

Hours:	Open daily.
Admission:	There is limited street parking. On the east side of the beach, parking is $3 for the day; $1 an hour, with 2 hours free with validation closer to the Maritime Museum; and $1 an hour on the wharf, with 2 hours free with validation from a restaurant or store. Swimming at Los Banos pool is $3 for adults; $1 for ages 16 and under. The wading pool is free.
Ages:	All

-----POTPOURRI-----

CIRCUS VARGAS

See the entry for CIRCUS VARGAS on page 134 for details.

MURALS

(800) 240-0999 or (805) 736-4567 / www.lompoc.com
throughout the city, Lompoc
(Exit Ocean Ave. S. on I St. The chamber of commerce is located on 111 South I St. [TG: 916 E1])

Mural, mural on the wall, which is the fairest one of all? Lompoc, dubbed "City of Murals in the Valley of Flowers," combines the best of both of these elements, and more, in the over sixty murals gracing the buildings throughout the city. I thought I'd have to drag the kids to view the murals and consider it a quick art experience. While I did make them accompany me, they became enamored with the paintings - with the variety of scenes and collages, characters, time periods, locations, styles, colors, and even sizes. The murals depict flowers, portraits, rocket launches, an old-fashioned train depot, and much more. For a self-guided "tour," pick up a free murals project brochure from the chamber of commerce, then drive around to admire and appreciate this unique outdoor art exhibit. Note: See the Calendar entry for details about the Flower Fields and Festival (pg. 584) and combine these two attractions in one visit.

Hours:	The murals can be seen during any daylight hours. The chamber of commerce is open Mon. - Fri., 9am - 5pm.
Admission:	Free
Ages:	4 years and up.

PAUL NELSON AQUATIC CENTER / COMMUNITY YOUTH CENTER

(805) 925-0951 / www.ci.santa-maria.ca.us
516 McClelland Street, Santa Maria
(Exit El Camino Real Fwy [101] W. on Main St., L. on Broadway, L. on Cook St., R. on McClelland. [TG: 796 H1])

Enjoy year-round swimming at this huge pool with a diving board and a short twisting water slide. An adjacent shallow wading pool features a little frog slide and a large mushroom-shaped shower that elicits giggles from young children. Parents can relax pool side in lounge chairs. The field beyond the fence has a grass area with basketball courts and a baseball field.

The indoor community youth center, geared for Jr. and Sr. high schoolers, has pool tables, air hockey, a few arcade games, basketball courts, exercise equipment, and other activities.

Hours: The pool is open year round for lap swimming and June through August, daily, for recreational swimming from 12:30pm - 3:30pm. The community center is open daily - the mornings are for adults and kids, but kids have it exclusively in the afternoons (after 2:30pm) until closing.

Admission: Swimming is $2.50 for adults; $1.25 for ages 6 - 16; seniors and ages 5 and under are free. Ask about purchasing a pool pass. The community center is free.

Ages: 1 year and up.

SANTA BARBARA COUNTY COURTHOUSE

(805) 962-6464 - courthouse; (805) 681-5650 - gardens / www.sbparks.com
1100 Anacapa Street, Santa Barbara
(Going S. on El Camino Real Fwy [101], exit N.E. Carillo St., L. on Santa Barbara St. It's bound by the streets of Santa Barbara, Anapamu, Anacapa and Figueroa. Going N. on 101, exit N. on Garden St., L. on Anapamu. Park wherever you can. [TG: 995 A3])

The verdict is in - this magnificent, historic courthouse is one of the city's most fascinating places to tour. The grandiose building, designed in Spanish-Moorish architecture, and its elegant surrounding gardens take up a city block.

Walk around and through the palace-like building on your own to admire the outside fountain, archways, graceful curved staircases inside, ornately-carved doors, colorful mosaic tiles, unusual iron and glass hanging lanterns, paintings, and decorative floors, walls, and ceilings. Note that the Courthouse is still used for trials and houses civic offices.

The free, forty-five-minute guided tour is a terrific option as the guide explains the history of California, particularly Santa Barbara, and the history of the Courthouse, including the explanations of the various artistic styles used throughout, especially the Muslim influence. The tour begins in the beautiful mural room, so nicknamed because the walls are covered with murals depicting Chumash Indians, Cabrillo, California under Mexican rule, the building of the mission, and the beginning of the California/American era. Make sure to look at the fancy ceiling beams. Meetings are still held in here. Going into the law library with its painted stars on the ceiling, then down massive hallways, and learning the meaning of the Latin inscriptions over the outside pointed archways are part of the tour, too. Other tour highlights (for us) included learning who Saint Barbara (the town's namesake) was; seeing, from across the courtyard, the jail and the solitary confinement quarters in a wing of the Courthouse; and looking at the stained glass window in the lobby. Note that parts of the tour incorporate walking in and out of the building as well as up and down stairs. Some outside ramps and an inside elevator are available.

While here, take a ride eighty feet up in the elevator, walk up a few stairs, and out onto the balcony of the Courthouse clock tower for a wonderful, panoramic view of Santa Barbara. See the mountains, the ocean, and all the red-tiled roofs in the vicinity.

The meticulously landscaped sunken garden in the center courtyard has an expansive lawn and bordering bushes, trees, and flowers. It's a peaceful haven for a picnic, and a relaxing place to ponder.

Hours: The Courthouse is open Mon. - Fri., 8am - 4:45pm; Sat. - Sun., 10am - 4:45pm. Closed Christmas. Tours are offered Mon., Tues., and Fri. at 10:30am, as well as Mon. - Sat. at 2pm.

Admission: Free

Ages: 8 years and up.

SANTA MARIA SPEEDWAY

$$$

(805) 922-2233 or (805) 466-4462 / www.santamariaspeedway.com
Hutton Road, Santa Maria
(Exit El Camino Real Fwy [101] W on Cuyama Hwy [166], R. on Hutton. [TG: 776 G1])

Factory stocks, street stocks, sprint cars, minis, and more take to the track here seasonally bringing excitement (and noise!) to spectators. The one-third mile clay surface oval track has a three-foot-high concrete crash wall encircling it and a row of trees at the ridgeline, behind the bleachers, that provide a natural windbreak.

Hours: April through October on Sat. nights the gates open at 4pm; qualifying is at 6pm; races are at 7pm.

Admission: $12 for adults; $10 for seniors; $3 for ages 6 - 12; children 5 and under are free.

Ages: 5 years and up.

SOLVANG

!/$$

(800) 468-6765 or (805) 688-6144 - visitor's center;
(805) 688-0091 - bike rentals. / www.solvangusa.com; www.solvangstreetcar.com
Mission Drive, Alisal Road, Atterdag Road, and Copenhagen Drive form the perimeters of the core of the village, Solvang
(Exit El Camino Real Fwy [101] E. on Hwy 246/Mission Dr. Note that the visitor's centers are located on the N.W. corner of Fifth St. and Mission Dr. and at 1639 Copenhagen Dr. [TG: 940 E1])

Velkommen! The word Solvang is Danish for "sunny field." This sunny field is now both an authentic Old World village and a tourist haven. Established in 1911, Solvang, which has become the Danish capitol of America, looks like a page out of one of Hans Christian Andersen's storybooks. Adults, and even kids, will notice and be enamored with the ethnic heritage and Scandinavian architecture including thatched roofs, colorful storefronts, window boxes filled with flowers, windmills, and decorative wood work. It truly is like being in a different world.

The over 300 antique shops, smorgasbords, clothing stores, bakeries, souvenir shops, cafes, cobbler shops, and restaurants are all within walking distance from one another. Browse the stores to look for unique gifts and collectibles such as cuckoo clocks, clogs, hand-crafted lace, glasswork, dolls, miniature ceramic windmills, family coat of arms, and lots more. Snack on an aebleskiver - a Danish pancake ball concoction made with powdered sugar and served with raspberry jam. Just a few of our favorite stops include Solvang Restaurant at 1672 Copenhagen Drive for great aebleskivers; Storybook Toys at 451 2nd Street for a choice selection of quality and educational toys; Ingebrog's Danish Chocolate at 1679 Copenhagen for delectable chocolates and rich ice cream; and the Book Loft at 1680 Mission Drive for new, used, and rare books. The bookstore is also host to the HANS CHRISTIAN ANDERSEN MUSEUM (see pg 497).

Besides driving and walking around the village, other modes of transportation include renting a tandem or two- to six-passenger surrey to pedal from Wheel Fun Rentals, 475 First Street, or taking a carriage ride. For the latter excursion, Belgian draft horses pull a replica 1915 Danish streetcar or "honen" (Danish for "hen") for twenty minutes through the heart of downtown Solvang. Carriages depart from the Visitor's Center on Copenhagen Drive.

Be on the lookout for the town's four windmills, the red and white Danish national flags, the half-scale model of Copenhagen's Little Mermaid (at the intersection of Mission and Alisal streets), and storks (not real ones) on roofs that are supposed to bring good luck. While in Solvang, you can also visit the ELVERHOJ MUSEUM (see pg. 496), the SOLVANG MOTORCYCLE MUSEUM (see pg. 505), PCPA THEATERFEST (see pg. 513) (during the summer only), and MISSION SANTA INES (see pg. 499). See the back of this book, under Index by City, for the numerous other nearby attractions besides just shopping and eating - although that works fine for our family! Also check the Calendar section for annual events. "Mange tak." (Many thanks.)

Hours: The shops are usually open daily, 10am - 6pm. The visitor's center is open Mon. - Fri., 10am - 4pm. Streetcars operate daily most of the year and weekends only in the wintertime.

Admission: Free entrance and parking to Solvang. Carriage rides are $3.50 for adults. Bike rentals run from $10 an hour for tandems to $25 an hour for six-passenger surreys.

Ages: All

-----*SHOWS AND THEATERS*-----

ARLINGTON THEATER AND CENTER FOR PERFORMING ARTS

(805) 963-4408   *$$$$$*

1317 State Street, Santa Barbara

(Exit El Camino Real Fwy [101] N. on Mission St., R. on State St. [TG: 996 A3])

Enter via a Spanish courtyard, through a lobby decorated with ceiling murals of fiesta dancers, and into the actual theater that was built to resemble a Spanish town, complete with elegant balconies and electronic "stars" twinkling overhead. The theater is home to the Santa Barbara Symphony which performs a repertoire of traditional choral and pops selections throughout the year, including the Classics and Family Series. It also plays host to Broadway performances, such as *Cats*. In between live shows, the theater shows first-run, blockbuster movies.

Hours: Call for specific dates and times.

Admission: Prices vary greatly depending on the show and date.

Ages: 8 years and up.

CIRCLE BAR B DINNER THEATER

(805) 965-9652 - dinner theater; (805) 968-3901 - horseback riding / www.circlebarb.com   *$$$$$*

1800 Refugio Road, Goleta

(Exit El Camino Real Fwy [101] near Refugio State Beach, N. on Refugio Rd., go about 3.5 miles up the canyon. [TG: 981 D3])

This rustic-looking, cabin-style dude ranch is tucked away in the middle of horse country in the mountains. The dinner theater, which is just a part of the ranch's offerings, presents three or four different performances a year that are often family-friendly. The shows are often musicals and are an hour-and-a-half long.

Guests eat outside on a patio overlooking the pool. (Bring a sweater in case it gets cool.) Menu selections include barbecue tri tip, Cornish game hen, or a veggie pasta, accompanied by rolls, salad, and dessert - all the fixin's. Bring your own beverage or order it here. After dinner, the group is then shepherded past the stables into the 100-seat Old Barn building that serves as the theater.

The ranch also offers horseback riding on trails that crisscross through nearly 1,000 acres of coastal countryside. Horseback riding costs $30 for an hour-and-a-half. Make a day of your outing by riding and then enjoying dinner and a show, or even spend the night!

Hours: The season runs April - November, with dinner starting Fri. at 7:15pm; Sat., 7pm; Sun., 1pm. The show begins one hour after meal times.

Admission: $35 for adults for dinner and show; $31 for seniors; children 6 years and under are free. If you are staying at the hotel, the cost is $11 just for the show.

Ages: 6 years and up.

ENSEMBLE THEATER COMPANY / ALHECAMA THEATER

(805) 962-8606 / www.ensembletheatre.com   *$$$$*

914 Santa Barbara Street, Santa Barbara

(Going S. on El Camino Real Fwy [101], exit N.E. Carillo St., R. on De La Vina, L. on Canon Perdido. Going N. on 101, exit N. on Garden St., R. on Canon Perdido. It's in Presidio State Park on Canon Perdido and Santa Barbara St. [TG: 996 B3])

This resident theater troupe performs about four plays or musicals a year in the intimate, 140-seat theater. At least one of the plays is family-appropriate. The Storybook Theater, which shares billing and production space at the theater, puts on two plays a year designed specifically for kids. Past play titles include *Snow White and the Seven Dwarfs* and *The Mask of Harlequin*.

Hours: Plays are performed on Tues. - Sat., at 8pm; Sun. at 2pm and sometimes at 7pm. Storybook Theater performs selected Sat. at noon and 2:30pm.

Admission: Plays range between $20 - $42, depending on the day, date, and time. Storybook performances are $9 for adults; $6 for ages 11 and under.

Ages: 5 years and up for plays; 2 - 11 years for Storybook performances.

THE GREAT AMERICAN MELODRAMA & VAUDEVILLE

(805) 489-2499 / www.americanmelodrama.com

1863 Pacific Boulevard Highway 1, Oceano

$$$$

(Exit El Camino Real Fwy [101] on Los Berros Rd./Oceano, L. on Los Berros, crossing under Hwy 101 about 5 miles, L. on Valley Rd. until it ends at Hwy 1, turn R. [TG: 714 E7])

For an evening of good old-fashioned, light-hearted family entertainment, come boo, hiss, and cheer for the villains and heros (and heroines), respectively. (Participation is a must!) The music clues the audience in - if they can't figure out for themselves - when to do these actions. Each silly storyline is accompanied by lots of music and singing.

Upbeat piano music greets you as soon as you enter through the doors to the melodrama, getting you in the mood for a rollicking good time. Chairs are crowded around small round tables on the sawdust-covered floor. Other seating is available on benches around the raised perimeter of the room. The setting is intimate enough that the actors perform on stage without microphones. The show starts off with a sing along - the words are printed in the newspaper playbill. The hour-and-a-half feature presentation is just plain fun for all ages. After the melodrama, enjoy the half-hour vaudeville revue, with its song, dance, and comedy routine.

During intermission, or before the main show, food and drinks are available from the servers, who are also the performers. The bill of fare includes hot dogs ($3), salad with chicken breast ($4.25), Polish sausage ($3.75), nachos with cheese ($2), popcorn ($1.50), and assorted candy ($1). Tip: If you are interested in getting dinner before you arrive, check out ROCK & ROLL DINER (see pg. 479) which is just down the street. Note: I know that this theater isn't in Santa Barbara County, but it's so close to the border and the format was too unique to pass up!

Hours: Show times are Wed. and Thurs., 7pm; Fri., 8pm; Sat., 4:30pm and 8:30pm; Sun., 6pm. Doors open a half hour before the show.

Admission: $13.50 - $16.50 for adults, depending on the time and seat; $12.50 - $15.50 for seniors; $3 discount for ages 12 and under. Prices are slightly higher for the Holiday Extravaganza. A $2 handling fee is charged for all phone reservations.

Ages: 5 years and up.

LOBERO THEATER

(805) 963-0761- box office; (805) 966-4946 - tours and other info. / www.lobero.com

33 E. Canon Perdido Street, Santa Barbara

$$$$

(Going S. on El Camino Real Fwy [101], exit N.E. Carillo St., R. on De La Vina, L. on Canon Perdido. Going N. on 101, exit N. on Garden St., L. on Canon Perdido. [TG: 996 A3])

The Lobero is quite a busy theater, as well as the one of the oldest California theaters in continuous operation. It hosts the STATE STREET BALLET (see pg. 513), West Coast Ballet (call [805] 687-6086 / www.wcballet.org for more information), Santa Barbara Chamber Orchestra, Santa Barbara Grand Opera, Sings Like Hell concert series, Speaking of Stories performance series, and everything else in between. Come see magic shows, ballet, concerts, dance programs, dramatic presentations, and other first-class performances. The theater also offers fifty-minute behind-the-scenes tours, by reservation only.

Hours: Call for performance schedules.

Admission: Tickets prices vary depending on show title and date.

Ages: Depends on performance.

PCPA THEATERFEST

(805) 928-7731; (800) 549-7272 or (805) 922-8313 - box office / www.pcpa.org

2 locations: Santa Maria - 800 S. College Drive at the Marian and Severson Theaters at the Allan Hancock College; Solvang - 420 2nd Street at the outdoor Festival Theater.

(Santa Maria: Going N. on El Camino Real Fwy [101], exit L. on Stowell Rd., R. on Bradley, L. into the campus parking lot, then immediately turn R. Going S. on 101, exit R. on Main St., L. on Bradley, past Jones St., into the college parking lot. Solvang: Exit Hwy 246/Mission Dr. S. on 5th St., L. on Oak, L. on 2nd St. Look for a parking lot. [TG: 796 J2; 940 E1])

$$$$

Put a star next to this entry because the Pacific Conservatory of the Performing Arts (PCPA) knows how to make a theater experience a memorable one! Both theater locations have intimate settings, so the audience feels close to the on-stage action and professional actors. Many of the nine yearly plays and musicals are family friendly. Past shows have included *Hello Dolly!, Peter Pan, Little Women*, and *Honk!* - a musical tale of the ugly ducking.

We were especially enchanted by the 750-plus seat Festival Theater in Solvang because the theater is outdoors. In the middle of this Danish town, under a canopy of trees and starlight, the magic of theater comes to life. Although the Solvang season runs mid-June through October, bring a blanket and/or jacket because the nights can get chilly. Note that last minute tickets are sometimes available.

The PCPA also has Education and Outreach programs and tours. One Outreach program entails Shakespeare performance workshops geared for junior and senior high students, where students put on the plays. Other programs take age-appropriate shows to classrooms or other facilities. Come early for the prologue or stay after the performance for a post-play discussion with the actors.

Hours: Call for show dates and times.

Admission: Prices range, depending on location and show time, from $16 - $22 for adults; $12.50 - $17.25 for seniors and ages 5 - 18 years. Thursday previews are less expensive. Children 4 and under are not permitted.

Ages: 8 years and up.

SANTA MARIA CIVIC THEATER

(805) 922-4442 / www.smct.org

1660 North McClelland Street, Santa Maria

(Exit El Camino Real [101] E. on Donovan Rd., R. on McClelland. [TG: 776 H5])

$$$

This 100-seat theater is host to non-professional actors who produce some good area theater. Some of the shows are family friendly; call first. Fairy Tales, the summer children's program, is delightful. The troupe's goal of making theater accessible is met successfully as children are introduced (or re-introduced), for free, to live theater. The actors are a combination of "old" pros and young thespians who put on colorful, fun, and participatory shows that kids get into wholeheartedly.

Hours: The regular shows usually begin at 8pm. Fairy Tales run for three consecutive long weekends in July on Fri. evenings, Sat. mornings and afternoons, and Sun. afternoons. Call for specific shows and times.

Admission: $10 per person for the regular shows; free for Fairy Tales.

Ages: 3 - 12 years for Fairy Tales; 7 years and up for regular performances.

STATE STREET BALLET

(805) 965-6066 or (805) 963-0761 / www.statestreetballet.com

33 E. Canon Perdido Street at the Lobero Theatre, Santa Barbara

(Going S. on El Camino Real Fwy [101], exit N.E. Carillo St., R. on De La Vina, L. on Canon Perdido. Going N. on 101, exit N. on Garden St., L. on Canon Perdido. [TG: 996 A3])

$$$$$

This professional company tours nationally and performs at "home," at the LOBERO THEATER (see pg. 512), presenting both classic and contemporary ballets. Make sure to catch at least one of four graceful and passionate shows performed each year. At Christmas time the holiday staple, *Nutcracker* is performed. Ask about the ballet's school and community outreach programs. For instance, students can be invited to performances during school hours when the troupe is in town or the performers will come to schools for an on-site performance. The public is sometimes invited to dress rehearsals.

Hours: Performances are usually given in November, December, February or March, and April; Fri. and Sat., 8pm; Sun., 2pm.

Admission: $28 - $40 for adults, depending on the date and the seats; $24 for seniors and students; $18 - $20 for children.

Ages: 6 years and up.

-----*TOURS*-----

BRAILLE INSTITUTE (Santa Barbara)

(805) 682-6222 / www.brailleinstitute.org

506 Chapala Street / 2031 De La Vina, Santa Barbara

(The Chapala St. address is a temporary "home" while De La Vina is the permanent one. Directions are to the De La Vina site: Exit El Camino Real Fwy [101] N. on Mission St., L. on Chapala, L. on Los Olivos, R. on De La Vina. [TG: 995 H2])

A one-hour tour of the Braille Institute facilities enables visitors to better understand how well the visually impaired can function in the world. The classrooms, library, art rooms, and computer labs are set up to enable the blind to gain life skills. Try the adaptive computer software which has zoom text and screen reader programs, or type something on the Braille embosser. Ask for permission to sit in on an orientation on how to use the white cane. Kids will definitely like the student store which sells talking watches and calculators, among other products. Note that mobile outreach programs are available to come to elementary schools.

Hours: Call to schedule a tour.

Admission: Free

Ages: 8 years old and up.

ENDEAVOUR CENTER

(805) 734-1030 or (805) 734-1747;

(805) 606-3595 - Vandenberg AFB Public Affairs Office / www.endeavours.org

1 Carob Street, Vandenberg Village, Lompoc

(Exit Lompoc Casmalia Rd [1], N.E. on Mountain View Blvd., R. on Carob. [TG: 875 J1])

The Endeavour Center endeavors to help kids gain a deeper understanding of our universe through a variety of space exploration programs.

One of the most popular programs is a field trip. The first part entails an almost two-hour tour of Vandenberg Air Force Base, beginning at 9am. The tour includes visiting its launch complexes, range support facilities, and the Heritage Museum. Note: Call first to see if the base is open for tours as their availability varies. After a sack lunch at a nearby park, head to the Endeavour Center for the last two hours of the program, which begins about noon. Program choices include Astronomy and Waves - gain understanding of astronomy terms, watch a video, see hands-on demonstrations, and construct a spectroscope; Human Space Exploration - see videos from aboard the Space Shuttle and other missions, construct a glider, and learn about astronaut suit designs and concepts of heat transfer; or Rocket Propulsion - see a video of rocket launches, learn about solid and liquid type rocket engines, and construct and launch model rockets. The entire field trip is geared for ages 10 and up, with a minimum of ten students and maximum of fifty. Students 9 years and under do not visit V.A.F.B, but participate in the second portion of the outing. Field trips are offered Tuesdays and Thursdays. For ages 10 and above, the cost is $8 per student for groups of twenty or more; $10 per student for groups of less than twenty, with a minimum charge of $150. For youths 9 years and under, the cost is $5 per person for groups of twenty or more; $8 for groups of less than twenty. The airplane, model rocket, and spectroscope kits are extra, usually about $5 per. Teachers can inquire about the usage of videos and literature available from the NASA Teacher Resource Center.

Weekend and summertime week-long space camps are packed with "hands-on, minds-on" learning and applications. What an intense, but fun, way to gain knowledge (and make new friends). Weekend camps start at

$150 per person. Another option is the Saturday Youth and Family Math / Science Day Seminars that run October through April from 9am to 2pm. Past topics have included Basic Rocketry and Flight; Robots; Computers and Networks; and Topics in Astronomy: Telescopes, the Big Bang, and Quark Stars. The classes, geared for ages 8 to 11 or 12 to 15, cost $30 per session. Rocket-themed birthday parties are offered which can include an age-appropriate rocketry class, use of launch control panels, space ice cream, and more. What a blast!

Hours: See above.
Admission: See above.
Ages: 7 years and up.

GOLETA SANITARY DISTRICT

(805) 967-4519 / www.goletasanitary.org
One William Moffett Place, Goleta
(Exit El Camino Real Fwy [101] S. on Fairview, R. on Fowler Rd., L. on Moffett. [TG: 994 D4])

Students can take a tour of this sewage treatment plant that complements school standards. They learn about the water cycle by first listening to a talk on "following" a water stream (such as flushed toilet water) to see what happens to the water along its passage and at its destination. This is a very realistic and functional tour! Then, they visit the lab to analyze water samples and to learn to recognize chemical properties and components. Last, they walk through the treatment plant and see the mechanics of how it all works. The minimum needed for a tour is ten students.

Hours: Tours are offered Mon. - Fri. Call to make a reservations.
Admission: Free
Ages: 4th graders and up.

SANTA BARBARA AVIATION EDUCATION CENTER

(805) 964-7622 / www.flysba.com
45 Hartley Place, Santa Barbara
(Exit El Camino Real [101] S. on Fairview Ave., R. on Hollister Ave, L. on Hartley. [TG: 994 C2])

Come learn about flying the friendly skies through a very-well presented tour at this airport and visitors center. The guided tour, which is the only way to see this facility, includes on-site classroom time, working on computers, and activities such as making and flying paper airplanes. There are also a few hands-on aviation exhibits such as a small wooden plane to climb aboard, a flight simulator, and a radio-controlled aircraft that students fly in a wind tunnel to get the feel for currents and navigation. The wind tunnel is an exact copy of the one in the Smithsonian Air and Space Museum.

The small exhibit hall also contains several model airplanes and lots of literature and videos (over 200 of them!) pertaining to flight. These are great resources for teachers. The age-appropriate tours are usually about an hour long, depending on the age and attention span of the attendees. Tours are given for a minimum of ten students and a maximum of fifty. In-class presentations are available upon request, too. Note that once a year the center hosts a wonderful, GATE certified class on aviation for area 6th graders who excel in math and science. The visitors center is also the home base for the Santa Barbara Radio Modelers and for the YOUNG EAGLES PROGRAM (Santa Barbara) (see pg. 521).

Since the visitors center, which is wheelchair and stroller accessible, is adjacent to the airport, guests can also watch small planes land and take off. Note that the Santa Barbara airport is in the city of Santa Barbara on paper, but it's in the heart of Goleta. (I am taking no political stance on this one.)

Hours: Tours are available on Tues., Wed., and Thurs., 9am - 4pm by appointment only. Call at least
              three weeks ahead of the time you'd like to visit.
Admission: Free
Ages: Kindergarten and up.

SANTA MARIA TIMES

(805) 925-2691 / www.santamariatimes.com

3200 Skyway Drive, Santa Maria

(Going S. on El Camino Real [101], exit W on Betteravia Rd, L. on Orcutt Exwy [135] R. on Skyway Dr. Going N. on 101, exit W. on Santa Maria Way, L. on Bradley Rd., R. on Lakeview Rd. which turns into Skyway. [TG: 816 F1])

Take a tour of this small-town newspaper to see how production is done. Visit various departments and watch how a page is put together using the cut and paste method on a computer screen. Watch, too, how an ad is created using similar methods while an artist explains the process. Depending on the time of your tour you can view the presses running, from a safe distance. See the papers coming off the conveyor and being set up on pallets. Try to set up a tour, which lasts about a half hour, in the afternoon when more of the staff are working. Morning tours will find a skeleton crew.

Hours: Tours are offered by appointment.

Admission: Free

Ages: 6 years and up.

-----TRANSPORTATION-----

AMTRAK

(800) USA RAIL (872-7245) / www.dot.ca.gov/hq/rail; www.amtrak.com

Ride the rails! See page xi (in the front) for more information.

BIKE MAPS (Santa Barbara County)

The web site www.labikepaths.com is a fantastic resource. It actually covers all of Southern California, not just Los Angeles, with links to specific counties for maps, bikeways, and other cycling information. Another helpful contact website and phone number is for the State of California Caltrans Office of Bicycle Facilities: (916) 653-0036 / www.dot.ca.gov/hq/tpp/offices/bike/contracts.htm. Two other contacts include Santa Barbara Traffic Solution (805) 963-SAVE (7283) / www.sbcag.org and Caltrans for the Central Coast (805) 549-3282.

BIKE TRAIL: CABRILLO BEACHWAY (BIKEWAY)

parallel to Cabrillo Boulevard, Santa Barbara

(Going S. on El Camino Real Fwy [101], exit S. on Castillo St., L. Cabrillo. Going N. 101, exit S. on Garden St. which dead ends into Cabrillo. [TG: 996 A6 - 996 E4])

This mostly flat, three-mile palm-lined path runs along the waterfront, from the LEADBETTER BEACH (see pg. 477) parking lot to the ANDREE CLARK BIRD REFUGE (see pg. 481) near the SANTA BARBARA ZOO (see pg. 524). Note: The paved path gets very crowded on the weekends, especially during the summer.

Hours: Open daily.

Admission: Free

Ages: 4 years and up.

BLUE EDGE PARASAILING

$$$$$

(805) 966-5206 / www.blueedgeparasailing.com

Stearns Wharf, Santa Barbara

(Going N. on El Camino Real Fwy [101], exit S. on Garden St., R. on Cabrillo Blvd. Going S. on 101, exit S. on Castillo St., L. on Cabrillo. [TG: 995 C5])

Give your kids a lift by taking them on a parasailing journey, 600 feet up in the air. The first time I went parasailing I felt like I was truly flying, and all the noises of the earth below faded away. Actual air time is about ten minutes, either by yourself or tandem, but you'll be in the boat for about an hour going out onto the waters and waiting for other passengers to take their turn. Bring your camera, and let whoever is flying up up and away take pictures with a disposable camera, too.

Hours: Open May through September daily; weekends only the rest of the year. Call for specific hours.

Admission: $65 per person or $110 for tandem.
Ages: 8 years and up

CAPTAIN DON'S WHALE WATCHING TOURS

(805) 969-5217 / www.captdon.com $$$$$

219 Stearns Wharf, Santa Barbara

(Going N. on El Camino Real Fwy [101], exit S. on Garden St., R. on Cabrillo Blvd. Going S. on 101, exit S. on Castillo St., L. on Cabrillo. [TG: 996 C5])

The double deck, 149-passenger boat is loaded with amenities, including full galley and bar, and is wheelchair and stroller accessible. Gray whales migrate February through May, so Captain Don's cruises up and down the coastline looking for (and finding) them. Dolphins and other sea mammals are usually seen as well. Humpback and blue whales migrate June through mid-September out near the Channel Islands, specifically Santa Cruz and Santa Rosa islands. The tour usually stops by the Painted Caves on Santa Cruz island, too.

Hours: The two-and-a-half-hour gray whale cruises are offered daily, 9am, noon, and 3pm. The five-hour blue and humpback cruises are offered Mon. - Fri., 8am; Sat. - Sun., 8am and 1:30pm.

Admission: Gray whale cruises are $30 for adults; $20 for ages 12 and under. Blue and humpback cruises are $69.50 for adults; $39.50 for ages 12 and under.

Ages: 6 years and up.

CONDOR CRUISES

(888) 77WHALE (779-4253) or (805) 962-1127 / www.condorcruises.com $$$$$

301 W. Cabrillo Boulevard, Santa Barbara

(Going N. on El Camino Real Fwy [101], exit S. on Garden St., R. on Cabrillo Blvd. Going S. on 101, exit S. on Castillo St., L. on Cabrillo. [TG: 996 B5])

Board this seventy-five-foot, hydrofoil-assisted, high-speed catamaran to look for gray whales from February through April. The two-and-a-half hour excursions are on the *Condor*, which has upper and lower decks and a full-service bar and galley. A naturalist explains what you see and why you are seeing it. From May to January, take a half-day trip to the Channel Islands to watch for blue whales and humpbacks as well as numerous other marine mammals. You'll also check out the Painted Cave on Santa Cruz Island. Two-hour sunset cruises are offered seasonally that can include dinner. Educators - ask about the floating marine lab classes offered throughout the year. They are a fantastic way for students to learn about the animals and plants just off the Santa Barbara coast. See SEA LANDING on page 519 as it is the reservations center for Condor Cruises.

Hours: Gray whale watching trips are given in season daily at 9am, noon, and 3pm. Cruises out to the islands are offered in season daily at 8am and 1pm. Call for sunset cruise hours as it depends on when the sun is setting.

Admission: Gray whale excursions are $32 for adults; $18 for ages 12 and under. Island excursions are $69.50 for adults; $39.50 for ages 5 - 12; children 4 and under are free. Sunset cruises range from $25 - $35 for adults (depending on if it's for cocktails or dinner); $20 - $30 for ages 12 and under.

Ages: 6 years and up for most cruises.

METROPOLITAN TRANSIT DISTRICT

(805) 683-3702 / www.sbmtd.gov $

1020 Chapala Street, Santa Barbara

(Going S. on El Camino Real Fwy [101], exit N.E. Carillo St., L. on Chapala. Going N. on 101, exit N. on Garden St., L. on Canon Perdido, R. on Chapala. [TG: 996 A4])

Catch the inexpensive Field Trip, the MTD service that runs from the waterfront to over ten highlights of Santa Barbara, including the Mission, the Botanic Garden, County Courthouse, and Museum of Art. The transit runs from Carpinteria to Goleta. The address given above is for the main station. Pick up a schedule here or on

any MTD bus.
- **Hours:** Open daily. Call for hours and scheduled stops.
- **Admission:** One-way fare is $1. Day passes are $3 and good on both the Downtown-Waterfront Shuttle and the Field Trip.
- **Ages:** All

PADDLE SPORTS OF SANTA BARBARA

(805) 899-4925 / www.kayaksb.com

$$$$

117-B Harbor Way, Santa Barbara

(Going N. on El Camino Real Fwy [101], exit S. on Garden St., R. on Cabrillo Blvd., L. on Harbor Way. Going S. on 101, exit S. on Castillo St., R. on Cabrillo, L. on Harbor Way. [TG: 996 B6])

Kayaks are Paddle Sport's specialty. The store offers a large variety of kayaks to rent - $20 for two hours for a single; $30 for a two-seater - plus kayaking lessons, classes, and summer camps. Take a trip to Santa Cruz Island, the largest of the eight Channel Islands, for $165 per person during the week, $179 on a weekend. This trip focuses on guided kayaking into and through sea caves, weather permitting. A naturalist will teach you about the geology, sea animals, and plant life in the area as well as the rich history of the Channel Islands. You even have the option of staying overnight here, at an additional charge.
- **Hours:** Open in the summer daily, 10am - 6pm. Open the rest of the year, Tues. - Fri., 11am - 6pm; Sat. - Sun., 10am - 6pm.
- **Admission:** Prices are listed above.
- **Ages:** Must be able to swim.

SANTA BARBARA JET BOATS

(888) 779-4285 or (805) 963-3564 / www.sealanding.com; www.truthaquatics.com

$$$$

301 W. Cabrillo Boulevard, Santa Barbara

(Going N. on El Camino Real Fwy [101], exit S. on Garden St., R. on Cabrillo Blvd. Going S. on 101, exit S. on Castillo St., L. on Cabrillo. [TG: 996 B5])

Operating out of SEA LANDING (see pg. 519), this company rents four-person jet boats ($120 an hour), two- and three-seater Sea-Doos ($85 - $95 an hour) and kayaks. Single kayaks are $15 for three hours and tandems are $25. Single kayaks are $30 for the day and tandems are $45.
- **Hours:** Usually open daily - call for reservations in the winter.
- **Admission:** See prices listed above.
- **Ages:** 8 years and up.

SANTA BARBARA OLD TOWN TROLLEY

(805) 965-0353 / www.sbtrolley.com

$$$$

22 State Street, Santa Barbara

(Exit El Camino Real Fwy [101] S. on Castillo St., L. on Cabrillo Blvd. The tour begins and ends at the foot of State Street at Stearns Wharf. [TG: 996 C5])

Ding, ding, ding goes the trolley! Come aboard and see the highlights of Santa Barbara while hearing its history and anecdotes about the town and some of its citizens. Take the ninety-minute narrated tour nonstop, or stop off at Stearns Wharf, the Mission, the Courthouse, downtown (to shop), and/or numerous other places, and re-board any time throughout the day. Remember, too, that for kids, a trolley ride is part of the excursion fun.
- **Hours:** Trolley tours operate daily, leaving every 90 minutes from each destination, starting at 10am to about 5pm.
- **Admission:** $14 for adults; $7 for ages 12 and under; infants are free if they are sitting on your lap.
- **Ages:** 4 years and up.

SANTA BARBARA SAILING CENTER / DOUBLE DOLPHIN CRUISE

(800) 350-9090 or (805) 962-2826 / www.sbsail.com

133 Harbor Way, Santa Barbara

(Going N. on El Camino Real Fwy [101], exit S. on Garden St., R. on Cabrillo Blvd., L. on Harbor Way. Going S. on 101, exit S. on Castillo St., R. on Cabrillo, L. on Harbor Way. [TG: 996 B6])

Anything water oriented is offered here. Single kayaks rent for $20 for two hours; double kayaks are $30. Peddle boats are $25 for an hour. For rowing champs, rent a rowing scull for $50 for two hours. Narrated whale-watching cruises are available seasonally, mid-February through mid-May for $32 for adults; $20 for ages 12 and under. On this tour also be on the lookout for dolphins, sea lions, and seals. Cruise to Santa Cruz Island, a three-hour crossing, and watch for flying fish, dolphins, and other sea animals. Once there and anchored, you are set to swim, snorkel, kayak ($10 extra), explore a deep sea cave, and have lunch. Bring your own picnic lunch or purchase food from the on-board snack bar. The latter, all-day cruise is $68 for adults; $38 for ages 12 and under.

Kids and adults can also learn the ropes of sailing by taking a class, so why *knot*? The center also offers classes on kayaking, plus kids camps, and more. Call for a full schedule.

Hours: Call for hours on what interests you.

Admission: Some prices are given above.

Ages: 6 years and up, depending on excursion.

SEA LANDING

(805) 963-3564 / www.sealanding.com; www.truthaquatics.com

301 W. Cabrillo Boulevard, Santa Barbara

(Going N. on El Camino Real Fwy [101], exit S. on Garden St., R. on Cabrillo Blvd. Going S. on 101, exit S. on Castillo St., L. on Cabrillo. [TG: 996 B5])

Sea Landing is the reservations center and headquarters for CONDOR CRUISES (see pg. 517), SANTA BARBARA JET BOATS (see pg. 518), STARDUST SPORTFISHING (see pg. 519), and TRUTH AQUATICS (see pg. 520).

STARDUST SPORTFISHING

(805) 963-3564 / www.stardustsportfishing.com

301 W. Cabrillo Boulevard, Santa Barbara

(Going N. on El Camino Real Fwy [101], exit S. on Garden St., R. on Cabrillo Blvd. Going S. on 101, exit S. on Castillo St., L. on Cabrillo. [TG: 996 B5])

Catch a big one or at least give it your best effort on a half-day outing at sea. Although all ages are welcome, something that kids, especially, look forward to are the summer Fish Camps. An "extra" crewman is aboard ship at this time to help out, teach fishermen wannabes how to tie knots, and to read marine conditions. The price of this excursion also includes bait, tackle, rod, and reel.

Hours: Excursions run most of the year, 9am - 3pm. They run in the summer, 7am - noon and 12:30pm - 5:30pm. The Fish Camps are offered in the summer on Wed. and Sun., 12:30pm - 5:30pm.

Admission: Sportfishing is $35 for adults; $30 for ages 12 and under. Fish Camps are $42 per person.

Ages: 8 years and up.

SUNSET KIDD SAILING

(805) 962-8222 / www.sunsetkidd.com

125 Harbor Way, Santa Barbara

(Going N. on El Camino Real Fwy [101], exit S. on Garden St., R. on Cabrillo Blvd., L. on Harbor Way. Going S. on 101, exit S. on Castillo St., R. on Cabrillo, L. on Harbor Way. [TG: 996 B6])

Sailing cruises have a whole different feel than that of a more typical, large, noisy passenger cruises. Experience the sea waters on a two-hour sail, whether your goal is whale watching, available mid-January through April, or just for pleasure.

Hours: Cruises usually set sail Mon. - Fri., 10am and 2pm; Sat. - Sun., 9am, noon, and 3pm.
Admission: $35 per person.
Ages: 8 years and up.

TRUTH AQUATICS

$$$$$

(805) 962-1127 or (805) 963-3564 / www.truthaquatics.com
301 W. Cabrillo Boulevard, Santa Barbara
(Going N. on El Camino Real Fwy [101], exit S. on Garden St., R. on Cabrillo Blvd. Going S. on 101, exit S. on Castillo St., L. on Cabrillo. [TG: 996 B5])

This company has a fleet of three boats that are primarily designed as dive boats, although anyone will enjoy a single- or multi-day excursion to the Channel Islands, particularly Anacapa and Santa Rosa islands. The company also specializes in kayaking trips around the islands and naturalist-guided hiking tours inland. Snorkeling and kayaking equipment rentals can be taken care of before your trip at SEA LANDING (see pg. 519), the reservation center for Truth Aquatics. See CHANNEL ISLANDS NATIONAL PARK (from Ventura), on page 533, for more information on the chain of islands just off the coast.
Hours: Trips to the Channel Islands usually depart at 7am and return at 5pm.
Admission: Prices start at $60 for adults; $45 for ages 12 and under. Rentals are extra.
Ages: 7 years and up.

VOYAGES OF REDISCOVERY (Santa Barbara County)

$$/$$$$$

(800) 401-7835 or (415) 331-3214
Santa Barbara

See VOYAGES OF REDISCOVERY (pg. 175) for details.

WHEEL FUN RENTALS

$$$

(805) 966-6733 / www.wheelfunrentals.com
22 State Street, Santa Barbara
(Going N. on El Camino Real Fwy [101], exit S. on Garden St., R. on Cabrillo Blvd. Going S. on 101, exit S. on Castillo St., L. on Cabrillo. It near the corner of State and Cabrillo. [TG: 996 C5])

If you forgot to bring your own, you can still have some *wheel* along Santa Barbara's bike paths and harbor by renting transportation with wheels. Mountain bikes are $8 an hour; tandems are $10; and surreys are $15 for a single, $20 for a double.
Hours: Call for hours.
Admission: Prices are listed above.
Ages: 3 years and up.

WINDHAVEN GLIDERS

$$$$$

(805) 688-2517 / www.gliderrides.com
Airport Road, Santa Ynez
(Exit El Camino Real Fwy [101] E. on Hwy 246/Mission Ave., R. on Airport Rd. [TG: 921 D6])

Talk about quietly soaring above it all! A breath-taking lesson (given for ages 14 years and up) or flight adds up to an unforgettable experience as you lift off and up in your two-seater plane. It's like sailing in the sky. It is *almost* as much fun to bring a blanket and some snacks to just watch the pilots and passengers.
Hours: Call for reservations, or for a schedule of flights.
Admission: $85 per person for a 2,500-foot altitude, 15 - 20 minute flight; $155 for 5,280 feet, 35 - 40 minutes.
Ages: 14 years and up to fly; all ages to watch.

YOUNG EAGLES PROGRAM (Santa Barbara)

(800) 564-6322 - national; / www.eaa.org

45 Harley Place Road, Santa Barbara

(Exit El Camino Real [101] S. on Fairview Ave., R. on Hollister Ave, L. on Hartley. [TG: 994 C2])

See the entry for YOUNG EAGLES PROGRAM (Pacoima) on page 177 for details.

Admission: Free

Ages: 8 - 17 years.

YOUNG EAGLES PROGRAM (Santa Maria)

(800) 564-6322 or (877) 806-8902 / www.eaa.org

3233 Skyway at Santa Maria Airport, Santa Maria

(Going S. on El Camino Real [101], exit W. on Betteravia Rd, L. on Orcutt Exwy [135] R. on Skyway Dr. Going N. on 101, exit W. on Santa Maria Way, L. on Bradley Rd., R. on Lakeview Rd. which turns into Skyway. [TG: 166 F1])

See the entry for YOUNG EAGLES PROGRAM (Pacoima) on page 177 for details.

Admission: Free

Ages: 8 - 17 years.

-----ZOOS AND ANIMALS-----

CABRILLO HIGH SCHOOL AQUARIUM

(805) 733-4538 / www.cabrillo-aquarium.org

4350 Constellation Road, Lompoc

(Exit Lompoc Casmalia Rd [1], N.E. on Constellation. [TG: 876 C6])

This is an impressive aquarium for a high school campus! The aquarium is comprised of several large tanks, a few smaller ones, a theater, computers, murals, and stuffed fish.

One tank holds jellyfish; actually they're called sea nettles, and they look other-worldly. The warm water reef tank is visually exciting because the coral habitat holds brilliantly-colored fish such as clown fish, yellow tangs, damselfish, rainbow wrasse, and firefish. The surge tank, which simulates the surging waves along the coast, contains bottom-dwelling horned sharks, Garibaldi, and a few other sea creatures. Crustaceans such as spiny lobsters and crabs are in another tank. The tropical marine life tank showcases puffer fish, angelfish, several wrasse, and brittle stars. Other containers hold bass, eels, perch, and sea anemones. An incubator is really a nursery for the main in-house food source - brine shrimp. A light shines through swell shark egg casings enabling visitors to see shark embryos. Marine life, such as sea cucumbers, sea stars, and sea urchins, are in a touch tank.

The outside of the state-of-the-art, thirty-five-seat theater resembles a weathered lighthouse. Inside, various films are shown on the screen that can also be used as touch screen. The murals, located in a city renowned for its murals, are depictions of Pacific Blue whales and of the local coastline. Aquatic-related photographs and artwork decorate the room. Fish "swimming" overhead include a full-sized dolphin and a twenty-foot model of a Great White Shark. Computers record every angle of the aquarium and are available for research. Community outreach programs are also available.

Hours: Usually open about once a month. Call for hours.

Admission: Free

Ages: 3 years and up.

FLAG IS UP FARMS

(888) U2-MONTY (826-6689) or (805) 688-4264 / www.montyroberts.com

901 E. Highway 246, Solvang

(Exit El Camino Real Fwy [101] E. on Hwy 246/Mission Dr. [TG: 920 B7])

Horse lovers will appreciate all that Flag is Up Farms has to offer, as will fans of the book and movie *The*

Horse Whisperer. Monty Roberts is the owner of the farm. He is the original horse whisperer, author of *The Man Who Listens to Horses*, and he runs the training center here for starting horses. The farm also offers rehabilitation, a breeding and foaling center, a half-mile race track, stalls, and a covered arena.

Visitors will see a variety of goings on, depending on the day and time of visit. Call first if you want to see activity on the track or see Monty, or another trainer, in action. We simply walked around the farm, admired the numerous horses, and went to the breeding facility where we saw mares, foals, and even two zebras (who are not in the breeding program).

Hours: Open daily. Call first (of course!)
Admission: Free just to walk around. Call about prices to watch certain activities.
Ages: 7 years and up.

FLYING V LLAMA RANCH

(805) 735-3577
6615 E. Highway 246, Lompoc
(Exit El Camino Real Fwy [101] W. on Hwy 246/Mission Dr. [TG: 919 C4])

Llamas have eyes on the sides of their heads so predators can't sneak up on them. They also have feet and toes, not hooves. These are just a few of the facts we learned on our fascinating forty-five-minute guided tour, which is the only way to see the over forty llamas here. Note: There is no minimum number of people needed for a tour.

We walked around the well-kept up ranch and into a few of the large, grassy enclosures. We were able to gently stroke and even brush some of these unique animals, which by the way, have surprisingly soft hair. Guests visit both the male and female llamas, kept in separate pens, and discover their different characteristics and temperaments.

Make sure to visit the on-site gift shop which sells llama products made from their soft wool.

Hours: Call to make a tour reservation.
Admission: $5 per person; children 6 years and under are free.
Ages: 6 years and up.

LIL ORPHAN HAMMIES

(805) 693-9953 / www.lilorphanhammies.com
Solvang

Here a piggy; there a piggy; everywhere a piggy piggy! This aptly-named potbellied pig sanctuary, located in a residential district, is home to numerous abandoned, abused, and neglected, mostly adult pigs. The hope is to adopt the pigs out, but the reality is that many will live out their lives here.

A majority of the pigs dwell in, or just outside, a colorfully decorated group of buildings that resemble dog houses, dubbed Pig Turd Alley. They can roll, grunt, and squeal here 'til their hearts content. Another large enclosure also affords the pigs plenty of dirt and shade. Some of the pigs roam the grounds, along with a few dogs, cats, and chickens.

All visitors must call ahead first to make reservations. Guided tours are given for those who go hog wild over learning more about the animals and what the sanctuary has to offer them.

Hours: Call for reservations.
Admission: Free; donations gladly accepted.
Ages: 4 years and up.

OSTRICH LAND

(805) 686-9696 / www.ostrichland.com
610 E. Hwy 246, Buellton
(Exit El Camino Real Fwy [101] E. on Hwy 246/Mission Dr. [TG: 920 A6])

What are the differences between an ostrich and an emu? Stop by and see for yourself! Ostrich Land has about forty ostriches roaming around in the enclosure just off the highway. A planned walkway around, and perhaps through, a part of the pen will allow visitors a closer peek (not a closer peck) for a nominal fee. The ten, or so, emus are currently a little more accessible. In fact, you can purchase emu feed for 25¢.

Ostriches, one of the world's largest birds, lay equally huge eggs: One ostrich egg is equivalent to about twenty-four chicken eggs. The produce stand/gift shop here, which is Ostrich Land's main business, offers fresh ostrich eggs, emu eggs (which are avocado green in color), ostrich meat, feathers, and other ostrich products. A small selection of seasonal fruits and vegetables are also available here. Note: You can pick your own strawberries, in season, or buy them pre-picked. A parting question - Do ostriches actually bury their heads in the sand?

Hours: Open daily, 10am - 6pm.
Admission: Free
Ages: 3 years and up.

QUICKSILVER RANCH

(805) 686-4002 / ariel.syv.com/qsminis
1555 Alamo Pintado Road, Solvang
(Exit El Camino Real Fwy [101] E. on Hwy 246/Mission Dr., N. on Alamo Pintado Rd. [TG: 920 H3])

Question: What's small and says "neigh"? Answer: Miniature horses. Quicksilver Ranch is a working breeding facility and home to over eighty miniature horses. (A horse must not exceed thirty-four inches to be registered as a miniature.) The small "so cute!" horses romp and graze in the twenty acres of lush, grassy enclosures. Even young visitors will enjoy strolling the grounds as they can get up close and personal with the animals because the pens are down-scaled. Oftentimes a handler brings out a horse to pet. Note: If you want to see baby miniature horses, twenty to thirty are usually born during the months of April, May, and June.

Forty-five-minute guided tours are offered for groups of twenty or more, for third graders and above, with advanced reservations. Guests learn about the history of the horses and their gentle nature; they see the trophy room; and more. Please keep in mind that this is not a petting zoo, so don't bring food to feed the horses. You'll drive past goats and full-size horses that live on adjacent ranches.

Hours: Open daily, 10am - 3pm. Closed Thanksgiving and Christmas.
Admission: Free. Tours are $3 per person.
Ages: 3 years and up.

RETURN TO FREEDOM WILD HORSE SANCTUARY

$$$

(805) 737-9246 / www.returntofreedom.org
Jalama Road, Lompoc
(Exit Cabrillo Hwy [1] S. on Jalama Rd. [TG: 365 F5])

Picture wild horses running with abandon through tall grasses, past oak trees, and over hills; their manes and tails flowing behind them. Welcome to Return to Freedom where about 100 wild mustangs, the last true vestiges of the American West, roam the grounds with their natural herds or family groups on this 310-acre ranch sanctuary. The sanctuary's goals are to preserve these majestic mustangs in their natural habitat and to educate visitors, via self discovery, through direct encounters with horses. Children and adults have the rare opportunity to observe the mustangs (and their colts) on their own turf, to gently and respectfully approach them, and to develop compassion as they learn the history (and hopefully the future) of the horses. Be prepared to do some walking and to have romanticized images of cowboy roundups revamped.

Most "tours" start in the barn area/learning center. Depending on the type of tour, visitors can watch a video about the sanctuary; see maps of where the horse herds are located; hear about the history of the horses, which are descendants of the Spanish conquistador's horses; learn about the government's role in the treatment of mustangs; and learn horse behavior such as grooming, communication, social structure, head tosses, and how a lead horse acts.

A few of the horses here are in open-air paddocks. Some of these animals have come from abusive owners or from rodeos. One horse, however, has had a starring role. The beautiful stallion used as the model for the animated movie *Spirit, Stallion of Cimarron* has been retired and now lives at the ranch. Other animals that consider the sanctuary home include burros and a few goats and chickens.

Time spent at the ranch ranges from a forty-five-minute introductory talk and walk around the ranch; to two hours of just being around the horses, studying them, perhaps interacting with them, and/or drawing them; to clinics that teach how to become sensitive to and skilled at managing horses. Bring a lunch to enjoy at the picnic tables. Ask about volunteering opportunities. And if wild horses can't drag you here, hop in your mini van!

Hours: Tours are by appointment only. The first Sat. is the only regularly scheduled visit.

Admission: Forty-five-minute intro talk and walk is $10 for adults; $5 for ages 5 and under. Three-hour, once-a-month "walks" where herd behavior is studied is $50 per person. A variety of other tours are available.

Ages: 6 years and up.

SANTA BARBARA POLO

(805) 684-6683 or 6684 / www.sbpolo.com

3375 Foothill Boulevard, Carpinteria

(Exit El Camino Real Fwy [101] N.E. on Santa Claus Ln./Padaro Ln., L. on Via Real, R. on Nidever Rd., which turns into Foothill. [TG: 997 H4])

Watching a polo game was an unexpectedly enthralling event. At the start, eight players, four per team, astride their thoroughbreds with long mallets in hand, loosely gathered around the mounted umpire who bowled in the ball. Whack! A player swung the mallet in an arch, connected with the ball and sent it down the field as the other players galloped in pursuit. Each horse and rider pair ran, pivoted, stopped, and maneuvered their way up and down the court with skill and finesse, racing each other side by side. FYI - the beautifully manicured field is three football fields in length.

We learned a new word, "chukker," which is the seven minutes of playing time per period. There are six chukkers per game, with four minutes in-between each one. At the ten-minute half-time, everyone is invited out onto the field to help replace the divots (and to socialize and run around).

Bring your own food to have a tailgate party or order food from the adjacent snack bar which offers burgers ($4.25), hot dogs, soda ($1.50), and more. The clubhouse restaurant, also attached to the stands, is for members only. Note that the club offers polo classes for adults and youth, as well as summer camps.

Hours: Polo season runs April through mid-October. Tournament games are usually played on Sun. at 1pm and 3pm. Practice games are often held on Wed. or Thurs.

Admission: $10 per person for tournament games; free for the practices.

Ages: 6 years and up.

SANTA BARBARA ZOO

(805) 962-5339 / www.santabarbarazoo.org

500 Ninos Drive, Santa Barbara

(Going N. on El Camino Real Fwy [101], exit S. on Hot Springs/Cabrillo Blvd., R. on Ninos Dr. Going S. on 101, exit S. on Milpas, L. on Cabrillo Blvd., L. on Ninos. [TG: 996 E4])

This mid-size zoo lives up to its official name of Zoological Gardens in that the over 500 animals in naturalistic settings dwell in and amongst a myriad of lush plants.

Brightly-colored macaws, although centralized in the parrot garden, are also found in several locations throughout the zoo. The flamingoes have their own lagoon area. Walk through the tropical aviary to view more beautiful birds. For $1 you can feed the red, purple, blue, and green lorikeets, or just go into their aviary and watch them land on your arm or head. Bring a camera!

The nocturnal hall contains a sloth and other nighttime animals. The aquarium and reptile complex houses some unique creatures such as snake-necked turtles and a matamata turtle with its snorkel-like nose and lizard-like head and neck. A python, some bats, various types of frogs, Madagascar hissing cockroaches, stingrays, and arowana fish - with their fish heads and eel-like bodies - are also in here.

Look at the sea lions, with both above and below ground viewing. Feeding time is usually between 1pm and 2pm. The playful River Otters are also fun to watch, especially at feeding time, which happens four times a day. You can hear the gibbons screeching and hooting before actually reaching their enclosure. The Lowland

Gorillas, meerkats, elephants, coatimundi, alligators, and monkeys are fascinating to observe and easy to see as their habitats are relatively small. Watch the big cats pace, play around, or indulge in their favorite activity - sleep. Don't miss the giraffes - one has a profoundly crooked neck.

A small playground is one of the attractions at the Kid's Marketplace. You can also pet and feed llamas, goats, and sheep through the fence here. A carousel with a few wooden animals to ride on costs 75¢ and is open on weekends only. For an additional $1.50 for adults and $1 for ages 2 through 12, hop on board a mini train (which is handicap accessible) for a ten-minute ride around the perimeter of the zoo. Picnic grounds are just around the corner and you are allowed to bring outside food inside.

Ask about the zoo's numerous age-appropriate workshops geared for tiny tots up to junior zookeepers. Other interactive zoo happenings include camp outs, which means spending the night at the zoo and meeting some of the animals, especially nocturnal ones, close up; breakfast with the animals, for members only; behind-the-scenes tours; discovery kits for classroom use; and "Theater Gone Wild." This theater group puts on performances both at the zoo, and at school or Scout facilities. Note that the ANDREE CLARK BIRD REFUGE (see pg. 481) is just outside the zoo perimeters. Have a *wild* time at the zoo!

Hours: Open daily, 10am - 5pm. Closed Thanksgiving and Christmas Day.

Admission: $8 for adults; $6 for seniors and ages 2 - 12; children under 2 are free. Parking is $2.

Ages: All

VENTURA COUNTY

Located between two major tourist markets, Los Angeles and Santa Barbara, Ventura County is a low-key, but worthy destination. As coastal fog along the shores of Oxnard and Ventura lift, the distant Channel Islands are unveiled. Take a cruise out to them. Walk along Main Street in Ventura for a cluster of attractions, as well as some terrific shopping. Inland and northward are the towns of Ojai, with its refined atmosphere, and Santa Paula, with its mid-west open-door policy, but with better weather than that part of the country.

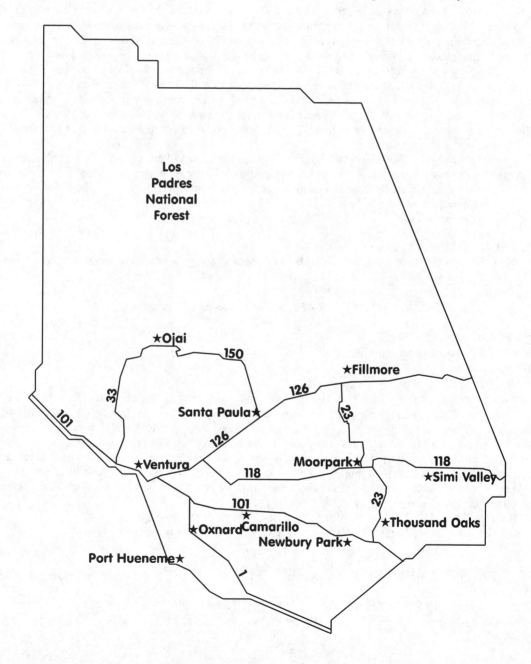

-----ARTS AND CRAFTS-----

CAROUSEL CERAMICS

(818) 879-8292

31149 Via Colinas, suite 604, Thousand Oaks

(Exit Ventura Fwy [101] N. on Lindero, L. on Via Colinas. It's in an industrial park, on a corner curve, next to Grason's art supply store. [TG: 557 E4])

$$$$

This workshop studio stocks the largest quantity of bisque, greenware, and plaster pieces I've ever seen. Two rooms are fully stocked with statues, figurines, picture frames, bowls, mugs, vases, dinner sets, and more. Long tables are completely set up for you to design and paint your piece. There are many finished samples at the studio that lend inspiration. Carousel, however, is not your typical paint-a-piece-in-one-session place. It is primarily a teaching studio where instructors give formal classes for groups or individuals. Just a few of the several classes offered throughout the year include acrylic painting on glass and painting wisteria or dogwood flowers on greenware. One-on-one tutoring is available for brush strokes, handmade flowers, airbrushing, drybrushing, glazing, and more. With such a variety of items to choose from, and all of this assistance being offered, even I could produce a work of art here! Come create a special gift, or make coming here a hobby and start your own heirloom collection.

Hours: Open Mon., Thurs., Fri., and Sat., 9am - 6pm; Tues., 10am - 9pm. (Closed Wed. and Sun.)

Admission: The cost of your piece, plus the brushes, paints, and other supplies you purchase. The owner will work out a price for those who want to use the store's supplies. Or, pay a yearly fee of $25 and paint without any hourly fee.

Ages: 5 years and up.

COLOR ME MINE (Ventura County)

(818) 707-6903; (877) COLOR ME (265-6763) - for a listing of all locations. / www.colormemine.com

706 Lindero Canyon Road, suite 728, Oak Park

(Exit Ventura Fwy [101] N. on Lindero Canyon. [TG: 557 G1])

$$$$

See the entry for COLOR ME MINE (Los Angeles County) on page 6 for details.

FIREFLY CERAMICS

(805) 650-1468 / www.fireflyceramics.net

1580 Saratoga Avenue, Unit-C, Ventura

(Exit Ventura Fwy [101] N. on Victoria, L. on Ralston, L. on Saratoga. [TG: 492 B4])

$$$$

Choices, choices - what to paint? What colors? Free-hand design or use a stencil? What size brush to use? To give or to keep? And painting your own ceramic piece is supposed to be a stress-free activity! Actually, this is a wonderful thing to do together as a family - it's time well spent with your child, and someone will get a unique item to use or display. Choose from an array of items, both decorative and practical, including dinnerware, animal banks, plant stakes, boxes, vases, figurines, and more. It will be glazed and fired and ready to pick up in just a few days. Pre-cut frames, plaques, clocks, and mirrors can be purchased to fill in with glass or tile pieces, also available at Firefly. Inquire about summer camp art classes and year-round school fields trips either here or at your classroom facility.

Hours: Open Mon., Wed. - Sat., 10am - 8pm; Sun., 10am - 4pm. Closed Tues.

Admission: The cost of the pieces, plus a studio fee of $7 for adults; $4 for ages 10 and under.

Ages: 4 years and up.

PAINT PALS CLUBHOUSE

(805) 581-4676

1716 Erringer Road, #106, Simi Valley

(Exit Simi Valley/San Fernando Valley Fwy [118] S. on Erringer Rd. It's on the N.E. corner of Heywood St. and Erringer. [TG: 498 A3])

$$$

Clubhouses weren't this much fun when I was a kid! The colorfully-decorated Paint Pals Clubhouse offers paint-your-own bisque, and a whole lot more. One section has shelves of items to paint, plus long tables and all the paint, brushes, smocks, and other materials needed. Popular items include sunflowers, pigs, jars with ceramic lids, magnets, and picture frames. Creating a masterpiece is a terrific activity. But, while moms (this one, anyway) sometimes take longer to do a project than kids do, there are plenty of other things here to keep the younger set busy. Karaoke is a popular option, and whether or not children can actually sing on key seems to be irrelevant. Next to the stage are costumes for dressing up. Toward the back of the store, and through a short tunnel of mirrors, is a small black light maze that my boys enjoyed going through. Kids can also play with soft foam blocks, make "pictures" in a shadow room, try to solve metal shape puzzles, and blow giant bubbles.

Hours: Open during the school year, Tues. - Thurs. and Sun.,10am - 6pm; Fri. - Sat., 10am - 6pm. Closed Mon., except holiday Mon. Open in the summer on Mon., 10am - 6pm, in addition to its other days and hours.

Admission: $1 per child (toddlers, too) entrance fee; free to adults. Items cost from $2.50 on up, which includes use of the paints and other supplies. Karaoke is 50¢ for one song; $1 for 3 songs.

Ages: 3 years and up.

-----EDIBLE ADVENTURES-----

CHUCK E. CHEESE
See the entry for CHUCK E. CHEESE on page 12 for details.

FARMER'S MARKETS
See the entry for FARMER'S MARKETS on page 14 for details.

FILLMORE & WESTERN RAILWAY
(800) 777-TRAIN (8724) / www.fwry.com
351 Santa Clara Avenue, Central Park Depot, Fillmore

See the entry for FILLMORE & WESTERN RAILWAY on page 554 for details.

OLIVIA'S DOLL HOUSE and TEA ROOM (Ventura County)
(805) 381-1553(661); 252-1404 - general number
Thousand Oaks Boulevard, #110, Thousand Oaks
(Exit Ventura Fwy [101] N. on Hampshire Rd., R. on Thousand Oaks Blvd. [TG: 557 B3])

See the entry for OLIVIA'S DOLL HOUSE and TEA ROOM (Los Angeles County) on page 19 for details.

$$$$$

UNDERWOOD FAMILY FARM
(805) 529-3690 or (805) 523-8552 - food farm;
(805) 523-2957 - animal farm / www.underwoodfamilyfarms.com
3370 Sunset Valley Road, Moorpark
(Exit 23 Fwy W. on Tierra Rejada Rd., L. on Sunset Valley Rd. (which used to be Moorpark Rd.) [TG: 496 H4])

$$

Tierra Rejada is both a huge working produce farm, as well as an animal farm. Let's talk food, first. There are two ways to enjoy the crops: 1) Stop by the on-site roadside market to purchase fresh produce (tasty, but boring), or 2) Let the kids pick their own fruits and vegetables. (Ya-hoo - we've got a winner!) There are rows and rows (and rows and rows) of seasonal crops including artichokes, strawberries, blackberries, peaches, squash, potatoes, green beans, apricots, apples, onions, garlic, tomatoes, eggplant, peppers, cabbages, pumpkins, melons, corn, and herbs. My boys were excited to eat strawberries they picked from the vines, carrots they pulled from the ground, beans they harvested from the stalks, and other good-for-you foods they won't normally eat, proving that kids really enjoy the fruits (and vegetables) of their labor.

Heavy-duty pull wagons are available to transport your prize pickings (or tired little ones) at no extra charge. A grassy picnic area, with tables, is located at the front of the farm, near the restroom facilities. Tips: Wear sunscreen and walking shoes; prepare to get a little muddy if you visit here after a rain; and bring a cooler to store your fresh produce.

The farm offers a variety of ninety-minute guided tours of the fields for groups of twenty or more. The tours entail learning about a designated crop (or crops) - care, growth cycle, and more - as well as picking some to take home, and a Clydesdale-drawn wagon ride. What a great combination of fun and education! Crops do grow seasonally, so call to see what is currently ripe. Add on a tour of the animal farm for an additional fee.

Tierra Rejada owns and operates the adjacent Farm Animal Center. This lovely landscaped area is a pleasant and fun way to spend an hour or so with your children. Wander around the pens to see sheep, bunnies, jersey cows, donkeys, alpacas, emus, and ponies. There is also a duck pond, chicken coop, bird aviary, incubation center with babies growing at various rates, and pygmy goats walking on skinny wooden ramps over your head - forty feet off the ground! Other attractions inside the fenced center include a moonbounce, a small playground with a slide and tunnel, haystacks to jump on (or off), pony rides (for 1 year up to 100 pounds), a petting corral, a sand box, a tiny looping trike trail (the bike is supplied), tractor-drawn hayrides, and a nice party area. Antique and modern farm equipment add to the atmosphere. Experience the animal farm on your own or take a guided tour. Tip: See the Calendar entry on page 602 for details about the Fall Harvest Festival. Note: There is an UNDERWOOD FARM MARKET with some animals in the nearby city of Somis. (See the below entry.)

Hours:	The food and animal farm are open April through October daily, 9am to 6pm; November and March, 9am - 5pm, weather permitting. Closed January and February.
Admission:	Crop prices are charged per pound and change per season/availability. Food tours are $7 per person including adults, although teachers are free. An hour mommy and me tour is $5 per child. Admission to the animal farm is $2 per person; children under 2 are free. Purchase tickets for the "extra" things to do - $1 for 1 ticket; $20 for 25 tickets. Pony rides are 4 tickets; the moonbounce is 3; the petting corral is 2; the trike trail is 2. Hayrides are $1.50 per person for a group of at least twenty people.
Ages:	All for a visit; 5 years and up for food tours; 2 - 10 years for the animal center.

UNDERWOOD FARM MARKET

(805) 386-4660 / www.underwoodfamilyfarms.com

!/$

5696 Los Angeles Avenue, Somis

(From the 23 Fwy/118 [Ronald Reagan Fwy] exit E. on Los Angeles Ave./118. [TG: 495 B4])

If you're in the area, stop at this roadside stand which sells fresh-picked, seasonal produce. The biggest draw for kids are the burros, jersey cows, rabbits, guinea pigs, alpacas (i.e. furry llamas that look like they're having a bad hair day), and most fascinating, the pygmy goats. The goats nimbly climb on very narrow wooden ramps that crisscross thirty feet above your head! An adjacent grassy area beckons picnickers. Kids can climb on the wooden vehicle stationed here. See the above entry for UNDERWOOD FAMILY FARM for a nearby, full-fledged, farm attraction.

Hours:	Open most of the year daily, 9am to 6pm; open in the winter daily, 9am to 5:30pm.
Admission:	Free
Ages:	2 - 12 years (although those overhead goats are quite cool for all ages).

-----*FAMILY PAY AND PLAY*-----

CHUCK E. CHEESE

See the entry for CHUCK E. CHEESE on page 12 for details.

GOLF 'N STUFF

(805) 644-7132 / www.golfnstuff.com

$$$

5555 Walker Drive, Ventura

(Exit Ventura Fwy [101] N. on Victoria Ave., take a quick L. on Walker St. The Golf 'N Stuff sign is visible from the freeway. [TG: 492 C5])

If you and the kids are in the mood for a little golf 'n stuff, here's the place for you. There are two, **miniature golf** courses with windmills, a tower, and other fanciful buildings, to putt around on at $7.50 per round for adults; $5.75 for seniors; children 5 years and under play for free. **Indy cars** ($5.50 for drivers) have a height requirement for drivers of 52", while **bumper cars** and **water boats** ($5 per ride) both have height requirements for drivers of 48". Play **laser tag** here, too, for $5.50 per game. The center also features arcade games and a full-service snack bar.

Hours: Open most of the year, Sun., 10am - 10pm (rides open until 9:30pm); Mon. - Thurs., 10am - noon (rides open 3pm - 9:30pm); Fri. - Sat., 10am - midnight. The park is open extended hours in the summer.

Admission: Prices are listed above or ask about package deals.

Ages: 4 years and up.

LAZERSTAR

(805) 388-0074 / www.lazerstar.org

1775 Daily Drive, Camarillo

(Exit Ventura Fwy [101] N. on Carmen, R. on Daily. [TG: 522 J2])

Reach for the stars at Lazerstar, a galactic adventure in laser tag. The large, noisy, dark lobby has numerous video games, including virtual reality games and arcade games, such as Wack-A-Mole and skee ball, along with a prize redemption center. A few smaller rooms, branching off the main lobby, are for eating or for hosting a party. The full-service snack bar sells hot dogs, pizza, and other food.

Two teams, of up to twenty individuals each, compete against each other armed with laser guns and a lighted vest. The foggy arena, illuminated only by black lights, has ceiling, walls, and barriers that are painted with fluorescent markings. Because the arena is so large (over 5,000 square feet), with numerous obstacles, expect to run around a lot during your fifteen-minute game. Stalk, dodge, hide, and fire laser beams in an effort to score against your opponents, while having fun, of course. When your mission is completed, return to Mission Command Center to pick up your score sheet because it details who scored on who and how many times. Tip: Ask Lazerstar about their great deals for team parties and their various monthly specials.

Hours: Open Mon. - Thurs., noon - 10pm; Fri., noon - midnight; Sat., 10am - midnight; Sun., 10am - 10pm. Open in the summer and on holidays Sun. - Thurs., 10am - 10pm; Fri. - Sat., 10am - midnight.

Admission: $6.50 per player for one game. Ask about specials.

Ages: 7 years and up.

SKATELAB

(805) 578-0040 / www.skatelab.com

4226 Valley Fair Street, Simi Valley

(Exit Ronald Reagan Fwy [118] S. on Tapo Canyon Blvd., L. on Cochran, R. on Tapo St., R. on Valley Fair. [TG: 498 F2])

Yeowser! This huge (20,000 square feet) indoor skate park has it all, and then some. It has a street section with two half pipes - one is six feet high and the other is four feet high -, plus grinding boxes, a really large bowl, and much more. It's definitely for the intermediate to advanced skater. All skaters 17 years and under must have a waiver signed by their parent or legal guardian at the time of registration. A helmet, and elbow and knee pads are mandatory. Rentals are available here.

Skatelab also has a museum devoted to skateboard paraphernalia, showing the history of the sport. It contains the largest collection of vintage skateboards around. I never knew there was so many "extras" in skateboarding! Your kids will think the stuff is so cool.

Hours: Open Mon., 7pm - 10pm; Tues. - Fri., 3pm - 10pm; Sat., 10am - 10pm; Sun., 10am - 5pm.

Admission: $8 a session, Mon. - Thurs.; $10, Fri. - Sun. Sessions are three hours long.

Ages: 7 years and up.

SKATE STREET

(888) 85 - SKATE (857-5283) / www.skatestreetusa.com

1954 Goodyear Avenue, Ventura

(Exit Ventura Fwy [101] S. on Telephone Rd., L. on Market St., just a few streets down and R. on Goodyear (this street sign is hard to see!). [TG: 492 A5])

This huge (29,000 square feet), airy, and very "tight" (according to skateboard lingo, this translates as "cool") indoor skate park became an instant favorite. It has several intense ramps, verts, half pipes and more crafted from a smooth wood-composite atop a cement floor. The street skate park caters to experienced skateboarders, in line roller-bladers, and even BMX riders. It also offers a section with less dramatic half pipes for those who haven't been skating (or biking) as long or who want to work (somewhat safely) on trickier maneuvers. Some of the inclines make me twinge, but the kids ate it up; and sometimes they just ate it. My middle child finally realized that not everyone else is watching him, at least not all the time, and he really got into it. The city scape murals and hard rock music add to the ambiance.

An observation area and two party rooms are on the second story. Vending machine snacks and beverages and a pro-shop are on the first floor. Note: All participants must wear a helmet. Those under 18 are also required to wear elbow and knee pads. Equipment is available for rent. Special sessions are available just for BMX riders. All participants under 18 years old *must* be accompanied by a parent the first time here to have a parent's signature and liability waiver on file, or have a parent's signature and a notary republic sign the waiver form. Note: There are special sessions for ages 13 years and under.

Hours: Open Mon. - Wed., noon - 10pm; Tues., noon - 6pm; Thurs. - Fri., noon - 9pm; Sat., 9am - 11pm; Sun., noon - 6pm. Summer and school vacation hours may differ. Each session is almost 3 hours long.

Admission: $12 per skater per session; $8 for members. The last 90 minutes costs only $7, or $5 for members. Rental equipment is $5 for everything. Membership is $45 for a year.

Ages: 7 years and up.

UNDER THE SEA (Thousand Oaks)

(805) 373-5580 / ww3.choicemall.com/underthesea

1182 E. Thousand Oaks Boulevard, Thousand Oaks

(Going W. on Ventura Fwy [101], exit N. on Hampshire Rd, L. on Thousand Oaks. Going E. on 101, exit N. on Moorpark Rd., R. on Thousand Oaks. [TG: 556 H1])

See the entry for UNDER THE SEA (Woodland Hills) on page 34 for details.

URBAN QUEST PAINTBALL

(805) 315-6091 / www.urbanquestpaintball.com

5011 W. Gonzales Road, Oxnard

(Exit Ventura Fwy [101] S. on Victoria Ave., R. on Gonzales and look for the Urban Quest sign. [TG: 521 J3])

The nine out-in-the-open fields of various sizes range from Urban - where buildings and piles of tires, as well as weeds and trees, make for interesting covers and surprise assaults - to Jungle, where the bush and trees are very dense. Some of the fields have bunkers, trenches, bamboo plants, and other obstacles, too. Games last about fifteen minutes, unless you get splatted with a paintball (i.e. hit); then you're out. Variation of games consist of Capture the Flag, Center Flag, or simply Elimination or Speedball. A covered picnic area, snacks, cold drinks, and lunch are available here. Equipment rental includes goggles, full face mask, camouflage clothing, air-rifle, 100 paintballs, and all-day air. A parental waiver, which is available on-line, must be signed for ages 17 and under.

Hours: Open Sat. - Sun., 9am - 4pm.

Admission: $20 for walk ons with own equipment; $40 for renting everything.

Ages: Must be 10 years or older.

-----GREAT OUTDOORS-----

CHANNEL ISLANDS NATIONAL PARK (from Ventura)

☼

$$$$$

(805) 658-5730 - National Park; (805) 642-7688 - recorded information for Island Packers; (805) 642-1393 - Island Packers reservations; (805) 987-1301 - Channel Islands Aviation / www.nps.gov/chis; www.islandpackers.com; www.flycia.com

The park headquarters is at 1901 Spinnaker Drive; Island Packers is at 1867 Spinnaker, Ventura (Going W. on Ventura Fwy [101], exit S.W. on Seaward Ave., L. on Harbor Blvd. Going S.E. on 101, exit at Seaward Ave. and go straight onto Harbor Blvd. From Harbor Blvd., go R. on Spinnaker Dr. - all the way to the end. [TG: 491 F7])

The Channel Islands comprise eight islands off Southern California, five of which make up Channel Islands National Park and marine sanctuary. Prepare your kids for a half or whole day excursion to an island by first obtaining information from the park service. The islands were originally the home of Chumash Indians. Then, hunters came and killed certain otter, seal, and sea lion species almost to extinction. Finally, ranchers settled here. Some parts of the islands are still privately owned. It's important to emphasize to your child that Channel Islands is a national preserve, so "take only memories, leave only footprints."

Climate on the islands is different from mainland climate, even during the summer. The harsher conditions have produced various terrains within the relatively small parcels of land, from sandy beaches to rocky hills. Cruise to the islands and explore nature at her best and wildest. Kids get especially excited about seeing the numerous seals and sea lions that are plentiful because they breed on many of the islands. Be on the lookout for blue sharks and dolphins and note that whale watching is included with all cruises from the end of December through March. Once on an island, be on the lookout for some unusual birds, and animals like the island fox. Bring jackets and your camera; wear sneakers; pack a water bottle; and have a terrific outing!

Here is a very brief overview of the islands (enough to whet your adventuring appetite), along with cruise prices from Island Packers:

Anacapa - This is the closest island to Ventura, only fourteen miles away. It is five miles long. On East Anacapa, climb up the 153 steps to a sweeping panoramic view. Enjoy a small visitor's center and nearly two miles of hiking trails. There is no beach here, but swimming is allowed at the landing cove on calm summer days, as is scuba and skin diving. Picnicking is welcomed. This is one of the most popular islands to visit. Round trip takes about seven hours, including about three hours on the island. Adult fare is $37; children 3 - 12 years are $20. A half-day cruise around the island, with no island landing, is about three-and-a-half hours long. Adult fare is $21; kids are $14. Take an express run - a five-hour day, including two hours on the island, for $32 for adults; $20 for kids. On days of low tide, visit the tidepools at West Anacapa. The price for this cruise is the same as an all-day cruise.

Santa Cruz - At twenty-four miles long, this is the largest island off California. Topography varies from sea caves and steep cliffs to rolling hills and grasslands. Offered year-round, round trip takes eight to nine hours, including about three-and-a-half hours on the island. Adult fare is $42; children 3 - 12 years are $25. Overnight camping here is $54 for adults; $40 for kids.

Santa Rosa - This island is fifteen miles long and, although eighty-five percent of it is grasslands, there are still canyons, volcanic formations, and fossil beds that vary the landscape. There is plenty to see and do here for those who thrive on being in the midst of nature. Offered April through November, round trip takes about twelve hours, including about four hours on the island. Adult fare is $62; children 3 - 12 years are $45. Overnight camping is $80 for adults; $70 for kids.

San Miguel - This eight-mile-long island has beaches and an incredible number of seals and sea lions. The most popular destination here is the Caliche Forest (i.e. mineral sand castings), which is a three-and-a-half-mile hike from the beach. Be prepared for strong winds, plus rain and fog any time of the year. The varying island terrains reflect the assault of weather upon San Miguel. Weekend camping, offered May through November, and round-trip transportation costs $90 for adults; $80 for children 3 - 12 years. Day trips leave only from the city of Santa Barbara, and entail spending the night before on the boat. The day visits to San Miguel, offered April, and June through October, are recommended for hardier kids.

Santa Barbara - This is the smallest island, only 640 acres, and is the farthest away from mainland

Ventura. It has steep cliffs, a small "museum," and hiking trails. There are no shade trees on the island, so load up with sunscreen. Round trip, offered April through November, takes about eleven hours, including about four hours on the island. Adult fare is $49; children 3 - 12 years are $35. Camping is $75 for adults; $65 for kids.

If you prefer to fly, check out Channel Islands Aviation located at the Camarillo Airport and at the Goleta airport. Following a half-hour scenic flight over Anacapa and Santa Cruz Islands, you'll land on Santa Rosa Island and be here for about five and a half hours. A ranger drives around the island where you'll see a century-old cattle ranch and other island highlights. You can hike around a bit, have a picnic lunch (which you supply), and explore more of the island before you fly back to Camarillo. Adult fare is $106 round trip; children 2 to 12 years cost $84. The aviation company flies to the island on Saturdays and every other Sunday. Horizons West Adventures, (562) 799-3880, offers three-day fly-in camping trips three times a month from March to November for about $400 per person - camping equipment and a tour guide are included. See TRUTH AQUATICS (pg. 520) and CONDOR CRUISES (pg. 517) for cruising to the islands via Santa Barbara.

Also check out CHANNEL ISLANDS NATIONAL PARK VISITOR CENTER (pg. 542) and VENTURA HARBOR and VILLAGE (pg. 549).

Hours: Listed under each island.
Admission: Listed under each island.
Ages: 6 years and up.

CHILDREN'S NATURE INSTITUTE (Ventura County)
(310) 364-3591 / www.childrensnatureinstitute.org

See the entry for CHILDREN'S NATURE INSTITUTE (Los Angeles County) on page 39 for details.

CONEJO COMMUNITY PARK and CONEJO VALLEY BOTANIC GARDEN
(805) 495-2163 / www.crpd.org; www.conejogarden.com
400 Gainsborough Road, Thousand Oaks
(Exit Ventura Fwy [101] N. on Lynn Rd., R. on Gainsborough Rd. [TG: 526 E6])

This nature park is delightful in size and scope. There are acres and acres of green rolling hills, and a creek running throughout. The creek, by itself, is a major attraction. My boys loved looking for crawdads and, of course, stepping on the rocks, with the possible thrill of slipping and getting a bit wet. Almost a full day's adventure can be had by climbing the gnarled, old oak trees. There are cement pathways throughout the park, making much of it stroller accessible. The ambiance here is peaceful, unless you bring your kids, of course!

The upper field sports a baseball diamond, while a basketball court is across the way. A playground is located in front of the community center building. A covered picnic area with barbecue pits, volleyball courts, a horseshoe pit, and shuffleboard court is also available here.

The adjoining botanic garden is thirty-three acres, although only part of it is open to walk through. One short path traverses through a variety of landscapes, looping around and covering most of the garden. Another nature trail goes up and around the hillside, following a creek through oak and willow trees before looping back around. I don't know how much actual plant knowledge my kids gained from our garden walk, but I'm always hopeful that just spending time in such an environment will help them develop an appreciation for the beautiful gift of nature. A Children's Discovery Garden is currently being constructed which will have a treehouse to climb up and in, a vegetable garden, a rose garden, large dinosaur topiaries, a hydroponic greenhouse display demonstrating photosynthesis, a butterfly garden and butterfly "house," a nature trail, and a trailer that will serve as a center and classroom.

Hours: The park is open daily, dawn - dusk. The community center is open Mon. - Fri., 9am - 7pm; Sat., 9am - 4pm; Sun., noon - 4pm.
Admission: Free
Ages: All

CONEJO CREEK NORTH PARK

(805) 495-6471 - park; (805) 449-2660 - library / www.crpd.org

1379 E. Janss Road, Thousand Oaks

(Exit the 23 Fwy E. on Janss Rd. [TG: 526 H5])

    Around the back of the library, near the freeway, is a long strip of land that is a delightful park. Trees block the view of the freeway, and some of its sound. A rock-lined creek runs through most of the park. (My boys could spend hours playing just here, and getting a little wet.) There are also walkways, a few nice playgrounds, sand volleyball courts, picnic shelters, grassy areas, shade trees, an ornamental fountain, and quite a few bridges, one of which leads directly to the library. A visit to the library and/or adjacent senior/teen community center can round out your trip.

    Hours: Open daily, sunrise - sunset. Call for library hours.

Admission: Free

     Ages: All

LAKE CASITAS RECREATION AREA

(805) 649-2233 - park; (805) 649-1122 - camping info / www.casitaswater.org

11311 Santa Ana Road, Ventura

(Exit the Ojai Fwy [33] E. on Casitas Vista Rd., R. on Santa Ana Rd. It's at the junction of Baldwin Rd. [150] and Santa Ana Rd. [TG: 450 G4])

    A day at Lake Casitas is pure pleasure. The main attractions at this beautiful huge lake, which is stocked seasonally with bass, rainbow trout, crappie, and catfish, have traditionally been fishing, biking, and camping. The bait and tackle shop, (805) 649-2043, has boats for rent. A four-passenger aluminum motorboat is $65 for the day and a ten-passenger pontoon boat is $65 an hour. Single kayaks are $12.50 and double kayaks are $17.50. No waterskiing is allowed. A fishing permit, $11.05, is needed for those 16 years and older. For $7 per student and $10 per adults, school groups can take a two-hour cruise on the wild side with a naturalist-guided Wildlife Discovery Cruise aboard a pontoon boat. Participants see and learn about a variety of waterfowl, such as the great blue heron, as well as the landlocked animals, such as deer, foxes, and perhaps a bobcat or coyote. Call (805) 649-3535 / www.earthconcerns.org for more information and reservations.

    Bike on the five miles, or so, of paved trail, plus a few dirt paths that run throughout the park. Cycles for Rent, (805) 652-0462, is located just inside the recreation area. Bike rentals start at $8 an hour for a mountain bike and $10 an hour for a tandem. Cycles is open April through September on weekends from 9am to 6pm. Over 450 campsites range from basic tent camping to full RV hookups. Each site has a picnic table and fire ring. Ask for a schedule of events, such as the Renaissance Fair, Pow Wows, Bass Tournaments, and more.

    Beat the summer heat with the lake's Blue Heron Water Playground, designed for children 10 years and under. Kids on the upper end of this spectrum, however, will probably find this wading pool too tame. This spacious, colorful water play area has six slides, chutes, climbing structures, wheels to turn to adjust the water spray, anchored squirt guns, and water spurting out of its pipes - all in only eighteen inches of water. Several lifeguards patrol the pool. Parents can cool off in the water or relax on the adjacent grassy areas that surround this aquatic playground. Note: If your younger child is not quite potty trained, swim diapers are available to purchase here for $10.

    Hours: The lake and most amenities are open daily, sunrise - sunset. The water playground is open on weekends only, May - mid-June and September 10:45am - 6pm. It is open daily during the summer, 10:45am - 6pm. Sessions are about an hour long.

Admission: Entrance to the lake is $6.50 per vehicle; $12 with a boat. Camping prices range from $16 - $44, plus a $6.50 reservation fee, depending on the site and time of year. The water playground is $2 per person per hour. For walk-ins (i.e. those not paying the vehicle entrance fee), the water playground costs $3 per person for the first session; $1.50 for additional sessions.

    Ages: 1 - 10 years for the water playground; 3 years and up for the rest of the park.

LAKE PIRU RECREATION AREA

(805) 521-1500 - lake and camping; (805) 521-1231 - bait shop / www.lake-piru.org
4780 Piru Canyon Road, Piru
(Exit Ventura Fwy [101] E. on Hwy 126 about 12 miles, N. when you seen the signs for Lake Piru and drive about 7 miles. [TG: 367 E7])

This lake is huge at over four miles long and about one mile wide - no wonder there are two floating restrooms (aptly titled the S.S. Reliefs) on it. Located at the foothill of mountains, Lake Piru offers year-round respite from "real" life. The marina offers boat rentals, such as pontoon ($135 per day), fourteen foot fishing boats ($28 for two hours), and more. If you want to go waterskiing, bring your own boat. No jet skis allowed. The lake is stocked with rainbow trout and bass, so reel 'em in. A California fishing license is needed for ages 16 and up. Ask about the annual fishing derby held in the spring. A bait and tackle shop are on the premises. Seasonally, the swim beach is open (using imported sand - so very chic!). Lifeguards are on duty in the summer.

Day use picnic areas have covered eating areas, a grassy lawn, and barbecue grills. A snack bar, general store, and the Condor Point Restaurant are open for business. Tent and RV camping sites are intertwined with shade trees and views of the lake. Note that Lake Piru is next to the Sespe Condor Sanctuary, so take a look at the birds flying overhead.

Hours: Open daily, sunrise - sunset.
Admission: $7.50 per vehicle. Camping for up to four people ranges from $18 - $32 depending on the season and hook-ups; $2 per person over that number. Daily boat permits are $7.50.
Ages: All

LIBBEY PARK

(805) 646-1872 / www.ci.ojai.ca.us/content/PublicWorks/libbeypark.html
Ojai Avenue & Signal Street, Ojai
(Exit Ventura Fwy [101] N. on Ojai Fwy [33], which turns into Ventura Ave. [33], stay R. on Ventura Ave. [33/150], stay R. on Ojai Ave. [150]. [TG: 441 H7])

This sprawling park is really a combination of several kinds of parks. The playground area, accessible from Ojai Avenue, is terrific. It has heavy-duty plastic tubes to crawl through and suspension bridges to cross, plus slides and swings. Kids love squishing the wonderfully fine sand between their bare toes. A thirty-five-foot long talking tube is mostly underground, with just the funnel-shaped ends above ground, at kid-level. Have your child talk into one end while you listen at the other.

An abundant number of tennis courts are here, some with stadium seating as this is the home of an annual spring tournament that attracts the country's top-ranked collegiate players. Amateurs can play on a first come, first serve basis. The lower courts have lights for nighttime play. The half-dome-shaped Libbey Bowl has graded seating for concerts, or for your young stars to make their (pretend) debut. The Ojai Music Festival takes place here as do many other musical forums.

Further back, or entering from Montgomery Street, is the nature section of the park. Kids naturally gravitate to the creek that is surrounded by glorious old oak and sycamore trees. For just a little while, you'll feel refreshingly removed from civilization. The OJAI VALLEY TRAIL (see pg. 553) also begins (or ends) here. Tip: Top off your time with a visit to the ice cream store across Ojai Street, in the Antique Mall.

Hours: The park is open daily, dawn - dusk.
Admission: Free
Ages: All

MARINA PARK

(805) 652-4550
Pierpont Boulevard, Ventura
(Exit Ventura Fwy [101] S. on Seward Ave., L. on Pierpont Blvd., which dead-ends into the park. [TG: 491 F5])

This very cool park is part beach, part grass. The beach part has rock jetties with a paved pathway that goes out to a point. Sand dunes along the path, with the ocean and sailboats parading in and out of the marina, make it ideal for taking pictures, or just for meditating. A small cove (with waves) for swimming, and a surfing area are here, too. A relatively large cement replica Spanish galleon, rigging and all, is on the beach and filled with sand. The "ship" has a zip line, or cable slide, that goes from the ship to a post about fifty feet away on the sand. The adjacent grassy knolls have a few palm trees (no shade trees), picnic tables, and a playground with swings, toddler swings, slides, and other apparatus. Note that VENTURA HARBOR (see pg. 549) is just around the corner.

Hours: Open daily, sunrise - sunset.
Admission: Free
Ages: All

MORANDA PARK
(805) 986-6542
Moranda Parkway, Port Hueneme
(Exit Ventura Fwy [101] S. on Ventura Rd., L. on Port Hueneme Rd., R. on Moranda Pkwy. [TG: 552 F6])

This hilly green park is spread out and diverse with eight tennis courts, two softball fields, horseshoe pits, a sand volleyball court, a basketball court, and a nice playground. A paved path goes around and through the park making it a great place to stroll, jog, or bike. Stop to play here, or have a picnic while exploring Oxnard and Ventura!

Hours: Open daily, dawn - dusk.
Admission: Free
Ages: All

OJAI SK8 PARK
(805) 646-1872 / ci.ojai.ca.us
414 E. Ojai Avenue, Ojai
(Exit Ventura Fwy [101] N. on Ojai Fwy [33], which turns into Ventura Ave. [33], stay R. on Ventura Ave. [33/150], stay R. on Ojai Ave. [150]. [TG: 441 H7])

This good-sized skate park has rails, ramps, pyramids, and other street elements that make it worth skating. The fixtures are on asphalt in a parking-lot-type of setting. The park has lights for nighttime action. There are certain hours set aside for BMX riders, and also for skaters in 6th grade and below. Parental waivers must be signed for ages 17 and under and a helmet and pads must be worn.

Hours: Open Mon., 10am - 6pm, 7pm - 11pm; Tues. - Wed., 10am - 5pm, 5pm - 7pm (BMX), Wed. also has a 7pm - 11pm session for skaters; Thurs., 2pm - 4pm; Fri., 10am - 5pm, 7pm - 11pm; Sat., 10am - 6pm, 7pm - 11pm; Sun., 10am - 6pm.
Admission: Skating during the day and BMXing is free; night skating (from 7pm) costs $3.
Ages: 7 years and up.

POINT MUGU STATE PARK
(805) 488-5223 or (310) 457-1324;
(800) 444-7275 - camping reservations / www.parks.ca.gov; www.beachcalifornia.com/mugu.html
9000 W. Pacific Coast Highway at Sycamore Cove and Sycamore Canyon, Malibu
(Exit P.C.H. north on Sycamore Canyon Rd. Another trailhead, the La Jolla Valley Loop Trail is reached by exiting P.C.H. north on La Jolla Canyon Rd. [TG: 585 A4])

This westernmost park in the Santa Monica Mountain Recreation Area consists of miles of beach and thirty more miles of inland hiking and biking trails. A passageway under the highway allows visitors access to both parts of the park. The beach is a popular spot for swimming, seasonal whale watching (end of December through March) and viewing flocks of monarch butterflies (November through December). The inland, mountainside trails vary in length, difficulty, and scenery. Some trail heads are found at the campground.

The La Jolla Valley Loop Trail is about seven miles round trip. It is a relatively easy walk (about ¾ of a mile) to a waterfall, then the trail gets more strenuous. This trail also leads past a small pond before entering valley grasslands. You can follow the Loop trail to reconnect to the canyon or continue to Mugu Peak Trail and the 1,266-foot summit (an additional three miles). Other trails offer high-walled canyons, oak trees groves, fields of wild flowers (in the spring), and more.

Camping is available in Sycamore Canyon, which is part of the Point Mugu State Park system. Most of the sites nestled in the mountainside have trees and are nice looking. Adjacent to the campground is the Sycamore Nature Center with exhibits housed in a 1928 mission-style bungalow. Beach camping is available just one mile north at the Thornhill Broome exit.

Hours: Open daily, 7am - sunset. The nature center is open Sat. and Sun., 10am - 3pm.

Admission: $3 per vehicle for day use. There is limited street parking available. Camping at Sycamore Canyon, which has showers and running water, starts at $12 a night. Camping at Thornhill Broome starts at $7 a night. A $7.50 camping reservation fee is also charged. Admission is free to the nature center.

Ages: All

RANCHO SIERRA VISTA / SATWIWA NATIVE AMERICAN CULTURE CENTER

(805) 370-2300 or (818) 597-9192 / www.nps.gov/samo
off Via Goleta Road, Newbury Park
(Heading N. on Ventura Fwy [101], exit S. on Lynn Rd., go about 5 miles, L. on Via Goleta. Heading S. on 101, exit S. on N. Wendy Dr., R. on Borchard Rd., L. on S. Reino Rd., R. on Lynn, L. on Via Goleta. From Via Goleta, go to the third parking area, as that's nearest to the cultural center and trailheads. [TG: 555 E4])

Since the cultural center is not visible from the parking area, you need to walk about a quarter of a mile on a tree-lined gravel road to reach it. A small garden, a large reconstructed Chumash ap (i.e. round house dwelling made of willow and tule) to walk through, and the center's building containing informational display panels and a few Native American artifacts are just the beginning. On Sundays the culture center plays host to traditionally-dressed Native Americans who tell stories or talk about aspects of their ancestor's life and culture; share tribal songs; demonstrate crafts; and/or lead workshops. Ask about special presentations and guided, educational hikes.

The two-mile Satwiwa loop trail, with its trailhead just outside the center, traverses amongst oak and sycamore trees and around the chaparral-covered hillsides that are particularly lovely after the winter rains and while the spring wildflowers are in bloom. This fairly easy hike is good for almost all ages. Tip: Bring your own water. Go just another mile, round trip, off the loop trail to connect to Boney Mountain trail, which crosses a stream several times to reach the seasonal waterfall. Several other trails intersperse throughout as this area extends into POINT MUGU STATE PARK (see pg. 537). You can even hike to the beach - about eight miles each way. A shorter, and bike/stroller friendly, option is the paved pathway that runs about three miles, one way.

Hours: The park is open daily, dawn - dusk. The Culture Center is open weekends during the summer, and Sun. the rest of the year, 10am - 5pm.

Admission: Free

Ages: 8 years and up.

SANTA MONICA MOUNTAINS NATIONAL PARK HEADQUARTERS/VISITORS CENTER

(805) 370-2301 - visitors center; (818) 597-9192 - park info / www.nps.gov/samo
401 W. Hillcrest Drive, Thousand Oaks
(Exit Ventura Fwy [101] N. on Lynn Rd., R. on Hillcrest, L. on McCloud, R. on Civic Center Dr. [TG: 526 E7])

From the thousands of acres of mountains to the coastline beaches to the inland grounds, the enormous Santa Monica Mountain National Park covers a major part of the wilderness and parkland in Southern California. This includes hiking, biking, and equestrian trails, plus camping, swimming, scenic drives, ranger-led programs, and more. The center has a few interpretative displays and a gift shop containing hiking and nature books. I am really writing about this place because maps and a calendar schedule of events for the numerous parks within the Santa Monica Mountains Park system can be found here. The parks, most of which can be found listed individually under the Great Outdoors Section, include Circle X Ranch, Coldwater Canyon Park, Franklin Canyon Ranch, Leo Carrillo State Park, Malibu Creek State Park, Malibu Lagoon State Beach, Paramount Ranch, Peter Strauss Ranch, Rancho Sierra Vista, Temescal Gateway Park, Topanga State Park, Will Rogers State Historical Park, and the U.C.L.A. Stunt Ranch.

Hours: Open daily, 9am - 5pm.
Admission: Free
Ages: 5 years and up.

WILDWOOD REGIONAL PARK

(805) 381-2741 or (805) 495-2163
W. Avenue de los Arboles, Thousand Oaks
(Exit Ventura Fwy [101] N. at Lynn Rd., L. at Avenida de los Arboles, all the way to the end. [TG: 526 B2])

Take a walk on the wild side at Wildwood Regional Park. The narrow, dirt trails and service roads are great for real hiking. There are two major trail heads that lead to an extensive trail system for hikers, bikers, and equestrians. Come prepared by bringing water bottles, sunscreen, and backpacks with food for designated picnic areas. Although hiking downhill is easy, plan twice as much time for the hike back up.

Some highlights along the somewhat shorter trails, which are still an almost all-day event, include the Nature Center, Little Falls, and Paradise Falls, which is a forty-foot waterfall that you'll hear before you actually reach it. As you walk along the creek or throughout the chaparral and woodlands, be on the lookout for wildlife, such as mule deers or lizards.

Hike here during the spring months and you'll see an abundance of wildflowers. I encourage you to get a trail map, as different routes have different highlights that you'll want to explore. The park offers wonderful, fun, and educational programs like Saturday Night S'Mores, Full Moon Hikes, and Outdoor Experiential Workshops. Enjoy nature, almost in your backyard!

Hours: Open daily, dawn - dusk.
Admission: Free. Some of the programs cost between $3 - $4.
Ages: 4 years and up. Kids will tire easily.

-----MALLS-----

THE OAKS - OK KIDS CLUB

(805) 495-2031 or (805) 376-3515 / www.shoptheoaksmall.com
222 W. Hillcrest Drive, Thousand Oaks
(Exit Ventura Fwy [101] N. on Lynn Rd., R. on Hillcrest. [TG: 556 E1])

A variety of half-hour shows are presented every week at the lower level court near Robinsons May. Shows could include marionettes, singers, dancers, magicians, and other entertainment. This mall often hosts special events, such as Kid's World in August. This particular event usually features hands-on exhibits, kids' concerts, small pet races, and a Safety Zone where kids learn about safety in an interactive manner. Note that this mall also features BUILD-A-BEAR WORKSHOP (see pg. 550) store, as well as many other fine stores and eateries.

Hours: Every Thurs. at 10:30am. No shows in December.
Admission: Free
Ages: 1½ - 7 years.

PACIFIC VIEW KID'S CLUB

(805) 642-0605 / www.shoppacificview.com
3301-1 E. Main Street, Ventura
(Going E. on Ventura Fwy [101], take Telephone Rd. exit, R. on Main. Going W. on Ventura, exit N.W. on Main. [TG: 491 H3])

Come sing a song a two, or just clap your hands along with the musical entertainment featured here every week. This is an ideal outing for younger kids. The club meets at the food court rotunda on the upper level. Sign your kids up to be a Kid's Club member because they will receive discounts at certain stores, a free birthday gift, and monthly event announcements. Note that the Farmer's Market meets outside the mall on Wednesdays from 9am to 1pm.

Hours: Shows are every Wed. at 10:30am.
Admission: Free
Ages: 2 - 6 years old.

-----MUSEUMS-----

ALBINGER ARCHAEOLOGICAL MUSEUM

(805) 648-5823 / www.vcmha.org
113 E. Main Street, Ventura
(Going W. on Ventura Fwy [101], exit N. on California Ave., L. on Main St. Going S.E. on 101, exit E. on Main. It's on the N. side of the street. [TG: 491 B2])

This small, one-room museum has a collection of archaeological finds spanning thirty-five centuries that have been uncovered from this site. Arrowheads, bottles, milling stones, bone whistles, and more are on display. When the kids have seen their fill, which was pretty immediate with my younger ones, head out the back door and look at the site of an actual dig. The foundations of an original Mission (church) are clearly marked here. My kids were more interested after I explained what we were looking at, and how archaeologists found the remains. (Digging in dirt is a popular pastime with our family, too.)

The enticing stone steps back here lead, disappointingly, to a small street, but at least we got in some exercise.

Hours: Open September through May, Wed. - Fri., 10am - 2pm; Sat. - Sun., 10am - 4pm. Open June through August, Wed. - Sun., 10am - 4pm. Closed New Year's Day, Easter, Thanksgiving, and Christmas.
Admission: Free; donations appreciated.
Ages: 6 years and up.

AVIATION MUSEUM OF SANTA PAULA

(805) 525-1109 / www.amszp.org
830 E. Santa Maria Street, Santa Paula
(Exit the Santa Paula Fwy [126] S. on Palm Ave., L. on Santa Maria St. [TG: 464 B6])

Take your child to new heights at this aviation museum, adjacent to the Santa Paula Airport. Watch small planes land and take off. The museum consists of a chain of hangars, each one featuring different exhibits. Inside the first hangar, displays pertain to the history of the Santa Paula airport, including a short video. Other hangars showcase restored vintage, military, classic, and experimental aircraft. More unusual exhibits (at least unusual for an aviation museum) are vintage and unusual radios, jukeboxes, antique and classic cars, vintage racing cars, paintings, photos, collectibles, and more. The museum's goal is to expand to include other hangars and incorporate more historical aircraft, especially from the various war eras. School and other group tours are offered during the week - call to make a reservation.

Enjoy the numerous classic airplanes that come in for a landing on the first Sunday, coinciding with the museum being open. What a great way to spend time with the whole family! Note: Grab a bite to eat at the on-site Logsdon's Restaurant and Lounge, which is open for breakfast, lunch, and dinner. Call (805) 525-1101 for more information. See SANTA PAULA AIRPORT / CP AVIATION, INC. (pg. 555) and YOUNG EAGLES PROGRAM - Santa Paula (pg. 556) if you're interested in taking airplane rides.

Hours: Open the first Sun. of every month, 10am - 3pm.
Admission: Free
Ages: 4 years and up.

CALIFORNIA OIL MUSEUM

(805) 933-0076 / www.oilmuseum.net

1001 E. Main Street, Santa Paula

(Exit the 126 Fwy, N. on State Route 150 [or 10ᵗʰ St.]. The Museum is on the N.E. corner of 10ᵗʰ and Main St. [TG: 464 C5])

The California Oil Museum is housed in the original headquarters of the Union Oil Company. The interior and exterior of the 1890 building has meticulously been restored to its original luster. Upon entering, kids can punch a keepsake time card in an old time card machine. The walls are covered with great pictures and murals regarding the history and technology of the oil industry.

Quite a few of the exhibits are interactive, such as the Lubricity Exhibit. Kids can turn the gears and see how much easier the figures on bicycles can pedal when the gears are oiled. They can push a button and watch a model rig "drill" for oil through the layers of the earth. With a touch of a button, the Centrifuge Exhibit spins to separate water and other substances from crude oil. A few touch screens here impart interesting information about how the oil industry affects so many aspects of our lives.

Since geology is vital to finding oil, several terrific geological displays are in the museum. Some of the fossils on display include shells, dinosaur bones, and shark teeth.

The upstairs, which can only be seen by a half-hour guided tour, is interesting to older kids. There are restored offices, bedrooms, a kitchen, and fireplaces with ornate tiles around them. A walk-in safe looks like a secret, hidden room.

Walk through the main building and outside to reach the Rig Room. Kids can see a full-size drilling rig, and a huge cable rig in action as the engine turns the sand wheel that turns the band wheel that moves the wooden walking beam and the huge drill bits. I hope you feel like we did when we visited the museum - like we struck oil!

Hours: Open Wed. - Sun., 10am - 4pm. Tours of the upstairs are offered during 11am - 2pm of regular museum hours. Closed major holidays.

Admission: $2 for adults; $1 for ages 6 - 18; children 5 and under are free. The tour of the upstairs costs an additional $1 per person. There is no admission charged for the museum the first Wed. of every month.

Ages: 4 years and up.

CAMARILLO RANCH MUSEUM

(805) 389-8182 / www.camarilloranch.org

201 Camarillo Ranch Road, Camarillo

(Going N. on Ventura Fwy [101] exit N. on Flynn Rd., R. on Mission Oaks Blvd., L. on Camarillo Ranch Rd. Going S. on 101, exit on Dawson and you'll be going S., turn R. on Petit St., R. on Dawson (back over the freeway), R. on Mission Oaks Blvd., L. on Camarillo. [TG: 524 G3])

This three-story, fifteen-room house is one of the most lovely restored Victorian homes I've had the pleasure of touring. The distinguished architecture - the archways, twelve-foot-high ceilings, octagon-shaped rooms, beautiful wood staircase, wrap around porch, and other special features - enhances the elegant furniture and colorful wallpaper and borders. The tour guide explained the past owners' history and all about the house, but truthfully, I mostly enjoyed just looking at all the rooms.

Adjacent to the house is the original mule barn, stables (one of which now houses a gift shop) as well as a huge Moreton Bay Fig tree, and beautifully landscaped grounds. Interesting to note is that the Ranch Museum is now surrounded by a business park, which seems out of place (or time).

Hours: Open Wed., noon - 4pm; Sat., 10am - 2pm; Sun., noon - 4pm. Group tours may be arranged at other times.

Admission: Free; donations appreciated.

Ages: 8 years and up.

CARNEGIE ART MUSEUM

(805) 385-8157 - exhibit info.;
(805) 385-8158 - receptionist during museum hours. / www.vcnet.com/carnart
424 S. 'C' Street, Oxnard
(Exit Ventura Fwy [101] S. on Hwy 1 [or Oxnard Blvd.], R. on 4th St. It's on the S. side of the street. [TG: 522 G6])

I mention this small, beautiful fine arts museum mainly because of the kid-friendly workshops offered. (Tell your kids the building is done in neo-classical design, though they'll just think the columns look really neat.) I take my kids through art museums, explaining what I can and hoping that some understanding and appreciation for art will take root. However, I think the best way to reach and teach our kids is through guided tours and hands-on workshops.

In a group tour here, kids learn about a particular style, artist, or medium, depending on the current exhibit. Then, they create their own art projects in a workshop taught by a local artist. Reservations are needed. Ask about other classes offered, too.

Come see the permanent and rotating exhibits of paintings, photographs, and sculptures at this Museum. Have your children draw a picture of their outing!

Hours: Open Thurs. - Sat., 10am - 5pm; Sun., 1am - 5pm. Closed during public holidays and during installation of new exhibits.

Admission: $3 for adults; $2 for seniors and students; $1 for ages 6 - 16; children 5 and under are free. The museum is free on Fri., 3pm - 6pm. Call for tour and class prices.

Ages: 6 years and up.

CEC/SEABEE MUSEUM

(805) 982-5163 or (805) 982-1249 / www.seabeehf.org
23rd Avenue and Dodson Street, Port Hueneme
(Exit the Ventura Fwy [101] S. on Ventura Rd., then just S. of Channel Islands Blvd. turn R. on 23rd Ave (it's Sunkist St. on the left). Park, tho, on San Pedro St., near building 11, near Pleasant Valley Gate. A van will drive you on base to the museum and back. [TG: 552 E3])

This huge museum, with a statue of a large bee with a machine gun, is dedicated to documenting, preserving, and maintaining public awareness of the contributions of the Seabees and Civil Engineer Corps. The mission statement is formal sounding, but the museum is incredibly rich with fascinating exhibits. There are life-size models and statues of men and women depicted in scenes of battle and peacetime, wearing authentic uniforms and costumes from around the world. Displays of weapons, medals, banners, photos, and equipment, such as gas masks, represent all facets of a Seabee's life in action.

Another wing has model boats and an underwater diving exhibit with small, model scuba divers. Kids can touch a full-size, old-fashioned diving suit and helmet. Wonderful dioramas, such as a Seabee's amphibious landing and establishment of camp, can be easily seen, thanks to viewing platforms.

The Cultural Artifacts section is interesting because of the number of exhibits and international content. On display are unusual musical instruments; foreign currency and coins; tools; Indian weapons, beadwork, drums, and other artifacts; an Alaska exhibit; a China exhibit; and so much more! Although nothing here is hands-on, my kids were captivated by the variety and uniqueness of the items. Each exhibit brought a yell of, "Hey, come over here and check this out!" It's the kind of museum, because of its size and the scope of displays, that you can visit again and again. Please note that reservations and a photo I.D. are required to visit the museum.

Hours: The museum is open to the public Wed., 10am - 11am and 1pm - 2pm; Fri., 1pm - 2pm. Closed federal holidays, Easter, and the week between Christmas and New Year's Day.

Admission: Free

Ages: 4 years and up.

CHANNEL ISLANDS NATIONAL PARK VISITOR CENTER

(805) 658-5730 / www.nps.gov/chis
1901 Spinnaker Drive, Ventura

(Going W. on Ventura Fwy [101], exit S.W. on Seaward Ave., L. on Harbor Blvd. Going S.E. on 101, exit at Seaward Ave. and go straight onto Harbor Blvd., R. on Spinnaker Dr. - all the way to the end. [TG: 491 F6])

The Channel Islands Visitor Center is worthy of a trip in itself. You'll pass by beaches and stores (see VENTURA HARBOR and VILLAGE on page 549), but pacify the kids with a, "We'll stop there on the way out." The Center is a good combination of museum, store, and resource center. The kids will head straight for the indoor tidepool (not a touch tank), which offers an up-close look at sea stars, anemones, and other small, ocean creatures. Other eye-catching displays are the taxidermied animals, such as birds in flight, a topographical model of the islands, a life-size replica of an elephant seal, and a cast of a pygmy mammoth skeleton. My boys also enjoyed sifting sand in the mini-sand pit and grinding pretend meal with a Chumash Indian stone mortar and pestle.

The twenty-five-minute movie, *A Treasure In the Sea,* is shown throughout the day, and is a fun way to learn more about sea life. Tidepool talks are available on weekends and holidays. Note that rangers come to local schools for presentations. (Also look under CHANNEL ISLANDS NATIONAL PARK (from Ventura) on page 533.)

    Hours: Open daily, 8:30am - 5pm. Closed Thanksgiving and Christmas.

  Admission: Free

     Ages: 2 years and up.

CHUMASH INTERPRETIVE CENTER / OAKBROOK REGIONAL PARK

(805) 492-8076 / www.designplace.com/chumash

3290 Lang Ranch Parkway, Thousand Oaks

(Exit Hwy 23 E. on Avenida De Los Arboles, R. on Westlake, then the first L. on Lang Ranch Pkwy. [TG: 527 C4])

Long ago, the Chumash Indians occupied this area of land, which is now Ventura County, and other surrounding areas. A small, one-room Interpretive Center features artifacts representative of the Chumash way of life. Pictures and native paintings decorate the walls. Some local plants, and the way they were used, are on display, such as yucca fibers braided into ropes, and sticks fashioned into weapons. Rabbit and bear furs can be touched, while other exhibits are behind glass. My kids liked the musical instruments, such as gourds and rattles, and I admired the jewelry made out of beads. Outside, kids can see a replicated Chumash village and sweat lodge. If kids can handle the one-and-a-half-mile walk, hike back to see the centuries-old pictographs, or rock paintings, visible from the caves/overhangs. (The pictographs might not look like much to kids, but their symbolism and preservation is important to Chumash heritage.) Sign up for a guided nature walk, given on Saturdays at 1pm. The cost is the same as admission to the center. Check out the Pow Wow held here over Memorial Day weekend. (See pg. 580.)

School or group tours are about three-and-a-half hours long, very informative, and one of the most effective ways to really see and understand what the Center has to offer. Listen to storytelling, play a few native games, and take a guided walk through the park and archaeological preserve, from a Chumash perspective. You'll learn about their way of life; inspect a re-created Chumash village complete with a large ap (i.e. round house), two smaller aps, the sweatlodge, and a ceremonial ground; and hear how different plants and trees were used. You'll also do some rock painting (i.e. pictograph), see a slide presentation, hear the history of the Chumash and an explanation of the museum exhibits, and make a craft to take home. As an alternative, one hour could be used as wildlife presentation, learning about the native animals and how to live with and respect them.

The park itself is beautiful, and can be visited without going into the Interpretive Center, although they do ask that you sign in. There are picnic tables, shady oak trees, and miles of hiking trails.

    Hours: The Center is open Tues. - Sat., 10am - 3pm. The park is open daily, dawn - dusk.

  Admission: Entrance to the park is free. Admission to the interpretive center is $5 for adults; $4 for seniors, students, and ages 5 - 12; children 4 and under are free. Tours are $4 per person; teachers are free.

     Ages: 7 years and up for the Center.

EARTH SCIENCE MUSEUM

(805) 642-3155
5019 Crooked Palm Road, Ventura
(Exit Ojai Fwy [33] W. on Shell Rd., L. on Ventura Ave., L. on Crooked Palm Rd. [TG: 471 C1])

This small museum is run by the Gem and Mineral Society and is open by appointment only. The "dinosaur petting zoo" consists of wonderful casts of dinosaur skulls, bones, and teeth that kids can touch. Other casts and real fossils include a ground sloth, mammoth tusk, sauropod ribs, skull of a cave bear, and lots more. The displays include nice pieces of various rocks and minerals, such as geodes, agates, and others; locally found fossils, including shells, eggs, and bird tracks; petrified wood; and lots of informational posters. Everything not behind glass can be handled. Tours are tailored toward your children's ages and attention spans, and the facts dispensed are fascinating. (i.e. A saber-tooth cat is not a tiger because it had no stripes.)

Hours: By appointment.
Admission: Free
Ages: 4 years and up.

GULL WINGS CHILDREN'S MUSEUM

(805) 483-3005 / www.gullwingsmuseum4kids.org
418 W. 4th Street, Oxnard
(Exit Ventura Fwy [101] S. on Hwy 1 [or Oxnard Blvd.], R. on 4th St. [TG: 522 G6])

Children's museums strive for the right combination of fun and education. Gull Wings has achieved a delightful balance of these goals. The long building has sectioned off "rooms," each one focusing on a different theme. The first room is a delightful toddlers' play area. The next one is set up like a farmer's market.

My kids played doctor and patient in the next room for over an hour. This complete medical room has gowns, a surgery table with play instruments, an X-ray set up, wheelchairs, and crutches. For hands-on health and science learning, there are plastic models of the body with removable parts, and cloth dolls that kids can unlayer to reveal muscles, bones, and organs.

Further back in the museum is a mini-market with shopping carts, a cash register, and bins of "food" for your little shoppers. A stage area has a town backdrop and props, like a fire hydrant and a boat, to help complete scenes for your kids act out. A cavern, for future geologists or paleontologists, contains rocks, fossils, and skulls to look at and/or touch. (The saber-tooth cat is a particular favorite). Kids can use a microscope to study other elements. Face painting and a glow-in-the-dark art nook brings out the creative genius in your offspring. Enter another dimension when you enter the outer space room. With the aid of a video camera and an unearthly backdrop, it appears as though you are on the moon.

Other highlights include computers with educational games; taking temporary shadow pictures against a photo-sensitive wall; a small space center with a control panel; a touch tank with sea stars, sea cucumbers, and sea urchins; and "driving" a kid-proofed Saturn car. Young drivers can get behind the wheel, shift gears, turn on headlights and, via a plexiglass hood, see the inner workings of an engine. A side door panel is also clear. Pet Corner has a few live animals that children can pet or hold, including turtles, garter snakes, a rat, and a guinea pig. Ask about the numerous craft and educational classes, as well as special family nights.

Hours: Open Tues. - Sat., 10am - 5pm.
Admission: $4 per person; children under 2 are free.
Ages: 1 to 13 years.

OJAI VALLEY HISTORICAL SOCIETY AND MUSEUM

(805) 640-1390
130 W. Ojai Avenue, Ojai
(Exit Ventura Fwy [101] N. on Ojai Fwy [33], which turns into Ventura Ave. [33], stay R. on Ventura Ave. [33/150], stay R. on Ojai Ave. [150]. [TG: 441 H7])

This museum, located inside an old chapel, has a mission - keeping historic Ojai alive by preserving the valley's cultural and natural heritage. Since most of the exhibits are encased in glass, my kids did a lot of nose pressing. They smudged up the cases containing Chumash Indian artifacts such as arrowheads, beadwork, and rattles made from turtle shells and sea shells. Another exhibit area with a lot of kid-appeal is the taxidermied animals. The stuffed animals on our hit parade include the black bear and the more unusual, platypus and bat. The museum also has a fine collection of taxidermied snakes.

Some of the fossils featured here include a big sea snail and an even bigger rock with at least a dozen sand dollars imbedded in it. (The buck stops here!) The museum has a fairly extensive shell collection, too. I only hope we can remember some of their names the next time we go to the beach.

    Hours: Open Wed. - Fri., 1pm - 4pm; Sat. - Sun., 10am - 4pm.

Admission: $3 for adults; $2 seniors; ages 18 and under are free.

    Ages: 3 years and up.

OLIVAS ADOBE HISTORICAL PARK

(805) 644-4346 / www.geocities.com/BourbonStreet/Dixie/9959/OlivasAdobeHistoricParkCenter.html

4200 Olivas Park Drive, Ventura

(Going S. on Ventura Fwy [101], exit S. on Harbor Blvd., L. on Olivas Park Dr. Going N.W. on 101, exit S. on Victoria, R. on Olivas Park Dr. [TG: 491 H7])

The Olivas Adobe is a restored two-story adobe home built in 1847 that once housed Senor Olivas, his wife, and their twenty-one children! It is representative of the rancho period in California's history and as such offers school tours geared for fourth graders, as well as to the general public. The residence has bedrooms, a living room, a large chapel room, and a kitchen to look into that are furnished just as they were over 100 years ago. The grounds are beautifully landscaped. The open courtyard, with its lovely bell gate entrance, contains a Spanish beehive oven and some farming equipment, and gives younger ones some running-around space. A small exhibit building, across from the rose garden, contains items that relate to this particular time period, such as saddles, pictures, and ranching equipment. While this is not an all day visit, kids enjoy the opportunity to "see" the past. Ask about the many special programs hosted by the park, such as concerts and candlelight tours at Christmastime.

    Hours: The grounds are open daily, 10am - 4pm. The Adobe, and tours of it, are available on Sat. and Sun., 10am - 4pm.

Admission: Free

    Ages: 6 years and up.

RONALD REAGAN PRESIDENTIAL LIBRARY AND MUSEUM

(800) 410-8354 or (805) 522-8444 / www.reagan.utexas.edu

40 Presidential Drive, Simi Valley

(From the Simi Valley/San Fernando Valley Fwy [118], exit S. on Madera Rd., R. on Presidential Dr. From the 23 Fwy, exit N.E. on Olsen Rd, which turns into Madera Rd., L. on Presidential Dr. [TG: 497 C4])

The massive, Spanish-style Ronald Reagan Library and Museum is alone on a hilltop. Remember those books that you read about kings and queens and their treasures? Walk down the hallway lined with incredible gifts from heads of states and feel like those storybook pages have come true. Treasures range from an exquisite hand-beaded blouse for the First Lady to an intricately carved, ivory-handled sword that has a gold sheath inlaid with jewels for the President. Note that the gifts of state do rotate.

Reagan's heritage and love of the West is evident throughout the museum. One room, in particular, is dedicated to the American west with displays of elaborate saddles, boots, spurs, statues, and an eye-catching cowboy hat with a real rattlesnake head on the band. Even the full-size replica of the Oval Office, which reflects each President's personal style, is decorated with western art.

Two theaters show twenty-minute-plus videos of the Reagan years that include inauguration speeches, tearing down the Berlin wall, and a remembrance of the Challenger crew. My kids were thoroughly captivated by the footage.

The next few galleries depict Reagan's road to the presidency via movie posters, uniforms, costumes, documents, and lots of photos. My oldest child was also impressed by a large nuclear cruise missile on display that was once deployed in Europe. One room contains signed sports paraphernalia. Another displays gifts that range from the elegant to the homemade, such as a jellybean-painted cane, and the Presidential Seal crafted from 6,500 silver nails - what a great kid's project this would make! There are pictures of Nancy Reagan, some of her gowns, and a whole wall devoted to her "Just Say No" campaign.

There are numerous touch screens throughout the museum so kids can learn about Reagan's views on issues by letting their fingers "do the walking." Visitors can become members of Reagan's cabinet (albeit temporarily) while sitting around a table in a re-created White House Room. His image and responses are shown on a big screen in the room. Travel to the Geneva Convention and witness a historic meeting between Gorbachev and Reagan as their images are projected on the screen above the chateau's fireplace.

Feeling presidential? Beginning spring, 2004, board a retired Air Force One plane used by seven past presidents, from Nixon to Bush. Dubbed the "flying White House," the plane will be enclosed in a glass-walled pavilion. The scintillating history of the plane will be told via displays panels, including a timeline by the entrance/exit. Walking through the plane, complete with a bowl of Reagan's favorite candy (jelly beans), visitors will hear an audio tour that re-creates the sound and conversations of a flight. Next to the plane will be a bullet-proof limousine used by Reagan, accompanied by police motorcycles, a chase car, and mannequins resembling Secret Service agents. Acquiring a Marine Corps One helicopter and F-14 escort jet are in the works to complete the exhibit. A separate, two-level structure will house a learning center consisting of an auditorium and more gallery space. A huge, decoratively spray-painted, chunk of the Berlin wall is also currently located out this way.

Note that the gift shop has great aids for teaching history. The Reagan Country Cafe is on-site and open the same hours as the museum.

Hours:	Open daily, 10am - 5pm. Closed New Year's Day, Thanksgiving, and Christmas.
Admission:	$5 for adults; $3 for seniors; children 15 and under are free. Call first to see if there is a separate admission charge to view the Air Force One exhibit and back galleries. (See C.E.E. L.A. for membership savings, page 86.)
Ages:	5 years and up.

SAN BUENAVENTURA MISSION

(805) 643-4318 / www.sanbuenaventuramission.org $

211 E. Main Street, Ventura

(Going W. on Ventura Fwy [101], exit N. on California Ave., L. on Main St. Going S.E. on 101, exit E. on Main. It's on the N. side of the street. [TG: 491 B2])

Built in 1792, and ninth in the chain of California missions, San Buenaventura exudes old-world charm. Although the mission is readily seen from the street, a tour through the rooms and grounds offer a better picture of life during this historical time period. You'll see a small courtyard, artifacts from mission days in the several rooms, and even a small cemetery around the side. Groups, with a minimum ten people, can take guided tours with reservations,. The tour, actually offered by the Ventura County Museum, includes information about the mission's past inhabitants and doing a thematic craft project.

Hours:	Open Mon. - Fri., 10am - 5pm; Sat., 9am - 5pm; Sun., 10am - 4pm. Closed major holidays.
Admission:	$1 for adults; 50¢ for children 16 and under.
Ages:	6 years and up.

STAGECOACH INN MUSEUM

(805) 498-9441 / www.stagecoachmuseum.org $

51 N. Ventu Park Road, Newbury Park

(Exit the Ventura Fwy [101] S. on Ventu Park Rd. [TG: 556 B1])

This beautiful 1870's hotel and stagecoach stop is both interesting and educational, and seen only by guided tour. The downstairs consists mainly of the parlor, dining room, and kitchen. The furniture, decor, and history are interesting to older kids, but younger kids get antsy.

Upstairs, however, it is a different story. A small "cowboy" bedroom has a saddle, bear skin rug, and other western paraphernalia. The Chumash Indian room has a collection of fossils, beadwork, baskets, and pictures. A child's room is filled with toys of yesteryear (no Nintendo!), and a bed that Todd Lincoln slept in. (I hope kids won't ask, "Who's that?") Oooooo - a man named Pierre was supposedly shot here and his ghost still haunts the Inn. Now, the Inn becomes fascinating to kids!

Outside the hotel, take a short nature trail that leads to other historic points of interest. The Carriage House contains stagecoaches, while further around the bend are the Pioneer Newbury House, the Spanish Adobe House, and a replica of the first schoolhouse in the area. All are open to tour. The Chumash Indian Hut and a beehive oven are also interesting. Explain to your kids that the oven is named for its design, not for cooking bees. Note that school tours are available upon request.

When the kids have seen all they want, head out to the small Stagecoach Park above the Inn. It's easier to drive to the park than to walk, as the entrance is on another street.

Hours: The Inn is open Wed. - Sun., 1pm - 4pm. The entire complex is open Sun., 1pm - 4pm.

Admission: $3 for adults; $2 for seniors; $1 for ages 5 - 12; children 4 and under are free. Closed New Year's Day, Easter, Thanksgiving, and Christmas.

Ages: 5 years and up.

STRATHERN HISTORICAL PARK AND MUSEUM

(805) 526-6453 / www.simihistory.com

137 Strathern Place, Simi Valley

(Exit Simi Valley/San Fernando Valley Fwy [118] S. on Madera Rd., R. on Strathern Place. [TG: 497 E2])

$$

This outside museum is several historical buildings inside a gated, over six-acre, park-like setting. Start your two-hour-plus guided tour at the visitor's center. Learn about the early days of Simi by first watching a fifteen-minute tape about the Valley's history. Some of the exhibits in here include maps and, a little more exciting, beekeeping equipment such as smokers and hoods. Next, walk through one of the very first local colony houses. Though the inside decor is from the 1930's, the building itself still retains its earlier, original charm. An adobe house, built in the early 1700's, displays an owner's furnishings from the 1950's. The Strathern House, which is a Victorian house built in 1893, has antique treasures throughout including furniture, clothing, and a pump organ.

The library contains some fossils, as well as books. The enclosed barn has eight stalls with different exhibits in each, such as kitchen gadgets, early laundry equipment, an old-fashioned switchboard, Chumash Indian artifacts, farm machinery, and old automobiles such as a truck, a tractor, and a Ford Model A. Another barn contains more farm equipment, such as hay wagons. Around the perimeters of the historical park are pieces of old (rusted) farming equipment, which adds to the rustic ambiance.

Hours: The grounds are open Tues. - Fri., 9am - 2pm; Sat. - Sun., 1pm - 4pm. The inside buildings, which can only be seen on a tour, are open Wed. at 1pm; Sat. - Sun., 1pm - 4pm, weather permitting. Open for large groups and for free school tours during the week upon request.

Admission: $3 per person.

Ages: 5 years and up.

VENTURA COUNTY MARITIME MUSEUM

(805) 984-6260

2731 S. Victoria Avenue, Oxnard

(Exit Ventura Fwy [101] S. on Victoria St. The museum is located at Channel Islands Harbor at the corner of Victoria St. and Channel Islands Blvd. [TG: 552 B2])

$

Explore the seas without leaving port! This good-sized, nautical museum has original paintings, and various sizes and styles of model ships behind glass cases. What detail! Marine artists from the 1700's to the present have their eye-catching work on display throughout the museum. If your child has the patience, or desire, a docent will gladly explain local nautical history, which gives more meaning to the exhibits. Ask about their tall ship expeditions and three-day at-sea excursions.

Hours: Open daily, 11am - 5pm.

Admission: Suggested donations of $3 for adults; $1 for children 11 and under.
Ages: 4 years and up.

VENTURA COUNTY MUSEUM OF HISTORY AND ART

(805) 653-0323 / www.vcmha.org   *$*
100 E. Main Street, Ventura

(Going W. on Ventura Fwy [101], exit N. on California Ave., L. on Main St. Going S.E. on 101, exit E. on Main. It's on the S. side of street. [TG: 491 B2])

This museum is a great introduction to art for children. The paintings and dioramas are beautiful, and the variety of exhibits is even better. As we followed along the building's circular layout, we saw a wonderful display of fossilized shells and bones. The outside patio area has an impressive collection of large farm machinery. Chumash Indian stone mortars and pestles are out here for kids to try. A section of the museum is set up chronologically, showing the beginnings of Ventura County, featuring Chumash artifacts, to the New West, which is represented by a 1910 car, an old vacuum cleaner, washer, and other household appliances.

The George Stuart Gallery room displays part of his over 200 historical figures. Marie Antoinette, American patriots, and others, are one-quarter life-size (three inches to the foot). The intricate art work and attention to detail makes the finished figures very lifelike. My kids were most intrigued with the models and pictures that explained how Mr. Stuart designs and constructs his figures. They now want to attempt to make similar figures at home.

The museum is well laid out and the kids enjoyed most of the exhibits - a good start for laying a foundation of art appreciation!

Hours: Open Tues. - Sun., 10am - 5pm. Closed Mon. The third Sun. is free admission from 1:30pm - 3pm.
Admission: $4 for adults; $3 for seniors; $1 ages 6 - 17; children 5 and under are free.
Ages: 4 years and up.

VINTAGE MUSEUM

(805) 486-5929 / www.chandlerwheels.com   *$$$*
1421 Emerson Avenue, Oxnard

(Exit Ventura Fwy [101] S. on Vineyard Ave., L. on Oxnard Blvd., L. on Woodley Rd., R. on Pacific, L. on Emerson. [TG: 552 J1])

Retired L.A. Times publisher Otis Chandler's extensive collection of motorcycles, race cars, and classic and antique cars are on display, all lined up, ready to hit the road. But they won't. They are kept in pristine condition for serious collectors and casual enthusiasts to admire.

The over thirty American classic cars include Dusenbergs, Packards, Lincolns, and Cadillacs. Just a few other automobiles in this collection include a 1905 Panhard, 1907 Renault, 1904 Mercedes Benz, and 550 Maranello. Five rare muscle cars are also here. More than sixty motorcycles are on exhibit, including numerous Harley Davidsons. Other vehicles are an Ahrens-Fox pumper fire truck, 1912 Packard Yosemite touring bus, and a 1894 Baldwin steam locomotive. Chandler's big-game hunting trophies are also on display.

Hours: Open one day a month, 10am - 2pm.
Admission: $7 per person.
Ages: Must be at least 10 years old.

WORLD WAR II AVIATION HERITAGE MUSEUM

(805) 482-0064 / www.orgsites.com/ca/caf-socal   *$$*
Eubanks Street at Camarillo Airport, Camarillo

(Exit Ventura Fwy [101] S. on Las Posas Rd., R. on Pleasant Valley Rd., R. on Eubanks. [TG: 523 J4])

Several World War II aircraft, and other items, are on display at this two-hangar museum. All of the artifacts on exhibit date from WWII and include helmets, flags, airplane parts, canteens, maps, posters, swords, remote-controlled planes, uniforms, a teletype machine, and more. Some of the planes are in flyable condition; some are in the process of being restored; and some can be boarded - all of which makes this museum-in-process a hit with visitors. Workers explain what they are doing to fix up planes and it really is interesting to see the metal sheets, rivets, and huge tires that are being used. Come see the Japanese Zero fighter, a Curtiss C-46 transport, a Grumman F8F Bearcat fighter, a North American SNJ Navy trainer, a B-25 Mitchell bomber, Hawker Hurricane, and other visiting planes.

Kids can climb in a cargo airplane cockpit, buckle up, don the heavy WWII helmets, and turn the knobs on the console. They are also invited to put on a headset and practice Morse code; pick up an old field telephone and pretend to call someone; look through a B-29 gunsight; walk through a plane that looks as it did when the Air Force Chief of Staff used it; and look under a B-25 bomber to see where torpedoes were once lodged. The docents are affable, knowledgeable, and ready to impart aviation facts whenever asked.

Outside, children may climb on a cannon that was originally from an aircraft carrier and look at a few jeeps located between hangars. As the museum is adjacent to the airport, you'll want to spend some time watching small planes take off and land. If you get hungry, jet on over to Way-Point Cafe, just off the runway, for inside and outside dining. The cafe is decorated with lots of aviation photos and a few pieces of airplane paraphernalia. At the end of the air field is Freedom Park, which has a large run-around field, a sports field, and small playground.

Hours: Open Tues. - Sun., 10am - 4pm. Closed Mon. and most major holidays. Hour-long guided tours are given on request.

Admission: $5 for adults; $2 for ages 10 - 16; children 9 and under are free.

Ages: 4 years and up.

-----PIERS AND SEAPORTS-----

CHANNEL ISLANDS HARBOR VILLAGE

!/$

(805) 985-5842

At the corner of Victoria Avenue and W. Channel Islands Boulevard, Oxnard

(Exit Ventura Fwy [101] S. on Victoria Ave. [TG: 552 B2])

Stroll and shop part of the day away in this quaint-looking, Victorian harbor village. While some stores cater to your taste buds, others have great gift-giving items for sale. Kids enjoy walking the village "streets" and taking in the sights. Stop in at the VENTURA COUNTY MARITIME MUSEUM (see pg. 547) sometime before you ship out.

Hours: Most stores are open daily, 10am - 6pm.

Admission: Free

Ages: All

VENTURA HARBOR and VILLAGE

!/$

(805) 642-8538 or (805) 644-0169 / www.venturaharborvillage.com

1559 Spinnaker Drive, Ventura

(Exit Ventura Fwy [101] S.W. on Seaward Ave., L. on Harbor Blvd., R. on Spinnaker Dr. [TG: 491 F7])

This harbor has a lot to offer. The picturesque "village" has over forty unusual gift shops, waterfront restaurants, and cafes. Come for lunch or, my personal favorite, dessert! Enjoy a stroll around and look at the boats, check out all the colorful ceramic tiled marine murals, or take a ride on the thirty-six horse carousel at $1.50 a ride. Every Saturday and Sunday, weather permitting, join in Kids Harborland, which includes pony rides ($4 for a few times around a sweep), and a petting zoo, a jump, and rock climbing wall, all available for an admission charge. The activities are offered noon to 4pm. Free outdoor concerts are also given on most weekends, usually on Sundays. A Fisherman's Market is held every Saturday from 8am to 11am in front of Andria's Restaurant. The harbor also sponsors numerous annual events, such as the Parade of Lights (pg. 616) in December, the tallships in February, and Seafest in June. Note that adults will probably enjoy the Comedy Club inside Hornblower's Restaurant, depending on who's headlining.

Your family can take a cruise (this is always such a treat for kids), walk on the rock jetties located down toward the Channel Islands Visitor Center, and/or play at the nearby MARINA PARK (see pg. 536) which has a playground, a cement ship, a walkway around a harbor, and more. By the way, the rock jetties are not for the faint of heart or for really young kids, as part of the "walkway" on the rocks is washed away. Bring your fishing poles if you have the time and patience. The beach is here, too, of course, along with picnic areas and barbecues. Enjoy your day here with all there is to do and *sea*! (Also see CHANNEL ISLANDS NATIONAL PARK (from Ventura) on page 533, and CHANNEL ISLANDS NATIONAL PARK VISITOR CENTER on page 542). Tip: The Ventura Trolley tours visitors around the entire city and all of the surrounding places of interest for only $1 per person. For cruise information, and rentals of kayaks and pedal boats, see BAY QUEEN HARBOR CRUISE (pg. 553).

   Hours: Most stores are open daily, 10am - 6pm. The carousel is open Mon. - Thurs., 10am - 7pm; Fri. - Sun., 10am - 9pm.

Admission: Technically free, but bring spending money.

      Ages: All

-----*POTPOURRI*-----

BART'S BOOKS

(805) 646-3755   *!/$*

302 W. Matilija, Ojai

(Exit Ventura Fwy [101] N. on Ojai Fwy [33], which turns into Ventura Ave. [33], stay R. on Ventura Ave. [33/150], stay R. on Ojai Ave. [150], quick L. on Canada, L. at Matilija. [TG: 441 H6])

   This unique, outdoor, used bookstore is worth at least a browse-through, weather permitting. Your reader-child will delight in this big, Bohemian-style store. It's like exploring an old, comfortable (albeit roofless) house, except that most of the "rooms" are created by bookshelves. There are hundreds of books here on every subject, including a small, but packed, children's section. Sit down on an assortment of benches and chairs, or in a recliner by a fireplace, and peruse your purchase.

   Books that are on shelves facing the outside of the store are available for purchase any time of day or night. The trusting (or hopeful) store sign reads: "When closed please throw coins in slot in the door for the amount marked on the book. Thank you." The atmosphere here is worth the trip.

   Hours: Open Mon., 11am - 5pm; Tues. - Sun., 10am - 5:30pm.

Admission: Free

      Ages: All readers.

BUILD-A-BEAR WORKSHOP (Thousand Oaks)

(805) 449-8704 - local; (877) 789-BEAR (2327) - national / www.buildabear.com   *$$$*

550 W. Hillcrest Drive at the Oaks mall, Thousand Oaks

(Exit Ventura Fwy [101] N. at Lynn Rd. It's at the upper level, near Macy's. [TG: 556 D1])

   See the entry for BUILD-A-BEAR WORKSHOP (Newport Beach) on page 250 for details.

   Hours: Open Mon. - Fri., 10am - 9pm; Sat., 10am - 8pm; Sun., 11am - 7pm.

CIRCUS VARGAS

   See the entry for CIRCUS VARGAS on page 134 for details.

PORT HUENEME LIGHTHOUSE

(310) 732-7310   *!*

250 N. Ventura Road, Port Hueneme

(Exit Ventura Fwy [101] S. on Victoria Ave., L. on Channel Islands Blvd., R. on Ventura Rd., R. on Port Hueneme. Note that the lighthouse tower is in a restricted port area on the corner roads. After you enter and park, you are taken to the lighthouse in a Coast Guard van. [TG: 552 D6])

   "Let your light shine before men" (and before ships). (Matthew 5:16a) A Victorian-style lighthouse was originally built on this site in 1874. The forty-eight-foot cement tower you now see was constructed in 1941 and its light still stands guard over this section of sea. While not particularly picturesque, the lure of actually going inside a lighthouse beacons, I mean beckons, many people. A few pieces of old lighthouse gear are on display and some old photographs of the tower line the walls. Walk up the three sets of stairs that wind around to reach the top, a domed chamber called the lantern room. The focal point is the old-fashioned lens - a beveled, brass-encased set of glass prisms. Up here, too, you can scan the horizon, just as lighthouse keepers of yesteryear. Visitors, often lighthouse afficionados, leave the place beaming.

Next door to the lighthouse is the Marine Institute that is only open the same hours as the lighthouse. The institute has several large tanks and a few smaller ones that contain fish and other sea creatures. Some of these animals have been rescued from the sea and some are grown here and then released. The marine biologist on hand shares information about the critters and allows visitors to touch some of them. A visit to the institute could be a highlight for your child.

Hours: Open the third Sat., 10am - 4pm.
Admission: Free
Ages: 8 years and up.

-----SHOWS AND THEATERS-----

PERFORMING ARTS CENTER
(805) 486-2424 / www.oxnardpacc.com
800 Hobson Way, at the Performing Arts Center, Oxnard
(Exit Ventura Fwy [101] S. on Hwy 1 [or Oxnard Blvd.], R. on 9th St., R. on Hobson. [TG: 522 F7])

$$$

Shows performed here at the 1,064-seat theater for the general public have included *Sesame Street*, *Nutcracker*, *Anne Frank, Snow White* (ballet), concerts, and numerous other top-notch performances. School groups often rent the theater for special performances put on by American Theater for Youth, or other touring groups. Call for a schedule.

Hours: Call for show dates and times.
Admission: Varies, depending on the show.
Ages: 3 years and up, depending on the show.

THOUSAND OAKS CIVIC ARTS PLAZA
(805) 449-ARTS (2787) / www.civicartsplaza.com
2100 E. Thousand Oaks Boulevard, Thousand Oaks
(Going W. on Ventura Fwy [101], exit N. on Hampshire Blvd., L. on Thousand Oaks. Going E. on 101, exit N. on Rancho Rd., R. on Thousand Oaks. [TG: 556 J2])

$$$

This arts plaza offers two theaters; the Scherr Forum Theatre, which seats 400 people, and the Kavli, which seats 1,800, as well as a packed calendar of events. Professional local and national touring production groups put on numerous, first-class shows ranging from ballet to comedies, juggling, musicals, distinguished speakers (such as David McCullough), concerts, symphonies, dance (such as the Moscow dance theater), dramas, and more. A variety of family and children's concerts are offered, as well as several different children's series. Past programs include Jim Gamble's Marionettes, *Do Jump! Acrobatic Theater, Freedom Train, The Music Man, Oregon Trail*, and *Sesame Street Live*. Call for a complete schedule.

Hours: Call for show dates and times.
Admission: Prices vary, depending on the show.
Ages: Varies, depending on the show.

-----*TOURS*-----

FILLMORE INSECTARY

(805) 524-2733

1003 Sespe Avenue, Fillmore

(Exit Ventura St. [126], N. on C St., R. on Sespe. [TG: 455 J6])

Here's the buzz - the insectary raises and releases beneficial insects, or mass-produced biological control agents, to help citrus growers. Three climate-controlled buildings house a variety of predatory mites that will feed on injurious mites. Visitors can see the little buggers, learn about them, how they are raised, and how they aid growers. Tours, technical or more visually-oriented, are offered for third graders and up.

> **Hours:** Call to schedule a tour.
> **Admission:** Free
> **Ages:** 3rd graders and up.

SIMI VALLEY COURTHOUSE

(805) 650-7599 - bar association/tour / www.vcba.org

3855 F Alamo Street, Simi Valley

(From Ventura County, exit Ventura Fwy [101] N. on Hwy 23, which turns into Hwy 118 - continue E., exit L. on Tapo Canyon Rd. under the fwy to head N., L. on Alamo, R. on Santa Lucia. From San Fernando Valley or L.A., exit 405 W. on Hwy 118, N. on Tapo Canyon Rd., L. on Alamo, R. on Santa Lucia.)

See the entry for VENTURA COUNTY COURTHOUSE below for details. This tour is two hours long.

> **Hours:** Tours are offered Wed. at 10am. with advanced reservations only.
> **Admission:** Free
> **Ages:** 6th , 8th, and 12th graders

VENTURA COUNTY COURTHOUSE

(805) 650-7599 - bar association/tour / www.vcba.org

800 S. Victoria Avenue, Ventura

(From Ventura Fwy [101], exit N. on Victoria. From Santa Paula Fwy [126], exit S. on Victoria. [TG: 492 C3])

Now kids can have their day in court! This two-and-a-half-hour tour, for groups between twenty to thirty-five people, explains the process of the Ventura County court system. The tour consists of seeing the courthouse, the administration building (where residents pay property taxes and obtain licenses), the sheriff department, and the jail. Here visitors learn what happens when an inmate is incarcerated - from frisking, to showers, to where they eat and sleep. At the courthouse, visitors see and learn about the law library, the ceremonial courtroom, the traffic court, and the jury room. When available, they'll have the opportunity to speak with judges, commissioners, attorneys, or other court personnel. They usually get to sit in on and observe a civil and/or criminal case, too.

A highlight of the tour is a grade-appropriate, mock trial of an actual court case. Participants read from scripts as they become members of the jury, lawyers, the bailiff, and even the judge (along with a robe and gavel). The tour ends with a video of the Sheriff's Detention Center. I think this is a fascinating tour, but I'll let you be the judge!

> **Hours:** Tours are given Tues. - Thurs. at 10:30am with advanced reservations only.
> **Admission:** Free
> **Ages:** 6th , 8th, and 12th graders.

-----TRANSPORTATION-----

AMTRAK
(800) USA RAIL (872-7245) / www.dot.ca.gov/hq/rail; www.amtrak.com

Ride the rails! See page xi (in the front) for more information.

BAY QUEEN HARBOR CRUISE
☀
$$
(805) 642-7753
1691 Spinnaker Drive, Ventura

(Going W. on Ventura Fwy [101], exit S.W. on Seaward Ave., L. on Harbor Blvd. Going S.E. on 101, exit at Seaward Ave. and go straight onto Harbor Blvd. From Harbor Blvd., go R. on Spinnaker Dr. [TG: 491 F7])

Enjoy a forty-minute cruise out of the harbor, past the boats and homes along the coastline. See VENTURA HARBOR and VILLAGE (pg. 549) for other things to do in this area. Kayak and pedal boat rentals are also available here.

Hours: Cruises depart Sat. - Sun., noon - 4pm, every hour on the hour.
Admission: Cruises are $6 for adults; $3 for ages 12 and under. Single kayaks are $12 an hour; doubles are $20. Pedal boats are $12 an hour.
Ages: All

BIKE MAPS (Ventura County)
The web site www.labikepaths.com is a fantastic resource. It actually covers all of Southern California, not just L.A., with links to specific counties for maps, bikeways, and other cycling information. Another helpful contact website and phone number is for the State of California Caltrans Office of Bicycle Facilities: (916) 653-0036; www.dot.ca.gov/hq/tpp/offices/bike/contracts.htm. Two other contacts include the Ventura County Transportation Commission at (805) 642-1591 / www.goventura.org and (800) 438-1112 - ask for a map.

BIKE TRAIL: OJAI VALLEY TRAIL / VENTURA RIVER TRAIL
☀
!/$
(805) 654-3951 - parks; (805) 646-8126 - Chamber of Commerce
One end begins on Ojai Avenue in Ojai; the other at San Buenaventura State Beach in Ventura. Or, start in the middle at Foster County Park in Casitas Springs

(The Ojai starting point is off State Highway 33/Ojai Ave. Catch the trail on the east side of town at Soule Park or just behind LIBBEY PARK [pg. 536]. You can also park your car at the park-and-ride lot at Ojai Ave. and Fox St. [TG: 441 H7]; To reach San Buenaventura State Beach, exit Ventura Fwy [101] S. on California St., L. on Harbor Blvd. To reach Foster Park, exit State Highway 33 at Casitas Vista Rd. and go underneath the freeway to the park. Foster is 6 miles N. of Ventura. [TG: 461 A6])

This scenic, paved route is about sixteen miles long one way. The Ojai Valley Trail, from Libbey Park to Foster Park, is about nine miles. Although it follows along the major street of Ventura Avenue (Highway 33), oak and sycamore trees adorn it, making it pretty while shading good portions of it, plus major sections are hidden from the main thoroughfare and give it a ride-in-the-country feel. The trail is frequented by bikers, skaters, strollers, equestrians, and joggers. The six-mile trail from Foster Park to the ocean, is not all easy on the eyes, as it goes through industrial areas, but pathway artists have enlivened it somewhat with murals. As you head toward your final destination, the Pacific Ocean, you'll connect with the Omer Rains Trail (i.e. Ventura River Trail) which goes along the coastline. Go north to reach Emma Wood State Beach or south to San Buenaventura Beach, (805) 648-4127, and the Ventura Pier. Note: The grade of the trail is a gentle slope from north to south, and therefore noticeably easier to pedal than vice versa.

Forgot your wheels? Bicycle rentals are available at Bicycles of Ojai, (805) 646-7736 at 108 Canada Street, Ojai for $6 an hour. Note: No child-size bikes are available here. Cycles 4 Rent, (805) 652-1114 at 239 W. Main Street, Ventura charges $6 to $9 an hour depending on the type of bike.

Hours: The trail is open daily, dawn - dusk.
Admission: Free at the Ojai end; $5 parking at San Buenaventura Beach; $2 parking at Foster Park during the week, $4 on the weekends.
Ages: 4 years and up, depending on how long and far you want to ride.

CHANNEL ISLAND'S LANDING

(805) 985-6059

3821 S. Victoria Avenue, Oxnard

(Exit Ventura Fwy [101] S. on Victoria Ave. [TG: 552 B4])

$$$$

Set sail on sailboats that rent for $18 to $25 an hour, or on an electric boat that seats up to ten people and rents for $40 an hour. (Somehow it doesn't sound right to say, "Set *sail* on an electric boat" - oh well!)

Hours: Open daily, 8:30am - 5pm.

Admission: Prices listed above.

Ages: All

CHANNEL ISLANDS MARINE FLOATING LAB

(805) 382-4563

4151 S. Victoria Avenue, Oxnard

(Exit Ventura Fwy [101] S. on Victoria Ave. to Channel Islands Harbor. The entrance is at Cisco's Sportfishing. [TG: 552 A2])

$$

This floating marine lab (i.e. boat) offers terrific in-harbor and out-of-harbor learning excursions. Students of all ages can book a "tour" here and receive hands-on teaching instruction via rotating learning stations as they gain knowledge about marine life, marine environments, and specifically, marine biology. What better way to involve and aid kids in understanding ocean life than for them to inspect it, even as close up as under a microscope when such as analyzing samples from the ocean floor; touch it, gently stroking such as tidepool creatures like sea stars, urchins, and more; explore it, by being on the ocean; and hear about it from naturalists.

The learning labs can be combined with whale watching when the whales migrate - January through March. Note that classes on board the boat are usually three-and-a-half hours long, but can be adjusted according to age and interest level. A shorter program is offered in partnership with the Ventura Maritime Museum. There is no minimum number of students - just a minimum fee. The maximum number is forty. Bring a lunch and enjoy it dockside.

Hours: Call to schedule a class.

Admission: About $400 for a three-plus-hour class. Call for other class prices.

Ages: Kindergartners and up.

FILLMORE & WESTERN RAILWAY

(800) 773-TRAIN (8724) or (805) 524-2546 / www.fwry.com

351 Santa Clara Avenue, Central Park Depot, Fillmore

(Exit State Route 126 N. on Central Ave. [TG: 456 A6])

$$$$

"More powerful than a locomotive"; *The Great Train Robbery*; and *The Little Engine That Could* - what does this potpourri of things bring to mind? A train ride, of course! Riding on a train is a real adventure for children. The countryside is scenic along this route with citrus groves and beautiful landscapes. This railway line is also a favorite Hollywood location, so many of the trains you'll see and ride on have appeared in movies and television shows. A snack bar and gift shop are on board.

There are several types of weekend excursions offered. The "regular" ride is two-and-a-half-hours round trip between Fillmore and Santa Paula, which includes a half-hour stopover in Santa Paula. Ride the rails in an open air railcar, a restored passenger coach (circa 1930), a 1929 parlour car, or a more modern car. Lunches are offered in the restored 1950's Streamlined diner before your ride or en route. Meal prices range between $5 to $12. Many specialty train rides are available, too, including Father's Day, Murder Mystery, Pumpkinliner, Santa Claus Express, and more. The Spaghetti Western ride, for instance, is offered on selected Fridays and includes the two-and-a-half hour ride, dinner (guess what they serve?), and entertainment by actors dressed in western attire. This is a memorable family outing. Ask about the hour-long-plus School Trains, where students ride the rails to the Fillmore Fish Hatchery (and back) as they learn about and see the workings of a train, vintage cars, the scenery, and more. See the Calendar entry for details about the annual Fillmore Spring RailFest (pg. 568).

Hours: Trains depart from Fillmore January through March on weekends at 2pm. They depart the rest of the year Sat. at 2pm; Sun., 11am, and 2pm. Spaghetti Western rides depart about 6pm. Call for other specialty rides.

Admission: Round-trip fare for the "normal" ride is $20 for adults; $18 for seniors; $8 for ages 4 - 12; $6 for ages 3 and under. Spaghetti Western rides are $49 for adults; $24 for ages 4 - 12; $6 for ages 3 and under. Call for prices for other specialty rides. School Trains are $7 per person.

Ages: 3 years and up.

JIM HALL RACING SCHOOL

$$$$$

(805) 654-1329 / www.jhrkartracing.com
675 N. Harbor Boulevard, Oxnard
(Going W. on Ventura Fwy [101], exit S. on Victoria, R. on Olivas Park Dr., L. on Harbor Blvd. Going S.E. on 101, exit at Seaward Ave. and go straight onto Harbor Blvd. [TG: 521 H5])

What child doesn't like racing around? Now he/she can learn how to do it in karts on the only paved beachside road course in America! Besides the adult classes, this racing school offers Day One Sprint Kart programs for ages 13 and up. Classes range from half-day instruction to a week, or more. Drivers learn safety (yea!), how to drive, braking techniques (this could be especially valuable in just a few years), and they'll even get timed. Watch out, Dale Ernhart, Jr.! Note that Ventura County beaches are just a few steps away from this school.

Hours: Call for class hours.

Admission: Varies, depending on the length of class. The Day One Sprint Kart program, which is four hours of instruction and driving, starts at $150.

Ages: 8 years and up.

METROLINK (Ventura County)

See the entry for METROLINK (Los Angeles County) on page 173 for details.

SANTA PAULA AIRPORT / CP AVIATION, INC.

$$$$$

(805) 525-2138 or (805) 933-1155 / www.cpaviation.com
830 E. Santa Maria Street, Santa Paula
(Exit the Santa Paula Fwy [126] S. on Palm Ave., L. on Santa Maria St. [TG: 464 B6])

This small airport is kid-friendly; partly because of its size, and partly because it's always fun to watch planes land and take off. Instead of just watching, however, why not take the kids up for a spin, literally! At the instructor's discretion, if your child is at least 12 years old (and doesn't get motion sickness), he/she can take an exhilarating half-hour aerobatic ride with loops, rolls, and G's (better than a roller coaster!) for $125 per person. For those who enjoy a calmer scenic ride, a Cessna 172, which seats three passengers, is only $55 (total) for a half-hour flight. Other aircraft are available for flights, too. Lunch at the airport restaurant will complete your lofty adventure.

If you're visiting on the first Sunday of the month, take a walk through the adjacent hangars that houses the AVIATION MUSEUM OF SANTA PAULA (see pg. 540). Also check the YOUNG EAGLES PROGRAM - Santa Paula (see pg. 556).

Hours: The airport is open daily. Call for hours for a flight.

Admission: Prices listed above.

Ages: 4 years and up for a look around the airport and a scenic flight.

VOYAGES OF REDISCOVERY (Ventura County)

$$/$$$$$

(800) 401-7835 or (415) 331-3214
Oxnard

See VOYAGES OF REDISCOVERY (pg. 175) for details.

YOUNG EAGLES PROGRAM (Camarillo)

(805) 647-6994 or (805) 482-0064 / www.youngeagles.com; www.eaa723.org
Eubanks Street, Camarillo Airport, Camarillo
(Exit Ventura Fwy [101] S. on Las Posas Rd., R. on Pleasant Valley Rd., R. on Eubanks. [TG: 523 J4])

See the entry for YOUNG EAGLES PROGRAM (Pacoima) on page 177 for details. Reservations are necessary! Also check out the WORLD WAR II AVIATION HERITAGE MUSEUM (see pg. 548) at the airport.

Hours: Offered the first Sat. of every month 9:30am - 11:30am.
Admission: Free
Ages: 8 - 17 years.

YOUNG EAGLES PROGRAM (Santa Paula)

(805) 647-6994 or (805) 525-1100 / www.youngeagles.com
830 E. Santa Maria Street, Santa Paula
(Exit the Santa Paula Fwy [126] S. on Palm Ave., L. on Santa Maria St. [TG: 464 B6])

See the entry for YOUNG EAGLES PROGRAM (Pacoima) on page 177 for details. Reservations are needed.

Hours: Offered the first Sun. of every month 10am - noon, which coincides with the AVIATION MUSEUM OF SANTA PAULA (see pg. 540) being open.
Admission: Free
Ages: 8 - 17 years.

-----ZOOS AND ANIMALS-----

AMERICA'S TEACHING ZOO

(805) 378-1441 / sunny.moorparkcollege.edu/~eatm
7075 Campus Road at Moorpark Community College, Moorpark
(Exit Simi Valley/San Fernando Valley Fwy [118] N. on Collins Dr. Continue all the way up Collins, behind the college, turn R. into the college and look for signs for the zoo. [TG: 477 A5])

Students attend this teaching zoo, that contains 130 exotic animals, to become zoo keepers, veterinarians, and animal trainers. My favorite aspect of this zoo is that the knowledgeable staff members (i.e. students) answer any and all of your child's questions. My kids and I learned so much here! As this is a teaching zoo and not just here for public enjoyment, many of the caged animals are in rows, making it difficult, or impossible, to see a lot of them. However, the animals that are readily viewed can be seen more up close than at a typical zoo. We saw llamas, baboons, a miniature horse, macaws, pot-bellied pigs, spider monkeys, lions, foxes, barn owls, hawks, eagles, tigers, Galapagos Island tortoises, birds in an aviary, and more.

Fifteen-minute demonstrations, featuring three to five animals per show, such as primates, hoofed animals, birds, or reptiles, are given on the hour on a small outdoor stage. The student trainers talk about the animal's habitats, nutrition, learned behavior, and training. Afterwards, sometimes, kids can touch the animals. One of the reptiles we saw and touched was a boa. We were amazed at its strength and its under-belly softness.

Don't miss the 3:45pm feeding of the carnivores! Actually, get there a little early and see animals being fed that aren't on the scheduled program. Trainers feed the tigers (go ahead - ask what they're eating) as they "show-off" the tigers' learned behavior. Forty-five-minute school tours are given during the week and include a few demonstrations or tour or both. See the Calendar entry for information on the Spring Spectacular (pg. 570). Ask about the week-long, summer Junior Zoo Safari for kids who like to work with animals. Note: Picnic tables are here for your lunching pleasure. There is also a park with a playground just down the street from the college on Campus Drive.

Hours: The Zoo is open weekends, 11am - 5pm. Trainer talks are given throughout the day. The demonstrations are every hour on the hour noon - 3pm, weather permitting. You can call to see what animals will be shown. Feeding of the carnivores is at 3:45pm.

Admission: $5 for adults; $3 for seniors and children 12 and under. School tours start at $100 for up to 30 people; additional people are $1 each.

Ages: All

FILLMORE FISH HATCHERY

(805) 524-0962

612 E. Telegraph Road, Fillmore

(Exit Hwy 23 R. on Ventura St. [126], which turns in to Telegraph. Look for signs. [TG: 456 H6])

Stop off and take a look around the fish hatchery to see hundreds of thousands of rainbow trout. This hatchery supplies fish to lakes and streams through San Luis Obispo, Santa Barbara, Los Angeles, and Ventura counties. The long narrow concrete tanks have compartments that are labeled with the various species names. Coin-operated fish food dispensers are here and the fish always seem to be hungry. Note: Just east down the road is Cornejo's produce stand offering great, in-season produce.

Hours: Open daily, 8am - 3:30pm

Admission: Free

Ages: 2 years and up.

PAINTED PONY FARM

(805) 525-9820

15315 Santa Paula Ojai Road, Santa Paula

(Exit Hwy 126 E. on Tenth St., veer R. at the fork and take Ojai Rd./Hwy. 150. [TG: 453 H2])

I don't think the ponies are really painted at this farm, but there are numerous animals to interact with here, including ponies. Different tours of the farm are offered. For instance, a "guided tour," with a minimum of twenty participants, includes a tour of the working farm, an opportunity to milk a goat, and to pet and feed the other farm animals. The cost is $1 per person and the petting farm is 50¢ per person. A "day on the farm," with a minimum of ten participants, is a two-hour program that includes all of the above, plus making and sampling goat's milk ice cream. The cost is $4.50 per person. Pony rides are offered on weekends for ages 1 and up for $3 per rider. Picnic facilities are on-site, too. Day camps for ages 5 to 10 are offered by reservations.

Hours: Open Tues. - Fri., 10am - 3pm; Sat., 10am - 5pm; Sun., 1pm - 5pm. Call to schedule a tour.

Admission: Prices are listed above.

Ages: 1 year up to about 12 years.

UNDERWOOD FAMILY FARM

(805) 523-8552 - food farm; (805) 523-2957 - animal farm / www.tierrarejadafamilyfarms.com

3370 Sunset Valley Road, Moorpark

See the entry for UNDERWOOD FAMILY FARM, on page 529, for details about its animal farm.

558

EDUCATIONAL PRESENTATIONS

This section is written for all kinds of educators as most of the programs / presentations travel to schools or other off-site facilities. It is by no means complete, just *some* of the treasures we've discovered.

AMUSEMENT PARKS
all counties

Amusement Parks are unexpected places to find educational classes. KNOTT'S BERRY FARM (pg. 193) has wonderful outreach programs, as well as over fifteen classes offered on-site. (Maybe you can squeeze in a ride or two!) Look under the Amusement Park section in each county for more information and ideas.

A VISIT WITH MR. LINCOLN
(949) 830-7239
all counties

John Kendall portrays Honest Abe, wearing his stove pipe hat and all. Looking every inch a president, he speaks about integrity, working hard for a worthy goal, and the power of a good character. He also recites the Gettysburg Address and tells students many historical facts and anecdotes of Abraham Lincoln's life. Mr. Kendall makes history come alive in a unique way. He speaks for forty-five- to sixty-minutes to individual classes and assemblies.

   Admission: $375 for one assembly.

      Ages: Kindergarten through 8th grade.

CALIFORNIA WEEKLY EXPLORER, INC.
(714) 730-5991 / www.californiaweekly.com
all counties

This company sends a knowledgeable staff member, or two, to your school for outstanding, interactive, and educational two-and-a-half-hour presentations. The six different presentations offered are called "walk throughs," as they walk students through particular time periods via costumes, role playing, skits, games, flags, props, music, hands-on quizzes, models, maps, and/or timelines. Each walk through is consistent with the California state framework and requires some prior preparation and memorization for participants.

Fourth graders (or so) can take Walk Through California, which covers state geography, history, and people, and/or Walk Along El Camino Real, which emphasizes missions and Native American cultures. Fifth graders (or so) are offered Walk Through the American Revolution, which focuses on participants in the Revolution, the document of the Declaration of Independence, and a greater understanding of freedom and the concept of liberty. Walk With Lewis and Clark, also geared for fifth grade students, presents Lewis and Clark, Jefferson, Sacagawea, and others, as well as the story of our country's expansion. Sixth graders (or so) can take a "trip" with Walk Through the Ancient World, which explores ancient Egypt, Greece, and Rome and the people (e.g. Julius Caesar, Socrates, Queen Cleopatra, Rameses II, and Homer) who made this time period so fascinating.

The program leaders do a great job of keeping children (and adults) interested and yes, even learning during the presentations. Programs are limited to thirty-five students.

      Hours: Programs are offered Mon. - Fri. Reservations are required.

   Admission: $290 for the first program; ask about discounts for same-day programs. All programs pay an additional travel fee of $45 - $115, depending on the zip code.

      Ages: 4th - 9th graders.

HISTORY-ALIVE
(626) 810-3397 / www.history-alive.com
all counties

This group is comprised of Living Legends presenters who "perform" for your class. Invite one of the following famous leaders to speak with your group: Patrick Henry, Benjamin Franklin, Thomas Jefferson, Harry S Truman, Golda Meir, Douglas MacArthur, Junipero Serra, Jedediah Smith, Betsy Ross, Susan B. Anthony, Louisa May Alcott, Thomas Paine, or Abraham Lincoln. The website has the various performer's phone numbers as well as their bios.

   Ages: Kindergartners and up.

ICARUS PUPPET COMPANY

(800) 449-4479 / www.icaruspuppet.org
San Diego County only

   This eleven-year-old company travels all over San Diego county entertaining audiences with the magic of puppetry. The shows are a dynamic blend of theater, puppetry, music, and mask-making. They also offer workshops.

   Admission: Between $200 - $450.
   Ages: Pre-school through 6th grade.

JIM WEISS - STORYTELLER EXTRAORDINARE

(800) 477-6234 / www.greathall.com
all counties

   Golden-voiced Jim Weiss, with Greathall Productions, is a nationally acclaimed storyteller. He's won over sixty-five prestigious awards from American Library Association, Parent's Choice Foundation, NAPPA, Oppenheim Toy Portfolio, and others. He retells (mostly) classic stories in voices and manners that kids of all ages enjoy. His tape/cd titles include *Arabian Nights, Greek Myths, Fairytales in Song and Dance, Sherlock Holmes, Shakespeare for Children, Three Musketeers*, and many more.

   As wonderful as he is to listen to on tape, he is even more enthralling in person. Jim does storytelling as well as workshops for both kids and adults on how to tell stories. He explains the twists and turns all good stories have, and teaches how to choose a topic, shape a story, map a plot, create and develop characters and their voices, use voice inflections masterfully, and lots more. He gears his presentations according to the age of his audience. Our school had him do a half-and-half presentation; half of the time was a workshop and the other half was storytelling. It was fascinating and educational for all ages!

   Admission: $500 for a two-hour presentation. Half-day and full-day workshop / presentations are also
                    available.
   Ages: All

MAD SCIENCE

(877) 900-9996 - call to find your local mad scientist! / www.madscience.org
all counties

   Bubbling potions, rocket launches, magnets, lasers, super bounce ball, cool chemical reactions, slime, and more hands-on learning fun is offered through Mad Science. Forty-five- to sixty-minute programs include after-school enrichment classes, summer camps, in-class workshops, school assembly demonstrations, and "edu-tainment" birthday parties. (That pretty much covers the gamut!) Programs are themed based and come with pre -and post-packages designed for teachers.

   Ages: Pre-school through 6th grade.

MUSEUMS
all counties

   Numerous museums have "traveling programs," designed specifically for coming to your choice of locale to present great, hands-on educational programs. Generally speaking, the art, science, and children's museums are the ones that offer this type of program. The following are just a sampling of places that have programs. For more information on them, and others, look under the Museums section:

CALIFORNIA SCIENCE CENTER (pg. 85)
DISCOVERY SCIENCE CENTER (pg. 238) - Offers a wonderful series of science classes at your location. Projects include owl pellet dissection, making seltzer-tablet rockets, squid dissection, creating a mini-terrarium, and Starlab, a portable planetarium. They also offer programs at the Science Center.
INTERNATIONAL PRINTING MUSEUM (pg. 99) - The extraordinary *History in Motion: A Museum on Wheels* presentation is one of the museum's specialities.
JURUPA MOUNTAINS CULTURAL CENTER (pg. 291) - They offer over twenty on-site programs, plus a few outreach programs.
CHILDREN'S MUSEUM AT LA HABRA (pg. 238)
RAYMOND M. ALF MUSEUM (pg. 116)

SCIENCE ADVENTURES

(800) 4SCIENCE (472-3623) or (800) 213-9796 / www.scienceadventures.net
all counties

Motorized cars, robots, launching rockets, X-treme science camps, physics, and more fun by doing projects are available through Science Adventures. They put on school presentations, after school classes, scouting programs, and birthday parties where participants build projects, conduct experiments, and play science-related games.
> **Admission:** Prices range widely. Two, forty-five performances are about $400. Their outstanding, week-long camps are $220 per person.
> **Ages:** Pre-school through 6th grade.

SHOWS AND THEATERS
all counties

This is another category that often has traveling shows - whether it's a play presented to children, or it is a theatrical workshop of some sort.

WAVES ON WHEELS

(805) 682-4711 / www.sbnature.org
Santa Barbara and Ventura counties only

The Santa Barbara Natural History Museum, Channel Islands National Marine Sanctuary, and County of Santa Barbara partner to make this mobile classroom available. Waves on Wheels, or W.O.W., offers an ocean of fun via a specially-equipped van filled with marine science activities. No live animals are brought to the locations. Each of the forty-five-minute programs, one for each grade level from kindergarten through sixth grade, correlate with state science standards. For instance, third graders learn about animal adaptation to the environment. Plastic models of sea creatures and real shells are used as well as scientific instruments to measure and study. Students learn research and methodology procedures, too. Summer camps are also available through this year-round program. So, do the Wave!
> **Hours:** Presentations are offered Tues. - Fri. Call for hours.
> **Admission:** $45 per class; $40 per class for 3 or more programs scheduled on the same day.
> **Ages:** K through 6th grade.

ZOOS AND ANIMALS
all counties

Many zoos have fantastic in-house programs as well as traveling presentations. Call the one nearest you for more information.

CALENDAR
(a listing of annual events)

Many places listed in the main section of this book offer special events throughout the year. Below is a calendar listing of other annual stand outs. If you are looking for more local events, like fairs and carnivals, check the front pages of your local phone book, call the Recreation Department of your local parks, or call your Chamber of Commerce. Also try this website: www.festivals.com. The prices and information quoted here are as of June 2003 - please keep in mind that some events change from year to year. **Please call an event a month in advance as dates sometimes fluctuate.**

JANUARY:

CABRILLO WHALE WATCH WEEKEND, Point Loma. (619) 557-5450 / www.nps.gov/cabr, Cabrillo Memorial Dr. at Cabrillo National Monument. On the third weekend in January come watch for Pacific gray whales as they migrate. Park rangers give presentations about marine life, exhibit booths are on site, and you can also tour the facilities or visit the tidepools. Open Sat. - Sun., 9am - 5pm. Admission is free; parking is $5.

CORONADO BUTTERFLY RESERVE, Goleta. (805) 966-4520 / www.sblandtrust.org/coronado.html, Coronado Drive off Hollister on the land trust for Santa Barbara County. Hundreds of Monarch butterflies come to this grove to rest as they migrate south. The public is welcome on this wooded and coastal land privately owned by a development company. Park near the "Reserve" sign, along the street, and hike on the path into the woods. Note that the small stream you need to cross gets a bit swollen after a rain. There is a section of roped off woods where, just beyond, the butterflies roost. They look like dead leaves when their wings are folded, but like a stunning orange and black mosaic as they flutter about. The butterflies arrive in mid-November and usually depart around the end of February.

DISNEY ON ICE. See December entry (pg. 613) for details.

HITS INDIO DESERT CIRCUIT, Indio. (760) 775-7731 / www.hitsshows.com, 81-500 Ave. 52 and Monroe St. at the HITS Desert Horse Park. For six weeks, horse-lovers can get an eyeful as more than 2,000 horses and riders, the top hunters and jumpers in North America, compete in America's largest horse show with over one million dollars as total prize money. Professional and amateur riders, both adults and juniors, compete in the show ring. Ask about kids' days and fiesta days. The circuit begins mid-January and ends mid-March. Open Wed. - Sun., 8am - 4pm. Admission is free from Wed. - Fri; $5 for ages 13 and over on the weekends.

HOLIDAY OF LIGHTS, Del Mar. See November entry (pg. 609) for details.

ICE SKATING. Huntington Beach, Irvine, W. Los Angeles, Woodland Hills. See November entry (pg. 609) for details.

NATIONS OF SAN DIEGO INTERNATIONAL DANCE FESTIVAL, San Diego. (619) 230-8623 / www.sandiegodance.org, 79 Horton Plaza at the San Diego Repertory Theatre/Lyceum Stage. For lovers of dance, this two-weekend festival hosted by San Diego Dance Alliance, featuring 100 dancers from 14 dance companies representing 14 countries, is a rhythmic and ethnic feast. One weekend showcases the same two-hour performance at each show and the next weekend features a different two-hour show. The theater lobby is transformed into a marketplace before the shows and during intermission. It offers food and arts and crafts from various countries. The shows are Fri., 8pm; Sat., 2pm and 8pm; Sun., 2pm. Admission per show is $15 - $25 for adults, depending on seating; $5 for ages 3 to 12.

POMONA VALLEY AIR FAIR, Upland. (909) 982-8048 or (909) 982-6121 / www.cableairport.com, 1749 W. 13th St. at Cable Airport. Fly bys, aerobatic maneuvers and demonstrations, remote control plane acrobatics, sky divers, a penny-a-pound 15-minute airplane rides, community performances (i.e. bands, gymnastics, etc.), an antique car show, vendors, and static displays are all part of this wonderful air fair. There isn't any seating (unless you bring your own), so just wing it! Open Sat., 8am - 4pm; Sun., 8am - 4pm. Admission is $10 for adults; $5 for ages 5 - 17; children 4 and under are free.

TOURNAMENT OF ROSES PARADE, Pasadena. (626) 449-ROSE (7673) - recording; (626) 449-4100 - real person / www.tournamentofroses.com, Pasadena City Hall. This two-hour, world-famous parade of fancifully, elegantly, decorated floral floats, plus bands and equestrian units, is held on New Year's Day. Camp out overnight on the streets to guarantee a viewing spot, (626) 744-4501 - police (ask about camping regulations on parade route); try your luck by arriving in the early morning hours on the actual day; or call Sharp Seating Company, (626) 795-4171 / www.sharpseating.com for grandstand seating. Prices for seats range from $35 - $80. Please make reservations at least two months in advance. The parade begins at 8am. Call for the parade route.

TOURNAMENT OF ROSES VIEWING OF FLOATS, Pasadena. (626) 449-ROSE (7673) or (626) 449-4100 / www.tournamentofroses.com, along Sierra Madre Blvd. and Washington Blvd., near Sierra Madre Villa Ave. The famous floats can be viewed up close for a few days after the parade. Arrive early, in hopes of bypassing some of the hordes of people, to let your kids walk around and "oooh" and "aaah" at the intricate workmanship. Bring your camera! It is a one-mile walk to view all the floats. Open Jan. 1, 1:30pm - 4:45pm and Jan 2, 9am - 4:45pm. Open Jan. 2, 7am - 9am for mobility-impaired and srs. Admission is $6 per person; children 2 and under are free. Expect to pay about $5 for parking.

UNIVERSAL CITYWALK'S ICE RINK / DRIVE-IN MOVIE, Universal City. See November entry (pg. 611) for details.

WHALE WATCHING. See the Transportation section in the main portion of the book for places to call to take a whale-watching cruise. The season goes from the end of December through March. Cruises are usually two and a half hours of looking for (and finding!) gray whales as they migrate to and from Baja. Also, be on the lookout for dolphins, pilot whales, and sea lions. Dress warmly.

FEBRUARY:

CALICO CIVIL WAR DAYS, Yermo. (800) TO CALICO (862-2542) / www.calicotown.com, 36600 Ghost Town Rd. at Calico Ghost Town. Over the three-day President's Day weekend, the North meets the South in Civil War reenactments complete with drills, music, living history displays, Confederate and Union camps, and two battles a day. Lincoln, Grant, and/or Lee might make an appearance, too. Open 9am - 5pm. Admission, which includes entrance to the Ghost Town, is $8 for adults; $5 for ages 6 - 15; children 5 and under are free. On-site camping (minimum 2 nights) is $15 a night; $28 a night for cabins.

CAMELLIA FESTIVAL, Temple City. (626) 287-9150, corner of Las Tunas Dr. and Golden West Ave. at Temple City Park. The festival, held the last weekend in February, is complete with carnival rides, and an art show on Sunday. The highlight, the festival parade, is held on Saturday. Camellia-covered floats (which must be finished only with parts of camellias), are designed and made by youth groups. Prizes, including a Sweepstakes Trophy, are given out. Over twenty marching bands and drill teams, plus other organizations that promote the welfare of children, such as Brownies and Cub Scouts, participate. Carnival rides are open Fri., 4pm - 10pm. The parade begins Sat. at 10pm and festivities, including the rides, go on to 10pm. The festival runs Sun., noon - 8pm. Admission is free. Certain activities cost.

CHINESE NEW YEAR CELEBRATION, Los Angeles. (213) 617-0396 / www.lachinesechamber.org; www.lagoldendragonparade.com, 600 - 900 block Broadway St. in Chinatown. This three-day celebration's main event is the elaborate Golden Dragon Parade on Saturday with floats, bands, and dragon dancers (in wonderful costumes), plus the Little King and Queen contest and the Children's Lantern Procession. Other goings-on include a street fair with arts and crafts, carnival rides, and live music. The New Year is celebrated on the first weekend of the Lunar New Year - "Gung Hay Fat Choy." (Happy New Year.) Open Fri., 5pm - 10pm, Sat., 11am - 10pm; Sun., 11am - 8pm. The parade is Sat., 2pm - 5pm. Admission is free, although certain activities cost.

CHINESE NEW YEAR FOOD AND CULTURE FAIR, San Diego. (619) 234-7844 or (619) 234-4447 / www.geocities.com/sandiegochinesecenter, 3rd and J Street, downtown San Diego. More than 20,000 people attend these two days of celebrating the Chinese culture. Enjoy demonstrations such as karate and acrobatics;

dances such as fire dances, Chinese folk dances, the lion dance, and the dragon dance (the dragon is thirty-five feet long!); a craft area where kids make a Chinese lantern and form a lantern parade; cooking demonstrations and wonderful food. Open Sat., 11am - 6pm; Sun., 11am - 4pm. Admission is free.

CIVIL WAR REENACTMENT. (714) 772-1363 / www.stcatherinesmilitary.com, 215 N. Harbor Blvd. at St. Catherine's Military School. Tours are given of the camp where participating students and adults live for the weekend, portraying Rebs and Yanks. A field hospital might be set up and "doctors" explain how medicine was practiced at the time; an officer might discuss the political events leading up to the war; and a camp cook might talk about supplies and feeding the troops. Teachers can request study guides. Two skirmishes a day, complete with cannons blasting, are reenacted - New Market and Appomattox or Shiloh. Open Sat. - Sun., 9:30am - 4:30pm. Skirmishes are usually at 11am and 2pm. Admission is $5 per day for adults; $3 for srs. and 12th graders and under.

COIN & COLLECTIBLES EXPO, Long Beach. (805) 962-9939 or (562) 436-3661 / www.longbeachshow.com, 100 S. Pine Ave. at the Long Beach Convention Center. A penny for your thoughts! Over 400 vendors buy and sell rare coins, paper money, foreign currency, collectible postcards, autographs, historical documents, jewelry, and stamps. A free coin and stamp are usually given out to younger children at the Young Numismatists and Young Stampers table, respectively. Open Thurs. - Sun., 10am - 7pm. Admission is $6 for adults for all four days; children 7 and under are free. Parking is $8.

CORONADO BUTTERFLY RESERVE, Goleta. See entry (pg. 563) in January.

DICKENS FESTIVAL, Riverside. (800) 430-4140 or (909) 781-3168 / www.dickensfest.com, Mission Inn Avenue between Lime and Orange. You'll have a Dickens of a time at this three-day festival! Walk the streets of a re-created London marketplace where the entertainment, costumes, and food are served up Victorian style. A mini fare for kids include making period crafts, storytelling, and scavenger hunt. Other activities and events included dramatic and musical presentations, a costume fashion show, educational workshops, eating fish n' chips, the Gordon Highlanders encampment (catch at least one drill and fire demonstration accompanied by pipes and drums), and even a night out on the town, such as a ball at Mr. Fessiwig's place where you can do the (Oliver) Twist. Open Fri. at 5:30pm for pub night (adults only - $25). Open Sat. - Sun., 10am - 6pm. Entrance to the marketplace is free. Some shows cost $5 per person.

FLYING LEAP STORYTELLING FESTIVAL. (805) 688-9533 or (800) 468-6765 / www.solvangusa.com, Storytellers from all over congregate to spin tales, swap stories, and put on programs full of laughter, drama, music, and passion about a given subject or storyline. First-timers and story afficionados will appreciate the tales. Sets, lasting about an hour, feature various storytellers, each with their own slant, heritage, and way of telling stories. Call for specific location, hours, and cost.

HITS INDIO DESERT CIRCUIT, Indio. See January entry (pg. 563) for details.

KUUMBA FEST, San Diego. (619) 544-1000 / www.sandiegorep.com, 79 Horton Plaza at the Lyceum Theatre. The San Diego Repertory Theatre celebrates Black History month with this three-day fest. Enjoy an ethnic marketplace, educational workshops, a pageant of Egyptian and Zulu monarchs, a fashion show, music, and arts and crafts. Call for dates, times, and prices.

LINCOLN CELEBRATION, San Juan Capistrano. (949) 234-1300 / www.missionsjc.com, on Ortega Hwy between Camino Capistrano St. and El Camino Real at Mission San Juan Capistrano. Meet President Lincoln, who seems to be everywhere on President's Weekend. Watch a reenactment of him signing documents deeding the mission to the church, and then check out the original documents here as well as other memorabilia. Other Civil War figures also roam the grounds. Open President's Day Mon., 10am - 4pm. Admission is $6 for adults; $5 for seniors; $4 for ages 3 - 11; children 2 and under are free.

PRESIDENT'S DAY, Simi Valley. (800) 410-8354 / www.reagan.utexas.edu, 40 Presidential Dr. at the Ronald Reagan Presidential Library and Museum. On President's Day Monday, Washington and Lincoln are only two of the president's honored. Roving president look-alikes could include Reagan (of course), Jefferson, Theodore Roosevelt, Washington, and Lincoln, as well as a few first ladies. Each year the specific activities change, but there are usually storytellers and few educational presentations for the family, as well as food booths. Open 10am - 5pm. Admission is $5 for adults; $3 for srs.; ages 15 and under are free.

PRESIDENT'S DAY, Yorba Linda. (800) 872-8865 / www.nixonfoundation.org, 18001 Yorba Linda Blvd. at the Richard Nixon Presidential Library and Birthplace. Presidential tributes begin on the Sunday before President's Day and continue on Monday. Actors portraying Lincoln and Washington tell stories about their lives and times, and pose for pictures. Explore the museum to experience another presidential era. Open Sun., 11am - 5pm; Mon., 10am - 5pm. Admission is $5.95 for adults; $3.95 for srs.; $2 for ages 8 - 11 years; children 7 and under are free. On Mon. admission is free.

RIVERSIDE COUNTY FAIR & NATIONAL DATE FESTIVAL, Indio. (800) 811-FAIR (3247) or (760) 863-8247 / www.datefest.org; www.indiochamber.org, 46350 Arabia St. at the Riverside County Fairgrounds. This ten-day county fair usually begins the Friday before President's Day. There are lots of special exhibits and activities, many with particular kid-appeal. These include the gem and mineral show, carnival-type rides, a model railroad, livestock shows, a petting zoo (we saw the usual array of farm animals as well as llamas, a zebra, and a kangaroo), camel rides, pony rides, and virtual reality rides. The camel and ostrich races (the animals are ridden bareback and also with "chariots") are some of the festival highlights. These races take place a few times a day, and you just never know what is going to happen with two such stubborn species of animals. On President's Day Monday there is a colorful parade with Queen Scheherazade. An hour-and-a-half musical pageant is put on nightly. The festival is open daily, 10am - 10pm. Admission is $7 for adults; $5 for srs.; $4 for ages 5 - 12; children 4 and under are free. Rides and some attractions have additional fees. Parking on the fairgrounds is $5.

SCOTTISH FESTIVAL, Long Beach. (562) 435-3511 / www.queenmary.com, 1126 Queens Hwy, adjacent to and on the Queen Mary. Wear a kilt and bring your bagpipes (although you don't have to) for this two-day event. Over fifty Scottish clans are on hand to entertain visitors with a parade (usually at noon), battle reenactments (on-going, but call), traditional and contemporary music, Highland games (e.g. tossing the caber, etc.), storytelling, vendors with Scottish wares, a parade of British automobiles, food, and much more. Open Sat. - Sun., 10am - 6pm. Admission, which includes entrance to the Queen Mary, is $17 for adults; $15 for srs. and military personnel; $13 for ages 3 - 11; children 2 and under are free. Parking is $8. Tips: Very limited free parking is available on Queensway Dr. and Harbor Plaza in front of the park. The games, which you may watch for free, take place at the park on the grassy lawn.

TET FESTIVAL, Westminster. (714) 206-6151 or (714) 890-1418 / www.thsv.org, 9301 Westminster Ave. at Garden Grove Park. This three-day festival celebrates the start of the Vietnamese lunar new year in a big way. A colorful parade with various costumes, flags, and floats kicks off the festival. Arts and crafts and food booths are just some of the fun "extras". Open Fri., 2pm - 10pm; Sat., 10am - 10pm; Sun., 10am - 9pm. Admission is $5 for adults; $4 for ages 3 - 12; children 2 and under are free.

VISIT WITH WASHINGTON AND LINCOLN, Los Angeles. (800) 204-3131 / www.forestlawn.com, 6300 Forest Lawn Dr. at Forest Lawn Memorial Park. Meet Betsy Ross, George Washington, and Abraham Lincoln (i.e. educators dressed in costume) who talk about "their" lives and their accomplishments for about thirty minutes each, near the Court of Liberty. Lincoln recites the Gettysburg Address, along with other speeches, and tells fascinating stories about himself. See the twenty-five-minute film called *Birth of Liberty* in the theater, then walk the grounds to see statues other famous people. This wonderful living history program is presented on two weekdays for up to 350 people, every half hour from 9:30am - 11:30am. Reservations are required, but a family could probably just add themselves to a group already there. Admission is free. See the Forest Lawn entry on page 135 for more details about the park.

WHALE WATCHING. See January entry (pg. 564) for details.

MARCH:

BIG TRAIN SHOW, Long Beach. (562) 435-3511 / www.bigtrainshow.com, 1126 Queens Highway at Queen Mary. Chug over to the weekend show that features operating train models interspersed with garden layouts, mountains, rivers, and bridges. Over a hundred vendors are on hand to sell train paraphernalia. Tours and workshops are offered so you can learn modeling tips and more. Open Sat. - Sun., 11am - 5pm. Admission is $10 for adults; $6 for ages 3 - 11; children 2 and under are free. Parking is $8.

BUNNY DAYS, Mission Viejo. (949) 768-0981 or (949) 460-2713 / www.saddlebackrecreation.com, 23941 Veterans Way at Oso Viejo Park. Join the Easter Bunny and friends the Saturday before Easter for egg hunts, carnival game booths, family crafts, a petting zoo, on-going entertainment, and big wheel races. Open Sat., 11am - 2pm. Admission and the egg hunts are free. Some activities cost.

CELEBRATION OF THE WHALES FESTIVAL, Oxnard. (805) 985-4852 / www.ci.oxnard.ca.us, between Fisherman's Wharf and Marine Emporium Landing. It's a whale of a sight! As the majestic ocean mammals migrate, look for them from the shore or take a cruise. This one-day festival includes kayak racing, tide-pool touch tanks, aquarium presentations, and other events and activities. Celebrate on Sun., 11am - 5pm. Admission is free.

CIVIL WAR CAMP, Santa Fe Springs. (562) 946-6476 / www.santafesprings.org, 12100 Mora Dr. at Heritage Park. For one day, join forces with the 1st N. Carolina Artillery and Calvary and the Taylor's/Hays Brigade. Troops, artillery drills, cannon firings, horses, Civil War surgeons demonstrating their skill on the wounded, and dancing Southern belles are all part of the reenactment. Open Sat., 10am - 4pm. Admission is free.

COWBOY POETRY AND MUSIC FESTIVAL, Santa Clarita. (661) 255-4910 or (661) 290-2997 - during the event. / www.santa-clarita.com, Arch St. and 12th St. at Melody Ranch Motion Picture Studio. Howdy-doo! Over 12,000 people attend this four-day event that acknowledges that cowboys are still heroes. Browse in shops at the historic Melody Ranch (which resembles a western town), grab some chuck wagon grub, and listen to some of the finest poetry, stories, and music that the west has to offer. Several specifically family-oriented programs are offered, including western farces and trick ropers. Off-site events include "gold" panning at Placerita Canyon Nature Center, watching old Western flicks on Friday night at the Saugus Train Station, and horseback riding at Mentryville Park. The festival just gets bigger and better every year! Tip: Dress up in western duds and don't forget to wear your Stetson. The festival grounds are only open Sat., 10am - 10pm; Sun., 10am - 5pm, but off-site activities run Thurs., 8pm - 9:30pm; Fri., 7pm - 10pm. Trail rides into the ranch begin at 8am on the weekend and cost $60. Admission to the festival is $10 for adults; $5 for ages 3 - 11, which includes a shuttle ride to the ranch. Note that while a majority of the shows are included in the admission price, certain shows are ticketed events and cost extra.

DISNEY ON ICE. See December entry (pg. 613) for details.

EASTER BUNNY CARNIVAL AND EGG HUNT, Rancho Margarita. (949) 589-4272, Antonio Parkway and Las Flores at Trabuco Mesa Park. Usually held the Saturday before Easter, this event (with over 2,000 participants last year and 17,000 plastic eggs!) is really *egg*citing. Start your morning off at 7am with a pancake breakfast - $3 for adults; $2.50 for ages 7 to 12. Then join in the Easter egg hunt designed for children 2 to 10 years old. (Each age group is then given a different starting time.) Don't forget your Easter basket! Visit the costumed characters of Mr. and Mrs. Bunny, the petting zoo, and the bounce house, plus make and decorate a child-size kite - all for free! There are also arts and crafts booths. At the on-site Baby Goods Swap Meet you can buy good quality used baby and children's clothes and toys. Hours for the *egg*stra special carnival and hunt are 9am - noon.

EASTER EGG HUNTS. Many parks and schools put on free Easter egg hunts and/or Easter craft activities the weekend or Saturday before Easter. Call the Recreation Department of your local park for more information.

FESTIVAL OF THE KITE, Redondo Beach. (310) 372-0308 / www.pierkites.com, 110 Fisherman's Wharf near the Redondo Beach Pier. On the second Sunday this month watch brilliantly colored kites of all shapes and sizes fly high above the shoreline. There are contests, activities for kids, and synchronized acrobatic flying teams. Come fly 11am - 7pm; beach activities are noon - 4pm. Admission is free.

FESTIVAL OF THE WHALES, Dana Point. (888) 440-4309 or (949) 496-2274 / www.festivalofwhales.org, 24200 Dana Point Harbor Dr. at the Ocean Institute. It's no fluke - this two-weekend festival celebrates the

California gray whales' migration. The whole family can enjoy a variety of events offered throughout Dana Point, such as parades, art shows, kite flying, sand castle workshops, tidepool explorations, street fairs, kid's coloring contests, film festivals, and whale-watching excursions. Have a whale of a time! Prices and hours vary depending on the event.

FIESTA DE LAS GOLONDRINAS (Festival of the Swallows), San Juan Capistrano. (949) 234-1300 or (949) 493-4700 / www.missionsjc.com; www.sanjuanchamber.com, This three-day festival, celebrating the return of the swallows from their annual migration to Argentina, takes place in different areas throughout San Juan Capistrano, including the mission. The swallows actually return to the mission every year on March 19th, so the festivities happen the weekend before this date and on the 19th. Some of the festivities include parades (like a children's pet parade), pageants, petting zoo, pony rides, carnival rides, carnival games, a kid's hat contest, arts and crafts, music, and more! The mission is open at 8am on the 19th as the birds usually arrive in the morning, closing at 5pm. Admission at the mission is $6 for adults; $5 for srs., $4 for ages 3 - 11; children 2 and under are free.

FILLMORE SPRING RAILFEST, Fillmore. (800) 773-TRAIN (8724) / www.fwry.com, off Hwy 126 on Central at Central Park. The Visitors Center has huge model train display and lots of paraphernalia and collectables. Antique tractors and equipment, engine demonstrations, craft booths, live entertainment, and barbecue cooking are part of the fun. Check out the open-top speeder cars used to maintain railroad tracks. Miniature live steamer rides cost a minimal fee. Periodically, gunslingers come into down, have a shootout, rob a bank, and make a getaway on a train. Ride an antique steam car for an hour, or go for a 2 ½-hour diesel excursion all the way to Santa Paula and back, including a half-hour stop over. Note: The Santa Paula ride has food services available. Admission is free. Train tickets are $15 for adults and srs.; $8 for ages 4 - 12 years; $5 for ages 3 and under. All aboard on Sat. - Sun., 9am - 5pm.

FLOWER FIELDS, Carlsbad. (760) 431-0352 / www.theflowerfields.com, 5704 Paseo del Norte, off Palomar Airport Rd. Early March through May, walk through fifty-three acres of rows of blooming ranunculus. The colors are amazing, and the trails lead to bluffs overlooking the shoreline. Call first to make sure the flowers are in full bloom. Guided educational tours are also available. On-site picnic tables, special kids' days with fun activities, and an antique wagon tractor ride ($2 for adults; $1 for kids) add to enjoyment. Open daily, 9am - dusk. Admission is $7 for adults; $6 for srs; $4 for ages 3 - 10; children 2 and under are free.

GEM SHOW, Costa Mesa. (760) 747-9215 / www.gemfaire.com; www.ocfair.com, 88 Fair Dr. at the Orange County Fairgrounds. This three-day show for rock hounds brings over fifty vendors that buy, sell, and trade a wonderful variety of rocks, minerals, beads, and jewelry. The event is held four times a year. Open Fri., noon - 7pm; Sat., 10am - 7pm; Sun., 10am - 5pm. Admission is $5 for adults; $4 for srs.; ages 12 and under are free.

GLORY OF EASTER, Garden Grove. (714) 54-GLORY (544-5679) / www.crystalcathedral.org, 12141 Lewis St. at the Crystal Cathedral. This ninety-minute, spectacular production with live animals and actors, celebrates the resurrection of Jesus Christ in a powerful way. The last days of his life; the events leading up to his death, including the crucifixion; and his resurrection are presented in a dramatic and realistic reenactment. The show runs for about fourteen nights, with the curtain rising at 6:30pm and at 8:30pm most nights (there are no shows on Mondays), and an additional show at 4:30pm on selected weekend days. Tickets are $30 - $40 for adults; $2 less for srs. and ages 12 and under. Ask about family night discounts, when tickets are $18 per person.

GREEN MEADOWS FARM (Irvine), Irvine. (800) 393-3276 / www.greenmeadowsproductions.com, 1 Irvine Park Dr. at Irvine Regional Park. From mid-March through mid-April take a guided, two-hour, walk around this unique, completely hands-on, petting farm. There are over 500 animals to see, touch, snuggle, and sometimes feed, such as rabbits, chicks, ducks, cows, pigs, sheep, goats, turkeys, and a buffalo. Spring is in the air, so kids are almost assured of seeing animal babies. Your admission price also includes milking a cow and taking a pony ride and a tractor-driven hayride. This is a wonderful, informative, and memorable field trip for kids and adults. A nice gift shop is here, too. Also see the May and September Green Meadows Farm entries. Open Mon. - Fri., 9:30am - noon (last tour); Sat., 10am - 2pm (last tour). Admission is $10 for ages 2 and up. Admission for groups of twenty or more is $8 per person. Reservations for groups are required.

GRUNION RUNS. up and down the coast. Call beaches, the Cabrillo Marine Aquarium (pg. 179), the Ocean Institute (pg. 244), or Birch Aquarium (pg. 462) for more details, dates, and times. Grunions are small, silvery fish that venture out of the waters from March to August to lay their eggs on sandy beaches. They are very particular about when they do this - after every full and new moon, and usually around midnight. You may catch them only on certain months and no nets or gloves are allowed; only bare hands. (Did I mention that the fish are slippery?) Eat what you catch, or let them go, and enjoy a unique night of grunion hunting. Cabrillo charges $5 for adults; $1 for srs. and children, which includes a slide presentation and instructions. Ages 16 and up must have a valid fishing license.

HARVEST FESTIVAL, Del Mar. (800) 321-1213 / www.harvestfestival.com, 2260 Jimmy Durante Blvd. at the Del Mar fairgrounds. See the October entry for Harvest Festival Ventura (pg. 603) for details.

HARVEST FESTIVAL, Pomona. (800) 321-1213 / www.harvestfestival.com, 1101 McKinley Ave. at Fairplex at the Pomona County Fairgrounds. See October entry for Harvest Festival Ventura (pg. 603) for details.

HITS INDIO DESERT CIRCUIT, Indio. See January entry (pg. 563) for details.

INDIO POWWOW, Indio. (800) 827-2946 or (760) 342-5000 / www.cabazonnation.com, 84245 Indio Springs Dr. at Fantasy Springs Casino. Hosted by the Cabazon Band of Mission Indians, this Pow Wow brings together Native Americans and non-Indians in a celebration of music, drums, dance, food, and arts and crafts. Don't miss the "grand entrance" where all the Indians, in full costume, dance as they come in. The Pow Wow is usually held the last weekend in March, Fri., 5pm - midnight (grand entrance at 7pm); Sat., 11am - midnight (grand entrance at 1pm and 7pm); Sun., 11am - 6pm (grand entrance at 1pm). Admission is $4 for adults; $3 for srs.; ages 12 and under are free.

IRISH FAIR AND FESTIVAL, Pomona. (310) 537-4240 / www.fairplex.com, 1101 W. McKinley Ave. at Fairplex. Coming to this weekend festival is like finding gold at the end of a rainbow. Six entertainment stages features Irish bands and Irish dancing. (I really enjoy the clogging.) Other activities and events include sheep herding demonstration, an Irish bred dog show, Leprechaun Village with rides for wee ones, food, a pony show, an Ancient Irish Village, a market place, a Celtic arts center, and Scottish games, including the original extreme sport - caber tossing. (Who thought of this sport?!) Other games include weight, stone, and hammer tossing. Open Sat. - Sun., 10am - 7pm. Admission is $12 for adults; $8 for srs.; ages 12 and under are free. Parking is $6.

LIFE OF CHRIST MOSAIC PROGRAM, Covina Hills. (800) 204-3131 / www.forestlawn.com, 21300 Via Verde at Forest Lawn Memorial Park. A costumed educator, representing Christ, talks for about forty-five minutes about "his" life and purpose. The talk is given in the forecourt of the Heritage Mausoleum. This living history program is given on a weekday at 10am. Reservations are necessary. Admission is free.

OCEAN BEACH KITE FESTIVAL, Ocean Beach. (619) 531-1527 / www.ci.san-diego.ca.us, between Santa Monica and Newport Sts. at Ocean Beach Elementary School and across the street at Ocean Beach Recreation Center. The first Saturday of the month offers a colorful, high-flying festival celebrating the joy of kiting. You are invited to build and decorate kites from 9am to 1pm. Judging commences from 1pm to 2pm and a parade goes from 2pm to 3pm. From then on, just fly 'em. There is also an on-going crafts fair. There is no charge for admission or for materials for kite making.

PAGEANT OF OUR LORD, Rolling Hills Estates. (310) 519-9406 / www.palosverdes.com/rhcovenant, 2222 Palos Verdes Dr. N. at Rolling Hills Covenant. Similar to Pageant of the Masters, but on a smaller scale and Christian-based, major works of art come to "life" as people dress up in costume and full make-up to impersonate, albeit statue-like, the people in the original paintings. Music accompanies each presentation. This is an amazingly powerful medium in which to express art. The program is offered for a few weeks in the evenings and on weekend afternoons in March. Admission is $8 - $15 for adults; $4 - $7 for ages 5 - 12; children 4 and under are not admitted.

POINT MUGU'S NAVAL AIR WEAPONS STATION'S AIR SHOW, Oxnard. (805) 989-8786 or (805) 989-8548 / www.nbvc.navy.mil, Las Posas near the Pacific Coast Highway intersection at the Naval Base Ventura County. At this three-day show, the air is filled with flight demonstrations including solo routines, formation flying, sometimes the famous Air Force Thunderbirds, and daring acrobatic stunts. The ground displays are equally exciting with exhibits of aircraft, a flight simulator, children's rides, food booths, and more. Bring suntan lotion! Gates are open Fri. at noon (the air show is at 3pm); Sat. - Sun. at 8am; demonstrations begin at 9:30am. Open-air, unreserved seating and parking are free. Reserved seats are between $4 - $35.

POPPY RESERVE, Lancaster. (661) 942-0662 - state park; (661) 724-1180 - recorded info from the poppy reserve / www.calparksmojave.com, 15101 W. Lancaster Rd. Do you hear echos of the wicked witch's voice in *The Wizard of Oz* cackling, "poppies, poppies"? During the months of March and April our bright orange California state flower blooms in this 1,758 + acre reserve, as do several other types of wildflowers. (You'll also notice wonderful patches of flowers along the roadside, too.) Call first to see how rains have affected the bloom schedule. Hike along the seven miles of hilly trails that run through the reserve, including a paved section for stroller/wheelchair access. Don't forget your camera!! Although poppies only bloom seasonally, the reserve is open year round sun-up to sundown. The Visitors' Center is just open seasonally - mid-March through April, Mon. - Fri., 10am - 4pm; Sat. - Sun., 10am - 5pm. It provides orientation to the reserve and educational information. Parking during poppy season is $4 a vehicle; $2 off season.

RENAISSANCE FESTIVAL OF PALM SPRINGS, Palm Springs. (800) 320-4736 / www.renaissanceinfo.com, Alejo and Palm Canyon Dr. in Frances Stevens Park. For three days experience a re-creation of a 15th/16th century European village and meet the type of people that lived there. Join in the merriment and dancing, music, magic, juggling, theater, crafts, and the food! Open Fri., 10am - 5pm; Sat., 10am - 9pm; Sun., 10am - 5pm. Admission is $10 for adults; $6 for srs. and ages 6 - 12; children 5 and under are free.

RIVERSIDE AIRPORT OPEN HOUSE AND AIR SHOW, Riverside. (909) 351-6113 or (909) 354-5274 / www.ci.riverside.ca.us, Arlington and Airport Drs. Army Golden Knights parachute team, Air force A-10 aerobatics team, and numerous other performances are part of this annual air show. Other activities and events include a Stealth Fighter fly-by, over thirty vintage aircraft plus military helicopters on display, twenty-minute helicopter rides ($40), and a car show with hot rods, cruisers, and custom cars. The Cafe is open. The Open House is Sat., 9am - 4pm. Admission is free. Parking is $5 per car.

SANTA BARBARA KITE FESTIVAL, Santa Barbara. (805) 682-2895 or (805) 966-2694, the lawn next to Garvin Theater at Santa Barbara City College's West Campus. A rainbow array of kites take to the skies, although some nose dive, at this annual one-day festival. Kites of all sizes, shapes, and colors fly in various competitions such as sport flying, highest flying, most beautiful, and largest kite. Prizes are awarded. The tail chase event is especially fun for kids as they try to catch the tail of a kite as it alternately dips, dives, and soars. Kites are available for purchase or bring your own. Fly some fun on Sun., 11am - 5pm. Free admission.

SHEEP SHEARING FESTIVAL, Santa Ana. (714) 835-7484 or (714) 953-8555 / www.santaanazoo.org, 1801 E. Chestnut Ave. at the Santa Ana Zoo. "Ewe" are wanted here for the shear joy of it! As a variety of sheep get their hair cut, visitors see shearing demonstrations, and spinners and weavers transform raw wool into refined yarn. The one-day festival runs from 10am - 12:30pm, although of course you are welcome to spend the rest of the day here. The festival is free with zoo admission, which is $5 for adults; $3 for srs. and ages 3 - 12.

SPRING SPECTACULAR, Moorpark. (805) 378-1441 / sunny.moorparkcollege.edu/~eatm, 7075 Campus Rd. at Moorpark College. Join in on three weekends of animal fun held at America's Teaching Zoo (see pg. 556). These weekends incorporate guest presentations and booths from various animal organizations; behind-the-scenes tours of animals not normally on exhibit; scripted shows with costumes; a kid's zone; educational animal programs and demonstrations; and an opportunity to see all the exotic animals. Open Sat. - Sun., 10am - 5pm. Admission is $8 for adults; $6 for srs. and ages 12 and under. Some activities may cost extra.

ST. PATRICK'S DAY PARADE AND FESTIVAL, San Diego. (858) 268-9111 / www.stpatsparade.org, Sixth and Maple near Balboa Park. The Saturday before St. Patty's day, think of little green men, and I don't mean Martians. Leprechauns, Celtic music, Irish folk dancing, marching bands, kiddie rides, arts and crafts booths, and food are top of the order for this one-day of shenanigans. Park near Balboa Park and take a free shuttle. The two-and-a-half-hour parade begins at 11am and goes along Fifth and Ivy up to Sixth Ave. and Maple. The festival is Sat., 10am - 5pm. Admission is free.

VISIT WITH FATHER SERRA, Long Beach. (800) 204-3131 / www.forestlawn.com, 1500 E. San Antonio Dr. at Forest Lawn Memorial Park. Learn California history from a founding father, or rather, a costumed actor who tells about Father Serra's life and time period from a "first person" perspective. This half-hour talk is interesting and educational. The presentation is on a weekday, geared for school kids. Call to make a reservation. Admission is free.

VISIT WITH MICHELANGELO AND LEONARDO DA VINCI, Glendale. (800) 204-3131 / www.forestlawn.com, 1712 S. Glendale Ave. at Forest Lawn Memorial Park. A costumed Michelangelo and Da Vinci talk to an audience of up to 350 people for about a half hour about "their" lives and achievements - history comes alive! Take a self guided tour around the premises to view "their" art. (Note: The art does contain some nudity.) See Forest Lawn, on page 135, for details about what else this park has to offer. This two-day, weekday, program is presented at 9:30am, 10:30am, and 11:30am. Reservations are necessary. Admission is free.

WHALE FEST CELEBRATION, Ventura. (805) 644-0169 / www.venturaharborvillage.com, Harbor Dr. at Harbor Village. This one-day festival celebrates the whales migrating to and from Baja. Besides watching for the whales from the village or via a cruise, there are tidepool touch tanks and other marine exhibits, as well as entertainment throughout the day. The festival is on a Sun., 11am - 4pm. Free admission.

WHALE FESTIVAL, Santa Barbara. (805) 897-3187 / www.sbwhalefestival.com, State Street and Cabrillo, near Stearns Wharf. I'm not just spouting off - the two-day whale festival is fun for the whole family. A kid's carnival area, arts and crafts show, marine education stations and exhibits, diving demonstrations, rescue/fire demonstration at sea, rubber duck races, storytelling, live entertainment, whale-watching cruises, and hopefully some whale sightings add to the festivities. The festival hours are Sat. - Sun., 10am - 5pm. Admission is free.

WHALE OF A DAY FESTIVAL, Rancho Palos Verdes. (310) 544-5264 / www.palosverdes.com/rpv, 31501 Palos Verdes Dr. W. at Pt. Vincente Interpretative Center. Bring your binoculars and look for the Pacific Gray Whales as they migrate. Other activities include storytelling, arts and crafts, and booths manned by representatives from Cabrillo Marine Aquarium, Marine Mammal Care Center, L.A. Zoo, and others. Tours of the Pt. Vincente Lighthouse are given on a first come first serve basis for ages 7 years and older. The festival commences Sat., 10am - 4pm. Admission is free. Parking is available at Long Point with free shuttles.

WHALE WATCHING. See January entry (pg. 564) for details.

APRIL:

AMERICA'S FAMILY PET EXPO, Costa Mesa. (800) 999-7295 or (626) 447-2222 / www.petexpo.com; www.ocfair.com, 88 Fair Dr. at Orange County Fairgrounds. Bark, meow, oink, baaa, sssss, neigh - this three-day weekend is for animals lovers. Over 1,000 animals - dogs, cats, reptiles, goats, mini horses, llamas, rabbits, pigs, fish, etc. - are at the expo. See bird shows, cat shows, a petting zoo, Frisbee dogs, celebrity animals, pet products, stage shows, and educational demonstrations. Check out the pet adoption services. (Animals are not for sale here.) Open Fri., 10am - 6pm; Sat., 9am - 7pm; Sun., 9am - 6pm. Admission per day is $8 for adults; $6 for srs.; $3 for ages 6 - 12; children 5 and under are free.

APRIL FOOLS JUGGLERS FESTIVAL, Isla Vista. / www.sbjuggle.org, Ocean Road at the University of California Santa Barbara. For over twenty years the campus juggling club has hosted this event, so juggle your schedule to try to attend. See beginner and advanced jugglers toss and catch various props - hats, juggling pins, balls, cigar boxes, and more. Also in attendance are clowns on unicycles, magicians, and prop vendors. Sometimes classes are offered. The Saturday show runs from 7:30pm - 9:30pm and costs $6 for adults; $4 for kids. The location of the shows are on, or nearby, the campus and vary from year to year. All profits go toward the Santa Barbara Rape Crisis Center. The Saturday and Sunday daytime events begin at about 10am, and are free to watch.

ARTWALK, San Diego. (619) 615-1090 / www.artwalkinfo.com, along India St. and Kettner Blvd. in Little Italy neighborhood, in downtown San Diego. Hundreds of visual and performing arts exhibitors strut their stuff in a weekend-long celebration of the arts. (Many events happen throughout the month, too.) In cooperation with

Museum of Contemporary Art, San Diego Area Dance Alliance, Children's Museum, San Diego Performing Arts League, etc., you'll see paintings, dance, ballet, poetry, photography, sculpture, opera, folkloric dance, divas, and more. Just a few specific activities for kids in the past have included writing poetry, creating an origami animal, making a 3-D paper model, and molding a sculpture. Open Sat. - Sun., noon - 6pm. Admission is free.

AVOCADO FESTIVAL, Fallbrook. (760) 728-5845 / www.fallbrookca.org/avofest.htm, Main St. Guacamole by the pound. Race cars made from avocados. Thousands of people thronging the streets. A flower show. Avocado croquet. A pit-spitting contest at the Avocado Olympics. These are glimpses of what the one-day festival has in store. Besides arts and crafts, kids activities, and agriculture displays, other happenings include packing house tours of the Del Rey Avocado Company, a walk through the Gem and Mineral Society Museum, and a vintage aircraft show at Fallbrook Air Park. Don't be green with envy; just get green with avocados. The festival is on a Sun. 9am - 5pm. Free admission.

BANNING HERITAGE DAYS, Wilmington. (310) 548-7777 / www.banningmuseum.org, 401 East M St. at the Banning Residence Museum. For one week, the museum becomes a living classroom for school groups on weekdays and for the public on the prior Sat. Intermingle with Victorian-dressed ladies and gentlemen and Civil War encampment reenactors; drill with the war regiment; learn new (actually, old) dance steps; practice tying sailor knots; pan for gold; play hoops and other 19th century games; learn animal husbandry; and take a self-guiding tour of the museum. The school program runs Mon. - Fri., 9am - 12:30pm. Tip: Bring a picnic lunch. Call way in advance for reservations. It's open to the public Sat., 11am - 4pm. Admission is free.

BLESSING OF THE ANIMALS, Los Angeles. (213) 625-5045 or (213) 485-8225 / www.ci.la.ca.us/ELP, 125 Paseo de la Plaza at El Pueblo de Los Angeles Historical Monument. This event is held on the Saturday before Easter. Children can dress up their pets - all domestic animals welcome - and bring them to the Plaza Church to be blessed by priests. Some participating zoos bring in more exotic animals. This is done to honor the animal's contributions to the world. It gets wild with all different kinds of animals "held" in children's arms! Open noon - 6pm with the procession and blessing at about 2pm. Admission is free.

CHILDREN'S DAY, Santa Fe Springs. (562) 946-6476 / www.santafesprings.org, 12100 Mora Dr. at Heritage Park. This day of old-fashioned fun is held around the Week of the Young Child. Kids can ride on a fire engine or on ponies; pet animals in the petting zoo; dress-up in old-fashioned clothing; make hats; try an obstacle course; get their faces painted; see reptiles; churn butter; pan for gold; and play turn-of-the-century games and crafts. Open Sat., noon - 4pm. Admission and activities are free.

CROSSROADS EUROPEAN RENAISSANCE FESTIVAL, Corona. (800) 320-4736 or (909) 735-0101 / www.renaissanceinfo.com, 14600 River Rd. at Archibald at Riverview Park. Peasants, lords and ladies, merchants, artisans, craftsmen, nobles, knights, travelers, and anyone else is invited to join in the weekend festivities. Archery competitions, horse shows, sheep shearing, weaving and spinning demonstrations, great food, and crafts of old are just part of the fun. Open mid-April through May, Sat. - Sun., 10am - 6pm. Admission is $12.50 for adults; $7 for srs. and ages 6 - 12; children 5 and under are free.

DEL MAR NATIONAL HORSE SHOW, Del Mar. (858) 755-1161 / www.delmarnational.com, 2260 Jimmy Durante Blvd. at the Del Mar fairgrounds. Saddle up for three weeks of exciting horse competition and Olympic selection. Each weekend features a main equestrian category: Western, Dressage, and Hunter/Jumper. Watch the horses being put through their paces during the week. Note: Check the website for exciting horse shows throughout the year. Open weekdays 8am - 5pm with free admission. Open weekends for shows (call for hours) - the cost is $8 - $15 for grandstand seats; $15 for box. Parking is $7.

EARTH DAY, San Diego. (619) 239-0512 / www.balboapark.org, Park Blvd. at Balboa Park. Celebrate the preservation of the environment in this one-day event. Several hundred organizations host booths and exhibits on organic materials; alternatives to lighting, power, and energy; and more. Kids (and parents) who attend Earth Day will hopefully become more planet smart. Activities begin at 10am and end at 5pm. Admission is free.

EASTER. Look at all the Easter-related activities in March, if Easter falls in April this year.

END OF THE TRAIL WORLD CHAMPIONSHIP COWBOY SHOOT OUT AND WILD WEST JUBILEE, Riverside. (877) 411-SASS (7277) or (714) 694-1800 / www.sassnet.com, River Rd. at Raahague's Ranch at the Prado Dam Recreation Area. For three days, hundreds of authentically-dressed Wild West competitors from all over compete in this action shooting contest, including a mounted shooting competition. Some of the shooting you can watch (wear protective eye gear), and most of it you can hear. Dress up, too, or you might feel out of place as the cowboy lifestyle is celebrated. The entire area is set up like an Old West town and features era-appropriate activities for the family such as chuck wagon races, trick ropers, cowboy poetry readings, and Wild West reenactments. Over 100 vendors are on site. Happy trails! The activities run 9am - 5pm. Admission is $10 a day for adults; children 11 and under are free. Parking is $2.

ESCONDIDO RENAISSANCE FAIRE AND SHAKESPEARE IN THE PARK, Escondido. (805) 496-6036 / www.goldcoastfestivals.com, 742 Clarence Ln. at Felicita Park. The age of chivalry is recreated in a natural setting. Experience the glories of the reign of Queen Elizabeth with battle pageants, jugglers, music in the streets, games, activities, a kid's play area, and entertainment from days of yore, including Shakespeare's plays. Open Sat. - Sun., 10am - 5pm. Admission is $10 for adults; $5 for ages 5 - 11; children 4 and under are free. Parking is $3.

FARM FEST, Santa Paula. (805) 525-9293 or (805) 658-7952 / hansentrust.ucdavis.edu, 14292 W. Telegraph Rd. at Faulkner Farm. If you have a brown thumb, come learn about gardening and more at the Farm Fest. The fest also features composting demonstrations, a storytelling area, and planting vegetables in containers. A 4-H petting zoo and display pens; weaving, spinning, and quilting demonstrations; farm equipment displays; living history by costumed docents; food vendors and a barbecue area; tours of the Faulkner House; and more are all included. Open the last Sat. in October, 10am - 4pm. Free admission.

FLOWER FIELDS, Carlsbad. See March entry (pg. 568) for details.

FREE CONE DAY. / www.benjerry.com/scoop_shops/free_cone_day/index.cfm, Life doesn't get any better than free ice cream. You get a scoop of any flavor of Ben & Jerry's ice cream for free on this one day. They call it Customer Appreciation Day, but we are the ones who say "thanks!" Call for the date and find out if your local store is participating.

FREE SCOOP NIGHT. / www.baskinrobbins.com, Here's the scoop: You get one scoop of any flavor of Baskin Robbins ice cream for free on this one evening - choices, choices! Check your local store or the web for the date and times.

GLORY OF EASTER, Garden Grove. See March entry (pg. 568) for details.

GREEN MEADOWS, Irvine. See March entry (pg. 568) for details.

IMAGINATION CELEBRATION, Orange County. (714) 540-4779 / www.icfestival.com, The Orange County Performing Arts Center is a main host for this forty-five day event that's held mid-April through May. At least fifty of Orange County's artistic and educational organizations bring performances, workshops, and exhibitions to over seventy family friendly events. This festival of arts for families takes place at malls, museums, parks, libraries, schools, etc. Some of the activities include puppet making, family art days, folk tales, band and theater performances, and dancing. Call for a schedule of events. Many events are free in this county wide celebration of imagination!

INTERNATIONAL SPEEDWAY, Costa Mesa. (949) 492-9933 / www.cmspeedway.com, 88 Fair Dr. at the Orange County Fairgrounds. The Speedway roars to life every Saturday night from April through October. Note: Racing in July is limited due to the Orange County Fair. This spectator sport of motorcycle racing can include sidecars, go karts, Quads, a kids' class (ages 6 to 12), and more. After the two-hour show, which can get long for younger ones, take the kids into the pits to get racer's autographs, or, when the bikes cool down, to sit on a cycle or two. Wear jeans and t-shirt (and bring a sweatshirt) as dirt tracks aren't noted for cleanliness. Gates open at 6:30pm; races start at 7:30pm. Admission is $10 - $12 for adults; $6 for srs. and ages 13 - 17; $3 for ages 6 - 12; children 5 and under are free. Parking is free.

KALEIDOSCOPE, Long Beach. (562) 985-2288 /
www.csulb.edu/web/divisions/students/Kaleidoscope/kaleidoscope03.html, 1250 Bellflower at California State
Long Beach campus. This open house, sponsored by the various departments of the college, is a wonderful, one-
day community event. There is face painting, cultural dances, an African marketplace, a Kid Zone, Earth Day
celebrations, a Cesar Chavez village, carnival, muscle car, push cart races, and more. Open 11am - 5pm.
Admission is free.

LAKESIDE RODEO & WESTERN DAYS, Lakeside. (619) 443-8561 or (619) 561-4331 - rodeo; (619) 561-
1031 - parade info / www.lakesiderodeo.com, 12854 Mapleview and Hwy 67 at the Lakeside Rodeo grounds.
Corral your young broncos and bring them to the two-and-a-half-hour rodeo show the last weekend in April.
This fantastic three-day rodeo features the major events - bull riding, team roping, calf roping, buckin' horses,
barrel racing, bareback riding, saddle broncs, and steer wrestling. On Saturday a down-home town parade
begins at 9:30am at Woodside and Main. Rodeo shows are Fri., 7:30pm; Sat., 2pm and 7:30pm; Sun., 2pm.
Tickets on Fri. are $6 per person or $25 for two adults and three kids 12 and under; weekend shows are $9 for
adults, $3 for ages 12 and under, or $11 - $13 for reserved seats.

LOS ANGELES TIMES FESTIVAL OF BOOKS, Westwood. (800) LATIMES (528-4637), ext. 7BOOK
(72665) / www.latimes.com/extras/festivalofbooks, U.C.L.A. campus. This weekend festival is absolutely the
place for book lovers of all ages. 150,000 people come to see the over 400 well-known authors, illustrators, and
celebrity authors that sign their books, do book readings, give seminars, and participate in panel discussions.
Hundreds of publishers, book stores, and other vendors have booths in which to sell their books, promote local
radio shows, and showcase Los Angeles attractions. Special programs on-going at the children's stages include
storytellers, clowns, musicians, crafts, character appearances (such as Barney), and much more. This is a "don't
miss" event. Open Sat., 10am - 6pm; Sun., 10am - 5pm. Admission is $7 per vehicle.

MOUNTAIN MAN DAYS (RENDEZVOUS), Banning. (909) 922-9200, 16th and Wilson at Gilman Historic
Ranch and Wagon Museum. This rendezvous is for school students only - lucky students! On Thursday and
Friday they can "meet" the trappers, mountain men, and cowboys of the Old West. Visit an 1700 to1800's-era
living history encampment and see clothing, tools, and equipment from this time period. Bring your gold dust
($) to use at the trading posts. Food and drink is available. Admission is $5 per student; $2.50 for chaperones.

PASADENA MODEL RAILROAD CLUB'S SPRING OPEN HOUSE, Pasadena. (877) 484-4664 /
www.pmrrc.org, 5458 Alhambra Ave. Over a period of several days, make tracks to see the largest model
railroad, which covers 5,000 square feet, as well as lots of other railroad paraphernalia. Call for hours.
Admission is $3 for adults; $1 for ages 10 - 17; free for ages 9 and under with an accompanying adult.

POINT MUGU'S NAVAL AIR WEAPONS STATION'S AIR SHOW, Oxnard. See March entry (pg. 569) for
details.

POPPY FESTIVAL, Lancaster. (661) 723-6077 / www.poppyfestival.com, 43011 N. 10th St W. at Lancaster
City Park. The poppy festival, located fifteen miles east of the poppy reserve, is held for one weekend in April.
The festival offers carnival rides, craft vendors, environmental displays, farmer's market area, live
entertainment, and more. Open Sat., 10am - 6pm; Sun., 10am - 6pm. Admission is $6 for adults; $3 for srs. and
ages 6 - 12; children 5 and under are free. Parking is $2.

POPPY RESERVE, Lancaster. See March entry (pg. 570) for details.

RAMONA OUTDOOR PLAY, Hemet. (800) 645-4465 / www.ramonabowl.com, 27400 Ramona Bowl Rd. All
the world's a stage, or at least this mountainside in Hemet. A cast of almost 400 (including children and
animals) use the mountainside as a stage to tell the romantic story of Ramona and her Indian hero, Alessandro.
The tale, which also reflects our early California heritage, is incredibly well told and fascinating. Going into its
81st year, this epic is performed for three weekends. Come early for lunch or to walk around the Mercado, a
Spanish marketplace with folk music, dancers, and artisans. Bring a jacket. Performances begin at 3:30pm. and
end at 6pm. Tickets range from $15 - $28, plus a $5 handling fee. Parking is $6

RENAISSANCE PLEASURE FAIRE, San Bernardino. (909) 880-0122 / www.renfair.com; www.recfair.com, 2525 Glen Helen Pkwy. at Glen Helen Regional Park. Heare ye, heare ye, this annual faire, one of the largest in Southern California, runs for eight weekends from April to June, bringing the Renaissance time to life, including wenches dressed accordingly, and bawdiness. Eat, drink, and be merry as you cheer on knights; play challenging games from times of yor; be entertained by juggling, dancing, and singing; and enjoy the delicious food and faire. The faire is open to the public Sat. - Sun., 10am - 6pm. Admission is $18.50 for adults; $16 for srs. and students; $8.50 for ages 5 - 11; children 4 and under are free. Parking is $8.

SANTA MARIA VALLEY STRAWBERRY FESTIVAL, Santa Maria. (800) 549-0036 or (805) 925-8824 / www.santamariafairpark.com, 937 S. Thornburg at the Santa Maria Fairgrounds. Bring your little shortcakes to this three-day festival to enjoy carnival rides, a petting zoo, train rides, kid's crafts, face painting, safety demonstrations by the police department, an ice sculpting demonstration, a monster truck show, and most importantly eating strawberries! Join in on pie eating contests, watch food preparation demonstrations with strawberries, and indulge in this sweet fruit presented in so many scrumptious ways. The festival is open Fri. - Sun., 11am - 10pm. Admission is $5 for adults; $3 for srs. and ages 6 - 11; children 5 and under are free. Parking is $3.

SCANDINAVIAN FESTIVAL, Thousand Oaks. (805) 493-3151 / www.clunet.edu, 60 W. Olsen Rd. at California Lutheran University. Valkommen! Enjoy a presentation/program of a 16th century Swedish royal court at this two-day festival, including a Viking encampment, folk dancing, a colorful parade with authentic costumes, arts and crafts booths, and a replica of Tivoli Gardens, though it's not quite as large as the one in Denmark. Kids will particularly enjoy the jugglers, puppet shows, magicians, clowns, and moon bounces. A smorgasbord is served here, too. The festival is open Sat., 10am - 5pm; Sun., noon - 5pm. Admission is $6 for adults; $1 for ages 6 - 12; children 5 and under are free. Certain activities cost extra.

SHAKESPEARE FESTIVAL PALMDALE, Palmdale. (888) 4-FILMAV (434-5628) or (661) 267-5685 / www.cityofpalmdale.org, 38334 10th St. East. This seven-day festival features performances that include Sonnet readers, madrigal singers, jugglers, and other pre-show performances. The four different, full-length performances vary in style - ballet, a modern-day version, and the original - and theme. Ask about the free language workshop to familiarize yourself with Shakespearian lingo and his influence on modern day verbiage. Enjoy English fair food. Performances are usually given at 7pm with a matinee Sun. at 2pm. (The matinee performance is usually an easier to understand play for kids.) Admission is $12 for adults; $10 for srs., students, and military; $8 for ages 12 and under.

SUNKIST ORANGE BLOSSOM FESTIVAL, Riverside. (909) 715-3400 / www.orangeblossomfestival.org, near Market and 10th Sts., 20 square blocks in historic downtown Riverside. *Orange* you glad you came to this weekend festival? It boasts several stages of live entertainment; a recreated living history town; a Technology Grove; a parade featuring floats, marching bands, and equestrian units on Sat. at 10am; tasty orange treats and cooking demonstrations; a children's grove with magic shows, carnival rides, craft activities, and a petting zoo; a fireworks display on Saturday night; and arts and crafts booths. Open Sat., 10am - 8pm; Sun., 10am - 7pm. Admission is free, although certain activities cost. Parking is $6.

TANAKA FARMS, Irvine. (949) 653-2100 or (949) 380-0379 / www.tanakafarms.com, 5380¾ University Dr. The time is ripe for tours of strawberry fields and to U-Pic them, too. Ninety-minutes-plus field trips, geared for pre-schoolers through fourth graders for groups of ten or more, can be made with advanced reservations for $10 per person. Tours include info on the plants, a wagon ride around the farm, and picking the delicious fruit. The fields are usually open mid-April through June daily, 9am - 5pm.

TOYOTA GRAND PRIX, Long Beach. (562) 981-2600 or (888) 82SPEED (827-7333) / www.longbeachgp.com, 3000 Pacific Ave. at Shoreline Dr. This top-of-the-line racing, three-day event includes practice and qualifying runs on Friday; celebrity racing and final qualifying runs on Saturday; and final Champ car racing on Sunday. See you at the races! Gates are open 7am - 6pm. Admission (unreserved seating) Fri. - Sat. is $30 for adults; Sun., $40; a three-day pass is $48. Children 12 and under are free with a paid adult.

Reserved seats on Sun. is $65 for adults; $47 for children; a three-day pass is $72 - $108 for adults; $53 - $82 for children.

TWENTYNINE PALMS WILD WEST GRAND PRIX, Twentynine Palms. (562) 428-4971 or (760) 367-3445 / www.obtel.com/race.html; www.29chamber.com, 3 miles east of town at the Moto Sports Arena. This AMA-sanctioned, District 37 competition Grand Prix Series dirt bike race features more than 1,300 participants in twelve events of different classes and skill levels across seven plus miles of desert. Top racers in the country compete on the course, and kids 4 to 11 can participate in a forty minute riding event around the track. Vendors round out the grand prix. Open Sat. - Sun., 6am - 10pm. Admission is $10 for adults; $5 for srs.; children 11 and under are free.

VAN OMMERING DAIRY, Lakeside. (619) 390-2929, 14950 El Monte Road. K through 6th graders are invited to take an hour-long tour of this family owned dairy. The tour starts in the commodities shed where seed is stored for the 600 cows that live on the premises. Guests then go through the showers (not literally!) where the cows are washed down before they're milked. From the milking barn, with all of its fascinating modern machinery, the tour visits the maternity pen. Kids are welcome to gently pet the newborns. Information is dispensed throughout the tour about the workings of a dairy, cows' eating habits, where the milk goes after it's outside the cows, and more. Visitors leave with lots of knowledge about these milk/meat/leather-producing animals, a greater understanding of how farmers' work affects everyone, and an informational pamphlet about the dairy industry. Note: The WILLIAMS WORM FARM (pg. 454) is right next door. Tours are offered April and May on Thurs. and Fri. at 9am, 10am, 11am, and noon. Groups from 15 to 100 people are welcome. Admission is free.

WHAT'S UP FOR KIDS EXPO, Torrance. (310) 544-1042 / www.whatsupforkids.com, 3330 Civic Center Dr. This one-day event is geared specifically for younger children. Some events and activities include live entertainment by popular children's singers and dancers, moon bounces, face painting, crafts, a safety expo, and lots of interactive exhibits, as well as parenting resources, products, and services. Open 10am - 3pm. Admission is free.

YOUTH EXPO, Costa Mesa. (714) 708-3247 / www.ocfair.com, 88 Fair Dr. at the Orange County Fairgrounds. This huge, three-day expo highlights the talents of Orange County kids from elementary through high school age. Their artistic endeavors are showcased in different buildings according to age groups and categories, such as fine arts, photography, woodworking, and ceramics. 4-H Club members also have wonderful exhibits. The Science Fair is a highlight which draws people from all over the United States who offer money and/or scholarships to students whose experimentally-based research designs are outstanding. The Expo is great for admiring other kids' works, and for sparking the creative genius in your child. Open Fri., 9am - 3pm (this day can get crowded with school tours); Sat. - Sun., 9am - 4pm. Admission is free.

MAY:

AIR SHOW, Chino. (909) 597-3722 / www.planesoffame.org, 7000 Merrill Ave. at the Air Museum Planes of Fame at Chino airport. Besides the in-air displays of classic and antique aircraft, trainer, liaison, fighter and bomber warbirds, flybys, and jet aircraft at this weekend event, a crowd favorite of aerobatic acts in the sky (e.g. wing walking, etc.) are featured. Several static (i.e. ground) displays include military aircraft, helicopters, fighter jets, and even a WWII bomber to tour through. Antique cars and vintage race cars will also be on display. Bring a picnic or purchase lunch from food vendors. Gates open at 8am; flying begins around 10am. Admission is $15 for adults (or $10 in advance); $5 for ages 5 - 11; children 4 and under are free. Tickets include entrance to the museum.

ARMED FORCES DAY FESTIVAL, Miramar. (858) 577-1000 / www.mccsmiramar.com, Marine Corps Air Station. This one-day event has a little something for everyone including a car show, craft fair, kiddie rides, Native American Pow Wow, a military history exposition, and military static displays such as planes, jets, helicopters, tanks, and more. The festival is open Sat., 10am - 4pm. Admission is free.

BUG FAIR, Los Angeles. (213) 763-3466 / www.nhm.org, 900 Exposition Blvd. at the Natural History Museum of Los Angeles. See page 109 for a description of the museum. This weekend fair really *bugs* me! Come and gawk at and even touch a wide variety of live insects, such as Madagascar hissing cockroaches, millipedes, and more. Over fifty vendors showcase every kind of insect product available including jewelry, t-shirts, toys, silkworms, live critters, a butterfly house, chocolate-covered crickets (poor Jimminy!), mounted insects, and lots more. The fair includes educational presentations and hands-on activities. Walk through the museum's Insect Zoo while here. Creep, crawl, or fly here on Sat. - Sun., 10am - 5pm. Admission to the fair includes admission to the museum: $8 for adults; $5.50 for srs. and students; $2 for ages 5 - 12; children 4 and under are free.

CALIFORNIA STRAWBERRY FESTIVAL, Oxnard. (888) 288-9242 or (805) 385-7578 / www.strawberry-fest.org, 3250 S. Rose Ave. at College Park. This big, juicy festival, held on the third weekend of May, offers unique strawberry culinary delights, an arts and crafts show with over 300 artisans, and contests, including a strawberry shortcake eating contest. Kids enjoy Strawberryland, in particular, because it has a petting zoo, puppet shows, clowns, hands-on arts and crafts, and carnival rides. Have a *berry* good time here! Open Sat., 10am - 7pm; Sun., 9:30am - 6:30pm. Admission is $9 for adults; $5 for srs. and ages 5 - 12; children 4 and under are free. Certain activities cost extra.

CHERRY FESTIVAL and CHERRY PICKING, Beaumont and Leona Valley. See June entry (pg. 582) for details.

CHILDREN'S DAY (or Kodomo no Hi), Los Angeles. (213) 628-2725 / www.jaccc.org, 244 S. San Pedro in Little Tokyo. This traditional Japanese celebration is for families, and particularly children ages 4 to 12. They are invited to participate in a running race, as well as making arts and crafts. Other attractions can include magic shows, sports clinics, kite-making, dancing, displays of traditional costumes, live entertainment, and more. Open Sat., 10am - 4pm. Admission is free, although certain activities cost.

CINCO DE MAYO CELEBRATION. The fifth of May, Mexican Independence Day, is celebrated throughout Southern California. The festival celebrates this Mexican holiday with several days of Mexican folk dancing, mariachi music, parades, puppet shows, booths, piñatas, and fun! In Los Angeles, for instance, call (213) 625-5045 or (213) 485-8225 / www.ci.la.ca.us/ELP, at El Pueblo de Los Angeles Historical Monument in downtown. In Santa Barbara County, call (805) 965-8561 / www.sbchamber.org, at De la Guerra Plaza. In San Diego County, call Bazaar del Mundo in Old Town San Diego, (619) 296-3161 / www.bazaardelmundo.com or www.fiestacincodemayo.com; Borrego Springs, (800) 559-5524 / www.borregosprings.org; or Oceanside, (760) 471-6549.

CROSSROADS EUROPEAN RENAISSANCE FESTIVAL, Corona. See April entry (pg. 572) for details.

EARLY CALIFORNIA DAYS, Long Beach. (562) 570-1755 / www.ci.long-beach.ca.us/park/facilities/rancholoscerritos.htm, 4600 Virginia Rd. at Rancho Los Cerritos. Blend Native American and Hispanic cultures, throw in Yankee seafaring elements, mix it together to re-create the period when California was under Mexican rule, and you'll get a old-time fiesta that's held bi-annually. Entertainment includes sea shanties, Hispanic songs and dances, roping, blacksmithing, hide scraping and leather working, rope weaving, and knot tying. Hands-on activities include rope making, adobe brick making, candle dipping, stick horse racing, and more. Open 12:30pm - 4:30pm. Admission is $3 per person; children 2 and under are free.

FARM DAYS, Valley Center. (760) 749-6297 / www.bellgardensfarm.com, 30841 Cole Grade Rd. at Bell Gardens. Some of the events and activities at this weekend, back-to-roots farm event include tractor parades, plowing demonstrations, tractor races, antique farm equipment on display, field demonstrations, blacksmith demonstrations, and much more. Look up Bell Gardens, on page 385, for more details about this great place. Open Sat. - Sun., 10am - 5pm. Free admission.

FELICITA PAGEANT, Escondido. (760) 745-1218 or (760) 745-4741 / www.felicitapageant.com, corner of Bear Valley Pkwy. and Mary Lane at Kit Carson Park. Felicita was the last Indian princess of the San Pasqual tribe. This romantic story tells of Felicita and her love, as well as the American versus Mexican Battle of San Pasqual. The outdoor pageant ends with California becoming a state. The play shows Fri. and Sat. night at 8pm; Sun., matinees. A BBQ dinner, available two hours before the program begins, is $15 per person. Admission is $15 for adults; $10 for srs. and students.

FERN STREET CIRCUS, San Diego. (619) 235-9756 / www.fernstreetcircus.com, Presidents Way and Park Blvd. in Balboa Park. Beginning with an interactive parade, this down home, yet professional circus aims to please and hits its mark. Aerial routines, jugglers, clowns, trampoline athletes, stilt walkers, music, theatrical lighting, acrobats, trapeze artists, and more send oohs and aaahs racing through the crowds. Ask about Fern Street's after-school program where they teach circus skills to youngsters. The circus runs for about a week with both day time and evening performances. Tickets are $10 for adults; $5 for ages 12 and under.

FREE COMIC BOOK DAY. / www.freecomicbookday.com, Sponsored by the Comic Book Industry, publishers such as Marvel, Dark Horse, DC, Image, and others prepare giveaway editions of their best titles for this one day. Some stores also host comic book creator appearances. Note that it is independent and specialty stores that participate. Call your local store for the date.

FRONTIER DAYS RODEO, Temecula. (909) 676-4718 / www.frontierdaysrodeo.com, near Winchester on Diaz Rd. at Northwest Sports Complex. The rodeo's in town and that's no bull. Main events include bull riding, calf roping, steer wrestling, barrel races, trick roping, rodeo clowns, team penning, and more. A children's rodeo includes mutton bustin'. A kid's fair area is also on the premises. P.R.C.A. Rodeos are held Sat. at 2pm and 7pm; Sun. at 2pm. Other happenings go on throughout the days. Admission to the matinee rodeos is $8 for adult; $10 for adults on Sat. night. Ages 5 - 12 are $5 for all shows; children 4 and under are free.

FULLERTON RAILROAD DAYS, Fullerton. (714) 278-0648 / www.trainweb.com/frpa, 124 E. Santa Fe Ave at the Fullerton Santa Fe Railroad Depot at the Fullerton Transportation Center. Usually held the first weekend in May, kids and adults go loco over going through a large steam locomotive, Amtrak passenger cars, and vintage private rail cars. More activities and events include model trains running in the huge and beautifully landscaped garden layout; more operating train layouts inside a circus tent; mini train rides; about 100 vendors selling train-related paraphernalia; and a food court. An antique fire truck and modern police car are on the grounds for show and tell. Open Sat., 9am - 6pm; Sun., 9am - 5pm. Admission is free.

GEM SHOW, Costa Mesa. See March entry (pg. 568) for details.

GREEN MEADOWS FARM (Los Angeles), Los Angeles. (800) 393-3276 / www.greenmeadowsproductions.com, 4235 Monterey Rd. at Ernest Debs Regional Park. The Farm is open May through June. See details in the March entry for Green Meadows Farm, Irvine (pg. 568).

GRUBSTAKE DAYS, Yucca Valley. (760) 365-6323 / www.yuccavalley.org, on Grand and Twenty-nine Palms Hwy. at Grubstake Grounds. This celebration commemorates the early mining background of the Morongo Basin. Favorite events include panning for gold, carnival rides and games, a street parade, Old West reenactments, motor sports, P.R.C.A. Rodeo, and demolition derbies ($10 for adults, $5 for ages 3 - 12; children 2 and under are free), and some equestrian events. Open Thurs., 4pm - 11pm; Fri., 4pm - midnight; Sat. - Sun., 10am parade - grounds open noon to midnight. Admission is free.

HEART OF THE FOREST RENAISSANCE FAIRE, Santa Barbara. (415) 897-4555 / www.forestfaire.com, on Hwy. 154 at San Marcos Pass in Live Oak Camp. Huzzah! For three weekends, make merry at an authentic re-creation of an English Market Faire during Elizabeth I's reign. Continuous performances on five stages and in the streets feature characters from the 16th century including Elizabethan improvisers, Shakespearean comedy, bawdy Italian theater, and English country song and dance. Kids will particularly enjoy children's theater with interactive performances, Punch and Judy puppet shows, storytelling, magic shows, games, parades, a petting farm, arts and crafts, and eating food with their fingers. Get into the spirit and come dressed in costume. Camping is available just down the road at Cachuma Lake Recreation Area. Tickets are $16 for adults; $13 for students, srs, and military; $6 for ages 5 - 11; children 4 and under are free. Advanced tickets are discounted. Parking is $4 or free with carpools of 4 or more.

I MADONNARI ART FESTIVAL, Santa Barbara. (805) 569-3873 / www.imadonnarifestival.com/im, at the corner of Los Olivos and Laguna sts. at Santa Barbara Mission. Since the 16th century, street painting, using chalk as a medium, has been an Italian tradition. Over 200 blank pavement squares in front of the mission will be filled in with colorful drawings by artists and aspiring artists of all ages over the three-day Memorial weekend. The professional works are indeed works of art. (Hope it doesn't rain!) The festival also includes live music and an Italian marketplace. Open Sat. - Sun., 11am - 6pm. Free admission. Young artists who want to paint a patch pay $10, which includes chalk.

IMAGINATION CELEBRATION, Orange County. See April entry (pg. 573) for details.

INTERNATIONAL MUSEUM DAY. / www.icom.museum, Here's a little known fact - May 18th is officially International Museum Day. Each year has a different theme. Many museum offer free admission, while others sponsor a family day of art and craft activities, storytelling, or other entertainment on or around that date. Call your local (or favorite) museum and see what they have to offer.

INTERNATIONAL SPEEDWAY, Costa Mesa. See April entry (pg. 573) for details.

LAKE CASITAS INTERTRIBAL POW WOW, Ojai. (805) 496-6036 / www.goldcoastfestivals.com, 11311 Santa Ana Rd. Enjoy this two-day weekend as more than forty American Indian tribes gather together to perform and compete (for cash prizes) in dance and music. Women's dances include traditional, shawl, jingle, and buckskin. Men compete in fancy, grass, traditional, and more. Special ceremonies plus arts and crafts booths (with beadwork, jewelry, and pottery), and even camping, fishing, and boating at the lake complete the festivities. Seating for the shows is limited, so bring your own chair. Open Sat. - Sun., 10am - 6pm. Admission is $10 for adults; $5 for ages 5 - 11; children 4 and under are free. Parking is $3.

LOCH PRADO SCOTTISH CLAN GATHERING AND HIGHLAND GAMES, Chino. (909) 597-4260 / www.co.san-bernardino.ca.us/parks/prado.htm, 16700 S. Euclid Ave. at Prado Regional Park. Enjoy the normal great regional park amenities with a Scottish twist. Enjoy Highland dancing, Scottish country dancing, fiddling, living history "experiences", pipes and drums, sheep dogs, a Scottish Marketplace, athletic games (such as tossing the caber), and Sunday Kirkin. (I think this means church.) Overnight camping is available. Sat. - Sun., 9am - 5pm. Admission to the park is $5. Call for admission to the games.

LOS RANCHEROS VISTADORES, Santa Ynez. (805) 688-4815 / www.missionsantaines.org, 1760 Mission Dr. at Mission Santa Ines. About 500 riders come to have their horses blessed by the padres at the mission on the Saturday afternoon of the Kentucky Derby. If you're in the area and a horse lover, it is a colorful procession to watch. There is no admission fee to watch the horses.

MEDIEVAL EVENT, Valley Center. (760) 789-2299 / www.historicenterprises.com; (760) 749-3333 / www.batesnutfarm.biz, 15954 Woods Valley Rd. at Bates Nut Farm. Knights on horseback, archers, dancing, period crafts, storytelling, music, and all the other sights and sounds of a working medieval camp are yours to enjoy. Note: This is not a Renaissance Fair and there isn't a jousting show; it's people going about their daily tasks around the time period of 1471. The camp is open Sat., 10am - 4pm. Admission is $5 for adults; $3 ages 5 - 10; children 4 and under are free.

MOTA DAY, Pasadena. (213) 740-8687 / www.gamblehouse.usc.edu; www.socalhistory.org, The five organizations that comprise MOTA - Museums Of The Arroyo - open their doors for free one Sunday a year and include fun family activities. The museums include Heritage Square Museum (pg. 95) at 3800 Homer St., Los Angeles; the Lummis Home and Garden at 200 E. Ave. 43; Southwest Museum (see pg. 119) at 234 Museum Dr.; Gamble House (see pg. 88) at 4 Westmoreland Pl.; and Pasadena Museum of History (see pg. 112) at 470 W. Walnut St. There is a free shuttle service between the museums. The museums are open 11am - 5pm.

NATURE'S CHILD OPEN HOUSE, San Dimas. (909) 599-7512, 1628 N. Sycamore Canyon Rd. at the San Dimas County Park Nature Center (see pg. 65). Over Memorial Day weekend enjoy Indian dances, nature hikes, face painting, pottery, weaving, beading, games, crafts, and Indian fry bread and sweet corn. The proceeds from the activities provide food and medical care for the animals in the center's sanctuary. Open Sat. - Sun., 10am - 4pm. Admission is free.

OJAI RENAISSANCE FAIR AND SHAKESPEARE BY THE LAKE, Lake Casitas. (805) 496-6036 / www.goldcoastfestivals.com, 11311 Santa Ana Rd. The age of chivalry is not dead! Enjoy a Renaissance weekend, via a recreated Elizabethan village, replete with games, three stages of entertainment, food (such as roasted turkey legs and sausages), and period-dressed performers and participants. A children's area has pony rides, jugglers, and more. Make sure you encourage the kids to watch a Shakespearean play or two, also. Tip: Bring your own chair or blanket. Open Sat. - Sun., 10am - 6pm. Admission is $15 for adults; $7 for ages 5 - 11; children 4 and under are free. Parking is $3.

OLD PASADENA SUMMER FEST, Pasadena. (626) 797-6803 / www.delmanoprod.com/lead.html, Central Park at Fair Oaks Ave. Memorialize the three-day Memorial Day weekend by participating in five events under this one banner. The Family Fest offers pony and train rides, a petting zoo, face painting, a moonbounce, a giant slide, swing chairs, a Ferris wheel, and hands-on cultural workshops. The Playboy Jazz Festival showcases top performers on stage - you can meet them and buy CDs afterward. Summer Art Festival features over 100 vendors promoting sculpture, hand-painted clothing, wooden toys, and demos. At Sports Zone watch extreme sporting events such as BMX racing and skateboarding and participate in basketball, baseball, and more. Indulge yourself in Taste of Summer in which local restaurants offer their tempting treats. Festival hours are 10am - 8pm. Admission is free, although certain activities cost.

OLD TOWN TEMECULA WESTERN DAYS CELEBRATION, Temecula. (909) 694-6412 / www.temeculacalifornia.com; www.cityoftemecula.org, Front St. and Main St. in Old Town. Kick up your heels in this wonderful old western-style town any day of the week, but particularly this weekend. Join in or watch gun fighters; a high noon shoot-out skit; Civil War reenactment encampment (with battles twice daily); stagecoach rides; historians and reenactors to talk with; a petting zoo; pony rides; vendor and craftsmen booths; street entertainment; contests; Old Town tours; and more. Come dressed in your best western duds. Open Sat. - Sun., 11am - 5pm. Admission is free.

OPEN HOUSE AT JET PROPULSION LABORATORY, Pasadena. (818) 354-0112 or (818) 354-4321 / www.jpl.nasa.gov, 4800 Oak Grove Dr. This annual open house is out of this world! The space research center offers a glimpse into outer space with over 30 exhibits including planetary imaging, spacecraft tracking, presentations, commercial technology booths that display state-of-the-art instruments and products, robotic demonstrations, thinking games for kids, and spacecraft models to build. Meet with scientists and engineers. This is a "don't miss" event. Note: The Open House is sometimes held in June. Open Sat. - Sun., 9am - 5pm. Admission is free.

POW WOW, Thousand Oaks. (805) 492-8076 / www.designplace.com/chumash, 3290 Lang Ranch Pkwy. at the Chumash Interpretive Center. On Memorial Day weekend this intertribal pow wow showcases fine Native American dancing, drumming, crafts, and face painting, as well as good food such as fry bread and Indian tacos. The Grand Entrance is at noon. Open Sat., 10am - 10pm; Sun., 10am - 6pm. Admission is $5 for adults; $3 for srs. and ages 6 - 16 years; children 5 and under are free.

RAMONA AIR FAIR, Ramona. (760) 788-6174 / www.ramonaairfair.org, Montecito Road at Ramona Airport. High-flying stunts by aerobatic planes; aerial fire fighting demonstrations; military flight demonstrations; a hot air balloon glow; antique and experimental planes in the air and on the ground; live family entertainment; fireworks; vendors; a pancake breakfast; skydivers; nighttime dancing; and more are yours at this three-day air fair located at a mountainous airport. Open Fri., 5pm - 10pm; Sat., 7am - 5pm; Sun., 7am - 4pm. Admission is $3 for adults; $1 for ages 6 - 12; children 5 years and under are free.

RAMONA OUTDOOR PLAY, Hemet. See April entry (pg. 574) for details.

RAMONA RODEO, Ramona. (760) 789-1311 or (760) 789-1484 / www.ramonarodeo.org; www.ramonachamber.com, 5th St. and Aqua Ln. Kick up your heels 'cause the rodeo's in town the second weekend in May! Rodeo shows include all the favorite featured events, plus a rodeo parade (Sat. at 10am), and numerous vendors. Sunday is kids' day with special activities such as "dummy" steer roping, rope tricks, and cowboy/cowgirl contests. Rodeo show hours are Fri., 7:30pm; Sat., at 2:30pm and 7:30pm; Sun., 2:30pm.

Arrive early. Admission is $10 on Fri., $12 - $15 on Sat.; $10 on Sun.; children 5 and under are free. Reserved seating is more, but worth it since shows can sell out. Parking is $2.

RENAISSANCE PLEASURE FAIRE, San Bernardino. See April entry (pg. 575) for details.

REPTILE SHOW, Long Beach. (562) 570-1745 / www.lbparks.org, 7550 E. Spring St. at El Dorado Nature Center. Members of the Herpetology (new word for the day) Society exhibit hundreds of snakes, lizards, and amphibians to look at and touch. Open Sat., 10am - 3pm. Admission is free. Parking is $5.

SAN BERNARDINO COUNTY FAIR, Victorville. (760) 951-2200 / www.sbcfair.com, 14800 7th St. For nine days, the desert really heats up with excitement when the county fair comes to town. 86 acres of carnival rides, attractions, farm animals, clowns, Destruction Derby, a rodeo, entertainment, and lots more fun. Open Mon. - Fri., 4pm - 11pm; Sat. - Sun., noon - 11pm. Admission is $6 for adults; $4 for srs.; $3 for ages 6 - 12; children 5 and under are free. Activities cost extra. Parking is $3.

SAN DIEGO WILD ANIMAL PARK, Escondido. (619) 234-6541 or (619) 231-1515 / www.sandiegozoo.org, 15500 San Pasqual Valley Rd. Get a little wild in the beginning of May as the Wild Animal Park celebrates founder's day and admission is free! Call for the exact date.

SCOTTISH FESTIVAL AND HIGHLAND GATHERING, Costa Mesa. (714) 708-3247 or (310) 370-9887 / www.ocfair.com, 88 Fair Dr. at the Orange County Fairgrounds. This Memorial weekend festival features everything Scottish - caber tossing, hammer throws, shot put, sheepdog herding, good food, opening and closing ceremonies, parades, and a lot of tartan. Bagpipes and Highland Fling dancers and country dancing also entertain you and the kids throughout the day. Open Sat. - Sun., 9am - 5pm. One-day admission is $14 for adults; $12 for srs. and students; $2 for ages 4 - 12; children 3 and under are free.

SPRING VILLAGE FAIRE, Carlsbad. (760) 931-8400 / www.carlsbad.org, at Carlsbad Village Dr. Held on the first Sunday in May, this is the one of the largest one-day fairs held in California. It has over 900 exhibitors, international food, and a variety of live entertainment. This type of fair is especially fun for shoppers of all ages as you never know what kind of unique items you might find (and *have* to purchase). It runs from 8am - 5pm. Admission is free, but bring spending money!

STORYTELLING FESTIVAL, Ojai. (805) 646-8907 / www.ptgo.org, at various locations, but mainly W. Ojai Ave. and Signal St. at Libbey Bowl. Once upon a time. . . . Enjoy stories from many lands including traditional folk tales, stories of suspense, adventure, and humor from re-known tellers of tales. Workshops are offered for those who want to hone their craft, as well as musical performances and children's activities. This four-day festival commences on Thurs. at 10am - 7:30pm; Fri., 10am - 10pm; Sat., 9am - 10pm; Sun., 9am - 3pm. Most events or sessions are $10 for adults; $8 for ages 3 - 12. Ask about passes.

STRAWBERRY FESTIVAL, Garden Grove. (714) 638-0981 or (714) 638-7950 / www.strawberryfestival.org; www.gardengrovechamber.org, 12862 Euclid Ave. and Stanford. This four-day event, usually held over Memorial Day weekend, features carnival rides, games, a parade (Saturday at 10am), arts and crafts booths, continuous entertainment at the amphitheater, dance recitals, a Berry Beautiful Baby Pageant, the annual redhead round-up, and lots and lots of strawberries! Open Fri., 1pm - 10pm ($15 for an all rides pass); Sat. - Sun., 10am - 10pm; Mon., 10am - 8:30pm. Admission is free, but certain activities cost.

STRAWBERRY PICKING, Carlsbad. Exit the 5 Fwy. E. on Cannon Rd. Pick your own sweet fruit from these strawberry fields mid-May through mid-August. The best bet is purchasing a $8 bucket, which holds about 5 ½ of the usual plastic green containers. Pre-picked strawberries are also available to purchase.

TANAKA FARMS, Irvine. See April entry (pg. 575) for details.

TURTLE AND TORTOISE SHOW, Long Beach. (562) 570-1745 / www.lbparks.org, 7550 E. Spring St. at the El Dorado Nature Center. Do you know the difference between a turtle or a tortoise? Find out here as members of the California Turtle and Tortoise Society bring their favorites, from the smallest turtle to the large Galapagos Island tortoise. All questions are welcome! This Sat. event is open 10am - 3pm. Admission is free. Parking is $5.

VISIT WITH MONTEZUMA, Los Angeles. (800) 204-3131 / www.forestlawn.com, 6300 Forest Lawn Dr. at Forest Lawn Memorial Park. A costumed Montezuma talks at the Plaza of Mexican Heritage to an audience of up to 350 people for about thirty minutes about "his" life and achievements - history comes alive! Mariachi music and a short, guided explanation of some of the artifacts from the Mexican museum follows the talk. This event repeats in October. This program takes place on select weekdays at 9:30am and 11am. Reservations are necessary. Admission is free.

WINGS OVER GILLESPIE, El Cajon. (888) 215-7000 or (619) 448-4505 / www.cafairgroup1.org, 1860 Joe Crosson Dr. at the Gillespie Field Airport. Several fly bys and aerial demonstrations, plus displays of more than seventy airplanes, including warbirds and vintage aircraft, decorate the air and airfield the first Friday through Sunday in May. Visitors may also tour through a grounded B-17, view antique cars and motorcycles, purchase memorabilia, and talk with aviation celebrities such as WWII Aces, original Flying Tigers, and Tuskegee Airmen. Students are particularly welcome on Friday when kids are given educational tours regarding the aircraft. The air show is open 8am - 5pm. Admission is $10 for adults; ages 12 and under are free.

JUNE:

ABSOLUT CHALK STREET PAINTING FESTIVAL, Pasadena. (626) 440-7379 or (626) 449-3689 / www.absolutchalk.com, 100 N. Garfield Ave., Pasadena City Hall at Centennial Square. Chalk it all up to having a good time! Over 600 artists draw marvelous, if temporary, masterpieces out of chalk on the sidewalks of Pasadena at this two-day festival in June or July. A children's chalk area is also set up. Live music and food complete the ambiance. Pull up a piece of sidewalk, Sat. - Sun., 10m - 6pm. Admission is free.

ADVENTURE PLAYGROUND, Huntington Beach. (714) 842-7442 - playground; (714) 374-1626 - recorded info; (714) 536-5486 / www.surfcity-hb.org, 7111 Talbot at Huntington Beach Central Park. Open mid-June through mid-August, young Huck Finns can use a raft (push poles are provided) in the shallow waters of a man-made lake. Kids will also love the slide (i.e. tarp-covered hill) which ends in a little mud pool; a rope bridge leading to a tire swing and mini zip line; sand box; and a work-in-progress kid-built "city" of shacks and clubhouses (only for ages 7 years and up). Lumber, hammers, and nails are provided. All guest must wear tennis shoes; no sandals or water shoes allowed. Note: Day campers usually invade during the morning hours. Open Mon. - Sat., 10am - 5pm. Admission is $1 for kids who are Huntington Beach residents; $2 for non-residents; free for adults.

CHERRY FESTIVAL and CHERRY PICKING, Beaumont and Cherry Valley. / www.beaumontcachamber.com, (909) 845-9541 - Beaumont Chamber of Commerce; (909) 845-3628 - Cherry Growers Association. I tell you no lie - June is a month ripe for cherry picking, but the season could start in mid-May and go as long as July, depending on the weather. Call first. The three-week, or so, season starts with a four-day festival ($1 admission) that includes a parade, carnival-type rides, game booths, amateur and professional live musical entertainment, and lots of family fun. One of our favorite places to pick cherries, and the place with the most acreage, is Wohlgemuth's Orchard, (909) 845-1548 / www.pickcherry.com, 1106 E. 11th St. in Beaumont. Admission to the orchards at Wohlgemuth's is $2 for adults; children 11 and under are free. Use the provided cans with ropes and hang them around your neck so cherries can be picked (and sampled) with both hands, working from the ground. Ladders aren't allowed or necessary. The per pound cost of cherries varies according to market value. There are also picnic tables under shade trees here, too. You may also purchase pre-picked cherries. Another place and number to try is Mile High Ranch, (909) 845-7344, at 13000 Mile High Road. Look for roadside signs along Live Oak Avenida, Brookside, and Cherry Ave., announcing other U-Pics. Note: Dowling Orchard, (909) 845-1217, is not a U-Pic, but it does offer just-picked cherries and a year-round produce market.

CHERRY PICKING, Leona Valley. (661) 266-7116 - Leona Valley Cherry Growers hotline; (661) 270-0615 / www.cherriesupic.com, Rancher's Market at 9001 Elizabeth Lake Rd. for a free map of the two dozen U-Pic orchards. The orchards here don't produce enough of the delicious crop for commercial sale, so the public wins by getting to harvest the cherries themselves! Put a bucket around your neck and start picking, although many orchards also sell pre-picked cherries. The weather-dependent, short season can start as early as May and can last through July. Different types of cherries, such as Bing, Rainier, Cashmere, Montmorency, Tartarians, etc., ripen at various times throughout the season. Call first! We especially enjoy Rhodes Orchard, (661) 270-1569, at 10600 Leona Ave. This large orchard of over 2,000 trees also has picnic tables on site and refreshments for sale (weekends only), a small farmer's market, and some of the best cherry prices around. Tip: If you pick a lot of cherries, purchase a cherry pitter!

CIVIL WAR REENACTMENT, Oak Glen. (909) 790-2364 - Riley's Farm and Orchard; (909) 797-4061 - at Riley's Log Cabin, S. Oak Glen Blvd. These adjacent peaceful farms erupt with a deluge of artillery during this weekend reenactment. Authentic encampments from the Civil War era feature men and women in period dress, pioneer cooking, bullet-making, blacksmithing demonstrations, and more. Along with battles, represented by "soldiers" with various units - the cavalry, dragoons, infantry, and more - are politicians, laundresses, nurses, and temperance workers. What a great way to combine education and fun! Call for dates and hours. Call for admission prices.

CIVIL WAR REENACTMENT AND ENCAMPMENT, Oak Glen. (909) 797-7534 or (909) 797-5145 / www.rileysfarm.com, 12261 S. Oak Glen Blvd. at Riley's Farm. (This is an adjacent farm to the ones mentioned above.) It's a warm weekend in 1864, give or take 137 + years and the army is on the move. 250 reenactors converge on Riley's Farm to show what life was like during the Civil War time period. Visit soldiers at their encampment; see battle skirmishes with infantry, calvary and artillery units; attend a Ladies Tea and period fashion show; and be immersed in this pivotal time, if only for a day or two. Farm Stays are offered for people who *really* want to live history - they may stay on the farm in rustic cabins for two nights, share in five meals, and be a participant (as part of the civilian attachment) in the reenactments, and maybe churn butter, knead bread, and help plow a field. Encampment hours are Sat. - Sun., 10am - 4:30pm. Admission is $5 for adults; $3 for ages 3 - 12. Overnight farm stays are $250 for adults; $185 for children 3 - 12 years.

COIN & COLLECTIBLES EXPO, Long Beach. See February entry (pg. 565) for details.

COLORADO LAGOON MODEL BOAT SHOP, Long Beach. (562) 570-1719 or (562) 570-1720 / www.lbparks.org, 5119 E. Colorado Ave. and Appian Way at Colorado Lagoon. Pre-packaged craft kits have their place in our instant-gratification society, but they have nothing on actually hand crafting a one-of-a-kind, wooden, 12" to 40"-long sailboat, which is balanced by a lead keel. Participants, who must be at least 7 years old, glue, sand, file, lacquer, and paint before the final rigging is done and they learn sailing lingo along the way. All materials, including hand tools, are provided. Boats take between five to seven days to complete, consecutively or in whatever increments you choose. Parents can drop kids off (or stay) anytime Mon. - Thurs., 10am - 4pm; Fri. 10am - 1:30pm. The small building "shop", staffed mostly by older kids, is a fenced in area just off the beach by the COLORADO LAGOON (see pg. 8). Bring a picnic lunch and suntan lotion. All participants can sail their finished products in the weekly regattas held on Fri. at 2pm. Help your kids chart their course to a great summer! Boats range from $15 for a 12", up to $40 for a 40".

DAIRY FESTIVAL AND TOUR, Chino. (909) 627-6177 / www.chinovalleychamber.com, at the corner of Central and Edison at the Chino Fairgrounds. Milk this festival for all it's worth! Contests here include cheese carving and milk drinking. Entertainment includes a petting zoo, kiddie rides, on-going entertainment, pony rides, hayrides, and best of all, a tour of Van Vliet Dairy. Hop on the provided bus to head over to the dairy for a one-hour tour. Watch cows being milked, learn how a dairy farm operates on a daily basis, and taste fresh cheese, yogurt, and ice cream. The festival usually runs the first Sat. in June, 9am - 4pm. Admission is free. Parking is $5 a car. A $5 wristband includes all the festival rides.

ELKS RODEO AND PARADE, Santa Maria. (805) 922-6006 or (805) 925-4125 / www.elks1538.com/rodeo.htm, Frontage Rd. at Elks Rodeo grounds. For four days experience the Old West with a roundup and professional cowboys who compete in calf roping, bull riding, saddle bronc riding, steer wrestling, barrel racing events. Don't forget to try some of Santa Maria's famous BBQ tri tips. The rodeo parade is held on Sat. at 9am. The rodeos are held on Thurs., 7pm - tickets are $6 for adults, children 11 and under are free; Fri., 7pm - tickets are $4 per person; Sat. and Sun. at 2pm - tickets are $10 for adults, $6 for ages 11 and under.

FAMILY ARTS FESTIVAL, Cerritos. (562) 916-8510 or (562) 916-1296 / www.cerritoscenter.com/friends.cfm, 12700 Center Court Dr. at the Cerritos Center for the Performing Arts. This one-day, free festival offers four stages of continuous entertainment which can include Taiko Drummers, country/western, salsa, ballet, jazz, storytelling, and lots more. The children's activities area includes face-painting, mask-making, and mural-making. Bring your own picnic food or purchase food from on-site vendors. The festival runs Sun., 11am - 4pm.

FIRE FIGHTER'S DESTRUCTION DERBY, El Cajon. (619) 541-2277 or (619) 448-8900 / www.burninstitute.org, Cajon Speedway near Gillespie Field. Starting out with a parade of Destruction Derby cars and fire apparatus at 6pm, the night progresses through several track races and then to the main event (around 10pm) - the Destruction Derby. Put your own pedal to the medal to come cheer your favorite car to the finish. The derby gets fired up at 6pm. on Sat. Tickets are about $10 for adults; $3 for ages 6 - 12; children 5 and under are free.

FLOWER FIELDS / FLOWER FESTIVAL, Lompoc. (800) 240-0999 or (805) 736-4567 / www.flowerfestival.org, The flower fields are usually in peak bloom June through August, so drive your car up and down the numerous roads, especially between Central and Ocean avenues traveling west, to get an eye full of color and nose full of fragrance. (The sweet peas are really aromatic.) Pick up a route map from the chamber of commerce at 111 South I St. Cut flowers and flowers grown for seed include larkspur, stock, marigolds, and many more. You'll also see vegetables and other produce. Stop and smell the flowers, but don't pick them. Make the most of your flower experience by also attending the five-day Flower Festival at Ryon Park in June. The parade, starting Saturday at 10am, goes along H and Ocean avenues. The creative floats must be constructed of flowers or natural materials. The parade also features equestrians, bands, drill teams, and clowns. The festival consists of carnival rides, food booths, an arts and crafts show, and a huge flower show as well as flower displays and demonstrations. One more thing - look up the entry on Lompoc murals (pg. 508). The flower fields are open daily. The Festival is open daily, but check for hours and specific exhibit times. Admission to the fields and the festival is free.

GREEK FEST, San Diego. (619) 297-4165 / www.goarch.org/en/parishes, 3655 Park Blvd. at St. Spyridon Church. Live (and lively) Greek music and dancing, home-made pastries and other Greek food, a tour of this Greek Orthodox church, booths, kids' carnival games, and more are offered at this two-day festival. Open Sat., 11am - 10pm; Sun., 11am - 9pm. Admission is $2 for adults; ages 11 and under are free.

GREEN MEADOWS, Los Angeles. See May entry (pg. 578) for details.

HO'OLAULE'A HAWAIIAN FESTIVAL OF THE VALLEY, Northridge. (818) 756-8616 / www.lacity.org/RAP, 10058 Reseda Blvd. at Northridge Park. Aloha! Concurrent festivals run the first weekend in June. The Hawaiian Festival features Pacific Island music, dance, and entertainment from Samoa, Mori, and Tahiti, plus traditional games, crafts, and Polynesian-type food. The community festival, a few booths away, features kiddie rides and games and more vendor booths. Both festivals run Sat. - Sun., 10am - 6pm. Admission is free.

HUCK FINN'S JUBILEE, Victorville. (909) 780-8810 / www.huckfinn.com, Ridgecrest Ave. in Mojave Narrows Regional Park. The huge, three-day jubilee always falls on Father's Day weekend. It kicks off with a fishing derby at 8am on Fri., followed by a weekend of river raft building contests, egg-tossing contests, a big-top circus, arm wrestling championships, a mountain man encampment, arts and crafts, a Huck Finn look-alike contest, hay rides, paddle boat rentals, rock wall climbing, horseback riding, country and blue grass music, and lots more down home fun. Put on a straw hat and join the throngs of people. Note: Camping is available here, too. Open Fri. - Sat., 7am - 11pm; Sun., 7:30am - 8pm. Admission $15 per day for adults; $5 each day for ages 6 - 11; children 5 and under are free. Parking is free.

INDIAN FAIR, San Diego. (619) 239-2001 / www.museumofman.org, 1350 El Prado at Museum of Man in Balboa Park. This weekend fair, attended by 1,000 artists and performers representing dozens of tribes, provides one of the largest forums for Native American artistry in the West Coast. It features costumed tribal dancers, traditional storytellers, and a market with arts, crafts, beadwork, pottery, and authentic cuisine. Open 10am - 4:30pm. Admission is $6 for adults; $3 for ages 6 - 17; children 5 and under are free.

INTERNATIONAL SPEEDWAY, Costa Mesa. See April entry (pg. 573) for details.

INTERTRIBAL POW WOW, Oceanside. (760) 724-8505 / www.slrmissionindians.org, 4050 Mission Ave. at Mission San Luis Rey de Franca. Join a weekend of tribal dancing, arts and crafts, and American Indian games and food. Open Sat., 10am - 11pm; Sun., 10am - 6pm. Admission is free.

IRISH FAIR AND MUSIC FESTIVAL, Encino. (310) 364-4566 / www.irishfair.org, Festival Fields at Woodley Park at Burbank and Woodley Ave. Top o' the mornin' to ye. This weekend Irish fair features top-name entertainment, such as Clancy, and Hal Roach; parades; traditional contests, such as fiddle playing and dancing; sheep-herding demonstrations; a dog show featuring Irish breeds; bagpipe music; vendors of Irish wares; and Leprechaun Kingdom for kids. The kingdom features storytelling, jugglers, pony rides, and carnival rides. Another favorite at the festival is a recreation of a medieval Irish village, Tara, where sword-yielding performers recount the village's legends and history. The festival runs Sat. - Sun., 10am - 6pm. Admission is $16 for adults; $13 for students and srs.; children 12 and under are free.

KIDS NATURE FESTIVAL, Pacific Palisades. (310) 998-1151 / www.childrensnatureinstitute.org, 15601 Sunset Blvd. in Temescal Gateway Park. Geared mostly for ages 2 to 10, this outdoor festival has a wonderful variety of things to do and see. Well-known children's bands perform periodically; craft booths are available; and live animals such as snakes, iguanas, millipedes, and tidepool creatures can be touched while some exotic animals such as a lynx, armadillo, and raccoon are shown and spoken of during wildlife presentations. Favorite activities include crawling through hoop tunnels, creating spider webs out of yarn, exploring a cave (made of disguised tents), getting faces painted, and making giant bubbles. On-site nature-themed booths and food vendors complete the festivities. Note: You are welcome to bring a picnic lunch. Open Sat., 10am - 4pm. Admission is $8 for adults; $7 for srs. and children 12 months - 12 years.

KINGSMEN SHAKESPEARE FESTIVAL, Thousand Oaks. (805) 493-3455 / www.kingsmenshakespeare.org, 60 Olsen Rd., California Lutheran University, Kingsmen Park. Two of Shakespeare's plays are featured, such as *Henry V* or *Twelfth Night,* during the six-weekend festival, as well as Elizabethan vendors, crafts, foods, and more. The festival usually runs Fri. - Sun., with performances starting at 8pm. Call for a schedule of pre and post-performance activities. Admission is $8 for adults; ages 17 and under are free. Lawn areas are available for rent for $35 and up.

MARIACHI USA FESTIVAL, Hollywood. (800) MARIACHI (627-4224) or (323) 848-7717 or (323) 850-2000 / www.mariachiusa.com; www.hollywoodbowl.org, 2301 N. Highland Ave. at the Hollywood Bowl. This event celebrates family, culture, and tradition. Bring a picnic dinner and enjoy Mariachi music, Ballet Folkloric, and a fireworks finale. The 4 ½ hour performances are given Sat. at 6pm. . Tip: Purchase tickets early as the concert is usually sold out. Admission is $10 - $127, depending on seating. Parking is $5 - $6.

MORRELL NUT & BERRY FARM, Solvang. (805) 688-8969, 1980 Alamo Pintado Road. Fresh off-the-vine raspberries and blackberries are yours for the picking at this U-Pic farm. (Dried walnuts are available in October.) Berry season runs June through September; call first. Come pick Thurs. - Tues. (closed Wed.), 10am - 6pm.

MUSICALS UNDER THE STARS, Vista. (760) 726-1340 / www.moonlightstage.com, 1200 Vale Terrace at Brengle Terrace Park at the Moonlight Amphitheater. Five Broadway musicals are performed at this outside amphitheater each summer, including one youth theater production. Past performances include *Annie*, *Singin in the Rain*, and *Children of Eden.* Come see a show under the stars (and moon). Productions run mid-June through mid-September. Call for specific dates and times. Tickets cost between $12 - $31 depending on age and seating.

OLD SANTA YNEZ DAYS, Santa Ynez. (805) 688-4878 or (805) 688-3448, Sagunto Street and the rest of the main part of town - you can't miss the happenings. The "Old West" comes to life as the small frontier town of Santa Ynez celebrates its birthday. Enjoy a parade with horses and Western carriages, plus cowboy shoot outs in the streets, kid's games, magic shows, food, arts and crafts, and entertainment.

OUTDOOR FAMILY FILM FESTIVALS, all over. Many parks offer free, nighttime, out-door family entertainment such as concerts or G or PG, movies. Bring a blanket, picnic dinner, and enjoy a show together! Call your local park for information.

PCPA THEATERFEST, Solvang. (800) 549-7272 or (805) 922-8313 / www.pcpa.org, 420 2nd Street at the outdoor Festival Theater. In the middle of the quaint town of Solvang, this 750-seat outdoor theater shows plays from mid-June through October. Come watch a musical under the canopy of trees and starlight and make sure you bring a jacket as summer night air can be chilly. The Theaterfest was a favorite activity for our family for the show and ambiance. See main entry (pg. 513) for more details. Call for a performance schedule. Tickets are $16 - $22 for adults; $12.50 - $17.50 for srs. and ages 5 - 18; children 4 and under are not permitted.

PEARSON PARK AMPHITHEATER, Anaheim. (714) 765-4422 or (714) 765-5274 / www.anaheim.net, Lemon and Sycamore sts. The terrific programs put on through the "Just For Kids" series throughout the summer are geared for kids 4 years old through 6th graders. The shows run approximately two hours. Past programs have included Make-a-Circus, magic shows, puppet shows, a wild west show, the mad scientist, and audience participation shows with songs or storytellers. Call for specific show information. Fri. shows start at 7pm; call for hours for Sat. shows. Tickets usually cost $2 for adults; $1 for srs. and ages 3 - 12; children 2 and under are free.

RAMONA AIR FAIR, Ramona. See May entry (pg. 580) for details.

REDLANDS BOWL SUMMER MUSIC FESTIVAL, Redlands. (909) 793-7316 / www.redlandsbowl.org; www.redlandsweb.com, Brookside Ave. between Eureka and Grant sts. Two nights a week, from late June through August, the bowl offers symphony music, jazz, and opera as well as musicals, ballet, and dance ensembles. These are great programs for the family! Programs are offered Tues. and Fri. evening at 8:15pm and are free - donations are appreciated. Free, forty-five minute music appreciation workshops are given for elementary-aged kids on Tues. at 3pm and Sat. at 10am.

RENAISSANCE PLEASURE FAIRE, San Bernardino. See April entry (pg. 575) for details.

SAN DIEGO COUNTY FAIR, Del Mar. (858) 793-5555 - recording; (858) 755-1161 - fairgrounds / www.sdfair.com, 2260 Jimmy Durante Blvd. at the Del Mar Fairgrounds. This major, three-week event features everything wonderful in a county fair - carnival rides, flower and garden shows, gem and minerals exhibits, farm animals, livestock judging, food, craft booths, and a festive atmosphere. Call for a schedule of events. Gates open daily at 10am. Admission is $10.50 for adults; $6 for srs.; $4.50 for ages 6 - 12 years; children 5 and under are free. Parking is $7. Certain activities cost extra.

SAN DIEGO SCOTTISH HIGHLAND GAMES AND GATHERING OF CLANS, Vista. (619) 645-8080 / www.sdhighlandgames.org, 1200 Vale Terrace at Brengle Terrace Park. For almost thirty years, fifty or so clans have come to participate and enjoy first class entertainment at this gathering. The last weekend in June is the one for Scottish merrymaking, which includes highland dancing, Celtic harping, bagpipe competitions, sheep dog herding trials, athletic competitions (such as caber tossing), and lots of good food. Open Sat. - Sun., 9am - 5pm. Admission is $10 for adults (per day); $8 for srs.; $5 for ages 6 - 16; children 5 and under are free. Ask about two-day passes. Parking is $3.

SAWDUST FESTIVAL, Laguna Beach. (949) 494-3030 / www.sawdustartfestival.org, 935 Laguna Canyon Rd. This three-acre, outdoor arts and crafts festival, with over 180 artisans, goes from the end of June through August (almost simultaneous with the Festival of Arts - see page 589). On-going demonstrations include ceramics such as throwing pots (so to speak), etching, glass blowing, and more. The Children's Art booth allows kids to create art projects - for free! Family-oriented daytime entertainment includes storytelling and juggling. Nighttime entertainment includes listening and dancing to bands. Restaurants and other food services are on-site. Tram service is free. The festival is open daily, 10am - 10pm. Admission is $6.50 for adults; $5.50 for srs.; $2 for ages 6 - 12; children 5 and under are free. A season pass is $10 per person.

SPECIAL OLYMPICS SOUTHERN CALIFORNIA GAMES, Long Beach. (310) 215-8380 / www.sosco.org, 1250 Bellflower Blvd. at California State Long Beach. "Let me win, but if I cannot win, let me be brave in the attempt." That is the Special Olympics motto. Come to cheer on hundreds of mentally retarded children and adults as they compete in Olympic-type sports of aquatics, basketball, golf, gymnastics, and more. These are gratifying events to witness. Take part in them if you can volunteer some time, too. The public will also enjoy live entertainment, community exhibits, games, and sports clinics at the Sports Expo Park. Fri. night Opening Ceremonies begin at 7pm; games run Sat. 8am - 4pm; Sun., 8am - 1:30pm, followed by the closing ceremony. Free admission.

STRAWBERRY PICKING, Carlsbad. See May entry (pg. 581) for details.

STREET PAINTING FESTIVAL, Temecula. (909) 694-6412 / www.temeculacalifornia.com, Old Town. Painting the streets is different than painting the town, especially when it's done with chalk. Come see great works of art on the asphalt, and come to see work that simply appeals to proud parents as the festival is open to all participants. Reserve a space or come to look. Entertainment is on-going. Open Sat. - Sun. - call for times. Free for artists and the public.

SUMMER AT THE FORD, Hollywood. (323) 461-3673 / www.fordamphitheatre.org, 2580 Cahuenga Blvd. E. at the John Anson Ford Amphitheater. This outdoor amphitheater presents wonderful, one-hour family performances on most Saturdays, June through September. Check the schedule for a complete listing, as family-friendly shows are also given sometimes during the week. Enjoy an intimate setting with shows that feature top-name entertainment in magic, puppetry, storytelling, music, dance, or plays designed with the whole family in mind. Stay after the show to have a picnic lunch that you may either bring or purchase on site. The cafe offers pizza, sandwiches, Cobb salad, nachos, and more. Shows on Sat. start at 10am. Call for a schedule of other show times and dates. Seats cost $5 for adults; children 12 and under are free. Ask about Family Day admission. Parking on site costs $5 - $8. Shuttle services from 1718 Cherokee in Hollywood are available.

SUMMER ORGAN FESTIVAL, San Diego. (619) 702-8138 / www.balboapark.org, Balboa Park at the Spreckels Organ Pavilion. Every Monday evening from mid-June through August enjoy the sounds of Scott Joplin, Charles Tournemire, Maurice Durufle, and others at the Organ Pavilion. Bring a picnic dinner (or at least dessert) to eat on the lawn and listen to the sounds of summer. Note that there are free outdoor concerts often given during the week, too. Concerts start at 7:30pm. Admission is free.

SUMMER SOLSTICE PARADE AND FESTIVAL, Santa Barbara. (8050 965-3396 / www.solsticeparade.com, State St. from Cota to Micheltorenia sts. For a really hot time, celebrate the summer solstice with a wacky, goofy, creative, colorful parade. Over 1,000 participants dress up in elaborate costumes, incorporating choreographed dancing, giant puppets, people-powered floats, and general silliness. Parade participants can attend workshops beforehand to create their ensembles and get help from artists in residence. Parade watchers grab curb space or set up lawn chairs along the street early. After the parade, people pour into Alameda Park for the festival which has musical entertainment, drummers, food and refreshment, arts and crafts, storytellers, short theater productions, air bounces, face painting, vendors, and an up-close view of the floats. The festitval is on the Sat. closest to summer solstic. The parade starts at noon; the festival goes from 1pm - 8pm. Only participants pay an entry fee; other admission is free.

SUMMER SOUNDS, Hollywood. (323) 850-2000 / www.hollywoodbowl.com, 2301 N. Highland, at the Hollywood Bowl. For six musically hot weeks, forty-five-minute, somewhat interactive, multi-cultural performances are given at the Bowl on the outside stage in the front Plaza entrance. Bring sunscreen. The performances, which are geared for young children, could incorporate dance, music, storytelling, etc. Past shows include Salsa, Call of Africa, Fiery Flamenco, and A Touch of Brass. An arts and craft project for ages 3 to 10 that pertains to the theme is offered with each performance under a shade awning in the parking lot. Each week brings a different show that is performed twice daily. Shows are Mon. - Fri. at 10am for children 4 and under; 11:15am for ages 5 - 10. Art projects are at 10am for older kids; 11am for younger kids. When the orchestra is rehearsing inside the Bowl for a later performance, Summer Sounds visitors are invited to watch the rehearsals at no additional cost. Call for a schedule if you're interested in incorporating the Bowl rehearsal with your experience here. Tickets for Summer Sounds are $5 per person for the seating area. There is a $2 materials fee for the art project. Parking is free.

SUNSET LUAU ON MISSION BAY, Pacific Beach. (858) 273-3303 / www.pacificbeach.org, between Garnet and Thomas Aves. on and near the boardwalk. You can easily be persuaded that Mission Bay is just like the islands as you enjoy a traditional Hawaiian buffet dinner at sunset. Eat roast Kalua pig, grilled mahi mahi, salads, desserts, and more on the beach. The Pride of Polynesia dancers perform a terrific Luau show. Aloha! Enjoy dinner and show Fri., 6pm - 9pm Admission is $35 for adults; $18 for ages 5 - 11; children 4 and under are free.

TANAKA FARMS, Irvine. See April entry (pg. 575) for details.

TEMECULA VALLEY BALLOON AND WINE FESTIVAL, Temecula. (909) 676-4713 / www.tvbwf.com, Warren Rd. at Lake Skinner Recreation Area. Rise and shine for this colorful three-day festival. On the weekends the balloons are filled with hot air starting at 6:30am, an event fascinating to watch. Lift-off is around 6:30am, with numerous balloons filling the sky in a kaleidoscope of color. Many of the balloons come back down around 8:30am. Other, less lofty, activities include live entertainment, arts and craft, and a kid's fair with kiddie rides, pony rides, a petting zoo, free tethered balloon rides, and more. The Friday and Saturday night "glows" (i.e. inflated, lighted balloons that glow in the evening sky) occur after sunset. Open Fri., 5pm - 9pm; Sat., 6am - 10:30pm; Sun., 6apm - 6pm. Admission Fri. is $7 for adults; Sat., $17; Sun., $15. Ages 7 - 12 are $5 per day; children 6 and under are free. Parking is $3. Certain activities cost extra. One hour balloon rides are also available for $145 per person. Advanced reservations are necessary - (800) 965-2122 / www.agrapeescape.com.

THRESHING BEE AND ANTIQUE ENGINE SHOW, Vista. (800) 587-2286 or (760) 941-1791 / www.agsem.com, 2040 N. Santa Fe Ave. at the Antique Gas & Steam Engine Museum. This show is held on two consecutive weekends in June, and again in October. Watch demonstrations of American crafts, farming, log sawing, and blacksmithing, plus see many of the restored tractors in a parade each day at 1pm; a very unusual-looking parade! Join in some of the activities such as hayrides and square dancing and taste the good, home-cooked food available for purchase. See the main entry (pg. 407) for more information about this museum. Open Sat. - Sun., 9am - 4:30pm. Admission is $7 for adults; $4 for ages 7 - 12; children 6 and under are free. Camping, with reservations, is $40 for the weekend and includes admission to the show.

VALLEY FAIR, Castaic. (818) 557-1600 / www.sfvalleyfair.org, 32132 Castaic Lake Dr. Highlights from the fair include carnival rides, a livestock auction (on Sun.), a petting zoo, exhibits of agricultural projects, entertainment, commercial vendors, and more. Students K - 5th grade, are especially invited to come for a "tour" on Fri. Call for details. Fair hours are Thurs. - Fri., 4pm - 11; Sat. - Sun., noon - 11pm. Admission is $6 for adults; $4 for srs. and ages 6 - 11; children 5 and under are free. Certain attractions and activities cost extra.

VAN NUYS AIRPORT AVIATION EXPO, Van Nuys. (818) 909-3529 / www.lawa.org, 8030 Balboa Blvd. Look - it's a bird, it's Superman, no - it's a plane! Actually this tremendous weekend expo features over sixty vintage and current military planes. Stunt pilots perform aerobatics and military jets fly overhead making a grand entrance. Besides the exciting air show, tour through several grounded planes (that could include a C-141, B-52, and others), and ride a simulator plane. Wear sun block! Open Sat. - Sun., 9am - 5pm. Admission is free.

WELBURN GOURD ART FESTIVAL, Fallbrook. (760) 728-4271 / www.welburngourdfarm.com, 40635-D De Luz Murrieta Rd. The largest supplier of hard-shelled gourds in the U.S. puts on a weekend festival that displays *gourd*eous works of art. The sheer number and variety of gourds, and the over fifty exhibitors who show their detailed and creative artistry, are fantastic. A Kid's Zone features some carnival rides, games, face painting, and a place to create their own gourd art. And don't squash your kid's hope - purchase a complete starter kit to take home. Polynesian-Hawaiian, African, and Native American music and dance add to the festivities. Note that full-day classes are available before the festival. The hours are Sat., 9am - 5pm; Sun., 9am - 4pm. Admission is $6 for adults; ages 12 and under are free.

WILL GEER THEATRICUM BOTANICUM, Topanga. (310) 455-3723 / www.theatricum.com, 1419 N. Topanga Blvd. This outdoor theater (dress warmly) produces summertime "edutainment." Family Fun Days run June through September. These are programs for young kids featuring name brand entertainment, such as the Parachute Express. Older audiences enjoy plays such as *The Merry Wives of Windsor* and *St. Joan*. See main entry on page 157. Show times vary. Ticket prices also vary depending on the show, although Kid's Koncerts are usually $7 per person. More mature productions are $13 - $20 for adults; $11 - $!4 for srs.; $7 for ages 6 - 12.

JULY:

ADVENTURE PLAYGROUND, Huntington Beach. See June entry (pg. 582) for details.

ALL NATIONS POW WOW, Big Bear City. (909) 584-7115 or (909) 790-1390; (909) 866-4607 - chamber of commerce, at the Los Vaqueros Rodeo arena, off Hwy. 38. This wonderful three-day gathering of the nations involves traditional tribal dances (the hoop dance is our favorite) in full regalia, usually accompanied by drums. Other music, plus arts and crafts and food booths are also on the grounds. Bring your own tribe! (i.e. family) Open Fri., 6pm - 10pm; Sat., 10am - 11pm, Sun., 10am - 6pm. Admission is $4 for adults; $3 for srs.; children 9 and under are free.

COLORADO LAGOON MODEL BOAT SHOP, Long Beach. See June entry (pg. 8) for details.

COMIC-CON, San Diego. (619) 414-1020 / www.comic-con.org, San Diego Convention Center. Simply *Marvel*ous! In*DC*ribable! This four-day, massive comic book convention features comics, graphic novels, original art, toys, movie memorabilia, games, trading cards, clothing, comic book characters, creators (for autographs), shows, and lots more. If a sci-fi movie has made it big during the year, there is paraphernalia and models from that movie. The Masquerade, when costumed participants dress up as their favorite comic book characters and compete on Saturday night, is a big event as well. Please note that there are certain elements of adult entertainment at the convention. Open Thurs. - Sat., 10am - 7pm; Sun., 10am - 5pm. Admission on Thurs. - Sat. is $25 for adults; $12 for ages 7 - 16. Admission on Sun is $15 for adults; $7 for ages 7 - 16. Children 6 and under are free.

FESTIVAL OF ARTS AND PAGEANT OF THE MASTERS, Laguna Beach. (949) 494-1145 / www.foapom.com, 650 Laguna Canyon Rd. at Irvine Bowl Park. This event runs from July through August, drawing thousands of visitors. More than 140 artisans and craftsmen display their work here - jewelry, wood crafts, paintings, and more - and at the nearby Sawdust Festival (pg. 586). Kids are particularly drawn to the ongoing demonstrations, such as print making, water color, and Japanese pottery making. Young aspiring artists should visit the Art Workshop, which is open daily, 11am to 5pm. It supplies free materials for paintings, instruments, paper hat making, and more. The Jr. Art Gallery is juried art work of over 150 school children from Orange County. Kids love looking at other kids' work. Bands play continuously. Call for a schedule of special events. Pageant of the Masters is people in full makeup and costumes who pose and re-create live "pictures" of well-known art works, both classic and contemporary. Each ninety-second picture is accompanied by a narration and full orchestral music. Note that some of the live art works contain nudity (i.e. real, semi-naked bodies). This one-and-a-half-hour production (with over 250 participants) is staged nightly at 8:30pm. Tickets range between $15 - $80 per person. Festival admission is included in the pageant tickets. The festival is open daily, 10am - 11:30pm. Admission to the festival is $5 for adults, for an unlimited number of visits during the run of the festival; $3 for srs.; children 12 and under are free. Metered parking is available on the streets, or take a shuttle for $1 from Lot 5. Certain activities cost extra.

FESTIVAL OF THE KITE, Redondo Beach. See March entry (pg. 567) for details. (This one takes place the last Sunday in July.)

FIRE EXPO, San Diego. (858) 541-2277 / www.burninstitute.org, Qualcomm Stadium. Did the title of this event spark your interest? Join firefighters in the largest fire expo in Southern California. For one-day, see live demonstrations of auto extrications and bomb robots; a canine dog demonstration; and a Burn Run where 70+ engines (one from each of the area's stations) converge in a siren blaring, lights flashing, parade at 2pm. Rides on fire engines, a rock climbing wall, firefighting displays, a kiddie carnival, and community service group booths add to this special event. Open 1pm - 7pm. Admission is free. Certain activities cost.

FIREWORKS and 4ᵗʰ OF JULY SHOWS, All over. Call the recreation departments at your local parks, or City Hall for information. Note: The Hollywood Bowl, (323) 850-2000 / www.hollywoodbowl.org, features a fireworks spectacular, along with outstanding lively music.

FLOWER FIELDS / FLOWER FESTIVAL, Lompoc. See June entry (pg. 584) for details.

FRENCH FESTIVAL, Santa Barbara. (805) 564-PARIS (7274) - festival; (8050 564-5418 - park / www.frenchfestival.com, 300 W. Alamar at Oak Park. Ooh la la! Join French compatriots across the sea in celebrating Bastille Day (the French Revolution) - or just come for the fun of it. Enjoy crepes, decadent pastries, French bread, quiche and escargot (don't tell the kids their more common name) at sidewalk cafes with Parisian ambiance. Continuos free entertainment on three stages include the cancan, Moroccan belly dancers, grand opera, Cajun and classical groups, folk dancing, jazz, and cabaret music. Look for artists wearing berets while painting at their easels, as well as mimes, jugglers, accordion players, puppet shows, and storytellers. Kids will also enjoy the large replica of the Eiffel Tower, the classic car show, the poodle parade on Sunday evening, and wading pool at the park. C'est magnifique! Open Sat. - Sun., 11am - 7pm. Free admission and parking.

GREEK FESTIVAL, Santa Barbara. (805) 683-4492 - church; (805) 564-5418 - park / www.saintbarbara.net, 300 W. Alamar at Oak Park. Come to my big fat Greek festival - well, it's not mine, but it is one of the largest Greek festivals around. Saint Barbara Greek Orthodox Church hosts this party. Baklava, shish-kabob, stuffed grape leaves, gyros, music, authentic Grecian dances, folk dance lessons and demonstrations, and lots of entertainment await festival goers. Open Sat. - Sun., 11am - 7pm. Admission is free.

HEROES AIR SHOW, Lake View Terrace. (818) 883-9248 / www.heroes-airshow.com, 11708 Foothill Blvd. at Hansen Dam Recreation Area. This one-day show is the premier air show exclusively for helicopters and flight teams, and their role in law enforcement, fire service, and search and rescue. See aerial demonstrations of rope/rescue techniques; take a helicopter ride (for a fee); look at the vintage fire engines, police cars, and emergency service vehicles that make up the "Rolling to the Rescue" exhibit; gather information at the Code 3 Career Fair; and enjoy the vendors and entertainment. Open Sat. 9am - 4pm. Free admission.

HOLY SPIRIT FESTIVAL, Artesia. (562) 865-4693 / www.artesiades.org, 11903 Ashworth Ave. at the D.E.S. Plaza. Held the last Friday through Monday in July, this four-day event celebrates several elements of the Portuguese culture. On Sunday, a grand religious procession is followed by marching bands, food booths (including a free lunch or dinner for every visitor), crowning of the festival queen, Mass, and entertainment. Monday night is the three-hour culmination of the festival with bloodless bullfights put on by professional matadors. (Velcro patches are worn by the bull to hold the Velcro tipped spears, but the danger to the matadors still remains.) The festival hours are Fri., 6pm - midnight; Sat., 5pm - midnight; Sun., 10am - midnight; Mon., 4pm - 9pm. Admission is free.

INTERNATIONAL SPEEDWAY, Costa Mesa. See April entry (pg. 573) for details.

KIDSWORLD, Santa Monica. (310) 394-1049 or (310) 394-5451 / www.santamonicaplace.com, 3ʳᵈ St. and Broadway at Santa Monica Place mall. From July through August, the mall has teamed up with L.A. Children's Museum, the Natural History Museum, and other organizations to present musical, theatrical, or educational shows every Friday at 11am and again at 1pm, plus craft activities every Saturday, noon to 4pm. Past shows have featured puppetry, music, song, dance, and storytelling. Both days' activities are geared for ages 7 years and under. Enjoy shopping or eating at the 140 shops and restaurants in the mall. Admission to the shows and crafts is free.

KINGSMEN SHAKESPEARE FESTIVAL, Thousand Oaks. See June entry (pg. 585) for details.

LA BREA TAR PITS EXCAVATION, Los Angeles. (323) 934-PAGE (7243) / www.tarpits.org, 5801 Wilshire Blvd. at the George C. Page Museum in Hancock Park. Can you dig it? Well, actually, you can't, but paleontologists can. July through mid-September they excavate Tar Pit 91 and recover fossils of Ice Age creatures, such as saber-tooth cats, dire wolves, and more. Peek into the pit from the observation area for a look into the past. Excavations take place Wed. - Sun., 10am - 4pm. Admission is free. Admission to the adjacent

George C. Page Museum, where recovered fossils are on display along with lots of other exhibits, is $6 for adults; $3.50 for srs. and students; $2 for ages 5 - 12; children 4 and under are free.

LONG BEACH SHAKESPEARE FESTIVAL, Long Beach. (562) 597-1301 / www.bardintheyard.com, Argonne and 23rd St. at Stearns Park. Fill your July weekends with culture. This particular group performs a variety of Shakespeare's plays outdoors each year with a pre-show (musicians and dancing) Sat. - Sun. at 4pm; the play at 5pm. Admission is free.

LOTUS FESTIVAL, Los Angeles. (213) 485-8745 or (213) 485-13010 / www.lacity.org, Park Ave. and Glendale Blvd. at Echo Park. A blend of Asian and Pacific Island cultures celebrate the symbolism of the lotus flower, which represents divine creative power and purity, at this old-LA. neighborhood park that contains a lake filled with an abundance of these flowers in bloom. What a beautiful sight! The lotus stay in bloom until late summer. The two-day festival also incorporates music, traditional food, martial arts exhibitions, Polynesian dancing, origami demonstrations, fireworks, dragon-boat races, and children's arts and crafts. Paddle boat rentals are available at the boathouse for $5 for half an hour. The festival is open Sat. - Sun., noon - 8pm. Admission is free, although some activities cost.

MORRELL NUT & BERRY FARM, Solvang. See June entry (pg. 585) for details.

MUSICALS UNDER THE STARS, Vista. See June entry (pg. 585) for details.

OJAI SHAKESPEARE FESTIVAL, Ojai. (805) 646-WILL (9455) / www.ojaishakespeare.org, Ojai Ave. at Libbey Park. To see or not to see, that is the question. Shakespearean plays, running from the end of July through the middle of August, are performed in the outdoor Libbey Bowl and are worthy to be seen. (Ask about the winter performances, too.) Sr. High intern students perform on Thurs. at 7:30pm and weekends at 4pm. Tickets are $8. Professional actors and musicians perform Fri. - Sun. at 7:30pm. Admission is $18 for adults; $15 for srs. and students.

OLD FORT MACARTHUR DAYS, San Pedro. (310) 548-2631 / www.ftmac.org, 3601 S. Gaffey St. at Angels Gate Park and Fort MacArthur Museum. Military encampments, set up chronologically, and reenactments, representing time periods from ancient days to modern times, are here on the weekend following the 4th of July. Observers can mingle with the soldiers and ask questions about their lives. Reenactments of historic military skirmishes can include the Indian wars, the Calvary, both World Wars, and/or the Korean War. There are also marching drills, rifle-loading drills, and firing demonstrations. On Sunday, some cannons are shot, too. Military vehicles are also on the grounds. Bring a sack lunch or purchase food from the vendors. See the Fort MacArthur Museum entry (pg88) for more details. Open 9am - 5pm, with skirmishes throughout the day. Admission per day is $10 for adults; $5 for ages 11 and under. This includes admission to the museum, as well.

OLD MINERS DAYS, Big Bear. (909) 866-4607 / www.bigbearchamber.com, in Meadow Park on Park Ave. This three-weekend event features a logger's jubilee, complete with tree cutting and log rolling contests; arts and crafts booths; children's games; cowboy poetry and music festival; pony rides; a Doo Dah parade featuring marchers in crazy costumes; and a grand finale parade. Parade entries range from elegant equestrian units, to floats, to old wagons (old flatbed wagons and the red Radio Flyer types, too), and clowns. Admission is free.

OLD SPANISH DAYS FIESTA, Santa Barbara. (800) 927-4688 or (805) 962-8101 / www.oldspanishdays-fiesta.org, multiple locations throughout Santa Barbara. This major five-day Santa Barbara party is kicked off Wed. night with "Little Fiesta" at Mission Santa Barbara, where a program of early Californian, Spanish and Mexican song and dance features dancers, clicking castanets, and more. Bring lawn chairs. A highlight of the fiesta is the Friday parade. Participants include the queen and her court, mounted color guards, marching bands, colorfully costumed equestrian riders, numerous antique carriages and wagons, Native American groups, Spanish Colonial re-enactors, costumed dancers and historical figures on elaborate floats decorated with fresh flowers. The parade begins at the corner of Cabrillo Blvd. and Castillo St. at noon. Grab a spot or, for reserved seating at $10 per person, call (805) 963-4408. On Saturday at 10am, the Children's Parade has niñas and niños in fiesta attire parade down State Street in home-constructed wagons and carts that are pushed and pulled by dogs, parents, and siblings. Open-air market places (in De La Guerra Plaza in downtown

Santa Barbara and other locations) feature music, dancing, and authentic Mexican and Spanish food. The carnival, located at Santa Barbara's City Colleges's La Playa West parking lot, is open 3pm to 10pm daily with its rides, midway games, and attractions. Other fair features include a weekend craft fair, and a tribute to Vaqueros (i.e. California's cowboys) at the Earl Warren Showgrounds via afternoon and nighttime rodeos with bull and bronc riding, barrel racing, team penning, steer wrestling, and stock horse classes. Watch cowkids do some mutton bustin' and wild cow milking. Admission to the rodeo is $10 for adults; $6 for children. Call (805) 967-6331/ www.earlwarren.com for more information. Nightlife at the sunken gardens of the County Court House showcases a free variety shows of mariachis, flamenco dancers, Mexican folklorico dancers in colorful regional costumes, and other Latin-flavored music. Bring blankets for lawn seating. Many events are free.

ORANGE COUNTY FAIR, Costa Mesa. (714) 708-FAIR (3247) or (714) 751-3247 / www.ocfair.com, 88 Fair Dr. at the Orange County Fairgrounds. This huge, twenty-one-day event is great fun for the whole family. There are lots of carnival rides and games; rodeos (that last a few hours); acrobats; headliner concerts; speedway racing; farm animals, featured in shows and races, and to pet; craft booths; exhibits; demonstrations, such as the firefighters combat challenge; and, of course great food. Each day brings new attractions and events. There is so much to see and do that one day might just not be enough! Call for information on discount days offered during the fair and for the calendar of special events. Open Tues. - Thurs., noon - midnight; Fri. - Sun., 10am - midnight; closed on Mon. Admission is $7 for adults; $6 for srs.; $3 for ages 6 - 12; children 5 and under are free. Discount tickets are available before the fair opens. Parking is $5; a carpool of 4 or more is $3.

PCPA THEATERFEST, Solvang. See June entry (pg. 513) for details.

PEARSON PARK AMPHITHEATER, Anaheim. See June entry (pg. 586) for details.

RASPBERRY PICKING, Oak Glen and Moorpark. The tastiest fruits are ones that have just been harvested. Raspberries are usually ripe from mid-July to mid-October. Here are a few places to call in the Oak Glen area: Los Rios Rancho - (909) 797-1005; Riley's Log Cabin Farm and Orchard - (909) 797-4061; Riley's Frontier Events - (909) 790-2364; Riley's Farm - (909) 797-5145 or (909) 797-7534; and Snow Line Orchard - (909) 797-3415. In Ventura County in Moorpark, call Underwood Family Farms at (805) 523-8552. The above entries are also listed in the main section of the book.

REDLANDS BOWL, Redlands. See June entry (pg. 586) for details.

REVOLUTIONARY WAR LIVING HISTORY ENCAMPMENT, Yorba Linda. (714) 993-3393 / www.nixonfoundation.org, 18001 Yorba Linda Blvd at the Richard Nixon Presidential Library and Birthplace. The British are coming . . . on a weekend near the 4th of July. See how townspeople and soldiers lived over 200 years ago as you visit with reenactors dressed in authentic period clothing and watch them cook, barter, work with wood, and even fight in mock skirmishes. Hear a reading of the Declaration of Independence and sign a giant copy of one. Spend some time inside the museum, too. Open 10am - 4:30pm. Admission is museum admission - $5.95 for adults; $2 for ages 8 - 11; children 7 and under are free.

RINGLING BROS. & BARNUM AND BAILEY CIRCUS, Anaheim, Long Beach, Los Angeles, and San Diego. Call (703) 448-4000 / www.ringling.com, This is a traditional month for "The Greatest Show on Earth" to come to town. Catch some of the most amazing animal and acrobatic acts ever performed!! Call ahead of time to find out when the parade of circus animals comes through the town. At some locations, come an hour early to participate in free pre-circus activities in the arenas, where visitors can try out a trapeze swing, ride a unicycle (with help), and be a part of a clown act. Tickets range from $11.50 - $32.50, depending on performance date and time, and your seat location.

SANTA BARBARA COUNTY FAIR, Santa Maria. (800) 549-0036 or (805) 925-8824 / www.santamariafairpark.com, 937 S. Thornburg at the Santa Maria Fairgrounds. Have some family fun at this five-day county fair with the petting zoo, agricultural and livestock exhibits, train rides, chimpanzee show (this may not be a yearly show), top-name entertainment, carnival rides, a Fair Queen Pageant for crowning the queen, dancing, booths, and much more. The fair hours are 11am - 10pm. Admission is $6 for adults; $3 for srs.

and ages 6 - 11; children 5 and under are free. Parking is $3. Ask about discount days for the carnival rides and other special events.

SANTA BARBARA NATIONAL HORSE SHOW, Santa Barbara. (805) 687-0766 / www.earlwarren.com, Calle Real and Las Positas Rd. at the Earl Warren Showgrounds. *Neigh* doubt about it - this is one of the most highly regarded horse shows. It takes place on two consecutive, four-day weekends in July. Classes and events include champion hunters and jumper, American saddle bred, Hackney ponies harnessed to their show buggies, walking horses that strut their stuff, and a Western Horse show. A flower show is going on at the exhibit halls during this time as well. Call for a schedule of events and for prices.

SAWDUST FESTIVAL, Laguna Beach. See June entry (pg. 586) for details.

SEA FESTIVAL, Long Beach. (562) 570-1728 or (562) 570-8920 / www.lbparks.org, mostly along Ocean Blvd and Appian Way. This month-long festival takes place in several areas near the shores of Long Beach. Participant and spectators, landlubbers and seafarers are welcome. Some of the events include a free fishing day for youths 15 years and under (with prizes!); a Chinese Dragon Boat Race and oriental cultural craft exhibition; swimming competitions; beach volleyball; a sand sculpture contest (build with your family 9am - 1:30pm, or just come to see finished masterpieces, 2pm - 4pm); day camps for people with disabilities; and boat races. Call for a schedule of events. Participant fees range according to event; spectators are usually admitted for free.

SHAKESPEARE FESTIVAL/L.A., Los Angeles. (213) 481-2273 / www.shakespearefestivalla.org, in the greater Los Angeles area. The bard is back! Each year's program features one play for a month's run at various outdoor locations throughout L.A. County. The actors and actresses are often name-recognizable performers. Call for hours and locations. Admission is a canned food donation. Inquire about the "Simply Shakespeare" readings by noted actors and the one-hour adaptations of the play specifically for students.

SHAKESPEARE FESTIVAL/L.A., Los Angeles. See June entry (pg. 593) for details.

STARLIGHT BOWL SUMMER CONCERT SERIES, Burbank. (818) 525-3721 / www.starlightbowl.com, 1249 Lockheed View Dr. Warm summer nights, music wafting through the air, surrounded by family and friends - this is the scene for summer concerts at the bowl. The concerts run the range of musical interests so check the schedule to see who's playing. The season starts with a 4th of July concert (and fireworks) and continue through mid-August. Concerts are given on Sun. from 6:30pm - 8:30pm. Gates open at 5:30pm, so bring a picnic dinner. Admission is $7 for adults; $4 for srs. and ages 3 - 12. Parking is $5.

ST. KATHERINE GREEK FESTIVAL, Redondo Beach. (310) 540-2434 / www.greek-fest.com, 722 Knob Hill. Held the first weekend of the month, this thirty-five-year old annual ethnic and religious festival recreates the atmosphere of a Greek village with costumed participants, live Greek music, fresh-baked pastries, cultural arts and crafts, and food booths. A small, kiddie area is on the premises, too. Tours of the church are also offered. I don't know - it's all Greek to me! Open Fri., 6pm - 10pm; Sat., noon - 10pm; Sun., noon - 9pm. Admission is free.

STRAWBERRY PICKING, Carlsbad. See May entry (pg. 581) for details.

SUMMER AT THE FORD, Hollywood. See June entry (pg. 587) for details.

SUMMER SOUNDS, Hollywood. See June entry (pg. 587) for details.

U.S. OPEN SANDCASTLE COMPETITION, Imperial Beach. (619) 424-6663 / www.usopensandcastle.com; www.ci.imperial-beach.ca.us, Imperial Beach Pier. Sign up as a competitor in this sandcastle competition, as there are various categories - age, amateur, masters, etc. - or just to watch other creative people at work. We are amazed at the fantastic designs the sculpturers dream up! A parade is held Sat. at 10am. Other activities include browsing around a street fair, with kiddie rides and arts and crafts, plus a children's sand-creation contest held Sat. afternoon, and fireworks at night. The adult contests begins around 7:30am Sun. Monetary prizes are awarded. Free admission to watch.

VENTURA COUNTY FAIR, Ventura. (805) 648-3376 / www.seasidepark.org, 10 W. Harbor Blvd. at Seaside Park. This major event is a week and a half long. The fair offers lots of carnival rides, plus rodeos, pig races, a petting zoo, pony rides, livestock and equestrian events, on-going first-class entertainment and concerts, and several buildings that have arts and crafts for sale, flower shows, fine arts, gems and minerals, and vendor demonstrations. Whew! The fair is open daily, 11am - 11pm. A fireworks show is put on nightly at 9:30pm. Admission is $7 for adults; $4 for srs. and ages 6 - 12; children 5 and under are free. Rides and certain activities cost extra. Parking is $5.

WILL GEER THEATRICUM BOTANICUM, Topanga. See June entry (pg. 588) for details.

AUGUST:

ADVENTURE PLAYGROUND, Huntington Beach. See June entry (pg. 582) for details.

AFRICAN MARKETPLACE AND CULTURAL FAIRE, Los Angeles. (323) 734-1164 or (213) 847-1540 / www.africanmarketplace.org, Exposition Park. This huge, three-weekend fair is international in scope and sequence. Focused on African influence around the world, there are numerous themed villages; a health fair; multiple performance stages with gospel, Latin jazz, reggae, blues, and other music; a Fine Art pavilion; over 200 importers and exporters and craft merchants; a technology village; athletic competitions such as a tennis tournament, soccer, and Celebrity Village games; a lot of ethnic restaurants; and a short film festival. A children's village and Little Africa youth village has carnival games, petting zoo, magicians, jugglers, drum and dance demonstrations and classes, and animation workshops. Open weekends (and a weekday or two) 10am - 9pm. Admission is $6 for adults; $3 for srs. and ages 9 and under.

ANTELOPE VALLEY FAIR, Lancaster. (661) 948-6060 / www.avfair.com, 155 E. Avenue I / 2551 W. Ave. H (starting 2004) at the fair grounds. This eleven day a*ffair* has all the good stuff - carnival rides, lots of livestock events, a parade, demonstrations from a variety of vendors, booths, great food, and entertainment, including headlining concerts. County fairs are a once-a-year treat. Open during the week around 4pm - midnight; weekends, noon - 1am. Admission is $6 for adults; $4 for srs. and ages 6 - 15; children 5 and under are free. Parking is $3.

APPLE PICKING - APPLE LANE ORCHARDS, Solvang. (805) 688-5481 / www.applelanefarm.com, 1200 Alamo Pintado Rd. at Apple Lane Orchards. U-Pic the apples, or just stop by for a bag of this fresh picked fruit. Varieties include gala, golden delicious, red delicious, fuji, and granny smith. You know what they say - "An apple a day . . . ." Class tours are available upon request. Open daily during harvest time which is August - October or so.

APPLE PICKING - BALLARD APPLE FARM, Solvang. (805) 693-1586 / www.ballardapplefarm.com, 2599 Baseline Ave. at Ballard Apple Farm. Royal galas, red delicious, golden delicious, and sommerfeld are the apple types available at this U-Pic farm. We liked the farm too, because of, well, the farm atmosphere. There were chickens and turkeys running around and a few other farm animals to look at and pet. Open in season, August - October or so, daily, 10am - 5pm.

CAMARILLO AIR SHOW, Camarillo. (805) 383-0686 or (805) 482-0064 / www.eaa723.org, Pleasant Valley at Camarillo Airport. Fly bys in the morning and demonstration flights, usually in the afternoon, are highlights of this air show. Other exhibits and activities include WWII warbirds, vintage aircraft, antique farm equipment, over a hundred home built airplanes, food vendors, and a kids area with a bounce, a maze, and more. Note: Check out the Commemorative Air Force World War II Flying Museum (pg. 413) which is on the airfield. Open Sat. - Sun., 8am - 5pm. Admission is $8 for adults; children 11 and under are free.

CHILDREN'S FESTIVAL OF THE ARTS, Hollywood. (323) 485-ARTS (2787) / www.hollywoodartscouncil.org, 6500 De Long Pre Ave. at the park. Expose kids to arts from around the world with this one-day festival. Attend art workshops and make masks, ribbon shakers, necklaces, puppets, and more. Costumed characters, face painters, and song and dance performances representing Africa, Philippines, America, and several other countries round out this event. Open Sun., noon - 4:30pm. Admission and the crafts are free.

CIVIL WAR REENACTMENT, Huntington Beach. (714) 962-5771 or (714) 536-5486 / www.hbvisit.com, Golden West Ave. in Huntington Beach Central Park. Live through the Civil War time period, if only for a day. Heralded as one of the best reenactments, come visit with soldiers from the North and South who are authentically dressed in uniform and stay in character throughout the duration. Watch mock battles and wander through the encampments. Open Sat. - Sun., 10am - 5pm. Battles are Sat., 1pm and 4pm; Sun., at 11am and 2pm. Admission is free.

COLORADO LAGOON MODEL BOAT SHOP, Long Beach. See June entry (pg. 8) for details.

FESTIVAL OF ARTS AND PAGEANT OF THE MASTERS, Laguna Beach. See July entry (pg. 589) for details.

FLOWER FIELDS / FLOWER FESTIVAL, Lompoc. See June entry (pg. 584) for details.

GREAT GREEK CATHEDRAL FEST, Los Angeles. (323) 737-2424 / www.greek-fest.com, 1324 S. Normandie Ave. at Saint Sophia Greek Orthodox Cathedral. This fest features authentic Greek food (sample souvlaki, baklava, gyros, and more), music, traditional folk dances, theatrical performances, game booths, and a tour of the cathedral. Open Sun., 11am - 10pm. Admission is $3 for adults; free for srs. and ages 11 and under.

HARVEST FESTIVAL, Long Beach. (800) 321-1213 / www.harvestfestival.com, 300 E. Ocean Blvd. at the Long Beach Convention Center. See October entry for Harvest Festival Ventura (pg. 603) for details. Hours here are Sat. - Sun., 10am - 7pm; Mon., 10am - 5pm.

INTERNATIONAL SPEEDWAY, Costa Mesa. See April entry (pg. 573) for details.

JPMORGAN CHASE OPEN, Carson. (310) 996-0313 / www.jpmorganchaseopen.com, 18400 Avalon Blvd., at the Home Depot Training Center. For one smashing week, top-seeded women tennis players come to tune-up for the U.S. Open in this intense tournament. Past participants include the Williams sisters, Lindsay Davenport, Mary Pierce, and lots more. Bring your sunscreen!

KIDSWORLD, Santa Monica. See July entry (pg. 590) for details.

KINGSMEN SHAKESPEARE FESTIVAL, Thousand Oaks. See June entry (pg. 585) for details.

LOS OLIVOS QUICK DRAW and ART AUCTION, Los Olivos. (805) 688-1222 / www.losolivos.com, Los Olivos Park. Not really similar to the quick draw of the Old West, talented artists at Los Olivos must complete a drawing, painting, or sculpture within forty-five minutes. (Bronzes are finished at the foundry.) You get caught up in the moment(s) and can't wait to see the outcome. A live auction (gavel and all) for the completed works immediately follows. Enjoy a barbecue in the park, musical entertainment, afternoon sculpture demonstrations, receptions at participating galleries, and browsing around the town. The Sat. festival begins at 9am, but the drawing doesn't actually commence until 11am. Free admission.

MORRELL NUT & BERRY FARM, Solvang. See June entry (pg. 585) for details.

MUD MANIA, Long Beach. (562) 570-1755 / www.lbparks.org/facilities/RanchoLosCerritos.htm, 4600 Virginia Rd. at Rancho Los Cerritos. Get down and dirty at this one-day event. Stomp around in an adobe mud pit, make real adobe bricks, play Tug O' War over a mud pit, and help whitewash the adobe oven. Tip: Bring a change of clothing. Cleaner activities include making bars of soap and crafting an adobe model out of cardstock. Refreshments and live musical entertainment round out the day. Open Sun., 12:30pm - 4:30pm. Admission is $5 for adults; $3 for ages 4 - 12; children 3 and under are free.

MUSICALS UNDER THE STARS, Vista. See June entry (pg. 585) for details.

NATIONAL CLOWN WEEK, San Diego. (619) 282-9668 / www.clowns.dreamstation.com, Don't stop clowning around! The San Diego All Star Clown Club performs the first week of August in several locations throughout San Diego County. The public is invited to most of these funny functions. Call or check the website for place and time.

NISEI WEEK JAPANESE FESTIVAL, Los Angeles. (213) 687-7193 or (213) 625-0414 / www.niseiweek.org, 369 E. First St. in Little Tokyo. This week-long festival, the biggest Japanese festival of the year, takes place at several locations throughout Little Tokyo. A sampling of events and exhibits include martial arts demonstrations, traditional Japanese dancing, games, arts and crafts, Yabusame archery on horseback, Taiko drumming (on huge drums), tofu tasting, calligraphy, bonsai arrangements, and a grand parade with floats. Most of the activities and programs occur on the weekends, Sat.,10am - 6pm; Sun., 10am - 4pm. Call for a schedule of events. Admission is free, although some activities cost.

OJAI SHAKESPEARE FESTIVAL, Ojai. See July entry (pg. 591) for details.

OLD SPANISH DAYS FIESTA, Santa Barbara. See July entry (pg. 591) for details.

PCPA THEATERFEST, Solvang. See June entry (pg. 513) for details.

PEAR PICKING, Leona Valley. 10600 Leona Ave. at Rose Orchard (661) 270-1569 and adjacent Bright Ranch (661) 270-0905. Delicious Asian pears ripen in late August, early September. The ranches have acres of U-Pic trees, although pre-picked pears are available also. Prices are usually lower than market prices and the fruit is much more flavorful than store-bought. Open daily, 8am - 4pm until sold out.

PEAR PICKING, Oak Glen. (909) 797-5145 / www.rileysfarm.com, 12261 S. Oak Glen Blvd. at Riley's Farm. Barlett pears are ready for picking here mid-August to mid-September.

PEARSON PARK AMPHITHEATER, Anaheim. See June entry (pg. 586) for details.

RANCHO MISSION VIEJO PRCA RODEO, San Juan Capistrano. (949) 240-3363 / www.rmvrodeo.com, at Ortega Hwy and Antonio Pkwy/La Patera at Oaks Blenheim Rancho Mission Viejo Riding Park. Ride 'em cowboy - the rodeo's back in town! See bareback riding, saddle bronc riding, bull riding, tie-down roping, steer wrestling, rodeo clowns, and more at this two-day, large purse (i.e. lots of prize money!) rodeo. Admission is $20 for adults; $10 for ages

RASPBERRY PICKING. See July entry (pg. 592) for details.

RENAISSANCE ART FESTIVAL, Long Beach. (562) 438-9903 / www.lbrenaissanceartsfest.com, Queens Highway at Queen Mary Special Events Park by the Queen Mary. Heralding all Lords and Ladies who wish to participate in two days of festivities that harken back to days of old! Renaissance period events and entertainers include jugglers, magicians, English royal court, and hands-on exhibits. Celtic reenactors, and musical entertainment. Hours are Sat. - Sun., 10am - 6pm. Admission per day is $10 for adults; $7 for srs.; $5 for ages 5 - 12; children 4 and under are free. Tickets bought in advance are less expensive.

RINGLING BROS. & BARNUM AND BAILEY CIRCUS, Anaheim, Long Beach, Los Angeles, and San Diego. See July entry (pg. 592) for details.

SAWDUST FESTIVAL, Laguna Beach. See June entry (pg. 586) for details.

SEA FESTIVAL, Long Beach. See July entry (pg. 593) for details.

SHAKESPEARE FESTIVAL/L.A.. See July entry (pg. 593) for details.

SOUTHERN CALIFORNIA INDIAN CENTER'S ANNUAL POW WOW, Costa Mesa. (714) 962-6673 / www.indiancenter.org, 88 Fair Dr. at the Orange County Fairgrounds at the Arlington Theater. Come see spectacular, traditional American Indian dancing with more than 1,000 dancers from 300+ tribes and nations. There is prize money involved. Also enjoy handcrafted arts and crafts, from over 100 vendors, plus storytelling, and a variety of food. Grand Entrances (with the members in full tribal regalia) are Fri., 6pm and 8pm; Sat., noon and 7pm; Sun., noon. The pow wow is open Fri., 2pm - 10pm; Sat., 9am - 10pm; Sun., 9am - 6pm. Admission is $7 for adults; $4 for srs. and ages 13 - 17; $2 for ages 6 - 12; children 5 and under are free.

STARLIGHT BOWL SUMMER CONCERT SERIES, Burbank. See July entry (pg. 593) for details.

STRAWBERRY PICKING, Carlsbad. See May entry (pg. 581) for details.

SUMMER AT THE FORD, Hollywood. See June entry (pg. 587) for details.

SUMMER SOUNDS, Hollywood. See July entry (pg. 587) for details.

VENTURA COUNTY FAIR, Ventura. See July entry (pg. 593) for details.

WESTERN DAYS, Yucaipa. (909) 797-1753 / www.parrishranch.com, 38651 Oak Glen Rd. at Parrish Ranch. Yee-ha! The Old West comes to life with staged gunfights, skits, yodeling Merle, country music, country crafts, Johnny Appleseed, and a Western-style barbecue. Join in the fun the third weekend in August from 10am - 6pm. Admission is free.

WILL GEER THEATRICUM BOTANICUM, Topanga. See June entry (pg. 588) for details.

WORLD BODYSURFING CHAMPIONSHIP, Oceanside. (760) 435-4014 / www.worldbodysurfing.com, near the pier. This three-day event has been an annual event for over two decades! Over 300 participants, including several from foreign countries, equipped with swim fins are judged on length of ride and style, such as barrel rolls and somersaults. Contestants must be at least 12 years old to enter. Held Fri., 7am - noon and Sat., 7am - 1pm; the semi-finals and finals are held on Sun., 7am - 3pm. Admission to watch is free; $25 to participate.

SEPTEMBER:

ANTELOPE VALLEY FAIR, Lancaster. See August entry (pg. 594) for details.

APPLE PICKING - CALICO RANCH, Julian. (858) 586-0392 - during the week. / www.julianfun.com, 4200 Wynola Road and Hwy 78/79. This twenty-acre apple orchard is one of the only U-Pic orchards left in the Julian area. It boasts of 130 different kinds of apples, although the rarer types have only one tree here. Visitors may enter the orchards to pick apples, or purchase a wide variety of just-picked apples, as well as gallons of fresh apple cider. Purchase pre-picked pecks at less per peck than personally picking them (say that five times fast), but then you lose out on the joy of actually picking the apples. The season is short, but tasty - it begins towards the end of September and most of the crop is gone by the beginning of November. The ranch is open seasonally Fri. - Sun., 9am - 5pm. $1 per person admission to the U-Pic orchards plus the cost of the apples.

APPLE PICKING - OAK GLEN, Oak Glen. See the main entry for Oak Glen on page 322. The season runs from mid-September through mid-November.

APPLE PICKING, Solvang. See August entry for Apple Picking - Ballard Apple Farms (pg. 594) and Apple Picking - Apple Valley Orchard (pg. 594) for details.

BARSTOW RODEO STAMPEDE, Barstow. (760) 252-3093 / www.barstowrodeo.com, Marine Corps Logistic Base (MCLB) Rodeo Grounds. Yee-ha! The last full weekend in this month brings a rodeo complete with bareback, saddle bronc, barrel racing, tie-down roping, team roping, steer wrestling, and championship bull riding. Watch the women's barrel race and the mutton bustin' for kids 10 years and under. The crowds go wild over the latter event especially! Open Fri. for barbecue and dance, around 5pm - 11pm; Sat. show is at 7:30pm; Sun., 5pm. Admission for the rodeo is $10 for adults; children 6 and under are free.

CABRILLO FESTIVAL, Point Loma. (619) 557-5450 / www.nps.gov/cabr, Cabrillo Memorial Dr. at Cabrillo National Monument. Journey back in time to commemorate the life and times of Juan Cabrillo, one of the first explorers of California. The weekend is filled with events and activities - listening to authentically-dressed Spanish soldiers give history talks; observing Native American basket making; sampling food from Mexico, Portugal, Spain, and Native America; enjoying the cultural music and dancing; watching a reenactment and drama of Cabrillo's landing called "Voyage of Cabrillo"; and partaking in the living history encampment; . Open Sat. - Sun., 9:30am - 5pm. Admission is free. Parking is $5.

CALIFORNIA INDIAN DAYS, San Diego. (619) 281-5964 / www.balboapark.org, Park Blvd. and President's Way in Balboa Park. Usually held on the third weekend of the month, the celebration showcases American Indian singers, fantastic dancers, and storytellers, as well as tribal arts and crafts to purchase or try making yourself. Open 10am - 6pm. Admission is free.

COIN & COLLECTIBLES EXPO, Long Beach. See February entry (pg. 565) for details.

DANISH DAYS, Solvang. (805) 688-6144 or (800) 468-6765 / www.solvangusa.com/html/danishdays.html, downtown Solvang. Velkommen! Danish Days are good not just for eating danish, although you must try the aebleskivers, but to celebrate this colorful heritage with old world customs and pageantry. Expect and enjoy lots of folk dancing by costumed participants; music; parades (one on Saturday afternoon and a children's one on Sunday); food; a Kids Korner at Solvang Park with games and shows; craft demonstrations, such as woodcarving, paper cutting, clog painting, and making Christmas ornaments; and everything else Danish that can be packed into this three-day festival. Two other note-worthy events that occur at this time are the wonderful PCPA outdoor theater presentations and a (free) visit to the Elverhoj Museum. Look in the Solvang entry (pg. 510) for more things to do while here. Open the third weekend in September, Fri. 4pm - 9pm; Sat., 8:30am - 7pm; Sun., 8:30am - 4:30pm. Free admission to most activities.

FLY IN, Santa Maria. (805) 922-8758 / www.smmof.org, Airpark Dr. behind the Radisson Hotel. The first day of the Fly In is free because although there is activity, this is arrival day for the planes and vendors. On the weekend, there is usually more than sixty aircraft, both static and in the air performing fly bys and some demonstrations; no aerobatics. See warbirds, commercial carriers, experimental craft, and military planes. Some military planes are available to climb aboard as are some military vehicles. Vendors are on the premises, too. Ironically a car shows takes place at the Santa Maria Museum of Flight (pg. 502), which is just down the runway. Admission to the Fly In includes admission to the museum, too. The Fly In is open Sat. - Sun., 9am - 5pm. Admission on Sat. is $6 for adults; $4 for ages 6 - 16; children 5 and under are free. Admission is $1 less on Sun.

FREE FISHING DAY, all over. The last weekend in September usually includes a free fishing day, meaning that no license is required. Call a park or your favorite fishing hole to see if they are participating in this "reel" deal.

GREEK FESTIVAL, Cardiff-by-the-Sea. (760) 942-0920 / www.greek-fest.com; www.yasas.com/festivals.html, 3459 Manchester Ave. Park at the adjoining Mira Costa College. Live Greek music and dancing, Greek cuisine (i.e. stuffed grape leaves, cheese pita, Greek caviar dip, Baklava, etc.), games, a bazaar, a live auction, and craft booths are a few of the goings-on at this weekend festival. Church tours of Saints Constantine and Helen Greek Orthodox Church are given at 1pm and 4pm each day. The festival is Sat., 11am - 10pm; Sun., 11am - 9pm. Admission is $2 for adults; free for children 11 and under.

GREEN MEADOWS FARM, Los Angeles. (800) 393-3276 / www.montecitohts.org/debs.htm, 4235 Monterey Rd. at Ernest Debs Regional Park. The Farm is here from the end of September through October. See details in the March entry for Green Meadows Farm, Irvine (pg. 568).

"HART" OF THE WEST, Newhall. (661) 259-0855 or (661) 222-7657 / www.hartmuseum.org, 24151 San Fernando Rd. at the William S. Hart Park and Museum. This celebration of "California is a nation" encompasses many facets of the Old West and usually takes place the last full weekend of the month. A pow wow, held at the large picnic area, begins around noon with the all tribes and nations procession, followed by the Blessing, and ongoing dancing (with narration and interpretation) from each of the Indian nations. Native American wares are for sale at booths. Mountain men, set up in encampments next to the pow wow, show how people lived in the mid 1800's, by using period tools, campfire cooking, and display booths. Some years, Civil War reenactments and skirmishes take place near the adjacent train depot. Sometimes President Lincoln shows up and recites the Gettysburg Address. A street fair is located just across the street. Parking is tight. See the entry for this museum (pg. 124) for more information. The celebration hours are Sat., 9am - 7pm; Sun., 9am - 6pm. Admission is free.

HARVEST FESTIVAL, Del Mar. (800) 321-1213 / www.harvestfestival.com, 2260 Jimmy Durante Blvd. at the Del Mar fairgrounds. See the October entry for Harvest Festival Ventura (pg. 603) for details.

INSECT FESTIVAL, Encinitas. (760) 436-3036 / www.qbgardens.com, 230 Quail Gardens Dr. at Quail Botanical Gardens. How about a bug cookie? Or, maybe bug jewelry? This three-day weekend fair also offers live insects and snakes on display, crafts, story time, nature walks at the gardens, and everything else that could bug guests. See the main entry for information on the gardens (pg. 399). Open Fri. - Sun., 10am - 4pm. Admission allows you to walk around the gardens, too - $8 for adults; $5 for srs.; $3 for ages 3 - 12.

INTERNATIONAL SPEEDWAY, Costa Mesa. See April entry (pg. 573) for details.

JULIAN GRAPE STOMP FESTA, Julian. (760) 765-2072 or (760) 765-1857 / www.julianfun.com, 1150 Julian Orchards at the Menghini Winery. For one juicy Sat. enjoy a bunch of fun and stomp around in a ton (literally) of grapes - and yes, this means you. Your feet are first sterilized in a vat of vodka and then you can squish the grapes between your toes. (This wine is not sold commercially!) Other activities include listening to Italian bands, dancing, playing Bocce ball (an Italian lawn game), participating in arts and crafts, and sampling wine (this last part is not for children, obviously). Open 11am - 7pm. Admission is $5 for adults; bambinos 4 and under are gratsi (free).

KELP FESTIVAL, Santa Monica. (310) 305-9645 / www.smbaykeeper.org, at Ocean Park Blvd. where the road meets the beach. This one day festival is co-hosted by the Santa Monica BayKeeper to promote awareness of the endangered kelp ecosystem. Environmental groups are on hand to give out information and to share exhibits with visitors. (Check out the birds with the wild bird group.) Entertainment includes pirates who put on stage shows, as well as Hawaiian dancers and Chumash Indian performances. Kids enjoy the games and activities offered. Kelp out on Sun., 11am - 4pm. Admission is free. Parking is $6.

KERN COUNTY AIR SHOW AND AEROSPACE EXPO, Ridgecrest/Inyokern. (760) 375-UP-UP (8787) / www.kerncountyairshow.com, Hwy. 178 at Inyokern Airport. Up, up and away to this two-day festival that takes visitors soaring to new heights. Activities and events include skydivers, hang gliders, numerous aerobatics, and several other types of aerial demonstrations; vintage warbirds and modern military planes both in the air and on the ground; fly bys; tethered hot air balloon rides, plus glider, and aircraft rides; food booths and vendors; continuous entertainment; a science expo; and a children's area with rides, clowns, face painting, and arts and crafts. Nighttime takes on a glow of its own with a hot air balloon glow (6:45pm), aerial pyrotechnics, and a fireworks finale. The Fri. hours are more preparatory with air show practices and such. Call for Sat. hours. Call for admission prices.

LOBSTER FESTIVAL, San Pedro. (310) 366-6472 / www.lobsterfest.com, Ports O' Call Village. "Here lobster, lobster." A Lobster Call is one of the activities at the three-day festival. (Do they really come?) On Saturday, see the LobsterDog Pet Parade, where pets, mostly dogs, are dressed up as lobsters or other sea creatures for prize money. Street performers, which are always entertaining to watch, and lots of musical performances, plus a kid's area with some games and crafts add to the fun. The *maine* attraction is, of course, the Maine lobster meals - 1.25 oz. of lobster (and a veggie and a roll) for about $11. Other food choices are available, too. Open Fri., 5pm - 11pm; Sat., 11am - 11pm; Sun., 11am - 7pm. Admission is $6 for adults; children 11 and under are free.

LOMBARDI'S RANCH, Saugus. See October entry (pg. 604) for details.

LOS ANGELES COUNTY FAIR, Pomona. (909) 623-3111 / www.fairplex.com, 1101 W. McKinley Ave. at Fairplex. Billed as the world's largest county fair, this three-week event is wonderful (and exhausting). It has lots of carnival rides and games, workshops, country contests, livestock shows, horse-racing, flower and garden shows, music, dancing, booths, and several long buildings filled with exhibits and truly unique items and products for sale. Come early and plan to spend the whole day - there is a lot to see and do (and buy!). Teachers - ask about the free Fairkids field trips. These field trips comes with curriculum that focus on particular aspects of the fair - animals and history, and allow students to enjoy a day at the fair. Call (909) 865-4075 for more information. Fair hours are Mon. - Thurs., 11am - 10pm; Fri., 11am - midnight; Sat., 10am - midnight; Sun., 10am - 11pm. Admission Mon. - Fri., $10 for adults; $8 for srs.; $5 for ages 6 to 12; children 5 and under are free. Sat. - Sun., $14 for adults; $10 for srs.; $7 for ages 6 - 12. Call to find out about discount admission days. Certain activities cost extra. Parking is $7.

MEXICAN INDEPENDENCE DAY FIESTA, San Diego. (619) 293-0117 or (619) 220-5422, 4002 Wallace St. at Old Town State Historic Park. San Diegans know how to fiesta as they celebrate this one-day event at the Plaza with games, contests, historic reenactments, and more. Fiesta hours are Sat., 11am - 4pm. Admission is free.

MORRELL NUT & BERRY FARM, Solvang. See June entry (pg. 585) for details.

MOUNTAIN MEN RENDEZVOUS, Poway. (858) 679-4313 / www.powaymidlandrr.org/rendezvous.htm, 14134 Midland Rd. in Old Poway Park. Be a part of history for a weekend as you walk among the twenty-five, or so, encampments and learn about the mountain men, cowboys, buckaroos, and more from the 1820s to 1890s lifestyle. Mock gunfights, Civil War-era cannons, train rides, crafts, an evening barn dance, train robberies, folk dancing performances, and more await you, pardner. Look up Old Poway Park (pg. 441) for more details on the park. Open Sat., 10am - 4pm; Sun., 10am - 2pm. Admission is free.

MULTI-CULTURAL DANCE AND MUSIC FESTIVAL, Santa Barbara. (805) 966-6950 / www.sbdancealliance.org, 300 at Oak Park. Africa, Argentina, Aztec, Egypt, Greece, Ireland, Israel, and Russian are just a few of the ethnicities represented by over fifty groups performing on two stages at this weekend festival. Come listen to music, watch dancers and learn dances. Lessons are offered on salsa, swing, African, and more. Kids enjoy the storytelling of tales from around the world; crafts, such as instrument-making and mask and puppet-making; and exotic food and merchandise to purchase. Open Sat. - Sun., 11am - 6pm. Admission is free.

MUSICALS UNDER THE STARS, Vista. See June entry (pg. 585) for details.

PACIFIC ISLANDER FESTIVAL, San Diego. (619) 699-8797 / www.pacificislanders.com, the location varies. This event invites the thousands of Melanesian, Micronesian, and Polynesian residents of Southern California to celebrate their heritage. Each community sets up their own village where singing and chanting, cultural dances, storytelling, crafts, foods, and even artifacts keep visitors entertained. Open Sat. - Sun., 9am - 5pm. Admission is free.

PCPA THEATERFEST, Solvang. See June entry (pg. 513) for details.

PIRATE FAIR, Oxnard. (805) 496-6036 / www.goldcoastfestivals.com, 3100 Harbor Blvd. Ahoy mateys! Walk the plank or bring your own motley crew to enjoy treasure hunts and two stages of entertainment featuring jugglers, sword fighters, fire eaters, battle reenactments, and merchants selling plunder. Dress up as a buccaneer, too, for the costume contests. Open Sat. - Sun., 10am - 6pm. Admission is $10 for adults; $5 for ages 5 - 11; children 4 and under are free.

PORTUGUESE BEND NATIONAL HORSE SHOW, Rolling Hills Estates. (310) 544-1047 or (310) 318-8258 / www.pcch.net, 25851 Hawthorne Blvd. at Ernie Howlett Park. For over forty years, this classy three-day show has featured numerous equestrian events in two sand rings. Past shows have also included, besides the main feature of horse competitions, a children's carnival, demonstrations by the Long Beach Mounted Police, puppet shows, pony rides, a moon bounce, food booths, and more. Feel free to bring a picnic lunch. Gates open and events begin Fri. - Sun. at 8am until 4pm. Admission is $5 for adults; $2 for ages 4 - 12; children 3 and under are free. Ask about reserved seating prices. Parking and shuttle service to the site is free.

POWAY DAYS RODEO, Poway. (760) 736-0594 or (858) 748-0016 / www.powayrodeo.com, on Tierra Bonita Rd. at the PVRA Arena. This "Brand Above the Rest" rodeo is yet another reason to come to Poway! The P.R.C.A. rodeos (i.e. Professional Rodeo Cowboys Association) are one of the best in the nation with cowboys competing in several categories. Favorites events include kid's mutton bustin', rodeo clown acts, and Jr. barrel races. Behind-the-scenes tours are offered an hour-and-a-half before the show. Pre-rodeo events, that happen days before the rodeo, such as a parade, petting zoo and penned bull in a parking lot, and pageant will have your kids hootin' and hollerin' for more. Rodeos are Fri and Sat. at 7:30pm, gates open at 5pm; Sun. at 2:30 pm, gates open at 12:30pm. Admission on Fri. and Sun. is $12 for adults; one free child, ages 6 - 12, with a paid adult; children 5 and under are free on Sat. The rodeo cost $15 per person.

RASPBERRY PICKING. See July entry (pg. 592) for details.

REVOLUTIONARY WEEKEND, Simi Valley. (800) 410-8354 / www.reagan.utexas.edu, 40 Presidential Dr. at the Ronald Reagan Presidential Library and Museum. The Brigade of the American Revolution camps at the museum and presents battle reenactments, demonstrations on the battle field and at home during the 1770's, and even some period dancing. Open Sat. - Sun., 10am - 5pm. Admission is $5 for adults; $3 for srs.; ages 15 and under are free. Price includes admission to the museum.

SEAFEST, Newport Beach. (949) 729-4400 / www.newportbeach.com; www.tasteofnewport.com, This two-weekend fest has two major events; a sand castle and sand sculpting contest, and Taste of Newport, which is a sampling of the many restaurants in the area, accompanied by live entertainment. Call about participating in the sandy events or just come to "sea" the most imaginative things created with sand. Admission to watch is free; Taste of Newport is $12 - $15 for adults; ages 12 and under are free.

STATER BROS. ROUTE 66 RENDEZVOUS, San Bernardino. (800) 867-8366 / www.route-66.org, downtown San Bernardino - call for exact locations. Let's go cruisin'! This four-day event draws car afficionados of all ages for some reved up contests and exhibits. Thursday night is the Neon Light Cruise Contest, which is free to attend. Friday from 3pm - 11pm experience hundreds of classic and cruise cars are on exhibit, plus vendors, rides, games, and other activities are on deck. Bands play continually. At night, 7pm - 10pm, is the popular Burnout and Flame Throwing Contest at Orange Show Speedway ($5 for spectators). Drivers, among with other things, stand on the brakes and spin the tires - smell the burning rubber and hear the tires squealing. Saturday, 9am - 11pm, enjoy the exhibits and other activities, plus a bike stunt show and kid's crafts. Sunday, 9am - 4pm, enjoy more festivities and watch the parade of champions, and the hottest ticket in town - the firefighters team competition.

TALLSHIPS FESTIVAL, Dana Point. (949) 496-2274 / www.tallshipsfestival.com; www.ocean-institute.org, 24200 Dana Point Harbor Dr. at the Ocean Institute. This festival, held the weekend after Labor Day, begins as majestic tall ships begin to sail into port on Friday at 5pm, entering through a gauntlet of "enemy" cannon blasts. Tour the ships and enjoy demonstrations and exhibits of the sailing arts, such as knot tying, scrimshaw, and wood carvings. Pirate encampment activities include sea chantey concerts, storytelling, mock trials and weddings, and perhaps, walkin' the plank. All this, plus music, crafts, and food make this festival worth *sea*ing. Don't forget to explore the touch tank in the Institute. Sunset cruises on board a tallship with mock cannon battle cruises are also available. If you don't take a cruise, watch the battles from the shoreline. Open Sat - Sun., 10am - 5pm. Free admission to the festival. Cruises are $40 for adults; $25 for ages 12 and under and include a tour of the ships.

VISIT WITH MONTEZUMA, Los Angeles. See May entry (pg. 582) for details.

WILL GEER THEATRICUM BOTANICUM, Topanga. See June entry (pg. 588) for details.

OCTOBER:

AMY'S FARM PUMPKIN TOUR, Chino. (909) 393-2936 / www.amysfarm.com, 7698 Eucalyptus Avenue. Take a tour of this working calf ranch with about 200 animals, learn about how pumpkins grow, and pick a pumpkin from the pumpkin patch. See the main entry of Amy's Farm Tours (pg. 348) for more details. Open the month of October for tours of at least ten people or more. Call to book a date and time. The pumpkin tour is $7 per person, or $5 for adults not picking a pumpkin.

APPLE PICKING - CALICO RANCH, Julian. See September entry (pg. 597) for details.

APPLE PICKING, Solvang. See August entry for Apple Picking - Ballard Apple Farms (pg. 594) and Apple Picking - Apple Valley Orchard (pg. 594) for details.

ARBORFEST, UGLY BUG FAIR & PLANT SALE, Fullerton. (714) 278-3579 / www.arboretum.fullerton.edu, 1900 Associated Rd. at Fullerton Arboretum. Pumpkins and bales of hay add to the atmosphere of celebrating harvest time for two days here in early October. There's an apple press to make cider, opportunities to make butter, "wash" clothes the old-fashioned way, watch lace being made, explore the Children's Garden, take a hay wagon ride; and look at bugs at the Ugly Bug Fair. The Heritage House is also open. The fest runs Sat. - Sun., 10am - 4pm. Admission is $5 for adults; ages 12 and under are free.

AVOCADO FESTIVAL, Carpinteria. (805) 684-0038 / www.avofest.com, Linden Ave. Holy guacamole! This festival has everything avocado, at least food-wise. Try avocado ice-cream, avocado Key lime tarts, roasted corn with avocado butter, or at least some guacamole from a huge vat. Over sixty bands provide entertainment on three stages. Arts and crafts booths as well as commercial booths and an expo tent offering educational information add to the weekend events. At the kids block party, young ones enjoy face painting, a petting zoo, make-and-take crafts, miniature golf, a rock climbing wall, storytelling, and theater performances. For the "best-dressed" avocado, try winning for best hair, funniest, or scariest. Open Fri., 4pm - 9pm; Sat., 10am - 9pm; Sun., 10am - 6pm. Admission is free.

BATES NUT FARM PUMPKIN PATCH, Valley Center. (760) 749-3333 / www.batesnutfarm.biz, 15954 Woods Valley Rd. This great farm (see the main entry on page 439) has an eight-acre (pre-cut) pumpkin patch, along with a straw maze ($1), petting farm, and large picnic area. Weekday educational programs are available for school groups. Weekend events include tractor-drawn hayrides ($1), a scarecrow contest, a moon bounce, pony rides ($3), arts and crafts, and more. Open daily during the month of October 9am - 5pm. Call first as some activities are only offered at certain times. Admission is free. Price per pumpkin is based on weight.

CALABASAS PUMPKIN FESTIVAL, Agoura. (818) 225-2227 / www.pumpkin-festival.com, 2813 Cornell Rd. at Paramount Ranch. Kick up your heels for a weekend of autumn country fun in a Wild West setting. On-going live entertainment includes country bands, kids dancing troupes, cloggers, and more. Join in a contest of pumpkin pie eating, pumpkin seed spitting, pumpkin carving, pumpkin bowling, and mechanical bull riding. Visit the Native American Indian Village and watch authentic dancers. Go through the corn maze. Shop at the numerous arts and crafts vendor booths. And don't forget to pick up a pumpkin or two. Open Sat. - Sun., 9am - 5pm. Admission is $9 for adults; $7 for srs. and ages 13 - 17; $5 for ages 4 - 12; children 3 and under are free. Parking is $5 and includes free shuttle service.

CALICO DAYS, Yermo. (800) TO-CALICO (862-2542) / www.calicotown.com, 36600 Ghost Town Rd. at Calico Ghost Town. During the three-day Columbus Day weekend relive Calico's glory days and enjoy a wild west parade, National Gunfight Stunt Championships and shootouts, old prospectors burro run, games from the 1880's, crafts, Native American dance exhibitions, and music. Walk around the town itself and enjoy its many attractions. See Calico Ghost Town (pg. 343) for more details. Open 9am - 5pm. Admission is $8 for adults; $5 for ages 6- 15 years; children 5 and under are free. On-site camping is also available.

CELEBRATION IN THE PARK, La Mirada. (562) 943-7277 / www.cityoflamirada.org, San Cristobal and San Esteban Drs. at the Neff House. For one day return to turn-of-the-century California at the historic Neff House. Learn to tan a hide (I don't mean spankings) and how to quilt; look at antique toys; try your hand (or face) at an authentic barbershop; enjoy a Victorian tea party; participate in traditional games; picnic on the grounds; and listen to live music. Open Sat., 10:30am- 4pm. Free admission.

COIN & COLLECTIBLES EXPO, Long Beach. See February entry (pg. 565) for details.

EDWARDS AIR FORCE BASE AIR SHOW, Kern County. (661) 277-3510 or (661) 277-3517 / www.edwards.af.mil, Rosamond Blvd. at Edwards Air Force Base. Come see an outstanding, two-day air show, complete with acrobatic teams, biplanes, wing-walking, military air-ground task force demonstrations, and much more. (Be prepared for crowds!) Bring folding chairs, water bottles, sunscreen, and hearing protection because some of the planes are loud. Gates open Sat. - Sun. at 8am; the show begins about 10am; events end at 4pm. Admission is free.

FALL FESTIVAL, Los Angeles. (323) 933-9211 or (323) 549-2140 / www.farmersmarketla.com, 3rd St. and Fairfax at Farmers Market. Enjoy this two-day, old-fashioned festival in the heart of historic L.A. See page 14 for info on Farmer's Market. Past activities and events have included a petting zoo; pumpkin patch; live country music; cooking, spinning, gardening, and pottery demonstrations; bobbing for apples; pie-eating contests; and more. Open Sat., 9am - 8pm; Sun., 10am - 7pm. Admission is free. Some activities may cost.

FALL HARVEST FESTIVAL, Moorpark. (805) 529-3690 / www.underwoodfamilyfarms.com, 3370 Sunset Valley Rd. at Underwood Family Farm. See page 529 for more details on this great farm. Take a wagon ride along the dirt trail through the pumpkin patch. Enjoy Clydesdale-drawn hayrides ($4 per person; ages 1 and under are free), pony rides, a large petting farm, a corn field maze, country games, and more. School tours vary in price from $4 to $7 per student. Farm fresh produce is available for purchase as well as gourds, squash, corn stalks, Indian corn, food, drinks, and more. Open for the month of October, 9am - 6pm. Admission is free - call for individual attraction prices.

FAULKNER FARM PUMPKIN PATCH and HARVEST FESTIVAL, Santa Paula. (805) 525-2226 / www.faulknerfarm.com, 14292 W. Telegraph Rd., off Briggs Rd. This seven-acre pumpkin farm, part of a larger working farm, offers a month of family fun in the country. One of the farm's major attractions is pumpkins ranging in size from mini up to 200 pounds. Afternoon weekday hayrides are $1 ($2 on weekends). Weekends offer a variety of rotating events and activities such as a petting zoo ($1 admission); face painting; western dancing; craft booths, live country and bluegrass entertainment; special farm demonstrations (i.e. milking cows, shearing sheep, etc.); spinning, weaving, and blacksmith demonstrations; an antique tractor show; pony rides ($4); entertainment by local school children; and a variety of fresh foods to purchase, such as jams and squash. Bring your own little *punkins* here, and have a picnic, too! Call to reserve a special school-group "tour," which includes educational information about pumpkins, a hayride, a pumpkin, and other goodies for $3.50 per person. The farm is open from in October daily, 10am - 5:30pm. Call for a specific calendar of events. Admission is free during the week; $1 per person on the weekends.

FLEET WEEK, San Diego. (800) FLEETWEEK (353-3893) or (619) 858-1545 / www.fleetweeksandiego.org, This tribute to the military includes over a week of activity including a parade of ships, fireworks, jeep races, submarine tours, and Naval ship tours. It coincides with the Miramar Air Show (pg. 605). Check the website for details on specific events, times, and places.

GEM-O-RAMA, Trona. (760) 372-5356 / www1.iwvisp.com/tronagemclub, 3½ hours north of L.A., near Ridgecrest. This two-day event, which occurs the second weekend in the month, is worth the trek! It's explanation deserves a full page, however space in this section is limited. A free gem and mineral show and a free bus trip around the chemical plant are the clean activities. Messy highlights include mineral collecting for two-and-a-half hours from gooey black mud for hanksite and borax crystals; collecting borax and halite from a blow hole; and trudging / wading knee to hip high in the salt lake, which crunches like new-fallen snow, for halite for four-and-half-hours. Bring sacrificial clothes and shoes, water (to use to wash off), gloves, a heavy hammer, a crowbar (for prying out the specimens), and large boxes lined with trash bags to bring home your treasures. What a unique opportunity to collect saline minerals! Activities begin at 8am on both days and end at 5pm on Sat., 4pm on Sun. Admission is $8 per vehicle on the Sat. mud trip; $8 for the Sat. blow hole; $10 for the Sun. halite lake - such a deal! Note that Pinnacles National Natural Landmark is down the road.

GEM SHOW, Costa Mesa. See March entry (pg. 568) for details.

GOLETA LEMON FESTIVAL, Goleta. (800) 646-5382 - chamber of commerce / www.lemonfestival.com, 7050 Phelps Road at Girsch Park. When life gives you lemons, make lemonade, or lemon chicken, lemon meringue pie, lemon cotton candy, and many other puckery creations. Besides citrus-flavored food, enjoy the petting zoo, blacksmith demonstrations, pony rides, Indy Slot car racing, fire engine rides, rock climbing wall, police and fire safety and action demonstration, arts and crafts, vending booths, and bands - country, folk, bluegrass, and pop. Open Sat., 10am - 9pm; Sun., 10am - 5pm. Admission is free.

GREEN MEADOWS, Los Angeles. See September entry (pg. 598) for details.

HALLOWEEN ALTERNATIVES. For alternatives to door-to-door trick or treating, check your local park, mall, or church as many of them offer carnival-type of fun, a safer atmosphere, and still plenty of candy!

HARVEST FESTIVAL, Anaheim. (800) 321-1213 / www.harvestfestival.com, 800 W. Katella Ave. at the Anaheim Convention Center. See below entry for details.

HARVEST FESTIVAL, San Diego. (800) 321-1213 / www.harvestfestival.com, See below entry for details.

HARVEST FESTIVAL, Ventura. (800) 321-1213 / www.harvestfestival.com, 10 W. Harbor at Seaside Park. This three-day event is the place to go for all your shopping needs and desires. Life in the nineteenth-century is the theme here, so an old-fashioned ambiance is prevalent through the festival. Over 250 craftsman and artisans sell unique items, from hand-carved train whistles to elegant jewelry, home decorating items, garden products, clothing, and everything in between. There is ongoing entertainment of craft demonstrations (which keeps kids intrigued) and live bands. Good food is on the premises, too. Open Fri., 11am - 8pm; Sat., 10am - 7pm; Sun., 10am - 5pm. Admission is $8.50 for adults; $7.50 for srs.; $4.50 for ages 6 - 12; children 5 and under are free. $1 off admission if you bring a can of food. Parking is $7.

INDUSTRY HILLS CHARITY PRO RODEO, City of Industry. (626) 961-6892 / www.industryhillsprorodeo.org, 16200 Temple Ave. at the Industry Hills Equestrian Center. Everyone benefits from this rodeo - several charities receive needed funds, top performers compete in the rodeo for a large purse, and guests have a great time! Besides the main event of the rodeo, visitors enjoy petting zoo, crafts, pony rides, clowns, Western theme booths, a visit by Smokey the Bear, entertainment, and food. Come before the weekend shows start to enjoy the pre-show fun. The rodeo commences Sat. at 6pm; Sun. at 2pm. Admission is $15 for adults; $10 for srs.; $6 for ages 3 - 11. Prices include parking. A dance, $10 per person, is given after the rodeo on Sat. evening.

INTERNATIONAL FESTIVAL OF MASKS, Los Angeles. (323) 937-4230 / www.cafam.org, 5814 Wilshire Blvd at Hancock Park. In association with the Craft and Folk Art Museum, contributors to this unusual festival include folkloric dancers from all over the world, ethnic musicians, theater, storytellers, mask makers, and mask vendors. Saturdays's mask parade is an absolute hit with kids. The festival is from 11am - 5pm. Admission is free.

KERN COUNTY AIR SHOW AND AEROSPACE EXPO, Ridgecrest. See September entry (pg. 599) for details.

KTLA KIDS DAY, Los Angeles. (888) LA-PARKS (527-2757) / www.laparks.org/ktla_kids/ktlakidsday.htm, 3990 S. Menlo Ave. at Exposition Park. Sometimes it seems like everyday is kids day! This event, sponsored by KTLA, features martial arts demonstrations, theatrical productions, dance and music performances, cartoon characters by Warner Bros., a mobile skate unit for skateboarders, arts and crafts, food vendors, and sports clinics, including USC and other Southern California athletes. An important emphasis is placed on safety with over fifty service providers offering information on education, safety (from the police and fire departments), arts, health, social services, and more. The festival is Sat., 10am - 4pm. Admission is free.

LIVE OAK CANYON CHRISTMAS TREE FARM, Redlands. (909) 795-TREE (8733) / www.liveoakcanyon.com, 32335 Live Oak Canyon Rd. This huge (at least in my city eyes) family-operated farm yields bushels of fun in the fall. A free petting zoo is on the grounds, with goats, sheep, pigs, donkeys, ponies, chickens, and ducks. Bring 25¢ to purchase feed. Tractor-drawn hayrides are usually available and are free. A giant hay "castle" is created from hundreds of bales of hay spread out as well as staggered on top of each other. Kids are welcome to climb up the castle "walls" for free and run through the maze burrowed through the bottom layers. Bring a sack lunch, or purchase food from a refreshment stand (usually open on weekends only), and eat at the numerous picnic tables scattered under shade trees. Special weekend events can include live music, pony rides, and other entertainment. Walk along the rows of the pumpkin patch, which feature fifteen acres of vine-cut pumpkins. There are also huge piles of pre-picked pumpkins that range from giant pumpkins (make pies for everyone in the neighborhood!), to sweet-tasting white pumpkins, to mini pumpkins. Wagons are available to help tote your load. An on-site store sells decorative fall items such as Indian corn (in all colors), corn stalks, scarecrows, pumpkin carving supplies, and numerous gourds, including the kind used by artists for making instruments, baskets, and other creative endeavors. Elementary-aged school tours are offered for students to learn about pumpkins and to make a gourd birdhouse. Tours starts at $4.50 per student (adults are free) and include a pumpkin and/or gourd to take home. Note: See this entry for December on page 610. Open end of September through October daily, 9am - 6pm. Admission is free.

LOMBARDI'S RANCH, Saugus. (661) 296-8697 / www.lombardiranch.com, 29527 Bouquet Canyon Rd. This family-owned and operated working farm opens its gates at the end of September and through the month of October. It offers forty-five-minute school tours during the week that include seeing and learning how pumpkins are grown, harvested, etc., and walking around the farm to see farm animals. The tours, which are $20 per group, are designed for ages 4 years and up and need a minimum of twelve people. Attractions here include a few vehicles to climb in (e.g. a paddy wagon and a real fire truck); a large fiberglass pumpkin slide; a walk through scarecrow alley (with over eighty scarecrows); bales of hay to sit on while munching on a hot dog (sold at the snack bar here); and hundreds of pumpkins (up to 150 lb.), squash, gourds, and Indian corn to purchase. Weekend activities include a petting zoo with goats, sheep, llama, etc. ($2 per person); wagon rides ($3); and face painting ($1 to $3). Ask about entering the scarecrow contest as it offers hundreds of dollars in cash prizes! Open daily, 9am - 6pm. The farm is also open August through September, and in November until Thanksgiving to sell fresh fruits and vegetables. Admission is free.

LONDON BRASS RUBBING CENTER, Long Beach. (562) 436-4047 / www.stlukeslb.org, 525 E. 7th Street at St. Luke's Episcopal Church. Cheerio! Your child will thoroughly enjoy making a medieval brass rubbing, offered October through November. (This has become one of our favorite fall activities.) On black background paper, use a wax rubbing crayon of gold, silver, or bronze to capture the intricate designs. The facsimiles of over sixty tombstones from England vary in size, and depict knights, Lords, ladies in fancy dress, griffons, Shakespeare, etc. Groups of at least ten people can incorporate a half-hour talk, given by a docent in period dress, to learn more medieval times and the stories of some of the engravings. A complete English tea can be added on to your time here, too, with advanced reservations and a group of at least ten people. The center is open to the public Thurs. - Sun., 10am - 4pm. It is open to groups during this time, too, as well as Tues. and Wed., 10am - 4pm. Teas are served upon request. The price to rub cost between $3 - $12, depending on the size of the brass plate. Groups between ten to twenty people pay $4.75 for a piece worth up to $7.50. Teas are $16.50 for adults; $9.50 for ages 17 and under. This price includes a rubbing and a half-hour lesson/talk, too.

MANZANITA HIGH MOUNTAIN RENDEZVOUS, Julian. (619) 390-0614 or (800) 488-1250 / www.sdcml.com, Mesa Grande Rd. at Santa Ysabel Ranch. Experience an authentic 1700's to 1840's Rocky Mountain fur traders encampment in a rustic mountain setting. Demonstrations of primitive survival skills such as cooking, tool making, tomahawk throwing, and black powder target shooting are given over a period of several days, but it's really a time of being immersed in this time period. Primitive and modern camping is available on site. This event is geared for fellow buckskinners and traders; the public welcome to visit, but not participate. Open 8am - 5pm. Admission is $3 for adults; ages 10 and under are free.

MCGRATH BROTHERS GREAT PACIFIC PUMPKINS, Ventura. (805) 648-1189 / ventura.K12.ca.us/resources/outdoors/id74.htm, 510 Olivas Park Dr. Open to the public and for school tours during the month of October, come walk the patch, take a tractor-drawn hayride, and purchase product from the produce stand. Tours, which last about an hour, are offered for pre-K to elementary-aged school kids to learn about the life cycle of a pumpkin. Visitors are then invited to look at the barnyard animals, take the hayride, and pick a pumpkin to take home. Open daily in October, Mon. - Fri., 8am - dusk; Sat. - Sun., 9am - dusk. Admission is free. Tours are $2 per child.

MCGRATH STREET PUMPKIN PATCH and GOURD FARM, Ventura. (805) 658-9972 / ventura.K12.ca.us/resources/outdoors/id74.htm, corner of Knoll Dr. and McGrath St. During the month of October, walk the fields and choose a vine-cut pumpkin from the patch. Multi-colored Indian corn and gourds (the hard-shell kind used by artists and musicians), are for sale here year round. Free, tractor-drawn hayrides are given on the weekends. A few animals are on the site to look at and gently pet. One weekend, a local school puts on a fair geared for younger children. Groups of ten or more can take a field trip during the week to learn all about pumpkins, Native Americans, and more. Tours are $2 per person. Call to make a reservation. Open daily, 9am - dusk. Admission is free.

MIRAMAR AIR SHOW, Miramar. (858) 577-1000 or (858) 577-1011; (858) 577-1016 for reserved seats / www.miramarairshow.com; www.mccsmiramar.com, Marine Corps Air Station. This three-day air show features the Blue Angels and military and civilian pilots performing thrilling aviation stunts and maneuvers. On the ground are over 100 displays of airplanes, helicopters, and military equipment, and some simulator rides. Gates open at 9am, the show runs Fri. - Sun., 10am - 4pm. A twilight show is given Sat., 5pm - 8pm, featuring aerial stunts and maneuvers, as well as a pyrotechnic display by the flying aircraft. Parking, admission, and blanket seating are free for all shows. Reserved seating ranges from $6 for adults, $3 for ages 3 - 11 for grandstand seats; to $50 for adults, $30 per child for tented patio seats, plus two meals and a program.

NATIONAL FIRE PREVENTION WEEK, all over. Call your local fire station to see if they are doing something special this week. Many offer tours of the fire engines and station houses, and sometimes kids can even dress up like firemen. The safety tips are lifesavers.

OKTOBERFEST, Torrance. (310) 327-4384 / www.alpinevillage.net, 833 W. Torrance Blvd. at Alpine Village. Bratwurst (yum!), live bands from Germany, watching a cow being milked, wood-sawing demonstrations, authentic German costumes, and beer - what more could a good German want? (Except maybe sauerkraut, pretzels, and sausages, which are also on hand.) This festival is open every Fri. - Sun. for a month, but only Sunday is really appropriate for children. Hours on Sun. are noon - 8pm. Admission is $5 for adults; ages 11 and under are free.

OLD TIME MELODRAMA AND OLIO, Julian. (760) 765-1857 / www.julianfun.com, 2129 Main St. at Julian Town Hall. Each weekend during the month of October, participate in a two-hour, old-time melodrama by booing the villain, cheering the hero, and sighing with the heroine. The shows feature local actors and incorporate a community sing-a-long. Shows are Fri. - Sat., 7:15pm; Sat. - Sun., 1:15pm. Admission is $5 for adults; $2 for ages 2 - 12.

ONCE UPON A STORY, San Juan Capistrano. (949) 493-5911 or (949) 768-1916 / www.storyfestival.com, at various locations around the city. Enjoy a weekend of tall tales and some great storytelling from some of the best storytellers in the country. Learn fundamentals of storytelling from masters in workshops, or come to just be entertained. Your kids might even get their fill of stories, for a day or two at least. Hours are Fri., 7:30pm; Sat., 10am - 10pm. Individually priced story sessions range from $3 to $10 per person. Ask for package deal pricing.

PACIFIC BEACHFEST, Pacific Beach. (858) 273-3303 / www.pacificbeach.org, between Garnet and Thomas Aves. on and near the boardwalk. This one-day, non-alcohol, event signifies the official end of summer in Southern California. Festival activities include kite flying, volleyball, sand castle building, and dancing to live bands. Purchase food from twenty Pacific Beach restaurants here, such as Asian chicken salads, jambalaya, feta cheese ravioli, and chocolate mousse cake. Kids can be kept busy with face painting, clowns, cookie decorating, and clay painting. Nearby museums participate by having booths for children here. A fire truck is also on hand to explore. A fireworks show from the Crystal Pier caps the day. Open 11am - 7:30pm. Admission is free. Some activities cost. Beach parking is limited.

PCPA THEATERFEST, Solvang. See June entry (pg. 513) for details.

PELTZER FARMS OLD FASHIONED PUMPKIN PATCH, Orange. (714) 289-1129 or (714) 289-0137 / www.peltzerfarms.com, 8415 E. Chapman Ave. This twenty-acre patch features pumpkins, naturally, plus a tractor-pulled hayride ($2), pony rides ($3), train rides ($2), a petting zoo ($3 per family of 4), and a cornfield maze. School tours are offered during the week for $5 - $6 per student. The patch is open daily during the month of October, 9am - 8pm. Admission is free.

PINERY PUMPKIN PATCH, Bonita and Rancho Bernardo. (858) 566-7466, Bonita at 5437 Bonita Rd., and Rancho Bernardo at 13421 Highland Valley Rd. These patches are open to the public during the month of October and are also offered to group and family tours (for eight or more people) during the week, with reservations. The tour, which is $6 per child (adults are free), includes a pumpkin ($4 value), a tractor pulled hayride (50¢), a coloring book on growing pumpkins, a walk through an eight-foot tall corn maze (50¢), and farm animals for viewing, not for petting. Open Mon. - Thurs., 9am - 6pm; Fri. - Sun., 9am - 8pm.

PIRATES FESTIVAL, San Juan Capistrano. (949) 234-1300 / www.missionsjc.com, corner of Ortega Hwy and Camino Capistrano at Mission San Juan Capistrano. Aaargh! Join other mateys for this one-day festival and dress up in yer best (or worst) because there is a costume contest. A re-enactment of the pirate raid on the Mission in 1818 (they lost), face painting, entertainment, and touring the mission are all part of this day. Open Sat., noon - 5pm. Admission is $6 for adults; $5 for seniors; $4 for ages 3 - 11; children 2 and under are free.

PORT HUENEME HARBOR DAYS, Oxnard. (805) 487-4470 / www.harbordays.org, Surfside Dr. at Ventura Rd. at Hueneme Beach. This celebratory weekend has been going on for almost fifty years! Join the arts and crafts festival; a parade complete with marching bands, floats, equestrians, and clowns; kite flying demonstrations; a fishing derby (on Sun. at 7am) with prizes; live entertainment; pony rides; scale model train rides; a moon bounce; a car show (on Sun.); food booths; and more. Tours of the lighthouse and of the CIMIRI Marine Conservation Laboratory are also offered. Open Sat. - Sun., 9am - 6pm. Admission is free.

PUMPKIN CITY'S PUMPKIN FARM, Laguna Hills. (949) 768-1103 or (949) 586-8282 - mall / www.shopsimon.com, 24155 Avenue De La Carlota at Laguna Hills Mall. This one-acre, fenced-in "farm" takes over part of the mall parking lot for the month of October. The ground is covered with hay, while tractors, cornstalks and bales of hay all around help enhance the autumn mood. There are Indian tepees to go in, a petting zoo to visit, and kids can take a ride on a pony, a scale train, an elephant (weekends only), and/or a few kiddie rides. Weekend entertainment is provided by costumed characters, country bands, and puppeteers. Group reservations are offered that include special rates on pumpkins and pony rides. And oh yes, there are thousands of pumpkins here of all shapes and sizes - mini pumpkins to ones that weigh up to 200 pounds! The farm is open daily, 9:30am - 9pm. Admission is free. "Extras" cost.

PUMPKIN FESTIVAL, Pomona. (909) 869-2215 or (909) 869-2200 / www.csupomona.edu, 3801 W. Temple Ave. at Cal Poly University. This two-day pumpkin festival is a very popular local event. Pick your own (precut) pumpkin off the vine ($4); pig out at a pancake breakfast ($4 per person); listen to live music; visit the Insect Fair at the Bronco student center which has over 200,000 preserved bugs on display ($4 for adults, $3 ages 12 and under); enter the petting zoo ($1 per person); ride a horse; go through a corn field maze; participate in games; and munch on food. Open 8am - 5pm. Admission is free.

PUMPKIN STATION, National City. (858) 566-7466, 2979 Plaza Bonita Rd. at Plaza Bonita Shopping Center. Hundreds of pumpkins, plus a few kiddie rides (i.e. trains, Bumble Bee, Swing, cars, and boats), carnival-type games, pony rides, and a petting zoo make this an attractive place to shop for a pumpkin and for fun. Open daily during the month of October, 10am - 8pm. Admission is free, but each activity costs.

RASPBERRY PICKING. See July entry (pg. 592) for details.

SAN DIEGO ZOO, San Diego. (619) 234-3153 or (619) 231-1515 / www.sandiegozoo.org, Park Blvd. in Balboa Park. The world-famous zoo is free for all ages on the first Monday of October in celebration of Founder's Day. Kids, ages 11 and under, are free for the entire month! What a way to celebrate! See the main entry (pg. 468) for more details.

SCANDINAVIAN FESTIVAL, Los Angeles. (323) 661-4273 / www.asfla.org, changing locations throughout Los Angeles. Quick - name all five Scandinavian countries. Even if you can't, enjoy a smorgasbord of folk dancing, colorful national costumes, children's corner, food, music, storytelling, crafts, and a parade - everything except the fjords. Open Sat., 11am - 7pm. Admission is $6 for adults; children 11 and under are free.

SOUTHERN CALIFORNIA FAIR, Perris. (909) 657-4221 / www.farmersfair.com, 18700 Lake Perris Dr. For nine days and nights, enjoy top-name entertainment, P.R.C.A. rodeos, livestock shows, monster trucks, demolition derby, petting zoo, extreme sports demonstrations, fishing demonstrations, carnival rides and games, and horticulture and fine art exhibits. Open daily, 11am - 11pm. Admission is $7 for adults; $6 for srs., $3 for ages 6 - 11; children 5 and under are free. Auto Club members are offered discounts Mon. - Fri. Rides and some activities cost extra. Parking is $5.

STAGECOACH DAYS, Banning. (909) 849-4695 / www.banningchamber.org, 22nd and Victory Sts. in A. C. Dysart Park. Commemorating the city as one of the major stops on the transcontinental stagecoach route, this four-day festival pulls out all the stops and features a carnival all four days, a P.R.C.A. rodeo on the weekends with all the major events, a parade on Saturday at 10am, plus shootouts, dances, and Old West themed contests throughout. Open Thurs. - Fri., 5:30pm - 10pm; Sat. - Sun., 11am - 11pm. Call for rodeo hours, times, and prices. Admission is a minimal cost.

TANAKA FARMS PUMPKIN PATCH, Irvine. (949) 653-2100 or (949) 380-0379 / www.tanakafarms.com, 5380¾ University Dr. This five-acre, U-Pic pumpkin patch is part of a larger, working farm. Walk the farm to see the rest of the fruits and vegetables currently growing. One-hour plus field trips, geared for pre-schoolers through fourth graders for groups of ten or more, can be made with advanced reservations. The cost is $10 per child and participants pick their own vegetables and pumpkins. There is also a small corn maze, petting zoo, and a wagon ride. The U-Pic is open daily during the month of October, 10am - 5pm. Pre-picked pumpkins (and other produce) is available daily, 10am - 6pm.

TEMECULA TRACTOR RACE, Temecula. (909) 676-4718 / www.temeculacalifornia.com, at Winchester and Diaz Rd. at Northwest Sports Park. This three-day event, which has been an annual event for over a quarter of a century, consists of getting down and dirty. Tractors, in all classes and categories (i.e. horsepower, pre-1940, diesel-powered, etc.), are raced around an oval track that has a 50' wide by 25" deep mud hole. Volleyball competitors (who play for cash prizes) play the sport here in the mud. Kids are not left out of the fun! An obstacle course with tires and ramps are set up to slosh through. Cleaner activities involve a rock climbing area, games booths, food booths, and a chili cook off. Open Fri., 1pm - dark - free admission. Open Sat. - Sun., 7:30am - 5pm for $10 for adults; $5 for ages 12 and under.

THRESHING BEE AND ANTIQUE ENGINE SHOW, Vista. See June entry (pg. 588) for details.

WESTERN DAYS RODEO, San Dimas. (909) 394-RODEO (7633) or (909) 592-3818 / www.sandimasrodeo.com, at Horsethief Canyon Park. Yee ha! This weekend P.R.C.A. rodeo features all a cowboys' (and cowgirls') favorite rodeo events. Come early for pre-rodeo activities, then enjoy the shows. Pre-show activities on Sat. and Sun. begin at 1pm; the shows starts at 2pm. Admission is $14 for adults; $7 for children.

WHOLESOME HERITAGE FARM PUMPKIN PATCH, Escondido. (760) 746-8822, 14305 San Pasqual Valley Road. This pumpkin patch is on a working twenty-five acre farm. (See pg. 470 for details about the farm.) Three acres of pumpkins grow and can be picked from the vine. Any age is welcome to take a tour which includes entrance into the petting zoo on the premises, a tour of the farm, and learning about pumpkins and their growth cycle. What a fun place to visit! Open the month of October - call for hours. Free admission. The tour is $4 per person.

WIDE SCREEN FILM FESTIVAL, Long Beach. (562) 985-7000 / www.carpenterarts.org, 6200 Atherton St. at the Carpenter Performing Arts Center. Classic motion pictures are shown in the original wide screen format for two weekends. Most screenings are preceded by a brief introduction by the film's director or a member of the cast. Many of the films are appropriate for children such as *Lady and the Tramp*, *20,000 Leagues Under the Sea,* and others. There are matinee and evening shows. Call for a schedule of times and prices.

NOVEMBER:

CORONADO BUTTERFLY RESERVE, Goleta. See entry (pg. 563) in January.

FALL VILLAGE FAIRE, Carlsbad. See May entry for Spring Village Faire, Carlsbad (pg. 581) for details.

FESTIVAL OF CULTURES, Pasadena. (800) 493-3276 / www.greenmeadowsproductions.com, 360 N. Arroyo Blvd. at Brookside Park, Rose Bowl. See below entry for details.

FESTIVAL OF CULTURES, Riverside. (800) 493-3276 / www.greenmeadowsproductions.com, 4600 Crestmore Rd. at Rancho Jurupa Regional Park. Hola, Jambo, Konichiwa - hello! Experience cultures from around the word - West Africa, Asia, Native American, and Mexican - through a series of twenty-minute interactive shows and hands-on programs. Shows include Wildlife of the World - see and touch different native species such as goats, sheep, iguanas, and snakes; Africa - native costumes and barefoot dancers, accompanied by drummers tell the story of their heritage through song and dance; Mexico - fancy feathered headdresses, as well as fancy footwork, are part of Mexican dancers' ancient traditions, and are part of the way they tell stories; Asia - gongs, flutes, drums, and masks are part of the Asian presentations, along with stories of their past; Native American - dances, chants, and storytelling are part of seeing and hearing about life in a village. Bring a picnic lunch to enjoy at the surrounding park. Open various days, 9:30am - 2pm. Admission is $8 per person; children 2 and under are free. Extra activities ($1 per) are archery, face painting, and feeding the animals.

GLORY OF CHRISTMAS, Garden Grove. See December entry (pg. 614) for details.

GREAT AMERICAN TRAIN SHOW, Pomona. (702) 252-0334 or (909) 623-3111 / www.gats.com; www.fairplex.com, 1101 W. McKinley Ave. at the Pomona Fairplex. Thousands of model trains are for sale and on display. Children are allowed to operate trains in the "play area". Models include old Lionel and American Flyer brands and state-of-the-art cars. Note: This show is held on different months every year. Open Sat. - Sun., 11am - 5pm. Admission is $7 for adults; ages 12 and under are free. Parking is $8.

GRIFFITH PARK LIGHT FESTIVAL, Los Angeles. (323) 913-4688, Riverside Dr (from Los Feliz Blvd off the I-5) and follow the signs for the drive through; park at the L.A. Zoo to walk through. Here's a bright idea - make this light festival an annual drive-through tradition! Turn off the headlights and gaze upon thousands of lights, from animated scenes depicting attractions around Southern California, reindeer, the Old West, and lots more, and go through decorated tunnels. Two tips: Go on a less crowded weekend night and, if possible, get in the left hand lane. Runs the day after Thanksgiving - Dec. 26, 5pm - 10pm. Admission is free.

HARVEST FAIR, San Bernardino. (909) 384-5426 / www.harvestfair.net, 8088 Palm Ln. Take a trip to the Old West for two weekends in November. There is so much to see and do - you might just need both weekends to do it all! Set up like an Old West Boom town, come to enjoy on-going cowboy stunt shows, gun slingers, square dancing, cloggers, bluegrass music, country music, an antique car show, carnival rides (the more modern kind), carnival game booths, pony rides, blacksmith demonstrations, Native American crafts, rope-making demonstrations, and lots more. Dress up or you might feel out of place! Open Sat. - Sun., 10am - 5pm. Admission is $3 for adults; children 6 and under are free. Activities cost extra.

HOLIDAY OF LIGHTS, Del Mar. (858) 793-5555 / www.sdfair.com, 2260 Jimmy Durante Blvd. at the Del Mar Fairgrounds. This dazzling drive-through light show extravaganza has more than 300 holiday displays that line the Del Mar Fairgrounds racetrack. Favorite displays include a waving snowman, an animated jumping horse, downhill skiers, a tail-wagging dragon in the lake, a Top Gun Santa, and the 125-foot tunnel of lights. Open Thanksgiving Day - Jan. 1, Sun. - Thurs., 5:30pm - 10pm; Fri. - Sat., 5:30pm - 11pm. Admission is $10 per vehicle for up to 5 people; $15 per van or car with 6 or more people.

HOLLYWOOD CHRISTMAS PARADE, Hollywood. (323) 469-2337 or (323) 469-8311 / www.hollywoodspectacular.com; www.hollywoodchamber.net, starting at Gower St. and Sunset Blvd; check to see this year's route. All the stars come out at night - I mean the stars of Hollywood - for this celebrity-packed parade that is put on the Sunday after Thanksgiving. There are fantastic floats, live bands, equestrian units, and of course, Santa Claus. The two-hour parade goes along a three-mile course through the streets of Hollywood. The parade goes from 6pm to 8pm. Reserved grandstand seating is $30 - $40 per person. Standing room is free, but it does get crowded, so get here early. All-day parking in nearby lots runs from $5 - $15.

HOW THE GRINCH STOLE CHRISTMAS, San Diego. (619) 239-2255 / www.theglobetheatres.org, Balboa Park at the Old Globe Theater. This Dr. Seuss-inspired production stars a fuzzy green villain who learns how to have a heart in the magical, musical world of Who-ville. Call for show times. Admission is $25 - $55 for adults; $25 for ages 3 - 17.

ICE SKATING. (800) 975-1885 / www.meetmeattheicerink.com, Huntington Beach - Pier Plaza; Irvine - 405 and 5 fwy junction at Irvine Spectrum. Ice skate on an outdoor rink without leaving the warmth and sunshine of Southern California, but still bundle up a little. The rink is ready for skaters mid-November through mid-January to practice their figure 8's or to just skate around. Usually open during the week, noon - 8pm; open weekends, 10am - 10pm. Admission is $10 for ninety minutes for adults; $7 for ages 9 and under. Skate rentals are $3.

ICE SKATING. (800) 975-1885 / www.meetmeattheicerink.com, W. Los Angeles - 10250 Santa Monica Blvd. at Westfield Shoppingtown Century City; Woodland Hills - 6100 Topanga Canyon Blvd. See the above entry for details. Admission is $12 for ninety minutes for adults; $9 for ages 9 and under. Skate rentals are $3.

INDIO POWWOW, Indio. See March entry (pg. 569) for details.

INTERTRIBAL MARKETPLACE, Highland Park. (323) 221-2164 / www.southwestmuseum.org, 234 Museum Dr. More than 150 nationally-known American Indian artists, traditional dancers, and storytellers, plus a plethora of ethnic food and craft demonstrations add up to a wonderful weekend marketplace. Explore the Southwest Museum (pg. 119) while you're here. Open Sat., 9am - 5pm; Sun., 10am - 5pm. Admission is $8 for adults; $6 for srs. and students; children 6 and under are free.

LIVE OAK CANYON CHRISTMAS TREE FARM, Redlands. (909) 795-TREE (8733) / www.liveoakcanyon.com, 32335 Live Oak Canyon Rd. Come join in the festivities celebrated here around Christmas time. Warm yourself by a large fire pit, visit with Santa Claus (on certain weekends), listen to carolers (usually on the weekends), and enjoy the hay bale maze, hay rides, pony rides, moon bounce, refreshment stands, and petting zoo. (See the October entry, on page 604, for more details on these attractions.) Walk among a twenty-five acre forest of home-grown Monterey Pines, Sierra Redwoods, and Aleppo Pines. Choose your own Christmas tree here (and have a worker cut it down), or purchase a fir tree shipped fresh from Oregon. A tented gift shop sells fresh wreaths, garland, and other decorations and gift items. Elementary-aged school tours are offered to learn about Christmas trees. Tours are $4.50 per student (adults are free) and include a tree seedling to take home. Open mid-November through to a few days before Christmas daily, 9am - 6pm. Admission is free. Certain activities cost.

LOGAN'S CANDY, Ontario. (909) 984-5410, 125 W. "B" St. This small retail candy store makes candy canes starting in November. A limited number of tours are offered to visitors to watch the fascinating process of striped candy become a sweet reality. During the half-hour tour, first stand outside and listen to a description of the procedure as you peer in through the storefront window. Flavoring is added and kneaded through a huge amber blob which is then stretched and pulled (think taffy pull) to form the white part of the cane. A smaller blob is dyed red. Next, go inside the store to see the two colors twisted together and shaped into variously-sized candy canes. This is one of our favorite seasonal excursions! Tours are given November through the third week in December, Mon. - Fri. at 5:30pm, 7pm, and 8:30pm. Reservations are needed. The cost is $2.25 per person and includes a small bag of candy.

LONDON BRASS RUBBING CENTER, Long Beach. See October entry (pg. 605) for details.

LOS ANGELES DREAMSHAPERS FESTIVAL. (888) 499-1270 / www.dreamshapers.org, Los Angeles - call for exact location. DreamShapers' storytellers take the stage to present folk, Native American, African American, Western, fairy, Islander, and personal tales. This one-day event is packed with a variety of stories, story swaps, and musical performances, as well as workshops for those who desire to tell better tall tales. Be entertained or come to learn on Sat., 9am - 9:30pm. Admission is $30 for the day or $10 per event.

MOTHER GOOSE PARADE, El Cajon. (619) 444-8712 / www.mothergooseparade.com, Main, Chambers, 2nd, and Madison Sts. This two-hour mother of parades has been going strong and gaining momentum since 1946. It features over 5,000 participants - bands, equestrian units, clown acts, and the best part of all - lots of floats depicting Mother Goose rhymes and fairy tales in a different theme each year. The parade takes place the Sun. before Thanksgiving beginning at about noon. Admission is free.

PASADENA MODEL RAILROAD CLUB'S OPEN HOUSE, Pasadena. See April entry (pg. 574) for details.

PILGRIM PLACE FESTIVAL, Claremont. (909) 621-9581 / www.pilgrimplace.org, 660 Avery Rd. This timely festival takes place on the second Friday and Saturday in November. Thanksgiving is a time to be thankful (and to eat), but do your kids know how this holiday began? Find out by watching the educational highlight here - an hour-long, live reenactment called, *The Pilgrim Story*. This play, which accurately and biblically retells an important story of our heritage, is performed at the outdoor stage at 1:45pm each day by the retired church professionals who live at this center. Call for special school performances, geared for 5th graders or so, given on the prior Tuesday and Wednesday at 10am. Bring a picnic lunch to enjoy at nearby parks. A favorite activity at the festival is called the Glue In. Tables full of recycled items are available for kids to glue onto a piece of cardboard to create a masterpiece (50¢). Other activities include riding the (motorized) Mayflower (50¢), taking a mini-train ride (50¢), visiting the on-site cultural museum, shopping at the bazaar and craft fair, face painting, eating good food, and going to the Wampanoag Indian Village for story time, and games. The festival runs from 10am - 4pm. Free admission and free, but hard-to-come-by, parking. Free shuttles are available.

POW WOW, Santa Fe Springs. (562) 946-6476 / www.santafesprings.org, 12100 Mora Dr. at Heritage Park. Share in two days of celebrating Native American cultures and intertribal gathering with traditional dancing, drumming, and singing, plus artifacts on display, Native American arts and crafts for sale, Indian fry bread, storytelling, and more. Open Sat., 11am - 9pm; Sun., 11am - 6pm. Admission is free.

RANCH DAYS, Riverside. (909) 369-6055, 4307 Briggs St. at the Jensen-Alvarado Ranch Historic Park. Celebrate Ranch Days with a lot of hoopla and activities include panning for gold, making your own soap, making ice cream, watching tortillas being made, and adobe bricks, among other things. Watch sheep shearing, branding, and spinning, weaving, and blacksmith demonstrations. Kick up your heels and keep time with the country music. See the Jensen-Alvarado Ranch (pg. 291) for details on the park. The party goes from 10am - 4pm. Admission is $4 for adults; $2 for ages 3 -12.

REINDEER ROMP, Los Angeles. (323) 644-6400 / www.lazoo.org, Griffith Park at the Los Angeles Zoo. Reindeer fly in to join their animal and human friends at the zoo during this season. Visitors can walk around the zoo, of course, as well as take a train ride (extra fee), make paper reindeer antlers, and enjoy special entertainment. Bring your herd! The reindeer are here the end of November through December. Admission is regular zoo admission - $8.25 for adults; $3.25 for ages 2 - 12.

SAWDUST WINTER FANTASY, Laguna Beach. (949) 494-3030 / www.sawdustartfestival.org, 935 Laguna Canyon Rd. Three acres of fun in the snow and other cool activities are offered for several consecutive weekends, beginning the one before Thanksgiving. (It is open the Friday after Thanksgiving, too.) Real snow is brought in daily so you can teach your little angels how to make snow angels. Family entertainment includes jugglers, balloon artists, storytellers, and carolers. Children's art activities, like mask making, are different each day and are free! Over 150 artists have booths here, with on-going crafting demonstration. Get your holiday shopping done and keep the kids happy - all at the same time! To complete the fantasy, Santa Claus makes his rounds. Open from 11am - 7pm. Admission is $4 for adults; $2 for ages 6 - 12; children 5 and under are free. A season pass is $5 per person. Parking fees vary depending on which lot you choose.

UNIVERSAL CITYWALK'S ICE RINK / DRIVE-IN MOVIE, Universal City. (818) 622- SKATE (75283) or (818) 622-4455 / www.citywalkhollywood.com, 1000 Universal Center Dr. at Universal CityWalk. Shopping, an ice rink, entertainment, Universal Studios, and movies all at one location! Prepare your ankles - the outdoor ice rink opens the end of November and shuts down (or melts) the beginning of January. It's usually open Mon. - Thurs., 4pm - 11pm; Fri., 3pm - 1am; Sat., 10am - 1am; Sun., 10am - 11:30pm. One-hour of skate time is $7.50 for adults; $6.50 for children. Skate rentals are $2.50. Enjoy rinkside gospel concerts, Santa and his band of singers, and other holidays specialties. The giant outdoor movie screen shows free films on some weekend evenings - call for a schedule and B.Y.O.C. (Bring Your Own Chair).

VETERANS DAY CELEBRATION, Chiriaco Summit. (760) 227-3483, 62510 Chiriaco Summit at the General Patton Memorial Museum. Veterans are remembered and celebrated during this one-day event. Entertainment includes a U.S.O. Show, an Army chorus, pipes and drums, military reenactments, fly overs, an appearance by General Patton "himself", and a walk through the museum. Open 9:30am - 4:30pm. The U.S.O. Show starts at 11am. Admission is $4 for adults; free for veterans in uniform ages and for ages 11 and under with a paying adult.

WINTERLIT CELEBRATION, Santa Monica. (310) / www.downtownsm.com; www.santamonicaplace.com, Third St. Promenade. Dramatically lit up Christmas trees, jutting icebergs, icicles dangling from light poles, and lots of twinkling lights are part of this illuminating celebration. The opening day festivities include a visit from Santa Claus, strolling carolers, and even a snowfall at Santa Monica Place. Winter lights transform this outdoor mall every night from Thanksgiving Saturday through the first week of January. Look up Third Street Promenade (pg. 76) for more details. Call for the opening date. Free admission.

DECEMBER:

ANNUAL BAY PARADE OF LIGHTS, San Diego. (619) 234-8791 or (619) 685-7818 / www.sdparadeoflights.org, San Diego Bay. Over 100 boats get decked out with lights and participate in a parade from Shelter Island, past the Embarcadero, Seaport Village, and then on to Coronado ending at the Navy carrier basin. The parade offers prizes to the "best of" in several categories. It runs on two consecutive Sun., 5:30pm - 9pm. Free viewing from the shore.

ARCTIC SNOW HILL / FESTIVAL OF LIGHTS AT SAN DIEGO WILD ANIMAL PARK, Escondido. (619) 234-6541 or (619) 231-1515 / www.sandiegozoo.org, 15500 San Pasqual Valley Rd. For a few weeks this month, see the Wild Animal Park in a whole new light! Animated figures move and light up the sky (and some enclosures) to celebrate the holiday season. Children 16 years and under can slip and slide down a 100-yard hill covered in freshly made snow. Both the snow play area and lights festival are open daily, 4pm - 8pm. Admission to these attractions is included with the price of admission to the Wild Animal Park.

BALBOA PARK DECEMBER NIGHTS, San Diego. (619) 239-0512 / www.balboapark.org, Park Blvd. and President's Way at Balboa Park. This festival marks the opening of the holiday season in San Diego as thousands of people join the celebration. The activities and events include looking at buildings glowing with Christmas lights, tasting holiday fare from around the world, listening to strolling carolers, participating in kid's crafts, enjoying free admission to the many museums here, watching the Santa Lucia procession, delighting in the Singing Christmas Story Tree at the organ pavilion, and applauding the holiday favorites performed at the Casa Del Prado Theatre. Usually open the first Fri. and Sat. of December, 5pm - 9pm. Admission is free.

BELMONT SHORE CHRISTMAS PARADE, Belmont Shore. (562) 434-3066 / www.belmontshore.org, 2nd St. between Bayshore and Livingston. This two-hour street parade starts about 6pm usually on the first Sat. in December and has over 100 entries, including bands, homemade floats, and Santa Claus. Call for exact date. Admission is free.

BETHLEHEM WALK, Escondido. (760) 745-5100, on the corner of 4th and Kalmia sts. at the First United Methodist Church of Escondido. Walk the streets of Bethlehem, or at least a re-creation of them. Visitors are escorted through a marketplace to experience the bartering of this ancient town and being hassled by soldiers, then onto the inn to try to get accommodations. Being redirected to the stable, guests then see Mary, Joseph, and baby Jesus, and the animals. Afterward, enjoy refreshments in the church's social hall. Reservations are (ironically) highly recommended and can be taken the Sun. after Thanksgiving. Open Fri., 5:30pm; Sat., 4:30pm; Sun., 4pm. Admission is free, but it is a ticketed/timed event to keep the tour numbers reasonable.

CHRISTMAS BOAT PARADE OF LIGHTS, Newport Beach. (949) 729-4400 / www.christmasboatparade.com, Newport Beach Harbor. The largest and oldest boat parade, with more than 200 participants, usually sets sail nightly, December 17 through December 21. Consider taking the kids on a cruise for a closer look at the beautiful boats. The ideal location for viewing is Balboa Island, but you should arrive before 5:30pm as parking is limited. If you are going to have dinner in this area, be sure to make reservations. The parade hours are from 6:30pm - 8:45pm.

CHRISTMAS BOAT PARADE OF LIGHTS, Oceanside. (760) 722-5751, Call to find out when and where, specifically, the boat parade will be held this year.

CHRISTMAS OPEN HOUSE AND PARADE, Coronado. (619) 437-8788 / www.coronadohistory.org, at First Street at the Ferry Landing Marketplace. Start off your holiday season with a bang as this one-day event, usually held on the first Friday in December, concludes with a fireworks display. Kids enjoy a parade along Orange Avenue, entertainment, holiday music (including Dickensian carolers), pony rides, snow play, and Santa's arrival by ferry (the reindeer are taking a rest). Call for specific hours. Admission is free.

CHRISTMAS PARADE, Fallbrook. (760) 728-5845 / www.fallbrookca.org, This one-day Christmas parade includes 120 groups of bands and decorated floats. Admission is free.

CORONADO BUTTERFLY RESERVE, Goleta. See entry (pg. 563) in January.

CRUISE OF LIGHTS, Huntington Beach. (714) 840-7542 / www.philharmonicsociety.org, Huntington Harbor. The Huntington Harbor Philharmonic Committee sponsors this event, raising money to donate to the youth music programs in Orange County. For ten days in the middle of December, forty-five-minute boat tours are given around the decorated homes of the harbor area. These homes have entered a competition, so you will see the creme de la creme, like the Sweepstakes winner, the Most Beautiful, the Most Traditional, etc. You'll also hear interesting commentary. Some boats along the way are also decked out in their Christmas best. Tours are offered every hour on the half hour from 5:30pm - 8:30pm. Tickets are $9 - $12 for adults, $7 for ages 2 to 12.

DISNEY ON ICE, Anaheim, Long Beach and Los Angeles. (714) 704-2400 / www.arrowheadpond.com - Arrowhead Pond in Anaheim; (213) 748-6136 / www.lacoliseum.com - L.A. Memorial Coliseum and Sports Arena; (562) 436-3636 / www.longbeachcc.com - Long Beach arena. / www.disneyonice.com, This ninety-minute, beautiful (and sometimes comical) show on ice usually features characters from Disney's newest film release. Some of the classic characters also make appearances. Tickets range from $10 - $50. Opening night tickets are usually less expensive.

DRIVE THROUGH NATIVITY, Chino Hills. (909) 517-1190 / www.cchministries.com, the corner of Chino Hills Pkwy. and Eucalyptus at Gordon Ranch Marketplace. Revisit Bethlehem, kind of. Slowly drive past (no walking allowed) nine scenes featuring live performers in still life poses, animals (i.e. camels, sheep, donkeys, etc.), and angels as they "reenact" the scenes of Jesus' birth. Open Sat. - Sun., 5pm - 10pm. Admission is free.

FAMILY CHRISTMAS TREE FARM, El Cajon. (619) 448-5331, 300 Pepper Dr. Select your own Monterey pine, or choose an already cut Noble, Douglas Fir or Grand Fir tree. A petting zoo, hayrides, and a small store with fresh winter greens are also on the premises. Open the day after Thanksgiving through December 22, daily, 9am - 9pm.

FESTIVAL OF CULTURES, Orange. (800) 493-3276 / www.greenmeadowsproductions.com, 701 S. Glassell St. at William Hart Park. See entry on page 608 for details.

FESTIVAL OF LIGHTS, Riverside. (909) 788-9556 / www.missioninnmuseum.com, Mission Inn Ave and Main St. The Main Street (therefore outdoor) mall is decked out with thousands of lights, including the historic Mission Inn. View Victorian Christmas animated scenes and characters and take a tour of the Inn. (The tour is $8 per person and advanced reservations are needed.) Add to the festivities by taking a horse-drawn carriage ride - call Carriages by Margaret at (909) 789-1620 / www.carriagesbymargaret.com.

FESTIVAL OF LIGHTS PARADE, Palm Springs. (760) 778-8415 / www.palm-springs.org, on Palm Canyon Dr. near Ramon Rd. The one-day holiday parade includes floats, bands, people, vehicles, and even animals festooned in white lights. Admission is free.

FIRST NIGHT, Escondido. (760) 639-0220 / www.firstnightescondido.com, Food and good clean fun (no alcohol allowed) are a great way to celebrate the New Year. This First Night celebration has thirteen stages for dance, including ballet, modern, and Asian-Pacific, and for music. See artist demonstrations such as gourd painting, glass etching, weavers, and more. Kids have special activities such as face painting, petting zoo, and such. Family fireworks are lit at 8pm; the fireworks extravaganza is at midnight.

FIRST NIGHT, Fullerton. (714) 738-6575 or (714) 738-6545 / www.firstnight.com, bordered by Lemon, Malden, Chapman, and Commonwealth sts. Bring in the New Year all night long! Activities include entrance to the Fullerton Museum Center, music and dancing in the streets, and a fun zone for kids that includes kid's karaoke, face painting, a petting zoo, and rides. Fireworks light up your life at midnight! First Night fun happens between 7pm - midnight. Tickets are $12 for adults; $8 for ages 11 and under.

FIRST NIGHT, San Diego. (619) 296-8731 / www.firstnight.com, Embarcadero Marina Park at Seaport Village. See above descriptions. This location includes llama rides, rock climbing, puppet shows, karaoke, Renaissance and Native American camps, and more.

FIRST NIGHT, Santa Fe Springs. (562) 863-4896 or (562) 868-0511, See above descriptions.

FIRST NIGHT, Whittier. (562) 464-3360 / www.firstnightwhittier.org, the bordering streets are Walnut, Philadelphia, Washington, and Pointer. See above description. This First Night starts at about 3pm with kids crafts, a snow play area and so much more, with the seventeen entertainment venues beginning around 6pm. See above entries for more description. Admission is $10 for adults; ages 10 and under are free.

FLOATING PARADE OF 1,000 LIGHTS, Long Beach. (562) 435-4093 / www.shorelineyachtclub.com, Come enjoy the boats on parade that are adorned with Christmas lights and decorations. Prizes are awarded in several categories. The best views are from Shoreline Village, particularly Parkers Lighthouse, although parking is at a premium.

GARDEN GROVE WINTERFEST CARNIVAL, Garden Grove. (714) 741-5000 / www.garden-grove.org, 9301 Westminster at Garden Grove Park. A lot of holiday fun is packed into the first Saturday of this month! Start off with a pancake breakfast and move on to the snow play area, pictures with Santa, games, inflatable bounces, and a crafts area where kids can make a variety of projects such as ornaments, wrapping paper, Christmas cards, and more. The carnival runs from 9am - 2pm. Admission includes pancake breakfast and activities - $8 for adults; $5 for ages 3 - 12; children 2 and under are free.

GLORY OF CHRISTMAS, Garden Grove. (714) 54-GLORY (544-5679) / www.crystalcathedral.org, 12141 Lewis St. at the Crystal Cathedral. Come see this ninety-minute, absolutely spectacular, musical production that is a reenactment of the miraculous birth of Jesus Christ. It's complete with live animals and angels soaring overhead. (Arrive a little early and see the animals in a farm enclosure towards the back of the parking lot.) Although show times vary they are usually at 6:30pm and 8:30pm nightly (no shows on Mon.), with additional shows at 4:30pm on selected Sat. and Sun. Tickets are $30 - $40 for adults; $2 less for srs. and ages 12 and under. Ask about family discount nights, when tickets are $18 per person.

GRIFFITH PARK LIGHT FESTIVAL, Los Angeles. See November entry (pg. 609) for details.

HARVEST FESTIVAL, Pomona. (800) 321-1213 / www.harvestfestival.com, 1101 McKinley Ave. at Fairplex at the Pomona County Fairgrounds. See October entry for Harvest Festival Ventura (pg. 603) for details.

HOLIDAY BOWL PARADE, San Diego. (619) 283-5808 / www.pacificlifeholidaybowl.com, Harbor Drive. Although football is the focal point of this one-day event, the colorful parade is also a highlight. Floats, inflatable balloons, numerous bands, and other entertainment await sports fans of all ages. The two-hour parade begins at 10am. Admission is free. Grandstand seating is $10.

HOLIDAY CHRISTMAS PARADE, Oxnard. (800) 269-6273 / www.oxnardtourism.com, The one-day hometown parade on this first Saturday in December includes floats, bands, entertainment, and awards ceremony. Admission is free.

HOLIDAY IN THE PARK, San Diego. (619) 220-5422 / www.parks.ca.gov, between San Diego Ave. and Twiggs St. in Old Town San Diego State Historic Park. Walk through the park to and enjoy on-going crafts for kids, live holiday music, walking tours of Old Town by lantern light, performances of a historic nativity play called *La Pastorela*, and goodies to purchase and eat. Look up the park on page 423. Open Fri. and Sat., 5:30pm - 9:30pm. Free admission.

HOLIDAY OF LIGHTS, Del Mar. See November entry (pg. 609) for details.

HOW THE GRINCH STOLE CHRISTMAS, San Diego. See November entry (pg. 609) for details.

ICE SKATING, Los Angeles. (213) 847-4970 or (213) 622-4083 / www.laparks.org, 532 S. Olive near Hill St. and 5th and 6th sts. at Pershing Square. Ice skate outside in sunny Southern California for the month of December through mid January. As the rink is sponsored by the L.A. Kings, free hockey clinics are given on certain weekends. Open Mon. - Thurs., noon - 9pm; Fri. - Sat., 11am - 10pm; Sun., 11am - 9pm. Admission is $7 an hour; $2.50 for skate rentals.

ICE SKATING. Huntington Beach, Irvine, W. Los Angeles, Woodland Hills. See November entry (pg. 609) for details.

LAS POSADAS, Long Beach. (562) 431-3541, 6400 Bixby Hill Rd. at Rancho Los Alamitos. See below description. The stable has live animals. Tour the museum rooms while enjoying seasonal music and refreshments. Open Sat., 2pm - 7:30pm; Sun., 2pm - 7pm. Call to make reservations. $10 - $15 per person.

LAS POSADAS, Los Angeles. (213) 625-5045 or (213) 625-7074 / www.ci.la.ca.us/ELP; www.olvera-street.com, Olvera Street. Guests join in a candlelight procession led by actors portraying Mary and Joseph as the couple searches for shelter. The Christmas pageant ends with a more modern celebration of breaking open a pinata. The procession starts at about 7pm. Admission is free.

LAS POSADAS, San Diego. (858) 459-2880 / www.bazaardelmundo.com, Juan St. at Old Town State Historic Park. Same description as above. Procession begins at 7pm. Admission is free.

LIGHTED STREETS, all over. Is there a street or two in your neighborhood that the owners have gone all out to decorate every year? One of our family traditions is to choose one special night during the Christmas season, go out to a restaurant, and walk up and down the festive streets to enjoy the lights and displays.

LIVE OAK CANYON CHRISTMAS TREE FARM, Redlands. See November entry (pg. 610) for details. Don't miss this one!

LIVING CHRISTMAS CAROL, Rancho Cucamonga. (909) 980-6450 / www.christmashouseinn.com, 9240 Archibald Ave. Ba humbug! In cahoots with Capers Production, the huge Victorian-style Christmas House bed and breakfast puts on an interactive play based on Dickens' *A Christmas Carol*. A storyteller (i.e. narrator/guide) greets participants at the door, explaining the premise of the play. Each group of fifteen people walk through eight rooms of the house (all of which have fireplaces), watching and even taking part in the different scenes playing in each one. Over thirty-five actors and actresses, whom visitors view close up, are involved in portraying Scrooge, his Christmas ghosts, the Cratchits, and townspeople. At the end, enjoy cider and warm cookies from Mrs. Cratchit in her kitchen and dance with Scrooge's nephews at the Christmas party. God bless us, every one! Groups of fifteen people depart every fifteen minutes for the hour-long play which runs Dec. 23 from 4pm - 8pm; Dec. 24, 1pm - 6pm. Advanced reservations are a must (and tickets sell out early.) Admission is $20 for adults; $10 for ages 3 - 12; children 2 and under are free. (No strollers allowed.)

LOGAN'S CANDY, Ontario. See November entry (pg. 610) for details.

LONG BEACH CHRISTMAS WATER PARADE, Long Beach. (562) 570-5333 or (562) 436-3645, Naples Canals. Boat-owners cover their boats with Christmas lights, and parade past decorated homes along the Naples canals. If you miss the boat parade, just seeing the homes along here is a special treat. Call for dates and hours. Admission is free.

LOS ANGELES HARBOR CHRISTMAS BOAT PARADE, San Pedro. (310) 832-7272 / www.sanpedrochamber.com, Ports O' Call. Owners go all out to decorate their boats and compete for the best in a wonderful parade that is put on the second Sat. of December.

MARINA DEL REY CHRISTMAS BOAT PARADE, Marina del Rey. (310) 823-5411or (310) 822-9455 / www.mdrlights.org, On the second Saturday of December over eighty boats, decorated to the hilt with Christmas lights and decorations, sail around the marina's main channel. The parade is exciting with winners chosen for Best Theme, Best Humor, Best Music, etc. The best views are from Burton Chase Park or Fisherman's Village.

MESSIAH SING-ALONG, Los Angeles. (213) 365-3500 / www.lamc.org, Dorothy Chandler Pavilion. Sing it out as you join in on one of the most acclaimed chorale presentations. Call for times, dates, and prices. Call your local orchestra as many others offer this same opportunity.

MISSION BAY CHRISTMAS BOAT PARADE OF LIGHTS, Mission Bay. (858) 488-0501 / www.mbyc.org, The lighted boat parade (the title of the event is self-explanatory) begins at Quivira Basin at 7pm and ends with lighting of the Sea World Sky Tower Tree of Lights at 9pm. The best viewing is along Crown Point, the east side of Vacation Island, or the west side of Fiesta Island. There is no admission.

MONARCH BUTTERFLIES, Ventura. (805) 658-4726 - the Office of Cultural Affairs for "tour" info / www.ci.ventura.ca.us, Camino Real Park. Thousands of Monarch butterflies arrive at the park during this month. Call for tour times and costs.

MUSEUMS, All over. Many of your favorite museums get all decked out for the holidays, particularly the historical homes. Many also offer holiday programs with special family activities.

NATIVITY PAGEANT, Solvang. (800) 549-7272 or (805) 688-6144 / www.solvangusa.com; www.pcpa.org, 420 2nd Street at the outdoor Festival Theater. The narrated nativity pageant is performed in Solvang's outdoor theater (dress warmly) on a Saturday evening in December. The program features a choir, characters in full costumes, and live animals. Free admission / first come first served.

NUTCRACKER. Numerous venues all over Southern California present this classic ballet to the timeless music of Tchaikovsky. This is an enchanting way to expose your children to the beauty of ballet and classical music because of the costumed characters and gripping storyline. Call your local theater.

OLD FASHIONED CHRISTMAS VILLAGE, La Mesa. (619) 462-3000 / www.lamesavillage.com, La Mesa Blvd. between Acacia Ave. and 4th St. Two Fri. and Sat. evenings in a row this winter wonderland boasts twinkling lights, holiday foods, Christmas music, and a children's carnival with hayrides, holiday crafts, puppet shows, and a visit from Santa. Open 6pm - 9pm. Free admission.

PARADE OF LIGHTS / STEARNS WHARF, Santa Barbara. (805) 564-5520, Cabrillo Street along the beach near Stearns Wharf. Watch the twenty, or so, decorated boats sail out of the harbor and parade up and down the shoreline, vying for prizes. The beaches north of Stearns Wharf offer the best vantage points. At the pier, usually around 3pm, is a huge mound of snow for kids to play in and carolers begin to sing holiday songs. The boat parade, which takes place on a Sunday, begins about 5:30pm. Admission is free.

PARADE OF LIGHTS, Ventura. (805) 642-7753 or (805) 985-4852 / www.venturaharborvillage.com, 1500 Spinnaker Dr. at Ventura Harbor Village. This festive boat parade is usually held the first or second weekend in December. Call for specific dates. Take the *Bay Queen*, a "California Sleigh Ride", during the month for an hour-and-a-half cruise, as it goes around the harbor to see homes that are decorated for the holidays. Also, call for the dates when a white Christmas is celebrated at the Village with snow brought in specially for kids.

PLANETARIUM SHOWS - CHRISTMAS SHOW / STAR OF BETHLEHEM. Look up planetariums in the main section of the book under Shows and Theaters, in your county. Many of them set the nighttime skies back to the time of Christ's birth during this month. Look at the Star of Bethlehem entry (pg. 617) to get a feel for most planetarium shows.

POINSETTIA FLOWER TOURS, Encinitas. (760) 753-6041 / www.encinitaschamber.com, at Paul Ecke Ranch. One day a year, usually the first Saturday in December, you are invited to take a "tour" of poinsettias at this famous ranch. See the original bright red colored ones and new varieties as you walk through the greenhouses and learn the history of this holiday plant. Make reservations early as this tour always sells out. Call for hours. Reservations are required. Admission is $15 per person.

RANCHO CHRISTMAS, Vista. (760) 724-4082 / www.sdcounty.ca.gov/parks; www.earlysandiego.org, 2210 N. Santa Fe Ave. at Rancho Guajome Adobe. Celebrate Christmas in an atmosphere of yesteryear. Kids crafts, such as candlemaking, dipping candy apples, and making corn husk angels, plus horse-drawn wagon rides, and other fun activities are all here. On Sat., the events culminate in the lighting of the luminaries and a caroling program. Look up Rancho Guajome Adobe (pg. 427) for more details. Open Sat., 10am - 6pm; Sun., 10am - 4pm. Admission is $5 for adults; $3 for ages 5 - 12; children 4 and under are free.

REINDEER ROMP, Los Angeles. See November entry (pg. 611) for details.

ROSE PARADE DECORATING, Various. (626) 449-4100 / www.tournamentofroses.com, Call to ask where your assistance might be needed in helping to decorate the Rose Parade floats. Children at least 13 years old and whose parents are Auto Club members can help decorate the AAA float. Call (714) 424-8190 for more information.

ROSE PARADE FLOAT VIEWING, Pasadena. (626) 449-4100 / www.tournamentofroses.com, Rosemont Pavilion - 700 Seco St.; Rose Palace - 835 S. Raymond Ave.; Brookside Pavilion - 1001 Rose Bowl Dr. at the Rose Bowl, which has access to those will physical disabilities, on the west side of the Rose Bowl Stadium; and Buena Vista Pavilion - 2144 Buena Vista in Duarte. Come see the famous floats as they are being made, from December 28 through December 31. Workers spend weeks meticulously decorating them using plants, seeds, tree bark, flowers, and single petals. Viewing times are from 9am - 9pm. Call to verify dates and times. Admission is $5.

SAN PASQUAL BATTLE REENACTMENT, San Pasqual. (760) 737-2201 / www.parks.ca.gov, 15808 San Pasqual Valley Rd. See the San Pasqual Battlefield State Historic Park (pg. 399). On a Sunday, reenactors dress up as mountain men and other pivitol figures from the mid 1800's and they pitch tents; provide music, crafts (i.e. adobe brick making, candle making, etc.), and dance of the era; and best of all, they reenact battles (even fire cannons!) at 11am and 2pm. Open 10am - 4pm. Admission is free.

STAR OF BETHLEHEM, Santa Ana. (714) 564-6356 / www.sac.edu/activities, 1530 W. 17th St. at Tessmann Planetarium (pg. 261) on Santa Ana College campus. For four nighttime shows and seven daytime shows, starting the end of November through the middle of December, the planetarium sky is reset to around the time of Jesus' birth. After an introduction of astronomy, the astronomer/narrator - via a slide show, Bible passages, and using the planetarium "skies"- discusses how (and when) this miraculous phenomena called the Star of Bethlehem came about, including possible origins of a nova, comet, star, meteorite, or aligning planets. I won't give away the ending. The one-hour presentation is educational, as well as a wonderful blend of science and faith. Nighttime shows start at 7:30pm; daytimes shows at 9:30am. Tickets are $3 per person. Reserve your space early as shows sell out.

TEMECULA'S ELECTRIC LIGHT PARADE, Temecula. (909) 694-6412 / www.cityoftemecula.org, A spectacular evening parade features floats, marching bands, and equestrian groups all lit up. The shows begins at 7pm. Admission is free.

TOURNAMENT OF ROSES FAMILY FESTIVAL, Pasadena. (626) 793-9911 - 24-hr. hotline; (626) 449-ROSE (7073); or (626) 449-4100 / www.tournamentofroses.com, 1001 Rose Bowl Dr. at the Rose Bowl. For three or four days before the big parade and football game, fans can participate in numerous activities inside, outside, and around the bowl. Come look at the Tournament of Roses Museum, which is a 10,000 square-foot tent that houses historic photographs, artifacts, and interactive exhibits. Take a tour of the stadium. Play at the Sports Village, where visitors take part in interactive contests such as kicking a field goal, running obstacle courses, cheerleading and coaching clinics, and visits by former Rose Bowl players. Experience Expo Village, which has free displays and activities for the family (past participants have included Legoland and the Sheriff's Department, among others). Eat at a food court. See the floats being decorated. (See Rose Parade Float Viewing on page 617 for details.) Bandfest, watching the high school marching bands from around the world practicing and performing, is $10 for adults; $5 for ages 4 - 12. Equestfest, located outside the bowl, is free. Here some of the parade's precision equestrian units are showcased, as well as exhibits, such as horse-drawn fire wagons, the unique camel and ostrich races, roping and riding demonstrations, country music, and a Civil War encampment. Ultimate fans can attend the Rose Bowl Kickoff Luncheon ($50 per person) and dine with everybody who's anybody in the Rose Parade or game, including the Rose Queen and her court, athletes, coaches, officials, and the grand marshal. Tickets are available through Ticketmaster at (213) 480-3232 or (714) 740-2000. Exact events and times change every year, so check the website to plan your outing. Call for prices on attractions.

TREE LIGHTING CEREMONY, Long Beach. (562) 435-3511 / www.queenmary.com, 1126 Queens Highway at the Queen Mary. "Deck the hull" with the tree lighting ceremony which includes a holiday sing-a-long. The ceremony goes from 6pm - 7:30pm, but the public may board at 4:30pm and take a look around the ship. Admission is free after 4:30pm and parking is reduced.

UNIVERSAL CITYWALK'S ICE RINK / DRIVE-IN MOVIE, Universal City. See November entry (pg. 611) for details.

UPTOWN HOLIDAY PARADE, Whittier. (562) 696-2662 or (562) 696-3872 / www.whittieruptown.org, This one-day uptown parade, for us downtown folks, features more than 120 entries including highschool bands, equestrian and marching units, floats, and Santa Claus. Admission is free.

VICTORIAN CHRISTMAS, Lake Forest. (949) 855-2028 / www.ocparks.com, 25151 Serrano Rd. at Heritage Hill Historical Park. On the first Saturday in December, experience Christmas as it was during the turn-of-the century. Walk through these four historic buildings, which are festooned with old-fashioned decorations. Over forty exhibits display and demonstrate homemade handicrafts like wooden carvings and lace making. A popular display is the antique engines which include a milking machine, a corn husker, and a corn grinder. A free children's crafts area is available for kids to make their own special creations. Genteel entertainment is provided, and Saint Nicholas also pays a visit. Open 10am - 4pm. Admission is $4 for adults; $3 for ages 3 - 12; children 2 and under are free.

VICTORIAN CHRISTMAS, Wilmington. (310) 548-7777 / www.banningmuseum.org, 401 E. M St. at the General Phineas Banning Residence Museum. Kick off the Yuletide season by immersing yourself in the 19th century on the first weekend in December at the Banning Museum. Docents greet you dressed in period costumes and show you around the beautifully decorated house/museum. The lavish Victorian adornments are quite lovely and the costumed carolers, bell ringers, and musicians complete the ambiance. You may even take a horse and trolley ride to and from the Drum Barracks Museum, which is just down the street. Open Sat. - Sun., 11am - 4pm. Admission is free. The decorated house is also open to tour through most of December at regular admission prices.

WILDLIGHTS, Palm Desert. (760) 346-5694 / www.livingdesert.org, 47900 Portola Ave. at the Living Desert Wildlife and Botanical Park. A special display, up for only six-weeks, features nearly a dozen, larger-than-life animal and other sculptures illuminated in lights. This can include a gigantic teddy bear, a thirty-foot snowman, assorted desert critters, and a golfing Santa. Live entertainment, good food, a huge model train exhibit, and a visit from Santa Claus (bring your own camera) add to the holiday festivities. The park is open 6pm - 9pm for these wild nights. (The animals are put to bed - it's a people-only party.) Admission is $6.50 for adults; $4.25 for children 11 and under.

WINTERLIT CELEBRATION, Santa Monica. See November entry (pg. 611) for details.

WINTER SNOW FROLIC, Temecula. (909) 694-6480 / www.cityoftemecula.org, 30875 Rancho Vista Rd. at the Temecula Community Rec Center. I'm dreaming of a white Christmas, so frolicking in tons of fresh snow helps the dream come true. Bring mittens and dress warmly. Start the day by having breakfast with Santa, then enjoy the snow, craft fair and rest of the fun. Breakfast seating is at 8am, 9am, 10am, and 11am. The snow fun goes from 9am - 1pm. Breakfast is $4 per person; admission to the snow and craft fair is free.

WINTER WONDERLAND, Corona del Mar. (949) 644-3151 / www.city.newport-beach.ca.us, between Iris and 5th Ave. at Grant Howald Park. If you don't feel like driving a few hours to the snow, just drive to Corona del Mar for this one-day event. Bring your mittens and have a great time building a snowman or ~~starting~~ having a snow ball fight with your kids. Food and beverages are available for purchase. Open 10am - 1pm. Admission is free.

IDEAS / RESOURCES
(General ideas of where else to go and what to do, plus where to find specific resource information.)

AIRPLANE or HELICOPTER RIDES -
Look in the phone book; call small, local airports for flight information; and/or check the Transportation section for specific flying venues.

ANIMALS (and fertilized chick eggs) -
AA Laboratories at 15075 Weststate in Westminster, (714) 893-5675 / www.egglab.com, sells fertilized eggs - $12.50 for a dozen chick eggs. They also have duck and quail eggs. Incubators rent for $10 a week - home births without the labor pains! Be forewarned, however, that very little instruction comes with your eggs and incubator. Tips: Go to the library to research the process by checking out picture books of developing chicks and ducks. Pick up an information sheet and feed at Blacksmith's Corner, (562) 531-0386 in Bellflower, or at a similar pet store near you. And yes, if you do not want to raise the birds, AA Labs will (usually) take them back and donate them to farms, zoos, etc.
Insect Lore, (800) LIVE BUG (548-3284) / www.insectlore.com. This catalog offers living science kits, giving families the opportunity to observe insects and other critters growing and transforming. Our favorite kits are the butterfly; earthworms and compost; praying mantis; silkworm; ladybird beetles (i.e. ladybugs, to lay people); and frog hatchery. Each kit comes with instructions, information, and eggs or embryos. The catalog also offers owl pellets to dissect, plus other science experiments, books, and visual aids.
Wagon Train Feed & Pet in Orange, (714) 639-7932 / www.wagontrain.net, is a small pet store that also sells chick, duck, and quail eggs, as well as incubators. (See the Pet Store entry in this section for more detail.)
Check out www.riovistaproducts.com/dealers/cal.html for a comprehensive listing of animal and pet stores and suppliers in your area.

ARCHERY -
Get on target and call the National Archery Association, (719) 866-4576 / www.usarchery.org, who refers callers to local clubs and places to practice. Look under the Great Outdoors section for local parks that offer archery ranges.

ARTS AND CRAFTS -
Many places, including libraries and bookstores, offer free or minimal fee classes / workshops for kids. Also check out craft and handy stores, such as:
Michaels, (800) MICHAEL (642-4235) / www.michaels.com - ask about Kids Club Saturdays
Home Depot, (800) 469-3376 / www.homedepot.com - most offer free Sat. workshops
Lakeshore Learning Materials stores, (800) 421-5354 / www.lakeshorelearning.com
Piecemakers Country Store, (714) 641-3112 / www.piecemakers.com
Zany Brainy, (877) WOW-KIDS (969-5437) / www.zanybrainy.com
Look under the Arts and Crafts section in the main part of the book, too.

AUDIO TAPES -
The following are some of our favorite, non-singing, tapes / cds:
Adventures in Odyssey, (800) A-FAMILY (232-6459) / www.family.org - Six tapes for about $25. Focus on the Family puts out this series consisting of twelve, half-hour-long, Biblically-based, radio dramas. The stories are centered around a fictional soda shop/Bible room/imagination station/kid's hang-out called Whit's End, and the people that live in the small (made-up) town of Odyssey. Each episode involves kids, families, dilemmas, solutions, morals, wit, and wisdom. I can't recommend these adventures highly enough!
Classical Kids Series - about $10.95 per tape. The tapes can be found in most larger retail record stores or ordered through catalogs such as Rainbow Re-Source Center, (888) 841-3456 / www.rainbowresource.com. Each hour-long tape in this wonderful series tells the story, told in play format, of a famous composer while the composer's music plays in the background. Titles include *Beethoven Lives Upstairs*, *Mozart's Magical Fantasy*, and *Tchaikovsky Discovers America*.

Focus on the Family Radio Theatre Drama, (800) A-FAMILY (232-6459) / www.family.org - Call for prices. Put out by Focus on the Family, as is the above-mentioned Adventures in Odyssey, this series presents fantastic dramatizations using a variety of voices, sound effects, and music. Titles include the *Chronicles of Narnia*, *Squanto*, *My Secret Garden*, *Ben Hur*, *A Christmas Carol*, and more.

Greathall Productions, (800) 477-6234 / www.greathall.com - about $9.95 per tape. Be enthralled by award-winning storyteller, Jim Weiss. Kids (and adults) of all ages will enjoy the masterful retelling of (mostly) classic stories. Tape titles include *Arabian Nights*, *Sherlock Holmes for Children*, *Three Musketeers*, *Giants!*, *Greek Myths*, *Shakespeare for Children*, and *Animal Tales*. Look up JIM WEISS under the Educational Presentations section in the main part of the book.

BASEBALL -

Call for a game schedule and ask about special days, such as fan appreciation day:

Angels at Edison International Field in Anaheim, (888) 796-HALO (4256) / www.angelsbaseball.com

Dodgers at Dodger Stadium in Los Angeles, (323) 224-1-HIT (448) / www.dodgers.com

Padres at PETCO Park in San Diego, (888) - MYPADRES (697-2373) / www.padres.com

Minor league games can be major league fun. Check out teams such as Bakersfield Blaze, (661) 322-1363 / www.bakersfieldblaze.com; High Desert Mavericks, (760) 246-6287 / www.hdmavs.com; Lake Elsinore Storm, (909) 245-4487 / www.stormbaseball.com; Lancaster Jethawks, (661) 726-5400 / www.jethawks.com; Rancho Cucamonga Quakes, (909) 481-5000 / www.rcquakes.com; and San Bernardino Stampede, (909) 888-9922 / www.stampedebaseball.com

High school and college games are exciting, too.

BASKETBALL -

Clippers at Staples Center in Los Angeles, (213) 742-7555 / www.clippers.com

Lakers at Staples Center in Los Angeles, (310) 426-6000 / www.lakers.com

Sparks (a women's pro team) at Staples Centers in Los Angeles, (310) 426-6031 / www.wnba.com/lasparks

Also check out high school and college games.

BATTING CAGES -

"Hey batter batter." Cages are great for hitting practice, in season or out.

BILLIARDS -

Many billiard parlors have a family-friendly atmosphere.

BOOKS -

Numerous book stores offer story times and/or craft times. Some of the bigger book stores, such as Barnes & Noble and Borders, have a huge children's selection, as well as a children's reading area. Many smaller bookstores cater specifically to kids and are delightful to browse through. Also look up Educational Toys, Books, and Games in this section. A & S Bargain Books has twenty-seven locations in Southern California that sell new books for bargain basement prices. Contact www.asbargainbooks.com for more information. Used book stores are a terrific bargain. To name just a few, try:

Acres of Books in Long Beach, (562) 437-6980 / www.acresofbooks.com - one of the largest used book stores in the world.

Book Baron in Anaheim, (714) 527-7022 / www.bookbaron.com - vintage and used books.

Book City in Hollywood, (323) 466-2525 / www.hollywoodbookcity.com and in Burbank, (818) 848-4417 - new and used books, and movie scripts.

Brindles in Tustin, (714) 731-5773 - new and used books.

Thrift stores and garage sales are another great resource for used books as are libraries, as they often host sales once or twice a year.

BOWLING -

Many alleys offer bumper bowling for kids, where the gutters are covered so kids almost always knock down a pin or two. (This sounds like something right up my alley, also.) Cosmic Bowling, sometimes known as Rock 'n Roll Bowl, is great fun, too. Usually played at nighttime, ordinary lights are turned out and neon lights take over. The pins, balls, and lanes glow in the dark and rock music and/or videos play. All this while trying to bowl! Call your local bowling alley.

CAMPING -

Campgrounds mentioned in this book are usually listed under the Great Outdoors section. Call Parknet, (800) 444-7275 / www.reserveamerica.com, to make camping reservations at any California State Park. Check your library or local book store for books written just on camping. A starting point are several books put out by Peterson (not me!) and the Guide to ACA-Accredited Camps in Southern California. Check out the American Camping Association at (800) 428-CAMP (2267) / www.acacamps.org or the National Camping Association at (800) 966-2267 / www.summercamp.org.

CELEBRITIES -

Call the Walk of Fame at Hollywood Chamber of Commerce, (323) 469-8311 / www.hollywoodchamber.net, to find out when the next celebrity will be honored with a ceremony dedicating his/her star along this famous "walk." Ceremonies occur almost monthly.

CIRCUS -

Check newspapers and sports arenas, or try the following numbers to see when the circus is coming to town. Ask about specials or opening day events:

Big Apple Circus, www.bigapplecircus.org - similar to Cirque Du Solei (see below), this top-notch circus which performs mainly in New York, but does travel, features acrobats and a storyline.

Carson & Barnes, (580) 326-3173 / www.carsonbarnescircus.com - features five rings of continual action, with hundreds of animals, international performers, and lots of razzle dazzle.

Circus Flora, (314) 533-1285 / www.circusflora.org - named for its African elephant, this circus which performs mainly in St. Louis, but does travel, specializes in new circus-style ensemble acts. An intimate show performed in a 1,500-seat Big Top.

Circus Vargas, (760) 248-6807 / www.circusvargas.com - this one-ring, 2,000-seat tent circus that performs primarily in California, has a small-town feel. See an elephants, horses, dogs, cats, and tigers, and human performers in a two-hour show.

Cirque Du Solei, www.cirquedusoleil.com - artsy and eccentric, much-acclaimed productions with frequent theme changes that focus on "impossible" body movements. Very unique! Note: No animals are used in this circus.

Fern Street Circus, (619) 235-9756 / www.fernstreetcircus.org - San Diego-based troupe with aerialists, clowns, and acrobats for whimsical entertainment; from a single clown to a three-ring circus. Ask about programs that teach children circus skills in San Diego.

Ringling Bros. & Barnum and Bailey Circus, (703) 448-4000 / www.ringling.com - "the greatest show on earth", this multi-ring circus is one of the best known in the Western world. It involves daring animal acts, clowns, and feats of skill presented with theatrical flare and state-of-the-art lighting. At some locations, arrive an hour before show time to get into the arena with the clowns and participate in some of the tricks - swinging on a trapeze swing, riding a unicycle (with lots of help), and more.

UniverSoul, (800) 316-7439 / www.universoulcircus.com - African-American-owned and operated touring circus performs traditional circus acts incorporating clowns and animals against a backdrop of rhythm and blues, urban, hip-hop, and gospel music.

CONSTRUCTION SITES -

If you're "toolin'" around, these sites can give your youngster constructive ideas to build on.

CONVENTION CENTERS -

as Kid's Stuff Expos, toy shows, circuses, and much more. Contact them intermittently to see what's going on:

Anaheim, (714) 765-8950 / www.anaheimconventioncenter.com
Long Beach, (562) 436-3661 or (562) 436-3636 / www.longbeachcc.com
Los Angeles, (213) 741-1151 / www.lacclink.com

Ontario, (909) 937-3000 / www.ontariocc.com
San Diego, (619) 525-5000 / www.sdccc.org
Santa Barbara, (805) 687-0766 / www.earlwarren.com

COOKING -

Kid's cooking classes are offered throughout the year through local parks and recreation departments. A few other suggestions are listed below:

Bristol Farms in Manhattan Beach, (310) 726-1350 / www.bristolfarms.com - three-hour classes offer a variety of subjects for kids 7-12 or teens 13-17. Contact them for other locations.

Let's Get Cooking in Westlake Village, (818) 991-3940 / www.letsgetcookin.com - once-a-month parent/child classes are held on Sat., as well as workshops for pre-teen/teen, and even classes for children ages 6 years and up. Cook up something new and wonderful if you have a birthday party here, too.

San Diego Culinary Institute in La Mesa, (619) 644-2100 /www.sdci-inc.com adult and teen cooking classes are available.

Sur La Table in Los Angeles (323) 954-9190; Newport Beach (949) 640-0200; and Santa Monica (310) 395-9712 - classes are offered for ages 6 - 12 and 12 - 16, depending on the location.

COUPONS -

Call the visitors center (or Chamber of Commerce) of the city you are planning to visit as they often offer discount coupons towards attractions. For instance, "The Family Values Coupon Book" for Orange County, features savings at over fifty area attractions, hotels, restaurants, and shops. Call (714) 765-8888 / www.anaheimoc.org for information. The San Diego Convention and Visitor's Bureau, (619) 236-1212 / www.sandiego.org, offers a free "value coupon" booklet that saves on main attractions, harbor cruises, restaurants, and more. Always check the internet for coupons, too.

CPR/FIRST AID CLASSES -

Call your local Red Cross or hospital for class information. This is a great class for you, your kids (when they are old enough) and for babysitters to take.

EDUCATIONAL TOYS, BOOKS, and GAMES -

There are numerous stores and catalogs that offer good quality, educational products. Some of our favorite stores include Bright Ideas for Learning (in Camarillo), F.A.O. Schwartz, Imaginarium, Lakeshore Learning, Learning Express, Parent Teacher Aids (in Simi Valley), and Zany Brainy, an immediate favorite, (877) WOW KIDS (969-5437) / www.zanybrainy.com. Look in your local telephone directory for the above listings, and look in the Yellow Pages for two other great resources - teacher supply stores and children's bookstores. Many museum gift shops offer a terrific line of educational (and fun) supplies. Also check out the following companies that offer catalogs and/or home workshops for their products:

Discovery Toys, (800) 426-4777 / www.discoverytoysinc.com - carries a fantastic line of toys, books, games, and computer software.

Dorling Kindersley Books, (212) 213-4800 / www.dk.com - offers outstanding books.

Usborne Books, (800) 475-4522 / www.edcpub.com - sells top-notch, visually-exciting books.

ETHNIC NEIGHBORHOODS -

Where can you take your family to experience another culture? Oftentimes, right in your own neighborhood, where people from other countries have settled and carved out a niche based on their homeland. Here are just a few options to check out, whether it's to try different foods or to shop for items not found in Target.

Armenian foods in Glendale, near Colorado St. and Glendale Ave.: Armenian cuisine, including several kabob places, pastries, lamb, quail, chicken, and more.

Chinatown in Los Angeles, along Broadway: Walk the streets to see a proliferation of red and gold colored buildings with pagoda-style roofs. See CHINATOWN (pg. \\CHINATOWN\\) for more details.

Korean neighborhoods abound in downtown Long Beach.

Little India in Artesia, on Pioneer Boulevard, between Ashworth and South sts: Aromatic restaurants, small grocery stores that carry an array of spices, and shops that prefer brightly-colored saris, among other items, beckon customers along this street.

Little Tokyo in Los Angeles, near 1st and Central sts: This area has the JAPANESE AMERICAN NATIONAL MUSEUM (pg. \\JAPANESEAMERICANNAT\\), lots of shops and restaurants, and many yearly activities.

EQUESTRIAN SHOWS -

English and Western riding, jumping, and prancing are all part of seeing a horse show. Call your local equestrian center for dates and times and/or check the Calendar section for special event shows.

FAIR GROUNDS -

Numerous events are held at the following locations throughout the year, such as gem shows, reptiles expos, fairs, cat shows, circuses, demolition derbies, Scottish games, horse shows, and lots more. Call for a schedule:

Los Angeles in Lancaster, (661) 948-6066 / www.avfair.com
Los Angeles in Pomona, (909) 623-3111 / www.fairplex.com
Orange in Costa Mesa, (714) 708-FAIR (3247) / www.ocfair.com
Riverside in Indio, (800) 811-FAIR (3247) or (760) 863-8247 / www.datefest.org
Riverside in Lake Perris, (909) 657-1569 / www.farmersfair.com
San Bernardino in Victorville, (760) 951-2200 / www.sbcfair.com
San Diego in Del Mar, (858) 755-1161 / www.sdfair.com
Santa Barbara in Santa Barbara, (805) 6887-0766 / www.earlwarren.com
Santa Barbara in Santa Maria, (800)-549-0036 / www.santamariafairpark.com
Ventura in Ventura, (805) 648-3376 / www.seasidepark.org

FARMER'S MARKETS -

See Edible Adventures in the main section of the book for details.

FILMING -

Interested in seeing actual filming? The L.A. Film Office, (323) 957-1000 / www.eidc.com, provides a free "shoot sheet" that lists expected location shots for any given day. The Los Angeles Convention and Visitor's Bureau, (213) 689-8822 / www.visitlanow.com, can help with directions.

FISHING -

Here's the hook - you have to look under the Great Outdoors section for places to go fish. Contact the Department of Fish and Game, (562) 590-4835 / www.dfg.ca.gov, for free information on fishing, including maps to local lakes, fishing events, hatcheries, stocking guides, fishing clinics, and regulations.

FOOTBALL -

Chargers at Qualcomm Stadium in San Diego, 877-CHARGERS (242-7437) / www.chargers.com
Los Angeles Avengers at Staples Center in Los Angeles, (888) AVENGERS (283-6437) / www.laavengers.com
Riptide at Sports Arena in San Diego (arena football), (619) 224-4625 / www.sandiegoarena.com
High school and college games are fun, too.

GYM CLASSES FOR KIDS -

Some suggestions are:

Creative Kids in Los Angeles, (310) 473-6090 - classes in gymnastics, music, art, fairytale theater, cooking, and more.

Gymboree, www.gymboree.com - check your local phone book for listings. Classes are offered for parents and their children - newborns through 4 years old - that include easy exercise, songs, bubbles, and visits from Gymbo, the clown.

My Gym, (800) 4-My-Gyms (469-4967) / www.my-gym.com - classes in tumbling, songs, games, and gymnastics are offered for the younger set. The franchises are everywhere in Southern California.

Y.M.C.A. - Fun fitness programs are available just for kids.

HOBBIES AND MODELS -

Kids like to collect - anything! For example - bottlecaps, dolls, miniatures (dollhouses), postcards, rocks, sports cards, and stamps. Other hobby ideas include model-making (i.e. cars, planes, rockets, and trains), creating jewelry, and sewing.

HOCKEY -

Ice Dogs at Long Beach Arena in Long Beach, (562) 423-3647/ www.icedogs.com
Kings at Staples Center in Los Angeles, (888) KINGSLA (546-4752) / www.lakings.com
Mighty Ducks at Arrowhead Pond in Anaheim, (714) 940-2101 / www.mightyducks.com
San Diego Gulls at the Sports Arena in San Diego, (619) 224-4625 / www.sandiegoarena.com

HORSEBACK RIDING -

Saddle up for a terrific family outing! Call your local equestrian center.

HOT AIR BALLOON RIDES -

Up, up and away! Hot air balloon rides are recommended for ages 8 and up, as younger children might get scared of the flames shooting out (i.e. the "hot air"); they might get bored; and they can't see very well over the basket. All ages, however, are enthralled by watching the balloon being inflated, either in the morning or at sunset! For a real colorful outing, look in the Calendar section or call the below numbers for Hot Air Balloon Festivals. Most of the companies listed fly over Del Mar, Palm Springs, and/or Temecula. Flights are about an hour and some include a champagne breakfast. Prices are per person. These are just a few names and numbers to get you started:

California Dreamin' in Encinitas, (800) 373-3359 / www.californiadreamin.com - between $128 - $138.
Fantasy Balloon Flights in Palm Springs, (800) GO ABOVE (462-2683) / www.fantasyballoonflights.com
    adults $150, kids 12 and under $125.
Skysurfer Balloon Company, (800) 660-6809 / www.sandiegohotairballoons.com - $120 - $130.
Sunrise Balloons, (800) 548-9912 / www.sunriseballoons.com - call for pricing.

ICE SKATING -

Go figure! Call, for instance, the arenas listed below:

Glacial Garden Skating Arena in Lakewood, (562) 429-1805 / www.glacialgardens.com - three rinks. They also offer broomball which is *fun*tastic! There is another location in Anaheim.
Disney Ice in Anaheim, (714) 535-7465 / www.disneyice.com - offers public sessions, plus figure skating and hockey classes. It's also the rink where the Mighty Ducks practice!
Also look up the Calendar section in December for Ice Skating listings.

JUNKYARDS -

One man's trash is another child's treasure. For kids who like to take things apart and make new creations, junkyards are inspiring places to investigate.

KITE FLYING -

Go fly a kite! Check the Calendar section for Kite Festivals.

LIBRARIES -

Your local library has a lot to offer. Get a group together and ask for a tour. Besides book, video, and cassette lending, many offer free storytelling on a regular basis and/or finger plays, puppet shows, magic shows, and crafts. Some libraries also encourage your bookworms by offering summer reading programs. A few times throughout the year libraries hold sales where book prices are practically a steal. *A Treasure Hunt in My Library*, by Candace Jackson, is an outstanding book, with curriculum, that takes kids on a tour of the library and teaches them how to use it. Order it through a bookstore or by contacting www.museummania.com.

MAGAZINES -

If you only receive one magazine, make it *Family Fun*. Put out by Disney, each edition is <u>packed</u> with do-able crafts, snacks, party ideas, games, activities, and family-friendly places to travel. Pick it up at the newsstand or call (800) 289-4849 / www.familyfun.com for subscription information. It is currently $14.95 for 10 issues.

MALLS -

Going to the mall <u>can</u> be a fun excursion with kids (honest!), especially if the mall has "extra" features, such as a merry-go-round or fountains, or, if it's spectacular in design, has unique shops and restaurants, etc. See the Malls section in the main part of the book for some of our top picks.

MONEY -

Collect money from foreign countries without the expense of traveling there. Call (800) CURRENCY (287-7362) / www.travelex.com to find the nearest Thomas Cook Foreign Exchange Currency. You may exchange any sum of money for currency from an unlimited number of countries, for only one transaction fee. The fee is usually a $5 service fee or 1% of the U.S. amount, whichever amount is greater.

MOVIE THEATERS -

An obvious choice, but movies, and especially matinees, can be a relatively inexpensive and fun treat. For instance:

Super Saver in Norwalk, (562) 868-9694 - showings on certain days of the week are only $2.50.

El Capitan Theater - see this in the main entry of the book on page \\ELCAPITAN\\.

Drive In Theaters include: Azusa Foothill in Azusa, (626) 334-0263; Pacific Vineland Theater in Pico Rivera, (562) 948-3671; South Bay Triple Drive-In/Swap Meet in San Diego, (619) 423-2727; Van Buren Arlington in Riverside (909) 688-2360; and Vineland Drive-In in City of Industry, (626) 961-9262 or (626) 369-7224.

The Bridge: Cinema De Lux in Los Angeles, (310) 568-9950 / www.thebridgecinema.com - Silver Screen Classics show once a month for $1. See page \\BRIDGECINEMADELUX\\ for details.

UltraStar Cinemas / www.ultrastarmovies.com - the theater has location in Riverside, San Bernardino, and San Diego counties. Early bird and discount Tuesdays are only $4 per person.

See the Shows and Theaters section in the main part of the book for IMAX Theaters.

MUSEUMS -

See the Museums legend for information and ideas on how to get the most out of a visit.

You can $ee L.A., or ¢.E.E. L.A. The Cultural Entertainment Events card (C.E.E.) offers entrance to seventeen top museums for only $43.95 a year for you and your family! These museums include Autry Museum, Hollywood Entertainment Museums, Bowers Kidseum, Petersen, and Richard Nixon. Call (818) 957-9400 / www.cee-la.com for more information. The card will also save you money on sporting and theater events.

PARKS -

Almost every local park offers classes or sports programs for free, or at a minimal cost. Ask about kid's cooking classes, sidewalk chalk art day, etc. For a comprehensive listing of California state parks, call (800) 777-0369 or (916) 653-6995 / www.parks.ca.gov.

PET STORES -

This is a fun, mini-outing. Ask about tours. Cuddly puppies and adorable rabbits are great, but so are unusual and exotic animals found at some of the stores listed below. Look in your phone book for fish and bird stores, too. Check out www.riovistaproducts.com/dealers/cal.html for a comprehensive listing of animal and pet stores and suppliers in your area.

Blacksmith's Corner in Bellflower, (562) 531-0386 - like visiting a mini farm, with its chickens, ducks, pheasants, etc.

La Habra Pets in La Habra, (562) 697-7110 - many exotic reptiles, such as ten-foot long snakes, a six-foot monitor lizard, and several others.

Prehistoric Pets in Fountain Valley, (714) 964-3525 / www.prehistoricpets.com - Incredible! See exotic snakes (some twenty-feet long) and monitor lizards from all over the world, plus a small fish pond in the middle of the store, and more.

Reptropolis in San Clemente, (949) 492-6598 - a variety of snakes, geckos, iguanas, tarantulas, turtles, and tortoises.

Wagon Train Feed & Pet, (714) 639-7932 / www.wagontrain.net - When we visited this small pet store it had chicks, ducks, a lamb, a pot-bellied pig, turtles, and chinchillas. The stop here was worth a peek and pet. Note: They also sell fertilized chick eggs and incubators.

PHOTO ALBUMS -

Tapped dry on how to put together a creative and memorable photo album? Many stores, such as Aaron Brothers and Michaels, offer acid-free products. Or, contact the magazines and multi-level company listed below for innovative ideas and other acid-free products:

Creative Keepsakes magazine, (888) 247-5282 / www.creatingkeepsakes.com - Browse through and implement the many ideas given here. Current subscription price is $24.97 for 6 issues.

Creative Memories (company), (800) 468-9335 / www.creative-memories.com - Call for information on purchasing craft scissors, and acid-free pages, stickers, cut outs, etc. Or, learn artistic techniques to organize and crop your photos by hosting or attending a workshop for you and your friends.

Memory Maker magazine, (800) 366-6465 / www.memorymakersmagazine.com - Pick up a copy of this beautifully laid out and inspirational magazine. Current subscription price is $45 for 8 issues.

PLAYGROUPS -

Check local parks, newspapers, and "Parenting" magazine for information on hooking up with a playgroup. This is a great way to share the joys and trials of raising children. Other resources include:

MOMS, e-mail:momsclub@aol.com - an international, non-profit support group specifically for stay-at-home moms. Weekly meetings consist of talking and eating together, listening to a speaker, and going on various outings. All age children are welcome at all meetings and activities. For information on a club near you, write to: MOMS Club, 25371 Rye Canyon, Valencia, CA 91355.

MOPS (Mothers Of Preschooler), (888) 910-6677 or (303) 733-5353 / www.mops.org - an international, Christian-based organization that has local meetings in almost every city. Moms usually meet at a church and talk, eat, listen to a speaker, and make a craft while their preschoolers are being cared for by a Moppet helper. Great organization! Call the headquarters to find a MOPS near you.

Tot Lot is a playgroup designed for preschoolers (and their parents) to meet and play together at community parks on a regular basis during the week, building those all-important socialization skills. Registration fees go towards crafts, snacks, and even field trips. Call, for example, Lakewood Recreation and Community Services, (562) 866-9771 / www.lakewoodcity.org for information on Tot Lot at Bolivar, Del Valle, and Mayfair parks. Call your local parks and recreation department to see what programs they offer.

RESTAURANTS -

See the Edible Adventures section in the main part of the book. Try eating at some unusual locations, such as at airports, on boats (such as the *Queen Mary*), etc. Take your kids out for ethnic foods, too.

ROCKETRY -

Southern California Rocket Association, (714) 529-1598 / home.earthlink.net/~mebowitz, can get you in touch with model rocketry classes (for ages 10 and older) and launch sites in Los Angeles and San Bernardino counties.

ROLLER SKATING -

Roll on the sidewalks, around parks, and at rinks. Try:

Surf City Skate Zone in Huntington Beach, (714) 842-9143 - offers roller skating and ice skating under one roof!

SOCCER -

Los Angeles Galaxy at the Home Depot Center in Carson, (877) - 3GALAXY (342-5299) or (310) 630-2200 / www.lagalaxy.com

Sockers at Sports Arena in San Diego (indoor soccer), (858) 836-GOAL (4625) / www.sockers.com

SPORTS ARENAS -

Many special events are held at sports arenas including sporting events like the Harlem Globetrotters and rodeos, concerts, Walt Disney's World on Ice, circuses, etc:

Anaheim at Arrowhead Pond, (714) 704-2400 / www.arrowheadpond.com

Carson at Home Depot Center, (310) 630-2060 / www.homedepotcenter.com

Long Beach at Long Beach Arena, (562) 436-3636 / www.longbeachcc.com

Los Angeles at L.A. Memorial Coliseum and Sports Arena, (213) 748-6136 / www.lacoliseum.com

Los Angeles at Staples Center, (213) 742-7340 / www.staplescenter.com

San Diego at Qualcomm Stadium, (619) 641-3131 / www.sandiego.gov/qualcomm

San Diego at Sports Arena, (619) 225-9813 / www.sandiegoarena.com

SPORTING EVENTS -

Check out high school and college events. These local games are a fun, inexpensive introduction to sports.

SUN CLOTHING -

SunGrubbies, (888) 970-1600 / www.sungrubbies.com and Sun Precautions, (800) 882-7860 / www.sunprecautions.com - Both companies make a full line of clothing especially designed to block out harmful rays from the sun.

SWAP MEETS / FLEA MARKETS -

Give your kids a dollar or two to call their own, as there are a lot of inexpensive toys or jewelry items for them to choose from at swap meets. Everyone goes home happy with their treasures! Here's a list of just a few good swap meets / flea markets. For a more complete listing and to locate a market near you, check www.fleamarketguide.com:

Alpine Village Swap Meet (outdoor) in Torrance, (323) 770-1961 / www.alpinevillage.net/swapmeet.htm - open Tues. - Sun., 8am - 2pm. Admission is free on Thurs.; 75¢ per person other days.

Anaheim Marketplace (indoor) in Anaheim, (714) 999-0888 / www.anaheimindoormarketplace.com - over 250 variety shops and a food court. They also have adjacent soccer fields and arcade games. Open Wed. - Mon., 10am - 7pm. Free admission.

Antelope Valley Swap Meet (outdoor) in Palmdale, (661) 273-0456 - open Sat., 7am - 4pm; Sun., 6am - 3pm.

Glendale Community College Flea Market (outdoor) in Glendale, (818) 240-1000/www.glendales.edu - A potpourri of new and old items. Open the 3rd Sun. of every month, 7am - 3pm. Free admission.

Kobey's Swap Meet (outdoor) at the sports arena parking lot in San Diego, (619) 226-0650 / www.kobeyswap.com - the equivalent of twelve footballs fields, this swap meet offers bargains on everything under the sun. Open Fri. - Sun., 7am - 3pm. Admission is 50¢ on Thurs. and Fri.; $1 on Sat. and Sun. No charge for children 11 years and under.

Orange County Marketplace (outdoor) in Costa Mesa, (949) 723-6616 or (949) 723-6660 / www.ocmarketplace.com - one of the best, with over 1,000 vendors, plus a food court. Open weekends, 7am - 3pm. (Some weekends in July are closed due to the Orange County Fair.) Admission is $2 for adults; children 11 years and under are free. (See pg. \\AUTOMOTIVEROAD\\ for a free car museum also at the Marketplace.

Pasadena City College Flea Market (outdoor), (626) 585-7906 / www.paccd.cc.ca.us/stulrnsv/flea - a mishmash mixture of merchandise from about 400 vendors - some great deals, some garage sale items. Open the first Sun. of every month, 8am - 3pm. Admission is free.

Roadium (outdoor) in Torrance, (323) 321-3902 / www.roadium.com - 450 merchants sell new items, some collectibles, bargains, garage-sale stuff, and food daily 7am - 3pm. Admission on Mon. and Fri., $1 for driver and 50¢ per person; Tues. and Thurs., 50¢ per person; Wed., $1.25 for adults; 75¢ for seniors and children; Sat. and Sun., $1.50 per car, plus $1 per person.

Rosebowl Flea Mart (outdoor) in Pasadena, (626) 577-3100 or (323) 560-7469 / www.rgcshows.com - more than 2,200 vendors offer everything you've ever seen and many things you've never heard of.

Held the second Sun. of each month. Admission is $20 from 6am - 7:30am; $15 from 7:30am - 9am; $7 from 9am until it closes. Parking is free.

San Bernardino Outdoor Market (outdoor) in San Bernardino, (909) 888-0394 / www.rgcshows.com - a large flea market held at the National Orange Showgrounds. Open Sun., 7am - 3pm. Admission and parking is free.

Santa Fe Springs Swap Meet (indoor) in Santa Fe Springs, (562) 921-9996 or (714) 523-3014 / www.sfswapmeet.com - over 500 vendors have been meeting here for thirty years to sell new wares. Live entertainment and food court open daily; a kiddie ride area open on the weekends. Open Wed., Thurs., and Sat., 6am - 3:30pm; Fri., 5pm - 10pm; Sun., 6am - 4pm. Admission for adults is 50¢ on Wed., free on Thurs., $1 Fri. - Sun. Children 11 and under are always free.

Saugus Speedway SwapMeet (outdoor) in Saugus, (661) 259-3886 / www.saugusspeedway.com - over 550 vendors, plus live entertainment, this huge swap meet is held every Sun., 7am - 3pm. The Tuesday swap meet, open 7am - 2pm, is smaller. Swap meets are held on Fri. only in the summer. Admission on Tues. is free; Sun., $1.50 for adults; children 11 years and under are free.

Street Fair by College of the Desert (outdoor) in Palm Desert, (760) 568-9921 / www.codstreetfair.com - new and used items, antiques, a Farmer's market, arts and crafts courtyard, jewelry, and more make this more of a street fair than swap meet ambiance. Held Sat. - Sun., 7am - 2pm; summer hours are 7am - noon. Admission is free.

Valley Indoor Swap Meet in Woodland Hills, (818) 340-9120 - new knickknacks, jewelry, clothes, accessories, plants, electronics, and more. Open Fri. - Sun., 10am - 6pm. Free admission.

Ventura Flea Market (outdoor) in Ventura, (805) 648-3376 / www.rgcshows.com - antiques, second hand, or used goods for sale. The flea market is held seven times a year at Seaside Park (i.e. Ventura County Fairgrounds). Call for dates. Admission is $5 for adults; children 11 and under are free. Parking is $7.

Tip: Also check out 99¢ Stores which are along the same lines, sans the atmosphere, as swap meets.

SWIMMING and WADING POOLS -
Community pools are open seasonally. Call your local park for information.

THEATER -
San Diego - Contact the San Diego Performing Arts League, (619) 238-0700 / www.sandiegoperforms.com, puts out a bimonthly booklet called *What's Playing?* It has a complete listing of the music, dance, and theater groups, plus specific show, dates, and prices in the San Diego area. $12 for a year's subscription.

Santa Barbara - Contact the Santa Barbara Performing Arts League at www.sbperformingartsleague.org for up-to-date listings.

THRIFT STORES -
Teach your children the gift of thrift! Give them a few dollars to buy a "new" article of clothing, a toy, or a book. Tip: Main Street, in the city of Ventura, has at least ten thrift stores in a row.

TICKETS -
Audiences Unlimited, (818) 506-0067 or (818) 753-3470 / www.tvtickets.com, offers free tickets to watch filming of almost all of the network television shows and many of their specials. For some shows, the minimum age for kids is 12 years old; for most, it's 18 years old. Call for a schedule or ask them to send you a monthly show schedule.

Times Arts Tix in San Diego next to Horton Plaza, (619) 497-5000 / www.sandiegoperforms.com, has half-price, day-of-performance, theater tickets available on a first-come, first-served, cash-only basis. Call for a listing of the day's shows.

Web TIX, operated by the Theatre League Alliance of Southern California / www.theatrela.org, allows day-of-show tickets (or even a few days before the show) to be purchased for 50% off the regular price. Check the website for a list of the shows and availability.

TOURS -

See Tours in the main section of the book. The following are general ideas of where you can go for group tours:

Animal Shelter	Dairy	Grocery Store	Pet Store
Airport	Dentist	Hospital	Police Station
Bakery	Factory	Hotel	Post Office
Bank	Fire Station	Newspaper Office	Printer
Chiropractor	Florist	Nurseries (plant)	Restaurant
College/University			

TOYS -

Look in this part of the book under Educational Toys, Books, and Games. Two other listings worth mentioning are:

U.S. Toy Company / Constructive Playthings in Garden Grove, (714) 636-7831 / www.ustoy.com - visit their store. They offer top-of-the-line toys, books, games, puzzles, etc., as well as lower priced, carnival-type "prizes." Contact this number - (800) 255-6124 / www.cptoys.com - for a catalog.

Oriental Trading Company, (800) 875-8480 / www.orientaltrading.com - This catalog company offers bulk and individual novelty items, usually priced at the lower end of the scale.

VOLUNTEERING -

Volunteering is a terrific way to spend time with your children while teaching them the real values of life - giving and serving. Check with local mission, churches, and temples, as many have regular times when they go to help feed the homeless. Here are just a few other volunteer agencies:

Adopt-a-Park and Adopt-a-Beach in Orange County, (714) 973-6855 or (714) 973-6871 / www.ocparks.com - Ongoing park and beach cleanups at more than 22 local sites for all age participants.

Children's Hunger Fund in Pacoima, (818) 899-5122 / www.chf2serve.org - Volunteers of all ages assemble care packages for disadvantaged children, Wed. and Sat., 9am - noon

Create-a-Smile in Santa Monica, (310) 392-6257 / www.create-a-smile.org - Families (children ages 11 and older) and their pets visit disabled, abused or ill children and adults in nursing homes and hospitals.

Doingsomething, (310) 335-0209 / www.doingsomethingla.org - Introduces volunteers to service organizations via a monthly newsletter ($15 per year) that includes many one-time projects for ages 8 and older including taking dogs for walks at a no-kill shelter, assembling holiday baskets, stocking food pantries, and more.

Florence Crittenton Services in Yorba Linda, (714) 680-9000 or (714) 680 - 8200 / www.kidsmatter.org - Abused children living here benefit from volunteers in numerous ways: Christmas gifts; coordinating on a holiday craft project to do with the kids; making holiday decorations; hosting a birthday party; etc.

Food Finders in Orange County, (562) 598-3003 / www.foodfinders.com - Families can donate, sort and deliver canned goods, toys, and food, year-round.

Habitat For Humanity, (229) 924-6935 x2553 / www.habitat.org - This non-profit organization is committed to providing low-income, owner-occupied housing by utilizing volunteer labor and donated materials. (Former President Jimmy Carter is one of the more prominent members.) Volunteers are needed to build homes and serve on committees such as finance, construction, and public relations. Kids must be at least 16 years old to work on construction sites, but younger children can help with off-site activities such as registration, making lunches, etc. Check web site for local affiliates or call information.

Heal the Bay, headquartered in Santa Monica, (800) HEAL BAY (432-5229) or (310) 453-0395 or (714) 536-5614 / www.healthebay.org - There's nothing like a day at the beach, especially if you're there to help make it cleaner. Clean up pollution in the Santa Monica Bay, San Pedro Bay, Orange County, and adjacent coastal waters. This program works in conjunction with Adopt-A-Beach and Coastal Clean Up.

Call (800) COAST-4U (262-7848) / www.coastal.ca.gov/publiced/pendx.html for the annual coastal clean up day and all the other ones in between.

Hugs for Health, (714) 832-HUGS (4847) / www.hugs4health.org - Hugs for the elderly are dispensed liberally through this program that operates mostly in senior-care facilities. All age huggers are welcome.

I Love a Clean San Diego, (858) 467-0103 / www.ilacsd.org - An educational and environmental group sponsoring beach clean-ups, storm drain stenciling, and graffiti removal.

Kids Giving to Kids, (714) 573-9474 or (310) 788-9474 / www.wishla.org or www.wishoc.org - Started by the Make-A-Wish Foundation, families can come up with creative fund-raising ideas to sponsor a wish for a child facing a life-threatening illness.

Kids Korps USA, (858) 259-3602 - North San Diego coastal / www.kidskorps.org. Young people, ages 5 - 18, can participate in a wealth of programs from preserving the environment to befriending those in need to helping animals and more. Every child who has a desire to do something to help can find an activity with Kids Korps.

Kids Who Care, (949) 459-9233 / www.kids-who-care.org - Ages 2 - 13 can serve in monthly activities, such as Salvation Army food distribution, volunteering at food banks, Angel Tree toy collection and distribution, gleaning in Irvine, beach and trail restoration, visiting senior centers, and more.

Los Angeles Midnight Mission, (213) 225-1180 / www.midnightmission.org - Volunteer to help set up, decorate, and help serve meals on Thanksgiving or another holiday.

Los Angeles Regional Foodbank in Los Angeles, (323) 234-3030 / www.lafoodbank.org - Ages 7 and up can help maintain 300 garden plots in a low income area, as well as participate in local food drive and food collection.

Move a Child Higher in La Canada / Flintridge, (626) 798-1222 / www.moveachildhigher - The Riding Club offers therapeutic horseback riding activities to children with disabilities. Volunteers, ages 13 and up, can exercise and groom the horses, and lead and walk alongside the riders.

Orange County Harvest in Orange County, (714) 708-1597 - Kindergartners and up are allowed to actually harvest and glean food from fields in Orange County. The food is delivered to Second Harvest Food Bank, (714) 771-1343 / www.feedoc.org, which in turn donates the produce to local food banks. Gleaning is usually done Tues. - Fri., 9am - 11am; Sat. - Sun., 1pm - 3pm. Pre-registration is required.

Points of Light Foundation, (800) 750-7653 / www.pointsoflight.org - The foundation points people to volunteer organizations in their area.

Ronald McDonald House in Orange County, (714) 639-3600 / www.rmhc.com and in San Diego, (858) 467-4750 / www.sdmcdonalds.com - This house provides a home-away-from-home for up to 20 families who have children receiving treatment for cancer and other serious illnesses at local medical facilities. Opportunities include making or sponsoring a meal, general housekeeping, and clerical opportunities. Note: There are other facilities throughout So. Cal.

Salvation Army, www.salvationarmy.socal.org - Volunteers are needed year round, but especially around Christmas time.

San Diego Bay Keeper, (800) 237-2583 / www.sdbaykeeper.org - This organization provides a listing of more than 40 coastal and inland cleanup sites throughout San Diego.

Second Harvest. See the above Orange County Harvest info.

St. Vincent de Paul in San Diego, (619) 233-8500 www.svdpv.org - Look up Tours in the main section of the book for details.

Tierra Del Sol Foundation, (818) 352-1419 / www.tierradelsol.org - Serves adults with developmental and often physical disabilities.

Trails4all, (714) 834-3136 / www.trails4all.org - Coordinates volunteers, who are at least 8 years old, to help with coastal cleanups, trail maintenance, and other activities that are group specific.

Volunteer Agencies, (800) 865-8683 for general information. Call (818) 908-5066 / www.vcla.net for volunteer opportunities in L.A. and San Fernando Valley. In Pasadena, call (626) 792-6819.

Volunteer Center of Greater Orange County, (714) 953-5757 / www.volunteercenter.org - A clearinghouse for a wide variety of age-appropriate opportunities, including feeding the homeless, visiting the elderly, planting trees, cleaning up parks, and removing graffiti. The center even has a guide book on family volunteer activities.

Volunteer Center of San Diego County, (858) 636-4131 or (800) VOLUNTEER (865-8683) / www.volunteersandiego.org - Includes a volunteer segment called SAVY (Students Actively Volunteering for You) for middle through highschoolers.

VolunteerMatch, www.volunteermatch.org - On-line website that matches volunteers with organizations that need them.

Youth Service America, 202-296-2992, www.ysa.org; www.servenet.org - A national organization "committed to making service the common experience and expectation of all young Americans."

WILDFLOWER HOTLINES -

Anza Borrego Desert State Park in Anza Borrego, (760) 767-4684 / www.anzaborrego.statepark.org

Joshua Tree National Park in Joshua Tree / Twentynine Palms, (760) 367-5500 / www.nps.gov/jotr

Mojave Desert Information Center, (760) 733-4040 / www.nps.gov/moja

Poppy Reserve in Lancaster, (661) 724-1180 or (661) 942-0662 / www.calparksmojave.com

Southern California Hotline, Theodore Payne Foundation, (818) 768-3533 / www.theodorepayne.org

ALPHABETICAL INDEX

INDEX BY CITY

INDEX BY PRICE

Free Occasionally - The following attractions have special days when no admission is charged:

FREE (!)

Los Angeles - !

1¢ to $5 ($)

$10.01 to $20 ($$$)

$20.01 to $40 ($$$$)

THEMATIC INDEX

Farms

Firefighting

Oceanography / Tidepools

Paleontology

Petting Zoos

ABOUT THE AUTHOR:

Fun and education are key words in our home. I enjoy home schooling my children; speaking to various groups; reading; hiking; traveling; writing; and whatever else God brings my family's way!

I would appreciate your ideas about this book. Do you have a wonderful place to go with kids that wasn't included in this edition? Please let me know and I'll share it in the next one. You can write to me at:

FUN PLACES TO GO WITH KIDS
P.O. Box 376
Lakewood, CA 90714 - 0376
(562) 867-5223
email: susan@funplaces.com

and educational
Fün ^Places to
go With Kids ^
and adults
in Southern California

$22.95

($20.95 includes tax, plus $2.00 shipping)

Please send copy(s) of this wonderful, innovative, well-written, absolutely fantastic, fun book to . . .

NAME _____

ADDRESS _____ CITY _____

STATE _____ ZIP _____ PHONE _____

ENCLOSED IS MY CHECK FOR $ _____ ($22.95 per book, which includes tax and shipping.)

Make check payable to: **Fun Places.**   Send to: **Fun Places Publishing**
P.O. Box 376
Lakewood, CA 90714-0376

- - - ✂ -

and educational
Fün ^Places to
go With Kids ^
and adults
in Southern California

$22.95

($20.95 includes tax, plus $2.00 shipping)

Please send copy(s) of this wonderful, innovative, well-written, absolutely fantastic, fun book to . . .

NAME _____

ADDRESS _____ CITY _____

STATE _____ ZIP _____ PHONE _____

ENCLOSED IS MY CHECK FOR $ _____ ($22.95 per book, which includes tax and shipping.)

Make check payable to: **Fun Places.**   Send to: **Fun Places Publishing**
P.O. Box 376
Lakewood, CA 90714-0376

FUN PLACES to go JOURNAL

Ever ask your child, "What do you remember most about the place we visited?" and he answers, "It was fun." Good. That's a good start. Ever try to probe a little deeper and still get the same response? If you have invested the time, energy, and money going on an outing with your child, you want to make sure he remembers where you've gone and what you've done, right? That's one of the many reasons we go on outings, field trips, or vacations with our kids. Aid your child in making memories by encouraging him to journal.

The *Fun Places to go Journal* gives your kids specific questions to answer, on pages bordered with fun figures. The one-page questions are for younger children, or a short excursion. The three pages of questions, pertaining to one outing, are for older children or a more in-depth field trip or vacation. There are plenty of pages for saving photographs, postcards, ticket stubs, and brochures. All the prep work is done for you! There are also several pages that have games to play such as crossword puzzles, word search, dot to dot, and more. The journal is a perfect supplement to this book and it comes with a host of practical ideas on how to incorporate education with fun .

and educational
Fün ^Places
to go
Jöurnal

$8.95
($7.95 includes tax, plus $1.00 shipping)

Please send copy(s) of this fun and educational aid to . . .

NAME _____

ADDRESS _____ CITY _____

STATE _____ ZIP _____ PHONE _____

ENCLOSED IS MY CHECK FOR $ _____ ($8.95 per journal, includes tax and shipping.)

Make check payable to: **Fun Places**. Send to: **Fun Places Publishing
P.O. Box 376
Lakewood, CA 90714-0376**

NOTES

NOTES

NOTES

NOTES